ROAD MAP SYMBOLS

- ┅━┅╾■╼┅━ Freeway, with tunnel and toll
- ┄┄┄┄┄┄ Freeway under construction
- ━[M31]━[31]━ Highway, sealed, with National Highway Route Marker
- ━[A1]━(1)━ Highway, sealed, with National Route Marker
- ━(5)━ Highway, sealed, with Metroad Route Marker
- ▪▪▪▪▪▪ Highway, unsealed
- ┄┄┄┄┄ Highway under construction
- ━[C141]━[26]━ Main road, sealed, with State Route Marker
- ┅┅┅▬▬ Main road, unsealed, with Tourist Route
- ┄┄┄┄ Main road under construction
- ──────── Secondary road, sealed, (suburbs maps only)
- ┄┄┄┄┄ Secondary road, unsealed, (suburbs maps only)
- ───←─── Other road, sealed, with traffic direction arrow
- ┄┄┄┄┄ Other road, unsealed
- ▬▬▬▬▬ Mall
- ┄┄┄┄┄ Vehicle track
- ········· Walking track
- ┝┿┿┿┿┿ Paratoo Railway, with station
- ┝┿┿┿┿┿ Flagstaff Underground railway, with station
- ▽──114──▽ Total kilometres between two points
- ▽──45──▽ Intermediate kilometres
- ─·─·─·─ State border
- ▬ ▬ ▬ Fruit fly exclusion zone boundary
- **SYDNEY** ◎ State capital city
- **GEELONG** ◎ Town, over 50 000 inhabitants
- **Bundaberg** ○ Town, 10 000–50 000 inhabitants
- **Katherine** ○ Town, 5 000–10 000 inhabitants
- Narrogin ○ Town, 1 000–5 000 inhabitants
- Robe ○ Town, 200–1 000 inhabitants
- Miena ○ Town, under 200 inhabitants
- BELCONNEN ○ Suburb, on state and region maps
- **Belconnen** Suburb, on suburban maps
- Williamsford Locality (area name)
- Alroy Downs □ Pastoral station homestead
- Borroloola ○ Major Aboriginal community
- Murgenella ○ Aboriginal community
- Fortesque Roadhouse ▣ Roadhouse
- ✈ Commercial airport
- • Place of interest
- ● Landmark feature
- ⁺ Hill, mountain, peak
- ⋈ Mine site
- ★ Lighthouse
- River, with waterfall
- Lake, reservoir
- Intermittent lake
- Mangroves
- Coastline, with rocks
- TO GOULBURN Route destination
- [386] Adjoining page number
- National park
- Other reserve
- Other named area
- Aboriginal / Torres Strait Islander land
- Prohibited area
- ❶ Text entry in A to Z listing

ROAD DISTANCE I⌷

	ADELAIDE						
Adelaide		2055	1170				
Albury	925	1440	352	3937	308	3583	565
Alice Springs	1548	2998	2658	1489	2255	3549	2931
Ballarat	618	1743	777	3645	112	3309	973
Bendigo	639	1619	653	3671	147	3335	849
Birdsville	1223	1463	2153	2246	2470	3293	2129
Brisbane	2055		1246	3406	1671	4289	984
Broken Hill	515	1545	1108	3128	825	2824	1154
Broome	4269	4646	4975	1874	4996	2237	5112
Cairns	3384	1699	2954	2885	3055	6050	2685
Canberra	1198	1246		4003	656	3741	292
Darwin	3037	3406	4003		3189	4043	4301
Geelong	832	1705	734	3842	72	3410	930
Geraldton	3135	4787	4329	3743	3853	422	4529
Kalgoorlie	2195	3634	3381	4021	2935	593	3451
Katherine	2723	3109	3683	314	3469	3729	3670
Mackay	2822	975	2216	2913	2318	5275	1948
Melbourne	732	1671	656	3789		3456	873
Mildura	395	1662	801	3444	549	3108	1023
Mount Gambier	452	2071	1114	3509	452	3161	1298
Newcastle	1580	850	423	3818	1036	4282	155
Perth	2716	4363	3741	4043	3456		3972
Port Augusta	318	1754	1343	2719	1058	2398	1574
Port Hedland	4348	5178	5542	2407	5066	1636	5742
Rockhampton	2488	641	1882	2954	1984	5199	1614
Sydney	1415	984	292	4301	873	3972	
Tennant Creek	2054	2457	3063	983	2792	4622	3050
Townsville	3214	1367	2608	2541	2710	5911	2340
Wagga Wagga	949	1342	253	3672	447	3668	472

Hobart to Launceston 200 kilometres

WILDLIFE-WATCHING SYMBOLS

These symbols are used on the **Wildlife-Watching** maps that appear in the **Features** section near the end of each State chapter.

🦡 bandicoots / quolls		🦘 kangaroos/wallabies	
🦇 bats		🐨 koalas	
🐦 birds		🦎 lizards	
🦋 Bogong moths		🐧 penguins	
🦋 butterflies		🦫 platypuses	
🐊 crocodiles		🐾 possums	
🐕 dingoes		🦫 quokkas	
🐬 dolphins		🦭 seals /sea lions	
dugongs		🐍 snakes	
🦔 echidnas		🦡 Tasmanian devils	
🐟 fish		tree kangaroos	
flying foxes		🐢 turtles	
🐸 frogs		🐋 whales	
gliders		🐗 wombats	
glow-worms			

EXPLORE
AUSTRALIA

EXPLORE AUSTRALIA

VIKING

CONTENTS

SOUTH AUSTRALIA

WESTERN AUSTRALIA

NORTHERN TERRITORY

JOURNEY THROUGH
AUSTRALIA

AUSTRALIA is a small, modern nation in a vast, ancient land. Covering an area
the size of Europe, Australia is the world's largest island continent. It is also the
oldest, flattest and – with the exception of Antarctica – the driest place on earth.
For about 70 000 years the continent was the preserve of around 600 groups
collectively known as Aboriginal people. Theirs is the longest continuous occupation
in human history. The British settled the east coast in 1788. Over the past two
hundred years the colonial prison outpost they established has been transformed
into a nation of nearly 20 million people.

FACT FILE

Total land area: 7 692 030 sq km

Length of coastline including islands: 59 740 km

Number of beaches: 7000

Longest river: Murray River – 2520 km

Highest mountain: Mount Kosciuszko – 2228 m

Largest lake: Lake Eyre – 9500 sq km

Hottest town: Marble Bar, WA – av. summer max. 41°C

Coldest region: Australian Alps – av. winter min. 5°C

Wettest place: Tully, Qld – av. annual median 4048 mm

Population: 19 500 000

Indigenous population: 427 000

Population born overseas: 24 per cent

Population residing in capital cities: 60 per cent

Land of contrast

The vast outback of red earth, vivid skies, weathered mountains and searing heat is unmistakably Australian. This landscape is a source of myth and legend for the first inhabitants and a symbol of the hardships endured by the early white settlers. In contrast, the lushly vegetated east coast, including the island of Tasmania, is a place of rugged peaks, wild rivers, waterfalls and ancient rainforests. Eucalypt forests, wetlands, river plains, snowfields and almost 60 000 kilometres of beaches, coastal cliffs, islands and reefs are other features that contribute to the complex story of the Australian landscape.

Unique wildlife

Much of the flora and fauna is unique and, like the landscape, extremely varied. The gum is the dominant tree in what is known colloquially as the bush, and boasts five hundred species alone. Our highest profile native animals are marsupials, which include the ever-popular koalas and kangaroos. Bar a few distant relatives bearing only the slightest family resemblance, there is nothing else like them on earth.

Cities on the coast

The harshness of the interior has kept most of the population near the relatively benign coastline. Most Australians live in cities and towns in the south-east and, to a lesser extent, the south-west of the continent. This preference has created unequal population figures across the six States and two Territories that make up a federated nation. Australia's most populated area, the State of New South Wales, has 6 500 000 residents, while the remote Northern Territory is home to just 192 000.

Relaxed lifestyle

Many Australians enjoy a way of life that is the envy of the rest of the world. Even the large cities, vital and modern as they are, feel relaxed, easy and overwhelmingly friendly. Accessible beaches and a typically sunny, warm climate have resulted in a lifestyle characterised by outdoor living, barbecues, friends and good health.

INDIGENOUS AUSTRALIA

Australia's indigenous people have the longest continuous history of any people in the world – between 50 000 and 70 000 years. There are two racially distinct groups: the Aboriginal people, who occupied the mainland and Tasmania, and the Torres Strait Islanders, from the islands off the tip of Cape York. At the time of white settlement the estimated 300 000 Aboriginal people comprised around 600 distinct societies. Today, the history of our indigenous people is central to any understanding of what we are as a nation. Increasingly, Aboriginal tourism, with its associated activities, is the most tangible bridge between Australian indigenous culture and the non-indigenous culture of locals and overseas visitors. Experiences of indigenous culture might include a bush tucker tour, travelling to a rock-art site, attendance at a dance performance or a visit to a cultural centre.

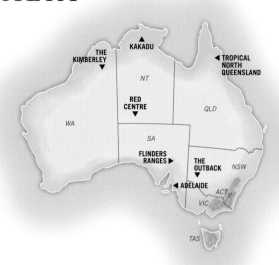

◀ TROPICAL NORTH QUEENSLAND
The distinctive art of the East Cape peoples in tropical north Queensland survives in the spectacular rock-art galleries near Laura. Near Cairns is the Tjapukai Aboriginal Cultural Park, an excellent centre featuring performance, demonstrations and art. There are flights from Cairns to the Torres Strait Islands; the best time to visit is July (even-numbered years) for the Torres Strait Cultural Festival. *See also: The Far North p. 461.*

KAKADU, NT ▶
The name Kakadu is derived from Gagudju, one of the three traditional owners and now managers of this World Heritage Area. The area – one of the most intensely populated before white settlement – has over 5000 rock-art sites, the largest collection in the world. There are numerous ways to explore the magnificent Aboriginal heritage of this area: start at the Bowali Visitor Centre, with its many historic displays and general tour information. *See also: Kakadu & Arnhem Land p. 402.*

TASMANIA'S ABORIGINAL PEOPLE
Tasmania's indigenous population, known as Palawa, migrated to the island about 35 000 years ago. On the eve of white settlement their population of over 4000 was divided between nine groups. White settlers drove the Palawa from their hunting grounds by use of violence and the spread of disease. The Black War, as it became known, culminated in the 1830s with the colonial government rounding up the 130 remaining survivors and banishing them to Flinders Island (see *Bass Strait Islands* p. 552). Many of Tasmania's traditional sites, from middens to rock art, lie in protected areas and are not easily accessible. The rich repository of sites in the Tasmanian wilderness played a significant part in the area's World Heritage listing. Kutikina Cave, with evidence of 20 000 years of occupation, can be reached via a rafting tour of the Franklin River.

▼ THE OUTBACK, NSW

Lake Mungo is Australia's most significant archaeological site. Burial sites, cooking hearths and campfires, preserved in lunar-like dunes, provide evidence of a period of human occupation dating back 60 000 years. Cultural tours operate from Mildura. Superb rock art is to be found at Mount Grenfell Historic Site (near Cobar), home of the Ngiyampaa, and in Mutawintji National Park, Wiljali country, where the traditional owners conduct regular tours of some of the more than 300 sites. *See also: The Outback p. 31.*

Heather Kemarre Shearer (1998)

▲ ADELAIDE, SA

Adelaide is home to two major centres dealing with Aboriginal culture. The Aboriginal-owned and-operated Tandanya houses a permanent collection of art, hosts contemporary art exhibitions and stages performance events. The South Australian Museum is home to the largest collection of Aboriginal cultural materials in the world. These items are presented in a series of sensitive and provocative displays in the new Aboriginal Cultures Gallery. *See also: Adelaide p. 239.*

◄ RED CENTRE, NT

The World Heritage Uluṟu–Kata Tjuṯa National Park is the traditional land of the Aṉangu, who help manage tours to art sites and other places of cultural and spiritual significance. To the north, in Alice Springs, which is Arrernte country, are a number of galleries and centres including the award-winning Aboriginal Art and Cultural Centre. Alice is also the base for tours to the surrounding country. *See also: The Red Centre p. 406.*

LINDERS RANGES, SA

se ancient hills are home to the yamathanha – meaning 'hills people', llective term for a number of traditional guage groups. Highlights of this rally rich and spiritually significant include the Yourambulla Caves, re there are rock shelters with charcoal vings and ochre paintings. A number tes surround the stunning visual trepiece of Wilpena Pound ('Wilpena' ves from an Adnyamathanha word ning 'cupped hands' or 'bent fingers'). *also: Flinders Ranges & Outback p. 252.*

TIME LINE: ABORIGINAL AUSTRALIA

70 000–50 000 BC *The first indigenous people cross from Indonesia to the New Guinea–Australia landmass*

35 000 BC *Aboriginal people reach Tasmania*

10 000 BC *Rising sea levels after the last Ice Age isolate Aboriginal people in Australia from Asia, and those in Tasmania from the mainland*

6000 BC *Distinct tribes and clans occupy the entire continent; economies adapt to different environments; religious beliefs and oral traditions derived from the Dreamtime indicate complex social organisation; extensive rock art appears*

1770 *The Tharawal of the Botany Bay region make contact with Captain Cook*

1778 *The Eora are displaced by the establishment of a penal colony at Sydney Cove*

1789 *A smallpox epidemic kills about half the Aboriginal population living in the vicinity of Sydney's penal colony*

1838 *Twelve whites massacre 28 Aboriginal people at Myall Creek*

1876 *Truganini, believed to be the last full-blooded Tasmanian Aboriginal person, dies*

1860–1900 *Protection Boards established across Australia; most Aboriginal people living on missions or government reserves*

1901 *The Commonwealth Constitution does not allow Federal parliament to legislate for Aboriginal people to be counted in the census*

1910 *Legislation in New South Wales increases government powers to remove Aboriginal children from their parents; similar provisions enacted in other States*

1967 *In a referendum, Australians vote with a 90 per cent majority to count Aboriginal people in the census*

1971 *Neville Bonner, the first Aboriginal parliamentarian, is elected to the Senate*

1972 *Aboriginal people erect a Tent Embassy outside Parliament House, Canberra, marking a new era of political activism*

1992 *In a decision known as Mabo, the High Court rejects the notion of terra nullius ('land belonging to no one') and affirms that Aboriginal people were in possession of the land before 1788*

1996 *In the Wik case, the High Court holds that pastoral leases granted by the Queensland Government did not extinguish native title*

1997 Bringing Them Home, *the report of a government inquiry into the Stolen Generation, is tabled in Federal parliament. The Howard government refuses to make a formal apology but the spirit of Reconciliation is embraced by many Australians.*

◄ THE KIMBERLEY, WA

The Kimberley retains a large Aboriginal population – at least 50 per cent of the total Kimberley population. This remote area has one of the country's most important collections of rock art, of which there are two main types: the Bradshaw and the more recent Wandjina. Tours of rock-art sites are available from some of the big stations in the area, and a variety of cultural tours operate from the region's community and cultural centres. *See also: The Kimberley p. 332.*

NEW ARRIVALS

Since the arrival of the First Fleet in 1788, the pace of development in Australia has been rapid and far-reaching. While not all our historic heritage has been preserved, what remains offers a substantial, if not comprehensive, interpretation of the unique and often remarkable events of Australian history. Convict settlements tell the story of the grim and unpromising early years; isolated townships provide evidence of courageous attempts to tame a harsh environment; and ornate Victorian architecture boasts of the greatest gold rush in history. A new appreciation of this unique heritage has resulted in the restoration of many historic sites over the past couple of decades, with locations now popular with a large number of visitors.

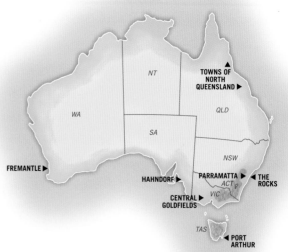

▲ THE ROCKS, NSW
The Rocks marks the site of the first European settlement in Australia and is probably the country's most intact historic precinct. A mix of early buildings – bond stores, maritime warehouses, churches, pubs, low-slung cottages and wharves – is crowded across the peninsula at the heart of Sydney's CBD. *See also: Sydney p. 3.*

HAHNDORF, SA ▶
This charming village forms an important part of one of the great stories of Australian history – immigration. Hahndorf was settled in the 1830s by Australia's first significant non-British immigrant group – German Lutheran peasants fleeing religious persecution. Today much of their culture is preserved through buildings, produce shops, restaurants and festivals. The nearby Barossa Valley also has a significant German heritage. *See also: Adelaide Hills p. 247.*

PORT ARTHUR, TAS. ▶
There is no other site in the world like Port Arthur. Built in the early 1800s by convicts as a prison for convicts, it is our most graphic reminder of why and how modern Australia came into being. The site comprises a clutch of sandstone buildings – a penitentiary, hospital, asylum and church among them – set along the dramatic coast of the Tasman Peninsula. *See also: The South-East p. 546.*

▲ FREMANTLE, WA

Fremantle is one of the world's best-preserved 19th-century ports and serves as a fascinating reminder of the significance of maritime history in an island nation. Established in 1829, Fremantle contains a range of buildings that includes public offices, warehouses, shipping-company headquarters, shopfronts and houses, many now open to the public as museums and galleries. *See also: Fremantle p. 321.*

▼ PARRAMATTA, NSW

Now an outer suburb of Sydney, Parramatta was originally preferred over Sydney Harbour by European settlers and officials, not least because of its proximity to farmland and distance from the convict population. Parramatta preserves important fragments of the earliest colonial years, including the country's oldest buildings – Elizabeth Farm, home to pastoralists John and Elizabeth Macarthur, and the first Government House. Both are open to the public. *See also: Sydney p. 3.*

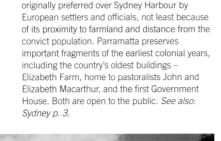

SINCE EUROPEAN DISCOVERY

1606 The Duyfken, *a Dutch ship, explores the western coast of Cape York Peninsula*

1616 Dirk Hartog on the Eendracht *lands on an island off the Western Australian coast*

1770 *James Cook takes possession of the east coast of New Holland for the British Crown*

1788 *The First Fleet establishes a British penal colony at Botany Bay*

1803 *Matthew Flinders completes the first circumnavigation of Australia and establishes it as a continent*

1803 *A British settlement is established on the River Derwent in Van Diemen's Land*

1813 *Wentworth, Blaxland and Lawson find a path across the Blue Mountains*

1824 *The Moreton Bay Penal Settlement is established near what will become Brisbane*

1829 *Western Australia is founded by British emigrants*

1835 *John Batman 'buys' the site of Melbourne from the Kulin people*

1836 *South Australia is proclaimed a British colony*

1840 *The British Government abolishes convict transportation to New South Wales after more than 84 000 convicts have arrived*

1851 *Gold is discovered in New South Wales and Victoria*

1901 *The six Australian colonies federate to form the Commonwealth of Australia*

1908 *Land known as Canberra, at the foothills of the Australian Alps, is chosen as the site of the national capital*

1914–18 *World War I: Australia fights against Germany with the loss of almost 62 000 Australian lives*

1929 *The Great Depression, triggered by the Wall Street crash, spreads to Australia*

1939–45 *World War II: Australia fights in Europe, Asia and the Pacific, with the loss of more than 39 000 Australian lives*

1951 *A referendum to outlaw the Communist Party of Australia is narrowly defeated*

1966 *The government begins dismantling restrictive immigration legislation known as the 'White Australia' policy*

1988 *Australia celebrates 200 years of European settlement*

▲ CENTRAL GOLDFIELDS, VIC.

Many areas in Australia experienced a gold rush in the second half of the 19th century, but nowhere were the yields as great and the effects as dramatic as in Victoria. The legacy is a series of towns – particularly Ballarat and Bendigo – boasting significant concentrations of rural Victorian-era architecture. Less conspicuous but also significant are the sites marking the history of the Chinese in Australia. *See also: The Goldfields p. 148.*

◀ TOWNS OF NORTH QUEENSLAND

Among others, the remote towns of Cooktown, Townsville, Charters Towers and Ravenswood are places where Australian themes of isolation, hardship and adaptation had their origins. Settled for a variety of reasons – to service farming communities or the gold rush, or as ports – they preserve significant recollections of the 19th century. Of particular interest are the architectural adaptations designed to cope with extreme environmental conditions. *See also: The Mid-Tropics p. 460 and The Far North p. 461.*

LIVEABLE CITIES

Although Australia is famed for its natural environment, most of its residents live in cities and large towns. The eight capital cities of the States and Territories vary sharply in size and character. Much of this has to do with the considerable distances that separate the cities, and the geographical conditions and historical circumstances that formed them. Some of the similarities come from a shared sense of what constitutes the good life and, hand-in-hand with this, a willingness to take of and embrace the superb natural landscapes in which the cities are located.

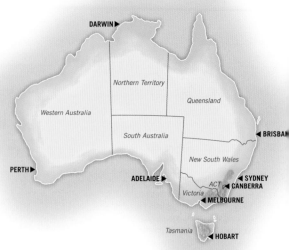

◀ MELBOURNE, VIC.

Southerly Melbourne with its unpredictable weather is the centre of style and substance. It is the birthplace of Australian art and literature and continues to foster the arts through its institutions and festivals. Melbourne boasts fine contemporary buildings, side by side with Victorian-era architecture that is second to none. It is the country's most educated, cosmopolitan and liberal city and its role as Australia's sporting capital is uncontested. *See also: Melbourne p. 131.*

▼ HOBART, TAS.

The sea and a sense of history dominate Hobart. Australia's second oldest city and the capital of the only island State, it preserves an intimate relationship with things maritime. Situated on the banks of the Derwent estuary and in the shadow of the frequently snow-covered Mount Wellington, the city has a pronounced European feel, although the rugged wilderness of the surrounding landscape marks it as distinctly Australian. *See also: Hobart p. 539.*

▲ CANBERRA, ACT

The national capital is also the country's most unusual city. Brought into being by an Act of Parliament and fully planned around its inland location at the foothills of the Australian Alps, it lacks the urban intensity, history and coastal flavour of the other cities. Yet Canberra makes up for this with a sense of restrained elegance, apparent in its wide boulevards, lakeside public buildings and extensive parklands. *See also: Canberra p. 114.*

▲ SYDNEY, NSW

Australia's oldest and largest city is the country's gateway to the world. It is loud, lively and bustling with folk from somewhere else. Set around the incomparable Sydney Harbour, bordered by bushland on three sides and the surf beaches of the Pacific on the fourth, it combines the excitement and facilities of an international city with the best of what the nation is so well known for – lifestyle. *See also: Sydney p. 3.*

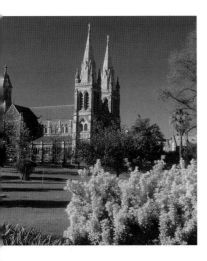

◀ **ADELAIDE, SA**

This charming, boutique-sized city, with its elegant 19th-century stone buildings, well-planned streets and squares, formal parklands and a European sense of scale, sits within reach of a remote and arid wilderness while enjoying a softer immediate setting of hills, plains and beaches. The city offers a range of diversions and amenities that include world-class festivals, excellent art and museum collections and an appreciation of top-quality food and wine. *See also: Adelaide p. 239.*

▲ **PERTH, WA**

This western outpost is closer to the cities of Asia than it is to Australia's population base on the eastern seaboard. Isolated from the mainstream, Perth, along with its home State, has earned itself a reputation for being aggressively individualist and forward-thinking. The manifestation of this is a big, bright and overwhelmingly modern city. Perth's considerable natural advantages include its unique Indian Ocean frontage; the Swan River, which cuts a course through the city; and a Mediterranean-style climate. *See also: Perth p. 315.*

▼ **DARWIN, NT**

Darwin, small and remote, remains a town of the frontier – robust, good humoured and eclectic. It is populated by indigenous Australians who have occupied the region for around 70 000 years; locals of European descent (including 'visitors who have never left'); southerners on secondment; and a large number of immigrants from nearby Asian countries. Despite the solidity of the city's structures, the partly shifting population makes for a sense of impermanence – against a backdrop of the Wet and Dry climate pattern, extreme tides and riotous tropical vegetation. *See also: Darwin p. 395.*

CITY FACT FILE

Adelaide
Population: 1 096 102
Date founded: 1836
Signature attraction: South Australian Museum
Top event: Adelaide Festival of the Arts

Brisbane
Population: 1 626 865
Date founded: 1825
Signature attraction: South Bank Parklands
Top event: Royal Brisbane Show – 'The Ekka'

Canberra
Population: 310 521
Date founded: 1908
Signature attraction: Parliament House
Top event: Floriade

Darwin
Population: 90 001
Date founded: 1839
Signature attraction: Mindil Beach Sunset Market
Top event: Darwin Beer Can Regatta

Hobart
Population: 194 228
Date founded: 1803
Signature attraction: Historic waterfront
Top event: 10 Days on the Island

Melbourne
Population: 3 466 025
Date founded: 1835
Signature attractions: Gardens and Victorian-era architecture
Top event: Melbourne Cup

Perth
Population: 1 381 127
Date founded: 1829
Signature attraction: Kings Park
Top event: Perth International Arts Festival

Sydney
Population: 4 085 578
Date founded: 1788
Signature attraction: Sydney Harbour
Top event: Gay and Lesbian Mardi Gras

BRISBANE, QLD ▲

This metropolis of the subtropics, Australia's third largest centre, is a city of light. The lazy curves of the Brisbane River, the glass and metal of the modern office towers, the sandstone of the colonial buildings and the lush foliage of the extensive parklands radiate with the sunshine and warmth that soak the city winter and summer. Open-air markets are a way of life here, with Eagle Street Pier hosting the lively Riverside Markets every Sunday. Needless to say this is a profoundly relaxed place: business-like yes, motivated of course, but never willing to ignore the considerable pleasures of its natural environment. *See also: Brisbane p. 439.*

NATURAL WONDERS

Australia is renowned for the beauty and diversity of its natural environment. As well as the vast tracts of desert that one would expect in the earth's oldest, driest and flattest continent, it is a place of lush forests, wild rivers, ancient mountains, dramatic alpine peaks, glacial lakes and a magnificent coastline. Two sites, the stunning Great Barrier Reef and the massive monolith of Uluru – both among the most recognised natural features in the world – have contributed greatly to the development of Australia as a major nature-travel destination. Other places, such as the remote wilds of Tasmania and the vast expanse of The Kimberley, are valued for their lonely beauty and remarkably unspoiled condition.

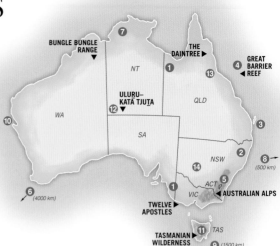

▼ AUSTRALIAN ALPS, NSW & VIC.

Few people realise that Australia has an alpine area more extensive that the snowfields of Austria and Switzerland combined. Straddling the Great Dividing Range, the Alps area is preserved in a series of connecting national parks. A landscape of glacial lakes, mighty rivers and rugged peaks make this one of the world's most spectacular alpine areas. *See also: Snowy Mountains p. 28 and The High Country p. 222.*

▲ THE DAINTREE, QLD

Part of the Wet Tropics World Heritage Area, the Daintree is popular place for exploring the dense and tangled primeval forests of tropical north Queensland. Phenomenally diverse and spectacularly beautiful, the forests are home to some of the world's most ancient plant species, as well as some of Australia's most brilliant birds and butterflies. *See also: The Far North p. 461.*

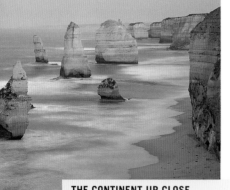

◄ TWELVE APOSTLES, VIC.

These massive limestone obelisks were once part of the original cliff-line, but have since become 'stranded' under the constant pressure of sea and wind erosion. Surrounded by swirling waves, and capturing the ever-changing coastal light, the Twelve Apostles are regarded as one of Australia's great scenic experiences. *See also: South-West Coast p. 143.*

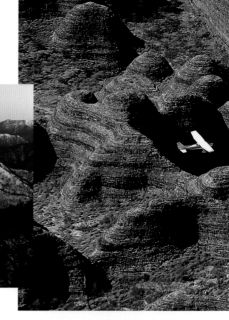

▲ BUNGLE BUNGLE RANGE, WA

These black-and-orange-striped, weathered mounds, which rise up out of the remote plains of The Kimberley in north-west Australia, were created 350 million years ago, and contain sedimentary layers said to be 1600 million years old. Palm-lined gorges and clear pools of water intersect the ancient domes. Travel into the area is by 4WD or scenic flight. *See also: The Kimberley p. 332.*

THE CONTINENT UP CLOSE

The character of the Australian landscape dates back 290 million years to a time when the continent was submerged under a huge ice cap. Since then, the deep valleys and high mountains of a glaciated landscape have been eroded away to a fairly uniform flatness (with some exceptions, spectacular for their shape – the Bungle Bungles and Uluru among them). The loss of high mountains brought a gradual increase in aridity. The formation of the rain clouds slowed and vast tracts of desert began to appear where lush forests had once stood. Today approximately 80 per cent of the continent is arid. There would probably be more arid land except for a dramatic geological episode 80 million years ago – the upthrust of the Great Dividing Range. This feature, stretching from north to south on the east of the continent, is where Australia's tallest peaks, grand forests and most significant rivers are found.

◀ TASMANIAN WILDERNESS

Covering nearly 20 percent of the total area of the island State, the Tasmanian wilderness is one of only three temperate wildernesses remaining in the Southern Hemisphere. It encompasses Australia's longest caves, ancient rocks, remote wild rivers, some of the world's oldest trees, and the stunning glaciated landscape of Cradle Mountain–Lake St Clair. *See also: The North-West p. 550 and South-West Wilderness p. 551.*

▲ GREAT BARRIER REEF, QLD

The world's largest reef is an enduring symbol of the rarity and beauty of Australia's natural environment. Stretching for 2000 km along the coast of Queensland, this maze of coral reefs and cays supports an astonishing diversity of life, from 1500 species of fish to sea mammals, turtles, sea grasses and molluscs. Brilliant colours, forms and textures have made these underwater landscapes one of the world's great diving destinations. *See also: Great Barrier Reef p. 455.*

◀ ULURU–KATA TJUTA, NT

These notable rock formations sit above an otherwise flat desert plain at the geographic heart of the continent. Uluru, with a height of 348 m and a base circumference of 9.4 km, is the largest monolith in the world. Neighbouring Kata Tjuta comprises 36 steep-sided domes that are possibly the eroded remains of a monolith many times the size of Uluru. *See also: The Red Centre p. 406.*

FOCUS ON WORLD HERITAGE

① *Australian Fossil Mammal Sites (Naracoorte & Riversleigh)*
Two sites that have yielded 20 million-year-old fossils of extinct Australian species. See also: The South-East p. 254 and Outback & Gulf Country p. 464.

② *Central Eastern Rainforest Reserves of Australia*
Large discontinuous patches of subtropical, warm temperate and Antarctic beech cool temperate rainforest. See also: Holiday Coast p. 17, Tropical North Coast p. 19, New England & the North-West p. 20 and Gold Coast & Hinterland p. 450.

③ *Fraser Island*
World's largest sand island, with complex dune system, freshwater dune lakes and rainforest. See also: Fraser Island & Coast p. 454.

④ *Great Barrier Reef*
World's largest reef, with the most diverse reef fauna. See also: Great Barrier Reef p. 455.

⑤ *Greater Blue Mountains Area*
A deeply incised plateau with dramatic cliffs and valleys and eucalypt forests. See also: Central Coast & Hawkesbury p. 16 and Blue Mountains p. 22.

⑥ *Heard and McDonald Islands*
An active volcano (on Heard), glacial landscapes and rare sub-Antarctic flora and fauna.

⑦ *Kakadu National Park*
Myriad natural environments and the world's oldest, most extensive rock art. See also: Kakadu & Arnhem Land p. 402.

⑧ *Lord Howe Island*
Home to a wealth of flora and fauna species, many unique to this remote volcanic island. See also: Lord Howe Island p. 18.

⑨ *Macquarie Island*
An island composed of oceanic crust and mantle rocks, home to 850 000 penguin pairs.

⑩ *Shark Bay*
Large population of sea mammals, and 3.5 billion-year-old stromatolites representing the oldest life on earth. See also: Outback Coast & Mid-West p. 331.

⑪ *Tasmanian Wilderness*
Forest, rivers, caves, glacial lakes, and 40 Aboriginal sites pointing to at least 30 000 years' occupation. See also: Midlands & the North p. 549, The North-West p. 550 and South-West Wilderness p. 551.

⑫ *Uluru–Kata Tjuta National Park*
Massive rock formations in the desert, with numerous Aboriginal sites. See also: The Red Centre p. 406.

⑬ *Wet Tropics of Queensland*
Ancient rainforests containing an almost complete evolutionary record of Earth's plant life. See also: The Mid-Tropics p. 460 and The Far North p. 461.

⑭ *Willandra Lakes*
Haunting landscape of ancient lunettes, and site of excavations that showed an Aboriginal presence dating back 60 000 years. See also: The Outback p. 31.

MAGNIFICENT COASTLINE

The outback may be the place of Australian myth and legend, but most Australians choose to live – and holiday – within reach of a beach. The superb scenery of almost 60 000 kilometres of coastline, which takes in the country's hundreds of offshore islands, ranges from the sultry mangrove inlets of the far north to the white sweeping sands of the Indian Ocean coast and the rugged cliffs and legendary surf of the continent's south. Going to the beach in Australia can mean an afternoon of bodysurfing in the suburbs; a sojourn in a international tropical resort; time out in a reclusive fishing community; a drive along dramatic clifftops; or an exploration of one of several coastal World Heritage areas of great beauty and environmental significance.

▲ GREAT OCEAN ROAD, VIC.
Australia's most scenic coastal road links the many towns and attractions of this popular holiday region. The diverse attractions include top surfing breaks and their attendant communities, thickly forested mountains, family beaches, restaurants to suit everyone, wildlife-watching and some remarkable historic maritime sites. *See also: South-West Coast p. 143.*

▲ SOUTH-WEST COAST, WA
This wild and rugged coastline stretches from Cape Naturaliste to Cape Leeuwin, where the Indian and Southern oceans meet. There are a couple of small holiday villages and the popular hinterland winegrowing area of Margaret River, but most of the coast, with its cliffs, limestone caves, sand dunes and forests, is untouched by development and preserved within the Leeuwin–Naturaliste National Park. The area is renowned for its world-class surfing breaks. *See also: The South-West p. 326.*

▲ GOLD COAST, QLD
Australia's largest and best-known international resort is centred on an outstanding subtropical coastline, legendary for its 35 beautiful beaches, great surf and year-round sunshine. Once a sleepy holiday backwater, the area is now a major urban centre offering everything from 18-hole golf to designer shopping, deep-sea fishing, fine dining and major theme park attractions. *See also: Gold Coast & Hinterland p. 450.*

COAST SAFETY
Swim between the flags on patrolled beaches; on unpatrolled beaches, take a walk and enjoy the scenery. Most beaches in popular areas, particularly near towns, are patrolled in the high season and some are patrolled year round. Surfers should always check conditions with locals before taking to the water, as should anglers. Between October and May the extremely dangerous box stinger inhabits the coastal waters of Queensland and other parts of northern Australia; beachgoers are advised not to enter the water during this period. Sharks are common in Australian waters and warnings should be heeded. In northern Australia saltwater crocodiles are found in the sea, estuaries and tidal rivers, and on land at the water's edge, and are extremely dangerous. Do not enter the water or remain at the water's edge in known crocodile areas and, if unsure, check with the locals. Avoid the hot Australian sun and the damage it can do. Don't sunbake in the middle of the day, wear a hat at all times, and apply sunblock every two hours.

◀ **EAST COAST, TAS.**
One of Australia's most relaxed, old-fashioned and least hurried coastal regions, the East Coast is a haven of tiny fishing villages, bushland, farmland and pristine beaches. Highlights include the history and scenic beauty of Maria Island, superb underwater scenery near Bicheno, and the magnificent Freycinet Peninsula in the national park. *See also: The East Coast p. 548.*

▲ **FLEURIEU PENINSULA, SA**
Just an hour or two from Adelaide, this is South Australia's premier coastal retreat. On the east coast lie surf beaches, conservation parks and the busy resort town of Victor Harbour; on the west, the calmer blue waters of Gulf St Vincent, a string of pretty, low-key holiday villages and some stunning coastal scenery. Nudging the coast are some spectacular rural landscapes, incorporating one of Australia's top wine and food districts. *See also: Fleurieu Peninsula p. 255.*

▲ **QUEENSLAND COAST**
The hundreds of beautiful islands that crowd the Queensland coast include the islands near Brisbane; the outstanding World Heritage-listed Fraser Island; and about 1000 Great Barrier Reef islands (of which 22 offer accommodation). There is an island to suit everyone's idea of a holiday in paradise, be it a lonely campsite beneath a palm, an environmental escape, a fishing, water-skiing and diving adventure, or a week by the pool with a book. *See also: Brisbane Islands p. 449, Fraser Island & Coast p. 454 and Great Barrier Reef p. 455.*

SYDNEY BEACHES, NSW ▶
Sydney's surf beaches are the envy of many a metropolis. Flanking the city to the north and south, generous in length and width and admirably patrolled for most of the year, they provide an easy escape from the bustle of city life for thousands of residents and holiday-makers alike. The jewel in the crown is the world-famous Bondi – a cultural institution as much as a patch of sand and surf. *See also: Sydney p. 3.*

TOP BEACHES

① *The Basin beaches, Rottnest Island, WA*
On the island's north side, reef-protected beaches offer a safe haven for holidaying families. See also: Rottnest Island p. 324.

② *Bells Beach, Torquay, Vic.*
Australia's top surfing destination and site of the legendary Bells Beach Classic each Easter. See also: South-West Coast p. 143.

③ *Booderee National Park beaches, Jervis Bay, NSW*
A series of near-deserted beaches, surrounded by native bush and boasting what is claimed to be the whitest sand in the world. See also: The South Coast p. 26.

④ *Cable Beach, Broome, WA*
A luxurious sweep of white sand fronting turquoise waters and forming the scenic centrepiece of Australia's most remote and exotic resort town. See also: The Kimberley p. 332.

⑤ *Cactus Beach, Penong, SA*
The three famous surfing breaks of this remote destination are strictly for surfers with frontier spirit and the skill to match. See also: Eyre Peninsula & Nullarbor p. 251.

⑥ *Four Mile Beach, Port Douglas, Qld*
A beach so beautiful that it helped turn a sleepy seaside village into an international resort. See also: The Far North p. 461.

⑦ *Noosa National Park beaches, Qld*
A subtropical wonderland of peaceful, pandanus-fringed coves providing a retreat from the otherwise busy Sunshine Coast. See also: Sunshine Coast p. 453.

⑧ *Watego Beach, Byron Bay, NSW*
Tune in and drop out at this popular north-facing surf beach in one of Australia's less conventional towns. See also: Tropical North Coast p. 19.

⑨ *Whitehaven, Whitsunday Island, Qld*
A paradise on an uninhabited island: 7 km long, protected by national park – and pristine. See also: Great Barrier Reef p. 455.

⑩ *Wineglass Bay, Freycinet Peninsula, Tas.*
Bushland in national park opens up to this magnificently sculpted, crescent-shaped beach. See also: The East Coast p. 548.

WILD AUSTRALIA

Australia has some of the world's most distinctive plants and animals. Pouched mammals, prehistoric reptiles, majestic gums and brilliant desert flowers are just a sample of the country's many strange and beautiful living things. Around a quarter of overseas visitors to the country rate the wildlife as a major attraction and at least a couple of our more famous creatures – kangaroos and koalas in particular – are regarded as national icons. Beyond the fascination of individual species, Australia offers a series of exceptionally well-preserved natural environments, from marine waters to deserts and rainforests, where animals and plants can be seen in their natural settings and as part of the complex communities to which they belong.

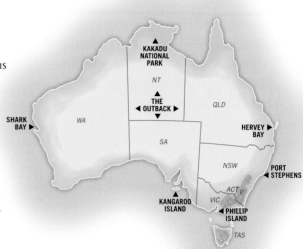

▼ SHARK BAY, WA

This World Heritage wonderland is best known for its bottlenose dolphins, which glide into the shallow waters of Monkey Mia and approach entranced visitors. Other highlights of this extraordinary area include the 230 bird species and a population of about 10 000 dugongs – the largest in the world. *See also: Outback Coast & Mid-West p. 331.*

▲ THE OUTBACK

Although referred to as the continent's 'Dead Heart', the vast areas of arid land at the centre of Australia support prolific and varied life including 2000 plant species and the highest concentration of reptiles in the world. Among its mammal species is the mighty red, the largest member of the kangaroo family with the male reaching two metres in height. *See also: The Outback p. 31, Flinders Ranges & Outback p. 252, The Kimberley p. 332, The Pilbara p. 334, The Red Centre p. 406 and Outback & Gulf Country p. 464.*

ISOLATION AND EVOLUTION

For 50 million years, wild Australia developed in isolation. The result is a unique set of plants and animals. Marsupials, represented by 180 species on this continent, are uncommon elsewhere. Likewise, the curious monotreme (an exclusive club with only platypuses and echidnas as members) is found nowhere else except New Guinea. When it comes to plants, only 15 per cent of our 28 000 indigenous species are found beyond Australia's shores. Aridity and poor soil have aided difference, with many species developing special characteristics to cope with harsh conditions. These adaptations have led to enormous biodiversity. Western Australia has about 11 000 wildflower species, giving the State one of the world's richest floras, while the rainforests of the east coast are among the most biologically complex places on Earth.

For more details on where to see wildlife, see the Wildlife-Watching features: NSW p. 72, Victoria p. 196, South Australia p. 280, Western Australia p. 364, Northern Territory p. 420, Queensland p. 501 and Tasmania p. 570.

▲ KAKADU NATIONAL PARK, NT

This large World Heritage-listed park is one of Australia's most biologically diverse and prolific regions. Around 1600 plant species thrive in Kakadu; they represent most of the native habitats of northern Australia. The wildlife is no less impressive and includes 280 bird species (one third of all Australian species), 123 reptile species, and 52 freshwater fish species. *See also: Kakadu & Arnhem Land p. 402.*

▼ KANGAROO ISLAND, SA

Isolation from the mainland has helped Australia's third largest island maintain an unusual concentration of wildlife. Highlights include a large colony of sea lions at Seal Bay; about 600 New Zealand fur seals at Cape du Couedic; 240 bird species; plenty of kangaroos, wallabies and possums; and koalas and platypuses. *See also: Kangaroo Island p. 256.*

◀ PORT STEPHENS, NSW

One of the largest koala colonies in Australia is to be found in the wild here at Tilligerry Habitat. Probably the country's best known native animal, these short, tailless marsupials are usually inactive for 20 hours a day and normally feed only on eucalypts. The waters of Port Stephens are home to around 160 bottlenose dolphins and serve as a thoroughfare for migrating humpback whales, which appear seasonally. *See also: Hunter Valley & Coast p. 14.*

◀ HERVEY BAY, QLD

Between August and October each year up to 400 humpback whales visit Hervey Bay, the whale-watching capital of Australia. It is believed that they pause here for rest and recreation on their 12 000-km journey between their breeding grounds in the Pacific Ocean and their feeding grounds in the Antarctic. Whale-watching cruises operate in the bay. *See also: Fraser Island & Coast p. 454.*

▲ PHILLIP ISLAND, VIC.

The little (fairy) penguins of Phillip Island are Victoria's best-known wildlife attraction. Each evening visitors can watch scores of these small creatures, measuring about 33 cm, returning to their sand burrows after a day of sea-fishing. Other island features include the koalas at the Koala Conservation Centre and the resident seals, which can be seen on a cruise to Seal Rocks or via satellite transmission at the Seal Rocks Sea Life Centre. *See also: Phillip Island & Gippsland p. 156.*

FLORAL EMBLEMS

Commonwealth of Australia

golden wattle (*Acacia pycnantha*)

New South Wales

waratah (*Telopea speciosissima*)

Australian Capital Territory

royal bluebell (*Wahlenbergia gloriosa*)

Victoria

common heath (*Epacris impressa*)

South Australia

Sturt's desert pea (*Swainsona formosa*)

Western Australia

red and green kangaroo paw (*Anigozanthos manglesii*)

Northern Territory

Sturt's desert rose (*Gossypium sturtianum*)

Queensland

Cooktown orchid (*Dendrobium phalaenopsis*)

Tasmania

Tasmanian blue gum (*Eucalyptus globulus*)

ADVENTURE HOLIDAYS

When it comes to adventure holidays and outdoor activities, Australia is a destination without peer. The continent's diverse and well-preserved environment of remote bush, snowfields, rugged cliffs, wild rivers, extensive coastline and underwater reefs is a mecca for the world's walkers, skiers, climbers, rafters, anglers and divers – and for all the first-time or would-be adventurers needing guidance. Many of these activities are offered within the boundaries of national parks and other conservation areas. Australia's regulated and well-organised tourism industry means that there are plenty of experienced operators offering training, tours, charters and equipment.

◄ GREAT BARRIER REEF, QLD

Novices and experienced divers alike come from around the world to test their skills in what is the most challenging and fascinating diving environment on earth. From Bundaberg to Cooktown, the facilities are extensive. The reef's islands, particularly the Whitsundays, are also known for their superb sailing opportunities. Most popular is bareboating, which involves hiring a fully equipped, easy-to-sail yacht (without a crew) for at least several days' touring. *See also: Great Barrier Reef p. 455.*

AUSTRALIAN ALPS, NSW & VIC. ►

This region, incorporating the ski slopes of Victoria and New South Wales, is the hallowed ground of winter sports enthusiasts including downhill and cross-country skiers. Less well known is the range of adventure activities available during the summer months; these include walking, caving, horseriding and whitewater rafting. *See also: Snowy Mountains p. 128 and The High Country p. 152.*

◄ TOP END, NT

The remote and sparsely populated tropical north attracts adventurers with a frontier spirit. Activities include barramundi fishing in the tidal rivers of the west coast or the crystal clear rivers of the east; deep-sea fishing via Darwin or the Gove Peninsula; canoeing in the gorges of Nitmiluk National Park; and 4WD expeditions in Litchfield National Park. *See also: Around Darwin p. 404, Gulf to Gulf p. 405 and Kakadu & Arnhem Land p. 402.*

SAFETY AND ENVIRONMENT

Adventure activities may involve risk that can prove fatal if participants are ill prepared. For the more hazardous sports, such as rock-climbing, cross-country skiing, sportfishing and diving, training with a professional operator is recommended, and even experienced participants should consider joining a tour or charter. Local visitor information centres and activity-based clubs can make recommendations. For bushwalking, a few rules stand fast. Always tell someone where you are going and when you expect to be back. For walks in national parks, get ranger advice about which walks suit your fitness. Always carry water – no matter how short the walk – and wear sturdy shoes and a hat. Observe fire warnings and fire bans. Walks of more than a day should be attempted only with a tour group or by experienced walkers. The flipside to many adventure activities in Australia is their potential for causing environmental damage. Participants can do their bit by observing the following: take only photographs (not flora, fauna or other matter) and stay on designated tracks.

▲ **OUTBACK COAST, WA**

Way off the beaten track, this remote coastal area has a range of adventure attractions that make the long journey worthwhile. The Ningaloo Reef, second only in scale and interest to the Great Barrier Reef, offers superb diving (where possibilities include swimming with whale sharks) and is also emerging as a popular sea-kayaking destination. Further south, Kalbarri National Park has 80 km of deep gorges for canoeing, as well as good walking tracks and top-class fishing off the coast. *See also: Outback Coast & Mid-West p. 331.*

▲ **SOUTHERN RIVERS, TAS.**

The wild rivers of the island State offer world-class whitewater rafting. The best known and probably most challenging run is the remote Franklin River in the depths of the south-west's World Heritage wilderness, where operators run tours of up to 12 days. Beginners should consider a one- or two-day tour of the gentler waters of the Picton River, to the south-east. *See also: The South-East p. 546 and South-West Wilderness p. 551.*

◀ **GRAMPIANS, VIC.**

Mount Arapiles, just to the west of the Grampians proper, is regarded as Australia's best rock-climbing venue. It has 3000 climbing routes across its surface, attracting enthusiasts from around the world. Rock-climbing, abseiling and bushwalking take place throughout the Grampians, as well as a range of other activities including ballooning via the town of Stawell. *See also: Grampians & Central West p. 144.*

TOP TRACKS

❶ *Australian Alps Walking Track, ACT, NSW & Vic.*
A 680-km track, usually completed in sections, taking in rivers, peaks and valleys. See also: Snowy Mountains p. 28 and The High Country p. 152.

❷ *Bibbulmun Track, WA*
A walk that traverses WA's spectacular south-west – 963 km from Kalamunda to Albany. See also: Darling Range & Swan Valley p. 325, The South-West p. 326 and Great Southern p. 327.

❸ *Blue Mountains, NSW*
Anything from an hour's stroll to a week-long trek, through some of Australia's most accessible bush. See also: Blue Mountains p. 22.

❹ *Flinders Ranges, SA*
A range of walks weaves across the ridges, gorges and river valleys of this ancient landscape. See also: Flinders Ranges & Outback p. 252.

❺ *Fraser Island, Qld*
Take a four-day, 76-km walk through this World Heritage island's sand-dune lake system. See also: Fraser Island & Coast p. 454.

❻ *Lamington National Park, Qld*
Around 160 km of walking tracks through primordial subtropical forests. See also: Gold Coast & Hinterland p. 450.

❼ *Larapinta Trail, NT*
A 220-km walking track along gorges, chasms, pools and arid habitats of the West MacDonnell Ranges. See also: The Red Centre p. 406.

❽ *Overland Track, Tas.*
Australia's best-known, spectacular long walk – 7 days from Cradle Mountain to Lake St Clair. See also: The North-West p. 550.

❾ *South Coast Track, Tas.*
A challenging 10-day hike that explores Tasmania's uninhabited south coast. See also: South-West Wilderness p. 551.

❿ *Wilsons Promontory, Vic.*
Pristine beaches and bush along 150 km of tracks in one of Australia's loveliest coastal parks. See also: Phillip Island & Gippsland p. 156.

◀ **BLUE MOUNTAINS, NSW**

The dense bush, misty valleys, deep canyons and rugged cliffs of this World Heritage Area make it a natural adventure playground for mountaineering enthusiasts. Rock-climbing, abseiling and canyoning are all on offer and the attendant facilities are excellent. Horseriding in the Megalong Valley is a gentler choice of activity, while the bushwalking throughout the mountain area is some of the best in the country. *See also: Blue Mountains p. 22.*

NEW SOUTH WALES

N ew South Wales, the first colony, dominated the early years of European settlement in Australia. The Premier State, as it styles itself, has a third of Australia's population (approximately 6 500 000 people), a bigger economy than any other State, and Australia's largest and most widely recognised city, Sydney.

Something for everyone

The 1000-km New South Wales coastline offers surfing beaches, and inlets, harbours, lakes and estuaries for fishing and boating. Inland, a steep escarpment rises to a succession of mountains and plateaus. The snowfields of the Australian Alps, rising to 2228 m at Mount Kosciuszko, attract skiers during winter. The high country gives way to the western slopes, a well-watered region of extensive grasslands supporting cattle, sheep and wheat, and to the dry western plains that cover nearly two-thirds of the State.

The climate is mainly temperate; only the north-west experiences extreme summer heat. On the coast, summers are warm and humid and winters pleasantly cool and generally dry. Winter frosts are widespread inland but only the Australian Alps receive regular snowfalls.

Economic backbone

New South Wales accounts for one-third of Australia's manufacturing, with the Port Kembla steel works providing the backbone of heavy industry. Vast black coal deposits near Gunnedah and

Idyllic Lord Howe Island, off the northern coast of New South Wales

Narrabri, and in the Hunter Valley and South Coast, contribute three-quarters of the State's income from mining. The rural economy rests on wheat and other cereals, wool, cattle and, more recently, cotton.

Tourism has grown rapidly. New South Wales is Australia's most visited State, with about 7 800 000 domestic and 2 280 000 international visitors each year. Many of these visits are for business, reflecting Sydney's growing importance in the globalised economy.

Historic building in the old mining town of Silverton, near Broken Hill

An ancient past

About 40 000 Aboriginal people lived in the area of New South Wales before white settlement. Evidence of Aboriginal occupation is everywhere: shell middens on the coast, canoe trees on the riverbanks, and numerous rock-art galleries. The discovery of a 60 000-year-old human skeleton at Lake Mungo in the dry west has forced a revision of the human history of the continent. Today about 100 000 Aboriginal and Torres Strait Islander people call the State home.

Nation or gaol?

Captain Cook claimed the eastern half of New Holland for the British Crown in 1770. Seventeen years later, eleven ships carrying 1487 people – 759 of them convicts – sailed from England to establish a penal colony in New South Wales. Captain Arthur Phillip, commander of the First Fleet, selected the site on Sydney Harbour known today as Circular Quay. In all, 72 326 male and 12 083 female convicts arrived from the United Kingdom. Transportation ceased in 1850 after the British government decided that New South Wales was more valuable as a destination for poor British emigrants, whose passages would be paid from the sale of colonial land.

Squatters and settlers

The colony struggled for thirty years until wool provided an export income. After 1813, squatters occupied the vast grasslands west of the Blue Mountains. Many Aboriginal people, deprived of their traditional hunting grounds, died from malnutrition, European diseases and at the hands of the white settlers. The most notorious massacre was at Myall Creek, near Glen Innes, in 1838 when white stockmen shot twenty-eight Aboriginal men, women and children and burned their bodies.

The discovery of gold north of Bathurst in 1851 brought many immigrants to New South Wales, including thousands of Chinese. In the second half of the 19th century, New South Wales lived off the sheep's back. Victoria, by encouraging industry through tariff protection, supplanted its mother colony – for a time – as the manufacturing and commercial centre of Australia.

Politics and power

Democracy was born in Australia with the election of twenty-four members in the thirty-six-seat New South Wales Legislative Council in 1843. Squatters dominated the first decade of the representative government but, after the advent of the fully elected Legislative Assembly in 1856, their influence declined. Universal male suffrage and the secret ballot followed two years later; women did not get the vote until 1902. The left-wing Labor Party has dominated in this State just as the conservative Liberal Party has been the party of power in Victoria.

Into the 21st century

Since New South Wales federated with the other five States to form the Commonwealth of Australia, the State has grown rapidly except during the depression years of the 1930s. Industrialisation and the mechanisation of farming have seen a large population shift to the cities since the 1920s.

Landmarks over the last fifty years have included the Snowy Mountains Scheme in the 1950s, the opening of the Sydney Opera House in 1973, the Bicentennial celebrations of 1988, the recent opening of Fox Studios Australia in Sydney to produce big-budget, high-tech films for international distribution, and the staging of the 2000 Olympic Games.

Yet the State's greatest achievement has been the expansion of its national parks. Many pristine beaches and waterways, foreshore bushland on Sydney Harbour, coastal rainforests, the wetlands and marshes of the western slopes and the austere and dramatically beautiful desert landscapes of the far west are now protected for the enjoyment of residents and visitors alike.

For more information on New South Wales, see Tourist Bureaus on p. 591.

SYDNEY

Breathtaking view from North Head to the Sydney Harbour Bridge

SYDNEY is Australia's largest city and boasts great restaurants, theatre, superb architecture, cultural diversity, and interesting historic sites. All this, set within a landscape of sweeping surf beaches, bushland, soaring cliffs and the glittering waters of Sydney Harbour, makes this city an irresistible destination.

VISITOR INFORMATION

Sydney Visitor Centre
Sailors' Home, 106 George St
The Rocks (02) 9255 1788

Sydney Visitor Centre Darling Harbour
33 Wheat Rd
(02) 9281 0788

Circular Quay Information Kiosk
cnr Alfred and Pitt sts 13 2077

Martin Place Information Kiosk
cnr Castlereagh St and Martin Pl.
(02) 9235 2424

Town Hall Information Kiosk
106 George St 13 2077

Manly Visitor Information Bureau
South Steyne (02) 9977 1088

www.visitnsw.com.au

With a population of 4 million and over 2 million international visitors per year, Sydney is regarded as one of the world's most beautiful cities. Its mild climate and sparkling harbour provide an outdoor playground for young and old, while the extensive parklands around the CBD make Sydney a rewarding city to explore.

GETTING AROUND

Airport shuttle bus
Airport Express (02) 9628 0027

Motoring organisation
National Roads & Motorists Association
(NRMA) 13 2132

Car rental
Avis 13 6333; Bayswater Car Rental
(02) 9360 3622; Budget 1300 362 848;
Hertz 13 3039; Thrifty 1300 367 227

Public transport
Bus, Train and Ferry Information Line 13 1500

Bus tours and specialty trips
Explorer Buses: red (city sights); blue (Bondi and
eastern suburbs); yellow (airport) 13 1500

Metro Monorail
(02) 8584 5288

Metro Light Rail
(02) 8584 5288

Taxis
ABC Taxis 13 2522; Legion Cabs
13 1451; Manly Cabs 13 1668; Premier Cabs
13 1017

Water Taxis
Harbour Shuttle (02) 9810 5010;
Water Taxis (02) 9955 3222

Cruises
Bounty Cruises (02) 9247 1789; Captain Cook
Cruises (02) 9206 1111; Matilda Cruises
(02) 9264 7377; Sydney Showboats
(02) 8296 7200

EXPLORING SYDNEY

Sydney is not a difficult city to negotiate despite the fact that many of its roads developed from the bullock tracks of the early colony. The transport system is large and well integrated, and a transport information phone number provides callers with tips on tickets, connections and timetables. Buy composite tickets and avoid the high cost of single fares. All the major attractions within the city can be reached easily on foot; to get to Darling Harbour take the monorail, light rail or ferry. For the many outlying attractions such as Manly, Taronga Zoo and the harbourside eastern suburbs, take a ferry ride and enjoy the harbour experience. If you are driving, an up-to-date road map is essential, given the number of changes to the network of late. Beware of having to use parking meters – they are very expensive. Inquire about the Explorer Buses that do circuits of the city attractions (red buses), the bay and beach attractions (blue), and the shuttle to the airport (yellow).

SYDNEY'S ICONS

The elegant soaring sails of the **Sydney Opera House** and the great arch of the **Sydney Harbour Bridge** dominate the harbour foreshore. Standing sentinel at the eastern end of Circular Quay, the Opera House is a breathtaking spectacle with its million white tiles

SYDNEY BY AREA

CITY CENTRE
MACQUARIE STREET & AROUND HYDE PARK
THE ROCKS
DARLING HARBOUR
THE EASTERN FRINGE
INNER EASTERN SUBURBS
OUTER EASTERN SUBURBS
SOUTHERN SHORES
WESTERN SUBURBS
NORTHERN SUBURBS

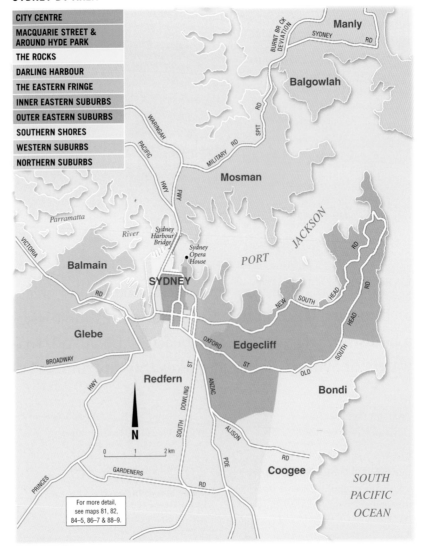

For more detail,
see maps 81, 82,
84–5, 86–7 & 88–9.

AMP Tower Centrepoint in its Olympic Glory

glinting in the sun and surrounded by the blue of the harbour. Its beauty belies its rather traumatic gestation period. The building was completed in 1973, but only after its Danish architect Jørn Utzon resigned in protest because of economically driven changes to his plans for the building's interior. Nevertheless, the Opera House is regarded as a stunning masterpiece and one of the great buildings of the 20th century. A guided tour of the building and its theatres is highly recommended.

The harbour bridge, opened in 1932, was designed by the engineer John Bradfield and is the second longest single span bridge in the world. (New York's Bayonne Bridge wins by a matter of centimetres.) Its broad deck is 134 metres above the water and carries 8 lanes for traffic, a double-track railway, a cycle lane and a pedestrian walkway offering stunning views. Pedestrian access is via Cumberland Street in The Rocks. The south-eastern Pylon Lookout contains the Harbour Bridge Exhibition featuring old photographs of this grand Sydney icon. It also offers magnificent harbour views from its viewing platform. The more adventurous can join a guided three-hour climb to the very top of the bridge. A headset links you to your guide and you wear a safety harness.

CITY CENTRE

To explore the city centre, start at **Circular Quay** on Sydney Cove, symbolic point of arrival for the city. Directly in front of the Quay is **Customs House**, an 1885 Classical Revival building, now home to a display of contemporary and indigenous art and culture, and interactive displays on Sydney's urban development.

Head east along Alfred Street, then take Phillip Street south towards the city. Along here you will find the **Justice and Police Museum**, which documents and displays the history of crime and punishment in Sydney – a limitless charter in this city of convict beginnings. On the intersection of Phillip and Bridge streets is the **Museum of Sydney**,

NOT TO BE MISSED IN SYDNEY
Map Ref.

AMP Tower Centrepoint — 81 E8
For a bird's eye view of the city

Art Gallery of New South Wales — 81 H7
One of the most comprehensive collections in the country

Australian National Maritime Museum — 81 B8
The maritime adventures of an island continent

Ferry Trip to Watsons Bay — 85 Q8
The foreshore of the eastern suburbs on display

Homebush Bay — 84 F8
Focus of the Sydney 2000 Olympic Games

Museum of Sydney — 81 F5
A thought-provoking survey of what has made Sydney the city it is

North Head — 85 R7
The best coastal views in Sydney

Sydney Opera House — 81 G3
An architectural giant of the 20th century

Oxford Street — 81 F10
Heartland of gay Sydney

Sydney Fish Market — 85 L10
Sydney seafood at its tastiest

TOP EVENTS

Sydney Festival (Jan.)
Arts, culture and summer fun

Gay and Lesbian Mardi Gras (Feb.)
Sydney's biggest party

Archibald Prize Exhibition (Mar.–Apr.)
National portrait prize – and the best gossip in Sydney

Australian Fashion Week (May)
The latest in Australian and international designs

Sydney Film Festival (June)
A winter retreat for filmophiles

City to Surf (July)
Challenging road race taking in Heartbreak Hill

Australian International Motor Show (Nov.)
Latest and futuristic models in a 10-day showcasing

For further details visit the web site
www.visitnsw.com.au

CLIMATE SYDNEY

	J	F	M	A	M	J	J	A	S	O	N	D
Max. °C	26	26	25	22	19	17	16	18	20	22	24	25
Min. °C	19	19	17	15	11	9	8	9	11	13	16	17
Rain mm	104	113	134	126	121	131	101	80	69	79	83	78
Raindays	12	12	13	12	12	12	10	10	11	12	11	12

built on the site of the first Government House. The amalgam of the old and the new is a theme of the innovative museum building – inside, the exhibitions chart the environmental, Aboriginal and European history of Sydney. Further down Bridge Street is the magnificent sandstone **Department of Lands** building (1887–90), with the niches in its facade filled with statues of prominent colonists. The length of Bridge Street, and the other small and irregular streets in the immediate area, offer some superb examples of ornate 19th-century architecture, with many of the buildings made from the distinctive Hawkesbury sandstone.

From Bridge Street, turn into Pitt Street to reach **Martin Place**, a sweeping pedestrian mall lined with some beautiful Victorian and Art Deco buildings. In the block between Pitt and George streets is the former General Post Office, which took 25 years to build and has now been transformed into **The Westin Sydney** hotel, with stunning interiors. Follow Pitt Street along to the main retail precinct of Sydney, which radiates out from the **Pitt Street Mall**. The magnificent arcade **The Strand**, opened in 1892, is a remnant of an era of grand jewel-like shopping arcades crammed with tiny boutiques and specialty shops. Access to the **AMP Tower Centrepoint** is around the corner on Market Street; here you can shop or take Sydney Sky-ride (a theme-park ride). An observation deck at 250 metres offers views to 85 kilometres on a clear day. Sculptures of athletes around the top of the tower made this Sydney landmark a focal point during the 2000 Olympics.

Continue west along Market Street, past the Pitt Street Mall to George Street and head south. Stop in at the **Sydney Hilton** to visit the Marble Bar, an 1893 bar designed in the Italian Renaissance style and rebuilt within the Hilton in the 1970s. Further along, more Italian opulence is to be found in the **Queen Victoria Building**, dubbed 'the most beautiful shopping centre in the world' by designer Pierre Cardin. The massive multiple-domed structure was built in 1898 as a produce market. Just across Druitt Street is the **Sydney Town Hall**,

constructed in the 1860s, on the site of a cemetery, to the designs of six different architects, which may explain its eclecticism. It houses a 19th-century organ with 8500 pipes and hosts regular concerts. Next door is **St Andrew's Cathedral**, Australia's oldest cathedral site, the foundation of which was laid in 1819; it contains memorials to Sydney's pioneers.

MACQUARIE STREET AND AROUND HYDE PARK

While The Rocks preserves much of the history of Sydney's early domestic, industrial and maritime history, it is **Macquarie Street** that holds the memory of the grand public endeavours of the Colonial Georgian and Victorian periods. At the harbour end of Macquarie Street is **Government House** (1837–45), set within the lush surroundings of the Royal Botanic Gardens. The magnificent state rooms, resplendent with 19th- and early 20th-century furnishings, may be seen on guided tours.

Further south, the **State Library of NSW** is the State's main reference library. In the old section of the building (1906) is the Mitchell Library, with its priceless collection of Australiana. Next door are three buildings, once all part of the original Sydney Hospital (dating from 1811), or the Rum Hospital as it was called, having being built by rum traders who performed the community service in exchange for the right to import that most valuable currency. The **Parliament of NSW** was the northern wing of the hospital, but became the seat of Government in the 1820s. Visitors can take a tour or view proceedings from the public galleries. The **Mint Museum**, now closed to the public, was the southern wing, but was appropriated in the 1850s when a building was needed to mint the gold from the NSW goldfields. Lying between the two is the present **Sydney Hospital**, built in 1894 after the original central building nearly collapsed as a result of the shoddy work of the rum builders. It is interesting to compare the elegance and restraint of the Georgian 'wings', with the fine display of the Victorian building.

Next stop is **Hyde Park Barracks Museum**, considered by many to be the finest example of Georgian Colonial architecture in the city. It was designed by Francis Greenway, completed in 1819, and used initially to house convicts. It now houses a fascinating museum of social and architectural history. Another Greenway building, **St James Church**, is to be found diagonally opposite in Queens Square. It was consecrated in 1824, making it Sydney's oldest church.

Macquarie Street veers east into College Street, where the soaring spires of **St Mary's Cathedral** are an impressive sight. The cathedral was built in 1882 by one of the world's chief proponents of the Gothic Revival style, William Wardell. Opposite, **Hyde Park** forms a small but important green corridor for the city centre. It was decreed and named in 1810 by Governor Macquarie and is now home to some interesting civic memorials, including the Art Deco **ANZAC Memorial** at its southern end. In Elizabeth Street, on the opposite side of Hyde Park, is **The Great Synagogue**, consecrated in 1878. Sydney's Jewish population was first established with the arrival of 16 Jewish convicts on the First Fleet.

Return to College Street and head south to the **Australian Museum**, Australia's oldest and most traditional museum, housing natural history displays, including one of the world's best indigenous Australian exhibitions, and the fascinating gallery Biodiversity – life supporting life.

THE ROCKS

The Rocks, with its winding streets and sandstone buildings, provides an intact and almost complete chronological overview of Sydney in the 19th century. Once the poorest area of Sydney, it now features the very popular weekend market, street entertainment, galleries, craft shops, traditional pubs and outdoor cafes. And of course there are the many historic sites of interest, best explored by picking up a copy of the excellent self-guide walking tour from the **Sydney Visitor Centre** in the old Sailors' Home in George Street.

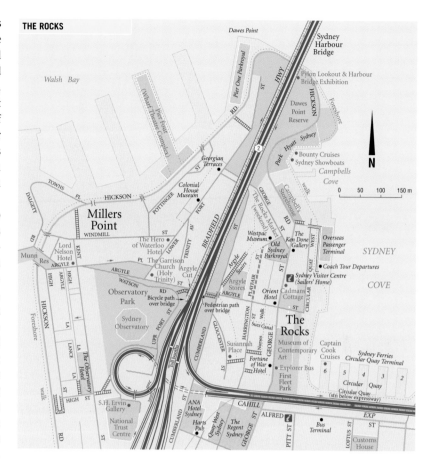

THE ROCKS

Down on the waterfront, **Campbell's Storehouse** has been a Sydney landmark since building began in 1839. A little further along the waterfront towards the city is **Cadmans Cottage**, built in 1816 and the oldest existing residence in Australia. It now houses an information centre for Sydney Harbour National Park. Nearby, lodged in an Art Deco building on the western flank of Circular Quay, is the **Museum of Contemporary Art**, the first institution in Australia dedicated to the contemporary visual arts. Behind the museum, up the hill in Gloucester Street, is **Susannah Place**, a block of terraces boasting continuous domestic occupancy from 1844–1990. Now a museum (open weekends), its displays evoke the domestic, working-class culture of the old Rocks. Nearby is Argyle Street, site of the **Argyle Stores** built in stages between 1826 and the 1880s, now a retail centre, and the **Argyle Cut**, a tunnel hewn from rock by the convicts.

THEATRES AND CINEMAS	Map Ref.
Belvoir Street Theatre An old tomato sauce factory in Surry Hills, now staging Sydney's most innovative theatre	85 M11
Capitol Theatre 1920s cinema designed as an Italian palace, hosts blockbuster musicals	81 D11
Concert Hall One of the best concert halls in the world, located at the Sydney Opera House	81 G3
Imax Theatre A giant screen and a crystal clear format	81 C9
State Theatre A 1929 temple to cinema-going, complete with golden baroque interiors	81 E8
Wharf Theatre Complex Spectacular old wharf at Walsh Bay with breathtaking views; home to Sydney Theatre and Sydney Dance Companies	81 D2

For a complete guide to what's on around Sydney, buy the *Sydney Morning Herald* on Friday for its lift-out 'Metro' section.

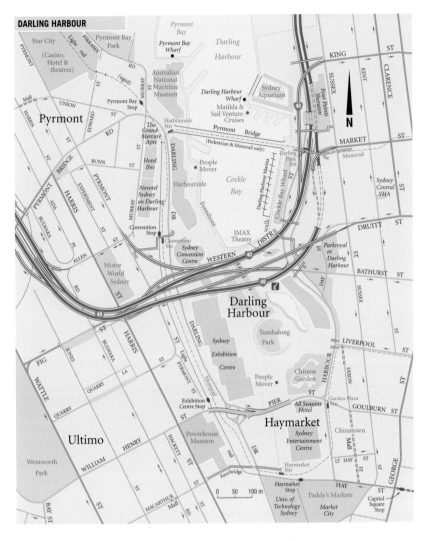

DARLING HARBOUR

RESTAURANTS AND CAFES

A restaurant guide is essential in Sydney. Best choices are the Sydney Morning Herald Good Food Guide, published by Anne O'Donovan, for a general run-down, and the SBS Eating Guide to Sydney, published by Allen & Unwin, for a roundup of the top choices in multicultural dining. The range in Sydney is incredible. Insiders' tips include: the cafes of Victoria Street, Kings Cross; the food halls of Chinatown, Haymarket; the stalls at the Sydney Fish Market; Norton Street, Leichhardt for Italian; Cleveland Street, Surry Hills for Lebanese; Liverpool Street in the city for Spanish; and the cafes at Hyde Park Barracks Museum, Centennial Park, the MCA, the Royal Botanic Gardens, the Art Gallery of New South Wales and the National Maritime Museum – for proof that good eating and tourist attractions are not necessarily mutually exclusive concepts.

From Argyle Street you can take the pedestrian footpath north along Cumberland Street, which crosses the Sydney Harbour Bridge. The quiet streets of **Millers Point**, to the west of the bridge, are where you will find some magnificent Georgian terraces, particularly in Lower Fort Street, and one of Sydney's oldest pubs, **The Hero of Waterloo Hotel**. Another historic pub is nearby, the **Lord Nelson Hotel** in Kent Street. Also in this area – on a more heavenly plane – is **The Garrison Church (Holy Trinity)**, and **Sydney Observatory** (1858), in Observatory Park, featuring night viewing and an astronomy museum. Nearby, housed in an old military hospital dating from 1815, are the offices of the **National Trust Centre** and the **S. H. Ervin Gallery** with its regular historical and contemporary cultural exhibitions.

DARLING HARBOUR

Darling Harbour is a major leisure precinct, with wonderful landscaped plazas and walkways and a whole series of stark structuralist buildings housing some of the city's major cultural and entertainment institutions. Ferries, the Monorail and the Light Rail provide the links from the city. Visitors to the area should inquire about composite tickets available for many of the attractions. At Darling Harbour, a fleet of People Movers, trucks styled to look like mini-trains, pick up and drop off at key points.

The National Trust-classified **Pyrmont Bridge** crosses Darling Harbour. Near the bridge's eastern end is the **Sydney Aquarium**. Here you will find underwater tunnels from which you can view an amazing array of sea life, including giant sharks and stingrays, and a host of other displays – from a tank of Australian fur seals to a living replica of the Great Barrier Reef. From the aquarium, walk south along the foreshore to **Cockle Bay Wharf**, a food and dining precinct with three levels of terraces, waterfront promenades, a food court, al fresco cafes and five-star restaurants. Nearby is the **IMAX Theatre**, featuring an 8-storey-high screen.

A short distance away (follow the signs) is one of Sydney's most tranquil little corners, the **Chinese Garden**. A gift from Guangdong Province in China, the garden incorporates a traditional design of lakes, waterfalls, pavilions and rare exotic species. From here, walk along Pier Street to reach **Chinatown**, Haymarket, the cultural and commercial heartland for Sydney's large Chinese population. The many Chinese restaurants and shops of the district cluster around the pedestrian mall of Dixon Street and spill over into the connecting streets. At the south end is **Paddy's Markets**, a rather suburbanised version of the magnificently rowdy fresh food markets that were once here.

Catch the Monorail or Light Rail or walk across to the **Powerhouse Museum**, off Harris Street. The museum is in a dramatically renovated and extended

old power station. The collection, housed here since 1988, provides a user-friendly, imaginative overview of the cultural, social, technological and scientific efforts and achievements of Australia and, in some instances, other parts of the world. Further north along Harris Street you can visit **Motor World Sydney**, where displays cover over a century of automotive history.

At the north-western corner of Darling Harbour is the **Australian National Maritime Museum**. This world-class institution houses a series of imaginative displays that chart what must be the single most important theme in the history of this island continent: all maritime traditions are covered, from the seagoing ways of the Aboriginal people to European exploration, transportation, war, trade, immigration and of course beach culture. From here take the People Mover or Monorail to **Harbourside**, a shopping centre with restaurants, inexpensive eateries and an exciting sound and visual experience – Cinimagic.

Nearby, on the western edge of Darling Harbour, **Star City**, Sydney's first and only legal casino, features interiors inspired by the Australian landscape, and bars, restaurants, shops, theatres and a hotel. Use the Light Rail to get there.

The Light Rail can be taken from Star City to the **Sydney Fish Market**, a short distance away in Pyrmont. This large, vibrant complex, with its many stalls selling an outstanding array of seafood, is a mecca for those pilgrims on the trail of Sydney's best gourmet experiences.

THE EASTERN FRINGE

The eastern fringe of the city centre includes the parklands of The Domain and the Royal Botanic Gardens, and is one of the most beautiful parts of Sydney. It is also an area that, in its essential character, has hardly changed since the early years of the colony, thanks to Governor Lachlan Macquarie who had the wit to claim the beautiful foreshore as parkland, thereby thwarting two centuries of potential development.

Start at the **Art Gallery of New South Wales** on Art Gallery Road in The Domain. The gallery is housed in a magnificent late-19th-century structure with the classical features so favoured for public buildings at the time. It houses major national and international collections, including the largest permanent collection of Aboriginal art in the world. Opposite is one of the two parts of **The Domain** where, during the Sydney Festival, huge opera, jazz and classical music concerts are held (they are free). The other part of The Domain runs north towards the harbour along Mrs Macquaries Road, past **Mrs Macquaries Chair**, which the Governor ordered to be carved out of the sandstone ledge for his wife, so that she could sit before her favourite harbour view. The road loops around the point, offering extraordinary glimpses of the inner city foreshore.

The **Royal Botanic Gardens** occupy a prime position on the shores of Farm Cove. The site of Sydney's first farm, they were declared in 1816, and have since been developed into a magnificent sweep of landscaped grounds, with some 17 000 native and exotic species and a series of fascinating botanic and historic attractions. The gardens' visitor facilities include an excellent cafe/restaurant, a garden shop, a People Mover for tired legs and an impressive self-guide audio trail. Follow the foreshore or catch a People Mover around to Bennelong Point, the site of the Sydney Opera House.

INNER EASTERN SUBURBS

The fascinating **Kings Cross** district marks the eastern border of the city. The 19th- and 20th-century houses and apartment blocks, set along European-style tree-lined avenues, have over many years been home to an incongruous mix of migrants, artists, intellectuals, the wealthy and the seriously disadvantaged. The area – something of an Australian Soho – is still one of the most culturally diverse sections of the city, and certainly one of its liveliest. Catch a train to Kings Cross Station or walk through **Woolloomooloo**, a small suburb with a maritime history evidenced today by its tiny cottages, once the homes of the wharf labourers, and the 1914 **Woolloomooloo Finger Wharf** on Cowper Wharf Road. Further along the same road is **Garden Island**, Sydney's naval base, usually closed to the public, but rows of navy ships can be seen berthed at the docks.

Take the **McElhone Stairs** to **Potts Point**, the 'upper class end of a lower class district', as used to be the case. The leafy avenue of Victoria Street has some spectacular examples of multi-storey Georgian and Victorian terraces, while Macleay Street is the site for a series of beautiful apartment blocks built in the first few decades of the 20th century, many of them boasting exquisite Art Deco features.

Sydney Opera House and city skyline

In Elizabeth Bay on Onslow Avenue is one of the district's few remaining mansions – **Elizabeth Bay House**, built in 1839 for the Colonial Secretary, to a design by prominent colonial architect, John Verde. This spectacular property, praised particularly for its vestibule with a domed ceiling and sweeping staircase, is fully furnished as a museum charting the life of the well-to-do classes in 19th-century Sydney.

Elizabeth Bay leads to the Darlinghurst Road end of Kings Cross, the district's strip of sleaze. Past the intersection of William Street is the lively cafe precinct of Victoria Street, and the **Sydney Jewish Museum** on Darlinghurst Road towards Oxford Street. The museum is a moving and impressive centre, which explores the history of Judaism, the Australian Jewish heritage and the terrible legacy of the Holocaust. Opposite, on the corner of Burton Street, behind massive stone walls, is the old **Darlinghurst Gaol**, built in the early 1800s, and an art college since 1921.

OUTER EASTERN SUBURBS

The eastern suburbs run along the South Head peninsula. Flanked by the harbour on one side and ocean on the other, and offering beautiful views and leafy surrounds, they represent Sydney's expensive strip of real estate. **Surry Hills** and **Paddington**, both slums just 30 years ago, have been revamped with the dollar of the young professional classes. Both feature an extraordinary range of 19th-century terrace housing, and streets that are in many instances completely intact from that era. Surry Hills has always veered on the side of the working class and its terraces are at the cramped end of the scale. One of its main attractions is the **Brett Whiteley Studio** in Raper Street, which houses many of the paintings of this famous Australian artist who died prematurely in 1992.

Among the galleries, shops and restaurants of Paddington, there are very interesting historic sites, including the massive **Victoria Barracks** in Oxford Street, built in the 1840s and considered one of the best examples of Imperial military architecture in the world. Pick up a copy of the National Trust's self-guide brochure *Paddington Walk*, and stroll along the north-facing hills of this expensive little pocket. Just beyond Paddington, off Oxford Street, is **Centennial Park**, 220 hectares of woodlands, lakes, trails and cultivated gardens.

The habourside suburbs are best seen from a Rose Bay–Watsons Bay ferry, which skirts along the foreshores of Darling Point, Potts Point and Vaucluse, providing views of the exclusive houses and gardens en route. **Vaucluse House**, located in Olola Avenue, Vaucluse, Australia's most expensive suburb, is one of the city's most important historic sites. The house belonged to W. C. Wentworth, one of three explorers to first cross the Blue Mountains, and a major public figure in the colony. He and his wife Sarah, both with solid convict connections, moved into the house in 1829, and over the years made a series of eccentric additions to the property to house their growing family. Set within a spectacular 19th-century landscaped garden, it is fully furnished and open to the public.

The last suburb on the peninsula is **Watsons Bay**, a maritime village, virtually unchanged this century except for the expensive makeovers to the tiny weatherboard cottages that line the impossibly narrow streets. This suburb of great charm has been one of Sydney's most popular places for a picnic and a walk for many years. To get here, you can catch the ferry from Circular Quay, then relax on the foreshore with fish and chips or take a stroll to the swimming beach of **Camp Cove**. Follow the path through the national park at the east end of the beach, out to the point of South Head; wander back along the ocean side of the peninsula. Along the clifftops you will pass **The Gap**, a notorious suicide spot, and **Macquarie Lighthouse**, which has been guiding ships through the heads since 1883.

SOUTHERN SHORES

Sydney's southern suburbs, best known for their spectacular beaches, also boast some of Australia's most important historic sites. The sweeping crescent of **Bondi Beach** marks the start of the southern beaches. With its excellent swimming, strolling and picnicking spots, it offers a summer haven only 7 kilometres from the city. The surrounding suburb is full of life, with many cafes, restaurants, interesting shops and Sunday markets. Further south, **Tamarama** is known for its in-crowd, while **Bronte** is more of a family affair, with spacious foreshore parklands. The magnificent 19th-century **Waverley Cemetery** sits on the hill past the southern end of the beach.

Further south is **Botany Bay**, the site of the first recorded European landing on the east coast of Australia. On its northern peninsula is **La Perouse**, reached from the city via Anzac Parade or Bunnerong Road. It is named for the French navigator who set up camp here in 1788, having being pipped to the colonisation post by the First Fleet, which had set down a few days earlier. Preserved by the Botany Bay National Park, the area contains the **La Perouse Monument**, **La Perouse Museum** and **Bare Island**, the last a curious 19th-century fortification built to protect the southern coastline from what the colonists were sure was an imminent Russian invasion. **Kurnell** lies across the bay on the southern peninsula and is where Captain Cook and the crew of the *Endeavour* stepped ashore in 1770. The event is commemorated and explained with displays in **The Discovery Centre**, which also has excellent exhibits on the Aboriginal culture and natural environment of the area.

The sunsoaked beachside suburb of **Cronulla** forms the southern border of Sydney. Catch a train from the city to Cronulla, then hop aboard a ferry to explore **Port Hacking**, or to take a ride to the **Royal National Park** across the water. The **Sydney Tramway Museum** is located inland at Loftus and reached via the Princes Highway. The museum has the largest collection of trams in the Southern Hemisphere and runs novelty tram trips.

WESTERN SUBURBS

Immediately to the west of the city are the suburbs of **Balmain** and **Glebe**. Both are essentially working-class districts that have found themselves elevated to 'desirable' by the increasing number of Sydneysiders who want to live where the action is. Glebe can be reached by one of the bus routes along Parramatta Road, whereas Balmain is best reached by ferry. They are wonderful places to explore on foot, full of aged sandstone churches, weatherboard cottages, Victorian terraces, the odd imposing mansion and networks of tiny streets, which every so often reveal glittering harbour views framed by rooftops and trees. Darling Street in Balmain is particularly

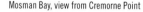

Mosman Bay, view from Cremorne Point

Manly Cove, Manly's harbourside beach

interesting for its many 19th-century public buildings. The shops, restaurants and cafes that fill the village-like centres of these suburbs are terrific, as are the lively weekend markets. Across Parramatta Road from Glebe is the **University of Sydney**, Australia's oldest university, famed for its ivy-covered 19th-century buildings and beautiful landscaping.

Homebush Bay on the southern shores of the Parramatta River is where you will find **Sydney Olympic Park**. Also of interest is the magnificent **Bicentennial Park**, with its 60 hectares of dryland and 40 hectares of conservation wetlands replicating the complex ecology of one Australia's most sensitive natural environments.

Parramatta, 22 kilometres west of the city centre, is a city within Sydney, yet retains its individuality and is the location of some of the nation's most historic sites. A good way to travel to Parramatta is along Parramatta River aboard a RiverCat from Circular Quay. Visit **Elizabeth Farm** (1793) in Alice

Street. Once the home of John and Elizabeth Macarthur, pioneers of the Australian wool industry, it incorporates the oldest European building in Australia. **Old Government House** (1799) is in Parramatta Park. It is Australia's oldest public building and has the country's best collection of Colonial furniture. Stroll along the **Parramatta River**, where there are some restaurants and pleasant scenery.

For an up-close encounter with Australian native wildlife and some exotic creatures, visit **Koala Park Sanctuary** at West Pennant Hills, **Featherdale Wildlife Park** at Doonside, and **Wonderland Sydney** at Eastern Creek. Wonderland is also an entertainment park with rides, games and large-scale daily shows.

NORTHERN SUBURBS

The northern suburbs of Sydney have for a long time represented the best of the good life, the place where a big cosmopolitan city meets a superb natural landscape of native bush, stunning surf beaches and tiny shell-like harbour coves.

The North Shore is reached via the Harbour Bridge or the Harbour Tunnel (both off the Cahill Expressway), with many areas accessible by ferry from Circular Quay. **Taronga Zoo** is best reached by ferry. From the wharf, visitors are whisked to the top of the hill via cable car, with knockout harbour views a part of the experience. The zoo, set within 30 hectares of harbourside bushland, was first opened in 1916. Its thousands of animals are housed within enclosures that are designed to be kind to animals and spectators alike. Of particular interest is the Free Flight Birdshow, an extraordinary display staged in an open amphitheatre, and the Friendship Farm, where children can meet tame animals.

Balmoral Beach, several suburbs north along Spit Road, is one of Sydney's loveliest harbourside beaches. Further north is Manly, Sydney's version of an old-fashioned, seaside, holiday village. Although well and truly a suburb, it has always had the laid-back festive atmosphere of a place 'a thousand miles from care' as the slogan goes. Catch the **Manly Ferry**, visit the old-fashioned fun park and take a stroll along **The Corso**, which crosses the narrow strip of land separating harbour and ocean. Swim at **Manly Beach**, one of Sydney's best, or walk south to the pretty rock pools of Fairy Bower Beach, and the protected waters of Shelly Beach. Visit **Oceanworld**, a top-class aquarium, or take a bus to North Head for a trip around Sydney's **Old Quarantine Station**.

A drive north along Pittwater Road reveals many of Sydney's picturesque northern beaches and it is tempting to stop at every one. At the northern end of Sydney's outer limits is an exclusive nest of suburbs set along the **Barrenjoey Peninsula**. These salt- and sun-saturated neighbourhoods – Avalon, Newport, Whale Beach and Palm Beach – boast beautiful surf beaches on one side and the calm stretch of Pittwater – perfect for water sports – on the other. Best known is **Palm Beach**, where you'll find good restaurants, walks, coastal lookouts, and ferry tours of Pittwater.

It is not surprising that Sydney, with its stunning harbour, cosmopolitan lifestyle, mild climate and diverse range of attractions and experiences, is a popular destination for both interstate and international visitors.

DAY TOURS FROM SYDNEY

Blue Mountains
Only 100 km from Sydney, the rugged cliffs and bush-lined valleys of the Blue Mountains provide the city with a superb nature retreat. Aboriginal cave art, heritage gardens, historic villages, walking trails and adventure sports are among the many attractions. *For more details see* Classic Tour *p. 77 and region coverage, p. 22.*

Southern Highlands
Nestled into the folds, hills and escarpments of the Great Dividing Range, the Southern Highlands offer rural scenery, historic townships, European-style gardens, festivals, and wonderful guesthouses and restaurants. *For more details see region coverage, p. 24.*

Ku-ring-gai Chase and Hawkesbury
North of Sydney, Ku-ring-gai Chase National Park encloses a magnificent stretch of bush set around the glittering waters of the mouth of the Hawkesbury River. Fishing, river cruises and bushwalking are popular activities. The Upper Hawkesbury, north-west of Sydney, is Australia's most historic rural area – a scenic river landscape dotted with charming Georgian villages. *For more details see region coverage, p. 16.*

South along the coast
Royal National Park, abutting Sydney's southern suburbs, encloses a landscape of sandstone outcrops, woodland, rainforest, cliffs and beaches – perfect for walks, fishing, wildlife-watching and camping. Beyond lies the city of Wollongong and pleasant resort towns set against a magnificent stretch of surf coast. *For more details see region coverage, p. 24.*

Hunter Valley
Around 60 wineries are to be found in the Lower Hunter area – Australia's oldest wine-growing district – radiating out from Cessnock, about 160 km from Sydney. Start your day tour at the wine centre in town. Book into one the district's many excellent restaurants or pack a picnic and enjoy a rustic landscape of rolling hills and neat rows of vines. *For more details see region coverage, p. 14.*

Activity on the northern beaches

HUNTER VALLEY & COAST

The Hunter is one of Australia's top wine-producing regions, but this is only a small part of its charm for visitors. Rich alluvial plains, historic towns, horse-breeding properties and tree-lined country avenues create one of the State's most attractive rural landscapes. In the north-east, the region is bound by the high cliffs and rainforest wilderness of Barrington Tops National Park. Over on the coast is Lake Macquarie, a saltwater paradise for boaters and anglers, while to its north lies Newcastle, Australia's second oldest city and major port and industrial centre. Further north again, past the 32-km stretch of Stockton Beach, is Port Stephens, a vast semi-enclosed body of water populated by dolphins and ringed by the white volcanic sands of near-perfect beaches.

EXPERIENCE IT!

① **Trek** the 4-hour-return Rocky Crossing Walk through subtropical rainforest in Barrington Tops National Park

② **Dine** at Chez Pok in Peppers Guest House (at Pokolbin), one of the Hunter's many fine restaurants

③ **Shop** for antiques, crafts and curios at heritage-listed Morpeth, Australia's oldest river port

④ **Take** a tour to see Aboriginal hand stencils at Wollombi

⑤ **Fish** the fresh waters of Lake Glenbawn near Scone

VISITOR INFORMATION

Hunter Valley (Cessnock): (02) 4990 4477

Newcastle: (02) 4974 2999

Port Stephens (Nelson Bay): (02) 4981 1579; 1800 808 900

www.winecountry.com.au

CLIMATE CESSNOCK

	J	F	M	A	M	J	J	A	S	O	N	D
Max. °C	31	31	29	26	21	19	18	19	23	25	29	30
Min. °C	17	17	16	12	7	7	4	6	9	12	14	16
Rain mm	80	84	79	64	59	59	45	41	43	57	60	76
Raindays	8	8	8	7	6	7	6	6	6	7	7	8

FOCUS ON

Top Wines

The Tyrrell family pioneered the wine industry in the Pokolbin district late in the 1850s. The McWilliams and the Draytons soon followed. Premium wines made from shiraz and semillon grapes grown on the lower Hunter's alluvial red soils are unique. A Hunter shiraz is dusty, mellow and soft on the palate. A Hunter semillon, Australia's most distinctive white, is bone-dry with a suggestion of citrus; try Tyrrells Vat 1 Semillon. In good years, Hunter chardonnay ranks with Australia's best; Tyrrells Vat 47 Chardonnay is notable. McWilliam's Mount Pleasant Elizabeth (semillon) and Philip (shiraz) are aged for 5 years before release and offer a relatively inexpensive introduction to the delights of Hunter reds and whites. McWilliam's more expensive Rosehill Shiraz provides a consistent example of a top-quality Hunter red. The Allandale and Capercaillie estates offer splendid chardonnay and semillon and very accessible shiraz. For a tiny winery producing superlative shiraz and chardonnay, look in on Thalgara.

Upper Hunter

This striking landscape of alluvial plains and rugged mountains supports 7 wineries, including the large estates of Rosemount and Arrowfield. The area just to the north, around Scone, is one of the world's largest thoroughbred horse breeding centres, and boasts some spectacular rural scenery.

Lower Hunter

The Lower Hunter is Australia's oldest and best known winegrowing district. Around 3000 ha of vines and over 60 wineries are set across rolling hills against the backdrop of the Broken Back Range. A day's tour should start at the wine and information centre in Cessnock. Excellent food and accommodation are available throughout the region.

Lake Macquarie

This is a magnificent saltwater expanse, four times the size of Sydney Harbour, offering every kind of water sport from angling to skiing, swimming, diving, sailing or kayaking. Don't miss Dobell House at Wangi Wangi (Sundays only), former home of prominent Australian painter William Dobell.

Barrington Tops National Park
Situated on one of the highest points of the Great Dividing Range (1600 m), Barrington Tops is the most southerly of the State's World Heritage Rainforest Reserves. Rugged basalt cliffs, cool-temperate and subtropical rainforests, gorges, waterfalls and a touch of light snow in winter make this stunning landscape a popular spot with walkers, campers and climbers.

Maitland
Situated on the Hunter River, Maitland was established in the 1820s to service the European settlers who cultivated the rich alluvial plains of the surrounding district. In the early 20th century, it boomed with the discovery of rich coal seams in the valley. Today it remains an elegant, prosperous-looking centre with intact streetscapes and a wealth of heritage buildings.

TOP EVENTS

Feb.	*Vintage Festival (Lower Hunter)*
Mar.	*Beaumont Street Jazz and Arts Festival (Newcastle)*
Apr.	*Heritage Afloat (Lake Macquarie)*
Apr.	*Harvest Festival (Cessnock)*
Apr.	*Heritage Month (Maitland)*
May	*Lovedale Long Lunch (Lovedale, near Cessnock)*
May	*Jazz Festival (Morpeth)*
Aug./ Sept.	*Cathedral Flower Festival (Newcastle)*
Sept.	*Garden Ramble (Maitland)*
Sept.	*Folk Festival (Wollombi)*
Oct.	*Jazz in the Vines (Cessnock)*
Oct.	*Opera in the Vineyards (Cessnock)*
Oct.	*Mattara Festival (Newcastle)*
Oct.	*Festival of Wine and Roses (Singleton)*
Dec.	*King Street Fair (Newcastle)*

Port Stephens
Port Stephens, reached via the township of Nelson Bay, is a haven of calm blue waters and sandy beaches, offering excellent boating, fishing and swimming. It is also something of a wildlife haven: about 160 bottlenose dolphins have permanent residence here, migrating whales can be seen in season from a cruise of Stockton Sand Dunes, and koalas can be spotted near Tilligerry Habitat.

For more detail see maps 96, 97, 102 & 105. For descriptions of ❶ towns see Towns from A to Z (p. 32).

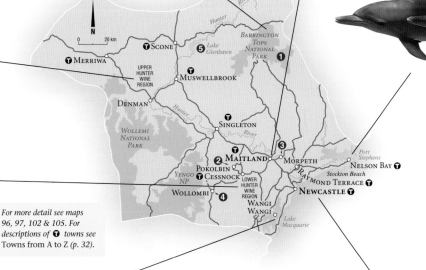

Newcastle
Australia's second oldest city was founded as a penal colony in 1804. Newcastle rises up the surrounding hills from a spectacular surf coastline, its buildings a pleasant chaos of architectural styles from different historical periods. The city boasts a range of attractions including good restaurants, a premier regional gallery and many historic sites.

CENTRAL COAST & HAWKESBURY

Within an hour of Sydney, visitors will discover a vast and largely unexplored wilderness, Australia's most historic farming district, the glittering waters and sandstone cliffs of one of the country's most popular national parks and a great sweep of magnificent coastline supporting lively holiday settlements. Explore these places as day trips from the city, or take a couple of days, book into a B&B, a caravan park or luxury resort, and discover the charms and diversity of Sydney's favourite weekend retreats.

TOP EVENTS

Jan.	*Entertainment on Waterfront Stage (The Entrance)*
May	*Bridge to Bridge Powerboat Classic (Windsor)*
June/ July	*Food, Wine and Chocolate Festivals (Terrigal)*
Mar.	*Central Coast Chilli Festival (Erina, near Terrigal)*
Sept.	*Hawkesbury District Orchid Spring Show (Richmond)*
Oct.– Nov.	*Fruits of the Hawkesbury Festival (Windsor, Richmond)*
Nov.	*Oyster and Wine Festival (Woy Woy)*
Dec.	*Tuggerah Lakes Mardi Gras Festival (The Entrance)*

EXPERIENCE IT!

❶ **Explore** Old Sydney Town and the Australian Reptile Park, both west of Gosford

❷ **Visit** the Bulgandry Aboriginal Engraving site in Brisbane Water National Park

❸ **Take** a drive through the bountiful fruit-growing district of the Yarramalong Valley

VISITOR INFORMATION

Terrigal: (02) 4385 4430;
1300 130 708
www.cctourism.com.au

Windsor: (02) 4577 2310
www.hawkesburyvalley.com

FOCUS ON

Fishing

Fishing is one of the area's great attractions. There are plenty of boat ramps and boat-hire outlets and no shortage of local bait and tackle suppliers. The trouble-free waters of the Hawkesbury are good for bream, luderick, mulloway and flathead, with bass in the upper reaches. Bream and whiting are a possibility for anglers in the calm stretches of Brisbane Water and Tuggerah Lake. On the coast, beach fishing yields bream, tailor and mulloway. There are excellent rock platforms, particularly around Terrigal (and including The Skillion), where anglers try for some of the big ocean fish, including tuna and kingfish.

Macquarie towns

In 1810 Governor Macquarie established a number of towns on the high ground of the fertile river plains north-west of Sydney. The area preserves some of Australia's oldest buildings and sites. Windsor's St Matthew's Church (pictured) is the oldest Anglican church in Australia, built in 1817. Even older is the surrounding cemetery. It contains graves dating back to 1810, some belonging to pioneers who arrived on the First Fleet.

For more detail see maps 86–7, 90–1 & 94. For descriptions of ❶ towns see Towns from A to Z (p. 32).

Wollemi National Park

This 500 000-ha wilderness includes areas still unmapped. The 1994 discovery of a new tree species in a rainforest gully was compared with finding a living dinosaur. Take the 1-km walk to the Glow Worm Tunnel, or visit the Colo River west of Wisemans Ferry, where there are walks, canoeing and camping.

CLIMATE GOSFORD

	J	F	M	A	M	J	J	A	S	O	N	D
Max. °C	27	27	26	24	20	18	17	19	21	24	25	27
Min. °C	16	17	15	12	8	6	4	5	7	11	13	15
Rain mm	139	148	150	136	119	128	79	76	69	83	92	102
Raindays	11	11	11	11	9	10	8	8	8	9	10	10

Central Coast

This holiday region contains a number of coastal communities fronting surf beaches and calm-water salt lakes. Choose cosmopolitan Terrigal, the family-friendly pace of The Entrance or the exclusivity of Pearl Beach near Woy Woy. National parks in the area provide a peaceful alternative to the busy beach scene.

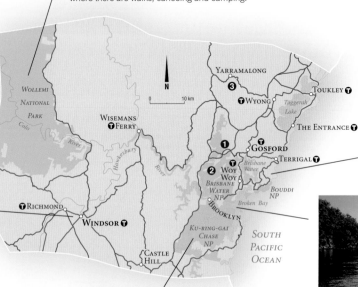

(Map labels: YARRAMALONG, WOLLEMI NATIONAL PARK, Colo, River, WISEMANS FERRY, Hawkesbury, River, WYONG, Tuggerah Lake, TOUKLEY, THE ENTRANCE, GOSFORD, Brisbane Water, TERRIGAL, WOY WOY, BRISBANE WATER NP, BOUDDI NP, Broken Bay, BROOKLYN, RICHMOND, WINDSOR, KU-RING-GAI CHASE NP, CASTLE HILL, SOUTH PACIFIC OCEAN, N, 0 10 km)

Ku-ring-gai Chase National Park

This 15 000-ha bush, river and sandstone landscape forms a scenic border on the northern edge of Sydney's suburbs. Attractions includes diverse flora (about 1000 species including the spectacular waratah), walks, views, access to the Hawkesbury River and engravings of the Guringgai people on the Basin Trail at West Head.

Lower Hawkesbury

The mouth of the Hawkesbury River opens up into a dazzling network of calm bush-lined waterways, which provide the perfect setting for a houseboat holiday or a day of boating and angling. Hop aboard Australia's last river postal run: the Riverboat Postman departs from Brooklyn at 9.30 a.m. on weekdays.

HOLIDAY COAST

This is classic Australian holiday territory: miles of perfect beaches; friendly seaside towns, both big and small; pristine areas of wilderness offering refuge from the holiday bustle; and a near-perfect subtropical climate. Choose between the tranquillity of a small fishing settlement – Seal Rocks, for example – and the resort-town excitement of somewhere like Coffs Harbour. As you would expect, the accommodation choices in the area are substantial, ranging from camping in the rainforests of the local national parks to well-serviced caravan parks, guesthouses and luxury resorts.

TOP EVENTS

Jan. Golden Lure Tournament (Port Macquarie)

Easter Arts and Crafts Exhibition (Dorrigo)

Easter Aquatic Festival (Taree)

June Non-Conventional Homes Eco Tour and Envirofair (Taree)

Aug. Jazz Festival (Bellingen)

Sept. Country Music Festival (Kempsey)

Oct. Global Carnival (Bellingen)

Oct. Food and Wine Fiesta (Coffs Harbour)

Oct. Oyster Festival (Forster)

EXPERIENCE IT!

❶ **Scuba-dive** at Broughton Island, 2 km offshore in Myall Lakes National Park

❷ **Dine** on oysters and watch the trawlers at Tuncurry's Wallis Lake Fishermen's Co-op

❸ **See** rare coastal rainforest at Sea Acres Rainforest Centre, south of Port Macquarie

VISITOR INFORMATION

Coffs Harbour: (02) 6652 1522; 1300 369 070

Port Macquarie: (02) 6583 1293; 1800 025 935
www.portmacquarieinfo.com.au

FOCUS ON

Beaches

The popularity of this area has everything to do with the quality of the beaches. Most towns are flanked by kilometres of perfect coast, which means a choice between a stretch of sand with a lively social scene, or one that offers seclusion. Elizabeth Beach (near Forster) is calm, seasonally patrolled and popular with families. Solitude seekers and nature lovers should explore the bays and coves protected by Crowdy Bay National Park. Further north, top spots include Crescent Head (popular with surfers, particularly long-board riders), South West Rocks, the beaches of Hat Head National Park and those around Coffs Harbour.

Dorrigo National Park
World Heritage-listed, this park preserves rugged escarpment country and the prehistoric growth of the country's most accessible temperate rainforest area. There are excellent walking tracks, lookouts and picnic areas, and opportunities to see lyrebirds and brush turkeys. The popular Skywalk is an elevated walkway through the dense canopy of rainforest.

For more detail see maps 95, 105 & 107. For descriptions of ❶ towns see Towns from A to Z (p. 32).

For more detail see maps 95, 105 & 107. For descriptions of ❶ towns see Towns from A to Z (p. 32).

CLIMATE PORT MACQUARIE

	J	F	M	A	M	J	J	A	S	O	N	D
Max. °C	26	26	25	23	21	18	18	19	20	22	23	25
Min. °C	18	18	17	14	11	8	7	8	10	13	15	17
Rain mm	156	177	175	169	146	133	98	84	83	96	101	127
Raindays	13	13	14	13	11	10	9	9	9	11	11	11

Map labels:
❶ DORRIGO / DORRIGO NP
❶ BELLINGEN
COFFS HARBOUR ❶
URUNGA ❶
❶ MACKSVILLE
NAMBUCCA HEADS ❶
SOUTH WEST ROCKS
HAT HEAD NP
KEMPSEY ❶
CRESCENT HEAD
SOUTH PACIFIC OCEAN
PORT MACQUARIE ❶
❶ WAUCHOPE ❸
KEW ❶
LAURIETON
CROWDY BAY NATIONAL PARK
❶ WINGHAM
TAREE ❶ ❷
GLOUCESTER
FORSTER–TUNCURRY ❶
❶ BULAHDELAH
❶ DUNGOG
ELIZABETH BEACH
❶ STROUD
SEAL ROCKS
MYALL LAKES NP
❶ Broughton Island
0 20 km
N

Bellingen
This inland township is situated on the Bellinger River in the rich dairy lands that were the setting for Peter Carey's *Oscar and Lucinda*. It offers charming 19th-century rural streetscapes, as well as a New Age character colourfully expressed in the art and craft stores, markets and cosy cafes.

Myall Lakes
The 'Murmuring Myalls' are 10 000 ha of connected lakes separated from the coast by a long line of windswept dunes. Hire a houseboat and explore the calm waters, or drop in for angling, windsurfing or canoeing. There are some spectacular beaches and lookouts along the adjoining coast.

Coffs Harbour
During the holiday season, the population of Coffs swells from about 22 000 to 100 000. Attractions include the Big Banana, marking one of the area's largest industries; the Pet Porpoise Pool, which features trained sea mammals; seasonal whale-watching; and Muttonbird Island for its large seasonal colony of short-tailed shearwaters (muttonbirds).

Ocean Drive
The 48-km Tourist Drive 10 between Kew and Port Macquarie offers golden beaches, rolling surf, rugged cliffs and tranquil coastal lakes. Take in the views from North Brother Mountain (pictured) in tiny Dooragan National Park and look for dolphins off the magnificent, 16-km-long Lighthouse Beach.

LORD HOWE ISLAND

The Lord Howe Group of Islands lies in subtropical waters about 500 km off the northern New South Wales coast. Listed as a World Heritage site, these volcanic remnants have great natural value and beauty, with sandy beaches, coral reefs, imposing forest-covered mountains and some of the rarest flora and fauna on earth. Fly from Sydney, Brisbane or Port Macquarie for wildlife-watching, walking, surfing, cruising, diving and relaxing in one of Australia's most unspoilt holiday environments. The narrow crescent-shaped main island is 11 km long and has a strict tourist capacity of 400, so book well in advance to avoid disappointment.

TOP EVENTS

Feb. Discovery Day Celebrations

Oct.– Gosford to Lord Howe Island
Nov. Yacht Race

Nov. Lord Howe Island Golf Open

EXPERIENCE IT!

❶ **Fish** or surf at Blinky Beach

❷ **Tee** off at one of the world's most scenic golf courses at the base of Mount Lidgbird

❸ **Enjoy** knockout views of The Lagoon along with fine food at the White Gallinule restaurant

Admiralty Islands
About 2 km offshore, travel north by scenic cruise past this group of eight rocky outcrops, a well-known breeding ground for large colonies of seabirds. Sooty terns (pictured) nest here in spring.

VISITOR INFORMATION
Lord Howe Island Visitor Centre
(02) 6563 2114

FOCUS ON

World Heritage features
The Lord Howe Group of Islands comprises a series of 7-million-year-old volcanic formations. Because of its isolation and the absence of humans until recently, Lord Howe has a significant natural history. Fifty-seven of the islands' 180 flowering plants and 54 fern species are not found elsewhere. At settlement (1834) there were 15 species of land birds, 14 of which were unique. Six species survive. Hundreds of thousands of seabirds roost on the islands. These include the world's largest colony of red-tailed tropic birds, as well as sooty terns, brown noddies, several shearwater species and the world's only providence petrel breeding colony.

CLIMATE

	J	F	M	A	M	J	J	A	S	O	N	D
Max. °C	25	26	25	23	21	19	19	20	21	22	24
Min. °C	20	20	20	18	16	14	13	13	14	15	17	19
Rain mm	108	114	122	149	160	177	178	141	135	127	116	117
Raindays	11	13	15	18	21	22	23	21	17	14	12	12

The Lagoon
A reef supporting many of the area's 98 coral species encloses the crystal waters of this 6-km-long lagoon on the western side of the main island. Spend the day sunbaking and swimming at Old Settlement Beach or go snorkelling at Escotts Hole, about 1 km out. Glass-bottomed boat and snorkelling tours are available.

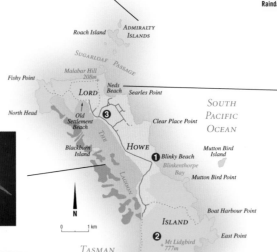

Roach Island

ADMIRALTY ISLANDS

SUGARLOAF PASSAGE

Malabar Hill 208m

Fishy Point

LORD
Neds Beach
Searles Point

North Head

Old Settlement Beach ❸

Clear Place Point

Blackburn Island

HOWE

❶ Blinky Beach
Blinkenthorpe Bay

Mutton Bird Island

Mutton Bird Point

SOUTH PACIFIC OCEAN

THE LAGOON

N
0   1 km

Boat Harbour Point

ISLAND

❷ Mt Lidgbird 777m

East Point

TASMAN SEA

Red Point

LORD HOWE ISLAND PERMANENT PARK PRESERVE NATURE RESERVE

Mt Gower 875m

South Head

King Point

Gower Island

Lord Howe Island
25 km
Balls Pyramid

Observatory Rock

Wheatsheaf Islet

Balls Pyramid

Neds Beach
Lush forests of kentia and banyan trees, two of the main island's most prolific and distinctive species, fringe this beautiful surf beach. Hand-feed the tropical fish, swim, surf the break, snorkel or take a 45-minute walk up Malabar Hill on the northern headland for superb island views.

Mount Gower
This 875-m mountain is the main island's highest point. Take a 9-hour guided walk to the summit through the island's endemic plants and areas of stunted rainforest – a fairytale world of gnarled trees, orchids and moss-covered basalt outcrops. Mists permitting, the view from the summit is spectacular.

Balls Pyramid
An extraordinary cathedral-shaped rocky island rising 551 m out of the sea 25 km south-east of the main island. Once nearly 6 km wide, this island's width has been eroded to only 400 m. The Pyramid is a major breeding ground for seabirds and can be seen by air charter or boat cruise. Deep-sea fishing in the vicinity is excellent.

TROPICAL NORTH COAST

Exquisite beaches, wide rivers, World Heritage forests and an alternative lifestyle culture are some of the features of this tropical paradise in the far north-east of the State. Popular activities include fishing, whitewater rafting, diving and surfing. Market shopping, festivals, scenic drives, excellent local restaurants and accommodation offering everything from rainforest retreats to beachfront B&Bs are attractions for the more sedentary traveller. The region is a magnet for visitors world-wide but avoids the trappings of most large-scale popular resorts. It remains non-commercial, culturally interesting as well as environmentally 'tuned in'.

TOP EVENTS

Jan. East Coast Sculpture Show (Thursday Plantation, near Ballina)

Easter East Coast Blues Festival (Byron Bay)

May Mardi Grass Festival (Nimbin)

July Grafton Cup

Aug. Tweed Valley Banana Festival and Harvest Week (Murwillumbah)

Sept. Rainforest Week (Tweed Heads)

Oct. Bounty Festival (Ballina)

Oct.– Nov. Jacaranda Festival (Grafton)

Oct. Seafood Expo (Yamba)

EXPERIENCE IT!

❶ **Dive** with turtles in the warm waters of Julian Rocks Aquatic Reserve, near Byron Bay

❷ **Visit** Tropical Fruit World, north of Murwillumbah, to see 500 varieties of tropical fruit

❸ **Take** the Tweed Range Scenic Drive (via Nimbin or Murwillumbah) for a 60-km tour of the Border Ranges World Heritage forests

VISITOR INFORMATION

Byron Bay: (02) 6685 8050

Grafton: (02) 6642 4677

www.tropicalnsw.com.au

FOCUS ON

Alternative lifestyle

This once sleepy dairy-farming and fishing district was colonised by alternative lifestyle enthusiasts some thirty years ago. The beautiful Byron Bay is known as the Cosmic Capital of Australia. Along with the town's new affluence you'll find health food outlets, alternative remedies and a colourful procession of residents, including refugee celebrities. Nimbin, the site of the 1973 counter-culture event, the Aquarius Festival, is still a place to 'drop in and drop out'. Organic food, markets, mudbrick buildings and murals are signature features. Other centres with an element of alternative style are The Channon (near Nimbin), Mullumbimby, Murwillumbah and Lismore.

Mount Warning National Park

The summit of Mount Warning is the first place in Australia to be lit by the sun in the morning. A bushwalking track leads up from the car park through pockets of subtropical and warm-temperate rainforest. The park, along with other north coast and hinterland reserves, is a World Heritage area, classified as part of the Central Eastern Rainforest Reserves.

CLIMATE BYRON BAY

	J	F	M	A	M	J	J	A	S	O	N	D
Max. °C	27	27	26	25	22	20	19	20	22	23	25	26
Min. °C	21	21	20	17	15	12	12	13	14	16	18	20
Rain mm	169	191	214	179	191	161	102	95	67	106	118	148
Raindays	14	16	17	15	14	12	10	9	9	11	12	13

Cape Byron

Cape Byron is the continent's most easterly point. Its dominant position makes it an excellent place to watch the 2000–3000 humpback whales which travel north along this coastline from late June or early July before heading south again in September. At the tip of the headland is the Cape Byron Lighthouse, said to be the most powerful in Australia.

Holiday coast

The bustling riverside settlement of Tweed Heads is great for active families while laid-back Byron Bay is perfect for surfers, singles and sophisticates. Camping and caravan facilities make Ballina and Evans Head appeal to those on a budget, while Iluka and Yamba draw visitors with a bent for angling, surfing and an old-fashioned holiday style.

Map labels:
QLD
TWEED HEADS ❶
MT WARNING NP ❸
BORDER RANGES NP ❷
MURWILLUMBAH ❶
MULLUMBIMBY ❶
BRUNSWICK HEADS ❶
KYOGLE ❶
RICHMOND RANGE NP
NIMBIN ❶
THE CHANNON ❶
Cape Byron ❶
BYRON BAY ❶
LENNOX HEAD ❶
LISMORE ❶
ALSTONVILLE ❶
CASINO ❶
BALLINA ❶
EVANS HEAD ❶
BUNDJALUNG NATIONAL PARK
MACLEAN ❶
Clarence River
ILUKA ❶
YAMBA ❶
SOUTH PACIFIC OCEAN
YURAYGIR NATIONAL PARK
GRAFTON ❶
N
0 20 km
WOOLGOOLGA ❶

For more detail see map 107. For descriptions of ❶ towns see Towns from A to Z (p. 32).

Grafton

This picturesque rural town, with a number of 19th-century buildings, is best known for its beautiful civic landscaping, particularly the mature jacaranda trees with their vivid purple springtime blossom. Located on the Clarence River, Grafton is also a busy centre for water sports, particularly whitewater rafting and canoeing.

NEW ENGLAND & THE NORTH-WEST

The New England district is some 200 km inland and approximately 1000 m above sea level. Chilly winters, golden autumns, heritage buildings and intensively farmed stretches of land contrast with the tropical coastal scenery of the nearby north coast. New England, however, also has superb tracts of native rainforest, including World Heritage-listed areas. To the west the country flattens out into plains with the occasional dramatic outcrop. Here you'll find historic towns in farmland, and the first red reaches of the outback. The region is also known for its fossicking opportunities – for everything from blue sapphires to rare black opals.

TOP EVENTS

Jan.	Country Music Festival (Tamworth)
Jan.	Great Inland Fishing Festival (Inverell)
Mar.	Autumn Festival (Armidale)
Apr.	Oracles of the Bush (bush poetry, Tenterfield)
May	Australian Celtic Festival (Glen Innes)
Oct.	Sapphire City Floral Festival (Inverell)
Oct.	Federation Festival (Tenterfield)
Oct.	Spring Wine Festival (Tenterfield)
Nov.	Golden Grain and Cotton Festival (Moree)

EXPERIENCE IT!

❶ **Drive** to the summit of Mt Kaputar for views of one-tenth of NSW

❷ **Take** a Woollool Woollool Aboriginal Cultural Tour from Tenterfield to see the Bald Rock monolith

❸ **Fish**, swim, water-ski, sail or picnic at Copeton Dam

VISITOR INFORMATION

Armidale: (02) 6772 4655; 1800 627 736
www.new-england.org/armidale
Tamworth: (02) 6755 4300
www.nnsw.com.au

FOCUS ON

Fossicking

The New England district is a fossicker's paradise. Quartz, jasper, serpentine and crystal are common finds, while sapphires, diamonds and gold present more of a challenge. Fossickers Way is a well-signposted tourist route that introduces visitors to the district, beginning at Nundle and travelling north as far as Glen Innes. The route passes through a number of towns including Inverell, the world's largest producer of sapphires. In the far west of the district, Lightning Ridge is well known as a source of the rare black opal. There are designated fossicking areas here, as well as underground mine tours.

CLIMATE ARMIDALE

	J	F	M	A	M	J	J	A	S	O	N	D
Max. °C	27	26	24	21	17	14	13	14	18	21	24	26
Min. °C	14	14	12	8	4	2	0	2	4	7	10	12
Rain mm	103	86	67	46	44	58	49	49	52	68	80	88
Raindays	10	10	10	8	8	10	9	9	8	9	9	10

Tenterfield

Visit the School of the Arts building, where in 1889 politician Henry Parkes advocated federation, earning the town the descriptor 'Birthplace of our Nation'. Or find Tenterfield Saddler, the shop that inspired singer and composer Peter Allen to write the song of the same name. Other attractions include magnificent autumn foliage and excellent heritage buildings.

New England National Park

Part of the World Heritage-listed Central Eastern Rainforest Reserves, this 71 000-ha park contains three distinct environments: subtropical rainforest, subalpine landscape and temperate forest. Much of the park is wilderness, for experienced walkers only; however, there are easy walks to the lookouts on the north-western (Armidale) side.

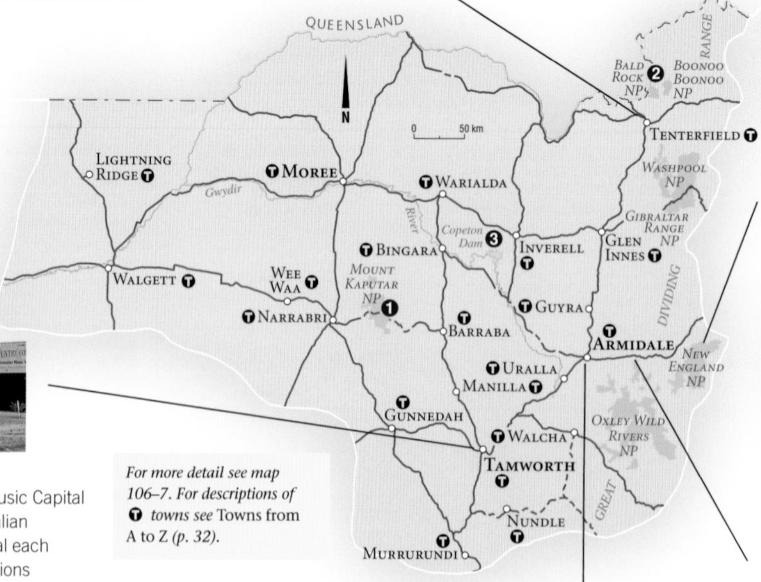

Tamworth

Australia's Country Music Capital hosts the huge Australian Country Music Festival each January. Other attractions include the 12-m high Golden Guitar (home of the Country Music Gallery of Stars, where you'll find wax replicas of favourite country artists), Country Music Hands of Fame (artists' handprints) and some superb heritage buildings.

For more detail see map 106–7. For descriptions of ❶ *towns see Towns from A to Z (p. 32).*

Armidale

Armidale, at the heart of New England, is a sophisticated university and cathedral town, with over 30 National Trust-listed buildings in gracious tree-lined streets. Visit the Aboriginal Cultural Centre and Keeping Place and the New England Regional Art Museum. The latter holds the multi-million dollar Hinton Collection, Australia's most significant provincial art holding.

Wollomombi Falls

Located in the Oxley Wild Rivers National Park, the stunning 220-m-high Wollomombi Falls are among the highest falls in the country. Other attractions of the park include camping, walks and superb escarpment scenery.

Map labels: QUEENSLAND · BALD ROCK NP · BOONOO BOONOO NP · LIGHTNING RIDGE · MOREE · WARIALDA · Gwydir · WASHPOOL NP · TENTERFIELD · River · Copeton Dam · GIBRALTAR RANGE NP · GLEN INNES · WALGETT · WEE WAA · BINGARA · INVERELL · MOUNT KAPUTAR NP · NARRABRI · GUYRA · BARRABA · ARMIDALE · NEW ENGLAND NP · URALLA · MANILLA · GUNNEDAH · OXLEY WILD RIVERS NP · WALCHA · TAMWORTH · NUNDLE · MURRURUNDI · DIVIDING RANGE · GREAT · N · 0 50 km

CENTRAL WEST

This land of open spaces straddles the western slopes of the Great Dividing Range and the expanse of the Western Plains. Cotton crops, vineyards, cattle and sheep draw on the rich volcanic soil and dominate the landscape, but nature exerts its presence often and, in the case of the strange formations of the Warrumbungles, with great spectacle. The history of the district is varied and well preserved, and appears most notably in the wonderful 19th-century goldmining settlements. Modern attractions include the Western Plains Zoo, and two major space observatories built to take advantage of the region's endless stretch of clear sky.

TOP EVENTS

Feb.– Mar. *Banjo Paterson Festival (Orange)*

Easter *Orana Country Music Festival (Dubbo)*

Apr. *Marti's Balloon Fiesta (Canowindra)*

Aug. *Jazz Festival (Dubbo)*

Sept. *Wine Festival (Mudgee)*

Oct. *Festival of the Stars (Coonabarabran)*

Oct. *Sakura Matsuri (Cherry Blossom Festival, Cowra)*

Oct. *Country Music Spectacular (Parkes)*

Nov. *Bathurst FAI 1000 Car Race*

EXPERIENCE IT!

❶ **Visit** *Siding Springs Observatory, west of Coonabarabran, home to Australia's largest telescope*

❷ **Go** *birdwatching at the 20 000-ha wetlands of Macquarie Marshes Nature Reserve*

❸ **Tour** *the Wellington Caves and see one of the world's largest stalagmites*

VISITOR INFORMATION

Bathurst: (02) 6332 1444;
1800 681 000
www.bathurstnsw.gov.au

Dubbo: (02) 6884 1422;
1800 674 443
www.dubbotourism.com.au

FOCUS ON

Mudgee and Gulgong wines

German settler Adam Roth planted vines at Mudgee in the 1850s. Thirteen wineries had been established by 1890 but just three survived the depression later in the decade. The red wine boom of the 1960s saw many new vineyards planted. The Mudgee and Gulgong area has 23 wineries offering tastings, and over 100 vineyards where plantings exceed 4000 ha. Warm summers favour the production of full-bodied shiraz and chardonnay that cellar well over four to five years (longer for shiraz from top vintages). Try Huntington's shiraz; the organic, preservative-free wines of Botobolar; Craigmoor's chardonnay; or the cabernet sauvignon from Thistle Hill.

Warrumbungle National Park

The Warrumbungles are extraordinary rock formations created by ancient volcanic activity. Best known is The Breadknife (pictured) which juts savagely out of the surrounding bushland. The surrounding 21 000-ha national park marks the area where the flora and fauna of the Western Plains merge with those of the Great Dividing Range.

CLIMATE DUBBO

	J	F	M	A	M	J	J	A	S	O	N	D
Max. °C	33	32	29	25	20	16	15	17	21	25	29	32
Min. °C	18	18	15	11	7	4	3	4	6	10	13	16
Rain mm	61	54	49	45	48	49	45	45	44	49	51	50
Raindays	6	5	5	5	6	8	8	8	7	7	6	6

Hill End

This small town remains largely unchanged since the 1870s gold boom. From the 1950s onwards, prominent Australian artists, most notably Russell Drysdale, were attracted by the aesthetic qualities of the town and surrounding landscape. The post office (pictured) is typical of Hill End's many historic buildings.

Western Plains Zoo

Five km from Dubbo, this excellent open range zoo covers 300 ha and is home to around 1400 animals representing 130 species. A series of environments recreate the natural habitats of the world's continents. Visitors can use their own car, hire a bicycle or use walking trails to all areas.

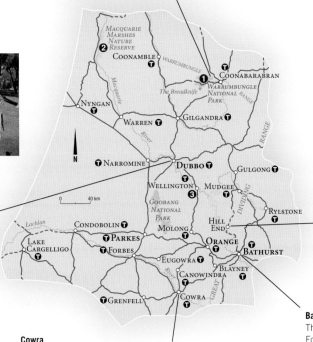

Bathurst

This is Australia's oldest inland settlement. Founded 1815, Bathurst is noted for its Colonial and Victorian architecture, including Miss Traill's House (c.1845), open to the public. Also of interest is Ben Chifley's Cottage (home of the wartime prime minister), the excellent regional art gallery and Mount Panorama, venue for the Bathurst 1000.

Cowra

In 1944, during World War II, 1000 Japanese soldiers tried to escape Cowra's POW camp, resulting in the death of 235 soldiers. The Japanese cemetery and a magnificent Japanese garden commemorate that history; they are linked by a 5-km avenue of cherry trees. These days Cowra is known for its gourmet produce and developing premium wine production.

For more detail see maps 90, 104, 106, 109 & 111. For descriptions of ❶ towns see Towns from A to Z (p. 32).

BLUE MOUNTAINS

The misty, bush-clad cliffs and valleys of the Blue Mountains are the eroded remains of a giant plateau that rose up out of a river delta 80 million years ago. Occupied for at least 20 000 years by Aboriginal peoples, the mountains proved an impenetrable barrier until 1813 to the European settlers of Sydney seeking westward expansion. These days the area provides an accessible and spectacularly beautiful nature retreat for the city's residents, with bushwalking, adventure sports, gourmet retreats and cool-climate gardens among the many attractions.

TOP EVENTS

Feb. *Blue Mountains Festival of Folk, Roots and Blues (Katoomba)*

Mar. *Blue Mountains Herb Fest (Medlow Bath)*

Apr. *Autumn Gardens Festival (Mt Wilson)*

May *Songs of the Wind Festival (throughout region)*

June *Winter Magic Festival (Katoomba)*

June– Aug. *Yulefest (throughout region)*

Sept.– Nov. *Spring Gardens Festival (throughout region)*

Oct. *Village Fair (Leura)*

Nov. *Rhododendron Festival (Blackheath)*

EXPERIENCE IT!

❶ *Go canyoning in the Grand Canyon, south-east of Blackheath*

❷ *Book a weekend at Cleopatra, a French-style gourmet retreat in Blackheath*

❸ *Descend the Giant Stairway into the Jamison Valley, south of Katoomba*

VISITOR INFORMATION

Blue Mountains Visitor Information Centre
Echo Point Rd, Katoomba and Glenbrook: 1300 653 408
www.bluemountainstourism.org.au

FOCUS ON

Gardens

Volcanic soil and cool-climate conditions have made the Blue Mountains one of the best known gardening regions in Australia. Visit Everglades near Leura, a 6-ha classically designed garden that melds with the surrounding bush. Mount Wilson is a tiny village of grand estates, nearly all with large historic gardens of formal lawns, cool-climate plantings, woodlands and huge European trees; many properties are open to the public. Mount Tomah Botanic Garden is the cool-climate annexe of Sydney's Botanic Garden. Here, specialist displays in terraces bring together thousands of worldwide rare species, including the Wollemi Pine, discovered 1994 in Wollemi National Park.

Grose Valley
A visit to the National Parks and Heritage Centre on Govetts Leap Road is a must for visitors who are keen to explore the network of trails overlooking and leading into the Grose Valley. The escarpment in this area east of Blackheath is particularly dramatic and the views are breathtaking.

CLIMATE KATOOMBA

	J	F	M	A	M	J	J	A	S	O	N	D
Max. °C	23	22	20	17	13	10	9	11	14	17	20	22
Min. °C	13	13	11	9	6	4	2	3	5	8	10	12
Rain mm	160	170	169	126	103	123	89	81	74	93	103	125
Raindays	13	12	13	10	9	9	9	9	9	9	10	11	12

For more detail see maps 90 & 92–3. For descriptions of ❶ towns see Towns from A to Z (p. 32). For touring details see Classic Tour (p. 77).

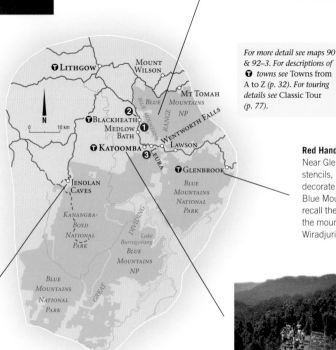

Red Hands Cave
Near Glenbrook, Aboriginal red-ochre hand stencils, between 500 and 1600 years old, decorate the walls of the Red Hands Cave in Blue Mountains National Park. The stencils recall the presence of the first inhabitants of the mountains, the people of the Dharug, Wiradjuri and Gandangara tribes.

Jenolan Caves
Formed 400 million years ago in a belt of limestone, this is one of the most extensive and complex underground limestone cave systems in the world. Of the 300 or so 'rooms', 9 are open to the public – by tour only.

Three Sisters and Echo Point
This feature has been carved by millions of years of erosion, although Aboriginal legend has it that the rock was formed when a father turned his daughters to stone to protect them from an evil figure. Nearby, visitors can ride into or across the Jamison Valley aboard the Scenic Railway or Scenic Skyway.

CAPITAL COUNTRY

This is a rich agricultural region, radiating out from the northern borders of the Australian Capital Territory. Set along the tableland of the Great Dividing Range, it is characterised by a landscape of undulating hills, golden plains and rocky outcrops. It is best known for its history of European settlement which, dating back to the 1820s, is recorded in the heritage architecture of the district's towns. Other attractions include boutique-style, cool-climate wineries and some beautiful areas of native landscape, which have survived early clearing and settlement. Most attractions are within an easy daytrip from Canberra.

TOP EVENTS

Feb. Australian Blues Music Festival (Goulburn)

Feb. Hilltops Flavours of the Harvest Festival (Young)

Mar. Country Weekend (Crookwell)

Mar. Weekend of Heritage (Goulburn)

Apr. Heritage Festival (Braidwood)

Oct. Days of Wine and Roses (throughout district)

Oct. Lilac City Festival (Goulburn)

Nov. Music at the Creek (Braidwood)

Nov.–Dec. National Cherry Festival (Young)

EXPERIENCE IT!

❶ **Explore** the dramatic Bungonia Gorge, in Bungonia State Reserve Area

❷ **Go** back in time at the Bywong Goldmining Town, a re-creation of an early mining settlement, north-west of Bungendore

❸ **Pick** cherries in season in the orchards of Young

VISITOR INFORMATION

Canberra: (02) 6205 0044
www.canberratourism.com.au

Goulburn: (02) 4823 4492;
1800 353 646

FOCUS ON

History

The first inhabitants of the area were the Ngaunawal, whose ancestors, archaeological evidence from Lake George suggests, may have arrived anywhere from 75 000 to 120 000 years ago. Europeans sighted the district in the late 1790s and the Goulburn plains were named in 1818. Settlers arrived between the 1820s and the 1850s, first attracted by the rich grazing land and later by the discovery of gold. Today a number of towns, including Yass, Young, Gunning, Bungendore and Braidwood, retain significant collections of heritage buildings and charming streetscapes. The district as whole provides an evocative glimpse of 19th-century life in rural Australia.

Yass

In 1821 the explorer Hamilton Hume declared the Yass district a place where 'sheep would thrive uncommonly well'. Hume's home, Cooma Cottage (pictured), built in 1835, is now open to the public. The town retains a strong 19th-century flavour, thanks to its intact shopfronts and early public buildings.

Capital wineries

The region's cool, dry climate has proved a bonus for local winegrowing. A number of small vineyards, most offering sales, are located on the north and north-east borders of the ACT. Look out for Murrumbateman Winery, Lark Hill and Brindabella Hills Winery.

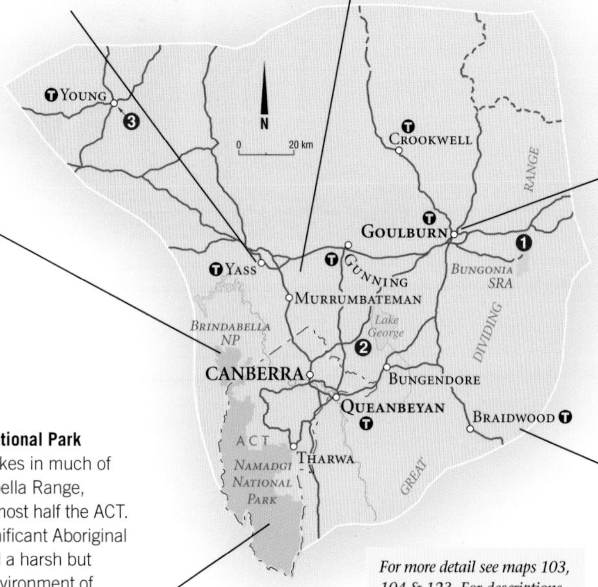

CLIMATE GOULBURN

	J	F	M	A	M	J	J	A	S	O	N	D
Max. °C	27	26	24	20	16	12	11	13	16	19	22	26
Min. °C	13	13	11	8	5	2	1	2	5	7	9	12
Rain mm	63	52	57	57	53	49	45	59	52	58	67	57
Raindays	10	9	9	9	11	11	12	12	11	12	12	9

Brindabella National Park

The lush Brindabella Range, the setting for stories by novelist Miles Franklin, provides a magnificent backdrop to the cleared hills and plains of the surrounding district. Four-wheel-drive access is recommended for this park. Camping, bushwalking and birdwatching are popular activities.

Namadgi National Park

Namadgi takes in much of the Brindabella Range, covering almost half the ACT. It offers significant Aboriginal rock art and a harsh but beautiful environment of mountains, valleys and bush. Camping, bushwalking and scenic touring are available. Access is along the Monaro Highway via Canberra.

Goulburn

Established 1833, this town displays elaborate 19th-century architecture, a legacy of early wool-growing wealth. Goulburn boasts two cathedrals and a regional art gallery. On the town's outskirts, The Big Merino (pictured) sells wool products.

Braidwood

Braidwood is a beautifully preserved 19th-century town. Its elegant Georgian buildings recall early agricultural settlement while ornate Victorian structures mark the town's goldmining boom. Today, art and craft, antiques, cafes and its reputation as a setting for films help underpin the local economy.

For more detail see maps 103, 104 & 123. For descriptions of ❶ towns see Towns from A to Z (p. 32).

Map labels: YOUNG, CROOKWELL, GOULBURN, YASS, GUNNING, MURRUMBATEMAN, BUNGONIA SRA, Lake George, BRINDABELLA NP, CANBERRA, BUNGENDORE, QUEANBEYAN, BRAIDWOOD, ACT, NAMADGI NATIONAL PARK, THARWA, RANGE, DIVIDING, GREAT, N, 0 20 km

SOUTHERN HIGHLANDS & ILLAWARRA

This region combines European-style rural scenery with a fine stretch of typically Australian coastline. The highlands, within the Great Dividing Range, is an area of Colonial sandstone buildings, traditional gardens, quaint villages and excellent B&Bs and guesthouses catering to the steady stream of visitors who, for well over a century, have been arriving from Sydney to seek the peace and clean air of a hillside retreat. Towards the coast, the rural landscape drops away into escarpments, woodland, rainforest and waterfalls, while on the coastal plains the scene is one of dairy farms, river valleys, surf beaches and rugged sea cliffs. Proximity to Sydney and the variety of landscapes makes this a first-rate touring region. Travel inland to the highlands, spend a night or two, and then work your way east for a return trip via the coast.

EXPERIENCE IT!

❶ **Fish**, swim, surf or stroll pristine shores at Seven Mile Beach National Park

❷ **Explore** the Wombeyan Caves (via Mittagong), one of the most extensive and complex cave systems in Australia

❸ **Sail** or windsurf the waters of the giant coastal lagoon of Lake Illawarra

❹ **Take** a drive up Mount Gibraltar, near Bowral, for splendid views across the Highlands and beyond

❺ **Scuba-dive** or snorkel at Bass Point, Shellharbour

VISITOR INFORMATION

Wollongong: 1800 240 737
www.tourismwollongong.com

Southern Highlands
Visitor Information Centre
Mittagong: (02) 4871 2888;
1300 657 559
www.highlandsnsw.com.au

Bradman Museum
'The Don', as Australia's most famous cricketer is known, was born in Cootamundra in 1908. In 1911 Bradman moved to Bowral, where he played on what is now known as the Bradman Oval. On retirement, he had a batting average of 99.94. Details of his life and career are displayed in this excellent museum.

CLIMATE BOWRAL

	J	F	M	A	M	J	J	A	S	O	N	D
Max. °C	25	25	23	20	16	13	12	13	16	19	21	24
Min. °C	13	13	11	7	4	2	1	2	4	7	9	11
Rain mm	88	80	110	88	77	84	45	63	57	84	100	73
Raindays	14	13	13	11	12	11	10	10	11	13	13	12

FOCUS ON

Towns of the Highlands

Bowral, with its historic streetscapes, restaurants and cafes, B&Bs and guesthouses and superb gardens, is the centre of the Southern Highlands holiday region. Historic Berrima, once the commercial heart of the district, now serves as a timepiece of Colonial Georgian Australia. Nearby Mittagong boasts lovely gardens, as well as good cafes and interesting shopfront architecture. Sutton Forest and Moss Vale are pretty towns with an air of the English countryside, while Bundanoon, further south, is known for its excellent guesthouses, health resort and views across Morton National Park. Away from the main tourist route are Robertson and Burrawang, peaceful settlements steeped in 19th-century history. Don't miss Ranelagh House in Robertson, designed in 1924 to resemble an English manor. The rolling hills of this district were the backdrop for the Australian film *Babe* (1996). To the south is Berry (established 1822), set in the dairy country of the Shoalhaven River district, and boasting charming heritage buildings, galleries, antique shops and guesthouses.

Berrima
Established in the 1830s, Berrima is Australia's best-preserved Georgian settlement. Architectural highlights include the gaol (1839) and Berrima Courthouse (1838), pictured here. A self-guide historical walking tour is available. Look out for Berkelouw's Book Barn, which has around 200 000 second-hand books.

Morton National Park
This vast tract of wilderness is best explored via the 14 designated walking tracks leading from the township of Bundanoon, including a night walk to Glow Worm Glen. Sandstone cliffs, wooded valleys, waterfalls and the winding tributaries of the Shoalhaven River are among the natural attractions.

Gardens of the highlands
The highlands are known for their traditional English-style gardens. In Bowral, the historic Corbett Gardens and the gardens of the Grand Mecure Hotel come alive at tulip time in spring. During September and October the many established private gardens of the region, mostly around Mittagong and Bowral, open their gates for vibrant springtime displays.

Royal National Park
The Royal, designated in 1879, was Australia's first national park. Features include Aboriginal rock engravings, beaches and waterholes, pockets of rainforest set amid stretches of woodland and heath, and some the State's most spectacular coastal scenery, seen from rugged sandstone cliffs. Camping, walks, cycling and picnic facilities are available.

For more detail see maps 99, 104 & 105. For descriptions of ❼ *towns see Towns from A to Z (p. 32).*

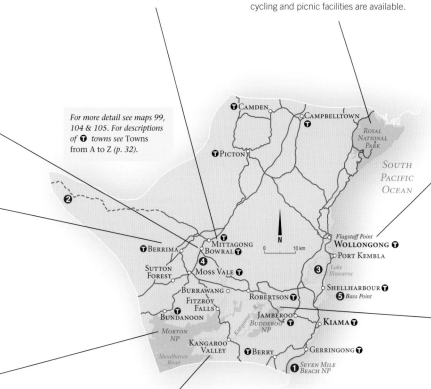

TOP EVENTS

Feb.	*Jazz Festival (Kiama)*
Mar.	*Southern Highlands Antique Fair (Bowral)*
Mar.	*Viva La Gong (Wollongong)*
Mar.	*Illawarra Folk Festival (Jamberoo)*
Apr.	*Autumn Gardens in the Southern Highlands*
Apr.	*Bundanoon is Brigadoon Highland Gathering (Bundanoon)*
Apr.	*National Parks ranger-guided walks (Morton and Budderoo national parks)*
Sept.– Oct.	*Tulip Time Festival (throughout Southern Highlands)*
Oct.	*Village Garden Ramble (Bundanoon)*
Oct.	*Seaside Festival (Kiama)*
Nov.	*Bong Bong Races (Bowral)*
Nov.	*Southern Highlands Jazz and Ragtime Festival (Bowral)*
Nov.	*Harbourfest (Port Kembla)*

Wollongong
Wollongong, an Aboriginal word for 'sound of the sea', is a major regional city set along a stretch of coast that includes 17 surf beaches. Visit the city's boat harbour, fish co-op and restaurants on Flagstaff Point; drive north through the old coal mines for coastal views; and to the south, see Nan Tien Temple, the largest Buddhist temple in the Southern Hemisphere.

Minnamurra Falls
The Minnamurra Falls, in Budderoo National Park, is one of several groups of falls formed by the massive sandstone escarpment that defines the edge of the Southern Highlands. Nearby is the Minnamurra Rainforest Centre, which incorporates a raised walkway leading into pockets of dense temperate and subtropical rainforest.

Kangaroo Valley
This valley, known for its stunning combination of rural and native scenery, is best explored from the scenic route (via Nowra Road) leading down from the highlands to the coast. Attractions include the historic townships of Kangaroo Valley and Berry, Hamden Bridge, which crosses the Kangaroo River, and the 80-m-high Fitzroy Falls (pictured).

THE SOUTH COAST

This long, beautiful stretch of sandy beaches, rivers, lakes, fishing villages, rolling hills, rugged escarpments and native forests has proved remarkably resilient to the excesses of coastal development. Whaling and wholesale logging have come and gone and sustainable tourism and dairying are the mainstays. Because the climate is cooler here, summer is the peak period. Even then the area has a laid-back feel. Weekend trips from Canberra are common, but visitors from Sydney or Melbourne usually stay for at least a week, to take full advantage of all the national parks and the surfing, fishing, walking and touring opportunities.

TOP EVENTS

Jan.   Blue Water Fishing Classic (Bermagui)

Mar.   Seaside Fair (Bermagui)

Easter Tilba Festival (Central Tilba)

Easter Blessing of the Fleet (Ulladulla)

Aug.   Festival of Food and Wine by the Sea (Ulladulla)

Oct.   Whale Festival (Eden)

Oct.   Country Music Festival (Merimbula)

Oct.   Jazz Festival (Moruya)

Oct.   Great Southern Blues Festival (Narooma)

EXPERIENCE IT!

❶ **Board** a charter and go deep-sea fishing offshore from Bermagui

❷ **Go** surfing at Tathra Beach and visit the historic Tathra Wharf

❸ **Eat** fresh Clyde River oysters on the waterfront at Batemans Bay

VISITOR INFORMATION

Batemans Bay: (02) 4472 6900; 1800 802 528

Eden: (02) 6496 1953; 1800 633 012

Nowra: (02) 4421 0778; 1800 024 261

www.southcoast.net.au

FOCUS ON

Aboriginal culture

Before European colonisation, the Yuin occupied the area from Jervis Bay to Twofold Bay, sustained by the produce of coast and rivers. Today the area remains steeped in Yuin history. At Wallaga Lake the Umbarra Cultural Centre offers tours, including one to the summit of Mount Dromedary (Gulaga), where, according to legend, the great creation spirit, Daramulun, ascended to the sky. Booderee National Park, within Jervis Bay Territory, is once again Yuin land after the successful 1995 land claim. Jointly managed by the Wreck Bay Aboriginal Community and Parks Australia, Booderee has numerous middens and significant sites, and an art and craft centre. The Murramarang Aboriginal Area, near Bawley Point, has a self-guide interpretive walk.

CLIMATE MERIMBULA

	J	F	M	A	M	J	J	A	S	O	N	D
Max. °C	24	25	23	21	19	16	16	17	18	20	21	23
Min. °C	15	15	14	11	8	6	4	5	7	9	12	14
Rain mm	80	71	95	71	70	64	37	45	52	77	85	65
Raindays	10	9	10	9	10	9	7	9	10	11	12	11

Central Tilba

This tiny National Trust village, in a spectacular mountain landscape, is a showpiece for late-19th-century rural architecture. It contains 25 timber structures of special interest, most of them built in the 1890s. Once a goldmining centre, the town now caters for tourists, with cafes, galleries and art and craft shops.

Jervis Bay

Part of this area is within Jervis Bay Territory and includes the national capital's seaport. The bay, in part bordered by NSW Jervis Bay National Park, is known for its dramatic underwater landscapes and its dolphins; diving and dolphin cruises are available. Nearby Booderee National Park protects important Aboriginal sites as well as beautiful beaches and bush.

For more detail see maps 99, 100 & 103. For descriptions of ❂ towns see Towns from A to Z (p. 32).

Map labels:
NOWRA
NSW JERVIS BAY NP
HUSKISSON
BOODEREE NP
Jervis Bay
JERVIS BAY
JERVIS BAY TERRITORY
ULLADULLA
BAWLEY POINT
MURRAMARANG NP
BATEMANS BAY
DEUA NATIONAL PARK
MORUYA
TASMAN SEA
EUROBODALLA NP
CENTRAL TILBA
Mt Dromedary
NAROOMA
Montague Island
TILBA TILBA
EUROBODALLA NP
WALLAGA LAKE NP
WADBILLIGA NP
BERMAGUI
MIMOSA ROCKS NP
BEGA
TATHRA
MERIMBULA
BOMBALA
BEN BOYD NP
EDEN
BOYDTOWN
BEN BOYD NP
VICTORIA
0   20 km

Eden

From the 1820s until the 1930s, this town served the huge whaling industry of these southern waters. Today Eden is a major whale-watching destination, particularly for humpbacks (October–November). Don't miss the Killer Whale Museum. Nearby are the beautiful Ben Boyd National Park (pictured) and historic Boydtown.

Montague Island

Montague Island, half an hour's boat ride from Narooma, is a wildlife paradise, with populations of 8000 pairs of little (fairy) penguins, 600 Australian fur seals, and various species of seabirds. It is also an excellent place to spot migrating humpbacks (September–November). Contact the national parks office in Narooma for tour details.

Mimosa Rocks National Park

The area covered by this national park is a traditional home of the Yuin. The park crosses a landscape of beaches, sea caves, cliffs, forests and wetlands. There are several secluded campsites, and swimming, walking, diving, fishing and birdwatching are among the activities on offer.

THE RIVERINA

The Riverina stretches across the flat, fertile plains of south central New South Wales. It is one of Australia's richest agricultural regions, watered by the Murrumbidgee River through a vast irrigation system. The spacious landscape, brilliantly clear skies and warm weather make touring the district a special pleasure. The towns of the region are busy, prosperous places, some bearing a strong Southern European character as a result of almost a century of settlement by immigrant farmers. Good restaurant and cafes, heritage buildings and excellent accommodation are to be found.

TOP EVENTS

Jan. *Australian Surf Carnival (Hay)*

Feb. *Tumbafest (food and wine, Tumbarumba)*

Mar. *John O'Brien Bush Festival (Narrandera)*

Easter *SunRice Festival (even-numbered years, Leeton)*

June *Taste of Riverina (alternates Griffith/Wagga)*

Aug. *Wattle Time (Cootamundra)*

Sept. *Jazz Festival (Wagga Wagga)*

Apr.– May *Festival of the Falling Leaf (Tumut)*

Nov. *Dog on the Tuckerbox Festival; Snake Gully Cup (Gundagai)*

EXPERIENCE IT!

❶ **Visit** the Dog on the Tuckerbox, five miles from Gundagai (8 km north)

❷ **Fish** for trout in the mountain streams around Tumut

❸ **Go** four-wheel driving across the Riverina outback, west of Hay

VISITOR INFORMATION

Wagga Wagga: (02) 6926 9621; 1800 648 144

www.riverinatourism.com.au

FOCUS ON

Regional produce

The region produces rice, citrus and stone fruit, grapes, poultry and vegetables in massive quantities, as well as gourmet products. It is Australia's biggest producer of rice; visit the Sunrice Country Visitors Centre in Leeton. For fruit products, tour the Berri Juice Factory at Leeton, the Catania Fruit Salad Farm at Hanwood (near Griffith) and the Fruits of Batlow Packing Complex at Batlow (known for its apples). In Leeton, Mick's Bake House makes excellent breads, while the Riverina Cheese Factory sells its produce at the Fresh Fruit Market. In Wagga, drop in to Tavenders Gourmet Produce for local lines.

CLIMATE TEMORA

	J	F	M	A	M	J	J	A	S	O	N	D
Max. °C	31	31	28	22	18	14	13	15	18	22	26	30
Min. °C	16	16	13	9	6	3	2	3	5	8	11	14
Rain mm	50	37	42	44	46	42	47	46	42	54	46	41
Raindays	6	5	5	6	9	10	13	12	9	9	7	6

Riverina wineries

The Riverina is responsible for 60 per cent of grapes grown in New South Wales. There are 14 wineries in the district, mostly around Griffith, including the De Bortoli, Miranda and McWilliams wineries. This region is best known for its rich botrytised semillon.

Griffith
The main township of the Riverina, Griffith was developed in response to the introduction of irrigation and was designed by Walter Burley Griffin, architect of Canberra. It is the centre for food and wine production in the region, and has good restaurants and cafes.

Hay
Hay lies at the centre of a huge stretch of semi-arid grazing country known as the Hay Plains (pictured). The town was established in 1859 and boasts an interesting collection of late 19th-century heritage buildings, including Bishop's Lodge (1888, in South Hay), a classic Australian homestead surrounded by a superb garden.

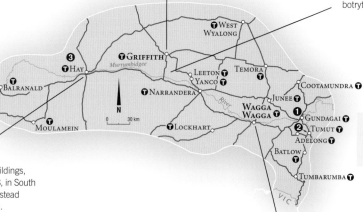

For more detail see maps 103 & 110–11. For descriptions of ❶ towns see Towns from A to Z (p. 32).

Wagga Wagga
Wagga, on the banks of the Murrumbidgee, is the State's largest inland city and a major centre for commerce, agriculture and education. Visit the two local wineries (one of which is a leading viticulture teaching facility), the Botanic Gardens, and the Regional Art Gallery, home of the National Art Glass Collection. River walks and cruises are popular activities.

SNOWY MOUNTAINS

Alpine New South Wales stretches from ACT to the border of Victoria along the spine of the Great Dividing Range. Kosciuszko National Park lies at the heart of the region, protecting the continent's highest mountain, its only glacial lakes, some of its rarest native species, and the headwaters of legendary rivers. Nestled within the folds of the landscape's peaks and valleys are a collection of world-class ski resorts that attract hundreds of thousands of skiers from across Australia and around the world each winter. In spring and summer a brilliant sweep of wildflowers cover the fields, mountain streams run full with melting snow, and tribes of bushwalkers, campers, anglers, scenic drivers and horseback and mountain-bike riders arrive to savour the warm-weather delights of this diverse and spectacular 'roof' of Australia.

EXPERIENCE IT!

❶ **Go** whitewater rafting on the headwaters of the Murray near Khancoban

❷ **Re-live** the adventures of legendary mountain horsemen on a horseriding tour via Adaminaby

❸ **Take** a 24-km-return walk from Charlotte Pass (via Jindabyne) along Australia's highest walking track, past the glacial Blue Lake

❹ **Tour** the historic sites of Cooma on the self-guide Lambie Town Walk

❺ **Visit** the Gaden Trout Hatchery near Jindabyne

VISITOR INFORMATION

Snowy Region Visitor Information Centre Jindabyne: (02) 6450 5600; 1800 636 525
www.snowymountains.com.au

CLIMATE THREDBO

	J	F	M	A	M	J	J	A	S	O	N	D
Max. °C	21	21	18	14	10	6	5	6	10	13	16	19
Min. °C	7	7	5	2	−1	−3	−4	−2	−1	1	3	5
Rain mm	116	84	113	119	172	160	161	186	208	207	159	119
Raindays	11	10	11	12	15	16	16	17	18	16	15	12

FOCUS ON

Ski resorts

The Snowy Mountain resorts are well equipped in terms of lessons, lifts, ski hire, transport, food, accommodation and entertainment. All ski resorts are in Kosciuszko National Park and most are 90–100 km south of Cooma. Perisher, Smiggin Holes, Mount Blue Cow and Guthega are collectively known as Perisher Blue Ski Resort, the largest in Australia, with 50 lifts and a variety of slopes. A good range of accommodation is available at Perisher and Smiggin Holes, but overnight parking is limited (many leave their cars at Bullocks Flat). Accommodation is limited at Guthega and not available at Blue Cow. Thredbo, the main village, has excellent skiing and tourist facilities. Charlotte Pass, 8 km from the Mount Kosciuszko summit, is Australia's highest settlement and provides access to some of the region's highest and most spectacular runs. In the north of the park, Mount Selwyn is a good place for families and beginners, and is one of the main centres for cross-country skiing.

Snowy River

This once mighty river was damned and diverted for the Snowy Mountains Scheme. Some 100 000 men from 30 countries worked for 25 years on the largest engineering project of its kind in Australia. Drop in at the Snowy Mountains Authority Information Centre in Cooma, or visit the power stations near Khancoban.

Alpine Way

Stretching 111 km from Jindabyne to Khancoban, this spectacular route traverses the national park, winding around the Thredbo slopes, passing through Dead Horse Gap and crossing the valley of the Murray headwaters. The route is best driven during spring and summer, although the winter scenery is superb.

Mount Kosciuszko

This is Australia's highest mountain, 2228 m above sea level. Explorer Paul Edmond de Strzelecki named the mountain in 1840 for the Polish patriot Tadeusz Kosciuszko. From Thredbo, the summit is easily reached via the Crackenback chairlift (operating all year), with a 12-km-return walk through wildflowers in spring and summer.

Thredbo

This charming alpine village with its peaked European-style lodges makes for an unusual sight in the Australian landscape. Packed and brimming with life during winter, it has year-round facilities and is also popular in the summer months with bushwalkers, wildflower enthusiasts, anglers and mountain-bike riders.

For more detail see maps 101 & 103. For descriptions of ❶ towns see Towns from A to Z *(p. 32).*

TOP EVENTS

Jan.	*Blues Festival (Thredbo)*
Mar.	*Tour de Snowy – women's cycling (throughout region)*
Mar.	*Strzelecki Polish Festival (Jindabyne)*
Mar.	*Global Music Festival (Thredbo)*
Easter	*Fair (Berridale)*
May	*Legends of Jazz (Thredbo)*
Sept.	*Shout About Trout (Jindabyne)*
Sept.	*Xtreme Winter Games (Perisher Blue)*
Oct.	*Coomafest (Cooma)*
Oct.	*Spring Festival (Khancoban)*
Nov.	*Snowy Mountains Trout Festival (throughout region)*
Dec.	*Monaro Wool Week (Cooma)*
Dec.	*Man from Snowy River Rodeo (Jindabyne)*

Yarrangobilly Caves
Located at the park's northern end, these caves with their underground pools, frozen waterfalls and weird web of limestone formations are said to be the most lavishly decorated in the country. Five out of 70 caves are open to the public. A naturally formed thermal pool offers year-round swimming.

Kosciuszko National Park
The State's largest park, declared 1967, takes in 690 000 ha of peaks, valleys, glacial lakes, woodlands and fields. The park protects many rare and unusual species, including the distinctive snow gum, the only native tree that can survive above 1800 m, and the pygmy possum (pictured), which lives above altitudes of 1400 m.

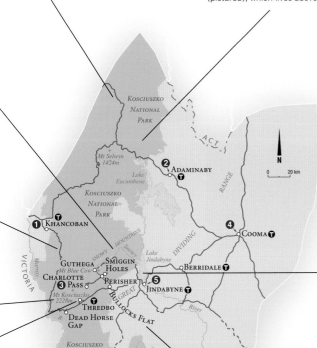

Lake Jindabyne
Created as part of the Snowy Mountain Scheme, this huge mountain lake, along with nearby Lake Eucumbene, has a reputation as one of the best inland fishing destinations in the State, particularly for trout fishing. Sailing, windsurfing and water-skiing are popular in summer.

Skitube
This European-style alpine train provides transport for skiers during winter and the chance for a scenic tour in summer. It leaves Bullocks Flat some 20 km south-east of Jindabyne, crosses the Thredbo River, climbs through stands of massive mountain ash, then disappears underground to link Perisher resort and the Mount Blue Cow ski area (pictured).

THE MURRAY

The Murray, Australia's most important river, runs for 2750 km from the peaks of the Snowy Mountains across three States. It was a great natural resource for the indigenous peoples, who settled the area in greater numbers than anywhere else on the continent. European settlers used the river as a major trade route and a centre for agricultural activity. More recently, the Murray has developed its leisure credentials, thanks to magnificent river red gum scenery and quiet sandy beaches (perfect for water sports), as well as a variety of introduced attractions ranging from excellent golf courses to vineyards and river cruises.

TOP EVENTS

Jan.	New Year's Day Power Boat Racing (Mulwala)
Jan.	Federation Festival (Corowa)
Feb.	Vintage Engine Rally (Barham)
Feb.	Riverboats, Food, Jazz and Wine (Echuca–Moama)
Easter	Jazz Festival (Deniliquin)
July	Winter Breakaway Festival (Corowa)
Sept.–Oct.	Play on the Plains Festival (Deniliquin)
Oct.	Food and Wine Festival (Albury)
Nov.	Festival of the Bogong Moth (Albury)

EXPERIENCE IT!

❶ **Hire** a houseboat or catch a paddle-steamer from the old river port settlement of Echuca (Vic.), the twin town of Moama

❷ **Swim** at one of the 25 river beaches at Tocumwal

❸ **Take** a river cruise at Wentworth

VISITOR INFORMATION

Albury: (02) 6041 3875; 1800 800 743

FOCUS ON

Golf

These days golf rivals agriculture as the activity for which the region is best known. Alongside the great stretches of cultivated land lie emerald-green fairways, most offering superb riverside scenery and excellent accommodation and club facilities, along with great golfing. The 36-hole Cobram-Barooga course is one of the district's best, as is Albury's Thurgoona Country Club, regularly rated among Australia's top 100 courses. There is a testing 27-hole course at Corowa, and a fine 18-hole course at the township of Howlong. Another favourite is the picturesque Tocumwal course, where kangaroos are on hand as spectators.

CLIMATE ALBURY

	J	F	M	A	M	J	J	A	S	O	N	D
Max.°C	31	31	28	23	16	13	12	14	17	21	25	28
Min. °C	14	15	12	8	5	3	2	4	5	8	10	13
Rain mm	23	26	36	46	72	59	83	85	73	73	39	67
Raindays	5	4	6	7	11	12	15	14	11	10	7	8

Deniliquin

Deniliquin, just to the north of the Murray, lies at the centre of one of the largest irrigation areas in the State. It is known for its massive rice export mill and its merino sheep studs, and is set amid a fine landscape of rural and river scenery.

Corowa

Corowa is the quintessential Australian river town with wide streets, turn-of-the-century architecture and an attractive riverside golf course. Federation got a jump-start here in 1893 at the Corowa Federation Conference, now commemorated in the Federation Museum. In 1889 Tom Roberts completed his iconographic work, Shearing of the Rams, at a sheep station nearby.

For more detail see map 110–11. For descriptions of ❶ towns see Towns from A to Z (p. 32).

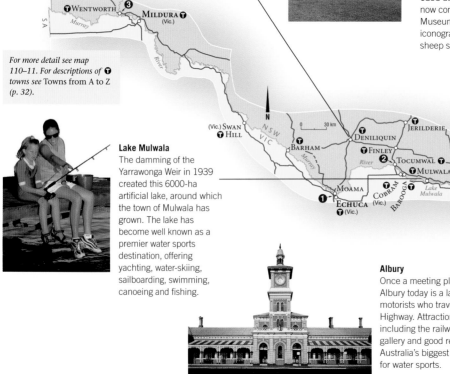

Lake Mulwala

The damming of the Yarrawonga Weir in 1939 created this 6000-ha artificial lake, around which the town of Mulwala has grown. The lake has become well known as a premier water sports destination, offering yachting, water-skiing, sailboarding, swimming, canoeing and fishing.

Albury

Once a meeting place for Aboriginal peoples of the area, Albury today is a large regional centre, familiar to motorists who travel the busy Sydney-to-Melbourne Hume Highway. Attractions include interesting heritage buildings including the railway station (pictured), a large regional art gallery and good restaurants. Lake Hume, one of Australia's biggest artificial lakes, is enormously popular for water sports.

THE OUTBACK

This vast, arid, sparsely populated landscape covers a good two-thirds of the country's most urbanised State. Mining and sheep farming, the main activities of human endeavour, keep life firmly rooted in a frontier past although such contemporary touches as the occasional film crew or espresso cafe are evident. One radical change has been the creation of a series of national parks over several decades. These parks preserve the region's stunning beauty, its natural heritage and its rich indigenous history. Conditions can be difficult out here. See page 599 for details on outback motoring.

TOP EVENTS

Mar.	*Outback and All That Jazz (Broken Hill)*
Mar./ Apr.	*St Patricks Race Day (Broken Hill)*
July	*Tibooburra Festival*
Aug.	*Festival of the Miner's Ghost (Cobar)*
Aug.	*Burke and Wills Fishing Challenge (Menindee)*
Sept.	*Mateship Festival (Bourke)*
Sept.– Oct.	*Darling River Surfboat Classic (Brewarrina)*
Oct.	*Rodeo (Bourke)*
Oct.	*Country Music Festival (Broken Hill)*

EXPERIENCE IT!

❶ **Go** *yachting, fishing, swimming, or camp, at lakes near Menindee*

❷ **Fossick** *for opals in the dugout town of White Cliffs*

❸ **Explore** *Willandra, once the west's best known sheep station, now part of Willandra National Park (via Hillston)*

VISITOR INFORMATION

Broken Hill: (08) 8087 6077

Bourke: (02) 6872 2280

www.outbacknsw.org.au

FOCUS ON

Willandra Lakes World Heritage Area

Willandra Lakes, covering 240 000 ha in the State's far west, comprises dry Pleistocene lakes formed over two million years ago. Fringed by huge dunes, the lakes bear evidence of major stages in the earth's evolution. Archaeological evidence also points to continuous Aboriginal occupation for about 50 000 years when the lakes were full and teeming with wildlife. The lakes dried around 12 000 years ago, but Aborigines continued to use the area. Human skeletons excavated there are believed to be about 60 000 years old. Mungo National Park covers 10 per cent of the area; the remainder is under pastoral lease.

Bourke

'If you know Bourke you know Australia', said Henry Lawson. Situated on the Darling River, the town began in the 1850s as a paddleboat destination. Later a service centre for a vast sheep-grazing area, Bourke has become synonymous with the outback. The town's colourful past is recalled in its heritage sites.

CLIMATE	**BROKEN HILL**											
	J	F	M	A	M	J	J	A	S	O	N	D
Max. °C	32	32	29	24	19	16	15	17	20	24	28	30
Min. °C	19	18	16	12	9	7	6	7	9	12	14	17
Rain mm	23	23	19	18	22	23	17	20	20	25	19	20
Raindays	3	3	3	4	5	5	5	5	4	4	3	3

For more detail see maps 108–9 & 110–11. For descriptions of ❶ towns see Towns from A to Z (p. 32).

Sturt National Park

Occupying 310 000 ha of Corner Country – the point where three States meet – Sturt offers varied landscapes of hill, rock and plain, congregations of native birds and animals, and wonderful wildflowers after rain. Camping is available; check in at the park centre, and take advantage of their tours.

Mutawintji National Park

Driving and walking allows visitors to enjoy sandstone cliffs, river red gums, gorges, rock pools and desert plains in this superb landscape. A program of tours and other activities provides a memorable insight into this area's Aboriginal heritage, which includes some of the State's best Aboriginal rock art.

Broken Hill

Broken Hill was established in the 1880s to service the mining of massive deposits of silver, lead and zinc in the Barrier Ranges. With its historic buildings, 20 or so art galleries and a constant stream of filmmakers and artists, it is an oasis of civilisation in a surreally sparse landscape.

Mungo National Park

Mungo is the focal point of Willandra Lakes World Heritage area. A 60-km signposted drive covers a large area, including remarkable sculptured dunes, The Walls of China. Aboriginal tours are run from Mildura (Victoria); further activities are available at the park headquarters, where non-campers can stay in former shearers' quarters.

Map labels: QUEENSLAND, SOUTH AUSTRALIA, STURT NATIONAL PARK, TIBOOBURRA ❶, WHITE CLIFFS ❷, MUTAWINTJI NP, WILCANNIA ❶, BROKEN HILL ❶, MENINDEE ❶, Menindee Lake, KINCHEGA NATIONAL PARK, MUNGO NATIONAL PARK, WILLANDRA NP ❸, HILLSTON ❶, BROKEN HILL, BREWARRINA ❶, BOURKE ❶, COBAR ❶, 0 100 km, N

NEW SOUTH WALES
TOWNS FROM A TO Z

Snow gums near Adaminaby

Adaminaby   Pop. 366

MAP REF. 101 H5, 103 D8, 126 E9, 235 L1

This small town was moved in the 1950s to its present site; the old site was flooded to form Lake Eucumbene as part of the Snowy Mountains Scheme. Located on the Snowy Mountains Hwy, the town is a good base for skiers and anglers. The ski area of Mt Selwyn (cross-country and downhill for families and beginners) is to the west. West and south of the town is Lake Eucumbene, with a range of holiday resorts and excellent fishing. **In town:** World's largest trout, Baker St. Nov.: Snowy Mountains Trout Festival (fishing competition, throughout region); Race Meeting. **In the area:** Power stations: tours, interactive displays; details from information centre. Fishing boat hire at: Old Adaminaby (8 km SW); Anglers Reach (16 km W); Buckenderra (39 km S). Horseriding, mountain-bike hire and fly-fishing tours. Historic goldmining site at Kiandra, 38 km NW. Yarrangobilly Caves and thermal pool, 59 km NW off Snowy Mountains Hwy in Kosciuszko National Park. **Visitor information:** The Pantry, 11 Denison St; (02) 6454 2453. Web site www.snowymountains.com.au **See also:** Snowy Mountains p. 28.

Adelong   Pop. 782

MAP REF. 103 B5, 104 D13

This picturesque tablelands town on the Snowy Mountains Hwy thrived after the discovery of reef gold in 1857. **In town:** National Trust-classified Tumut St: old Bank of NSW (1882), now a B&B; Beaufort House (1915), originally established as a hotel, now has hotel accommodation and gallery; Gold Fields Galleries, for art and craft; restored Old Pharmacy, now a guest house and restaurant. Village Walk: includes police station (1861) in Campbell St, St James Catholic Church (1868) in Gundagai St, and ends at Adelong Falls Reserve; brochures available. Dec.: Home, Craft and Garden Fair. **In the area:** Adelong Falls Reserve, 1 km N on Tumblong–Gundagai Rd, where Reefer Battery operated until 1910, driven by water from falls (ruins still visible); picnic area, three marked walking trails, gold fossicking. **Visitor information:** York's Newsagency, 52 Tumut St; (02) 6946 2051. **See also:** The Riverina p. 27.

Albury   Pop. 41 491

MAP REF. 111 Q13, 233 P4, 234 C1

Albury–Wodonga is situated beside the Murray River, 572 km SW of Sydney. Once the meeting-place for local Aboriginal groups, today the region is a convenient stopover on the Sydney–Melbourne Hume Hwy. The 1936 building of the Hume Weir created Lake Hume, one of the most extensive artificial lakes in Australia. **In town:** Albury Regional Museum, in former Turk's Head Inn, Wodonga Pl.: display on Australia's largest post-war migrant centre at Bonegilla (Vic.). Botanical Gardens (1871), cnr Wodonga Pl. and Dean St. The Parklands (comprising Hovell Tree Reserve, Noreuil and Australia parks), on western side of Wodonga Pl. at town entrance: riverside walks, swimming, kiosk and picnic areas. Noreuil Park is departure point for Murray River cruises on the PS *Cumberoona*. Albury Regional Art Centre, Dean St, has extensive Sir Russell Drysdale collection. 360° views from Albury Monument Hill at end of Dean St. Performing Arts Centre, Civic Centre, Swift St. Kids Play World, Young St, indoor play centre and cafe. Local dairy products at Haberfield's Milk Dairy Shop, Hovell St (tours). Rotary Community Market, Sun., Tax Office car park, Townsend St. Feb.–Mar.: Festival of Sport. Oct.: Food and Wine Festival. Nov.: Festival of the Bogong Moth. **In the area:** Lake Hume, 14 km E, a paradise for all water sports. Hume Weir Trout Farm, nearby, offers trout feeding and fishing. Upstream of weir, operating Wymah Ferry. Ettamogah Wildlife Sanctuary, 12 km NE on Hume Hwy. Nearby, cartoonist Ken Maynard's Ettamogah Pub. Cooper's Ettamogah Winery, 3 km further along hwy. Australian Newsprint Mill, 15 km N (tours by appt). Linbrae Camel Farm, 16 km N off Urana Rd: winery and river treks. Thurgoona, 9 km NW, home to Thurgoona Country Club, one of the top 100 golf courses in Australia. Jindera Pioneer Museum, 14 km NW, featuring traditional general store.

Howlong, 26 km w, excellent 18-hole golf course. Hume and Hovell Walking Track from Albury to Gunning, 440 km, 23-day trek for long-distance walkers; contact Department of Lands, Sydney; (02) 9228 6111. A section of this track and other trails are part of the Albury–Wodonga Trail System; for information contact Albury–Wodonga Regional Parklands. Hot-air ballooning, skydiving, trail-riding, fishing tours, canoe hire, and tours to wineries and Mad Dan Morgan (the infamous bushranger) country. Bogong Mountains, gateway to Victorian snowfields and high country, 130 km s. **Visitor information:** Lincoln Causeway, Wodonga; (02) 6041 3875, freecall 1800 800 743. Web site www.albury.wodonga. com **See also:** The Murray p. 30.

Alstonville   Pop. 4725

MAP REF. 107 Q3, 525 Q12

Nestled in lush surroundings at the top of the Ballina Cutting between Ballina and Lismore, Alstonville is known for its immaculate gardens and its purple tibouchina trees, which blossom in Mar. Surrounding properties produce potatoes, sugarcane, coffee, tropical fruits, macadamia nuts and avocados. **In town:** Lumley Park, Bruxner Hwy, features open-air pioneer transport museum. In Budgen Ave: Kolinda Gallery and Ward's Antiques for local art and craft. Elizabeth Ann Brown Park, Main St, a rainforest park with picnic facilities. **In the area:** Summerland House With No Steps, 3 km s, has a nursery, gardens, crafts, tropical fruit processing factory, fruit sales and tearooms, all run by disabled people. Nearby, Victoria Park, boardwalk and picnic area. **Visitor information:** Ballina Visitor Information Centre, cnr Las Balsas Plaza and River St, Ballina; (02) 6686 3484. Web site www.tropicalnsw.com.au **See also:** Tropical North Coast p. 19.

Armidale   Pop. 21 330

MAP REF. 107 L9

Midway between Sydney and Brisbane in the New England Ranges (altitude 980 m), this university city is the centre of the New England district and has more than 30 National Trust-classified buildings. **In town:** Armidale Heritage Trolley Tours: 2-hr tour includes Railway Museum and University of New England; departs information centre daily. In Kentucky St: New England Regional Art Museum, contains Hinton Collection, Australia's most

valuable provincial art collection; Aboriginal Cultural Centre and Keeping Place: museum, education centre, craft displays. Newling Gallery in Old Teachers College, Faulkner St, exhibitions by local artists. Pioneer relics in National Trust-classified Folk Museum, cnr Faulkner and Rusden sts. Railway Museum, adjacent to station in Brown St (open by appt or as part of trolley tour). In Dangar St: Gothic Revival-style St Mary's Roman Catholic Cathedral (1912); St Peter's Anglican Cathedral (1875), built of 'Armidale blues' bricks. The Stables (1872), Moore St, now craft shop. Courthouse (1860) and Imperial Hotel (1890) in Beardy St. Central Park, Dangar St, has useful relief map of area. Self-guide heritage walk (3 km) and heritage drive (25 km) of city; brochures available. Markets in Mall, last Sun. each month. Mar.: Autumn Festival. **In the area:** Excellent trout fishing. University of New England, 5 km NW: features historic Booloominbah homestead, now administration building (tours Mon., bookings essential); Antiquities Museum; Zoology Museum, and kangaroo and deer park. Dumaresq Dam, 15 km NE: walking tracks, non-power boating, swimming and trout fishing (Oct.–June). At former mining town of Hillgrove, 31 km E: Rural Life and History Museum with goldmining equipment (check opening times); self-guide walk through old town site (brochure available). Oxley Wild Rivers National Park: Wollomombi Falls (40 km E), one of highest falls in State, plunging 220 m; Dangars Falls (21 km SE), 120 m waterfall in spectacular gorge setting. National Trust-owned Saumarez homestead (1888), 5 km s, tours of house, self-guide farm and garden tours (homestead closed mid-June to end Aug.). Mount Yarrowyck Nature Reserve, 27 km w, 3-km walk to Aboriginal heritage sites. **Visitor information:** 82 Marsh St; (02) 6772 4655, freecall 1800 627 736. Web site www.newengland.org/armidale **See also:** New England & the North-West p. 20.

Ballina   Pop. 16 056

MAP REF. 107 Q3, 525 R12

Ballina is a fishing town at the mouth of the Richmond River in northern NSW. Ideal year-round temperatures, golden beaches, and picturesque farmlands make the area a popular family holiday destination. Cedar-cutters were among the first European settlers. By 1900 a dairy-farming industry was

established alongside sugarcane plantations. **In town:** Naval and Maritime Museum, Regatta Ave, behind information centre, features a restored Las Balsas Expedition raft that sailed from South America in 1973. Kerry Saxby Walkway, from behind information centre to river mouth; brochure available. The Big Prawn Complex, Pacific Hwy: fresh seafood, opal and gem museum, and art and craft. Summerland Antiques, Pacific Hwy, and Heath's Collectables, Southern Cross Dr., for antiques and bric-a-brac. *Richmond Princess* and *Bennelong* river cruises. Shaws Bay, off Compton Dr., swimming and ideal picnic spot. Shelly Beach, off Shelly Beach Rd: rock pools, wading pool for toddlers; beachside cafe; dolphins year-round; humpback whales June–July and Sept.–Oct. Markets at Outdoor Entertainment Reserve, Canal Rd, 3rd Sun. each month. Oct.: Bounty Festival. **In the area:** Self-guide driving tours, incl. River Drive; leaflets available. Deep-sea fishing, whale-watching and 4WD eco tours. Thursday Plantation Tea Tree Oil, 3 km w: tours; East Coast Sculpture Show held Jan. **Visitor information:** cnr Las Balsas Plaza and River St; (02) 6686 3484. Web site www.ballina. tropicalnsw.com.au **See also:** Tropical North Coast p. 19.

Balranald   Pop. 1419

MAP REF. 110 H8, 231 N6

Balranald is set in wool, cattle, wheat, fruit and timber country on the Murrumbidgee River, 438 km NW of Melbourne. **In town:** Historical Museum in Heritage Park, Market St, includes gaol, Murray pine school house, museum with local history displays (open Wed. 2–4 p.m.), picnic/barbecue facilities and information centre. Picturesque Memorial Drive. Self-guide town walk; brochure available. Easter: Homebush Gymkhana. Dec.: Christmas Festival (on Christmas Eve). **In the area:** Balranald Weir (when water is low-level) for picnics, barbecues and fishing. Yanga Lake, 7 km SE, offers good fishing and water sports. Historic Homebush Hotel (1878), 25 km N. Redbank Weir, 58 km NE on Homebush–Oxley Rd for barbecues and picnics. World Heritage-listed Mungo National Park, 150 km NW, features The Walls of China (sand dunes); record of 50 000 years of Aboriginal life; maps available. **Visitor information:** Heritage Park, Market St; (03) 5020 1599. **See also:** The Riverina p. 27; National Parks p. 74.

Barham
Pop. 1167

MAP REF. 110 I12, 229 Q2, 231 Q13, 232 B1

Barham and its twin town Koondrook (in Vic., across the Murray) are centres for the timber, cattle, fat lamb, dairying and tourism industries. **In town:** Self-guide historic walks, brochure available. Barham Lakes Complex, Murray St: artificial lakes, walking track and picnic/barbecue facilities. Feb.: Border Vintage Engine Rally. Aug.: The Country Music Stampede. Sept.: Pro-Am Golf Tournament. **In the area:** Around Koondrook, historic sawmilling town and river port: self-guide historic walk, brochure available; Redgum Forest to Furniture, 4 manufacturers in Grigg and Punt rds; Gannawarra Wetlander Cruises, 15 km S; Kerang Ibis Rookery, 28 km SW on Murray Valley Hwy; State Forest, East Barham Rd. At Murrabit, 20 km NW, market, 1st Sat. each month. Feb.: Flywheelers Rally (restored machinery show). May: Tentpegging Championships. **Visitor information:** Golden Rivers Tourism, 25 Murray St; (03) 5453 3100, freecall 1800 621 8820. Web site www.goldenrivers.com **See also:** The Murray p. 30.

Barooga
Pop. 999

MAP REF. 111 M13, 233 J3

A rapidly growing town near Cobram (Vic.), Barooga's beautiful setting and abundant wildlife make it a popular holiday town. **In town:** Sandy beaches along Murray River. In Vermont St: Dalveile Gallery, features antique oil lamp collection; Botanical Gardens. Binghi Boomerang Factory, Tocumwal Rd. Excellent 36-hole golf course. Lions Market, Vermont St, 3rd Sat. each month. Jan., Easter, June, Aug.: major golf events. **In the area:** Citrus- and grape-growing. Brentwood Fruit Juices, 6 km E, tours. **Visitor information:** Cobram Barooga Visitors Centre, 2 Station St, Cobram; (03) 5872 2132, freecall 1800 607 607. **See also:** The Murray p. 30.

Barraba
Pop. 1267

MAP REF. 106 I8

Surrounded by magnificent mountain scenery on the Manilla River in the Nandewar Range, Barraba is an agricultural and pastoral centre, and an ideal base for exploring the eastern section of the Nandewar Mountains. **In town:** Nandewar Historical Museum, Queen St (open by appt). Clay Pan and Fuller Gallery, Queen St, for art, craft and pottery. Heritage-listed Thomas Jones and Son pipe organ in Anglican church, Fitzroy St. Jan.: Australia's Smallest Country Music Festival (quite large). Nov.: Barrarbor Cultural Festival (celebrating music and trees). Dec.: Horton Valley Rodeo. **In the area:** Birdwatching trails, 171 species incl. the rare regent honeyeater; leaflet available. Adam's Lookout, 4 km N, for views of town. Horton River Falls, 38 km W, for scenery, swimming and bushwalking. Barraba Track and Mt Kaputar National Park, 48 km W, for scenery, swimming and bushwalking (4WD and walking-track access only). Split Rock Dam and The Glen Riddle Recreation Reserve, 15 km SE: boating, fishing, water-skiing and picnicking. Ironbark Creek, 18 km E, for gold fossicking. **Visitor information:** 116 Queen St; (02) 6782 1255. **See also:** New England & the North-West p. 20.

Batemans Bay
Pop. 9568

MAP REF. 103 H7, 127 N7

Crayfish and oysters are the specialty of this holiday town on the Princes Hwy 285 km S of Sydney. Located at the estuary of the Clyde River, Batemans Bay provides access to the river and the Pacific Ocean. **In town:** *Clyde Princess* and MV *Merinda* river cruises (depart Ferry Wharf). On Beach Rd: 27-hole golf course; Birdland Animal Park with rainforest trail. Houseboat hire. Fishing charters available. Market at High School, Glenella Rd, 3rd Sun. each month. **In the area:** Murramarang National Park, 10 km NE, a coastal park noted for its mostly undisturbed coastline and kangaroos. Just north of park, Murramarang Aboriginal Area, 39 km NE near Bawley Point, protects 12 000-yr-old Aboriginal sites; self-guide walk. Durras Lake, 8 km NE, for fishing and swimming. Historic Nelligen, 10 km NW, on Clyde River; Country Music Festival here each Jan. At Mogo, 8 km S: art and craft; Mogo Goldfields Park with working goldmine; Old Mogo Town, 19th-century re-created goldmining town; Mogo Zoo. Calligraphy Gallery, 12 km SE, for local art. Surfing at Malua Bay, 14 km SE. **Visitor information:** Eurobodalla Coast Visitors Centre, cnr Princes Hwy and Beach Rd; (02) 4472 6900, freecall 1800 802 528. Web site www.naturecoast-tourism.com.au **See also:** The South Coast p. 26.

Bathurst
Pop. 26 029

MAP REF. 90 B4, 104 H6

Bathurst, 211 km W of Sydney on the Macquarie River, is the centre of a pastoral and fruit- and grain-growing district. The birthplace of former Prime Minister J. B. Chifley, it is better known today for its motor-racing circuit, Mount Panorama. Town has an abundance of Georgian and Victorian architecture; elegant lampposts in main street. **In town:** Self-guide historical walking tour and Rotary Heritage self-drive tour (leaflets available). Ben Chifley Home, Busby St. In Russell St: Historical Society Museum in East Wing of courthouse; Miss Traill's House (c. 1845), contains 100-year one-family collection, recording history of town and reflects family's passion for horse-breeding and racing. Bathurst Regional Art Gallery, Keppel St. Machattie Park, bounded by Keppel, William and George sts, Victorian-era gardens with sculptures and glasshouses. Oct.: Bathurst (Super-tourers) Car Races. Nov.: FAI 1000 (V8 Supercar Race). **In the area:** Southwest at Mt Panorama on Panorama Ave: Bathurst Goldfields, a reconstruction of historic goldmining area; National Motor Racing Museum at Mt Panorama Motor Racing Circuit; views from summit of Mt Panorama; nearby, McPhillamy Park features Sir Joseph Banks Nature Reserve. Abercrombie Caves, 72 km S on Bathurst–Goulburn Rd: limestone cave system featuring largest natural limestone bridge in Southern Hemisphere; guided and self-guide tours; Carols in the Caves held here in Dec. Abercrombie House (1870s), 6 km W on Ophir Rd, baronial-style Gothic mansion. Wallaby Rocks, 40 km N, wall of rock rising from Turon River, ideal swimming and picnic spot. Sofala, historic gold town, 42 km N, setting for scenes from *The Cars That Ate Paris* (1974) and *Sirens* (1994). Hill End Historic Site, 86 km NW, former goldfield with many original buildings; area has inspired painters Russell Drysdale, Donald Friend, John Olsen and Brett Whiteley; National Parks and Wildlife Service Visitor Centre in old Hill End Hospital, incl. historical display and information on panning and fossicking (equipment for hire). Old gold towns nearby incl. Peel, Wattle Flat, Rockley, O'Connell and Trunkey. Bathurst Sheep and Cattle Drome at Rossmore Park, 6 km NE on Limekilns Rd: performing sheep and cattle, milking, shearing and sheepdog demonstrations. **Visitor information:** 28 William St; (02) 6332 1444, freecall 1800 681 000. Web site www.bathurstnsw.gov.au **See also:** Central West p. 21.

Batlow
Pop. 1069

MAP REF. 103 B6, 104 D13, 126 A4

This timber-milling and former gold-mining town is situated in the Great Dividing Range 28 km S of Tumut, in a district known for its apples, pears and berry fruits. **In town:** Historical Society Museum, Mayday Rd. Fruits of Batlow Packing Complex, Old Tumbarumba Rd (tours by appt). Cascade Fuchsia Nursery, Fosters Rd (open Oct.–Apr.). Superb views of town and Snowy Mountains from Weemala Lookout, H. V. Smith Dr. Apr.: Apple Harvest Festival. Sept.: Daffodil Show. **In the area:** Hume and Hovell Lookout, 6 km E, for views over Blowering Reservoir; picnic area at site where explorers paused in 1824. Blowering Reservoir, 20 km E. Springfield Orchard, 6 km N on Tumut Rd, grows 16 apple varieties; picnic/barbecue facilities. Pick-your-own berry fruits and cherries at farms on Tumut Rd. Access points for short-section walks on 440-km Gunning–Albury Hume and Hovell Walking Track. Batlow District Drive, south of town, links walks and forest parks in Bago State Forest; brochure available. Spectacular Buddong Falls, 25 km S; fine weather access only. **Visitor information:** Old Butter Factory, Adelong Rd, Tumut; (02) 6947 1849. Web site www.tumut.nsw.gov.au/trrc **See also:** The Riverina p. 27.

Bega
Pop. 4190

MAP REF. 100 F7, 103 G10, 235 Q6

It is possible to surf and ski on the same day from Bega, set as it is between the beach and the Kosciuszko snow resorts. The town is near the junction of the Princes and Snowy Mountains hwys, which link Sydney, Melbourne and Canberra. **In town:** Bega Family Museum, cnr Bega and Auckland sts. Feb.: Far South Coast National Show. Mar.: Cheese Pro-Am. Oct.: Bega Valley Art Awards. Dec.: Showjumping Cup. **In the area:** Fine views from Dr George Lookout (8 km NE) and Bega Valley Lookout (3 km N). Bega Cheese Heritage Centre, 3 km N, reproduction of original cheese factory with displays of old

cheese-making techniques. See cows being milked at Brogo Valley Rotolactor, 18 km N (by appt only; fee applies). Mumbulla Falls, 19 km NE, rock pools, natural waterslides, boardwalks, viewing platforms, picnic area. Grevillea Estate Winery, 5 km W on Buckajo Rd, see cows being milked in dairy, 3 p.m. daily. Historic village of Candelo, 24 km SW, old-world charm untouched by time; market (largest on south coast) held 1st Sun. each month. Brogo Dam, 30 km NW, wildlife, bass-fishing, swimming, picnic area, boat-ramp, canoe-hire. **Visitor information:** 91 Gipps St; (02) 6492 2045, freecall 1800 633 012. Web site www.sapphirecoast.com.au **See also:** The South Coast p. 26.

Bellingen
Pop. 2690

MAP REF. 107 P8

Bellingen is an attractive tree-lined town on the banks of the Bellinger River in the rich dairylands of the Bellinger Valley. In pioneer days it was a timber-getting and ship-building centre. More recently, it has become a haven for alternative-lifestylers, incl. farmers and artisans. The area is also known as the setting for Peter Carey's *Oscar and Lucinda*. **In town:** Much of town classified by Heritage Commission. In Hyde St: Bellingen Museum, has pioneer memorabilia (check opening times); restored Hammond and Wheatley Emporium; Sweetwater Gallery. Local art and craft at The Yellow Shed, cnr Hyde and Prince sts, and at The Old Butter Factory (1906), Doepel La. Canoe hire. Markets at Bellingen Park, Church St, 3rd Sat. each month. Aug.: Jazz Festival. Oct.: Global Carnival. **In the area:** Riverside walks and canoeing on Bellinger River. Bike tours into forest areas, maps available; state forests for bushwalking and horseriding. Scenic Bellingen Bat Island in river, with flying fox colony. Raleigh Vineyard and Winery, 11 km E. Picnicking at Thora, 14 km NW, at foot of Dorrigo Plateau. Trout fishing in streams on Dorrigo Plateau (area between Dorrigo and Urunga). Scenic drive north-east through farmlands and wooded valleys, across Never Never Creek to the Promised Land (brochure available); swimming holes and picnic areas; road continues to Dorrigo National Park. Gambaarri Aboriginal Cultural Tours to same area. **Visitor information:** Pacific Hwy, Urunga; (02) 6655 5711. Web site www.bellingen. nsw.gov.au/tourism/bellinger.html **See also:** Holiday Coast p. 17.

Bermagui
Pop. 1196

MAP REF. 100 H4, 103 H9, 127 M13, 235 R4

Fishing – lake, estuary, deep-sea and big-game – is excellent in this delightful small port, 13 km from the Princes Hwy. It was much publicised for its fishing by American novelist/sportsman Zane Grey in the 1930s. Because of its proximity to the Continental Shelf, the town hosts numerous game-fishing tournaments Nov.–June. The town's harbour is the safest on the south coast. **In town:** Diving, deep-sea and game-fishing charters. Fresh fish and prawns at Fish Co-op at harbourside. Humpback whale-, southern right whale- and dolphin-watching cruises depart from harbour Sept.–Nov. Craft market, last Sun. each month. Jan.: Blue Water Fishing Classic. Feb.: International Dog Show. Mar.: Seaside Fair; Tag and Release Game-Fishing Tournament. Easter: Four Winds Easter Concerts; Victorian Game-Fishing Tournament. **In the area:** Beautiful rock pools, particularly Blue Pool; rugged coastline and unspoiled countryside. Safe swimming at Horseshoe Bay Beach. Good surfing at Beares, Mooreheads, Cuttagee and Haywards beaches. Coastal walk (8 km) to Wallaga Lake, through wetland reserves and remnants of Montreal Goldfields. At Wallaga Lake, 8 km N: Camel Rock, unusual rock formation on shoreline; Umbarra Cultural Centre, offering Aboriginal cultural tours of natural features incl. the lake and Mount Dromedary (Gulaga); Wallaga Lake National Park, for boating, fishing, swimming, bushwalking and picnicking, and walking trail to summit of Mt Dromedary. Cobargo, 20 km W on Princes Hwy, an unspoiled historic working village with art galleries, wood and leather crafts, iron forge, pottery and tearooms; country market, 4th Sat. each month in RSL Hall grounds. **Visitor information:** Lamont St; (02) 6493 3054. Web site www.sapphirecoast.com.au **See also:** The South Coast p. 26.

Berridale
Pop. 1295

MAP REF. 101 I10, 103 D9, 126 E12, 235 L4

This small town is near Lake Eucumbene, Lake Jindabyne and the ski fields of southern NSW. **In town:** St Marys Church (1860), Mary St, off Kosciuszko Rd. Berridale School (1883), Oliver St. In Exchange Sq.: Berridale Inn (1863) and Berridale Store (1863). Easter: Fair. **In the area:** On Old Dalgety Rd: Snowy River

Winery, 12 km s, has tastings and restaurant. At Dalgety, 18 km s, historic Buckley's Crossing Hotel (1889) marks spot where cattle used to cross the Snowy River. Snowy River Ag Barn and Fibre Centre, 21 km s. Eucumbene Trout Farm, 19 km N, has sales, horseriding and tours. **Visitor information:** Berridale Store, 38 Jindabyne Rd; (02) 6456 3206. **See also:** Snowy Mountains p. 28.

Berrima   Pop. 815

MAP REF. 99 B6, 103 H3, 105 J10

A superbly preserved 1830s village, Berrima is on the Old Hume Hwy in the Southern Highlands. **In town:** Self-guide historical walk, brochure available. Many old buildings restored as craft and antique shops, restaurants and galleries. In Market Pl.: White Horse Inn (1832), now a restaurant; historical museum; Australian Alpaca Centre, selling knitwear. The Surveyor General (1835), Old Hume Hwy, Australia's oldest continually licensed hotel. Gaol (1839), Argyle St, still in use. Courthouse (1838), Wilshire St, finest building in town, first trial by jury in Australia held here in 1841, now a museum with displays and video of early Berrima. **In the area:** Berkelouw's Book Barn, 3 km N, has over 200 000 secondhand books. Joadja Winery, 8 km NW. Amber Park Emu and Ostrich Farm, 11 km NW. **Visitor information:** Berrima Courthouse Museum, cnr Wilshire & Argyle sts; (02) 4871 1505. Web site www.highlandsnsw.com.au **See also:** Southern Highlands & Illawarra p. 24.

Berry   Pop. 1604

MAP REF. 99 F11, 103 I4, 105 K11

Old English trees add to the charm of this town on the Princes Hwy, 18 km NE of Nowra. Situated in rich dairy country, it was founded by David Berry, whose brother Alexander was the first European settler in the Shoalhaven area. **In town:** Many National Trust-classified buildings incl. Historical Museum, Queen St. Variety of antique shops and galleries. Markets: 1st Sun. each month at showground; 3rd Sun. each month at the Great Southern Hotel, Queen St. Feb.: Agricultural Show. **In the area:** At Coolangatta, 11 km SE, convict-built cottages, winery and accommodation on site of first European settlement in area in 1822. Wineries open for tastings and sales: Jasper Valley Wines, 4 km s; The Silos Winery, 6 km s;

Coolangatta Estate, 11 km SE. Kangaroo Valley, 27 km NW, historic town in scenic setting. **Visitor information:** Shoalhaven Visitors Centre, cnr Princes Hwy and Pleasant Way, Nowra; (02) 4421 0778. Web site www.shoalhaven.nsw.gov.au **See also:** Southern Highlands & Illawarra p. 24.

Bingara   Pop. 1236

MAP REF. 106 I6

Around this fascinating town, garnets, rhodonite, jasper, tourmaline and gold may be found in the creeks and rivers (maps available). **In town:** Self-guide historical/scenic town drive and town walks, brochures available. Stamper battery at site of former All Nations Gold Mine, top of Hill St. National Trust-classified Museum (1860) in slab building thought to be town's first hotel, displays gems and minerals, 19th-century furniture and photographs, and working smithy. Murray Cod Hatchery, Bandalong St (open by appt). Gwydir River Rides (trail rides), Maitland St. Walking track along Gwydir River. Easter: Gold Rush Festival; Easterfish. Aug.: Orange Festival (incl. street markets). Dec.: Country Christmas Carnival. **In the area:** Birdwatching, details from information centre. Rocky Creek glacial area, 37 km SW, unusual conglomerate rock formations. Sawn Rocks, 70 km SW, pipe-shaped volcanic rock formations. At Upper Bingara, 24 km s: remains of old gold and copper mines; Three Creeks Tourist Goldmine, a working mine where visitors can pan for gold. **Visitor information:** 64 Maitland St; (02) 6724 0066. **See also:** New England & the North-West p. 20.

Blackheath   Pop. 4119

MAP REF. 90 H6, 92 C5, 105 J7

This pretty resort town, the highest in the Blue Mountains, has breathtaking views. Known for its comfortable guesthouses and annual Rhododendron Festival, it is a popular retreat for Sydneysiders. **In town:** Statue commemorating the popular myth of Govett (a 'daring bushranger'), centre of town. Cleopatra, French-style gourmet retreat, Cleopatra St. Market at Community Centre, Great Western Hwy, 3rd Sun. each month. Nov.: Rhododendron Festival. **In the area:** Rhododendrons and azaleas at Bacchante Gardens, 1.5 km N. Pulpit Rock Reserve and Lookout, 6 km NE off Hat Hill Rd. On Govetts Leap Rd: at National Parks and Wildlife Heritage

Centre (2.4 km E), interpretive display on geology, wildlife and Aboriginal and European history of the mountains; starting point for Fairfax Heritage Track walk (1 hr return); Govetts Leap Lookout (3 km E). Evans Lookout, 6 km E, offers views of the Grose Valley and 190-m Bridal Veil Falls, the longest single-drop falls in the mountains. Turn off Evans Lookout Rd for Neates Glen and 5-hr circuit walk to Grand Canyon. Mermaid Cave, 4 km s on Megalong Rd. Shipley Tea Rooms, 4.6 km s on Shipley Rd, for art exhibitions (open weekends). Hargraves Lookout on Panorama Point Rd, 2.8 km SW of Shipley Tea Rooms; Mt Blackheath Lookout on Mt Blackheath Rd, 3.6 km N of tearooms. Horseriding at Werriberri Trail Rides in Megalong Valley, 9 km s; at nearby Megalong Australian Heritage Centre, horseriding and tourist farm. Mount Victoria, 6 km NW: craft shops, museum and Mt Vic Flicks historic cinema (open Thurs.–Sun. and school holidays). At Medlow Bath, 5 km s: Hydro Majestic Hotel, once a health resort; Blue Mountains Herb Fest held here in Mar. **Visitor information:** Echo Point Rd, Katoomba; 1300 653 408. Web site www.bluemountainstourism.org.au. **See also:** Blue Mountains p. 22; Wildlife-Watching p. 72; National Parks p. 74; Classic Tour p. 77.

Blayney   Pop. 2672

MAP REF. 104 G6

A major regional centre on the Mid Western Hwy between Cowra and Bathurst. **In town:** Buildings classified by National Trust. Avenues of deciduous trees, particularly beautiful in autumn. In Adelaide St: On Adelaide, for local craft; The Cottage, for local craft and visitor information; Heritage Park, with small wetland area. Mar.: Agricultural Show. **In the area:** Carcoar Dam, 12 km SW, for water sports; camping and picnic/barbecue facilities nearby. National Trust-classified village of Carcoar, 14 km SW, scene of NSW's first bank hold-up in 1863. At Newbridge, 20 km E, historic buildings and craft outlets. Abercrombie Caves, 50 km SE: set in a 220-hectare reserve featuring the largest natural arch in the Southern Hemisphere, tours; Carols in the Caves held in Dec. Local art and craft at Taroona Wool Park (5 km NE) and Cottesbrook Gallery (15 km NE), both on Mid Western Hwy. At Millthorpe, National Trust-classified village, 11 km NW: quaint shop fronts; art and craft shops; historic churches; Golden Memories Museum, a huge complex with blacksmith's shop and old-style kitchen. **Visitor information:** Adelaide St; (02) 6368 3534. **See also:** Central West p. 21.

Bombala Pop. 1380

MAP REF. 100 A9, 103 E11, 235 N7

This small town on the Monaro Hwy, 83 km S of Cooma, is the centre for the surrounding wool, beef cattle, fat lamb, vegetable and softwood timber-producing area. The Bombala River is also known for an abundance of platypuses and good trout fishing. **In town:** Self-guide historical walk (1 hr) includes courthouse (1882), cnr High and Dickinson sts; School of Art (1871), Caveat St (leaflet available). Toorallie Woollen Mill, Maybe St (check opening times). Endeavour Reserve, Caveat St, has 2-km return walking track. Bicentennial Park, Mahratta St, with pleasant river walk. In Railway Park, Monaro Hwy: historic engine shed (open by appt.); Lavender House, local lavender produce, museum of local artifacts and farm implements. Jan.: Wool and Wood Festival. Nov.: Riverside Festival. **In the area:** Fly-fishing and trout fishing, maps available. Platypus Sanctuary, 3 km S, just off Monaro Hwy on road to Delegate. On Monaro Hwy, Burnima Homestead (1880s), 6 km N (open by appt). Early Settlers Hut at Delegate, 36 km SW. Scenic drives (gold-fossicking along route) to Bendoc Mines in Vic., 57 km SW. Coolumbooka Nature Reserve, 15 km NE. **Visitor information:** Mobil Service Station, 161 Maybe St; (02) 6458 3047. **See also:** The South Coast p. 26.

Bourke Pop. 2775

MAP REF. 109 N5

Anything 'Back o' Bourke' is the real outback. Bourke claims to be the largest centre for wool shipment in the world, servicing a vast area of sheep country that produces up to 25 000 bales of wool a year. In recent times, citrus fruits, table grapes and cotton have been successful because of Darling River irrigation. **In town:** Many colonial buildings; self-drive historical mud-map tours, leaflet available. Old Railway Station, Anson St, has displays of Aboriginal artifacts, and local history and products. In Cobar Rd: Fred Hollows' grave and memorial in cemetery; Cotton Gin, tours in season.

Bridge (1883) over Darling River, first lift-up bridge in NSW. Lock and weir, only such structure on Darling. Replica of historic wharf, Sturt St, a reminder of days when Bourke was a busy paddle-steamer port. Paddleboat rides on river, details from information centre. Minibus tours of historic Bourke and of fruit and cotton farms; bookings essential, details from information centre. Easter: Fishing Competition. Sept.: Mateship Festival; Police and Community Outback Trek. Oct.: Rodeo. **In the area:** At airport, 5 km N, ultralight scenic flights, details from information centre. Replica of Fort Bourke Stockade, 20 km SW, memorial to early explorer Major Thomas Mitchell. Mt Gundabooka, 74 km S, wildlife sanctuary featuring caves with Aboriginal art (tours, contact National Parks and Wildlife Service; (08) 8088 5933). Mt Oxley, 40 km SE, views of plains from summit. **Visitor information:** Old Railway Station, Anson Street; (02) 6872 2280. Web site www.outbackonline.net/bourke **See also:** The Outback p. 31.

Bowral Pop. 8705

MAP REF. 99 C6, 103 I3, 105 J10

Bowral nestles below Mount Gibraltar, 107 km S of Sydney. Originally a popular summer retreat for wealthy Sydney residents, who left a legacy of mansions and beautiful gardens, Bowral is now the commercial centre of the Southern Highlands. **In town:** For Tulip Time displays: Corbett Gardens, Merrigang St; garden of Grand Mecure Hotel, Kangaloon St. Bradman Oval, near house where cricketer Sir Donald Bradman spent his youth, and Bradman Museum, St Jude St. Historic buildings, mostly in Wingecarribee and Bendooley sts. Specialty shopping and antiques, especially in Bong Bong St. Market, 3rd Sun. each month at Rudolf Steiner School, Lyell Ave. Mar.: Southern Highlands Antique Fair. Apr.: Autumn Gardens in the Southern Highlands. Sept.–Oct.: Tulip Time Festival; District Art Society Exhibition. Nov.: Bong Bong Races; Southern Highlands Jazz and Ragtime Festival. **In the area:** Magnificent private gardens open seasonally. Lookout on Mt Gibraltar, 2 km N; also bushwalking trails. **Visitor information:** Southern Highlands Visitor Information Centre, 62–70 Main St, Mittagong; (02) 4871 2888 or 1300 657 559. Web site www. highlandsnsw.com.au **See also:** Southern Highlands & Illawarra p. 24.

Braidwood Pop. 940

MAP REF. 103 G6, 104 H13, 127 L4

Braidwood, 86 km S of Goulburn, has been declared an historic town by the National Trust. Gazetted in 1839, it was a pastoral centre before the discovery of gold in 1851, after which it became the southern goldfields' principal town. Much of the architecture from this period has survived. *Ned Kelly* (1969), *The Year My Voice Broke* (1986) and *On Our Selection* (1994) were all filmed here. **In town:** Museum, Wallace St, displays of local Aboriginal history, Chinese settlement and goldmining artifacts (open Fri.–Mon., daily during school holidays). Historic buildings incl.: St Andrews Church, Elrington St; St Bedes, and Royal Mail Hotel with beautiful iron lacework, both in Wallace St. Self-guide tour of historic buildings, leaflets available. Galleries; craft and antique shops. Apr.: Heritage Festival. Nov.: Music at the Creek; The Quilt Event. **In the area:** Scenic drives, brochure available. Catch and buy at Rainbow Valley Trout Farm at Mongarlowe, 14 km E. The Big Hole, a large sink hole, and the Marble Arch rock formation, 45 km S near Gundillion. **Visitor information:** National Theatre, Wallace St; (02) 4842 1144. **See also:** Capital Country p. 23.

Brewarrina Pop. 1113

MAP REF. 109 Q5

Located 97 km E of Bourke, Brewarrina developed in the 1860s as a river-crossing for stock, later becoming a thriving river port. Today, the main industries include wool and wheat production. **In town:** Aboriginal stone fish-traps in Barwon River, once a significant food source for local Aborigines. In Bathurst St: Aboriginal Cultural Museum, displays aspects of Aboriginal life from Dreamtime to present (open Mon.–Fri.); Settlers Museum, shows 1800s river and town life (open by appt). Many 19th-century buildings. Self-guide drive, brochure available. Wildlife park, Doyle St. Apr.: Agricultural Show. Sept–Oct.: Darling River Outback Surfboat Classic. **In the area:** Fishing in the Barwon River. Start of Darling River Run (self-drive tour), brochure available. Narran Lake, 40 km NE, features native birdlife and other fauna. **Visitor information:** Shire Offices, Bathurst St; (02) 6839 2799. Web site www.outbacknsw.org.au **See also:** The Outback p. 31.

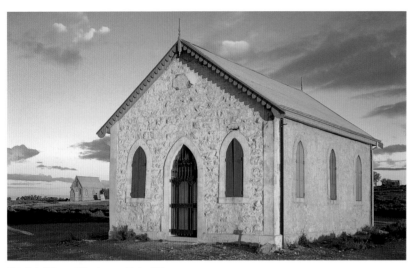

Historic buildings at Silverton near Broken Hill

Broken Hill   Pop. 20 963

MAP REF. 108 B12

This artificial oasis in the vast arid lands of far western NSW was created to serve the miners working in the rich silver-lead-zinc mines of the Barrier Range. The mines produce around 2 million tonnes of ore annually. The city's water supply comes from local storage schemes and the Menindee Lakes on the Darling River. Note that Broken Hill operates on Central Standard Time, half an hour behind the rest of NSW. **In town:** Silver Trail self-guide historical town drive, booklet available. National Trust-classified historic streetscape, Argent St. Railway, Mineral and Train Museum, cnr Blende and Bromide sts. Albert Kersten Geocentre, cnr Crystal and Bromide sts. White's Mineral Art and Mining Museum, Allendale St. Joe Keenan's Lookout, Marks St, for view of town and mine dumps. Many art galleries, incl. Broken Hill City Art Gallery, cnr Blende and Chloride sts. Broken Hill is home of Brushmen of the Bush, a group of artists that includes Pro Hart and Jack Absalom. Thankakali Aboriginal Arts and Crafts, cnr Buck and Beryl sts: works created on premises; artists will explain works and symbols; sales. School of the Air, cnr McCulloch and Lane sts (open by appt, book at information centre). Delprat's Underground Tourist Mine, access via Iodide St, daily 2-hr tours (check times). Muslim mosque, Buck St, built by Afghan community in 1891. Zinc Twin Lakes, off Wentworth Rd, South Broken Hill. Mar.: Outback and All That Jazz. Mar. or Apr.: St Patrick's Race Day. Sept.: Silver City Show. Oct.: Country Music Festival. **In the area:** Royal Flying Doctor Service, 10 km s (book visits at information centre). Mutawintji National Park, 130 km NE, features magnificent scenery and Aboriginal historic site, rich in rock engravings and paintings; access to site on 2-hr tour, twice weekly Apr.–Nov.; contact National Parks and Wildlife Service on (08) 8088 5933 to check road conditions and book tour. Stone sculptures on hillside in Living Desert, 5 km N on Nine Mile Rd, leaflet available. Wildlife-watching on Sundown Nature Trail (2.8-km return), begins 9 km N on Tibooburra Rd (take water); leaflet available. National Trust-classified Silverton, 27 km NW, where silver chlorides were discovered 1883; Silverton Hotel (1880), regularly features in films, documentaries and advertisements (film set photographs displayed on walls); Silverton Heritage Walking Trail (self-guide leaflet available); Silverton Gaol (1889); Nelson's Pioneer Museum; Silverton Camel Farm offers 15-min ride around outskirts of town. Mundi Mundi Plain Lookout, further 10 km N, desolate landscape was setting for *Mad Max II* (1981), *Young Einstein* (1988) and *The Adventures of Priscilla, Queen of the Desert* (1994). Daydream Mine, 13 km NE of Silverton, operated in 1880s, 45-min guided tours weekdays (10 a.m.–3.30 p.m.). **Visitor information:** cnr Blende and Bromide sts; (08) 8087 6077. Web site www.murrayoutback.org.au **See also:** The Outback p. 31.

Brunswick Heads   Pop. 1835

MAP REF. 107 Q2, 525 Q12

This town at the mouth of the Brunswick River is the base for a large commercial fishing fleet. **In town:** Canoe and paddleboat hire at The Pirate Ship on river, off Mullumbimby St. Surfing and swimming. Market at Banner Park, Fawcett St, 1st Sat. each month. Jan.: Fish and Chips (wood chop) Festival. Easter: Blessing of the Fleet; Fishing Competition. **In the area:** New Brighton Hotel, an old pub with character, 7 km NW at Billinudgel. **Visitor information:** 80 Jonson St, Byron Bay; (02) 6685 8050. Web site www.tropicalnsw.com.au **See also:** Tropical North Coast p. 19.

Bulahdelah   Pop. 1113

MAP REF. 105 O3

Situated on the Pacific Hwy at the foot of Alum Mountain, Bulahdelah is a good base for bushwalking and houseboating. The town is surrounded by State forests and the beautiful Myall Lakes. Nov.: Show and Rodeo. **In the area:** Lovely Bulahdelah Mountain Park, has picnic/barbecue facilities, remains of alunite mining machinery, rare orchids and walking track. In Bulahdelah State Forest, 14 km N off the Lakes Way, is State's tallest known tree, a flooded gum (*Eucalyptus grandis*). At Wootton, 15 km N, walking trail along a reconstructed timber railway to historic trestle bridge, picnic/barbecue facilities nearby. Myall Lakes National Park, 12 km E: contains network (10 000 ha) of coastal lakes; ideal for water sports; houseboat hire; bushwalking and camping in rainforest; diving at Broughton Island, 2 km offshore. Fishing village of Seal Rocks, 40 km E: beaches; camping areas; Sugarloaf Point Lighthouse (1875), grounds (check times), whale-spotting near base of lighthouse (June–Aug.). Whoota Whoota Lookout, 43 km NE in Wallingat State Forest, for magnificent views of coast and lakes. **Visitor information:** Pacific Hwy; (02) 4997 4981. Web site www.greatlakes.org.au **See also:** Holiday Coast p. 17; National Parks p. 74.

Bundanoon   Pop. 1763

MAP REF. 99 A9, 103 H3, 105 J10

This town is 30 km SW of Mittagong. The area is well known for its deep gullies and views over the mountains and gorges of Morton National Park. Drive and walk to several lookouts. Bundanoon was once a honeymoon resort; today it boasts an English-style pub, delightful guesthouses, a health resort, and a train stop in the heart of town. Market at Memorial Hall,

Railway Ave, 1st Sun. each month. Apr.: Bundanoon is Brigadoon Annual Highland Gathering. Oct.: Village Garden Ramble. **In the area:** Bundanoon section of Morton National Park has spectacular lookouts, walking tracks and glow worms visible at night in Glow Worm Glen (access is from the end of William St, a 25-min walk, or Riverview Rd, a 40-min walk); ranger-guided walks in park in Apr. Exeter, a small village 7 km N; Old English Fayre held in Nov.; fine horse studs in the area. **Visitor information:** Southern Highlands Visitor Information Centre, 62–70 Main St, Mittagong; (02) 4871 2888 or 1300 657 559. Web site www.highlandsnsw.com.au **See also:** Southern Highlands & Illawarra p. 24; National Parks p. 74.

Byron Bay
Pop. 6130

MAP REF. 107 R2, 525 R12

Before European settlement, Byron Bay was the meeting place for local Aboriginal people celebrating the abundance of seafood and game in the coastal strip. Today it is a mecca for surfers, backpackers and family holiday-makers. Nearby Watego Beach is a north-facing eastern seaboard beach, making it popular with surfers. Cape Byron is the most easterly point on the Australian mainland, its working lighthouse majestic atop 100-m-high cliffs. **In town:** Country-town-like atmosphere with trendy cafes and shops selling everything from lentil burgers to hemp clothing. Also popular for discount surfboards, jewellery, clothing, handmade glassware and timber furniture. Dairy products, coffee, macadamia nuts and tropical fruits are produced locally. Market in Butler St, 1st Sun. each month. Easter: East Coast Blues Festival. Nov.: Buzz Film Festival. **In the area:** Bushwalking, horseriding, fishing, swimming, diving, kite-flying, skydiving. On Cape Byron, 3 km SE: Cape Byron Lighthouse, visitor centre with cultural and natural history of area; humpback whales pass June–July and Sept.–Oct.; dolphin-watching year-round. Offshore Julian Rocks Aquatic Reserve, 3 km S, protects 450 underwater species; diving. Broken Head Nature Reserve, 9 km S, for rainforest, secluded beaches and dolphin-watching. Bangalow, 10 km SW: rustic village with magnificent scenery; art, craft and antique shops; walking tracks; market 4th Sun. each month. **Visitor information:** 80 Jonson St; (02) 6685 8050. Web site www.tropicalnsw.com.au **See also:** Tropical North Coast p.19; Wildlife-Watching p. 72.

Camden
Pop. 10 896

MAP REF. 91 K10, 99 F1, 103 I1, 105 K8

In 1805 John Macarthur was granted 5000 acres (2023 ha) at the Cowpastures; he named the area Camden Park. It was here his wife Elizabeth conducted her famous sheep-breeding experiments. The town of Camden dates from 1840, and is 60 km SW of Sydney on Camden Valley Way. **In town:** Self-guide walk and scenic drive, brochures available. Historic buildings, incl.: Belgenny Farm (1819) and Camden Park House (1834), open one weekend in Sept. only, both part of Macarthur's Camden Estate, Elizabeth Macarthur Ave; Church of St John the Evangelist (1840–49), John St; Camelot, designed by J. Horbury Hunt, and Kirkham Stables (1816), both in Kirkham La. Camden History Museum, John St. Market, 3rd Sat. each month at Onslow Park, 1 km S on Cawdor Rd. Feb.: Heritage Wine and Food Fair. Sept.: Camden Park House Open Weekend. **In the area:** At Narellan, 3 km NE, Museum of Aviation. Oran Park Raceway, 4 km NE, venue for bike, car and truck racing. Kirkham Estate Winery, 1 km N on Camden Valley Way, has regular jazz evenings. Struggletown Fine Arts Complex, 3 km N. Historic Gledswood homestead and winery, 10 km N; unique opportunity to experience a working colonial farm. Vicarys Winery, 25 km N (open daily). Camden Aerodrome, 3 km NW, for ballooning and gliding; vintage aircraft on display. Global Ballooning, 1-hr hot-air balloon flights over Camden Valley, bookings essential; (02) 4655 6440. Markets held at Cobbitty, 11 km NW, 1st Sat. each month. Wollondilly Heritage Centre and slab-built St Matthew's Church (1838) at The Oaks, 16 km W. Burragorang Lookout, 24 km W, for views over Lake Burragorang. Further west, Yerranderie, fascinating old silver-mining town; reached by 6-hr 4WD journey from Camden or 30-min plane flight. **Visitor information:** Oxley Cottage, Camden Valley Way; (02) 4658 1370. **See also:** Southern Highlands & Illawarra p. 24.

Campbelltown
Pop. 11 409

MAP REF. 91 L11, 99 G1, 105 K8

Founded in 1820 by Governor Macquarie and given his wife's maiden name, Campbelltown is a rapidly growing city 50 km SW of Sydney. It is also the location for the legend of Fisher's ghost. In 1826, an ex-convict, Frederick Fisher, disappeared. A farmer claimed to have seen the ghost of Fisher pointing at the creek bank where his body was subsequently found. **In town:** Self-guide heritage walks, leaflet available. Campbelltown City Bicentennial Art Gallery and Japanese Gardens, Art Gallery Rd, cnr Camden and Appin rds. Historic buildings: Glenalvon (1840) and Richmond Villa (1830–40), Lithgow St; colonial houses, 284–298 Queen St; St Peter's Church (1823), Cordeaux St; Old St John's Church, cnr Broughton and George sts, with grave of James Ruse; Emily Cottage (1840), cnr Menangle and Camden rds; and Campbelltown Art and Craft Society (licensed as Farrier's Arms Inn in 1843), Courthouse (1888) and Fisher's Ghost Restaurant, formerly Kendall's Millhouse (1844), all in Queen St. Stables Museum, Lithgow St, has display of historic farm machinery and household goods. Apr.: Agricultural Show. Nov.: Festival of Fisher's Ghost. **In the area:** Winery tours, horseriding and go-kart racing. Eschol Park House (1820), 15 km N. Steam and Machinery Museum, 5 km SW on Menangle Rd. At Menangle, 9 km SW: The Store (1904), old-style country store selling everything from antiques to ice-creams; St James' Church (1876). Mount Annan Botanic Gardens, 3 km W, magnificent display of Australian native plants. At Appin, coal-mining town, 16 km S: monument to explorers Hume and Hovell who began their 1824 expedition to Port Phillip from this district; weekend markets in 10 locations, leaflet available; celebration of Scottish links through Highland Gathering and Pioneer Festival each Nov. **Visitor information:** Art Gallery Rd; (02) 4645 8921. Web site www.mycommunity.com.au/campbelltown **See also:** Southern Highlands & Illawarra p. 24.

Canowindra
Pop. 1656

MAP REF. 104 E7

Bushranger Ben Hall and his gang commandeered this township in 1863. Canowindra today is known as a centre for balloon flights. In 1956, fish fossils of world significance, 360 million years old, were discovered 9 km SW; another major dig took place in 1993. Situated on the Belubula River, Canowindra is noted for its curving main street and fine buildings; the entire commercial section in Gaskill St has been classified by the National Trust as a Heritage Conservation Area.

In town: In Gaskill St: Age of Fishes Museum, display includes fossils from area; local memorabilia museum (open Sun. p.m.); antique shops. Gondwana Dreaming Fossil Historical Digs; digs at 3 sites can be arranged. Hot-air balloon rides, Mar.–Nov. (weather permitting). Historical tourist drive and riverbank self-guide walks, brochures available. Apr.: Marti's Balloon Fiesta. Easter: Model Aircraft Championships. Sept.: Agricultural Show. **In the area:** Numerous wineries and vineyards, incl. Hamiltons Bluff, 1 km N and Wallington Wines and Swinging Bridge, 10 km NW. **Visitor information:** Canowindra Newsagency, 45 Gaskill St; (02) 6344 1618. **See also:** Central West p. 21.

Casino Pop. 9990

MAP REF. 107 P3, 525 P12

Situated beside the Richmond River, this typical country town with its wide streets and verandahed hotels is an important commercial centre for the surrounding beef-cattle region. **In town:** Self-guide heritage and scenic walks and drives, brochures available. In Walker St: Bicentennial Mural; Casino Folk Museum (open Wed. p.m. and Sun. a.m.). Many fine buildings incl. public school and courthouse, both in Walker St; St Mark's Church of England, West St; and Cecil Hotel, post office and Tattersall's Hotel, all in Barker St. Mini railway, West St, operates each Sun. Adjacent, Jabiru–Geneebeinga Wetlands. Eight parks in town and attractive picnic spots beside Richmond River. Tours of meat works, by appt only. May: Beef Week Festival. June: Primex (primary industry exhibition). Aug.: Gold Cup (horseracing). Oct.: Agricultural Show. **In the area:** Fossicking for gold, labradorite and smoky and clear quartz. Freshwater fishing on Cooke's Weir and Richmond River. **Visitor information:** Centre St; (02) 6662 3566. Web site www.richmondnet.com.au/casino **See also:** Tropical North Coast p. 19.

Cessnock Pop. 14 860

MAP REF. 97 B10, 102 E11, 105 M4

Many excellent Hunter River table wines are produced in the Cessnock district. The economy of the city, formerly based on coal mining, is now centred on wine and tourism. **In town:** Galleries, antique and craft shops. Feb.: Vintage Festival (throughout region). Apr.: Harvest Festival (throughout region). Sept.: Budfest Festival (food, wine, street parade). Oct.: Jazz in the Vines; Opera in the Vineyards. **In the area:** Over 60 wineries in Lower Hunter area, most open for tastings and sales (see Hunter Valley map p. 102). At 6 venues in Lovedale, 10 km N, Long Lunch in May. At Rothbury, 11 km N: hot-air ballooning; Charlicia Alpacas, Talga Rd, offers alpaca-patting, rugs and garments for sale, picnic/barbecue facilities. Local art at Branxton Inn and Gallery, 22 km N at Branxton. Rusa Park Zoo, an exotic wildlife park at Nulkaba, 7 km NW. At Pokolbin, 13 km NW: Hunter Valley Aqua Golf, Broke Rd; Hunter Valley Cheese Factory at McGuigan Cellars complex, McDonalds Rd, for tastings, sales and viewing of processes; dining at Chez Pok, Peppers Guest House, Eckerts Rd. Picturesque village of Wollombi, 29 km SW, once Aboriginal meeting place, has wealth of historic buildings, incl. beautiful St John's Anglican Church (1846); courthouse (1866), now Endeavour Museum (open Sun.); old-style combined general store and post office; tours of Aboriginal cave paintings (inquire at general store); Undercliff Winery and Studio (for etchings); Folk Festival (music, theatre, Aboriginal culture) in Sept. Watagan Mountains and State Forest, 33 km SE: splendid views and picnic/barbecue facilities at Heaton, Hunter's and McLean's lookouts. Bimbadeen Lookout over Hunter Valley, 10 km E. German Tourist and Holiday Estate, 10 km NE, has pottery, art gallery, Windarra Winery and restaurant. Richmond Vale Railway Museum, 17 km NE, offers steam-train rides (open 1st, 2nd and 3rd Sun. each month). Local art at Butterflies Gallery, 17 km NE (open Fri.–Tues.). **Visitor information:** Turner Park, Aberdare Rd; (02) 4990 4477. **See also:** Hunter Valley & Coast p. 14.

Cobar Pop. 4524

MAP REF. 109 N10

A mining town with wide tree-lined streets, Cobar is 723 km NW of Sydney. The town is at the junction of Kidman Way and the Barrier Hwy, the main road into the NSW, Qld and NT outback. Since the opening of the CSA copper mine in the 1960s, and the introduction of a channel water supply, the town has become a green oasis. The Elura silver-lead-zinc mine opened in 1983, and the Peak goldmine in 1992 (Golden Walk tour of Peak mine, brochure available). Wool is the other primary industry. **In town:** Self-guide heritage walks (brochure available) and heritage bus tours of town and surroundings. Great Cobar Outback Heritage Centre, Barrier Hwy, features pastoral and mining displays. Fine early architecture, incl. courthouse and police station, Barton St; St Laurence O'Toole Catholic Church, Prince St; Great Western Hotel, Marshall St, with longest iron-lace verandah in NSW. Commonwealth Meteorological Station, Louth Rd (open by appt). Market, last Sat. each month at railway station. May: Agricultural Show. Aug.: Festival of the Miner's Ghost. **In the area:** Aboriginal cave paintings at Mount Grenfell Historic Site, turn-off 40 km W on Barrier Hwy, near Mount Grenfell homestead; picnic area nearby. Historic, deserted mining town of Mount Drysdale, 34 km N; tours available. **Visitor information:** Great Cobar Outback Heritage Centre, Barrier Hwy; (02) 6836 2448. Web site www.outbacknsw.org.au **See also:** The Outback p. 31.

Coffs Harbour Pop. 22 177

MAP REF. 107 P8

One of the larger centres on the Holiday Coast, this subtropical holiday town is 555 km N of Sydney on the Pacific Hwy. The surrounding district produces timber, bananas, vegetables, dairy products and fish. Coffs Harbour is really two towns – one on the highway and the other near the harbour and railway station. **In town:** Coffs Harbour Explorer offers bus tours of town and surroundings. Self-guide walks, incl. Jetty Walk and Coffs Creek Walk, brochures available. In High St: Historic Pier Hotel (1908, rebuilt 1920s); jetty (1892, rebuilt 1997); Coffs Harbour Museum. The Marina: departure point for fishing charters and scuba-diving; whale-watching trips to the Solitary Islands (June–Nov.). A walk along northern sea wall of harbour leads to Muttonbird Island Nature Reserve, a vantage point to see migration of humpback whales June–Nov., and to see short-tailed shearwaters (muttonbirds) Aug.–Apr. North of jetty, Pet Porpoise Pool, Orlando St: performing porpoises and seals; research and nursery facilities. Aquajet Waterslide, Park Beach Rd. North Coast Regional Botanical Gardens complex, Hardacre St, has splendid rainforest and prolific birdlife. Sun. markets at jetty. Oct.: Food and Wine Fiesta. Dec.: Pittwater to Coffs Harbour Yacht Classic. **In the area:** Whitewater rafting (on Nymboida River and Goolang Creek), canoeing, reef fishing, diving, horseriding through rainforest, Harley rides and 4WD tours; Gambaari Aboriginal Cultural Tour of coastal area; self-guide tours through Wedding Bells State Forest and the Dorrigo region (4WD only), brochures available. Clog-making and Dutch village at Clog Barn on Pacific Hwy, 2 km N. The Big Banana, 4 km N along Pacific Hwy, concrete landmark in form of huge banana with displays on banana industry; skywalk through banana plantation alongside. Big Banana Theme Park features Aboriginal Dreamtime Cave experience, 'realistic' bunyip, and ice-skating rink. World of Horticulture, with monorail, is nearby. Coffs Harbour Zoo, 14 km N. Bruxner Park Flora Reserve, Korora, 9 km NW, a dense tropical jungle area of vines, ferns and orchids; bushwalking tracks and picnic area at Park Creek. Georges Gold Mine tours, 38 km W. **Visitor information:** cnr Marcia St and Rose Ave; (02) 6652 1522, freecall 1300 369 070. **See also:** Holiday Coast p. 17; Wildlife-Watching p. 72.

Condobolin   Pop. 3100

MAP REF. 104 A5, 111 Q3

On the Lachlan River, 475 km W of Sydney, Condobolin is the centre of a red-soil plains district producing wheat, wool, beef cattle, fat lambs, fruit and mixed farm products. Apr.: Centre Trek (car rally). Aug.: Agricultural Show. Oct.: Art Exhibition. Dec.: Rodeo. **In the area:** Aboriginal relics, 40 km W, incl. monument marking burial place of one of the last Lachlan group elders. Gum Bend Lake, 5 km W, good for fishing and water sports. Agricultural research station, 10 km E (open weekdays). Mt Tilga, 8 km N, said to be geographic centre of NSW; steep climb (approx. 2 km) to summit, but view is worth it. **Visitor information:** Shire Offices, 58–64 Molong St; (02) 6895 4444. **See also:** Central West p. 21.

Cooma   Pop. 7150

MAP REF. 100 A2, 103 E9, 126 G11, 235 M3

This modern tourist centre at the junction of the Monaro and Snowy Mountains hwys, on the Southern Tablelands of NSW, was once dubbed Australia's most cosmopolitan town. Thousands of migrants from many different countries worked in the region on the Snowy Mountains Scheme. It is a busy tourist centre year-round, and the jumping-off point for the Snowies.

Siding Spring Observatory, near Coonabarabran, has Australia's largest optical telescope

Motorists should check tyres and stock up on petrol and provisions before setting off for the alpine country. **In town:** Self-guide Lambie Town Walk includes National Trust-classified buildings in Lambie St, a street lined with huge oaks, pines and elms (brochure available). In Vale St: Old Gaol (tours, check times); courthouse (1887), designed by noted colonial architect James Barnet. Cooma Hospital (1867), Bombala St. St Paul's Church, Commissioner St, constructed with local alpine ash and granite with beautiful stained-glass windows; first service held here 1869. In Centennial Park, Sharp St: International Avenue of Flags, with flags of 27 countries unfurled in 1959 to commemorate 10th anniversary of Snowy Mountains Hydro-electric Authority and in recognition of workers' nationalities; The Time Walk, district's history depicted in 40 ceramic mosaics. Also in Sharp St, Southern Cloud Park, features Southern Cloud Memorial, a display of remains of *Southern Cloud* aircraft, crashed here 1931 and found 1958. Snowy Mountains Authority Information Centre, Monaro Hwy, has displays and films on Snowy Mountains Scheme. Alongside, Snowy Memorial, commemorating 121 people killed working on the scheme. Nanny Goat Hill Lookout, Massie St, offers views of town. Loegoss Gallery and The Little Gallery, both in Sharp St. Raglan Gallery and Cultural Centre, Lambie St, originally an inn built 1854: works by local artists; local history display. Bike track between Lambie St and Rotary Oval follows Cooma Creek. Historical railcar trips from Cooma to Bunyan (weekends, details

from information centre). Market, 3rd Sun. each month in Centennial Park. Jan.: Rodeo. Mar.: Agricultural Show. Oct.: Coomafest. Dec.: Monaro Wool Week. **In the area:** Mt Gladstone Lookout, 6.5 km W: spectacular views; mountain-bike trails; Austrian Teahouse. Lama World, 19 km W on Snowy Mountains Hwy, cafe and shop open daily; tours and llama 'bushwalks' (bookings essential, (02) 6452 4593). Kosciuszko Memorial, 2.5 km N, donated in 1988 by the Polish Government, commemorating Tadeuz Kosciuszko (champion of the underprivileged) after whom Australia's highest mountain was named. Transylvania Winery, 14 km N on Monaro Hwy. Tuross Falls, in Wadbilliga National Park, 30 km E; 4WD access only to falls. **Visitor information:** 119 Sharp St; (02) 6450 1742, freecall 1800 636 525. **See also:** Snowy Mountains p. 28.

Coonabarabran   Pop. 3012

MAP REF. 106 F11

A tourist-conscious town in the Warrumbungle Mountains on the Castlereagh River, 465 km NW of Sydney, near Warrumbungle National Park. **In town:** Crystal Kingdom, Newell Hwy, exhibits unique collection of minerals from Warrumbungle Range. At information centre, Australian Museum Diprotodon Display, featuring local prehistoric animal remains incl. a massive diprotodon skeleton. Easter: Carnival (includes market Easter Sat.). Oct.: Festival of the Stars (includes Coona Cup Racing Carnival). **In the area:** Aboriginal cultural and ecological tours. Signposted scenic drives, self-guide brochures available. On National Park Rd: Skywatch Night and Day Observatory, 2 km NW, has interactive display, planetarium, night sky-viewing through telescopes, and 18-hole Astro Mini Golf (with space themes); Siding Springs Observatory, 28 km W, has Australia's largest optical telescope (3.9 m) (open day in Oct.), permanent hands-on exhibition 'Exploring the Universe', science shop and cafe. Warrumbungle National Park, 35 km W, features volcanic plug The Breadknife (a 90-m-high rock wall), bushwalking, rock-climbing, wildflowers, nature study and camping facilities (guided walks in school holidays or by appt). Pilliga Pottery and Bush Cafe, 34 km NW, off Newell Hwy, terracotta pottery, showrooms and tearooms in bushland setting. Pilliga Scrub, 'A million wild acres', near Baradine, 44 km NW: 450 000-ha forest (biggest in NSW) of white cypress and ironbark with plains of dense heath and scrub; koala habitat; picnic areas (good koala-spotting at The Alloes); forest drives and walking tracks, maps available. Impressive sandstone caves, 35 km NE (not signposted; directions from information centre). **Visitor information:** Newell Hwy; (02) 6842 1441. Web site www.lisp.com.au/coonabarabran **See also:** Central West p. 21.

Coonamble   Pop. 2754

MAP REF. 106 C10

This town on the Castlereagh Hwy is situated on the Western Plains, 518 km NW of Sydney. The district produces wheat, wool, fat lamb, beef, cypress pine and hardwood timber. **In town:** Historical Museum, in former police station and stables, Aberford St (open weekdays 10 a.m.–4 p.m.). Historical town walk, self-guide brochure available. May: Agricultural Show. June: Rodeo and Campdraft. Oct.: Gold Cup Race Meeting. Nov.: Country Music Festival. **In the area:** Hot bore baths, maps available. Warrana Creek Weir, on southern outskirts of town, for boating, swimming and fishing. Macquarie Marshes, 80 km W, sanctuary for waterbirds. At Gulargambone, 45 km S: restored steam train in Memorial Park; Gular Crays, Armitree St, large yabby hatchery, tours, cooking ideas. **Visitor information:** Shire Council, Castlereagh St; (02) 6827 1900. **See also:** Central West p. 21.

Cootamundra   Pop. 5879

MAP REF. 103 B3, 104 D10

This town on the Olympic Way, 427 km SW of Sydney, is less than 2 hours' drive from Canberra, and is well known for the Cootamundra wattle (Acacia baileyana). The town is a large stock-selling centre for the surrounding pastoral and agricultural holdings. **In town:** Self-guide 'Two Foot Tour' around town, brochure available. Local crafts at information centre and at the Art and Craft Centre, Hovell St. Birthplace of Sir Donald Bradman, town's most famous son, at 89 Adams St. Memorabilia Cottage, next to Bradman's birthplace, displays local historical material. Captains Walk, Jubilee Park, Wallendoon St, bronze sculptures of past cricket captains. Cootamundra Public School Museum, Cooper St (check opening times). Pioneer Park, bushland with 1.3-km walking trail, on northern outskirts of town. Rotary markets at Albert Park, Bourke St, last Sun. each month. Aug.: Wattle Time. Oct.: Agricultural Show. **In the area:** At Murrumburrah, 5 km NE: Harden–Murrumburrah Historical Museum (open weekends); local craft; picnic areas; Picnic Races held here in Nov. Between Cootamundra and Wallendbeen, 19 km NE, The Milestones, sculptures representing the significance of wheat to this district. Wineries in the Harden area, 37 km NE; cellar-door sales. Kamilaroi Cottage Violets, 25 km N, violet farm (tours by appt). Yandilla Mustard Seed Oil, 26 km N (tours by appt). **Visitor information:** Railway Station, Hovell St; (02) 6942 4212, freecall 1800 350 203. **See also:** The Riverina p. 27.

Corowa   Pop. 5161

MAP REF. 111 O13, 233 M3

Birthplace of Australia's Federation, Corowa took its name from currawa, an Aboriginal word describing the pine trees that once grew there in profusion. A typical Australian country town, Corowa's wide main street, Sanger St, lined with turn-of-the-century veranda-hed buildings, runs down to the banks of the Murray River. Tom Roberts' painting Shearing of the Rams, in National Gallery of Victoria, was completed in 1889 at Brocklesby Station, near town. **In town:** Federation Museum, Queen St. Self-guide historical walk (guide on request for groups). Excellent 27-hole golf course. Gliding joyflights and skydiving at aerodrome off Redlands Rd (weekends,

weather permitting). Market in Sanger St, 1st Sun. each month. Jan.: Federation Festival. Easter: Billy Cart Races. July: Winter Breakaway Festival. **In the area:** All Saints Estate, 5 km SE at Wahgunyah, historic and fascinating winery in Victoria's Rutherglen district, features redbrick castle (1878) and Winemakers Hall of Fame. **Visitor information:** 88 Sanger St; (02) 6033 3221. **See also:** The Murray p. 30.

Cowra   Pop. 8544

MAP REF. 104 F8

The peaceful air of this town on the Lachlan River belies its dramatic history. On 5 August 1944, over 1000 Japanese prisoners attempted to escape from a nearby POW camp. Four Australian soldiers and 231 Japanese prisoners died in the struggle. Blessed with rich soil and irrigated from the river, Cowra is now promoted as a destination for lovers of food and wine – asparagus, trout, beef, lamb and smallgoods are some of the quality local produce. **In town:** Australia's World Peace Bell, Darling St. Information centre has fascinating POW interpretive display; adjacent, Cowra Rose Garden. Italian POW monument, Kendal St, built in recognition of Italians who died in WW II; Italian POWs interned at Cowra formed a strong Cowra–Italy friendship (another Italian monument located at POW camp outside town). Lachlan Valley Railway and Steam Museum, Campbell St, has displays and train rides (check times). Colemane's Country Corner, cnr Mulyan and Cooyal sts, a country music museum. Cowra Mill Winery, Vaux St, winery in former flour mill (1861). Aboriginal murals on pylons of bridge over Lachlan River, by local artist Kym Freeman. Cowra Heritage Walk, self-guide brochure available. Mar.: Festival of International Understanding (incl. ringing of World Peace Bell). July: Picnic Races. Oct.: Sakura Matsuri (Cherry Blossom Festival). Nov.: Chardonnay Festival. **In the area:** Australian and Japanese War Cemeteries, 5 km N, beside Cowra–Canowindra Rd (Australian soldiers who died are buried in Australian War Cemetery; Japanese soldiers who died during escape, and Japanese internees who died in Australia during WW II, are buried in Japanese War Cemetery). Sakura Ave, 5 km of flowering cherry trees, links cemeteries with POW camp and Japanese Garden which is setting for the Cultural Centre, traditional tea house, bonsai house, pottery and display of Japanese artifacts. Historic Croote Cottage, 25 km NW at Gooloogong, built by convicts and raided by bushrangers (open by appt). Conimbla National Park, 27 km W. Darby Falls Observatory, 25 km SE, where amateur astronomer has telescopes available nightly. Lake Wyangala and Grabine Lakeside State Park, 40 km SE, ideal for water sports and fishing. Cowra museums (war, rail and rural museums in one complex), 5 km E on Sydney Rd. Self-guide drives, incl. a wine-lovers' drive, through surrounding countryside; brochure available. Numerous wineries open for tastings; details from information centre. **Visitor information:** Olympic Park, Mid Western Hwy; (02) 6342 4333. Web site www.cowra.org **See also:** Central West p. 21.

Crookwell
Pop. 2016

MAP REF. 103 F3, 104 H10

Located 46 km NW of Goulburn, Crookwell is the centre of a rich agricultural and pastoral district, producing wool, beef, fat lambs, apples and pears, and is the State's major supplier of certified seed potatoes. **In town:** Weaving Mill and Gallery, Denison La. (open Wed.–Sun.). Self-drive bushranger trails, brochure available. Market at Uniting Church, Goulburn St, 1st Sat. each month. Mar.: Country Weekend. Spring and autumn: Open Gardens Weekend (dates from information centre). **In the area:** Historic villages associated with gold, coppermining and bushranging, incl. Tuena, Peelwood, Laggan, Bigga, Binda (all north of town) and Roslyn (south, and birthplace of poet Dame Mary Gilmore). Redground Lookout, 8 km NW. Willow Vale Mill, 9 km NE at Laggan, restored flour mill with restaurant and accommodation. Wombeyan Caves, 60 km NE, 5 caves open to public. Snowy Mountain Lookout, 42 km NW. Upper reaches of Lake Wyangala and Grabine Lakeside State Park, 65 km NW, for water-skiing, picnicking, fishing, bushwalking and camping. **Visitor information:** 106 Goulburn St; (02) 4832 1988. **See also:** Capital Country p. 23.

Culcairn
Pop. 1164

MAP REF. 111 Q12, 233 Q1

Dating back to 1880 and planned to service the Sydney–Melbourne railway, Culcairn today reflects the district's rural prosperity. Bushranger Dan Morgan began his life of crime at Round Hill Station, with a hold-up on 19 June 1864. The town owes its tree-lined streets and parks to its underground water supply (discovered 1926). **In town:** Historic Culcairn Hotel (1891), Railway Pde. Many National Trust-classified buildings on Railway Pde and Olympic Way. Also in Railway Pde, French's Furniture, for rustic Australian-style furniture. Local crafts at N & H Crafts, Balfour St. Centenary Mural, Main St. Artesian pumping station, Gordon St. **In the area:** John McLean's Grave, 3 km E; a price was put on Morgan's head after he shot McLean. Round Hill Station, Holbrook Rd. At Walla Walla, 18 km SW: Old Schoolhouse (1875), museum and largest Lutheran church (1924) in NSW. Morgan's Lookout, 18 km NW. Premier Yabbies, 7 km S, hatchery and catch-your-own (closed Tues.). Pioneer Museum at Jindera, 42 km S. **Visitor information:** Post Office, 33a Balfour St; (02) 6029 8521. **See also:** The Murray p. 30.

Deniliquin
Pop. 7816

MAP REF. 111 L11

At the centre of the most extensive irrigation area in Australia, Deniliquin has the largest rice export mill in the world. The town is beside the Edward River, 750 km SW of Sydney. The northern part of the district is known for its merino sheep studs, incl. Wanganella and Boonoke. **In town:** Historical and nature walk, self-guide brochure available. National Trust-classified Old George Street Public School (1879), George St, now houses Peppin Heritage Centre, a museum dedicated to the Peppin family's development of merino sheep industry last century, and history of local rice and irrigation industry. Other National Trust-classified buildings: Courthouse (1883), Poictiers St; former Anglican church (1887), now Multi Arts Centre, Cressy St, surrounded by Waring Gardens; former Police Inspectors Residence (1880s), MacCauley St, now home to Deniliquin Historical Society (check opening times). Sun Rice Centre, Rice Mill Rd, has visitors centre and presentations (weekdays). Blake Botanic Reserve, cnr Harfleur and Fowler sts, community project to present local flora in natural environments. Island Sanctuary, off Cressy St footbridge, features kangaroos and birdlife. River beaches, incl. McLean and Willoughby's beaches. Market, 4th Sat. each month.

Soroptomist Market, in McFaulls Park, Civic Centre, 2nd Sun. in Mar. and Oct. Jan.: Sun Festival. Easter: Jazz Festival. Sept.–Oct.: Play on the Plains Festival. **In the area:** Pioneer Tourist Park, 2 km N: art and craft gallery; nursery; blacksmith shop; antique steam and pump display; mini rural museum. Bird Observatory Tower at Mathoura, 34 km S. Irrigation works at Lawsons Syphon, 7 km E and Stevens Weir, 25 km W. Conargo Pub, 25 km NE, authentic bush pub with photograph gallery depicting history of merino wool in the area. **Visitor information:** Peppin Heritage Centre, George St; (03) 5881 2878, freecall 1800 650 712. **See also:** The Murray p. 30.

Dorrigo
Pop. 1013

MAP REF. 107 O8

This important timber town, on the eastern edge of the Dorrigo Plateau, is surrounded by magnificent river, mountain and forest scenery. Today, Dorrigo is recognised as a place to enjoy country cooking and browse through art and craft shops. **In town:** Historical Museum, Cudgery St (check opening times). For local crafts: Calico Cottage, Hickory St, and The Art Place and Country Crafts, Cudgery St. Wood Fired Bakery, Hickory St. Market at Showground, Armidale Rd, 1st Sat. each month. Easter: Arts and Crafts Exhibition. Oct.: Spring Festival. **In the area:** Trout fishing and white-water rafting. Scenic drives, brochures available. Dangar Falls, 2 km N, viewing platform over wall of water 30 m high. Ebor Falls, 46 km W, in Guy Fawkes River National Park, where river plunges off the tablelands; cliff-top viewing platforms above. Cathedral Rock National Park, 56 km SW, picnicking and walks (incl. 2-hr loop walk to summit of Cathedral Rock for 360° views of tableland). L. P. Dutton Trout Hatchery near Ebor, 63 km SW. Point Lookout, 74 km SW, in New England National Park, for views over head of Bellinger Valley, across to ocean. Dorrigo National Park, 3 km E, features luxuriant rainforest waterfalls; variety of birds incl. bowerbirds and lyrebirds; Rainforest Centre, with picnic facilities, cafe, video theatre and exhibitions; Skywalk, boardwalk offering views over canopy of World Heritage-listed rainforest; Walk with the Birds Birdwalk. Griffiths Lookout, 6 km S, for sweeping views of ranges. **Visitor information:** Hickory St; (02) 6657 2486. **See also:** Holiday Coast p. 17; Wildlife-Watching p. 72; National Parks p. 74.

Dubbo

Pop. 30 102

MAP REF. 104 E2

This pleasant city on the banks of the Macquarie River, 420 km NW of Sydney, is recognised as the regional capital of western NSW. **In town:** In Macquarie St: Old Dubbo Gaol, features original gallows and solitary confinement cells, and animatronic robots telling story of convicts; Dubbo Museum; Indiginart, Aboriginal art and craft from central/western New South Wales. Dubbo Art Gallery, Darling St, constantly developing collection of 'Animals in Art', generally on display during school holidays (open Wed.–Mon.). Market at Dubbo Showgrounds, 2nd Sun. each month. Easter: Orana Country Music Easter Festival. May: Agricultural Show. June: Eisteddfod. Aug.: Jazz Festival. **In the area:** Western Plains Zoo, 5 km S, Australia's first open-range zoo: over 1400 animals from 5 continents, set in more than 300 ha of bushland; program of keeper talks and early morning walks; accommodation. Tracker Riley Cycleway from Dubbo to zoo (5 km); inquire at information centre for directions and bicycle hire. Heritage drives, self-guide brochures available. Macquarie River cruises. Military Museum, 8 km S, with open-air exhibits. Dundullimal homestead (1840s), 7 km SE on Obley Rd, restored squatter's slab-style homestead, with working saddler and blacksmith, animals and Woolshed Cafe. Wellington Caves and phosphate mine, 58 km SE: huge stalagmite; unique limestone coral; fossils; guided tours. Opposite caves, Japanese gardens, a gift from sister city of Osawano. Burrendong Arboretum, 80 km SE: 160 ha preserving endangered plants; constructed rainforest with water features, paths and bridges. Lake Burrendong for water sports; picnic/barbecue and camping facilities. Golfworld, 3 km N in Fitzroy St, has driving range and mini-golf course. Jinchilla Gardens and Gallery, 12 km N, off Gilgandra Rd. **Visitor information:** cnr Erskine and Macquarie sts; (02) 6884 1422, freecall 1800 674 443. Web site www.dubbotourism.com.au **See also:** Central West p. 21.

Dungog

Pop. 2181

MAP REF. 97 A1, 105 N3

Dungog was established in 1838 as a military post to prevent bushranging. On the upper reaches of the Williams River, the town is on a main route to Barrington Tops National Park, making it an ideal base for bushwalkers. Apr.: Rodeo. Sept.: Spring Festival. Nov.: Agricultural Show. **In the area:** Chichester Dam, 23 km N, in picturesque mountain setting; picnic spots in Duncan Park, nearby. Telegherry Forest Park, 30 km N, with walks along Telegherry River and picnic, swimming and camping spots. World Heritage-listed Barrington Tops National Park, 40 km N, has unusual native flora and varied wildlife; good bushwalking, incl. Jerusalem Creek Trail to waterfalls; forest drives. Superb views from Mt Allyn (1100 m), 40 km NW. Clarence Town historic village, 24 km SE, one of the first European settlements in Australia. **Visitor information:** cnr Brown and Dowling sts; (02) 4992 2212. Web site www.dungong.nsw.gov.au **See also:** Holiday Coast p. 17; National Parks p. 74.

Eden

Pop. 3106

MAP REF. 100 F11, 103 G11, 235 Q8

Eden is a quiet former whaling town on Twofold Bay, 512 km S of Sydney, with an outstanding natural harbour. Fishing and timber-getting are the main industries. **In town:** Eden Killer Whale Museum, Imlay St, features skeleton of 'Tom the killer whale', who helped early whalers find their prey. Whale-watching (particularly humpbacks) Oct.–Nov., from platforms on Showground Rd along Aslings Beach. Mar.: Amateur Fish Club Competition. Oct.: Eden Whale Festival. **In the area:** Whale-watching and other bay cruises. At Jiggamy Farm, near Pambula Lake, 9 km N, Aboriginal cultural and bush tucker experience at Monarroo Bubbaroo Guddoo Keeping Place. Ben Boyd National Park, extending north and south of Eden, has outstanding scenery and fishing, swimming, wreck-diving, bushwalking and camping; in park are Boyd's Tower (1840s) at Red Point (32 km SE), and the Pinnacles, red and white earth formations (8 km N). On park perimeter, 9 km S, on shores of Twofold Bay, former rival settlement of Boydtown has convict-built Seahorse Inn (still licensed), safe beach and excellent fishing. Davidson Whaling Station Historic Site on Kiah Inlet, 30 km SE. Harris Daishowa Chipmill Visitors Centre, Jews Head, 34 km SE, has logging and milling displays (open daily, tours Thurs. 10.30 a.m.). Scenic drive and easy rainforest walk at Nadgee State Forest, 35 km SE. Green Cape Lighthouse, 45 km SE, tours. Good fishing and 4WD tracks at Wonboyn Lake, 40 km S; scenic area between Ben Boyd National Park and Nadgee Nature Reserve. **Visitor information:** Princes Hwy; (02) 6496 1953, freecall 1800 633 012. Web site www.sapphirecoast.com.au **See also:** The South Coast p. 26; National Parks p. 74.

Eugowra

Pop. 612

MAP REF. 104 E6

Eugowra is situated in the rich basin of the Lachlan River. It was nearby on the Orange–Forbes Road that 'the great gold-escort robbery' occurred in 1862. Today, Eugowra is known for its crafts. **In town:** Eugowra Museum, displaying Aboriginal artifacts, gemstones, early farm equipment and wagons. Nangar Gems, Norton St, for sapphires, opals, emeralds and garnets. **In the area:** Escort Rock, 3 km E, where bushranger Frank Gardiner and gang (incl. Ben Hall) hid before ambush of Forbes gold escort; plaque on road gives details, unlocked gate allows entry. Nanami Lane Lavender Farm, 19 km SE. **Visitor information:** Orange Information Centre, Civic Square, Byng St, Orange; (02) 6393 8226. **See also:** Central West p. 21.

Evans Head

Pop. 2613

MAP REF. 107 Q4, 525 Q13

Situated off the Pacific Hwy via Woodburn, this holiday and fishing town is the centre of the NSW prawning industry. It has extensive surf beaches and sandy river flats. Rock, beach, river and ocean fishing, boating and windsurfing are popular. Markets, cnr Oak and Park sts, 4th Sat. each month. July: Fishing Classic. Aug.: Bowling Carnival. **In the area:** At Bundjalung National Park, just south: Aboriginal relics, fishing, swimming and bushwalking. Broadwater National Park, 5 km N, for bushwalking, birdwatching, fishing and swimming. At Woodburn, 11 km NW, Riverside Park beside Richmond River; further 14 km S at New Italy, monument and remains of settlement, result of the ill-fated Marquis de Ray expedition in 1880. In New Italy Complex, Guuragai Aboriginal Arts and Crafts offers quality works and information about Aboriginal culture. **Visitor information:** The Professionals Real Estate, 9 Oak St; (02) 6682 4611. Web site www.tropicalnsw.com.au **See also:** Tropical North Coast p. 19.

Finley
Pop. 2137

MAP REF. 111 M12, 232 I1

This town on the Newell Hwy, 21 km from the Vic. border, is the centre of the Berriquin irrigation scheme. **In town:** Mary Lawson Wayside Rest, Log Cabin (replica) and museum, Murray St (Newell Hwy), has rural heritage display. Finley Lake, north of town on Newell Hwy: boating, sailboarding, picnic areas. Jan.: Rodeo and Country Music Festival. Sept.: Agricultural Show. **In the area:** Historic town of Berrigan, 22 km E, known for its connections with horse-racing. Near Berrigan, Sojourn Station Art Studio (3 km SE) and Grassleigh Woodturning (15 km NE). **Visitor information:** Mary Lawson Wayside Rest, Murray St; (03) 5883 2195. **See also:** The Murray p. 30.

Forbes
Pop. 7467

MAP REF. 104 D6

Bushranger Ben Hall was shot by police in 1865 outside this former gold-mining town 386 km W of Sydney beside the Lachlan River. Today industries include an abattoir, feed lots, pet food manufacture, and export of beef and hay. **In town:** Many historic buildings, especially in Camp and Lachlan sts. Bushranger Hall of Fame in Albion Hotel, Lachlan St. Historical town walk, brochure available. Historical museum, Cross St, featuring relics associated with colonial life and with Ben Hall. Cemetery, Bogan Gate Rd, has graves of Ben Hall, Kate Foster (Ned Kelly's sister), and Rebecca Shields (Captain Cook's niece). Memorial in King George V Park, Lawler St, where 'German Harry' discovered gold in 1861. In Dowling St park, memorial marks spot where explorer John Oxley first passed through Forbes. Fossil sites on town outskirts, details from information centre. Markets in Lawler St, last Sat. each month. Jan.: Jazz Festival; Flatlands Hang-Gliding Championships. Mar.: Ben Hall Bike Show. Sept.: Agricultural Show. Oct.: Carnivale (balloon spectacular). **In the area:** Sandhills Vineyard, 5 km E off Orange Rd. Lachlan Vintage Village, 1 km S, historic buildings re-create district life 1860–1900, incl. gold rush era. Gum Swamp Sanctuary for birdlife and other fauna, 4 km S. **Visitor information:** Old Railway Station, Union St; (02) 6852 4155. Web site www.forbes.nsw.gov.au/fbsinfo **See also:** Central West p. 21.

Forster
Pop. 10 443

MAP REF. 105 P2

A holiday area in the Great Lakes district, Forster is connected by a bridge to its twin town Tuncurry, across Wallis Lake. The area is well known for its fishing and is a major producer of oysters. Launch and boat hire for lake and deep-sea fishing. **In town:** Forster Arts and Craft Centre, Breese Pde. Tobwabba Art Studio, cnr Breckenridge and Little sts, specialises in urban coastal Aboriginal art, from paintings on canvas to decorative tiles. Wallis Lake Fishermen's Co-op, Wharf St (Tuncurry), for fresh and cooked oysters and ocean fish. Dolphin-spotting cruises and lake cruises available. Dolphins also seen from Tuncurry Breakwall and Bennetts Head. Pebbly Beach Bicentennial Walk, gentle 2-km walk to Bennetts Head, begins at baths off North St. Apr.: Australian Ironman Triathlon. Oct.: Oyster Festival. Nov.: Half Ironman Triathlon. **In the area:** 4WD nature and eco tours of Great Lakes area, includes bushwalks. Curtis Collection Museum of vintage cars, 3 km S. Cape Hawke, 8 km S, take steep 400-m track to summit for views of Wallis Lake, Seal Rocks and inland to Great Dividing Range. The Green Cathedral, at Tiona on shores of Wallis Lake, 13 km S, open-air church with pews and altar, sheltered by cabbage tree palm canopy. Booti Booti National Park, 17 km S (access from The Lakes Way), includes Elizabeth, Boomerang and Blueys beaches, for surfing, swimming and fishing. Smiths Lake, 30 km S, sheltered lake for safe swimming. Sugar Creek Toymakers, 38 km S at Bungwahl. **Visitor information:** Little St; (02) 6554 8799. Web site www.greatlakes.org.au **See also:** Holiday Coast p. 17.

Gerringong
Pop. 2891

MAP REF. 99 G10, 105 K11

Spectacular views of white sand and rolling breakers can be seen from this town, 10 km S of Kiama on the Illawarra Coast. **In town:** Heritage museum, Blackwood St (check opening times). **In the area:** Surfing, fishing and swimming at local beaches. Gerroa and Seven Mile beaches, 3 km S, world-famous for windsurfing. Memorial to pioneer aviator Sir Charles Kingsford Smith at northern end of Seven Mile Beach, site of his 1933 take-off in the *Southern Cross*. Bushwalks through Seven Mile Beach National Park,

13 km S, brochures available; camping and picnic areas. **Visitor information:** Blowhole Pt Rd, Kiama; (02) 4232 3322. Web site www.kiama.com.au **See also:** Southern Highlands & Illawarra p. 24.

Gilgandra
Pop. 2822

MAP REF. 106 D13

An historic town at the junction of three highways, Gilgandra is the centre for the surrounding wool and farming country. It was the home of the 1915 Coo-ee March, which left for Sydney to recruit more soldiers for WW I. The area is also known for its windmills, which once provided sub-artesian water. **In town:** Heritage Museum at information centre, Newell Hwy, displays Coo-ee March memorabilia. Film *The Chant of Jimmy Blacksmith* was based on Breelong Massacre, which took place near Gilgandra; related items in museum. Also on Newell Hwy: Orana Cactus World; Rural Museum, featuring antique farm machinery (check opening times). Hitchen House Museum, Miller St, has memorabilia from world wars I and II, and Vietnam. At Gil Nursery, Eiraben St, model railway exhibition. The Observatory and Display Centre, cnr Wamboin and Willie sts. Tourist drives around town and to Flora Reserve, brochures available. Easter: Vintage Farm and Steam Rally. May: Agricultural Show. Oct.: Coo-ee Festival. **In the area:** Gilgandra Flora Reserve, 14 km NE, has wildflowers in spring. **Visitor information:** Cultural Heritage Museum, Coo-ee March Memorial Park, Newell Hwy; (02) 6847 2045. **See also:** Central West p. 21.

Glen Innes
Pop. 6101

MAP REF. 107 L6

Gazetted 1852, this highland town was the scene of many bushranging exploits. In a beautiful setting, at an elevation of 1073 m, it is now the centre of a rich farming district where sapphire mining is important. **In town:** Many historic public buildings, particularly in Grey St; self-guide walks, brochures available. Centennial Parklands with Martin's Lookout, Meade St, now site of Celtic monument 'Australian Standing Stones'; Crofters Cottage, adjacent, provides explanation. Cooramah Aboriginal Cultural Centre, cnr McKenzie St and New England Hwy, for Aboriginal art and craft, historic artifacts, restaurant with bush tucker. Land of the Beardies History

House, cnr Ferguson St and West Ave, a folk museum in town's first hospital and set in extensive grounds, with reconstructed slab hut, period room settings and pioneer relics. Market in Grey St, 2nd Sun. each month. Feb.: Show. Mar.: Minerama Gem Festival. May: Australian Celtic Festival. Nov.: Land of the Beardies Bush Festival. **In the area:** Scenic mountain and riverside country. Good fishing for trout, perch and cod; fishing safaris at Deepwater, 40 km N. Fossicking for sapphire, topaz and quartz; includes Emmaville, old mining town 39 km NW, and Torrington 66 km NW (also has unique rock formations). Horse treks, with accommodation at historic pubs. Convict-carved tunnel, halfway between Glen Innes and Grafton, on Old Grafton Rd. Gibraltar Range National Park, 70 km NE: impressive falls; The Needles and Anvil Rock granite formations. World Heritage-listed Washpool National Park, 75 km NE, a rainforest wilderness area. At The Willows, 45 km NW: farm and Aboriginal tourism centre with activities reflecting traditional lifestyle (permit from Cooramah Centre in town); fishing, bushwalking, camping, 4WD tracks. Unusual balancing rock formations at Stonehenge, 18 km S. Guy Fawkes River National Park, 77 km SE, wild river area: bushwalking, canoeing and fishing. **Visitor information:** 152 Church St; (02) 6732 2397. **See also:** New England & the North-West p. 20.

Glenbrook   Pop. 5059

MAP REF. 91 J7, 93 Q9

Glenbrook began as a water-stop for the steam engines that came up the Lapstone Zig Zag Railway line. **In town:** Lapstone Zig Zag Walking Track (3 km return), northern outskirts of town, follows cutting for original Lapstone Zig Zag Railway; features Lennox Bridge, Knapsack Bridge and numerous lookouts. Nearby monument to John Whitton, who had a key role in railway development. Market at Community Hall, Great Western Hwy, 1st Sun. each month (not Jan.). Sept.–Oct.: Legacy Gardens Festival. Nov.: Spring Festival. **In the area:** Convict-built Lennox Bridge, 5 km NW on Mitchells Pass Rd, oldest surviving bridge on the mainland. Wascoe Siding Miniature Railway (operates 1st Sun. each month), 2.5 km W off Great Western Hwy. In Blue Mountains National Park: Euroka Clearing, 4 km S, popular for camping and eastern grey

kangaroos; Red Hands Cave, 15 km S, historic Aboriginal handprint stencils. At Linden, 20 km W: Kings Cave; nearby, Caleys Repulse Cairn, commemorating early surveyor George Caley. Faulconbridge, 16 km NW: Corridor of Oaks, trees planted by recent Australian Prime Ministers; grave of Sir Henry Parkes, 'father' of Federation; Norman Lindsay Gallery and Museum (open daily). At Springwood, 12 km NW: Ivy Markets at Civic Centre, Macquarie Rd, 2nd Sat. each month (not Jan.); Blue Gum Market at school in Macquarie Rd, 4th Sat. each month; Hawkesbury Lookout, further 10 km NE on Hawkesbury Rd, offers views across plains to Penrith. **Visitor information:** Great Western Hwy, Glenbrook; freecall 1300 653 408. Web site www.bluemountainstourism.org.au **See also:** Blue Mountains p. 22; Wildlife-Watching p. 72; National Parks p. 74; Classic Tour p. 77.

Gloucester   Pop. 2634

MAP REF. 105 N1

This town lies at the foot of a range of monolithic hills, The Bucketts, at the junction of three tributaries of the Manning River. Set in dairy, timber and beef-cattle country, Gloucester is known for its gourmet-quality Barrington beef and perch. **In town:** Heritage walk, brochure available. Belbouri Aboriginal Art Centre, Hume St. Market at Billabong Park, Denison St, Sat. of long weekends. May: Shakespeare Festival. Sept.: Mountain Man Triathlon (kayaking, mountain-biking and running). **In the area:** Excellent fishing for trout and perch. The Bucketts Walk (1 hr 30 min return), just west of town, leads up Bucketts Mountain Range offering good views. Scenic flights from aerodrome, 4 km S. Views from Mograni Lookout (5 km E), Kia-ora Lookout (4 km N) and Berrico Trig Station (14 km W). Goldtown, at Copeland, 16 km W, former site of Mountain Maid Goldmine (1876), now largely covered with rainforest: underground mine tours; gold-panning; historical museum (check opening times). Barrington Tops Forest Drive from Gloucester to Scone (sections of road may be covered with ice and snow in winter), features rainforest walks, picnic spots and views; self-guide drive and walk brochures available. Farm tours by appt. **Visitor information:** 27 Denison St; (02) 6558 1408. Web site www.gloucester. org.au **See also:** Holiday Coast p. 17.

Gosford   Pop. 25 690

MAP REF. 91 P4, 94 F6, 105 M6

Gosford, part of the scenic Central Coast, is 85 km N of Sydney on the beautiful Brisbane Water. Sept.: Springtime Flora Festival. Oct.: Mangrove Mountain District Country Fair; Gosford City Arts Festival. Oct.–Nov.: Gosford to Lord Howe Island Yacht Race. **In the area:** Central Coast Winery, 11 km NE. Gosford City Arts Centre, Webb St, 3 km E, has local art and craft and Japanese Garden. Brooklyn, 32 km S, access to Lower Hawkesbury for houseboating, fishing and river cruises; Riverboat Postman leaves Brooklyn weekdays for cruise and postal delivery. Ku-ring-gai Chase National Park, along shores of Lower Hawkesbury; excellent walks, Aboriginal engravings, views, wildlife. Henry Kendall Cottage (1838), 3 km SW in Henry Kendall St, where poet lived 1874–75; picnic/barbecue facilities in pleasant grounds. Australian Reptile Park and Wildlife Sanctuary, at Somersby, 15 km SW, features a snake house with taipans and pythons, goannas and a platypus. Adjacent is Old Sydney Town, a reconstruction of early pioneer settlement. Somersby Falls, near Old Sydney Town, ideal picnic spot. Forest of Tranquillity at Ourimbah, 14 km NW, walking trails through rainforest; Firefly Festival held here mid-Nov.–mid-Dec. **Visitor information:** 200 Mann St; (02) 4385 4430, freecall 1300 130 708. Web site www.cctourism.com.au **See also:** Central Coast & Hawkesbury p. 16; National Parks p. 74.

Goulburn   Pop. 21 293

MAP REF. 103 G3, 104 H11

This history-rich city is just off the Hume Hwy, 202 km SW of Sydney. It is the centre of a wealthy farming district at the junction of the Wollondilly and Mulwaree rivers. **In town:** National Trust-classified coach-house Riversdale (1840), Maud St. St Clair History House (c.1843), Sloane St, a 20-room mansion restored by local historical society. Garroorigang, Braidwood Rd, South Goulburn (1857), private home in almost original condition. Old Goulburn Brewery Hotel, Bungonia Rd. Goulburn Courthouse, Montague St, features Italianate dome. In Bourke St: Regional Art Gallery; St Saviour's Cathedral. Cathedral of St Peter and St Paul, cnr Bourke and Verner sts. Two-foot Walking

Tour (2 hrs) of historic town buildings, brochure available. Fibre Design gallery, Montague St. The Big Merino, a 15-m sculptured relief, Hume Hwy, has displays of wool products and Australiana for sale. South Hill, Garoorigang Rd, features woollen art. Picnic/barbecue facilities at Marsden Weir. Rocky Hill War Memorial, Memorial Dr., city's best-known landmark. East Goulburn Markets, 3rd Sat. each month. Feb.: Australian Blues Music Festival. Mar.: Rose Show; Weekend of Heritage. Oct.: Lilac City Festival. **In the area:** Shearing and sheep-dog demonstrations (by appt) at Pelican Sheep Station, 10 km S. Geologically interesting Bungonia State Recreation Area, 35 km E; walks, incl. one through the spectacular Bungonia Gorge, brochures available. Lake George, 40 km SW, 25-km-long lake that regularly fills and empties; picnics. **Visitor information:** 201 Sloane St; (02) 4823 4492, freecall 1800 353 646. **See also:** Capital Country p. 23.

Grafton Pop. 16 562

MAP REF. 107 P6

A garden city, noted for its riverbank parks and its jacaranda, wheel and flame trees, Grafton is at the junction of the Pacific and Gwydir hwys, 665 km N of Sydney. **In town:** Numerous National Trust-classified buildings. Schaeffer House (1900), Fitzroy St, now district historical museum. Stately Prentice House, Fitzroy St, houses a fine regional art gallery. Susan Island in Clarence River, a rainforest recreation reserve and home to large fruit bat colony. Rivercat for self-drive hire or skippered cruises. Alumy Greek Markets, Southgate Rd, last Sat. each month; Southside Markets, cnr Spring and New sts, South Grafton, 3rd Sat. each month. July: Grafton Cup. Oct.: Bridge to Bridge Ski Race. Oct.–Nov.: Jacaranda Festival. Nov.: Bridge to Bridge Sailing Classic. **In the area:** Canoeing and rafting on wild rivers. National parks within hour's drive: Yuraygir (50 km E), Bundjalung (70 km N), Washpool (88 km NW) and Gibraltar Range (92 km NW). National Trust-classified Ulmarra village, 12 km NE, a turn-of-the-century river port. House-boat hire at Brushgrove, 20 km NE. Weekend gliding at Eatonsville, 18 km NW. **Visitor information:** cnr Spring St and Pacific Hwy, South Grafton; (02) 6642 4677. Web site www.tropicalnsw. com.au **See also:** Tropical North Coast p. 19.

Goulburn Courthouse, a testimony to the wealth of the district

Grenfell Pop. 1956

MAP REF. 103 B1, 104 D8

Birthplace of writer Henry Lawson, this small town is 377 km W of Sydney, on the Mid Western Hwy. **In town:** Henry Lawson Obelisk, next to Lawson Park on road south to Young, on site of house where poet is believed to have been born in 1867. Bust of Henry Lawson, Main St. Historic George St has many buildings dating back to 1860s. Guide to Historic Buildings of Grenfell (walk) and Tour of Grenfell Town (drive); brochures available. Museum, Camp St (open weekends). Off Mid Western Hwy, O'Brien's Reef Lookout, gold discovery site, has walkway and picnic facilities; endemic garden and iris garden adjacent to lookout (access from O'Brien St). Grenfell House (1907), Weddin St, former convent, now tea-rooms and B&B. Easter: Guinea Pig Races. June: Henry Lawson Festival of Arts. Oct.: Iris Festival. Nov.: Grenfell Guineas (horseracing). **In the area:** Weddin Mountains National Park, 18 km SW, for bushwalking, camping and picnicking; area used as hideout by bushrangers Ben Hall and others; easy walk to Ben Hall's Cave and to Seaton's Farm, an historic homestead in park; self–guide drive/walk, brochure available. Site of Ben Hall's farmhouse and stockyards, 25 km W, on Sandy Creek Rd, off Mid Western Hwy. Lirambenda Riding School and Animal Farm, 20 km S. Adelargo Drive, features Cypress Valley Ostrich Facility, 30 km NE on Peaks Creek Rd; self-guide brochure available. Company Dam Nature Reserve, 1 km NW, for bushwalking. Old Richmond Cottage, 30 km W at Quandialla, for tours of cottage gardens, bush stories, poetry readings and devonshire teas (by appt only). **Visitor information:** CWA Wool & Craft Centre, 68 Main St; (02) 6343 1612. **See also:** Central West p. 21.

Griffith Pop. 14 209

MAP REF. 111 N7

A thriving city developed as a result of irrigation, Griffith was designed by Walter Burley Griffin, architect of Canberra, and named after Sir Arthur Griffith, the first Minister for Public Works in the NSW government. Rice is the most profitable industry, followed by citrus fruits, grapes, vegetables, eggs and poultry. Griffith is also a wine-producing area; there are over a dozen wineries in the district, while the Murrumbidgee Irrigation Area produces more than 70 per cent of the State's wines. **In town:** Two Foot Tour and self-drive tour, brochures available. Riverina Grove, Whybrow St, local jar produce (tastings). In Banna Ave: Regional Theatre has stage curtain designed and created by 300 residents, to reflect city, surrounding villages and industries; Regional Art Gallery, has monthly exhibitions. Griffith Cottage Gallery, Bridge Rd. Crafty Spot, Benerembah St. Market, each Sun. in Wakaden St. Easter: Festival of Griffith. June: Taste of Riverina (alternates with Wagga). Oct.: Festival of Gardens. **In the area:** Pioneer Park Museum, 2 km N, set in 18 ha of bushland features drop-log buildings, early 20th-century memora-bilia and Bagtown Village, re-created to show development of area. Belle Amour (5 km N) and Casuarina (11 km N), private gardens open Sept.–May (check

Canola, one of the crops grown around Gunnedah

opening times). Lake Wyangan, 10 km NW, for water sports. Bagtown Cemetery, 5 km S, a reminder of pioneering days. Catania Fruit Salad Farm, 8 km S on Cox Rd at Hanwood, horticultural farm offering demonstrations (guided tours daily, 1.30 p.m.). Cocoparra National Park, 25 km NE, for wildflowers and birdlife. Many wineries in area, incl. Miranda, De Bortoli and McWilliams; most open for tastings and cellar-door sales. **Visitor information:** cnr Banna and Jondaryan aves; (02) 6962 4145, freecall 1800 648 144. Web site www.riverinatourism.com.au **See also:** The Riverina p. 27.

Gulgong   Pop. 2018

MAP REF. 104 H2

This old goldmining town, 29 km NW of Mudgee, is known as 'the town on the [original] $10 note'. In the 1870s it was packed with fortune hunters. The town's narrow streets are lined with clapboard and iron buildings from the gold era, decorated with their original iron lace. **In town:** Henry Lawson Centre, Mayne St, boasts largest collection of Lawson memorabilia outside Sydney's Mitchell Library. Historic buildings on Two Foot Tour (brochures available) include: Prince of Wales Opera House, Mayne St; Ten Dollar Town Motel (formerly Royal Hotel), cnr Mayne and Medley sts; American Tobacco Warehouse and Fancy Goods Emporium, Mayne St; Pioneers Museum, cnr Herbert and Bayly sts. Red Hill, off White St, site of original gold strike, features restored stamper mill, poppet head, memorial of Henry Lawson. Jan.: Folk Festival. June: Henry Lawson Festival. Oct.: Heritage Weekend. **In the area:** A number of wineries. At Ulan, 22 km NE: Ulan Coal Mine, viewing areas overlook large open-cut mine; Hands on the Rock, Aboriginal rock art. In

Goulburn River National Park, The Drip, 50-m curtains of water dripping through rocks alongside Goulburn River. Talbragar Fossil Fish Beds, 35 km NE, one of few Jurassic Period fossil deposits in Australia. **Visitor information:** 109 Herbert St; (02) 6374 1202. **See also:** Central West p. 21.

Gundagai   Pop. 2064

MAP REF. 103 B5, 104 D12

Much celebrated in song and verse, this town on the Murrumbidgee River at the foot of Mt Parnassus, 398 km SW of Sydney, has become part of Australian folklore. Its history includes Australia's worst flood disaster in 1852 when 89 people drowned; nearby gold rushes; and many bushranging attacks. Today it is the centre of a rich pastoral and agricultural district that produces wool, wheat, fruit and vegetables. **In town:** Marble carving of cathedral, comprising over 20 000 pieces, by Frank Rusconi (sculptor of tucker box dog) on display in information centre, Sheridan St. Also in Sheridan St: Gabriel Gallery, with its outstanding collection of early photographs, letters and possessions of poet Henry Lawson; National Trust-classified courthouse (1859), scene of historic trials, incl. that of notorious bushranger Captain Moonlite; National Trust-classified Prince Alfred Bridge (1866), longest timber viaduct in Australia. Historical museum, Homer St. National Trust-classified St John's Anglican Church (1861), cnr Otway and Punch sts. Excellent views from Mt Parnassus Lookout, Hanley St, and Rotary Lookout, Luke St, South Gundagai. Oct.: Spring Flower Show. Nov.: Dog on the Tucker Box Festival; Snake Gully Cup. **In the area:** The Dog on the Tucker Box, 'five miles from Gundagai' (8 km N), monument to pioneer teamsters and their dogs, celebrated in song by Jack

O'Hagan; statues of Dad and Dave, characters from writings of Steele Rudd; kiosk; fernery; ruins of Five Mile Pub. Asparagus plantation at Jugiong, 41 km NE (sales daily Oct.–Dec.). **Visitor information:** 249 Sheridan St; (02) 6944 1341. **See also:** The Riverina p. 27.

Gunnedah   Pop. 8315

MAP REF. 106 H10

Gunnedah, on the banks of the Namoi River, is in rich pastoral and agricultural country and is one of the largest stock-marketing centres in NSW. Other industries include a brickworks, a tannery, flour mills and open-cut and underground coal mines. **In town:** Self-drive town tour and Bindea Town Walk; brochures available. In Anzac Park, South St: Water Tower Museum; Dorothea MacKellar Memorial statue (MacKellar was an Australian poet and author of 'My Country'). Opposite at information centre, MacKellar memorabilia. Rural Museum, Mullaley Rd. Red Chief Memorial to an Aboriginal warrior of Gunn-e-dar group, State Office building in Abbott St. Old Bank Gallery, Conadilly St. Creative Arts Centre, Chandos St. Eighth Division Memorial Avenue of flowering gums. Market, 3rd Sat. each month in Wolsely Park, Conadilly St. Sheep and cattle sales at Saleyards, Boggabri Rd, each Tues. Jan.: National Tomato Competition. Apr.: Grey Mardi Gras (celebration for senior citizens). Aug.: Ag Quip (Agricultural Field Days). Sept.: Vintage Car Swap Meet. **In the area:** Porcupine Lookout, 3 km SE, offers views over town and surrounding agricultural area. Lake Keepit Dam and State Recreation Centre, 34 km NE, for water sports, bushwalking, gliding club, picnicking, camping, caravan park. Waterways Wildlife Park, 7 km W on Mullaley Rd. 150° East Time Meridian, 28 km W. **Visitor information:** Anzac Park, South St; (02) 6740 2230. Web site www.infogunnedah.com.au **See also:** New England & the North-West p. 20.

Gunning   Pop. 486

MAP REF. 103 E4, 104 G11

This town, on the Old Hume Hwy between Goulburn and Yass, is in the centre of pastoral country. **In town:** In Yass St: Pye Cottage, a slab-style pioneer cottage; historic post office; Telegraph Hotel; old courthouse; Do Duck Inn (now B&B). Feb.: Agricultural Show. Oct.: Festival. **In the area:** Greendale Pioneer

Cemetery, Gunning–Boorowa Rd. Hume and Hovell Walking Track extends 440 km, from Gunning to Albury, a 23-day trek for long-distance walkers; half-day, one-day and weekend walks at various points along route (contact Department of Land and Water Conservation, Wagga Wagga; (02) 6921 2503). **Visitor information:** Gunning Motel, Yass St; (02) 4845 1191. **See also:** Capital Country p. 23.

Guyra   Pop. 1801

MAP REF. 107 L8

Guyra is Aboriginal for 'fish may be caught', and local streams are excellent for fishing. At 1320 m, this small town in the Great Dividing Range is one of the highest in NSW. The area has a rich mining history, but is known today for its fat lambs, beef, wool and potatoes. **In town:** In Bradley St: Historical Society Museum (open by appt); Railway Station, with large display of antique machinery. Waterbirds at Mother of Ducks Lagoon, McKie Pde. Jan.: Lamb and Potato Festival (includes Hydrangea Festival). Feb.: Agricultural Show. Apr.: Rugby Seven Carnival. Nov.: Rodeo. **In the area:** Chandler's Peak, 20 km E, for spectacular views. Llangothlin Handcraft Hall on Hwy, 10 km N. Thunderbolt's Cave, 10 km S. **Visitor information:** Crystal Trout Caravan Park, New England Hwy; (02) 6779 1241. **See also:** New England & the North-West p. 20.

Hay   Pop. 2896

MAP REF. 111 K8

Hay, established 1859, was named after the politician and pastoralist Sir John Hay. The commercial centre for a huge area of semi-arid grazing country, Hay is on the banks of the Murrumbidgee River at the junction of the Cobb, Mid Western and Sturt hwys. Increasing irrigation from the Murrumbidgee has led to an expansion in rice- vegetable- and fruit-growing. The area supports a strong beef industry and world-famous sheep studs. **In town:** Self-guide historical town walk and scenic drive, brochures available. In Lachlan St: historical buildings, incl. post office (1881), Shire office (1877), and Lands office (1896), buildings designed for the harsh outback environment; Witcombe Fountain (1883) and plaque, commemorating journey of explorer Charles Sturt along Murrumbidgee and Murray rivers 1829–30; coach-house in main shopping area, featuring original Cobb & Co. coach on Deniliquin–Hay–Wilcannia run until 1901. Hay Gaol Museum, Church St, has pioneer relics. Restored courthouse (1892), Moppett St. Restored railway station (1882), Murray St, houses POW Internment Camp Interpretive Centre: documents WW II internment of over 3000 prisoners of war in Hay. Australian Shearer's Hall of Fame, Alma St, working museum documenting wool industry. Hay Park, cnr Moppett and Pine sts. Nature walk along banks of river, southern end of town off Brunker St. Sandy river beaches for swimming, boating and fishing. Hay Wetlands, north-western edge of town; breeding ground for many inland bird species; directions from information centre. Bishop's Lodge, South Hay (1888), restored as museum, exhibition gallery and conference centre; Spring Market here 3rd Sun. in Oct. Jan.: Surf Carnival. Mar.: Riverina Stud Merino Field Day. May: Sheep Show. Sept.: Agricultural Show. **In the area:** Ruberto's Winery, Sturt Hwy, South Hay. Sunset viewing area, 16 km N on Booligal Rd. John Oxley Memorial at Booligal, 78 km N on Lachlan River; town mentioned in Banjo Paterson's poem 'Hay and Hell and Booligal'. Weir on Murrumbidgee River, 12 km W. Further west, vast river plains popular for 4WD tours. Villages of Maude (53 km W), with attractive picnic areas near weir, and Oxley (87 km NW), with river red gums and prolific wildlife (best seen at dusk). **Visitor information:** 407 Moppett St; (02) 6993 4045. Web site www.riverinatourism.com.au **See also:** The Riverina p. 27.

Henty   Pop. 878

MAP REF. 104 A13, 111 Q11

The historic pastoral township of Henty is in the heart of Morgan Country (named after the infamous, ill-fated bushranger Dan Morgan). Henty is almost midway between Albury–Wodonga and Wagga Wagga. **In town:** Headlie Taylor Header Memorial, Henty Park, off Allen St, a tribute to mechanical header-harvester (invented 1914) that revolutionised the grain industry. Mini Museum under supermarket in Sladen St, has town and commercial memorabilia. Sept.: Machinery Field Days. **In the area:** Sergeant Smith Memorial Stone, 2 km W on Pleasant Hills Rd, marks site where Dan Morgan fatally wounded a policeman. Doodle Cooma Swamp (2000 ha), breeding area for waterbirds, is visible from memorial stone. At Pleasant Hills, 27 km W, unique headstones on graves of German descendants in area. Buckargingah Woolshed, built of chocks and logs (no nails), 11 km E on Cookardinia Rd. Vintage Day held in Yerong Creek, 17 km N, each Oct. **Visitor information:** Dales Supermarket, 13 Sladen St; (02) 6929 3302. **See also:** The Murray p. 30.

Holbrook   Pop. 1331

MAP REF. 111 R12, 233 R1

This small town is a well-known stock-breeding centre, 521 km SW of Sydney, on the Hume Hwy. **In town:** Bronze statue of Commander N. D. Holbrook and his submarine, in Holbrook Park, Hume Hwy; submarine is a scale model of one in which Holbrook won the VC in WW I; town (formerly Germanton) was renamed in his honour. Adjacent to park, 30 m submarine formerly called the Otway, decommissioned in 1995. Woolpack Inn Museum, in former hotel (1860), Albury St, features 20 rooms furnished in turn-of-the-century style, bakery, horse-drawn vehicles and farm equipment. Ten Mile Creek, behind museum, for picnics. Apr.: Beef Fest (even-numbered years). Nov.: Agricultural Show. **In the area:** Ultralight Centre, 3 km N at Holbrook Airport; flights and instruction available. Hume and Hovell Walking Track, access from Woomargama, 15 km S; brochure available. **Visitor information:** Woolpack Inn Museum, 83 Albury St (Hume Hwy); (02) 6036 2131. **See also:** The Murray p. 30.

Huskisson   Pop. 3350

MAP REF. 103 I4, 105 K12, 127 R1

Huskisson is 24 km SE of Nowra, on the shores of Jervis Bay, which is renowned for its clear water and is frequently used for underwater film sequences. **In town:** Lady Denman Heritage Complex, Woollamia Rd, provides history of wooden shipbuilding at Huskisson; also in Complex, Laddie Timbery's Aboriginal Art and Craft Centre, bush tucker demonstrations and talks on request; Museum of Jervis Bay Science and the Sea has fine maritime and surveying collections. Diving and dolphin-watching cruises (dolphin population in bay). Market, 2nd Sun. each month at White Sands Park. Easter: White Sands Carnival. **In the area:** Water sports, particularly diving. Excellent fishing. Barry's Bush Tucker Tours, guided native walks, Aboriginal history, bush tucker. NSW Jervis Bay National Park, north and south of town: walking tracks; mangrove boardwalk. Booderee National Park, south of town: Aboriginal sites; Cape St George Lighthouse; Booderee Botanic Gardens; boat-launching facilities; magnificent beaches. **Visitor information:** Shoalhaven Visitors Centre, cnr Princes Hwy and Pleasant Way, Nowra; (02) 4421 0778, freecall 1800 024 261. Web site www.shoalhaven.nsw.gov.au **See also:** The South Coast p. 26; National Parks p. 74.

Iluka
Pop. 1863

MAP REF. 107 Q5

A coastal resort alongside the mouth of the Clarence River, Iluka is well known for its fishing. A deep-sea fishing fleet operates from the harbour. **In town:** Daily passenger ferry services to Yamba. River cruises from Boatshed, Wed. and Fri. July: Amateur Fishing Classic. **In the area:** World Heritage-listed Iluka Rainforest, in Bundjalung National Park, at northern edge of town; park has a variety of birdlife, and offers excellent fishing, swimming, surfing, canoeing, walking and camping. Woombah Coffee Plantation, 14 km W, world's southernmost coffee plantation (tours by appt). **Visitor information:** Lower Clarence Visitors Centre, Ferry Park, Pacific Hwy, Maclean; (02) 6645 4121. **See also:** Tropical North Coast p. 19.

Inverell
Pop. 9378

MAP REF. 107 K6

Known as 'Sapphire City', this town, 67 km W of Glen Innes, is surrounded by fertile farming land and rich mineral deposits. Zircons, sapphires, industrial diamonds and tin are mined in the area. **In town:** National Trust-classified courthouse, Otho St. Pioneer Village, Tingha Rd, has buildings dating from 1840, moved from their original sites, incl. Grove homestead, Paddy's Pub and Mt Drummond Woolshed. Visitor Centre and Mining Museum in Water Towers Complex, Campbell St. Art Society Gallery, Evans St. Gem Centre, Byron St. Transport Museum, Taylor Ave, displays rare vehicles. Town Stroll (self-guide), and Town and Country Drive; leaflets available. Hobby Market, 1st Sun. each month; Sapphire City market, 3rd Sun. each month. Jan.: Great Inland Fishing

Festival. Mar.: Art Exhibition. Oct.: Sapphire City Floral Festival. **In the area:** Gem-fossicking areas. Lake Inverell Reserve, 3 km E. Draught Horse Centre, Fishers Rd, 4 km E, with 6 breeds, has display of harness and memorabilia. See working sapphire mine at DeJon Sapphire Centre, 19 km E on Glen Innes Rd. Smith's Mining and Natural History Museum, 36 km SE at Green Valley Farm. Lookout, 2 km W, excellent views. Goonoowigall Bushland Reserve, 5 km S. Gilgai Winery, 12 km S. Copeton Dam State Recreation Area, northern foreshore 17 km S, for boating, water-skiing, swimming, fishing, bushwalking, rock-climbing, adventure playgrounds, water slides and picnic/barbecue facilities; on western shore of dam, golf course where kangaroos graze at dusk. Honey Farm and Bottle Museum, 8 km SW, see bees working under glass. Memorial marks site of 1838 Myall Creek massacre of Aborigines (for which perpetrators were punished), 35 km SW on Delungra–Bingara Rd. Gwydir Ranch 4WD Park, 28 km W. Pindari Dam, 58 km N, offers fishing, swimming, camping and picnic/barbecue facilities. Kwiambal National Park, 90 km N: Macintyre Falls; Ashford Caves (bat nurseries, view with torch); swimming, bushwalking, camping; kangaroos, emus and koalas. **Visitor information:** Water Towers Complex, Campbell St; (02) 6722 1693. Web site www.northnet.com.au/~inverell **See also:** New England & the North-West p. 20.

Jamberoo
Pop. 883

MAP REF. 99 G9, 105 K10

Jamberoo, 10 km W of Kiama, is in one of the most picturesque areas of the NSW coast, with lush pastures surrounded by towering escarpments. The district is well known for the quality of its dairy products. **In town:** Jamberoo Hotel, Allowrie St, features bush bands Sun. p.m. Market, Kevin Walsh Oval, last Sun. each month. Sept.: Illawarra Folk Festival. **In the area:** Jamberoo Recreation Park, 3 km N, family fun park. Saddleback Lookout, 7 km S, for 180° views of coast; starting point for Hoddles Trail, a 1-hr walk to Barren Grounds escarpment, excellent views. Walking trails and birdwatching in Barren Grounds Bird Observatory and Nature Reserve, 10 km SW on Drualla Rd; wildlife-watching

activities and workshops available (bookings essential). Minnamurra Rainforest Centre, 4 km W: elevated boardwalk through rainforest; paved walkway to Minnamurra Falls. **Visitor information:** Kiama Visitors Centre, Blowhole Point Rd, Kiama; (02) 4232 3322. Web site www.kiama.com.au **See also:** Southern Highlands & Illawarra p. 24; Wildlife-Watching p. 72.

Jerilderie
Pop. 871

MAP REF. 111 M11

This town on the Newell Hwy was held by the Kelly gang for two days in 1879 when they captured the police station, cut the telegraph wires and robbed the bank. Today it is the centre of an important merino stud area and an expanding vegetable industry. **In town:** Telegraph Office Museum, Powell St; next door, The Willows historic home (1878), has craft and tearoom. Original courthouse (1874), now library, Newell Hwy. Doll World, Bolton St, displays large world-wide collection. Lake Jerilderie for water sports; adjacent, Luke Park features Steel Wings, one of the largest windmills in Southern Hemisphere. Opposite park, Mini Heritage Steam Rail (2nd and 5th Sun. each month). **In the area:** Coleambally, 62 km N, centre of Coleambally Irrigation Area, features Wineglass Water Tower, Brolga Pl. **Visitor information:** The Willows, 11 Powell St; (03) 5886 1666. **See also:** The Murray p. 30.

Jindabyne
Pop. 1670

MAP REF. 101 G11, 103 D9, 126 C12, 235 K4

Now on the shores of Lake Jindabyne in the Snowy Mountains foothills, the original Jindabyne was beside the Snowy River. From 1962, residents moved to Snowy Mountains Hydro-Electric Authority's new site. The river was then dammed to form a water-storage area for the Snowy Mountains Scheme. At an altitude of 930 m, Jindabyne attracts skiers in winter and anglers, water-sports enthusiasts and bushwalkers in summer. **In town:** Snowy Region Visitor Centre, Kosciuszko Rd. Walkway and cycleway around lake's foreshore, from Banjo Paterson Park on Kosciuszko Rd to Snowline Caravan Park. Mar.: Strzelecki Polish Festival; Tour de Snowy (women's cycling, throughout the region) Sept.: Shout About Trout. Nov.: Snowy Mountains Trout Festival (fishing competition, throughout region). Dec.: Man from Snowy River Rodeo; Lake Jindabyne Sailing Club Hobie Cat Races. **In the area:** Alpine Way, 111-km road through mountains to Khancoban, offers superb scenic touring in summer. Scenic walks of varying lengths, brochure and map available. Lake Jindabyne, well stocked with trout, also ideal for boating, water-skiing and other water sports; lake cruises in summer. Crackenback Cottage, 12 km SW, has craft, maze and restaurant. Winter shuttle-bus service to Bullocks Flat and Thredbo. At Bullocks Flat, 20 km SW, terminal for Skitube, a European-style alpine train to Perisher and Mt Blue Cow (operates daily year-round). Perisher, Smiggin Holes, Mount Blue Cow and Guthega, known collectively as Perisher Blue, largest ski resort in Australia. Xtreme Winter Games held here in Sept. Charlotte Pass, 45 km W, highest slopes in Australia, for experienced skiers. Craigie Lookout, 40 km SW, for views of Snowy River Valley. Gaden Trout Hatchery, 10 km NW (tours daily; barbecues alongside Thredbo River). At Sawpit Creek, 14 km NW: Kosciuszko Education Centre has interactive displays and children's environment programs; at picnic area, start of Palliabo (walking) Track. Snowy Valley Lookout, 8 km N, view of Lake Jindabyne. Kunama Galleries, 7 km NE. **Visitor information:** Snowy Region Visitor Centre, Kosciuszko Rd; (02) 6450 5600, freecall 1800 636 525. Web site www.snowymountains.com.au **See also:** Snowy Mountains p. 28; National Parks p. 74.

Junee

Pop. 3681

MAP REF. 103 A4, 104 C11, 111 R9

Junee is an important railhead and commercial centre, 482 km SW of Sydney on the Olympic Way. **In town:** Monte Cristo homestead, overlooking town, a restored Colonial mansion with carriage collection. 19th-century railway refreshment rooms, Railway Sq., now cafe and information centre. Roundhouse Museum, Harold St, features original workshop, locomotives, model train and memorabilia (check opening times). Historical Museum, Lorne St (check opening times). **In the area:** Clock Museum, 17 km NE at Illabo. Turn-off at Bethungra for Bethungra Dam, ideal for canoeing and sailing. Bethungra Rail Spiral, unique engineering feat, 33 km NE. **Visitor information:** Railway Sq.; (02) 6924 2522. **See also:** The Riverina p. 27.

Cascades near Katoomba in the Blue Mountains

Katoomba

Pop. 11 795

MAP REF. 90 H7, 92 E9, 105 J7

Katoomba is the main residential and tourist centre of the Blue Mountains. Nearby, the smaller towns of Leura and Wentworth Falls have many interesting features and superb mountain scenery. Developed as a coal mine last century, Katoomba soon attracted wealthy Sydney holiday-makers. The coal mine foundered, but Katoomba developed as a tourist destination. **In town:** Maxvision Cinema, Great Western Hwy (access through Civic Pl.), daily screenings of *The Edge* (images of the Blue Mountains) on a six-storey-high screen. Markets at Civic Centre, Katoomba St, 1st and 3rd Sat. each month. Feb.: Blue Mountains Festival of Folk, Roots and Blues. May: Songs of the Wind Festival (throughout region). June: Winter Magic Festival. June–Aug.: Yulefest (throughout region). Sept.–Nov.: Spring Gardens Festival (throughout region). **In the area:** Excellent bushwalking, cycling, abseiling and 4WD tracks. West of town off highway, Explorers Tree (with carved initials). *South of town:* Echo Point, best place to view the famous Three Sisters rock formation (floodlit at night); Orphan Rock and Katoomba Falls, also floodlit; Giant Stairway bushwalk. Blue Mountains Scenic World, cnr Violet St and Cliff Dr.: Skyway, first horizontal passenger-carrying ropeway in Australia, travels 350 m across gorge; Scenic Railway, built late 1800s to transport coal and miners, is reputed to be world's steepest railway. *At and around Leura, 3 km E:* Leura Mall, beautiful tree-lined main street; gardens; specialty shops, galleries and restaurants. Everglades Gardens, Everglades Ave, celebrated 1930s garden, includes gallery devoted to its creator, Danish master gardener Paul Sorensen. Leuralla, Olympian Pde, an historic Art Deco mansion with major collection of toys, dolls, trains and railway memorabilia. Cascades, just south of town, where Leura Creek cascades into the valley. Dramatic views from Sublime Point; Cliff Drive offers spectacular views at lookouts and picnic spots. Walking tracks along cliff tops and descending into Jamison Valley. Market at public school, Great Western Highway, 1st Sun. each month. Sept.–Oct.: Legacy Gardens Festival. Oct.: Village Fair; Greystanes Spring Gardens. *At Wentworth Falls, 7 km E:* Conservation Hut Cafe, an eco-designed cafe with splendid views; Valley of the Waters Picnic Area. Kings Tableland Observatory (open evenings Fri.–Sun.). *At Hazelbrook, a further 10 km E:* Selwood Science and Puzzles has puzzle room, science kits, bookshop and local artwork. Feb.: Regatta Day (on Wentworth Falls Lake). *At Jenolan Caves, 75 km SW:* Some of the most splendid underground caves and above-ground arches in Australia, in flora and fauna reserve. *At Yerranderie, 200 km S via Oberon:* Silver-mining ghost town in 2430-ha wildlife reserve (4WD access only); historic buildings include museum and quaint hostel-style accommodation. **Visitor information:** Echo Point Rd; 1300 653 408. Web site www.bluemountainstourism.org.au **See also:** Blue Mountains p. 22; Wildlife-Watching p. 72; National Parks p. 74; Classic Tour p. 77.

Kempsey Pop. 8630

MAP REF. 95 G3, 107 O11

Kempsey, situated in the Macleay River Valley, 428 km N of Sydney, is the centre of a growing district of dairying, horticulture, tourism and light industry, incl. the Akubra hat factory. **In town:** Historical walks, brochures available. Wigay Aboriginal Cultural Park, Sea Street, Aboriginal cultural experience, incl. introduction to bush tucker. Macleay River Historical Society Museum and Settlers Cottage, Pacific Hwy, South Kempsey. Video of Akubra hat-making at information centre. Markets at racecourse, North St, 1st Sat. each month. May: Agricultural Show; South West Rocks Fishing Classic. July: Off-road Race. Sept.: Country Music Festival. **In the area:** Walks in nature reserves, and self-guide scenic and historical drives, brochures available. At Frederickton, 8 km NE, Blues Festival in Jan. At Gladstone, 15 km NE, Pumpkin Festival in Apr. At South West Rocks, 37 km NE: good beach; maritime history display at restored Boatmans Cottage (1902); handfeeding of fish at Everglades Aquarium; water sports, dive centre, camping, boat hire. Nearby, Trial Bay Gaol (1886), public works prison until 1903, reopened to hold 'enemy aliens' in WW II; Smoky Cape Lighthouse (1889), not open to public, but excellent views from headland; Gaol Break Festival held at Easter. Barnett's Rainbow Beach Oyster Barn, 31 km NE, direct purchases; see oysters being processed. Hat Head National Park, 32 km E, a coastal park with magnificent dunes and unspoiled beaches; birdwatching, snorkelling, swimming and walking tracks (brochures available); whale-watching from Korogoro Point (May–July and Sept.–Oct.). Crescent Head, 20 km SE, popular seaside holiday town; good board-riding; Aboriginal bora ring, old ceremonial ground, 23 km SE. Fish Rock Cave, noted for diving, just off Smoky Cape. At Kundabung, 12 km S, Australasian bull-riding titles in Oct. Brandybrook Lavender Farm, at Clybucca, 23 km N. At Turners Flat, 15 km NW, M. A. J. Artworks has porcelain tableware. Bellbrook, 47 km NW, a National Trust-classified village. **Visitor information:** Cultural Centre, Pacific Hwy, South Kempsey; (02) 6563 1555, freecall 1800 642 480. Web site www.kempsey.midcoast.com.au **See also:** Holiday Coast p. 17.

Khancoban Pop. 379

MAP REF. 101 A9, 103 B9, 234 I3

Set in the lush green Upper Murray Valley at the western end of the Alpine Way, 108 km NW of Jindabyne, this town was built by the Snowy Mountains Authority. **In town:** Lady Hudson Rose Garden, Mitchell Ave. National Parks and Wildlife Service, Scott St, displays and videos of Snowy Mountains Scheme and Kosciuszko National Park. Easter: Festival and Fireworks. Oct.: Spring Festival. **In the area:** Trout fishing, bushwalking, water sports, whitewater rafting; fishing tours. Permit required for vehicles entering national park. On Alpine Way: Murray 1 Power Station and Visitor Centre, 10 km SE, has interactive display, and tours for booked groups; further 1 km SE, power station viewing area; spectacular mountain views from Scammell's Spur Lookout, 20 km SE; Olsen's Lookout, turn-off 29 km SE, magnificent views of main range; Geehi Rest Area, 32 km SE, wheelchair access walking track and toilets, brilliant spring and autumn wildflowers; Tom Groggin Rest Area, 50 km SE, close to source of Murray River. **Visitor information:** National Parks and Wildlife Service, Scott St; (02) 6076 9373. Web site www.snowymountains.com.au **See also:** Snowy Mountains p. 28.

Kiama Pop. 11 711

MAP REF. 99 H9, 105 K10

The spectacular blowhole is the major attraction of this holiday town. Discovered by explorer George Bass in 1797, it sprays water up to heights of 60 m and is floodlit each evening. Kiama is the centre of a prosperous dairying and mixed farming district. **In town:** Terrace houses, specialty and craft shops in Collins St. Family History Centre, Railway Pde, contains world-wide collection of records for tracing family history. Heritage walk, leaflet available. At Blowhole Point: Blowhole; Pilots Cottage Historical Museum; constructed rock pool; pelicans; cafe. Beaches for surfing, swimming and fishing. Market, 3rd Sun. each month. Feb.: Jazz Festival; Seven-a-Side Rugby Competition. June: Folk Music Festival. Oct.: Seaside Festival. **In the area:** Scenic drives, brochures available. Little Blowhole, 2 km S, off Tingira Cres. Cathedral Rocks, 3 km N at Jones Beach, a scenic rocky outcrop, best at dawn. **Visitor information:** Blowhole Point Rd; (02) 4232 3322. **See also:** Southern Highlands & Illawarra p. 24.

Kyogle Pop. 2866

MAP REF. 107 P2, 525 P12

Kyogle makes a good base for exploring nearby mountains. It is also the centre of a lush dairy and mixed-farming area on the upper reaches of the Richmond River. **In town:** Captain Cook Memorial Lookout, Fairy St. July: Fairymount Festival. Oct.: Show. Nov.: Charity Golf Tournament. **In the area:** World Heritage-listed Border Ranges National Park, 27 km N, with forestry road access, walking tracks, camping and views of Mt Warning and Tweed Valley; in eastern section, Tweed Range Scenic Drive (64 km) through pristine rainforest with deep gorges, creeks and waterfalls, brochure available. Rodeo in Mar. at Wiangaree, 15 km N. Scenic forest drive via Mt Lindesay, 45 km NW on NSW–Qld border, offers magnificent views, brochure available. Toonumbar Dam, 31 km W, with bushwalking and picnic/barbecue facilities nearby; at Bells Bay, 2 km from dam, excellent bass-fishing and camping. Picnic spots include Roseberry Forest Park, 23 km N; Sheepstation Creek, in Border Ranges National Park. **Visitor information:** Kyogle Council, Stratheden St; (02) 6632 1611. Web site www.tropicalnsw.com.au **See also:** Tropical North Coast p. 19; National Parks p. 74.

Lake Cargelligo Pop. 1218

MAP REF. 111 O4

With the same name as the lake alongside, Lake Cargelligo, 586 km W of Sydney, serves the surrounding agricultural and pastoral district. **In town:** The large lake is ideal for fishing (silver perch, golden perch and redfin), boating, sailing, water-skiing and swimming. It is also home to many bird species, incl. the rare black cockatoo. Information centre, Foster St, has large gem collection. June: Blue Water Art and Craft Festival. Sept.: Lake Show. Oct.: Rodeo. Dec.: Lake Festivale. **In the area:** Lake Brewster, 41 km W: 1500 ha; birdwatchers' paradise; fishing and picnic area; no guns, dogs or boats. Willandra National Park, 163 km W, once a huge sheep station; station buildings preserved; 4WD only. Nombinnie Nature Reserve, 45 km N, birdwatching, bushwalks, abundant spring wildflowers (Sept.–Dec.). **Visitor information:** 1 Foster St; (02) 6898 1501. **See also:** Central West p. 21.

Laurieton Pop. 5823

MAP REF. 95 F10, 107 O11

The villages of Laurieton, North Haven and Dunbogan are around an inlet at the Camden Haven River mouth, 34 km S of Port Macquarie. This tidal inlet is ideal for estuary fishing. **In town:** Historical Museum, in old post office, Laurie St (open by appt). **In the area:** Oysters, lobsters, crabs, bream and flathead in local rivers and lakes. Seafront is a well-known fishing spot. Bushwalks along seafront and around lakes. Kattang Nature Reserve, 5 km E, for coastal views and wildflowers. Crowdy Bay National Park, 5 km S: prolific birdlife and magnificent ocean beach; at Diamond Head, hut in which Kylie Tennant wrote *The Man and the Headland;* walking tracks offer stunning ocean views, brochures available. Viewing platforms on North Brother Mountain, in Dooragan National Park, 6 km W. Big Fella Gum Tree, 18 km SW, one of three massive trees in Middle Brother State Forest. At Kendall, 10 km W, art and craft galleries incl. Craft Co-op in railway station; markets in Logans Crossing Rd, 1st and 3rd Sun. each month. Norfolk Punch Factory, 20 km W, see traditional English punch being made, tastings; historic kitchen appliances. Taramac Macadamia Farm, 23 km W (closed Mon. and Fri.). **Visitor information:** Pacific Hwy, Kew; (02) 6559 4400. **See also:** Holiday Coast p. 17.

Leeton Pop. 6615

MAP REF. 111 O8

Located 560 km SW of Sydney, Leeton was the first of the planned towns in the Murrumbidgee Irrigation Area and was designed by American architect Walter Burley Griffin. Fruit, rice and wine grapes are grown in the area. **In town:** Information centre (1913), Yanco Ave, a beautifully restored building with photographic displays, local artwork and heritage garden. Art Deco streetscape incl. Roxy Theatre and historic Hydro Hotel (1919), Chelmsford Pl. SunRice Country Visitors Centre (weekdays) at rice mill, Calrose St. National Foods Juice Factory, Brady Way, tours (weekdays). Mick's Bake House, Pine Ave, for bread products. Riverina Cheese Factory, Massey Ave, has sales outlet at Fresh Fruit Market, Kurrajong Ave. Easter: SunRice Festival (even-numbered years). **In the area:** Near town, tastings and tours at Toorak and Lillypilly Estate wineries. Fivebough Swamp, 2 km N, a waterbird sanctuary. Gliding and hot-air ballooning at Brobenah airfield, 9 km N. Whitton Courthouse and Historical Museum, 23 km W. Gogeldrie Weir, 23 km SW, for fishing. Murrumbidgee State Forest, 12 km S, scenic drives; self-guide brochure available. **Visitor information:** 10 Yanco Ave; (02) 6953 6481. Web site www.leeton.nsw.gov.au **See also:** The Riverina p. 27.

Lennox Head Pop. 4511

MAP REF. 107 R3, 525 R12

Just north of Ballina, Lennox Head has a charming seaside village atmosphere. The area is well known for beautiful Seven Mile Beach. **In town:** Freshwater Lake Ainsworth, popular with windsurfers. Market on shores of lake, 2nd and 5th Sun. of month. **In the area:** Swimming, surfing, windsurfing, catamaraning, sailboarding, snorkelling, scenic walks and rainforests. Pat Morton Lookout, 1 km S: whale-watching June–July and Sept.–Oct.; below is world-renowned surfing spot 'The Point'. **Visitor information:** Ballina Visitor Information Centre, cnr Las Balsas Plaza and River St, Ballina; (02) 6686 3484. Web site www.tropicalnsw.com.au **See also:** Tropical North Coast p. 19.

Lightning Ridge Pop. 1814

MAP REF. 106 B5

Lightning Ridge is a small opal-mining town in the world-renowned black opal fields, 74 km N of Walgett. **In town:** Displays of art and craft, incl. opal jewellery and gem opals. Underground mine tours. In Opal St: Bottle House Museum, has collection of bottles, minerals and mining relics; John Murray Art has paintings and photographs. In Pandora St: Gemopal Pottery; Goondee Aboriginal Keeping Place, featuring Aboriginal artifacts and educational tours of premises. Local craft market in Morilla St, each Fri. Easter: Great Goat Race; Rodeo. June: Opal Open Pistol Shoot. July: Opal and Gem Festival. **In the area:** Designated fossicking areas, details at information centre. Opal-cutting demonstrations and daily underground working-mine tours at the Big Opal on Three Mile Rd, southern outskirts of town. Walk-In-Mine, 2 km N, off Bald Hill Rd; Cactus Nursery nearby. Hot Artesian Bore Baths, 2 km NE. Fauna Orphanage, Opal St, 3 km S. Opal fields: Grawin, 65 km W and Sheepyards, 76 km W; details at information centre. **Visitor information:** Fred Reece Way; (02) 6829 0565, freecall 1800 639 545. **See also:** New England & the North-West p. 20.

Lismore Pop. 28 380

MAP REF. 107 Q3, 525 Q12

Regional centre of the Northern Rivers district, Lismore is situated beside Wilsons River, 821 km N of Sydney. **In town:** Rotary Rainforest Reserve, Rotary Dr., 6-ha tropical rainforest with boardwalk. Indoor rainforest walk, and local art and craft displays at information centre. Picnic areas and mini steam-train rides in surrounding Heritage Park, cnr Ballina and Molesworth sts. Cedar Log Memorial, Ballina St. In Molesworth St: Richmond River Historical Museum; Lismore Regional Art Gallery. Robinson's Lookout, Robinson Ave. Claude Riley Memorial Lookout, New Ballina Rd. Wilsons Park, Wyrallah St, East Lismore. River cruises on MV *Bennelong*, The Wharf, Magellan St. Heritage Walk, self-guide brochure available. Heritage Park market, 5th Sun. each month; Car Boot Markets, Shopping Square, Uralba St, 1st and 3rd Sun. each month. May: Trinity Arts Festival. June: Lantern Parade. Sept.: Cup Day. Oct.: North Coast National Show. **In the area:** At Alphadale, 11 km E: Macadamia Magic, a macadamia processing plant and tourist complex; Stephen Morris Glassware. Boatharbour Reserve, 5 km N on Bangalow Rd, has 17 ha of remnant rainforest, wildlife sanctuary, picnic area and walking tracks (maps available). Rocky Creek Dam, 25 km N, has platypus-viewing platform. Minyon Falls and Peates Mountain Lookout in Whian Whian State Forest, 25 km N. Three World Heritage-listed areas: Border Ranges National Park, 40 km N of Kyogle, Nightcap National Park, 27 km N, with spectacular Protesters Falls, and Mt Warning National Park near Murwillumbah, 105 km NE; check road conditions at information centre. Lismore Lake, 3 km S: good lagoon for swimming; picnic/barbecue facilities; adventure park. Tucki Tucki Koala Reserve, 15 km S, adjacent to Lismore–Woodburn Rd; Aboriginal ceremonial ground nearby. **Visitor information:** cnr Ballina and Molesworth sts; (02) 6622 0122. Web site www.liscity.nsw.gov.au **See also:** Tropical North Coast p. 19; National Parks p. 74.

Lithgow Pop. 11 441

MAP REF. 90 G5, 104 I6

This coal-mining city on the north-west fringes of the Blue Mountains is a must for railway enthusiasts. The city has two power stations and several large factories; the countryside is beautiful. **In town:** Museum in 1841 Eskbank House, Bennett St: 19th-century furniture and vehicles; displays on industrial history of area; open Thurs.–Sun. Blast Furnace Park, a wetland restoration area off Inch St, with ruins of Australia's first blast furnace complex. State Mine Railway Heritage Park, State Mine Gully Rd, features mining and railway equipment, and historic mining buildings (check opening times). Small Arms Museum, Methven St (check opening times). Art and Craft in the Park, at Queen Elizabeth Park, one Sat. each month, Aug.–May (check dates). Oct.: National Go-Kart Championships. **In the area:** Zig Zag Railway, 10 km E via Bells Line of Road, built 1869 and later restored, offers train trips, 1 hr 40 min return. Mount Wilson, 35 km E, 19th-century village with large houses and superb gardens, many open to public; Autumn Gardens Festival in Apr.; Cathedral of Ferns, fern forest past village. Mt Tomah Botanic Garden, 35 km E. Glow Worm Tunnel, 37 km N in Wollemi National Park; 1-km walk to glow-worms in disused rail tunnel (take a torch). Lake Wallace at Wallerawang, 11 km NW, for sailing and trout fishing. Mt Piper Power Station, 21 km NW (tours weekdays). Archvale Rainbow Trout Farm, 7 km W, for fishing and trout sales. Lake Lyell, 9 km W, for powerboating, water-skiing and trout fishing. Hassans Walls Lookout, 5 km S via Hassans Walls Rd. At Hartley, 14 km SE: many historic buildings; village is administered by National Parks and Wildlife Service. In Kanangra–Boyd National Park, 92 km S: Jenolan Caves; Kanangra Walls, series of cliffs and valleys (check road conditions). **Visitor information:** 1 Cooerwull Rd; (02) 6353 1859. **See also:** Blue Mountains p. 22; Wildlife-Watching p. 72; Classic Tour p. 77.

Lockhart Pop. 882

MAP REF. 111 P10

This pleasant historic town, situated 65 km SW of Wagga Wagga, was known as Green's Gunyah. **In town:** National Trust-listed: Green St, turn-of-the-century streetscape with wide shopfront verandahs; Showground grandstand (1906).

Greens Gunyah Museum, cnr Green and Urana sts, historical items and craft. Mar.: Verandah Town Music Festival. Oct.: Picnic Races. **In the area:** Galore Hill, 16 km N: caves where bushranger Mad Dog Morgan hid; walking tracks (brochures available) and lookouts; picnic/barbecue facilities. **Visitor information:** Lockhart Roadhouse, 57 Urana St; (02) 6920 5531. **See also:** The Riverina p. 27.

Macksville Pop. 2712

MAP REF. 107 P9

Macksville is an attractive town beside the Nambucca River, south of Nambucca Heads. **In town:** In River St: Mary Boulton Pioneer Cottage, replica of pioneer home, incl. horse-drawn vehicles; Star Hotel (1885). Craft markets on riverbank, 4th Sat. each month. Easter: Patchwork and Quilt Display. Apr.: Nambucca River Show. May: Egg-Throwing Championships; Trek to 'the pub with no beer'. Oct.: Pro-Ag Field Day. Nov.: Macksville Gift (Australia's second oldest footrace). **In the area:** Forest drives, brochures available. Holiday Coast Country Crafts, 4 km N on Pacific Hwy. Ngurrala Arts and Crafts Gallery, 8 km N on Wirrimbi Rd, Aboriginal works, brochure available (open Mon.–Wed.). At Bowraville ('the verandah-post town'), 16 km NW: National Trust-classified main street; Joseph and Eliza Newman Folk Museum; Red Cedars Gallery; Bawrrung Cultural Centre (closed Sat.); Sat. markets; regular racedays at picturesque racecourse; Back to Bowra Festival each Oct. Bakers Creek Station, 30 km W, for horseriding, fishing, rainforest walking, canoeing and picnicking; accommodation. Cosmopolitan Hotel (1903), 'the pub with no beer', made famous by song, at Taylors Arm, 26 km SW. Yarahappini Mt Lookout, 10 km S, for 360° views. Quantum Creations, 15 km S at Eungai Creek, for pottery and sculpture. Horseriding in Ingalba State Forest, 10 km SE. Scotts Head, 18 km SE, for surfing, swimming and fishing; dolphins offshore. **Visitor information:** 4 Pacific Hwy, Nambucca Heads; (02) 6568 6954. **See also:** Holiday Coast p. 17

Maclean Pop. 3157

MAP REF. 107 P5

Maclean, on the Clarence River, about 740 km N of Sydney, is known as 'the Scottish town'. Fishing fleets from this pretty town and from nearby Yamba and

Iluka catch about 20 per cent of the State's seafood. It is also a centre for river-prawning, sugarcane and mixed-farm crops. **In town:** Self-guide historic buildings walk, brochure available. In River St: Scottish Corner; Civic Hall (1903). Free Presbyterian Church (1864), cnr Wharf and River sts. Bicentennial Museum and adjacent Stone Cottage (1879), Wharf St, on road to Maclean Lookout and Pinnacle Rocks. Market, 2nd Sat. each month. Easter: Highland Gathering. Aug.: Aquatic Powerboat Regatta. Sept.: Cane Harvest Festival. **In the area:** 24-hr ferry service, 10 km SW, crosses river to Lawrence. Houseboat hire at Brushgrove, 21 km SW. Yuraygir National Park, 24 km SE, features clay formations, rock formations and sand dunes. **Visitor information:** Lower Clarence Visitors Centre, Ferry Park, Pacific Hwy; (02) 6645 4121. Web site www.tropicalnsw.com.au **See also:** Tropical North Coast p. 19.

Maitland Pop. 50 108

MAP REF. 97 C7, 105 M4

Maitland is on the Hunter River, 32 km NW of Newcastle. The city's winding High St is a National Trust Conservation Area: most of the buildings date back to the 1800s. Settled by Europeans in the 1820s, when convicts were cedar-cutters, it was a flourishing township by the 1840s. **In town:** Self-guide heritage walks, incl. one designed for children; brochures available. National Trust properties in Church St: Georgian-style Grossmann House (1862), now a folk museum, and Brough House (1870), housing city's art collection, are mirror images. Cintra, Regent St, a Victorian mansion offering weekend B&B. Aberglasslyn House (1840), Aberglasslyn La., now a B&B, tours for booked groups or by appt. Former Maitland Gaol, John St, East Maitland, significant historic site, tours daily. Market, 1st Sun. each month at Showground. Feb.: Vintage Festival, (throughout region); Agricultural Show. Mar.: Craft-a-Fair. Apr.: Heritage Month; Hunter Valley Steamfest. Sept.: Garden Ramble. **In the area:** At National Trust-classified Morpeth, 5 km NE: historic buildings with superb iron lace, incl. St James Church (1830s); self-guide heritage walk, brochure available; Jazz Festival held in May; Craft Crawl in July; Weird and Wonderful Novelty Teapot Exhibition in Aug. Scenic drive to Walka Waterworks, 3 km N, former pumping

Menindee Lake guarantees Broken Hill's water supply

station, now excellent recreation area. Signposted scenic drive to historic settlement of Paterson, 16 km N. Tocal Agricultural College, 14 km N, set in historic Georgian-style homestead (1820s), open by appt and on Tocal Field Days (1st weekend in May). At Lochinvar, 13 km W, Windermere Colonial homestead, sandstone residence built by convicts 1820s; open by appt. **Visitor information:** Ministers Park, cnr New England Hwy and High St; (02) 4933 2611. Web site www.maitlandtourism. nsw.gov.au **See also:** Hunter Valley & Coast p. 14.

Manilla
Pop. 2073

MAP REF. 107 J9

This small town, 42 km NW of Tamworth, is known for its meadery, one of two in the State. **In town:** Dutton's Meadery, Barraba St, has tastings and sales of honey and mead. In picturesque Manilla St: antique and coffee shops; Royce Cottage Historical Museum. Mar.: NSW Hanggliding Championships. June: Lake Keepit Kool Sailing Regatta. Oct.: Festival of Spring Flowers. **In the area:** Manilla Ski Gardens on Lake Keepit, 20 km SW. Warrabah National Park, 40 km NE, a peaceful riverside retreat. Swimming, fishing and canoeing on Namoi and Manilla rivers. **Visitor information:** cnr Murray and Peel sts, Tamworth; (02) 6755 4300. **See also:** New England & the North-West p. 20.

Menindee
Pop. 385

MAP REF. 108 E13, 110 E1

The ill-fated Burke and Wills stayed at this small town, 111 km SE of Broken Hill,

in 1860 on their journey north. The nearby lake system contrasts with the semi-arid countryside. **In town:** Maiden's Hotel, Yartla St, where Burke and Wills lodged. Ah Chung's Bakehouse Gallery, Menindee St. May: Inland Speedboat Championships. Aug.: Burke and Wills Fishing Challenge. **In the area:** Yachting, fishing, swimming, water sports and camping on lakes. Menindee Lake, 1 km NW, part of water-storage scheme for Broken Hill. Menindee Lake Lookout, 10 km N. Copi Hollow, 18 km N, attracts water-skiers and power-boat enthusiasts. Kinchega National Park, 1 km W, has prolific wildlife, visitors centre (15 km W), wreck of paddle-steamer *Providence* on Darling River (10 km W), and restored shearers' quarters. **Visitor information:** Railway Station, Maiden St; (08) 8091 4274. Web site www.outbacknsw.org.au **See also:** The Outback p. 31.

Merimbula
Pop. 4383

MAP REF. 100 F9, 103 G11, 235 Q7

Excellent surfing, fishing and prawning at this small sea and lake town. **In town:** Aquarium at Merimbula Wharf, Lake St. Old School Museum, Main St. June: Jazz Festival. Oct.: Country Music Festival. **In the area:** Scenic flights, lake cruises, whale-watching Oct.–Nov. and boat hire. Magic Mountain Family Recreation Park, 5 km N on Sapphire Coast Dr. Tura Beach, 5 km NE. Yellow Pinch Wildlife Park, 5 km E. Historic Pambula, 7 km SW, (sister village); fine fishing and surfing; market 2nd Sun. each month. Walking track and lookout at nearby Pambula Beach, 10 km S; kangaroos and wallabies on foreshore early morning and dusk.

Visitor information: Beach St; (02) 6495 1129, freecall 1800 663 012. Web site www.sapphirecoast.com.au **See also:** The South Coast p. 26.

Merriwa
Pop. 937

MAP REF. 105 J2

This small town in the western Hunter region is noted for its early colonial buildings. **In town:** Self-guide historical walk, brochure available. Historical Museum in stone cottage (1857), Bettington St (check opening times). Bottle Museum, Vennacher St. May: Polocrosse Carnival. June: Festival of Fleeces (incl. fireworks). **In the area:** Goulburn River National Park, 35 km S. Convict-built Flags Rd, to Gungal, 25 km SE. Cassilis, 45 km NW, has historic sandstone buildings. Coolah Tops National Park, 107 km NW: lookouts, waterfalls, glider possums, large snowgums; access by 4WD (alternative sealed-road access via Coolah). Official gem-fossicking area, 27 km SW. **Visitor information:** Shire Council, Vennacher St; (02) 6548 2607. Web site www. infohunt.nsw.gov.au/merriwa **See also:** Hunter Valley & Coast p. 14.

Mittagong
Pop. 6088

MAP REF. 99 C6, 103 I2, 105 J10

The gateway to the Southern Highlands, Mittagong is 110 km S of Sydney. **In town:** Historic cemeteries and buildings. Lake Alexandra, Queen St. Market, 3rd Sat. each month at Uniting Church Hall, cnr Albert and Alice sts. Apr.: Autumn Gardens in the Southern Highlands. Sept.–Oct.: Tulip Time Festival (throughout region). **In the area:** Box Vale walking track begins northern end of Welby, 4 km NW. Wombeyan Caves, 60 km NW; reached by scenic, narrow road (not suitable for caravans); tours daily. **Visitor information:** Southern Highlands Visitor Information Centre, 62–70 Main St; (02) 4871 2888 or 1300 657 559. Web site www.highlandsnsw. com.au **See also:** Southern Highlands & Illawarra p. 24.

Molong
Pop. 1604

MAP REF. 104 F5

Molong is a charming rural town on the Mitchell Hwy, 35 km NW of Orange. **In town:** Yarn Market, Craft Cottage and Coach House Gallery, Bank St. **In the area:** Grave of Yuranigh, Aboriginal guide of explorer Sir Thomas Mitchell, 2 km E.

Mitchell's Monument, 21 km S, marks site of explorer's base camp. **Visitor information:** Orange Visitor Information Centre, Civic Square, Byng St, Orange; (02) 6393 8226 or Railway Station Complex, Mitchell Hwy, Molong. **See also:** Central West p. 21.

Moree
Pop. 9270

MAP REF. 106 G5

Situated at the junction of Mehi and Gwydir rivers, 640 km NW of Sydney, this town is the centre of a cotton-, wheat- and olive-growing region. It is best known for its artesian spa baths, said to relieve arthritis and rheumatism. **In town:** Spa complex, cnr Anne and Gosport sts. National Trust-classified Moree Lands Office (1894), cnr Frome and Heber sts; opposite, Moree Plains Regional Gallery. Barry Roberts historical walk, self-guide brochure available. Yurundiali Aboriginal Corporation, Endeavour La., operates a screen-print clothing factory (tours by appt). The Big Plane, Amaroo Dr., a DC3 transport plane at Amaroo Tavern. Market, 1st Sun. each month at Jellicoe Park. Easter: Carnival of Sport. Nov.: Golden Grain and Cotton Festival. **In the area:** At Trawalla, 35 km E, large pecan nut farm; tours. Inspection of cotton gins during harvesting (Apr.–July). **Visitor information:** Lyle Houlihan Park, cnr Newell and Gwydir hwys; (02) 6757 3350. Web site www.moreeon-line.net.au **See also:** New England & the North-West p. 20.

Moruya
Pop. 2602

MAP REF. 103 H7, 127 M8

Many well-known dairying estates were founded near this town, once a gateway to the Araluen and Braidwood goldfields. Situated on the Moruya River, 322 km S of Sydney, it is now a dairying and oyster-farming centre. Granite used in the Sydney Harbour Bridge was quarried in the district. **In town:** Eurobodalla Historic Museum, in town centre, depicts gold discovery at Mogo, and district history. Courthouse (1880), Princes Hwy. St Marys Catholic Church (1889), Queen St. Markets in Main St, each Sat. Oct.: Jazz Festival. **In the area:** Good fishing, surfing and water sports. Black swan and sea-eagle colonies up-river at Yarragee. Deua National Park, 20 km W, for flora and fauna; Hanging Mountain and lookout. Nerrigundah, 44 km SW, former goldmining town. At Bodalla,

24 km S: Coomerang House, home of 19th-century industrialist and dairy farmer Thomas Sutcliffe Mort; Mort Memorial Church and historic cemetery. **Visitor information:** cnr Princes Hwy and Beach Rd, Batemans Bay; (02) 4472 6900, freecall 1800 802 528 or Narooma; (02) 4476 2881, freecall 1800 240 003. Web site www.naturecoast-tourism.com. au **See also:** The South Coast p. 26.

Moss Vale
Pop. 6108

MAP REF. 99 B7, 103 I3, 105 J10

The industrial and agricultural centre of the Southern Highlands, this town stands on part of land granted to Charles Throsby 1819. **In town:** Leighton Gardens, Main St. Historic walk, brochure available. Southern Highlands Country Fair, 4th Sun. each month, at showground. Mar.: Agricultural Show. Apr.: Autumn Gardens in the Southern Highlands. Sept.–Oct.: Tulip Time Festival (throughout Southern Highlands). **In the area:** Cecil Hoskins Nature Reserve, 3 km NE, has abundance of birdlife. At Sutton Forest, 6 km SW, A Little Piece of Scotland, for all things Scottish; Sutton Forest Village Market, 3rd Sun. each month at Village Hall. Horse studs in surrounding countryside. **Visitor information:** Southern Highlands Visitor Information Centre, 62–70 Main St, Mittagong; (02) 4871 2888, or 1300 657 559. Web site www. highlandsnsw.com.au **See also:** Southern Highlands & Illawarra p. 24.

Moulamein
Pop. 459

MAP REF. 110 I10, 231 P9

This town on the Edward River is the oldest in the Riverina. It was a river crossing for drovers and a busy inland port. Today, Moulamein is a service centre for its wheat district and popular for river fishing. **In town:** Old Wharf (1850s), Morago St. Restored courthouse (1845), Nyang St (key from Shire Offices). Riverside picnic areas. Lake Moulamein, Brougham St. Easter: Yabby Races. Dec.: Horseracing Cup. **Visitor information:** The Business Centre, Morago St; (03) 5887 5354 (weekdays) or 25 Murray St, Barham; (03) 5453 3100 (weekends). **See also:** The Riverina p. 27.

Mudgee
Pop. 8195

MAP REF. 104 H3

This attractive town, with wide streets and gracious Victorian buildings, is the

centre of one of the largest premium wine-producing regions in Australia. Located on the Cudgegong River, 264 km NW of Sydney, its produce includes wine grapes (shiraz), fine wool, livestock and gourmet foods. The landscape attracts many artists. **In town:** Self-guide historical town walks, brochure available. Many National Trust-classified buildings. In Market St: St John's Church of England (1860); St Mary's Roman Catholic Church; railway station; town hall; Colonial Inn Museum. Honey Haven, cnr Hill End and Gulgong rds. Market, 1st and 2nd Sat. each month. Sept.: Wine Festival. **In the area:** Site of Old Bark School, attended by Henry Lawson, 6 km N; adjacent, Eurunderee Provisional School with historical displays of school life (check opening times). Munghorn Gap Nature Reserve, 34 km NE, features sandstone outcrops, 160 bird species, walking tracks and picnic areas. Water sports and trout fishing at Windamere Dam, 24 km SE; camping facilities. Pick-Your-Own Farm, 12 km S, has variety of fruit and vegetables (Oct.–May). Mt Vincent Mead, Common Rd, 4 km SW, produces alcholic mead from honey (tastings and sales). Fragrant Farm, garden and craft shop, 8 km SW. Hargraves, 39 km SW, old goldmining town; gold-panning tours (inquire at Hargraves General Store at Bushlands Caravan Park). Over 100 vineyards in area; 23 offer tastings, incl. Poets Corner Wines, Huntington Estate, Botobolar; signposted self-guide drives. **Visitor information:** 84 Market St; (02) 6372 1020. **See also:** Central West p. 21.

Mullumbimby
Pop. 2870

MAP REF. 107 Q2, 525 Q12

Situated in lush subtropical country, Mullumbimby is some 850 km NE of Sydney. **In town:** Art Gallery, cnr Burringbar and Stuart sts. Antiques gallery in National Trust-classified Cedar House (1908), Dalley St. Brunswick Valley Historical Museum, in old post office (1907), Stuart St. Brunswick Valley Heritage Park, Tyagarah St, features rainforest plants. Market, 3rd Sat. each month at museum. Sept.: Chincogan Fiesta. **In the area:** Wanganui Gorge, 20 km W, 4-km bushwalk through gorge. Crystal Castle, 7 km SW, large display of natural quartz. Skydiving and paragliding at airstrip at Tyagarah, 13 km SE on Pacific Hwy.

Visitor information: 80 Jonson St, Byron Bay; (02) 6685 8050. Web site www.tropicalnsw.com.au **See also:** Tropical North Coast p. 19.

Mulwala   Pop. 1593

MAP REF. 111 N13, 233 L3

This town is on the foreshores of Lake Mulwala, an artificial lake of over 6000 ha, formed by the damming of the Murray River at Yarrawonga Weir in 1939 for irrigation. **In town:** Yachting, water-skiing, sailboarding, swimming, canoeing and fishing. Everglade and Swamp Tours to waterbird rookeries and native animal habitats, bookings essential. Linley Park Animal Farm, Corowa Rd, has native and exotic animals, and horse and ponyrides (open long weekends and school holidays). Pioneer Museum, Melbourne St, featuring historic farming exhibits (open Wed.–Sun.). Tunzafun Amusement Park, Melbourne St, for mini-golf, mini-train and dodgem cars. Cruises on Lake Mulwala. Jan.: New Year's Day Power Boat Racing. **Visitor information:** Irvine Pde, Yarrawonga; (03) 5744 1989. **See also:** The Murray p. 30.

Murrurundi   Pop. 902

MAP REF. 107 J13

This picturesque town on the New England Hwy, is set in a lush valley on the Pages River. **In town:** St Joseph's Catholic Church, Polding St, has 1000-piece Italian marble altar. Self-guide historical town walk, brochure from Murrurundi Museum, Mayne St (check opening times). Paradise Park, Paradise Rd, is horseshoe-shaped and surrounded by mountains; kangaroos at dusk. Just behind park, difficult walk 'Through the Eye of the Needle', small gap in rocks to squeeze through; excellent view from top of rock formation. Apr.: Sheepdog Trials. Sept.: Billycart Competition. Oct.: Bushman's Carnival. **In the area:** Chilcott's Creek, 15 km N, where huge diprotodon remains were found; now in Australian Museum (Sydney). Wallabadah Rocks, 26 km NE, a large plug of an extinct volcano (959 m high); flowering orchids in Oct. Burning Mountain, 20 km S at Wingen, a deep coal seam that has been smouldering at least 5000 years. **Visitor information:** Council Offices, 47 Mayne St; (02) 6546 6205. **See also:** New England & the North-West p. 20.

Murwillumbah   Pop. 7657

MAP REF. 107 Q1, 525 Q11

Situated on the banks of the Tweed River, 31 km S of the Qld border in the beautiful Tweed Valley, Murwillumbah's local industries include cattle-raising and the growing of sugarcane, tropical fruits, tea and coffee. **In town:** World Heritage Rainforest Centre, cnr Pacific Hwy and Alma St, has displays on local vegetation and wildlife. Tweed River Regional Art Gallery, Tumbulgum Rd, home to Doug Moran National Portrait Prize. Tweed River Historical Society Museum, cnr Queensland Rd and Bent St, has displays of local history (check times). Market in Main St, 1st Sat. each month. Market in Showground, 4th Sun. each month. May: Fish 'n' Nana Festival. Aug.: Tweed Valley Banana Festival and Harvest Week. **In the area:** Houseboat hire, on Pacific Hwy, 1 km N of information centre. Lisnager homestead (1902), just past Showground on northern edge of town (open Sun. 10 a.m.–3 p.m.). Condong Sugar Mill, 5 km N (open July–Dec.). Tropical Fruit World, 15 km N. Treetops Environment Centre, 8 km NE, features furniture crafted from salvaged timber. Madura Tea Estates, 12 km NE. At Tyalgum, 16 km E, Music Festival in Sept. Hare Krishna Community Farm at Eungella, 10 km W; visitors welcome. Pioneer Plantation, Pottsville Rd, Mooball, 19 km SE, a working banana plantation: farm animals; native gardens; nectar-feeding birds; tours, incl. 6WD trip to top of Banana Mountain. World Heritage-listed national parks within radius of 50 km: Nightcap National Park (road access to Mt Nardi); Border Ranges National Park (walking tracks, lookouts, Antarctic Beech Picnic Area and 60-km Tweed Range Scenic Drive); Mt Warning National Park. **Visitor information:** World Heritage Rainforest Centre, cnr Pacific Hwy and Alma St; (02) 6672 1340. Web site www.tropicalnsw.com.au **See also:** Tropical North Coast p. 19; National Parks p. 74.

Muswellbrook   Pop. 10 541

MAP REF. 105 K2

In the Upper Hunter Valley, Muswellbrook is a centre for surrounding agriculture and has a large open-cut coal-mining industry. **In town:** Art Gallery in old town hall, Bridge St. Upper Hunter Wine Centre, Loxton House, Bridge St. Historical town walk, self-guide brochure available. Mar.: Agricultural Show. Oct.– Nov.: Spring Carnival. **In the area:** 7 local wineries open for tastings and sales, incl. Rosemount Estate (35 km SW) and Arrowfield Wines (28 km S). Wollemi National Park, 30 km SW, features Aboriginal carvings and paintings. Sandy Hollow, 36 km SW, Bush Ride in Apr. Bayswater Power Station, 16 km S (tours Tues. and Fri.). **Visitor information:** 87 Hill St; (02) 6541 4050, freecall 1800 065 773. Web site www.infohunt. nsw.gov.au/muswell **See also:** Hunter Valley and Coast p. 14.

Nambucca Heads   Pop. 6253

MAP REF. 107 P9

At the mouth of the Nambucca River, 552 km N of Sydney, this beautifully sited town is ideal for boating, fishing, surfing, water-skiing and swimming. **In town:** Copenhagen Mill and Shipyard Foreshore Walk, signposted historical walk. Headland Historical Museum, Headland Reserve. Model Train Museum, Pelican Cres. Stringer Art Gallery, Ridge St, for local art. Crafters Cottage, Ridge St. Mosaic sculpture, Bowra St. V-Wall Breakwater, Wellington Dr., add your own graffiti. Stuart Island Golf Club, mid-river, on Australia's only island set aside for a golf course. Gordon Park Rainforest, between town centre and Inner Harbour. Market, 2nd Sun. each month at Nambucca Plaza. Easter: Country Music Festival. June: Ken Howard Memorial Bowls Competition. Aug.: VW Spectacular (odd-numbered years). Oct.: Show 'n' Shine Hot Rod Exhibition. **In the area:** Breathtaking views from several lookouts. Scuba-diving training and charters. Wooden toys at Swiss Toymaker, 5 km N on Pacific Hwy (closed Sun.). At Valla Beach, 10 km N: Valla Art and Craft Gallery; Valla Smokehouse, gourmet smoked products; Australiana Workshop; Gallery of Hidden Treasures. **Visitor information:** 4 Pacific Hwy; (02) 6568 6954. Web site www.midcoast.com.au/~nambuct **See also:** Holiday Coast p. 17.

Narooma   Pop. 3389

MAP REF. 100 I2, 103 H9, 127 N11, 235 R2

This popular fishing resort at the mouth of the Wagonga Inlet on the Princes Hwy, 360 km S of Sydney, is well known for its natural beauty. **In town:** Scenic cruises on *Wagonga Princess;* whale-watching cruises (mid-Sept.–mid-Nov.); Montague

Fishing boats at Wagonga Inlet, Narooma

Island trips with National Parks guide to see little (fairy) penguin colony and Australian and New Zealand fur seals (year-round, bookings essential); scuba-diving to shipwrecks. Oct.: Great Southern Blues Festival. **In the area:** Scenic golf course on cliff-top, Ballingalla St. Mystery Bay near Lake Corunna, 17 km S, haunt of lapidary collectors, strange rock formations. Other inlets and lakes north and south of town. Central Tilba (founded 1895), 17 km SW just off Princes Hwy: classified as 'unusual mountain village' by National Trust; old buildings, incl. ABC Cheese Factory in original 19th-century condition; new buildings to National Trust specifications; quality arts and crafts; Tilba Festival each Easter. Nearby, Tilba Valley Vineyard. At Tilba Tilba, further 2 km S, Foxglove Spires, historic cottage surrounded by a 3.5-ha garden. At Wallaga Lake, 22 km SW, Umbarra Aboriginal Cultural Centre: local artifacts; hands-on cultural activities; tours to Aboriginal sites. **Visitor information:** Princes Hwy; (02) 4476 2881, freecall 1800 240 003. Web site www. naturecoast-tourism.com.au **See also:** The South Coast p. 26; Wildlife-Watching p. 72.

Narrabri   Pop. 6419

MAP REF. 106 G8

Situated between the Nandewar Range, incl. Mt Kaputar National Park and the extensive Pilliga scrub country, Narrabri is a major cotton-producing centre. **In town:** Historic buildings, incl. courthouse (1886), Maitland St. Self-guide town walk/drive, leaflets available. Riverside picnic area, Tibbereena St.

Apr.: Agricultural Show. June: Farm-craft. Oct.: Spring Festival. **In the area:** Tours of cotton fields and gin processing plants (Apr.–June). CSIRO Australia Telescope, 25 km W: six giant radio telescopes; visitors centre (open Mon.–Fri.). Yarrie Lake, 32 km W, for birdwatching, water-skiing and windsurfing. Mt Kaputar National Park, 53 km E in dramatic volcanic mountain country; huge 360° views from peak (drive to summit, or 3.5-km walk from main carpark); Sawn Rocks, wilderness area in northern section (via Bingara Rd), has spectacular basaltic formation; bright pink slug endemic to Nandewar Range. **Visitor information:** Newell Hwy; (02) 6799 6760. Web site www.tournarrabri.nsw.gov.au **See also:** New England & the North-West p. 20.

Narrandera   Pop. 4678

MAP REF. 111 P9

This historic town on the Murrumbidgee River, at the junction of the Newell and Sturt hwys, is an urban conservation area with several National Trust-classified buildings. Located 570 km SW of Sydney, it is the gateway to the Murrumbidgee Irrigation Area. **In town:** Lake Talbot Aquatic Playground, Lake Dr. Antiques in Larmer St. NSW Forestry Tree Nursery, Broad St (closed weekends). On Newell Hwy: Tiger Moth Memorial; Parkside Cottage Museum; information centre with 5.8-m playable guitar at Narrandera Park. My Dolls, Dangar Dr., doll and teddy bear collection. Two Foot town heritage tour, Bundidgerry Walking Track through Nature Reserve (koalas), and Blue Arrow scenic drive; pamphlets available. Mar.: John O'Brien Bush Festival.

Aug.: Camellia Show. Oct.: Tree-mendous Festival. **In the area:** Inland Fisheries Research Station, 6 km SE, has visitors centre (open Mon.–Fri.). Berembed Weir, 40 km SE, for picnicking, fishing and boating. Craig Top Deer Farm, 8 km NW (tours daily). **Visitor information:** Narrandera Park, Newell Hwy; (02) 6959 1766, freecall 1800 672 392. Web site www.riverinatourism.com.au **See also:** The Riverina p. 27.

Narromine   Pop. 3486

MAP REF. 104 D2

This town on the Macquarie River, 457 km NW of Sydney, is the centre of an area well known for quality agricultural products, incl. citrus fruit, tomatoes, corn, lamb, beef and cotton. It is also an outstanding gliding area. **In town:** At information centre, photographic history of area. On Mitchell Hwy: Waterslide at Rose Gardens Caravan Park, eastern edge of town; at airport, western side of town, gliding and ultralight flying and Aviation Museum, with vintage aircraft and memorabilia. Market at Tom Perry Park, 1st Sun. every 2nd month. Nov.: Festival of Flight. **In the area:** Water-skiing along the Macquarie River. Tours of Highland View, large lime orchard, 3 km NW on Mitchell Hwy. Tours of cotton gins, details from information centre. Swane's Rose Nursery, 5 km W. Narromine Iris Farm, 3 km S on Torringley Rd; over 600 varieties. Gui Gui Weir, 44 km N, for swimming, fishing and picnics. **Visitor information:** 37 Burraway St; (02) 6889 4596. Web site www.narromine.nsw.gov. au **See also:** Central West p. 21.

Nelson Bay   Pop. 7001

MAP REF. 97 H2, 105 O4

This town's beautiful bay is the main anchorage of Port Stephens, about 60 km N of Newcastle. **In town:** Restored Inner Lighthouse, Nelson Head, includes museum. Self-guide heritage walk from Dutchmans Bay to Little Beach (brochure available); dolphin-watching cruises; whale-watching cruises (May–July, Sept.–Nov., check with information centre); cruises on harbour, Myall River and to Broughton Island; dive charters; 4WD tours along coastal dunes; canoe, aquabike and boat hire. Shell Museum, Sandy Point Rd, Corlette. Craft market in Neil Carroll Park, Victoria Pde, 1st and 3rd Sun. each month (every Sun. in school holidays); markets in Lutheran

Church grounds, 1st Sat. each month. Game-fishing tournaments (details from information centre). Jan.: Blessing of the Fleet. Nov.: Regional Boat Show. **In the area:** Native Flora Reserve at Little Beach, 1 km E. Gan Gan Lookout, 2 km SW on Nelson Bay Rd. Toboggan Hill Park, 5 km SW, has toboggan runs, mini-golf course, indoor wall-climbing and fun shed. On Nelson Bay Rd: Port Stephens Winery, 10 km SW (Jazz at the Winery in Mar.); Oakvale Farm and Fauna World, 16 km SW at Salt Ash. Tomago House (1843), 30 km SW on Tomago Rd (open Sun.). Stockton Sand Dunes, accessible by 4WD (or safari) from Anna Bay or Williamtown, 38 km SW, huge dune area popular for sandboarding and whale-watching. At Shoal Bay, 2 km NE, Jazz, Wine and Food Fair in June. Tomaree National Park, stretches along coast from Shoal Bay (3 km NE) to Anna Bay (10 km SW); signposted walk around headland; Fort Tomaree Lookout for 360° views (signposted walkway to top). Across bay (70 km by road), Yacaaba Lookout also offers 360° views. **Visitor information:** Port Stephens Visitor Information Centre, Victoria Pde; (02) 4981 1579. Web site www.portstephens. org.au **See also:** Hunter Valley & Coast p. 14; Wildlife-Watching p. 72.

Newcastle — Pop. 270 324

MAP REF. 96, 97 G7, 105 N4

This large and vibrant city, 158 km N of Sydney, overlooks a spectacular harbour and is bordered by some of the finest surfing beaches in the world. After the 1989 earthquake, some rebuilding was necessary. Newcastle is popular for the magnificent coastline and the picturesque villages and vineyards of the nearby Hunter Valley region. **In town:** Queens Wharf, on Wharf Rd, centrepoint of foreshore redevelopment, has indoor and outdoor restaurants; 'boutique' brewery; observation tower linked by walkway to the City Mall, a part of Hunter St. Victorian-era terrace houses along nearby city streets. Regional Museum, Hunter St, includes interactive 'Supernova' museum for children. Regional Art Gallery, Laman St. Historic customs house (1877) in Watt St, now a bar and restaurant. City Hall (1929), King St. In King Edward Park, situated on waterfront: sunken gardens; ocean views; band rotunda (1898); obelisk (1850), marks site of Newcastle's first windmill; Soldiers Baths (1880s), off Shortland Espl., a public pool; Bogey

Hole, hole cut in rocks by convict labour, also a public pool. Merewether Baths, off Scenic Dr., largest ocean baths in Southern Hemisphere. River and harbour cruises. Fort Scratchley, Nobbys Rd, perched high above Newcastle Harbour, features network of tunnels, gun emplacements and fascinating Military and Maritime museums. Blackbutt Reserve, off Carnley Ave in suburb of New Lambton, 182 ha of bushland with duck ponds, native animal enclosures, walking trails and picnic/barbecue facilities. Self-guide walks, incl. Town Walk, and Shipwreck Walk along foreshore; maps available. Jan.: National Maritime Regatta. Mar.: Surfest; Beaumont Street Jazz and Arts Festival. Aug.: Conservatorium Keyboard Festival. Aug. or Sept.: Cathedral Flower Festival (music, flower displays). Sept.: Hamilton Fiesta; Cathedral Music Festival. Oct.: Mattara Festival. Dec.: King Street Fair. **In the area:** Many fine surf beaches. Lake Macquarie, 20 km S, a huge aquatic playground with well-maintained parks lining foreshore: lake cruises from Toronto Wharf and Belmont Public Wharf; Dobell House, Dobell Dr., Wangi Wangi, home of artist Sir William Dobell, has collection of his work and memorabilia (open Sun.); power station tours at Eraring (bookings essential); Lake Macquarie Heritage Afloat Fest held Apr. Munmorah State Recreation Area, a coastal recreation area south of Swansea. Shortland Wetlands, 15 km W, a bird and reptile habitat, with walking, cycling and canoeing trails. About 50 km NW is Australia's notable wine region, the Hunter Valley. Fighter World, museum and high-tech exhibition at Williamtown RAAF base, 20 km N. Yuelarbah Track, part of Great North Walk from Sydney to Newcastle, 25 km from Lake Macquarie to Newcastle harbour; pamphlet available. **Visitor information:** Wheeler Place, 363 Hunter St; (02) 4974 2999. Web site www.newcastletourism.com **See also:** Hunter Valley & Coast p. 14.

Nimbin — Pop. 319

MAP REF. 107 Q2, 525 Q12

The 1973 Aquarius Festival established Nimbin as the alternative culture capital of Australia. Today Nimbin's friendly atmosphere, and the buildings that reflect the community's beliefs, attract alternative-lifestylers. **In town:** In Cullen St: shops in psychedelic colours, featuring homemade products and local art and craft; Triple Blah Theatrette, showing

short films; Choices Cafe, offering views over the valley; Nimbin Museum, dedicated to hippy culture and history of St Aquarius; town hall mural featuring Aboriginal art; Rainbow Power Company, Alternative Way, alternative power supplier, now exporting (tours). Market, Sat. at Alternative Way; Aquarius Fair, 3rd Sun. each month at Nimbin Community Centre, Cullen St, outlet for local craftspeople. May: Mardi Grass Festival, organised by the Nimbin HEMP (Help End Marijuana Prohibition) Embassy. Sept.: Agricultural Show. **In the area:** Eco-tours; spectacular volcanic Nimbin Rocks, 3 km S, on Lismore Rd. At The Channon, 15 km SE: 'alternative' craft market in Coronation Park, 2nd Sun. each month; Opera at The Channon in Aug.; Music Bowl Live Band Concert each Nov. World Heritage-listed Nightcap National Park, 5 km NE, features Protesters Falls (9.5 km NE), named after the 1979 anti-logging protest, which led to the area being gazetted a national park. To the west, access to 60-km Tweed Range Scenic Drive. **Visitor information:** Lismore Visitor Information Centre, cnr Ballina and Molesworth sts, Lismore; (02) 6622 0122. Web site www.liscity.nsw.gov.au **See also:** Tropical North Coast p. 19.

Nowra — Pop. 17 614

MAP REF. 99 E12, 103 I4, 105 K11

Nowra is the principal town of the Shoalhaven district, a popular tourist area on the south coast. Bomaderry is on the northern side of the river. **In town:** Historic Houses Trust property Meroogal (1885), cnr Worrigee and West sts (open Sat. p.m. and Sun.). Shoalhaven Historical Museum, cnr Plunkett and Kinghorne sts, in old police station. On Shoalhaven River: fishing, water-skiing, canoeing, sailing, and cruises on MV *Christine* (depart Nowra Wharf, Riverview Rd, check times). Hanging Rock, via Junction St, has fine views. Nowra Animal Park, Rockhill Rd. Bens Walk, alongside river; Bomaderry Creek Walk from Bomaderry, self-guide pamphlets available. Market, 3rd Sun. each month. Oct.: Spring Festival. **In the area:** Many beautiful beaches within 30 km of town. Cambewarra Estate winery (open weekends and public holidays), 5 km N on Illaroo Rd. Australian Naval Aviation Museum, 7 km SW at HMAS *Albatross*. Cambewarra Lookout, 12 km NW, for spectacular views of Shoalhaven River. At Kangaroo Valley, 23 km NW: historic buildings incl. Friendly Inn (National Trust-classified); Pioneer Settlement Reserve, reconstruction of 1880s dairy farm; Hampden Bridge (1898), oldest suspension bridge in Australia; Kangaroo Valley Fruit World, a working fruit farm; canoeing and kayaking safaris to Kangaroo River and Shoalhaven Gorge; superb rural valley scenery along Nowra Rd. Fitzroy Falls in Morton National Park, 38 km NW; also in park (turn-off at Kangaroo Valley), Tallowa Dam water catchment area, 42 km NW, ideal for picnicking. Bundanon, National Estate-listed historic homestead, 21 km W, given to the nation by artist Arthur Boyd and his wife Yvonne; Bundanon collection and Boyd's studio, open 1st Sun. each month (obtain tickets from information centre, advance bookings essential). Marayong Emu Farm, Falls Creek, 11 km S. At Culburra, 21 km SE: nearby Lake Wollumboola and coastal beaches for surfing, swimming, prawning and fishing; beach patrolled in summer; Open Fishing Carnival held Jan. Fresh fish and oyster sales at Greenwell Point, 14 km E. **Visitor information:** Shoalhaven Visitors Centre, cnr Princes Hwy and Pleasant Way, Nowra; (02) 4421 0778, freecall 1800 024 261. Web site www.shoalhaven. nsw.gov.au **See also:** The South Coast p. 26.

Nundle   Pop. 270

MAP REF. 107 K12

The history of this small town began in the 1850s gold rush. Skirted by the Peel River and well known for its fishing, Nundle is situated 56 km SE of Tamworth, at the foot of the Great Dividing Range in a sheep, cattle, wheat and timber district. **In town:** In Jenkins St: Courthouse (1880); historic Peel Inn (1860s). Goldmining display in restored coffin factory, Gill St. Aug.–Sept. and Dec.: Camp Drafting and Dog Trials. **In the area:** Hanging Rock and Sheba Dams Reserve, 11 km W, for picnicking, bushwalking and camping. Mineral fossicking at Hanging Rock (good samples of scheelite can be found); gold-panning on Peel River. Chaffey Reservoir, 11 km N, for fishing, sailing and picnicking; Dulegal Arboretum on foreshore. Fossicker's Way tour through scenic New England countryside, brochure available. **Visitor information:** cnr Peel and Murray sts, Tamworth; (02) 6755 4300. **See also:** New England & the North-West p. 20.

Picturesque Lake Canobolas near Orange

Nyngan   Pop. 2240

MAP REF. 109 R10

The centre of a sheep, wheat and wool district, Nyngan is 603 km NW of Sydney beside the Bogan River. **In town:** Historical town drive and Levee Tour (levee built after 1990 floods), brochures available. Historic buildings, especially in Cobar and Pangee sts. In Pangee St: Bicentennial Mural Wall; Flood Museum at railway station, has local memorabilia (open Mon.–Sat.). Railway Overbridge, heritage-classified footbridge, lookout over town. Cobb & Co Coach Yard, cnr Nymagee St and Monagee Rd, has old coaches, working forge, museum. Apr.: Anzac Day Race Meeting; Agricultural Show. Aug.: Dog Trials. Sept: Spring into Nyngan (festival). **In the area:** Cairn on private property, 65 km S, marking geographic centre of NSW. Grave of Richard Cunningham, 70 km S, botanist with explorer Major Mitchell's party, speared by Aborigines in 1835. Water-bird sanctuary and breeding ground in Macquarie Marshes, 64 km N. **Visitor information:** Shire Offices, Cobar St; (02) 6832 1503. Web site www.nyngan.com **See also:** Central West p. 21.

Orange   Pop. 30 705

MAP REF. 104 G6

This prosperous city is set in rich red volcanic soil on the slopes of Mt Canobolas, 264 km NW of Sydney. Orange is known for its food and wines, parks and gardens, and goldmining history. An obelisk marks the birthplace of poet A. B. (Banjo) Paterson; his birthday is celebrated with a festival. **In town:** Historic Cook Park, Summer St, has begonia house (flowers Feb.–May), duck pond, fernery and picnic area; self-guide walk through park (brochure available). Botanic Gardens, Kearneys Drive. Museum, McNamara St. Civic Gardens, Byng St, comprises Regional Art Gallery, City Library, information centre and Civic Theatre. Self-guide historical walk, brochure available. Sun. market, Kmart carpark. Feb.–Mar.: Banjo Paterson Festival. Apr.: Food of Orange District Week. **In the area:** Campbell's Corner, 8 km S on Pinnacle Rd, a roadside picnic/barbecue spot. Lucknow, 10 km SE, old goldmining town. Ophir gold-fields, 27 km N, site of first discovery of payable gold in Australia 1851, features fossicking centre, picnic area, walking trails to historic tunnels (brochures available), and tours of working gold-mine. At Borenore, 15 km W, National Field Days Oct.–Nov. Borenore Caves, 17 km W, have picnic/barbecue facilities. Lake Canobolas Park, 8 km SW via Cargo Rd, has recreation and camping area, deer park, children's playground, picnic/barbecue facilities; trout fishing in Lake Canobolas. Mt Canobolas Park, a 1500-ha bird and animal sanctuary, 14 km SW. Cadia Mines, 25 km SE, largest gold and copper mine in the State; check annual open day. Several wineries open for tastings and sales (check times). **Visitor information:** Civic Square, Byng St; (02) 6393 8226. **See also:** Central West p. 21.

Parkes
Pop. 10 094

MAP REF. 104 D5

The settlement of Bushmans was renamed after the visit of Sir Henry Parkes (1815–96), a major player in the lead-up to Australian Federation. Situated 364 km W of Sydney on the Newell Hwy, Parkes is the commercial and industrial centre of an important agricultural area. **In town:** Self-guide tourist drive (90 min). Self-guide historical walks include one of town's oldest houses, Balmoral, noted for its iron lacework; brochures available. Motor Museum, cnr Bogan and Dalton sts, displays vintage and veteran vehicles, and local art and craft. Henry Parkes Historical Museum, Clarinda St, has memorabilia and 1000-volume personal library of Sir Henry Parkes. In north Parkes: imposing views of town from Memorial Hill, at eastern end of Bushman St; Pioneer Park Museum, Pioneer St, in historic school and church, has displays of early farm machinery and transport; Kelly Reserve (Newell Hwy), playground and picnic/barbecue facilities in bush setting; Bushmans Hill Reserve (Newell Hwy), at site of old goldmine. Jan.: Elvis Revival. Easter: Sports Festival. June: Picnic Races. Oct.: Country Music Spectacular. **In the area:** Australia Telescope Visitors Centre, 23 km N, has aids that explain use of giant saucer-shaped telescope. At Peak Hill, 48 km N: Peak Hill working goldmine; lookout. **Visitor information:** Kelly Reserve, Newell Hwy; (02) 6862 4365. **See also:** Central West p. 21.

Picton
Pop. 2668

MAP REF. 91 J12, 99 E2, 103 I2, 105 K9

Picton, named after Sir Thomas Picton, hero of Waterloo, is 80 km SW of Sydney. The old buildings and quiet hills of this small town are evocative of an earlier era. **In town:** Historic buildings: splendid railway viaduct (1862) over Stonequarry Creek, Webster St; St Mark's Church (1848), Menangle St; George IV Inn, Argyle St, incorporating Scharer's Little Brewery. Self-guide historical walk, brochure available. Ghost tours around Picton, Fri. and Sat. nights. Country markets in Menangle Rd, 4th Sat. each month. Jan.: Rodeo. Oct.: Music Festival; Agricultural Show; White Waratah Festival. **In the area:** Sydney Skydiving Centre, 5 km E. On Remembrance Dr.: Jarvisfield (1865), 2 km N, home of pioneer landholders, now clubhouse

of Antill Park Golf Club; Wool Away! Woolshed, 3 km N, has bush dances Fri. and Sat. nights. At Thirlmere, 5 km SW: NSW Rail Transport Museum; steam-train rides to Buxton each Sun. (Buxton Rail Craft Markets, 3rd Sun. each month); Festival of Steam 1st Sun. in Mar. Further 3 km SW, Thirlmere Lakes National Park protects five linked freshwater lakes; scenic drive around lakes. Wirrimbirra Sanctuary, 13 km SW, native flora and fauna; overnight cabins. Dingo Sanctuary, 15 km S (open Sat. and Sun.). Bridge-swinging (bungee jumping) at Maldon Suspension Bridge, 5 km SE. **Visitor information:** Old Post Office, cnr Argyle and Menangle sts; (02) 4677 3962. **See also:** Southern Highlands & Illawarra p. 24.

Port Macquarie
Pop. 33 709

MAP REF. 95 G7, 107 P12

Founded as a convict settlement in 1821, and one of the oldest towns in the State, Port Macquarie is now a major holiday resort, situated at the mouth of the Hastings River, 423 km N of Sydney. **In town:** Award-winning Hastings Historical Museum, Clarence St, displays of convict and pioneer relics in 15 rooms of building (1835–40). Convict-built St Thomas' Church (1824–28), Hay St, designed by convict architect Thomas Owen, 3rd oldest surviving church in Australia. Port Macquarie Historic Courthouse (1869), cnr Hay and Clarence sts (closed Sun.). Mid-North Coast Maritime Museum, William St, features shipwreck relics, model ships and early photographs. At end of Horton St: historic cemetery dating from 1842; Kooloonbung Creek Nature Reserve, 50 ha of bushland with boardwalks. Roto House and Macquarie Nature Reserve, Lord St, a koala hospital and study centre. Port Macquarie Observatory, William St. Maritime museum, William St. Fantasy Glades, Pacific Dr., with rainforest gardens and picnic/barbecue facilities. Billabong Koala and Aussie Wildlife Park (Billabong Dr.) and Kingfisher Park (Kingfisher Rd), for close-up look at Australian animals. Town Beach, has surf at one end, sheltered coves at other. Peppermint Park has slides and roller-blading. River cruises daily. Walk following coastal headlands from breakwall to lighthouse (8 km). Hydro-golf, Boundary St, a golf course incorporating water targets. Market in Findlay Ave, 2nd and 4th Sun. each month. Jan.: Golden Lure Tournament

(deep-sea fishing). **In the area:** Excellent fishing and all water sports. Charter fishing; Harley Davidson motor-bike tours; horseriding; abseiling; skirmish (paintball game); skydiving. Sea Acres Rainforest Centre, 4 km S, elevated 1.3 km boardwalk through canopy; tours. At Lighthouse Beach, 10 km S, 16-km expanse of white sand; camel rides; dolphin-watching from shore; breathtaking views from grounds of Tacking Point Lighthouse at northern end of beach (lighthouse not open to public). Lake Cathie, 16 km S, holiday town between surf beach and tidal lake, for swimming and fishing. Scenic drives to Ellenborough Falls, 85 km SW and to Wauchope and Timbertown, 20 km W; 4WD tours into hinterland; bus tours of surrounding area (brochures available). Cassegrain Winery, 13 km W; Discovery Concert held here under the stars each Oct. **Visitor information:** cnr Clarence and Hay sts; (02) 6583 1293, freecall 1800 025 935. Web site www. portmacquarieinfo.com.au **See also:** Holiday Coast p. 17.

Queanbeyan
Pop. 25 689

MAP REF. 103 E5, 104 G13, 123 G4, 126 H3

Adjoining Canberra, Queanbeyan has a special relationship with the Australian capital. The town, proclaimed 1838, is named from a squattage held by an ex-convict innkeeper, Timothy Beard, and called 'Quinbean' ('clear waters'). **In town:** Self-guide walks through town, brochure available. History Museum, Farrer Pl. Byrne's Mill (1883), now a restaurant, Collett St. Byrne's Mill House, cnr Collett and Morisset sts, now Queanbeyan Books and Prints. Queanbeyan Art Society Inc., Trinculo Pl., exhibits local art and craft. Railway Historical Society Steam Train rides, depart station in Henderson St, check details. Cottage markets, 2nd Sun. each month (except Jan.). Mar.: Festival of Traditions; Psychic Fair (meetings of psychics, palmists and tarot-card readers). Oct.: Sporting Weekend Spectacular. Nov.: Agricultural Show. **In the area:** Molonglo Gorge, 2 km N, for bushwalking. At Bungendore, 26 km NE: historic village square contains Colonial-style shops; Bungendore Woodworks Gallery sells local art and craft; Country Muster in Feb. Lark Hill Winery, 7 km N of Bungendore, tastings and sales. Historic Bywong Goldmining Town, 31 km NE, a re-creation of early mining settlement. Googong Dam, 10 km S, for fishing;

bushwalking and wildlife refuge. London Bridge Woolshed and Shearers' Quarters, 24 km S; walk 1 km to limestone formation. **Visitor information:** cnr Farrer Pl. and Lowe St; (02) 6298 0241. Web site www.canberratourism.com.au **See also:** Capital Country p. 23.

Raymond Terrace Pop. 12 332

MAP REF. 97 E6, 105 N4

This town, set on the banks of the Hunter and William rivers, was an important wool-shipping centre in the 1840s. Several historic buildings remain. **In town:** Significant buildings: courthouse (1838, cnr William St and Pacific Hwy), still in use; Anglican church and rectory (1830s, Glenelg St), built of hand-hewn sandstone; numerous buildings in historic King St, along waterfront. Sketchley Cottage, on Pacific Hwy, a museum of memorabilia (open Sun.). **In the area:** Hunter Region Botanic Gardens, 3 km S on Pacific Hwy at Motto Farm, has over 2000 native plants and several theme gardens. Fighter World, RAAF Base Williamtown, 16 km NE. Tilligerry Habitat, 34 km N, eco-tourism centre with Aboriginal culture and guided walks to see koalas. Convict-built Tanilba House (1831), 36 km N (check times). Koala Reserve, 40 km N, boardwalk through koala colony. **Visitor information:** 240 Pacific Hwy; (02) 4987 1211. Web site www. portstephens. org.au **See also:** Hunter Valley & Coast p. 14.

Richmond Pop. 7972

MAP REF. 91 K6, 105 K7

One of the five Macquarie towns and sister town to Windsor, 6 km E, Richmond was proclaimed in 1810. **In town:** Historic buildings: Hobartville (privately owned), Castlereagh Rd; Toxana (1841), Windsor St, now an art gallery (open Thurs. and Sat.); St Peter's Church (1841), also in Windsor St, and adjacent graves of notable pioneers, incl. William Cox and Australia's convict chronicler Margaret Catchpole. Lions Club Markets, Richmond Park, Windsor St, Sat. every 6 weeks; Bellbird Craft Markets, March St, 1st Sat. each month. Sept.: Hawkesbury District Orchid Spring Show; Hawkesbury Waratah Festival. Oct.–Nov.: Fruits of the Hawkesbury Festival. **In the area:** RAAF base, 3 km E on Windsor–Richmond Rd, oldest Air Force establishment in Australia; used for civilian flying from 1915. University

of Western Sydney, 3 km S; foundation stone laid in 1895. Vale of Avoca Lookout, 20 km W, for stunning views over Grose Valley. Bellbird Hill Lookout at Kurrajong Heights, 13 km NW, for views across to Sydney skyline. Markets each Sat. at Bilpin, 31 km NW. Mountain Lagoon, 40 km NW, bushwalking, cabins; brochures available. Hawkesbury Lookout, 15 km SW. **Visitor information:** Tourism Hawkesbury, Bicentenary Park, Ham Common, Clarendon; (02) 4588 5895. Web site www.hawkesburyvalley.com **See also:** Central Coast & Hawkesbury p. 16.

Robertson Pop. 922

MAP REF. 99 E8, 103 I3, 105 K10

The link between the Southern Highlands and the coast, Robertson sits at the top of the Macquarie Pass. Vantage points offer spectacular views of the coast. Robertson is also the centre of the largest potato-growing district in NSW. This idyllic countryside featured in the film *Babe* (1996). **In town:** Manor-style Ranelagh House (1924), 3 km E on Illawarra Hwy. The Cockatoo Run heritage railway (Port Kembla to Robertson, Tues., Thurs., Sat., Sun. Mar.–Nov.). Market, 2nd Sun. each month, at Robertson School of Arts. Mar.: Agricultural Show. **In the area:** Burrawang, 6 km W, 19th-century village with historic general store. In Morton National Park: Belmore Falls, 10 km SW; Fitzroy Falls, 15 km SW; NPWS Visitor Centre at the town of Fitzroy Falls; ranger-guided walks in park in Apr. Manning Lookout over Kangaroo Valley, 16 km SW. Robertson Rainforest, 2 km S. Carrington Falls, in Budderoo National Park, 10 km SE; ranger-guided walks in park in Apr. **Visitor information:** Southern Highlands Visitor Information Centre, 62–70 Main St, Mittagong; (02) 4871 2888 or 1300 657 559. Web site www.highlandsnsw.com.au **See also:** Southern Highlands & Illawarra p. 24; National Parks p. 74.

Rylstone Pop. 723

MAP REF. 104 I4

This historic town is west of the Great Dividing Range on the Cudgegong River, 275 km NW of Sydney. **In town:** Historic buildings, especially in Louee St, incl. Bridge View Inn information centre and restaurant (formerly bank), and post office. Self-guide historical town walk, brochure available. Feb.: Rylstone–Kandos

Agricultural Show. **In the area:** Many camping spots and fishing areas on Capertee, Cudgegong and Turon rivers. Signposted scenic drives, brochure available. Bicentennial Museum (open weekends) at Kandos, 3 km S. Lake Windamere, 19 km W, for water sports and fishing; camping and picnic/barbecue facilities; Fishing Festival at Easter. Fern Tree Gully, 16 km N, tree ferns in subtropical forest. Military Vehicle Museum, 20 km N. Dunn's Swamp, 18 km E, for camping, fishing and bushwalking. Glen Davis, 56 km SE on Capertee River, surrounded by sheer cliff faces; nearby, Wollemi National Park, for wilderness bushwalking and excellent canoeing. **Visitor information:** Bridge View Inn, Louee St; (02) 6379 1132. Web site www.rylstone.com **See also:** Central West p. 21.

Scone Pop. 3468

MAP REF. 105 K1

This town, set in beautiful country on the New England Hwy, 280 km N of Sydney, is the world's second largest thoroughbred and horse-breeding centre. **In town:** In Kelly St: *Mare and Foal*, Elizabeth Park, life-size bronze sculpture by Gabriel Sterk; Australian Stock Horse Museum. Historical Society Museum, Kingdon St (open Wed. and Sun.). Market at information centre, last Sun. each month. May: Horse Festival. Sept.–Oct.: Hunter Valley Horse Expo. Nov.: Rodeo. **In the area:** Several wineries open for tastings. Tours of thoroughbred studs and sheep station. Lake Glenbawn, 15 km E, for water sports, good bass fishing, lakeside horserides (summer), picnic/barbecue facilities and camping. At Moonan Flat, 50 km NE: Victoria Hotel (1865), Cobb & Co. coach stop during gold-rush era, reputedly patronised by bushranger Captain Thunderbolt; Jazz by the River each Oct. Burning Mountain at Wingen, 20 km N, a deep coal seam that has been smouldering for at least 5000 years. **Visitor information:** cnr Susan and Kelly sts; (02) 6545 1526. Web site www.infohunt. nsw.gov.au/scone **See also:** Hunter Valley & Coast p. 14.

Shellharbour Pop. 3697

MAP REF. 99 H8, 105 K10

This attractive holiday resort, 7 km S of Lake Illawarra, is one of the oldest settlements on the South Coast and was a thriving port in the 1830s. **In town:** Illawarra Light Railway Museum, Russell St, has train and tram rides, stationary engines and other artifacts. Jan.: Australia Day Breakfast by the Lake. Sept.: Festival of the Forest. **In the area:** Killalea Recreation Park, 3 km S, foreshore picnic area; beach here is ideal for surfing, diving, snorkelling and fishing. Blackbutt Forest Reserve, 2 km W, remnant of coastal plain forest in urban area, has walking trails with views of Lake Illawarra and Illawarra Escarpment. BMX circuit at Croom Regional Sporting Complex, 8 km W. Bass Point Aquatic and Marine Reserve, 5 km SE, has picnic area with views; good scuba-diving, snorkelling, fishing and surfing offshore. Lake Illawarra, 7 km N, boat hire. **Visitor information:** Shellharbour Square, Blackbutt; (02) 4221 6169. **See also:** Southern Highlands & Illawarra p. 24.

Singleton   Pop. 12 519
MAP REF. 105 L3

Set on the Hunter River in rich grazing land, Singleton is the geographical heart of the Hunter Valley. New wealth has come from the huge open-cut coal mines. **In town:** Town walk, brochure available. Monolithic sundial on riverbank in James Cook Park, Ryan Ave. Markets in Burdekin Park, New England Hwy, 4th Sun. each month. Oct.: Festival of Wine and Roses. **In the area:** Industry and wine tours, details from information centre. Royal Australian Infantry Corps Museum, 5 km S, traces development of the infantry corp. Village Fair in Sept. at Broke, 26 km S. Broke–Fordwich winery area of Hunter Valley, brochure available. Yengo National Park, 15 km S, features extensive Aboriginal carvings and paintings; tours. Wollemi National Park, 15 km SW, a large wilderness park. Pick your own oranges at Hillside Orange Orchard, 25 km SW on Windsor–Putty Rd. Lake St Clair, 25 km N, has extensive recreational and waterway facilities, camping on shore; nearby, magnificent views of Mt Royal Range. **Visitor information:** 33 George St; (02) 6571 5888, freecall 1800 449 888. Web site www. singleton.nsw.gov.au **See also:** Hunter Valley & Coast p. 14.

Stroud   Pop. 598
MAP REF. 105 N3

There are many historic buildings in this delightful town, 75 km N of Newcastle. **In town:** Self-guide town walk covers 32 historic sites, brochure available. In Cowper St: St John's Anglican Church, convict-built of local clay bricks (1833), has beautiful stained glass windows and cedar furnishings; Rectory of St John's (1836); Stroud House (1832); Parish House (1837); courthouse, post office and Quambi House. Underground silo (one of 8 built 1841) at Silo Hill Reserve, off Broadway St. July: International Brick and Rolling-pin Throwing. Sept.–Oct.: Rodeo. Nov.: Branch Picnic Races. **Visitor information:** Stroud Newsagency, Cowper St; (02) 4994 5117. Web site www.greatlakes.org.au **See also:** Holiday Coast p. 17.

Tamworth   Pop. 31 865
MAP REF. 107 J11

This prosperous city at the junction of the New England and Oxley hwys is the country music capital of Australia, as well as being the heart of many other cultural activities. Thousands of fans flock here for the long-established 10-day Tamworth Country Music Festival. With its attractive public buildings and parks and gardens, Tamworth is also the commercial capital of northern NSW. **In town:** Country Music Hands of Fame cornerstone at Hands of Fame Park, Kable Ave, has hand imprints of country music stars. National Trust-classified Calala Cottage, Denison St, home of Tamworth's first mayor. City Gallery, Marius St, exhibits works by Turner, Hans Heysen and Will Ashton; National Fibre Collection. Oxley Park Wildlife Sanctuary, north off Brisbane St. Oxley Lookout for views of city and rich Peel Valley, at top of White St; lookout is starting point for Kamilaroi walking track (6.2 km), brochure available. Powerstation Museum, cnr Peel and Darling sts, traces Tamworth's history as first city in Southern Hemisphere to have electric street lighting. At Tamworth RSL Club, Kable St: Tamworth Country Theatre, all-star live radio broadcasts, 3rd Sat. each month (bookings at information centre); Country Music Jamboree (Thurs., from 7.30 p.m.). Various line-dancing venues. Stamp and Coin Market, 1st Sat. each month at St Paul's Church, Church St. Market, 2nd Sun. each month at Showground Pavilion. Main St Markets, 3rd Sun. each month at Peel St Blvd. Jan.: Country Music Festival; National Pro Rodeo. May: Gold Cup Race Meeting. June: Fireside Bush Poetry Festival. **In the area:** Golden Guitar Complex, 6 km S on New England Hwy: fascinating gemstone collection; 12-metre Golden Guitar; Gallery of Stars Wax Museum; Great Australian Ice-creamery; well-known Longyard Hotel. Opposite is Country Music Roll of Renown at Radio Centre, dedicated to contributing country music artists. Lake Keepit State Recreation Area, 57 km NW, for water sports; good visitor facilities. Fossicker's Way tour through scenic countryside begins at historic goldmining town of Nundle, 63 km SE; brochures available. **Visitor information:** cnr Murray and Peel sts; (02) 6755 4300. Web site www.tamworthonline.com.au **See also:** New England & the North-West p. 20.

Taree   Pop. 16 702
MAP REF. 95 C13, 105 O1, 107 N13

Taree on the Pacific Hwy, 310 km N of Sydney, serves as the commercial hub of the Manning River district. **In town:** Self-guide historical walks through eastern and western sections of town, brochures available. Houseboat and dinghy hire, Crescent Ave. Taree Craft Centre, next to information centre, Old Pacific Hwy, Taree North. Manning Regional Art Gallery, MacQuarie St (check opening times). Jan.: Craftathon. Easter: Aquatic Festival. Apr.–May: Eisteddfod. June: Non-Conventional Homes Eco Tour and Envirofair. **In the area:** Weekly markets, details from information centre; many art and craft galleries. 4 national parks and 11 nature reserves; horseriding, and 4WD and mountain-bike tours. Forest drives and walking trails in Manning Valley, brochures available. Joyflights over Manning Valley, depart airport, northern outskirts of town on Lansdowne Rd. Deep Water Shark Gallery, Peverill St, Tinonee, 8 km SW, for Aboriginal art and craft. Good surfing beaches on coast 16 km E. Manning River, a 150-km navigable waterway, with beaches, good fishing and holiday spots. The Big Buzz Funpark, 15 km S on Lakes Way, Rainbow Flat. Rainforest Nature Walk at Hallidays Point, 25 km SE, self-guide leaflet available. Crowdy Bay National Park, 40 km NE, offers wildflowers in spring, fishing, swimming, bushwalking and camping. Coorabakh National Park, 20 km NE on the Pacific Hwy, features scenic drive to Vincent's Lookout, Waitui Falls and Big Nellie Mountain (volcanic plug). High Adventure Air Park, 38 km NE on Pacific Hwy, a light airsports centre. **Visitor information:**

Hat Head National Park near Taree

Manning Valley Visitor Information Centre, Old Pacific Hwy, Taree North; (02) 6552 1900, freecall 1800 801 522. Web site www.gtcc.nsw.gov.au/tourism **See also:** Holiday Coast p. 17.

Tathra Pop. 1684

MAP REF. 100 G8, 103 G10, 235 R6

Tathra is centrally located 18 km SE of Bega on the south coast of NSW, midway between Merimbula and Bermagui. Tathra is ideal for a family holiday, with its patrolled 3-km-long surf beach, safe swimming for small children at Mogareeka Inlet (the sandy mouth of the Bega River), and good fishing spots. Diving and deep-sea fishing charters at Kianinny Bay. **In town:** National Trust-classified historic wharf (1860s), Wharf Rd, has fishing platform and seafood cafe. Above wharf, Maritime Museum traces history of wharf and has replicas of early vessels. Oct.: Amateur Fishing Competition. **In the area:** Bournda National Park, 11 km S, for camping and bushwalking; at Lake Wallagoot in park, wetland area, birdwatching, fishing, prawning, swimming, water sports, boat hire. Mimosa Rocks National Park, 17 km N, a picturesque coastal park named after the steamship *Mimosa*, wrecked on volcanic rock in 1863. **Visitor information:** Tathra Wharf, Wharf Rd; (02) 6494 4062, freecall 1800 633 012. Web site www.sapphirecoast.com.au **See also:** The South Coast p. 26.

Temora Pop. 4125

MAP REF. 103 A2, 104 C10, 111 R8

Temora is the commercial centre for the rich agricultural district of northern and western Riverina, which produces wheat, oats, canola, triticale, wool and meat stocks. The 1880s gold rush left a legacy of fine buildings. **In town:** Heritage walk and drives, brochures available. Temora Rural Museum, Wagga Rd, has working displays, and rock and mineral collection (open p.m.). Skydive Centre, Aerodrome Rd, instruction and adventure jumps (open weekends). Quota Markets, Pale Face Park, last Sat. each month. Feb.: Golden Gift (foot race). Mar.: Temora Rural Museum Exhibition Day. Oct.: Antique Engine Field Day and Swap Meet. Nov.: Battle of the Bands (youth band competition). **In the area:** Lake Centenary, 3 km N, for boating, swimming and picnics. Paragon Gold Mine at Gidginbung, 15 km N (open by appt). **Visitor information:** 296 Hoskins St; (02) 6978 0500. Web site www.temora.nsw.gov.au **See also:** The Riverina p. 27.

Tenterfield Pop. 3205

MAP REF. 107 M4, 525 N13

The countryside around Tenterfield, at the northern end of the New England highlands in northern NSW, offers a contrast of mountains and rural landscapes. Primarily a sheep- and cattle-grazing area, other industries include logging and sawmilling, and tourism. Autumn in Tenterfield is spectacular. **In town:** Centenary Cottage (1871), Logan St, has local history collection. Early residential buildings in Logan St. Self-guide historical town walk, leaflet available. Sir Henry Parkes Library and Museum in School of Arts (1876), Rouse St, features relics relating to Sir Henry Parkes, who made his famous Federation speech there in 1889. In High St, handmade saddles at Tenterfield Saddler, the place that inspired the Peter Allen song of the same name. Cobb & Co. coach tours. Railway Markets at Railway Station, Railway Pde, 1st Sat. every 2nd month (beginning Feb.). Apr.: Oracles of the Bush (Australian culture and bush poetry festival). Oct.: Federation Festival; Spring Wine Festival; Highland Gathering. Nov.: Campdraft. **In the area:** Mt McKenzie Granite Drive, 30-km circular route from Molesworth St (in town), incl. Ghost Gully. Bluff Rock, 10 km S on New England Hwy, unusual granite outcrop. Thunderbolt's Hideout, 11 km NE, reputed haunt of bushranger Captain Thunderbolt. Gold mine at Drake, 31 km NE. Boonoo Boonoo Falls (210-m drop), in Boonoo Boonoo National Park, 32 km NE. Good views from summit of Bald Rock, largest granite monolith in Australia, 35 km N in Bald Rock National Park; Woollool Woollool Aboriginal Culture Tours to Bald Rock (daily). Girraween National Park (in Qld) renowned for wildflowers and massive granite outcrops. **Visitor information:** 157 Rouse St; (02) 6736 1082. Web site www.tenterfield.com **See also:** New England & the North-West p. 20.

Terrigal Pop. 8894

MAP REF. 91 Q4, 94 H5, 105 M6

Excellent surfing, boutiques and restaurants are attractions of this popular holiday town on the Central Coast. June or July: Food, Wine and Chocolate Festivals. **In the area:** The Skillion, 3 km SE, a headland offering coastal views. Several good surfing beaches: Wamberal Beach (3 km N); Shelly Beach (13 km N); Avoca Beach (7.5 km S). Central Park Family Fun Centre, 6 km N at Forresters Beach, has waterslide, fun cars and barbecues. Ken Duncan Gallery, Oak Rd, Matcham, 8 km NW, has largest privately owned photographic collection in Australia. Fragrant Garden, Portsmouth Rd, Erina, 4 km W, has display garden, gift shop and cafe; Central Coast Chilli

Festival in Mar. Secluded beaches and pockets of rainforest at Bouddi National Park, 17 km S. Sea kayaking tours available. **Visitor information:** Central Coast Tourism, Rotary Park, Terrigal Dr.; (02) 4385 4430, freecall 1300 130 708. Web site www.cctourism.com.au **See also:** Central Coast & Hawkesbury p. 16.

The Entrance   Pop. 5348

MAP REF. 91 Q3, 94 H2, 105 M6

Blessed with clean beaches, this beautiful lakeside and ocean town between Sydney and Newcastle is the aquatic playground of these two cities. **In town:** Pelican feeding at 3.30 p.m. in Memorial Park, Marine Pde. Town Mall: 180 shops, pavement restaurants, playground for children and Sat. craft market. Art and craft market, each Sun. in Bayview Ave. Jan.: Entertainment on Waterfront Stage. Dec.: Tuggerah Lakes Mardi Gras Festival. **In the area:** Bike tracks and horseriding. Fishing on lakes (Tuggerah, Budgewoi and Munmorah) and ocean beach; prawning on lakes in summer. Water sports on Lake Tuggerah. Extensive shell collection at Shell Museum, 1 km N at Dunleith Caravan Park. Bushwalking trails in Wyrrabalong National Park, 6 km N. Crackneck Point Lookout, 6 km S, for coastal views. **Visitor information:** Central Coast Tourism, Memorial Park, Marine Pde; (02) 4334 4213, freecall 1800 033 502. Web site www.cctourism.com.au **See also:** Central Coast & Hawkesbury p. 16.

Thredbo   Pop. 224

MAP REF. 101 C13, 103 C10

This popular mountain village lies in Kosciuszko National Park between Jindabyne and Khancoban. Its history began in 1962 with a State government lease for resort development. In summer Thredbo attracts anglers, mountain-bikers and bushwalkers; a chairlift places visitors within walking distance of Australia's highest summit, Mt Kosciuszko (2228 m). Winter snows transform Thredbo into one of the State's premier ski resorts; the ski season runs from the June long weekend to the October long weekend. **In town:** Chairlifts (incl. quad lifts) for access to marked downhill ski trails for beginners to advanced; cross-country skiing, ski school and ski hire. In summer and early autumn: inline skate hire for use at the resort; Thredbo Bobsled rides; canoe hire for use in the resort ponds; walks around the village, incl. Meadows Nature

Walk through ti-trees, and Thredbo Village Walk for the diversity of alpine architecture; mountain-bike riding on the Village Bike Track and various other tracks around Thredbo (bike hire available); Australian Institute of Sport Alpine Training Centre, used by athletes for high-altitude training, has quality sporting facilities. Jan.: Blues Festival. Mar.: Tour de Snowy (women's cycling, throughout region); Global Music Festival. May: Legends of Jazz. **In the area:** Skiers can access Perisher and Mt Blue Cow ski fields via the Skitube from Bullocks Flat, 15 km NE. Crackenback chairlift operates year-round from the resort to Eagles Nest Mountain Hut; from here, in summer, a 12-km return walk on alpine walkway leads to Mt Kosciuszko via Kosciuszko Lookout. Alternatively, return from Eagles Nest to Thredbo on Merritts Nature Walk. Guided alpine walks also available. Trout fishing on Thredbo River and at Lake Jindabyne, 34 km NE. Pilot Lookout, 10 km SE, magnificent view dominated by The Pilot (1828 m) and on the Vic. side of border, The Cobberas (1883 m). Horseriding and station accommodation at historic Tom Groggin, 24 km SW. **Visitor information:** Friday Dr.; (02) 6459 4198 or Snowy Region Visitor Centre, Kosciuszko Rd, Jindabyne; (02) 6450 5600, freecall 1800 636 525. Web site www.snowymountains.com.au **See also:** Snowy Mountains p. 28.

Tibooburra   Pop. 214

MAP REF. 108 D3

The name of this former gold town, 333 km N of Broken Hill, comes from an Aboriginal word meaning 'heaps of rocks'. The town is surrounded by granite outcrops and was previously known as The Granites. **In town:** In Briscoe St: courthouse (1887), houses National Parks and Wildlife Service Pastoralist Museum; Family Hotel (1882); Tibooburra Hotel (1883); Tibooburra Aboriginal Land Council 'Keeping Place', display includes tribal headdress; School of the Air (tours during term time). July: Tibooburra Festival. Oct.: Gymkhana and Rodeo (long weekend). Dec.: Night Rodeo. **In the area:** Check road conditions before travelling; read section on Outback Motoring p. 599. Self-guide historical Goldmining Walk and Granite Scenic Walk in Sturt National Park, adjacent to town; park has 4 camping grounds and is a semi-desert area noted for its wildlife and geological features;

Explorers Tree, at western end of park, tree faintly blazed by explorer Charles Sturt; outdoor pastoralist museum at Mt Wood (27 km E). Cameron Corner, 133 km NW, where three States meet. At former gold township of Milparinka, 40 km S: Albert Hotel (closed), restored courthouse, remains of old police station, bank, general store and post office. Depot Glen Billabong, 14 km NW of Milparinka, where Sturt was marooned for 6 months in 1845; 1 km further east, grave of James Poole, a member of Sturt's 1845 expedition. Further 7 km N of Depot Glen is Mt Poole, where Poole's Cairn commemorates Charles Sturt's expedition. **Visitor information:** National Parks and Wildlife Service, Briscoe St; (08) 8091 3308. Web site www.outbacknsw.org.au **See also:** The Outback p. 31.

Tocumwal   Pop. 1453

MAP REF. 111 M12, 232 I2

This Murray River town on the Newell Hwy is ideal for golf, boating, fishing, swimming, water-skiing and camping. **In town:** In Foreshore Park, Deniliquin Rd: large fibreglass Murray cod; Foreshore Markets (dates from information centre). Miniature World of Trains, cnr Deniliquin Rd and Bridge St, has model-train display. River cruises, walks, drives and bike tracks; self-guide brochures available. Mar.: Pioneer Skills Day. Easter: Easter Eggs-Travaganza. June: Country Craft Fiesta. Oct.: Open Garden Weekend. **In the area:** Around 25 beaches in vicinity of town, some with picnic areas. Picturesque golf course with resident kangaroos. Aerodrome, 5 km NE, largest RAAF base in Australia during World War II, now home to international Sportavia Soaring Centre (glider joy-flights and learn-to-glide packages). The Rocks and Blowhole, 8.5 km NE on Rocks Rd, associated with local Aboriginal legend; adjacent to working granite quarry. **Visitor information:** Foreshore Park, Murray St; (03) 5874 2131, freecall 1800 677 271. Web site www. tocumwalgolf.com.au **See also:** The Murray p. 30.

Toukley   Pop. 4983

MAP REF. 91 Q2, 97 H13, 105 M6

Situated on the peninsula between Tuggerah and Budgewoi lakes, this coastal hamlet offers unspoilt beaches and breathtaking scenery. **In town:** Local art and visitor information, Art Centre,

Wallarah Rd. Open-air markets, each Sun. at Shopping Centre car park, Yarralla Rd. Sept.: Gathering of the Clans (Scottish festival). Oct.: Cycle Classic. **In the area:** Lakes, venue for all water sports. In summer, prawning from lake foreshores. Rock pool at Cabbage Tree Bay, 5 km E. Norah Head Lighthouse, 5 km E. Many bushwalking trails in magnificent Munmorah State Recreation Area, 10 km N, and in Red Gum Forest in Wyrrabalong National Park, 4 km S. **Visitor information:** Central Coast Tourism, Rotary Park, Terrigal Dr., Terrigal; (02) 4385 4430, freecall 1300 130 708. Web site www.cctourism.com.au **See also:** Central Coast & Hawkesbury p. 16.

Tumbarumba
Pop. 1502

MAP REF. 103 B7

A former goldmining town in the western foothills of the Snowy Mountains, 504 km SW of Sydney, Tumbarumba is an ideal base for day trips to the Snowy Mountains. **In town:** Bicentennial Botanic Gardens, Prince St. Wool and Craft Centre, Bridge St, incl. Historical Society Museum, which features a working model of water-powered timber mill. Jan.: New Year's Day Rodeo. Feb.: Tumbafest (food and wine festival). Nov.: Heritage Week. **In the area:** Whitewater rafting, trout fishing, paragliding, gem-fossicking, mountain-bike trails, horse trail-rides. Site of old Union Jack Mining Area, 3 km N. Pioneer Women's Hut, 8 km NW on Wagga Rd, a fascinating domestic, rural history museum (open Wed., Sat. and Sun.). Paddy's River Falls, 16 km S, cascades drop 60 m; nearby, walking track and picnic area. Henry Angel Trackhead, 7 km SE on Tooma Rd, starting point for section of Hume and Hovell Walking Track; facilities for campers and picnickers. At Tooma, 34 km SE: historic hotel, tearooms and store. **Visitor information:** This 'n' That, 31 Albury St; (02) 6948 3444. **See also:** The Riverina p. 27.

Tumut
Pop. 5915

MAP REF. 103 C5, 104 D12, 126 A2

Situated on the Snowy Mountains Hwy, 424 km SW of Sydney, Tumut attracts visitors all year. Close to ski resorts and the Snowy Mountains Hydro-electric Scheme, it is also well known for spectacular mountain scenery. **In town:** Historical and tree-identifying walks, brochures available. Old Butter Factory

Tourist Complex, Adelong Rd, for local art and craft and information centre. Fishing at Tumut-U-Fish, Fitzroy St. Millet broom factory, Snowy Mountains Hwy. Bakehouse Gallery, Wynyard St. Powered hang-gliding at airport, 6 km E off Snowy Mountains Hwy. River walk along Tumut River, from Elm Dr. Tours to power stations: Tumut 3 (45 km S) and Tumut 2 (115 km S); brochure available. Apr.–May: Festival of the Falling Leaf. **In the area:** Excellent fishing in Tumut and Goobraganda rivers. Whitewater rafting, canoeing, horseriding, abseiling, hang-gliding and scenic flights. Two access points (for shorter walks) on Hume and Hovell Walking Track. Triton Trout Farm, 19 km E, fish sales (open Wed.–Mon.). Largest African violet farm in Australia, 7 km S on Tumut Plains Rd (open Tues.–Sun.). Blowering Reservoir, 10 km S, centre for water sports, fishing for rainbow trout, brown trout and perch; lookout over dam wall. Blowering Cliffs walk (5 km) in Kosciuszko National Park, 19 km S; outstanding granite cliffs overlooking reservoir. Talbingo Dam and Reservoir, 40 km S, tall dam in steep wooded country. Historic goldmining site at Kiandra, 95 km S. **Visitor information:** Old Butter Factory Tourist Complex, Adelong Rd (Snowy Mountains Hwy); (02) 6947 1849. **See also:** The Riverina p. 27.

Tweed Heads
Pop. 37 775

MAP REF. 107 Q1, 518 I11, 525 Q11

Tweed Heads, the State's most northern town, and its twin town Coolangatta (Qld), are popular holiday destinations at the southern end of the Gold Coast. **In town:** World's first laser-beam lighthouse on Point Danger, nearby, cliff-edge walk (dolphins may be seen offshore) and picnic spots. Tweed cruise boats, operating from River Tce, visit locations along Tweed River. Fishing and diving charters, and houseboats for hire. Sun. craft market, Florence St. Jan.: Jet Sprint Racing. June: Wintersun Carnival; Greenback Fishing Competition. Sept.: Rainforest Week (promotes ecosystem awareness). Nov.: Agricultural Show. **In the area:** Idyllic beaches, reserves and coastal towns on Tweed Coast, particularly Kingscliff, 14 km S. Minjungbal Aboriginal Cultural Centre, just over Boyds Bay Bridge, features Aboriginal ceremonial bora ring, museum, and mangrove and rainforest walk. Melaleuca Station, 9 km S on Pacific

Hwy at Chinderah, a re-created 1930s railway station in tea-tree plantation, has train rides, tea-tree oil distillation plant and animal nursery. Tropical Fruit World, 15 km S on Pacific Hwy (tours of plantation). John Hogan Rainforest at Urliup, 17 km SW, spectacular palm rainforest; walks and picnics. **Visitor information:** 4 Wharf St; (07) 5536 4244. Web site www.tactic.nsw.gov.au **See also:** Tropical North Coast p. 19.

Ulladulla
Pop. 8384

MAP REF. 103 I6, 105 J13, 127 P4

This fishing town is the main centre on this section of the South Coast: a stretch of beautiful coast, lakes, lagoons and white sandy beaches. **In town:** Old building (c. 1868) houses Millard's Cottage Restaurant, Princes Hwy. Funland, Princes Hwy, large indoor family fun park. At Warden Head, lighthouse, views and walking tracks. Coomie Nulunga Cultural Trail (30 min), starts Deering St, opposite Lighthouse Oval carpark. Native plants, birdlife and walks at South Pacific Heathland Reserve, Dowling St. Ulladulla Wildflower Reserve, Warden St. Coastal Patrol Markets, 2nd Sun. each month at harbour wharf. Easter: Blessing of the Fleet. Aug.: Festival of Food and Wine by the Sea. **In the area:** At historic Milton, 7 km NW on Princes Hwy: art galleries and outdoor cafes; Village Markets on hwy, 1st Sat. each month; Scarecrow Festival held Apr.; Settlers Fair held Oct. Pointer Gap Lookout, 20 km NW, for coastal views. Mollymook, 2 km N, for surfing and excellent fishing. Narrawallee Beach, 4 km N. Nearby Narrawallee Inlet has calm, shallow water ideal for children. Sussex Inlet, 47 km N, holds fishing carnival in May. Lakes Conjola (23 km NW) and Burrill (5 km SW), ideal for swimming, fishing and water-skiing. Pigeon House in beautiful Morton National Park, 25 km NW, walk to summit for breathtaking views (3-hr return). **Visitor information:** Civic Centre, Princes Hwy; (02) 4455 1269, freecall 1800 024 261. Web site www.shoalhaven.nsw.gov.au **See also:** The South Coast p. 26.

Uralla
Pop. 2460

MAP REF. 107 L9

Rich gold discoveries were made near this charming New England town in the 1850s. **In town:** Self-guide Heritage Walking Tour, brochure available. In Bridge St: Hassett's Military Museum, displays military history and memorabilia; statue of Thunderbolt, 'gentleman' bushranger shot dead by a local policeman in 1870 at nearby Kentucky Creek (see grave in old Uralla Cemetery, John St). McCrossin's Mill (1870), Salisbury St, now a museum: goldfields history displays; re-created joss house honouring Chinese gold-seekers; Thunderbolt exhibits; collection of Thunderbolt paintings. Old Uralla courthouse, Hill St, now library. New England Brass and Iron Lace Foundry, operating since 1872 (check times). Market, 2nd Sat. each month. Apr.: New England Grand Parade (racing of classic cars). Nov.: Thunderbolt Country Fair. **In the area:** Dangars Lagoon, 5 km SE on Walcha Rd, a bird sanctuary and hide. Mt Yarrowyck Aboriginal rock-art site, 23 km NW off Bundarra Rd. Gold-fossicking, 5 km SW. Thunderbolt's Rock, 6 km S, used by the bushranger as lookout; climb with care. Tourist Drive 19 (signposted) includes historic Gostwyck Church (11 km SE) and Dangars Falls and Gorge (40 km S); brochure available. **Visitor information:** 104 Bridge St; (02) 6778 4496. Web site www.new-england.org/uralla **See also:** New England & the North-West p. 20.

Urunga   Pop. 2716

MAP REF. 107 P9

Located at the junction of the Bellinger and Kalang rivers, 28 km S of Coffs Harbour, Urunga is one of the best fishing spots on the north coast. **In town:** Water sports and fishing. In Morgo St: Oceanview Hotel (1927), original furniture; Urunga Museum (check times); safe lagoon swimming for children, with picnic reserve. On Anchor's Wharf, riverside restaurant and boat hire. Water Rat River Cruises. The Honey Place, Pacific Hwy, a huge concrete replica of old-style straw beehive, has a glass beehive display, honey-tasting, gallery and gardens. July: Bowling Club Carnival. **In the area:** Beautiful beach for surfing and swimming at Hungry Head, 3 km S. At Raleigh, 4 km N: Prince of Peace Anglican Church (1900), winery, horseriding and go-kart complex. Bongil Bongil National Park at Mylestom, 15 km N, 10 km of coastal beaches with good fishing and swimming. **Visitor information:** Pacific Hwy; (02) 6655 5711. Web site www.bellingen.nsw.gov. au/tourism/bellinger.html **See also:** Holiday Coast p. 17.

Pandanus palms line the foreshore near Tweed Heads

Wagga Wagga   Pop. 42 848

MAP REF. 104 B12, 111 R10

This prosperous city – the largest inland city in NSW – is 478 km SW of Sydney, just off the Hume Hwy. Wagga Wagga is known for industry, commerce, education, agriculture, its two military bases and its cultural pursuits and performing arts. **In town:** Botanic Gardens and mini-zoo on Willans Hill; a miniature railway in gardens (check times). Regional Art Gallery, cnr Baylis and Morrow sts, features National Art Glass Collection and incorporates Museum of the Riverina. Tavenders Gourmet Produce, Australian Arcade, Fitzmaurice St, for regional gourmet products. Mar.: Australian Veterans Games (even-numbered years). June: Taste of Riverina (alternates with Griffith). Sept.: Jazz Festival. **In the area:** River cruises and walking tracks, details from information centre. Lake Albert, 7 km S, for water sports. RAAF Museum, 10 km E. Wagga Wagga Winery, 15 km NE; tasting area and restaurant have early Australian theme. Charles Sturt Winery at Charles Sturt University (Riverina Campus), 6 km NW. Aurora Clydesdale Stud and Pioneer Farm, 9 km W of Collingullie on Sturt Hwy. Self-drive tours of military base at Kapooka, 9 km SW, brochures available. The Rock, 32 km SW, a small town noted for its unusual scenery; walking trails through reserve lead to summit of The Rock. **Visitor information:** cnr Tarcutta & Morrow sts; (02) 6926 9621, freecall 1800 648 144. Web site www.tourismwaggawagga.com.au **See also:** The Riverina p. 27.

Walcha   Pop. 1623

MAP REF. 107 L10

This town on the eastern slopes of the Great Dividing Range was settled by Europeans in 1832. **In town:** Walking tour, includes sculptures and 'Lamington Capital of the World', brochures available. Pioneer Cottage and Museum, Derby St, features first Tiger Moth plane used for crop-dusting in Australia, and a replica of blacksmith's shop. Courthouse (1878), cnr Derby and Apsley sts. In South St: Anglican Church (1862); St Patricks Church (1881). Amaroo Museum and Cultural Centre, Derby St: Aboriginal art and craft; artists working on site; cultural information; visitors welcome to tour centre. Old School Gallery in Fitzroy St. Mar.: Agricultural Show. Sept.: Timber Expo (even-numbered years). Oct.: Ride the Rim (mountain-bike ride). **In the area:** Trout fishing. Oxley Wild Rivers National Park, encompasses a high plateau, deep gorges and numerous waterfalls, incl. Apsley (20 km E) where 7 platforms and a bridge provide access to both sides of gorge and waterfall; Tia Falls area (35 km E) also developed for visitors; 4WD access to Riverside and Youdales Hut, where there are unique campsites. **Visitor information:** 106E Fitzroy St; (02) 6777 1075. **See also:** New England & the North-West p. 20.

Walgett   Pop. 1970

MAP REF. 106 C7

Walgett is at the junction of the Barwon and Namoi rivers, 272 km NW of Dubbo. With its airport and railhead, it is also the gateway to the Lightning Ridge opal fields. **In town:** First European settler's grave on banks of Namoi River, northern end of town. Tracker Walford Track, signposted 1.5-km scenic walk from levee bank at end of Warrena St. Hot artesian springs pool at swimming pool, Montkeila St (open in summer; key from information centre in winter). May: Agricultural Show. **In the area:** Good fishing year-round; contact information centre for details of reserved land and permits. At Come-by-Chance, 65 km SE, Picnic Races in Sept. Grawin, Glengarry and Sheepyard opal fields, 70 km W, brochures available. (Motorists are warned water is scarce; adequate supply should be carried.) One of largest inland lakes in Australia, Narran Lake, 96 km W via Cumborah Rd, is a wildlife sanctuary (no facilities for private visits). **Visitor information:** Shire Offices, 77 Fox St; (02) 6828 1399. **See also:** New England & the North-West p. 20.

Warialda   Pop. 1287

MAP REF. 106 I5

Warialda, on the Gwydir Hwy, 61 km NW of Inverell, is in a rich farming district. **In town:** Historic buildings, especially on Stephen and Hope sts. Self-guide historical town walk. Historic Carinda House, Stephen St, now craft shop. Historic graves (from 1850s) in bushland setting at Pioneer Cemetery, Queen and Stephen sts. Well's Family Gem and Mineral Collection in Heritage Centre, Hope St. Koorilgur Nature Walk (3.6 km), features wildflowers and birdlife, self-guide brochure available. May: Agricultural Show. Oct.: Flower Show. **In the area:** Good picnic spots, camping, fossicking, wildflowers and wildlife at Cranky Rock Nature Reserve, 8 km E. **Visitor information:** Heritage Centre, Hope St; (02) 6729 0046. **See also:** New England & the North-West p. 20.

Warren   Pop. 1909

MAP REF. 106 B13

The centre for the surrounding wool and cotton district, Warren is on the Oxley Hwy, 126 km NW of Dubbo. Located beside the Macquarie River, it is popular with anglers. **In town:** Historical and nature walks, brochures available. In Burton St: Macquarie Park, on banks of river; The Craft Shop for local craft.

Tiger Bay Wildlife Reserve, a wetlands reserve at northern outskirts of town on Oxley Hwy. May: Golden Fleece Race Day. Sept.: Macquarie Merino Field Days. Nov.: Cotton Cup Racing Carnival. **In the area:** Excellent racecourse, 3 km W, location for race days. **Visitor information:** 6 Burton St; (02) 6847 3181. Web site www.ilanet.net.au/clients/warren **See also:** Central West p. 21.

Wauchope   Pop. 4693

MAP REF. 95 E8, 107 O12

A major re-creation of a typical 1880s timber town at nearby Timbertown has put Wauchope on the tourist map. The town is the centre of a timber-getting, dairying, beef-cattle and mixed-farming area on the Oxley Hwy, 19 km W of Port Macquarie. Mar.: Lasiandra Festival. Apr.: Show; Demolition Derby; Rusty Iron Rally. May: Timbertown Empire Day Celebrations. Oct.: Colonial Carnival. **In the area:** Timbertown, re-created village, 3 km W on edge of Broken Bago State Forest, features craft gallery and leather goods outlet, working bullock team, horse-drawn wagons, smithy, woodturner, steam-powered train and sleeper-cutting demonstrations. Adjacent, small church houses Historical Society Museum. Broken Bago Winery, 8 km SW. Old Bottlebutt, 6 km S, largest known bloodwood tree in State. The Big Bull, 2 km E off Oxley Hwy, has dairy-farming display, hay rides and animal nursery. Billabong Animal Park, 10 km E. **Visitor information:** High St; (02) 6586 4055, freecall 1800 025 935. Web site www.portmacquarieinfo.com.au **See also:** Holiday Coast p. 17.

Wee Waa   Pop. 1860

MAP REF. 106 F8

This small town near the Namoi River is the centre of a major cotton-growing district. **In town:** Guided tours (Apr.–Aug.) to Merah North Cotton Gin (9 km) and cotton farms. Apr.: Agricultural Show. **In the area:** Cuttabri Wine Shanty, 25 km SW, an original Cobb & Co. coach stop between Wee Waa and Pilliga. Cubbaroo Winery, 48 km W. Yarrie Lake, 24 km S, for boating and birdwatching. **Visitor information:** Newell Hwy, Narrabri; (02) 6799 6760. Web site www.tournarrabri.nsw.gov.au **See also:** New England & the North-West p. 20.

Wellington   Pop. 4920

MAP REF. 104 F3

Limestone caves are one of the interesting features of this town at the junction of the Macquarie and Bell rivers, 362 km NW of Sydney. **In town:** Self-guide town walk, brochures available. Historical Museum in old bank (1883), cnr Percy and Warne sts. Orana Aboriginal Corporation, Swift St, authentic Aboriginal ceramics, paintings, clothing and artifacts. Mar.: The Wellington Boot (horseraces); Vintage Fair. Aug.: Eisteddfod. Oct.: Festivale. **In the area:** Wellington Caves, 9 km S, features Cathedral Cave and Gaden Cave with rare cave coral and phosphate mine (guided tours). Nearby, aviary, opal shop, Japanese Gardens, picnic/barbecue facilities and kiosk. Markeita Cellars, 16 km S in village of Neurea. Rabbit Farm, 20 km SW, has shearing demonstrations of angoras; also alpacas. At Burrendong and Mookerawa state parks, 32 km SE: Lake Burrendong, for water sports, fishing, camping, cabins, spectacular lake views from main wall; Burrendong Arboretum for birdwatching and walking tracks. Bakers Swamp Art Gallery, 22 km S on Mitchell Hwy, local artists. Further 6 km S, Eris Fleming Gallery. Glenfinlass Wines, 8 km SW on Parkes Rd. Nangara Gallery, 26 km SW, Aboriginal art and craft. From Mt Arthur Reserve, 3 km W of town, walks to lookout at summit of Mt Binjang; maps available. **Visitor information:** Cameron Park, Nanima Cr.; (02) 6845 1733. **See also:** Central West p. 21.

Wentworth   Pop. 1504

MAP REF. 110 D6, 230 F2

This historic town at the junction of the Murray and Darling rivers was once a busy riverboat and customs port; today it is a quiet holiday town. **In town:** In Beverley St: Grandma's Place (museum); Old Wentworth Gaol (1881). Courthouse (1870s), Darling St. Historic convent (1912), Cadell St. Historic PS *Ruby*, in Fotherby Park, Wentworth St. River cruises on MV *Loyalty*, depart from end Darling St. Lock 10, weir and park for picnics. Easter: Henley on the Darling (rowing regatta). Nov.: Wentworth Cup (on Melbourne Cup Day). **In the area:** Heritage and nature driving trails. Houseboat hire. Harry Nana Aboriginal Cultural Tours to sites in area, details from information centre. Perry Sandhills, 5 km NW off Silver City Hwy. Model aircraft display at Yelta (Vic.), 12 km SE. At Dareton,

12 km E, Tulklana Kumbi, Aboriginal art gallery. At Buronga, 26 km E: Australian Inland Botanical Gardens, River Rd; Orange World and Stanley Wine Co. both on Silver City Hwy. World Heritage-listed Mungo National Park, 157 km NE, features The Walls of China (sand dunes); record of 50 000 years of Aboriginal life; maps available. **Visitor information:** 28 Darling St; (03) 5027 3624. Web site www.walkabout.com.au **See also:** The Murray p. 30; National Parks p. 74.

West Wyalong Pop. 3419
MAP REF. 104 B8, 111 Q6

This former goldmining town, at the junction of the Mid Western and Newell hwys, celebrated its centenary in 1994. It is the business centre of a prosperous wheat, wool and mixed-farming area, and gateway to the Riverina and central west regions of the State. **In town:** On Newell Hwy: Aboriginal Artifacts Gallery (open Mon.–Fri.); Bland District Historical Museum, with scale model of a goldmine. Sept.: Agricultural Show. **In the area:** Bird sanctuary and fishing at Lake Cowal, 48 km NE via Clear Ridge. Weethalle Whistlestop, 65 km W on Hay Rd, for Devonshire teas, art and craft. At Barmedman, 32 km SE, Mineral Water Pool, believed to help arthritis and rheumatism. **Visitor information:** McCann Park, Newell Hwy; (02) 6972 3645. **See also:** The Riverina p. 27.

White Cliffs Pop. 207
MAP REF. 108 F8

In White Cliffs, 93 km NW of Wilcannia, pioneering is a way of life. The first opal field lease was granted 1890; in the boom years that followed, the fields supported 4500 people. Precious opal is still mined today. Jewelled opal 'pineapples' are found only in this area. Road access to the town is via a graded gravel road (sealed in parts), suitable for conventional cars and caravans when driven with care in dry weather. **In town:** Guided tours of town, incl. historic features and opportunity to fossick for opal. Self-guide Heritage Trail, map available. *In town centre:* Historic buildings incl. old police station (1897), public school (1900) and post office (1900); camping, barbecue facilities and swimming pool in Reserve; pioneer cemetery. *Just south of town centre:* Solar power station (tours); rugged outback golf course. *On the southern outskirts (Smith's Hill):* Top Level Opals; Outback

Treasures (opal jewellery and Aboriginal art); Underground Dugout Motel. *On the eastern outskirts (Turley's Hill):* Eagles Gallery, underground complex with local art and craft (open on request); Jock's Place, dugout home and museum; P. J.'s Underground B&B. *On the northern outskirts:* Wellington's Underground Art Gallery; Brian Moore's Opal Showroom. May: Gymkhana and Rodeo. **In the area:** Mutawintji National Park, 90 km SW, guided tours of Aboriginal rock-art sites in cooler months (extremely hot in summer). **Visitor information:** Karara Rd; (08) 8091 6611. Web site www.outbacknsw.org.au **See also:** The Outback p. 31.

Wilcannia Pop. 688
MAP REF. 108 G10

Situated 196 km NE of Broken Hill, and proclaimed a town in 1864, Wilcannia was a key inland port in the days of paddle-steamers. Today it is the service centre for a far-flung rural population. **In town:** Self-guide historical tour (brochure available) introduces several fine sandstone buildings, incl. post office (1877), prison and courthouse (1880), and Athenaeum Chambers (1890), all in Reid St. Opening bridge (1895) across Darling River; paddle-steamer wharf upstream. **In the area:** At Tilpa, 140 km NE, historic hotel (continuous licence since 1894) on banks of Darling River. Willandra National Park, 290 km SE, site of historic sheep station; 4WD only. **Visitor information:** Shire Offices, Reid St; (08) 8091 5909. Web site www.outbacknsw.org.au **See also:** The Outback p. 31.

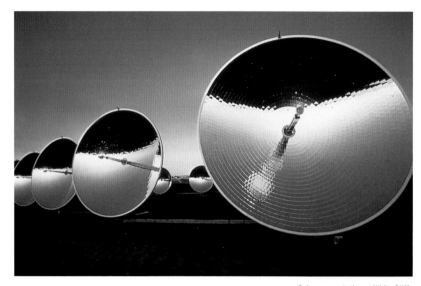

Solar power station at White Cliffs

Windsor Pop. 13 345
MAP REF. 91 L6, 105 K7

A town for lovers of history and early architecture, Windsor is one of the oldest in Australia, situated 56 km NW of Sydney. **In town:** Self-guide tourist walk/drive, brochures available. St Matthew's Church, Moses St, oldest Anglican Church in Australia, designed by Francis Greenway and convict-built in 1817; graveyard is older. Courthouse, Court St, another Greenway building. In Thompson Sq.: The Doctor's House (1844), privately owned; Hawkesbury Museum, formerly Daniel O'Connell Inn (1843). Other fine buildings in historic George St and Thompson Sq. Markets, each Sun. in Windsor Mall. May: Bridge to Bridge Power Boat Classic. Oct.: Bridge to Bridge Canoe Classic. Oct.–Nov.: Fruits of the Hawkesbury Festival. Nov.: Bridge to Bridge Water Ski Classic. **In the area:** Self-guide tourist drives, incl. Grand Circular Tourist Drive; brochures available. Rouse Hill Estate (1813), 15 km E on Windsor Rd: historic rural property; guided tours Thurs. and Sun., bookings essential. Cattai National Park, 14 km NE, has historic homestead, picnic/barbecue facilities and camping area. Hawkesbury Heritage Farm, 6 km N: Rose Cottage, considered oldest timber dwelling in Australia; wagon and buggy collection; picnic/barbecue facilities; open Thurs.–Sun. At Ebenezer, 11 km N: Tizzana Winery; Uniting Church (early Presbyterian church, 1809); old cemetery and school-house (1817). Wollemi National Park, 26 km N via Colo: spectacular Colo River; abseiling and canoeing; 4WD touring. **Visitor information:** Hawkesbury Museum, 7 Thompson Sq.; (02) 4577 2310. Web site www.hawkesburyvalley.com **See also:** Central Coast & Hawkesbury p. 16; Wildlife-Watching p. 72.

Wingham   Pop. 4446

MAP REF. 95 B13, 105 O1, 107 N13

Dating back to 1836, Heritage-listed Wingham is the oldest town along the Manning River. Timber-milling was once the main activity, but has been overtaken by beef cattle and dairy farming. **In town:** Manning Valley Historical Museum, part of attractive village square bounded by Isabella, Bent, Farquhar and Wynter sts. Historical walk through town, self-guide brochure from museum. Market, 2nd Sat. each month in Wynter St (a.m.). Jan.: Summer Rodeo. Mar.: Agricultural Show. May: Manning Valley Beef Week. Nov.: Show and Rodeo. **In the area:** Wingham Brush, Farquhar St, close to town centre, part of last 10 ha of subtropical flood-plain rainforest in NSW: orchids, ferns, Moreton Bay fig trees, grey-headed flying foxes and 100 bird species. On Tourist Drive 8, Ellenborough Falls, 40 km N, 160-m single drop. **Visitor information:** Manning Valley Visitor Information Centre, Old Pacific Hwy, Taree North; (02) 6552 1900, freecall 1800 801 522. Web site www.gtcc.nsw.gov.au/tourism **See also:** Holiday Coast p. 17.

Wisemans Ferry   Pop. 150

MAP REF. 91 M3, 105 L6

Situated beside the Hawkesbury River, 66 km NW of Sydney, Wisemans Ferry is an important area for water sports. Two car ferries cross the river. **In town:** Wisemans Ferry Inn, Old Northern Rd, was named after innkeeper and founder of original ferry service, and is said to be haunted by his wife, whom he allegedly pushed down the front steps of the inn to her death. **In the area:** Dharug National Park, on northern side of river: Aboriginal rock engravings; convict-built Old Great North Rd, great engineering feat of early colony; walking and cycling tracks along lower section (closed to vehicles) from ferry. **Visitor information:** Bicentenary Park, Ham Common, Richmond Rd, Clarendon; (02) 4588 5895. Web site www.hawkesburyvalley.com **See also:** Central Coast & Hawkesbury p. 16.

Wollongong   Pop. 219 761

MAP REF. 98, 99 H6, 105 K10

The area surrounding Wollongong, the third largest city in NSW, contains some of the South Coast's most spectacular scenery. **In town:** Guided walk and guided 4WD tour, details from information centre. Illawarra Historical Society Museum, Market St, incl. handicraft room and Victorian parlour (check times). Wollongong City Gallery, cnr Burelli and Kembla sts. Mall in Crown St, with soaring steel arches and water displays. Wollongong Botanic Gardens in Northfields Ave, Keiraville. Rhododendron Park, Parrish Ave, Mt Pleasant. Surfing beaches and rock pools, to north and south. Foreshore parks for picnicking. Wollongong Harbour, home to fishing fleet. On Endeavour Dr., Flagstaff Point: fish market; historic lighthouse (1872). On Port Kembla Harbour foreshore, at southern end of city, is highly automated BHP steel mill, an export coal loader and largest grain-handling facility in NSW. Market, each Thurs. and Sat. at southern end of Harbour St. Mar.: Viva La Gong. **In the area:** Nan Tien Temple, 5 km SW, Berkeley Rd, Berkeley, largest Buddhist temple in Southern Hemisphere, with range of programs (closed Mon.). Lake Illawarra, 5 km S, stretching from South Pacific Ocean to foothills of Illawarra Range, has good prawning, fishing and sailing; boat hire. At Port Kembla, 10 km S: Australia's Industry World, tours (check times) and visitor centre; Harbourfest in Nov. Illawarra Escarpment, forming western backdrop to city, has lookouts at Stanwell Tops, Sublime Point, Mount Keira and Mount Kembla. Bulli Lookout, at top of escarpment in Bulli Pass Scenic Reserve, a steep, scenic drive with stunning coastal views. At University of Wollongong Campus East, Squires Way, Fairy Meadow, 2 km N: Science Centre, activities for all ages. Symbio Wildlife Gardens, 32 km N at Stanwell Tops, features koalas, eagle-flying, wombats, reptiles, cow- and goat-milking. Royal National Park, 35 km N, oldest national park in Australia; walks, camping, fishing, beaches and extaordinary coastal scenery. Lawrence Hargrave Memorial and Lookout at Bald Hill, 36 km N, site of aviator Hargrave's first attempt at flight in early 1900s; now popular for hang-gliding. Mount Kembla, 10 km W, scene of tragic 1902 mining disaster: monument in church; original miners' huts; several historic buildings incl. former post office, now Historical Museum featuring pioneer kitchen, blacksmith's shop and reconstruction of Mount Kembla disaster. **Visitor information:** cnr Crown & Kembla sts; (02) 4228 0300, freecall 1800 240 737. Web site www. tourismwollongong.com **See also:** Southern Highlands & Illawarra p. 24; National Parks p. 74.

Woolgoolga   Pop. 3772

MAP REF. 107 P7

This charming seaside town on the Pacific Hwy, 25 km N of Coffs Harbour, is popular with beach and offshore anglers. The banana industry became established in the district in the 1930s, attracting a sizeable population of Indian migrants. **In town:** Guru Nanak Sikh Temple, River St, Art Gallery, Turon Pde, exhibits local works. Market, Beach St, 2nd Sat. each month. **In the area:** Clean, sandy beaches. Yuraygir National Park, 10 km N, for bushwalking, canoeing, fishing, surfing, swimming, picnicking and camping on unspoiled coastline. Yarrawarra Aboriginal Cultural Centre and Tours, Red Rock Rd, Corindi Beach, 10 km N: locally produced art, craft, books and CDs; Bush Tucker Cafe; tours. Wedding Bells State Forest, 14 km NW. **Visitor information:** cnr Marcia St & Rose Ave, Coffs Harbour; (02) 6652 1522. **See also:** Tropical North Coast p. 19.

Woy Woy   Pop. 11 038

MAP REF. 91 P4, 94 F8, 105 L6

Woy Woy, 90 km N of Sydney and 6 km S of Gosford, is the centre for the holiday villages and national parks near the magnificent Brisbane Water and Broken Bay. Markets at Ettalong Beach, 3 km S on Ocean View Rd, each Sat. and Sun., and Mon. of long weekends. Nov.: Oyster and Wine Festival. **In the area:** Boating, fishing and swimming on Brisbane Water, Broken Bay and Hawkesbury River. Mt Ettalong Lookout, 6 km S, for coastal views. Pearl Beach (12 km S), ideal for a stroll at sunset. Brisbane Water National Park, 3 km SW: spring wildflowers, bushwalks and birdlife; Staples Lookout (7 km W), for coastal views; Bulgandry Aboriginal engravings (9 km W); Warrah Lookout, for views and wildflowers. Bouddi National Park, 12 km E, has good fishing, bushwalks and swimming areas; wreck of PS *Maitland* at Maitland Bay, an unspoiled coastal environment. Near entrance to park, Marie Byles Lookout offers good views of Sydney. Wreck of WW I ship *Parramatta*, Hawkesbury River near Milson Island; accessible only by boat. **Visitor information:** Shop 1, 18–22 The Boulevarde; (02) 4385 4430, freecall 1300 130 708. Web site www.cctourism. com.au **See also:** Central Coast & Hawkesbury p. 16; National Parks p. 74.

Wyong   Pop. 6216
MAP REF. 91 P2, 94 F1, 105 M6

Wyong is on the Pacific Hwy between Tuggerah Lakes and the State Forests of Watagan, Olney and Ourimbah. **In town:** District Museum, Cape Rd, has displays relating to early ferry services across lakes, and forest logging. Country Fair, 3rd Sun. each month, at racecourse on Racecourse Rd. Mar.: Wyong Shire Festival of the Arts. Oct.: Cycle Classic. **In the area:** Hinterland popular for bushwalking and camping. Burbank Nursery, 3 km S at Tuggerah, features 20 ha of azaleas (flowering Sept.). Fowlers Lookout over forest, 10 km SW. Macadamia Nut Plantation, 18 km W in beautiful Yarramalong Valley. The Durren Pottery, 20 km NW, uses local clay (open by appt). Bumble Hill Studio, 30 km NW at Kulnura, for ceramics, glasswork and paintings (open Fri.–Sun.). Frazer Park, 28 km NE, a recreational park in a natural bush setting. Within the State forests to the north: Mandalong Lookout, Muirs Lookout and picnic area in Olney State Forest; Wishing Well, destination for Watagan Mountains Walking Trail in Watagan State Forest; Flat Rock Lookout and picnic area in Corrabare State Forest. **Visitor information:** Central Coast Tourism, Rotary Park, Terrigal Dr., Terrigal; (02) 4385 4430, freecall 1300 130 708. Web site www. cctourism.com.au **See also:** Central Coast & Hawkesbury p. 16.

Yamba   Pop. 4721
MAP REF. 107 Q5

This prawning and fishing town at the mouth of the Clarence River offers sea, lake and river fishing. It is the largest coastal resort in the Clarence Valley. **In town:** Story House Museum, River St, for early records. Views from base of lighthouse, via steep Pilot St. Yamba Boatharbour Marina, off Yamba Rd; departure point for daily ferry services to Iluka, river cruises (Thurs. and Sun.), deep-sea fishing charters and whale-watching trips; houseboat hire. Market, 4th Sun. each month, at oval on River St. Oct.: Family Fishing Festival; Seafood Expo. **In the area:** Lake Woolowyah, 4 km S, for fishing and prawning. Yuraygir National Park, 5 km S, for swimming, fishing and bushwalking in area dominated by sand ridges and banksia heath. The Blue Pool, 5 km S at Angourie, a freshwater pool, 50 m from ocean, depth and origin unknown; popular swimming and picnic spot. **Visitor information:** Lower Clarence Visitors Centre, Ferry Park, Pacific Hwy, Maclean; (02) 6645 4121. Web site www. tropicalnsw. com.au **See also:** Tropical North Coast p. 19.

Yanco   Pop. 576
MAP REF. 111 O8

Located 8 km S of Leeton, this town is where Sir Samuel McCaughey developed his own irrigation scheme, which led to the establishment of the Murrumbidgee Irrigation Area. **In town:** In Binya St: Powerhouse Museum (last Sun. each month or by appt); McCaughey Aquatic Park. Village Markets, Yanco Hall, Main Ave, last Sun. each month (a.m.). May: Murrumbidgee Farm Fair. **In the area:** Yanco Weir, 1 km N, for fishing. McCaughey's mansion, 3 km S, now an agricultural high school; nearby Yanco Agricultural Institute, open to public. Extensive red gum forests along the Murrumbidgee River; well-marked forest drives lead to sandy beaches and many pleasant fishing spots. **Visitor information:** 10 Yanco Ave, Leeton; (02) 6953 6481. Web site www.leeton.nsw. gov.au **See also:** The Riverina p. 27.

Yass   Pop. 4840
MAP REF. 103 D4, 104 F11

Near the junction of the Hume and Barton highways, this interesting old town is set in rolling countryside on the Yass River, 280 km SW of Sydney and 55 km from Canberra. **In town:** Self-guide town walk and drive, maps available. Grave of explorer Hamilton Hume in Yass Cemetery (signposted from Rossi St). National Trust-owned Cooma Cottage (c. 1835), 3 km E, where Hume lived for almost 40 years (closed Tues.). Hamilton Hume Museum, Comur St. Railway Museum, Lead St, history of Yass Tramway (open Sun.). Market, 2nd Sat. each month. Mar.: Picnic Races. Apr.: Agricultural Show and Rodeo. Nov.: Rodeo. Dec.: Cup Raceday. **In the area:** Binalong Motor Museum and Southern Cross Glass, 37 km NW. At Bookham, 30 km W: Markets, 2nd Sun. each month; Sheep Show and Country Fair in Apr. At Wee Jasper, 50 km SW: Goodradigbee River for trout fishing; Micalong Creek; Carey's Caves, with superb limestone formations (guided tours); access point for Hume and Hovell Walking Track. Burrinjuck Waters State Park, 54 km SW off Hume Hwy, for bushwalking, cruises, water sports and fishing; Burrinjuck Ski Classic in Nov., water level permitting. In Brindabella National Park, 61 km SW: birdwatching, camping and bushwalking in alpine surrounds; 4WD only, via Wee Jasper. Wineries in Murrumbateman area, 20 km S, on Barton Hwy; Days of Wine and Roses in Oct. **Visitor information:** Coronation Park, Comur St; (02) 6226 2557. **See also:** Capital Country p. 23.

Young   Pop. 6798
MAP REF. 103 C2, 104 D9

Attractive former goldmining town in the western foothills of the Great Dividing Range, 395 km SW of Sydney. Today the area produces cherries, prunes and other stone fruits, flour and fabricated steel. **In town:** Lambing Flat Folk Museum, Campbell St, for town history, incl. 'roll-up' flag carried by miners during infamous anti-Chinese Lambing Flat riots of 1861. Burrangong Art Gallery, Olympic Hwy. Blackguard Gully with historic pug-mill, on Boorowa Rd, a reconstruction showing early goldmining methods; gold-fossicking alongside gully (hire equipment from museum). The Price of Peace Garden and Cafe, Willawong St, overlooking town. Feb.: Hilltops Flavours of the Harvest Festival. Nov.–Dec.: National Cherry Festival. **In the area:** Orchards open in season (pick your own cherries); list from information centre. Wineries open for tastings and sales. J. D.'s Jam Factory, north-western outskirts of town on Grenfell Rd; tours, tastings and Devonshire teas. Chinaman's Dam recreation area, 4 km SE, has picnic/barbecue facilities, playground and scenic walks. At Murringo, 21 km E: several historic buildings; glassblower and engraver. Yandilla Mustard Seed Oil, 20 km S. **Visitor information:** 2 Short St; (02) 6382 3394, freecall 1800 628 233. **See also:** Capital Country p. 23.

WILDLIFE-WATCHING

Australian fur seals near Montague Island

IN SYDNEY

Australia's largest city is not the perfect environment for native animals, though several species have found a niche. For a colourful and noisy spectacle visit the seaside suburb of **Manly**, where thousands of raucous rainbow lorikeets arrive each evening to roost in the Norfolk pines along the ocean-beach foreshore.

Sydney's other winged residents are somewhat quieter. A large colony of flying foxes – up to 50 000 in summer months – lives in Ku-ring-gai Flying Fox Reserve in Sydney's northern suburbs. The reserve itself is not open to the public, although the bats can still be seen from Rosedale Road bridge in **Gordon**. After spending the day hanging in trees, they take to the air at dusk along particular 'flight paths' to feed on flowering trees.

AROUND SYDNEY

Royal National Park south of Sydney provides a green buffer against the city's southern suburbs, and many birds thrive here. Sulphur-crested cockatoos are happy to make their presence known, though it is worth keeping an eye out for quieter birds, such as heath wrens, satin bowerbirds, lyrebirds and top-knot pigeons. Diamond pythons, eastern water dragons and lace monitors can be seen by observant reptile-watchers.

The famous **Blue Mountains National Park** is a prime location for eastern grey kangaroos. A large mob lives around Euroka Clearing at the eastern end of the park near Glenbrook. While they are most active at dawn and dusk, there are usually eastern greys about at any time of day.

North of Blue Mountains National Park, in the adjoining **Wollemi National Park**, is the Glow Worm Tunnel, home to the iridescent larvae of the fungus gnat. A kilometre-long walk will take you to the tunnel entrance,

after which you will need a torch to negotiate the uneven and sometimes slippery ground inside. To see the glow-worms, turn off your torch and wait quietly for a few minutes. Tiny blue spots of light will gradually become visible on the damp walls of the tunnel.

IN THE NORTH-EAST OF THE STATE

Humpback whales are regular visitors to the waters off **Cape Byron**, near Byron Bay township, following the demise of the east-coast whaling industry in 1963. Between two and three thousand now migrate from Antarctica to their northern breeding grounds, passing the cape in June and July. They return either pregnant or with newborn calves between September and October. A calm ocean and a pair of binoculars will increase your chances of witnessing humpback whale acrobatics.

Further south is **Muttonbird Island Nature Reserve**. The island, linked to the city of Coffs Harbour by bridge, has a sizeable population of short-tailed shearwaters (muttonbirds), between August and April each year. Dawn and dusk are the best times to look skywards as the shearwaters fly out and return from fishing excursions. Also keep an eye on the ocean for passing humpback whales from June to November.

Just inland from Coffs Harbour is the rainforest of **Dorrigo National Park**. Brush turkeys are a common sight around the park's picnic areas; these bald-headed ground dwellers are brash characters, very much at home among human visitors. The Walk with the Birds Boardwalk is a good way to see other forest birds, including yellow robins, thornbills and riflebirds. The Lyrebird Link Track provides an opportunity to see one of Dorrigo's numerous lyrebirds. Another park resident is the regent bowerbird; the male is well known for its habit of collecting blue objects to decorate its bower in the hope of attracting a mate.

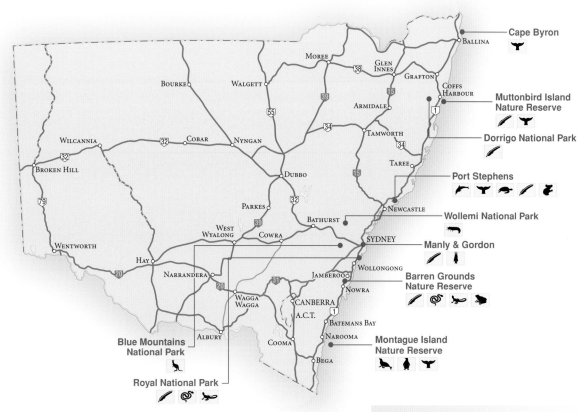

ON THE CENTRAL COAST

The deep, clean waters around **Port Stephens** are a great place to see bottlenose dolphins at play. Fortunately the 160 or so resident dolphins seem to enjoy some 'people-watching' themselves. They will often ride on bow waves of dolphin-viewing boats, turning on their sides to glance at the excited humans aboard.

Cruises operate out of Nelson Bay, within Port Stephens, to view migrating humpback whales in season (June–July, September–November). Watching these marine entertainers as they tail-slap, pectoral fin-wave and launch their 30-tonne bodies clear of the water is a memorable experience. Turtles, sea eagles and short-tailed shearwaters (muttonbirds) are also likely to make an appearance. Later in the season minke whales follow shoals of pilchards along the coast.

There is a large population of koalas on Tilligerry Peninsula: visit Tilligerry Habitat on Tanilba Bay or, across the peninsula, the Koala Reserve for a stroll through a koala colony.

ON THE SOUTH COAST

Thirty minutes by boat from the coastal town of Narooma is **Montague Island Nature Reserve**, home to hundreds of Australian fur seals. August to December are the best times to view and photograph large numbers of these protected sea mammals as they sun themselves on the rocks. Montague Island is one of the few 'haul-out' sites for these seals on the Australian coastline; boat tours operate to the colony on a daily basis.

A second boat tour heads for the penguin parade. Each evening at dusk the island's little (fairy) penguins return from their daily fishing excursion at sea. June to March are the best times to see the birds emerge from the waves and waddle up the beach to their burrows. Between mid-September and mid-November the tour-boat skippers watch for migrating whales as there is a good chance of spotting a humpback at this time of year.

IN THE SOUTHERN HIGHLANDS

Within **Barren Grounds Nature Reserve** near Jamberoo is a bird observatory that offers some unique wildlife-watching experiences. This non-profit environmental education venture, set up by Birds Australia, hosts regular nature-based weekend activities.

Popular workshops include a lyrebird-watching weekend in winter, when the birds' courtship displays and songs are at their finest. The Birds for Beginners weekends combine birdwatching with useful information, while the Slither and Croaker weekend concentrates on searching for reptiles and frogs. There is also a bird-banding workshop where visitors can watch birds being trapped, banded, measured and released. Phone (02) 4236 0195 for bookings. The observatory has several good walking tracks for birdwatchers to view yellow-tailed black cockatoos, beautiful firetails, yellow robins and the endangered ground parrot.

For more information on wildlife-watching in national parks contact the National Parks and Wildlife Service, 102 George St, The Rocks, NSW 2000; 1300 361 967 within NSW, or (02) 9253 4600. Web site www.npws.nsw.gov.au

NATIONAL PARKS

Club Lake in Kosciuszko National Park

AROUND SYDNEY

Sydney Harbour National Park is made up of pockets of bushland and other open space encircling Sydney Harbour and is the closest national park to the city. One way to explore the park is to follow the Manly-to-Spit walk, which meanders through bushland on the northern edges of the harbour. Harbour islands offer secluded picnic destinations and there are regular visits to Fort Denison from Circular Quay.

On the southern edge of Sydney is **Botany Bay National Park**. The northern section contains the sandy beaches of La Perouse, the historic fort on Bare Island (guided tours) and a maritime museum. The southern section at Kurnell protects the site of Captain Cook's first Australian landing in 1770; the Discovery Centre provides an insight into the history of the area.

The **Royal National Park**, just 32 kilometres south of Sydney, was the first national park to be proclaimed in Australia. It was established in 1879 and has over 15 000 hectares of sandstone plateau country, broken along the coastline by fine surf beaches. The Hacking River runs almost the entire length of the park. Boats may be hired at Audley and visitors can row in leisurely fashion along the river.

Lane Cove National Park, located within the northern urban area of Sydney, offers good walks and is extremely popular with families. There are many picnic areas next to the river, some of which can be reserved. The river is good for boating (non-powered only), while a wildlife shelter and wildlife shop are popular features.

Further inland, west of Sydney, are splendid parks nestling in the mountains that overawed European explorers. Year after year visitors return to the **Blue Mountains National Park**, where blue mists shroud the immense valleys of the Grose and Coxs rivers, creating ever-changing patterns of green, blue and purple. At Katoomba, weathered sandstone pillars rise like church spires: these are the Three Sisters, the most popular tourist attraction in the Blue Mountains. The Grose and Jamison valleys offer walks with spectacular views. Aboriginal hand stencils can be seen in Red Hands Cave near Glenbrook.

Just north of Sydney are two prominent national parks, on the southern and northern shores of the Hawkesbury River: **Ku-ring-gai Chase** and **Brisbane Water national parks**. These parks have sheltered creeks and inlets, ideal for boating, and bushland walking tracks through colourful wildflowers.

Ku-ring-gai Chase, established in 1894 and only 24 kilometres from Sydney, hugs the shores of Cowan Creek, Broken Bay and Pittwater. The eucalypt forest, scrub and heath are home to a wide range of animal life, including the shy swamp wallaby, the elusive lyrebird, honey-eaters, waterbirds, colourful parrots and lorikeets. Walking tracks lead to Aboriginal hand stencils and rock engravings.

Brisbane Water also has sandstone landscapes rich in Aboriginal art. There are scenic views from Warrah Trig and Staples Lookout, while Somersby Falls and Girrakool picnic areas mark the beginning of rainforest walks.

Nearby on the coast is **Bouddi National Park** which protects the coast and bush at the eastern entrance to Broken Bay and the coastal foreshore from Killcare Heights to McMasters Beach; it also covers a large offshore area near the beautiful Maitland Bay. Walking tracks lead to secluded, unspoiled beaches and pockets of rainforest.

Upstream along the Hawkesbury River is **Dharug National Park**, its sandstone cliffs rising high above the meandering river. A network of walking tracks includes a section of the convict-built Old Great North Road.

IN THE NORTH-EAST OF THE STATE

The largest coastal lake system in New South Wales is protected by the **Myall Lakes National Park**, an important waterbird habitat. Water is the focus of tourist activities: you can enjoy sailing and canoeing on the quiet lake waters, or surfing, scuba-diving and beach fishing off the shores of the Pacific Ocean.

Barrington Tops, one of the State's most popular national parks, is a World Heritage-listed Area with a section set aside as wilderness. It has a mountainous plateau (1600 metres), providing spectacular views of the surrounding Hunter Valley and, in the distance, the Pacific Ocean, but visitors should be prepared for sudden bad weather. The stands of snow gums here give way, at about 1000 metres, to forests of Antarctic beech, with lichens, mosses and tree ferns. The lowest areas of the park feature subtropical rainforests, rivers, waterfalls and rapids. Many of the walking tracks in the park are suitable for families. Longer walks, ranging from 4 to 5 hours to overnight, are suitable for more experienced bushwalkers.

The World Heritage-listed **New England National Park**, which preserves one of the largest remaining areas of rainforest in New South Wales, is 576 kilometres north-east of Sydney. The park covers three distinct zones: subalpine with tall snow gums; temperate forests of ancient moss-covered Antarctic beeches; and true subtropical rainforests, rich in ferns, vines and orchids. The park has a diverse range of flora and fauna, including the rare rufous scrub-bird. Some 20 kilometres of walking tracks (on the north-western side of the park) reveal to visitors the charm of the rainforest, while the trackless wilderness attracts more experienced bushwalkers. Nearby, the World Heritage-listed **Dorrigo National Park** protects some of the rainforests of northern New South Wales. At the Dorrigo Rainforest Centre, visitors can experience the

sights, sounds and smells of rainforests. The Skywalk provides magnificent views over the rainforest canopy to the Bellinger Valley and Pacific Ocean beyond.

Yuraygir and **Bundjalung national parks**, to the south and north respectively of the Clarence River on the far north coast, are a water wonderland with isolated beaches, quiet lakes and striking scenery. The parks deserve their reputation as prime areas for fishing. Surfing is also popular; waterways invite exploration by canoe; and the estuaries offer safe swimming. Heathwalking offers opportunities for birdwatching and nature photography, particularly in spring when both parks explode in a spectacle of colour.

In the far north of the State, **Border Ranges**, **Mount Warning** and **Nightcap national parks** offer the visitor vistas of World Heritage-listed rainforest. Border Ranges National Park includes the rim of the ancient volcano once centred on Mount Warning to the east. The best access is via the spectacular Tweed Range Scenic Drive. Stunning escarpments, waterfalls, and walking tracks from picnic areas abound in the eastern part.

Known to Aboriginal people as 'Wollumbin', the cloud-catcher, Mount Warning (1157 metres) dominates the landscape and catches the first rays of the rising sun on the continent. A walk through Breakfast Creek rainforest leads to a steep climb to the summit. Nightcap National Park is part of the volcanic remnants of Mount Warning and includes Protesters Falls, named after the 1979 anti-logging protest.

Further inland are two well-known national parks: Warrumbungle and Mount Kaputar. **Warrumbungle National Park**, on the western side of the Great Divide, is 491 kilometres north-west of Sydney. Here is some of the most spectacular scenery in the nation: sheltered gorges, rocky spires and volcanic peaks. At Warrumbungle, east meets west: the dry western plains and moist eastern coast combine to give high peaks covered with gums and lower forests filled with fragrant native trees and shrubs. In the spring and summer months the colourful displays of wildflowers and the calls of brightly plumaged birds lure many visitors. There are also easy access tracks for families and the disabled.

Mount Kaputar National Park, near Narrabri, is one of Australia's most accessible wilderness areas. Several lookouts can be reached by car or are only a short walk from your car. The park's vegetation ranges from dry sclerophyll forest to subalpine, and the park is rich in flora and fauna. One of the highlights is Sawn Rocks, a 40-metre-high rock formation resembling a series of organ pipes.

IN THE SOUTH-EAST OF THE STATE

Parks in the southern part of the State include **Morton National Park**, particularly known for the Fitzroy and Belmore falls, and **Budderoo National Park**, which includes the award-winning Minnamurra Rainforest Centre, where an elevated boardwalk takes you into the rainforest canopy. Both parks offer ranger-guided walks in April.

Over 9000 hectares of rocky but beautiful coastline flanking Twofold Bay make up **Ben Boyd National Park**. Flowering heaths and colourful banksias add to the area's attraction. Boyd's Tower, constructed in the 1840s, is a prominent feature of the park.

Booderee National Park on the South Coast falls within the (Federal) Jervis Bay Territory. Skirting Jervis Bay and including the bay itself, is **NSW Jervis Bay National Park**. This park falls across a beautiful bush-clad landscape and encircles clear waters and white beaches. Highlights include

Wildflowers in Ku-ring-gai Chase National Park

wildlife and some of the most dramatic underwater landcape in NSW (scuba and snorkelling available).

The largest national park in New South Wales is **Kosciuszko**. It includes mainland Australia's only glacial lakes, as well as limestone caves, grasslands, heaths and woodlands. Situated 450 kilometres south-west of Sydney, this park is significant because it embraces a large area of the continent's largest alpine region and contains Australia's highest mountains as well as the sources of the Murray, Snowy and Murrumbidgee rivers. The most extensive snow fields of the nation are here, around Thredbo, Perisher, Smiggin Holes, Mount Blue Cow, Mount Selwyn and Charlotte Pass. There are easy grades, and slopes for expert skiers. Although Kosciuszko is associated with winter sports, it is also a superb summer retreat of lakes and wildflowers. It is a popular venue for those who enjoy camping, fishing, boating and bushwalking. Yarrangobilly Caves in the park are open year-round, subject to winter road conditions. Yarrangobilly boasts five tourist caves — one with wheelchair access — a naturally heated thermal pool, nature trails and picnic facilities.

IN THE WEST OF THE STATE

In the far west of New South Wales are four outstanding national parks. **Kinchega**, 110 kilometres south-east of Broken Hill, contains the beautiful saucer-shaped overflow lakes of the Darling River. The lakes provide an important breeding ground for waterbirds, including herons, ibises, spoonbills and black swans. Walking tracks pass through river red gum forests, and scenic drives follow the river and the lake shores.

North-east of Wentworth is the World Heritage-listed **Mungo National Park**, part of the Willandra Lakes World Heritage Area. The shores of the now dry lake hold a continuous record of Aboriginal life dating back more than 50 000 years. The remarkable Walls of China, a great crescent of dunes, stretches along the eastern shore of the lake bed. Visitors can enjoy a daytrip, camp or stay in the shearers' quarters accommodation. Self-guide walking tracks and a 60-kilometre self-guide drive tour give visitors the opportunity to see and learn about the many attractions of the park.

Mutawintji National Park, 130 kilometres north-east of Broken Hill, offers breathtaking gorge and desert-plain scenery, and a rich heritage of Aboriginal art, some of it accessible by guided tour only.

The State's most remote national park is **Sturt**, 1400 kilometres from Sydney and 330 kilometres north of Broken Hill. This is an ideal place for getting away from it all and experiencing the real outback. The park comprises scenic red sand dunes, rocky ridges, ephemeral lakes and Mitchell grass plains. Visitors must come well prepared but may camp in the park and enjoy walks and the abundant native fauna. Wildflowers, which include the scarlet and black Sturt's desert pea, are abundant in good seasons. Fort Grey, where Sturt's party built a stockade to protect their supplies, is worth a visit, even though there is little evidence of his occupation today.

For further information about the national parks of New South Wales, contact the National Parks and Wildlife Service, 102 George St, The Rocks, NSW 2000; 1300 361 967 within NSW, or (02) 9253 4600. The National Parks and Wildlife Service has produced an excellent booklet, *Visitor Guide to National Parks in NSW*, which can be obtained free from its visitor centres and offices, or by mail. Web site www.npws.nsw.gov.au

Classic Tour

Blue Mountains Experience

Glenbrook to Mount Tomah (188 km)

Y ou will find drama and interest around every bend on this Blue Mountains tour. Take a day or three to experience the natural beauty of the mountains – from the grandeur of the escarpment and its thundering waterfalls, to the detail of gorgeous red waratahs and delicate orchids. Perceived by early European settlers as a barrier to valuable western pastures, the towering sandstone cliffs and deep valleys were finally traversed by explorers Blaxland, Wentworth and Lawson in 1813. Within two years, a ridge-top track had been completed using convict labour. Today, the Great Western Highway follows a similar route.

① Red Hands

The Blue Mountains Experience begins at the Blue Mountains Visitor Information Centre on the Great Western Highway in Glenbrook, 66 km west of Sydney. Your first stop is the **Red Hands Cave**, one of the best-preserved examples of Aboriginal hand stencils and prints in the Sydney region. The images on the cave wall – believed to be between 500 and 1600 years old – were made using the hand as a stencil and blowing a spray of ochre from the mouth. Three Aboriginal groups, the Duruk, the Wiradjuri and the Gandangera, occupied or were familiar with the mountains for at least 20 000 years before European settlement.

To reach the cave, turn left into Ross Street just after the information centre and follow the signs through Glenbrook to the Blue Mountains National Park. From the entrance, continue to the Oaks Picnic Area (the road is unsealed after 2.5 kilometres); turn right for the Red Hands Picnic Area. A 300-metre walking track leads to the cave.

If you wish to incorporate some wildlife-watching into your Blue Mountains tour, turn right just after the Iron Barks Picnic Area on your way back to the park entrance. Keep right at the fork in the road. The road descends into the natural amphitheatre of Euroka Clearing. Eastern grey kangaroos are commonly seen grazing on the pastures, and the birdlife is prolific.

② Historic link

After rejoining the highway, watch for the turn-off to **Lennox Bridge** coming up soon on your right. This solid arched bridge, the oldest on the Australian mainland, was hewn by convicts from local sandstone in 1833, forming an essential link on the road across the mountains.

③ Artist's hideaway

Back on the highway, continue through the villages of Blaxland, Warrimoo, Valley Heights and Springwood. On the outskirts of Faulconbridge, take the signposted turn-off to the **Norman Lindsay Gallery and Museum**. Norman Lindsay (1879–1969) lived and worked in this stone cottage for most of his long, creative life. You might recognise the house as the setting for the film *Sirens* (1993). Today, it displays a collection of Lindsay's work, including his famous depictions of female nudes, as well as puppets representing characters from his classic children's book, *The Magic Pudding* (1918). The studio remains much as the artist left it – an unfinished painting is surrounded with favourite brushes and half-squeezed tubes of paint.

Norman Lindsay Gallery and Museum
14 Norman Lindsay Cres.
Faulconbridge
Phone: (02) 4751 1067
Open: 10 a.m.–4 p.m. daily

④ Scenic overview

The highway then follows a narrow ridgeline through the mountain hamlets of Linden, Woodford, Hazelbrook, Lawson and Bullaburra. At certain points, there are sweeping views across the Blue Mountains National Park. From the town of Wentworth Falls, take Falls Road to **Wentworth Falls Picnic Area**. A 500-metre track leads to Princes Rock Lookout for superb views of Wentworth Falls, Jamison Valley and King's Tableland. You might also like to take the 1-kilometre circuit trail, which extends down into the valley to Weeping Rock, past patterned rocks with mysterious face-like features.

⑤ Valley of the Waters

Return along Falls Road as far as Fletcher Street and turn left to the Conservation Hut Cafe and **Valley of the Waters Picnic Area**. Follow the 500-metre walking track to

Valley of the Waters

Norman Lindsay Gallery and Museum

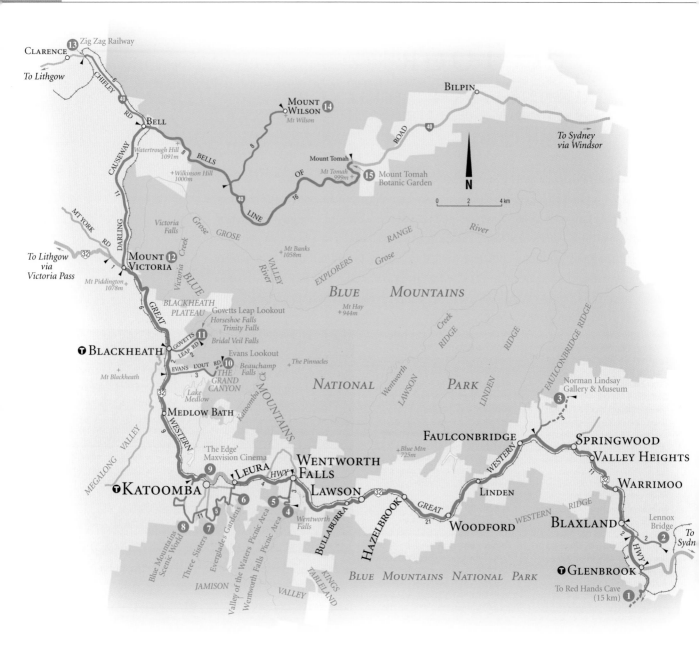

Queen Victoria and Empress lookouts for panoramic views over distant mountains and valleys. To join the more challenging Valley of the Waters Nature Track, continue until you reach a small creek and track junction. This 4-kilometre circuit takes in fern-fringed Asmodeus Pool and the windswept heights of Edinburgh Castle Rock.

6 Ornamental windows

After returning to the highway, you will soon reach the turn-off to Leura Mall, starting point of Tourist Drive 5 . This picture-postcard street is lined with antique stores, galleries, gift shops and cafes. To visit **Everglades Gardens**, turn left from the mall into Craigend Street and right at Everglades Avenue. This splendid example of 1930s garden

design is a testimony to its creator, Danish master gardener, Paul Sorensen. Rest by the grotto pool or view Jamison Valley through ornamental garden windows. The Art Deco interior of Van de Velde House is also open to the public and now houses a tearoom.

Everglades Gardens
37 Everglades Ave
Leura
Phone: (02) 4784 1938
Open: 10 a.m.–5 p.m. daily
(spring/summer);
10 a.m.–4 p.m. daily
(autumn/winter)

7 Three Sisters

Join Tourist Drive 5 , which leads past pretty Leura Falls and along the cliff tops to Echo Point, viewing area

for the famous **Three Sisters** rock formation. This scenic highlight is a busy stopping point for visitors. King parrots, galahs, gang gangs and crimson rosellas gather around the Echo Point Visitor Information Centre, adding to the colour and sense of activity. If quiet contemplation is more your style, take time to explore the network of marked trails around the escarpment.

8 In suspense

Continue along Tourist Drive 5 to **Katoomba Scenic Railway**. The railway was built in the 1880s to haul coal from tunnel mouth to cliff top. In 1945 the colliery closed, and the steepest incline railway in the world became a popular tourist attraction. The **Scenic Skyway** departs from the same point,

transporting passengers a distance of 350 metres in a cable-car suspended almost 300 metres above the Jamison Valley floor.

Katoomba Scenic Railway and Skyway (at Blue Mountains Scenic World)
Cnr Violet St and Cliff Dr.
Katoomba
Phone: (02) 4782 2699
Open: 9 a.m.–5 p.m. daily

9 Take the plunge

Tourist Drive 5 rejoins the highway on the western edge of Katoomba. Take care as you turn right along the highway back towards Leura. After about 1 kilometre, turn left and follow the signs to **'The Edge' Maxvision Cinema**, where fast-moving images are projected onto

Three Sisters

a larger-than-life screen (18 metres x 24 metres). Here you can soar over mist-filled valleys, scale vertical cliffs and plunge over waterfalls … all without leaving your seat.

'The Edge' Cinemas
225–237 Great Western Hwy (access through Civic Pl.)
Katoomba
Phone: (02) 4782 8900
Open: 6 screenings daily

⑩ Through the canyon
Follow the highway through Medlow Bath and turn right onto Evans Lookout Road, just before Blackheath. Continue 3 kilometres for superb views of the Grose Valley from **Evans Lookout**. Alternatively, park your car at Neates Glen (2 kilometres along the road) and take the Grand Canyon Walk, an adventurous 5-kilometre track that leads past moss-covered rocks, through a tunnel and under rocky overhangs. The enclosed canyon atmosphere provides a wonderful contrast to the vistas that unfold at Evans Lookout up ahead. Sturdy shoes and steady footing are essential for this walk; after heavy rains, contact the Heritage Centre (see below) to check track conditions.

⑪ The leap
From Blackheath, take a right-hand turn off the highway onto Govetts Leap Road and head towards the the National Parks and Wildlife Service Heritage Centre and **Govetts Leap Lookout**. The Heritage Centre, managed by the National Parks and Wildlife Service, has an interactive display on the geology, wildlife, and Aboriginal and European history of the mountains. Inquire here about ranger-guided bushwalks and special holiday programmes.

The 1.8-kilometre Fairfax Heritage Track, specially designed to suit wheelchairs and prams, extends from the Heritage Centre to Govetts Leap Lookout. This view of the Grose Valley and Bridal Veil Waterfall is one of the Blue Mountains' greatest sights. In 1836, Charles Darwin described the vista as 'perhaps even more stupendous' than that obtained from Wentworth Falls. Darwin noted that 'the gulf was filled with a thin blue haze which … added to the apparent depth … at which the forest was stretched out beneath our feet.'

National Parks and Wildlife Service Heritage Centre
Govetts Leap Rd
Blackheath
Phone: (02) 4787 8877
Open: 9 a.m.–4.30 p.m. daily

⑫ Above the pass
After Blackheath, continue along the highway to historic **Mount Victoria**, perched above the western escarpment. The 19th-century Refreshment Rooms at the Railway Station, once the rest-stop on a busy passenger line, now house a treasure trove of historic artifacts.

Between 1814 and 1920, several attempts were made to find the best route down into the valley. These old roads now form a network of walking tracks which can be accessed via Mt York Road, on the right side of the highway just before it descends through Victoria Pass. The track head is about 2 kilometres from the highway.

Mt Victoria and District Museum
Refreshment Rooms,
Railway Station
Station St
Mount Victoria

Phone: (02) 4787 1190
Open: 2 p.m.–5 p.m. Sat., Sun., public and school holidays

⑬ Zig Zag
Depart the Great Western Highway at Mount Victoria. Follow the Darling Causeway to Bell and turn left along Chifley Road to **Zig Zag Railway**. Another longer but more interesting option is to continue along the Great Western Highway from Mount Victoria, and approach the Zig Zag Railway via Hartley and Lithgow (40 kilometres). The historic site of Hartley, which features a Greek Revival sandstone courthouse (1837), is a fascinating attraction in its own right.

The Zig Zag Railway, built between 1866 and 1869, has been described as one of the engineering wonders of the 19th century. Built to bring the Great Western Railway Line from the top of the Blue Mountains down the steep mountainside into the Lithgow Valley, it comprises a series of gently sloping ramps in Z-formation. The Zig Zag is no longer part of the Lithgow railway line, but visitors can experience the past on a steam train which operates on the restored Zig Zag track.

Zig Zag Railway
Bells Line of Road
Clarence
Phone: (02) 6353 1795
Open: steam train operates weekends, Wednesdays, public and most school holidays (departs 11 a.m., 1 p.m. and 3 p.m.); vintage rail motor trip and depot tour operates during the week, except Wednesdays (departs 11 a.m., 1 p.m. and 3 p.m.)

⑭ Glorious gardens
From Bell, take the Bells Line of Road towards Bilpin. Those with an interest in gardens would be

well-advised to take a short diversion to **Mount Wilson**, famous for its English-style private gardens. Many of these gardens, established by Sydney's leisured elite in the 19th century, are now open to the public on a regular basis. For open hours, visit the Blue Mountains Visitor Information Centres in Glenbrook, or at Echo Point, Katoomba, or call 1300 653 408.

⑮ Seasonal colours
Located further along the Bells Line of Road, **Mount Tomah Botanic Garden** features 28 hectares of magnificent colour: protea and heath in winter, cherry blossoms, bulbs, rhododendrons and azaleas in spring, alpine flowers in summer and shades of russet foliage in autumn. At 1000 metres above sea level, Mount Tomah specialises in cool-climate plants from around the world. On a clear day, views extend 180 kilometres across the canyon country towards the Hunter Valley.

Mount Tomah Botanic Garden
Bells Line of Road
Mount Tomah
Phone: (02) 4567 2154
Open: 10 a.m.–4 p.m. daily, Mar.–Sept.; 10 a.m.–5 p.m. daily, Oct.–Feb.

Returning to Sydney
From Mount Tomah, the road descends past the orchards and roadside fruit stalls of Bilpin, through the foothills and onto the plains of the Hawkesbury River. To return to Sydney, continue through Richmond and Windsor and along Route ⑩ (111 kilometres).

NEW SOUTH WALES
LOCATION MAP

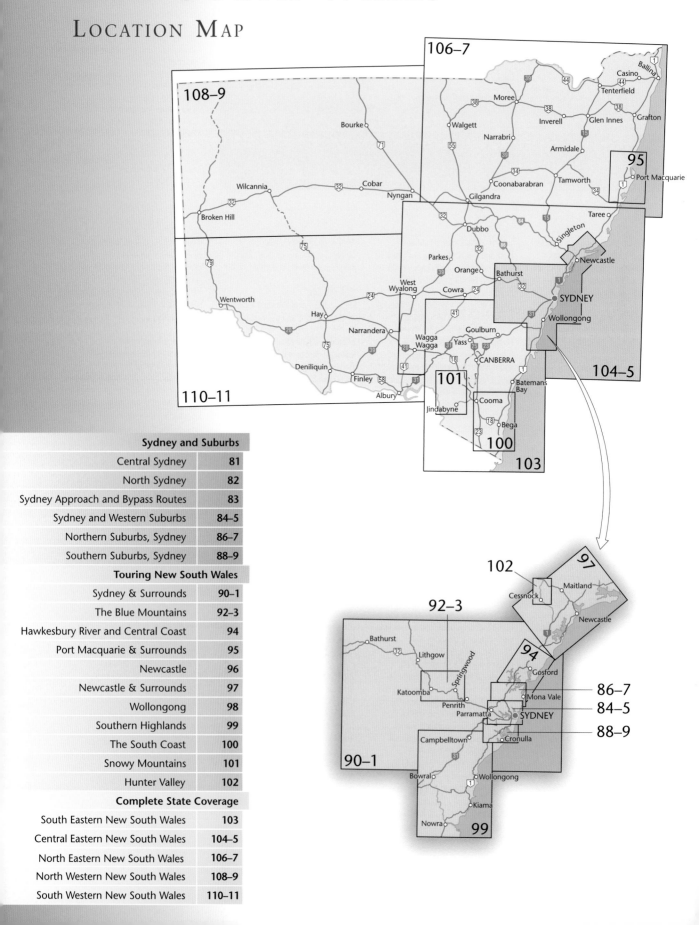

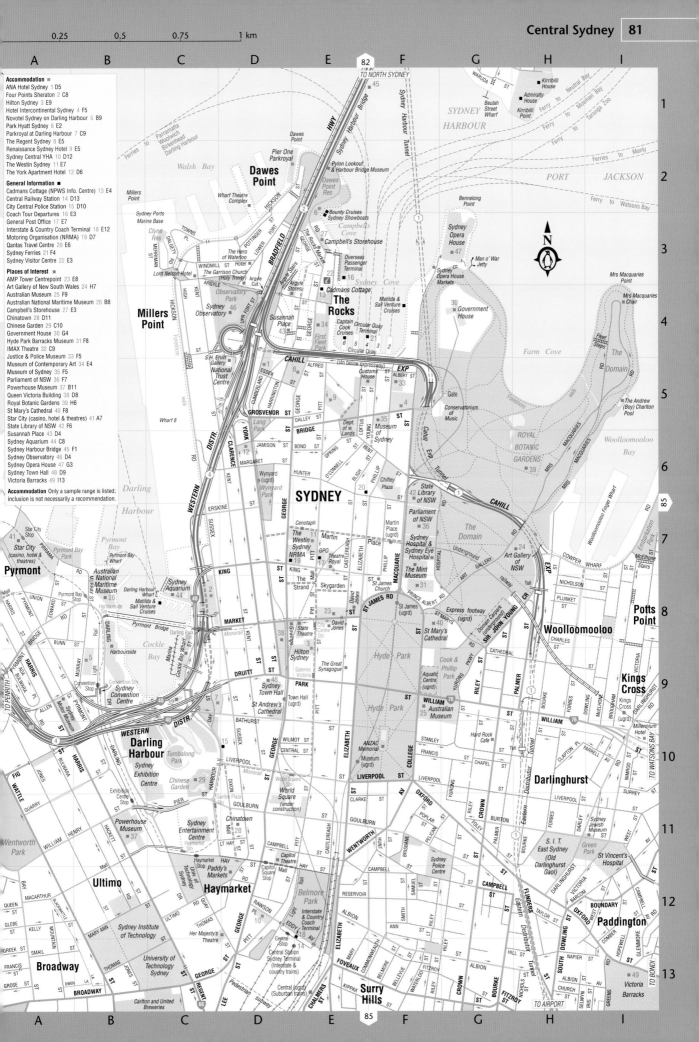

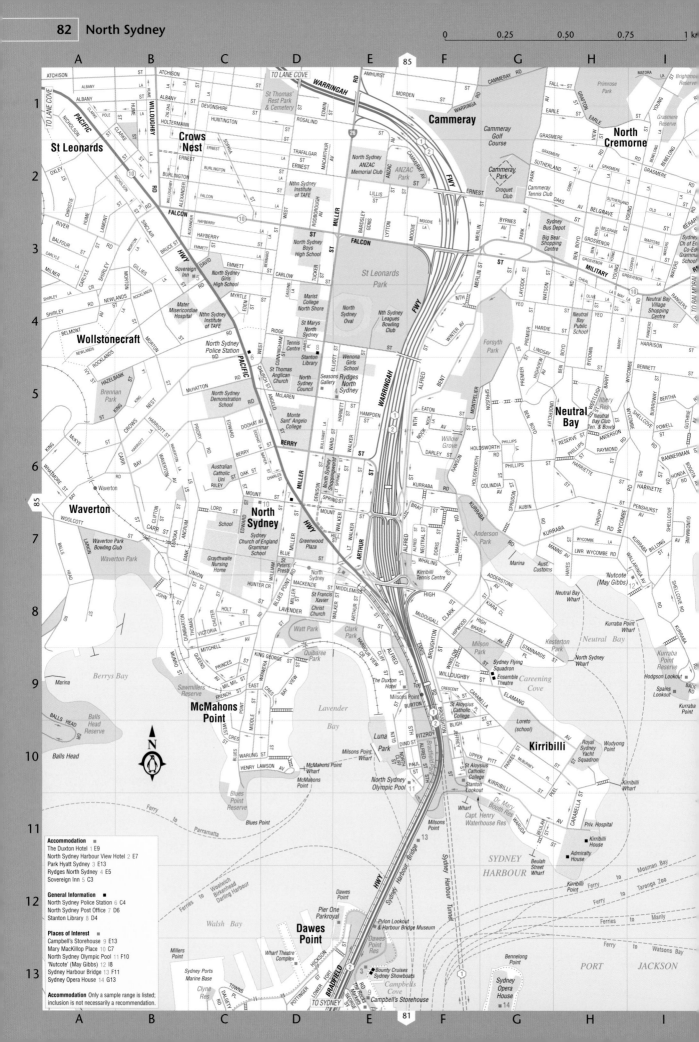

St Leonards

Crows Nest

Cammeray

North Cremorne

Wollstonecraft

St Leonards Park

Neutral Bay

Waverton

North Sydney

Kirribilli

McMahons Point

Lavender Bay

Neutral Bay

Balls Head

Berrys Bay

Luna Park

Dawes Point

SYDNEY HARBOUR

Walsh Bay

PORT JACKSON

Sydney Opera House

Accommodation
The Duxton Hotel 1 E9
North Sydney Harbour View Hotel 2 E7
Park Hyatt Sydney 3 E13
Rydges North Sydney 4 E5
Sovereign Inn 5 C3

General Information
North Sydney Police Station 6 C4
North Sydney Post Office 7 D6
Stanton Library 8 D4

Places of Interest
Campbell's Storehouse 9 E13
Mary MacKillop Place 10 C7
North Sydney Olympic Pool 11 F10
'Nutcote' (May Gibbs) 12 I8
Sydney Harbour Bridge 13 F11
Sydney Opera House 14 G13

Accommodation Only a sample range is listed;
inclusion is not necessarily a recommendation.

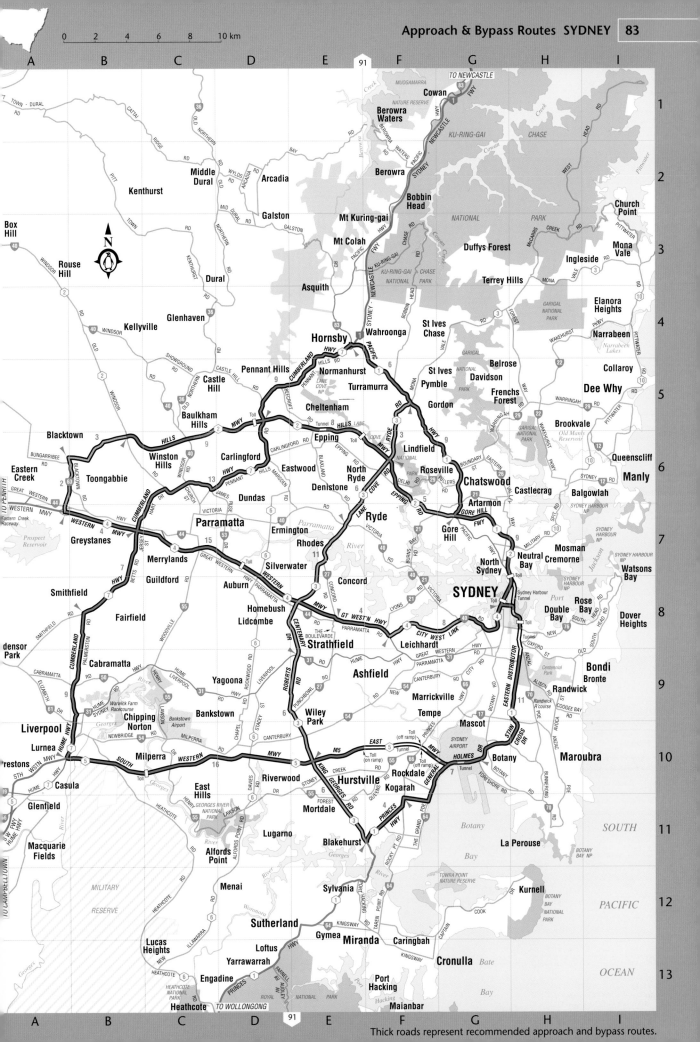

Thick roads represent recommended approach and bypass routes.

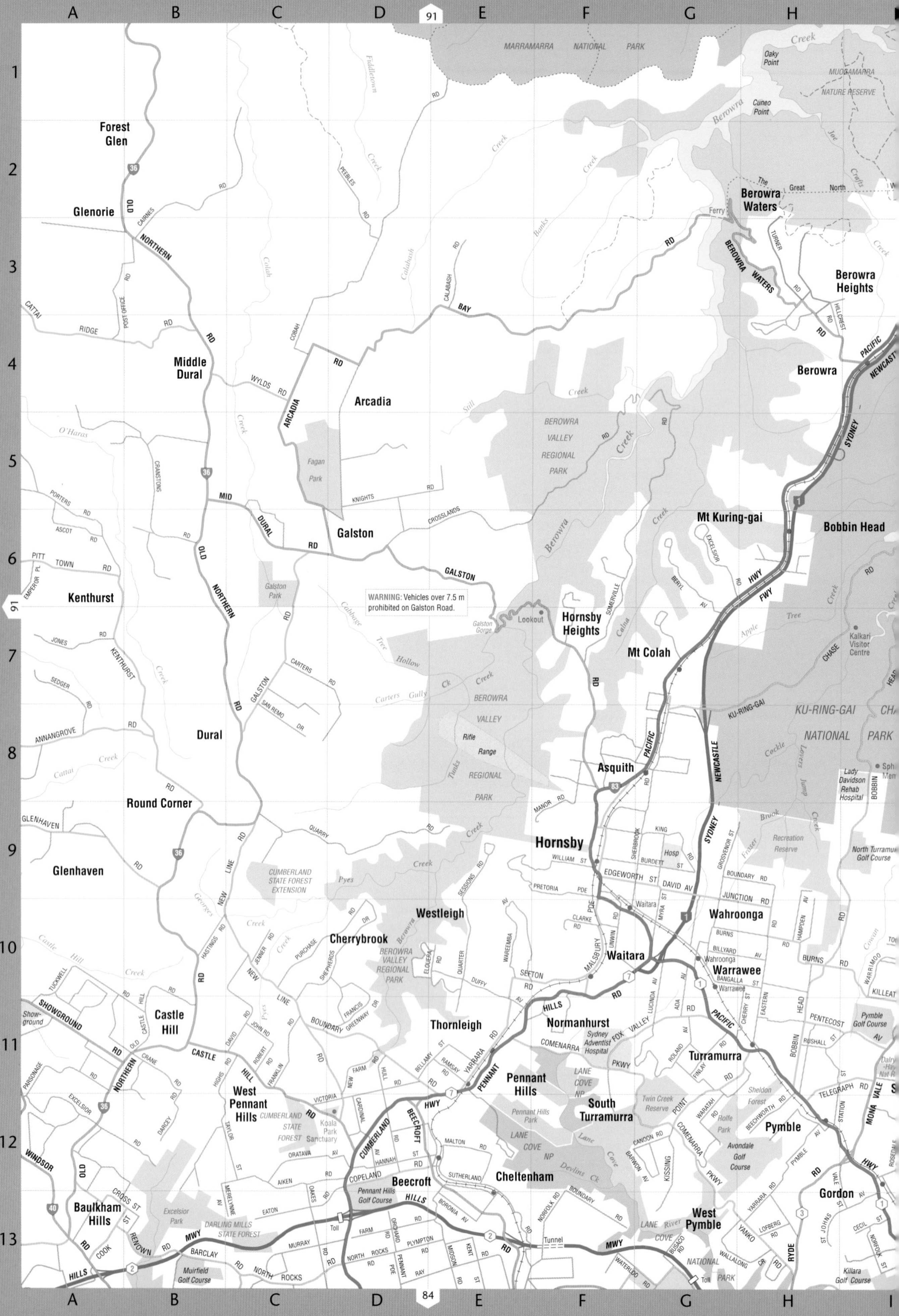

A B C D 91 E F G H

1

MARRAMARRA   NATIONAL   PARK

Oaky
Point

MUOGAMARRA
NATURE RESERVE

Creek

Forest
Glen

2

Berowra

The

Cuneo
Point

Berowra
Waters

36

PEEBLES

Glenorie

OLD

Ferry

BEROWRA WATERS

Berowra
Heights

3

NORTHERN

RD

Calabash

CABBAGE

RD

POST OFFICE

Colah

Calabash

BAY

HILLCREST

RD

PACIFIC

4

Middle
Dural

WYLDS

RD

Arcadia

Creek

Berowra

NEWCASTLE

SYDNEY

CATTAI

RIDGE

RD

ARCADIA

RD

BEROWRA
VALLEY
REGIONAL
PARK

Creek

O'Haras

CRANSTONS

5

Fagan
Park

Creek

RD

36

MID

KNIGHTS

CROSSLANDS

Mt Kuring-gai

Bobbin Head

PORTERS

RD

DURAL

EXCELSIOR

1

6

PITT

TOWN

RD

Galston

GALSTON

RD

Somerville

BERYL

HWY

FWY

EMPEROR PL

Kenthurst

OLD

Galston
Park

WARNING: Vehicles over 7.5 m
prohibited on Galston Road.

AV

Tree

Apple

Kalkari
Visitor
Centre

7

JONES

RD

NORTHERN

RD

CARTERS

RD

Galston
Gorge

Lookout

Hornsby
Heights

CHASE

KU-RING-GAI

SEDGER

KENTHURST

GALSTON

SAN REMO

DR

Carters

Gully

Hollow

Ck

Creek

Mt Colah

KU-RING-GAI

NATIONAL

PARK

8

ANNANGROVE

Dural

BEROWRA

VALLEY

Rifle

Range

RD

Asquith

83

PACIFIC

NEWCASTLE

Cockle

Lady
Davidson
Rehab
Hospital

Sph
Men

Cattai

Creek

Tanks

REGIONAL

MANOR

RD

SYDNEY

BOBBI

9

Round Corner

36

NEW

LINE

QUARRY

PARK

Creek

RD

Hornsby

WILLIAM

ST

SHERBROOK

KING

Hosp

BURDETT

RD

North Turramurra
Golf Course

GLENHAVEN

Pyes

Creek

EDGEWORTH ST

DAVID AV

JUNCTION

RD

Recreation
Reserve

Glenhaven

RD

Castle

Hill

CUMBERLAND
STATE FOREST
EXTENSION

PRETORIA

PDE

Waitara

MYRA

ST

1

Wahroonga

HAMPDEN

AV

10

Creek

Westleigh

PDE

CLARKE

ST

Waitara

BILLYARD

AV

BURNS

Tod

TUCKWELL

Cherrybrook

DR

BEROWRA
VALLEY
REGIONAL
PARK

ELOUERA

MALSBURY

Wahroonga

Warrawee

Warrawee

KILLEAT

SHOWGROUND

HASTINGS

PURCHASE

SHEPHERDS

DUFFY

QUARTER

WAHROONGA

SEFTON

RD

BANGALLA

PENTECOST

11

CASTLE

NEW

LINE

Thornleigh

HILLS

Normanhurst

Turramurra

PARSONAGE

West
Pennant
Hills

FRANCIS

BOUNDARY

GREENWAY

RELLAMY

RAMSAY

ST

COMENARRA

Sydney
Adventist
Hospital

FOX

VALLEY

PKWY

ROLAND

FINLAY

BOBBIN

ROSHALL

EXCELSIOR

CASTLE

HILL

RD

ROBERT

FARM

HILL

YARRARA

LANE
COVE
NP

WARATAH

STATION

Pymble
Golf Course

AV

12

36

TAYLOR

Koala
Park
Sanctuary

VICTORIA

CARDINAL

Pennant
Hills
Park

PENNANT

South
Turramurra

Twin Creek
Reserve

Rolfe
Park

Pymble

WINDSOR

OLD

CUMBERLAND
STATE
FOREST

ORATAVA

AV

CUMBERLAND

BEECROFT

MALTON

RD

LANE

SUTHERLAND

Cheltenham

CANYON RD

BARWON

Avondale
Golf
Course

PYMBLE

MONA VALE

TELEGRAPH

Baulkham
Hills

46

AIKEN

OAKES

COPELAND

Beecroft

HILLS

BORONIA

COVE

NP

Devlins

Ck

West
Pymble

YARRARA

LOFBERG

Gordon

3

13

RD

COOK

RENOWN

MWY

BARCLAY

Muirfield
Golf Course

DARLING MILLS
STATE FOREST

MURRAY

NORTH ROCKS

Toll

FARM

ORCHARD

PLYMPTON

2

RD

Tunnel

MWY

Toll

Killara
Golf Course

HILLS

2

NORTH

ROCKS

PDE

RAY

ST

KENT

ST

MISSIO

NORFOLK

RD

WATERLOO

RD

WALLALONG

RYDE

NATIONAL

A B C D 84 E F G H

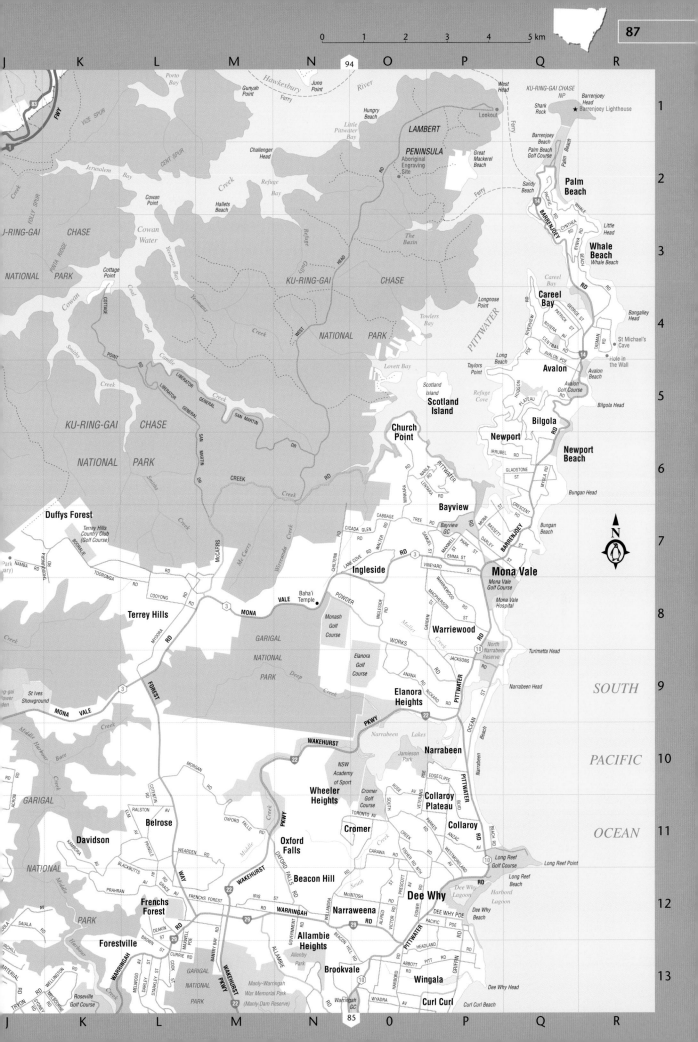

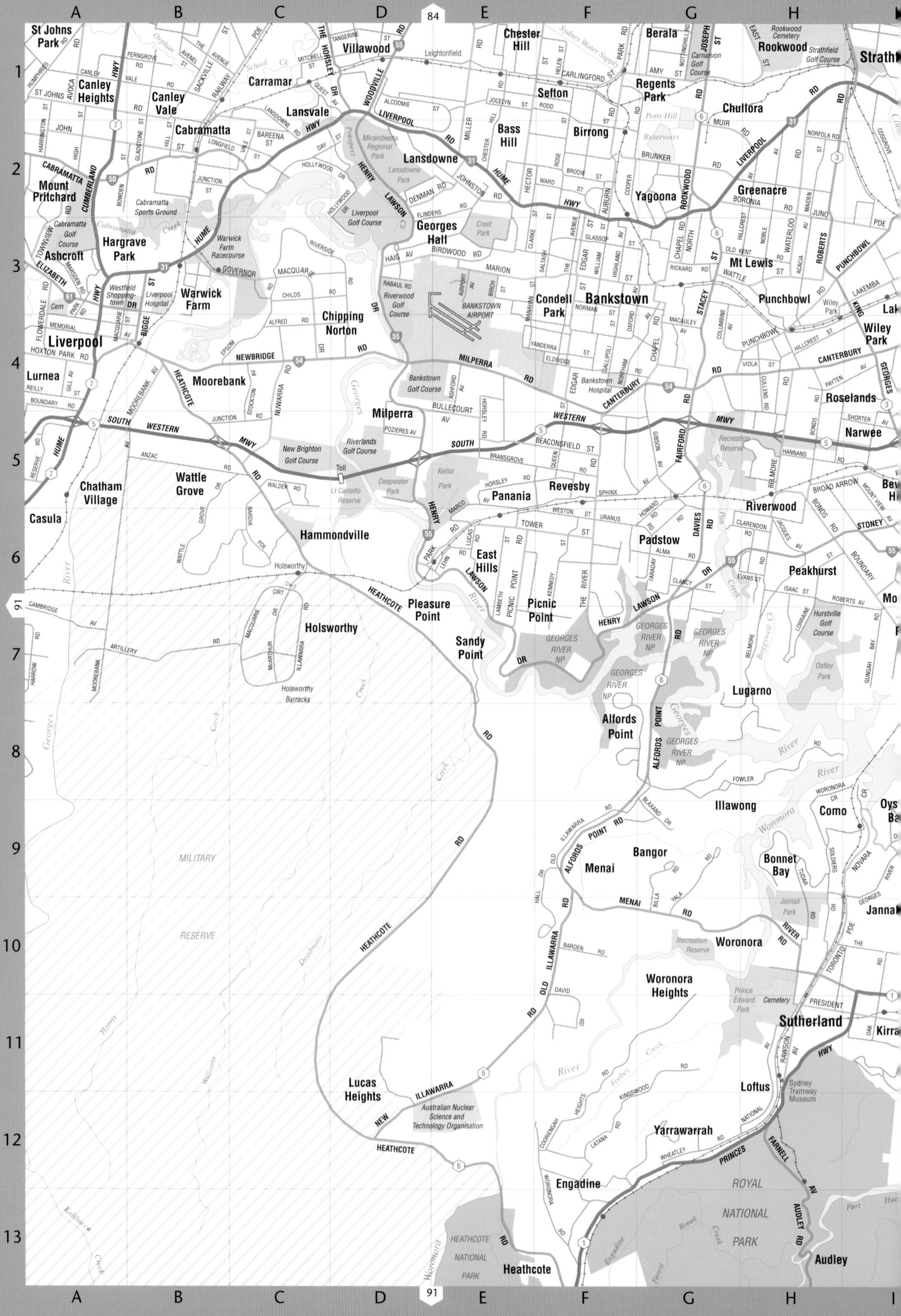

St Johns Park
Canley Heights
Canley Vale
Cabramatta
Carramar
Lansvale
Villawood
Chester Hill
Berala
Rookwood
Strath

Sefton
Regents Park
Chullora
Mount Pritchard
Cabramatta Sports Ground
Lansdowne
Bass Hill
Birrong
Greenacre

Ashcroft
Hargrave Park
Warwick Farm Racecourse
Liverpool Golf Course
Georges Hall
Crest Park
Condell Park
Bankstown
Mt Lewis
Punchbowl
Wiley Park
Lakemba

Liverpool
Warwick Farm
Chipping Norton
Riverwood Golf Course
Bankstown Airport
Roselands
Narwee

Lurnea
Moorebank
Bankstown Golf Course
Bankstown Hospital
Revesby
Riverwood
Bev

Casula
Chatham Village
Wattle Grove
New Brighton Golf Course
Riverlands Golf Course
Deepwater Park
Kelso Park
Panania
Padstow
Peakhurst

Hammondville
Pleasure Point
East Hills
Picnic Point
Lugarno

Holsworthy
Sandy Point
Georges River NP
Alfords Point
Illawong
Como
Oys Ba

MILITARY RESERVE
Menai
Bangor
Bonnet Bay
Janna

Woronora
Woronora Heights

Lucas Heights
Australian Nuclear Science and Technology Organisation
Sutherland
Loftus
Sydney Tramway Museum

Yarrawarrah
Engadine
Heathcote
ROYAL NATIONAL PARK
Audley

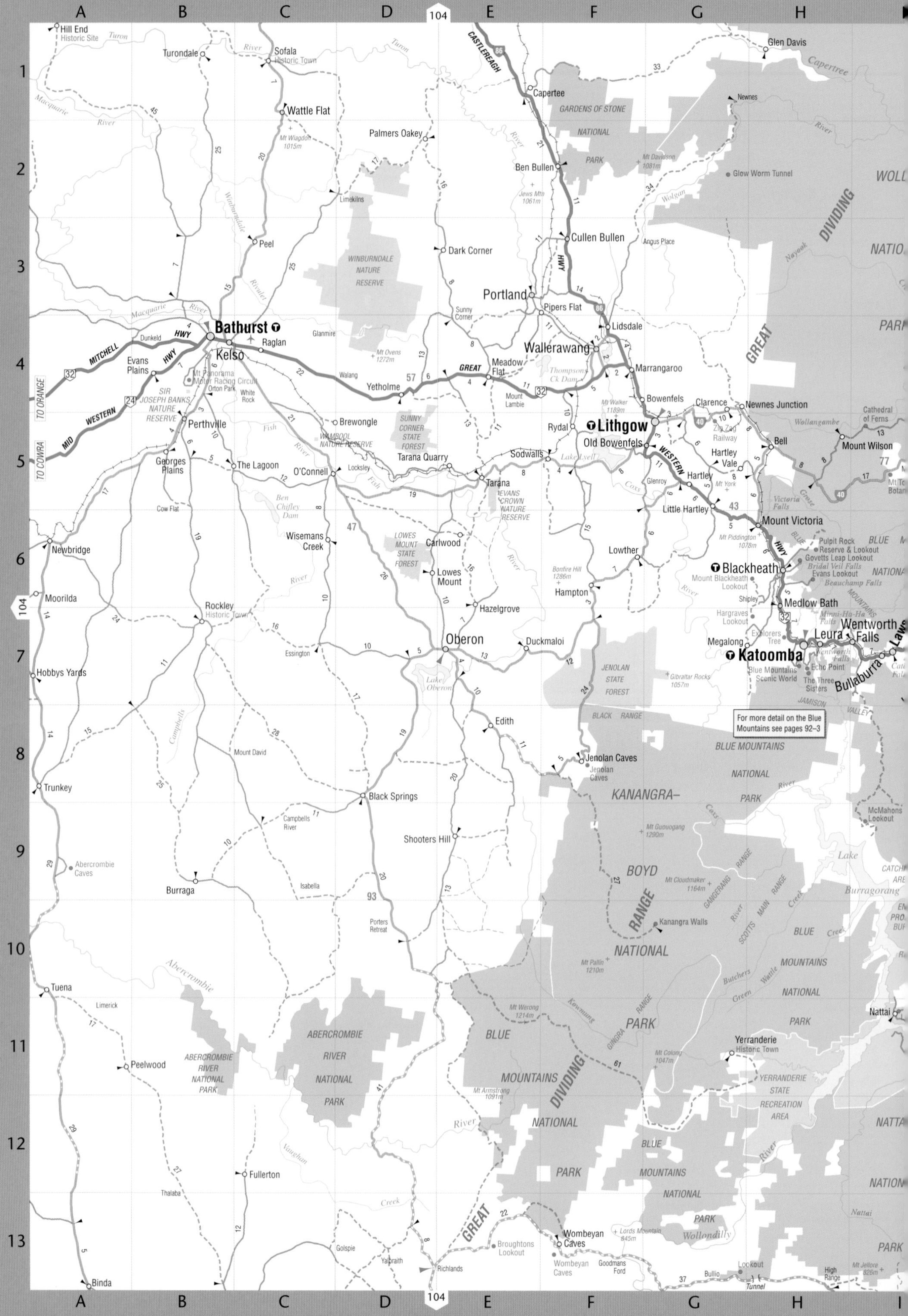

Hill End Historic Site
Turondale
Sofala Historic Town
Wattle Flat
Palmers Oakey
Limekilns
Peel
Dark Corner
Ben Bullen
Cullen Bullen
Angus Place
Glow Worm Tunnel
Newnes
Glen Davis
GARDENS OF STONE NATIONAL PARK
WOLLEMI
WINBURNDALE NATURE RESERVE
Portland
Pipers Flat
Lidsdale
Glanmire
Mt Ovens 1272m
Sunny Corner
Meadow Flat
Wallerawang
Thompson Ck Dam
Marrangaroo
GREAT DIVIDING
NATIO
Bathurst
Raglan
Kelso
Dunkeld
Evans Plains
MITCHELL HWY
WESTERN HWY
MID WESTERN HWY
TO ORANGE
TO COWRA
SIR JOSEPH BANKS NATURE RESERVE
Perthville
Mt Panorama Motor Racing Circuit
Orton Park
White Rock
Walang
Yetholme
Mount Lambie
Mt Walker 1189m
Bowenfels
Clarence
Newnes Junction
Cathedral of Ferns
Zig Zag Railway
Rydal
Lithgow
Old Bowenfels
Hartley Vale
Bell
Mt Wilson
GREAT
WESTERN
Brewongle
SUNNY CORNER STATE FOREST
WAMBOOL NATURE RESERVE
Tarana Quarry
Sodwalls
Lake Lyell
Glenroy
Hartley
Mt York
Victoria Falls
Georges Plains
The Lagoon
O'Connell
Locksley
Fish
Tarana
EVANS CROWN NATURE RESERVE
Coxs
Little Hartley
Mount Victoria
BLUE
Cow Flat
Ben Chifley Dam
Wisemans Creek
Carlwood
Mt Piddington 1078m
Pulpit Rock Reserve & Lookout
Govetts Leap Lookout
Evans Lookout
Bridal Veil Falls
Beauchamp Falls
Newbridge
LOWES MOUNT STATE FOREST
Lowes Mount
Lowther
Bonfire Hill 1286m
Hampton
Blackheath
Mount Blackheath Lookout
Shipley
Minni-Ha-Ha Falls
Moorilda
Rockley Historic Town
Hazelgrove
Hargraves Lookout
Megalong
Explorers Tree
Medlow Bath
Hobbys Yards
Essington
Oberon
Duckmaloi
Blue Mountains Scenic World
Echo Point
The Three Sisters
Leura
Wentworth Falls
Katoomba
Lawson
Bullaburra
JAMISON VALLEY
Edith
JENOLAN STATE FOREST
Gibraltar Rocks 1057m
BLACK RANGE
BLUE MOUNTAINS
Trunkey
Mount David
Black Springs
Jenolan Caves
KANANGRA–
NATIONAL PARK
Abercrombie Caves
Campbells River
Shooters Hill
BOYD RANGE
Mt Guouogang 1290m
Mt Cloudmaker 1164m
McMahons Lookout
Lake
Burragorang
CATCH
Burraga
Isabella
Porters Retreat
93
Kanangra Walls
NATIONAL PARK
Mt Paralln 1210m
Green
BLUE MOUNTAINS NATIONAL PARK
Tuena
Limerick
Mt Wareng 1214m
Nattai
Peelwood
ABERCROMBIE RIVER NATIONAL PARK
BLUE
Mt Colong 1047m
Yerranderie Historic Town
YERRANDERIE STATE RECREATION AREA
Fullerton
Mt Armstrong 1091m
MOUNTAINS
DIVIDING
Thalaba
BLUE
MOUNTAINS
NATIONAL
PARK
Wollondilly
Binda
Golspie
Yalbraith
Richlands
GREAT
Wombeyan Caves
Broughtons Lookout
Wombeyan Caves
Goodmans Ford
Lords Mountain 845m
Bullio
High Range
Mt Jellore 926m
NATTAI
Tunnel

0 5 10 15 20 25 30 km

J K L 105 M N O P 97 Q R

1
TO NEWCASTLE
Buckelly
OLNEY STATE
Muirs Lookout
Morisset Brightwaters Nords Wharf
Mandalong Gwandalan
Sunshine
Catherine Hill Bay
Cedar Brush
Cedar Brush Creek
Ravensdale
Dooralong
Wyee
Mannering Park
MUNMORAH STATE RECREATION AREA
YENGO
HOWES RANGE
Higher Macdonald
PRIESTS RIDGE
Lake Munmorah

2
NATIONAL
PUTTY
Webbs Ridge
Kulnura
Yarramalong
Little Jilliby
Jilliby
BUDGEWOI
GOROKAN
NORAVILLE
TOUKLEY
NORAH HEAD
PARK
Upper Macdonald
WYONG STATE FOREST
Wyong Creek
WYONG
TUGGERAH
Budgewoi Lake
Tuggerah Lake

3
St Albans
Upper Mangrove Creek
Mangrove Mountain
Peats Ridge
Palm Grove
Palmdale
Somersby
NARARA
OURIMBAH
TUMBI UMBI
LISAROW
MATCHAM
THE ENTRANCE NORTH
THE ENTRANCE
LONG JETTY
TOOWOON BAY
BATEAU BAY
WYRRABALONG NATIONAL PARK
FORRESTERS BEACH
WOMERAH RANGE
PARR STATE RECREATION AREA
Ten Mile Hollow
DHARUG
POPRAN NATIONAL PARK
BRISBANE WATER NATIONAL PARK
NEWCASTLE
Fowlers Lookout

4
Webbs Creek
Wisemans Ferry
Laughtondale
Lower Mangrove
Old Sydney Town
Glenworth Valley
Calga
Australian Reptile Park & Wildlife Sanctuary
GOSFORD
POINT CLARE
KINCUMBER
WOY WOY
ETTALONG UMINA
WAMBERAL
TERRIGAL
ERINA
The Skillion
AVOCA BEACH
MACMASTERS BEACH
Upper Colo
Colo
Leets Vale
Maroota
Spencer
Mount White
Gunderman
SYDNEY
BRISBANE Water
Brisbane Water
BOUDDI NATIONAL PARK

5
Blaxlands Ridge
Comleroy Road
Bellbird Hill Lookout
Glossodia
Kurmond
Ebenezer
Cattai
Sackville North
Kurrajong
Bowen Mountain
Freemans Reach
Wilberforce
Cattai
Glenorie
Cowan
MARRAMARRA NATIONAL PARK
Mooney Mooney
Brooklyn
Patonga
Warrah Lookout
Broken Bay
KILLCARE
WAGSTAFFE
BOUDDI NP
SOUTH

6
Kurrajong Heights
North Richmond
Agnes Banks
Richmond
Clarendon
Pitt Town
Maraylya
McGraths Hill
Windsor
Hawkesbury Museum
Londonderry
Galston
BEROWRA
PALM BEACH
WHALE BEACH
AVALON
NEWPORT
KU-RING-GAI CHASE NATIONAL PARK
Pittwater
CENTRAL
Grose Vale
Glenhaven
Kenthurst
Annangrove

7
Springwood
Winmalee
Valley Heights
Warrimoo
Vineyard
Riverstone
Rouse Hill Estate
SCHOFIELDS
GLENHAVEN
CASTLE HILL
HORNSBY
ST IVES
PYMBLE
TERREY HILLS
FRENCHS FOREST
MONA VALE
ELANORA HEIGHTS
NARRABEEN
COLLAROY
DEE WHY
LANE COVE MWY
HILLS MWY
Marsden Park
QUAKERS HILL

8
Blaxland
Glenbrook
PENRITH
KINGSWOOD
MOUNT DRUITT
ROOTY HILL
BLACKTOWN
Featherdale Wildlife Park
EASTERN CREEK
PARRAMATTA
RYDE
GLADESVILLE
HOMEBUSH BAY
BALMAIN
LANE COVE
NORTH SYDNEY
CHATSWOOD
BALGOWLAH
MANLY
WATSONS BAY
MOSMAN
SYDNEY HARBOUR NP
SYDNEY
PADDINGTON
DOVER HEIGHTS
ST MARYS
WESTERN
Wonderland Sydney
Erskine Park
HORSLEY PARK
CECIL PARK
MERRYLANDS
FAIRFIELD
STRATHFIELD
Prospect Reservoir
PACIFIC

9
Mulgoa
Wallacia
Luddenham
Badgerys Creek
CABRAMATTA
LIVERPOOL
MILPERRA
BANKSTOWN
REVESBY
BEXLEY
BELFIELD
MARRICKVILLE
BONDI
COOGEE
KINGSFORD
MAROUBRA
BOTANY
SYDNEY AIRPORT
HURSTVILLE
PEAKHURST
BRIGHTON LE SANDS
LA PEROUSE
KURNELL
GEORGES RIVER NP
Austral
Rossmore
Bringelly
LEPPINGTON
Catherine Field
MACQUARIE FIELDS
BLAKEHURST
SYLVANIA
Botany Bay
BENTS BASIN SRA

10
Theresa Park
Cobbitty
Oran Park (Raceway)
MINTO
MILITARY RESERVE
SUTHERLAND
MIRANDA
CRONULLA
BOTANY BAY NATIONAL PARK
Bate Bay
OCEAN
Brownlow Hill
NARELLAN
CAMDEN
GRASMERE
LEUMEAH
CAMPBELLTOWN
HEATHCOTE
Audley
BUNDEENA
Port Hacking

11
The Oaks
Mount Hunter
Cawdor
Menangle Park
Menangle
Wedderburn
HEATHCOTE NATIONAL PARK
Waterfall
Maianbar
ROYAL NATIONAL PARK
Wattamolla
Mowbray Park
Woronora Reservoir

12
Picton
Maldon
Douglas Park
Appin
DHARAWAL STATE RECREATION AREA
Helensburgh
Garie Beach
Otford
Stanwell Tops
Lawrence Hargrave Memorial & Lookout
Stanwell Park
Tahmoor
Wilton
Appin Falls
DHARAWAL NATURE RESERVE
Lake Cataract
WESTERN
SOUTHERN FWY
N

13
Bargo
Yanderra top
Yerrinbool
Nepean River
Cordeaux Reservoir
Avon Reservoir
TO SHELLHARBOUR
Coalcliff
Clifton
Scarborough
Wombarra
Coledale
Austinmer
Thirroul
BULLI
GORRIMAL
Sublime Point Lookout
PRINCES

For more detail on the Hawkesbury River & Central Coast see page 94

For more detail on Sydney Suburbs see pages 84–9

For more detail on the Southern Highlands see page 99

J K 99 L M N O P Q R

A B C D E F G H I

90

BELLS LINE OF RD 40

1

DARLING

Walls Lookout

Rigby Hill
924m

Grose

King George Brook

RANGE

Victoria
Falls

2

CAUSEWAY

VICTORIA FALLS RD

Victoria Falls
Lookout

Baltzer Lookout

River

Mt Banks
1058m

Creek

Explorers Brook

EXPLORERS

3

TO LITHGOW

Sunset Rock

+ Mt Victoria
1044m

Mount Victoria

Bennett Lookout

Anvil Rock

Hat Hill Creek

Grose

Edgeworth David Hill
864m

Mt Hay
944m

BLUE MOUNTAINS

RANGE

only

MOUNT VICTORIA: A blend of weatherboard and sandstone colonial buildings, Mount Victoria is an historic village with craft shops, an historical museum and a quaint cinema, Mt Vic Flicks.

Mt Piddington
1078m

BLUE

Victoria Creek

Pulpit Rock
Reserve & Lookout

BUSHWALKS:
There are a number of scenic walks throughout the Blue M
These include:

1. The Fairfax Heritage Track (2 km, approx. 1 hour return)
starts at Heritage Centre, finishes at Govetts Leap; several
wheelchair access.

2. Three Sisters Walk (approx. half hour return): Easy walk
the Information Centre at Echo Point, view of the Three Sis

3. Govetts Leap to Evans Lookout (approx. 4 hours return):
difficulty; a clifftop walk with spectacular views across the

4. Valley of the Waters Nature Track (approx. 3 hours return
difficulty; waterfall circuit from the Conservation Hut Cafe a
Falls.

5. National Pass Circuit (approx. 4 hours return): Difficult;
clifftop and waterfall circuit from the Conservation Hut Cafe
Wentworth Falls.

4

BLACKHEATH

GREAT

32

PLATEAU

HAT HILL RD

Hat Hill
1033m

Cripps Lookout

Horseshoe Falls
Trinity Falls

Govetts
Leap
Lookout

Bacchante
Gardens

NPWS
Heritage Centre

GOVETTS LEAP RD

Bridal Veil
Falls

Luchetti
Lookout

Lockley
Pylon

Govetts

Fortress Hill
950m

LYCON
PLATEAU

The Pinnacles

Urella

MOUNT HAY RD

4WD

NATIONAL PARK

Bro

Wirralie

5

Blackheath

RD

SHIPLEY

5

Govetts
Statue

Blackheath

EVANS LOOKOUT RD

WESTERN

18

Evans
Lookout

THE GRAND

Beauchamp Falls

Arethusa Falls

MOUNTAINS

Flat Top
928m

4WD

Flat Top

only

Brook

GARDENS: The Blue Mountains region is justly famous f
its beautiful gardens. One of the most famous is the Ever
Gardens, created by the Danish landscaper Paul Sorensen
daily. The Bacchante Gardens, at Blackheath, lovely all-ye
round, are at their peak in late spring; open daily.

6

Stony

Creek

VALLEY

Mount Blackheath
Lookout

+ Mt Blackheath

Mermaid Cave

Lake
Greaves

Lake
Medlow

Walls
Cave

THE GRAND CANYON

RD

Katoomba Falls

Creek

90

7

MEGALONG VALLEY RD

Shipley
Tea Rooms

Shipley

Medlow Bath

Hydro Majestic
Hotel

4WD

Minni-Ha-Ha
Falls

RD

Wentworth
Falls Lake

DIVIDING

LEURA: Home to some of Australia's most beautiful gardens. The village with its unhurried atmosphere also offers beautifully restored historic buildings, charming tea houses, craft shops and galleries displaying the work of local artists.

8

KANIMBLA

Sugarloaf
Peak

Hargraves Lookout

Cascade
Creek
Dams

BARTON ST

3

The Edge
Maxvision Cinema

Leura

HWY

Wentworth

BLAXLAND

4

RD

FALLS

**Wentworth
Falls**

Conservation
Hut Cafe

RAILWAY

14

32

Lawso

Bullab

GENEVIEVE RD

9

Explorers Tree

Werriberri Trail Rides

Megalong Australian
Heritage Centre

+ Megalong Head

Megalong

NARROW NECK

CLIFF

DR

KATOOMBA ST

MEGALONG ST

Katoomba

Leura Mall

Leura
Falls

Cascades

Leura
Falls

Gordon
Falls

Everglades Gardens

Pool of Siloam

Valley of the
Falls Picnic Area

Wentworth Fall
Picnic Area

Wentworth
Falls

Creek

5

Sublime
Point

Kings Table
883m

QUEEN

KATOOMBA SCENIC RAILWAY AND SKYWAY: The Scenic Railway was built in the 1880s by the founder of the Katoomba coalmine to bring out the coal and transport the miners. Reputed to be the steepest in the world, it descends into the Jamison Valley at an average incline of 45 degrees through a sunlit, tree-clad gorge approximately 445 m in length.
The Scenic Skyway is the first horizontal passenger-carrying ropeway in Australia. It travels about 350 m across the mountain gorge above Cooks Crossing and provides stunning views of Katoomba Falls, Orphan Rock and Jamison Valley.
The Scenic Railway and Skyway are both located at Blue Mountains Scenic World.

10

Billy Healy Hill
637m

Megalong Ck

Foot

Track

Chaplowe

Blue Mountains
Scenic World

Katoomba
Falls

Visitor
Information

Echo Point

The Three
Sisters

Giant Stairway

THE THREE SISTERS: A major attraction of the Blue Mountains and one of Australia's best known rock formations. This trio of rocky pinnacles is floodlit at night.

Queen Victoria
Hospital

KINGS

KEDUMBA

4WD

ELIZABETH

11

+ Pinnacle Hill

Six

MEGALONG

NECK

Mitchells

Castle Head
986m

Castle

Track

FIRE

GREAT

JAMISON VALLEY

River

Jamison

KINGS

4WD

only

TABLELAND

12

Euroka

NARROW

4WD

Ruined

Katoomba

Mt Solitary
965m

Cedar

BLUE MOUNTAINS

Greenfields
Lookover

Melvilles
Lookdown

Creek

Kedumba

VALLEY

ERSKINE

13

Coxs River

NATIONAL PARK

CEDAR VALLEY

Creek

KEDUMBA VALLEY

4WD only

RD

River

A B C D E F G H I

90

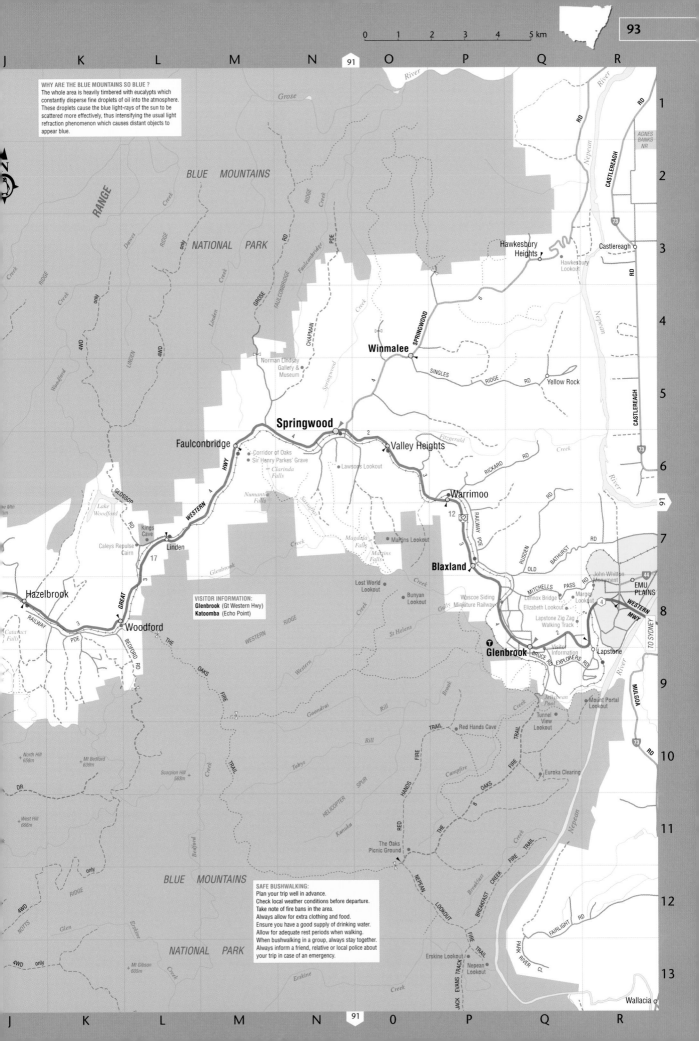

0 1 2 3 4 5 km

WHY ARE THE BLUE MOUNTAINS SO BLUE ?
The whole area is heavily timbered with eucalypts which constantly disperse fine droplets of oil into the atmosphere. These droplets cause the blue light-rays of the sun to be scattered more effectively, thus intensifying the usual light refraction phenomenon which causes distant objects to appear blue.

BLUE MOUNTAINS

RANGE

NATIONAL PARK

Hawkesbury Heights

Hawkesbury Lookout

Castlereagh

AGNES BANKS NR

CASTLEREAGH

Winmalee

Norman Lindsay Gallery & Museum

Yellow Rock

Springwood

Faulconbridge

Valley Heights

Corridor of Oaks
Sir Henry Parkes' Grave

Clarinda Falls

Lawsons Lookout

Warrimoo

Numantia Falls

Magdala Falls

Martins Lookout

Blaxland

Kings Cave

Caleys Repulse Cairn

Linden

Martins Falls

VISITOR INFORMATION:
Glenbrook (Gt Western Hwy)
Katoomba (Echo Point)

Lost World Lookout

Bunyan Lookout

Wascoe Siding Miniature Railway

John Whitton Monument

EMU PLAINS

Lennox Bridge
Elizabeth Lookout

Lapstone Zig Zag Walking Track

Hazelbrook

Woodford

Glenbrook

Visitor Information

Lapstone

TO SYDNEY

Cataract Falls

THE OAKS

WESTERN

St Helens

Jellybean Pool

MULGOA

Mount Portal Lookout

North Hill 658m

Mt Bedford 639m

Scorpion Hill 563m

Tunnel View Lookout

Red Hands Cave

Euroka Clearing

West Hill 666m

BLUE MOUNTAINS

SAFE BUSHWALKING:
Plan your trip well in advance.
Check local weather conditions before departure.
Take note of fire bans in the area.
Always allow for extra clothing and food.
Ensure you have a good supply of drinking water.
Allow for adequate rest periods when walking.
When bushwalking in a group, always stay together.
Always inform a friend, relative or local police about your trip in case of an emergency.

The Oaks Picnic Ground

NATIONAL PARK

Mt Gibson 605m

Erskine Lookout

Nepean Lookout

Wallacia

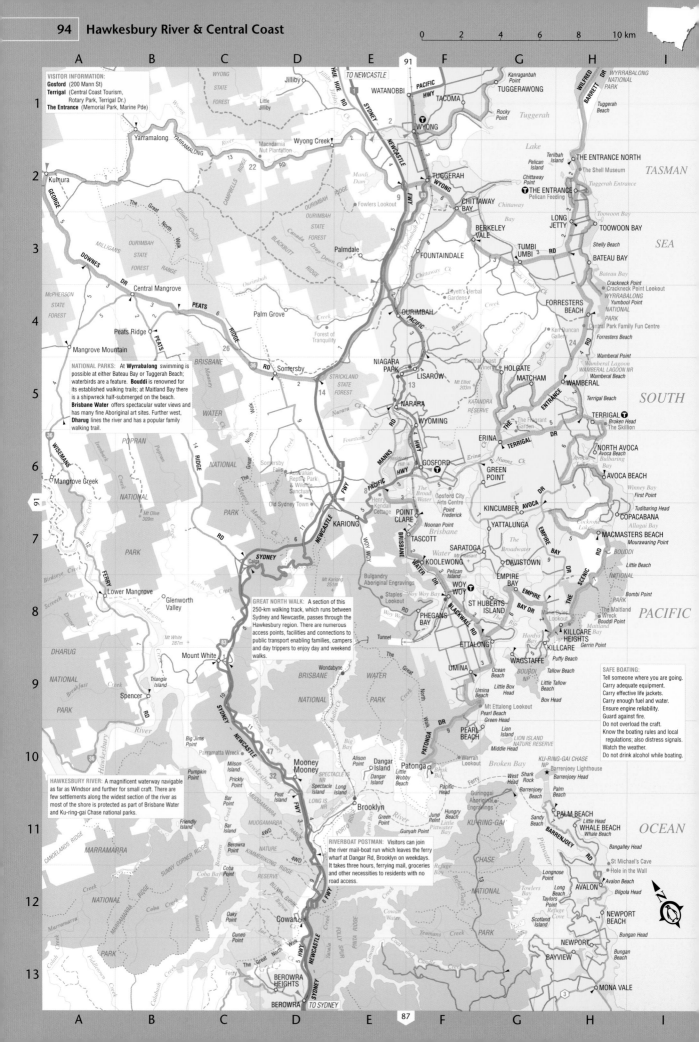

0 2 4 6 8 10 km

VISITOR INFORMATION:
Gosford (200 Mann St)
Terrigal (Central Coast Tourism, Rotary Park, Terrigal Dr.)
The Entrance (Memorial Park, Marine Pde)

NATIONAL PARKS: At **Wyrrabalong** swimming is possible at either Bateau Bay or Tuggerah Beach; waterbirds are a feature. **Bouddi** is renowned for its established walking trails; at Maitland Bay there is a shipwreck half-submerged on the beach. **Brisbane Water** offers spectacular water views and has many fine Aboriginal art sites. Further west, **Dharug** lines the river and has a popular family walking trail.

GREAT NORTH WALK: A section of this 250-km walking track, which runs between Sydney and Newcastle, passes through the Hawkesbury region. There are numerous access points, facilities and connections to public transport enabling families, campers and day trippers to enjoy day and weekend walks.

HAWKESBURY RIVER: A magnificent waterway navigable as far as Windsor and further for small craft. There are few settlements along the widest section of the river as most of the shore is protected as part of Brisbane Water and Ku-ring-gai Chase national parks.

RIVERBOAT POSTMAN: Visitors can join the river mail-boat run which leaves the ferry wharf at Dangar Rd, Brooklyn on weekdays. It takes three hours, ferrying mail, groceries and other necessities to residents with no road access.

SAFE BOATING:
Tell someone where you are going.
Carry adequate equipment.
Carry effective life jackets.
Carry enough fuel and water.
Ensure engine reliability.
Guard against fire.
Do not overload the craft.
Know the boating rules and local regulations; also distress signals.
Watch the weather.
Do not drink alcohol while boating.

TASMAN

SEA

SOUTH

PACIFIC

OCEAN

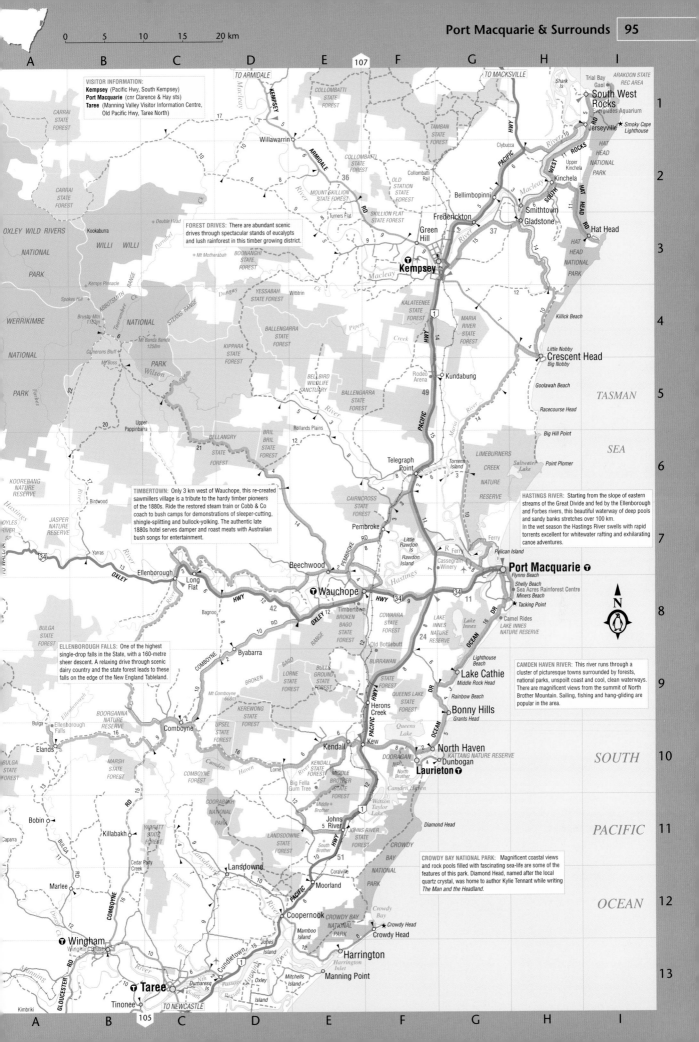

0 5 10 15 20 km

VISITOR INFORMATION:
Kempsey (Pacific Hwy, South Kempsey)
Port Macquarie (cnr Clarence & Hay sts)
Taree (Manning Valley Visitor Information Centre, Old Pacific Hwy, Taree North)

FOREST DRIVES: There are abundant scenic drives through spectacular stands of eucalypts and lush rainforest in this timber growing district.

TIMBERTOWN: Only 3 km west of Wauchope, this re-created sawmillers village is a tribute to the hardy timber pioneers of the 1880s. Ride the restored steam train or Cobb & Co coach to bush camps for demonstrations of sleeper-cutting, shingle-splitting and bullock-yolking. The authentic late 1880s hotel serves damper and roast meats with Australian bush songs for entertainment.

HASTINGS RIVER: Starting from the slope of eastern streams of the Great Divide and fed by the Ellenborough and Forbes rivers, this beautiful waterway of deep pools and sandy banks stretches over 100 km.
In the wet season the Hastings River swells with rapid torrents excellent for whitewater rafting and exhilarating canoe adventures.

ELLENBOROUGH FALLS: One of the highest single-drop falls in the State, with a 160-metre sheer descent. A relaxing drive through scenic dairy country and the state forest leads to these falls on the edge of the New England Tableland.

CAMDEN HAVEN RIVER: This river runs through a cluster of picturesque towns surrounded by forests, national parks, unspoilt coast and cool, clean waterways. There are magnificent views from the summit of North Brother Mountain. Sailing, fishing and hang-gliding are popular in the area.

CROWDY BAY NATIONAL PARK: Magnificent coastal views and rock pools filled with fascinating sea-life are some of the features of this park. Diamond Head, named after the local quartz crystal, was home to author Kylie Tennant while writing *The Man and the Headland.*

TASMAN

SEA

SOUTH

PACIFIC

OCEAN

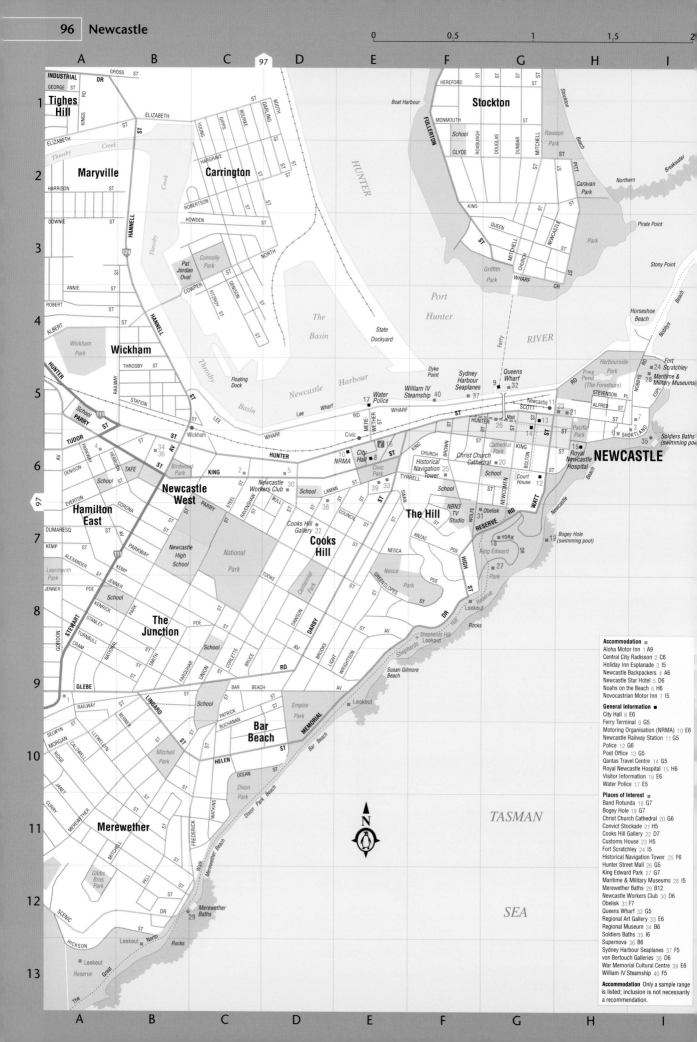

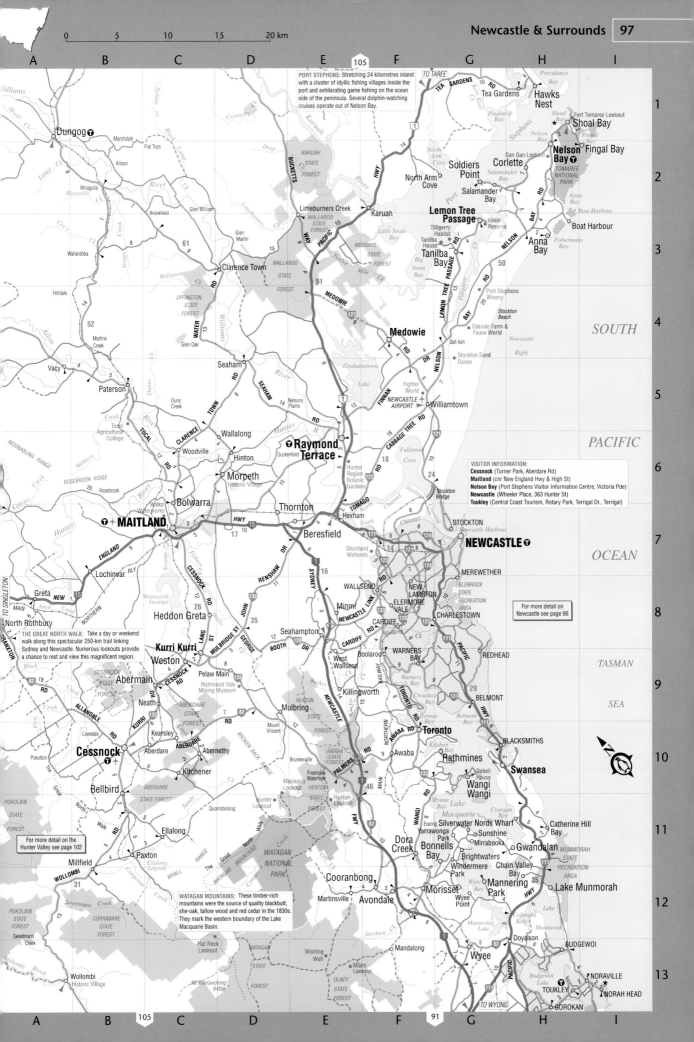

0 5 10 15 20 km

A B C D E F G H I

PORT STEPHENS: Stretching 24 kilometres inland with a cluster of idyllic fishing villages inside the port and exhilarating game fishing on the ocean side of the peninsula. Several dolphin-watching cruises operate out of Nelson Bay.

TO TAREE

TEA GARDENS RD

Tea Gardens

Hawks Nest

Providence Bay

Fort Tomaree Lookout

Shoal Bay

Shoal Bay

1

PACIFIC HWY

Corlette

Nelson Bay

Fingal Bay

North Arm Cove

Soldiers Point

Salamander Bay

Gan Gan Lookout

TOMAREE NATIONAL PARK

Anna Bay

Boat Harbour

Fishermans Bay

2

Limeburners Creek

Karuah

Lemon Tree Passage

Koala Reserve

Tilligerry Habitat

Tanilba House

Tanilba Bay

Big Swan Bay

Little Swan Bay

Port Stephens Winery

LEMON TREE PASSAGE RD

NELSON BAY RD

50

Anna Bay

3

WALLAROO STATE FOREST

MEDOWIE STATE FOREST

Twelve Mile Ck

51

MEDOWIE RD

121

9

Medowie

NELSON RD

Salt Ash

Oakvale Farm & Fauna World

Stockton Beach

Stockton Sand Dunes

Newcastle Bight

SOUTH

4

WATER RD

UFFINGTON STATE FOREST

52

Martins Creek

Glen Oak

Seaham

Nelsons Plains

Grahamstown Lake

Williamtown

Fighter World

NEWCASTLE AIRPORT

FINNAN RD

5

Vacy

Paterson

Duns Creek

Wallalong

Hinton

SEAHAM RD

Hunter River

Duckenfield

Raymond Terrace

Hunter Region Botanic Gardens

CABBAGE TREE RD

Fullerton Cove

121

PACIFIC

6

Total Agricultural College

Woodville

Morpeth Historic Village

CLARENCE TOWN RD

TOCAL RD

Bolwarra

Walka Waterworks

Thornton

Tomago

Hexham

TOMAGO RD

122

24

Stockton Bridge

Stockton Channel

VISITOR INFORMATION:
Cessnock (Turner Park, Aberdare Rd)
Maitland (cnr New England Hwy & High St)
Nelson Bay (Port Stephens Visitor Information Centre, Victoria Pde)
Newcastle (Wheeler Place, 363 Hunter St)
Toukley (Central Coast Tourism, Rotary Park, Terrigal Dr., Terrigal)

MAITLAND

NEW ENGLAND HWY

17 10

Beresfield

15

Shortland Wetlands

STOCKTON

Newcastle Harbour

NEWCASTLE

OCEAN

7

Lochinvar

Greta

NEW MAIN RD

NORTHERN

Wentworth Swamps

Heddon Greta

CESSNOCK RD

RENSHAW DR

JOHN RENSHAW DR

132

SYDNEY

16

Minmi

Wallsend

NEWCASTLE LINK RD

133

NEW LAMBTON

ELERMORE VALE

MEREWETHER

GLENROCK STATE RECREATION AREA

128

124

For more detail on Newcastle see page 96

8

TO SINGLETON

North Rothbury

82

18

CESSNOCK STATE FOREST

Kurri Kurri

Weston

Abermain

Neath

LANG ST

MULBRIDGE ST

GEORGE BOOTH DR

Pelaw Main

Richmond Vale Mining Museum

35

Seahampton

Cardiff

CARDIFF

West Wallsend

Boolaroo

WARNERS BAY

CHARLESTOWN

REDHEAD

TASMAN

123

THE GREAT NORTH WALK: Take a day or weekend walk along this spectacular 250-km trail linking Sydney and Newcastle. Numerous lookouts provide a chance to rest and view this magnificent region.

ALLANDALE RD

Lovedale

Cessnock

Kearsley

Aberdare

ABERDARE RD

Abernethy

Kitchener

Mount Vincent

Mulbring

HEATON STATE FOREST

ABERDARE STATE FOREST

Killingworth

TORONTO RD

Warners Bay

Croudace Bay

131

BELMONT

29

BLACKSMITHS

Belmont Bay

Killaben Bay

SEA

9

Pokolbin

Bellbird

Brunkerville

Maclean's Lookout

AWABA RD

Awaba

AWABA STATE FOREST

Toronto

PALMERS RD

Rathmines

Dobell House

Myuna Bay

Swansea

10

POKOLBIN STATE FOREST

For more detail on the Hunter Valley see page 102

Ellalong

Freemans Waterhole

Heaton Lookout

NEWCASTLE FWY

46

MAIN RD

WANGI RD

Wangi Wangi

Silverwater

Eraring

Nords Wharf

Catherine Hill Bay

Lake Macquarie

11

Millfield

Paxton

The Great North Walk

WATAGAN MOUNTAINS NATIONAL PARK

WATAGAN STATE FOREST

WATAGAN MOUNTAINS: These timber-rich mountains were the source of quality blackbutt, she-oak, tallow wood and red cedar in the 1830s. They mark the western boundary of the Lake Macquarie Basin.

Cooranbong

Dora Creek

Bonnells Bay

Brightwaters

Windermere Park

Yarrawonga Park

Mirrabooka

Sunshine

Chain Valley Bay

Mannering Park

Lake Munmorah

MUNMORAH STATE RECREATION AREA

12

WOLLOMBI RD

31

POKOLBIN STATE FOREST

CORRABARE STATE FOREST

Flat Rock Lookout

Martinsville

Avondale

Morisset

Wyee Point

Mannering Lake

Colongra Lake

BUDGEWOI

13

Wollombi Historic Village

Mt. Warrawolong 640m

OLNEY STATE FOREST

Wishing Well

Muirs Lookout

Mandalong

Wyee

Doyalson

TOUKLEY

TO WYONG

GOROKAN

NORAVILLE

NORAH HEAD

Budgewoi Lake

SOUTH PACIFIC OCEAN

TASMAN SEA

A B C D E F G H I

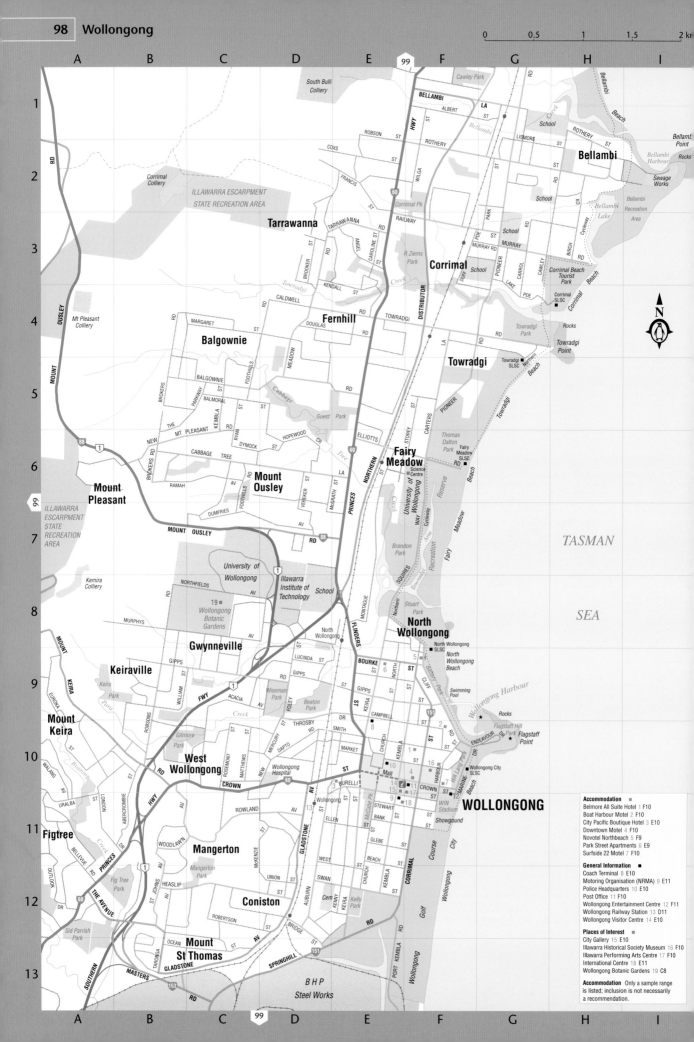

0   0.5   1   1.5   2 km

N

Accommodation ▦
Belmore All Suite Hotel 1 F10
Boat Harbour Motel 2 F10
City Pacific Boutique Hotel 3 E10
Downtown Motel 4 F10
Novotel Northbeach 5 F9
Park Street Apartments 6 E9
Surfside 22 Motel 7 F10

General Information ▣
Coach Terminal 8 E10
Motoring Organisation (NRMA) 9 E11
Police Headquarters 10 E10
Post Office 11 F10
Wollongong Entertainment Centre 12 F11
Wollongong Railway Station 13 D11
Wollongong Visitor Centre 14 E10

Places of Interest ▣
City Gallery 15 E10
Illawarra Historical Society Museum 16 F10
Illawarra Performing Arts Centre 17 F10
International Centre 18 E11
Wollongong Botanic Gardens 19 C8

Accommodation Only a sample range
is listed; inclusion is not necessarily
a recommendation.

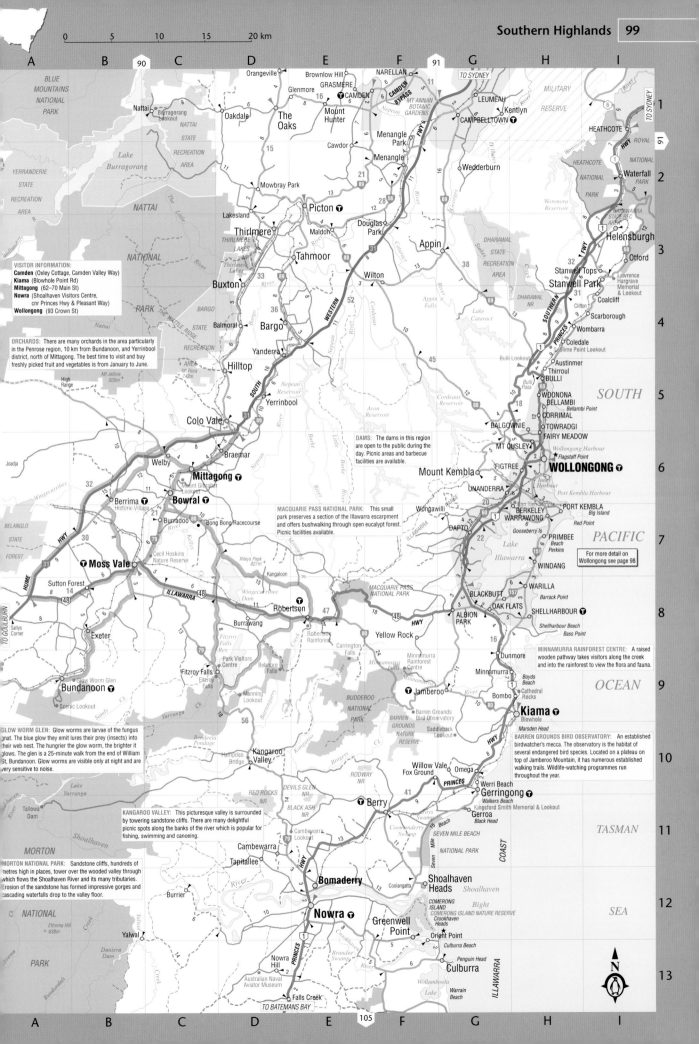

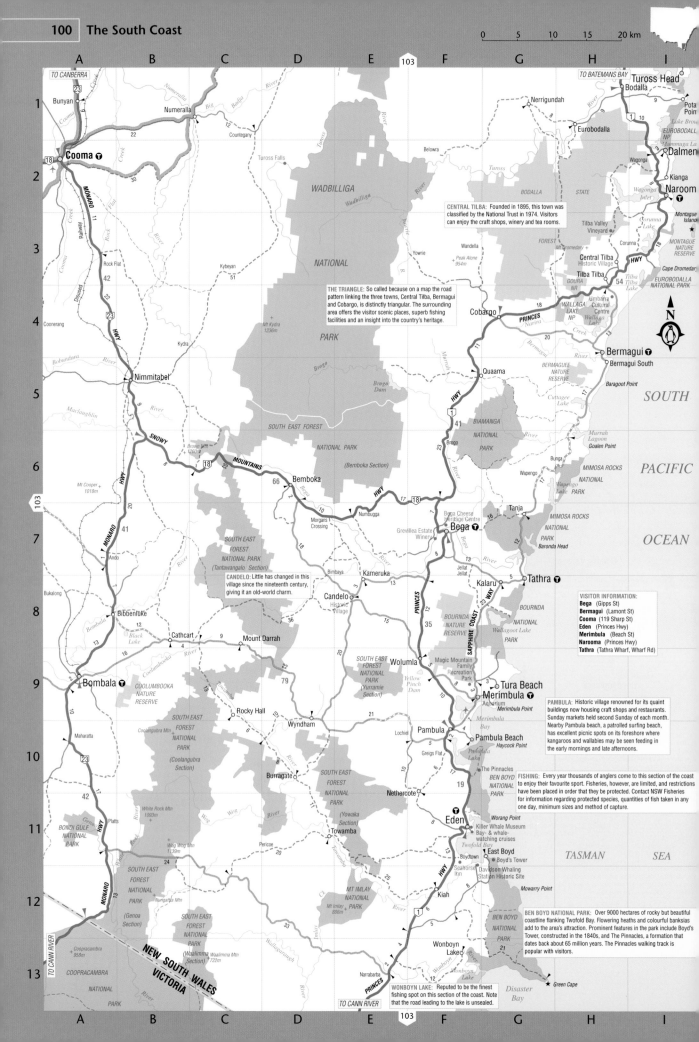

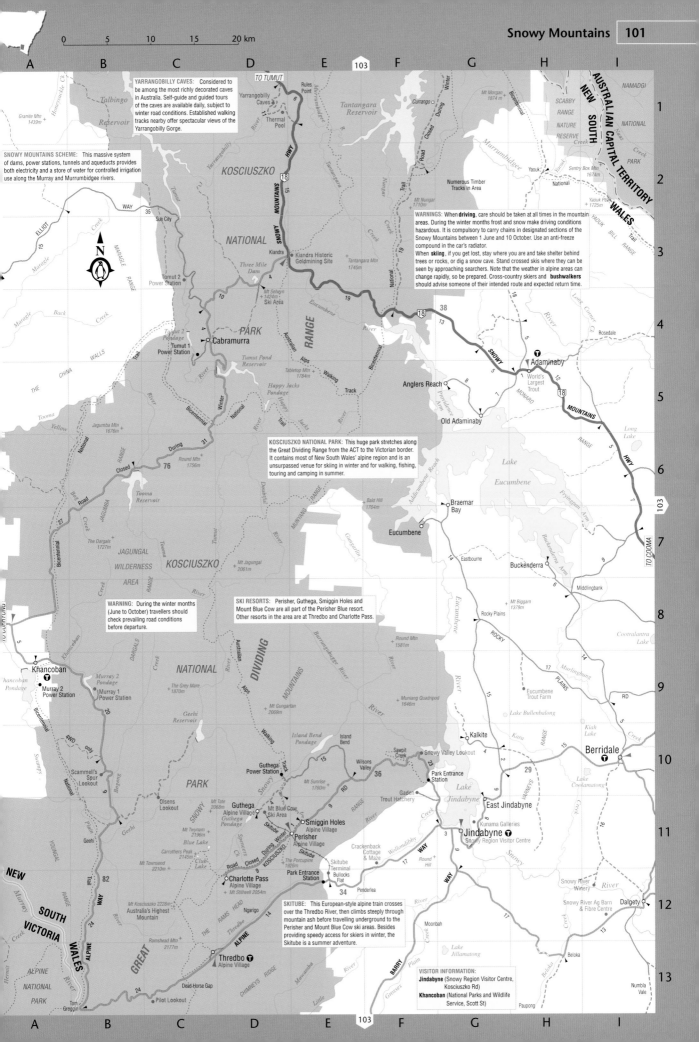

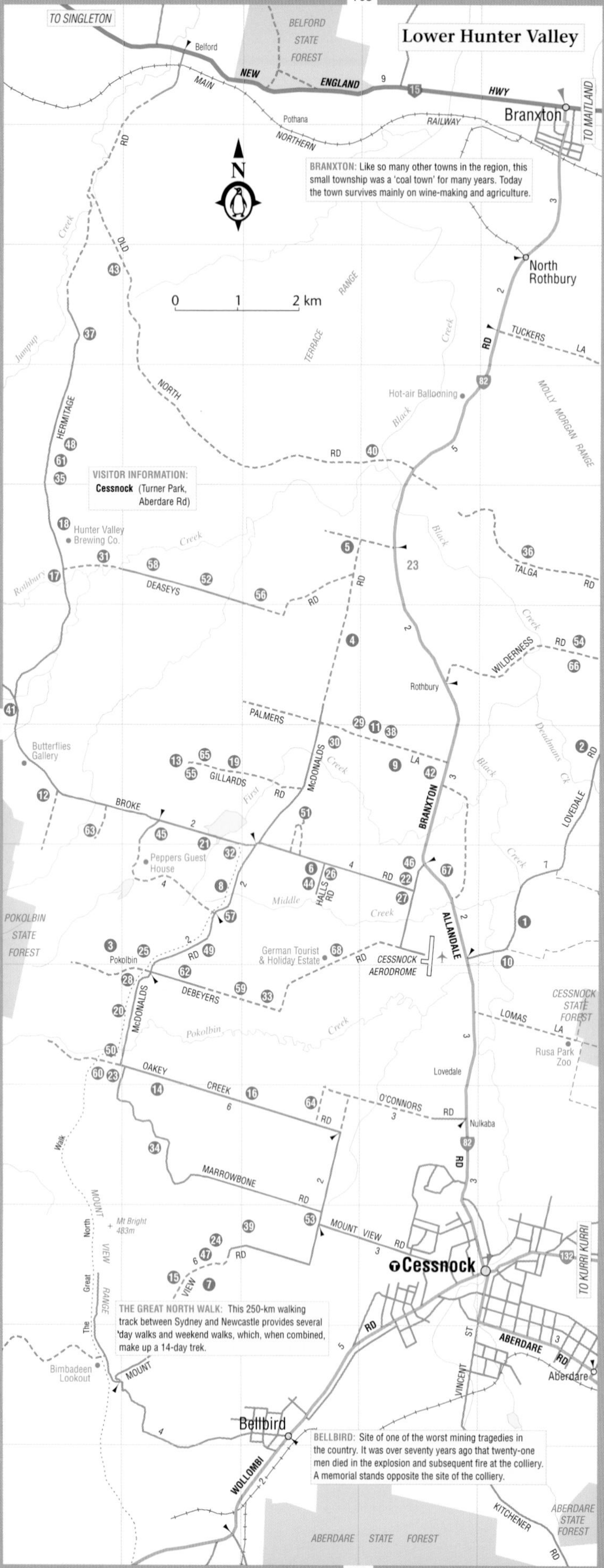

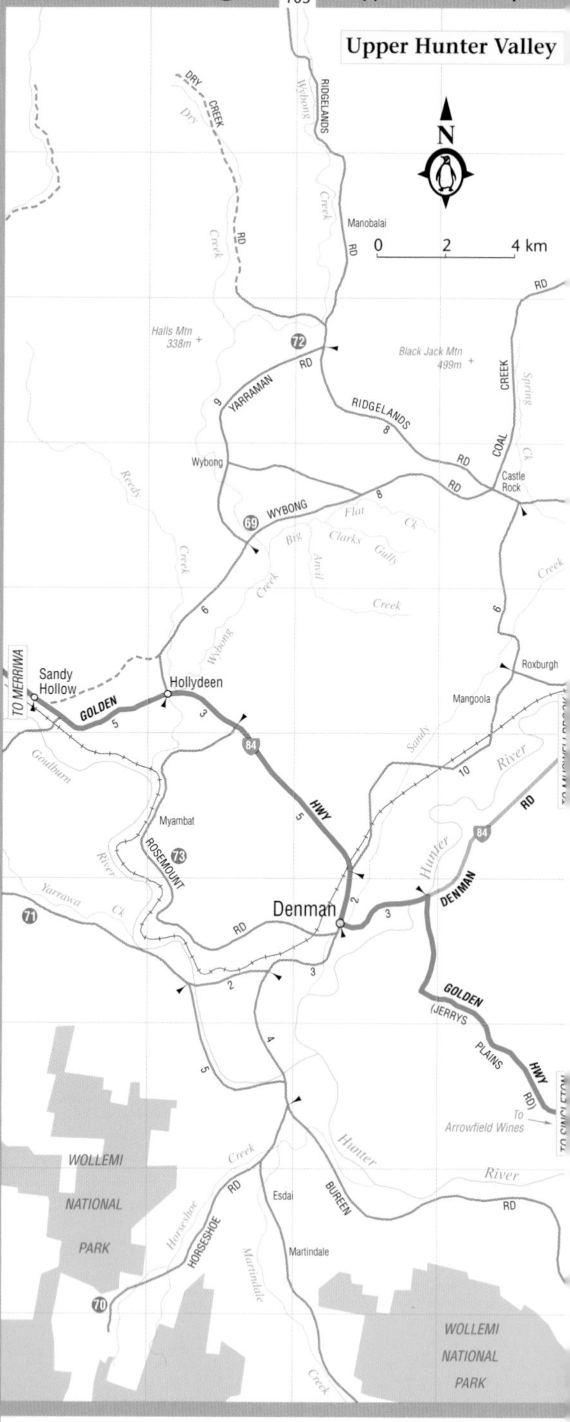

Lower Hunter Valley
TO SINGLETON
Belford
BELFORD STATE FOREST
NEW ENGLAND HWY
MAIN NORTHERN RAILWAY
Pothana
Branxton
TO MAITLAND
BRANXTON: Like so many other towns in the region, this small township was a 'coal town' for many years. Today the town survives mainly on wine-making and agriculture.
North Rothbury
TUCKERS LA
Hot-air Ballooning
MOLLY MORGAN RANGE
VISITOR INFORMATION:
Cessnock (Turner Park, Aberdare Rd)
Hunter Valley Brewing Co.
DEASEYS RD
TALGA RD
WILDERNESS RD
Rothbury
PALMERS LA
Butterflies Gallery
GILLARDS RD
McDONALDS RD
BRANXTON
BROKE RD
Peppers Guest House
HALLS RD
ALLANDALE
LOVEDALE
POKOLBIN STATE FOREST
Pokolbin
German Tourist & Holiday Estate
CESSNOCK AERODROME
DEBEYERS RD
LOMAS LA
CESSNOCK STATE FOREST
Rusa Park Zoo
OAKEY CREEK
Lovedale
O'CONNORS RD
Nulkaba
MARROWBONE RD
MOUNT VIEW RD
Mt Bright 483m
MOUNT VIEW RANGE
The Great North Walk
Cessnock
TO KURRI KURRI
THE GREAT NORTH WALK: This 250-km walking track between Sydney and Newcastle provides several day walks and weekend walks, which, when combined, make up a 14-day trek.
Bimbadeen Lookout
ABERDARE RD
Aberdare
VINCENT ST
Bellbird
BELLBIRD: Site of one of the worst mining tragedies in the country. It was over seventy years ago that twenty-one men died in the explosion and subsequent fire at the colliery. A memorial stands opposite the site of the colliery.
WOLLOMBI RD
KITCHENER RD
ABERDARE STATE FOREST
0 1 2 km

Upper Hunter Valley
DRY CREEK RD
RIDGELANDS RD
Manobalai
0 2 4 km
Halls Mtn 338m
Black Jack Mtn 499m
YARRAMAN RD
COAL CREEK RD
Wybong
WYBONG
Castle Rock
Roxburgh
Mangoola
TO MERRIWA
Sandy Hollow
GOLDEN
Hollydeen
HWY
Myambat
ROSEMOUNT
Denman
DENMAN
GOLDEN (JERRYS PLAINS RD) HWY
To Arrowfield Wines
WOLLEMI NATIONAL PARK
HORSESHOE RD
Esdai
BUREEN RD
Martindale
Hunter River

WINERIES: ❶

LOWER HUNTER VALLEY

Allandale Winery 1 E8
Allanmere Wines 2 E7
Audrey Wilkinson Vineyard 3 A8
Bimbadgen Estate Winery 4 C6
Blueberry Vineyard 5 C5
The Boutique Wine Centre 6 C8
Briar Ridge Vineyard 7 B11
Brokenwood 8 B8
Calais Estate 9 D7
Capercaillie Wine Co. 10 E8
Carindale Wines 11 D7
Chateau Francois 12 A7
Constable & Hershon Vineyards 13 B7
Drayton's Family Wines 14 B10
Farrell's Limestone Ck Vineyard 15 B11
Golden Grape Estate 16 C10
Hardys Hunter Ridge 17 A5
Hermitage Rd Cellars & Winery 18 A5
Honeytree Estate Wines 19 B7
Hungerford Hill Wines 20 A9
Hunter Cellars 21 B7
Hunter Valley Wine Society 22 D8
Ivanhoe Wines 23 A9
Jackson's Hill Vineyard 24 B11
JYT Wine Co. 25 B8
Kevin Sobels Wines 26 C8
Lake's Folly Vineyard 27 D8
Lindemans Ben Ean 28 B9
Little's Winery 29 C6
Maling Family Estate 30 C7
Marsh Estate 31 A5
McGuigan Cellars 32 B8
McLeish Estate 33 C9
McWilliam's Mount Pleasant Estate 34 B10
Mistletoe Wines 35 A4
Molly Morgan Vineyard 36 E5
Montagne View Estate 37 A3
Moorebank Vineyard 38 D7
Mount View Estate 39 C11
Murray Robson Winery 40 D4
Oakvale Winery 41 A6
Peacock Hill Vineyard 42 D7
Pendarves Estate 43 A3
Pepper Tree Wines 44 C8
Peppers Creek Winery 45 B7
Petersons House 46 D8
Petersons Wines 47 B11
Piggs Peake Winery 48 A4
Pokolbin Estate Vineyard 49 B8
Reg Drayton Wines 50 A9
Rothbury Estate 51 C7
Rothvale Wines 52 B5
Saddler's Creek Wines 53 C11
Sandalyn Estate 54 E6
Scarborough Wine Co. 55 B7
Sutherland Wines 56 C5
Tamburlaine Wines 57 B8
Terrace Vale Wines 58 B5
Thalgara Estate 59 B9
Tinkler's Vineyard 60 A9
Tintilla Vineyard 61 A4
Tulloch Wines 62 B9
Tyrrell's Wines 63 A7
Van De Scheur Wines 64 C10
Vinden Estate Wines 65 B7
Warrarong Estate 66 E6
Wilderness Estate Wines 67 D8
Windarra Winery 68 C8

UPPER HUNTER VALLEY

Cruikshank Callatoota Estate 69 G4
Horseshoe Vineyard 70 F9
James Estate 71 F7
Reynold's Yarraman 72 H3
Rosemount Estate 73 G6

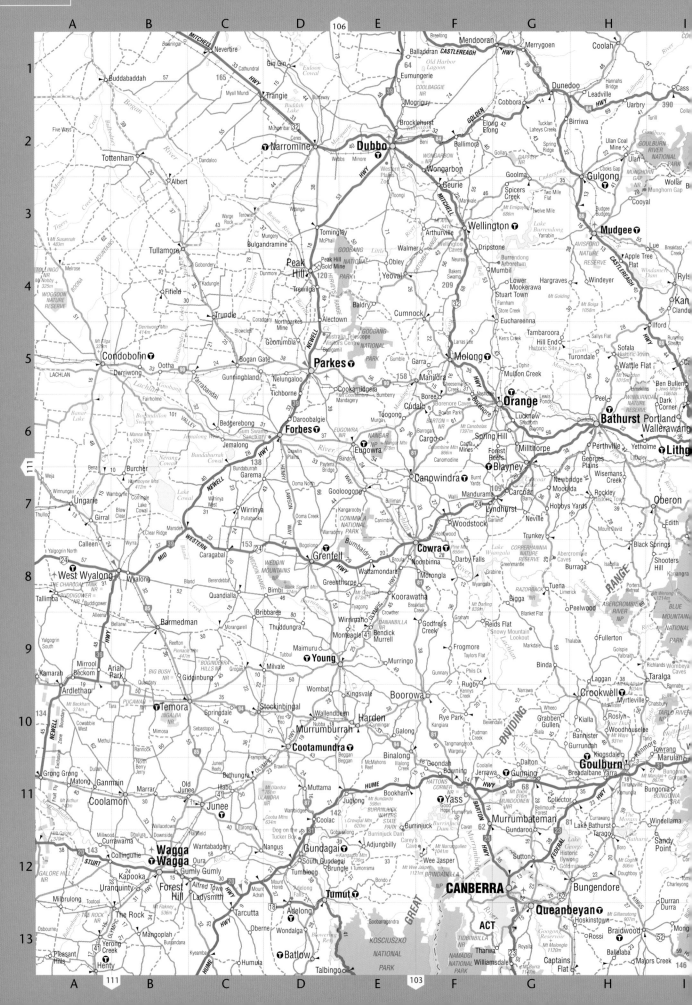

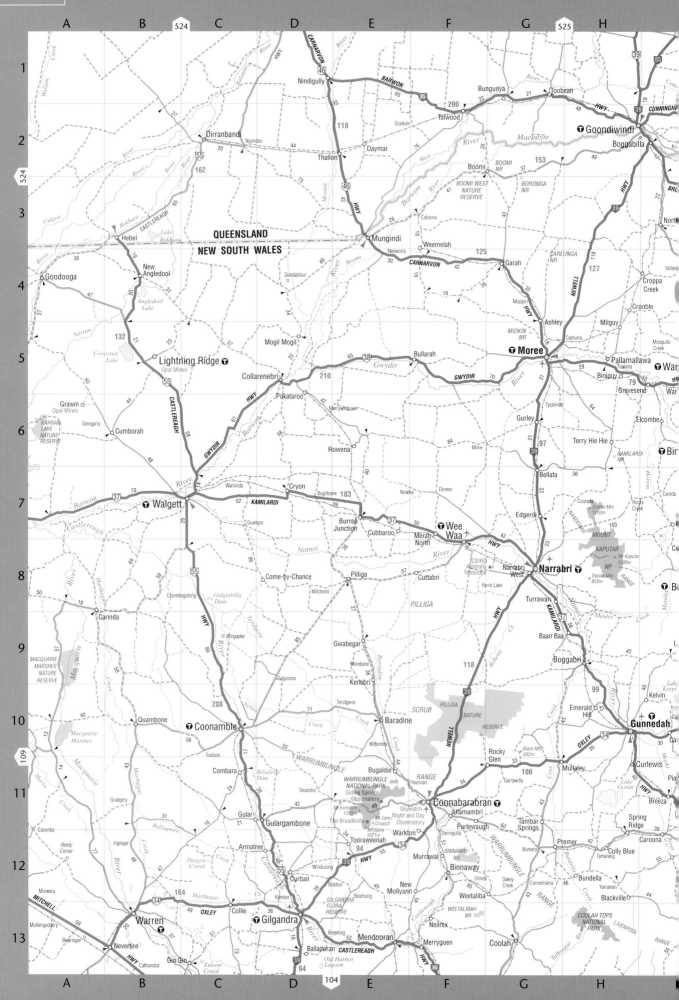

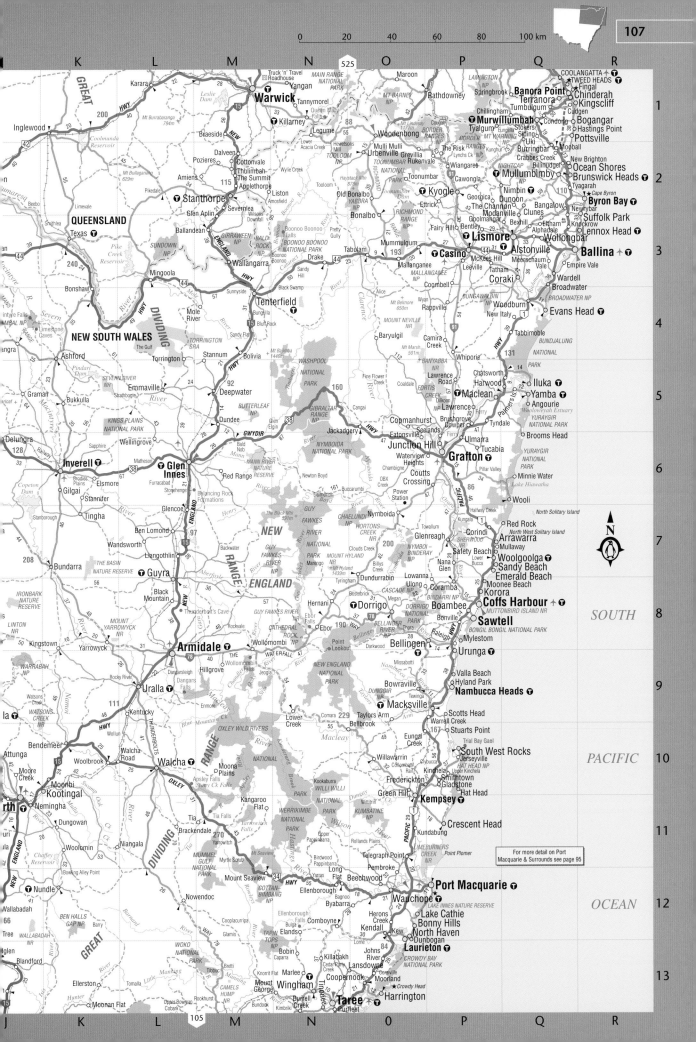

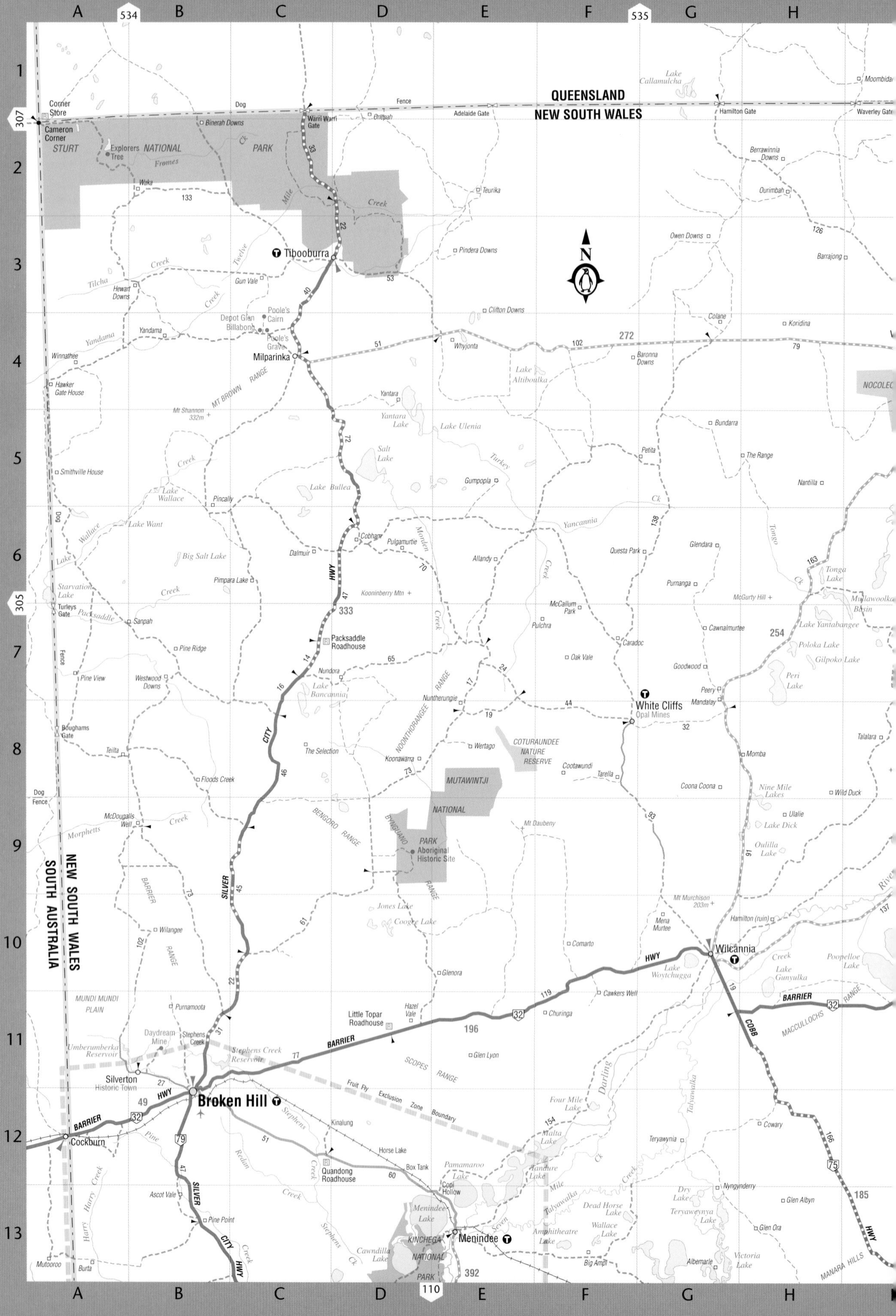

534   535

QUEENSLAND
NEW SOUTH WALES

307

305

N

Corner Store
Cameron Corner
STURT
Explorers Tree
NATIONAL PARK
Frome's
Binerah Downs
Dog
Fence
Warri Warri Gate
Olepah
Adelaide Gate
Hamilton Gate
Waverley Gate
Lake Callamulcha
Moombidary
Berrawinnia Downs
Ourimbah
Owen Downs
Barrajong
126

Woka
133
Teurika
Pindera Downs

Tibooburra
Gun Vale
Twelve
Mile
Creek
53
Clifton Downs
Colane
Koridina

Tilcha
Hewart Downs
Poole's Cairn
Depot Glen Billabong
Poole's Grave
Milparinka
Whyjonta
Lake Altiboulka
51
102
272
79
Baronna Downs
NOCOLEC

Winnathee
Hawker Gate House
Mt Brown
Mt Shannon 332m
MT BROWN RANGE
Yantara
Yantara Lake
Lake Ulenia
Turkey
Bundarra
Petita
The Range
Nantilla

Smithville House
Lake Wallace
Pincally
Lake Bullea
Salt Lake
Gumpopla
Yancannia
Glendara
138
Tonga
163
Tonga Lake
Mullawoolka Basin

Dog
Lake
Big Salt Lake
Creek
Dalmuir
Cobham
Pulgamurtie
Morden
Allandy
Questa Park
Purnanga
McGurty Hill
254
Lake Yantabangee
Poloka Lake
Gilpoko Lake
Peri Lake

Starvation Lake
Turleys Gate
Packsaddle
Sanpah
Pimpara Lake
HWY
47
333
Kooninberry Mtn
70
McCallum Park
Pulchra
Caradoc
Cawnalmurtee
Glendara

Pine Ridge
Packsaddle Roadhouse
65
Oak Vale
24
Goodwood
Peery

Boughams Gate
Pine View
Fence
Teilta
14
16
Nundora
Lake Bancannia
Nuntherungie
NOONTHORANGEE RANGE
17
19
44
White Cliffs
Opal Mines
32
Mandalay
Talalara
Momba

CITY
46
The Selection
Koonawarra
Wertago
73
COTURAUNDEE NATURE RESERVE
Cootawundi
Tarella
Coona Coona
Nine Mile Lakes
Ulalie
Lake Dick
Wild Duck

McDougalls Well
Floods Creek
BENGORO RANGE
MUTAWINTJI
NATIONAL
Mt Daubeny
93
Oulilla Lake
91

Morphetts
Dog Fence
SILVER
45
BYNGUANO RANGE
PARK
Aboriginal Historic Site
Hamilton (ruin)
Mt Murchison 203m
River
137

SOUTH AUSTRALIA
NEW SOUTH WALES
BARRIER RANGE
73
61
Jones Lake
Coogee Lake
Glenora
Comarto
Mena Murtee
Wilcannia
HWY
Lake Woytchugga
Creek
Lake Gunyulka
Poopelloe Lake

MUNDI MUNDI PLAIN
Purnamoota
22
31
Little Topar Roadhouse
Hazel Vale
119
Cawkers Well
Churinga
19
BARRIER
COBB
32
MACCULLOCHS RANGE

Umberumberka Reservoir
Daydream Mine
Stephens Creek
Stephens Creek Reservoir
77
BARRIER
196
32
Glen Lyon
SCOPES RANGE
Four Mile Lake
166

Silverton Historic Town
27
HWY
49
Broken Hill
Kinalung
Fruit Fly Exclusion Zone Boundary
Malta Lake
154
Teryawynia
Cowary
75
185

Cockburn
BARRIER
32
79
Pine
Redan
Horse Lake
Box Tank
60
Quandong Roadhouse
Copi Hollow
Pamamaroo Lake
Tandure Lake
Dry Lake
Dead Horse Lake
Nyngynderry
Glen Albyn

47
SILVER
Ascot Vale
Pine Point
Kinchega
Menindee
Cawndilla Lake
NATIONAL PARK
392
Amphitheatre Lake
Big Ampi
Teryaweynya Lake
Wallace Lake
Albemarle
Victoria Lake
Glen Ora
MANARA HILLS

Mutooroo
Burta
CITY HWY
110

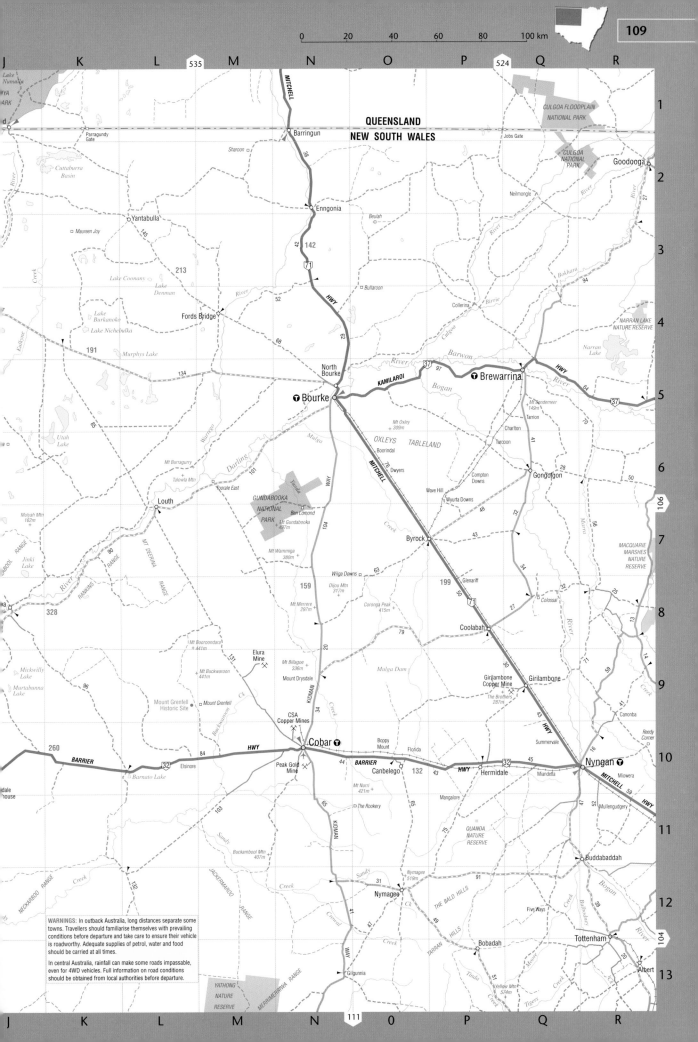

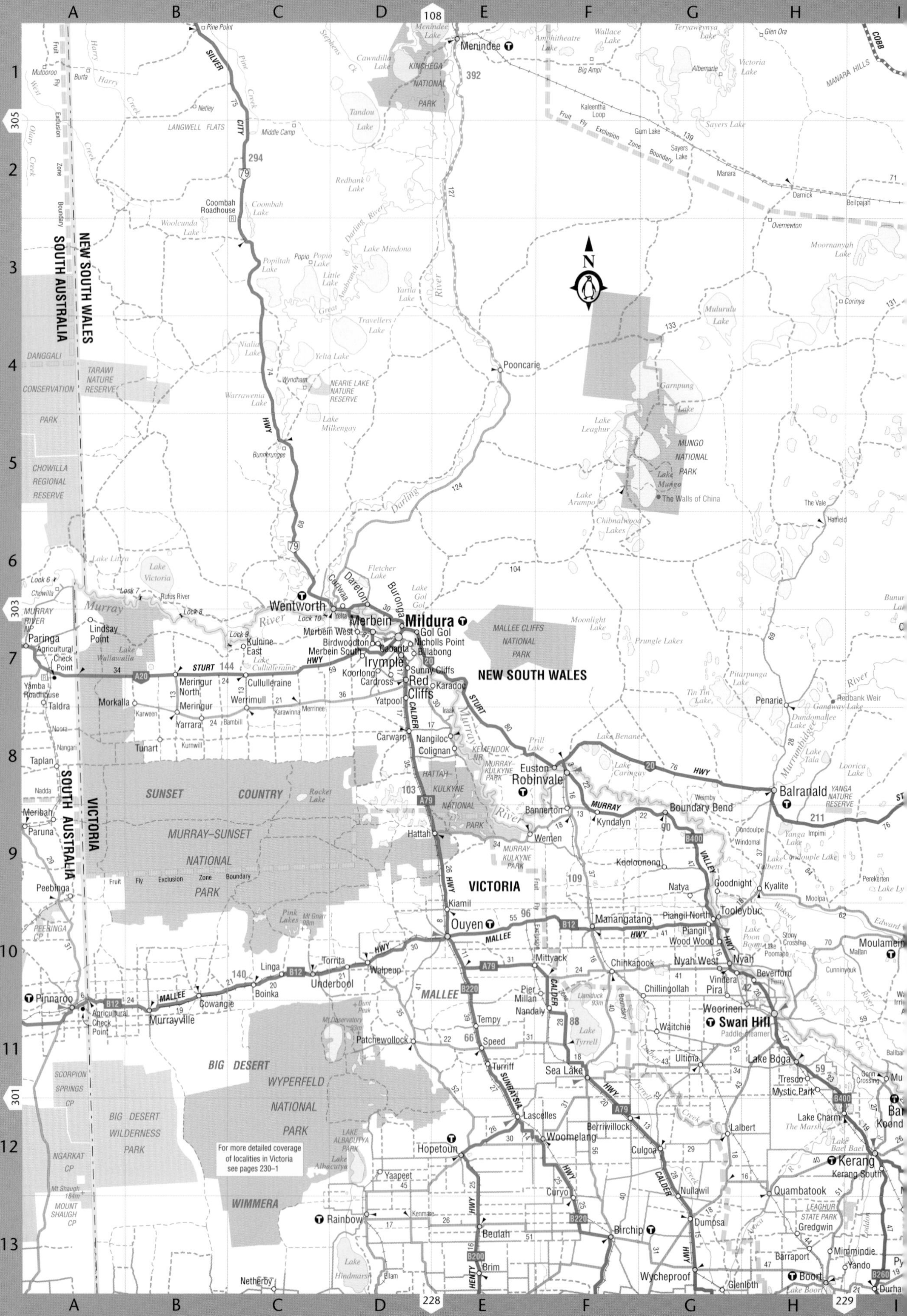

A B C D E F G H I

1 2 3 4 5 6 7 8 9 10 11 12 13

108
305
303
301

228 229

Pine Point
SILVER CITY
Menindee
Menindee Lake
KINCHEGA NATIONAL PARK
392
Amphitheatre Lake
Wallace Lake
Big Ampi
Albemarle
Victoria Lake
Glen Ora
MANARA HILLS
COBB

Mutooroo
Burta
Fruit
Fly
Harry
West
Olary Creek
Exclusion Zone
Boundary
SOUTH AUSTRALIA
NEW SOUTH WALES

Netley
Harry
Creek
75
Pine Creek
79
294
Middle Camp
LANGWELL FLATS
Coombah Roadhouse
Woolcunda Lake
Coombah Lake

Stephens Ck
Cawndilla Lake
Tandou Lake
Redbank Lake
Darling River
127
Kaleentha Loop
Fruit Fly Exclusion Zone Boundary
Gum Lake
139
Savers Lake
Sayers Lake
Manara
Teryaweynya Lake
Moornanyah Lake
Darnick
Beilpajah
71

Popiah Lake
Popio Lake
Little Lake
Great Anabranch
Yartla Lake
Lake Mindona
Mulurulu Lake
Corinya
131

DANGGALI CONSERVATION PARK
TARAWI NATURE RESERVE
Nialia Lake
Wyndham
74
Yelta Lake
Warrawenia Lake
NEARIE LAKE NATURE RESERVE
Lake Milkengay
Pooncarie
Garnpung Lake
Lake Leaghur
Lake Mungo
MUNGO NATIONAL PARK

CHOWILLA REGIONAL RESERVE
68
124
Bunnerungee
Lake Arumpo
The Walls of China
Chibnalwood Lakes
Moonlight Lake
The Vale
Hatfield

Lake Littra
Lake Victoria
Fletcher Lake
Darling River
Lake Gol Gol
104
Prungle Lakes

Lock 6
Chowilla
Lock 7
Rufus River
Lock 8
Murray River NP
Murray River
Wentworth
Lock 10
Curlwaa
Dareton
30
Buronga
MALLEE CLIFFS NATIONAL PARK
Penarie
Redbank Weir
Dundomalee Lake
Ganawulla Lake

Paringa
Lindsay Point
Lock 9
Lake Wallawalla
Kulnine East
Merbein West
Merbein
Merbein South
Birdwoodton
Gol Gol
Nicholls Point
Billabong
Mildura
NEW SOUTH WALES
Tin Tin Lake
Pitarpunga Lake

Agricultural Check Point
Yamba Roadhouse
34
Taldra
A20
STURT 144
Meringur North
Cullulleraine
Koorlong
Cardross
Irymple
Sunny Cliffs
Karadoc
Red Cliffs
Murrumbidgee
Loorica Lake
Lake Tala
211

Noora
Nangari
Morkalla
Karween
Werrimull
21
Merrinee
Yatpool
CALDER
17
Iraak
80
STURT
KEMENDOK NR
Lake Benanee
ST

Meribah
Paruna
Meringur
Yarrara
Kurnwill
Tunart
36
Carwarp
Nangiloc
Colignan
HATTAH-KULKYNE PARK
Euston
Robinvale
20
76
HWY
Balranald
YANGA NATURE RESERVE

SUNSET COUNTRY
Rocket Lake
MURRAY-SUNSET NATIONAL PARK
103
A79
HATTAH-KULKYNE NATIONAL PARK
Bannerton
Kyndalyn
MURRAY
Boundary Bend
B400
VALLEY
Ondoulpe
Windomal
Yanga Lake

Peebinga
Fruit Fly Exclusion Zone Boundary
Pink Lakes
Mt Gnarr
Hattah
34
MURRAY-KULKYNE PARK
VICTORIA
109
Wemen
Kooloonong
90
Natya
Goodnight
Kyalite
Perekerten

Meribah
Paruna
29
Kiamil
8
Ouyen
MALLEE
55
96
Manangatang
Piangil North
Piangil
Wood Wood
Tooleybuc
62
Moolpa
Moulamein

Pinnaroo
B12
MALLEE
Gowangie
Linga
140
Torrita
Walpeup
30
HWY
11
Mittyack
16
Chinkapook
Nyah West
Nyah
Beverford
Cunninyuk

Murrayville
Boinka
Underbool
B12
20
B220
Pier Millan
CALDER
24
Chillingollah
41
Vinifera
Pira
Woorinen
Matlan

BIG DESERT
Mt Observatory
Dunt Peak
Tempy
39
Nandaly
Lunduck
88
Lake Tyrrell
Waitchie
Ultima
Swan Hill
Paddle-steamer
Lake Boga
Tresco
59
Mu

SCORPION SPRINGS CP
Patchewollock
22
66
Speed
31
Sea Lake
SUNRAYSIA
18
HWY
Lalbert
Mystic Park
B400
Ba

WYPERFELD NATIONAL PARK
BIG DESERT WILDERNESS PARK
Lake Albacutya
Lake Albacutya Park
Lascelles
26
30
Woomelang
Berriwillock
A79
Culgoa
29
Lake Charm
The Marsh
Kerang
Kerang South

NGARKAT CP
Mt Shaugh
MOUNT SHAUGH CP
WIMMERA
For more detailed coverage of localities in Victoria see pages 230-1
Hopetoun
Yaapeet
45
Curyo
25
Nullawil
18
Quambatook
LEAGHUR STATE PARK
Gredgwin

Rainbow
17
Netherby
Kenmare
26
Beulah
51
Birchip
Dumosa
Wycheproof
HENTY
B200
B220
CALDER
Glenloth
Barrapon
Mimmindie
Yando
Boort
Durha
B260

AUSTRALIAN CAPITAL TERRITORY

The Australian Capital Territory, occupying 2400 square kilometres, lies in the valley of the Molonglo River and at the foothills of the Great Dividing Range. The capital city Canberra and its suburbs take up approximately a quarter of the Territory; Namadgi National Park protects the bush and mountain landscape of the remaining area.

From sheep station to seat of government

The ACT was formed through a series of political acts rather than as a process of natural expansion. The Commonwealth Constitution Act of 1901, which united the six colonies within the Commonwealth of Australia, required that there be a seat of Federal Government. Over the next nine years, two Royal Commissions and various parliamentary committees considered the claims of established towns and cities to become the new capital. They finally decided on a new site – sheep station land at Limestone Plains – a few miles west of Queanbeyan.

Meeting place

The site of the future capital was first occupied by two groups of Aboriginal people, the Ngunnawal and the Ngario. The large campsites found along the banks of the Molonglo indicate a substantial Aboriginal population in the area. In summer, the tribes left the hot plains of the region for the high country to the west, to feast on bogong moths.

In 1820 Charles Throsby Smith was the first European to explore the area. Four years later, Joshua Moore took up 1000 acres (400 hectares) on the banks of the Molonglo River, a tributary of the Murrumbidgee River. He named his property Canberry, an Aboriginal word meaning 'meeting place'. Another early European settler was Robert Campbell, who in 1825 also acquired land on the Molonglo. His family became the district's most prominent clan in the years before the site was chosen for the capital.

A capital plan

In 1912 Walter Burley Griffin and Marion Mahony Griffin, American architects from Chicago, won an international competition for the design of the capital city. Their geometrical design, inspired by the plan of Washington DC, was based on a triangle. The plan incorporated vistas: boulevards lined with trees and monumental buildings; spacious parks; and residential and commercial areas extending to the hills beyond. Canberra to this day is one of only a few completely planned cities in the world.

Growth was slow in the capital in the 1930s and 1940s. Many Federal Government departments and their public servants remained in Melbourne or Sydney. By the 1950s the population had struggled to reach 25 000. But after the filling of Lake Burley Griffin in 1965, grand buildings were constructed along its shore: the National Library (1968), the High Court (1980), the National Gallery (1982) and the new Parliament House (1988). The Australian National University was expanded and parklands matured. Office blocks appeared and government departments and their personnel transferred – often reluctantly – to the new capital. All these developments have gradually completed the mosaic of Walter and Marion Griffin's extraordinary design.

Today the residents of the ACT enjoy the highest standard of living of any Australian State or Territory. As well as a gracious environment, Canberra offers amenities and facilities far beyond those of any other similar-sized city in the world.

For more information on the Australian Capital Territory, see Tourist Bureaus on p. 591.

Canberra in autumn

CANBERRA

Canberra is awash with colour during Floriade

CANBERRA, capital of Australia and seat of Federal Government, is a model metropolis. Planned for spaciousness and style, its unique concentric circular streets are set graciously on the shores of Lake Burley Griffin and surrounded by rolling hills.

VISITOR INFORMATION
Canberra Visitors Centre
Northbourne Ave, Dickson
(02) 6205 0044
www.canberratourism.com.au
Jolimont Centre
Northbourne Ave, City
(for brochures)
Canberra Getaways
1800 100 660
(for bookings)

The cultural as well as the political life of the country is on show in Canberra. This small city, with a population of only 310 521, claims some of the nation's most significant institutions, including a magnificent art gallery and one of the best war museums in the world. Grand public buildings and monuments, many architecturally renowned, complement the order and beauty of the city's original design.

Many visitors come to see the national collections or to see federal politics in action, but Canberra has much more to offer. It has superb parklands and thousands of hectares of natural bushland to explore, cool-climate wineries and top class restaurants, a full calendar of cultural and sporting events, and excellent attractions for children.

EXPLORING CANBERRA

Canberra is a city with a very high rate of car usage and it is easy to see why: wide, traffic-free roads serve single-system public transport (bus only) that can be variable at off-peak times. For a convenient way to get around the main attractions, catch a double-decker City Sightseeing bus departing from the Melbourne Building. The road infrastructure in Canberra is probably the best in Australia and visitors will find that they can cover long distances in a short time. Clean air, wide streets and plenty of parkland make Canberra a great place to explore by foot or bicycle. A boat cruise of Lake Burley Griffin is an essential visitor experience; tours depart from the Royal Canberra Yacht Club at Lotus Bay.

PARLIAMENTARY TRIANGLE AND BEYOND

The Parliamentary Triangle incorporates Canberra's important buildings, dotted around Lake Burley Griffin. The triangle's apex is Capital Hill, with Commonwealth and Kings avenues as the side perimeters, and Constitution Avenue as the base. The grandest boulevard in Australia, Anzac Parade, crosses Constitution Avenue at right angles.

A good starting point for exploring Canberra is the **National Capital Exhibition** on Barrine Drive, at Regatta Point on the north side of the lake. Here you can see exhibits on the history and development of the city, and look out across the lake at the parliamentary precinct. From here, cross Commonwealth Avenue Bridge and on the left is the **Captain Cook Memorial Water Jet**.

Directly ahead lies **Parliament House**, Australia's most expensive building and Canberra's centrepiece. Designed by the American-based company Mitchell, Giurgola and Thorpe (who won an international competition from 329 entries), the building was completed in 1988, at a cost of $1.1 billion. It has 4500 rooms including a series of public places that reflect the major themes of Australian life. There are more than 3000 artworks, some of which are displayed in the

public spaces. Take a free tour of the building or schedule your visit to coincide with a sitting of either of the two Houses of Parliament, the Senate or the House of Representatives, and watch from the public galleries.

In front of the new Parliament House lies **Old Parliament House** (a couple of minutes' drive along King George Terrace or a quick walk along Federation Mall). Designed in 1927 by John Smith Murdoch, it was intended only as the provisional home for the parliament, but served this purpose for some 60 years. Now it offers a fascinating recollection of the events and intrigues of Australian political life. Tours are available and a special feature is the sound and light show, *Order! Order!* in the old House of Representatives chamber. In addition, its restored public spaces with their superb Art Deco detail now house the National Portrait Gallery, where changing exhibitions acquaint visitors with the people of Australia's history. Around the building

GETTING AROUND

Motoring organisation
National Roads and Motoring Association (NRMA) 13 2132

Car rental
Avis 13 6333; Budget (02) 6257 1305;
Capital Car Rentals (02) 6282 7272;
Hertz 13 3039; Thrifty 1300 367 227;
Rumbles (02) 6280 7444

Public transport
ACTION Buses 13 1710

Lake cruises
Canberra Steam Boat Cruises 0149 418 846;
Lakeside Boat Hiring and Charters 0408 828 357;
Southern Cross Cruises (02) 6273 1784

Bicycle hire
Mr Spokes Bike Hire (02) 6257 1188
(near Acton Ferry Terminal)

Taxis
Canberra Cabs 13 2227

CLIMATE CANBERRA

	J	F	M	A	M	J	J	A	S	O	N	D
Max. °C	28	27	24	20	15	12	11	12	16	19	23	26
Min. °C	13	13	11	7	3	1	0	1	3	6	9	11
Rain (mm)	58	56	53	49	49	37	40	48	52	68	62	53
Raindays	8	7	7	8	9	9	10	11	10	11	10	8

CANBERRA BY AREA

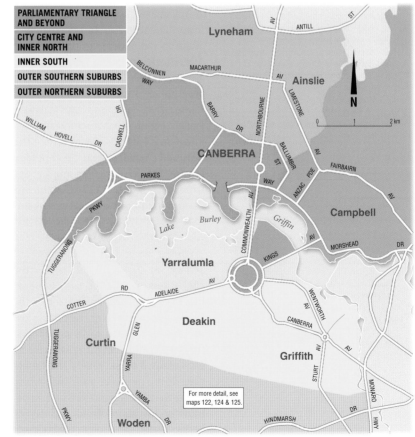

PARLIAMENTARY TRIANGLE AND BEYOND
CITY CENTRE AND INNER NORTH
INNER SOUTH
OUTER SOUTHERN SUBURBS
OUTER NORTHERN SUBURBS

For more detail, see maps 122, 124 & 125.

Calthorpes' House

RESTAURANTS AND CAFES

*For a small city, Canberra has a large number of restaurants of very high quality. The main eating districts are **Dickson, Kingston, Manuka** and the **city centre**, but many of the small shopping centres in the inner-city suburbs have at least one or two eateries apiece. Special mentions go to **Juniperberry Restaurant** (lunch in the Sculpture Garden at the National Gallery of Australia), **A Foreign Affair** (brilliant Italian cooking in Manuka), **The Atlantic** (modern Australian in Manuka), **The Chairman and Yip** (modern Asian in the city centre), and **Artespresso** (modern Australian in Kingston). Capital Taste, by Mary Brander, is published by Wakefield Press and provides a comprehensive overview of everything to do with food in Canberra.*

ENTERTAINMENT

*Pick up a copy of the Canberra Times on Thursday for its lift-out entertainment guide 'Times Out'. There is usually a good selection of live music around town, ranging from rock concerts at the **ANU Union** to a spot of mellow jazz or soul at **Tilley's Devine** in Lyneham. The main theatre venue is the **Canberra Theatre Centre** in the city, with a couple of smaller venues around town such as **Gorman House Markets**, catering to more eclectic tastes. For a quiet drink try the large hotels including the **Hyatt**, housed in magnificent 1920s Art Deco surrounds. The **Casino Canberra** in Binara Street is a boutique-style casino, its elegance enhanced by the absence of poker machines.*

are the beautiful gardens of Old Parliament House, and adjacent in Queen Victoria Terrace is the **National Archives of Australia**, housed in one of Canberra's original buildings and its first GPO.

Travel north along Parkes Place West to reach the **National Library of Australia**, established in 1901. The present building – a grand neo-classical structure built in 1968 – contains some 6 million books, as well as newspapers, periodicals, films, historical documents and photographs. There is an extensive collection of Australiana, including the diaries of Captain Cook's *Endeavour* voyages, and beautiful artworks, most notably the stained-glass windows by Leonard French. A short distance south-east along King Edward Terrace is **Questacon – The National Science and Technology Centre**. This futuristic building features hands-on displays and experiments (everything from earthquakes to lightning strikes) within five galleries that wind around a circular rampway.

Further along, just off King Edward Terrace on Parkes Place East, is the **High Court of Australia**, Australia's final court of appeal and interpreter of the Constitution. The court was established in 1903 and moved to its present site in 1980. The building is notable for its glass-encased public gallery and timber courtrooms; murals by artist Jan Senberg reflect the history, functions and operations of the court. From Monday to Friday, visitors can explore the building,

drop in on a case, and talk to the knowledgeable attendants. Across the road is the **National Gallery of Australia**, established in 1911 and housed here since 1982. The national collection provides a brilliant overview of Australian art, incorporating an extensive Aboriginal collection and works from all the major Australian artists since European settlement. The overseas collection is equally impressive and includes Jackson Pollock's *Blue Poles*, a controversial purchase. One of the best gallery features is the Sculpture Garden, a series of native garden 'rooms' housing some 50 sculptures.

Cross Kings Avenue Bridge and turn left along Russell Drive (which becomes Constitution Avenue); just before Anzac Parade turn left into Wendouree Drive. Here you will find **Blundell's Cottage**, built in 1858 for Robert Campbell's ploughman. The cottage re-creates the struggle of the labouring classes in those early farming years. Retrace your steps, continuing along Constitution Avenue. After crossing Anzac Parade you will encounter more early history at **St John the Baptist Church and Schoolhouse Museum**. Both buildings date back to the 1840s; the schoolhouse serves as a museum re-creating an original classroom.

Return to Anzac Parade; at its northern end lies the **Australian War Memorial**. Opened in 1941, the War Memorial honours war victims through the Roll of Honour, with 100 000 names

The National Carillon at Lake Burley Griffin

of Australians killed in war; the Pool of Reflection; the Hall of Memory; and the Tomb of the Unknown Soldier. It is probably the world's largest war museum, with its collection of an estimated four million items including weapons, documents and paintings by some of Australia's well-known artists. It also offers the Bradbury Aircraft Hall, refurbished in 2000 to house real-life war planes; Anzac Hall where you'll find large relics like a Japanese midget submarine, artillery and tanks; the Sculpture Garden; and the Research Centre, which has on-line access for visitors to look up family history (appointments not necessary).

From here turn away from the city into Fairbairn Avenue. A couple of kilometres along on the left is Mount Ainslie Drive, which leads to **Mount Ainslie Lookout** with its superb views over the Parliamentary Triangle and beyond. Further along Fairbairn Avenue turn right into Northcott Drive, the location of **Duntroon House**. Built by Robert Campbell in 1833, with later additions in 1862, this was the first substantial house in the area and has a lovely garden with plantings dating back to the 19th century. The gardens are open to the public; tours of the house by appointment only.

CITY CENTRE AND INNER NORTH

Compared with the splendour of the Parliamentary Triangle, the centre of Canberra looks modest. Nevertheless, there are attractions around the city centre and nearby district immediately to the north of the lake. Start at **Civic Square**, site of the **Legislative Assembly of the ACT**, the seat of government for Canberra as opposed to that of the nation. The **Canberra Theatre Centre**, the **Canberra Museum and Gallery** and many of the city's private enterprise offices and legal offices are also here. Nearby is the **Canberra Centre**, the main shopping precinct for the city and site of the magnificent old St Kilda merry-go-round, and **Garema Place**, with its cafes frequented by locals.

The 145-hectare native-landscaped grounds of the **Australian National**

NOT TO BE MISSED IN CANBERRA	Map Ref.
Australian Institute of Sport Tour the complex where top athletes train	124 F7
Australian National Botanic Gardens The most comprehensive display of native Australian plants anywhere	124 F9
Australian War Memorial An outstanding monument honouring Australia's wartime efforts	122 H4
Lanyon Homestead A gracious homestead with a permanent collection of paintings by Sidney Nolan	123 E7
National Gallery of Australia An excellent collection in one of the best art spaces in Australia	122 F9
National Museum of Australia Explore the nation's history and icons at the city's newest attraction	122 B7
Old Parliament House Sound and light show and National Portrait Gallery	122 D9
Parliament House Completed in 1988 – now the city's centrepiece	122 C11
Questacon – The National Science & Technology Centre A state-of-the-art, hands-on science centre for the whole family	122 D8
Telstra Tower Lookout Superb views of Canberra and surrounds	124 F9

LAKESIDE AND RIVERSIDE RETREATS	Map Ref.
Casuarina Sands Where the Cotter and Murrumbidgee rivers meet	123 C4
Commonwealth Park Formal gardens and parkland on the lake	122 D5
Jerrabomberra Wetlands A nesting ground for waterbirds on the lake's southern shores	124 I11
Kambah Pool A beach and bushland retreat on the Murrumbidgee River	123 D5
Weston Park A peaceful woodland and lakeside recreation area	124 E10

Questacon – The National Science and Technology Centre

SHOPPING	Map Ref.
Canberra Centre, City Centre Around 150 small shops and a couple of compact department stores	122 E4
Kingston Village For old-fashioned specialty shopping	124 H11
Manuka Village For upmarket clothes, homewares and jewellery	124 G12
Manuka Plaza Supermarkets and specialty shops	124 G12
Suburban Malls Belconnen (Westfield Shopping Centre) Woden (Woden Plaza) Tuggeranong (Tuggeranong Hyperdome)	124 E6 125 C4 125 B9

MARKETS	Map Ref.
Belconnen Fresh Food Markets, Belconnen Fresh fruit and vegetables, produce, cooking demonstrations	124 D6
Fyshwick Markets, Fyshwick The city's fresh produce markets (Thurs.–Sun.)	125 H3
Gorman House Markets, Braddon Fresh food, art and craft, home-baked produce and a great upbeat atmosphere near the city centre (Sat.)	122 F3
Hall Markets, Hall Fresh produce, plants, recycled timber furniture, home-made designer clothing, non-commercial hand-made goods (1st Sun. each month, closed Jan.)	124 D2
Old Bus Depot Markets, Kingston Food, clothes, crafts and plenty of New Age therapies (Sun.)	122 G12

University hug the eastern edge of the inner city. A major attraction nearby on McCoy Circuit is **ScreenSound Australia**, dedicated to the preservation of Australia's film and sound archive – everything from *Dad and Dave* to *Dame Edna*. Housed in an Art Deco building, formerly the Institute of Anatomy, the museum and archive has regularly updated displays and a 1930s cinema running old film footage.

From here turn south down Edinburgh Avenue, right into Parkes Way and then left down Lennox Crossing to the newly constructed **National Museum of Australia**. More than twenty years in the planning, it is the new home for the Australian Institute of Aboriginal and Torres Strait Islander Studies, and contains an extraordinary collection of artifacts, tools and bark paintings. The museum also features displays, videos and gardens that document Australia's development from European settlement through to Federation and beyond.

Return to Parkes Way and travel west, turning right into Clunies Ross Street for **CSIRO Discovery** (enter at Julius Road), which showcases Australian scientific research with exhibitions and working displays. Then travel south-west along Clunies Ross Street and turn right onto Black Mountain Drive for access to **Black Mountain**. The **Australian National Botanic Gardens** lie on the mountain's lower slopes. Envisaged by Walter Burley Griffin as a retreat for city dwellers, the gardens boast the largest collection of native plant species in the country. The species are organised into groups re-creating Australia's major ecosystems. Highlights are the Rainforest Gully, representing the major rainforest types of Australia's entire east coast, the Aboriginal Plant Use Walk, demonstrating a number of species used for food and medicine by Aboriginal people, and for young children, an interpretive walk inspired by the sculptures of David Miller. Continue along Black Mountain Drive to reach the **Telstra Tower**, a 195-metre communications tower with a viewing platform, an exhibition hall and a restaurant.

Return to Clunies Ross Street, which becomes Lady Denman Drive under the Parkes Way Bridge. Continue along Lady Denman Drive to the **National Aquarium and Wildlife Park**. The aquarium features an underwater tunnel that allows you to see an amazing collection of freshwater fish species through walls and ceiling of glass, while the wildlife sanctuary has native bushland where all the Australian favourites are on display.

INNER SOUTH

Beyond the Parliamentary Triangle lie Canberra's most desirable suburbs – the quiet, leafy streets of the inner south, containing official residences, Art Deco bungalows, the diplomatic precinct, the Royal Australian Mint and a couple of charming urban villages.

The Lodge, on Adelaide Avenue immediately south-west of Parliament House, was built in 1926 as the official residence of the prime minister. Public access is only possible occasionally. Likewise at **Yarralumla**, the Governor's residence on Dunrossil Drive, accessed by continuing along Adelaide Avenue, which becomes Cotter Road, and turning right. This 1820s building, now the official residence of the Governor-General, was part of a sheep station; there are views of the grounds from a lookout on Lady Denman Drive.

The **Royal Australian Mint** can be found on Denison Street in nearby Deakin: return to Adelaide Avenue and turn right into Kent Street. The mint, opened in 1965, produces around two million coins a day. Visitors can see the production process from the visitors' gallery, or view the exhibits that detail the history of money minting.

Return to Adelaide Avenue and head towards the city, turning right along Hopetoun Crescent for a tour of the diplomatic precinct. Here, as well as throughout the nearby suburbs of Forrest and Red Hill (follow the signs for Tourist Drive 6), you will find most of Australia's diplomatic missions. Many of these have been built to represent the culture of their country of origin, and together provide a concentrated overview of worldwide architectural practice, with everything from American Colonialism to Eastern mysticism.

Hopetoun Crescent leads into Mugga Way, Red Hill and **Calthorpes' House**, a 1927 Spanish Mission-style house containing original furnishings and providing a fascinating glimpse of middle-class domestic life in the fledgling capital. Turn left into Flinders Way for the old-style inner-city shopping areas of **Manuka** and **Kingston**, both offering interesting shopping and an impressive range of cafes and restaurants. The **Canberra Railway Museum** is near the Kingston shops on Cunningham Avenue, off Wentworth Avenue. It houses

Australia's oldest steam locomotive (1878), as well as other engines and some 40 carriages (open weekends and public holidays).

OUTER SOUTHERN SUBURBS

The long corridor of new suburbs south of the city are set against the superb Brindabella Range, merging harmoniously with the surrounding native bushland and pine forests. Follow Adelaide Avenue onto Cotter Road, travelling south out of the city. To visit the numerous attractions, follow the signs for Tourist Drive 5 around the outer edges of the southern suburbs. First stop is **Mount Stromlo Observatory**, which was established in 1924 and houses a huge telescope that charts the night skies; visitors can tour the large research telescopes and learn about the wonders of the galaxy at the hands-on visitors centre. Next, look out for the right-hand turn-off to **Cotter Dam and Reserve**, a popular recreation area with swimming, camping and picnic facilities.

Continue along Tourist Drive 5 and take the left-hand turn-off to the **Canberra Deep Space Communications Complex** at Tidbinbilla. Look out for the aluminum communications dishes along the way. Opened in 1965, it is one of only three facilities forming NASA's deep space network, and it assists, by way of deep space tracking, some of the world's most significant space operations, such as the Mars

MONUMENTS	Map Ref.
Australian–American Memorial Celebrates America's WW II contribution to Australia's defence	122 H8
Anzac Parade Memorials Dramatic monuments commemorating the war efforts of 11 different groups	122 G5
Captain Cook Memorial Water Jet A 150-metre water jet and terrestrial globe	122 D7
National Carillon Three-column belltower – a gift from the British Government to mark Canberra's Jubilee	122 F8
National Jewish Memorial Centre Synagogue and memorial to World War II veterans	122 D12

SPORT

Spectator
*The national basketball team, the Canberra Cannons, plays home games at the **Australian Institute of Sport** (AIS) Arena; the Rugby League side, the Raiders, can be seen at the **Bruce Stadium**, as can the Rugby Union side, the ACT Brumbies.*

Participator
*Canberra has nine golf courses offering very cheap rates; the private, as well as public, courses generally welcome visitors. Swimming pools are to be found at the AIS, **Phillip**, the city and **Manuka** (among others). There are around 900 kilometres of cycling tracks throughout the city and suburbs with the most popular being around Lake Burley Griffin.*

Old Parliament House, home of the National Portrait Gallery

Parliament House

DAY TOURS FROM CANBERRA

Historic towns
A number of towns within easy driving distance of Canberra are noted for their heritage buildings and are filled with a sense of the area's agricultural and goldmining history. These towns include Goulburn, Braidwood, Bungendore, Yass and Young; most are within an hour or so of the capital.

Namadgi National Park
Covering over 45 per cent of the ACT, Namadgi protects a superb alpine environment of mountains and native forests and offers scenic drives as well as a retreat for the bushwalkers, wildlife watchers and trout fishers of Canberra. Start at the visitor centre near Tharwa, about 30 kilometres south of the city.

Wine district
The wineries of the Canberra district are few, but have a big reputation for the quality of the cool-climate varieties they produce. Most are located to the immediate north and north-east of the Territory (pick up a map from the Canberra Visitors Centre), and are open daily for tastings and sales.

For more details on all of the above see Capital Country in New South Wales region coverage, p. 14.

Pathfinder mission. There is an excellent museum and display area on site with films, astronaut suits and space food along with a plethora of hard facts on space exploration and technology.

Nearby is the **Tidbinbilla Nature Reserve** (look out for the native-animal carving at the entrance), 5500 hectares of bushland offering refuge for many species of native wildlife. There are 12 well-signed walking tracks, beautiful picnic spots with free wood barbecues and an excellent information centre and cafe. Just past the reserve on the right is the turn-off to **Corin Forest Mountain Recreation**, great for children with its 800-metre alpine slide, flying foxes, supervised winter snowplay, and picnic spots. Continue to tiny historic **Tharwa**; just south of the town is the **Cuppacumbalong Craft Centre**. In a beautiful 19th-century garden on the Murrumbidgee riverbank, this old homestead has become the showroom for quality works by Canberra's craftspeople.

From the Craft Centre you can follow the tourist route to **Namadgi National Park**, a stretch of alpine wilderness with a visitor centre near Tharwa. Alternatively, head back towards the city via **Lanyon Homestead** and the satellite centre of Tuggeranong. Lanyon is one of Australia's most beautiful 19th-century homesteads. Set in a peaceful hollow along the banks of the Murrumbidgee and just shielded from the suburban sprawl, the homestead and its glorious gardens provide a glimpse of the 1850s when sheep-farming was to the district what politics is today. Part of the homestead has been restored and re-furnished in the style of the period, while another section houses the **Nolan Gallery**, featuring important works by the prominent Australian artist Sidney Nolan.

Return to the city along Tharwa Drive, which leads onto the Monaro Highway.

OUTER NORTHERN SUBURBS

The edge of the northern suburbs is no more than 15 minutes away from the centre of the city, which means that the excellent attractions in the area, many with appeal for children, can be covered in a day.

The **Australian Institute of Sport** is to be found on Leverrier Crescent in Bruce (follow the signs from Northbourne Avenue for Belconnen). The institute opened in 1981 with a charter to provide top-class facilities for Australia's elite athletes. Members of the institute, some of them well known, lead the tours. Highlights include the interactive museum **Sportex** – where you can pit your fitness levels against those recorded by our Olympians – and access to the venues where athletes on six-day-a-week training programs demonstrate the less glamorous side of sporting fame.

Near the northern end of Northbourne Avenue in Hawdon Place (right-hand turn into Antill Street just past the **Canberra Visitors Centre**), is the **Canberra Planetarium and Observatory**, featuring research-grade telescopes for night-time viewing. Back on Northbourne Avenue, turn left onto Barton Highway. First stop along the highway is the **National Dinosaur Museum** at Nicholls, which boasts a 300-exhibit display, including ten full-size replica skeletons. Close by, on the perimeter of the Gold Creek Country Club, is **Cockington Green**. Just off Gold Creek Road, it offers a detailed miniature re-creation of an English rural village, complete with tiny folk going about their business. In addition, there is an interesting collection of re-creations (also knee-high) of Australian and overseas buildings of architectural and historical merit.

Forming part of Gold Creek village is **Federation Square**, which boasts excellent specialty shops, a walk-in bird aviary, the nearby **Australian Reptile Centre Canberra**, and the historic settlement of **Ginninderra Village**, its craft studios and art galleries set among historic buildings dating from the late 19th century.

AUSTRALIAN CAPITAL TERRITORY
LOCATION MAP

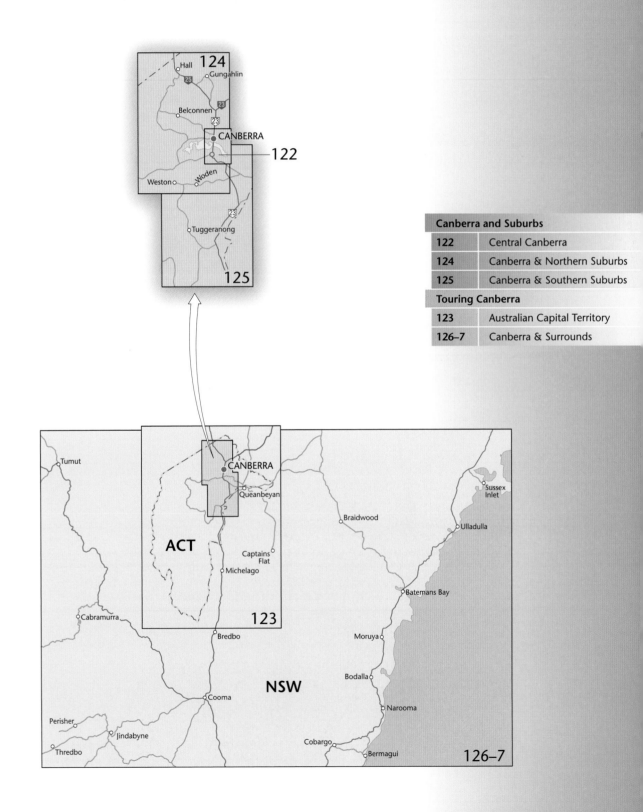

Canberra and Suburbs	
122	Central Canberra
124	Canberra & Northern Suburbs
125	Canberra & Southern Suburbs
Touring Canberra	
123	Australian Capital Territory
126–7	Canberra & Surrounds

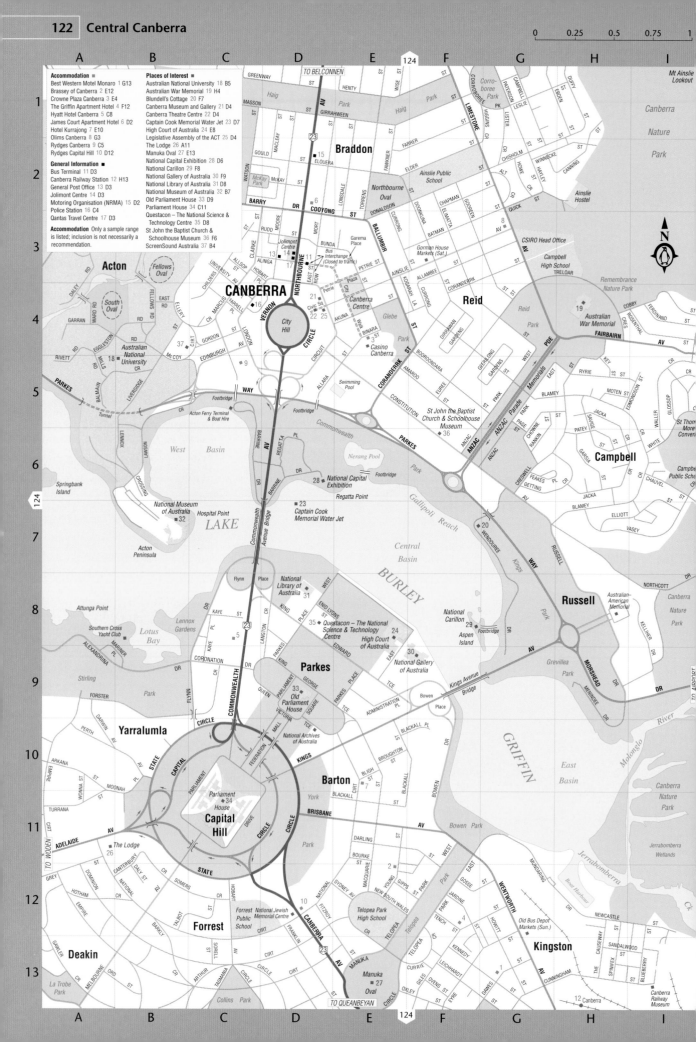

0   0.25   0.5   0.75   1

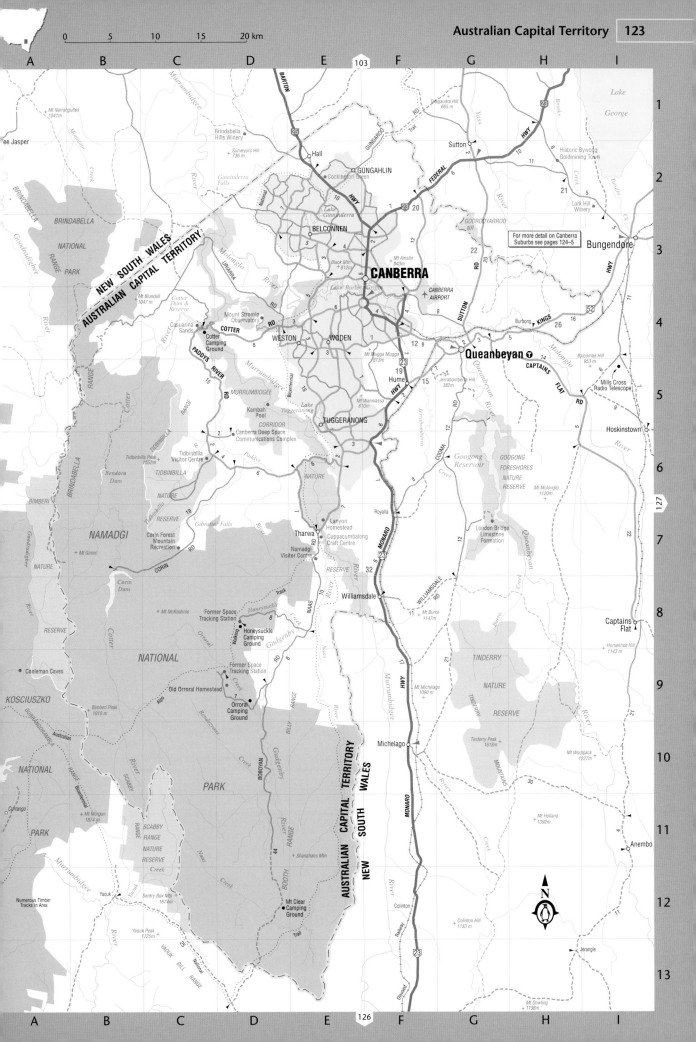

0 5 10 15 20 km

A B C D E F G H I

NEW SOUTH WALES
AUSTRALIAN CAPITAL TERRITORY

Lee Jasper

+ Mt Narrangullen 1041m

Murrumbidgee

Murrumbidgee

BARTON

Brindabella Hills Winery

Surveyors Hill 736 m

Hall

GUNDAROO

Taagandra Hill 665 m

Lake George

Brooks

HWY 23

Sutton

Historic Byrong Goldmining Town

1

BRINDABELLA

NATIONAL

RANGE PARK

Ginninderra Falls

GUNGAHLIN

Cockington Green

National

Lake Ginninderra

BELCONNEN

FEDERAL HWY

GOORODYARROO NR

Yass River

21

Lark Hill Winery

2

Goodradigbee

River

Mt Blundall 1047 m

URIARRA

Molonglo

Cotter Dam & Reserve

Casuarina Sands

Mount Stromlo Observatory

RD

COTTER

Black Mtn 812m

+ Mt Ainslie 843m

CANBERRA

SUTTON RD

22

For more detail on Canberra Suburbs see pages 124–5

Bungendore

HWY

3

BRINDABELLA RANGE

Cotter Camping Ground

PADDYS RIVER RD

15

WESTON

3

WOODEN

CANBERRA AIRPORT

Burbong

KINGS HWY

26

16

52

4

Goodradigbee River

MURRUMBIDGEE

MURRUMBIDGEE RD

Bicentennial

15

Lake Tuggeranong

Mt Mugga Mugga 813m

12 8

Queanbeyan

Molonglo

Balcombe Hill 953m

Mills Cross Radio Telescope

CAPTAINS FLAT RD

5

BIMBERI

Kambah Pool

Canberra Deep Space Communications Complex

2

Hume

HWY

19

15

Jerrabomberra Hill 382m

14

CAPTAINS

Hoskinstown

River

6

Tidbinbilla Peak 1562m

Tidbinbilla Visitor Centre

4

Paddys

TUGGERANONG

3

2

2

5

127

NAMADGI

NATURE

RESERVE

TIDBINBILLA

NATURE

RESERVE

19

Gibraltar Falls

River

7

Lanyon Homestead

Cuppacumbalong Craft Centre

Tharwa

Royalla

London Bridge Limestone Formation

12

Mt Molonglo 1120m

GOOGONG FORESHORES NATURE RESERVE

Googong Reservoir

22

7

+ Mt Ginini

CORIN RD

Corin Forest Mountain Recreation

Namadgi Visitor Centre

RESERVE

32

Queanbeyan

Captains Flat

Horseshoe Hill 1143 m

8

Corin Dam

+ Mt McKeahnie

Former Space Tracking Station

Honeysuckle Camping Ground

Honeysuckle

Walang

Track

Gudgenby

NAAS

Williamsdale

WILLIAMSDALE RD

11

Mt Burta 1147m

21

TINDERRY

NATURE

Mt Michelago 1090 m

RESERVE

9

KOSCIUSZKO

Cooleman Caves

Bimberi Peak 1910 m

Former Space Tracking Station

Old Orroral Homestead

7

Orroral Camping Ground

Cotter River

Orroral

Creek

BOBOYAN RD

Gudgenby River

BILLY RANGE

MONARO HWY

Michelago

Tinderry Peak 1618m

Mt Woolpack 1227m

10

NATIONAL

GUDGENBY RANGE NATURE RESERVE

Australian

PARK

SCABBY RANGE

RANGE

44

Shanahans Mtn

BOOTH RANGE

MONARO HWY

Murrumbidgee River

30

Mt Holland 1392m

Anembo

11

Cufrango

+ Mt Morgan 1874 m

NATURE RESERVE

SCABBY RANGE

Naas Creek

Creek

AUSTRALIAN CAPITAL TERRITORY

NEW SOUTH WALES

Mt Clear Camping Ground

Colinton

Colinton Hill 1133 m

N

12

Numerous Timber Tracks in Area

Yaouk

Yaouk

Sentry Box Mtn 1674m

Yaouk Peak 1725m+

25

YAOUK BILL RANGE

National

Trail

Railway

Diesel

23

Mt Dowling 1198m

Jerangle

13

A B C D E F G H I

103

25

23 20

23

23

23

126

0 1 2 3 4 km

A B C D E F G H I

1
2
3
4
5
6
7
8
9
10
11
12
13

NEW SOUTH WALES
AUSTRALIAN CAPITAL TERRITORY

Hall
Kinlyside
Casey
Ngunnawal
Amaroo
Gungahlin
Nicholls
Palmerston
Gold Creek Country Club
Federation Square
Cockington Green
Ginninderra Village
Australian Reptile Centre Canberra
National Dinosaur Museum
Gungahlin Lakes Golf Course
Gungahlin Pond
Crace
Canberra Nature Park
Gungahlin Cemetery
Treloar Technology Centre
Mitchell
Sandford
Kenny

Dunlop
Charnwood
Fraser
Spence
Evatt
Melba
Flynn
Macgregor
Latham
Florey
McKellar
Giralang
Kaleen
Holt
Higgins
Scullin
Page
Belconnen
Lawson
Ginninderra
University of Canberra
Belconnen Naval Station
Maribyrnong
Hawker
Bruce
Canberra Nature Park
Australian Institute of Sport
Weetangera
Macquarie
Cook
Aranda
Yowani Golf Course
National Tennis & Squash Centre
Canberra Racecourse
Exhibition Park
Flemington
Federal
Downer
Watson
Hackett
Lyneham
Dickson
Canberra Planetarium & Observatory
O'Connor
Ainslie
Turner
Braddon
Mt Ainslie Lookout
Reid
Canberra Nature Park
Canberra War Memorial
Fairbairn
Campbell
Duntroon
Russell
Morshead

Black Mtn 812m
Telstra Tower Lookout
Black Mountain
CSIRO Discovery Centre
Australian National University
Australian National Botanic Gardens
CANBERRA
Acton
Parkes
Coppins Crossing
Stromlo Forest
National Aquarium & Wildlife Park
Scrivener Dam
'Yarralumla' Government House
Royal Canberra Golf Course
Black Mountain Peninsula
Weston Park
Springbank Island
Spinnaker Island
Lake Burley Griffin
National Library
High Court
National Gallery of Australia
Commonwealth
Capital Circle
Parliament House
Yarralumla
The Lodge
Forrest
Kingston
Canberra Railway Museum
Barton
Kings
Manuka
Griffith
Narrabundah
Capital Golf Course

Mount Stromlo Observatory
Mt Stromlo 782m
Stromlo Forest
Equestrian Park
Canberra Nature Park
Duffy
Curtin
Deakin
Hughes
Federal Golf Course
Red Hill 720m
Red Hill
Holder
Weston
Lyons
Woden
Phillip
Garran
Stirling

For more detail on Central Canberra see page 122

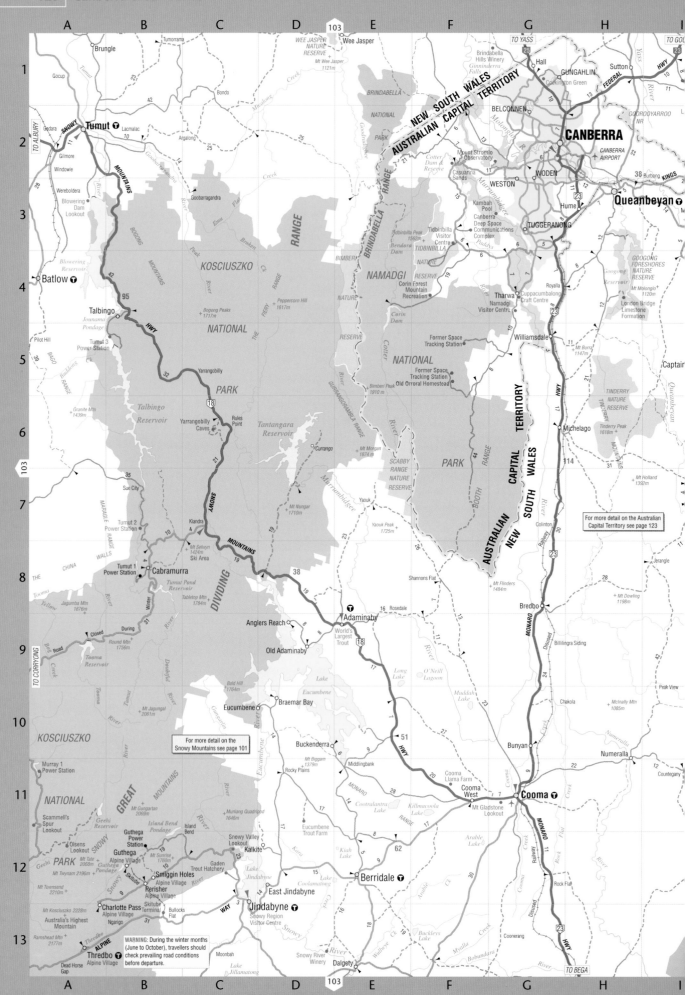

0 5 10 15 20 km

TO NOWRA

NSW JERVIS BAY NP
Callala Bay
Huskisson
Tomerong
St Georges Basin
Wandandian
Vincentia
Basin View
Erowal Bay
Hyams Beach
NSW JERVIS BAY NP
Jervis Bay
Sussex Inlet
Sanctuary Point
JERVIS BAY TERRITORY
Green Patch
BOODEREE NATIONAL PARK
Conjola
CUDMIRRAH NATIONAL PARK
Berrara
Swanhaven
Cudmirrah
Fishermans Paradise
Bendalong
Manyana
Yatte Yattah
Lake Conjola
Cunjurong
Pointer Gap Lookout
CONJOLA Lake NP
NARRAWALLEE CREEK NR
Milton
Narrawallee
Kings Point
Mollymook
Ulladulla
Burrill Lake
Lake Tabourie
Termeil
ILLAWARRA
Bawley Point
MURRAMARANG ABORIGINAL RESERVE
East Lynne
Kioloa
Benandarah
Pebbly Beach
Nelligen
Depot Beach
Cullendulla
Long Beach
Durras
Runnyford
MURRAMARANG NATIONAL PARK
Batemans Bay
Shell Museum
Batehaven
Surf Beach
Mogo
Malua Bay
Rosedale
Bimbimbie
Tomakin
Mossy Point
Broulee
Mogendoura
Yarragee Gundary
Mullenderee
Moruya
Kiora
Moruya Heads
The Anchorage
Congo
EUROBODALLA NATIONAL PARK
Bergalia
Meringo
Coila Lake
Turlinjah
Tuross Lake
SOUTH
PACIFIC
Tuross Head
Bodalla
Nerrigundah
Potato Point
Eurobodalla
Lake Brou
EUROBODALLA NP
Mummuga Lake
Wagonga
Dalmeny
OCEAN
Kianga
BODALLA STATE FOREST
Narooma
COAST
SEA
Tilba Valley Vineyard
Corunna Lake
Montague Island
MONTAGUE ISLAND NATURE RESERVE
Corunna
Central Tilba Historic Village
Tilba Tilba
EUROBODALLA NATIONAL PARK
GOURA NR
Tilba Tilba Lake
WALLAGA LAKE NP
Wallaga Lake
Cobargo
SOUTH
TO BEGA
Quaama
Bermagui
Bermagui South
BERMAGUEE NATURE RESERVE

MORTON
NATIONAL
PARK

Sandy Point
Nerriga
Bulea Brook
Sassafras
Mt Tianjara 768m
Corang
Mt Corang 863m
Freeman Creek
BUDAWANG RANGE
Pigeon House Mtn 719m
Mt Mogood 391m
BUDAWANG NATIONAL PARK
Currockbilly Mtn 823m

Boro
Mt Fairy
Lower Boro
Mt Coghill 806m
Doughboy
Durran Durra
Charleyong
Tomboye
Braidwood Historic Town
Mongarlowe
Mt Gillamatong 907m
Reidsdale
Ballalaba
Majors Creek
Currowan Corner Upper
Monga
Clyde Mtn 850m
Shallow Crossing
Araluen North
Araluen
Togannoggera
Oranmeir
Benandarah
The Big Hole and Marble Arch
Gundillion
Wandera Mtn 580m
DEUA
NATIONAL
PARK
Mt Donovan 784m
Bendethera Mtn 997m
SWAMPS RESERVE
Jinden
Nerrigundah
Belowra
Yowrie
Wandella
Peak Alone 954m
Mt Dromedary 806m
BODALLA
FOREST

VICTORIA

V ictoria is Australia's second smallest State with an area of 227 420 square kilometres, just 3 per cent of the continent's total landmass. It has, however, a remarkably diverse landscape, industry, culture and population.

Small State, rich resources

Eastern Victoria is dominated by the Great Dividing Range. Heavy rainfalls provide winter snow for the ski resorts and water for the rivers flowing inland. The Murray River, rising in the high country, flows northwest through farming and grazing country to the semi-arid plains of the Mallee. The Goulburn River passes through central Victoria before joining the Murray. Irrigation schemes on the banks of these two rivers support orchards and grape-growing.

The semi-arid Mallee country of north-west Victoria supports wheat and sheep. South of the majestic granite Grampians, the golden-brown Wimmera landscape gives way to the rich wool country of the Western District. Victoria's wild southwest coast is known for its shipwrecks and dramatic sea-stranded sandstone formations, most notably the Twelve Apostles.

Gippsland, in eastern Victoria, supports dairying in the lush foothills of the high country. The vast brown coal deposits of central Gippsland generate electricity to power Victorian industry. The stunning beaches, inlets, lakes and lagoons of the coast are renowned for commercial fishing and summer tourism.

A bad deal

The Koories, as the Aboriginal people of southeast Australia are collectively known, arrived at least 40 000 years before the Europeans. As many as 50 000,

Errinundra National Park, East Gippsland

organised into over 30 different dialect groups, enjoyed a more sedentary lifestyle than groups in the drier regions of the continent. Different groups established complex fishing economies, quarried and traded stone for weapons and tools and, in the Grampians, created extraordinary galleries of rock art.

In May 1835, John Batman crossed Bass Strait from Van Diemen's Land in search of grazing land and, with blankets and tomahawks, 'bought' 243 000 hectares of land around Port Phillip from the tribes of the Kulin, the nation of people who lived in much of central Victoria.

Coolart Homestead (1895) on the Mornington Peninsula

Third time lucky

Before the arrival of Batman, the British government made two attempts to settle the Port Phillip district in a bid to stop other European powers occupying the south-east corner of the continent. Both attempts at settlement failed because of poor soil and lack of water.

A superintendent administered the Port Phillip District, originally part of New South Wales, from 1839 to 1851. A campaign for separation from New South Wales culminated in the creation of the colony of Victoria on 1 July 1851. Victoria became a separate State at the time of Federation, in 1901.

Gold!

Gold was discovered just weeks after Victoria became a separate colony. Capital and immigrants poured in from around the world. Australia experienced its first and only civil insurrection as miners joined the Eureka Rebellion in 1854 to protest against the inequities of the goldfields licensing system.

Violence against Chinese miners and the subsequent restriction of Chinese immigration were among the era's less glorious events.

Wool from the Western District added to Victoria's wealth and, as gold petered out, investors turned to manufacturing, commerce and real estate. By 1880 Melbourne had become the financial and commercial centre of the colonies, as well as a showcase for the ornate, monumental architecture of the period.

The golden age ended in the 1890s when rising interest rates and British bank failures stemmed the flow of money to Victoria. Falling prices for wool and other commodities, industrial unrest and the collapse of the building industry ushered in a decade of depression.

Changing the stock

Victoria's population throughout its establishment years was drawn overwhelmingly from Anglo-Celtic stock. This changed after World War II as thousands of Italians, Greeks and other displaced Europeans (as well as many British) poured into the State as part of an Australia-wide immigration program.

The next thirty years would see the immigrant base swell with arrivals from Turkey, Lebanon, South America and Asia. Today, one in four Victorians was born overseas and the population can claim the heritage of 100 different nations. Cultural diversity has become one of the State's defining features, not only in Melbourne, with its prominent Greek, Italian, Spanish, Vietnamese and Turkish neighbourhoods, but in country areas as well. Immigrants have laid out their orchards, market gardens, olive groves and vineyards alongside the traditional wheatfields and sheep and cattle properties of the Anglo-Celts. Many Victorians prominent in science, education, the arts, business, the media, politics and sport are of post-war immigrant origin.

The pursuit of leisure

Along with multiculturalism and conservative politics (conservative governments have ruled Victoria for 82 years out of 100) the State is known for its cultural and leisure activities. Melbourne stages Australia's biggest writers' festival, one of the world's top comedy festivals and the Australian Open, one of the four Grand Slam tennis tournaments. The State has 332 museums and galleries and around 21 per cent of Victorians visit a gallery each year. Victorians also love their sport and about 35 per cent of the population attends at least one Australian Rules football game each year. Known as the Garden State for many years, Victoria today attracts over 40 per cent of its population to its peerless public gardens, a legacy of the State's early wealth.

For more information on Victoria, see Tourist Bureaus on p. 591.

MELBOURNE

Melbourne skyline and Yarra River at sunset

DESCRIBED as the world's most livable city, Melbourne is a vibrant and multicultural metropolis offering great restaurants, excellent shopping and world-class sporting venues. Add stunning new buildings, tree-lined boulevards and magnificent public gardens, and you will have some idea of the city.

VISITOR INFORMATION

Melbourne Visitor Information Centre
Melbourne Town Hall,
cnr Swanston and Little Collins sts
Melbourne (03) 9658 9658
Information booths
Flinders St Station & Bourke St Mall,
Melbourne
Victorian Tourism Information Service
13 2842
www.melbourne.vic.gov.au

There's always something happening in Melbourne. The major festivals include the Melbourne Festival (an arts festival), the Comedy Festival, the Food and Wine Festival and the Film Festival. For sports enthusiasts, the year starts with the Australian Open tennis; the Australian Formula One Grand Prix follows; the cricket season leads into the football season, then there is the Spring Racing Carnival (horseracing), culminating with the Melbourne Cup in November. The year ends with a cricket Test Match that traditionally begins on Boxing Day at the Melbourne Cricket Ground (MCG).

Melbourne is a multicultural city, with residents from many countries,

Riverside scene

NOT TO BE MISSED IN MELBOURNE — Map Ref.

Melbourne Aquarium — 202 C9
The magic of marine life

Melbourne Museum — 202 F3
A superb introduction to Melbourne and Australia

Melbourne Zoo — 204 G9
An essential stop for animal lovers

Queen Victoria Market — 202 B4
Always bustling, noisy and fun

Rialto Towers — 202 C8
Stunning 360° views of the city from the Observation Deck of Australia's tallest building

Royal Botanic Gardens — 202 I12
Considered to be among the best in the world

Scienceworks — 204 E11
Exciting and award-winning interactive science and technology museum, with new Planetarium

Southgate & Crown Entertainment Complex — 202 C10, E9
Something for everyone – shop, wine and dine or have a flutter

Williamstown — 204 F13
Take a ferry from St Kilda to this historic area

particularly Asia and Greece; it has one of the largest Greek-speaking populations in the world. This cosmopolitan influence is reflected in Melbourne's bustling markets, delicatessens and restaurants. Eating out is a great Melbourne pastime.

Situated at the head of Port Phillip and centred on the north bank of the Yarra River, Melbourne's population is about 3.4 million. The suburbs spread in all directions, particularly down the east coast of the bay and towards the Dandenongs, the picturesque mountains east of Melbourne. The Yarra River has become a focus for Melburnians: there are barbecues and picnic tables overlooking the river near the Botanic Gardens, and a bike path runs along the riverbank from the city into the Yarra Valley. The Yarra is an integral part of the Moomba Festival in March, with dragonboat racing, fireworks and waterskiing drawing huge crowds. The popular Southgate and the Crown Entertainment Complex are the stars of

the south bank, along with the beautiful riverside public gardens.

EXPLORING MELBOURNE

The city centre is easy to explore, with its wide streets laid out in a grid system. Public transport is excellent, particularly the tram system. There are free City Circle trams around the perimeter of the central grid, in both directions. Normal tram services criss-cross the city on their way to the suburbs. Tickets are available at railway stations and shops displaying a Metcard flag throughout Melbourne, as well as a limited choice from vending machines on the trams; tickets are valid for suburban trains, trams and buses.

There are two main railway stations: Spencer Street services country and suburban destinations, while Flinders Street is the main terminus for the suburban lines. Trains from Flinders Street go round an underground loop that can be used instead of the City Circle tram to explore Melbourne. Buses cover major routes that are not reached by trams or trains.

A good way to explore the city is on the City Wanderer (summer only) or the City Explorer, the former extending as far as the Westgate Bridge and Williamstown. View more than 50 attractions from their upper decks or, alternatively, break your journey at any point and rejoin later. Both buses operate daily and tickets are available from the Visitor Information Centre, or your bus driver.

The city centre has plenty of parking, mainly as short-term parking meters and undercover carparks. At peak times it can

MELBOURNE BY AREA

CITY CENTRE
DOCKLANDS DEVELOPMENT
SOUTH OF THE RIVER
INNER SOUTH-EAST
INNER NORTH
BAYSIDE
SOUTH-WESTERN SUBURBS
EASTERN SUBURBS

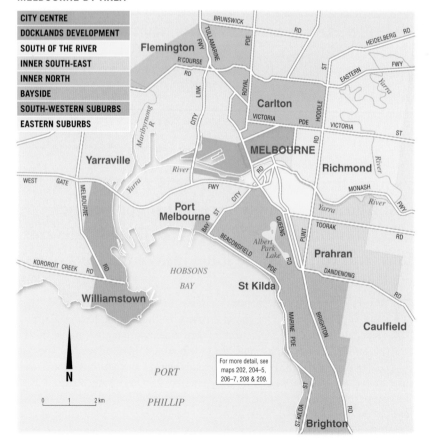

For more detail, see maps 202, 204–5, 206–7, 208 & 209.

Victorian Arts Centre spire

be difficult to find an unoccupied meter, and inexpensive long-term parking is not so easy to locate centrally. Outside the centre, however, there is usually no problem finding a parking spot.

The Yarra River has a variety of tour boats, including water taxis and ferries. Many are moored at Southgate or Princes Bridge, and destinations include Williamstown and St Kilda. There are sightseeing trips around the bay and the river, and along the Maribyrnong River departing from Dynon Bridge in Footscray.

Cycling is popular, particularly alongside the Yarra River, and you can hire a bicycle at Princes Bridge to explore the Yarra Bike Trail.

CITY CENTRE

Flinders Street Station, on the corner of Flinders and Swanston streets, is an excellent place to begin. A busy terminus, it is a popular meeting place. Diagonally opposite is **St Paul's Anglican Cathedral**, built 1880–91. This Gothic-style building has a sandstone exterior whilst the interior is banded with limestone and bluestone.

The area between St Paul's and the Yarra River is **Federation Square**, intended to be a contemporary focus for the city, with the Museum of Australian Art and the Australian Centre for the Moving Image. **Young & Jacksons Hotel** is also on this intersection. It was once notorious for *Chloe*, a nude painting that shocked Victorians at the turn of the century. *Chloe* now hangs upstairs.

Take the free burgundy-and-cream-coloured City Circle tram (they depart about every 10 minutes between 10 a.m. and 6 p.m.) west down Flinders Street to the Old Customs House. Restored to its original grandeur, the Long Room in particular is worth a look as it is a magnificent example of Victorian architecture, with a superb tessellated tile floor, wonderful Ionic columns and architraves. The Old Customs House is now the **Immigration Museum**. You can search genealogical records and passenger lists at the Discovery Centre for information on migrant forebears.

On the river just south-west of this spot is the **Melbourne Aquarium**,

GETTING AROUND

Airport shuttle bus
Skybus (03) 9335 3066

CityLink
A toll road linking the Tullamarine, West Gate and Monash Freeways. There are no toll booths. Travellers can buy an e-TAG or a Day Pass, or pay by credit card afterwards, within 24 hours of making a journey: 13 2629

Motoring organisation
Royal Automobile Club of Victoria (RACV) 13 1955

Car rental
Avis 13 6333; Budget 1300 362 848; Delta 13 1390; Hertz 13 3039; Thrifty 1300 367 227

Public transport
The Met (trams, including free City Circle trams, suburban trains) 13 1638

Tourist bus
City Explorer, City Wanderer (03) 9563 9788

Taxis
Black Cabs Combined 13 2227; Embassy 13 1755; Melbourne Combined (wheelchair only) 13 6133; North Suburban 13 1119; Silver Top 13 1008; West Suburban (03) 9386 2986

Water taxi
Melbourne Water Taxi (Yarra River); (03) 9686 0914

Yarra River boat trips
Melbourne River Cruises (03) 9614 1215; Southbank Cruises (03) 9546 9944; Williamstown Bay and River Cruises (03) 9397 2255; Penguin Waters Cruises (03) 9645 0533

Bicycle hire
Bike Now Hire (03) 9696 8588; Fitzroy Cycles (03) 9639 3511; The Freedom Machine (03) 9826 2597; St Kilda Cycles (03) 9534 3074

HISTORY

Melbourne was founded in 1835, when John Batman and John Pascoe Fawkner sailed from Tasmania and settled at the mouth of the Yarra River. Gold was discovered in 1851 in Victoria, and Melbourne grew quickly over the next 30 years, as wealth poured into it. Many of its gracious wide streets were laid out at this time, resulting in a legacy of elegant mansions and well-proportioned terrace houses, with cast-iron verandahs and balconies, that give charm to Melbourne's streetscape today. The trams that are so much a part of Melbourne were horsedrawn at first, and electrified in the early 1900s.

CLIMATE MELBOURNE

	J	F	M	A	M	J	J	A	S	O	N	D
Max. °C	26	26	24	20	17	14	13	15	17	20	22	24
Min. °C	14	14	13	11	8	7	6	7	8	9	11	13
Rain mm	48	47	52	57	58	49	49	50	59	67	60	59
Raindays	8	7	9	12	14	14	15	16	15	14	12	11

Southgate sculpture

where state-of-the-art technology allows visitors to see an underwater world of approximately 270 marine species from the Southern Ocean and Australia's inland waterways.

From the Aquarium, take the City Circle tram to Spencer Street. As the tram turns into Spencer Street, you can see, through the arches of the railway bridge, the **World Trade Centre** and **Melbourne Convention Centre**, which host trade displays. Tucked behind these is the **Victoria Police Museum**, in the Victoria Police Centre on Flinders Street. This museum houses memorabilia from some of Victoria's most famous criminal cases, including Ned Kelly's armour, and displays of state-of-the-art police equipment. Rejoin the City Circle tram (or walk) to the Collins Street stop in Spencer Street. Walk a block along Collins Street to the **Rialto Towers**, and take the lift to its Observation Deck on level 55 for a magnificent view of the city. A 20-minute film of major Melbourne and Victorian tourist attractions is shown here every half-hour. The elaborate Rialto Towers building and its neighbours on Collins Street were retained as a facade to this towering hotel and office complex, the tallest building in Australia.

Rejoin the tram again on its clockwise route to **Flagstaff Gardens**. These were the city's first public gardens, and were used as a signalling station to inform settlers of the arrival and departure of ships at Williamstown. Before this the area was a pioneer graveyard; today it is a pleasant place to relax under shady trees. Facing the park, in King Street, you can see **St James' Old Cathedral** (1839). Built of sandstone and bluestone, it contains two unusual pews set high in the walls, resembling boxes at a theatre; Victoria's first Governor, Governor La Trobe, sat in one and faced the Chief Justice of Victoria.

The old **Royal Mint Building** on the corner of La Trobe and William streets, a splendid building built in 1872, is home to the Royal Historical Society of Victoria. Its wrought-iron gates still bear elaborate coats of arms. Further down William Street is the **Supreme Court of Victoria** and the Law Courts.

Continue down La Trobe Street to **Melbourne Central**, a huge retail complex featuring a 20-storey glass cone that encloses an historic shot tower – where lead shot was made by dropping molten metal into water – and a large clock with an 'Australiana' theme which attracts visitors on the hour to see its display. **Daimaru**, a well-known department store, is here and you can reach Melbourne's best-known department store, **Myer**, through a walkway over Lonsdale Street.

The **State Library of Victoria**, with its magnificent domed roof, is on the corner of La Trobe and Swanston streets. Just behind the library, in Russell Street, is the temporary home of the National Gallery of Victoria under renovation until 2002. Just north of the crossroads on Swanston Street is the unusual facade of **Storey Hall**, part of RMIT University. Two doors along, the RMIT Gallery has changing exhibitions of contemporary art.

Nearby, left down Russell Street, is the **Old Melbourne Gaol**, a grim reminder of the past with its chillingly

Flinders Street Station

macabre exhibits, including the gallows where bushranger Ned Kelly swung. The gaol's claustrophobic atmosphere becomes even more dramatic during after-dark tours. A little further along La Trobe Street, on the corner of Exhibition Street, is the National Philatelic Centre and **Post Master Gallery**, for those interested in stamps.

The tram then takes you to Victoria Parade near the corner of Nicholson Street. A short walk along Victoria Parade leads to Gisborne Street and the Eastern Hill Fire Station – headquarters of the Melbourne Fire Brigade, which houses the **Fire Services Museum** (open Friday and Sunday). In Melbourne's early days, the site was one of the highest spots, and a fire-watch could be kept from the lookout tower. **St Patrick's Cathedral** also fronts Gisborne Street. Built of massive bluestone, it dominates the north-east corner of the city. Further south is Parliament Place, and on your left the elegant **Tasma Terrace**, which houses the head office of the National Trust where you can gather information on their properties.

Continue south to Spring Street, the centre of State government. At the top of Bourke Street is the **Parliament of Victoria**, a classical-style building;

when Parliament is not sitting there are free guided tours. Across the street is **The Windsor Hotel**, the grandest of Melbourne's hotels; a block to the north is the beautifully restored **Princess Theatre**. The **Old Treasury Museum** stands just south of MacArthur Street. Built in 1853, it has been refurbished and houses Melbourne Exhibition, an exhibition on Melbourne's fine architecture and colourful social history; and Built on Gold, a display in the historic basement gold vaults. Nearby are the **Treasury Gardens**, a delightful park full of huge old trees; beside its lake is the J. F. Kennedy Memorial.

From Spring Street wander west down Collins Street. You will pass **The Melbourne Club**, mecca to the Establishment, on your right. Opposite is **Collins Place**, an impressive multi-storey complex with many shops and a Sunday market. Continue down the hill past the exclusive shops until you reach **St Michael's Uniting Church** and, opposite this, the **Grand Hyatt Melbourne** hotel complex, with its interesting food hall and shopping plaza. **The Scots Church** is just over the road and, if you continue west, the graceful porticoed **Melbourne Baptist Church** is a little further on.

MELBOURNE ON FOOT

Aboriginal Heritage Walk
With an Aboriginal guide, explore the culture of the Bunurong and Woiwurrung people in their traditional camping place, now the Royal Botanic Gardens; bookings essential; charge applies

Art and About
Tours through Melbourne's cultural precincts and galleries (Mon.–Fri.); bookings essential

Chinatown Heritage Walk
Includes Chinese Museum; bookings essential; charge applies

Chocolate Indulgence
Walk around major chocolate outlets; bookings essential; charge applies

City Pub Walks
Young locals introduce you to Melbourne nightlife; bookings essential; charge applies

Melbourne Cemetery
Melbourne's history brought to life; bookings essential; charge applies

Murders and Mysteries Tour
Night tour examining some of the murders and unsolved mysteries around Melbourne; bookings essential; charge applies

Queen Victoria Market – Foodies Dream Tour
Tour of this famous market; bookings essential; charge applies

Royal Botanic Gardens
Guided walk, free of charge

For further information, contact the **Melbourne Visitor Information Centre**

Boxing Day Test Match, Melbourne Cricket Ground

SPORT

Spectator

*The **Melbourne Cricket Ground**, on Brunton Avenue, is the venue for Australian Football League (AFL), and cricket including One Day International Series Cricket and a Test Match that begins on Boxing Day each year. The adjacent **Melbourne Park**, which hosts the Australian Open tennis in January, offers two world-class facilities: the centre court, known as the Rod Laver Arena, and the Vodafone Arena, which hosts sporting events including tennis, basketball and cycling (as well as concerts and ice spectaculars). The Australian Formula One Grand Prix is raced in **Albert Park**, around the lake, every March. On winter weekends you'll see football supporters dressed to cheer their Australian Rules team – Melbourne has nine teams, with a new football venue, **Colonial Stadium**. In late October is the Spring Racing Carnival, culminating in the nation-stopping Melbourne Cup at **Flemington** on the first Tuesday in November. Albert Park's **Melbourne Sports and Aquatic Centre** is a state-of-the-art venue for swimming events.*

Participator

*Melbourne Park Tennis in Batman Avenue (closed mid-December to early February) is a splendid place for tennis players. For swimming, go to Albert Park's **Melbourne Sports and Aquatic Centre**, where you can also play squash, table tennis, badminton and basketball, or to the **City Baths** in Swanston Street. Golfers will enjoy Melbourne's 'sand-belt' courses, considered to be some of the best in the world. **Royal Melbourne** is rated as Australia's foremost layout, while **Kingston Heath**, **Huntingdale** and **Victoria** are all among Australia's top 20. The city's park areas, beaches and riverside offer a wide choice of attractive locations for cycling, rollerblading, walking and jogging. For rock-climbers there is **The Mill Indoor Rock Climbing Centre** in Collingwood, where beginners receive belay instruction.*

The **Melbourne Town Hall** stands on the corner of Collins and Swanston streets (as does a statue dear to Melburnians, the statue of the famous explorers Burke and Wills); the Melbourne Visitor Information Centre is in the town hall. On the right, just before the next major intersection, is the **Block Arcade** on Collins Street. This elegant precinct is the oldest arcade in Australia, and has a mosaic floor, glass and iron-lace roof and stylish shops. The arcade leads to Block Place and Little Collins Street and another gracious arcade, the **Royal Arcade**, where large gilded statues of Gog and Magog strike the hour. Do not miss the magnificent **ANZ Bank** building on the corner of Collins and Queen streets, a wonderful example of 19th-century Gothic Revival architecture, with an elaborate carved facade. Its palatial banking hall, with gold leaf, pilasters and mouldings, is a reminder of a vanished era. Inside are historical displays in the **ANZ Banking Museum** (open Monday to Friday).

Turn right along Bourke Street. It becomes a mall at Elizabeth Street, and you can sit and watch the buskers. Be careful when crossing the mall, though, as trams run through it. The mall has humorous sculptures, and a Half-Tix booth where you can buy reduced-price theatre tickets for the day's performances. There is also a visitor information booth, and shopping and sightseeing tram tours depart from here (bookings are essential). As well, the mall is home to the **General Post Office** and two department stores, **Myer** and **David Jones**. These huge shops extend over several blocks, and vie with each other for fine window displays, especially at Christmas.

Further along Bourke Street, towards Parliament of Victoria, you will find a mixture of bookshops and bistros. The coffee bar at **Pellegrini's** is an old favourite, while on the Spring Street corner is the up-beat **Hard Rock Cafe**. For a different perspective, walk along Little Bourke Street, one block north. Between Spring and Swanston streets is Melbourne's **Chinatown**, packed with fascinating restaurants and shops. In the heart of Chinatown, at Cohen Place off Little Bourke Street, the colourful **Chinese Museum** is worth a visit. You can see a 92-metre-long dragon that walks Melbourne's streets at Moomba and Chinese New Year, and the basement has a fascinating glimpse of life on the goldfields for Chinese immigrants in the 19th century.

For a different cultural experience, visit Lonsdale Street between Swanston and Russell streets. Cafes playing Greek music and shops selling pastries make this a mini-Athens. Further east towards Spring Street is the **Koorie Heritage Centre**, which provides an insight into Aboriginal cultural life in Victoria. You will find commercial galleries of Aboriginal art at the top end of Flinders Lane.

DOCKLANDS DEVELOPMENT

The vast area that was Melbourne's docklands is being redeveloped, and will be a major new waterfront area, with a promenade, parks, restaurants and sporting facilities, and a mixture of houses and businesses surrounding a marina.

Closest to the city is the **Colonial Stadium**, with a retractable roof and seating for 52 000. The stadium converts from a sporting area to an entertainment venue, and promises to be an exciting addition to the varied life of the city.

SOUTH OF THE RIVER

The south side of the Yarra River has many attractions. The *Polly Woodside* is a restored 1885 square-rigged sailing ship that stands in a wooden-walled dry dock. It is run by the National Trust, and there is an interesting maritime museum here. Next to the *Polly Woodside* is the **Melbourne Exhibition Centre**, with its striking entrance angled upward over the water. Walking east along the riverbank, you reach the **Crown Entertainment Complex**, which contains a casino as well as shops, restaurants, nightclubs and cinemas. Walk into the

magnificent atrium at its east end (the Crown Towers hotel) where music, lights and water are choreographed in a dazzling display. Continuing east you reach **Southgate**, an exciting development of restaurants, shops, wine bars and outdoor eating areas. Melburnians flock to this spot to sip cappuccinos as they watch the world go by. Many river cruises and ferries depart from the dock here.

The Southgate promenade ends at St Kilda Road, where the arts precinct begins. The **Melbourne Concert Hall** is used for classical music and large concerts. It also houses the **Performing Arts Museum** archives. Alongside the Concert Hall, the **Victorian Arts Centre**, with its distinctive spire that is lit at night, contains three theatres: the State Theatre, used for opera, ballet and large musicals; the Playhouse, for drama; and the George Fairfax Studio, for experimental productions. The Performing Arts Museum has regularly changing exhibitions in the foyer of the Victorian Arts Centre, the George Adams Gallery and the Vic Walk. Next door to the Victorian Arts Centre is the massive bluestone **National Gallery of Victoria**, which is undergoing major renovations until 2002. Some of its collection is on display at the former Museum of Victoria in Russell Street, while some is touring Victoria's regional centres.

SHOPPING	Map Ref.
Department Stores, City David Jones, Myer and Daimaru	202 D6, D7
Collins Street, City Melbourne's most elegant shopping boulevard	202 E7
Block Arcade, City Brings old-world charm to shopping	202 D7
Southgate, Southbank Has a vibrant mix of clothes and gifts	202 E9
Chapel Street, Prahran The fashion heart of Melbourne	204 H12
Toorak Road, Toorak Where you will find the top labels	204 I12
Bridge Road, Richmond Pick up a bargain at the designers' warehouse outlets	204 I10
High Street, Armadale Rugs, jewellery and antiques	204 I12

St Kilda Pier and kiosk

PARKS AND GARDENS	Map Ref.

Melburnians are extremely proud of their extensive parks and public gardens, some of which are listed below.

Albert Park	204 H12
Venue of the Formula One Grand Prix, with lake, cafes and playground	

Brimbank Park	204 B5
Showcase for native plants; children's farm	

Burnley Gardens	205 J11
Horticultural gardens with superb displays	

Carlton Gardens	202 F3
Site of the Royal Exhibition Building	

Eltham Lower Park	205 N6
Miniature steam-train rides	

Fawkner Park	204 H11
Oasis in 19th-century tradition	

Fitzroy Gardens	202 H6
With Captain Cook's Cottage; the Fairy Tree; and Model Tudor Village	

Flagstaff Gardens	202 B6
Historical associations and shady trees	

Gasworks Park	204 G12
Sculptures, playground and native garden in a park setting	

Jells Park	206 I7
127 hectares with the large Wildlife Lake; watch the waterbirds	

Kings Domain	202 G10
Huge park south of the river containing the Sidney Myer Music Bowl and Shrine of Remembrance	

Museum of Modern Art at Heide	205 L7
Sculpture gardens around museum lead down to the Yarra River	

Royal Botanic Gardens	202 I12
Melbourne's showpiece	

Royal Park	204 G9
Large park with many sporting facilities and the Melbourne Zoo	

Treasury Gardens	202 G7
At dusk you can see many possums	

Wattle Park	205 M11
Bushland retreat with many native birds	

Westerfolds Park	205 M6
Large park beside the Yarra River	

Yarra Bend Park	204 I9
Last refuge of bushland in inner-city Melbourne; boathouses with canoe hire	

Nearby, in Sturt Street, **The C.U.B. Malthouse** contains two more theatres.

Across St Kilda Road from the National Gallery of Victoria is the **Floral Clock**; behind it stretches a superb series of parks. **Alexandra Gardens** is on the water's edge, **Queen Victoria Gardens** in front of you and the trees of **Kings Domain** behind. In the latter is the **Sidney Myer Music Bowl**, used in summer for outdoor concerts; **Government House**, with its prominent white tower (open to visitors on the third Sunday in October); and the majestic, pyramid-style **Shrine of Remembrance**, which dominates St Kilda Road. Kings Domain is also home to **La Trobe's Cottage**, on Dallas Brooks Drive. This quaint cottage was Victoria's first Government House. It was imported from England by the first Governor (La Trobe) in prefabricated sections. It is now a National Trust property, furnished with many of La Trobe's belongings. Adjacent is the **Australian Centre for Contemporary Art**.

Immediately east are the wonderful **Royal Botanic Gardens**, established in 1846 and covering more than 35 hectares. There are several entrances, but the most interesting is **Observatory Gate** in Birdwood Avenue. With lush, landscaped gardens and lawns, attractive trees and shrubs and ornamental lakes, the gardens are a peaceful retreat. The rainforest fern-gully is home to fruit bats. In the gardens are tearooms, a cafe, a gift shop and a garden shop, a Visitors Centre – guided walks depart from here at 11 a.m. and 2 p.m. daily, Sunday to Friday – and the restored Old Observatory which offers star-viewing as part of its night tours. On summer evenings, the gardens host various theatrical performances and a moonlit cinema. Alexandra Avenue, on the river side of the Botanic Gardens, is one of Melbourne's prettiest streets. Barbecues are dotted along the riverbank and provide a focus for Melburnians to gather and watch the rowing crews at training.

INNER SOUTH-EAST

Toorak and **South Yarra** are areas of fine shopping, great food and vibrant life, with expensive houses tucked away.

Fawkner Park, off Toorak Road, offers a refuge in 19th-century tradition, with orderly avenues, playing ovals and lawns. Take a tram along **Toorak Road** – known for its elegant boutiques carrying designer labels, expensive restaurants and gourmet food shops – to the **Como Centre**, at the Chapel Street intersection, which has a large food plaza, shops and a cinema.

Chapel Street is the haunt of the younger crowd, and is lined with bistros, cafes and trendy fashion outlets. The **Jam Factory** is a shopping precinct developed within an old factory. On the opposite side of Chapel Street, on the corner of Commercial Road, the traditional **Prahran Market** springs to life on Tuesdays, and Thursdays to Saturdays. A block south is **Greville Street**, a funky mix of clubs and shops.

High Street is the next main road crossing Chapel Street, and a tram will take you east along High Street to **Armadale**, centre of the antique trade. There are also art and craft galleries, and designer clothes shops stretching for several blocks along High Street. Turning north along Orrong or Kooyong roads will bring you back to Toorak; the area bounded by Malvern Road to the south, and the river to the north, is full of imposing gates and high walls screening huge mansions.

The National Trust mansion **Como** is at the north end of Williams Road. It is set in pleasant gardens and is a perfect example of 19th-century Colonial grandeur. Parkland stretches from the house down to the river, and from here you can see **Herring Island**. A constructed island, formed when the river's path was altered, it is now an environmental sculpture park, but is accessible only by water. A punt service operates from Como Landing at weekends, 12 noon to 6 p.m.

INNER NORTH

The suburbs of **North Melbourne**, **Carlton** and **Fitzroy** are mainly residential, but with many interesting sights. Carlton has one of the largest concentrations of Victorian houses in Melbourne. Its shady wide streets and

West Gate Bridge

squares of restored terraces can make you forget you are within walking distance of a modern city. **Brunswick Street** in Fitzroy is, by contrast, alive with young style: boutiques and bookshops sit next to pubs and restaurants. At the city end is the **Mary MacKillop Foundation**, where there is information about Australia's beatified nun.

From Brunswick Street you can cut through to **Carlton Gardens**, and its domed **Royal Exhibition Building**. Built for the Great Exhibition of 1880, trade and public exhibitions are still held here. In Carlton Gardens you will also find the new **Melbourne Museum**. Adjacent is the **IMAX Theatre** where you can enjoy movies on an immense screen. **Lygon Street** lies a block west of Carlton Gardens. Known locally as 'little Italy', it is lined with restaurants, delicatessens, bookshops and boutiques. Also on Lygon Street is the **Trades Hall** building (1859), the world's oldest operating trade union building.

Carlton is the home of the **University of Melbourne**. In its grounds – a mixture of original ivy-clad buildings and modern blocks – are three museums. The **Ian Potter Museum of Art** is on Swanston Street and the **Grainger Museum**, a collection of memorabilia, including instruments, belonging to the composer Percy Grainger, is on Royal Parade. The **Medical History Museum** is in the Medical building near the corner of Grattan Street and Royal Parade. Nearby is the leafy suburb of **Parkville**, another pocket of gracious Victorian terraces.

South of the university on Victoria Street is the **Queen Victoria Market** – a Melbourne institution. Here you will find a huge variety of all sorts of food – meat, vegetables, breads and cheeses – plus clothing, plants and souvenirs. It is open Tuesdays and Thursdays to Sundays.

Further north lies **Royal Park**, home of many sporting facilities and the **Melbourne Zoo**. The zoo prides itself on making the enclosures as large and natural as possible. See the magnificent collection of butterflies in the walk-through butterfly house, and lions at play from the safety of a 'people cage' – an enclosed bridge that takes you through the lions' enclosure. The primates have also been housed in extensive, natural environments into which humans gaze from small galleries. To finish your tour of the northern suburbs, take a cruise on the **Maribyrnong River**; boats leave from near the Dynon Bridge, Footscray.

BAYSIDE

Melbourne's seaside suburbs are diverse. Directly south-west out of the city along City Road is **Port Melbourne**. Once a working-class area with light industry, this area is being redeveloped and the houses restored. **Station Pier**, now the departure point for the *Spirit of Tasmania*, was the introduction to Australia for many thousands of migrants.

Beaconsfield Parade, which runs along the Port Phillip foreshore, takes you to the suburb of **South Melbourne** with its leafy streets and trendy outdoor cafes.

RESTAURANTS AND CAFES	Map Ref.
Melbourne prides itself on the variety and standard of its restaurants and cafes. Many restaurants are BYO – bring your own wine or beer (there is usually a small charge for corkage).	
Southgate & Crown Entertainment Complex A variety of modern cafes, bistros, takeaways and restaurants along the riverbank	202 C10, E9
Little Bourke Street, City The heart of Chinatown, with terrific Chinese restaurants at all price ranges	202 E6
Lygon Street, Carlton Italian pasta, pizza and gelati, in traditional style	202 E4
Victoria Street, Abbotsford A bustling road full of inexpensive Vietnamese establishments	204 I9
Brunswick Street, Fitzroy Trendy cafes and bistros	204 H10
Toorak Road & Chapel Street, Prahran The place to be seen, in drop-dead stylish surroundings	204 I11
Swan Street, Richmond For authentic Greek cuisine	204 H11
Acland Street, St Kilda Cafe society and luxury cakes	204 H13
Fitzroy Street, St Kilda Almost a hundred restaurants in this cosmopolitan strip	204 H13

Entrance to Luna Park, St Kilda

The Chinese Temple of See Yup Society in Clarendon Street, a 19th-century temple, is still a place of worship. Further around the bay from South Melbourne lies **Albert Park**. The Albert Park Lake, formed by draining a swamp, is covered with small boats at weekends, with joggers, walkers and cyclists circling its perimeter all week. The park is the venue for the Australian Formula One Grand Prix each March, but the grandstands are temporary so for much of the year there is comparatively little evidence of Formula One. The park is home to many sports, with facilities for badminton, table tennis and soccer, and the **Melbourne Sports and Aquatic Centre**, the nation's largest integrated sport and leisure facility.

Next around the bay is the cosmopolitan **St Kilda**. Roller-bladers weave between walkers, and the **St Kilda Pier** is always busy. On the foreshore you will find **South Pacific St Kilda**, a fitness complex with heated indoor seawater pool, spa, shops and restaurant. Other restaurants overlook the foreshore, and in nearby **Fitzroy Street**, grand old hotels have been restored as stylish cafes, cinemas and restaurants. Adjacent to the beach are the funfair **Luna Park** and the enormous **Palais Theatre**. And on Sundays art and craft stalls appear on **The Esplanade**, which winds around to **Acland Street**, famous for its luscious cakes. Around the corner is the **St Kilda Botanical Garden**, with tropical fernhouse, lake, rose garden and children's playground. A short distance away is the **Jewish Museum of Australia**, in Alma Road.

South of St Kilda lie **Hampton** and **Brighton**. Brighton Beach has a colourful line of bathing boxes, and is a favourite with Melburnians in summer. **Elwood**, the next suburb, is a quiet family area. Inshore, at Hotham Street in **Elsternwick** stands **Rippon Lea**, a National Trust property. This Romanesque mansion, open daily, has beautiful English-style landscaped gardens. Yet further around the bay is **Black Rock** with its family atmosphere, and the additional attraction of HMVS *Cerberus* offshore. The *Cerberus* was commissioned by Victoria in 1866, to counter the threat of a Russian attack. Its naval career over, it was scuttled as a breakwater in 1926.

SOUTH-WESTERN SUBURBS

South-west of the city lies Melbourne's oldest suburb, **Williamstown**. To reach it, take a ferry or the West Gate Freeway. The **West Gate Bridge** is a marvel of modern engineering, taking you over the wide river to **Spotswood**. The award-winning science and technology museum, **Scienceworks**, is here. There are hands-on, high-tech exhibitions, a new Planetarium, Australia's first plane and car, and the opportunity to see the Victorian sewage pumping station that serviced Melbourne. Scienceworks is fascinating and well worth a visit.

The route to Williamstown takes you through **Newport**, where there is a **Railway Museum** on Champion Road. Open only weekend afternoons, it contains an extraordinary collection of old steam locomotives. Williamstown itself, a former maritime village, has many quaint seafront pubs, churches and cottages. It was somewhat cut off from Melbourne until the West Gate Bridge was built, and retains an independent atmosphere. At weekends you can tour **HMAS** *Castlemaine*, a World War II minesweeper restored by the Maritime Trust, and see model ships, early costumes and relics at the **Maritime Museum**.

EASTERN SUBURBS

The **Fitzroy Gardens**, on Wellington Parade, is a good spot to begin an exploration of Melbourne's east. A Model Tudor Village, the Fairy Tree – with its carved trunk – and Captain Cook's Cottage are just some of its attractions. The cottage, the home of Captain Cook's family in Yorkshire,

was re-erected here in 1934 to commemorate Melbourne's centenary.

Across Wellington Parade is the tiny suburb of **Jolimont** and the **Melbourne Cricket Ground** – the MCG. Holding about 100 000 people, this complex is the focus for much of Melbourne's sport, and major concerts are held here too. Outside the Members' entrance is the **Australian Gallery of Sport**, which celebrates Australian sporting history. There is also an **Olympic Museum** and, in the Members' Pavilion, a **Melbourne Cricket Club Museum**. A footbridge over the railway takes you to **Melbourne Park**, home of the Australian Open tennis tournament; the **Melbourne Sports and Entertainment Centre** (known as the Glasshouse) is close by.

Four major roads head east out from the city centre, each catering to particular tastes. The most southerly, **Swan Street**, is a centre for Greek culture and home to a horticultural college whose gardens are superb. Parallel to Swan Street is **Bridge Road**, a mecca for the fashion-conscious, with its many designer-label factory outlets. Further north again, **Victoria Street** is the

Vietnamese area of Melbourne, and dozens of restaurants offer affordable and interesting food. Finally, **Johnston Street** takes you over the Yarra River into Studley Park and the huge **Yarra Bend Park** which runs north past the Eastern Freeway. **Raheen**, a grand mansion on Studley Park Road, is now owned privately but was originally built as the Catholic archbishop's palace. Turn down Yarra Boulevard to drive along the river. **Studley Park Boathouse** is a pleasant spot for a rest, and you can hire a canoe here. North-east over the Eastern Freeway is the **Museum of Modern Art at Heide**; set in the tranquil parklands of Bulleen, and one of Australia's most renowned art spaces, it houses a collection of the great Australian Modernists and new artists.

The magnificent, wide, tree-lined avenues; the understorey of Victorian-era facades; the shopping and eating precincts both riverside and in the inner suburbs; the huge areas of beautiful parkland in the heart of the city; the international cultural and sporting events: all justify Melbourne's plaudit as the 'world's most livable city'.

DAY TOURS FROM MELBOURNE

The Dandenongs
These scenic hills at the far edge of Melbourne's eastern suburbs, 50 km from the city, are an easy and popular daytrip. Native rainforests of mountain ash and giant ferns, extensive cool-climate gardens, the popular steam train Puffing Billy and cafes, galleries and craft shops are among the many attractions. *For more details see region coverage, p. 151.*

Yarra Valley and Healesville
High quality cool-climate wines are produced across what is fast becoming one of Australia's best-known wine areas. Pick up a brochure from the information centre in Healesville and map out your wine-tasting tour. Worthy of its own daytrip is the superb Healesville Sanctuary, featuring around 200 native animal species in a bushland setting. *For more details see region coverage, p. 151.*

Mornington Peninsula
Fine-food producers, around 40 cool-climate wineries, three distinct coastal fronts, exclusive holiday villages, quiet coastal national parks, 20 golf courses and a long list of attractions for children are some of the features of this major holiday centre, 100 kilometres from Melbourne. *For more details see region coverage, p. 155.*

Phillip Island
The nightly Penguin Parade on Phillip Island is one of Victoria's signature attractions; bookings are advised. Other wildlife-watching opportunities include the huge seal colony on Seal Rocks (via a cruise), the Seal Rocks Sea Life Centre at The Nobbies, and the Koala Conservation Centre. Phillip Island is 142 kilometres from the city. *For more details see region coverage, p. 156.*

Werribee Park
This large estate is 35 kilometres from Melbourne in the outer western suburbs. It features a 60-roomed 1870s mansion, opulently furnished in the style and time of the original occupants; The Mansion Hotel offering luxury accommodation; Victoria's Open Range Zoo, where the free-roaming animals are seen from aboard a safari bus; and the Victoria State Rose Garden. *For more details see region coverage, p. 142.*

Sovereign Hill
This award-winning recreation of a 19th-century goldmining village, just over 100 kilometres from Melbourne, recreates the detail and drama of life during one of the nation's most exciting periods of history. Stay into the evening for the on-site show that re-enacts the events of the Eureka Rebellion, Australia's major armed civil uprising. *For more details see region coverage, p. 148.*

Bellarine Peninsula
The Bellarine, a quick 100 kilometres from Melbourne, separates the waters of Port Phillip from the famously rugged coastline of Victoria's south-west coast. It features the historic buildings, streets and waterfront of Geelong, Victoria's second largest city, as well as distinctive coastal villages and excellent beaches, golf courses and wineries. *For more details see region coverage, p. 142.*

Mount Macedon and Hanging Rock
Country mansions and superb 19th- and 20th-century European-style gardens sit comfortably in a native bush and volcanic landscape 70 kilometres from Melbourne. Wineries, cafes, nurseries, galleries and the mysteriously beautiful Hanging Rock also feature. *For more details see region coverage, p. 150.*

Spa country
For a few hours of health-giving indulgence visit the historic spa complex at Hepburn Springs. Afterwards explore the colourful shops of Daylesford, enjoy a meal at one of the region's excellent eateries, or take a peaceful forest drive. Hepburn Springs is 110 kilometres from Melbourne. *For more details see region coverage, p. 150.*

WERRIBEE & BELLARINE PENINSULA

The Bellarine Peninsula lies at the western entrance to Port Phillip, connected by car ferry to the Mornington Peninsula. Geelong, at the base of the peninsula, is a large regional city with strong links to the great days of the wool industry. Beyond Geelong are resort towns that offer surfing, swimming, sailing, scuba-diving, golf, tennis and bushland walks. Visitors can dine opulently in Queenscliff or take the sea air from a caravan at Point Lonsdale. Wine buffs will be delighted with the pinot noirs and chardonnays offered for tasting at the wineries on the peninsula and around Geelong.

TOP EVENTS

Jan.	*Waterfront Festival (Geelong)*
Feb.	*Australian International Air Show (Avalon Airfield, near Geelong, odd-numbered years)*
Feb.–Mar.	*Spray Farm Winery Summer Concert Series (near Drysdale)*
Mar.	*Highland Gathering (Geelong)*
Apr.	*Alternative Farmvision (Geelong)*
June	*National Celtic Folk Festival (Geelong)*
Sept.	*Momenta Arts (Geelong)*
Oct.	*Racing Carnival (horseracing, Geelong)*
Nov.	*Music Festival (Queenscliff)*

EXPERIENCE IT!

❶ See native birds in wetland and grassland at Serendip Sanctuary, north of Lara

❷ Enjoy the promenade at Geelong's Eastern Beach and swim in the restored 1930s sea baths

❸ Play at Barwon Heads Golf Club, one of Victoria's top three public courses

VISITOR INFORMATION

Geelong: (03) 5222 2900; 1800 620 888
Queenscliff: (03) 5258 4843

FOCUS ON

Holiday havens

Just an hour or so from Melbourne, this district is enormously popular with Melburnians for a weekend away. Queenscliff offers luxurious accommodation and fine dining; the Maritime Centre displays the region's historic relationship with the sea. The tiny historic town of Point Lonsdale has great views of the turbulent entrance to Port Phillip. Ocean Grove, the peninsula's biggest town, is popular with retirees, surfers and scuba divers. A bridge across the estuary leads to Barwon Heads, setting for the television series *SeaChange*. This is a small town with an excellent surfing beach and good accommodation and restaurants.

The You Yangs

These granite tors rising suddenly from the Werribee Plain are visible from Melbourne's bayside suburbs. There is a fairly easy 3.2-km-return walk from the car park to the top of Flinders Peak (347 m). The view on a clear day extends to Mount Macedon, Geelong and Melbourne's tall buildings.

For more detail see maps 208, 215 & 217. For descriptions of ❶ towns see Towns from A to Z (p. 158).

CLIMATE GEELONG

	J	F	M	A	M	J	J	A	S	O	N	D
Max. °C	25	26	24	20	17	14	14	15	17	19	21	24
Min. °C	14	14	13	10	8	6	5	6	7	8	10	12
Rain mm	44	38	35	39	47	43	42	47	53	63	52	48
Raindays	8	6	9	12	14	16	16	17	16	15	13	10

Geelong

The National Wool Museum records the development of Victoria's second city as a port for the wealthy wool industry of the Western District. Geelong has over 100 National Trust-classified buildings and a lively waterfront where attractions include delightful bollards – colourful, oversized figures representing local personalities.

Werribee Park

The Chirnside family built a 60-roomed Italianate mansion here in the 1870s. It survives as a museum, grandly furnished to recreate the lifestyle of a wealthy family in Victoria's boom years. Other attractions are the Victoria State Rose Garden, and Victoria's Open Range Zoo, home to many exotic animal species.

Bellarine wineries

The vineyards planted around Geelong in the 1850s were uprooted during the 1870s phylloxera outbreak. The industry was revitalised in the 1960s. There are now some 20 wineries, with a number offering sales. Scotchmans Hill has views to the coast and a growing reputation for its pinot noir and chardonnay.

Queenscliff's historic hotels

Queenscliff was established as a fishing village in the 1850s and today has attractive historic buildings and a picturesque waterfront. It is known for its grand Victorian-era hotels, namely Mietta's Queenscliff (pictured), Vue Grand and Ozone. With their highly regarded restaurants and sense of luxury, they offer a great weekend away.

SOUTH-WEST COAST

The south-west coast of Victoria is one of Australia's great scenic destinations. The Great Ocean Road, the region's main touring route, weaves a breathtaking course across a coastal landscape of rugged cliffs and unique geological formations, quiet bays and wild surf beaches, rainforests and waterfalls. En route is a string of charming holiday towns, with many attractions, including heritage sites and wildlife. Inland, the geological theme continues in the craters and lakes of the region's volcanic landscape. The accommodation choices throughout the region include everything from gourmet retreats to B&Bs, hillside cabins and remote camping spots.

TOP EVENTS

Jan. Pier to Pub Swim; Mountain to Surf Footrace (Lorne)

Feb. Food and Wine Festival (Heywood, near Portland)

Mar. Folk Festival (Port Fairy)

Easter Bells Beach Surfing Classic (Torquay)

Apr. Country Music Festival (Colac)

May Racing Carnival (horseracing, Warrnambool)

July Fun 4 Kids (children's festival, Warrnambool)

Sept. Angair Wildflower Festival (Anglesea)

Dec. Falls Festival (Lorne)

EXPERIENCE IT!

❶ **Spot** southern right whales at Logans Beach, Warrnambool (June to September)

❷ **Walk** the Alan Marshall Memorial Walking Track to the summit of Mt Noorat, near Terang

❸ **Take** a boat trip at Cape Bridgewater to see Australian fur seals at play

VISITOR INFORMATION

Lorne: (03) 5289 1152
Warrnambool: (03) 5564 7837
www.greatoceanrd.org.au

FOCUS ON

Maritime history

There are about 160 wrecks along the vital though treacherous south-west coast shipping route. Victoria's Historic Shipwreck Trail, between Moonlight Head (in Port Campbell National Park) and Port Fairy, marks 25 sites with plaques telling the history of the wrecks. Not to be missed is the evocative *Loch Ard* site, near Port Campbell. Maritime history is preserved in the superb streetscape of Port Fairy, an 1830s whaling port, and in the 200 heritage buildings of Portland, Victoria's first settlement. At Flagstaff Hill Maritime Museum in Warrnambool you'll find a completely rebuilt 19th-century maritime village, and a collection of seafaring treasures.

CLIMATE WARRNAMBOOL

	J	F	M	A	M	J	J	A	S	O	N	D
Max. °C	24	23	22	20	17	15	14	15	16	18	20	22
Min. °C	13	14	13	11	9	7	6	7	8	9	10	12
Rain mm	33	34	48	60	78	77	88	86	74	67	55	44
Raindays	8	8	10	13	17	17	20	19	17	15	13	11

Mount Eccles National Park

Mount Eccles is at the far edge of the 20 000-year-old volcanic landscape that extends west from Melbourne. Geological features of the park include a complex cave system, scoria cones and a large lake (suitable for swimming), enclosed within three volcanic craters. There are excellent walking trails and camping is available.

For more detail see maps 216–17 & 226.
For descriptions of ❶ towns see Towns from A to Z (p. 158). For touring details see Classic Tour (p. 198).

Surf coast

Torquay is Victoria's premier surfing town. This is where young surfers start out and old surfers settle down, where surfing is business as well as fun. Factory outlets offer great bargains on surf gear and the local Surfworld Surfing Museum celebrates the wonders of the wave. Bells and Jan Juc beaches are just around the corner.

The Twelve Apostles

These spectacular sandstone stacks were part of the original cliffs until wind and water carved them into their present shape and left them stranded in wild surf off the shoreline. Preserved within Port Campbell National Park, they are one of Australia's most photographed sights and the region's signature attraction.

The Otways

Ancient southern temperate rainforest is preserved in the hills and gullies of this magical landscape. Follow a rainforest boardwalk at Maits Rest in Otway National Park, drive along the 20-km scenic Turtons Track, north-east of Apollo Bay, and visit historic Cape Otway Lighthouse.

Lorne

This popular resort village is the inner city of the south-west coast: it has excellent cafes and restaurants and a lively summertime crowd. As well, it offers good beaches and surfing opportunities. Nearby, in Angahook–Lorne State Park (pictured), beautiful forests and waterfalls provide time out for walkers and nature lovers.

GRAMPIANS & CENTRAL WEST

Victoria's central west is a mix of ancient mountains, semi-arid plains and classic farming landscapes. In the south, the rugged 400 million-year-old blue-grey shapes of the Grampians rise from the cleared plains, a dense and awe-inspiring environment of forests, fern gullies, soaring cliffs, waterfalls, creeks, lakes and swampland. In the many rock shelters of the area, details of pre-European Aboriginal life are impressively recorded. Anglo-Celtic settlement has made its mark with the hundred of thousands of hectares of wheat crops and sheep paddocks that dominate what is Australia's richest farming country, while the proliferation of olive groves and vineyards signal a more Mediterranean landscape. In the north, the timeless pink-tinged salt lakes and claypans mark the limits of agricultural expansion and a return to a native landscape.

TOP EVENTS

Jan.	Champagne Picnic Races (Great Western, near Ararat)
Feb.	Grampians Jazz Festival (Halls Gap)
Feb.	Country Muster (Penshurst, near Hamilton)
Mar.	Jailhouse Rock Festival (Ararat)
Mar.	Vintage Car Rally (Casterton)
Easter	Easter Gift (professional foot race, Stawell)
Easter	Y-Fest (wide-ranging festival, Warracknabeal)
Apr.	Wimmera German Fest (Dimboola)
May	Grampians Gourmet Weekend (Halls Gap)
July	Kelpie Working Dog Auction (Casterton)
Sept.	Cymbidium Orchid Festival (Ararat)
Oct.	Golden Gateway Festival (Ararat)
Oct.	Southern Grampians Open Gardens (Cavendish, near Hamilton)
Oct.	Spring Garden Festival (Horsham)
Nov.	Kannamaroo Rock 'n' Roll Festival (Horsham)

VISITOR INFORMATION

Halls Gap: (03) 5356 4616

Hamilton: (03) 5572 3746; 1800 807 056

Horsham: (03) 5382 1832; 1800 633 218

www.grampians.org.au

Mount Arapiles
Mount Arapiles, part of the Mount Arapiles–Tooan State Park, is regarded as Australia's best rock-climbing venue. It attracts interstate and international enthusiasts with its 2000 rock-climbing routes marked out across 365 m of sandstone cliffs. Courses and tours are available.

CLIMATE STAWELL

	J	F	M	A	M	J	J	A	S	O	N	D
Max. °C	28	28	25	20	16	13	12	14	16	19	22	26
Min. °C	13	13	12	9	7	4	4	5	6	8	9	11
Rain mm	37	28	37	46	63	46	67	63	60	61	40	28
Raindays	6	4	7	9	12	14	18	17	13	11	9	7

Grampians day drive
From Halls Gap, drive to Boroka Lookout, Reed Lookout and Mackenzie Falls (pictured). Pause for lunch at Zumsteins, an historic site, picnic area and home to a large kangaroo population. Return to Halls Gap via Silverband Falls and through the stringybark forests and tree ferns at Delleys Dell.

FOCUS ON

Aboriginal culture in the Grampians

The Djab Wurrung and Jardwadjali peoples shared the territory they called Gariwerd, for at least 5000 years before European settlement, though some evidence points to 30 000 years of habitation. The Brambuk Aboriginal Cultural Centre at Halls Gap, run by five Koorie communities, is an excellent first stop for information about the region's heritage. There is a ceremonial ground for cultural demonstrations, including performances of Koorie dance and music, while traditional bush tucker is served in the cafe. There are 100 recorded rock-art sites in the region, representing more than 80 per cent of all sites found in Victoria. A Brambuk-guided tour of some of the sites (most are in Grampians National Park) is probably the most rewarding way to experience the meaning and nature of the art. Notable 'shelter' sites include: Gulgurn Manja, featuring over 190 kangaroo, emu and handprint motifs; and Ngamadidj, a site consisting of 16 figures painted with white clay. Bunjil's Rock Shelter is just outside the park.

Halls Gap
Halls Gap, 24 km south-west of Stawell and surrounded by Grampians National Park, is the gateway to the central Grampians. This little village is connected to a network of scenic drives and walking tracks into the mountains. The area attracts bushwalkers, campers, abseilers and, between August and October, wildflower enthusiasts.

Byaduk Caves
These caves, located in Mt Napier State Park, are part of a giant 24-km flow, and evidence of the volcanic activity that shaped the region's landscape. The caves, one of which is open, are a wonderland of ropey lava, columns, stalactites and stalagmites. A map of permitted areas is essential (available from Hamilton's information centre).

EXPERIENCE IT!

❶ Take *a dawn balloon flight from Stawell over the Grampians*

❷ Visit *the Historical Centre and the North Western Agricultural Machinery Museum at Warracknabeal, to get a picture of pioneering life*

❸ Swim *in summer at Lake Bellfield, just south of Halls Gap*

❹ Choose *one of the short walks through the eastern part of Little Desert National Park, near Nhill*

❺ Drive *to the top of One Tree Hill at Ararat for a 360º view of the region*

The olive groves of Laharum
Mount Zero Olives at Laharum, 30 km south of Horsham, is the largest olive plantation in the Southern Hemisphere (55 000 trees on 730 ha). The first trees were planted in 1943, after WW II had stopped olive oil imports. Buy oil, vinegar and lentils, and stay overnight.

The wheat belt
The plains of the Wimmera yield huge crops of wheat, barley and canola. Towns of interest include historic Warracknabeal and Jeparit, birthplace of Australia's longest-serving prime minister, Sir Robert Menzies. Dimboola and Nhill provide access to the sandhills, floodplains and wildflower displays of Little Desert National Park.

For more detail see maps 220, 226–7 & 228–9. For descriptions of ❶ towns see Towns from A to Z *(p. 158).*

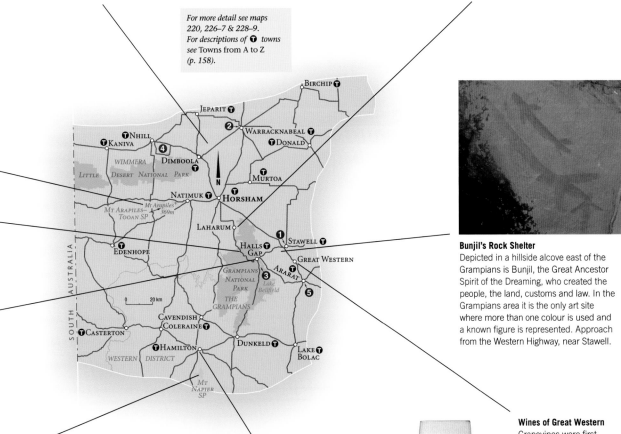

Bunjil's Rock Shelter
Depicted in a hillside alcove east of the Grampians is Bunjil, the Great Ancestor Spirit of the Dreaming, who created the people, the land, customs and law. In the Grampians area it is the only art site where more than one colour is used and a known figure is represented. Approach from the Western Highway, near Stawell.

Hamilton
Hamilton is the commercial hub of the wool-rich Western District. Gracious houses and churches on its tree-lined streets testify to over a century of prosperity. The town boasts botanic gardens (pictured) and an excellent gallery. Close to town are historic homesteads in magnificent gardens; these properties are generally open in spring.

Wines of Great Western
Grapevines were first planted at Seppelt's Great Western vineyards in 1865. Seppelt Winery is best known for its red and white sparkling wines, cellared in 1.6 km of National Trust-classified tunnels dug by miners late in the 19th century. Other wineries in the area include Best's and Garden Gully.

MALLEE COUNTRY

The Murray River is the lifeblood of the semi-arid mallee country of north-west Victoria. After several attempts, Australia's first large-scale irrigation scheme was established in Mildura by two Canadian brothers, the Chaffeys, around 1900. Since then, water from the Murray has allowed the cultivation of citrus fruit, olives, avocados and grapes and the development of the major riverside settlements of Mildura and Swan Hill. Despite intensive farming, vast spaces of mallee and semi-arid country intercut by lakes and rivers is preserved in accessible national parks and reserves.

TOP EVENTS

Mar.	*Arts Festival (Mildura)*
Mar.	*Redgum Festival (Swan Hill)*
July	*International Balloon Fiesta (Mildura)*
July	*Italian Festa (Swan Hill)*
Aug.	*Great Australian Vanilla Slice Triumph (Ouyen)*
Sept.	*Country Music Festival (Mildura)*
Sept.	*Big Lizzie Festival of Vintage Tractors (Mildura)*
Oct.	*Mallee Wildflower Festival (Ouyen)*
Nov.	*Sunraysia Jazz and Wine Festival (Mildura)*

EXPERIENCE IT!

❶ **Board** *a paddle-boat in Swan Hill to see where Major Mitchell named the town for the region's black swans*

❷ **Photograph** *the Pink Lakes from a walking trail in Murray–Sunset National Park*

❸ **Dine** *at Stefano's in Mildura, home to television chef Stefano di Pieri*

VISITOR INFORMATION

Mildura: (03) 5021 4424;
1800 039 043

Swan Hill: (03) 5032 3033;
1800 625 373

www.murrayoutback.org.au

FOCUS ON

Murray and mallee wildlife

Despite the degree of settlement, the region has abundant wildlife. Most notable is the birdlife: spoonbills, herons, eagles, mallee fowl, harriers and kites are to be found in parks and on roadsides and riverbanks. Hattah–Kulkyne National Park protects around 200 bird species as well as the red kangaroo, comparatively rare in Victoria. The Murray–Sunset National Park – true desert country in parts – includes riverine plains. It supports an array of native fauna, including mallee fowl and the rare black-eared miner. Wyperfeld National Park is a wildlife haven: follow the Brambruk Nature Trail for kangaroos and the prolific birdlife.

Mildura

With its museums and galleries, excellent dining and surrounding wineries and orchards, Mildura is like a colourful Mediterranean oasis. Go to the zoo, visit Rio Vista museum (pictured), once home of William Chaffey, or book a day tour, with indigenous guides, to Mungo National Park in NSW (see The Outback in New South Wales, p. 31).

CLIMATE MILDURA

	J	F	M	A	M	J	J	A	S	O	N	D
Max. °C	32	31	28	23	19	16	15	17	20	24	27	30
Min. °C	17	16	14	10	8	5	4	5	7	10	12	15
Rain mm	22	22	19	20	27	23	27	27	29	32	25	22
Raindays	4	3	4	4	7	8	10	9	8	7	6	4

River district wines

The winegrowing areas of Mildura and Swan Hill have long been the Australian industry's heartland, producing 37 per cent of the total output – most for the bulk market, although prestige production is rising. The dozen or so wineries include the large Lindemans Karadoc.

Hattah–Kulkyne National Park

This magnificent park covers 48 000 ha of low scrub and native pine. A network of creeks and lakes is fed by overflow from the Murray. The larger lakes abound in birdlife and are perfect for canoeing.

Wyperfeld National Park

A park of brilliant sunsets, huge open spaces and spring wildflowers, Wyperfeld is explored via walks from Wonga Campground and Interpretative Display Centre, 50 km west of Hopetoun. The park is home to the endangered mallee fowl (pictured), a turkey-size bird that makes nesting mounds up to 5 m across.

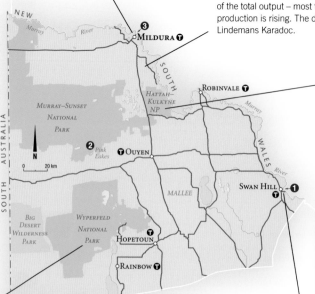

For more detail see maps 228 & 230–1. For descriptions of ❶ towns see Towns from A to Z (p. 158).

Swan Hill Pioneer Settlement

This 7-ha park offers a lively experience of river port life in early Australia. The re-creation features aspects of local Aboriginal culture as well as the production and sale of 19th-century goods by staff in period dress. Ride on yesteryear's transport, or book for the popular Sound and Light Tour.

GOULBURN & MURRAY

The Goulburn River is the backbone of Victoria's central northern region. Rising in the Yarra Ranges, the Goulburn runs north into the Murray River near Echuca (an Aboriginal word meaning 'meeting of the waters'). Victoria's richest farming country is north of Nagambie in the Goulburn Valley. The canneries of Shepparton, the region's hub, process much of the harvest grown on irrigated land. In the central reaches of the Murray are attractions of great historical interest, particularly the paddle-steamers at Echuca. As well, there are ecologically significant wetlands with ancient river gums, and opportunities for freshwater fishing.

TOP EVENTS

Jan. Peaches and Cream Festival (Cobram, odd-numbered years)

Feb. Aquatic Festival (Cohuna)

Feb. Riverboats, Food, Jazz, and Wine Festival (Echuca)

Feb. Southern 80 Ski Race (Torrumbarry Weir to Echuca)

Mar. Goulburn Valley Vintage Festival (Nagambie)

Apr. Barmah Muster (Barmah State Forest, near Echuca)

June Steam, Horse and Vintage Car Rally (Echuca)

Oct. Port of Echuca Steam Heritage Festival

Nov. Sun Country Dolls, Bears and Collectibles Show (Cobram)

EXPERIENCE IT!

❶ **Take** time in Yarrawonga at the Tudor House Clock Museum's display of hundreds of timepieces

❷ **Cruise** the Murray aboard a paddle-steamer from the Port of Echuca

❸ **Head** for Australia's largest cactus collection, the 2-ha Cactus Country, at Strathmerton

VISITOR INFORMATION

Echuca: (03) 5480 7555; 1800 677 679
www.echucamoama.com

Shepparton: (03) 5831 4400;
1800 808 839

FOCUS ON

Food and wine

Irrigation has transformed the once dusty Goulburn Valley into the fruit bowl of Victoria. Orchards, market gardens and farms supply the canneries in Shepparton, which are among the largest in the Southern Hemisphere. The valley is dotted with outlets for venison, poultry, smoked trout, berries, organic vegetables, honey, jams, preserves, fruit juices, mustards, pickles, vinegar and liquored truffles. The region's nine wineries make reliable reds and distinctive whites. Near Nagambie, Mitchelton Wines is known for marsannes and rieslings grown on sandy, riverine soils. At nearby Avenel, Plunkett Wines make long-finishing chardonnay from grapes grown high in the Strathbogie Ranges.

CLIMATE ECHUCA

	J	F	M	A	M	J	J	A	S	O	N	D
Max. °C	31	31	27	22	18	14	13	15	18	22	26	29
Min. °C	15	15	13	9	7	5	4	5	6	9	11	14
Rain mm	27	27	32	33	42	43	41	43	40	43	32	29
Raindays	4	4	5	6	9	10	11	11	10	9	6	5

Barmah State Park and State Forest

These adjacent areas form the State's biggest river red gum forest. Ulupna Island and Barmah Lake have camping facilities, walks and beach access; bush camping is permitted elsewhere. A 60-km scenic drive takes in sites of historical interest. The Dharnya Centre interprets the culture of the Yorta Yorta people.

For more detail see maps 229 & 232–3. For descriptions of ❶ towns see Towns from A to Z (p. 158).

Cobram

This lovely fruit-growing town is surrounded by peach, nectarine, pear and orange orchards. The town also offers access to a number of wide sandy beaches on the Murray, perfect for swimming, fishing, picnicking and water sports. Camping facilities are available, and across the river in NSW is the renowned 36-hole Cobram–Barooga Golf Club.

Port of Echuca

The historic port of Echuca with its impressive red-gum wharf recalls the second half of the 19th century, when the Murray carried wool and other goods from farms and stations. A number of beautifully restored paddle-steamers are moored here.

Chateau Tahbilk

Chateau Tahbilk (1860) was established on the sandy loam of the Goulburn River south of Nagambie. One of Australia's most beautiful wine properties, it has a National Trust-classified cellar which, with other buildings, is a working example of early Australian winegrowing. Chateau Tahbilk produces top quality wines and has won over 1000 awards.

Tatura

Internment camps were set up around this small farming town during WW II for German POWs and Australians thought to be German sympathisers. Tatura's museum (open weekends and public holidays) has relevant photographs and memorabilia, and a German cemetery is adjacent to the town cemetery.

THE GOLDFIELDS

The Goldfields region of Central Victoria is the historic jewel of rural Australia. The discovery of gold near Ballarat in 1851 transformed a sleepy farming district into a rowdy, anarchic, cosmopolitan and fantastically wealthy goldmining frontier as immigrants from all over the world poured in to try their luck. Development took place on a massive scale between the 1850s and 1890s. Today the area preserves an intense concentration of Victorian architecture, in both the grand public buildings, parks and gardens of Ballarat and Bendigo and the more modest but charming streetscapes of smaller towns such as Castlemaine, Creswick, Clunes, Maldon and St Arnaud. The region's many galleries, museums, working mines and interpretative centres recall all the drama and detail of the goldfields history, while stylish B&Bs, hotels, restaurants and cafes supply visitors with modern comforts.

TOP EVENTS

Jan.	Organs of the Ballarat Goldfields
Jan.	Highland Gathering (Maryborough)
Feb.	Gold King Festival (Buninyong, near Ballarat)
Mar.	Begonia Festival (Ballarat)
Easter	Fair (Bendigo, features Chinese dragon)
Easter	Fair (Maldon)
Apr.	Pyrenees Vignerons' Gourmet Food and Wine Race Meeting (Avoca)
Apr.	State Festival (Castlemaine, odd-numbered years)
Apr.	Food, Wine and Jazz Festival (Smeaton, near Creswick)
July	Winter Festival (Ballarat)
Aug.–Sept.	Golden Wattle Festival (Maryborough)
Aug.–Nov.	Royal South Street Eisteddfod (Ballarat)
Oct.	Vintage Car Hill Climb (Maldon)
Nov.	Festival of Gardens (Castlemaine, odd-numbered years)
Dec.	Tram Spectacular (Bendigo)

VISITOR INFORMATION

Ballarat: (03) 5320 5741; 1800 648 450

Bendigo: (03) 5444 4445; 1800 813 153

www.goldfields.org.au

Backblocks of the goldfields

Some of the quieter towns are tucked away in a rural pocket north-west of Bendigo. In Dunolly, where 126 nuggets were found in the town itself, see replicas at the Goldfields Historic and Arts Society. St Arnaud boasts the beautiful Queen Mary Gardens and a number of old pubs and verandah-fronted shops. There are eucalyptus distilleries at Inglewood and Wedderburn.

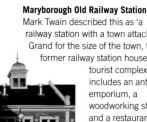

Maryborough Old Railway Station

Mark Twain described this as 'a railway station with a town attached'. Grand for the size of the town, this former railway station houses a tourist complex that includes an antique emporium, a woodworking shop, and a restaurant and cafe.

CLIMATE BENDIGO												
	J	F	M	A	M	J	J	A	S	O	N	D
Max. °C	29	29	25	21	16	13	12	14	16	20	24	26
Min. °C	14	15	13	9	7	4	3	5	6	8	11	13
Rain mm	34	32	36	41	55	60	56	58	54	53	38	33
Raindays	5	4	5	7	10	12	13	13	11	10	7	6

FOCUS ON

Gold-rush history

Sovereign Hill in Ballarat is one of the country's best historic theme parks. It offers a complete recreation of life on the 1850s goldfields. The nearby Gold Museum, part of the Sovereign Hill complex, features displays of gold nuggets and coins and changing exhibits on the history of gold. The Eureka Stockade Centre, also in Ballarat, offers interpretative displays on Australia's only armed insurrection, which took place in 1854. See the original Eureka Flag at the Ballarat Fine Art Gallery, which also houses historic collections of Australian and gold-rush art. In Eureka Street is the tiny Montrose Cottage (1856), an ex-miner's house furnished in the style of the period; here a moving museum display recalls the lives and contribution of women in the gold-rush era. In Bendigo, the Central Deborah Gold Mine offers tours 80m down a 410-m-deep reef mine and excellent displays on goldmining techniques.

Maldon

The 1860s streets of Maldon are shaded by European trees and lined with old buildings of local stone. Declared a Notable Town by the National Trust, Maldon has historic B&Bs and a tourist steam railway. Take in the view from the Anzac Hill lookout.

Sovereign Hill

One of Victoria's top tourist attractions, Ballarat's Sovereign Hill is a living museum. Blacksmiths, bakers, innkeepers and storekeepers in period dress ply their trades amid the tents while miners pan for gold. In the evenings, 'Blood on the Southern Cross', a sound and light re-enactment of the Eureka Rebellion, is played out across the town streets.

Whipstick State Park

This 2300-ha park, 21 km north of Bendigo, conserves distinctive whipstick mallee forest and protects abundant birdlife. There are picnic areas, walking tracks and designated gold-fossicking areas.

EXPERIENCE IT!

❶ **Book** a weekend's indulgence at the Warrenmang Vineyard Resort, north-west of Avoca in the Pyrenees wine district

❷ **Enjoy** the begonias in March at Ballarat's historic Botanic Gardens on the shores of Lake Wendouree

❸ **Learn** more about Australia's often maligned native dog at the Dingo Farm near Castlemaine

❹ **See** potters in action at the long-established Bendigo Pottery

❺ **Ride** a camel at Sedgwick's Camel Farm, south-east of Bendigo (weekends; weekdays by appointment)

Bendigo's Chinese sites

The restored Joss House (pictured), on the city's northern outskirts, and the Golden Dragon Museum in Bridge Street are reminders of the substantial presence of Chinese on the goldfields. The museum has an excellent display of Chinese regalia. A ceremonial archway leads to the Garden of Joy, built 1996 to represent the Chinese landscape in miniature.

Pall Mall, Bendigo

The tree-lined French-style boulevard of Pall Mall is probably country Australia's most impressive street, with many of its buildings dating back to the gold rush. Don't miss the grand Shamrock Hotel, opened 1897. City heritage tours are available aboard Vintage Trams.

CHARLTON

WEDDERBURN

ST ARNAUD

INGLEWOOD

WHIPSTICK SP

❹ BENDIGO

N

0   20 km

DUNOLLY

MALDON ❺

❶ MARYBOROUGH

PYRENEES WINE REGION

AVOCA

CASTLEMAINE
❸

CLUNES

CRESWICK

BEAUFORT

BALLARAT

❷

SKIPTON

For more detail see maps 218, 219, 220–1, 227 & 229. For descriptions of ❶ *towns see* Towns from A to Z *(p. 158).*

Castlemaine

This historic goldmining town has a community of painters, potters, instrument makers and other craftspeople. The original market building (1862), with its classical Roman facade, now houses visitor information and a gold-diggings interpretive centre. Don't miss the 1860s Buda Historic Home, with its heritage-listed garden.

Ballarat's gardens and gallery

A large part of Ballarat's visual charm is its beautiful parks and gardens with begonias, the city's floral emblem, a common theme. Australia's oldest and largest provincial gallery is in Ballarat's elegant Lydiard Street. Paintings by Tom Roberts, Sir Sidney Nolan, Russell Drysdale and Fred Williams feature, as well as more contemporary works and exhibitions.

SPA & GARDEN COUNTRY

Ancient volcanic eruptions, lava flows and erosion have formed a stunning mountain landscape rising out of the coastal plains to the north-west of Melbourne. Gold and timber attracted the first European settlers to the district. Soon afterwards, Melbourne's elite arrived to take the health-giving waters at the mineral springs in the area and to establish their grand, European-style country gardens on the basalt-rich soil. Today the district retains the air of a 19th-century hills retreat, with historic spa towns, mansions, gardens, galleries, craft shops, forest walks and drives, and gracious guesthouses and B&Bs.

TOP EVENTS

Jan. Picnic Races
(Hanging Rock, near Mount Macedon)

Jan. Lavandula Harvest Festival
(Shepherds Flat, near Hepburn Springs)

Feb. Country Music Festival (Kyneton)

May Hepburn Swiss-Italian Festival
(Daylesford)

July Fine Food and Wine Fayre
(Glenlyon, near Daylesford)

Sept. Daffodil and Arts Festival (Kyneton)

Oct. Macedon Ranges Budburst Wine Festival
(throughout wine district)

Dec. Highland Gathering (Daylesford)

Dec. Five Mile Creek Festival (Woodend)

EXPERIENCE IT!

❶ **Visit** one of the region's wineries to taste chardonnay, riesling or pinot noir; brochures available from Woodend.

❷ **Dine** at the award-winning Lake House in Daylesford

❸ **Shop** for cool-climate plants at the nurseries of Macedon

VISITOR INFORMATION

Daylesford: (03) 5348 1339
Woodend: (03) 5427 2033

FOCUS ON

Country gardens

Gardens flourish in the volcanic soil and cool, moist climate of the spa country. There are botanic gardens in Daylesford and Malmsbury. Around the village of Mount Macedon classic mountainside gardens surround large houses; check with visitor information for their spring and autumn open days. Cope-Williams Vineyard at Romsey is well known for its English-style garden and cricket green, while at Blackwood the beautiful Garden of St Erth offers 2 ha of exotic and native species (closed Wed. and Thurs.). For something special, visit the Lavandula Lavender Farm near Hepburn Springs, where the lavender crop sits well beside cottage-style plantings.

CLIMATE KYNETON

	J	F	M	A	M	J	J	A	S	O	N	D
Max. °C	27	27	24	18	14	11	10	12	15	18	22	25
Min. °C	10	10	8	6	4	2	2	2	3	5	7	9
Rain mm	37	39	47	54	75	90	82	84	74	69	52	50
Raindays	5	5	6	9	12	15	16	16	13	11	9	7

Daylesford and Hepburn Springs

The spa complex at Hepburn Springs offers heated spas, flotation tanks, saunas and massages. The adjacent town of Daylesford is an attractive weekend destination with galleries, antique shops, heritage buildings and B&Bs. Worth a visit is the Convent Gallery (pictured), a 19th-century former convent that houses notable local artwork, sculpture and jewellery.

For more detail see maps 210–11 & 221. For descriptions of ❶ towns see Towns from A to Z (p. 158).

Hanging Rock

This impressive rock formation, north of the village of Mount Macedon, was created by the erosion of solidified lava. The spot was inspiration for Joan Lindsay's novel *Picnic at Hanging Rock* and a setting for the subsequent film. Walking tracks lead up to a superb view, with glimpses of koalas along the way.

Wombat Forest Drive

Start this 65-km-return forest drive (gravel and sealed road) at Blackwood. The waters of Lyonville Mineral Springs, in a glade on the Loddon River, are rich in potassium and calcium. Trentham Falls (pictured) is an ideal spot for a picnic.

Lerderderg Gorge and State Park

The Lerderderg River has cut a deep gorge through sandstone and slate in this 13 400 ha park. Rugged treed ridges enclose much of the river. Also a feature are quiet forest pools and wetland. Explore on foot, or take a scenic drive via O'Briens Road (turn off south of Blackwood).

Organ Pipes National Park

Lava flows created a 20-m wall of basalt columns in a gorge in this 121-ha park near Sunbury. The 'organ pipes' can be seen from the carpark, or close up via an easy walking trail. A regeneration program is gradually bringing this once denuded area back to its native state.

YARRA & DANDENONGS

Wineries, fine-food outlets, historic gardens, ancient forests, snowfields and excellent activities for children are some of the diverse attractions that make this region so popular with daytrippers and weekenders alike. The scenic Yarra Valley, about an hour's drive from Melbourne, is one of Australia's best producers of cool-climate wines. The Dandenong Ranges, east of the city, offer an intoxicating mix of native mountainside forests and remarkable European-style gardens. Between the two areas, some of the State's most magnificent forests and a series of charming villages form a gateway to Victoria's beautiful alpine country.

TOP EVENTS

Jan.   Upper Yarra Draughthorse Festival (Warburton)

Feb.   Coldstream Country and Western Festival (Healesville)

Mar.   Grape Grazing Festival (throughout Yarra Valley wine district)

Apr.   Great Train Race (Emerald)

Apr.   Musica Viva Yarra Valley Festival (at Domain Chandon, near Yarra Glen)

July   Winterfest (Warburton)

Aug.– Rhododendron Festival
Nov.   (Olinda)

Sept.– Tesselaar's Tulip Festival
Oct.   (Silvan, near Olinda)

Nov.   Gateway Festival (Healesville)

EXPERIENCE IT!

❶ **Enjoy** fine Italian fare at the De Bortoli estate, north of Yarra Glen

❷ **Follow** the Yarra Valley Regional Food Trail for berries, trout, chocolates and cheese (brochure at Healesville's information centre)

❸ **See** winter snow on Mount Donna Buang, near Warburton

VISITOR INFORMATION

Healesville: (03) 5962 2600

Dandenong Ranges Tourism
Upper Ferntree Gully: (03) 9758 7522
www.yarrarangestourism.com

FOCUS ON

Tours of the forest

This area has some of the State's best forest scenery. Bushwalkers, horseriders and cyclists can travel the 38-km Warburton Rail Trail starting in Lilydale. The Beeches, via Marysville, is a 5-km stroll through forests of ancient beech and mountain ash. The less energetic can take a forest drive through or around the Yarra Ranges National Park: the Black Spur (between Healesville and Marysville); Acheron Way (from Warburton to Marysville); or Lady Talbot Drive (from Marysville and return). For something special, visit Mount Donna Buang Rainforest Gallery (9 km from Warburton), which includes a viewing platform and rainforest walkway.

CLIMATE HEALESVILLE

	J	F	M	A	M	J	J	A	S	O	N	D
Max. °C	26	26	24	19	16	12	12	14	16	19	22	24
Min. °C	11	12	11	9	7	4	4	5	6	8	9	11
Rain mm	58	68	64	91	96	82	87	98	94	106	93	86
Raindays	7	7	8	11	14	14	16	17	15	14	12	10

Gardens of the Dandenongs

Mountain ash forests and fern gullies frame the historic cool-climate gardens of one of Australia's best-known gardening regions. Many of the private gardens are open daily. Non-private gardens include the National Rhododendron Gardens and the R. J. Hamer Forest Arboretum (both near Olinda), the William Ricketts Sanctuary (Mount Dandenong) and the Alfred Nicholas Memorial Gardens (Sherbrooke); small fees may apply.

Yarra Valley wineries

The 30 or so wineries of this charming district produce high-quality chardonnay, cabernet sauvignon and pinot noir. Visit Domain Chandon, built by French champagne makers Moet et Chandon; the magnificent tasting-room offers fine views of the vine-covered plains and hilly backdrop. Early-morning balloon flights provide another perspective.

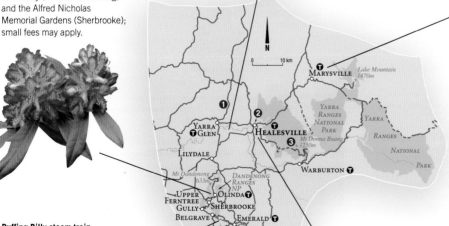

Marysville and Lake Mountain

This beautiful sub-alpine village with its excellent cafes and art and crafts outlets is the centre for forest walks and provides access to the magnificent Steavenson Falls. Lake Mountain, 19 km east, is a popular tobogganing and cross-country skiing resort in winter.

Puffing Billy steam train

In the early 1900s four railways were established to develop rural areas near Melbourne; only the Puffing Billy line survives. Now one of the State's top attractions, the little train with its open carriages and restaurant car travels 25 km through the tree ferns, from Belgrave to Gembrook and back again.

For more detail see maps 207 & 211. For descriptions of ❶ towns see Towns from A to Z (p. 158).

Healesville Sanctuary

Spread across 32 ha of bushland, this world-renowned native animal sanctuary has over 200 animal and bird species, many in natural habitats. Special features include talks by keepers, a nocturnal viewing area, bird of prey displays and the platypus exhibit.

THE HIGH COUNTRY

The Victorian Alps is a continuation of the Great Dividing Range, which runs along Australia's east coast. Mount Hotham and Falls Creek, both on the Bogong High Plains, offer some of the State's most challenging skiing. Fast-flowing trout streams originate in these mountains and feed into the upper reaches of the Murray River. The foothills to the north-west of the High Country are used for farming and grazing. In this area there are several old goldfield towns (for example Beechworth) of great charm and historical interest. Lake Eildon, Victoria's largest constructed lake, stores water flowing west from the near-wilderness of Alpine National Park. The Hume Highway traverses the plains west of the Strathbogie Ranges, passing towns raided by the Kelly gang in the 1870s. Just west of Wodonga, grapes from the hot, alluvial flats on the south side of the Murray are made into the widely known fortified wines of Rutherglen.

FOCUS ON

Ski country

Victoria's ski resorts are within easy distance of Melbourne. The main resort mountains and their distances from Melbourne are Mount Buller (221 km via Mansfield), Mount Buffalo (331 km via Myrtleford), Mount Hotham (363 km via Bright) and Falls Creek (367 km via Mount Beauty). The ski season starts officially on the Queen's Birthday weekend early in June and ends on the first weekend in October. Snowsport conditions, however, depend on the weather. All resorts offer protected runs for beginners and cross-country skiing. Mount Hotham, known as the 'powder snow capital' of Australia, has the most challenging runs for experienced downhill skiers and snowboarders. Life in the high country does not stop when the snow melts. The adventurous can try mountain bike riding, tandem paragliding, abseiling or caving. Mountain lakes and streams offer trout fishing, swimming, sailing and canoeing. Trails across the mountains, ablaze with wildflowers in summer, can be explored on horseback or foot. The less energetic can just breathe the crystalline air and gaze across hazy blue ridges.

TOP EVENTS

Mar.	*Man from Snowy River Festival (Corryong)*
Mar.	*Harvest Festival (Mansfield)*
Mar.	*Tobacco, Hops and Timber Festival (Myrtleford)*
Mar.	*Tastes of Rutherglen (district wineries)*
Easter	*Golden Horseshoes Festival (Beechworth)*
Apr.	*Music Muster (Mount Beauty)*
Apr.	*Autumn Festival (Bright)*
June	*Winery Walkabout (Rutherglen wineries)*
July	*Winter Wonderland Festival (Bright)*
Aug.	*International Kangaroo Hoppet (cross-country ski race, Falls Creek)*
Sept.	*Wine Show (Rutherglen)*
Oct.	*Alpine Spring Festival (Bright)*
Oct.	*Great Alpine Bike Ride (Myrtleford to Bright)*
Nov.	*Gang Gang Mountain Bike Festival (Mount Beauty)*
Nov.	*Brown Brothers Wine and Food Weekend (Milawa)*
Nov.	*Wangaratta Festival of Jazz*
Dec.	*Golden Spurs Rodeo (Myrtleford)*

Kelly country

A giant effigy of Ned Kelly (pictured) greets visitors to Glenrowan. After killing three local policemen in 1878, the Kelly gang hid for two years in the Warby Range (near Wangaratta), raiding nearby towns. Ned was captured in 1880 after a shootout in Siege Street, Glenrowan, and was later hanged. Visit the Ned Kelly Memorial Museum and Homestead in Gladstone Street.

VISITOR INFORMATION

Albury–Wodonga: (02) 6041 3875; 1800 800 743

Bright: (03) 5755 2275; 1800 500 117

Wangaratta: (02) 5721 5711; 1800 801 065

CLIMATE	**HOTHAM HEIGHTS**											
	J	F	M	A	M	J	J	A	S	O	N	D
Max. °C	18	19	15	10	6	3	1	3	5	9	13	15
Min. °C	8	9	7	4	1	−2	−4	−2	−1	1	4	5
Rain mm	88	59	121	154	195	175	266	256	210	179	168	172
Raindays	10	7	12	12	15	16	19	19	17	15	15	14

Historic Beechworth

The National Trust has classified over 30 buildings, some built of honey-coloured granite, in what is now one of Australia's best-preserved gold rush towns. Dine in a stately former bank, visit the powder magazine, and wander through an evocative cemetery (pictured) for Chinese goldminers who never returned to their ancestral land.

Lake Eildon

Created by damming the Goulburn River in the 1950s, this lake, with six times the capacity of Sydney Harbour, is popular with water sports enthusiasts, anglers and houseboat holidaymakers. The surrounding Lake Eildon National Park offers bushwalking, camping, and 4WD tracks through the foothills of the Victorian Alps.

EXPERIENCE IT!

❶ Go abseiling, rock-climbing, kayaking or bushwalking with experts in the wilderness of Alpine National Park

❷ Indulge in a weekend of fine dining at Howqua Dale Gourmet Retreat near Howqua

❸ Ride the high country on horseback, via the mountain town of Corryong

❹ Visit the childhood home of novelist Henry Handel Richardson and see a remarkable grapevine at historic Chiltern

❺ Shop for gourmet cheese at Milawa and taste excellent fortified wines nearby

The Upper Murray

The Murray River rises in rugged alpine country in north-east Victoria on the border of New South Wales. The swift mountain streams that feed the Murray are a paradise for trout fishermen. The river and its rapids can be negotiated by canoe on half-day, weekend or four-day adventure tours. The heavily timbered Burrowa–Pine Mountain National Park, which has waterfalls, lyrebirds, wallabies and wombats, will challenge most bushwalkers. Access is via the town of Corryong.

The Great Alpine Road

This road travels some 307 km (a 5-hour journey) through the high country and beyond. Beginning in Wangaratta, it traverses the hop fields and walnut groves around Myrtleford and Bright. It climbs into the Alps, passing through the vast 645 000-ha Alpine National Park including one of Victoria's favourite downhill skiing areas, Mount Hotham, and descends through rugged gorge country to Bairnsdale and the East Gippsland lakes.

Wines of Rutherglen

Vines on alluvial flats in a shallow loop of the Murray River produce some of the world's great fortified wines. The region is known for tokays and muscats, big reds and, more recently, lighter reds such as gamay. There are over a dozen wineries near Rutherglen; look out for All Saints (with a National Trust-classified building), Pfeiffer, Chambers and Campbells.

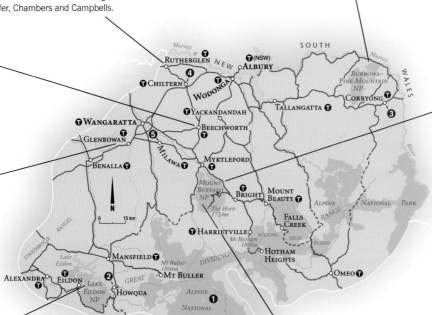

For more detail see maps 211, 222–3, 233 & 234. For descriptions of ❶ towns see Towns from A to Z (p. 158).

Mount Buffalo National Park

This 31 000-ha national park is the State's oldest, declared in 1898. A plateau of boulders and tors includes The Horn (pictured), the highest point, for great views at sunrise. Walking tracks are set among streams, waterfalls, and snow gum and mountain ash forest. There is summer camping, swimming and canoeing at Lake Catani. In winter, the Mount Buffalo ski area is popular with families.

EAST GIPPSLAND

Australia's largest system of inland waterways, the remote splendour of Ninety Mile Beach, and scenic foothills of the high country are the natural features that make East Gippsland one of Victoria's top holiday destinations. These diverse landscapes offer extraordinary touring opportunities. Other recreational activities include fishing, sailing, swimming, surfing and, in the foothills, whitewater rafting, abseiling and caving. Accommodation can be had in caravan parks, motels, B&Bs and on houseboats, or in the camping grounds of the beautiful coastal and mountain national parks.

TOP EVENTS

Jan.	Lakes Summer Festival (Lakes Entrance)
Feb.	Bruthen Blues Bash (near Bairnsdale)
Feb.	Jazz Festival (Paynesville)
Mar.	Marlay Point–Paynesville Overnight Yacht Race (from Marlay Point, near Sale)
Easter	Rodeo (Buchan)
Easter	Festival of the Great Southern Ocean (Mallacoota)
Apr.	Australian Line Dancing Championships (Bairnsdale)
June	Gippsland Wool and Fibre Fair (Bairnsdale)
Oct.	International Festival of the Lakes (Lakes Entrance)

EXPERIENCE IT!

❶ Swim in the rock pools of the Mitchell River Gorge, in Mitchell River National Park

❷ Stay at the remote Point Hicks Lightstation in Croajingolong National Park

❸ Tour the Royal and Fairy caves in Buchan Caves Reserve

VISITOR INFORMATION

Lakes Entrance: (03) 5155 1966; 1800 637 060

Orbost: (03) 5154 2424; 1800 637 060

www.lakesandwilderness.com.au

FOCUS ON

Fishing

Fishing is a huge drawcard in East Gippsland. Fish for trout in the mountain streams and rivers – such as the Delegate River – or head for the coast. The lakes, rivers and inlets around Paynesville, Marlo, Bemm River and Mallacoota are great for bream, trevally and flathead. Boat angling is the best choice here, although land-based angling will yield results. Ninety Mile Beach and the remote beaches of The Lakes National Park provide some of the best surf fishing in the State, with salmon, tailor and flathead among the prospects.

CLIMATE LAKES ENTRANCE

	J	F	M	A	M	J	J	A	S	O	N	D
Max. °C	24	24	22	20	17	15	15	16	17	19	20	22
Min. °C	14	15	13	11	8	6	5	6	7	9	11	13
Rain mm	57	35	55	61	79	65	55	57	57	61	73	74
Raindays	8	7	10	10	12	13	12	14	13	13	13	11

Snowy River National Park

The much-celebrated Snowy River begins as a trickle near Mt Kosciuszko and passes through wild limestone gorge and forest country before reaching a coastal lagoon. McKillops Bridge (via Buchan) is a beautiful area with camping and barbecue facilities, swimming spots and some good short walks.

For more detail see maps 225 & 234–5. For descriptions of ❶ towns see Towns from A to Z (p. 158).

Mallacoota

Surrounded by the remote ocean beaches, estuarine waterways and unspoilt bush of Croajingolong National Park, this old-fashioned resort offers one of the best fishing, walking, boating, swimming and nature-watching holidays in Victoria. The town hosts a popular arts festival at Easter.

Bataluk Cultural Trail

This driving tour starts at the visitor centre in Sale and links sites significant to the Gunai (Kurani) people, who travelled the area for at least 18 000 years before European settlement. Features include Buchan Caves (pictured), and the legend-rich Den of Nargun (a cave) in Mitchell River National Park.

Large lakes and a long beach

Gippsland Lakes, a vast natural resort, is contained on the coastal side by a strip of sand and channels and the remote Ninety Mile Beach. At the system's centre, the water-bound Lakes National Park offers birdwatching, walking, swimming and camping. Access is via boat from Paynesville or road and foot from Loch Sport.

Lakes Entrance

Lakes Entrance (pictured), at the head of the Lakes, is a great base for fishing and boating and offers accommodation at all levels. For a holiday afloat, book a self-drive cruiser from nearby Metung. There are several wineries in the area. Wyanga Park Winery offers a lakes cruise from town to its cellar door and restaurant.

MORNINGTON PENINSULA

This broad peninsula separating Port Phillip and Western Port has a long history as a summer retreat for Melburnians. It offers a clutch of well-serviced seaside towns with access to three seafronts: the sheltered 'front' beaches of Port Phillip, the wild 'back' beaches on Bass Strait, and the relatively unpopulated surf beaches of Western Port. During winter, holidaymakers turn their attention to the region's scenic countryside and its impressive collection of cool-climate vineyards and gourmet food producers. In any season, popular activities are walking, fishing, golfing (a choice of 20 courses), and grazing at the many restaurants, pubs and cafes.

TOP EVENTS

Jan.   Swim Classic (Portsea)

Jan.   Sail Melbourne
(coastal towns throughout region)

Mar.   Maize Maze Festival
(Arthurs Seat, near Dromana)

Mar.   Pinot Week (throughout wine district)

Mar.   Cool Climate Wine Show (Red Hill)

Mar.   Street Festival (Sorrento)

June   Queen's Birthday Wine Weekend
(throughout wine district)

Oct.   Mornington Food and Wine Festival
(throughout wine district)

Nov.   Film Festival (Rosebud)

EXPERIENCE IT!

❶ Shop till you drop at the popular community market at Red Hill (first Sat. of month, Sept.–May)

❷ Canter on the sands or take an equine winery tour with Gunnamatta Trail Rides, via Rye

❸ Visit McCrae Homestead, the cottage home of 19th-century artist Georgiana McCrae, at McCrae

VISITOR INFORMATION

Mornington Peninsula Visitor Centre
Dromana: (03) 5987 3078;
1800 804 009

FOCUS ON

Wineries

The grape came relatively late to the Mornington Peninsula: the longest surviving vineyard, Elgee Park, north of Merricks, was established early in the 1970s. Viticulture exploded during the 1980 and 1990s; now there are nearly 40 wineries on the Mornington Peninsula, most clustered around Red Hill. The vineyards are in a cool climate, tend to be small and set in postcard landscapes, concentrate on the classic varieties of pinot noir and chardonnay, and produce fairly expensive wines. Stonier's Winery, Tucks Ridge and Main Ridge Estate are a few of the names to look out for.

CLIMATE MORNINGTON

	J	F	M	A	M	J	J	A	S	O	N	D
Max. °C	25	25	23	19	16	14	13	14	16	18	20	23
Min. °C	13	14	13	11	9	7	7	7	8	10	11	12
Rain mm	46	43	50	62	71	71	69	71	72	70	60	55
Raindays	7	7	8	11	14	15	15	15	14	13	11	8

French Island

Half this sparsely inhabited island, a 15-min ferry ride from Stony Point, is national park. It supports 600 indigenous plant species, a large koala population and 234 bird species. There is no car access: explore by foot, hire a bicycle or book a tour. Camping and guesthouse accommodation is available.

Sorrento sojourns

The Queenscliff–Sorrento car ferry crosses Port Phillip several times a day, offering visitors a tour of the two quite distinct peninsulas – Bellarine and Mornington – without a long drive by land. Dolphin cruises, some of which offer a swim with Port Phillip's bottlenose population, operate in summer.

Portsea

Near the north-west tip of the peninsula, this village has been long favoured by Melbourne's wealthy. It has large houses, some of which have their own private boathouses (pictured), elegant hotels, comfortable motels and B&Bs, good dining and a legendary pub. Further west, don't miss Fort Nepean, once an important defence site, and London Bridge, a rock formation off Portsea Surf Beach.

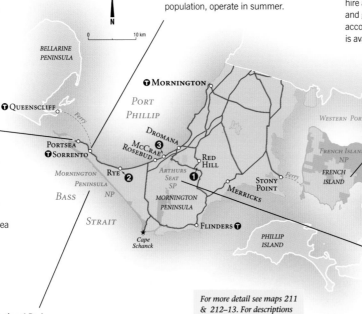

For more detail see maps 211 & 212–13. For descriptions of ❶ towns see Towns from A to Z *(p. 158).*

Mornington Peninsula National Park

This park extends along the south coast of the peninsula where the Bass Strait surf pounds windswept beaches and headlands. A 32-km walking track runs from Portsea Surf Beach right along the coast to Cape Schanck, with its historic lighthouse (1858), at the peninsula's southern tip.

Arthurs Seat

Just inland from Dromana off the Nepean Highway, in a state park of the same name, Arthurs Seat offers superb views back over Melbourne and the bay. The 300-m summit is reached by chairlift. Nearby is Arthurs Seat Maze, which features a series of themed gardens and mazes including the largest Maize Maze in the Southern Hemisphere.

PHILLIP ISLAND & GIPPSLAND

This is an area as diverse as it is beautiful. Along the coast, wild beaches and calm inlets give way to historic fishing, mining and farming towns, and spectacular stretches of bushland, much of it protected by national park. Wildlife thrives, most famously in the penguin and seal colonies of Phillip Island. Inland, the forested ridge country of the Strzelecki Ranges meets the central Gippsland plain where Australia's largest deposits of brown coal are mined to fuel the power stations that generate most of Victoria's electricity. Throughout much of the district, well-watered fields and rolling hills support one of Australia's biggest dairy industries and burgeoning wine and gourmet food production. In the north, gentle foothills rise to the high country of the Great Dividing Range, offering skiing in winter and walking tracks through grasslands and alpine flowers in summer.

TOP EVENTS

Jan.	King of the Mountain Woodchop (Erica, near Walhalla)
Jan.	South Gippsland Food and Wine Festival (Leongatha)
Feb.–Mar.	Music in the Park (Traralgon)
Mar.	Jazz Festival (Inverloch)
Mar.	Potato Festival (Koo-wee-rup)
Mar.	Jazz Festival (Moe)
Mar.	Blue Rock Classic (cross-country horse race, Moe)
Mar.	Fishing Contest (Port Albert)
Easter	Coal Skip Fill (Wonthaggi)
Easter	Tarra Festival (Yarram)
Apr.	World Superbike Championships (Phillip Island)
Sept.	Daffodil and Floral Festival (Leongatha)
Oct.	Grand Prix Motorcycle Race (Phillip Island)
Nov.	Seabank Fishing Competition (Yarram)

VISITOR INFORMATION

Phillip Island (Newhaven):
(03) 5956 7447; 1300 366 422

Traralgon: (03) 5174 3199;
1800 621 409

South Gippsland Visitor
Information Centre
Korumburra: (03) 5655 2233;
1800 630 704

www.phillipisland.net.au

Gourmet Deli Trail

Tour for trout, venison, fine cheeses, baked goods, berries, potatoes, herbs and wine on the Gourmet Deli Trail. The extensive area covered includes the towns of Warragul, Foster and Wonthaggi and annotated maps are available from information centres. There are a dozen or so cool-climate wineries; try Bass Phillip's pinot noir at Leongatha.

CLIMATE LEONGATHA

	J	F	M	A	M	J	J	A	S	O	N	D
Max. °C	25	25	23	19	16	14	13	14	16	19	21	23
Min. °C	12	12	11	9	7	5	5	5	7	8	9	11
Rain mm	59	61	71	88	85	95	83	95	88	96	81	68
Raindays	10	9	11	15	17	18	18	20	17	16	14	11

FOCUS ON

Phillip Island wildlife

The Penguin Parade on Summerland Beach in Phillip Island Nature Park is a major international tourist attraction. Just after sunset, little (fairy) penguins, the world's smallest at 33 cm tall, come home to their burrows in the sand dunes after a day in the sea. To protect the penguins, visitors are restricted to designated viewing areas and no cameras are allowed. Bookings are essential during peak holiday periods. The Visitor Centre also offers a simulated underwater tour showing the penguins foraging for food and avoiding predators. Seal Rocks, 2 km offshore, is home to thousands of sunbaking, sea-frolicking seals. These creatures can be viewed up close from aboard a seal-watching cruise boat, or on a visit to the Seal Rocks Sea Life Centre near The Nobbies, where real-time images of the seals are relayed onto giant screens. Another popular resident species on the island is the koala. Visit the Koala Conservation Centre and take a walking tour across the park's network of raised walkways.

The Grand Ridge Road

Join The Grand Ridge Road (Tourist Route 93) at tiny Seaview. This mostly gravel road travels 132 km along the spine of the Strzelecki Ranges, offering spectacular views. The drive passes Tarra–Bulga National Park (pictured), where ash, myrtle beech, sassafras, and tree ferns form an exquisite 'cathedral', full of birdsong.

Phillip Island

Although best known for its little (fairy) penguins (pictured), Phillip Island has other impressive attractions. The main town, Cowes, has sheltered beaches, safe for swimming and water sports. Visitors can walk around the island's highest point, Cape Woolamai, visit an historic home on Churchill Island (road access), or attend the Grand Prix Motorcycle Race (each October).

EXPERIENCE IT!

❶ Tour *the State Coal Mine at Wonthaggi with an old-time miner as a guide*

❷ Take *a 3-hour tourist train ride along an historic Gippsland route, beginning at Leongatha*

❸ Fish *at Anderson Inlet near Inverloch, one of the State's best fishing spots*

❹ Spend *a day at Korumburra's Coal Creek Heritage Village, a re-creation of a 19th-century coalmining town*

❺ Stop *to smell the roses in spring at the Rose Garden, Commercial Road, Morwell*

Baw Baw National Park

The Aboriginal word for echo gives the name to this alpine park. In the highest part of the park, Mount Baw Baw (via Moe) has ski facilities and is seldom crowded. The eastern section (via Erica and Walhalla) is popular in summer with walkers, wildflower enthusiasts and campers.

Walhalla

Tourist Route 91, from Moe or Traralgon, leads to the perfectly preserved former goldmining town of Walhalla, situated in a steep, narrow valley. Historic buildings of gold-boom days include the post office, old bakery, museum and Windsor House (pictured). Take the signposted town walk, or a 45-min ride on the Walhalla Goldfields Railway (weekends and holidays), or inspect the Long Tunnel Mine (open most days).

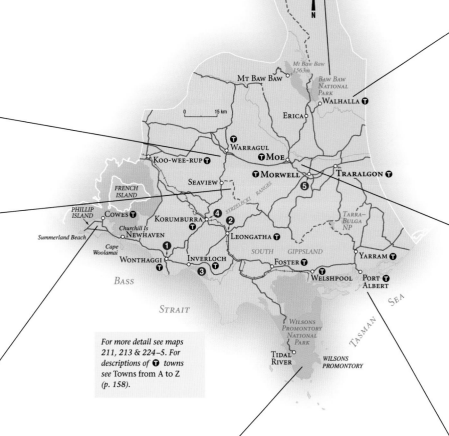

For more detail see maps 211, 213 & 224–5. For descriptions of ❶ *towns see* Towns from A to Z (p. 158).

The power track

At the centre of the Latrobe Valley lies one of the world's largest brown coal deposits. The PowerWorks museum at Morwell explains the processes that supply 85 per cent of Victoria's electricity. Tours of the open mines and power stations operate daily from the museum.

Wilsons Promontory

The Prom is a remote and beautiful landscape supporting diverse native flora and fauna in a near wilderness. The 30-km scenic access road ends at Tidal River, where there are cabins and camping facilities. Access to 150 km of walking tracks across bays and bush is from Tidal River and other points along the road.

Port Albert

This quaint fishing village, near the ruins of an 1840s port, sits on a narrow spit of land beside sheltered waters. About 40 old buildings survive. The town is a major centre for fishing, with plentiful snapper, whiting, flathead, bream and trevally in the shallow waters offshore.

VICTORIA
TOWNS FROM A TO Z

Goulburn River near Alexandra, late afternoon

Alexandra
Pop. 1859

MAP REF. 211 O1, 233 J11

Alexandra is a farming and holiday centre, 26 km W of Eildon. The nearby Goulburn River is an important trout fishery. **In town:** Timber and Tramway Museum in former railway station, Station St. In Downey St: National Trust-classified post office and adjacent law courts; Alexandra Potters (closed Sun.). Rotary Park, Grant St. Bush Market, Perkins St, 2nd Sat. each month (Sept.–June). Jan., Mar., Oct. and Nov.: Picnic Race Races. Easter: Art Show. June: Truck, Bus and Ute Show. Oct.: Open Gardens Weekend. Nov.: Agricultural Show; Rose Festival. **In the area:** Trout-fishing in Goulburn, Acheron and Rubicon rivers. Self-guide tourist drives, brochure available. Excellent walks at Lake Eildon National Park, 16 km E. Bonnie Doon, 37 km NE near Lake Eildon, a good base for trail-riding, bushwalking, water sports and scenic drives. McKenzie Nature Reserve, southern edge of town, virgin bushland with winter and spring orchids. Coach Stop Gallery, 8 km S. At Taggerty, 18 km S: Willowbank Gallery; bush market 4th Sat. each month. Cathedral Range State Park, 3 km S of Taggerty, for camping, bushwalking and rock climbing. **Visitor information:** 45a Grant St; (03) 5772 1100, freecall 1800 652 298. **See also:** The High Country p. 152.

Anglesea
Pop. 1995

MAP REF. 210 E12, 217 N8, 227 Q9

This attractive seaside town on the Great Ocean Road offers excellent swimming and surfing. The golf course is well known for its tame kangaroos. **In town:** Melaleuca Gallery, Great Ocean Rd. Coogoorah Park, on Anglesea River, a bushland reserve with waterways, islands, boardwalks, bridges and picnic areas. Viewing platform, behind town in Coalmine Rd, overlooks open-cut brown-coal mine and power station. Sept.: Angair Wildflower Festival. **In the area:** J. E. Loveridge Lookout, 1 km W. Point Roadknight beach, 2 km SW. Angahook–Lorne State Park, access from Anglesea or Aireys Inlet (11 km SW on Great Ocean Rd). At Aireys Inlet: lighthouse and horseriding. Further south, Memorial Arch, commemorating construction of Great Ocean Rd. 35-km Surf Coast Walk, from Jan Juc (south of Torquay) to Moggs Creek (south of Aireys Inlet); brochure available. Ironbark Basin Reserve, 7 km NW north off Point Addis Rd, for walks, birdlife and cliff-top views of coastline. Point Addis Koorie Cultural Walk, brochure available. **Visitor information:** Jums Barbecued Chickens, 77 Great Ocean Rd; (03) 5263 2390. Web site www.greatoceanrd.org.au **See also:** South-West Coast p. 143.

Apollo Bay
Pop. 979

MAP REF. 217 J12, 227 N12

The Great Ocean Road leads to this centre for dairying, fishing and commercial abalone diving. The wooded mountainous hinterland offers memorable scenery and there is excellent sea and river fishing. The rugged and beautiful coastline has been the scene of many shipwrecks. **In town:** Self-guide walks, leaflet available. Bass Strait Shell Museum, Noel St. Old Cable Station Museum, Great Ocean Rd (2–5 p.m. weekends, school and public holidays). Market on foreshore each Sat. Mar.: Music Festival. Dec.: Aquathon (swimming and running race). **In the area:** Historical and scenic guided and self-guide drive, walking and mountain-bike tours; details from information centre. Carisbrook Falls, 14 km NE on Great Ocean Rd; nearby walking tracks to spectacular views. Turtons Track, 21 km NE, 20-km scenic road through Otway State Forest. Grey River Scenic Reserve, 24 km NE. Marriners Lookout, 1.5 km NW, for views across Skenes Creek and Apollo Bay. Crows Nest Lookout, 5 km NW, on Tuxion Rd. Paradise Scenic Reserve in beautiful Barham River Valley, 10 km NW. Beauchamp Falls, 20 km NW; scenic walk from picnic area to falls. Triplet Falls, 70 km NW via Ferguson in former timber-milling country; 450 m or 900 m walks with steep steps. In Otway National Park, 13 km SW: excellent bushwalking through park to sea; scenic Elliot River and adjacent Shelly Beach; Maits Rest rainforest boardwalk; 300-yr-old National Trust-registered native beech tree; historic Cape Otway Lighthouse (1848), 34 km SW. Melba Gully State Park, 56 km W near Lavers Hill, features fern gullies, myrtle beech trees, glow-worm habitat; self-guide rainforest walk.

Visitor information: 100 Great Ocean Rd; (03) 5237 6529. Web site www. greatoceanrd.org.au **See also:** South-West Coast p. 143.

Ararat   Pop. 6890

MAP REF. 220 B8, 227 K2, 229 K13

The short-lived Ararat gold boom came in 1857. Sheep farming then became the basis of the town's economy. Today the town is the commercial centre of prosperous farming, fine merino wool production, and winegrowing. The district's first vines were planted by French settlers in 1863 and Great Western, 17 km NW of Ararat, gave its name to some of Australia's most famous wines. **In town:** Historical walk/drive, brochures available. Beautiful bluestone buildings in Barkly St: post office, town hall, civic square and war memorial. Also in Barkly St, Ararat Art Gallery, a regional gallery specialising in wool and fibre pieces by leading artists. Oth Art gallery, Birdwood Ave. Chinese Gold Discovery Memorial, Lambert St. Langi Morgala Folk Museum, Queen St, displays Aboriginal weapons and artifacts. Alexandra Park and Botanical Gardens, Vincent St, features orchid glasshouse display, walk-in fernery and herb garden. J-Ward, Old Ararat Gaol, off Lowe St; guided tours. Gum San ('Hill of Gold') Chinese Museum, Western Hwy, commemorates 600 Chinese miners who discovered gold (1857) on Canton Lead. Mar.: Jailhouse Rock Festival. Sept.: Cymbidium Orchid Festival. Oct.: Orchid Festival; Golden Gateway Festival. **In the area:** Green Hill Lake, a constructed lake 4 km E off Western Hwy, ideal for fishing and water sports. Langi Ghiran State Park, 14 km E off Western Hwy, has scenic walks and children's playground. At Buangor, 23 km SE, century-old Buangor Hotel and old Cobb & Co. changing station (c. 1860); 18 km further on, Mt Buangor State Park includes Fern Tree Waterfalls. One Tree Hill Lookout, 5 km NW, for 360° views. Wineries, most open for tastings and sales, *north-west of town:* Garden Gully Vineyard, 15 km; Seppelt Great Western Winery, 17 km, established 1865 and specialising in dry red and sparkling wines (underground cellars National Trust-classified); Champagne Picnic Races in Jan.; Best's Wines, 19 km; *east of town:* Kimbarra Wines, 1.5 km; Mt Langi Ghiran Wines, 20 km; *south of town:* Montara Winery, 3 km; *west of town:* Cathcart Ridge Winery, 6 km; The Gap, 35 km. **Visitor information:** Old Railway Station, 91 High St; (03) 5352 2096, freecall 1800 657 158. Web site www. ararat.asn.au/tourism.htm **See also:** Grampians & Central West p. 144.

Avoca   Pop. 968

MAP REF. 220 H6, 229 M12

Located at the junction of the Sunraysia and Pyrenees hwys, Avoca was established with the discovery of gold in 1852. The surrounding Pyrenee Range foothills offer attractive bushwalking and sightings of kangaroos, wallabies and koalas. **In town:** Self-guide walk, leaflet available. Early National Trust-classified bluestone buildings: old gaol, Davy St; powder magazine, Camp St; courthouse (now a museum) and one of State's earliest pharmacies, Lalor's (1854), operating on original site, in High St. Also in High St.: bakery in old State Bank building; Albion House; and The Avoca Museum. Pyrenees Waterfalls and picnic area, Vinoca Rd. Market at RSL Hall, High St, 2nd Sat. each month. Mar. and Apr.: Petanque Tournaments (French bowls). Apr.: Pyrenees Vignerons' Gourmet Food and Wine Race Meeting. Oct.: Avoca Cup (horse race). **In the area:** Mt Lonarch Arts, 10 km S, gallery and studio. Cemetery, northern outskirts of town, has early Chinese burial sites. At Elmhurst, 26 km SW, Oasis Crystal Gallery for local art and craft. Fishing: Avoca River, near town; Wimmera River 42 km W. A number of wineries in the area; details from information centre. Warrenmang Vineyard Resort, 22 km NW, restaurant serving regional produce. **Visitor information:** 120 High St; (03) 5465 3767. Web site www. goldfields.org.au **See also:** The Goldfields p. 148.

Bacchus Marsh   Pop. 11 279

MAP REF. 210 G5, 221 Q13, 224 A3, 227 R4

The Avenue of Honour provide an impressive entrance from the east to Bacchus Marsh, 49 km W of Melbourne. This long-established town is in a fertile valley, once marshland, between the Werribee and Lerderderg Rivers. **In town:** Manor House, Manor St, home of town's founder, Captain Bacchus; privately owned. In Main St: original blacksmith's shop and cottage; courthouse, lockup and National Bank (all National Trust-classified); Border Inn (1850), thought to have been State's first service stop for Cobb & Co. coaches travelling to goldfields. In Gisborne Rd: Holy Trinity Anglican Church (1877); Express Building Art Gallery. Ra Ceramics and Crafts, Station St. Big Apple Tourist Orchard, Avenue of Honour. June: Rotary Art Show. Nov.: Cup Day in the Park. Dec.: Woodchop. **In the area:** Lerderderg Gorge, 10 km N in Lerderderg State Park, for picnics, bushwalking and swimming; scenic drive through park along O'Briens Rd. Long Forest Flora Reserve, 2 km NE, features bull mallee, some specimens centuries old. Merrimu Reservoir and Wombat State Forest, both about 10 km NE. At Melton, 14 km E, Willows historic homestead. Maddingley open-cut coal mine, 3 km S. At Brisbane Ranges National Park, 16 km SW: steep-sided Anakie Gorge, walking tracks and wildflowers in spring. Werribee Gorge, 10 km W, day walks and picnic area. At Ballan, 20 km NW, Vintage Machinery and Vehicle Rally in Feb. At Blackwood, 31 km NW: Mineral Springs Reserve; Garden of St Erth (closed Wed., Thurs.); start of 53-km-return scenic drive through Wombat State Forest; Shindig Festival on Australia Day Sat. (Jan.); Easter Festival. Wineries and vineyards: St Anne's Vineyard on Western Fwy, 6 km W, has a bluestone cellar built from remains of old Ballarat gaol; Craiglee Winery and Goonawarra Vineyard, Sunbury, 47 km NE; Wildwood Vineyard, Bulla, 9 km SE. **Visitor information:** Blackwood General Store, 7 Martin St, Blackwood; (03) 5368 6525, freecall 1800 659 667. **See also:** Spa & Garden Country p. 150.

Bairnsdale   Pop. 10 890

MAP REF. 225 P4, 234 F13

Located on the Mitchell River flats, this East Gippsland trade centre and holiday town is at the junction of Princes Hwy, Great Alpine Rd and the road east to Lakes Entrance, making it a good base for touring the region. **In town:** Self-guide heritage walks. Historical Museum (1891), Macarthur St, contains items of local historic interest. St Mary's Church, Main St, features wall and ceiling murals by Italian artist Francesco Floreani. Krowathunkooloong, Aboriginal Keeping Place and Museum, Dalmahoy St, houses history, heritage and culture of East Gippsland Koories; canoe tree in Howitt Park, Princes Hwy, 170-year-old 4-m-long scar — both included in Bataluk Cultural Trail (driving tour), brochure available. Adjacent to post office, Port of Bairnsdale site and river walk. Boardwalk across part of McLeod Morass, a bird wetland habitat on southern outskirts of town, access from Macarthur St. Market at Howitt Park, Princes Hwy, 4th Sun. each month.

Apr.: Australian Line Dancing Championships; East Gippsland Agricultural Field Days. May: Australasian Street Grand Prix. June: Gippsland Wool and Fibre Fair. Nov.: Agricultural Show. **In the area:** Self-guide scenic drives and walks, and 4WD tours; details from information centre. Mitchell River empties into Lake King at Eagle Point, 12 km S, where it forms silt jetties that stretch 8 km into lake; view from Eagle Point Bluff; Australian Powerboat Racing Carnival here at Easter. Jolly Jumbuk Country Craft Centre, 5 km E on Princes Hwy, woollen products for sale. Nicholson River Winery, 10 km E. Metung, 30 km SE, a picturesque fishing village on shores of Lake King. At Bruthen, 24 km NW, Blues Bash held in Feb. Historic Dargo township, 93 km NW; Dargo Valley Winery has accommodation and sales. Scenic drive through high plains to Hotham Heights, 80 km N of Dargo (unsealed road, check conditions); stunning in spring when wattles bloom. Mitchell River National Park, near Lindenow, 15 km W, features excellent bushwalking tracks and Den of Nargun, Aboriginal cultural site in gorge and part of Bataluk Cultural Trail. **Visitor information:** 240 Main St; (03) 5152 3444. Web site www.lakesandwilderness. com.au **See also:** East Gippsland p. 154.

Ballarat   Pop. 64 831

MAP REF. 210 C4, 219, 221 K11, 227 O3, 232 A13

Ballarat, 110 km west of Melbourne, is Victoria's largest inland city. The city centre retains much of the charm of the gold-boom era, with many splendid original buildings still standing. Ballarat was a small township in 1851 when its rich alluvial goldfields were discovered. Within two years it had a population of nearly 40 000. A major civil battle occurred here in 1854, when miners refused to pay Government licence fees and fought police and troops at the Eureka Stockade. Today Ballarat features many galleries, museums and antique and craft shops. It has excellent recreational facilities and beautiful gardens and parks. The begonia is the city's floral emblem. **In town:** In Lydiard St: Fine Art Gallery, Australia's largest and oldest regional gallery, has comprehensive collection of Australian art including works by Lindsay family; Her Majesty's Theatre (1875), oldest intact, purpose-built theatre in Australia; Craig's Royal Hotel and George Hotel for old-world surroundings.

Lake Wendouree, used for water sports, and paddle-steamer tours with historical commentary. At Botanic Gardens adjoining the lake: Robert Clarke Horticultural Centre, showcase for begonias; Adam Lindsay Gordon Cottage; Tramway Museum, featuring vintage trams; Prime Ministers' Avenue, displaying busts of Australian prime ministers; elegant statuary pavilion nearby. Vintage Tramway, via Wendouree Pde (rides weekends, public and school holidays). In Eureka St: award-winning historic Montrose Cottage (1856), first masonry cottage built on the goldfields, has museum displaying history of women in the gold rush; unique $4 million Eureka Stockade Centre, with information about the famous battle. Ballarat Wildlife and Reptile Park, cnr York and Fussell sts, features native animals in natural habitat. Sovereign Hill, Main St, a major tourist attraction: world-class reconstruction of a goldmining settlement; features orientation centre and working displays; 'Blood on the Southern Cross', a nightly sight-and-sound spectacular re-creating the Eureka rebellion; Proctor's Wheelwright Factory, a working replica of wooden carriage-wheel production; panning for gold; re-created shops and businesses; barbecue facilities, kiosk, restaurant and licensed hotel; accommodation. Adjoining Sovereign Hill, the Gold Museum features exhibits of gold history, large collection of gold coins and display on the uses of gold. Trash and Trivia Market at Showgrounds, Creswick Rd, each Sun. Pleasant Street Market, 4th Sun. each month. Jan.: Organs of the Ballarat Goldfields. Feb.: Super Southern Swap Meet. Mar.: Begonia Festival; Antique Fair. Apr.: Eureka Jazz Festival. July: Winter Festival. Aug.–Nov.: Royal South Street Eisteddfod. Nov.: Springfest Extravaganza; Ballarat Cup. **In the area:** On western edge of city, Avenue of Honour (22 km) and Arch of Victory, honouring those who fought in WW I. Kirks and Gong Gong reservoirs, both 5 km NE, for picnics. Kryal Castle, 9 km E, reconstruction of a medieval castle offering family entertainment. Lake Burrumbeet, 22 km NW, for water sports and excellent trout fishing; scenic picnic spots on shore. At Yendon, 15 km SW, Yuulong Lavender Estate (check opening times). Yellowglen Winery, 24 km SW at Smythesdale. Berringa Mines Historic Reserve, 8 km SE of Smythesdale. At Buninyong, 13 km S: Flora and Bird Park, with raised walkway and 60 parrot aviaries; Clayfire Gallery; Timeless Timber Gallery;

market 1st Sun. each month; in Feb., Gold King Festival celebrates early history of town. Enfield State Park, 16 km S near Enfield, features 61 species of orchid and some remains of goldworkings. Mt Buninyong Lookout, 13 km SE, for good views. Lal Lal Falls (30 m) on Moorabool River, 18 km SE. Nearby, Lal Lal Blast Furnace, beautiful 19th-century archaeological remains. **Visitor information:** cnr Sturt and Albert sts; (03) 5320 5741, freecall 1800 648 450. Web site www.ballarat.com **See also:** The Goldfields p. 148.

Beaufort   Pop. 1039

MAP REF. 220 F10, 227 M3

This small town on the Western Hwy, midway between Ballarat and Ararat, has gold-rush history: the discovery of gold at Fiery Creek swelled its population in the late 1850s to nearly 100 000. Today Beaufort is primarily a centre for the surrounding pastoral and agricultural district. **In town:** Historic courthouse, Livingstone St, open by appt. Early 20th-century band rotunda, Neill St. **In the area:** Mt Cole State Forest, 16 km NW via Raglan, for bushwalks, flora and fauna, picnic and camping facilities. At Lake Goldsmith, 14 km S, Steam Rally held in May and November. **Visitor information:** Beaufort Resource Centre, 72 Neill St; (03) 5349 3004. **See also:** The Goldfields p. 148.

Beechworth   Pop. 2953

MAP REF. 233 O6, 234 A3

Once the centre of the great Ovens goldmining region, Beechworth lies 24 km off the Hume Fwy, between Wangaratta and Wodonga. This is one of Victoria's best-preserved and most beautiful gold towns, magnificently sited in the foothills of the Alps. The whole town has been classified as historically important by the National Trust. The rich alluvial goldfield at Woolshed Creek was discovered during the 1850s, and 4 121 918 ounces of gold was mined in 14 years. A story is told of Daniel Cameron, campaigning to represent the Ovens Valley community: he rode through the town at the head of a procession of miners, on a horse shod with golden shoes. Sceptics claim they were merely gilded, but the tale indicates what Beechworth was like during the boom, when its population was 42 000 and it boasted 61 hotels and a theatre at which international celebrities performed. **In town:** Local honey-coloured

The lively main street of Sovereign Hill, Ballarat

granite in fine 1850s government buildings (especially in Camp and Ford sts), and in the powder magazine (1860) in Gorge Rd on northern outskirts. In Albert Rd: Harness and Carriage Museum, run by National Trust; Tanswell's Hotel, restored lacework building; Ned Kelly's cell, under Shire Offices; Beechworth Gaol (1859), still used as a prison. In Ford St: historic former Bank of Australasia, now a restaurant; Berringa Antiques and Buckland Gallery. In Camp St: Beechworth Galleries and Beechworth Bakery. In Loch St: Robert O'Hara Burke Memorial Museum, displays relics of gold rush and features 16 mini-shops depicting town's main street as it was more than 100 years ago. Bicycle hire, horseriding and maps for walking tours and gem/gold fossicking available. Market at Town Hall gardens, Ford St, 4 times a year (check dates). Feb.: Drive Back in Time (vintage car rally). Easter: Golden Horseshoes Festival. Nov.: Celtic Festival. **In the area:** Cemetery on northern outskirts of town:Chinese burning towers; Chinese cemetery. Beechworth Historic Park (surrounds town): Woolshed Falls historical walk through former alluvial goldmining sites; Gorge Scenic Drive (5 km) starts north of town; gold-fossicking in designated areas. Fletcher Dam, Beechworth Forest Drive, 3 km SE towards historic village of Stanley. Kelly's Lookout, Woolshed Creek, about 4 km N. Mt Pilot Lookout, 5 km N, for views of Murray Valley; signposted Aboriginal cave paintings nearby. **Visitor information:** Ford St; (03) 5728 3233. Web site www.beechworth.com **See also:** The High Country p. 152.

Benalla   Pop. 8582

MAP REF. 222 A2, 233 K7

This small city, just off the Hume Fwy, is 40 km sw of Wangaratta. In the late 1870s Benalla experienced the activities of the notorious Kelly gang, captured at nearby Glenrowan in 1880. Benalla is also the home town of Sir Edward ('Weary') Dunlop, and Michael J. Savage, NZ Prime Minister in the 1940s. **In town:** Lake Benalla, created in Broken River: good recreation and picnic facilities; haven for birds; self-guide walk around lake, brochure available. In Bridge St: Botanical Gardens, with splendid rose gardens and memorial statue in honour of Sir Edward ('Weary') Dunlop; Art Gallery, on shores of lake, features important Ledger Collection of Australian paintings. In Mair St: a 3-dimensional ceramic mural; The Creators Gallery at information centre, for paintings, pottery and craft; Costume and Pioneer Museum, has Ned Kelly's cummerbund on display. At aerodrome on northern outskirts: centre for Gliding Club of Victoria; hot-air ballooning and glider flights. Market, Fawckner Dr., 4th Sat. each month. Easter: Art Show; Garden Expo. Nov.: Rose Festival; Agricultural Show. **In the area:** Reef Hills Regional Park, 4 km S on Midland Hwy: 2040 ha of forest with wide variety of native flora and fauna. At Swanpool, 23 km S, 1950s-style cinema showing classic films. Pleasant day trip south-east to King Valley and spectacular Paradise Falls. Winton Motor Raceway, 10 km NE. **Visitor information:** 14 Mair St; (03) 5762 1749. Web site www.benalla.net.au **See also:** The High Country p. 152.

Bendigo   Pop. 59 936

MAP REF. 218, 221 P2, 229 Q9, 232 C8

One of Victoria's best-known goldmining cities, and sited at the junction of four highways, Bendigo is central for trips to gold towns nearby. The gold rush began here in 1851 and production continued for 100 years. The affluence of the period can be seen today in splendid public and commercial buildings. **In town:** Self-guide heritage walk, brochure available. Bus tours, in red London-style buses, of major attractions. Shamrock Hotel (1897), cnr Pall Mall and Williamson St, Bendigo's well-known landmark (tours). Sacred Heart Cathedral, largest outside Melbourne, Wattle St. Alexandra Fountain at Charing Cross. In Pall Mall: renaissance-style post office (1887), now information centre; and law courts (1896). In View St: Bendigo Art Gallery (1890); Capital Theatre (1873); and National Trust-classified Dudley House (1859). Central Deborah Gold Mine, Violet St, in working order; surface interpretive display and underground tours. Vintage Trams (taped commentary), run from mine on 8-km city trip (includes stop at Tram Depot Museum displaying 30 vintage trams). Golden Dragon Museum, Bridge St, features Chinese history of goldfields, exceptional display of Chinese processional regalia (incl. world's oldest imperial dragon 'Loong' and longest imperial dragon 'Sun Loong'). Garden of Joy, classical Chinese gardens adjacent to museum. Lookout tower, cascade and Conservatory Gardens in Rosalind Park, Barnard St. Discovery Science and Technology Centre, Railway Pl., has more than 100 hands-on displays.

Bendigo Woollen Mills, Lansell St West (tours). Markets each Sun. at Showgrounds, Holmes St, and cnr Rotis and Strickland rds; craft market, Pall Mall Rd, 4th Sun. each month. Mar.: Easter Festival: Madison 10 000 Cycling Race. Easter: Fair (first held 1871; features Chinese dragon). Apr.: Bendigo by Bike; Chrysanthemum Championships; Wine Festival. July: National Model Engineers Annual Exhibition. Oct.: Bendigo Heritage Uncorked; Orchid Club Spring Show. Nov.: National Swap Meet (Australia's largest meet for vintage cars and bikes); Racing Carnival. Dec.: Tram Spectacular. **In the area:** Excellent wineries, art, ceramics and antiques. Guided goldfields prospecting tours and self-guide Goldfields Tourist Route; details from information centre. Fortuna Villa mansion (1871), Chum St, 2 km S (open Sun.). One Tree Hill observation tower, 4 km S, panoramic views. At Mandurang, 8 km SE: historic wineries; Orchid Nursery; Tannery Lane Pottery; Rupertswood Country Home Open Garden (check open weekends). Arakoon Resort, 18 km SE, aquatic fun park (check opening times). Sedgwick's Camel Farm, 20 km SE at Sedgwick, offers rides and treks (weekends; weekdays by appt). Bendigo Cactus Gardens (established 1937), National Trust-classified, 3 km NE at White Hills. At Epsom, 6 km NE: Bendigo Pottery, Australia's oldest working pottery (potters at work, cafe and sales); Living Wings and Things (wildlife display, adjacent to pottery); National

Trust-classified Chinese Joss House, 1 km N at Emu Point, temple built by Chinese miners. Iron Bark Riding Centre, 4 km N. At Whipstick State Park, 21 km N: wildlife, old goldmining areas (take care around old gold workings), bushwalking, cycling, gold-panning in gullies after rains; nearby, Hartland's Eucalyptus Factory and Historic Farm (tours Sun.), built 1890 to process eucalyptus oil obtained from surrounding scrub. At Eaglehawk, 6.5 km NW, site of goldrush in 1852: reminders of mining days; fine examples of 19th-century architecture, many National Trust-classified; self-guide heritage tour, brochure available; Dahlia and Arts Festival held each Mar. Balgownie Estate winery, 10 km NW (open Mon.–Sat.). Chateau Leamon winery, 10 km SW (open Wed.–Mon.). Goldfields Mohair Farm at Lockwood, 11 km SW (open daily, guided tours Mon.–Fri.). **Visitor information:** Old Post Office, 51–67 Pall Mall; (03) 5444 4445, freecall 1800 813 153. Web site www.bendigotourism.com **See also:** The Goldfields p. 148.

Birchip — Pop. 800

MAP REF. 110 F13, 229 K4

On the main rail link between Melbourne and Mildura, Birchip gets its water supply from the Wimmera–Mallee stock and domestic channel system. **In town:** In Cumming Ave: Big Red (Mallee bull); Historical Society Museum in old courthouse (open by appt). **In the**

area: Shire's sites of historic interest are marked; leaflet available. Junction of two major irrigation channels constructed in early 1900s, 1 km N. Sections of original Dog Fence, a vermin-proof barrier constructed in 1883 between Murray River near Swan Hill and South Australian border, 20 km N. Tchum Lakes, 9 km E, facilities for motor boats, caravans and camping. **Visitor information:** Shire Offices, 22 Cumming Ave; (03) 5492 2200. **See also:** Grampians & Central West p. 144.

Boort — Pop. 805

MAP REF. 110 H13, 229 O5

A pleasant rural and holiday town on the shores of Lake Boort: water sports, redfin-fishing; beaches; good picnic facilities. There is prolific native birdlife in the area; each spring several species raise their young around the lake. **Visitor information:** Boort Lake Caravan Park, Durham Ox Rd; (03) 5455 2064. **See also:** Goulburn & Murray p. 147; Wildlife-Watching p. 196.

Bright — Pop. 1898

MAP REF. 223 L5, 233 P8, 234 C6

In the beautiful Ovens Valley and at the foothills of the Victorian Alps, Bright is an attractive tourist centre. The town provides access to the ski resorts of Mt Hotham, Mt Buffalo and Falls Creek; ski-hire shops in the town stay open late during ski season. The discovery of gold led to the formation of the town; remains of alluvial goldfields can still be seen. The area is excellent for bushwalking, horseriding, mountain-bike riding and trout-fishing, and is a photographer's delight in autumn. **In town:** Avenues of deciduous trees, planted in 1930s, particularly beautiful in autumn. In Gavan St: Gallery 90; local art and craft at information centre; Centenary Park with deep weir (ideal for swimming in summer), children's playground and picnic facilities. Bright Art Gallery and Cultural Centre, Mountbatten Ave. Historical Museum, old railway station, Station Ave. Lotsafun Amusement Park, entrance Mill Rd. Ovens River flows through town; picnic and camping spots alongside. Variety of safe, well-marked walking tracks in Bright area, including Canyon Walk along Ovens River where remains of gold workings can be seen; leaflets available.

Splendid views from Mount Buffalo National Park, near Bright

Hang-gliding, paragliding and 4WD tours. Craft market, Burke St, 3rd Sat. each month. Apr.: Autumn Festival. July: Winter Wonderland Festival. Oct.: Alpine Spring Festival. **In the area:** Wandiligong, National Trust-classified hamlet in scenic valley, 6 km SE; linked to Bright by road, and walking and cycle track; hedge maze. Scenic drives to: Tower Hill Lookout, 4 km NW; Huggins Lookout, 2 km S; Clearspot (stunning views), 13 km S; from Great Alpine Rd south-east to Mt Hotham, superb views of Mt Feathertop, the Razor Back and Mt Bogong. At Porepunkah, 6 km NW at junction of Ovens and Buckland rivers, Boyntons of Bright winery; further 10 km, Snowline Deer and Emu Farm in Hughes Lane, Eurobin. In Mount Buffalo National Park: Mount Buffalo Chalet, 33 km W; wildlife including ringtail possums at Lake Catani, wombats and crimson rosellas; 100 km of walking tracks. **Visitor information:** 119 Gavan St; (03) 5755 2275, freecall 1800 500 117. **See also:** The High Country p. 152; National Parks p. 193; Wildlife-Watching p. 196.

Buchan Pop. 134

MAP REF. 103 B13, 234 I11

This small town, in Gippsland mountain country north-east of Bairnsdale, is well known for its limestone caves. **In town:** Daily tours of Royal and Fairy Caves, (adventure tours also available); spring-fed swimming pool at Buchan Caves Reserve. Conorville Heritage Model Village, Main St: model buildings from 1780 to 1914, incl. miniature sculptures of people; also full-sized furnished 1840s bark-house replica. Feb.: Canni Creek Races. Easter: Rodeo. Nov.: Flowers and Craft Show. **In the area:** 4WD and rafting trips; self-drive Forest Snowy Drive east of town, brochure available. Schoolhouse (1865), at Suggan Buggan, 64 km N. South of Suggan Buggan, Eagle Loft Gallery for local art and craft. Alpine National Park, surrounding Suggan Buggan, for spectacular mountain scenery. Outstanding views from lookout over Little River Gorge, 70 km N on road to McKillops Bridge (large bridge over Snowy River); Little River Falls near gorge. **Visitor information:** General Store, Main St; (03) 5155 9202. Web site www.lakesandwilderness.com.au **See also:** East Gippsland p. 154.

McKillops Bridge, north of Buchan

Camperdown Pop. 3153

MAP REF. 216 F6, 227 L8

This south-western town on the Princes Hwy has gracious buildings and avenues of elms. The centre for a rich pastoral district, Camperdown is also a base for fishing in the crater lakes nearby. **In town:** Historical Heritage Trail, brochure available. Clock tower (1896), cnr Manifold and Pike sts. Also in Manifold St: Historical Society Museum; courthouse; post office. Craft market at Finlay Ave or Theatre Royal, 1st Sun. each month. July: One Act Play Festival. **In the area:** At Mt Noorat, near Noorat, 21 km W: Alan Marshall Memorial Walking Track, off Glenormiston Rd, 3-km summit and return (1 hr) or crater-rim 1.5-km circuit (30 min.); excellent views over Western District. Mt Leura, 1 km S, extinct volcano next to the perfect cone of Mt Sugarloaf; lookout offers views over crater lakes and volcanoes, north across plains to the Grampians. At Cobden, 13 km S, Cobden Miniature Trains, operates 3rd Sun. each month. Lake Corangamite, 13 km E, Victoria's largest salt lake. Excellent fishing lakes incl. Bullen Merri, 3 km W; and Purrumbete, 15 km SE, well-stocked with Quinnat salmon, also has excellent water-sports facilities, picnic spots and caravan park. **Visitor information:** Old Courthouse, Manifold St; (03) 5593 3390. **See also:** South-West Coast p. 143.

Cann River Pop. 246

MAP REF. 103 E13, 235 N11

A popular stop for Sydney–Melbourne motorists using the Princes Hwy. Excellent fishing, and bushwalking and camping in the rugged hinterland. **In the area:** Lind National Park, 15 km W, includes Euchre Valley Nature Drive through warm-temperate rainforest, brochures from Parks Victoria. Coopracambra National Park, 30 km N near NSW border. Croajingolong National Park, main access 45 km S, stretches from Sydenham Inlet to NSW border; incorporates Point Hicks Lighthouse Reserve at Point Hicks, and Tamboon, Wingan and Mallacoota inlets. Accommodation at Point Hicks Lightstation. **Visitor information:** Snowy River–Orbost Visitor Centre, 13 Lochiel St, Orbost; (03) 5154 2424, freecall 1800 637 060, or Parks Victoria; 13 1963 (ask for Cann River office). Web site www.lakesandwilderness.com.au **See also:** East Gippsland p. 154.

Casterton Pop. 1731

MAP REF. 226 C4

Given the Roman name meaning 'walled city' because of lush hills surrounding the valley, Casterton is on the Glenelg Hwy, 42 km E of the South Australian border. The Glenelg River flows through the town. Overlooking the town is a large illuminated scout emblem carved into a hillside. **In town:** Signposted town walk, brochure available. Historical museum in old railway buildings, cnr Jackson and Clarke sts (open by appt).

Alma and Judith Zaadstra Fine Art Gallery, Henty St. On eastern edge of town, Mickle Lookout. Mar.: Vintage Car Rally; Polocrosse Championships. May: Race Cup (horseracing). July: Kelpie Working Dog Auction. Aug.: Woodturning Demonstration Exhibition. Nov.: Street-car Drag Racing. Dec.: Christmas Lights Festival (bus tours available). **In the area:** Long Lead Swamp, 11 km W on Penola Rd, has waterbirds, kangaroos and emus, and trail-bike track. National Trust-classified Warrock Homestead (1843), 26 km N, unique collection of 33 buildings erected by founder, George Robertson; open working day on Easter Sun. Bilston's Tree, 30 km N on Glenmia Rd, 50 m high and arguably world's largest red gum. Baileys Rocks, 50 km N in Dergholm State Park, unique green-coloured giant granite boulders. Other interesting geological formations: The Hummocks, 12 km NE; The Bluff, 20 km SW, exposed geological formations dating back 150 million years; nearby, slab cottage (1870), school (1875) and picnic facilities (open Sun. and public holidays). **Visitor information:** Shiels Tce; (03) 5581 2070. Web site www.grampians. org.au **See also:** Grampians & Central West p. 144.

Castlemaine   Pop. 6690

MAP REF. 221 O6, 229 Q11, 232 C10

At the intersection of the Pyrenees and Midland hwys, 119 km from Melbourne, Castlemaine epitomises the goldmining towns of north-western Victoria. In the 1850s and 1860s enormous quantities of gold were found in its surface fields. Castlemaine grew rapidly and many of its fine old buildings were constructed then. **In town:** Midland Hotel, Templeton St, and Imperial Hotel, Lyttleton St, have splendid iron lacework verandahs. Also in Lyttleton St: courthouse, town hall, regional art gallery and museum. Theatre Royal, Hargraves St. Buda Historic Home and Garden, Urquhart St, home from early 1860s of silversmith and jeweller Ernest Leviny and his family, with preserved home and gardens of the era. Restored 19th-century Castlemaine Market Building (1862-63), Mostyn St, has Diggings Interpretive Centre and regular exhibitions. Botanic Gardens, Parker St, designed by Baron von Mueller, who also designed the Royal Botanic Gardens in Melbourne. Old Castlemaine Gaol, Bowden St. Apr.: Castlemaine State Festival (odd-numbered years).

Nov.: Festival of Gardens (odd-numbered years). **In the area:** Mt Alexander Diggers Trails, for gold rush sites; booklet available. At Wesley Hill, 2.5 km E, market each Sat. At Harcourt, 9 km NE: Skydancers Orchid and Butterfly Gardens, a nursery and butterfly house; Harcourt Valley Vineyard (Wine Festival each Easter Sunday); Blackjack Vineyards; Mt Alexander wineries; Spring Orchid Festival each October; Apple Festival each March. On Mt Alexander, 19 km NE, koala reserve. Historic Forest Creek Gold Mine, on road to Chewton (4 km SE), tours and gold panning. At Chewton: Wattle Gully goldmine; Dingo Farm (puppy time July–Aug.); market each Sat. At Fryerstown, 11 km SE: ruins of Duke of Cornwall mine; Herons Reef Cultural Heritage Gold Diggings (tours, check opening times). Chinese cemetery and mineral springs at Vaughan, 14 km S. Big Tree, a giant red gum over 500 years old, 14 km SW at Guildford. At Newstead, 16 km SW: winery, pottery. At Strathlea, Kyirong Emu farm, 24 km SW on Strathlea Rd, (by appt). **Visitor information:** Old Market, Mostyn St; (03) 5470 6200, freecall 1800 171 888. Web site www. mountalexander.vic.gov.au/tourism **See also:** The Goldfields p. 148.

Charlton   Pop. 1096

MAP REF. 229 M6

A supply centre for a rich wheat district, Charlton is set on the banks of the Avoca River, at the intersection of the Calder and Borung hwys in north-central Victoria. **In town:** Fishing in Avoca River; Travellers Rest picnic area, on banks of river. Walking track along river, from town to weir (4 km return). Easter: Lions Market. Oct.: Art Show. **In the area:** Wooroonook Lake, 12 km W, for swimming and boating. Bish Deer Farm, further 18 km W. At Wycheproof, 30 km NW: Mt Wycheproof, 43 m high and smallest mountain in world; Centenary Park and Willandra Historical Museum. Wychitella State Forest, 27 km E, for a variety of native flora and fauna, including the mallee fowl. **Visitor information:** Buloke Shire Council, 1 High St; (03) 5491 1755. **See also:** The Goldfields p. 148.

Chiltern   Pop. 1080

MAP REF. 111 P13, 233 O4, 234 A2

Halfway between Wangaratta and Wodonga, Chiltern is 1 km off the Hume

Fwy. It was once a goldmining boom town with 14 suburbs. Many of its buildings are National Trust-classified. **In town:** In Conness St: Athenaeum Museum (1866), features heritage display; Dow's Pharmacy (1868), National Trust-owned chemist shop with its original features; Stephen's Motor Museum, for motoring memorabilia. In Main St: Famous Grapevine, formerly Grape Vine Hotel, boasts the largest grapevine in Australia (in Guinness Book of Records, planted 1867); National Trust-classified Federal Standard newspaper office, dates from goldmining era (1860–61) (open by appt for groups). Picnic/barbecue facilities at Lake Anderson, via Main St. Walking track from lake-shore over bridge to National Trust-classified 'Lake View', Victoria St, home of author Henry Handel Richardson (open p.m.only, weekends, public and school holidays). Self-guide historical walk, leaflet avaiable. Aug.: Antique Fair. Oct.: Art Show. **In the area:** Chiltern Box-Ironbark National Park, surrounding town, for spring wildflowers, bushwalking and picnicking; tourist drives and guided walks available. Magenta open-cut mine, 2 km E. Near Barnawartha, 10 km NE, Koendidda historic homestead and gardens and B&B. Pioneer Cemetery, 2 km N. **Visitor information:** 30 Main St; (03) 5726 1611. **See also:** The High Country p. 152.

Clunes   Pop. 846

MAP REF. 210 C2, 221 J8, 227 O2, 229 O13, 232 A11

The first registered gold strike in the State was made at Clunes on 7 July 1851. The town, 36 km N of Ballarat, has several National Trust-classified bluestone buildings. Fraser St is especially elegant. Surrounding the town are a number of extinct volcanoes, and a good view of these can be obtained about 3 km S, on the road to Ballarat. **In town:** In Bailey St: town hall and courthouse (1870); Bottle Museum in former South Clunes State School; Queens Park, established over 100 years ago on banks of Creswick Creek; old post office (1873), now second-hand bookshop (open weekends). Butter Factory Gallery, Cameron St, sculpture and art gallery. In Fraser St: The Weavery, handwoven fabrics; Museum, open weekends, public and school holidays. Nov.: Agricultural Show. **In the area:** Clunes Homestead Furniture, 1 km NW on Talbot Rd. At Talbot, historic town 18 km NW: many 1860–70 buildings, particularly in Camp St and Scandinavian Cres.; Arts and Historical Museum in former Primitive Methodist Church (1870); Bull and Mouth restaurant in old bluestone building (1860s), formerly hotel. At Mt Beckworth, 8 km W, scenic reserve. **Visitor information:** Clunes Museum, Fraser St; (03) 5345 3592. **See also:** The Goldfields p. 148.

Cobram   Pop. 3865

MAP REF. 111 M13, 233 J3

Wide sandy beaches are a feature of the Murray River here, so picnicking, fishing and water sports are popular. This is an area of fast-growing industry and is also fruit-growing country; the clingstone peach was developed here. **In town:** At information centre, Punt Rd, award-winning local gourmet jar produce. Log Cabin, opposite information centre, historic cottage built in Yarrawonga 1875 and moved piece by piece. Rotary dairy, 200 cows, on outskirts of town; open at milking time, 4–5 p.m. daily. Market in Punt Rd, 1st Sat. each month. Jan.: Peaches and Cream Festival (odd-numbered years). May: Rotary Art Show. June: Antique Fair. Oct.: Agricultural Show: Open Gardens Display. Nov.: Sun Country Dolls, Bears and Collectibles Show; Harness Racing Meeting. **In the area:** Wineries open for tastings and sales include: Heritage Farm Wines, 5 km W on Murray Valley Hwy, with 116-m wood-carving depicting scenes of early Murray River life; Monichino Wines, 30 km W on Berry's Rd, Katunga; Strathkellar Wines, 8 km E and Fyffefield Wines, 15 km E, both on Murray Valley Hwy. Strawberry-picking in season, 5 km W at Koonoomoo. At Strathmerton, 16 km W: Cactus Country, Australia's largest cacti gardens. Just east of town, Quinn Island on Murray River; self-guide nature walk. At Barooga (NSW) 4 km NE: 36-hole Cobram–Barooga Golf Club; Binghi Boomerang Factory. Sportavia Soaring Centre at Tocumwal airport, 20 km NW. **Visitor information:** The Old Grain Store, cnr Station St and Punt Rd; (03) 5872 2132, freecall 1800 607 607. **See also:** Goulburn & Murray p. 147.

Cohuna   Pop. 1979

MAP REF. 111 J12, 229 Q3, 232 C2

Located on the Murray Valley Hwy, Cohuna is surrounded by dairy farms. The town is beside Gunbower Island, formed by the Murray River and Gunbower Creek. This island is covered in red gum

Chiltern's verandahed streetscape

and box forest, which provides a home for abundant birdlife and kangaroos and emus. A large part of the island has breeding rookeries during flood periods. **In town:** Cohuna Historical Museum, Sampson St. Feb.: Aquatic Festival; Bridge to Bridge Swim. Mar.: Agricultural Show. **In the area:** 2-hr cruises in the *Wetlander* along Gunbower Creek. On Gunbower Island: birdlife, picnic/barbecue facilities and walking tracks (map at local shops). Major Mitchell Trail, 1700-km signposted trail that retraces this explorer's footsteps from Mildura to Wodonga via Portland; from Cohuna, signposted trail along Gunbower Creek, down to Mt Hope. Kow Swamp, 23 km S, a bird sanctuary; picnic spots and good fishing at Box Bridge. Mt Hope (110 m), about 28 km S, for good views and spring wildflowers. Cohuna Grove Cottage, 4 km SE on Murray Valley Hwy, local art and craft. Kraft factory and shop (open a.m. Mon.–Fri.), 16 km SE at Leitchville. Torrumbarry Weir, 40 km SE; during winter, entire weir structure is removed; in summer, water-skiing above the weir. Mathers Waterwheel Museum, 9 km W on Brays Rd, has memorabilia. **Visitor information:** Golden River Tourism, 25 Murray St, Barham; (03) 5453 3100. **See also:** Goulburn & Murray p. 147.

Colac   Pop. 9793

MAP REF. 210 B11, 216 I7, 227 N9

Colac is situated on the eastern edge of the volcanic plain that covers much of the Western District of Victoria. It is the centre of a prosperous agricultural area

and is sited on the shores of Lake Colac, which has good fishing and a variety of water sports. **In town:** In Gellibrand St: Historical Centre (open Thurs., Fri., Sun. p.m.); Botanic Gardens. Barongarook Creek has prolific birdlife and walking track, leading from Princes Hwy to Lake Colac on northern outskirts of town (good redfin-fishing in lake). Self-guide town walk leaflet and information on full-day mountain scenic drive available. At information centre, recreation area with picnic/barbecue facilities. Market in Memorial Sq, Murray St, 3rd Sun. each month. Feb.: Otway Harvest Festival. Apr.: Country Music Festival. Oct.: Garden Expo; Go Colac, Go Country Festival (includes Ferret Cup). **In the area:** Irrewarra Homestead, 10 km N on Colac–Ballarat Rd; natural ice-creams. Red Rock Lookout, 22 km N near Alvie; 30 volcanic lakes can be seen from here, including Lake Corangamite, Victoria's largest saltwater lake. Floating Island Reserve, 18 km W off Princes Hwy, a lagoon with islands that change position. Burtons Lookout, 13 km S, views of Otway hinterland; Wanawong Gardens at lookout. Red Rock Winery, 15 km S (check opening times). Gellibrand Pottery, 30 km S. Otway Ranges, about 30 km S, features beautiful winding roads, lush mountain scenery, and waterfalls. Tarndwarncoort Homestead, 15 km E, has wool display and sales. At Birregurra, 20 km E, interesting old buildings. **Visitor information:** cnr Murray and Queen sts; (03) 5231 3730. **See also:** South-West Coast p. 143.

Coleraine Pop. 1084

MAP REF. 226 E4

Situated 34 km NW of Hamilton, the Coleraine area was first settled by Europeans in 1838 for pastoral grazing. Today the primary products are fine-wool and beef. **In town:** Historic railway station, Pilleau St, now information centre; local arts and crafts. In Whyte St, both open by appt: Matthew Cooke's Blacksmiths Shop (1888), and Historical Society in Old Courthouse. Also in Whyte St: Chocolate Factory, open daily for tastings; Eucalyptus Discovery Centre. At Point's Arboretum, southern outskirts of town on Coleraine–Portland Rd: largest number of eucalyptus species in Australia; also other native plants; prolific birdlife; lookout and picnic area. Apr.: Autumn Festival. Aug.: Art Show. **In the area:** Self-guide scenic day trips, brochure available. Historic homesteads: National Trust-classified Warrock Homestead (1843), 20 km W towards Casterton; Glendinning Homestead with wildlife sanctuary near Balmoral, 49 km N. Gardens of Glendinning Homestead and Mistydown Perennials (also at Balmoral); brochure available (check opening times). Wannon Falls, 14 km SE, and Nigretta Falls, 24 km SE. **Visitor information:** Old Railway Station, Pilleau St; (03) 5575 2733. **See also:** Grampians & Central West p. 144.

Corryong Pop. 1215

MAP REF. 103 B8, 234 G2

Corryong is situated at the gateway to the Snowy Mountains. The district offers superb mountain scenery and excellent trout-fishing in the Murray River and its tributaries. **In town:** Two Feet Tour, brochure available. The grave of Jack Riley, reputedly 'the Man from Snowy River', is in Corryong cemetery. The Man from Snowy River Folk Museum, Hanson St, features Riley's hut and classic clothing and ski collections. Large wooden galleon, Murray River Hwy. Mar.: Man from Snowy River Festival. Apr.: Bush Festival. **In the area:** Horse trail rides and 4WD tours; details from information centre. Scenic drive west from Corryong. Scenic views: Players Hill Lookout, 1 km SE; Mt Mittamatite and Emberys Lookout, 10 km N; lookout with views over Kosciuszko National Park at Towong, 12 km NE; Sassafras Gap, 66 km S. Canoeing and mountain-bike excursions

from Walwa, 47 km NW. Emu Farm, 4 km W on Murray Valley Hwy. At Burrowa–Pine Mountain National Park, 27 km W: Cudgewa Bluff Falls, excellent scenery and bushwalking tracks. At Nariel, 45 km SW: trout-fishing in Nariel Creek; Folk Music Festival in Dec. Upper Murray Fish Farm, 38 km S. **Visitor information:** Hanson St; (02) 6076 2277. **See also:** The High Country p. 152.

Cowes Pop. 3060

MAP REF. 211 L12, 213 O11, 224 E9

This is the main town on Phillip Island, a popular resort area in Western Port linked to the mainland by a bridge at San Remo. Cowes is on the northern side of the island; it has safe beaches for children, and a popular jetty for fishing and swimming. **In town:** Market, Settlement Rd, each Sun. Apr.: World Superbike Championships. May: Motor Racing. Oct.: Grand Prix Motorcycle Race. **In the area:** Summerland Beach, on southern shore, about 11 km SW, famous for its nightly penguin parade (no cameras beyond the Visitor Centre). Colonies of fur seals year-round on Seal Rocks, 2 km offshore (tours), also short-tailed shearwaters (muttonbirds) Oct.–Apr.; Seal Rocks Sea Life Centre at nearby Nobbies offers marine displays and activities, and seal-watching. Phillip Island Vineyard and Winery, 9 km SW on Berrys Beach Rd, for tastings, sales and casual dining. Rhyll swamp and bird sanctuary, 8 km E. On Phillip Island Rd: Phillip Island Wildlife Park has native fauna in natural environment, 3 km S; Koala Conservation Centre features elevated boardwalk. Grand Prix Circuit and Visitor Centre, 6 km SE on Back Beach Rd, venue for Grand Prix Motorcycle Race. A Maze 'N Things, 7 km SE: large timber maze, optical illusion rooms, maxi mini golf. Cape Woolamai, 16 km SE: 2- and 4-hr walks from surf beach, around southern end of cape, past The Pinnacles. Australian Dairy Centre at Newhaven, 16 km SE, museum and cheese factory. On Churchill Island, 2 km from Newhaven (road bridge access), historic homestead and walking tracks. Feed pelicans, 11.30 a.m. on foreshore opposite San Remo Fishing Co-op. Wildlife Wonderland, 9 km from San Remo, including the Giant Earthworm Museum and Wombat World. Walks on island, maps available. **Visitor information:** 895 Phillip Island Rd, Newhaven; (03) 5956 7447 or freecall

1300 366 422 (tickets for Phillip Island attractions available here). Web site www.phillipislandgippsland.com **See also:** Phillip Island & Gippsland p. 156; Wildlife-Watching p. 196.

Creswick Pop. 2327

MAP REF. 210 C3, 221 K9, 227 O2, 229 O13, 232 A12

Creswick is situated 18 km N of Ballarat on the Midland Hwy. One of the richest alluvial goldfields in the world was discovered here. **In town:** Mullock heaps on Ullina Rd (take care around old gold workings). Historical Museum, Albert St. Gold Battery, Battery Cres. Cemetery, Clunes Rd, with early miners' graves and Chinese section. In Melbourne Rd: Koala Park; St Georges Lake. Oct.: Brackenbury Classic Fun Run. **In the area:** Creswick Landcare Nursery, 1 km E. World of Dinosaurs, 1.5 km E off Midland Hwy, has life-size models. Gold panning in Slaty Creek, 4 km E. Tangled Maze, a maze formed by climbing plants, 5 km E. At Smeaton, 16 km NE: Smeaton House (1850s); Anderson's Mill (1860s), Food, Wine and Jazz Festival here each Apr.; Tuki Trout Farm. **Visitor information:** Vincent St, Daylesford; (03) 5348 1339. Web site www.goldfields.org.au **See also:** The Goldfields p. 148.

Daylesford Pop. 3287

MAP REF. 210 E2, 221 N9, 227 Q2, 229 Q13, 232 B12

Daylesford and Hepburn Springs, 4 km N, together constitute a spa town, with 65 documented mineral springs, many with hand pumps. Daylesford rambles up the side of Wombat Hill; at the top are the Botanical Gardens and a lookout tower. **In town:** Hepburn Springs Spa Complex, in the Mineral Springs Reserve, Forest Ave, offers baths, pool, flotation tanks, massage and a sauna. Convent Gallery with beautiful gardens, in former girls' school (1891), Daly St. In Vincent St: Alpha Hall Galleria, in former silent movie house (open Thurs.– Mon.); historical museum in former School of Mines (open weekends). Central Springs Spa Reserve and Lake Daylesford, Central Springs Rd; Tipperary Walking Track from here to Mineral Springs Reserve, leaflet available. Lake House on shore of Lake Daylesford, restaurant and accommodation. Market near railway station, Sun. a.m.; during market, Central Highlands Tourist Railway runs rail-motor between

The Pinnacles, on Cape Woolamai, south-east of Cowes

Daylesford and Musk, 7 km SE, and gangers' trolleys operate to Wombat Forest every Sun. Jan.: Daylesford Gift (horse race). Apr.: Fair. May: Hepburn Swiss-Italian Festival. Nov.: Agricultural Show. Dec.: Highland Gathering. **In the area:** Wombat Forest Drive, 65-km-return: waterfalls, springs and picnic areas; brochure available. Lyonville Mineral Springs, 15 km SE. Trentham Falls, 21 km SE. At Glenlyon, 8 km NE: Glenlyon Sports Day in Jan.; Fine Food and Wine Fayre in July. Loddon Falls, 10 km NE. Breakneck Gorge, 5 km N. Mt Franklin, an extinct volcano, 13 km N. Near Shepherds Flat, 10 km N, Lavandula Lavender Farm: sales, cottage garden; Lavandula Harvest Festival held Jan. Yandoit, a settlement of Swiss–Italian heritage, 18 km NW. Sailors Falls, 5 km S. **Visitor information:** Vincent St; (03) 5348 1339. **See also:** Spa & Garden Country p. 150.

Derrinallum   Pop. 265

MAP REF. 216 F2, 227 L6

A small rural town servicing the local farming community and surrounded by volcanic plains. **In the area:** Significant dry-stone walls, immediately west of town. Mt Elephant, 2 km SW, a scoria cone of volcanic origin rising high above surrounding plains. At Darlington, 19 km SW: Elephant Bridge Hotel, a 2-storey bluestone building, National Trust-classified. Lake Tooliorook, 6 km SE, for fishing and water sports. **Visitor information:** Old Courthouse, Manifold St, Camperdown; (03) 5593 2288. **See also:** South-West Coast p. 143.

Dimboola   Pop. 1557

MAP REF. 228 F7

This is a peaceful town on the tree-lined Wimmera River, 36 km NW of Horsham. **In town:** Walking track along Wimmera River. Apr.: Wimmera German Fest. Oct.: Agricultural Show. Nov.: Rowing Regatta. **In the area:** At Little Desert National Park, 6 km SW: self-guide walks, incl. Pomponderoo Hill Nature Walk (1 km) from Horseshoe Bend picnic and camping area at river's edge; short-beaked echidnas; occasional sightings of endangered mallee fowl. At Wail, 11 km SE, well-stocked Natural Resource League forest nursery (open Mon.–Fri.). Ebenezer Mission Station (founded 1859), near Antwerp on Jeparit Rd, 15 km N: historic site with ruins and restored church. Pink Lake, coloured salt lake, 9 km NW. At Kiata, 26 km W, mallee fowl can be seen in Lowan Sanctuary all year. **Visitor information:** Megan's Corner, 119 Lloyd St; (03) 5389 1290. **See also:** Grampians & Central West p. 144.

Donald   Pop. 1383

MAP REF. 229 K7

Donald is situated on the Richardson River, at the junction of the Sunraysia and Borung hwys. **In town:** In Wood St: historic police station (1874); shepherd's hut (1850). Steam Train Park, cnr Hammill and Walker sts, site of old J524 class steam locomotive. Agricultural museum, Hammill St. Historic water pump by lake in caravan park. Bullocks Head Lookout, Byrne St, beside Richardson River. Good fishing in river.

Scilleys Island has walking tracks and wildlife; access by footbridge from Sunraysia Hwy. Kooka's Country Cookies, Sunraysia Hwy, has tours and sales. Self-guide walks, brochure available. Market in Byrne St, 3rd Sat. each month. June: Scottish Dancing Country Weekend. Labour Day Weekend Lawn Tennis Championship. **In the area:** Glengar River Sanctuary, 2 km NE on Borung Hwy, contains grave of first woman settler in district. Mt Jeffcott, 20 km NE, for flora, kangaroos and views of Lake Buloke, 10 km N, a wetlands area. Watchem Lake, 35 km N, good fishing and water sports. Lake Batyo Catyo and Richardson River Weir offer good fishing, both 20 km S. **Visitor information:** Bev and Guildy's Cafe, 75 Wood St; (03) 5497 1300. **See also:** Grampians & Central West p. 144.

Drysdale   Pop. 1474

MAP REF. 210 H9, 224 B6

This is primarily a service centre for the local farming community on the Bellarine Peninsula. **In town:** In High St: Old Courthouse Museum, home of the Bellarine Historical Society; Drysdale Community Crafts. Community Market at Recreation Reserve, Duke St, every 3rd Sun. (Sept.–Apr.). **In the area:** Lake Lorne picnic area, 1 km SW. Nearby Bellarine Peninsula Railway offers steam-train rides between Drysdale and Queenscliff, weekends and summer holidays; locomotives and carriages dating back to 1870s on display. Soho Nursery and Fine Arts Gallery, 6 km E. Local wineries include: Scotchmans Hill Winery, 8 km NE on Scotchmans Road; historic Spray Farm Winery, Portarlington Rd (open weekends and public holidays), has Summer Concert Series Feb.–Mar. in natural amphitheatre. At Portarlington, a popular seaside resort 8 km NE: flour mill (1857), restored by National Trust, with historical displays; Lavender Cottage Gallery; safe bay for children to swim. At St Leonards, a small beach resort, 13 km E: Edwards Point Wildlife Reserve; memorial commemorates landing by Matthew Flinders in 1802, and John Batman in 1835. **Visitor information:** A Maze'N Things, 1570 Bellarine Hwy, cnr Grubb Rd, Wallington; (03) 5250 2669. Web site www.greatoceanrd.org.au **See also:** Werribee & Bellarine Peninsula p. 142.

Dunkeld
Pop. 444

MAP REF. 226 H4

On the Glenelg Hwy, 32 km NE of Hamilton, Dunkeld is the southern gateway to the Grampians and is convenient for trips to the Chimney Pots, a landmark in the Grampians National Park, 25 km N. **In town:** Self-guide historical walk or drive, leaflet available. Museum in old church, Templeton St, features history of area's Aborigines, local wool industry and explorer Major Mitchell's journeys; open weekends or by appt. Arboretum, Old Ararat Rd, has exotic species from around the world, brochure available. Nov.: Dunkeld Cup (horse race). **In the area:** Walking tracks to top of Mt Sturgeon (3 km N) and Mt Abrupt (8 km N); both climbs steep, but good views. Easier walk to Mt Piccaninny, 4.5 km N. Freshwater Lake Reserve, 8 km N. **Visitor information:** Glenelg Hwy; (03) 5577 2558. **See also:** Grampians & Central West p. 144.

Dunolly
Pop. 668

MAP REF. 221 J3, 229 O10

A small town in north-central Victoria on the Goldfields Tourist Route. 'Welcome Stranger', considered to be the largest nugget ever discovered, was found 15 km NW at Moliagul. The district has produced more nuggets than any other goldfield in Australia; 126 were unearthed in the town itself. **In town:** Restored courthouse, Market St, has display relating to historic gold discoveries in area (open by appt). Next door, original lockup (1859) and stables. In Broadway: handsome original buildings; Goldfields Historical and Arts Society collection, includes replicas of town's spectacular nuggets (open weekends). **In the area:** Self-guide bike rides and gold-themed tours of region, leaflets available. Countryside abounds with spring wildflowers and native fauna. Gold-panning in local creeks. Laanecoorie Reservoir, 16 km E, for swimming, boating, water-skiing, camping and picnic facilities. Tarnagulla, 16 km NE, a small mining town with splendid Victorian architecture; mine (not open to public) and flora reserve nearby. At Moliagul, 15 km NW: monuments mark spot where 'Welcome Stranger' nugget found in 1869; birthplace of Rev. John Flynn, founder of Royal Flying Doctor Service; Welcome Stranger Discovery Walk, leaflet available.

Visitor information: cnr Bull & Market sts; (03) 5468 1032. Web site www.goldfields.org.au **See also:** The Goldfields p. 148.

Echuca
Pop. 10 014

MAP REF. 111 K13, 232 E4

Echuca and its twin town Moama, across the river in NSW, are at the junction of the Murray, Campaspe and Goulburn rivers. Now a city and once Australia's largest inland port, Echuca took its name from an Aboriginal word meaning 'meeting of the waters', while Moama means 'place of the dead'. An historic iron bridge joins the two. **In town:** Port of Echuca, restored to the period of its heyday with its massive red gum wharf; paddle-steamer *Pevensey* (renamed *Philadelphia* for TV mini-series *All the Rivers Run*); D26 logging barge, PS *Alexander Arbuthnot*; PS *Adelaide*; all available for cruises. Also in Murray Esplanade: Star Hotel, underground bar with escape tunnel; Bridge Hotel, built by Henry Hopwood, founder of Echuca, who ran original punt service; Red Gum Works, has woodturning demonstrations; award-winning Sharp's Magic Movie House and Penny Arcade; carriage rides; port tour. In High St: Echuca Historical Society Museum (1867) in former police station; World in Wax museum. National Holden Museum, Warren St. Port of Call Wine Centre, Redcliffe St. Cruises on paddlewheelers *Canberra* and *Pride of the Murray*; accommodation and cruises on paddle-steamer *Emmylou*; MV *Mary Ann* cruising restaurant. Boat hire. Feb.: Southern 80 Ski Race from Torrumbarry Weir to Echuca; Riverboats, Food, Jazz and Wine Festival. June: Steam, Horse and Vintage Car Rally. Oct.: Port of Echuca Steam Heritage Festival. **In the area:** Gourmet produce available; details from information centre. Camping, fishing, water sports and bushwalking. In Moama (NSW): Gumnutland model village; Silverstone Go-Kart Track; Horseshoe Lagoon reserve. At Barmah State Park and State Forest, 39 km NE: Dharnya Centre, has excellent display of culture of local Yorta Yorta people; wetlands cruises, fishing, swimming, canoes and barbecue pontoons for hire at Barmah Lake; 60-km scenic and heritage drive. Ulupna Island, in eastern section of park (near Strathmerton), has river beaches and camping. Barmah Muster

(cattle muster) held in State Forest in Apr. Near Mathoura, 40 km N: Moira Forest Walkway and Bird Observatory. Picnic Point recreational area, 11 km E of Mathoura. **Visitor information:** 2 Heygarth St; (03) 5480 7555, freecall 1800 677 679. Web site www.echuca moama.com **See also:** Goulburn & Murray p. 147; Wildlife-Watching p. 196.

Edenhope
Pop. 776

MAP REF. 228 C11

On the Wimmera Hwy, just 30 km from the border with South Australia, Edenhope is situated on the shores of Lake Wallace, a haven for waterbirds. When full, the lake is popular for water sports and fishing. **In town:** Cairn, beside lake in Lake St, commemorating visit of first all-Aboriginal cricket team to England. Feb.: Henley-on-Lake Wallace. Mar.: Gourmet Food Day; Races. **In the area:** At Harrow, one of Victoria's oldest inland towns, 32 km SE: historic buildings incl. Hermitage Hotel (1851) and log gaol (1862); cemetery contains grave of first Aboriginal cricketer, Johnny Mullagh; National Bush Billy-cart Championship in Mar. Rocklands Reservoir, part of Wimmera–Mallee irrigation system, for fishing and boating; 65 km E. About 50 km W, over SA border, Naracoorte Caves Conservation Park. **Visitor information:** 98 Elizabeth St; (03) 5585 1509. **See also:** Grampians & Central West p. 144.

Eildon
Pop. 703

MAP REF. 211 P2, 222 A12, 233 K11

Built to irrigate a vast stretch of northern Victoria and to provide hydro-electric power, Lake Eildon is the State's largest constructed lake and is a popular resort area, surrounded by the beautiful foot-hills of the Alps. Self-guide walks and drives, and horseriding. Excellent recreational facilities around the foreshores, two major boat harbours, launching ramps, picnic grounds and many lookout points. Power boat and houseboat hire at boat harbours. Dec.: Christmas Eve Gala Night. **In the area:** Signposted Lake Eildon Wall Lookout, 1 km N. Lake cruises from Eildon Boat Harbour. Eildon Pondage and Goulburn River, for excellent fishing (no closed season for trout in Lake Eildon). Lake Eildon National Park, surrounding town: has walking tracks incl. popular Candelbark Gully Nature Walk; camping and picnicking at Jerusalem Inlet; scenic drive to spot in park 16 km NW. Mt Pinninger (503 m), 3 km E, for views of Mt Buller, the Alps and lake. Snobs Creek Fish Hatchery, 6 km SW; millions of trout bred to stock waterways. Just past hatchery, Snobs Creek Falls. Eildon Deer Park nearby, on Goulburn Valley Hwy. Rubicon Falls, 18 km SW via Thornton. **Visitor information:** Main St; (03) 5774 2909, freecall 1800 003 713. Web site www.lakeeildon. com **See also:** The High Country p. 152.

Emerald
Pop. 4673

MAP REF. 211 M7, 214 C13, 224 F5

The Puffing Billy steam railway runs from Belgrave to Gembrook via Emerald, the first European settlement in the Dandenong Ranges. **In town:** Many galleries and craft shops. At Emerald Lake, on Emerald Lake Rd: Environmental Centre, walking tracks, barbecues, paddleboats, model railway, kiosk and tearooms; scenic trails. Apr.: Great Train Race (runners attempt to race Puffing Billy from Belgrave to Emerald Lake Park). **In the area:** Many scenic walking tracks, brochures available. At Menzies Creek, 4 km NW: Puffing Billy Steam Museum (open weekends, and public holidays and Wed.); Cotswold House, fine food and views; Cardinia Reservoir Park, for good views, picnic spots and native fauna including kangaroos roaming freely; nearby Lake Aura Vale, for sailing and picnics. Sherbrooke Art Gallery in Monbulk Rd, Belgrave, 11 km NW. Australian Rainbow Trout Farm at Macclesfield, 8 km N. At Gembrook, 14 km E: The Motorist Cafe and Museum, Main St, heritage vehicles; market last Sat. each month at railway station. Bimbimbie Wildlife Park at Mount Burnett, 12 km SE. Trail horseriding available at Sherbrooke Equestrian Park, 3 km W on Wellington Rd. **Visitor information:** Dandenong Ranges Information Centre, 1211 Burwood Hwy, Upper Ferntree Gully; (03) 9758 7522. Web site www.dandenongrangestourism.asn.au **See also:** Yarra & Dandenongs p. 151.

Euroa
Pop. 2697

MAP REF. 232 I8

A small town 151 km NE of Melbourne, just off the Hume Fwy, Euroa is a good base for exploring the Strathbogie Ranges and tablelands. The Kelly gang staged a daring robbery here in 1878, rounding up some 50 hostages and making off with money and gold worth almost £2000.

Puffing Billy makes its way through the Dandenongs, near Emerald

In town: Several historic buildings, including National Bank and post office in Binney St. In Kirkland Ave: Seven Creeks Park for fishing; Farmers Arms Historical Museum, includes Ned Kelly and Eliza Forlonge history (open Fri.–Mon. p.m.). Miniature steam-train rides, Turnbull St (last Sun. each month). Parachuting School, Drysdale Rd (open weekends). Wildflower walks in spring, leaflet available; open gardens spring and autumn. Oct.: Agricultural Show; Wool Week. **In the area:** Forlonge Memorial, off Strathbogie Road, 10 km SE, commemorates Eliza Forlonge, who with her sister imported first merino sheep into Victoria. Scenic drive to Gooram Falls (20 km SE) and around Strathbogie Ranges. Polly McQuinns, historic river crossing and reservoir, 20 km SE on Strathbogie Rd. Balloon Flights Victoria, 10 km SW. At Longwood, 14 km SW: historic buildings, especially White Heart Hotel; Lavender Art Gallery; horse-drawn carriage rides. At Locksley, 20 km SW, gliding and parachuting. Mt Wombat Lookout, 25 km SW, spectacular views of surrounding country and Alps. Faithfull Creek Waterfall, 9 km NE. At Violet Town, 24 km NE, Stone Crop art gallery. **Visitor information:** Strathbogie Ranges Tourism Information Service at BP Service Centre, Tarcombe St; (03) 5795 3677. **See also:** Goulburn & Murray p. 147.

Flinders
Pop. 501

MAP REF. 211 J12, 213 J11, 224 D9

Flinders is the most southerly town on the Mornington Peninsula. There are spectacular clifftop views across the bay to French Island and The Nobbies and Seal Rocks on Phillip Island. **In town:** Several historic buildings, incl. Bimbi (1870s), the earliest remaining dwelling in Flinders; and Wilga (1880s), fine Victorian-era home; both in King St. Flinders Golf Links, Wood St, on West Head with views across Bass Strait. Mar.: Pinot Week (throughout wine district). **In the area:** A number of wineries with tastings and sales. Ace Hi horseriding and wildlife park, 11 km W. Cape Schanck lighthouse (1859), 15 km W. At Main Ridge, 11 km NW: Sunny Ridge Strawberry Farm, Mornington–Flinders Rd, pick-your-own berries in season; Pig and Whistle, English-style pub, Purves Rd. At Red Hill 17 km N: The Cherry Farm, Arkwells Lane, picturesque setting, pick-your-own cherries and berries; variety of galleries on Mornington–Flinders Rd; community market first Sat. of month (Sep.–May); Red Hill Truck Show and Festival in Jan; Cool Climate Wine Show in Mar. At Shoreham, 6 km NE, Ashcombe Maze and Water Gardens, Red Hill Rd, hedge mazes surrounded by gardens (closed Aug.). The Barn Art and Craft Centre at Merricks, 13 km NE on Bittern–Dromana Rd, has numerous local craft displays (open Wed.–Mon.). At Balnarring 17 km NE: Emu Plains Market, 3rd Sat. each month, (Nov.–May); Coolart Homestead, with historical displays, gardens, wetlands bird observation area. At Stony Point, 26 km NE, ferry to French Island: walks, cycling (bike hire) tours (bookings essential), no car access; guesthouses and camping; in French Island National Park, abundant flora and fauna incl. koalas. Surfing at Point Leo, 5 km E of Shoreham. **Visitor information:** Nepean Hwy, Dromana; (03) 5987 3078, freecall 1800 804 009. Web site www.travelbook.com.au/vic/mornpen/ index.html **See also:** Mornington Peninsula p. 155; National Parks p. 193.

Foster   Pop. 1049
MAP REF. 225 J10

A picturesque, small town within easy reach of Corner Inlet, Waratah Bay and Wilsons Promontory, and about 170 km E of Melbourne. **In town:** In Main St: Historical Museum, in old post office; Stockyard Gallery. Kaffir Hill Walk from town car park, scenic walk past old gold-mining sites. Feb.: Agricultural Show. **In the area:** A number of wineries in the area, incl. Windy Peak Winery, 10 km S. Gourmet Deli Trail; brochure available. Foster North Lookout, 6 km NW. Scenic drive to Fish Creek, 11 km SW; 2 km SE of town, Fish Creek Potters. Cape Liptrap, 46 km SW, views of rugged coastline and Bass Strait. Good surf beach at Sandy Point, 22 km S; surrounding protected waters of Shallow Inlet popular for fishing, windsurfing and swimming. Wilsons Promontory National Park, 32 km S: spectacular scenery; abundant flora and fauna; magnificent beaches; many walks; camping and cabins at Tidal River. Turtons Creek, 18 km N, old gold-rich area; lyrebirds sometimes seen in tree-fern gullies nearby. Pleasant beaches: Waratah Bay, 34 km SW; Walkerville, 36 km SW; Port Franklin, 12 km SE. **Visitor information:** Stockyard Gallery, Main St; (03) 5682 1125, freecall 1800 630 704. Web site www.phillipislandgippsland.com **See also:** Phillip Island & Gippsland p. 156; National Parks p. 193; Wildlife-Watching p. 196.

Geelong   Pop. 125 382
MAP REF. 210 F9, 215, 217 O5, 224 A6, 227 R7

Geelong, on Corio Bay, is the largest provincial city in Victoria. It is a major centre for manufacturing and processing, and has traditionally sold and stored wool. The Corio Bay area was first settled by Europeans in the 1830s and, apart from a gold-rush exodus, Geelong has prospered steadily. It is a pleasant and well-laid-out city with lovely views across the bay. **In town:** National Wool Museum, in historic bluestone woolstore cnr Moorabool and Brougham sts, features sound and audio-visual displays, re-created shearers' quarters and mill-worker's cottage. Interesting buildings (more than 100 with National Trust classifications) include Merchiston Hall (1856), Osborne House (1858), and Corio Villa (1856). Open to the public: The Heights (1855), 14-roomed prefabricated timber mansion in delightful gardens, Aphrasia St, Newtown; Barwon Grange (1855), Fernleigh St, Newtown. Christ Church, Moorabool St, oldest Anglican church in Vic. in continuous use. Customs House, Brougham St. Ford Discovery Centre, cnr Brougham and Gheringhap sts, history of Ford cars, with interactive displays (closed Tues). In Little Malop St: Geelong Art Gallery, large regional gallery; Performing Arts Centre. Wintergarden, McKillop St, historic building housing gallery, nursery, antiques and gift shop. Pottage Crafts, Moorabool St. Waterfront Geelong, restored promenade on Eastern Beach; swimming in fully restored 1930s sea-baths. Beachfront Scenic Drive. Botanic Gardens, Garden St in Eastern Park, overlooking Corio Bay. Johnstone Park, cnr Mercer and Gheringhap sts. Queens Park, Queens Park Rd, Newtown, has walks to Buckley Falls. Balyang Bird Sanctuary, Shannon Ave, Newtown. Extensive walking tracks and bike paths alongside Barwon River. Boat ramps on Corio Bay beaches. Good river and bay fishing. Steampacket Gardens Market on foreshore at Eastern Beach, 1st Sun. each month. Jan.: Waterfront Festival. Feb.: Australian International Air Show (at Avalon Airfield, odd-numbered years). Mar.: Highland Gathering. Apr.: Alternative Farmvision. June: National Celtic Folk Festival. Sept.: Momenta Arts. Oct.: Agricultural Show; Racing Carnival. **In the area:** Around 20 wineries (details from information centre). Norlane Water World, 7 km N. You Yangs, 20 km N, a range of distinctive granite hills in You Yangs Regional Park, has walking tracks, picnic grounds and information centre. Nearby, Serendip Sanctuary, a wildlife research station open to public, has nature trails, bird hides and visitors' centre. Anakie, 29 km N: Mt Anakie Winery and Staughton Vale winery, both north of town on Staughton Vale Rd. Steiglitz, 10 km NW of town, once a gold town, now almost deserted, has restored courthouse (1875), open Sun. Brisbane Ranges National Park, 34 km N: has many species of ferns and flowering plants, and native fauna, including koalas; Discovery Walk leads to Anakie Gorge (leaflet available). Nearby Fairy Park, with miniature houses and scenes from fairytales. Fyansford, 4 km W on outskirts of city, one of oldest settlements in region: historic buildings including Swan Inn, Balmoral Hotel (1854) and Fyansford Hotel; information board at Common Reserve has interpretative material on history, flora and fauna of region; Monash Bridge across Moorabool River thought to be one of first reinforced-concrete bridges in Vic. Brownhill Observation Tower, 10 km SW at Ceres, excellent view of surrounding areas. At Moriac, 22 km SW, horse-drawn caravan hire. At Werribee Park, 40 km NE off Princes Hwy: 60-roomed 1870s mansion; luxury accommodation; Victoria State Rose Garden; Victoria's Open Range Zoo, home to free-roaming native and exotic animals. **Visitor information:** National Wool Museum, 26–32 Moorabool St; (03) 5222 2900, freecall 1800 620 888. Web site www.greatoceanrd.org.au **See also:** Werribee & Bellarine Peninsula p. 142; Wildlife-Watching p. 196.

Glenrowan   Pop. 343
MAP REF. 222 D1, 233 M6

Glenrowan, 220 km NE of Melbourne, is the site of the defeat of Ned Kelly and his gang by the police in 1880. **In town:** Self-guide Historic Ned Kelly Trail, brochures available. Historic Siege St, site of Kelly's last stand against police. In Gladstone St (Old Hume Hwy): Ned Kelly Memorial Museum and Homestead; Kate's Cottage, gifts and souvenirs behind huge 6-m high statue of Ned Kelly set in cottage gardens; Kellyland, computer-animated show of Ned Kelly's capture; Cobb and Co and Museum. White Cottage Herb Garden, Hill St. **In the area:** Nearby wineries: Baileys of Glenrowan, Taminick Gap Rd (just NW of town); Auldstone Cellars and Booths Taminick Cellars, both on Booths Rd, Taminick, 10 km NW; HJT Vineyards, Keenan Rd (near Lake Mokoan). **Visitor information:** Kate's Cottage, Gladstone St (Old Hume Hwy); (03) 5766 2448. **See also:** The High Country p. 152.

Halls Gap   Pop. 256
MAP REF. 226 I1, 228 I12

In the heart of the Grampians, this little village is adjacent to Lake Bellfield and surrounded by the Grampians National Park and a network of scenic roads. **In town:** Long-billed corellas arrive each evening to roost opposite shops. Feb.:

Grampians Jazz Festival. May: Grampians Gourmet Weekend. Oct.: Wildflower Exhibition. **In the area:** The region is noted for its wildflowers. Bushwalking, camping, rock climbing and abseiling in national park, one of largest in State; park information centre, 2.5 km S on Dunkeld Rd. Brambuk Aboriginal Cultural Centre, 2 km S: displays; art exhibitions; information on shelters, art and other significant sites; tours of rock art. Lake Bellfield, 8 km S, for swimming, canoeing and picnics. The Gap Vineyard, 2 km E. Lake Fyans, 17 km E, for swimming, fishing, yachting and water-skiing. At Roses Gap Recreation Park, Roses Gap Rd, 21 km N in Northern Grampians section of park: scenic walks, fitness track, accommodation and camping. Also within Grampians National Park: Boroka Lookout, Reed Lookout and The Balconies, 12 km NW; Mackenzie Falls, 17 km NW; eastern grey kangaroos at Zumsteins picnic area, 22 km NW; school holiday activities. Half-day scenic drive through park; details from information centre. Wartook Pottery and Restaurant, 20 km NW. **Visitor information:** Dunkeld Rd; (03) 5356 4616. Web site www.grampians.org.au **See also:** Grampians & Central West p. 144; National Parks p. 193; Wildlife-Watching p. 196.

Hamilton   Pop. 9248

MAP REF. 226 F5

Hamilton is a prosperous and stylish city less than an hour's drive from the coastal centres of Portland, Port Fairy and Warrnambool to the south and the Grampians to the north. **In town:** Big Woolbales Complex, Coleraine Rd, focuses on wool industry, and has woolshed memorabilia and craft centre. Hamilton Country Spun Woollen Mill and Factory, Peck St, has sales and tours (Mon.–Fri.). HIRL (Hamilton Institute of Rural Learning), North Boundary Rd, has nature trail and breeding area for eastern barred bandicoots (open Mon.–Wed.). Historical and scenic walks and drives, brochures available. Land-care tours, bookings essential (contact information centre). Hamilton Art Gallery, Brown St, fine regional gallery, contains Herbert Shaw Collection. Lake Hamilton, Ballarat Rd, for water sports and fishing; sandy beach, jogging and cycling tracks and picnic facilities. On banks of lake, Sir Reginald Ansett Transport Museum, Glenelg Hwy, has historical collection and

Werribee Park, located between Melbourne and Geelong

memorabilia; Ansett transport industry began in Hamilton 1931. Botanical Gardens (established 1870), French St, has native animal enclosure, free-flight aviary and historic band rotunda. Hamilton Pastoral Museum, in former St Luke's Lutheran Church, on Glenelg Hwy (check times). Hamilton History Centre, Gray St, features histories of early Western District families. Hamilton is the starting point for Mary MacKillop Pilgrims Drive; grave of Mary's father in cemetery on Henty Hwy. Feb.: Beef Expo. Apr.: Southern Grampians Autumn Festival (even-numbered years); Races (horseracing). July: Eisteddfod. Aug.: Sheepvention (sheep and wool inventions and farmdog championships). **In the area:** Nigretta Falls, 15 km NW, has viewing platform nearby. Wannon Falls, 19 km W. Mt Eccles National Park, 35 km S near Macarthur, features 3 extinct volcanoes: Mt Eccles (with crater Lake Surprise, camping and koalas), Mt Rouse (at Penshurst), and Mt Napier (not accessible). At Penshurst, 31 km SE, Country Muster each Feb. Byaduk Caves (lava caves) at western entrance to Mt Napier State Park; one cave open to public. Grampians tour (day trip from Hamilton) to Dunkeld, Grampians National Park, Halls Gap, Ararat and back via Glenthompson. At Cavendish, 25 km N: 3 beautiful private gardens; Southern Grampians Open Gardens in Oct., brochure available. **Visitor information:** Lonsdale St; (03) 5572 3746, freecall 1800 807 056. Web site www.grampians.org.au **See also:** Grampians & Central West p. 144.

Harrietville   Pop. 186

MAP REF. 223 M8, 233 Q9, 234 C7

This former goldmining village, tucked into the foothills of Mt Hotham and Mt Feathertop, is a convenient accommodation centre for skiers at Mt Hotham and summer holidaymakers. **In town:** On Great Alpine Rd: Pioneer Park, an open-air museum and picnic area; Tavare Park, with swing bridge and picnic/barbecue facilities. Bush market, 2nd Sun. in Jan. and Easter Sun. Jan.: Classical Music Competition; Ride-on Mower Grand Prix. **In the area:** Lavender Farm, at northern edge of town on Great Alpine Rd (closed in winter). Summer bushwalking in high mountain country of Alpine National Park, which surrounds town (note that weather conditions can be harsh and change suddenly); walking tracks to Mt Feathertop (1922 m), 20 km return; Mt Hotham (1868 m), 65 km return. Hotham Heights Alpine Village, 31 km SE, has summer bushwalking (Australian Alps Walking Track passes through village) in Bogong High Plains and Dargo High Plains, and winter downhill and cross-country skiing. Dinner Plain Alpine Village, 43 km SE, has summer bushwalking and horseriding, and winter cross-country skiing. Bright Waters Trout Farm and, nearby, Mountain Fresh Trout Farm, 5 km N, offer fishing and educational displays. **Visitor information:** General Store, Great Alpine Rd; (03) 5759 2553. **See also:** The High Country p. 152.

Close encounter with a falcon at Healesville Sanctuary

Healesville   Pop. 6368

MAP REF. 211 N5, 214 E6, 224 F3

Surrounded by mountain forest country, Healesville is a short drive from Melbourne along the Maroondah Hwy. It has been a popular resort town since the turn of the century and the area offers excellent bushwalks and scenic drives. **In town:** Open-air trolley rides, Healesville railway station to Yarra Glen (Sun. and public holidays). Market, River St, 1st Sun. each month. Feb.: Coldstream Country and Western Festival. Mar.: Australian Car Rally Championship; Grape Grazing Festival (throughout wine district). Nov.: Gateway Festival. **In the area:** World-famous Healesville Sanctuary, 4 km s on Badger Creek Rd: 32-ha reserve housing native birds and animals in largely natural bushland setting; displays enable animals to be seen close up; picnic/barbecue facilities, kiosk and bistro. En route to Healesville Sanctuary: HCP Antique Emporium, a large, undercover antique market; Hedgend Maze, Albert Rd; pottery, lapidary and art gallery at Nigel Court; Corranderrk Aboriginal Cemetery, 3 km s. Mallesons Lookout, 8 km s, views of Yarra Valley through to Melbourne. Yarra Ranges National Park, just east of town: majestic mountain ash forests and fern gullies; within park, superb drive through tall forest over Black Spur, picnic facilities at top; Badger Weir Park, 7 km SE, majestic park in natural setting; Tuscany Gallery, 5 km E; Donnelly's Weir Park, 4 km N, start of 5000-km Bicentennial National Trail to Cooktown (Qld) for horseriders and walkers; Mt St Leonard, 14 km N, fine views from summit. Maroondah Reservoir Park, 3 km NE: magnificent park in forested setting, walking tracks and lookout nearby.

At Toolangi, 20 km NW: Singing Garden of C. J. Dennis, a beautiful, formal garden; Sculpture Studio, sculpture from recycled timbers, and pottery. Around 30 wineries in the area open for tastings and sales; Yarra Valley wine tours. Yarra Valley Regional Food Trail; brochure available. **Visitor information:** Yarra Valley Visitor Information Centre, Old Courthouse, Harker St; (03) 5962 2600. **See also:** Yarra & Dandenongs p. 151; Wildlife-Watching p. 196.

Heathcote   Pop. 1565

MAP REF. 232 E9

In attractive countryside on the McIvor Hwy, Heathcote is set along the McIvor Creek, 47 km SE of Bendigo. **In town:** Courthouse Crafts, in old courthouse, High St, has historical display, art and craft. Pink Cliffs, Pink Cliffs Rd, off Hospital Rd, brilliant mineral staining created by eroded spoil from gold sluices. Old Heathcote Hospital (1859), Hospital St. McIvor Range Reserve, off Barrack St. Heathcote Winery, High St. Easter: Rodeo. Nov.: Agricultural Show. **In the area:** Bushwalking tracks in surrounding forests, details from information centre. Lake Eppalock, 10 km W, one of the State's largest lakes; Eppalock Gold Cup (power boat race) each Feb. Mount Ida Lookout, 4 km N, excellent views. Central Victorian Yabby Farm, 5 km S: catch-your-own, farm tours, picnic/barbecue facilities. Wineries nearby: Zuber Estate, 2 km N; Wild Duck Creek Estate, 10 km W; Jasper Hill and Huntleigh Vineyards, 6 km N; McIvor Creek Wines, 5 km SE; and Eppalock Ridge Vineyards, 22 km NW. **Visitor information:** Cnr High and Barrack sts; (03) 5433 3121. **See also:** Goulburn & Murray p. 147.

Hopetoun   Pop. 670

MAP REF. 110 E12, 228 H3, 230 H13

This small Mallee town, south-east of Wyperfeld National Park, was named after the first Governor-General of Australia. The Earl of Hopetoun frequently visited Edward Lascelles, who was largely responsible for opening up the Mallee area. **In town:** In Evelyn St, 2 National Trust-classified homes: Hopetoun House (1891) built for Lascelles; Corrong Homestead (1846), home of first European settler in area, Peter McGinnis. Mallee Mural and leadlight window in Shire Offices, Lascelles St, depict Mallee history. Lake Lascelles, end Austin St, for boating, swimming and picnics. Oct.: Agricultural Show. **In the area:** Wyperfeld National Park, 50 km W: information centre at Wonga Campground in park, Brambruk Nature Walk, occasional sightings of threatened mallee fowl. At Patchewollock, 35 km NW, Easter Sports and Camel Cup (part of Warracknabeal Y-Fest). **Visitor information:** Gateway Beet, 75 Lascelles St; (03) 5083 3001. Web site www.murrayoutback.org.au **See also:** Mallee Country p. 146; National Parks p. 193; Wildlife-Watching p. 196

Horsham   Pop. 12 591

MAP REF. 228 G9

Situated at the junction of the Western, Wimmera and Henty hwys, Horsham is the chief town of the Wimmera region. It is a popular base for tours to Little Desert National Park, the Grampians and Mt Arapiles. **In town:** Botanic Gardens, cnr Baker and Firebrace sts. Horsham Regional Art Gallery, Wilson St, features Mack Jost collection of Australian art. May Park, Dimboola Rd. In Golf Course Rd: Horsham Rocks and Gems and Country Crafts; The Wool Factory, producing extra-fine wool from Saxon-Merino sheep (tours daily). Attractive picnic spots and viewing places for spectacular sunsets alongside Wimmera River. Historic River Walk and self-guide town tour, brochures available. Market, at showgrounds, McPherson St, 2nd Sun. each month. Mar.: Wimmera Machinery Field Days; Fishing Competition; Art Is (community festival). Sept.: Agricultural Show. Oct.: Spring Garden Festival. Nov.: Kannamaroo Rock'n'Roll Festival. **In the area:** Water sports and good fishing for redfin and trout in lakes in area, including: Green

Lake, 13 km SE; Pine Lake, 16 km SE; Taylors Lake, 18 km SE; Toolondo Reservoir, 44 km SW, home of the fighting brown trout; and Rocklands Reservoir, 90 km S, on Glenelg River, built to supplement Wimmera–Mallee irrigation scheme. Mount Zero Olives at Laharum, 30 km S, largest olive grove in the Southern Hemisphere: tastings; oil, lentils and vinegar for sale; accommodation. Black Range Cashmere and Thryptomene Farm, 40 km S; 4WD tours available, bookings essential, contact information centre. Grampians National Park, 50 km SE, for Aboriginal rock-art sites, rugged sandstone ranges, wildflowers, waterfalls and wildlife. At Jung, 10 km NE, market last Sat. each month. Do See View Farm, 15 km NW: operating farm, native flower walk, Clydesdale horses, blacksmith's shop. Little Desert National Park, 40 km NW. **Visitor information:** 20 O'Callaghan Pde; (03) 5382 1832, freecall 1800 633 218. Web site www.grampians.org.au **See also:** Grampians & Central West p. 144.

Inglewood   Pop. 699

MAP REF. 229 O8, 232 A7

North along the Calder Hwy from Bendigo is the 'Golden Triangle' town of Inglewood. Sizeable gold nuggets were found in this area during the gold rush and are still being unearthed. Inglewood is also known as the birthplace of Australian aviator Sir Reginald Ansett. **In town:** Old eucalyptus oil distillery, Calder Hwy, northern end of town. Old courthouse, Southey St, has historical memorabilia (open by appt). In Verdon St: Tivey House (1883) and town hall (1887) with chiming clock. Blue Mallee Crafts, Brooke St. Old Inglewood Cemetery, Calder Hwy. Oct.: Blue Eucalyptus Festival (even-numbered years). **In the area:** Blanche Barkly Winery, 10 km SW on Kingower–Rheola Rd; Passing Clouds winery, 11 km W at Kingower; Kangderaar Vineyard, 15 km SW at Rheola. Kooyoora State Park, 16 km W, features well-known Melville Caves, once haunt of notorious bush-ranger Captain Melville. At Bridgewater on Loddon, 8 km SE: fishing, water-skiing, parachute jumping at weekends; Old Loddon Vines vineyard, Water Wheel Vineyards; horse-drawn caravans for hire. **Visitor information:** Loddon Shire Council, High St, Wedderburn; (03) 5494 1200. **See also:** The Goldfields p. 148.

Inverloch   Pop. 2448

MAP REF. 224 G10

This is a small seaside resort on Anderson Inlet, east of Wonthaggi. It has long stretches of beach with good surf and excellent fishing. **In town:** In the Esplanade: Environment Centre, for books and natural products; Shell Museum. Mar.: Jazz Festival. **In the area:** Adjacent to town, Anderson Inlet, most southerly habitat of mangroves; nearby, Townsend Bluff and Maher's Landing for birdwatching. Inverloch–Cape Paterson scenic road to the south-west through Bunurong Marine Park, offers splendid coastal views. At Cape Paterson, spear fishing and surfing. Tarwin River, 20 km SE, offers good fishing. Beaches, natural bushland and wildlife at Venus Bay nearby. **Visitor information:** Community Centre, 3 Reilly St; (03) 5674 1169. Web site www.phillipislandgippsland.com **See also:** Phillip Island & Gippsland p. 156.

Jeparit   Pop. 403

MAP REF. 228 F6

This little town in the Wimmera, 37 km N of Dimboola, is 5 km SE of Lake Hindmarsh, the largest natural freshwater lake in Victoria. Sir Robert Menzies, long-serving Prime Minister, was born here 1894. **In town:** Sir Robert Menzies Spire, Sands Ave. Menzies Square, cnr Charles and Roy sts, site of dwelling where Menzies was born. Wimmera–Mallee Pioneer Museum, Charles St, at southern entrance to town: 4-ha complex of colonial buildings furnished in period-style, and displays of restored farm machinery; Wimmera River walk (6 km return) from museum, brochures available. Mar.: Museum Open Day. Oct.: Agricultural Show. **In the area:** Safe beaches, fishing, water-skiing, sailing and camping at Lake Hindmarsh, 5 km NW. Wildflowers, native fauna and walking tracks at Wyperfeld National Park, 44 km N. **Visitor information:** Wimmera–Mallee Pioneer Museum, Dimboola Rd; (03) 5397 2101. **See also:** Mallee Country p. 146.

Kaniva   Pop. 765

MAP REF. 228 C7

Kaniva in the west Wimmera, 43 km from Bordertown, SA, is just north of Little Desert National Park, noted for its spring wildflowers. **In town:** Historical town walks, brochure available. Shoe Museum (shoes displayed in various shop windows). Historical museum, Commercial St, has large local history collection (open by appt). On western outskirts of town, Rotary Fauna Park with nature walk and bird hide. Tours to Little Desert, Big Desert and farms; details from information centre. **In the area:** Billy-Ho Bush Walk, a 3-km self-guide walk in Little Desert National Park, begins some 10 km S; numbered pegs allow identification of various species of desert flora, brochure available. Mooree Reserve, 20 km SW. At Serviceton, 25 km W, National Trust-classified railway station (1889) (key from Serviceton General Store). **Visitor information:** Apricot House, 41 Commercial St; (03) 5392 2418. **See also:** Grampians & Central West p. 144.

Kerang   Pop. 3883

MAP REF. 110 I12, 229 P3, 231 P13, 232 A2

Some 30 km from the Murray River and 60 km from Swan Hill, Kerang is the centre of a productive rural area and lies at the southern end of a chain of lakes and marshes. Some of the world's largest breeding-grounds for ibis and other waterfowl are found in these marshes. The ibis is closely protected because of its value in controlling locusts and other pests. **In town:** Lester Lookout Tower, cnr Murray Valley Hwy and Shadforth St, houses Gemstone Museum. Historical Museum, Riverwood Dr., features cars and farm machinery. Easter: Quilters Exhibition. Oct.: Woodworking Expo. **In the area:** Apex Park recreation area near the first of the three Reedy Lakes (8 km NW); the second has a large ibis rookery. Lakes Meran, Reedy, Kangaroo and Charm for water sports; and others have excellent fishing. Gunbower State Forest, 25 km N: significant red gum habitat, flora and fauna. At Murrabit, 27 km N on the Murray and surrounded by picturesque river forests: historic building and sawmill; country market, 1st Sat. each month. Lake Boga, 42 km NW, for good sandy beaches and water sports. At Easter, Australian Tractor Pull Championship at Quambatook, 40 km SW. **Visitor information:** Wellington St; (03) 5452 1860. **See also:** Goulburn & Murray p. 147.

Kilmore   Pop. 2710

MAP REF. 211 J2, 232 F11

Kilmore, 60 km north of Melbourne on the Northern Hwy, is Victoria's oldest inland town, settled by Europeans in

1841. It is known for its historic buildings and its horseracing. **In town:** Fine old buildings, including Whitburgh Cottage (1857), Piper St; Post Office, Sydney St, and Court House, Powlett St, (both 1860s); several Sydney St shops and hotels (1850s). Old Kilmore Gaol, Sutherland St, has restaurant, tours (closed Mon). Hudson Park, cnr Sydney and Foote sts, has cable-tram rides and picnic/barbecue facilities. Market at Old Kilmore Gaol, 2nd Sat. each month. June: Celtic Festival. **In the area:** Tramways Museum at Bylands, just south of town: extensive display of cable cars and early electric trams; tram rides. At Broadford, 14 km NW: historic precinct in High St; Scottish Festival each Oct.; Hells Angels Concert each Dec. Nearby: Mt Piper Walking Track (1 hr return, wildlife and wildflowers); Strath Creek, for Strath Creek Falls and drive through Valley of a Thousand Hills. **Visitor information:** Library, 12 Sydney St; (03) 5782 1322. **See also:** Spa & Garden Country p. 150.

Koo-wee-rup   Pop. 1118

MAP REF. 211 M10, 224 F7

Well known for its Potato Festival, this town near Western Port is in Australia's largest asparagus-growing district. **In town:** Historical Society Museum, Rossiter Rd (open Sun.). Mar.: Potato Festival. **In the area:** Bunyip Byways Tourist Trails, maps available. Bayles Flora and Fauna Park, 8 km NE. At Tynong, 20 km NE: Victoria's Farm Shed (farm animals and shearing displays); Gumbaya Park, in landscaped bushland. At Pakenham, 13 km N: Military Vehicle Museum, Army Rd; Berwick–Pakenham Historical Society Museum, John St. At Cardinia, 11 km NW, Australian Pioneer Farm offers opportunity to shear sheep and milk cows. Royal Botanic Gardens, 22 km NW at Cranbourne, native gardens. Fishing and boating at Tooradin, 10 km W, on Sawtell's Inlet. On South Gippsland Hwy towards Tooradin: Harewood House (1850s), has original furnishings (open weekends); Swamp Observation Tower offers views of surrounding swamp and Western Port. Market, 4th Sun. each month, at Grantville, 30 km S. **Visitor information:** Newsagency, 277 Rossiter Rd; (03) 5997 1456. Web site www.phillipislandgippsland. com **See also:** Phillip Island & Gippsland p. 156.

Korumburra   Pop. 2739

MAP REF. 211 O12, 224 H8

Korumburra is known for a large species of a local worm, the giant Gippsland earthworm. Situated on the South Gippsland Hwy, the town is 118 km SE of Melbourne. The area surrounding the town is given to dairying and agriculture, and the countryside is hilly. **In town:** Coal Creek Heritage Village, cnr South Gippsland Hwy and Silkstone Rd, a re-creation of 19th-century coalmining village on original site of Coal Creek mine. **In the area:** Food and wine along Gourmet Deli Trail; brochure available. South Gippsland Railway tourist train offers 40-km rides linking Leongatha, Korumburra, Loch and Nyora (check departure times). Gooseneck Pottery, 9 km SE at Ruby. At Loch, 14 km NW: antiques, art and craft. At Poowong, 18 km NW: Poowong Pioneer Chapel, fine example of German architecture; Mudlark Pottery. At Arawata, 12 km NE, Quilters' Barn, for craft, coffee shop and accommodation. **Visitor information:** South Gippsland Visitor Information Centre, cnr South Gippsland Hwy and Silkstone Rd; (03) 5655 2233, freecall 1800 630 704. Web site www.phillipislandgippsland.com **See also:** Phillip Island & Gippsland p. 156.

Kyabram   Pop. 5738

MAP REF. 232 G5

A prosperous town in the Murray–Goulburn area, just 40 km NW of Shepparton, Kyabram is located in a dairying and fruit-growing district. **In town:** Community-owned waterfowl and fauna park on Lake Rd has five ponds with waterbirds and 15-ha of open-range parklands with native fauna. The Stables, adjacent to fauna park, for pottery and crafts. Mar.: Rodeo. Oct.: Bush Market Day. **Visitor information:** Kyabram Fauna Park, 75 Lake Rd; (03) 5852 2883. **See also:** Goulburn & Murray p. 147.

Kyneton   Pop. 3757

MAP REF. 210 G1, 227 R1, 229 R12, 232 D11

About an hour from Melbourne along the Calder Hwy, Kyneton is a well-preserved, attractive town with several interesting bluestone buildings. Farms around the town prospered during the gold rushes, supplying fresh food to the Ballarat and Bendigo diggings. **In town:** In Piper St: Kyneton Museum in former bank (c.1865), drop-log cottage in grounds (open Fri.–Sun.); Steam Mill, restored to operational condition (check opening times); Meskills Woolstore, has spinning mill, and yarn and garments for sale. Botanic Gardens, Clowes St, 8-ha area above river with 500 specimen trees. Historic buildings: town's churches; mechanics institute, Mollison St; old police depot, Jenning St. Campaspe River Walk, leaflet available. Feb.: Country Music Festival. Mar.: Autumn Flower Show. Sept.: Daffodil and Arts Festival. Nov.: Kyneton Cup (horse race). **In the area:** Two two-storey bluestone mills both on Calder Hwy, one on each side of town. Upper Coliban, Lauriston and Malmsbury reservoirs, all nearby. At Malmsbury, 10 km NW: historic bluestone railway viaduct; historic Botanic Gardens; Bleak House (1850s), with rose garden; The Mill (1861), National Trust-classified, has gallery, restaurant and accommodation; wineries in the area. At Trentham, 22 km SW: historic foundry; Minifie's Berry Farm, pick-your-own in season; Firth Park in Wombat State Forest. Carlsruhe Gallery and Campaspe Art Gallery at Carlsruhe, 5 km SE. Art and craft gallery at Tylden, 13 km W. Trentham Falls, 20 km SE. Turpins and Cascade falls with picnic area and walk, 22 km N near Metcalfe. **Visitor information:** Jean Haynes Playground, High St; (03) 5422 6110. **See also:** Spa & Garden Country p. 150.

Lake Bolac   Pop. 235

MAP REF. 227 J5

This small town on the Glenelg Hwy, 102 km W of Ballarat, is on the shores of a 1460-ha freshwater lake. The lake has a sandy 20-km shoreline and is good for fishing (eels, trout, perch and yellowbelly), boating and swimming. There are several boat-launching ramps. Easter: Yachting Regatta. **Visitor information:** Lake Bolac Motel, Glenelg Hwy; (03) 5350 2218. **See also:** Grampians & Central West p. 144.

Lakes Entrance   Pop. 5248

MAP REF. 225 R5, 234 H13

This popular holiday town is at the eastern end of the Gippsland Lakes, an inland network of waterways, covering an area of more than 400 sq. km. The lakes are separated from the ocean by a thin sliver of sand dunes forming a large part of Ninety Mile Beach, which stretches south to Seaspray. A bridge across the Cunningham Arm gives access to the surf beach from Lakes Entrance. The town caters for both seaside recreation and exploration of the mountain country to the north. It is the home port for a large fishing fleet and many pleasure craft. **In town:** Fisherman's Co-operative, Bullock Island, has viewing platform and fish for sale. Seashell Museum, The Esplanade. Jan.: Lakes Summer Festival. Oct.: International Festival of the Lakes. Dec.: New Year's Eve Fireworks. **In the area:** Sightseeing cruises of lakes; boat hire; fishing charters; beach fishing; joy flights; Bataluk Cultural Trail, which covers Aboriginal heritage in the East Gippsland area, self-guide brochure available. Lake Bunga, 3 km E, has nature trail on foreshore. Kinkuna Country Family Fun Park, 3.5 km E on Princes Hwy. East Gippsland Carriage Co., 30 km E, has carriage tours. Lake Tyers (6–23 km NE, depending on access point): sheltered waters ideal for fishing, swimming and boating; cruises depart from Fishermans Landing; Lake Tyers Forest Park, for walking, wildlife, picnicking and camping. Braeburne Park Orchards, 6 km N. Woodsedge Art Centre, 8 km N on Baades Rd; gallery, furniture workshop and glass-blowing demonstrations. Wyanga Park Winery, 10 km N; also reached by boat trip from town. Nyerimilang Heritage Park, 10 km NW: 1920s homestead, farm buildings and East Gippsland Botanic Gardens; Rose Pruning Day here in July features demonstrations (clippings given to the public). At Swan Reach, 14 km NW: Rosewood Pottery; Malcolm Cameron Studio Gallery (open weekends). Nicholson River Winery, 22 km NW. Good views from Jemmy's Point, 1 km W. At Metung, 15 km W: Chainsaw Sculpture Gallery has chainsaw sculpture and display of Annemieke Mein's embroidery art; boat hire, incl. cruisers; marina regatta in Jan. each year. **Visitor information:** Lakes and Wilderness Tourism, cnr Esplanade and Marine Pde; (03) 5155 1966, freecall 1800 637 060. Web site: www.lakesandwilderness.com.au **See also:** East Gippsland p. 154.

Leongatha   Pop. 4144

MAP REF. 211 P13, 224 H9

Located near the foothills of the Strzelecki Ranges, Leongatha is a large dairying area and a good base for Wilsons Promontory, the seaside and fishing resorts on the coast. **In town:** In McCartin St: Historic Society Museum (check opening times); Art and Craft Gallery. Mushroom Crafts and Pottery, Bair St. Jan.: South Gippsland Food and Wine Festival. Feb.: Cycling Carnival; South Gippsland Golf Classic.

Fishing boats at Lakes Entrance

Mar.: Riverfest. Sept.: Daffodil and Floral Festival; Rotary Art Show. **In the area:** Food and wine along gourmet Deli trail; brochure available. Canoeing and abseiling adventures. South Gippsland Railway tourist train, from Leongatha to Korumburra, Loch and Nyora (check departure times). Firelight Museum, 9 km N, features antique lamps and firearms. Mossvale Park, 16 km NE: impressive park plantation of exotic trees, good picnic/barbecue facilities; soundshell is venue for Victorian State Orchestra performance each Feb. At Mirboo North, 26 km NE: Grand Ridge Brewing Company, viewing of beer-brewing process and sales; Colonial Bank Antiques; Erinae Lavender Garden and Tea Rooms. Brackenhurst Rotary Dairy, 5 km E on Christoffersens Rd: 300 cows (milked from 3.30 p.m. daily); museum. Craft shop at Meeniyan, 16 km SE. Bass Phillip Wines, 15 km SW on Hunts Road. Gooseneck Pottery, 9 km NW at Ruby. **Visitor information:** CAB, Michael Place Complex; (03) 5662 2111 (weekdays). Web site www.phillipisland gippsland.com **See also:** Phillip Island & Gippsland p. 156.

Lorne   Pop. 1082

MAP REF. 210 D13, 217 L9, 227 P10

The approaches to Lorne along the Great Ocean Road are quite spectacular. The town is one of Victoria's most attractive and lively coastal resorts. It has a year-round mild climate and the superb mountain scenery of the Otways nearby. Captain Loutit, of the schooner *Apollo*, named the district Loutit Bay. The village of Lorne was established in 1871, became popular with pastoralists from inland areas, and developed in the style of an

English seaside resort. When the Great Ocean Road opened in 1932, Lorne grew; however, the area has remained relatively unspoiled, with good beaches, surfing, and excellent bushwalking in the hills. **In town:** Teddy's Lookout, at edge of George St behind town, has excellent bay views. Foreshore reserve. Shipwreck Walk along beach. Paddleboats for hire. Qdos Contemporary Art Gallery, Allenvale Rd. Lorne Fisheries on pier; daily supplies from local fleet. Jan.: Pier to Pub Swim; Mountain to Surf Foot Race. Dec.: Falls Festival. **In the area:** Surrounding town: Angahook–Lorne State Park, features Erskine Falls (9 km NW of town) and many walking tracks, incl. one to Kalimna and Phantom waterfalls from Sheoak Picnic area (about 4 km from town). Scenic drives: west in the Otway Ranges; south-west or north-east along Great Ocean Rd. Cumberland River Valley, 4 km SW, has walking tracks and camping. Mt Defiance, 10 km SW; narrow stretch of the road with excellent roadside viewing-point. Wye River, 17 km SW, for fishing and surfing. Gentle Annie Berry Gardens, 26 km NW via Deans Marsh, pick-your-own (open Nov.–Apr.). **Visitor information:** 144 Mountjoy Pde; (03) 5289 1152. Web site www.greatoceanrd.org.au **See also:** South-West Coast p. 143.

Maffra   Pop. 4033

MAP REF. 225 M5

The area around Maffra supports intensive farming, made possible by the Macalister Irrigation Scheme. **In town:** Maffra Sugar Beet Historic Museum, River St (open Sun. p.m.). Mineral and gemstone display at information centre, Johnson St. All Seasons Herb Gardens, Foster St. Feb.:

Railway station at Maldon, a National Trust-classified town

Scotfest. Mar.: Gippsland Harvest Festival; Mardi Gras. Easter: Tennis Tournament. **In the area:** 'Traralgon to Stratford' brochure available, describes attractions in area. Lake Glenmaggie, 21 km N of Heyfield, popular water-sports venue. Spectacular scenic drives north along forest road (closed in winter), which follows Macalister Valley to Licola (54 km N of Heyfield), and to Mt Tamboritha (20 km NE of Licola) in Alpine National Park; or to Jamieson (145 km NW of Heyfield, check road conditions), with access to snow-fields or Lake Eildon. 4WD tours into high country (bookings essential, at information centre). At Briagolong, 26 km NE, historic hotel and mechanics institute. Lake Tali Karng, in Alpine National Park, 60 km NE of Licola, is a popular bushwalking destination in season. At Stratford, 9 km E: Avon River for picnics; Aboriginal Bataluk Cultural Trail (driving tour); Shakespeare Celebration here in May. Australian Wildlife Art Gallery and Sculpture, 25 km E, on Princes Hwy near Munro. Trail-riding tours in surrounding area. **Visitor information:** Courthouse, 8 Johnson St; (03) 5141 1811. **See also:** East Gippsland p. 154.

Maldon   Pop. 1255

MAP REF. 221 M5, 229 P11, 232 B10

In 1996 the National Trust declared Maldon a Notable Town, the first in Australia. Situated 18 km NW of Castlemaine in central Victoria, Maldon is very popular with tourists, especially during the Easter Fair, and in spring wildflower season. Quartz reef goldmines in the area were among Victoria's richest, and at one stage 20 000 men worked on the

Tarrangower diggings. Enthusiasts still search for gold in the area. **In town:** Anzac Hill, southern end of High St, for good view of town. Many notable buildings, some of local stone: Maldon Hospital (1860), cnr Adair and Chapel sts; post office (1870), High St; old council offices, High St (now Museum); Dabb's General Store, with restored shopfront, Main St. National Trust properties: former Denominational (Penny) School, Camp St; Welsh Congregational Church, cnr Camp and Church sts. The Beehive Chimney (1862), south end of Church St. Victorian Goldfields Railway runs steam trains from railway station, Hornsby St (Sun., Wed., public and school holidays). Town walking tour, leaflet available. Feb.: Camp Draft. Easter: Fair. Oct.: Vintage Car Hill Climb. Oct.–Nov.: Folk Festival. **In the area:** Bushwalks and intriguing rock formations. Views from Mt Tarrangower Lookout Tower, 2 km W. Carman's Tunnel, 2 km SW, a reminder of hardships of goldmining days. Cairn Curran Reservoir, 10 km SW, for water sports and fishing; picnic facilities, sailing club near spillway. 'Porcupine Township', 3 km NE, a reconstructed gold-mining town. Goldmining dredge beside road to Bendigo, 4 km NE. Nuggetty Ranges and Mt Moorol, 2 km N. **Visitor information:** High St; (03) 5475 2569. Web site www.mountalexander.vic.gov.au/tourism **See also:** The Goldfields p. 148.

Mallacoota   Pop. 982

MAP REF. 103 G13, 235 Q11

In far east Gippsland, at the mouth of a deep inlet, Mallacoota is a seaside and fishing township and a popular holiday centre with a good swimming beach and

Foreshore Reserve. **In town:** Easter: Festival of the Great Southern Ocean. **In the area:** Birdwatching; lake and river cruises; scenic drives and walks; network of bushwalking tracks; leaflets available from Parks Victoria, cnr Allan and Buckland drs. In Croajingolong National Park (a World Biosphere Reserve), surrounding town: over 300 bird species; glossy-black cockatoos along walking track to Genoa Peak, magnificent views from peak; camping areas with walking trails; excellent surf fishing from remote beaches. Gabo Island Lightstation Reserve, 11 km W, scenic day trip or stay in Lightkeeper's Residence. Gipsy Point, 16 km NW, a quiet holiday retreat over-looking Genoa River. Bastion Point, 2 km SE, and Betka, 5 km S, are good surfing beaches. **Visitor information:** Snowy River–Orbost Visitor Centre, 13 Lochiel St, Orbost; (03) 5154 2424, freecall 1800 637 060 or call Parks Victoria, 13 1963 (ask for Mallacoota office). Web site www.lakesandwilderness.com.au **See also:** East Gippsland p. 154; National Parks p. 193; Wildlife-Watching p. 196.

Mansfield   Pop. 2526

MAP REF. 222 C10, 233 L10

A popular town at the junction of the Midland and Maroondah hwys, Mansfield is 3 km E from the northern arm of Lake Eildon. It is the nearest sizeable town to Mt Buller and Mt Stirling ski areas. **In town:** Self-guide historical walk, brochure available. Troopers' Monument, cnr High St and Midland Hwy, monument to police officers shot by Ned Kelly at Stringybark Creek, near Tolmie, in 1878; graves in Mansfield cemetery. Nearby, National Trust-classified courthouse. Highton Manor (1896), Highton La. Balloon trips leave from Highton Manor, advance bookings essential, details from information centre. Bush market, 4 times a year (check date). Balloon Festival (check dates). Mar.: Harvest Festival. Nov.: Mountain Country Festival. **In the area:** Camel treks and horse trail-riding. Road over mountains to Whitfield in the King River Valley (62 km NE) passes through spectacular scenery, incl. Powers Lookout, 48 km NE, for views over King River Valley (was vantage point for bushranger Harry Power). Lake William Hovell, 85 km NE, for boating and fishing. Mt Samaria State Park, 14 km N, for scenic drives, camping and bushwalking. At Lake

Nillahcootie, 20 km NW: boating, fishing, canoeing and sailing. Houseboat hire, water sports and fishing at Lake Eildon, 15 km S. To the south, Delatite, Howqua, Jamieson and Goulburn rivers for trout fishing and gold-fossicking. Near Howqua, 26 km S, Howqua Dale Gourmet Retreat. Historic buildings at old goldmining town of Jamieson, 37 km S on Jamieson River. Mt Skene, 48 km SE of Jamieson, has wildflowers Dec.–Feb. (road closed in winter). Delatite Winery, on Stoneys Rd, 7 km SE. At Merrijig, 19 km SE, Rodeo each Mar. Craig's Hut, 50 km E, used for filming *The Man from Snowy River* (no vehicle access in winter). Alpine National Park, 60 km E, bushwalking and 4WD tracks. **Visitor information:** Old Railway Station, Maroondah Hwy; (03) 5775 1464. **See also:** The High Country p. 152.

Maryborough　　Pop. 7381

MAP REF. 221 J5, 229 O11

Sheep farming, the gold rush and secondary industry have contributed to the development of this small city on the northern slopes of the Great Dividing Range, 70 km N of Ballarat. Maryborough is in the centre of an agricultural and forest area. **In town:** Pioneer Memorial Tower, Bristol Hill. Worsley Cottage (1894), Palmerston St, an historical museum (open Sun.). Old railway station (1890), Station St, now houses information centre, antique emporium gallery and woodwork shop. Central Goldfields Art Gallery, in old fire station, Neill St. Phillips Gardens, Alma St. Imposing Civic Square buildings, Clarendon St, incl. Town Hall. Self-guide Historic Buildings Drive, brochure available. Markets, Maryborough–Dunolly Rd, 1st and 3rd Sun. each month. Jan.: Highland Gathering. Aug.–Sept.: Golden Wattle Festival (includes Gumleaf-Playing Championship). Oct.: Gourmet, Grapes and Gardens Weekend. Nov.: Energy Breakthrough (energy expo). **In the area:** Self-guide Golden Way Tourist Drive, brochures available. Aboriginal wells, 4 km S. At Carisbrook, 7 km E, Tourist Market, 1st Sun. each month in Chaplins Rd. **Visitor information:** Railway Station Complex, Station St; (03) 5460 4511, freecall 1800 356 511. Web site www.goldfields. org.au **See also:** The Goldfields p. 148.

Autumn trees, Marysville

Marysville　　Pop. 626

MAP REF. 211 O4, 214 I3, 224 G2, 233 J13

This peaceful year-round resort owes its existence to gold, as its site was on the route to the Woods Point goldfields, and to timber milling. The town, 34 km NE of Healesville off the Maroondah Hwy, is surrounded by attractive forest-clad mountain country. **In town:** In Murchison St: Old Fashioned Lolly Shop; Country Touch pottery; Hidden Talents, local art and crafts. Bruno's Art and Sculpture Garden, Falls Rd. Sawyer's Marysville Museum, Darwin St, features vintage cars and accessories. Nicholl's Lookout, Cumberland Rd, for excellent views. Market, Murchison St, 2nd Sun. each month. **In the area:** Numerous bushwalking tracks lead to beauty spots: 3-min walk to Steavenson Falls from Falls Rd (walk and falls illuminated at night); 4-km loop walk in Cumberland Memorial Scenic Reserve, 16 km E; 2-hr walk to Keppel's Lookout; 30-min walk to Mt Gordon (begins 2 km W of town); 5-km Beeches Walk through ancient beech and mountain ash forests. Lady Talbot Forest Drive through surrounding area, brochure available. Lake Mountain, 19 km E: accessible walking and cross-country skiing trails and tobogganing. Big River State

Forest, 30 km E: camping, good fishing and gold-fossicking. At Buxton, 11 km N: zoo; trout farm; Australian Bush Pioneer's Farm, at foot of Mt Cathedral; nearby, Cathedral Range State Park. **Visitor information:** 17 Murchison St; (03) 5963 4567. Web site www.mmtourism.com.au **See also:** Yarra & Dandenongs p. 151.

Milawa　　Pop. 120

MAP REF. 222 G1, 233 N6

Milawa is 16 km SE of Wangaratta on what is known as the Snow Road, which links Oxley, Milawa and Markwood with Wangaratta to the west and the Great Alpine Rd to the east. Brown Brothers Vineyard has operated here since 1889, producing quality wines. **In town:** Milawa Mustards, off Snow Rd, has a wide range of mustards and attractive cottage garden. Milawa Cheese Company, Factory Rd, for specialist cheeses. Nov.: Brown Brothers Wine and Food Weekend. **In the area:** Numerous wineries, details from information centre. At Oxley, 4 km W: Blue Ox Blueberry Farm; Churchworks; Earthly Gems; King River Cafe. At Whitfield, 46 km S, and Cheshunt, 51 km S, King Valley Virgin Wine, Food and Arts Festival in Nov. **Visitor information:** Wangaratta and Region Visitors Information Centre, cnr Handley St and Tone Rd, Wangaratta; (03) 5721 5711. **See also:** The High Country p. 152.

Mildura　　Pop. 24 142

MAP REF. 110 D7, 230 G3

Sunny mild winters and picturesque locations on the banks of the Murray River make the Mildura area popular with tourists. Mildura, 557 km N of Melbourne, is a pleasant city that developed with the expansion of irrigation. Alfred Deakin, statesman and advocate of irrigation, persuaded the Chaffey brothers, Canadian-born irrigation experts, to visit this region. They selected Mildura as the first site for development. After setbacks the citrus industry was established by 1900 and, with the locking of the Murray completed in 1928, Mildura soon became a city. **In town:** In Deakin Ave: The Alfred Deakin Centre, has interactive exhibitions and displays of region; statue of W. B. Chaffey, Mildura's first mayor. Mildura Arts Centre complex, Cureton Ave, includes Rio Vista, original Chaffey home, now museum displaying colonial household items; Sculpture Trail in gardens surrounding the centre. Langtree Hall

(1889), Walnut Ave, is Mildura's public hall (open Tues.–Sun). Paddle-steamers leave from Mildura Wharf, end of Madden Ave, for river trips: PS *Melbourne*, 2-hr round trips; PS *Avoca*, luncheon and dinner cruises; PS *Coonawarra*, 3-, 5- and 6-day cruises; PV *Rothbury*, day cruise to Trentham Winery (each Thurs.). Snakes and Ladders, 17th St, fun park featuring dunny collection. Mildura Lock Island and Weir. Aquacoaster waterslide, cnr Seventh St and Orange Ave. Stefano's in Grand Hotel, Seventh St, Italian restaurant run by television personality, Stefano di Pieri. Dolls on the Avenue, Benetook Ave. Pioneer Cottage, Hunter St. The Citrus Shop, Deakin Ave, for local citrus products. Mar.: Arts Festival. July: International Balloon Fiesta; Golf Week; Racing Cup Carnival. Sept.: Country Music Festival; Big Lizzie Festival of Vintage Tractors. Oct.: Sunraysia Oasis Rose Festival. Nov.: Sunraysia Jazz and Wine Festival; World Jet Sprint Boat Championships. **In the area:** Many vineyards: Lindemans Karadoc Winery, 20 km S, largest winery in Southern Hemisphere; Milburn Park Winery, south off Calder Hwy; Trentham Estate, south off Sturt Hwy; Mildara Wines, 9 km W. Woodsie's Gem Shop and Murray Gum Pottery, 6 km SW. Sunbeam Dried Fruits, 6 km S at Irymple (tours). Red Cliffs, 15 km S, important area for citrus and dried fruit industries; 'Big Lizzie' steam traction engine in town. Bushwalking and birdwatching in Hattah–Kulkyne National Park, 70 km S. Angus Park Promotion Centre, 10 km SE, dried fruits and confectionery. In NSW: Orange World, 6 km N, offers tours of citrus areas; Australian Inland Botanic Gardens, 6 km N (open Sun.–Fri); Mungo National Park, 104 km NE, World Heritage Area with Walls of China, a huge crescent of dunes (day tours from Mildura, with indigenous guides). In Vic.: Tulkland Kumbi Aboriginal Galleries, 18 km N (open Mon.–Fri); Golden River Zoo, 3 km NW, with native and exotic species in natural surroundings. Several self-guide drives, maps available. **Visitor information:** The Alfred Deakin Centre, 180–190 Deakin Ave; (03) 5021 4424, freecall 1800 039 043. Web site www.murrayoutback. org.au **See also:** NSW National Parks p. 74; Mallee Country p. 146.

Moe   Pop. 15 558

MAP REF. 211 R10, 225 J7

Situated on the Princes Hwy, 134 km SE of Melbourne, Moe is a rapidly growing city in the La Trobe Valley and a gateway to the alpine region. **In town:** Pioneer township, Lloyd St, re-creation of 19th-century community with over 30 restored buildings and fine collection of fully restored horse-drawn vehicles. Cinderella Dolls, Andrew St. Picturesque race track, Waterloo Rd. Self-guide walks, brochure available. Craft and produce market at Heritage Park, 2nd Sun. each month. Jan.: Modelling and Hobby Exhibition. Feb.: Woodworking Festival. Mar.: Jazz Festival; Blue Rock Classic (cross-country horse race). Oct.: Moe Cup (horse race). **In the area:** Edward Hunter Heritage Bush Reserve, 3 km S via Coalville St. Trafalgar Lookout and Narracan Falls near Trafalgar, 10 km W. Blue Rock Dam, 20 km NW, for fishing, swimming and sailing. Walhalla Mountain River Trail (Tourist Route 91) leads to picturesque old mining township of Walhalla (check road conditions in winter). Mt Baw Baw, 77 km N, for cross-country and downhill skiing (Alpine Village has 8 lifts and accommodation); Baw Baw plateau is excellent for bushwalking, with abundant wildflowers in summer. At Thorpdale (known for its potatoes), 22 km SW: potato bread from bakery, Potato Festival each Mar. **Visitor information:** Gippsland Heritage Park, Lloyd St; (03) 5127 3082. Web site www. phillipislandgippsland.com **See also:** Phillip Island & Gippsland p. 156.

Mornington   Pop. 13 692

MAP REF. 211 K10, 213 J3, 224 D7

Mornington retains its small-town character while being easily accessible from Melbourne. It is an excellent base for exploring the Mornington Peninsula. **In town:** Historic Mornington pier, first built in 1850s. Studio City Pop and Media Museum, Cool Stores, Moorooduc Hwy: film, television, radio and pop-music memorabilia. Mornington Peninsula Regional Gallery, Dunns Rd, has print and drawing collections, including works by Dobell, Drysdale and Nolan (open Tues.–Sat.). Motorised trolley rides operate from Bungower Rd level crossing each Sun. p.m. In Tyabb Rd: National Antique Centre; World of Motorcycles Museum. Local historical display, housed in old post office, cnr Main St and The Esplanade. Self-guide town walk, brochures available. Street market on Main St each Wed., and Mornington Racecourse craft market on 2nd Sun. each month. Nov.: Tea Tree Festival. **In the area:** Ballam Park (1845), 14 km NE on Cranbourne Rd at Frankston, French farmhouse-style homestead (open Sun.). At Baxter, 14 km NE: Mulberry Hill, Golf Links Rd, former home of artist Sir Daryl Lindsay and Joan Lindsay, author of *Picnic at Hanging Rock* (open Sun. p.m.). At Tyabb, 16 km E, Tyabb Packing House, Mornington–Tyabb Rd, for antiques and collectables. Several wineries between Tyabb and Hastings, with sales, including Barak Estate, Ermes Estate, Stumpy Gully Vineyard and Moorooduc Estate. Several festivals celebrate Peninsula produce, incl. Pinot Week in Mar., Queen's Birthday Wine Weekend in June and Mornington Food and Wine Festival in Oct. At Hastings, 21 km SE on Western Port: fauna park; wetlands area and 2-km coastal wetlands walk through most southerly mangroves in world. Coastline between Mornington and Mount Martha (7 km S), features sheltered sandy bays. At Mount Martha, historic The Briars (1866): significant collection of Napoleonic artifacts and furniture; gardens; wetland areas and bird hides; bushland walks. At Dromana, 16 km SW: 20-min. scenic chairlift ride up the mountain to Arthurs Seat State Park (check operating times); picnic facilities at top, as well as several walks; historic Seawinds Park, with gardens, sculptures, short walks and sweeping views; Arthurs Seat Maze, with gardens, a variety of mazes and Maize Maze Festival in Mar.; Pine Ridge Car and Folk Museum; riding school for horserides. **Visitor information:** Nepean Hwy, Dromana; (03) 5987 3078, freecall 1800 804 009. **See also:** Mornington Peninsula p. 155.

Morwell   Pop. 13 823

MAP REF. 225 J7

Morwell, an industrial town 150 km SE of Melbourne, is situated in the heart of the La Trobe Valley, which contains one of the world's largest deposits of brown coal. **In town:** PowerWorks, Ridge Rd, dynamic displays on electrical industry; tours of mines and power stations daily. In Commercial Rd: La Trobe Regional Gallery; Rose Garden, with over 200 varieties. Market, La Trobe Rd, each Sun. **In the area:** Scenic day tours, brochure available. Views of La Trobe Valley from routes along Strzelecki Ranges and Baw Baw mountains. Hazelwood Pondage, 5 km S, has warm water, ideal for year-round water sports. Morwell National Park, 12 km S, has good walking tracks. At Yinnar, 12 km SW, Arts Resource

Boat harbour at Mornington

Collective in old butter factory. Narracan Falls, 27 km W. Lake Narracan, 15 km NW, for fishing and waterskiing. **Visitor information:** PowerWorks Visitors Centre, Ridge Rd; (03) 5135 3415. Web site www.phillipislandgippsland.com **See also:** Phillip Island & Gippsland p. 156.

Mount Beauty   Pop. 1649

MAP REF. 223 N5, 233 Q8, 234 D6

Situated in the Upper Kiewa Valley, 338 km NE of Melbourne, Mount Beauty was originally an accommodation town for workers on the 1940s Kiewa Hydro-electric Scheme. An ideal holiday centre, the town lies at the foot of Mount Bogong, Victoria's highest mountain (1986 m). It offers ski hire, coach services and parking for Falls Creek skiers. In summer, the area is a premier mountain-bike location; the town also services high plains bushwalkers. **In town:** Heritage Museum, at information centre. Markets, Main St, each Sat. Mar.: Conquestathon Fun Climb of Mt Bogong. Apr.: Music Muster. Nov.: Gang Gang Mountain Bike Festival. **In the area:** Good water sports and fishing at Mount Beauty Pondage, 250 m N of Main St. Bogong, 15 km SE; walks around nearby Lake Guy. Scenic drive to Falls Creek, 30 km SE, and the Bogong High Plains (not accessible in winter beyond Falls Creek); at Falls Creek, winter skiing and International Kangaroo Hoppet (cross-country ski race) each Aug. Tawonga Gap, 13 km NW, features lookout over 2 valleys. Walks, mountain-bike hire, horseriding and hang-gliding. **Visitor information:** Kiewa Valley Hwy; (03) 5754 1962. Web site www.mtbeauty.com **See also:** The High Country p. 152.

Murtoa   Pop. 839

MAP REF. 228 I9

Murtoa, a wheat-belt town, is situated around picturesque Lake Marma, 31 km E of Horsham on the Wimmera Hwy. **In town:** Huge wheat-storage silos and facilities. Many buildings c. 1880. Original shopping centre (c. 1900), McDonald St. Four-storey railway water tower (1886), Soldiers Ave, now a museum with James Hill's 1885–1930 taxidermy collection of some 500 birds and animals (open Sun. p.m.). Lake Marma: walking track; birdwatching; spectacular sunsets. Stick Shed (1941) built from 640 unmilled tree trunks, Wimmera Hwy on eastern side of town. Jan.: New Year's Day Race Meeting. June: Murtoa Cup (horse race). Oct.: Big Weekend (includes Agricultural Show, race meeting, Arts Show, vintage machinery demonstrations and Poets on the Pier). **In the area:** Barrabool Forest Reserve, 7 km S, has wildflowers in spring (difficult access in winter). **Visitor information:** Marma Gully Antiques, 50 Marma St; (03) 5385 2422. **See also:** Grampians & Central West p. 144.

Myrtleford   Pop. 2705

MAP REF. 223 J2, 233 O7, 234 B5

On the Great Alpine Rd, 46 km SE of Wangaratta, the town of Myrtleford is surrounded by an area that produces hops, timber, vegetables, fruit, chestnuts and wine. It also has large walnut groves. **In town:** The Phoenix Tree, in Lions Park on highway, sculptured butt of a red gum, crafted by Hans Knorr. The Big Tree, Smith St, a huge old red gum. Town's original school, Albert St, now restored (open Thurs., Sun. or by appt). Myrtleford Mart, Myrtle St, for bric-a-brac. Swing bridge over Myrtle Creek, Standish St. Reform Hill Lookout, end of Halls Rd; scenic walking track from Elgin St leads to lookout. Rotary Park, Myrtle St, and Apex Park, Standish St, both delightful picnic spots and rest areas. Jan Mitchell Art Gallery, Power St. Michelini Wines, Great Alpine Rd. Street Life market, Great Alpine Rd, each Sat. (Jan.–Apr.). Mar.: Tobacco, Hops and Timber Festival. Oct.: International Festival (even-numbered years); Great Alpine Bike Ride. Dec.: Golden Spurs Rodeo. **In the area:** Wineries: Rosewhite Vineyards and Winery, 8 km SE, Happy Valley Rd (open weekends, public holidays and Jan.); at Gapsted, 8 km NW, Victorian Alps Winery. Also at Gapsted, Valley Nut Groves has tours and sales. Near Eurobin, 16 km SE: Red Deer and Emu Farm; Leita Berry Farm, for homemade jams and berries in season (Dec.–Mar.); Bisinella Rose Farm. Nug Nug Quarter Horse Stud and Dingo Breeding, 16 km S (open by appt). Good fishing at Lake Buffalo (25 km S), Ovens River and Buffalo River. **Visitor information:** Ponderosa Cabin, 29–31 Clyde St; (03) 5752 1727. **See also:** The High Country p. 152.

Nagambie   Pop. 1335

MAP REF. 232 G8

Between Seymour and Shepparton on the Goulburn Valley Hwy, Nagambie is on the shores of Lake Nagambie, created by the construction of the Goulburn Weir in 1891. Rowing regattas, and speedboat and water-ski tournaments are held here. **In town:** Several National Trust-classified buildings. In High St: Colonial Doll Shop; The Nut House, for Australian products. Boat hire. Self-guide walking tour, brochure available. Mar.: Goulburn Valley Vintage Festival. Nov.: Shiraz Challenge (competition for the best shiraz). Dec.: Rowing Regatta. **In the area:** David Traeger Wines, on Goulburn Valley Hwy, southern side of town. Museum and National Trust-classified buildings at Chateau Tahbilk Wines, 6 km SW. Mitchelton Wines, 10 km SW off Goulburn Valley Hwy, also has 60-m observation tower and cruises on the Goulburn River (check times). Days Mill, 18 km N of Murchison, flour mill with buildings dating from 1865. Plunkett Wines and Cafe at Avenel, 20 km SE. Self-guide bicycle tours of surrounding area, brochures available. **Visitor information:** 145 High St; (03) 5794 2647, freecall 1800 444 647. Web site www.mcmedia. com.au/nagambie **See also:** Goulburn & Murray p. 147.

Natimuk Pop. 479

MAP REF. 228 F9

This Wimmera town, 27 km W of Horsham, is close to the striking Mt Arapiles, a 369-m sandstone monolith that has been described as 'Victoria's Ayers Rock'. A drive to the summit, in Mount Arapiles–Tooan State Park, reveals a scenic lookout. The mountain was first climbed by Major Mitchell in 1836, and today, with over 2000 marked climbing routes, is popular with rock-climbing enthusiasts. Brigitte Muir, the first Australian woman to climb Mt Everest, trained here. **In town:** In Main St: Arapiles Historical Society Museum, in old courthouse (open by appt); Arapiles Craft Shop. Self-guide heritage trail, brochures available. **In the area:** Lake Natimuk, 2 km N, for water sports. Duffholme Museum, 21 km W. Mount Arapiles–Tooan State Park, 12 km SW. Toolondo Reservoir, 30 km S, for excellent trout fishing. Banksia Hill Flower Farm, 10 km E. **Visitor information:** National Hotel, Main St; (03) 5387 1300. **See also:** Grampians & Central West p. 144.

Nhill Pop. 1890

MAP REF. 228 D7

The name of this town may be derived from the Aboriginal word *nyell*, meaning 'white mist on water'. A small wheat town on the Western Hwy, exactly halfway between Melbourne and Adelaide, it claims to have the largest single-bin silo in the Southern Hemisphere (in Davis Ave). The town is the starting point for tours of the Little Desert. **In town:** Historical Society Museum, McPherson St (open by appt). In Victoria St: cottage of John Shaw Neilson, lyric poet (in Jaypex Park, open by appt); boardwalk from Jaypex Park to Nhill Lake, with bird hide; Draughthorse Memorial to Clydesdales used in opening up Wimmera region (in Goldsworthy Park); Lowana Craft Shop, for local craft. National Trust-classified post office (1888), Nelson St. Self-guide historical walk and drive, brochures available. Miniature Railway, at various locations, see by appt. Mar.: Country Music Festival. Oct.: Garden Walk. **In the area:** Little Desert National Park, 18 km S. Nearby, Little Desert Lodge operates day tours of Little Desert; Little Desert Wildflower Exhibition here in Oct. Mallee Dam, 20 km SW, is important location for native birdwatching and has bird hide.

From Kiata picnic and camping area, 20 km SE, short walks through eastern section of park. Big Desert Wilderness Park, 52 km NW via Yanac, on track north to Murrayville; explore this remote park by walking tracks and 4WD (but roads impassable in wet weather, check conditions); tours. **Visitor information:** Victoria St; (03) 5391 3086. **See also:** Grampians & Central West p. 144; National Parks p. 193; Wildlife-Watching p. 196.

Numurkah Pop. 3128

MAP REF. 111 M13, 232 I4

Numurkah, 37 km N of Shepparton on the Goulburn Valley Hwy, is half an hour from sandy beaches and excellent fishing spots on the Murray River. The town is in an irrigation area concentrating on dairying, and was developed through the Murray Valley Soldier Settlement Scheme. **In town:** In Melville St: Steam and Vintage Machinery Display; historical museum (open Sun. p.m.). Marie's House of Dolls, Meiklejohn St. Mar.: Art Show. Apr.: Splashdown (fishing competition). Sept.: Kart Titles (go-kart championships). **In the area:** Glenarron, 8 km N, a tourist dairy farm. Monichino's Winery at Katunga, 11 km N. At Strathmerton, 26 km N, Cactus Country, cactus and succulent garden (2 ha). Ulupna Island flora and fauna reserve, 21 km N near Strathmerton, has large koala population; Red Gum Wildlife Tours of Ulupna Island. Barmah State Park, 40 km NW, large red gum forest; safari tours. Morgan's Beach Caravan Park, at edge of forest on bank of Murray River, offers bushwalking and horseriding (horses for hire, facilities for visitors' horses). Historic buildings on banks of Broken Creek at Nathalia, 24 km W. At Wunghnu 5 km S: Institute Tavern in restored Mechanics Institute (c. 1880); Tractor Pull Festival at Easter. Crafty Characters Cottage at Brookfield, 6 km SE (open Sat. or by appt). **Visitor information:** 25 Quinn St; (03) 5862 3458. **See also:** Goulburn & Murray p. 147.

Ocean Grove Pop. 9144

MAP REF. 210 G10, 217 P6, 224 A7, 227 R8

At the mouth of the Barwon River, Ocean Grove offers fishing and surfing. Nearby Barwon Heads offers safe family relaxation on the shores of its protected river. The towns are linked by a bridge over the Barwon River estuary, and are popular in

summer as they are the closest ocean beaches to Geelong, 26 km NW. **In town:** Ocean Grove Nature Reserve, Grubb Rd. **In the area:** Barwon Heads, 3 km S: location for television series *SeaChange*; Barwon Heads Golf Club, one of top 3 public courses in State. Jirrahlinga Koala and Wildlife Sanctuary, Taits Rd. Mangrove swamps in Lake Connewarre State Game Reserve, 7 km N. At Wallington, 8 km N: A Maze'N Things, timber maze with mini-golf and cafe; Koombahla Park Equestrian Centre; Country Connection Adventure Park; Bellarine Adventure Golf. **Visitor information:** A Maze'N Things, 1570 Bellarine Hwy (at Grubb Rd), Wallington; (03) 5250 2669. Web site www.greatoceanrd.org.au **See also:** Werribee & Bellarine Peninsula p. 142.

Olinda Pop. 949

MAP REF. 207 P6, 211 M7, 214 B11, 224 E4

This picturesque town in the centre of the Dandenong Ranges is well known for its gardens and galleries. There are a number of tea rooms and cafes in the area: Devonshire teas are a tradition. **In town:** Galleries, incl. Touchstone Gallery, Monash Ave; Olinda Art Gallery, Parsons La. Feb.: Jazz Festival. Aug.–Nov.: Rhododendron Festival. **In the area:** On Olinda–Monbulk Rd: National Rhododendron Gardens, superb displays of rhododendrons and azaleas in season; R. J. Hamer Arboretum, walking tracks among 100 ha of rare and exotic trees; Cloudehill Gardens, has excellent landscaped gardens and twilight concerts in summer. Nearby, walks and picnic areas among mountain-ash forest in Dandenong Ranges National Park; lyrebirds occasionally seen along walking tracks; rosellas feed from your hand. At Sherbrooke, 4 km S, Alfred Nicholas Gardens, featuring quaint ornamental lake and boathouse; George Tindale Memorial Garden, flowering plants under mountain ashes. At Upwey, 28 km S, Burrinja Gallery, memorial to artist Lin Onus, has Aboriginal and Oceanic sculptures and paintings. Mount Dandenong Lookout, 2 km N, spectacular views over Melbourne. William Ricketts Sanctuary, 3 km N, sculptures by the well-known Australian artist and conservationist, in bushland setting. Kawarra Australian Plant Garden, 4.5 km N at Kalorama, extensive native plant collection. At Wandin North, 15 km NE, Mont De Lancey (1882):

Cloudehill Gardens, Olinda

historic house and garden; museum; chapel; open Wed.–Sun. and public holidays. At Silvan, 15 km NE: tulip farms; Silvan Reservoir, surrounding area has walking tracks and picnic facilities; Silvan Winery, open for tastings on weekends and public holidays; Tesselaar's Tulip Festival each Sept.–Oct. At Kallista, 6 km S, Grants Picnic Ground, good spot to feed rosellas; craft market here 1st Sat. each month. **Visitor information:** Dandenong Ranges Information Centre, 1211 Burwood Hwy, Upper Ferntree Gully; (03) 9758 7522. Web site www.dandenongrangestourism.asn.au **See also:** Yarra & Dandenongs p. 151; National Parks p. 193.

Omeo
Pop. 298

MAP REF. 103 A12, 234 F8

The high plains around historic Omeo (an Aboriginal word meaning 'mountains') were opened up in 1835 when overlanders from the Monaro region moved stock south to these summer pastures. The town, set in the Victorian Alps at an altitude of 643 m, is a base for winter traffic approaching Mt Hotham and Dinner Plain along the Great Alpine Rd from Bairnsdale, 121 km S, and for summer and autumn bushwalking expeditions to the Bogong High Plains. Omeo was damaged by earthquakes in 1885 and 1892 and was half destroyed by the 1939 Black Friday bushfires. Nevertheless, several old buildings remain. **In town:** In the A. M. Pearson Historical Park, Day Ave: old courthouse (1861), now museum; present courthouse (1892); log gaol (1858); stables; blacksmiths. Also in Day Ave: post office (1891); Commercial Bank (1890);

Colonial Bank (1889); school (1866); 19th-century timber buildings including DNRE office, CWA Hall and Petersens Gallery; Cuckoo Clocks, has traditional German clocks and artifacts. Pioneer Cemetery, cnr Great Alpine Rd and Omeo Hwy. Dec.–Jan.: Omeo Plains Mountain Festival. Mar.: Picnic Races. Easter: Rodeo and Market. Nov.: Agricultural and Pastoral Show. **In the area:** High-country horseback and 4WD tours; llama tours; bushwalking; trout fishing; water-skiing and whitewater rafting (in spring) on Mitta Mitta and Cobungra rivers; scenic drives, brochure available; wineries and riverside drive. Omeo has a gold-rush history; high cliffs left after sluicing for gold, stone walls and tunnel openings can be seen at the Oriental Claims, 1.5 km W on Great Alpine Rd; walks; gold-panning popular along Livingstone Creek. Remains of State's first hydro-electric plant (power for Cassilis goldfield), 25 km W off Victoria Falls Rd. At Cassilis, 15 km S: Mt Markey Winery, Cassilis Rd; markets held next to historic cemetery (check dates). Blue Duck Inn (1890s) is a base for fishing at Anglers Rest, 29 km NW. Just beyond Benambra, 21 km NE, Lake Omeo, huge scenic salt lake in extinct volcano, has abundant bird life. Taylors Crossing suspension bridge, part of Australian Alps Walking Track, 44 km NE, off Tablelands Rd. National Trust-classified Hinnomunjie Bridge over Mitta Mitta River, 37 km N. Scenic drives: Tambo River valley between Swifts Creek and Bruthen (97 km S), beautiful in autumn; to Benambra then Corryong, 144 km NE; Omeo Hwy through Mitta Mitta to Tallangatta (172 km NW); from Omeo through Dinner Plain to Mt Hotham. Note: scenic drives cross State forests (be

alert for timber trucks) or alpine areas (check road conditions in winter). **Visitor information:** German Cuckoo Clock Shop, Day Ave (Great Alpine Rd); (03) 5159 1552. Web site www.omeo.net/region **See also:** The High Country p. 152.

Orbost
Pop. 2150

MAP REF. 235 J12

Situated on the banks of the legendary Snowy River, Orbost is on the Princes Hwy, surrounded by spectacular coastal and mountain territory. **In town:** Information centre, Lochiel St, has audiovisual display explaining complex rainforest ecology. In Forest Rd: Old Pump House, behind relocated 1872 Slab Hut; Historical Museum; Croajingolong Mohair Farm, sells garments, yarns, fleeces, fabrics and leather goods; Snowy River Country Craft; Lorna's doll display. Netherbyre Gemstone and Art Gallery, cnr Browning and Carlyle sts. Jan.: Australian Wood Design Exhibition. Nov.: Craft Expo. **In the area:** Raymond Creek Falls, 42 km N, 40-min-return walk to falls; further 1-hr walk to Snowy River; check road conditions. Beautiful Bonang Rd, unsealed in parts, leads north-east through mountains to Delegate in NSW. Walking in Snowy River National Park, 25 km NW, and Errinundra National Park, 54 km NE. Latter has rainforest boardwalk; check road conditions in wet weather; 4WD tours. Tranquil Valley Tavern, on banks of Delegate River near NSW border, about 115 km NE. Spectacular drive to Buchan, 58 km NW, leads to Little River Falls and McKillops Bridge on the Snowy River. Scenic coastal drive to Marlo (where Snowy River meets the sea) and Cape Conran (30 km E) starts just west of Orbost, returns to Princes Hwy near Cabbage Tree Creek. Cabbage Tree Palms Flora Reserve, 27 km E. At Marlo, popular fishing spot 14 km S: galleries; Slab Hut; Bush Races in Jan.; Triathlon in Jan. or Mar. Bemm River Scenic Reserve, 40 km E off Princes Hwy: 1-km signposted Rainforest Walk; picnic facilities. Bemm River, on Sydenham Inlet, 58 km E, popular for bream anglers. Baldwin Spencer Trail, a 262-km scenic driving circuit following route of explorer; incorporates Snowy River estuary and Errinundra National Park. **Visitor information:** 13 Lochiel St; (03) 5154 2424, freecall 1800 637 060. Web site www.lakesandwilderness.com.au **See also:** East Gippsland p. 154.

Ouyen
Pop. 1251

MAP REF. 110 E10, 230 H9

At the junction of the Calder and Mallee hwys, Ouyen is 107 km s of Mildura, north-east of the Big Desert area. **In town:** Apr.: Autumn Art Show. Aug.: Great Australian Vanilla Slice Triumph. Oct.: Mallee Wildflower Festival. **In the area:** Hattah–Kulkyne National Park, 34 km N, with abundant wildlife, bird-watching, bushwalking, canoeing, and wildflowers in spring. Murray–Sunset National Park, 60 km W; good walks; pink lakes are outstanding subjects for photography. At Patchewollock, 41 km SW, Easter Sports (with camel-racing). At Speed, 39 km s, Mallee Machinery Field Days each Aug. **Visitor information:** Mallee Tourism, Oke St; (03) 5092 1000. Web site www.murrayoutback.org.au **See also:** Mallee Country p. 146.

Paynesville
Pop. 2661

MAP REF. 225 Q5

A popular tourist resort 18 km SE of Bairnsdale on the McMillan Straits, Paynesville is a mecca for fishing, boating, yachting, speedboat racing and water-skiing. **In town:** In the Esplanade: St Peter-by-the-Lake church (1961), incorporating seafaring symbols; Community Craft Centre. Market at Gilsenan Reserve, 2nd Sun. each month. Feb.: Jazz Festival. Mar.: Marlay Point–Paynesville Overnight Yacht Race. **In the area:** At Eagle Point, 2 km NW, Australian Power Boat Racing Championships held each Easter. Rotamah Island Bird Observatory, 8 km s by boat. Ninety Mile Beach, 10 km s by boat; ferry crosses Straits to Raymond Island. On Raymond Island: Koala Reserve; Riviera Meadows, an animal farm specialising in miniature breeds. The Lakes National Park, to the east, 5 km by boat to Sperm Whale Head; otherwise via Loch Sport. Lake cruises and organised scenic tours of lakes. Boat charter and hire. Dolphins in lakes. **Visitor information:** Community Craft Centre, Esplanade; (03) 5156 7479. Web site: www.lakesandwilderness.com.au **See also:** East Gippsland p. 154.

Port Albert
Pop. 248

MAP REF. 225 L10

This tiny town on the south-east coast, 120 km SE of Morwell, was the first established port in Victoria. Sailing boats from Europe and America once docked at the jetty here. Boats from China brought thousands to the Gippsland goldfields. Originally established for trade with Tasmania, Port Albert was the supply port for Gippsland until the Melbourne–Sale railway was completed (1878). Today, Port Albert is a commercial fishing port, its sheltered waters popular with anglers and boat owners. Ninety Mile Beach, popular with surfers and anglers, begins north-east of the town. **In town:** Historic buildings in Tarraville Rd: original government offices and stores; Bank of Victoria (1861), now Maritime Museum with photographs and relics of the area. Warren Curry Art Gallery, also in Tarraville Rd, features Australian country-town streetscapes. Port Albert Hotel, Wharf St, first licensed in 1842 and one of the oldest hotels still operating in State. Mar.: Fishing Contest. **In the area:** At Tarraville, 5 km NE: Christ Church (1856), first church in Gippsland. Beaches patrolled in summer: Manns (swimming), 10 km NE; Woodside (surfing) on Ninety Mile Beach, 34 km NE. Wildlife sanctuary on St Margaret Island, 12 km E. **Visitor information:** The Court House, Rodgers St, Yarram; (03) 5182 6553. Web site www.phillipislandgippsland.com **See also:** Phillip Island & Gippsland p. 156.

Port Campbell
Pop. 281

MAP REF. 216 E10, 227 K11

This small crayfishing village and seaside resort is situated in the centre of Port Campbell National Park and on a spectacular stretch of the Great Ocean Rd. **In town:** Historical Museum, Lord St (open school holidays). Loch Ard Shipwreck Museum, Lord St, has relics from the *Loch Ard* wrecked in 1878 at nearby Loch Ard Gorge. Signposted self-guide Discovery Walk (2.5 km). Good fishing from rocks and pier; boat charters for fishing and diving. Market, Lord St, each Sun. in summer. **In the area:** Mutton Bird Island, just off coast, attracts short-tailed shearwaters (muttonbirds) Sept.–Apr.; best viewing at dawn and dusk. Port Campbell National Park surrounds town; its coastal features include London Bridge, one section of which has now fallen down (6 km W), The Arch (5 km W), Loch Ard Gorge (7 km SE) and world-famous Twelve Apostles (12 km SE). Walking tracks in park (Parks brochure available), scenic drives, and historic shipwreck sites (for divers only). Historic Shipwreck Trail, between Moonlight Head (in park) and Port Fairy, 25 wreck sites marked by plaques. Glenample, 12 km E on Great Ocean Rd, first homestead in area; survivors of Loch Ard recuperated there (check opening times). Gibson Steps, 13 km SE, cut into limestone cliff face, provide access to beach and Twelve Apostles. Otway Deer and Wildlife Park, 20 km E. Picturesque road leads north to pretty Timboon, 19 km N, centre of dairy area. Nearby, pick-your-own berries (in season) at Berry World. Just south of Timboon is Timboon Farmhouse Cheese, for tastings and sales. **Visitor information:** 26 Morris St; (03) 5598 6089. Web site www.greatoceanrd.org.au **See also:** South-West Coast p. 143; Wildlife-Watching p. 196.

Port Fairy
Pop. 2625

MAP REF. 226 G9

The home port for a large fishing fleet, old-world Port Fairy is 28 km W of Warrnambool, with ocean and river as its borders. With a whaling history, at one time it was one of the largest ports in Australia. Over 50 of its cottages and bluestone buildings are National Trust-classified. **In town:** Self-guide historical walks, brochures available. History Centre, Gipps St, in old courthouse. Battery Hill, end Griffith St, old fort and signal station at mouth of river. National Trust-classified buildings: splendid timber home of Captain Mills, Gipps St; Mott's Cottage, Sackville St. Other attractive buildings: Old Caledonian Inn, Bank St; Seacombe House and ANZ Bank building, Cox St; St John's Church of England (1856), Regent St; Gazette Office (1849), Sackville St. Hot Glass Studio, Regent St. Mar.: Folk Festival. Oct.: Spring Music Festival. Dec.: Moyneyana Festival (holiday and family festival). **In the area:** Mahogany Walk to Warrnambool, 6–7 hrs one-way (return by bus); brochures available. Griffiths Island, connected to east of town by causeway, has lighthouse and short-tailed shearwater (muttonbird) rookeries; spectacular nightly return of the short-tailed shearwaters to island (Sept.–Apr). Australia's only mainland colony of short-tailed shearwaters at Pea Soup Beach and South Beach, on southern edge of town. Lady Julia Percy Island, 22 km off coast, home of fur seals; accessible only by experienced boat operators in calm weather. Lake Yambuk, 17 km W. Mt Eccles National Park, 56 km NW, ancient volcanic landscape with complex cave system, scoria cones and crater lake.

Tower Hill State Game Reserve, 14 km E, fascinating area with an extinct volcano and crater lake with islands; nature walk starts at Natural History Centre in reserve. Historic Shipwreck Trail, between Port Fairy and Moonlight Head, 25 wreck sites marked by plaques. **Visitor information:** 22 Bank St; (03) 5568 2682. Web site www.greatoceanrd.org.au **See also:** South-West Coast p. 143.

Portland   Pop. 9664

MAP REF. 226 D9

Situated 72 km E of the South Australian border, Portland is the most western of Victoria's major coastal towns and the only deep-water port between Melbourne and Adelaide. It was the first permanent settlement in Victoria, founded 1834 by the Hentys. Today it is an industrial and commercial centre, and a popular year-round destination with beaches, surfing, fishing and outstanding coastal and forest scenery. **In town:** Number of self-guide and guided walks in and around Portland, incl. the Walk in the Footsteps of Mary MacKillop, around sites significant during this beatified nun's time in Portland (also guided tours). Portland Maritime Discovery Centre at information centre, Lee Breakwater Rd: 13-m sperm whale skeleton (sit inside); original lifeboat used to rescue 19 survivors from shipwreck of *Admella* (1859). Adjacent is wreck of *Regia*, in 2 m of water. Botanical Gardens (1857), Cliff St. More than 200 early buildings, some National Trust-classified: customs house and courthouse in Cliff St; Steam Packet Inn (1842) and Mac's Hotel in Bentinck St. History House, Charles St, an historical museum and family research centre in old town hall (1863). Edward Henty's homestead Burswood, Cape Nelson Rd. Fawthrop Lagoon, Glenelg St, has prolific birdlife. Powerhouse Car Museum, Percy St. 360° views from Watertower Lookout, Clifton Crt, 133 steps (displays of memorabilia on the way); excellent for whale-watching (also from Portland Battery, Battery Hill). Portland Aluminium Smelter (guided tours, check times). Kingsley Winery (tastings and sales), Bancroft St. Feb.: Go Kart Street Grand Prix; Yachting Regatta. Nov.: Three Bays Marathon. **In the area:** Cape Nelson State Park, 11 km SW, offers spectacular coastal scenery and National Trust-classified lighthouse (check opening times). Discovery Bay Coastal Park, 19 km W, has rugged coastline and habitat for endangered hooded plover. Barrett's

Moyne River borders the coastal fishing village of Port Fairy

Gorae West Wines, 20 km W. Safe swimming and surfing at Cape Bridgewater, 21 km SW; nearby, petrified forest (formed by sand engulfing an ancient forest), blowholes and freshwater springs; 2-hr return walk (or take boat trip) to see up to 650 Australian fur seals from viewing platform; walks to Cape Duquesne and Discovery Bay, both further west. For the more energetic, the 250-km Great South West Walk, a scenic circular track from information centre through national parks and State forests to Discovery Bay and Cape Nelson (can be covered in easy stages). Mt Richmond National Park, 25 km NW. Lower Glenelg National Park, 44 km NW via Kentbruck, has spectacular gorges, wildflowers, native birds and animals, and excellent fishing. Along coastal road is charming hamlet of Nelson, 70 km NW; here, launch trips to Glenelg River mouth (at Discovery Bay), also good water-skiing area. Nearby Princess Margaret Rose Cave (tours). Narrawong State Forest, 18 km NE. At Heywood, 28 km N: Bower Birds Nest Museum; Food and Wine Festival in Feb. **Visitor information:** Lee Breakwater Rd; (03) 5523 2671, freecall 1800 035 567. Web site www.greatoceanrd.org.au **See also:** South-West Coast p. 143.

Pyramid Hill   Pop. 527

MAP REF. 110 I13, 229 Q5, 232 B4

A small town 32 km SW of Cohuna and 101 km N of Bendigo, Pyramid Hill was named for its unusually shaped hill, 187 m high. **In town:** Historical Museum, McKay St (open Sun. or by appt). Climb to top of Pyramid Hill: views of surrounding irrigation and wheat district and wildflowers in spring; Braille walking trail for the visually

impaired. Trips to Pyramid Hill Salt mines, 10 km SW, bookings essential; contact information centre. Oct.: Pioneer Machinery Display; Agricultural Show. Nov.: Sidewalk Sale (local produce and festival events). **In the area:** Terrick Terrick State Park, 20 km SE: large Murray Pine forest reserve with numerous granite outcrops (southernmost outcrop called Mitiamo Rock); walks; variety of birdlife and other fauna. Mt Hope, 16 km NE, named by explorer Major Mitchell, has wildflowers in spring. **Visitor information:** Newsagency, 12–14 Kelly St; (03) 5455 7036. **See also:** Goulburn & Murray p. 147.

Queenscliff   Pop. 3832

MAP REF. 210 H10, 212 B5, 217 R6, 224 B7

Queenscliff, 30 km SE of Geelong on the Bellarine Peninsula, was established as a commercial fishing centre in the 1850s and still has a large fishing fleet based in its harbour. The town looks out across the famous and treacherous Rip at the entrance to Port Phillip. **In town:** Queenscliff Maritime Centre, Weeroona Pde, explores town's long association with the sea. Adjacent, Marine Studies Centre offers summer holiday programme for visitors. Fort Queenscliff (1882), King St, built during the Crimean War, includes Black Lighthouse (1861), White Lighthouse (1862). Other historic buildings include: Vue Grand Hotel, Hesse St; Ozone and Mietta's Queenscliff hotels, Gellibrand St. Historical tours leave from pier. In Hesse St: Queenscliff Arcade, for local art and craft; Seaview Gallery in Seaview House. In Hobson St: Hobson's Choice Gallery; The Grand Ballroom Gallery. Bellarine Peninsula

Railway operates steam train between Queenscliff (station in Symonds St) and Drysdale (8 km NW) on weekends and summer holidays; also display of historic locomotives and carriages at station. Regular passenger ferry service between Queenscliff and Portsea across bay (summer and school holidays). Daily vehicle and passenger ferry service between Queenscliff and Sorrento (about 45 min.). Fishing charters, seal- and dolphin-watching trips, and swimming with dolphins and seals; details from information centre. Market at Princes Park, Gellibrand St, last Sun. of month (Sept.–May). Nov.: Music Festival. **In the area:** Point Lonsdale, 6 km SW, seaside holiday and tourist resort with views of entrance to Port Phillip; market 2nd Sun. each month. Marine life viewing at Harold Holt Marine Reserve, which includes Mud Island and coastal reserves. Lake Victoria, 1 km W of Point Lonsdale. At Wallington, 15 km NW: A Maze'N Things; horseriding at Australian Equestrian Academy; Country Connection Adventure Park; pick-your-own fruit and vegetable farms (in season); Strawberry Fair in Nov. **Visitor information:** 55 Hesse St; (03) 5258 4843. Web site www.greatoceanrd.org.au **See also:** Werribee & Bellarine Peninsula p. 142.

Rainbow   Pop. 562

MAP REF. 110 D13, 228 F4

This Wimmera township, 69 km N of Dimboola, is near Lake Hindmarsh, popular for fishing, boating and water-skiing. **In town:** Murals on buildings, Federal St; self-guide mural walk, brochure available. Pasco's Cash Store (1928), Federal St, an original country general store. National Trust-classified Yurunga Homestead (1910), Gray St (on northern edge of town), has large collection of antiques and original fittings. Oct.: Iris Festival; Agricultural Show (includes harness racing). **In the area:** Historic fisherman's hut, 10 km SW at Lake Hindmarsh. Lutheran church (1901), 10 km W at Pella, has old pipe organ, only one other of its kind in State. Lake Albacutya Park, 12 km N, lake only fills when Lake Hindmarsh overflows. Wyperfeld National Park, 30 km N via sealed road north from Yaapeet: walks, bike trails and car tours, extended 4WD tours, brochures available at park entrance. **Visitor information:** Shell Service Station, cnr Federal and Tavern sts; (03) 5395 1026. Web site www.murrayoutback.org.au **See also:** Mallee Country p. 146.

Robinvale   Pop. 1758

MAP REF. 110 F8, 231 J6

This small riverside town on the NSW border, 83 km SE of Mildura, is almost entirely surrounded by bends in the Murray River. The area around town produces wine grapes and fruit for drying. Water sports and fishing are popular along the river. **In town:** In Moore St: McWilliams Wines; Lexia Room, features historical exhibits. In Bromley Rd: Rural Life Museum (open by appt); at information centre, local almonds for sale. Mar.: 80 Ski Classic; Tennis Tournament. **In the area:** Euston Weir and lock on Murray, 3 km downstream. Robinvale Wines, Greek-style winery, 5 km S on Sea Lake Rd. Hattah–Kulkyne National Park, 66 km SW, walks and drives, brochures available. **Visitor information:** Kyndalyn Park Information Centre, Bromley Rd; (03) 5026 1388. Web site www.murrayoutback.org.au **See also:** Mallee Country p. 146.

Rochester   Pop. 2553

MAP REF. 232 E6

On the Campaspe River, 29 km S of Echuca, Rochester is the centre for a rich dairying and tomato-growing area. A busy town, it has some attractive older buildings and a large dairy factory. **In town:** In Moore St: The 'Oppy' Museum (open Mon.–Fri.); opposite, statue of Sir Hubert Opperman, champion cyclist; antique shop. Historical Plaque Trail, Cemetery Walk and Campaspe River Walk; brochures available. **In the area:** Random House homestead, in 4 ha of gardens beside river in Bridge Rd, on eastern edge of town. Campaspe Siphon, 3 km N, an engineering achievement, where the Waranga–Western irrigation channel runs under the Campaspe River. District channels are popular with anglers for redfin and carp. Lakes popular for fishing and water sports incl. Greens Lake and Lake Cooper (14 km SE). At Elmore, 17 km S: Campaspe Run Rural Discovery Centre, tells story of Koorie and European settler history and heritage; Elmore Field Days held in Oct. **Visitor information:** Railway Station, Moore St; (03) 5484 1860. **See also:** Goulburn & Murray p. 147.

Rushworth   Pop. 976

MAP REF. 232 G7

Rushworth, 20 km W of Murchison, off the Goulburn Valley Hwy, still shows traces of its gold-rush days. Many original buildings still stand, witness to the days when Rushworth was the commercial centre for the surrounding mining district. **In town:** Nearly all the High St buildings are National Trust-classified: St Pauls Church of England; band rotunda; former Imperial Hotel (now a private residence); Glasgow Buildings; the Whistle Stop. Also in High St, History Museum in Mechanics Institute (1913) (open by appt). **In the area:** Rushworth State Forest, 3 km S, largest natural ironbark forest in world. At Whroo Historic Area, 7 km S: Balaclava Hill open-cut goldmine, camping, visitor centre display, Whroo cemetery and Aboriginal waterhole (all with visitor access). Further south, remnants of deserted goldmining towns Angustown, Bailieston and Graytown. At Murchison, 20 km E: Italian War Memorial and chapel; Meteorite Park, site of meteorite fall in 1969; nearby, Longleat Winery and Campbell's Bend picnic reserve. At Waranga Basin, 6 km NE: water sports, fishing, camping and excellent picnic facilities. **Visitor information:** Shire of Campaspe, 33 High St; (03) 5856 1207. **See also:** Goulburn & Murray p. 147.

Rutherglen   Pop. 1904

MAP REF. 111 O13, 233 N4

Rutherglen is the centre of one of the most important winegrowing areas in Victoria. A cluster of vineyards surrounds the town, with winegrowing country stretching south to the Milawa area. Many of the local wineries are best known for their fortified wines. **In town:** Main St, a fully preserved example of late-19th-century small-town architecture. Historical walking, bike or drive tour of town, maps available. Common School Museum, just behind Main St, for local memorabilia in restored 1800s schoolroom. Walkabout Cellars, Main St. Bush market in Main St, 4th Sun. each month. Mar.: Tastes of Rutherglen. Easter: Easter in Rutherglen. June: Winery Walkabout; Country Fair. Sept.: Wine Show. Nov.: Campbell's Spring Picnic; Tour de Muscat (cycling). **In the area:** National Trust-classified castle-like building at All Saints Estate, 10 km NW; All Saints Live Concert here in Jan. Other wineries incl. Anderson, Bullers (with bird park), Campbells, Chambers Rosewood, Cofield, Fairfield, Gehrig Estate, Jones, Morris, Mount Prior, Pfeiffer, St Leonards, Stanton and Killeen, Sutherland Smith and Warrabilla; check

The impressive All Saints Estate Winery, near Rutherglen

opening times. Old customs house at Wahgunyah, 10 km NW, relic of days when duty was payable on goods from NSW. Lake Moodemere Vineyards, 6 km W. Further 2 km W is Lake Moodemere, good for water sports, with canoe trees around lake; fauna reserve nearby. **Visitor information:** cnr Drummond and Main sts; (02) 6032 9166. **See also:** The High Country p. 152.

St Arnaud Pop. 2638

MAP REF. 229 L9

This old goldmining town is on the Sunraysia Hwy between Donald and Avoca, and is surrounded by forest and hill country. Many of the iron-lacework buildings are National Trust-classified and together form a nationally recognised historic streetscape. **In town:** In Napier St: notable Queen Mary Gardens; Shire Hall (1902); courthouse (1866); Crown Lands Office (1876); Old Post Office (1866), now B&B and restaurant. Police lock-up (1862), Jennings St. Oct.: Agricultural Show. Nov.: Festival. **In the area:** Good fishing in Avoca River and at Teddington Reservoir, 28 km S. St Peter's Church (1869), made of pebbles, at Carapooee, 11 km SE. Self-guide drive in surrounding area, map available. **Visitor information:** The Old Post Office, 2 Napier St; (03) 5495 2313. **See also:** The Goldfields p. 148.

Sale Pop. 13 366

MAP REF. 225 N6

Sale is the main administrative city in Gippsland. In nearby Bass Strait, there is a concentration of offshore oil development. Just over 200 km E of Melbourne on the Princes Hwy, Sale is convenient for

exploring the Gippsland Lakes area, which extends from Wilsons Promontory to Lakes Entrance, and is bordered to the north by the Great Dividing Range and, most of the way along the coast, by Ninety Mile Beach. **In town:** Port of Sale, thriving during the days of the paddle-steamers. In Foster St: Lake Guthridge, with fauna park and adventure playground; historical museum; Gippsland Regional Arts Gallery; bronze of Mary MacKillop in St Mary's Church. Also in Foster St, Ramahyuck Aboriginal Corporation, has locally produced art and craft, and is part of Bataluk Cultural Trail (driving tour) which begins at information centre; Howitt Bike Trail also begins in Sale; details and brochures available for both. Attractive buildings: Our Lady of Sion Convent; clock tower; Victoria Hall; Criterion Hotel, with beautiful lacework verandahs. RAAF base, Raglan St, home of the famous Roulettes aerobatic team. Sale Common and State Game Refuge, protected wetlands area with boardwalk, on south-east edge of town. Jan.: Bush Races (bush horse race). Feb.: Sale Cup (horse race). Nov.: Agricultural Show. **In the area:** Holey Plains State Park, 14 km SW, has fossils in limestone quarry wall, and swimming lake. Vintage Tractor Pull each Mar. at Longford, 7 km S. Seaspray, 32 km S on Ninety Mile Beach, offers excellent surfing and fishing; as do Golden and Paradise beaches, 35 km SE, and Loch Sport, a further 30 km; nearby, The Lakes National Park and Rotamah Island Bird Observatory, 15 km from Loch Sport. Marlay Point, 25 km E on shores of Lake Wellington, has extensive boat launching facilities; yacht club here sponsors overnight yacht race to Paynesville each Mar. Popular rivers for fishing include

the Avon, close to Marlay Point, and the Macalister, Thomson and La Trobe, especially at Swing Bridge (1883), 5 km S of Sale. **Visitor information:** Central Gippsland Information Centre, Princes Hwy; (03) 5144 1108, freecall 1800 677 520. Web site www.wellington.vic.gov.au **See also:** East Gippsland p. 154.

Seymour Pop. 6294

MAP REF. 232 G10

Seymour is a commercial, industrial and agricultural town on the Goulburn River, 89 km N of Melbourne. The area was recommended for a military base by Lord Kitchener during his 1909 visit. Nearby Puckapunyal was an important training place for troops during WW II and is still a major army base. **In town:** In Emily St: Royal Hotel, featured in Russell Drysdale's famous 1941 painting 'Moody's Pub'; The Old Courthouse (1864), for local art; Fine Art Gallery in The Old Post Office; Old Goulburn Bridge (1891), preserved as historic relic; walking track alongside Goulburn River. Goulburn Park, cnr Progress and Guild sts, for picnics and swimming. Seymour Railway Heritage Centre, Railway Pl., has restored steam engine and carriages (by appt). Self-guide historical walk, brochure available. Mobby's Market, Wimble St, every 2nd Sun. Feb.: Alternative Farming Expo. Mar.: Rafting Festival. Oct.: Seymour Cup. **In the area:** Wineries: Somerset Crossing Vineyards, 2 km S; Hankin's Wines, 5 km NW on Northwood Rd; Hayward's Winery, 12 km SE near Trawool. Army Tank Museum at Puckapunyal army base, 10 km W. Historic railway station in scenic Trawool Valley, 5 km SE. At Mangalore, 5 km N, National Air Show held Easter Sunday. **Visitor information:** The Old Courthouse, Emily St; (03) 5799 0233. Web site www.mitchellshire.vic.gov.au **See also:** Goulburn & Murray p. 147.

Shepparton Pop. 31 945

MAP REF. 232 I6

The 'capital' of the rich Goulburn Valley, this thriving city, 172 km N of Melbourne, has 4000 ha of orchards within a 10-km radius and 4000 ha of market gardens along nearby river flats. The area is irrigated by the Goulburn Irrigation Scheme. **In town:** Art Gallery, Welsford St, features Australian paintings and ceramics. Parkside Gardens and Aboriginal Keeping Place, Parkside Dr., has displays and dioramas (check opening times). Historical

Museum in Historical Precinct, High St (open even-dated Sun. p.m.). Emerald Bank Heritage Farm, Goulburn Valley Hwy, shows 1930s farming. Redbyrne Pottery, Old Dookie Rd. Victoria Park Lake, Tom Collins Dr. SPC cannery, Andrew Fairley Ave: direct sales; and guided tours during fruit season (Jan.–Apr.). Reedy Swamp Walk, at end of Wanganui Rd, for prolific birdlife. Fruit Connection, at rest stop on causeway, has arts and crafts. Trash and treasure market, Melbourne Rd, each Sun.; craft market in Queens Gardens, Wyndham St, 3rd Sun. each month. Jan.: International Dairy Week. Feb.: Bush Market Day. Nov.: Spring Car Nationals (car competitions). **In the area:** Several vineyards in surrounding region. Tallarook State Forest, 5 km SW. At Tatura, 17 km SW: museum has displays on local WW II internment camps; German cemetery adjacent to town cemetery; Taste of Tatura here each Mar. At Kialla, 5 km S: Boxwood Pottery, Elm Vale Nursery. Mud Factory Pottery, 6 km S on Goulburn Valley Hwy. Belstack Strawberry Farm, on Goulburn Valley Hwy, Kialla West, 9 km S (by appt); Belstack Strawberry Fair in Nov. Ardmona Kids Town, 3 km W on Midland Hwy. At Mooroopna, 5 km W: craft market, 1st Sun. each month; Fruit Salad Day in Feb.; Lemnos-Campbells soup cannery and Ardmona fruit cannery have direct sales. **Visitor information:** 534 Wyndham St; (03) 5831 4400, freecall 1800 808 839. **See also:** Goulburn & Murray p. 147.

Skipton   Pop. 453

MAP REF. 220 F13, 227 M4

This township on the Glenelg Hwy, 51 km SW of Ballarat, is situated in an important pastoral and agricultural district. The town was a major centre for merino sheep sales in the 1850s. **In town:** Eel factory, Cleveland St, nets eels in region's lakes and rivers and exports them, mainly to Germany. National Trust-classified bluestone Presbyterian Church (1872), Montgomery St, has unusual gargoyles. May and Nov.: Lake Goldsmith Steam Rally (vintage vehicles). Dec.: Rose Festival. **In the area:** Mooromong, 11 km NW, notable historic homestead (open by appt). Mt Widderin Cave, 6 km S, volcanic cave with large underground chamber that was once a dance venue (tours by appt). Kaolin Mine, 10 km E (open by appt). **Visitor information:** Roadhouse, Glenelg Hwy; (03) 5340 2131. **See also:** The Goldfields p. 148.

Sorrento   Pop. 1328

MAP REF. 210 I11, 212 D7, 217 R7, 224 B8

Situated on a thin strip of land between Port Phillip and Bass Strait, Sorrento was the site of Victoria's first European settlement in 1803. Initially abandoned through lack of water, the area has been a popular seaside holiday destination since the 1870s. The town is close to historic Point Nepean and to major surf and bayside beaches. **In town:** Collins Settlement Historic Site on Sullivan Bay, marking the State's first European settlement, includes early graves. Several self-guide walks around town; brochures available. Sorrento Hotel, Hotham Rd; Continental Hotel, Ocean Beach Rd; and Koonya Hotel, The Esplanade; all fine early Victorian architecture. Nepean Historical Society Museum and Heritage Gallery, Melbourne Rd, houses collection of artifacts and memorabilia in the National Trust-classified Mechanics Institute (1877). Adjacent is wattle and daub Watt's Cottage (1869) and the Pioneer Memorial Garden. A vehicular and passenger ferry operates between Sorrento and resort town of Queenscliff across the bay; ferries depart adjacent to Sorrento pier and return daily. Craft market at Sorrento Primary school, cnr Kerferd and Coppin rds, last Sat. each month. Mar.: Street Festival. **In the area:** Cruises to fabricated Pope's Eye Marine Reserve, where gannets nest; dolphin cruises (some with swimming) and seal cruises. Portsea, 4 km NW, opulent holiday town with safe swimming on its bayside beach and good jetty-fishing. Portsea Swim Classic held here in Jan. Mornington Peninsula National Park, including Sorrento, Rye and Portsea back beaches, features: wild coastline and excellent surfing; London Bridge, at Portsea back beach, a unique rock formation; Point Nepean; Fort Nepean, the fort's guns fired the first allied shots in both world wars (access to the point and the fort by daily transport service departing Portsea, except on Bike and Hike Day, 4th weekend of each month, when the 10-km return trip is made on foot or by bicycle); former Quarantine Station (1859) on Point Nepean (tour includes quarantine and army health services museums each Sun. and public holidays). At Blairgowrie, 4 km E, swim-with-dolphins tours (Sept.– May). At Rye, 8 km E, horseriding. At the bayside resort town of Rosebud, 15 km E: summer fishing launches, depart from Rosebud pier;

safe family beaches; Film Festival in Nov. McCrae Homestead (1844), 17 km E, drop-slab National Trust property (open p.m.). **Visitor information:** St Albans Way (near Sorrento Aquarium); (03) 5984 5678. **See also:** Mornington Peninsula p. 155; Wildlife-Watching p. 196.

Stawell   Pop. 6272

MAP REF. 220 A5, 229 J11

North-east of Halls Gap and 129 km NW of Ballarat on the Western Hwy, Stawell is well sited for tours to the Grampians. It is the home of the Stawell Easter Gift, Australia's best-known professional foot race. **In town:** Self-guide historic city tour, maps available. Big Hill, local landmark and goldmining site; at summit, Pioneers Lookout indicates positions of famous mines. Old cyanide vats, Leviathans Rd, last used in 1935 to extract gold from tailings. Casper's World in Miniature Tourist Park, London Rd: scale working models of famous world features such as Eiffel Tower; dioramas; commentaries. In Main St: Stawell Gift Hall of Fame Museum, Central Park; Fraser Park, has various items of mining equipment on display. Pleasant Creek Court House Museum, Western Hwy. Stawell Ironbark Forest, northern outskirts of town, off Newington Rd, has spring wildflowers, incl. rare orchids. Market, Sloane St, 1st Sun. each month. Easter: Stawell Easter Gift (professional foot race); Easter Festival. **In the area:** Scenic flights, 4WD tours and balloon flights. Bunjil's Shelter, 11 km S off Pomonal Rd, Aboriginal rock paintings in ochre. The Sisters Rocks, 3 km SE, huge granite tors beside Western Hwy. Wineries at Great Western, Ararat and Halls Gap. At Great Western, a picturesque wine village 19 km SE: The Diggings pottery; Champagne Picnic Races in Jan. Overdale Station, 10 km E on Landsborough Rd, guided tours by appt. National Trust property, Tottington Woolshed, 55 km NE on road to St Arnaud, rare example of 19th-century woolshed. Deep Lead Flora and Fauna Reserve, 6 km W, off Western Hwy. Lake Fyans, 17 km SW, for sailing. Lake Bellfield, 30 km SW, offers fishing, canoeing and kayaking. Lake Wartook, in Grampians National Park, 60 km W and Lake Lonsdale, 12 km NW, for all water sports. **Visitor information:** Stawell and Grampians Visitor Information Centre, 50–52 Western Hwy; (03) 5358 2314, freecall 1800 246 880.

Web site www.grampians.org.au **See also:** Grampians & Central West p. 144; National Parks p. 193.

Swan Hill   Pop. 9385

MAP REF. 110 H11, 231 N11

In 1836 explorer Thomas Mitchell named this spot Swan Hill because the black swans kept him awake all night. The township became a busy 19th-century river port and today it is a pleasant city and major holiday centre on the Murray Valley Hwy, 335 km NW of Melbourne. The climate is mild and sunny, and the river and nearby lakes offer good fishing, boating and water sports. **In town:** Australia's first heritage museum, The Pioneer Settlement, at end of Gray St on Little Murray River: local Aboriginal culture; 19th-century town life; staff in period costume; yesteryear transport; Sound and Light tour (bookings essential); daily Murray cruises on paddlesteamer, PS *Pyap*. Regional Gallery of Contemporary Art, opposite Pioneer Settlement. Huge Burke and Wills Fig Tree, Curlewis St, commemorates explorers' visit. Self-guide walk, brochure available. Market, Curlewis St, 3rd Sun. each month. Mar.: Redgum Festival. June: Racing Cup Carnival. July: Italian Festa. **In the area:** Lakeside Nursery and Gardens, 10 km NW, with over 300 roses. Buller's winery at Beverford, 11 km NW. Historic Tyntyndyer Homestead (c. 1846), National Trust-classified, 20 km NW on Murray Valley Hwy (open public and school holidays or by appt). Market at Nyah, 27 km NW, 2nd Sat. each month. Pheasant farm and aviaries at Nowie North, 32 km NW. At Tooleybuc, 46 km N (in NSW): tranquil riverside atmosphere, fishing, picnicking, riverside walks, Bridgekeepers Cottage for craft and dolls. Murray Downs Homestead, 2 km NE over bridge into NSW on Moulamein Rd, is historic sheep, cattle and irrigation property (check opening times); daily river cruises from Murray Downs River Cruises wharf on MV *Kookaburra*. At Lake Boga, 17 km SE: re-built Catalina flying boat and museum in original communications war bunker; Imperial Egg Gallery, collection of egg artwork; lake nearby for water sports, with Yacht Club Regatta each Easter. Best's St Andrew's Vineyard near Lake Boga. **Visitor information:** 306 Campbell St; (03) 5032 3033, freecall 1800 625 373. Web site www.murrayoutback.org.au **See also:** Mallee Country p. 146.

Tallangatta   Pop. 952

MAP REF. 233 Q5, 234 D2

When the old town of Tallangatta was submerged in 1956 for the construction of the Hume Weir, many of its buildings were moved 8 km W to the shores of Lake Hume. Today, situated 42 km SE of Wodonga on the Murray Valley Hwy, the town enjoys this large lake and its attractive beach. Tallangatta is directly north of Victoria's beautiful alpine region. **In town:** The Hub, Towong St, for art and craft; also houses Lord's Hut, only remaining slab hut in district. Self-guide walks and drives; leaflets available. Apr.: Dairy Festival. Oct. or Nov.: Art Exhibition; Fifties Festival. **In the area:** Laurel Hill Trout Farm at Eskdale, 33 km S. Scenic drives incl.: to Cravensville; from Mitta Mitta along Omeo Hwy; to Tawonga and Mount Beauty. At Mitta Mitta, 60 km S: remnants of large open-cut gold mine; Baratralia Emu Farm. Australian Alps Walking Track passes over Mt Wills, 48 km S of Mitta Mitta. Lake Dartmouth, 58 km SE, for good trout fishing and boating. Traron Alpacas, 15 km E at Bullioh, has alpacas and other animals, yarns and garments for sale, and Paulownia trees (Chinese trees grown for shade or fodder). Gold-panning tours to Granya, 28 km NE. **Visitor information:** The Hub, 35–37 Towong St; (02) 6071 2611. **See also:** The High Country p. 152.

Terang   Pop. 1867

MAP REF. 216 D6, 227 K8

Terang, located on the Princes Hwy in a predominantly dairy-farming area, is a well-laid-out town with grand avenues of deciduous trees, recognised by the National Trust. The town is well known for its horseracing facilities and events. **In town:** Early 20th-century commercial architecture. In High St: Gothic-style sandstone Presbyterian church; cottage crafts shop in old courthouse. District Historical Museum, Princes Hwy, features old railway station and memorabilia. Self-guide historical town walk, brochure available. Lions walking track (4.8 km) beside dry lake beds and National Trust-classified trees (entrance behind Civic Centre, High St). Jan.: New Year's Day Family Picnic; Australian Stockhorse Weekend. **In the area:** Intricately constructed dry-stone walls, built 1860s. Lake Keilambete, 4 km NW, 2.5 times saltier than the sea, reputed to have therapeutic properties, contact information centre.

Noorat, 6 km N, birthplace of Alan Marshall, author of *I Can Jump Puddles*; Alan Marshall Walking Track, a gentle climb to summit of extinct volcano with excellent views of crater, surrounding district and across to Grampians. Noorat Agricultural Show in Nov. Glenormiston Agricultural College, 4 km further N, tastefully developed around historic mansion. Model Barn Australia, 5 km E on Robertson Rd, collection of model cars, boats and planes (open by appt). Ralph Illidge Wildlife Sanctuary, 17 km S. Demo Dairy, 3 km W on Princes Hwy, demonstrates dairy-farming practices (open 1st Mon. each month). Hopkins Falls, 33 km W, spectacular after good rains. **Visitor information:** Clarke Saddlery, 105 High St; (03) 5592 1164. Web site www.ansonic.com.au/tdpa **See also:** South-West Coast p. 143.

Torquay   Pop. 5984

MAP REF. 210 F11, 217 O7, 227 Q9

This popular resort is 21 km S of Geelong, close to the Bells and Jan Juc surfing beaches. The Torquay Surf Lifesaving Club is the largest in the State. Torquay also marks the eastern end of the Great Ocean Road, a spectacular drive south-west to Anglesea and beyond. **In town:** On Surfcoast Hwy: Mary Elliott Pottery; surfing products and Surfworld Australia. Craft Cottage, Anderson St. Barbara Peake's Studio, Sarabande Cr. Pieces Gallery, Bell St. Large sundial, Fishermans Beach foreshore. Tiger Moth World vintage aeroplane flights, Blackgate Rd, offers joyflights. Easter: Bells Beach Surfing Classic. **In the area:** Bicycle track along Surfcoast Hwy, Grovedale to Anglesea; walks and scenic drives; brochures available. Horserides at Sea Mist Stud, 22 km NW on Wensleydale Station Rd, Winchelsea. Museum of early Australian horse-drawn carriages near Bellbrae, 5 km W. At Bellbrae: Pottery Studios, Fast 'n' Fun, radio-controlled models, Spring Creek Trail Rides. **Visitor information:** Surfworld Australia, Surf Coast Plaza, cnr Surfcoast Hwy and Beach Rd; (03) 5261 4219. Web site www.greatoceanrd. org.au **See also:** South-West Coast p. 143.

Traralgon   Pop. 18 993

MAP REF. 225 K7

Situated on the Princes Hwy, 172 km SE of Melbourne, Traralgon is one of the La Trobe Valley's main cities. **In town:** Walking tours and heritage drive, leaflets

Airworld Aviation Museum near Wangaratta

available. Old post office and courthouse, cnr Franklin and Kay sts. On Princes Hwy: band rotunda and miniature railway at Victory Park. Jan.: International Junior Tennis Championships. Feb.–Mar.: Music in the Park. Nov.: Traralgon Cup (horse races). **In the area:** Walhalla Mountain Rivers Trail (Tourist Route 91) winds through scenic hills to north. Loy Yang power station, 5 km S (tours, contact Morwell visitor centre). At Toongabbie, 19 km NE, Festival of Roses held in Nov. **Visitor information:** The Old Church, Southside Central, Princes Hwy; (03) 5174 3199, freecall 1800 621 409. Web site www.phillipislandgippsland.com **See also:** Phillip Island & Gippsland p. 156.

Walhalla

Pop. 15

MAP REF. 225 K5

This tiny goldmining town is tucked away in dense mountain country in Gippsland. The Walhalla Mountain Rivers Trail (Tourist Route 91), from Moe or Traralgon, takes in spectacular scenery. Walhalla is set in a narrow, steep valley, with sides so sheer that some cemetery graves were dug lengthways into the hillside. It was connected to electricity in 1998. **In town:** Historic buildings and relics of gold-boom days. Signposted heritage town walk. Excellent local walks, including to cricket ground, on top of 200-m hill, and historic cemetery. Long Tunnel Gold Mine, one of the most successful in the State (open most days, guided tours, check times). Rotunda (1896). Old Fire Station (1901), hand-operated fire engine and fire

memorabilia. Post office (1886). Old bakery (1865), oldest surviving building in town, near hotel. Museum (1894), gold-era memorabilia. Windsor House (1890). Walhalla Goldfields Railway, runs Sat., Sun. and public holidays. Gold-panning in Stringers Creek, which runs through town. **In the area:** 4WD tours to gold-era 'suburbs'. Australian Alps Walking Track (655 km) begins at Walhalla. Deloraine Gardens, terraced gardens just north of town. Walking and downhill and cross-country skiing in Baw Baw National Park, on western outskirts of town. Access to Aberfeldy River picnic and camping area on eastern side of park. Rawson, 8 km SW, built for construction of nearby Thomson Dam; Mountain Trail Rides. At Erica, 12 km SW: timber industry display at Erica Hotel; Mountain Saddle Safaris; King of the Mountain Woodchop held each Jan. Thomson River, 4 km S, for excellent fishing, canoeing and white-water rafting (rafting tours). Moondarra State Park, 30 km S. Boola Boola Winery, 5 km SE on Tyers Rd. **Visitor information:** Regional Visitor Information Centre, The Old Church, Southside Central, Princes Hwy, Traralgon; (03) 5174 3199, freecall 1800 621 409. Web site www. phillipislandgippsland.com **See also:** Phillip Island & Gippsland p. 156.

Wangaratta

Pop. 15 527

MAP REF. 233 M6

Wangaratta's proximity to the high country, winery regions and the Murray River, make it an ideal base for exploring

north-eastern Victoria. The surrounding fertile area produces wool, wheat, tobacco, kiwifruit, walnuts, chestnuts, hops and wine grapes. **In town:** Numerous bike trails, leaflet available. In cemetery, Tone Rd, grave of bushranger Daniel 'Mad Dog' Morgan; his headless body was buried here, the head having been sent to Melbourne for examination. At information centre, cnr Tone Rd and Handley St: Mrs Stell's House in Miniature (one-sixth scale 1950s-style mansion); history of Kelly Gang. Paddys market at Council car park, Ovens St, each Sun. a.m. Oct.: Agricultural Show. Nov.: Festival of Jazz and Blues. **In the area:** Scenic drive, 307 km, along Great Alpine Rd through Alps to Bairnsdale. Airworld Aviation Museum, 7 km S, said to be Australia's largest collection of antique civil aircraft in flying condition. Road to Moyhu, 27 km S, leads to beautiful King Valley and Paradise Falls. Network of minor roads allows exploration of unspoiled area and tiny townships of Whitfield (50 km S), Cheshunt and Carboor. King Valley scenic drive runs beside King River to Whitfield and Powers Lookout (74 km S). Newton's Prickle Berry Farm at Whitfield. At Warby Range State Park, 12 km W: good vantage points, picnic spots and variety of bird and plant life. Interesting old gold township Eldorado, 20 km NE: has largest gold dredge in the Southern Hemisphere, built in 1936; historical museum; potteries. Nearby, Reids Creek, popular with anglers, gem-fossickers and gold-panners. Wombi Toys at Whorouly, 25 km SE. **Visitor information:** cnr Tone Rd and Handley St; (03) 5721 5711, freecall 1800 801 065. **See also:** The High Country p. 152.

Warburton

Pop. 2446

MAP REF. 211 O6, 214 H9, 224 G3

Warburton was established with the 1880s gold finds; however, by 1900 it had become a popular tourist town with fine guest houses. It is surrounded by the Great Dividing Range foothills and is a 90-min. drive from Melbourne. **In town:** At information centre, Warburton Hwy: 6 m-diameter old-style operating waterwheel; historical display; arts and crafts; wood-fired bakery. Riverside Walk (5 km return), access behind information centre. River Walk (9 km return), from Signs Bridge on Warburton Hwy. Jan.: Upper Yarra Draughthorse Festival. June: Film Festival. July: Winterfest (wood festival).

Nov.: Strawberry Festival. **In the area:** Bushwalks, horseriding, birdwatching and fishing; opportunities to spot platypuses; details from information centre. Multi-use Rail Trails follow former railway tracks, leaflet available. Tommy Finn's Trout Farm, 2 km W. Yarra Junction Historical Museum, 10 km W. Mt Donna Buang, 17 km NW in Yarra Ranges National Park, popular daytrip from Melbourne, often snow-covered in winter; lyrebirds, increasing in number, may be seen at dawn and dusk in summer; Donna Buang Rainforest Gallery has treetop viewing platform and walkway; popular night walks. Upper Yarra Dam, 23 km NE. Along Warburton Hwy, attractive vineyards: Yarra Burn Winery, McWilliams Lillydale Vineyard, Five Oaks Vineyard and Brahams Creek Winery. The Acheron Way begins 1 km E of Warburton, giving access to views of Mt Donna Buang, Mt Victoria and Ben Cairn on the scenic 37-km drive north to St Fillans and Marysville. Walk into History, from Powelltown (25 km S) to Warburton East, leaflet available (branch of Centenary Trail). Between Powelltown and Noojee, rainforest gully walk to Ada Tree, a giant mountain ash. Yellingbo State Fauna Reserve, 25 km SW. **Visitor information:** Warburton Waterwheel, 3400 Warburton Hwy; (03) 5966 5996. **See also:** Yarra & Dandenongs p. 151.

Warracknabeal   Pop. 2493

MAP REF. 228 H6

Situated at the intersection of the Borung and Henty hwys, 378 km NW of Melbourne, Warracknabeal is in the centre of a rich grain-growing area. The Aboriginal name means 'the place of the big red gums shading the watercourse'. **In town:** Historical Centre, Scott St, includes pharmaceutical collection, clocks, and antique furnishings of child's nursery (open p.m.). Black Arrow Tour of historic buildings (self-guide drive or walk) and other walks incl. the Yarriambiack Creek Walk; leaflets available. National Trust-classified buildings: post office (1907) and Warracknabeal Hotel (1872), with beautiful iron lacework, both in Scott St; original log lock-up (1872), Devereaux St, built when town acquired a policeman. Lions Park, on Yarriambiack Creek: picnic spots; flora and fauna park. Easter: Y-Fest (golf, horseracing, vintage machinery, country music, Patchewollock Sports and Camel Cup). **In the area:** North Western

Agricultural Machinery Museum, 3 km S on Henty Hwy, displays of farm machinery from last 100 years. **Visitor information:** 119 Scott St; (03) 5398 1632. **See also:** Grampians & Central West p. 144.

Warragul   Pop. 9011

MAP REF. 211 P10, 224 H6

Much of Melbourne's milk comes from this prosperous dairy-farming area 106 km SE of Melbourne. It is also an important commercial centre. **In town:** West Gippsland Arts Centre, Civic Pl. Lillico Garden Railway, Copelands Rd. Mar.: Gippsland Field Days. **In the area:** Gourmet Deli Trail, brochure available. Wild Dog Winery, 5 km S on Warragul–Korumburra Rd (open daily by appt). Grand Ridge Road (Tourist Route 93), 132 km, starts at Seaview, 17 km S, and leads to Tarra–Bulga National Park via Strzelecki Ranges. Near Drouin, 8 km W: Oakbank Angoras and Alpacas; Fruit and Berry Farm. Gumbaya Park, 35 km W, a family fun park. Wildflower sanctuary at Labertouche, 16 km NW. At Neerim South, 17 km N: Tarago River Cheese Company; picnic/barbecue facilities at nearby Tarago Reservoir; scenic drives through nearby mountain country. Further 12 km N at Nayook: Fruit and Berry Farm; Country Farm Perennials Nursery and Gardens. At Noojee, 10 km NE of Nayook: Alpine Trout Farm; trestle bridge. Darnum Musical Village, 8 km E on Princes Hwy, complex of buildings housing collection of musical instruments dating back to 1400s; visitors can play them. Yarragon, 13 km SE, has good shopping for antiques, crafts, gourmet food and boutique wines; Dairy Fest held in Nov. At Childers, 31 km SE: Sunny Creek Fruit and Berry Farm; Windrush Cottage. Mt Worth State Park, 19 km SE. Nature reserves and picnic spots: Glen Cromie (Drouin West), Glen Nayook (south of Nayook) and Toorongo Falls (just north of Noojee). **Visitor information:** The Old Church, Southside Central, Princes Hwy, Traralgon; (03) 5174 3199, freecall 1800 621 409. Web site www.phillipislandgippsland.com **See also:** Phillip Island & Gippsland p. 156.

Warrnambool   Pop. 26 052

MAP REF. 216 A8, 226 I9

Warrnambool is 257 km SW of Melbourne on Lady Bay, where the Princes Hwy meets the Great Ocean Road.

This beautiful seaside city has first-class sporting, cultural and entertainment facilities and well-maintained parks and gardens. Over 100 ships were wrecked on the coast near Warrnambool, the best known being the *Loch Ard* in 1878 which claimed all but two of those on board. **In town:** Self-guide Heritage Walk, 3 km, brochure available. Flagstaff Hill Maritime Museum, Merri St: a reconstructed 19th-century Maritime Village; Flagstaff Hill tapestry, with themes of Aboriginal history, sealing, whaling, exploration, immigration and settlement; famous earthenware Loch Ard Peacock, recovered from *Loch Ard* wreck. In Timor St: Performing Arts Centre; Art Gallery. In Gilles St: Customs House Gallery; History House, with local memorabilia (open 1st Sun. each month or by appt). Botanic Gardens, Botanic Rd, designed by Guilfoyle in 1879. Fletcher Jones Gardens, Raglan Pde. Lake Pertobe Adventure Playground, Pertobe Rd; swimming beach opposite. Portuguese Padrao, Cannon Hill, monument to Portuguese explorers. The Potter's Wheel, Liebig St. Thunder Point Reserve, end Macdonald St. Middle Island, off Pickering Point, colony of little (fairy) penguins, Aboriginal middens. Unusual Wollaston Bridge (over 100 years old), on northern outskirts of town. Kid's Country Treasure Map (available at information centre) provides informative way for the whole family to enjoy Warrnambool. Horseriding trail rides, mainly on beach. Cruises on Hopkins River. National Trust-classified Hopkins River Boathouse, off Otway Rd. Blue Hole, at mouth of river, for fishing, surfing and rock pools. Sun. market at showgrounds, Koroit St. Feb.: Wunta Fiesta (family entertainment and stalls); Tarerer Festival (celebration of indigenous culture and music). May: Racing Carnival (horseracing). July: Fun 4 Kids (children's festival). Oct.: Melbourne–Warrnambool Cycling Classic; Spring Orchid Show. **In the area:** Visit of rare southern right whales, usually June–Sept. (viewing platform just east of town at Logans Beach). Allansford Cheeseworld, 10 km E, for tasting and sales. At Cudgee, 17 km E, Cudgee Creek Wildlife Park: deer; crocodiles and other native fauna; aviary; barbecue facilities. In late spring, early summer at Hopkins Falls, 13 km NE, see hundreds of baby eels migrating up falls. Warrnambool Trout Farm, 4 km N on Wollaston Rd: catch-your-own; fish cleaned by staff; fish-feeding;

Lake Pertobe, Warrnambool

seafood product sales. At Koroit, 18 km NW: National Trust-classified historic buildings, botanic gardens. Mahogany Walk from Warrnambool–Port Fairy (22 km), along beach dunes. Helicopter and joy flights along coast. **Visitor information:** 600 Raglan Pde; (03) 5564 7837. Web site www.greatoceanrd.org.au **See also:** South-West Coast p. 143; Wildlife-Watching p. 196.

Wedderburn   Pop. 708

MAP REF. 229 N7

Once one of Victoria's richest gold-mining towns in the 'Golden Triangle', Wedderburn is on the Calder Hwy, 74 km NW of Bendigo. Many large nuggets have been unearthed in the area, and gold is still found here. **In town:** At northern edge of town: Hard Hill area, former gold diggings, Government Battery and working eucalyptus distillery, Wilson St; Kuku-Yalanji, Wallaby Dr., an Aboriginal art and craft gallery. In High St: Coach House Cafe and Museum, original 1910 building furnished and stocked as it was then; coach-building factory; old bakery, converted into a pottery. Self-guide town walks, brochure available. Mar.: Gold Festival. Aug.: Wool Expo. Sept.: Historic Engine Exhibition. **In the area:** Fossickers Drive, takes in goldmining and Aboriginal sites, wineries, Melville Caves and bushwalk starting points; brochure available. Mount Korong, 16 km SE, for rock-scrambling and bush-walking. Wychitella Forest Reserve, 16 km N, wildlife sanctuary in mallee forest. At Korong Vale, 13 km NW, The Chandelier Man, manufacturer of crystal chandeliers. **Visitor information:**

Shire Offices, High St; (03) 5494 1200. **See also:** The Goldfields p. 148.

Welshpool   Pop. 138

MAP REF. 225 K10

Welshpool is a small dairying town and nearby Port Welshpool is a deep-sea port servicing fishing and oil industries. Barry Beach Marine Terminal, 8 km S of the South Gippsland Hwy, services the offshore oil rigs in Bass Strait. **In the area:** Excellent fishing and boating. At Port Welshpool, Maritime Museum. Agnes Falls, 19 km NW, highest falls in State. Scenic drive west with views from Mt Fatigue, off South Gippsland Hwy. Near Toora, 11 km W, Franklin River Reserve has nature walk. **Visitor information:** cnr South Gippsland Hwy and Silkstone Rd, Korumburra; (03) 5655 2233, freecall 1800 630 704. Web site www.phillipislandgippsland.com **See also:** Phillip Island & Gippsland p. 156.

Winchelsea   Pop. 1027

MAP REF. 210 D10, 217 L6, 227 P8

This town is on the Barwon River, 37 km W of Geelong. It originated as a watering-place for travellers on the road to Colac from Geelong. **In town:** On Princes Hwy: Barwon Bridge, with its graceful stone arches, opened 1867 to handle increasing westward traffic; Alexandra's Antiques and Art Gallery; Barwon Hotel (1842), housing museum of Australiana; Old Shire Hall, beautiful restored bluestone building, about 1900, now popular tearooms with craft and woodwork for sale in gallery; old library (1893), now art gallery. **In the area:** National Trust property, Barwon Park Homestead, 3 km N

on Inverleigh Rd (open Sun. and Wed.). Country Dahlias gardens, 5 km S on Mathieson Rd (open Feb.–Apr.). Killarney Park Lavender Farm, 6 km S (open Sept.–May). **Visitor information:** Old Shire Art Gallery, Princes Hwy; (03) 5267 2769. **See also:** South-West Coast p. 143.

Wodonga   Pop. 25 825

MAP REF. 111 P13, 233 P4, 234 B2

Wodonga and its twin, Albury (NSW), sit astride the Murray in north-east Victoria. Albury–Wodonga, with the attractions of the Murray and nearby Lake Hume, makes a good base for a holiday. **In town:** National Museum of Australian Pottery, South St, displays work of 19th-century potters. Gateway Village, Lincoln Causeway, incl. working craft shops, information centre and restaurant. Behind village, self-guide Wiradjuri Walkabout river walk highlights Aboriginal culture; canoe trees, fish and tortoise carvings in trunks; brochure available. Also on Lincoln Causeway: Palatinat Boutique Brewery; Harveys Fish Farm, offers catch-your-own Australian native fish; minigolf; water playground and restaurant. Sumsion Gardens, Church St, a beautiful lakeside park. In Melrose Dr., largest outdoor tennis centre in Australia. Border Country Fair at Gateway Village, 2nd Sun. each month. Feb.: Sports Festival. Mar.: Wodonga Show. Oct.: Wine and Food Festival. Nov.: World Cup Show Jumping. **In the area:** Winery and fishing tours, hot-air ballooning, trail-riding and canoe hire; details from information centre. Kids Play World, indoor play centre with cafe and restaurant, Young St, Albury. Jindera Museum, 16 km NW of Albury, pioneer museum with old-style store and storekeeper's house. At Bonegilla, 12 km W of Wodonga, Festival held in Oct. (odd-numbered years). Military Museum, 4 km SE at Bandiana. Hume Weir, 15 km E; Hume Weir Trout Farm. Mt Granya State Park, 56 km E, offers spectacular views of alps. Nearby touring areas include: Upper Murray, mountain valleys of north-east Victoria; Murray Valley; Riverina district. **Visitor information:** Gateway Information Centre, Lincoln Causeway; (02) 6041 3875, freecall 1800 800 743. Web site http://albury.wodonga.com/tourism **See also:** The High Country p. 152.

Wonthaggi   Pop. 5887

MAP REF. 224 G10

Once the main supplier of coal to the Victorian Railways, Wonthaggi, 8 km from Cape Paterson in Gippsland, is South Gippsland's largest town. It began as a tent town in 1909 when the coal mines were opened up by the State government following industrial unrest in the NSW coalfields. The mines operated until 1968. **In town:** Easter: Coal Skip Fill. **In the area:** Gourmet Deli Trail, brochure available. State Coal Mine, 1.5 km S on Cape Paterson Rd, features tours of reopened Eastern Area Mine, with experienced former coalminer as guide, and museum of mining activities. Cape Paterson, 8 km S in Bunurong Marine Park, for surfing, swimming, snorkelling and scuba-diving. Scenic drive to beaches at Inverloch, 12 km SE. George Bass Coastal Walk from Kilcunda, 11 km NW, and other walks; brochures available. **Visitor information:** Watts St; (03) 5672 2484. Web site www.phillipislandgippsland.com **See also:** Phillip Island & Gippsland p. 156.

Woodend   Pop. 2974

MAP REF. 210 G2, 224 A1, 227 R2, 232 D12

Woodend is situated on the Calder Hwy, an hour's drive north of Melbourne. During the gold rushes (1850s), travellers sought refuge from mud, bogs and bushrangers at the 'wood's end' around Five Mile Creek. The main danger today is 'black ice' in winter; hazard warning lights are installed on the Calder Hwy. **In town:** On Calder Hwy: Bluestone bridge (1862) crossing Five Mile Creek, on northern outskirts of town; St Mary's Anglican Church (1864); clock tower, built as WW I memorial; Insectarium of Victoria, insect and invertebrate research

and interpretation centre. Courthouse (1870), Forest St (check opening times). The Bulb Shop, High St, has rare bulbs. Craft market, 3rd Sun. each month (Oct.–May). Oct.: Macedon Ranges Budburst Festival (throughout wine district). Dec.: Five Mile Creek Festival. **In the area:** Black gum trees (*Eucalyptus aggregata*); Woodend region is only place in State where these trees are found. Hanging Rock, 8 km NE, a massive rock formation featuring in *Picnic at Hanging Rock*, film of Joan Lindsay's novel, and film by the same name; Picnic Cafe; picnic races held nearby on New Year's Day and Australia Day; vintage car rally each Feb. At Lancefield, 25 km NE: historic buildings, wineries, horseriding; Woodchopping Competition in Mar.; Dog Show in Dec. At Monegeetta, 15 km S of Lancefield, Mintaro homestead (1882), replica (but smaller) of Melbourne's Government House (not open to the public). Mt Macedon (1013 m), 10 km E on Mount Macedon Rd, has huge WW I memorial cross at summit; area around renowned for its beautiful gardens, many open autumn and spring. The Camels Hump, 12 km E off Mount Macedon Rd, has 12-km signposted walk to summit. At Romsey, 19 km E, Cape Williams Vineyard: English-style garden; cricket green. Scenic drives and bushwalks in Macedon Regional Park. At Macedon, 8 km SE: Church of the Resurrection has stained-glass windows designed by Leonard French; excellent plant nurseries. At Gisborne, 16 km SE: Gisborne Steam Park; craft outlets. Barringo Wildlife Reserve at New Gisborne, 17 km SE. Llapaca Picnics, 20 km W on McGiffords Rd, Fernhill: organised scenic walk; picnic supplied, and carried by llama or alpaca (by appt, contact information centre). At Carlsruhe, 10 km NW: galleries, crafts and antiques. Over 15 wineries in region (maps available): close to town is Hanging Rock Winery, at Newham (10 km NE). **Visitor information:** High St, beside Five Mile Creek; (03) 5427 2033. **See also:** Spa & Garden Country p. 150.

Yackandandah   Pop. 592

MAP REF. 233 P5, 234 B3

Located about 28 km S of Wodonga, this exceptionally attractive town, with avenues of English trees and traditional verandahed buildings, is National Trust-classified. Yackandandah is in the heart of the north-east goldfields (gold was discovered here in 1852), but today it

is better known for its historic buildings. **In town:** Original buildings in High St: post office; several banks and general stores; Bank of Victoria (1865), now historical museum (open Sun. and school holidays). Self-guide walking tour, brochure available. Also in High St: Ray Riddington's Premier Store and Gallery; The Old Stone Bridge (1857). Art and craft: Yackandandah Workshop, cnr Kars and Hammond sts; Wildon Thyme, High St. Numerous antique shops, incl. Finders Bric-a-Brac and Old Wares, Frankly Speaking (both in High St); Vintage Sounds Restorations, Windham St (old and antique gramophones, telephones and radios). Rosedale Garden and Tea Rooms, Kars St. Jan.: Lavender Harvest Festival. Mar.: Folk Festival. June: Vintage Engine Swap Meet. **In the area:** Tours of Kars Reef Goldmine, and gold-panning (licence required); details from information centre. Creeks in Yackandandah area still yield alluvial gold to amateur prospectors. Lavender Patch Plant Farm, 4 km W on Beechworth Rd. Picturesque Indigo Valley, 6 km NW; scenic drive leads along valley floor to Barnawatha. At Allans Flat, 10 km NE: The Vienna Patisserie, for coffee, ice-cream and Austrian cakes (closed Tues.); Park Wines; Schmidt's Strawberry Winery. At Leneva, 16 km NE, Wombat Valley Tramways small-gauge railway (Easter or by appt for groups). Kirbys Flat Pottery and Gallery, 4 km S on Kirbys Flat Rd (open weekends or by appt weekdays). **Visitor information:** The Athenaeum, High St; (02) 6027 1988. **See also:** The High Country p. 152.

Yarra Glen   Pop. 1232

MAP REF. 211 M5, 214 B6, 224 E3

Yarra Glen is situated in the heart of the picturesque Yarra Valley wine country, a favourite touring destination from Melbourne. **In town:** National Trust-classified Yarra Glen Grand hotel (1888), Bell St. Craft Market at racecourse, 1st Sun. each month. Mar.: Grape Grazing Festival (throughout wine district). May: Yarra Valley Expo. **In the area:** Yarra Valley Regional Food Trail, brochure available. Hot-air balloon flights and champagne breakfast, details from information centre. Gulf Station (1854), 2 km NE, National Trust-owned pastoral property, virtually unchanged since pioneering days; farming implements, original breeds of cattle, sheep, horses, turkeys and ducks; open Wed.–Sun. and public holidays. At Dixons Creek, 9 km NE: De Bortoli Wines &

The Old Stone Bridge, Yackandandah

Restaurant has excellent Yarra Valley views; Allinda Winery (open Sat., Sun., public holidays). Fergusson Winery and Restaurant, 7 km N of Yarra Glen in Wills Rd. Domaine Chandon, 9 km SE, renowned champagne makers: tasting room with valley views; Musica Viva Yarra Valley Festival here in Apr. Several other wineries in area, and also in Panton Hill–St Andrews area to the west. Kinglake National Park, 26 km N: walking tracks, waterfalls, lyrebirds and wombats, and picnic areas. Ponyland Equestrian Centre, 7 km W: trail rides, riding lessons, overnight and weekend rides. Sugarloaf Reservoir Park, 10 km W: sailing, fishing, walking, barbecues and picnic areas. Yarra Valley Dairy, 4 km S, specialty cheeses and clotted cream. **Visitor information:** Yarra Valley Visitor Information Centre, Old Courthouse, Harker Street; Healesville; (03) 5962 2600. **See also:** Yarra & Dandenongs p. 151.

Yarram   Pop. 1807

MAP REF. 225 L9

This established South Gippsland town, 225 km by road from Melbourne, has interesting original buildings and a golf course inhabited by relatively tame kangaroos. Situated between the Strzelecki Ranges and Bass Strait, it is a gateway to both rainforest and the coast. **In town:** Restored Regent Theatre (1930), Commercial Rd; cinema operates weekends and school holidays. Easter: Tarra Festival. Nov.: Seabank Fishing Contest. **In the area:** Good bush camping, details from information centre. Historic towns: Alberton, 6 km S, has early settlers' graves in cemetery. Beaches patrolled in summer: Woodside, 29 km E; Seaspray, 68 km NE.

Fishing beaches: Manns, 16 km SE; McLoughlins, 29 km E. Native animal zoo, 19 km E at Woodside. Australian Omega Navigation Facility with 432-m-high steel tower, 30 km N. In the Strzelecki Ranges, 27 km NW: Tarra–Bulga National Park, has hilly, beautiful rainforest, dense mountain ash, myrtle and sassafras, spectacular fern glades, splendid river and mountain views, the occasional koala as well as rosellas and lyrebirds; wagon rides through ranges; Tarra Bulga Visitor Centre at Balook, Grand Ridge Rd, has interpretive displays. In the Tarra Valley, north-west of town: Eilean Donan Gardens and Riverbank Nursery; splendid gardens; 2 caravan parks; horseriding nearby. 46-km circuit drive from Yarram through Hiawatha: Minnie Ha Ha Falls on Albert River; nearby, picnic facilities and camping; gypsy wagons for hire. Won Wron Forest, 16 km N on Hyland Hwy, has spring wildflowers. **Visitor information:** The Court House, Rodgers St; (03) 5182 6553. Web site www.phillipislandgippsland.com **See also:** Phillip Island & Gippsland p. 156.

Yarrawonga   Pop. 3435

MAP REF. 111 N13, 233 K3

A pleasant stretch of the Murray and the attractive Lake Mulwala have made this border town and Mulwala (in NSW) extremely popular holiday resorts. The 6000-ha lake was created in 1939 during the building of the Yarrawonga Weir, which controls the irrigation waters in the Murray Valley. **In town:** Around lake and along river: sandy beaches and still waters, ideal for water sports; abundant birdlife. Yarrawonga and Mulwala foreshore areas: shady willows, water-slides, barbecues and

boat ramps. At information centre, Irvine Pde: Old Yarra Mine Shaft has large collection of gems, minerals and fossils. Canning A.R.T.S. Gallery, Belmore St, has art and craft, incl. local art. Tudor House Clock Museum, Lynch St. Bush market at railway station, Sharp St, 2nd and 4th Sun. each month. Rotary Market at Showgrounds, 3rd Sun. each month. Jan.: Rowing Regatta; Powerboat Racing; Rockalonga Concert. Oct.: Linga Longa Festival. Dec.: Murray Marathon. **In the area:** Daily cruises on *Paradise Queen* or *Lady Murray*, depart Bank St. Canoe and boat hire, horseriding. Ovens River and winery tours, bookings at information centre. Fishing in Murray River. Fyffefield Winery, 19 km W on Murray Valley Hwy. **Visitor information:** Irvine Pde; (03) 5744 1989. **See also:** Goulburn & Murray p. 147.

Yea   Pop. 960

MAP REF. 211 M1, 232 I11

This town, 58 km N of Yarra Glen, stands beside the Yea River, a tributary of the Goulburn River. Set in pastoral and dairy-farming land, it is well situated for touring around Mansfield, Eildon and the mountains, gorge country between Yea and Tallarook, and south-east to Marysville. There are beautiful gorges and fern gullies close to the Yea–Tallarook Rd. **In town:** Heritage Walk, brochure available. In High St: Beaufort Manor (1870s); General Store (1887), now a restaurant. On eastern outskirts of town, Wetlands Walk, glider possums and a variety of birds. Market, Main St, 1st Sat. each month (Sept.–May, a.m.). Mar.: Autumn Fest. Nov.: Agricultural Show. **In the area:** Many scenic drives (best time is Aug.–Sept., when wattles are in bloom), leaflets available. In Murrindindi Reserve, 11 km SE: Murrindindi Cascades and wildlife including wombats, platypuses, lyrebirds. Pick-your-own fruit at Berry King Farm, Two Hills Rd, 28 km S at Glenburn. Kinglake National Park, 30 km S, for waterfalls, tall eucalypts, fern gullies and impressive views. Spectacular Wilhelmina Falls, 32 km S via Melba Hwy. Flowerdale Winery, 23 km SW on Whittlesea–Yea Rd. Ibis rookery at Kerrisdale, 17 km W. Grotto, a beautiful old church, in the hills 27 km N at Caveat. Mineral springs at Dropmore, 47 km N off back road to Euroa. Several good campsites along Goulburn River. **Visitor information:** Old Railway Station, Maroondah Highway, Mansfield; (03) 5797 2663. **See also:** Goulburn & Murray p. 147.

NATIONAL PARKS

Dramatic rock formations in Grampians National Park

AROUND MELBOURNE

At **Organ Pipes National Park**, only 20 kilometres north-west of Melbourne, there are fascinating rock formations: hexagonal basalt columns rising more than 20 metres above Jacksons Creek. These 'organ pipes' were formed when lava cooled in an ancient river bed. While this is the best-known feature of the 121-hectare park, the area is also excellent for picnics, walks and bird-observing. Nearby is the 800-hectare **Woodlands Historic Park**, which features the Woodlands Homestead, brought from Britain as a timber kit home and erected here in 1843. A favourite of bushwalkers, 40 kilometres north-east of Melbourne, is **Kinglake National Park**, where wooded valleys, fern gullies and timbered ridges provide a perfect setting for two beautiful waterfalls, Masons and Wombelano falls. From a lookout, visitors can enjoy a view of the Yarra Valley, Port Phillip Bay and the You Yangs. Rugged **Brisbane Ranges National Park**, 80 km west of Melbourne, is excellent for walks, picnics and wildlife.

Just 35 kilometres east of Melbourne is the green wonderland of the 3215-hectare **Dandenong Ranges National Park**. This park includes tree-fern gullies in which huge fronds of ferns form a canopy overhead, screening the sun and creating a cool, moist environment in which mosses, delicate ferns and flowers, including over 30 orchid species, all thrive. There are more than 20 native animal species, including echidnas, platypuses, ringtail possums and sugar gliders; kookaburras, rosellas and cockatoos often visit picnic areas. The spectacular rufous fantail can be seen in the summer months. There are over 100 bird species, but make sure you identify them by sight, because the lyrebird can mimic many of their calls.

Mornington Peninsula National Park has a total area of 2686 hectares and stretches from Point Nepean to Cape Schanck. Highlights of Point Nepean are Fort Nepean, the cemetery with burials dating from the 1850s, and the fascinating Cheviot Hill and Pisterman's Track walks. Note that vehicles are not permitted to the tip of Point Nepean – visitors can walk, cycle or take the transporter. For more than 100 years, this section of the park was out of bounds to the general public due to its defence status. In the Cape Schanck section, a staircase leads down the spectacular cliff to the beach below.

Nearby **French Island National Park** is accessible by passenger ferry (no car access) at Stony Point on Mornington Peninsula. The park has echindas, potaroos, a large koala population and abundant birdlife. As well, there are over 500 plant species and nearly 100 orchids, some of which are found only on the island. Visitors can book a tour, hire a bicycle or walk. Accommodation and camping are available.

Yarra Ranges National Park is north-east of Melbourne. The majestic eucalypts and lush tree-fern glades of the Black Spur on the Maroondah Highway form a dramatic gateway to Marysville, Lake Mountain, Alexandra and Eildon. Further south, along the Yarra Valley via Warburton, is the sub-alpine environment of Mt Donna Buang. The park includes some of Melbourne's water catchment areas, generally closed to public access. The moist forests of the Yarra Ranges are of national botanical significance, and they provide vital habitats for unique animals. In particular, the forests of mountain ash – the world's tallest flowering plant – provide the habitat for Leadbeater's possum, an endangered species that is hollow-dependent. Long thought to be extinct, Leadbeater's possum was rediscovered in these forests in 1961.

COASTAL PARKS

Wilsons Promontory National Park in Gippsland is the best-known coastal park and one of the most popular in Victoria. The Prom, as it is known, has something for everyone. Amenities and accommodation, including camping and caravan sites and cabins, are located at Tidal River, as are the visitor information centre and park office. Leaflets for 150 kilometres of walking tracks are available here, and visitors should also inquire about the long but rewarding Lighthouse Walk (walker accommodation is available at the lighthouse). Other natural attractions include secluded bays and magnificent stretches of beach, granite outcrops, and spectacular wildflowers that begin blooming in late winter and continue through spring. Wilsons Promontory is very popular, particularly in summer. Campsites are available only by ballot for the Christmas and Easter holiday periods.

The unusual rock structures found at **Port Campbell National Park** – including The Twelve Apostles, The Arch and Loch Ard Gorge – are majestic formations sculpted out of soft limestone cliffs by the relentless sea. While it is the spectacular coastal scenery that makes this park so popular, it is also an interesting park for birds, with around 100 species being recorded. The park was a popular place with Aboriginal people too, if the number of shell middens along the coast is an indication. And it is especially notorious for being part of the 'Shipwreck Coast'. Further west is **Discovery Bay Coastal Park**, which offers a rugged coastline and a broad range of fauna environments. The park is an important habitat for the endangered hooded plover, which nests in exposed situations above high-tide line.

Closer to Melbourne are the beautiful, lush tree-fern gullies and towering mountain-ash forests of **Otway National Park** and **Melba Gully State Park** near Lavers Hill. Because of the treacherous waters of Bass Strait, a lighthouse was the first piece of 'civilisation'

Tidal River in Wilsons Promontory National Park

at Cape Otway; it was opened in 1848. Cottages adjacent to the lighthouse can be booked for accommodation. Activities include year-round sightseeing, and camping, surfing, fishing and walking are best in spring and summer.

Eastern Victoria, with its mild and fairly wet climate, has vast areas of dense forest. These are attractive to bushwalkers and campers, who will find here a wide range of trees — mainly eucalypts, but also native pines, banksias and paperbarks.

Some of the most attractive coastal scenery close to any major regional centre can be found in and around **The Lakes National Park**. The park is surrounded by the extensive Gippsland Lakes system, ideal for sailing, boating and fishing. The 2390-hectare park harbours a large population of kangaroos and more than 140 bird species. Camp areas, picnic spots and a network of walking tracks cater for those who are land-based.

Croajingolong National Park has 87 500 hectares of coastline and hinterland stretching from Sydenham Inlet to the New South Wales border. The area contains remote rainforest, woodland, ocean beaches, rocky promontories, inlets and coves. Several rare species of wildlife can be found here, such as the smoky mouse and the ground parrot, and in spring the visitor will see an array of wildflowers. There is a wide range of activities for visitors at Croajingolong, with camping areas, a holiday centre at Mallacoota, and other towns along the Princes Highway offering accommodation and food.

IN THE NORTH-EAST OF THE STATE

The **Alpine National Park**, created in December 1989 and currently covering approximately 645 000 hectares, is the State's largest national park. Stretching along the Great Dividing Range, the park links with Kosciuszko National Park in New South Wales and its neighbour Namadgi National Park in the Australian Capital Territory in a grouping of national parks that encompasses almost all of south-east Australia's alpine areas. The park protects the habitats of a variety of flora and fauna, including the rare mountain pygmy possum (the world's only exclusively sub-alpine marsupial). The Alps are renowned for their sublime landscapes, features characterised by Mount Bogong and Mount Feathertop (Victoria's highest mountains) and the unique Bogong High Plains. During spring and summer the high plains are carpeted with wildflowers; more than 1100 native plant species are found in the park, including 12 found nowhere else in the world. The park is ideal for bushwalking, horseriding, four-wheel driving and cross-country skiing. Both Falls Creek and Mount Hotham ski resorts are surrounded by the Alpine National Park. In the summer months most roads provide easy access for vehicles, allowing a range of scenic drives with short walks to lookouts and other points of interest. Some huts in the park, popular places for walkers to visit, are being restored for their historic value.

Mount Buffalo National Park, north-west of Bright, encompasses Mount Buffalo plateau with its granite tors and rounded boulders. In milder weather, the park, with its bubbling streams and cascading waterfalls, offers visitors over 80 kilometres of marked walking tracks. The wildflowers on the undulating snow plains are at their best between November and March. Wombats, wallabies, lyrebirds, rosellas and gang-gang cockatoos may be seen. In winter, skiers can enjoy excellent cross-country and beginners' downhill skiing.

Canoeists will enjoy shooting the rapids or exploring the gorges of **Snowy River National Park** or **Mitchell River National Park**, both in East Gippsland, while bushwalkers can hike through beautiful forests.

Baw Baw National Park covers the granite Baw Baw plateau at the southern end of Victoria's high country, and sections of the Thomson and Aberfeldy river valleys. This park offers good cross-country skiing in winter: Baw Baw Alpine Village abuts the park. Numerous walking tracks are popular in summer, including a 20-kilometre section of the Australian Alps Walking Track, which extends from Walhalla to Canberra. In summer, visitors can take short walks to the track and to the plateau, or follow cross-country ski trails. Colourful wildflowers bloom on the plateau in summer. The park is home to Leadbeater's possum and the Baw Baw frog (both endangered species), as well as wombats, wallabies, echidnas, platypuses, gliders and several types of snakes and lizards. Crimson rosellas, yellow-tailed black cockatoos, gang-gangs and lyrebirds are common.

Lake Eildon National Park centres on Lake Eildon, and offers boating, sailing, water skiing, fishing and swimming, and a number of walking tracks, including a nature trail. The park's western boundary provides scenic views over nearby peaks and Coller Bay. There are many kangaroos and wallabies in the park. Crimson rosellas, cockatoos, galahs and kookaburras visit the camping grounds, and around the lake there are cormorants, pelicans, ducks, swans, herons and ibis.

IN THE WEST OF THE STATE

The 167 200-hectare **Grampians National Park** offers marvellous scenery, wildlife and tourist facilities. The park is famous for rugged sandstone ranges, waterfalls, wildflowers and varied birds and mammals, as well as Aboriginal rock-art sites. The peaks rise to over 1000 metres and form the western limit of the Great Dividing Range. The Grampians are best seen on foot: there are many walking tracks, from short well-marked trails in the Wonderland section near Halls Gap, to challenging walks across the sub-alpine landscape of the Major Mitchell Plateau.

Mount Eccles National Park, in south-west Victoria, is one of several parks that contain rock formations of great geological interest. An extinct volcano, a lava canal, lava cave and the Stony Rises are exceptional features. In the middle of the crater of Mount Eccles is the appropriately named Lake Surprise. South-west of this park is **Lower Glenelg National Park**, surrounding the tranquil Glenelg River and offering good walks and fishing.

Little Desert National Park is neither little (at 132 647 hectares) nor a desert. It is best known for its amazing displays of wildflowers in spring, boasting more than 600 flowering-plant species including more than 40 ground orchids. Another special feature of the Little Desert is that mallee fowl are found here. The males of the species build large mounds to incubate their eggs.

Wyperfeld National Park in the north-west contains hundreds of species of plants and birdlife, and is a great park to visit in the spring, autumn and winter. In good rainfall years there are colourful spring wildflowers, and in the autumn and winter the visitor will enjoy crisp, clear days – perfect for bushwalking and birdwatching.

The vast **Murray–Sunset National Park** contains semi-arid environments from riverine floodplains to heathlands, salt lakes and woodlands, which support a tremendous variety of wildlife, particularly birdlife. It is the second largest national park in the State covering 633 000 hectares. This park is also best visited in the cooler months of the year.

Another park in the north-west of the State is **Hattah–Kulkyne National Park**. Typically, summers here are long, hot and dry; rainfall is usually less than 300 millimetres per year. The animals of this area have evolved strategies for avoiding or tolerating heat and dryness: some burrow, others just rest during the heat of the day; some birds catch thermals to cooler air. After rainfall and flooding from the Murray River, the serenely beautiful Hattah Lakes system transforms the park into a bird haven and a wonderful wildflower landscape.

Although it is Australia's smallest mainland State, Victoria has over 100 national, State, wilderness and regional parks. Victoria's parks protect representative samples of most of the State's land and vegetation types: from alps, grasslands and mallee to rainforests, tall forests, coasts, volcanic plains and heathlands. Spring and summer are the best seasons to visit parks noted for their wildflowers. For more information on Victoria's national parks, contact the Parks Victoria Information Centre; 13 1963. Web site www.parkweb.vic.gov.au

The Cathedral, Mount Buffalo

WILDLIFE-WATCHING

Eastern grey kangaroos can be seen in the Grampians

IN MELBOURNE

Thanks to Melbourne's wonderful gardens and reserves, native animals can still be seen in the city. The lake in the **Botanic Gardens**, in the inner suburb of South Yarra, is a habitat for black swans, cormorants, ducks, moorhens and coots. An indigenous fruit bat, the grey-headed flying-fox, also roosts in the gardens.

Melbourne's possums have adapted well to their urban environment. There are two varieties: the ringtail with its white-tipped tail, and the larger brushtail possum. Brushtails are the more brash of the two, and can often be seen rummaging after dark in the **Fitzroy** and **Alexandra gardens**.

Melbourne is on the shores of **Port Phillip**, which is home to schools of bottlenose dolphins and seals. Dolphin- and seal-viewing boat tours operate from the bayside towns of Sorrento and Queenscliff. Cruises also leave for **Pope's Eye Marine Reserve**, within the bay, to view Australasian gannets.

AROUND MELBOURNE

The most famous penguin-watching spot is a couple of hours south of Melbourne at **Phillip Island**. At Summerland Beach the little (fairy) penguins come ashore each evening to their burrows in the sand dunes. At the visitors centre, nesting penguins can be spied on through peepholes in their specially designed nesting boxes. From May to July, these birds can be seen nest-building; from August to January, eggs are laid and chicks raised. February to April are good months to see the penguins moulting.

Koalas can also be seen in their natural habitat from raised walkways at the Koala Conservation Centre on the island. Cruise trips leave from Cowes to **Seal Rocks** on the south-western tip of the island, allowing close-up views of Australia's largest colony of breeding fur seals. At the Seal Rocks Sea Life Centre, visitors can see live images of the seals relayed onto giant screens. At **San Remo**, pelicans get a fish meal daily on the waterfront.

South-west of Melbourne near Lara is **Serendip Sancturary**. This grassland and wetland habitat has viewing hides and is a good location to see native birds. Visitors can see waterbirds such as spoonbills, grebes and ducks, as well as several species of birds of prey.

ON THE SOUTH-WEST COAST

Just off the coast near Port Campbell is **Mutton Bird Island**, a bird colony free from introduced predators. Thousands of migratory short-tailed shearwaters (muttonbirds) arrive from the north Pacific and nest on the island between September and April.

The most famous visitors to the south-west coast are southern right whales. After spending the summer months in the plankton-rich sub-Antarctic waters, they return to breeding grounds at **Logans Beach** just east of Warrnambool between June and September. Southern right whales are slowly increasing in numbers after being decimated by commercial whaling earlier in the century.

IN THE GRAMPIANS

The rugged sandstone ranges of the Grampians offer some of the best opportunities for wildlife-watching in south-western Victoria. Koalas can be seen around **Halls Gap**, and flocks of long-billed corellas arrive each evening to roost in the eucalypts. Eastern grey kangaroos are common in grassland around the town, particularly at dawn and dusk. For a closer look at our national symbol, visit **Zumsteins picnic area** in Grampians National Park. Kangaroos graze freely throughout the day. During school holidays, night wildlife-watching walks are conducted – several species are likely to be seen by torchlight, including gliders, owls, kangaroos, ringtail and brushtail possums, and wallabies.

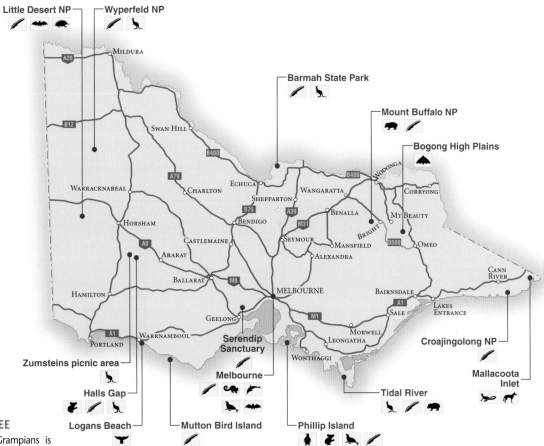

IN THE MALLEE

North of the Grampians is
Wyperfeld National Park. Follow
the Lake Brambruk Nature Walk to see emus, kangaroos,
soaring wedge-tailed eagles, and the endangered regent parrot. Wyperfeld's
best-known bird is the threatened mallee fowl. The male builds a large
nesting mound comprising a core of organic material covered by a layer of
sand. With a little patience there is a good chance of seeing a mallee fowl at
its mound, particularly October–March. **Little Desert National Park** also has
mallee fowl, along with small insectivorous bats which can be seen flying on
summer evenings, and a healthy population of short-beaked echidnas.

AROUND THE MURRAY

Barmah State Park in north-central Victoria provides a unique bird habitat.
Floods are common between July and October; a good time for boat tours
to look for waterbirds. Eastern grey kangaroos can be readily seen
throughout the forest, though you will need a torch and some patience to
glimpse the less-common nocturnal marsupials.

IN THE NORTH-EASTERN HIGHLANDS

One of Victoria's most popular native species is the common wombat, and
a good place to see this burrowing marsupial is in **Mount Buffalo National
Park**. They venture out at dusk to graze on snow grass flats. The chalet within
the park attracts the colourful crimson rosellas. An equally colourful but much
smaller park resident is the flame robin, the male having a bright red breast.

The Bogong moth played an important part in the lives of local
Aborigines before European settlement. Each summer Aboriginal groups
trekked to the high country to feast on the insects. Thousands of the moths
still inhabit the **Bogong High Plains** in summer, and the best places to find
them are in rock crevices.

ON THE EASTERN COAST

The Mallacoota region offers wildlife-watchers a good chance to see large
tree goannas, particularly along the picnic sites at **Mallacoota Inlet**. The
elusive dingo can occasionally be spotted along beaches in the area, and

WILDLIFE-WATCHING ETHICS

*Do not disturb wildlife or wildlife habitats. Keep the impact of
your presence to a minimum. Use available cover or hides
wherever possible.*

*Do not feed wildlife, even in urban areas.
(Note: supervised feeding is allowed at some locations)*

*Be careful not to introduce exotic plants and animals –
definitely no pets.*

Stay on defined trails.

their tracks can be seen in the sand. There is a large bird population in
Croajingolong National Park – over 300 species. Glossy black cockatoos
are attracted to the native casuarina trees along the walking track to Genoa
Peak within the park. King parrots and lyrebirds can also be seen.

AT WILSONS PROM

Wilsons Promontory National Park has no shortage of wildlife. Eastern grey
kangaroos and emus graze on grassland at **Tidal River**, and blond-coloured
wombats emerge at dusk at Norman Beach. This is also a good area for
short-tailed shearwaters (muttonbirds). Kookaburras and flame robins are
easily seen, while Easter is prime-time for flocks of rainbow lorikeets as they
arrive to feed on flowering coastal banksias.

For a good introduction to Victorian wildlife visit Healesville Sanctuary, just
east of Melbourne. The Department of Natural Resources and Environment
publishes an excellent guide titled *Wildlife Watching in Victoria*. For more
information on wildlife-watching in national parks, contact the Parks
Victoria Information Line; 13 1963. Web site www.parkweb.vic.gov.au

CLASSIC TOUR
GREAT OCEAN TOUR
Geelong to Port Fairy (345 km)

T he Great Ocean Road winds through some of the most dramatic scenery in Australia. It is a journey of contrasts, with a magnificent vista around every corner: massive rock formations sculpted by the waves, stunning surf beaches, and ancient rainforests. Shortly after Port Campbell, the route passes Victoria's top whale-watching spot en route to the quaint fishing village of Port Fairy. You should allow about three days to complete the tour and return to Geelong. There are numerous holiday cottages, B & Bs, motels and camping grounds all along the coast – Apollo Bay and Port Fairy would make ideal overnight stops.

1 Port city
The tour begins in **Geelong**, set on the shores of Corio Bay, 72 kilometres from Melbourne. This large, industrial, port city has exported wool and other produce from Victoria's rich western district since the 1830s. Some of the historic bluestone warehouses remain along the waterfront, and one of these has been restored to house the fascinating National Wool Museum. Geelong's attractive waterfront, stretching from Cunningham Pier to the art deco pavilion at Eastern Beach, is an ideal stopping place – cafes, restaurants and grassy picnic spots overlook the bay.

Loch Ard Gorge

National Wool Museum
26 Moorabool Street
Geelong
Open: 9.30 a.m.–5 p.m. daily
Phone: (03) 5227 0701

2 Making waves
Take the Princes Highway and join the Surf Coast Highway on the southern outskirts of Geelong. Your next destination is **Torquay**, mecca for surf enthusiasts and home of the Surfworld Surfing Museum. Visitors to the museum can make waves (in an 8-metre tank), listen to their favourite surf music and view the historic surfboard collection. Many big-name manufacturers of surfing gear are based here, including Rip Curl, Quicksilver and Rojo. If you are in the market for some discount beach gear, take a wander through the busy factory outlets adjacent to the museum.

Surfworld Australia
Beach Road
Torquay
Open: 9 a.m.–5 p.m. weekdays;
10 a.m.–4 p.m. weekends/
public holidays
Phone: (03) 5261 4606

3 Hang ten
After Torquay, the Surf Coast Highway becomes the Great Ocean Road. Two kilometres from town, turn left along **Bells Beach** Road to the world-famous surf beach of the same name. Over Easter, this is the setting for one of the coveted international titles, the Bells Beach Surfing Classic. From the cliff-top car park you can usually see distinct swell lines moving towards the shore. On a good day the waves are an impressive 3–4 metres high.

If you are tempted to test the water yourself, the company, Go Ride a Wave operates regular 2-hour classes for beginners at Anglesea and Torquay; phone (03) 5263 2111 for details.

4 Kangaroos
From Bells Beach Road, take Jarosite Road to return to the Great Ocean Road and head towards **Anglesea**. The beach at Anglesea is patrolled during the summer school holidays and on weekends from November to the end of Easter (see signs on beach for details of patrol times). If you want to stretch your legs, turn left down Purnell Street, soon after you enter town, and stop at the car park. A 3.5-kilometre circuit walk extends from here, along the cliff-top and back through heathland alongside the Anglesea Recreation Reserve.

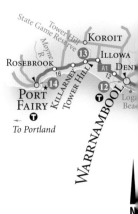

SOUTH

Southern right whale

No trip to Anglesea is complete without a visit to the golf course, where kangaroos graze the greens. From the Great Ocean Road, turn right along Noble Street after crossing the bridge and follow the signs to Anglesea Golf Club.

5 History of the road

Return to the Great Ocean Road and turn right towards Lorne. Soon after leaving Anglesea, you crest Point Roadknight and are rewarded with a spectacular view of the coastline stretching out ahead.

After passing through Aireys Inlet, you come to the **Memorial Arch**, dedicated to those who died in World War I. The Great Ocean Road was initially a post-war project devised to employ returned soldiers; these men were later joined by the unemployed during the Great Depression of the 1930s. The connection with World War I is evident in many of the names given to features along the route – Artillery Rocks and Shrapnel Gully are two examples. It is hard to comprehend that picks, shovels and crowbars were the main tools used to carve the road out of the rocky coastline.

6 Waterfalls

As you continue towards Lorne, the road hugs the cliffs and shoreline, with a dramatic meeting of land and sea at each bend. Lorne is a popular holiday town on the shores of Loutit Bay – and scenic, with the Otway Ranges forming a striking backdrop. The main street is a cosmopolitan mix of cafes, restaurants and shops, an ideal place to stop. Enjoy a caffe latte or an ice-cream, and watch the throng of holidaymakers.

Nearby, in the leafy, emerald folds of the Otway Ranges, is **Erskine Falls**. Take the signposted turn-off from the centre of town and follow the road as it winds up through the forest. After 8 kilometres, branch off to the Erskine Falls car park. From here it is only a short walk through the rainforest to a viewing platform overlooking the falls; follow the steps down the side of the gully to see the falls from beneath.

7 Rainforest rest

Return to the Great Ocean Road and continue south-west towards Apollo Bay. The route winds along the shore and there are lookouts at Mount Defiance, Wye River and Cape Patton. After 45 kilometres of superb coastal scenery, you arrive at Apollo Bay, where rolling hills extend down to the sea. The town is the base for the local fishing fleet, and you can buy fresh seafood down at the harbour.

After Apollo Bay, the Great Ocean Road leaves the coast, temporarily, to wind through the cool green of Otway National Park. The road is lined with a forest of tree ferns and giant mountain ash trees. No drive along the Great Ocean Road is complete without pausing at one of the beautiful pockets of rainforest, either **Maits Rest** or Melba Gully State Park (near Lavers Hill). Maits Rest is 17 kilometres from Apollo Bay on the left. An easy 40-minute boardwalk circuit leads into the heart of a mossy gully, past tree ferns and ancient myrtle beech trees.

8 To the lighthouse

Continue along the Great Ocean Road for a few kilometres before turning left along Lighthouse Road to Cape Otway. The **Cape Otway Lighthouse** stands dramatically on a cliff 100 metres above the sea. Built by convicts in 1848, this remote lighthouse was accessible only by sea, until the road was completed in 1937. It is now open to the public and the historic keeper's quarters are available for accommodation (bookings must be made well in advance).

Cape Otway Lighthouse
Lighthouse Road
Cape Otway
Open: 9 a.m.–4.30 p.m. daily
Phone: (03) 5237 9240

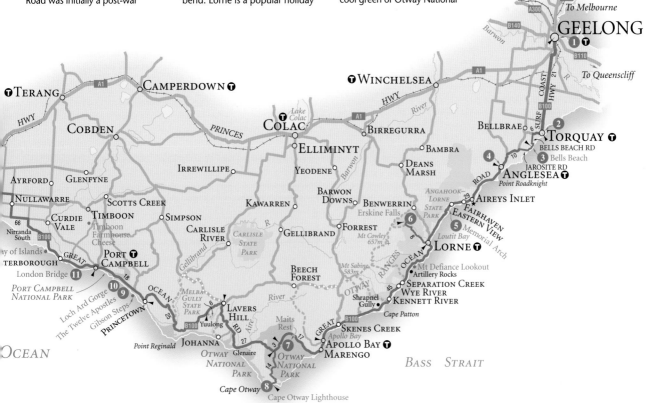

The Twelve Apostles

9 The Twelve Apostles

Return to the Great Ocean Road and continue on towards Lavers Hill. The road winds inland for 29 kilometres before reaching Lavers Hill, where you can turn left to visit the other beautiful pocket of rainforest, Melba Gully State Park. Follow the signs to the car park. A boardwalk winds through the damp, mysterious world of the rainforest, across the Johanna River and past a 300-year-old tree with its impressive 27-metre girth.

After almost 40 kilometres of forest and farmland, the Great Ocean Road returns to the coast near Princetown. From this point, the road runs parallel to the precipitous cliff-line of Port Campbell National Park. Over the years, strong waves have eroded the limestone headlands, creating huge rock stacks. For your first views of these dramatic rock formations, pull in at the lookout above Gibson Steps. If you are feeling energetic, take the steps to the base of the cliff and enjoy a stroll along the magnificent beach – the sheer size of the formations and the height of the cliff are even more apparent.

Shortly after Gibson Steps, prepare to turn left to **The Twelve Apostles** lookout. The view of these famous rock forms is one of the great highlights of the Great Ocean Road. The Twelve Apostles have a sculptural quality that makes them irresistible to amateur and professional photographers alike.

10 Shipwreck coast

Return to the Great Ocean Road and take the signposted turn-off to **Loch Ard Gorge**. The narrow gorge, which is a short walk down steep steps from the car park, was named after the ill-fated clipper *Loch Ard*, which was dashed against the rocks in 1878. Of the 54 people on board, only two survived: Tom Pearce, a crew member only 18 years old, and Eva Carmichael, a passenger of the same age, who was eventually washed into the gorge and saved by Tom. The cemetery above the gorge contains the graves of those who drowned.

11 London Bridge

Return to the Great Ocean Road and continue through the town of Port Campbell before taking the signposted turn-off to another famous sight, **London Bridge**. This was, until recently, a bridge with two 'spans' along which visitors could walk, as the water foamed beneath. In 1990 one span collapsed, leaving a couple of tourists stranded; they had to be rescued by helicopter.

12 Whale-watching

Just after Peterborough, as the Great Ocean Road turns inland again, the Bay of Islands can be seen. It contains smaller rock stacks than The Twelve Apostles, but nevertheless is a delightful sight. The tour continues though dairy country to join the Princes Highway just before **Warrnambool**.

If you are touring between June and September, a detour to Logans Beach is a must. Southern right whales swim from their Antarctic feeding grounds to give birth just off the beach here, and visitors are often rewarded with the sight of huge cows swimming with their calves. The turn-off along Simpson Street to Logans Beach is signposted during the whale-watching season.

Return to the Princes Highway and continue to the centre of Warrnambool. Turn left down Banyan Street to visit Flagstaff Hill Maritime Museum. The museum is a re-creation of a 19th-century port based around an original lighthouse. There are displays of Aboriginal history and other displays of shipwreck artifacts, restored ships, a working blacksmith and a shipwright.

Flagstaff Hill Maritime Museum
Merri Street
Warrnambool
Open: 9 a.m.– 5 p.m. daily
Phone: (03) 5564 7841

13 Extinct volcano

Twelve kilometres west of Warrnambool, to the right of the Princes Highway, is **Tower Hill State Game Reserve**, an extinct volcano with a lake in its crater. At one stage the area around the lake was heavily over-grazed, but extensive revegetation in recent years has resulted in a haven for birdlife (around 200 species). The reserve is also a habitat for many kangaroos, koalas and emus. A one-way road circles the lake, past lookout points and pleasant picnic areas.

14 Fishing village

The final leg of the tour takes you a further 16 kilometres along the Princes Highway to **Port Fairy**, one of Victoria's earliest ports. The town is an enchanting mixture of historic whitewashed houses and a busy waterfront. Over 50 of the town's buildings have been classified by the National Trust. You can buy fresh seafood from the jetty on the Moyne River where the local fishing fleet moors. Alternatively, if you have come equipped, there is surf fishing on East Beach and estuary fishing on the river. For the birdwatcher, Griffiths Island, at the head of the river, is home to a huge colony of short-tailed shearwaters (muttonbirds). Between September and April as many as 15 000 birds can be seen flying in to roost every evening.

Returning to Geelong
The most direct route back to Geelong is via the Princes Highway (213 kilometres). If you have the time, there are various interesting alternative routes. One option is to retrace your steps back to the Great Ocean Road and take one of the many roads leading inland to the Princes Highway, through the dairy country around Cobden; consider stopping at Timboon Farmhouse Cheese to taste the local produce en route. Another option is to return to Lavers Hill and wind your way back to the Princes Highway through the forests of the Otway Ranges, but beware of logging trucks and take care to avoid unsealed roads after rain.

Otway rainforest

VICTORIA
LOCATION MAP

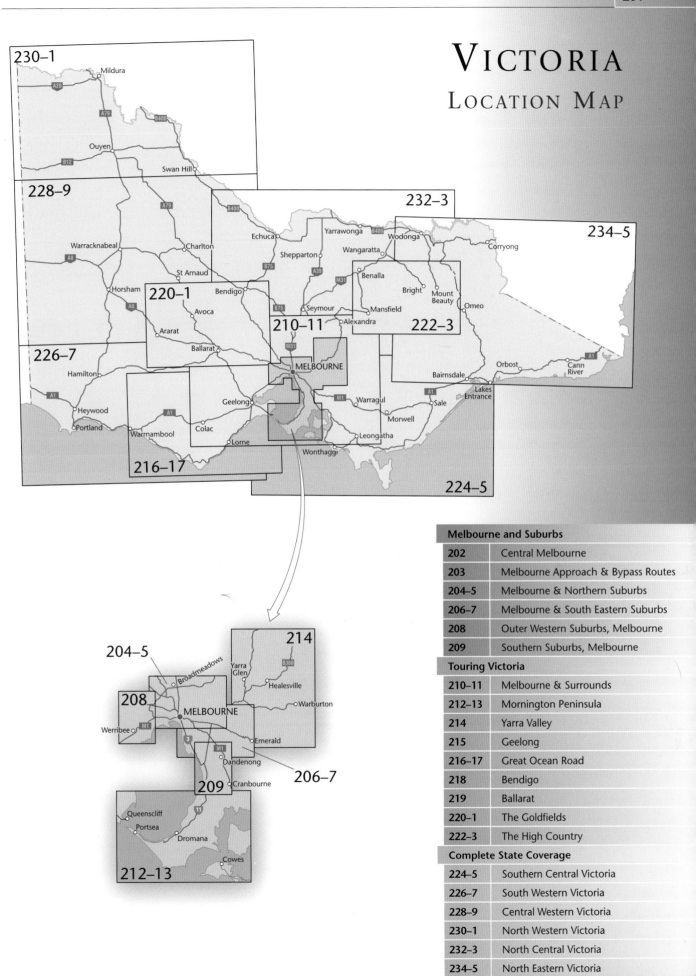

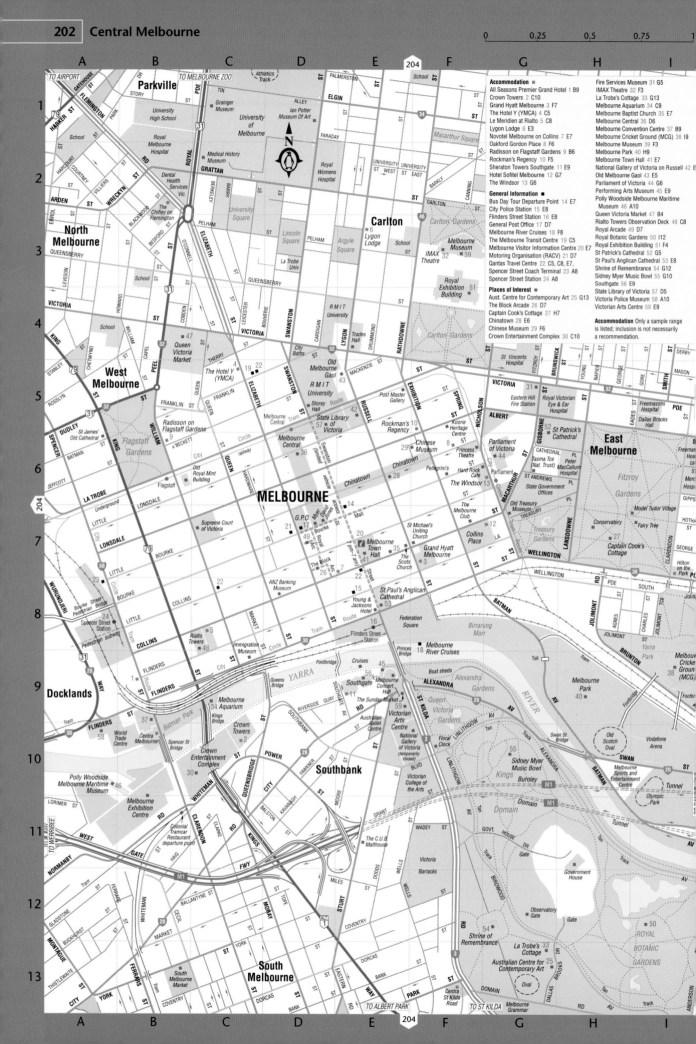

Accommodation ■
All Seasons Premier Grand Hotel 1 B9
Crown Towers 2 C10
Grand Hyatt Melbourne 3 F7
The Hotel Y (YMCA) 4 C5
Le Meridien at Rialto 5 C8
Lygon Lodge 6 E3
Novotel Melbourne on Collins 7 E7
Oakford Gordon Place 8 F6
Radisson on Flagstaff Gardens 9 B6
Rockman's Regency 10 F5
Sheraton Towers Southgate 11 E9
Hotel Sofitel Melbourne 12 G7
The Windsor 13 G6

General Information ■
Bus Day Tour Departure Point 14 E7
City Police Station 15 E8
Flinders Street Station 16 E8
General Post Office 17 D7
Melbourne River Cruises 18 F8
The Melbourne Transit Centre 19 C5
Melbourne Visitor Information Centre 20 E7
Motoring Organisation (RACV) 21 D7
Qantas Travel Centre 22 C5, C8, E7,
Spencer Street Coach Terminal 23 A8
Spencer Street Station 24 A8

Places of Interest ■
Aust. Centre for Contemporary Art 25 G13
The Block Arcade 26 D7
Captain Cook's Cottage 27 H7
Chinatown 28 E6
Chinese Museum 29 F6
Crown Entertainment Complex 30 C10

Fire Services Museum 31 G5
IMAX Theatre 32 F3
La Trobe's Cottage 33 G13
Melbourne Aquarium 34 C9
Melbourne Baptist Church 35 C8
Melbourne Central 36 D6
Melbourne Convention Centre 37 B9
Melbourne Cricket Ground (MCG) 38 I9
Melbourne Museum 39 F3
Melbourne Park 40 H9
Melbourne Town Hall 41 E7
National Gallery of Victoria on Russell 42 E8
Old Melbourne Gaol 43 E5
Parliament of Victoria 44 G6
Performing Arts Museum 45 E9
Polly Woodside Melbourne Maritime
    Museum 46 A10
Queen Victoria Market 47 B4
Rialto Towers Observation Deck 48 C8
Royal Arcade 49 D7
Royal Botanic Gardens 50 I12
Royal Exhibition Building 51 F4
St Patrick's Cathedral 52 G5
St Paul's Anglican Cathedral 53 E8
Shrine of Remembrance 54 G12
Sidney Myer Music Bowl 55 G10
Southgate 56 E9
State Library of Victoria 57 D5
Victoria Police Museum 58 A10
Victorian Arts Centre 59 E9

Accommodation Only a sample range
is listed; inclusion is not necessarily
a recommendation.

Thick roads represent recommended approach and bypass routes.

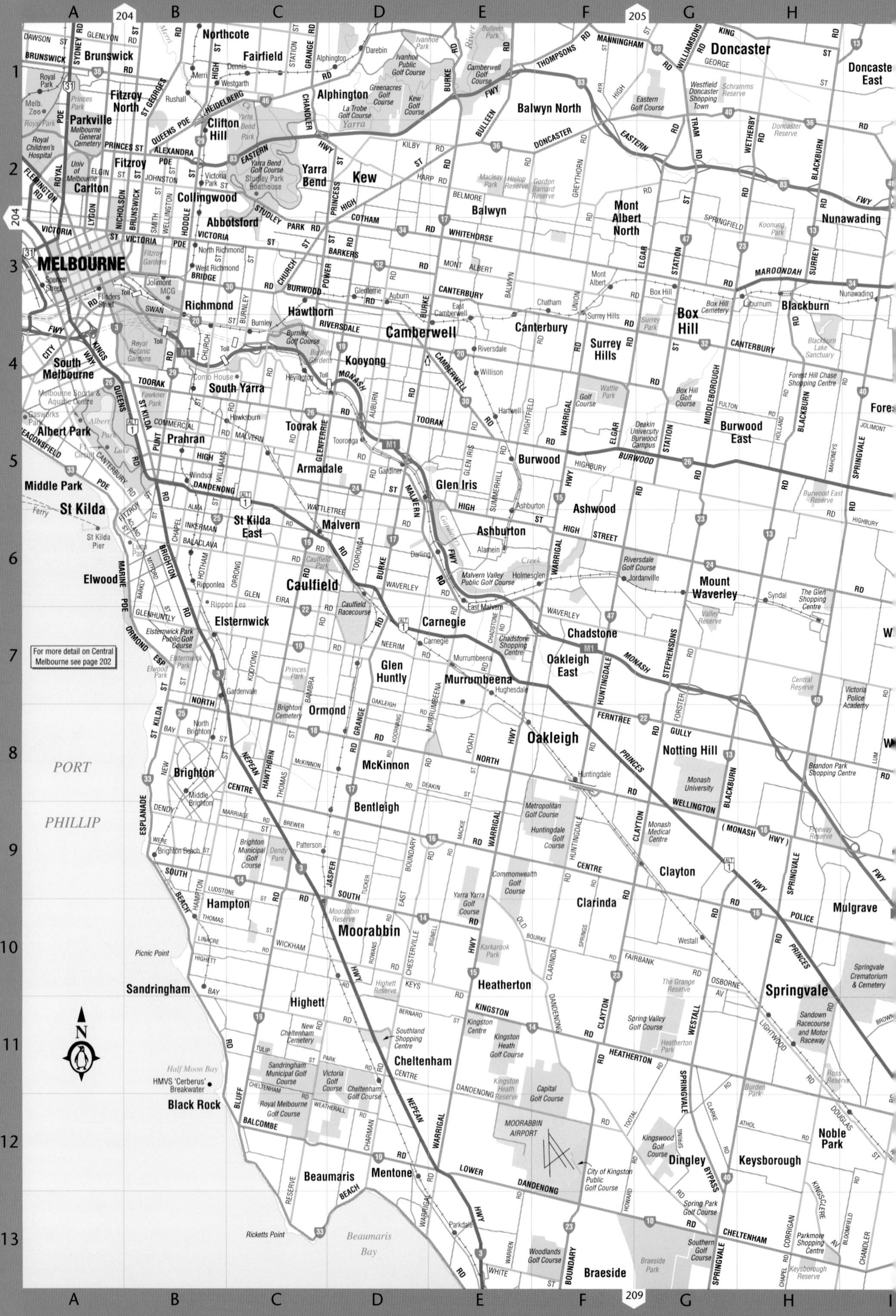

Brunswick
Northcote
Fairfield
Alphington
Darebin
Ivanhoe
Doncaster
Doncaster East
Fitzroy North
Parkville
Clifton Hill
Yarra Bend
Kew
Balwyn North
Fitzroy
Carlton
Collingwood
Abbotsford
Balwyn
Mont Albert North
Nunawading
MELBOURNE
Richmond
Hawthorn
Camberwell
Canterbury
Box Hill
Blackburn
South Melbourne
Burnley
Kooyong
Surrey Hills
Burwood East
Albert Park
South Yarra
Toorak
Burwood
Prahran
Armadale
Glen Iris
Ashwood
Middle Park
St Kilda
Windsor
St Kilda East
Malvern
Ashburton
Mount Waverley
Elwood
Balaclava
Caulfield
Carnegie
Chadstone
Elsternwick
Glen Huntly
Murrumbeena
Oakleigh East
Oakleigh
Notting Hill
Ormond
McKinnon
Clayton
Brighton
Bentleigh
Clarinda
Hampton
Moorabbin
Heatherton
Springvale
Sandringham
Highett
Cheltenham
Kingston
Mulgrave
Black Rock
Beaumaris
Mentone
Braeside
Dingley
Keysborough
Noble Park

PORT PHILLIP

For more detail on Central Melbourne see page 202

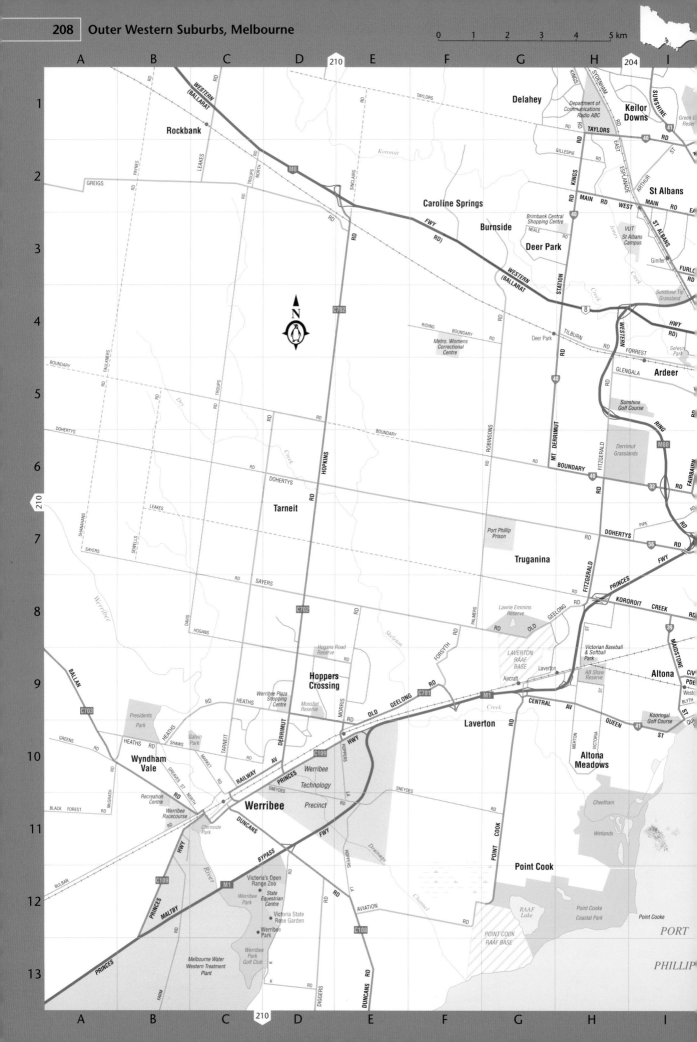

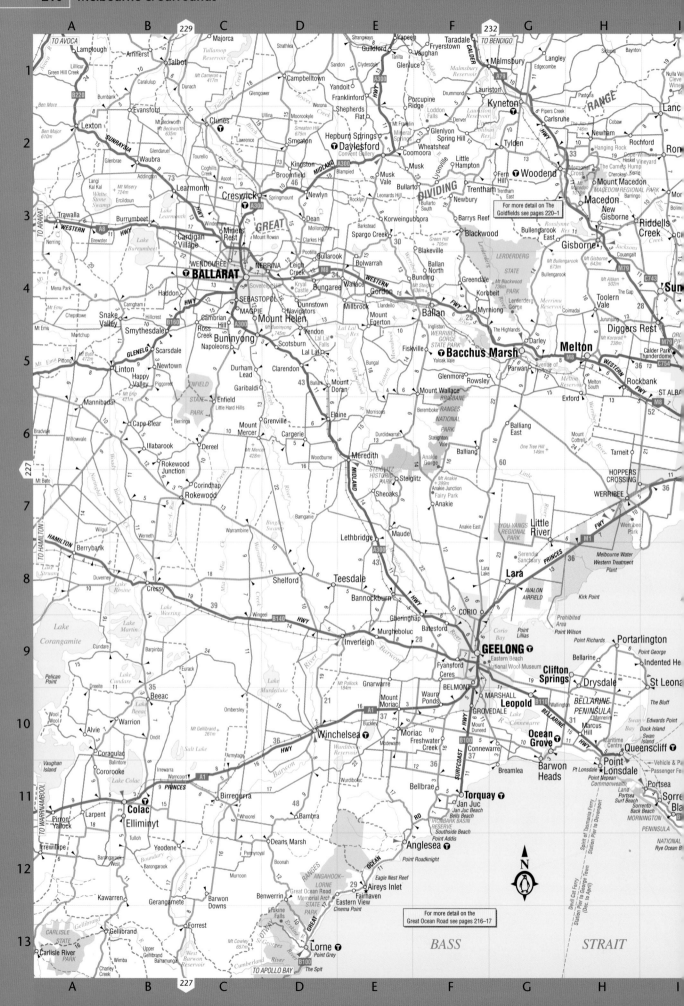

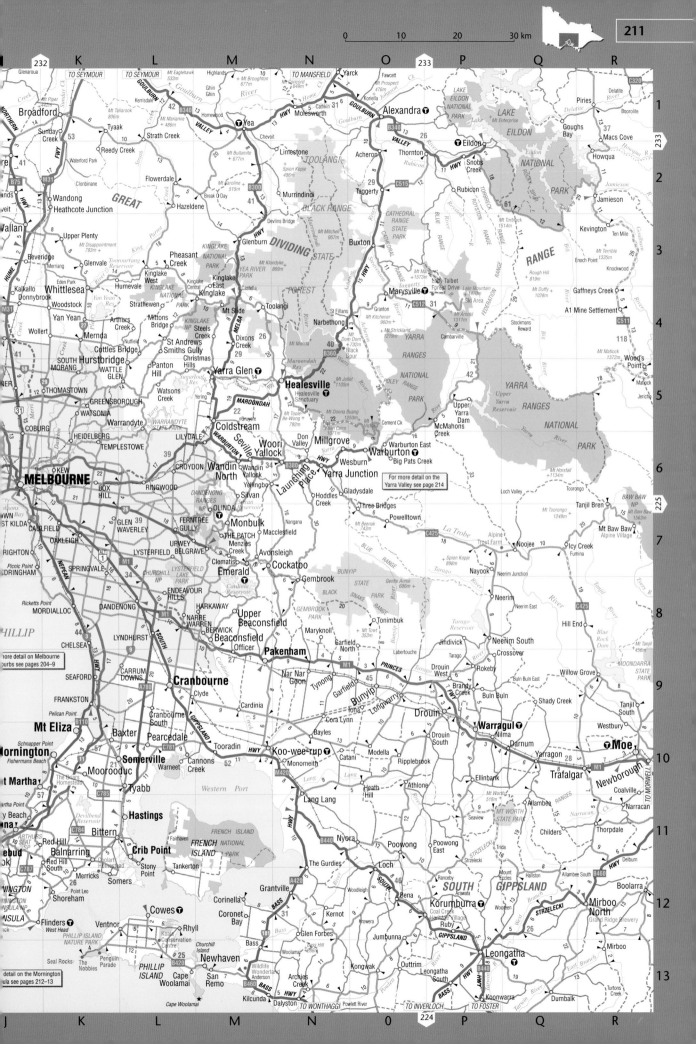

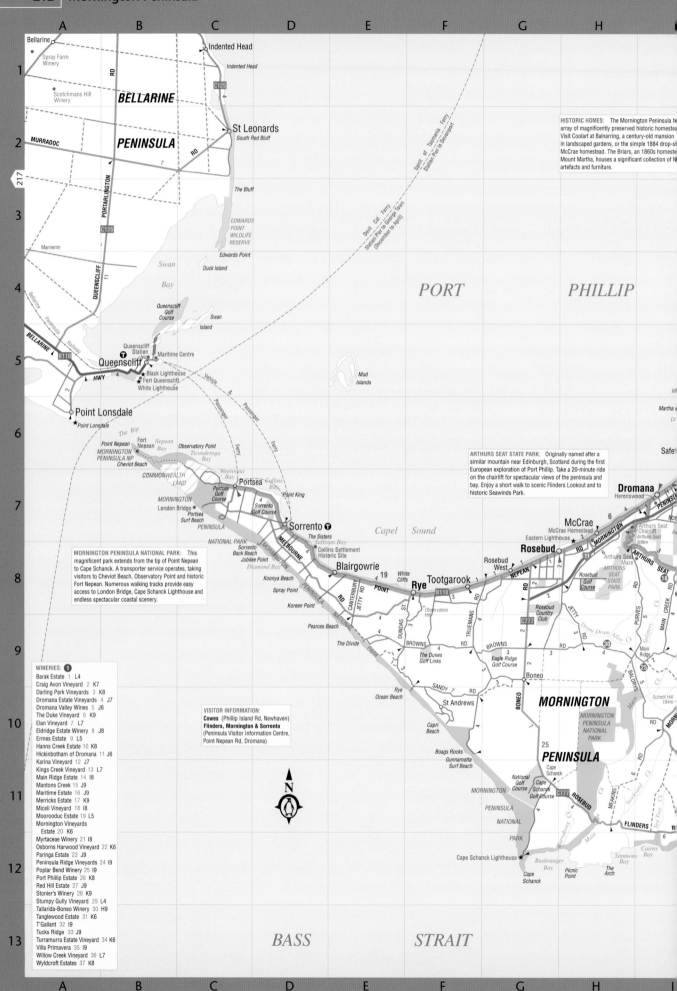

HISTORIC HOMES: The Mornington Peninsula h[...] array of magnificently preserved historic homeste[...] Visit Coolart at Balnarring, a century-old mansion [...] in landscaped gardens, or the simple 1884 drop-s[...] McCrae homestead. The Briars, an 1860s homeste[...] Mount Martha, houses a significant collection of M[...] artefacts and furniture.

ARTHURS SEAT STATE PARK: Originally named after a similar mountain near Edinburgh, Scotland during the first European exploration of Port Phillip. Take a 20-minute ride on the chairlift for spectacular views of the peninsula and bay. Enjoy a short walk to scenic Flinders Lookout and to historic Seawinds Park.

MORNINGTON PENINSULA NATIONAL PARK: This magnificent park extends from the tip of Point Nepean to Cape Schanck. A transporter service operates, taking visitors to Cheviot Beach, Observatory Point and historic Fort Nepean. Numerous walking tracks provide easy access to London Bridge, Cape Schanck Lighthouse and endless spectacular coastal scenery.

WINERIES: ❶
Barak Estate 1 L4
Craig Avon Vineyard 2 K7
Darling Park Vineyards 3 K8
Dromana Estate Vineyards 4 J7
Dromana Valley Wines 5 J6
The Duke Vineyard 6 K9
Elan Vineyard 7 L7
Eldridge Estate Winery 8 J8
Ermes Estate 9 L5
Hanns Creek Estate 10 K8
Hickinbotham of Dromana 11 J6
Karina Vineyard 12 J7
Kings Creek Vineyard 13 L7
Main Ridge Estate 14 I8
Mantons Creek 15 J9
Maritime Estate 16 J9
Merricks Estate 17 K9
Miceli Vineyard 18 I8
Moorooduc Estate 19 L5
Mornington Vineyards
   Estate 20 K6
Myrtaceae Winery 21 I8
Osborns Harwood Vineyard 22 K6
Paringa Estate 23 J9
Peninsula Ridge Vineyards 24 I9
Poplar Bend Winery 25 I9
Port Phillip Estate 26 K8
Red Hill Estate 27 J9
Stonier's Winery 28 K9
Stumpy Gully Vineyard 29 L4
Tallarida-Boneo Winery 30 H9
Tanglewood Estate 31 K6
T'Gallant 32 I9
Tucks Ridge 33 J9
Turramurra Estate Vineyard 34 K6
Villa Primavera 35 I9
Willow Creek Vineyard 36 L7
Wyldcroft Estates 37 K8

VISITOR INFORMATION:
Cowes (Phillip Island Rd, Newhaven)
Flinders, Mornington & Sorrento
(Peninsula Visitor Information Centre,
Point Nepean Rd, Dromana)

N

0 2 4 6 8 10 km

K L M N O P Q R

FRANKSTON

TO MELBOURNE

CRANBOURNE

TO DANDENONG

Cranbourne
South

BROWNS

Five Ways

LANGWARRIN

Daveys
Bay

Ballam Park
Homestead

Devon Meadows

Pelican Point

Canadian
Bay

Langwarrin
Flora &
Fauna
Reserve

ROBINSONS

Mt Eliza

WARRANDYTE

Baxter

BAXTER - TOORADIN

Pearcedale

BAXTER - TOORADIN

Tooradin

Sunnyside
Beach

Mornington
Golf Course

Mt Eliza
160m

Baxter
Park

Cannons
Creek

TO KORUMBURRA

Schnapper
Point

Railway

Somerville

Warneet

Blind
Bight

Studio City
Pop & Media
Museum

ERAMOSA
ROAD
WEST

ERAMOSA
ROAD
EAST

Quail
Island

Watson
Inlet

Mornington
Racecourse
Civic
Reserve
Craft Market

Mornington

TYABB

Moorooduc

Bembridge
9 Hole
Golf Course

WESTERN   PORT

The Briars
Homestead

Devilbend
Golf Course
& Rec Res

Tyabb

Scrub Point

FRENCH ISLAND: Named in 1802 by Captain Bauclin,
leader of a French scientific expedition, this naturally
protected island provides the perfect habitat for rare
white-breasted sea eagles, potoroos and koalas.

Devilbend
Reservoir

Western
Port
Airfield

BHP Steel
Western
Port
Works

BAYVIEW

GRAYDENS

FRENCH ISLAND

NATIONAL PARK

Bittern
Reservoir

HODGINS

Long Point

Long Island

Hastings

Hastings
Bight

Fairhaven

Sandstone
Island

Mt Wellington
98m

BITTERN

Warringine

The Pinnacles
66m

FRENCH

Balnarring
Racecourse

Bittern

WOOLLEYS

Emu Plains
Market

DISNEY

Crib
Point

ISLAND

Red Hill

BITTERN   DROMANA

Crib Point

Passenger

Tankerton

Balnarring

Stony Point

Tankerton
Jetty

Red Hill South

Merricks

HMAS
CERBERUS
NAVAL
BASE

Ferry

Tortoise
Head

STANLEYS

Coolart
Reserve

Sandy
Point

Balnarring
Beach

Somers
Beach

Somers

Merricks
Beach

Point
Summer

South
Beach

Western
Park
Beach

Sandy Point

Long Point

Point Leo

Ashcombe
Maze

FLINDERS

Point Leo

Shoreham

Passenger

ASHCOMBE MAZE: Wander through the large green hedge maze with
one kilometre of pathways, or wind your way through the beautiful
rose maze of over 1200 colourful and fragrant roses. The tea room
and extensive gardens provide perfect places for relaxation.

Shoreham
Beach

Rocks

Seal

Cowes

Cowes
Golf Course

Observation Point

Penguin
Rock

CHURCH
ST

Rhyll Inlet

Flinders

WESTERN   PORT

VENTNOR
RD

COWES

RHYLL
RD

Rhyll

Kennon
Cove

McHaffie
Point

Bird
Sanctuary

Fishermans Point

West Head

Ventnor

Phillip Island
Wildlife Park

Koala
Res

PHILLIP ISLAND
NATURE PARK

PHILLIP   ISLAND

Five
Ways

Conservation
Centre

Churchill
Island

IP ISLAND: This year-round tourist destination with
rse coastline is an excellent weekend getaway. Visit
ged terrain of The Nobbies and view the seal colony
Rocks. Wander through various sections of Phillip
Nature Park. Every evening the little (fairy) penguins
up Summerland Beach providing a delightful natural
e spectacle.

BACK   BEACH

A Maze N Things

Cat Bay

Phillip Island
Vineyard & Winery

Swan
Lake

Australian
Dairy
Centre

Newhaven

Point Grant

Penguin
Reserve

Penguin
Parade
Summerland
Beach

Berrys
Beach

PYRAMID ROCK

Grand Prix Circuit
& Visitor Centre

PHILLIP
ISLAND

San Remo

Phillip Is
Airfield

Cape Woolamai

The Nobbies

The Blowhole

Seal Rocks

Seal Rocks
Sea Life Centre

Berrys
Beach

Cunningham
Bay

PHILLIP ISLAND
NATURE PARK

Storm
Bay

Pyramid Rock

Swan
Bay

Woody Point

K L M N O P Q R

0 2 4 6 8 10 km

TO YEA

TO ALEXANDRA

KINGLAKE NATIONAL PARK: Home to numerous lyrebirds and wombats, Kinglake National Park was established to protect the wet eucalypt forests on the Great Dividing Range. Tranquil walks through fern gullies and forested spurs take you to the Wombelano Falls.

TOOLANGI–BLACK RANGES: Toolangi, once home of C.J. Dennis, author of *The Sentimental Bloke*, is a mountainous berry-producing area nestled in the Black Ranges State Forest. Picturesque roadways provide easy access to the spectacular Wilhelmina Falls and Murrindindi Cascades. There are excellent riding tours available in the area, taking you along rugged mountain tracks and tranquil river paths. Trout and blackfish can be caught in the Murrindindi River.

GULF STATION: Now owned by the National Trust, Gulf Station at Yarra Glen is one of Victoria's oldest pastoral properties, dating back to the 1850s. Visitors can step back in time and explore the original timber buildings and cottage gardens.

HEALESVILLE SANCTUARY: Home to over 200 of Australia's unique birds, animals and reptiles, including some endangered species. Open every day of the year, the sanctuary is recognised as Victoria's top wildlife park. Spend the day venturing among friendly kangaroos, emus and wombats in 31 hectares of natural bushland.

SILVAN RESERVOIR: Located on the edge of beautiful Olinda, Stonyford picnic ground at Silvan Reservoir provides excellent barbecue facilities. Stop along the Monbulk Road for breathtaking views of the region.

PUFFING BILLY: This superbly restored vintage steam train ambles its way from the ferny stands of Belgrave through the cool rainforest to Gembrook.

VISITOR INFORMATION:
Healesville (Yarra Valley Visitor Information, Harker St)
Marysville (Murchison St)
Warburton (3400 Warburton Hwy)

WINERIES: 1

Allinda Winery 1 C5
Badgers Brook Winery 2 D7
Bianchet Winery 3 A7
Brahams Creek Winery 4 H8
Britannia Falls Winery 5 G9
Coldstream Hills 6 D8
De Bortoli Wines 7 C4
Domaine Chandon 8 C6
Eyton on Yarra 9 D7
Fergusson Winery & Restaurant 10 C5
Five Oaks Vineyard 11 C10
Kellybrook Winery & Restaurant 12 A7
Lirralirra Estate 13 A8
Long Gully Estate 14 D5
Lovey's Estate 15 C5
McWilliams Lillydale Vineyards 16 D9
Oakridge Estate 17 C7
Paternoster 18 D13
St Huberts Vineyard 19 C7
Shantell Vineyard 20 C4
Steels Creek Estate 21 B4
Tarrawarra Estate 22 D6
Warramate Vineyard 23 D7
Yarra Burn Winery & Restaurant 24 F9
Yarra Ridge 25 B6
Yarra Track Winery 26 C6
Yering Station-Yarrabank Vineyards 27 B6

Pheasant Creek
Glenburn
Mt Despair 884m
Buxton
Buxton Trout Farm
Kinglake Central
Kinglake East
Castella
Toolangi
Marysville
Mount Slide
Steels Creek
Dixons Creek
Narbethong
Mittons Bridge
Christmas Hills
Yarra Glen
Healesville
Badger Creek
Coldstream
Gruyere
Lilydale
Wandin North
Seville
Woori Yallock
Launching Place
Millgrove
Warburton East
Warburton
Wesburn
Wandin Yallock
Yarra Junction
Big Pats Creek
Mt Evelyn
Monbulk
Yellingbo
Hoddles Creek
Gladysdale
Three Bridges
Kalorama
Silvan
Olinda
Sherbrooke
Monbulk
Macclesfield
The Patch
Belgrave
Selby
Menzies Creek
Avonsleigh
Clematis
Emerald
Cockatoo
Gembrook

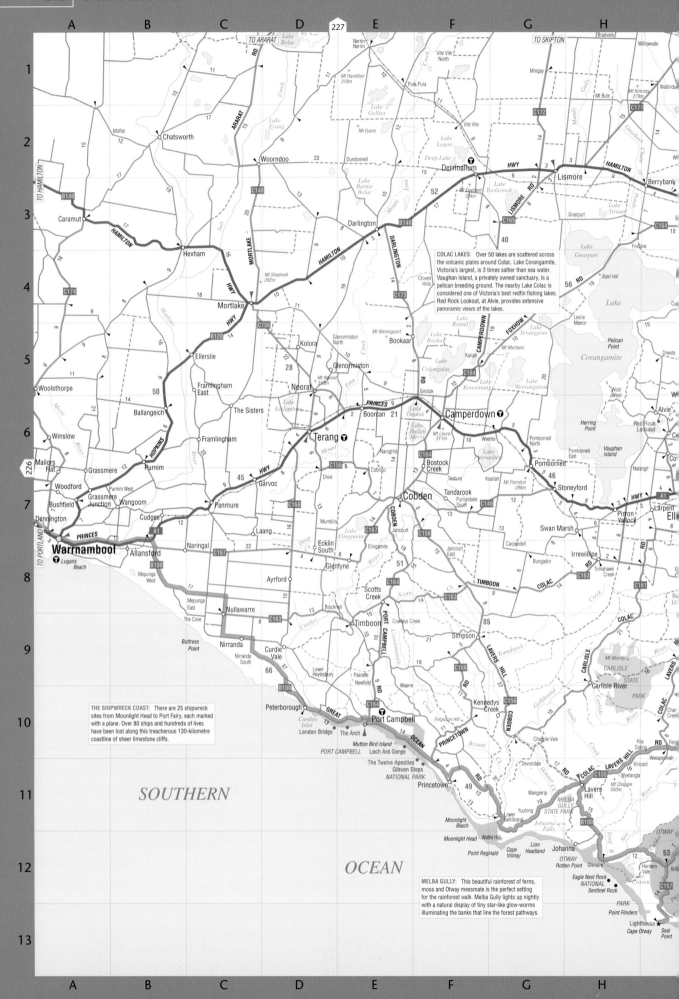

COLAC LAKES: Over 50 lakes are scattered across the volcanic plains around Colac. Lake Corangamite, Victoria's largest, is 3 times saltier than sea water. Vaughan Island, a privately owned sanctuary, is a pelican breeding ground. The nearby Lake Colac is considered one of Victoria's best redfin fishing lakes. Red Rock Lookout, at Alvie, provides extensive panoramic views of the lakes.

THE SHIPWRECK COAST: There are 25 shipwreck sites from Moonlight Head to Port Fairy, each marked with a plane. Over 80 ships and hundreds of lives have been lost along this treacherous 130-kilometre coastline of sheer limestone cliffs.

MELBA GULLY: This beautiful rainforest of ferns, moss and Otway messmate is the perfect setting for the rainforest walk. Melba Gully lights up nightly with a natural display of tiny star-like glow-worms illuminating the banks that line the forest pathways.

SOUTHERN

OCEAN

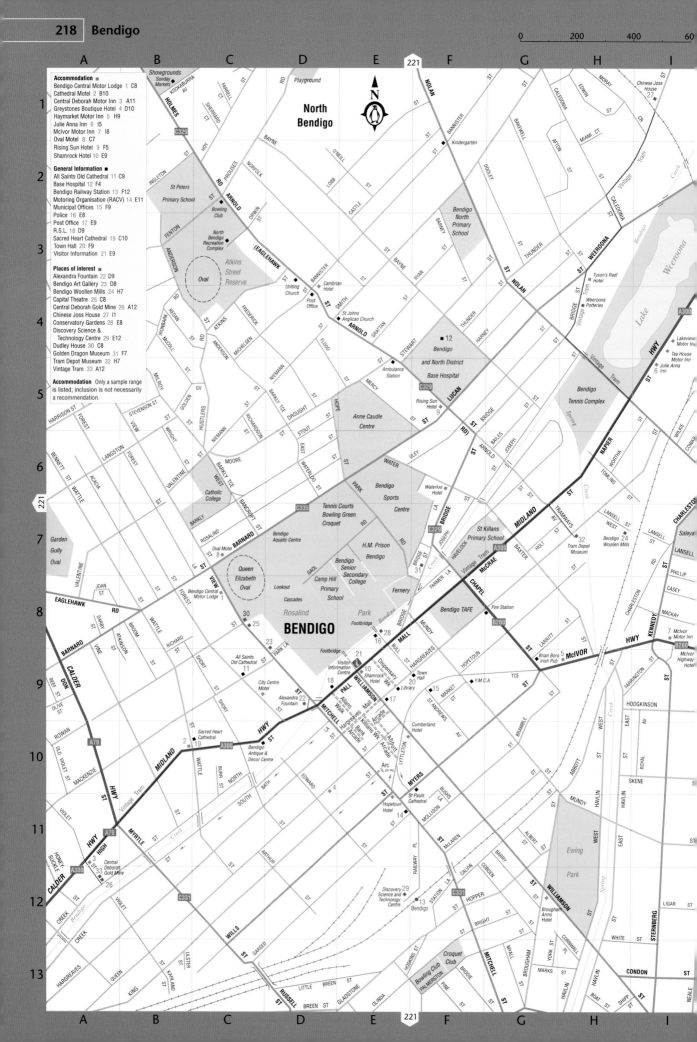

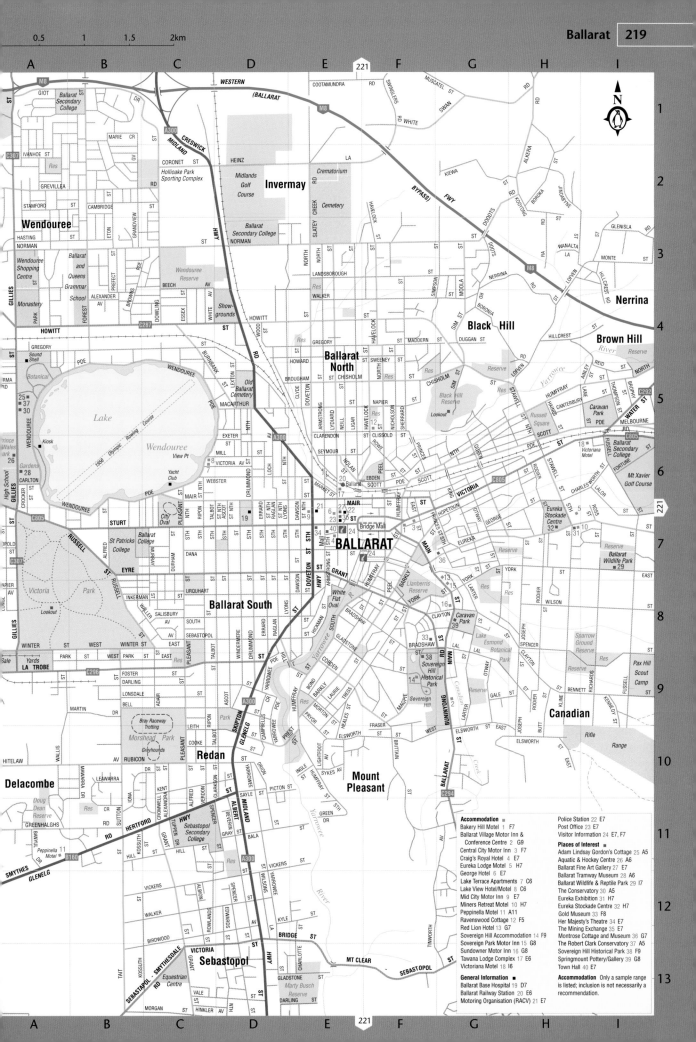

Accommodation
Bakery Hill Motel 1 F7
Ballarat Village Motor Inn & Conference Centre 2 G9
Central City Motor Inn 3 F7
Craig's Royal Hotel 4 E7
Eureka Lodge Motel 5 H7
George Hotel 6 E7
Lake Terrace Apartments 7 C6
Lake View Hotel/Motel 8 C6
Mid City Motor Inn 9 E7
Miners Retreat Motel 10 H7
Peppinella Motel 11 A11
Ravenswood Cottage 12 F5
Red Lion Hotel 13 G7
Sovereign Hill Accommodation 14 F9
Sovereign Park Motor Inn 15 G8
Sundowner Motor Inn 16 G8
Tawana Lodge Complex 17 E6
Victoriana Motel 18 I6

General Information
Ballarat Base Hospital 19 D7
Ballarat Railway Station 20 E6
Motoring Organisation (RACV) 21 E7

Police Station 22 E7
Post Office 23 E7
Visitor Information 24 E7, F7

Places of Interest
Adam Lindsay Gordon's Cottage 25 A5
Aquatic & Hockey Centre 26 A6
Ballarat Fine Art Gallery 27 E7
Ballarat Tramway Museum 28 A6
Ballarat Wildlife & Reptile Park 29 I7
The Conservatory 30 A5
Eureka Exhibition 31 H7
Eureka Stockade Centre 32 H7
Gold Museum 33 F8
Her Majesty's Theatre 34 E7
The Mining Exchange 35 E7
Montrose Cottage and Museum 36 G7
The Robert Clark Conservatory 37 A5
Sovereign Hill Historical Park 38 F9
Springmount Pottery/Gallery 39 G8
Town Hall 40 E7

Accommodation Only a sample range is listed; inclusion is not necessarily a recommendation.

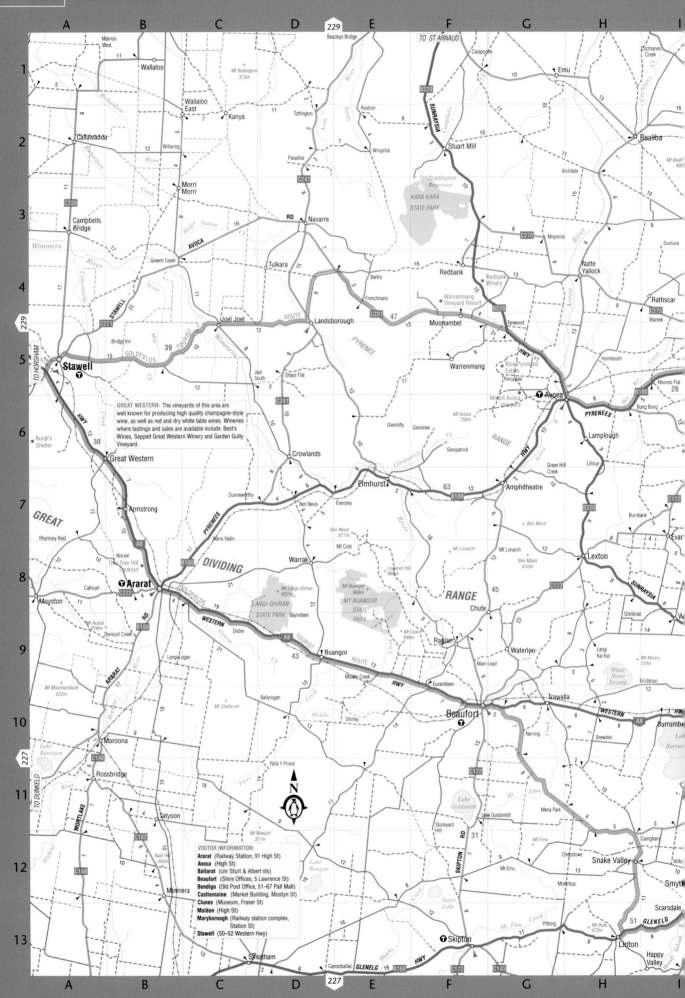

GREAT WESTERN: The vineyards of this area are well known for producing high quality champagne-style wine, as well as red and dry white table wines. Wineries where tastings and sales are available include: Best's Wines, Seppelt Great Western Winery and Garden Gully Vineyard.

VISITOR INFORMATION:
Ararat (Railway Station, 91 High St)
Avoca (High St)
Ballarat (cnr Sturt & Albert sts)
Beaufort (Shire Offices, 5 Lawrence St)
Bendigo (Old Post Office, 51–67 Pall Mall)
Castlemaine (Market Building, Mostyn St)
Clunes (Museum, Fraser St)
Maldon (High St)
Maryborough (Railway station complex, Station St)
Stawell (50–52 Western Hwy)

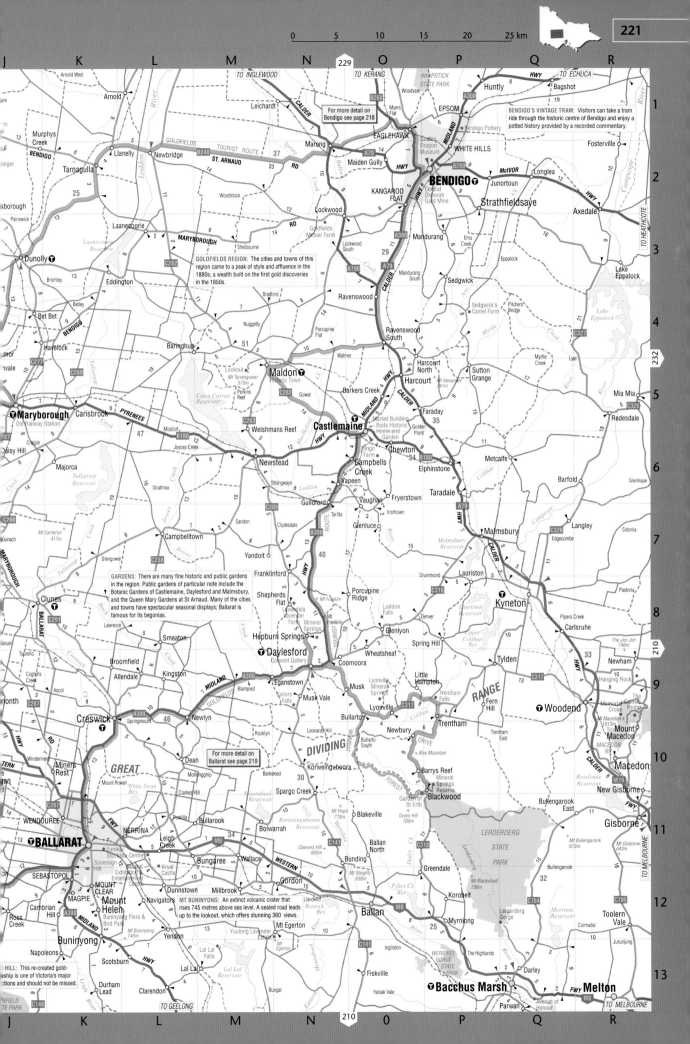

0 5 10 15 20 25 km

229

TO INGLEWOOD

TO KERANG

TO ECHUCA

For more detail on Bendigo see page 218

BENDIGO'S VINTAGE TRAM: Visitors can take a tram ride through the historic centre of Bendigo and enjoy a potted history provided by a recorded commentary.

GOLDFIELDS TOURIST ROUTE

ST. ARNAUD RD

MARYBOROUGH

GOLDFIELDS REGION: The cities and towns of this region came to a peak of style and affluence in the 1880s, a wealth built on the first gold discoveries in the 1850s.

Arnold West
Arnold
Leichardt
Woodvale
Huntly
Bagshot
Fosterville

Murphys Creek
Llanelly
Newbridge
Marong
Maiden Gully
EAGLEHAWK
EPSOM
Bendigo Pottery
WHITE HILLS
Golden Dragon Museum

Tarnagulla
Laanecoorie
Woodstock
Lockwood
KANGAROO FLAT
BENDIGO
Central Deborah Gold Mine
Strathfieldsaye
Longlea
Junortoun
Axedale

Painswick
Laanecoorie Reservoir
Shelbourne
Bradford
Lockwood South
Mandurang
Mandurang South
Sedgwick
Emu Creek
Eppalock
Lake Eppalock

Dunolly
Bromley
Eddington
Betley
Nuggetty
Ravenswood
Sedgwick's Camel Farm
Pilchers Bridge

Bet Bet
Havelock
Baringhup
Porcupine Flat
Walmer
Ravenswood South
Harcourt North
Sutton Grange
Myrtle Creek
Lyal
Mia Mia
Redesdale

Maryborough
Carisbrook
Moolort
Maldon
Mt Tarrengower 570m
Perkins Reef
Barkers Creek
Harcourt
Mt Alexander 741m
Faraday
Golden Point

Daisy Hill
Craigie
Welshmans Reef
Gowar
Market Building
Buda Historic Home and Garden
Dingo Farm
Chewton
Metcalfe
Barfold
Glenhope

Majorca
Strathlea
Newstead
Campbells Creek
Yapeen
Elphinstone
Taradale
Langley
Sidonia

Campbelltown
Yandoit
Guildford
Vaughan
Fryerstown
Glenluce
Malmsbury
Edgecombe

GARDENS: There are many fine historic and public gardens in the region. Public gardens of particular note include the Botanic Gardens of Castlemaine, Daylesford and Malmsbury, and the Queen Mary Gardens at St Arnaud. Many of the cities and towns have spectacular seasonal displays; Ballarat is famous for its begonias.

Clunes
Glengower
Franklinford
Clydesdale
Tarilla
Porcupine Ridge
Drummond
Lauriston
Kyneton
Pipers Creek
Carlsruhe

Lawrence
Shepherds Flat
Mt Franklin
Lauriston Reservoir
Newham

Smeaton
Hepburn Springs
Mineral Springs
Glenlyon
Spring Hill
Tylden
Hanging Rock

Broomfield
Allendale
Kingston
Daylesford
Convent Gallery
Wheatsheaf
RANGE
Fern Hill
Woodend
Memorial Cross

Coghills Creek
Ascot
Newlyn
Coomoora
Musk
Lyonville Mineral Springs
Little Hampton
Trentham Falls
Mount Macedon

Creswick
Springmount
Rocklyn
Lyonville
Bullarto
Newbury
Trentham
New Gisborne

Miners Rest
Dean
Korweinguboora
Bullarto South
Blue Mountain
Gisborne

GREAT DIVIDING RANGE
Mount Rowan
Mollongghip
Barkstead
Barrys Reef
Blackwood
Garden of St Erth
Green Hill 705m
LERDERDERG STATE PARK

WENDOUREE
Nerrina
Bolwarrah
Spargo Creek
Blakeville
Greendale
Bullengarook East

BALLARAT
Eureka Stockade Centre
Sovereign Hill
Ballarat Exhibition Entertainment Centre
Bungaree
Wallace
Bunding
Ballan North
Bullengarook
Gisborne

SEBASTOPOL
MOUNT CLEAR
MAGPIE
Kryal Castle
Millbrook
Gordon
Ballan
Korobeit
Lerderderg Gorge
Merrimu Reservoir
Toolern Vale

Cambrian Hill
Mount Helen
Dunnstown
Mt Egerton
Myrniong
Bacchus Marsh
Melton

MT BUNINYONG: An extinct volcanic crater that rises 745 metres above sea level. A sealed road leads up to the lookout, which offers stunning 360 views.

Buninyong
Yendon
Yuulong Lavender Estate
Ingliston
WERRIBEE GORGE STATE PARK

Napoleons
Scotsburn
Lal Lal Falls
Lal Lal Reservoir
Bungal
Darley

TO GEELONG

TO MELBOURNE

210

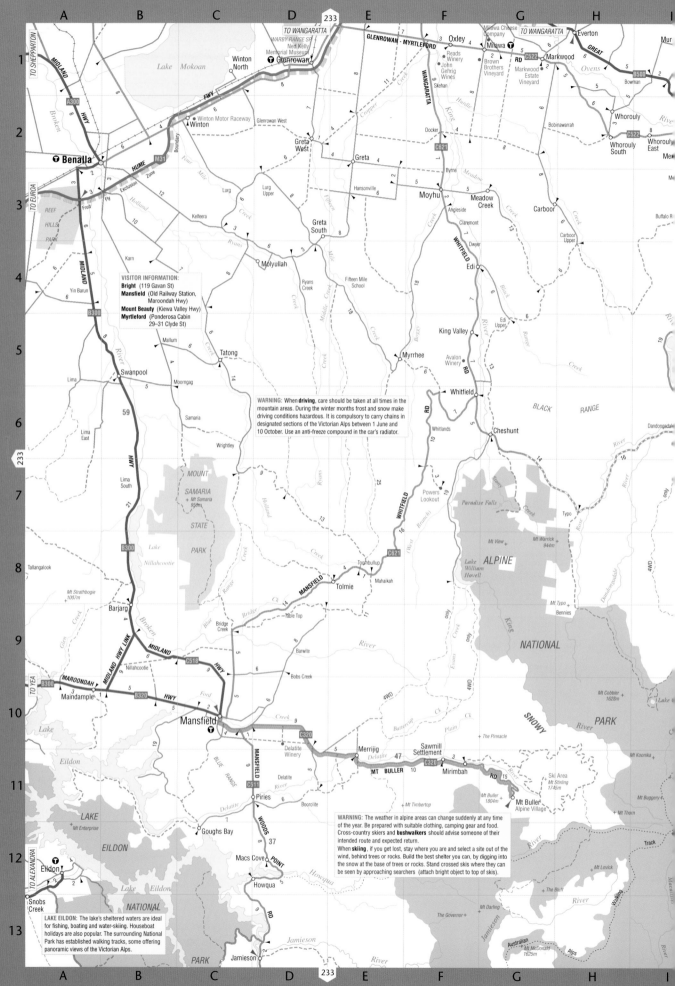

VISITOR INFORMATION:
Bright (119 Gavan St)
Mansfield (Old Railway Station, Maroondah Hwy)
Mount Beauty (Kiewa Valley Hwy)
Myrtleford (Ponderosa Cabin 29–31 Clyde St)

WARNING: When **driving**, care should be taken at all times in the mountain areas. During the winter months frost and snow make driving conditions hazardous. It is compulsory to carry chains in designated sections of the Victorian Alps between 1 June and 10 October. Use an anti-freeze compound in the car's radiator.

WARNING: The weather in alpine areas can change suddenly at any time of the year. Be prepared with suitable clothing, camping gear and food. Cross-country skiers and **bushwalkers** should advise someone of their intended route and expected return.
When **skiing**, if you get lost, stay where you are and select a site out of the wind, behind trees or rocks. Build the best shelter you can, by digging into the snow at the base of trees or rocks. Stand crossed skis where they can be seen by approaching searchers (attach bright object to top of skis).

LAKE EILDON: The lake's sheltered waters are ideal for fishing, boating and water-skiing. Houseboat holidays are also popular. The surrounding National Park has established walking tracks, some offering panoramic views of the Victorian Alps.

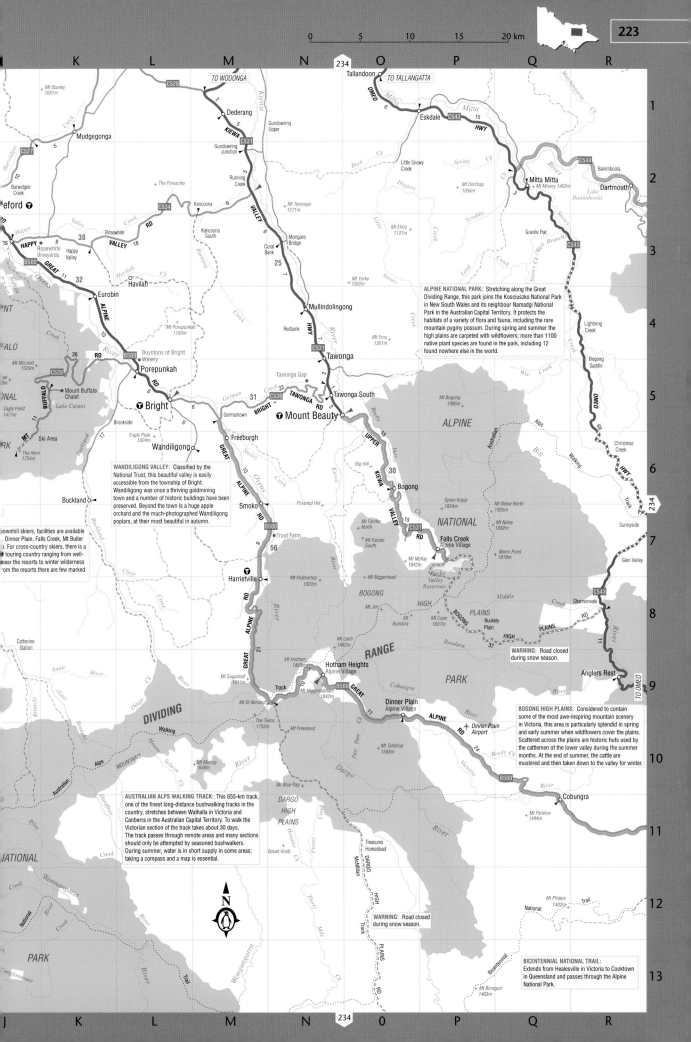

0 5 10 15 20 km

K **L** **M** **N** **O** **P** **Q** **R**

Mt Stanley 1051m +

Mudgegonga

C527
eford ⊕

C528 **TO WODONGA**

Dederang

KIEWA 5

Gundowring Upper

Gundowring Junction

C531

Running Creek

+ *The Pinnacles*

C534 Kancoona

6

Kancoona South

Rosewhite

Creek

C527 10

Barwidgee Creek

Happy

38 9

HAPPY Rosewhite Vineyards

B500 **GREAT** 11 32

Havilah

Eurobin

ALPINE 10

Porepunkah

C535 **BUFFALO** 26 **RD**

Boyntons of Bright Winery

B500 **RD** 6

+ *Mt Porepunkah 1193m*

⊕ **Bright**

Brookside

BRIGHT – TAWONGA RD 31

Germantown

6 6

Wandiligong

Freeburgh

GREAT

Buckland

ALPINE 10

Smoko

RD

B500

• Trout Farm

9

56

Harrietville ⊕

Mt Feathertop 1922m +

+ *Mt Niggerhead*

Gundowring Upper

KIEWA **VALLEY** 18

Kancoona

6

Coral Bank

Mongans Bridge

25

Redbank

Mullindolingong

HWY C531

Tawonga

2

Tawonga Gap

22 1

TAWONGA RD

Tawonga South

⊕ **Mount Beauty**

UPPER 15

Big Hill

KIEWA 30

Bogong

VALLEY 15

C531

RD

Mt Fainter North +

+ *Mt Fainter South*

+ *Mt McKay 1842m*

Falls Creek Alpine Village

Rocky Valley Reservoir

BOGONG

Mt Jim +

+ *Mt Bundara*

HIGH

RANGE

Mt Loch 1862m +

Mt Hotham 1868m +

Hotham Heights Alpine Village

Mt Higginbotham 1842m +

B500 **GREAT**

Track

Mt Sugarloaf 1541m +

+ *Mt St Bernard*

GREAT

ALPINE 21

RD

The Twins 1703m +

+ *Mt Freezeout*

10

Dinner Plain Alpine Village

11

ALPINE **RD**

Dinner Plain Airport

+ *Mt Tabletop 1588m*

B500

24

Cobungra

+ *Mt Parslow 1494m*

DIVIDING

Catherine Station

Annie River

Dingo Ck

MOUNTAINS

Walking

+ *Mt Murray 1640m*

DARGO

HIGH

PLAINS

Mt Blue Rag +

Treasures Homestead

DARGO

HIGH

PLAINS

RD

+ *Mt Phipps 1402m*

National

Trail

+ *Mt Birregun 1463m*

Bicentennial

PARK

Mt Stanley 1051m

Tallandoon

OMEO **TO TALLANGATTA**

6

Eskdale C543 15 **HWY**

Mitta Mitta

+ *Mt Misery 1403m*

3

Granite Flat

C543

+ *Mt Dorchap 1056m*

Little Snowy Creek

Spring Ck

Mitta

River

C544

Banimboola

Dartmouth

Lake Banimboola

+ *Mt Elmo 1101m*

Diggers Creek

Scrubbs

+ *Mt Yorke 1262m*

+ *Mt Emu 1361m*

Lightning Creek

Bogong Saddle

OMEO

HWY

69

Christmas Creek

234

Sunnyside

Glen Valley

C543

Shannonvale

11

Anglers Rest

TO OMEO 234

+ *Mt Bogong 1986m*

ALPINE

NATIONAL

Spion Kopje 1834m +

+ *Mt Nelse North 1885m*

+ *Mt Nelse 1882m*

+ *Marm Point 1819m*

PLAINS

Middle Creek

Buckety Plain

HIGH **PLAINS**

BOGONG **HIGH**

PARK

River

Reedy Ck

River

ALPINE NATIONAL PARK: Stretching along the Great Dividing Range, this park joins the Kosciuszko National Park in New South Wales and its neighbour Namadgi National Park in the Australian Capital Territory. It protects the habitats of a variety of flora and fauna, including the rare mountain pygmy possum. During spring and summer the high plains are carpeted with wildflowers; more than 1100 native plant species are found in the park, including 12 found nowhere else in the world.

WANDILIGONG VALLEY: Classified by the National Trust, this beautiful valley is easily accessible from the township of Bright. Wandiligong was once a thriving goldmining town and a number of historic buildings have been preserved. Beyond the town is a huge apple orchard and the much-photographed Wandiligong poplars, at their most beautiful in autumn.

ownhill skiers, facilities are available Dinner Plain, Falls Creek, Mt Buller . For cross-country skiers, there is a touring country ranging from well-near the resorts to winter wilderness om the resorts there are few marked

AUSTRALIAN ALPS WALKING TRACK: This 655-km track, one of the finest long-distance bushwalking tracks in the country, stretches between Walhalla in Victoria and Canberra in the Australian Capital Territory. To walk the Victorian section of the track takes about 30 days. The track passes through remote areas and many sections should only be attempted by seasoned bushwalkers. During summer, water is in short supply in some areas; taking a compass and a map is essential.

BOGONG HIGH PLAINS: Considered to contain some of the most awe-inspiring mountain scenery in Victoria, this area is particularly splendid in spring and early summer when wildflowers cover the plains. Scattered across the plains are historic huts used by the cattlemen of the lower valley during the summer months. At the end of summer, the cattle are mustered and then taken down to the valley for winter.

WARNING: Road closed during snow season.

WARNING: Road closed during snow season.

BICENTENNIAL NATIONAL TRAIL: Extends from Healesville in Victoria to Cooktown in Queensland and passes through the Alpine National Park.

N

J **K** **L** **M** **N** **O** **P** **Q** **R**

1 2 3 4 5 6 7 8 9 10 11 12 13

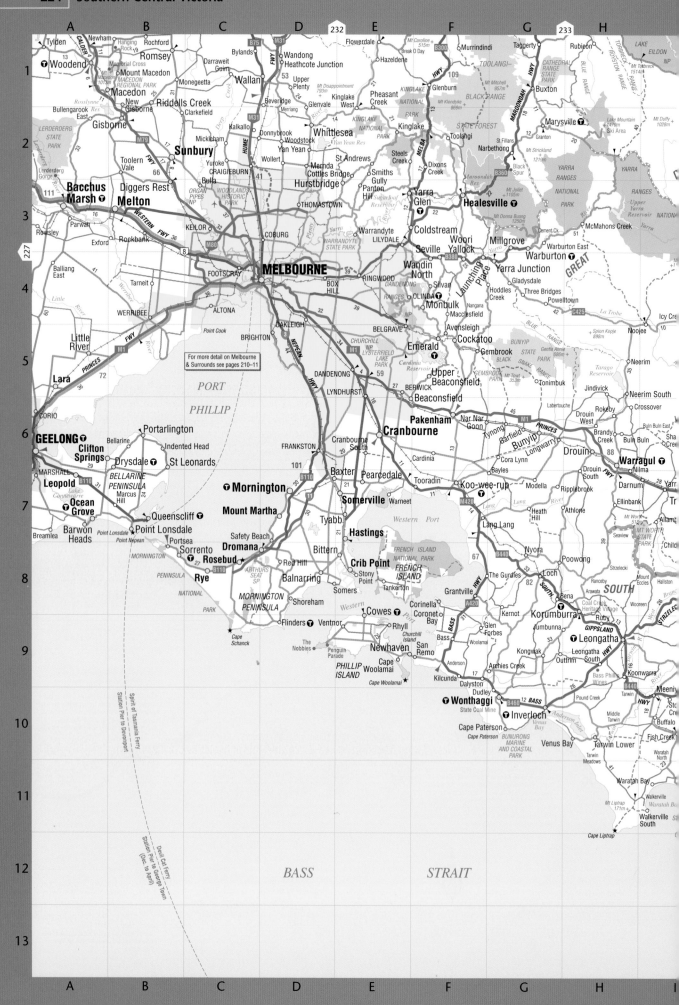

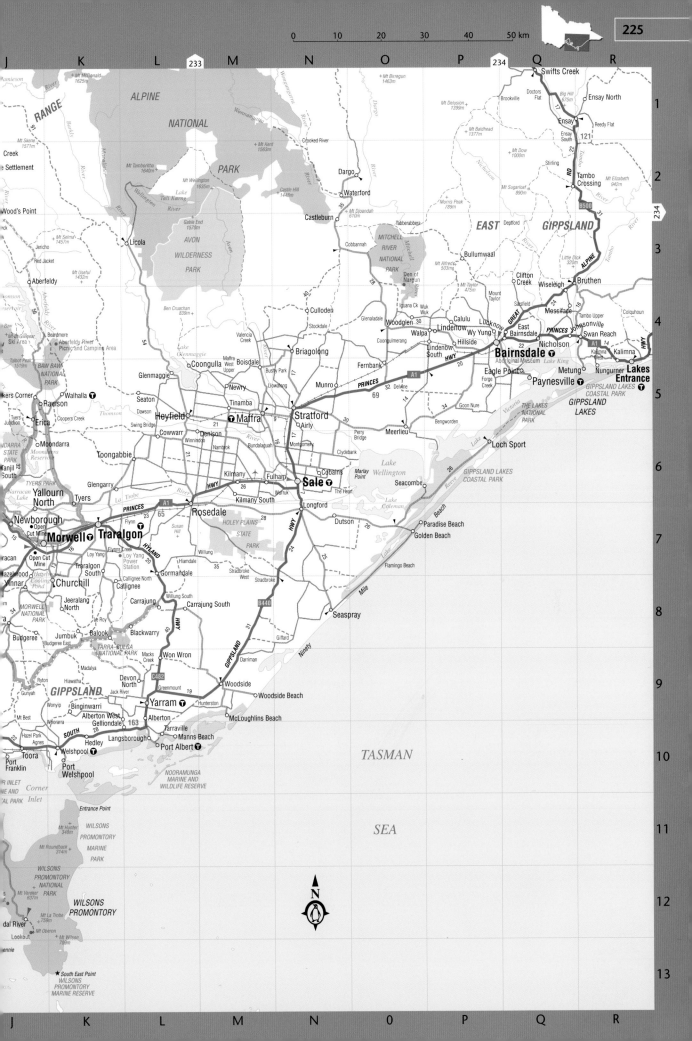

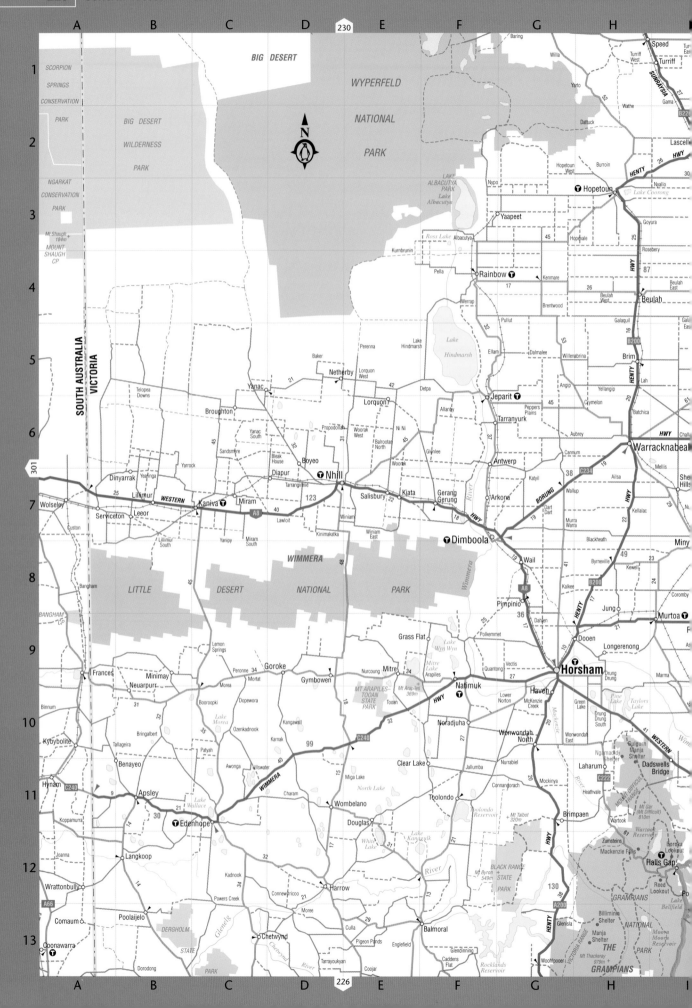

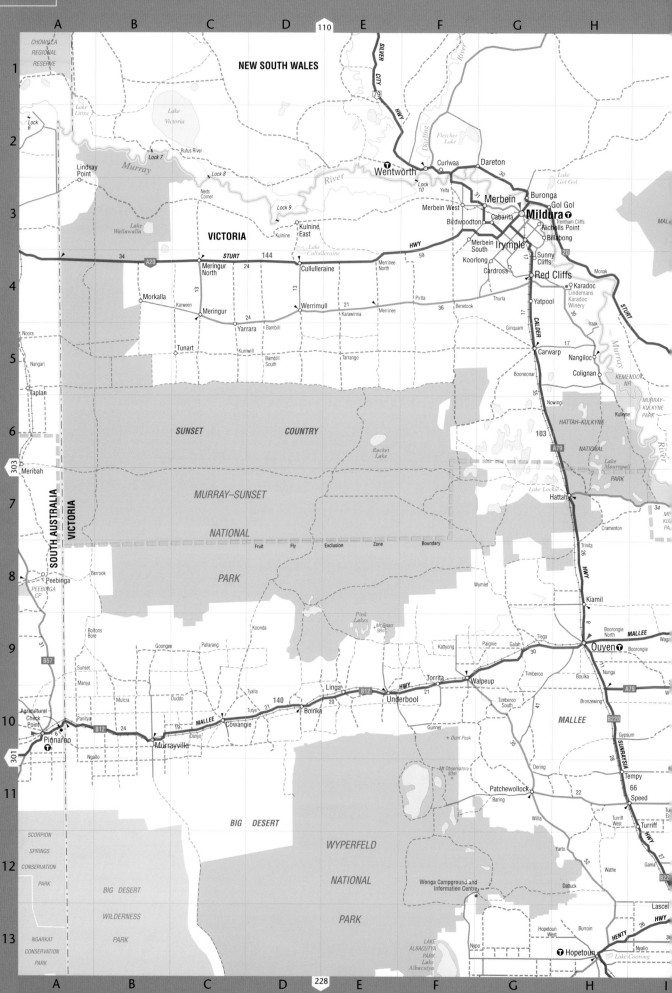

SILVER CITY HWY 79

NEW SOUTH WALES

CHOWILLA REGIONAL RESERVE

Lock 6

Lake Littra

Lake Victoria

Murray

Lindsay Point

Rufus River

Lock 7

Lock 8

Neds Corner

Lock 9

Kulnine

Kulnine East

Lake Cullulleraine

VICTORIA

Lake Wallawalla

Darling River

Fletcher Lake

Wentworth

Curlwaa

Dareton

Lock 10

Yelta

Merbein

Merbein West

Birdwoodton

Cabarita

Buronga

Gol Gol

Mildura

Trentham Cliffs

Nicholls Point

Billabong

Lake Gol Gol

MALe

34 A20 STURT 144

Meringur North 24

Cullulleraine

Merrinee North

HWY 59

Merbein South

Koorlong

Cardross

Irymple

Sunny Cliffs

Red Cliffs

STURT 20

Monak

Murray

Morkalla

Karween

Meringur 13

Werrimull

21

Karawinna

Merrinee

Pirlta

36

Benetook

Thurla

Yatpool

Karadoc

Lindemans Karadoc Winery

Iraak

KEMENDOK NR

Yarrara

Bambill

24

Tunart

Kurnwill

Bambill South

Tarrango

Carwarp

Boonoonar

Nowingi

Nangiloc

Colignan

17

CALDER

35

103 A79

HATTAH-KULKYNE

NATIONAL

Lake Mournpall

PARK

MURRAY-KULKYNE PARK

Kulkyne

River

Noora

Nangari

Taplan

303

Meribah

SOUTH AUSTRALIA   VICTORIA

B57

31

Berrook

Peebinga

PEEBINGA CP

SUNSET COUNTRY

Rocket Lake

MURRAY–SUNSET

NATIONAL

Fruit Fly Exclusion Zone Boundary

PARK

Lake Lockie

Hattah

Cramenton

34

Mt KU KU PA

Trinita

HWY 26

Kiamil

8

Boorongie North

MALLEE

Boorongie

Ouyen

Nunga

A79

W

Boltons Bore

Goongee

Pallarang

Sunset

Manya

Koonda

Pink Lakes

Mt Gnarr 98m

Wymlet

Kattyong

Paignie

Galah

Tiega

30

Timberoo

Boulka

Murrayville

Ngallo

Pinnaroo

301

Agricultural Check Point

6

Panitya

24

Danyo

T9

MALLEE

Cowangie

Tutye 21

20

140

Boinka

Linga

B12

Underbool

HWY

Torrita

Walpeup

Timberoo South

Gunner

Dunt Peak

41

Dering

35

Bronzewing

MALLEE

B220

SUNRAYSIA

28

Gypsum

Tempy

66

Speed

Mt Observatory 93m

Patchewollock

Baring

Willa

22

Turriff West

Turriff

HWY

27

SCORPION SPRINGS CONSERVATION PARK

BIG DESERT

WYPERFELD

NATIONAL

PARK

BIG DESERT

WILDERNESS PARK

NGARKAT CONSERVATION PARK

Wonga Campground and Information Centre

Dattuck

Yarto

Wathe

52

Gama

B22

Lascel

HENTY HWY 26

Hopetoun West

Burroin

Nypo

Hopetoun

LAKE ALBACUTYA PARK

Lake Albacutya

Nyallo

Lake Coorong

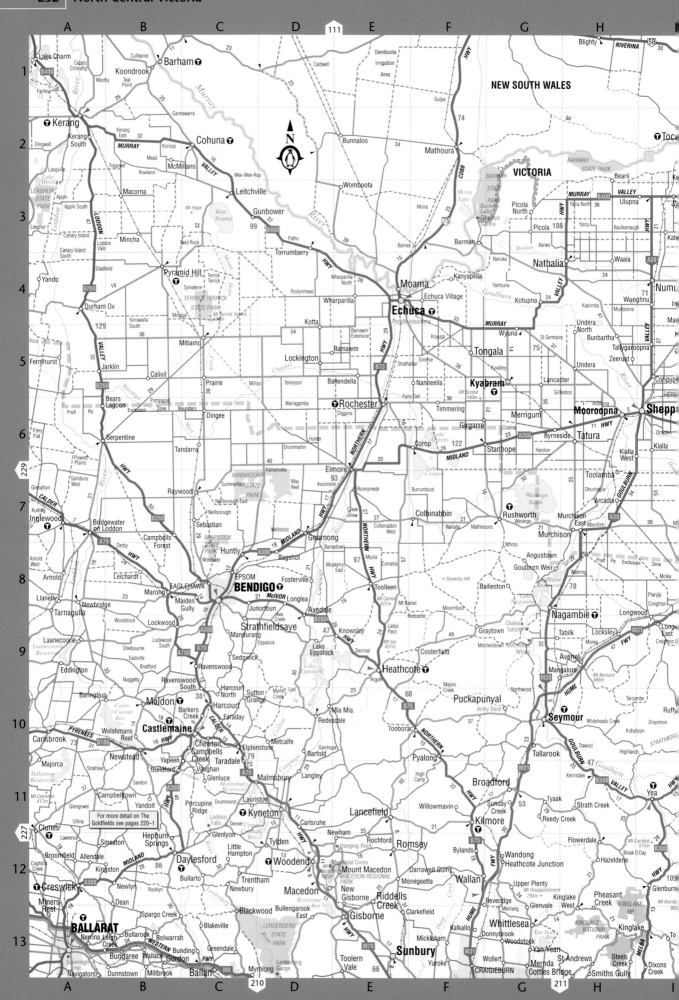

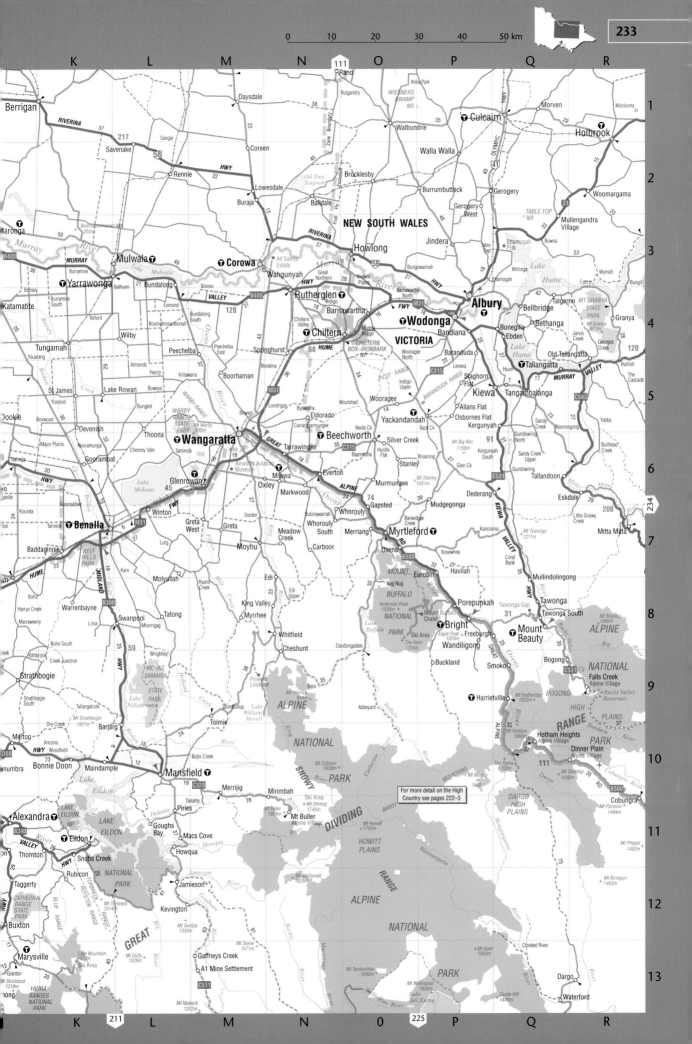

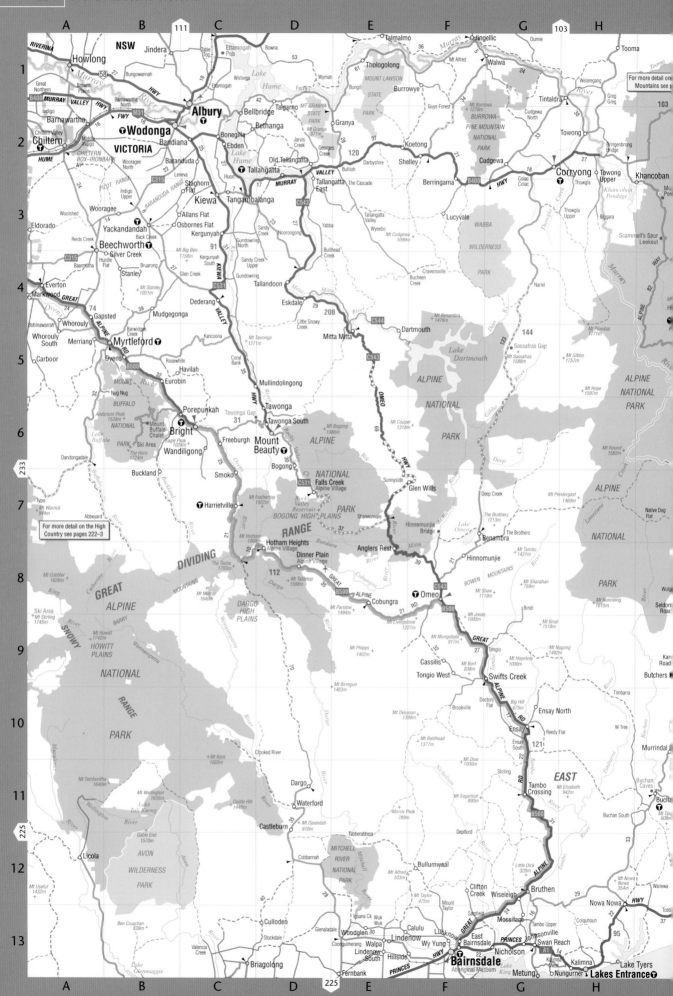

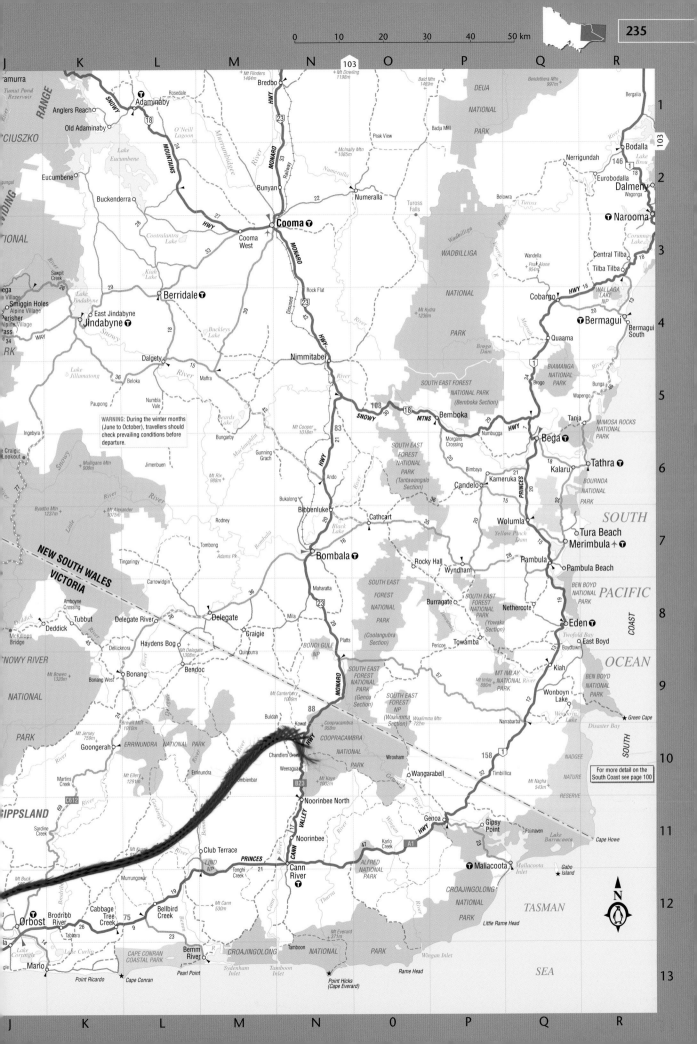

SOUTH AUSTRALIA

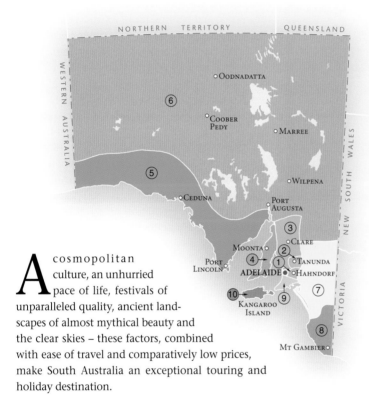

A cosmopolitan culture, an unhurried pace of life, festivals of unparalleled quality, ancient land-scapes of almost mythical beauty and the clear skies – these factors, combined with ease of travel and comparatively low prices, make South Australia an exceptional touring and holiday destination.

From desert to sea

South Australia is the driest State in the world's driest continent after Antarctica. It lies mid-way across the south end of the continent and has an area of just under a million square kilometres.

The 3700-kilometre coastline offers a diversity of scenery, ranging from seaside cliffs edging the Nullarbor Plain to the blue-green shallows of Gulf St Vincent, the wetlands and sandhills of The Coorong, and the bush-fringed wild beaches of Kangaroo Island.

South Australia's most spectacular mountain range, the Flinders Ranges, extend north-east from the head of Spencer Gulf. The beauty of this eroded landscape is equalled only by its geological significance as one of the oldest landscapes on earth.

The range country gives way to vast salt lakes. Lake Eyre, the largest, is 15 metres below sea level and is dry for most of the time. A vast sand and gibber desert extends north and west of the great salt lakes to the borders of Western Australia and the Northern Territory. Much of this area receives less than 150 millimetres of rain annually.

Most of the State's agricultural activity, including its huge and well-known wine industry is located along the fertile plains and hills of the south-east corner of the State, which is also where the Murray River's South Australian journey begins and ends.

Living on the land

Aboriginal people have inhabited the land known today as South Australia for at least 40 000 years.

Bethany Wines in the Barossa Valley

Anthropologists estimate the Aboriginal population at the time of European settlement at about 15 000, divided into 50 or so groups. The Aboriginal peoples were nomadic hunters and gatherers but their material culture varied with their geographical habitat. In the arid western desert, very small groups moved constantly between waterholes, hunting wildlife. The groups living in the central lakes district benefited from the great north–south trading route that ran the length of the continent, while the peoples of the more temperate and the coastal regions hunted game, fished, gathered wild fruit and nuts and made reed baskets.

German-style house built in Hahndorf in the 1840s

Whaleboat down the Murray

The first Europeans sighted the coast of South Australia in 1627 when a Dutch ship, the *Gulden Zeepaard* (Golden Seahorse), sailed into the Great Australian Bight while on a voyage to the East Indies. A few years later Abel Tasman mapped part of the South Australian coast, and Flinders and Baudin made separate surveys in 1802. Charles Sturt reached South Australia overland in 1829–30 by sailing a whaleboat down the Murray River.

Under the gum tree

Early in the 1830s a group of English businessmen formed the South Australian Land Company to establish a colony in South Australia. The objective was to create 'a virtuous and enlightened society'. They envisaged an agrarian paradise funded by land sales and populated by free settlers rather than convicts. The British Government passed the South Australian Act in 1834, authorising the colony. In November 1836 Surveyor-General Colonel Light surveyed the site of Adelaide in preparation for his famously elegant plan for the city. The following month, in a ceremony conducted under a gum tree at Glenelg, Governor Hindmarsh proclaimed South Australia a colony.

Representative government arrived in South Australia in 1851 with the establishment of a Legislative Council. Responsible government was established in 1856 with the creation of a Legislative Assembly. South Australia became one of the six Australian States, with Federation in 1901.

New ideas

South Australia, with its history of enlightened democracy, has been described as a laboratory for new social and political ideas. Australia's first significant non-British immigrant group found its home in South Australia: a group of 517 German immigrants, most of them Lutheran peasants fleeing religious persecution, arrived in 1838 and began laying down roots and traditions still evident in South Australian life and society today. South Australian women were given the right to vote and stand for Parliament in 1896. Australia's first Aboriginal governor, Sir Douglas Nicholls, was appointed in 1976 and Australia's first female governor, Dame Roma Mitchell, was appointed in 1991. In the 1970s, South Australia's reputation as a leader in social change and policy skyrocketed with the election of Don Dunstan as premier (1970–79). A self-confessed rebel, Dunstan oversaw radical changes in such areas as consumer protection, the environment, Aboriginal land rights and homosexual law.

Land of plenty

South Australia today has a population of 1 500 000. The State that the first settlers imagined as a paradise for landholders and farmers is now heavily urbanised, with about 70 per cent of the population living in Adelaide. Discoveries of rich mineral deposits from the 1840s onwards shifted the economic focus away from agricultural self-sufficiency to mining and export activities. With this, the importance of the major towns and the capital increased. Nevertheless, the agrarian spirit lives on. South Australia, despite its low rainfall and its focus on heavy industry and mining, remains a place of produce. It boasts fine vineyards, orchards, olive and almond groves, shimmering wheat fields and abundantly stocked coastal waters.

For more information on South Australia, see Tourist Bureaus on p. 591.

ADELAIDE

St Peter's Cathedral and Pennington Gardens

ADELAIDE is set on the wide curves of the River Torrens between the Mount Lofty Ranges and Gulf St Vincent. Its immediate location belies the fact that beyond the rolling hills lie great tracts of desert – Adelaide is the capital of the driest State in the world's second-driest continent.

It is a well-planned city, thanks to Colonel Light, the first Surveyor-General. It is the only major metropolis in the world where the city's centre is completely encircled by parkland. It has a population of almost 1.1 million, but feels smaller and, despite its bustle and cosmopolitan character, it remains a friendly and open place. The city offers visitors a regular calendar of festivals, a well-preserved history, a large and varied arts program, the warmth and light of the South Australian outdoors, and excellent wining and dining.

EXPLORING ADELAIDE
Adelaide's city centre is compact and easily negotiated on foot. For those

GETTING AROUND

Airport shuttle bus
Transit Regency Coaches (08) 8381 5311

Motoring organisation
*Royal Automobile Association of South Australia
(RAA) (08) 8202 4600*

Car rental
*Avis 13 6333; Budget 1300 362 848;
Hertz 13 3039; Thrifty 1300 367 227*

Public transport
*Passenger Transport Information Hotline
(08) 8210 1000*

Taxis
*Suburban Transport Services (08) 8212 2766;
United Yellow Cabs 13 2227*

Torrens River cruises
Popeye Motor Launches (08) 8295 4747

Port Adelaide cruises
Port Adelaide River Cruises (08) 8341 1194

Bicycle hire
*Contact Bicycle SA for operators
(08) 8232 2644*

who like some help getting around, or those wishing to travel further out, there is a safe, clean and efficient public transport system. The **Explorer Tram** offers visitors the chance to tour the city's attractions at a leisurely pace and with the benefit of a recorded commentary. This tram replica has many stopping points and visitors can board and alight as they wish. A fleet of **Popeye** motor launches cruise the River Torrens and also provide an ideal means of transport to the Adelaide Zoo. The **Trans Adelaide's O-Bahn** is the longest guided busway in the world. The busway runs alongside the river, from the city to Modbury, through its own landscaped park. The historic **Glenelg tram** is the most famous of Adelaide's tourist rides. It departs Victoria Square regularly for a return trip to Adelaide's premier seaside suburb. The **MV Port Princess**, operating from Port Adelaide, carries visitors down the Port Adelaide River, taking in historic sites and beaches and providing a chance to see dolphins. Car travel is recommended

for touring some of the farther-flung regions; the roads are excellent and, provided you have a road map, navigation should not be a problem.

CITY CENTRE

The centre of Adelaide is a well-planned area of wide streets, low buildings and plenty of open public areas. An exploration of the city should start at **Rundle Mall**, the city's major shopping precinct. It is a pleasant tree-lined area where shoppers can sit and watch the passing parade and regular street entertainment. There are department stores, boutique outlets, and arcades off the mall. The historic **Adelaide Arcade** (1885) is a fine example of the highly decorative style of Victorian retail architecture.

From Rundle Mall enter King William Street and head south. On the right-hand side is **Edmund Wright House** (1878) distinguished by its elaborate Renaissance facade. Travelling exhibitions from the National Museum of Australia are held here and it is also the home of the State History Centre. Further along and across

ADELAIDE BY AREA

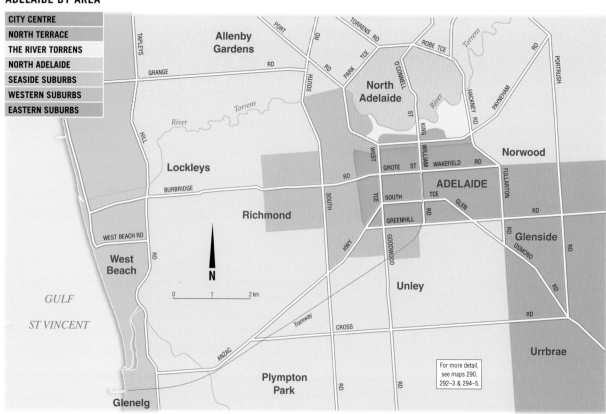

CITY CENTRE
NORTH TERRACE
THE RIVER TORRENS
NORTH ADELAIDE
SEASIDE SUBURBS
WESTERN SUBURBS
EASTERN SUBURBS

For more detail, see maps 290, 292–3 & 294–5.

Palm House in the Botanic Gardens

NOT TO BE MISSED IN ADELAIDE

	Map Ref.
Adelaide Casino	290 E8
In a beautifully restored railway station	
Adelaide Festival Centre	290 E7
One of the best performance venues in the world	
Art Gallery of South Australia	290 F8
A superb overview of Australian art	
Botanic Gardens	290 G7
Join a free tour of these beautiful formal gardens on the edge of the CBD	
Central Market	290 D10
Bustling market with local produce	
Glenelg	292 C10
Board a tram to this seaside resort with its old-world feel	
Light's Vision	290 D6
Share Light's vision of the city from this spot	
Rundle Street	290 E8
Enjoy the vibrant, cosmopolitan cafe strip	
St Peter's Cathedral	290 E6
Visit one of Australia's finest cathedrals	

Pirie Street is the **Adelaide Town Hall** (1863), also in the Renaissance style and modelled on buildings in Genoa and Florence; it is much admired for its magnificent tower and classic portico entrance. King William Street opens out into Victoria Square, an elegant public space that captures something of the essence of Light's vision of an ordered, open city. The historic **General Post Office** and **Treasury Building**, which claim the north-west and north-east corners respectively, are well worth a look. The General Post Office was constructed in 1867 and is a fairly typical, large, Victorian-era building. The Treasury, parts of which date back to 1839, now houses a museum that charts the fascinating history of exploration and surveying in South Australia. On the eastern side of Victoria Square, in Wakefield Street, is **St Francis Xavier's Cathedral**. Dating from 1856, it is Australia's oldest Catholic cathedral.

Head west across Victoria Square into Grote Street to reach the **Central Market**. This busy marketplace has some of the best (and cheapest) fresh food anywhere in Australia, with vendors specialising in superb local produce such as olive oil, nuts, herbs and smallgoods. Cafes and restaurants in the area offer cuisines from around the world. Nearby is **Chinatown** with its good produce shops and restaurants; also nearby is

Gouger Street, a must for the legendary seafood of South Australia (you will be amazed at the prices).

Just north of here and towards Hindley Street is the precinct known locally as the West End. This area has some interesting old buildings including **Her Majesty's Theatre** on Grote Street; **Queen's Theatre** in Waymouth Street, Australia's oldest mainland theatre; and old **Wests Coffee Palace Building** in the heart of Hindley Street. **Hindley Street**, the western extension of Rundle Mall, is the city's liveliest precinct. Here you will find nightclubs and bars as well as an extensive selection of ethnic restaurants, with a heavy concentration on Middle Eastern Food.

The area around the eastern end of **Rundle Street** is known as the **East End**, the city's busy cafe precinct. This is where Adelaide looks and feels like a large Mediterranean town, with acres of outdoor tables, wide pavements, plenty of streetlife and even the odd grapevine bedecking a verandah here and there. By contrast you will also find here an English pub, a cigar bar and an Imax Cinema. The shops in this area generally tend towards the out-of-the-ordinary in terms of their products, be it music, books, clothes or flowers. One block south of the East End Markets, in Grenfell Street, is **Tandanya – National Aboriginal Cultural Institute**. This was

TOP EVENTS

Schützenfest (Jan.)
Celebration of South Australia's German heritage

Tour Down Under (Jan.)
Cycling event featuring the world's top pros

Womadelaide (Feb., odd-numbered years)
Vibrant world music in Botanic Park

Adelaide Festival of the Arts and Adelaide Fringe Festival (Feb.–Mar., even-numbered years)
Highly regarded international festival

Glendi Festival (Mar.)
Greek culture, food, song and dance

500 in Adelaide (Apr.)
V8 supercar race on a modified Grand Prix circuit

Tasting Australia (Oct., odd-numbered years)
Sample the latest innovations in food and wine

For further details visit the web site
www.visit-southaustralia.com.au

CLIMATE ADELAIDE

	J	F	M	A	M	J	J	A	S	O	N	D
Max. °C	29	29	26	22	19	16	15	16	18	21	24	27
Min. °C	17	17	15	13	10	9	8	8	9	11	13	15
Rain mm	20	21	24	44	68	72	67	62	51	44	31	26
Raindays	4	4	5	9	13	15	16	16	13	11	8	6

the first institution in Australia devoted to Aboriginal culture. It houses a permanent collection of Aboriginal art, hosts a range of exhibitions of artworks and artifacts and offers performance space for dance and theatre.

NORTH TERRACE

Many of the city's most important cultural institutions sit shoulder to shoulder on this gracious tree-lined boulevard. Visitors can stroll easily between churches, galleries and museums, and still have the energy for a flutter at the casino as the day ends. The **Botanic Hotel** (1878), at the eastern end, is the grandest of Adelaide's historic hotels. Fully and faithfully restored, it offers fine or casual dining. A short stroll, heading west, is **Ayers House** (1855), an elegant 19th-century residence and one of the first grand homes to be built in Adelaide. Originally owned by Henry Ayers, seven times premier and early mining magnate, Ayers House is open to the public and contains a small museum and a restaurant. The **University of Adelaide** is another North Terrace cultural landmark, offering a mix of classic and contemporary architecture set in superbly landscaped grounds that stretch from North Terrace down to the River Torrens. On campus is the **Museum of Classical Archaeology**, which boasts a collection of more than 500 objects, some of which date to the third millennium B.C.; behind the museum lies **Elder Hall**, a fine concert venue with a spectacular pipe organ.

Alongside the museum is the **Art Gallery of South Australia**, which was established in 1871 and houses a collection that offers a stunning overview of the history of Australian art from the 18th century on. Of particular interest are the works of many distinguished artists from South Australia, including Margaret Preston and Stella Bowen. Next door, the **South Australian Museum** has the world's largest collection of anthropological Aboriginal artifacts, arranged in the new Aboriginal Cultures Gallery, as well as an extraordinary

range of artifacts from the Pacific Islands and Ancient Egypt.

The **State Library** is situated around the corner from North Terrace in Kintore Avenue. The Mortlock Library within houses an important South Australian collection of books, maps and other archives. The Institute, also part of the library, is responsible for the Bradman Collection, comprising more than 100 items of cricket memorabilia belonging to that giant of test cricket, Don Bradman, or 'The Don' as he is known. Behind the library is the **Migration Museum**, located in the magnificent old buildings of what was once the Destitute Asylum. The exhibits chart the hopes and fears of generations of migrants, the social policies that helped or hindered them, and the material circumstances of their lives before, during and after arrival.

Near the corner of King William Street and North Terrace lies **Government House**. Construction of the building began in 1839, and constant renovations and enlargements took place throughout the 19th century; it stands today as Adelaide's oldest building. Across King William Street is **Parliament House**, South Australia's seat of government. The west wing of the building was completed in 1889, while the east wing did not open until 1939. The most striking feature of this classically inspired building are the ten Corinthian columns at the front, a popular adornment for large public buildings in Australia towards the end of the 19th century.

Back behind Parliament House lies **Adelaide Casino**, looking increasingly elegant when compared with the Las Vegas-like ventures that have sprung up in some east-coast cities. Housed within the beautifully restored old Adelaide Railway Station, the casino prides itself on being at the boutique end of the market. It forms the eastern end of a large entertainment complex that includes the **Adelaide Convention Centre**, **Exhibition Hall** and the appropriately luxurious **Hyatt Regency**. **Holy Trinity Church** (on the south side of North Terrace) is the oldest church in South Australia; construction began in 1838, just two years after the arrival of the Europeans. It provides a

Light's Vision on Montefiore Hill

wonderful example of very early South Australian colonial architecture. Further along are the **Lion Arts Centre** and **Jam Factory Craft and Design Centre**, near the corner of North Terrace and Morphett Street. Together, these two institutions offer something of an overview of the cultural life of South Australia. There are performance and gallery spaces, a cinema, and tours around studios where you can see artists working at their various crafts.

THE RIVER TORRENS

Since the days of early settlement, the River Torrens has provided an essential focus for a city set 10 kilometres from the coastline. Flanked by parkland and a series of must-see attractions, the river has developed as the chief artery of central Adelaide's leisure and entertainment activity. An extensive network of trails and paths provides scenic opportunities for cycling and walking. **Elder Park**, on the southern riverbank, is a popular picnic spot and its 1882 Rotunda is an Adelaide icon.

The **Adelaide Festival Centre** graces the rise of Elder Park and provides superb views across the river. It serves as a central venue during the Adelaide Festival and is considered to have some of the finest performance space in the world. There is a spectacular environmental sculpture in the Southern Plaza, and the many contemporary tapestries and paintings throughout the building are well worth a look. The South Australian Theatre Museum, also housed here, has a display charting the history of the performing arts.

East of Elder Park are the **Botanic Gardens**, 16 hectares of native and exotic plant species set among artificial lakes and attractions such as the **Palm House** (an extensive 19th-century glasshouse) and the **Bicentennial Conservatory** (considered to be the largest in the Southern Hemisphere). The National Wine Centre is also located in the gardens and offers an insight into

ENTERTAINMENT

*In Adelaide you immediately notice the number and quality of the city's old pubs. Some are friendly 'locals' where you can get a local beer on tap and join in a conversation, particularly if you mention Australian Rules Football. Others incorporate restaurants, wine bars and dance floors. The **Stag Hotel** in Rundle Street is in a beautifully restored heritage building with a restaurant and bar, and the **Austral Hotel** in Rundle Street is also well worth a look. The best bar in town for its general ambience and its offerings of local wines is in the old **Botanic Hotel** on the corner of North Terrace and East Terrace. The nearby **Adelaide Casino**, centrally located on North Terrace, is a good spot for a bit of after-dinner fun, or drop in at the **Oxford Hotel** or the **Royal Oak Hotel**, both in O'Connell Street, North Adelaide.*

*Thanks to the demands of its enormous arts festival, Adelaide has many excellent performance-arts spaces, ranging from dugout warehouses to the acoustic perfection of the **Adelaide Festival Centre** spaces. Adelaide has its own theatre company, an internationally renowned classical music quartet, a symphony orchestra and one of Australia's most innovative modern dance companies. For cinema goers, the city offers an **Imax Theatre** as well as big blockbuster complexes and smaller arthouse cinemas, some of them tourist attractions in their own right. For a full guide to what's on, there is a lift-out entertainment guide in the Adelaide Advertiser on Thursdays.*

ADELAIDE ON FOOT

Botanic Gardens
Guided walks (including Aboriginal trails);
self-guide walks

City Parks
Walking and cycling trails in parkland
around city and along the River Torrens

East End
Self-guide heritage walk, 'Light on Adelaide',
produced by the National Trust

Glenelg
Self-guide heritage walk in
Your Guide to Glenelg booklet

North Adelaide
Self-guide heritage walk in
O'Connell Street brochure

Port Adelaide
Self-guide heritage walk

St Kilda
Various guided and self-guide walks through
mangrove area near town; bookings essential

For further information
and bookings, contact the
South Australian Visitor & Travel Centre

SPORT

Spectator
Adelaide Oval, on King William Road, is a
venue for interstate and international cricket
matches and Australian Rules Football
(also played at the Football Park Stadium in
West Lakes). The Memorial Drive Tennis
Courts have hosted international players since
1929. There is horseracing at Victoria Park,
Morphettville and Cheltenham and
greyhound racing at Angle Park.

Participator
Pools, water slides, fountains, river rapids,
waterfalls, and gym, spa and sauna facilities
are a feature of the Adelaide Aquatic Centre.
The City of Adelaide Golf Links in North
Adelaide commands splendid views of the city.
The parkland along the River Torrens is a
perfect place for cycling, walking and jogging.

all the wine regions of Australia. During February, in odd-numbered years, the gardens host Womadelaide, a popular World Music event. Further north is the **Adelaide Zoo**, which runs along the banks of the River Torrens and can be reached via one of the fleet of Popeye river launches from an Elder Park landing stage. Reptiles and mammals from around the world can be seen. Of special interest is the large variety of native birdlife, including many unusual land and water species.

NORTH ADELAIDE

North Adelaide is set in the large belt of parkland that surrounds the city centre. Head north along King William Road and across the Adelaide Bridge to reach this pretty historic inner suburb, and explore some of the attractions along the way. On the western side of King William Road is the **Adelaide Oval**, said to be one of the most picturesque sporting ovals in the world. The Adelaide Oval Cricket Museum is housed in one of the grandstands, and is a must for enthusiasts. Just off Montefiore Road on Montefiore Hill is **Light's Vision**, where the figure of Colonel Light is immortalised in bronze. From this vantage point visitors can gaze over the city of Adelaide with its broad streets and rolling parklands, and see the lay of the land as Light did when he stood on this spot to map out the city. **St Peter's Cathedral** (foundation stone laid in 1869) in King William Road, is one of Australia's finest ecclesiastical buildings, an exceptional example of the Gothic Revival craze that swept through the colonial cities during this period. **Pennington Gardens** provide a perfect backdrop, and make a lovely spot for a picnic. There are many fine old colonial buildings in North Adelaide, from the stately homes and grand hotels with lacework balconies to the tiny stone cottages. In particular, the area around O'Connnell Street, which is the northern extension of King William Road, preserves many fine examples of 19th-century public architecture. It is also one of Adelaide's best shopping and dining precincts.

SEASIDE SUBURBS

The sheltering curve of Gulf St Vincent creates a massive body of calm, clean water fronted by more than 60 kilometres of quiet sandy beaches within the Adelaide metropolitan area. Add to this a near-perfect climate of dry, warm days, and you have a city with great

Central Market, well stocked with fresh produce

The Rotunda in Elder Park

seaside value. This magnificent suburban coastline provides everything you need for a family day out or a more extended stay. There are boats for hire, jetties to fish from, cafes and restaurants offering a wide range of cuisine, promenades and piers for those evening strolls and, if it should rain, there are plenty of indoor attractions for entertainment.

Glenelg, the most famous and easily reached Adelaide beach, is a must for the family – particularly if a visit to **Magic Mountain**, the giant seaside waterslide and amusement centre on Anzac Highway, is on the agenda. A popular way to reach Glenelg from the city is to take the tram south-west from Victoria Square right to the edge of the beach. Lunch at the magnificent **Stamford Grand**, perhaps, and stroll along the foreshore to see the grand old houses dating back to the time when Glenelg was established as a resort for Adelaide's wealthy. Take a look at the excellent replica of HMS *Buffalo*, the boat that brought the first European settlers to found a new colony. Attached is a museum where the seafaring tales are retold through the exhibits of illustrations, maps, logbooks and other fascinating relics. Or visit the **Old Gum Tree** in MacFarlane Street, where the first Europeans came ashore and later proclaimed the colony of South Australia.

Continuing north along the coast are **Henley Beach** and **Semaphore**, sharing a relaxed, small seaside village atmosphere, with their generous piers, cafes, and fish and chip shops. Just north of Henley Beach is the suburb of Grange where you will find **Sturt House** (1840), once home to Captain Charles Sturt, who pursued (unsuccessfully) the mythical inland sea, and mapped (successfully) much of Australia's eastern inland river system. The furnished cottage recreates for the visitor an idea of colonial Adelaide. Further north is the **Semaphore Railway**, 2 kilometres of coast-hugging railway line, which takes visitors from **Fort Glanville**, the oldest fort in South Australia, to Semaphore.

If you travel a couple of kilometres inland from here you will reach **Port Adelaide**. This area at the mouth of the Adelaide River was the centre for export trade in Adelaide throughout much of the 19th century, and it remains a well-preserved reminder of the waterfront architecture and culture of that era. There are many significant buildings, including the police station, courthouse, town hall, and various shipping and transport buildings. The **South Australian Maritime Museum** in Lipson Street offers a wealth of memorabilia, chronicling a time when the sea was South Australia's only link with the rest of the world. There is a re-creation of 19th-century dock life, hands-on replicas of parts of old sailing boats, and a re-creation of the third-class quarters on an immigrant ship of the 1850s. Also in Lipson Street is the **Port Dock Railway Museum**, housing the largest under-cover collection of locomotives, carriages and freight vehicles in Australia. Back towards the water, at the end of Commercial Road, is the **South Australian Military Museum**. There are cruises and fishing trips available from Queens Wharf and McLaren Wharf near the **Fishermans Wharf Market**. A few blocks north in Ocean Steamers Road is the **Aviation Museum** which houses the Woomera rocket collection.

St Kilda is located to the north of the city on the outer edge of Torrens Reach. This area is known for its mangrove vegetation and there is an excellent

SHOPPING	Map Ref.
East End, Rundle Street Has experienced a retail rebirth; offers good, but not expensive, boutique shopping	290 G8
Glen Osmond Road, Eastwood Offers a wide variety of top-label fashions at reduced prices	290 F11
King William Road, Hyde Park Many stylish specialty shops, cafes and boutiques	292 I6
Magill Road, Stepney For antiques and second-hand treasures	293 J4
Melbourne Street, North Adelaide Some of the city's most exclusive shops	290 E5
The Parade, Norwood A boulevard bursting with great delis, coffee shops, home design stores and bookshops	293 J5

MARKETS	Map Ref.
Brickworks Market, Thebarton Sells produce and bric-a-brac (Fri.–Sun.)	292 F4
Central Market Some of the best local produce in Australia (Tues. & Thurs.–Sat.)	290 D10
Fishermans Wharf Market, Port Adelaide Offers produce and quality bric-a-brac (Sun.)	294 C11
Junction Markets, Kilburn A popular market featuring fresh produce (Sat. & Sun.)	294 H11
Orange Lane Market, Norwood Features second-hand goods, homemade produce and local crafts (Sat. & Sun.)	293 K4
Torrens Island Open Market, Moorhouse Road Fresh fish can be bought direct from the boats (Sun.)	294 D8

Sculpture in plaza adjacent to Adelaide Festival Centre

DAY TOURS FROM ADELAIDE

Barossa Valley

Australia's best known wine-growing district, the Barossa, about 70 kilometres north of Adelaide, boasts about 50 wineries, including some of the top names in the business. The district is also celebrated for strong German traditions expressed in the local food, architecture and many cultural events. *For more details see region coverage, p. 248.*

Clare Valley

Boutique wineries, historic mining villages, attractive 19th-century architecture and excellent food and accommodation make this scenic area, 160 kilometres north of Adelaide, a favourite weekend retreat from the city. *For more details see region coverage, p. 249.*

Fleurieu Peninsula

The calm waters of Gulf St Vincent and the surf beaches of Victor Harbor provide irresistible seaside destinations close to the capital. Inland, just 43 kilometres from Adelaide, the 53 wineries around McLaren Vale form one of the country's top wine-producing regions. *For more details see region coverage, p. 255.*

Adelaide Hills

History, wineries, gourmet produce, native wildlife and cultivated gardens have made this beautiful semi-rural area a perennially popular daytrip with visitors from Adelaide, just 28 kilometres away. *For more details see region coverage, p. 247.*

1.7-kilometre walk along the **St Kilda Mangrove Trail Boardwalk**. While there, stop at the **Australian Electric Transport Museum** which charts the history of the time (1908–58) when trams were the main form of transport in Adelaide. The **St Kilda Adventure Playground** at the end of St Kilda Road is an engineering feat with flying foxes, swings, dips and ships, and is probably one of the best of its kind in Australia.

WESTERN SUBURBS

The inner western suburbs have their share of attractions. The **Historic Adelaide Gaol** is adjacent to Bonython Park, a stroll away from the city. Built in 1840 and last used in 1988, the gaol is open on Sundays and provides a rare glimpse of colonial penal architecture. In Thebarton, and offering a great family day, is **Mount Thebarton Snow and Ice**. This ice arena boasts the world's first artificial ski slope and a large skating rink. An outing for the young, and the young at heart, is **Kart-Mania** at Richmond, providing safe indoor 'kart' racing and interactive computer games. Another high-tech attraction is the **Investigator Science and Technology Centre** at Wayville, on the inner south-west corner of the city. Packed with hands-on displays, this centre combines a genuine opportunity

for some science education with a healthy dose of pleasure.

EASTERN SUBURBS

Heritage lovers might like to head south-east to the suburb of Springfield, where the magnificent **Carrick Hill** is open to the public. The house, built to look like an English manor, was home to Sir Edward Hayward, a prominent retailer. It contains an impressive art collection, plenty of solid oak and English furniture, and is set in a lovely formal garden created in 1939 and inspired by some of the great gardens of England. North-east in Magill is the **Penfolds Magill Estate**, the original vineyard and winery of one of Australia's best-known wine companies, and producer of the nation's most famous red, Grange Hermitage. Tours are available, and occasionally wine clinics are held, where you can bring your aged bottles in for an update and reseal. The tasting and sales facility is in the former distillery, and the restaurant on the property is one of the best in Adelaide.

Surrounded by parkland, Adelaide, with its elegant stone buildings and wide avenues, combines the vitality of a large modern city with an easy-going Australian lifestyle.

ADELAIDE HILLS

This magnificent landscape of hills and valleys rises in the east above the coastal plains of Adelaide. It is well known for its interesting mix of Australian bushland and European-style farmland, as well as its historic villages, gardens, museums, galleries, vineyards, lookouts and native fauna. The city, only 20 minutes away, is a suitable base for those who wish to take a few days to tour the district. Alternatively, book into a local B&B or guesthouse and get the full rustic experience of this scenic pocket of South Australia.

TOP EVENTS

Mar.   Adelaide Hills Harvest Festival

Easter Oakbank Easter Racing Carnival

Apr.   Mount Lofty Spring Bulb Festival (Stirling)

May   Autumn Leaves Festival (Aldgate)

Sept. Bay to Birdwood Run (vintage vehicles, even-numbered years)

Sept. Hills Affare (wine and food, Stirling)

Oct.   Heysen Festival (Hahndorf)

Nov.   Rock and Roll Rendezvous (Birdwood)

Nov.   Great Train Race (Mount Barker)

EXPERIENCE IT!

❶ Board the steam train at Mount Barker for a trip to Victor Harbor

❷ Journey back in time along the guided trail at the Jupiter Creek Gold Fields near Echunga

❸ Climb the biggest rocking-horse in the world at The Toy Factory, Gumeracha

VISITOR INFORMATION

Adelaide Hills Visitors Centre
Hahndorf: (08) 8388 1185
www.visitadelaidehills.com.au

FOCUS ON

Food and wine

The Adelaide Hills is becoming increasingly well known for its excellent regional produce and as a touring destination for those with gourmet expectations. Best experiences include a visit to Petaluma's Bridgewater Mill for tastings and sales of Petaluma wines, or lunch at the restaurant attached. In Hahndorf you can sample German-style produce at Hahndorf's Smallgoods, taste wine and cheese at Hillstowe Wines and buy berry produce at Beerenberg Strawberry Farm. Mount Barker's gourmet outlets include Brezel Bakehouse and Springs Smoked Seafoods, while near Birdwood you can buy German breads at the Lobethal Bakery, visit the Netherhill Strawberry Farm and taste the grapes at Chain of Ponds Wines.

CLIMATE **MOUNT BARKER**

	J	F	M	A	M	J	J	A	S	O	N	D
Max. °C	27	27	25	20	16	14	13	14	16	19	22	25
Min. °C	12	12	10	8	7	5	4	5	6	7	9	10
Rain mm	26	26	31	59	89	100	106	102	86	68	40	34
Raindays	6	5	7	11	15	16	17	18	15	13	9	7

Birdwood National Motor Museum
The largest museum of its kind in the Southern Hemisphere, this museum has over 300 vintage exhibits tracing the history of motoring.

Mount Lofty Lookout
Spectacular views of Adelaide and the Hills may be enjoyed from the lookout at the 727-metre summit of Mount Lofty. Drop into the information centre to plan your day and enjoy 'food with a view' in the adjacent restaurant and cafe.

Cleland Wildlife Park
Within Cleland Conservation Park, this excellent wildlife park features a large collection of everybody's favourite marsupials, as well as aviaries and nocturnal walks. Combine your visit with a picnic in the adjacent Mount Lofty Botanic Gardens.

For more detail see map 296. For descriptions of ❶ towns see Towns from A to Z *(p. 257).*

Belair National Park
South Australia's oldest national park, established in 1891, offers a natural landscape of eucalypt forests and brilliant flowering native species. Garden lovers will enjoy a stroll through the gardens of the governor's old summer residence (pictured), which dates back to 1859.

Hahndorf
This distinctive town was settled in the 1830s by Prussian refugees. Its heritage is preserved in classic buildings and German-style shops, museums and cafes. Visit The Cedars, former home of artist Hans Heysen, and see local artworks in the splendid Hahndorf Academy.

BAROSSA VALLEY

The Barossa is Australia's best known wine-producing area. Along with nearby Eden Valley, it offers a landscape of vine-covered hills dotted with historic villages, stone cottages, and the grand buildings of old wine estates. It is also a place of rich culture. These traditions are based on a 150-year history of German settlement and can be seen in every aspect of life, from the spires of the Lutheran churches to the local German breads and pastries. Only an hour from Adelaide, and boasting some of the best restaurants and accommodation of any regional area, the Barossa is a popular weekend destination.

TOP EVENTS

Feb. *Barossa Under the Stars (Tanunda)*

Feb. *Oompah Festival (Tanunda)*

Mar. *Tanunda Show and Essenfest (Tanunda)*

Apr. *Barossa Vintage Festival (throughout region, odd-numbered years)*

May *Barossa Balloon Regatta (Nuriootpa)*

Sept. *Spring into the Barossa (throughout region)*

Oct. *Barossa International Music Festival (throughout region)*

Oct. *Brass Band Contest (Tanunda)*

EXPERIENCE IT!

❶ **Take** a tour of the historic Lutheran churches of Tanunda

❷ **Travel** Menglers Hill Road Scenic Drive between Angaston and Tanunda to appreciate the rustic charms of the region

❸ **Dine** at Vintners Bar and Grill in Angaston, one of the many excellent restaurants

VISITOR INFORMATION

Barossa Wine and Visitor Centre
Tanunda: (08) 8563 0600
www.barossa-region.org

FOCUS ON

Gourmet tradition

Whereas many parts of Australia have developed gourmet credentials over the last decade or so, the Barossa has a culinary heritage that goes back 150 years. German-style baking is a highlight: try the Lyndoch Bakery, or the Apex Bakery in Tanunda, established 70 years ago. Old-fashioned ice-cream is made and served at Tanunda's Nice Ice and in Angaston you'll find the shopfront for Australia's biggest processor of dried fruit – Angus Park Fruit Company. Maggie Beer's Farm Shop at Nuriootpa sells the products that have made her name, while Angaston Gourmet Foods is a great place for all the region's best products.

CLIMATE NURIOOTPA

	J	F	M	A	M	J	J	A	S	O	N	D
Max. °C	29	29	26	21	17	14	13	14	17	20	24	26
Min. °C	14	14	12	9	7	5	4	5	6	8	10	12
Rain mm	19	19	22	38	55	56	66	64	60	49	29	24
Raindays	5	4	5	8	12	13	16	16	13	11	8	6

Barossa wineries
The Barossa is one of the oldest and largest wine areas in Australia and is best known for its riesling and shiraz. The biennial Barossa Vintage Festival (pictured) is a time of great activity and colour.

Seppeltsfield
Seppelts estate, established in the 1850s, is one of the grandest in the country. Elegant bluestone buildings are surrounded by superb gardens and an avenue of date palms. Don't miss the hilltop mausoleum built in the style of a Doric temple. Tours available.

Kaiser Stuhl Conservation Park
This rugged mountainside park offers a view of what the Barossa would have looked like before European settlement. A couple of excellent walking trails allow visitors to explore the varied terrain as well as offering a glimpse of local wildlife.

STOCKWELL

SEPPELTSFIELD ☉   NURIOOTPA ☉
☉ TANUNDA   ANGASTON ☉
      ❶   ❷ ❸

GAWLER ☉   KAISER STUHL CP   KEYNETON

NORTH MOUNT LOFTY RANGES

LYNDOCH ☉

EDEN VALLEY

N

0   10 km

SPRINGTON

MOUNT PLEASANT

For more detail see maps 296 & 300. For descriptions of ☉ towns see Towns from A to Z (p. 257).

Gawler
This heritage-listed town was a 19th-century market centre for the rural area north of Adelaide. It preserves magnificent buildings, from mansions to 1840s cottages, and is admired for its original design, which features civic squares, wide streets and reserves.

Eden Valley wineries
This elevated wine-growing area is regarded as a distinct region. A small number of wineries are open for tastings. In Springton, find the Herbig Tree, a giant red gum that was temporary home to a German family in the 1850s.

CLARE VALLEY & THE MID-NORTH

The Mid-North was settled in the 1840s as a major coppermining and agricultural district. The area is renowned for its scenic beauty – old stone cottages and a spread of rolling hills and vineyards. The wineries of the Clare Valley are the prime regional attraction, followed by the coppermining sites preserved in the area – said to be among the most important historic industrial sites in Australia. These attractions, plus galleries, antique and craft stores, and B&Bs and restaurants, make this peaceful region a great choice for a daytrip or a weekend away.

TOP EVENTS

Mar. Twilight Jazz Affair (Burra)
Easter Easter Races (Clare)
Apr. Picnic Races (Burra)
Apr. Spanish Festival (Clare)
May Antique Fair (Burra)
May Gourmet Weekend (Clare)
Aug. Balaklava Cup (horseracing, Balaklava)
Oct. Spring Garden Festival (Clare)

EXPERIENCE IT!

❶ **Buy** local gourmet produce, including olive oil, from Clare retailers

❷ **Picnic** at Burra Gorge, 27 kilometres south-east of Burra

❸ **Cycle** or walk the Riesling Trail, a scenic 27-kilometre path following the old railway line between Clare and Auburn

VISITOR INFORMATION

Clare: (08) 8842 2131
Burra: (08) 8892 2154
www.classiccountry.org.au

FOCUS ON

History

Historically, this is one of the most interesting and well-preserved areas of rural South Australia. In 1839 Edward Eyre explored the Clare Valley and his favourable reports led quickly to pastoral settlement. Places of interest include historic buildings in many towns, particularly in Clare and Mintaro streetscapes. North-west of Clare is Bungaree, a Merino sheep station established 1841. Copper was discovered in the region in 1842 and soon vast mines and major settlements were established. Mining history is preserved in Burra and Kapunda; in both places you'll find accommodation and numerous sites that recall the mining boom of the mid to late 19th century.

CLIMATE CLARE

	J	F	M	A	M	J	J	A	S	O	N	D
Max. °C	30	29	27	22	17	14	13	15	18	21	25	27
Min. °C	13	13	12	8	6	4	3	4	5	7	10	12
Rain mm	25	24	25	47	73	80	82	80	73	57	37	29
Raindays	4	4	5	8	12	14	15	15	13	11	7	6

For more detail see maps 296, 303 & 305. For descriptions of ❶ towns see Towns from A to Z (p. 257).

Clare Valley wineries
This winegrowing district extends for 35 kilometres across the fertile valley. Although the climate is generally Mediterranean, many Clare Valley wines have cool-climate characteristics. The region is known for quality, and its rieslings are widely regarded as among the best in Australia. There are about 30 wineries, ranging from big names to charming boutique-style establishments.

Sevenhill
Austrian Jesuit priests established Clare's first winery here in the early 1850s to ensure a steady supply of altar wine. There have been seven Jesuit winemakers since then, and the range now includes good table wine. Next to the cellars, St Aloysius Church (completed 1875) is worth a visit.

Burra
Located in the sparse landscape of the Bald Hills Range, this former coppermining centre is a mid-19th-century timepiece. It comprises public buildings, shops, miners' cottages, miners' dugouts and the open-cut mine (pictured). Museums chart the area's history, and mine site tours are available. Many cottages have been converted to visitor accommodation.

Mintaro
Mintaro is an almost intact 19th-century South Australian village with attractive stone buildings, many of them incorporating the region's unique slate. Mintaro General Store (pictured) is typical of local heritage charm. South-east is Martindale Hall, an 1879 mansion used for the film *Picnic at Hanging Rock* (1975) and now open as a hotel.

YORKE PENINSULA

Yorke Peninsula, only an hour and a half from Adelaide, is a popular holiday destination. Flanked by the mostly calm waters of Gulf St Vincent on one side and Spencer Gulf on the other, it is known for its great range of seaside activities including fishing, diving and surfing, and for its spectacular coastal scenery. The area was put on the map in the late 1850s by the discovery of rich copper-ore deposits. Many of the now peaceful resort towns along the coast were once busy ports. Today the area is one of the world's richest barley- and wheat-growing regions.

TOP EVENTS

Jan. Festival of the Crab (Port Germein)

Easter Bowling Carnival (Kadina)

Apr. Prawnfest (odd-numbered years, Wallaroo)

May Mine Shafters B&S Ball (Kadina and Wallaroo)

May Kernewek Lowender (odd-numbered years, Kadina, Moonta and Wallaroo)

Sept. Blessing of the Fleet (Port Pirie)

Oct. Gala Day (Edithburgh)

Oct. Yorke Surfing Classic (Innes National Park)

Oct. Festival of Country Music (Port Pirie)

EXPERIENCE IT!

❶ Go diving and follow the Wardang Island Maritime Heritage Trail to eight shipwrecks

❷ Travel the countryside in a fully self-contained Gipsy Wagon from Brentwood

❸ Visit State-heritage Moonta Mines and see a miner's cottage, a museum and a mine railway

VISITOR INFORMATION

Harvest Corner Information Centre
Minlaton: (08) 8853 2600
www.yorkepeninsula.com.au

FOCUS ON

Fishing

Yorke Peninsula is one of the State's top fishing destinations, with jetties at Wallaroo, Moonta Bay, Edithburgh, Stansbury and Port Victoria. The rocky points and sandy coves of the region also provide excellent opportunities for land-based anglers. Snapper, squid, tommy ruff, garfish and whiting are among the more commonly caught species. Reef-fishing is also popular. Browns Beach, on the western side of Innes National Park, is renowned for its big hauls of salmon. Near Goose Island, just north of Wardang Island on the west coast, are two reefs that offer excellent boat-fishing for a variety of species.

CLIMATE KADINA

	J	F	M	A	M	J	J	A	S	O	N	D
Max. °C	30	30	28	23	19	16	15	17	19	23	26	28
Min. °C	16	16	14	11	9	7	6	7	8	10	12	14
Rain mm	15	18	19	33	46	51	49	45	39	33	22	18
Raindays	3	3	4	6	10	11	13	13	10	8	5	4

Port Victoria

This town was once the main port of call for the clippers and windjammers that transported grain to the Northern Hemisphere, a history recorded in the local Maritime Museum. Port Victoria is now a resort town, offering access to swimming beaches and to Wardang Island, a popular diving spot with an underwater heritage trail featuring eight wrecks.

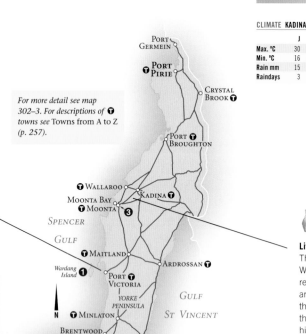

For more detail see map 302–3. For descriptions of ❶ towns see Towns from A to Z (p. 257).

Little Cornwall

This is a collective name for Wallaroo, Moonta and Kadina and refers to the Cornish immigrants who arrived in the early 1860s to mine the substantial copper deposits of the region. The towns preserve some historic architecture – the legacy of early wealth – as well as having museums and festivals that recall the rich local history.

Innes National Park

At the southern tip of the peninsula, Innes National Park protects salt lakes, low mallee scrub, wildflowers, sandy beaches and rugged cliffs. Browns Beach and Pondalowie Bay are popular for surfing, diving and fishing. A 1904 shipwreck can be glimpsed on Ethel Beach, and the interesting remains of Inneston mining town (pictured) are on the eastern side of the park.

Edithburgh

The town's jetty was once the site of a large shipping operation, when thousands of tonnes of salt were harvested from the nearby lakes and exported. Edithburgh is now a popular resort town. Attractions include a tidal pool for safe swimming, good diving locations and access to Troubridge Island, home to populations of little (fairy) penguins, black-faced shags and crested terns.

EYRE PENINSULA & NULLARBOR

This region offers vast distances and spectacular scenery. It stretches 1000 kilometres from the large town of Whyalla to the remote border of Western Australia, taking in the calm waters of Spencer Gulf and the wild Southern Ocean in the Great Australian Bight. Fishing and surfing spots here are among the best in the world. Wildlife, wildflowers, coastal scrub and low hills dominate the eastern reaches; in the west, vast treeless plains and the spectacular sea cliffs of the Nullarbor Plain take over. Travel in the cooler months to avoid extreme heat and take precautions when crossing the Nullarbor.

TOP EVENTS

Jan.	*Tunarama Festival (Port Lincoln)*
Feb.	*Lincoln Week Yachting Regatta (Port Lincoln)*
Apr.	*Australian Amateur Snapper Fishing Championship (Whyalla)*
Apr.	*World Championship Kalamazoo Classic (Cummins)*
Apr.	*Cup Race Meeting (Streaky Bay)*
Aug.	*Agricultural Show (Whyalla)*
Sept.	*Agricultural Show (Ceduna)*
Oct.	*Oyster-Fest (Ceduna)*
Nov.	*Camel Cup Races (Streaky Bay)*

EXPERIENCE IT!

1 **Fish** *from a charter around the Sir Joseph Banks Group of Islands, via Tumby Bay*

2 **Swim** *with sea-lions and dolphins at Baird Bay, near Streaky Bay*

3 **Visit** *Australia's largest permanently land-locked ship at the Whyalla Maritime Museum*

VISITOR INFORMATION

Port Lincoln: (08) 8683 3544
Ceduna: 1800 639 413
www.epta.com.au

FOCUS ON

Wildlife

This sparsely settled district remains a wildlife haven. White-bellied sea eagles, ospreys, pied and sooty oystercatchers and silver and Pacific gulls are just some of the birds found on the coastline. Sir Joseph Banks Group of Islands, via Tumby Bay, is Australia's largest breeding ground for Cape Barren geese; other creatures in this marine conservation park are New Zealand fur seals, sea-lions and dolphins. Point Labatt, near Streaky Bay, is home to Australia's only resident mainland colony of sea-lions, while Head of Bight offers the ultimate wildlife experience – a view of southern right whales in their breeding grounds (June to October).

Nullarbor Plain

The Nullarbor, Latin for 'treeless', is a plain of 250 000 square kilometres, resting on a massive area of limestone riddled with underground caves. Along the coast a long line of sheer-faced cliffs drop suddenly into the wild waters of the Great Australian Bight. Between June and October a popular activity is whale-watching, from cliffs 300 kilometres west of Ceduna.

CLIMATE PORT LINCOLN

	J	F	M	A	M	J	J	A	S	O	N	D
Max. °C	25	25	24	22	19	17	16	17	18	20	22	24
Min. °C	15	16	15	13	11	9	8	8	9	11	12	14
Rain mm	13	15	20	37	57	75	79	69	50	35	22	19
Raindays	4	4	5	10	14	16	18	17	14	11	7	6

Spencer Gulf coast

Here calm waters serve peaceful holiday villages, as well as the northerly regional centre of Whyalla. At Port Lincoln in the south, the huge natural harbour is home to Australia's foremost tuna fleet. Beaches, boat hire, museums, golf, walks and drives are all on offer, but the biggest drawcard is fishing – jetty angling or game-fishing – in some of the best grounds in Australia.

For more detail see maps 302 & 310–11. For descriptions of **o** *towns see Towns from A to Z (p. 257).*

WA
NULLARBOR PLAIN
NULLARBOR NP
Head of Bight
GREAT AUSTRALIAN BIGHT
PENONG
CEDUNA **o**
N
0   60 km
STREAKY **o** BAY
Point Labatt **o** BAIRD BAY
o ELLISTON
WUDINNA **o**
KIMBA **o**
3 **o** WHYALLA
COWELL **o**
CUMMINS
Spencer Gulf
o COFFIN BAY
COFFIN BAY NP
TUMBY BAY **o**
1 *Sir Joseph Banks Group*
SIR JOSEPH BANKS GROUP
PORT CP
o LINCOLN
o

Surf coast

Renowned surf beaches nestle in along this remote coastline, mainly between Ceduna and the tiny settlement of Penong 73 kilometres away. The best known beach is Cactus, just south of Penong, which boasts three world-famous surfing breaks.

Note: Sharks have been known to frequent these waters – seek local advice.

Coffin Bay National Park

This park protects a pristine coastal wilderness of exposed cliffs, small coves and beaches and abundant wildlife. Bush camping, surfing, wildflower-viewing (in spring), walking and fishing are all popular activities. Many of the vehicle tracks are four-wheel-drive only, but for conventional vehicles there is a popular scenic tour called the Yangie Trail, beginning at Coffin Bay township.

FLINDERS RANGES & OUTBACK

This vast, varied region, covering about 70 per cent of the State, offers spectacular scenery and abundant flora and fauna. While many attractions are easily reached along well-maintained roads, other spots are remote and require special preparations and, in some cases, a four-wheel drive vehicle. Always check weather conditions ahead. Camping and caravanning holidays are very popular in these parts, a fact reflected by the high quality of many facilities. Fees are charged for entry to national parks; a pass should be bought in advance for the desert parks in the north. Conditions apply to travel in Aboriginal lands.

TOP EVENTS

Easter Opal Festival (Coober Pedy)

Apr. Antique and Craft Fair (Port Augusta)

May Race Meeting and Gymkhana (Oodnadatta)

June Glendi Festival (Greek culture, Coober Pedy)

July Australian Camel Cup (Marree)

Aug. Races (Innamincka)

Sept. Art Exhibition (Hawker)

Sept. Opal Festival (Andamooka)

EXPERIENCE IT!

❶ **Take** a Ridgetop Tour via Arkaroola for a taste of the ancient world of the Flinders Ranges

❷ **Admire** desert flora at Port Augusta's Australian Arid Lands Botanic Gardens

❸ **Visit** Kanyaka Homestead Historic Site, south of Hawker

VISITOR INFORMATION

Wadlata Outback Centre
Port Augusta: (08) 8641 0793
www.flinders.outback.on.net

FOCUS ON

Ancient landforms

Traces of the first life on earth, marine animal fossils, have been found in the Flinders Ranges. There are numerous places to experience the geological and scenic wonders of these ancient peaks and valleys. In the south around Wilpena, attractions include the Great Wall of China (a massive limestone ridge) and Bunyeroo and Brachina gorges, where an interpretative walk retraces 1000 million years of fossil history. In the north, in and around the Gammon Ranges National Park, visit the Bararrana, Wearing, Mount Chambers, Big Moro, Italowie and Weetootla gorges, and the Bolla Bollana and Nooldoonooldoona waterholes.

Coober Pedy

This town is famous for its opal production (70 per cent of world's supply), and for buildings constructed underground to protect residents against extreme temperatures. Visit the museums and mines, try your hand at prospecting, and shop for opals.

Lake Eyre

Australia's largest salt lake, in Lake Eyre National Park, is also the continent's lowest lying land at 15 metres below sea level. A few times each century the dry lake fills and hundreds of thousands of birds flock to the area to feed and breed.

Innamincka and Cooper Creek

Near Innamincka is the part of Cooper Creek where the Burke and Wills expedition ended in tragedy. Memorials include the Dig Tree, across the Queensland border. The nearby Coongie Lakes form a remarkable wetland in the midst of gibber plains.

CLIMATE HAWKER

	J	F	M	A	M	J	J	A	S	O	N	D
Max. °C	34	33	30	25	20	16	16	18	21	26	29	32
Min. °C	17	18	15	11	7	5	4	4	7	10	13	16
Rain mm	20	21	17	20	31	39	35	33	28	24	22	21
Raindays	3	2	2	3	5	7	7	7	6	5	4	3

Yourambulla Caves

One of several Aboriginal rock-art sites in the Flinders Ranges, these caves are reached via a 15-minute walk off the road south of Hawker. The images are characterised by the use of black and yellow pigment rather than the common red ochre.

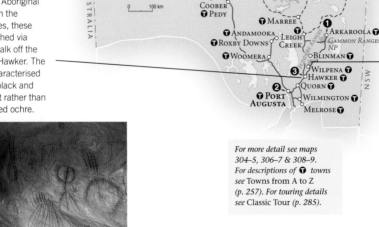

For more detail see maps 304–5, 306–7 & 308–9. For descriptions of ❂ towns see Towns from A to Z (p. 257). For touring details see Classic Tour (p. 285).

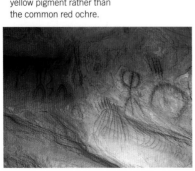

Wildflowers of the ranges

In spring, rainfall permitting, native flowers carpet the semi-arid landscape of the Flinders Ranges. Stunning displays can be seen throughout the region, including around the popular Wilpena Pound in Flinders Ranges National Park. Favourites include Sturt's nightshade, silver tails, yellow buttons and the brilliant Sturt's desert pea (pictured).

THE MURRAY

The Murray River runs through South Australia for 650 kilometres. It crosses a variety of landscapes that include rugged cliff-lined river valleys, mallee scrub, red gum forests, lagoons, orchards and vineyards. The river empties into massive Lake Alexandrina on the coast and feeds the wondrous Coorong wetlands. Its rich history of trade and agriculture has been preserved in the many river towns along the way. As South Australia's only river of significance, it provides a welcome focus in a State known for its aridity. Over the years the Murray has become a popular alternative to a seaside destination.

TOP EVENTS

Jan.	*Apex Fisherama (Loxton)*
Feb.	*Mardi Gras (Loxton)*
Mar.	*Rotary Food Fair (Waikerie)*
Mar.	*Riverland Run, Rally and Rock (Renmark)*
May	*Riverland Rock 'n' Roll Festival (Waikerie)*
June	*SA Country Music Festival (Barmera)*
Oct.	*Rose Festival (Renmark)*
Nov.	*Steam Rally Festival (Murray Bridge)*
Nov.– Dec.	*Loxton Lights Up (Christmas lights)*

EXPERIENCE IT!

1. **Visit** *the Monarto Zoological Park at Murray Bridge*

2. **Captain** *your own houseboat for a few days of river sightseeing*

3. **Discover** *the rich Aboriginal history of the Coorong at the museum at Camp Coorong*

VISITOR INFORMATION

Murray Bridge Information Centre: (08) 8539 1142
Riverland Information Centres
Berri, Loxton, Renmark: 1300 657 625

FOCUS ON

Paddle-steamers

Paddle-steamers were first used in South Australia when the *Mary Ann* was launched at Mannum in 1853. Carrying goods and passengers, they were vital in the development of the all-important trade route that ran from the mouth of the river into New South Wales and Victoria. Two of the original boats, the PS *Mayflower* and the PS *Marion*, operate as day-cruisers, departing from Morgan and Mannum respectively. Longer tours are available on the PS *River Murray Princess* – the largest paddleboat ever built in the Southern Hemisphere – and the *Proud Mary*, which specialises in nature tours.

CLIMATE **RENMARK**												
	J	F	M	A	M	J	J	A	S	O	N	D
Max. °C	32	32	29	24	20	17	16	18	21	25	28	30
Min. °C	17	17	14	11	8	6	5	6	8	11	13	15
Rain mm	16	19	14	18	25	25	23	25	28	28	21	18
Raindays	3	3	3	4	6	8	8	8	7	6	4	4

Morgan

Morgan's days as a busy river port may be over, but a rich heritage of sites and buildings preserve something of the excitement of river trading in the late 19th century. Look out for the wharves (built in 1877), the customs house and courthouse. For an insight into the history of these buildings drop in to the Port of Morgan Historical Museum in the old railway buildings.

Riverland produce

The Riverland is the fruit bowl of South Australia, producing over 90 per cent of the State's citrus, stone fruit and nuts. Winegrowing is also a feature: tastings and sales are available at half-a-dozen estates, including Angoves near Renmark and Banrock Station Wine and Wetland centre at Kingston-on-Murray.

Camping and watersports

From Murray Bridge to Renmark there are caravan parks and camping grounds with river frontage and access to a wide range of watersports, including canoeing, fishing and swimming. The Murray River National Park provides a couple of quiet spots at the north-east end of the river for those who like their recreation in a park setting.

The Coorong

The Coorong, a shallow lagoon in Coorong National Park, is one of Australia's significant wetland areas. It stretches 135 kilometres along the coast, separated from the Southern Ocean by the dunes of Younghusband Peninsula. Apart from its spectacular scenery, The Coorong is best known for its abundant birdlife, with over 240 species recorded. Popular activities include fishing, camping and walking.

For more detail see maps 301 & 303. For descriptions of ❶ towns see Towns from A to Z (p. 257).

THE SOUTH-EAST

Beginning 300 kilometres to the east of Adelaide and stretching across to the Victorian border along the Princes Highway, the South-East is a major holiday centre. It is best known for its coastline of historic fishing villages and stunning beach scenery, and for the prestigious wineries of the Coonawarra district. Other attractions include the World Heritage-listed Naracoorte Caves and the large regional centre of Mount Gambier set in pine forests on the edge of an ancient volcano. The district makes for a great long weekend away or an ideal place to break the journey between Melbourne and Adelaide.

TOP EVENTS

Jan.	Cape Jaffa Seafood and Wine Festival
Jan.	Fishing Contest; Lobster Festival (Kingston S.E.)
Jan.	Bayside Festival (Port MacDonnell)
Jan.	Vigneron Cup (Penola)
Feb.	Country Music Festival (Mount Gambier)
May	Arts Festival (Penola)
May	Generations in Jazz (Mount Gambier)
Nov.	Cabernet Celebrations (Coonawarra)
Nov.	Spring Village Fair and Blessing of the Fleet (Robe)

EXPERIENCE IT!

❶ **Go** birdwatching at Bool Lagoon Game Reserve, one of the region's largest wetlands

❷ **Walk** the massive dunes of Canunda National Park

❸ **Visit** the Mary MacKillop Interpretative Centre at Penola to learn about this unusual pioneer

VISITOR INFORMATION

Lady Nelson Visitor and Discovery Centre Mount Gambier: (08) 8724 9750 www.seol.net.au/tse

FOCUS ON

Seaside towns

The South-East includes some of the State's most scenic coast, where golden beaches frame the blue-green waters of the Southern Ocean. Quiet resort towns, such as Robe, offer good swimming, surfing and fishing. Nearby lies Kingston S.E., a major lobster port (look out for the unusual lighthouse and the Big Lobster), and Cape Jaffa, site of wrecks well known to divers. Further south is Beachport, settled as a whaling station in the 1830s. The town's long jetty is a popular fishing spot. Port MacDonnell, near the Victorian border, boasts the State's largest lobster fleet.

CLIMATE MOUNT GAMBIER

	J	F	M	A	M	J	J	A	S	O	N	D
Max. °C	24	25	23	20	17	14	14	15	16	19	21	23
Min. °C	12	12	11	9	8	6	5	6	7	8	9	11
Rain mm	32	29	36	63	84	97	107	100	77	63	46	41
Raindays	7	7	9	13	17	18	20	20	17	15	11	9

Robe

Settled in the 1840s, Robe is one of South Australia's oldest and best-preserved towns. It boasts a fine collection of stone cottages, shops, public buildings and hotels, many of them National Trust-classified. Set around Guichen Bay at the heart of spectacular coastal landscape, Robe combines a quaint fishing village atmosphere with excellent facilities for holidaymakers.

For more detail see map 301. For descriptions of ❶ *towns see* Towns from A to Z *(p. 257).*

KINGSTON S.E.
Cape Jaffa
NARACOORTE
BOOL LAGOON GAME RESERVE
NARACOORTE CAVES CP
Bool Lagoon
ROBE
COONAWARRA
PENOLA
BEACHPORT
MILLICENT
CANUNDA NATIONAL PARK
MOUNT GAMBIER
PORT MACDONNELL
VICTORIA
N
0   20 km

Naracoorte Caves

Along with Queensland's Riversleigh Fossil Field, this is one of Australia's most significant cave systems, a fact reflected by its World Heritage listing. There are 60 known caves, several of which are open to the public. At the excellent Wonambi Fossil Centre, displays show how fossils found in the caves have played a key role in charting the continent's evolutionary history.

Coonawarra

Coonawarra is Australia's most valuable piece of wine real estate. Just 12 kilometres long and 2 kilometres wide, its soil is rich terra rossa, which produces wine of the highest quality. The region's cabernet sauvignon, in particular, is outstanding. Established names include Wynns, Mildara, Petaluma and Rouge Homme. Over 20 wineries offer cellar-door sales and tastings.

Mount Gambier

This major regional centre is near the State border, roughly half way between Adelaide and Melbourne. It is set on the slopes of an extinct volcano near the intensely coloured Blue Lake. There are a number of caves in the area, including the Engelbrecht Caves (popular with divers) and the Umpherston Sinkhole.

FLEURIEU PENINSULA

This peninsula is one of South Australia's most popular and accessible holiday destinations. It is known for its wineries, magnificent coastline, scenic landscapes and gourmet produce. Some of the Fleurieu's rural villages date back 160 years. Many of the attractions are only an hour or so from Adelaide and visitors can schedule day tours using the city as a base. Travellers heading for the Victor Harbor district, on the far side of the peninsula, might consider booking a night or two of accommodation to take account of longer distances.

TOP EVENTS

Jan.   Granite Island Regatta (Victor Harbor)
Jan.   Milang to Goolwa Freshwater Sailing Classic
May   Vintage Affair (Langhorne Creek)
June   Sea and Vines Festival (McLaren Vale)
June   Whale Season Launch (Victor Harbor)
July   Almond Blossom Festival (Willunga)
Aug.   Collectors, Hobbies and Antique Fair (Strathalbyn)
Oct.   Wine Bushing Festival (McLaren Vale)
Oct.   Folk and Music Festival (Victor Harbor)

EXPERIENCE IT!

1 **Lunch** amid the vines at the Salopian Inn, McLaren Vale

2 **Cruise** from the river port of Goolwa to the mouth of the Murray

3 **Ride** the horse-drawn tram from the township of Victor Harbor to Granite Island, to see fairy penguins

VISITOR INFORMATION

McLaren Vale and Fleurieu Visitor Centre
McLaren Vale: (08) 8323 9944
Victor Harbor: (08) 8552 5738
www.fleurieu.com.au/tourism

FOCUS ON

Wine districts

The McLaren Vale winegrowing district, just 45 minutes from Adelaide, has 53 wineries offering tastings, set against a landscape of weathered hills and rolling acres of almond and olive groves. With a viticultural history dating back to 1838, the region is highly regarded, particularly for its full-bodied reds and notably its shiraz. It supports a wide range of wineries from boutique outfits to some of the big players. In the highly productive Langhorne Creek area a few wineries offer tastings, although many of the grapes grown here are used by wineries in other regions around the country.

McLaren Vale

This is the heart of the winegrowing region. Several wineries are near the town's centre, as are the olive and almond groves, where visitors can buy local produce. Maps are available at the visitor information centre in the main street.

CLIMATE VICTOR HARBOR

	J	F	M	A	M	J	J	A	S	O	N	D
Max. °C	24	24	23	21	19	16	15	16	18	20	22	23
Min. °C	16	16	15	12	10	8	8	8	9	11	12	14
Rain mm	22	20	23	43	62	71	74	67	55	46	28	23
Raindays	4	4	6	10	14	15	16	16	14	11	8	6

Strathalbyn

Picturesque Strathalbyn was settled in 1839 by Scottish immigrants and is a heritage town. The thirty or so listed buildings are fine examples of the State's 19th-century rural architecture. Shop here for antiques, bric-a-brac and arts and crafts.

Gulf St Vincent coast

Enjoy the scenery at Second Valley and Cape Jervis or go snorkelling at Port Noarlunga. Bathe at one of a number of family beaches, or wine and dine on superb local produce at the Star of Greece at Port Willunga.

PORT NOARLUNGA
OLD NOARLUNGA
McLAREN VALE
PORT WILLUNGA
ALDINGA BEACH
WILLUNGA
STRATHALBYN
GULF ST VINCENT
MOUNT COMPASS
LANGHORNE CREEK
YANKALILLA
MILANG
SECOND VALLEY
PORT ELLIOT
GOOLWA
CAPE JERVIS
FLEURIEU PENINSULA
VICTOR HARBOR
DEEP CREEK CP
Granite Island
N
0   10 km

SOUTHERN OCEAN

For more detail see maps 297 & 303. For descriptions of ● towns see Towns from A to Z (p. 257).

Victor Harbor

Located on the Southern Ocean side of the peninsula, historic Victor Harbor has long been a popular holiday resort. Attractions include the horse-drawn tram, heritage sites, penguins, dolphins, whales and the bush trails in wilderness parks west of town.

Mount Compass Gourmet Trail

Mount Compass is the centre of gourmet food production in this region, with trout, berry, deer, pheasant and marron farms open for viewing and sales. Pick up a touring map from the visitor information centre in McLaren Vale.

KANGAROO ISLAND

Australia's third largest island is located in the remote Southern Ocean, 16 kilometres off the tip of the Fleurieu Peninsula. Its most popular attraction is a large local population of native creatures who live undisturbed in pristine natural habitats. Other attractions include coastal scenery, maritime history and a range of fine regional foods. The island is reached by vehicular ferry from Cape Jervis or by plane from Adelaide. Daytrips are popular, but there is plenty of accommodation for those who wish to stay longer.

TOP EVENTS

Feb. Racing Carnival (Kingscote)

Feb. Street Fair (Kingscote)

Easter Easter Fair (Parndana)

Easter Easter Art Exhibition (Penneshaw)

Oct. Agricultural Show (Kingscote)

Nov. Floraison (Flowering of the Vineyards, Emu Bay)

EXPERIENCE IT!

❶ **Taste** the island's gourmet produce by visiting producers located inland from Kingscote

❷ **Swim** safely at the tidal pool at Emu Bay or the rock pool at Stokes Bay

❸ **Canoe** the waters or walk the bush tracks of Antechamber Bay

VISITOR INFORMATION

Kangaroo Island Visitor Information Centre
Penneshaw: (08) 8553 1185
www.tourkangarooisland.com.au

FOCUS ON

Wildlife-Watching

As a result of its isolation from the mainland, Kangaroo Island has one of Australia's most impressive concentrations of wildlife still in its native habitat. Seal Bay is home to a colony of sea lions, while at Cape du Couedic in Flinders Chase National Park, there is a 600-strong colony of New Zealand fur seals. This national park is also the best place to see such land animals as kangaroos, tammar wallabies, brushtail possums and the occasional koala or platypus. Little (fairy) penguins can be seen on tours operating from Kingscote or Penneshaw. There is a large and varied bird population (240 species) across the island, with Murray Lagoon (en route to Seal Bay) particularly good for waterbirds.

Cape Borda Lighthouse

The unusually shaped lighthouse, built in 1858, was converted to automatic operation in 1989. Guided tours are conducted regularly and accommodation is available in the old lighthouse keeper's residence.

Kingscote

The island's largest town and the site of the South Australia's first settlement (1836). Attractions include a nearby colony of little (fairy) penguins, Hope Cottage Folk Museum (an 1850s historic house), the State's oldest cemetery and a very good fishing jetty.

CLIMATE KINGSCOTE												
	J	F	M	A	M	J	J	A	S	O	N	D
Max. °C	25	24	23	21	18	16	15	15	17	19	21	23
Min. °C	15	16	14	13	11	9	8	8	9	10	12	14
Rain mm	15	17	18	37	60	72	78	65	46	36	23	19
Raindays	3	3	5	9	13	15	18	16	13	10	6	5

For more detail see maps 297 & 302. For descriptions of ❶ towns see Towns from A to Z (p. 257).

Flinders Chase National Park

This park is known for its wonderfully varied springtime wildflowers, its wildlife (including a New Zealand fur seal colony at Cape du Couedic), and its unusual geological formations, most notably Admirals Arch and Remarkable Rocks (pictured). There are walking trails and camping is available at designated sites. Accommodation is available in the former keeper's residence at Cape du Couedic.

Seal Bay Conservation Park

Some 500 Australian sea lions can be seen feeding their young and resting between fishing expeditions at this popular beachside wildlife colony. See the creatures from a boardwalk, or up close on a ranger-guided tour.

South Australia
Towns from A to Z

Aldinga Beach
Pop. 4638

MAP REF. 297 E4, 298 A11, 301 B3, 303 K10

This holiday town 49 km S of Adelaide, near the Fleurieu Peninsula, is known for its good fishing, surfing and diving. **In town:** Gnome Caves, Aldinga Beach Rd, for children. Aldinga Market, Old Coach Rd, 1st Sat. each month. **In the area:** Self-guide historic walk around Aldinga and Willunga, brochure available. Aldinga Bay Winery, 3 km SE. At Aldinga, 4 km NE: St Ann's Anglican Church (1866); Uniting Church (1863). McLaren Vale, 16 km NE, centre of wine-growing region; more than 50 wineries. Sellicks Beach, 8 km S, boat access and good fishing. Maslin Beach, 10 km N, Australia's first nude bathing beach. At Port Willunga, 3 km NW: wreck of *Star of Greece* (1888) visible at low tide; Star of Greece Cafe, overlooking wreck. Bush trails through Aldinga Scrub Conservation Park, 1.6 km from Aldinga, brochures available. Off-shore, Aldinga Aquatic Reserve has a rare reef formation and good diving. Lookout, 6 km SW, views of Gulf St Vincent. Lookout, 23 km SW, views of Myponga Reservoir. **Visitor information:** Aldinga Bay Holiday Village, 209 Esplanade; (08) 8556 5019. **See also:** Fleurieu Peninsula p. 255.

Andamooka
Pop. 506

MAP REF. 304 G4

Andamooka, surrounded by opal fields, is about 600 km N of Adelaide, to the west of the saltpan Lake Torrens. The road to Andamooka from the turn-off at Roxby Downs is now sealed. The town is off the beaten track, summer conditions are harsh, the weather is severe and water is precious. Many people live in dugouts to avoid the heat. Visitors need a precious-stone prospecting permit from the Mines Department in Adelaide before staking out a claim. Looking for opals on mullock dumps requires permission from claim owners. There are tours, including underground, and showrooms with opals for sale. **In town:** Andamooka Heritage

Historic cottage in Angaston

Trail and other self-guide walks/drives, brochures available. In Main St: Duke's Bottle House, made of empty beer bottles; Andamooka Gems and Trains, mineral specimens, model railway; quaint 1930s miners' cottages, next to creek bed. Market, Sun. of long weekends (May, June, Oct.). Art and craft market, 1st Sun. each month. Easter: Family Fun Day. Sept.: Opal Festival. **In the area:** Self-guide walk/drive, brochure available. **Visitor information:** 275 Opal Creek Boulevard; (08) 8672 7007. **See also:** Flinders Ranges & Outback p. 252.

Angaston
Pop. 1862

MAP REF. 296 G4, 300 I5, 303 M8

Angaston is high in the Barossa Valley; within 79 km of the coast, it is 361 m above sea level. The town is named after 1830s Barossa Valley settler, George Fife Angas. **In town:** Angas Park Fruit Co., Murray St, dried fruit and nuts. Angaston Gourmet Foods in Murray St for local produce. A & H Doddridge Blacksmith Shop (1873), Murray St, once the industrial heart of the village, now restored, tools of trade on display. For excellent dining, Vintners Bar and Grill, Nuriootpa Rd. For local art and craft, Bethany Arts and Crafts, Washington St. The Lego Man, Jubilee Ave, collection of Lego models dating back to 1959. Apr.: Barossa Vintage Festival (odd-numbered years). Aug.–Sept.: Spring into the Barossa. Oct.: Barossa International Music Festival. **In the area:** Good view of Barossa Valley from Mengler's Hill Lookout, 8 km SW, via scenic drive. Kaiser Stuhl Conservation Park, 10 km S, for rugged bushland, walks and wildlife. Saltram Wine Estate, 1 km W. Yalumba Winery, 2 km S. Collingrove homestead (1850), 7 km SE, National Trust property once owned by Angas pioneering family; viewing and accommodation (meals by prior arrangement only). Henschke Cellars, 10 km SE. Eden Valley and Mountadam wineries at Eden Valley, 19 km SE. At Springton, 27 km SE: Karl Seppelt Grand Cru Estate; Herbig Tree, large hollow river red gum, first home of the Herbig family (information board, historic photos); Herbig Homestead Heritage Centre (open by appt); Merindah Mohair Farm. Yookamurra Sanctuary, 54 km NE, for local wildlife and plant species (check opening times); guided walks and tours and accommodation (bookings essential). **Visitor information:** Barossa Wine and Visitor Information Centre, 66 Murray St, Tanunda; (08) 8563 0600, freecall 1800 812 662. **See also:** Barossa Valley p. 248.

Ardrossan

Pop. 1081

MAP REF. 303 J7

Ardrossan, 148 km NW of Adelaide, is the largest port on Yorke Peninsula's east coast. An important outlet for wheat, barley and dolomite, it is an attractive town with excellent crabbing (blue crabs) and fishing from the jetty. **In town:** Ardrossan and District Historical Museum, Fifth St. The stump jump plough (late 1800s) was invented here; restored plough on display on cliffs in East Tce. **In the area:** Salt and dolomite mines. BHP Lookout, 2 km S, excellent views of Gulf St Vincent. For keen divers, *Zanoni* wreck off coast, 20 km SE (permission essential, from Department for Environment, Heritage and Aboriginal Affairs, Heritage South Australia, (08) 8204 9245). Clinton Conservation Park, 40 km N, tidal shallows attract migratory waterbirds. **Visitor information:** Ardrossan Bakery, 39 First St; (08) 8837 3015. Web site www.classiccountry. org.au/ardrossan.html **See also:** Yorke Peninsula p. 250.

Arkaroola

Pop. 24

MAP REF. 299 H1, 305 M3

Arkaroola is a remote settlement in the northern Flinders Ranges, about 660 km N of Adelaide. It is set on Arkaroola Wilderness Sanctuary, a privately owned property of 61 000 ha. The area is crossed by incredible quartzite ridges, deep gorges and rich mineral deposits, and is a haven for birdlife and rare marsupials. **In town:** Astronomical Observatory, access by tour only. Guided bush tucker, bush medicine and Dreamtime walking tour. Various self-guide walks. **In the area:** At nearby Gammon Ranges National Park, ruins of Cornish-style Bolla Bollana Smelters (1861). Scenic waterholes Bolla Bollana, and Nooldoonooldoona, 12 km NW. Weetootla Gorge, 31 km SW, permanent springs. Italowie Gorge, 42 km SW, 4WD vehicles required; experienced bushwalkers only. Big Moro Gorge, with rock pools, 59 km S (Aboriginal Land Permit required for entry, contact Nepabunna Community Council, (08) 8648 3764); access to gorge may require 4WD. Mt Chambers Gorge, 98 km S, has Aboriginal rock carvings. Marked walking trails, self-guide brochures available. 4WD tours: Ridgetop Tour, spectacular 42-km trip across Australia's most rugged mountains including Mt Painter and Mt Gee, breathtaking views of Yudnamutana Gorge and Lake Frome (salt lake); other 'tagalong' tours (your own 4WD in an organised convoy). Scenic flights, guided tours. **Visitor information:** Arkaroola Village, Port Augusta; (08) 8431 7900. Web site www.arkaroola.on.net **See also:** Flinders Ranges & Outback p. 252; National Parks p. 282; Classic Tour p. 285.

Balaklava

Pop. 1441

MAP REF. 303 K6

Balaklava, on the banks of the River Wakefield 91 km N of Adelaide, was named after a battle in the Crimean War. **In town:** National Trust Museum, May Tce, has relics of district's early days of European settlement (check opening times). Court House Gallery and Shop, Edith Tce, community art gallery. Urlwin Park Agricultural Museum, Short Tce. Lions Club Walking Trail along Wakefield River, brochure available. Racecourse, Racecourse Rd, major country racecourse. Aug.: Balaklava Cup. Sept.: Agricultural Show. Oct.: Garden and Gallery Festival (even-numbered years). **In the area:** Weekend glider joy-flights. Devils Gardens, 7 km NE on Auburn Rd, and The Rocks Reserve, 10 km E; both with picnic facilities. Beachside town of Port Wakefield, 26 km W at head of Gulf St Vincent. **Visitor information:** Country Gardens Coffee Shoppe, 14 Edith Tce; (08) 8862 2123. Web site www. classiccountry.org.au/balaklava.html **See also:** Clare Valley & the Mid-North p. 249.

Barmera

Pop. 1837

MAP REF. 303 P7

The sloping shores of Lake Bonney make a delightful setting for this Riverland town, 214 km NE of Adelaide. Lake Bonney is ideal for swimming, water-skiing, sailing, boating and fishing. The surrounding irrigated areas are mainly vineyards but there are also apricot and peach orchards and citrus groves. Soldier settlement after WW I marked the start of the town. **In town:** Donald Campbell Obelisk, Queen Elizabeth Dr., commemorates Campbell's attempt on world water-speed record in 1964. Rocky's Country Hall of Fame, Barwell Ave. Bonneyview Wines, Sturt Hwy, has restaurant and wine-tasting. Canoe tours, jetski hire. Easter: Lake Bonney Yachting Regatta. June: SA Country Music Festival and Awards. Oct.: Sheepdog trials. Dec.: Christmas Pageant and Fireworks. **In the area:** At Kingston-on-Murray 10 km W, visit Banrock Station Wine and Wetland Centre. North Lake, 10 km NW, ruins of Napper's Old Accommodation House (1850) preserved by National Trust. Loch Luna Game Reserve, 16 km NW. At Overland Corner, 19 km NW on Morgan Rd: hotel (1859), now also National Trust museum; self-guide historical walk. Highway Fern Haven, 5 km E on Sturt Hwy, rare ferns in tropical setting. At Cobdogla, 5 km W: Irrigation and Steam Museum, with the only working Humphrey Pump in the world, photos and memorabilia of Loveday Internment Camp, steam rides (check open times); self-guide drive to remains of internment camp, 3 km SW; Chambers Creek, for canoeing and prolific birdlife; Easter Sunday Craft Expo. Moorook Game Reserve, 16 km SW, includes Wachtels Lagoon with birdlife and walking trail. Nearby, Yatco Lagoon abounds with a variety of birdlife. **Visitor information:** Barwell Ave; (08) 8588 2289. **See also:** The Murray p. 253.

Beachport

Pop. 441

MAP REF. 301 F11

First settled as a whaling station in the 1830s, Beachport is 51 km S of Robe. Rivoli Bay nearby provides safe swimming as well as shelter for lobster boats. One of the State's longest jetties stretches into Rivoli Bay and is popular with anglers. **In town:** Old Wool and Grain Store, Railway Tce, now National Trust Museum with whaling, shipping and local history exhibits. Artifacts Museum, McCourt St, Aboriginal heritage displays. Centenary Park, in town centre, has barbecues, tennis courts, playgrounds and skateboard track. Heritage walk, maps from National Trust Museum; other walking trails, maps from District Council. Oct.: Festival by the Sea. **In the area:** At Lake George, 4 km N: waterbirds, windsurfing and fishing. Beachport Conservation Park, between Lake George and the Southern Ocean, features Aboriginal shell middens and Jack and Hilda McArthur Walk; 1.2-km signposted flora trail around Wolley Lake (accessed from Five Mile Drift Rd). Bowman Scenic Drive from base of lighthouse to Woolleys Rock (5 km N) for spectacular views of Southern Ocean; on the way, swim in Pool of Siloam, a lake with high salt content

Aroona Valley, south of Blinman

and reputed therapeutic benefits. Woakwine Cutting, 10 km N on Robe Rd, extraordinary drainage project, with observation platform and machinery exhibit. **Visitor information:** Millicent Rd; (08) 8735 8029. **See also:** The South-East p. 254.

Berri   Pop. 3912

MAP REF. 303 Q7

The commercial centre of the Riverland region, Berri is 227 km NE of Adelaide. Once a wood-refuelling stop for paddle-steamers and barges that plied the Murray River. This is fruit- and vine-growing country, dotted with peaceful picnic and fishing areas. **In town:** Earth Works, Sturt Hwy, for local art and craft. Berri Art Gallery, Wilson St. Water Tower Lookout (17 m), Fiedler St, for panoramic views of river and town. Nearby, sculpture and cave memorial to Jimmy James, Aboriginal tracker. Houseboats and canoes for hire, contact information centre. Feb.: Rodeo; Speedboat Spectacular (subject to river condition). Easter: Carnival. Nov.: Art and Craft Fair. **In the area:** On Sturt Hwy: dried fruit and confectionery at Angas Park Kiosk, 3 km W; Berri Estates winery and distillery, largest winemaking facility in Southern Hemisphere, 13 km W. Murray River National Park, 10 km SW, features Kia Kia Nature Trail for bushwalkers. Martin's Bend, 2 km E, popular for water-skiing and picnicking. Berrivale Orchards, 4 km N on Sturt Hwy, has

educational audiovisual on Riverland's history and various stages in fruit-processing (open Mon.–Fri., Sat. a.m.). Wilabalangaloo flora and fauna reserve, 5 km N, off Sturt Hwy: walking trails, spectacular scenery, museum and paddle-wheeler (check opening times). Rollerama roller-skating centre nearby. At Monash, 12 km NW on Morgan Rd: Monash Adventure Playground, features maze, flying fox, rope bridge. Nearby, Norman's Winery. **Visitor information:** Riverland Information Centre, 24 Vaughan Tce; 1300 657 625. **See also:** The Murray p. 253.

Birdwood   Pop. 668

MAP REF. 296 F8, 301 C1, 303 L9

Established by German settlers in 1848, this small town is in the northern part of the popular Adelaide Hills district. It is best known as the site of the largest motor museum in the Southern Hemisphere. **In town:** In Shannon St: National Motor Museum, housed in 1852 flour mill, has notable collection of vintage cars and motorcycles; Top of Times Gallery (in same complex), features changing exhibitions of local artists; many historic buildings, including 1850s German-style cottages (brochure available). Sept.: Bay to Birdwood Run (even-numbered years, vintage vehicles). Nov.: Rock and Roll Rendezvous. **In the area:** At Lobethal, 13 km SW: Motorcycle and Heritage Museum with large collection of vintage machines;

historic German-style cottages and 1842 Lutheran Seminary; Lobethal Bakery, long-established business specialising in German-style breads; Bushland Park with picnic area; Fairyland Village featuring characters from German fairytales. The Toy Factory, 7 km W at Gumeracha, home to giant rocking-horse, offers displays and sales in nature park environment. Chain of Ponds Wines, 9 km W, boutique winery with sales, restaurant and B&B. Netherhill Strawberry Farm, 11 km SW: berry products, fruit-picking in season; gardens, picnic facilities and walks. Gorge Wildlife Park, 19 km W, features native wildlife in superb natural setting. Torrens Gorge, 25 km W, spectacular cliffs and streams, popular for picnics. Mar.: Hills Harvest Festival (several locations in district). **Visitor information:** Top of The Torrens Gallery, Shannon Street; (08) 8568 6677. **See also:** Adelaide Hills p. 247.

Blinman   Pop. 30

MAP REF. 305 K6

Blinman, 478 km N of Adelaide and 30 km from the Flinders Ranges National Park, is the sole survivor of numerous mining townships surveyed in the area in the 19th century. The town was a thriving coppermining centre from 1860–75 and 1882–1907. Blinman's population peaked at 1500 in 1869. **In town:** Historic buildings in Mine Rd: pug and pine miners' cottages (c. 1870), school (1883), police station and cells (1885), memorial hall (1896), hotel (1869). May: Land Rover Jamboree. Oct.: Picnic Gymkhana and Races. **In the area:** Mawson (bike) Trail (Adelaide to Blinman) ends here, brochures from Recreation SA, (08) 8416 6677. Blinman Mine Historic Site, just NE of town: 1-km self-guide walk (approx. 1 hr), signs explaining history and geology of the site, brochure available. Great Wall of China, limestone ridge, 10 km S on Wilpena Rd. Further south, beautiful Aroona Valley and ruins of old Aroona homestead; nearby Brachina Gorge. Scenic Glass Gorge, beautiful wildflowers in spring, and Parachilna Gorge, both between Blinman and Parachilna; nearby, the Blinman Pools, fed by a permanent spring. Scenic drive east through Eregunda Valley, then north-east to Mt Chambers Gorge with its rock pools and Aboriginal carvings, then north-west to view spectacular Big Moro Gorge off Arkaroola Rd (Aboriginal Land Permit required, contact Nepabunna Land Council, (08) 8648 3764; access to gorge may require 4WD). **Visitor information:** Post Office, Mine Rd; (08) 8648 4874. **See also:** Flinders Ranges & Outback p. 252; National Parks p. 282; Classic Tour p. 285.

Bordertown · Pop. 2337

MAP REF. 301 H6

Bordertown is a quiet town on the Dukes Hwy, 274 km SE of Adelaide. In 1852 it became an important supply centre for the goldfields of western Victoria. Today the area produces wool, cereals, meat and vegetables. **In town:** Robert J. L. Hawke, former Australian Prime Minister, was born here. His childhood home, in Farquhar St, includes memorabilia (open Mon.–Fri.). Apex park, Woolshed St. **In the area:** Bordertown Wildlife Park, Dukes Hwy, has native birds and animals, including pure white kangaroos. Historic Clayton Farm, 3 km S, features vintage farm machinery and thatched buildings (open p.m. Sun.–Fri.). Clayton Farm Vintage Field Day, held Oct. long weekend. At Mundulla, 10 km SW: Mundulla Hotel (1884), National Trust building with restaurant, tearooms and craft shop. At Padthaway, 42 km SW, 1882 homestead housing Padthaway Estate winery (meals and accommodation). Nearby, picnic areas among magnificent red gums and stringybarks at Padthaway Conservation Park. Bangham Conservation Park, 30 km SE, near the town of Frances, significant habitat for the red-tailed black cockatoo. **Visitor information:** 81 North Terrace; (08) 8752 0700. **See also:** The Murray p. 253.

Burra · Pop. 1008

MAP REF. 303 L5

Nestled in Bald Hills Range, 154 km N of Adelaide, this former coppermining centre is one of the country's best-preserved mining towns. Copper was discovered in 1845 and extraction valued almost $10 million before the mine closed in 1877. The district of Burra Burra is now noted for stud merino sheep. *Breaker Morant* was filmed here in 1980. **In town:** Burra Heritage Passport allows a walk or drive around 11 km of heritage buildings, museums, mine shafts and lookout points. Daily bus tours of town and its mining history; bookings essential. Antique shops, Commercial St. Burra Creek miners' dugouts, alongside Blyth St, where over 1500 people lived during the boom; 2 dugouts preserved. Cemetery, off Spring St. Heritage and cemetery walks, details from information centre. Burra Mine Open Air Museum, off Market St, with Enginehouse Museum built 1858 and reconstructed 1986 near archaeological excavation of 30-m entry tunnel to Morphett's Shaft; also features ore dressing tower, powder magazine and offers views of open-cut mine and town. Market Square Museum, opposite information centre. Malowen Lowarth Cottage, Kingston St, old miner's cottage. In Bridge Tce: underground cellars of old Unicorn Brewery; Paxton Square Cottages (1850), 33 two-, three- and four-roomed cottages built for Cornish miners, now visitor accommodation. In Burra North: antique shops; police lockup and stables (1849), Tregony St; Redruth Gaol (1857), off Tregony St; Ryan's Deer Farm, opposite gaol, includes animal nursery; Bon Accord Mine buildings (1846), Railway Tce, now a museum complex. Picturesque spots on Burra Creek for swimming, canoeing and picnicking. Feb.: Rock'n'Roll Festival. Mar.: Twilight Jazz Affair. Apr.: Picnic Races. May: Antique Fair. **In the area:** Chatswood Farm Gallery, 14 km S at Hanson. Scenic 90-km Dares Hill Drive, begins 30 km N near Hallett (maps available). Barracas Park Alpacas, eastern outskirts of town (off Paradise St). Burra Trail Rides, 4 km E. Mongolata gold mine, 27 km E, tours by appt. Burra Gorge, 27 km SE. **Visitor information:** Visitor Centre, 2 Market Sq.; (08) 8892 2154. Web site www.weblogic.com.au/burra/ **See also:** Clare Valley & the Mid-North p. 249.

Ceduna · Pop. 2599

MAP REF. 311 N9

Near the junction of the Flinders and Eyre hwys, Ceduna is the last major town before you cross the Nullarbor east–west; the place to check your car and stock up on food and water before the long drive. Ceduna is set on Murat Bay with its sandy coves, sheltered bays and offshore islands. It is an ideal base for swimming, diving, fishing, water-skiing, windsurfing and boating. Sharks have been known to frequent these waters – seek local advice. The port at Thevenard, 3 km SW, handles bulk grain, gypsum and salt. The fishing fleet is noted for its large whiting hauls. Snapper, salmon, tommy ruff and crab are other catches. There was a whaling station on St Peter Island in the 1850s. According to map references in Swift's Gulliver's Travels, the tiny people of Lilliput might well have lived on St Peter Is. (visible from Thevenard) or the Isles of St Francis. **In town:** Old Schoolhouse National Trust Museum, Park Tce, pioneering items and artifacts from atomic testing at Maralinga (open Mon.–Sat.). Sea Dragon Art Gallery, cnr Day and O'Loughlin Tce, works by local artists (check opening times). Easter: Horseracing Carnival. Sept.: Agricultural Show. Oct.: Oyster-Fest. **In the area:** Paul's Fish Factory at Thevenard Boat Haven, fresh seafood (best prior to 9 a.m.). At Denial Bay, 13 km W: McKenzie Ruins, site of original settlement; Clear Water Oyster Farm, tours. Picnicking, surfing and fishing: west of town at Denial Bay and Davenport Creek, with its pure white sandhills; and to the south-east at Decres Bay, Laura Bay and Smoky Bay (boat charter for diving and fishing from Ceduna). Whales can be seen June–Oct. along coast west of Ceduna particularly at Head of Bight, 300 km W (daytrips; contact information centre). At Penong, 73 km W: more than 40 windmills draw town's water from underground; Penong Woolshed museum with local crafts; Goanywea camel day-rides and safaris (May–Oct.). Sand dunes and good surf at Cactus Beach, 94 km W. Prominent headland at Point Brown, 56 km SE, noted for its surf beaches, salmon fishing and coastal walks. **Visitor information:** Ceduna Gateway Visitor Information Centre, 58 Poynton St (closed p.m. weekends); (08) 8625 2780, freecall 1800 639 413. Web site www.epta.com.au **See also:** Eyre Peninsula & Nullarbor p. 251; Wildlife-Watching p. 280.

Clare · Pop. 2815

MAP REF. 303 L5

Set in rich agricultural and pastoral country, this charming town was first settled by Europeans in 1842; it was named after County Clare in Ireland. The area is famed for its prize-winning table wines. Gourmet produce such as olive oil, wheat, barley, honey, stud sheep and wool are other important regional industries. The first vines were planted by Jesuit priests at Sevenhill in the early 1850s; today Sevenhill Cellars still produces table and sacramental wines. **In town:** Gift Horse Gallery, 130 Main Rd. National Trust museum in old police station (1850), cnr Victoria Rd and Neagles Rock

Rd (open weekends and holidays). Stately Wolta Wolta homestead (1846), West Tce, built by pastoralist John Hope, still owned by Hope family; rebuilt after Ash Wednesday fires (open by appt). Lookouts at Billy Goat Hill, from Wright St; Neagles Rock, Neagles Rock Rd. Maynard Memorial Park, Pioneer Ave. Town walk, self-guide leaflets available. Mar.: Clare Valley Cup. Easter: Easter Races. Apr.: Spanish Festival. May: Gourmet Weekend. Oct.: Spring Garden Festival. **In the area:** More than 30 wineries (most open for inspection and cellar-door sales, check opening times); *around Clare:* Tim Adams Wines, Leasingham Wines, Jim Barry Wines, Knappstein Wines, Emerald Estate, Eldredge Wines; *in Polish Hill River district, 12 km SE:* Pike's Polish Hill River Estate, Paulett Wines and The Wilson Vineyard; *at Mintaro, 19 km SE:* Mintaro Cellars and Reilly's Cottage; *at Sevenhill, 7 km S:* Sevenhill Cellars established early 1850s and featuring monastery buildings, including historic St Aloysius Church, Stringy Brae Wines, Waninga Wines, Skillogalee Wines, Jeanneret Wines and Mitchell Winery; *around Penwortham, 10 km S:* Penwortham Wines and Pearson Wines; *around Watervale, 12 km S:* Clos Clare, Crabtree of Watervale, Olssen Wines, Stephen John Wines, Quelltaler Estate and Tim Gramp Wines; *around Auburn, 26 km S:* Taylors Wines and Grosset Wines. Also at Watervale, 12 km S, Murray Edwards Studio. Also at Auburn, 26 km S: Riesling Trail, 27-km-long scenic bike and walking path along old Clare railway line between Clare and Auburn; birthplace of poet C. J. Dennis in 1876; many historic buildings (accommodation in some), maintained by National Trust (self-guide walk leaflets available); Auburn Railway Station (1918) transformed into Mt Horrocks Wines cellar-door outlet; Taylors Wines. At Blyth, 13 km W: flora and fauna in Padnainda Reserve; Medika Gallery, originally a Lutheran church (1886), specialising in Australian bird and flower paintings. Scenic drive 12 km S to Spring Gully Conservation Park featuring rare red stringybarks. Bungaree Station homestead (1841), historic merino sheep station 12 km N: group tours, accommodation. Geralka Rural Farm, 25 km N, working farm (tours). **Visitor information:** Town Hall, 229 Main North Rd; (08) 8842 2131. Web site www.classiccountry.org.au/clare.html **See also:** Clare Valley & the Mid-North p. 249.

Underground home at Coober Pedy

Coffin Bay
Pop. 396

MAP REF. 302 C8

A picturesque holiday town and fishing village, on the shores of a beautiful estuary 51 km NW of Port Lincoln, Coffin Bay offers sailing, water-skiing, swimming and fishing. The coastal scenery is magnificent. Oysters cultivated in Coffin Bay are among the best in the country. The bay's name was bestowed by Matthew Flinders in 1802 to honour his friend Sir Isaac Coffin. **In town:** Oyster Farm, also known for its lobster, The Esplanade. Oyster Walk, 12-km walkway along foreshore from lookout (excellent view of Coffin Bay) to Long Beach; brochure available. Charter boats and boat hire. **In the area:** Coffin Bay National Park and Kellidie Bay Conservation Park surround township; abundant wildflowers in both parks in spring. Yangie Trail drive, 10 km S via Yangie Bay Lookout (magnificent coastal views to Point Avoid). Farm Beach, 50 km N; further 5 km N, Gallipoli Beach, location for film Gallipoli (1981). Further 50 km N, scenic stretch of Flinders Hwy between Mount Hope and Sheringa. **Visitor information:** Beachcomber Agencies, The Esplanade; (08) 8685 4057. Web site www.epta.com.au **See also:** Eyre Peninsula & Nullarbor p. 251.

Coober Pedy
Pop. 2762

MAP REF. 309 R11

In the heart of South Australia's outback, 845 km N of Adelaide on the Stuart Hwy, is the opal-mining town of Coober Pedy. This is the last stop for petrol between Cadney Homestead (151 km N) and Glendambo (252 km S) on the Stuart Hwy.

The name Coober Pedy is Aboriginal for 'white man's hole in the ground': many people live in dugouts (at a constant 24°C) for protection from the severe summer temperatures (often reaching 45°C), and the cold winter nights. The countryside is desolate and harsh, and the town has reticulated water from a bore 23 km N. Opals were discovered here in 1915; today there are thousands of mines. **In town:** Demonstrations of opals being cut and polished; jewellery and stones for sale. On eastern edge of town: Big Winch Lookout, Italian Club Rd; Old Timers Mine, Crowders Gully Rd, a mine museum and interpretive centre with self-guide walks. In Hutchison St: Umoona underground mine and museum, has interpretive section and underground mine tours; underground churches, including St Peter and St Pauls; Desert Cave, an international underground hotel with shopping complex. Underground Catacomb Church, Catacomb Rd. Guided tours of mines and town. Easter: Opal Festival. June: Glendi Festival (celebration of Greek culture). Sept.: Horse races. **In the area:** Opal fields pocked with diggings; beware of unprotected mine shafts. Avoid entering any field area unless escorted by someone who knows the area. For safety reasons, visitors to the mines are advised to join a tour. Trespassers on claims can be fined a minimum of $1000. Opal Quest Mine, 2 km SW, tours. Underground Pottery, 2 km W, features local pottery. The Breakaways, 30 km N: 40-sq. km reserve featuring unique landscape, used as backdrop in many films and commercials (passes to reserve from information centre and other outlets in town); return via road past part of dog fence, a 5300-km fence stretching across Australia, built to protect sheep properties in the south from wild dogs. Arckaringa Hills, 234 km N, richly coloured hills in an area known as the Painted Desert; also noted for its flora and fauna. At William Creek, 170 km E: hotel; Race Meeting and Gymkhana held weekend before Easter. **Visitor information:** Council Offices, Hutchison St; (08) 8672 5298, freecall 1800 637 076. Web site www.opalcapitaloftheworld.com.au **See also:** Flinders Ranges & Outback p. 252.

Coonalpyn   Pop. 233

MAP REF. 301 F4, 303 O12

This tiny town, 180 km SE of Adelaide, is a good place to break your journey along the Dukes Hwy. In the cooler months it is also a base from which to explore the Mt Boothby (30 km SW) and Carcuma (20 km NE) conservation parks, and to see grey kangaroos, echidnas, emus and mallee fowl. Summer access to both parks is discouraged because of heat and fire danger. Check bushfire danger and fire restrictions before entering parks; for Mt Boothby Conservation Park, (08) 8575 1200; for Carcuma Conservation Park, (08) 8576 3690. **In town:** Dog Exercise Park, signed on hwy, safe stop for pets. Tunnel Vision, under railway line in subway leading to Dog Park, mural depicting town's history. Daisy Patch Nursery, cnr George and Richards tces, for native plants. Oct.: Agricultural and Horticultural Show (includes Antique Tractor Pull). **In the area:** Scenic 26-km loop drive, maps available. Tintinara homestead, 37 km S, historic buildings. **Visitor information:** Peg's Place, 27 Dukes Hwy; (08) 8571 1272. **See also:** The Murray p. 253.

Coonawarra   Pop. 40

MAP REF. 228 A13, 301 H10

The European settlement of Coonawarra goes back to 1890 when John Riddoch subdivided 2000 acres (800 ha) of his vast landholding for orchards and vineyards. Although the vines flourished and excellent wines were made, demand was not high until the 1950s and 1960s, when the region became an important winegrowing area. The terra rossa soil and dedicated viticulturalists and winemakers combine to produce award-winning white and red table wines. **In town:** Art gallery at Chardonnay Lodge, Penola Rd. Nov.: Cabernet Celebrations. **In the area:**

Wineries, most open for tastings and sales, including (N to S): S. Kidman Wines, Rymill Winery, Redman Wines, Brands Laira Wines, Wynns Coonawarra Estate, Rouge Homme Wines, Zema Estate, Mildara Wines, Majella Wines, St Mary's Vineyard (15 km E), Katnook Estate, Highbank Wines, Leconfield Coonawarra, Bowen Estate, Balnaves of Coonawarra, The Blok Estate, Hollick Wines, Wetherall Wines, Punters Corner, Lindemans Wines. **Visitor information:** 27 Arthur St, Penola; (08) 8737 2855. **See also:** The South-East p. 254.

Cowell   Pop. 748

MAP REF. 302 G5

A pleasant township 108 km S of Whyalla, Cowell is on the almost landlocked Franklin Harbor. One of the world's major jade deposits is in the district. The sandy beach at Cowell is safe for swimming; fishing is excellent. Oyster farming is a local industry and fresh oysters can be purchased year-round. **In town:** Old post office and attached residence (1888), Main St, now Franklin Harbor National Trust Historical Museum. On Lincoln Hwy: open-air agricultural museum; Cowell Jade Motel, has displays and sales of local jade jewellery. Boats for hire. **In the area:** Franklin Harbor Conservation Park, south of town, has good fishing spots. Swimming and excellent fishing locations abound, including around Gibbon Point, 15 km S. Arno Bay, 48 km S, popular holiday town with sandy beaches and jetty for fishing. **Visitor information:** Council Offices, Main St; (08) 8629 2019. Web site www.epta.com.au **See also:** Eyre Peninsula & Nullarbor p. 251.

Crystal Brook   Pop. 1323

MAP REF. 303 J4

Once part of a vast sheep station, this town, 25 km SE of Port Pirie, is now a service centre for the sheep, beef and cereal industries of the region. **In town:** National Trust Museum, Brandis St, has local history collection in first two-storeyed building in town, originally a butcher's shop and bakery; underground bakehouse behind building. Crystal Crafts, Bowman St, for local craft. Picnicking in creekside parks. Aug.: Agricultural Show. **In the area:** Bowman Park, 5 km E: surrounds ruins of Bowman family property Crystal Brook Run (1847); Steakhouse Restaurant and opportunities

for wildlife-watching. Heysen Walking Trail through Bowman Park. At Gladstone, set in rich rural country in Rocky River Valley 21 km NE: tours of Gladstone gaol (1881); Trend Drinks Factory, home of Old Style Ginger Beer (tours). At Laura, boyhood town of C. J. Dennis the author of *The Songs of a Sentimental Bloke*, 32 km N: cottage crafts; art galleries; historic buildings; self-guide walking tour, leaflet at Biles Art Gallery, Herbert St (open Sat., Sun., public holidays); Beetaloo Valley and Reservoir (west of Laura), pleasant picnic spot Apr.–Nov. and venue for Folk Fair in Apr. Near Wirrabara, 50 km N: scenic walks through pine forests; picnic grounds; Old Tree Nursery, est. 1877. At Redhill, 25 km S: riverside walk; museum; craft shop; antique shop. Koolunga, 10 km E of Redhill, has cottage industry (potters and painters) outlets and picnic areas. Salt lakes around Snowtown, 50 km S. Nearby on Lochiel–Ninnes Rd, lookout with superb views of inland lakes and countryside. **Visitor information:** Port Pirie Regional Tourism and Arts Centre, 3 Mary Elie St; (08) 8633 8700, freecall 1800 000 424. **See also:** Yorke Peninsula p. 250.

Edithburgh   Pop. 400

MAP REF. 302 I10

Located on the foreshore at the south-eastern tip of Yorke Peninsula, Edithburgh overlooks Gulf St Vincent and Troubridge Island. **In town:** Native Flora Park, Ansty Tce. In Edith St: Edithburgh Museum, features historical maritime collection (check opening times). In Blanche St: Bakehouse Arts and Crafts, for local crafts; 9-hole golf course. Town jetty, end of Edith St, built 1873, popular with anglers. Boat ramp adjacent caravan park. Natural tidal pool, excellent for swimming. Fishing and offshore diving tours; diving trail to Clan Ranald wreck, brochures available. Nature walks; south to Sultana Point and north to Coobowie, brochures available. Oct.: Gala Day. **In the area:** Nearby Sultana Point, 2 km S, for fishing and swimming. Scenic drive south-west along coast to Innes National Park. Coobowie, 5 km N, a popular coastal town. Tours to Troubridge Island Conservation Park (30 min. by boat), home to penguins, black-faced shags and crested terns. **Visitor information:** Edithburgh Caravan Park; (08) 8852 6056. Web site www.classiccountry.org.au/edithburgh.html **See also:** Yorke Peninsula p. 250.

Elliston
Pop. 217

MAP REF. 302 A5

Nestled in a range of hills on the shore of Waterloo Bay, 332 km SW of Port Augusta, Elliston is the centre for a cereal-growing, mixed-farming and fishing community. Known for its rugged and scenic coastline, excellent fishing and safe swimming beaches, Elliston is a popular holiday destination. **In town:** Town hall mural, Main St, representing history of town and district. **In the area:** Just north of town: clifftop walk at Waterloo Bay; good surfing near Anxious Bay. Walkers Rocks, 15 km N, has good beaches, rock fishing and camping area. Talia Caves, 40 km N. Camel Beach, 50 km N, good salmon-fishing. Lock's Well Beach and Sheringa Beach to south, for surf fishing. Scenic drives north and south of town offer views of coastline; good views also from Cummings Monument Lookout, just off hwy near Kiana, 52 km S. Flinders Is. 35 km offshore (limited accommodation). **Visitor information:** District Council, Beach Tce; (08) 8687 9177. Web site www.epta.com.au **See also:** Eyre Peninsula & Nullarbor p. 251.

Gawler
Pop. 15 484

MAP REF. 296 D5, 303 L8

Settled by Europeans in 1839, Gawler, 40 km NE of Adelaide, is a historic town and the centre for a thriving agricultural district. It is also the gateway to the famous Barossa Valley. **In town:** Self-guide historical walks/drives, brochures available. Historic buildings: Gawler Mill, Bridge St; old telegraph station, Murray St. Eagle Foundry (1870), King St, once a busy manufacturer of castings for agricultural implements and cast-iron lacework, now B&B. Para Para (1862), Penrith Ave, historic residence (not open to the public). Anglican Church, has interesting pipe organ (open Sun. or by appt). Church Hill Heritage Area (adjacent to Murray St), provides a fascinating 'snapshot' of town planning in the 1830s. Dead Man's Pass Reserve, end Murray St, has picnic facilities and walking trails. Gawler South Markets, each Thurs., Adelaide Rd. June: Horse Trials. Aug.: Agricultural Show. **In the area:** Restored Willaston post office, 2 km N. Roseworthy Agricultural Museum, 15 km N on Roseworthy campus of University of Adelaide, is a dryland farming museum featuring vintage farm implements, engines and working tractors (open Wed. and 3rd Sun. each month, tours by appt). Astronomical Society of SA's observatory at Stockport, 30 km N, has public viewing nights. Scholz Park Museum (open by appt), 54 km N, at Riverton. Wellington Hotel at Waterloo, 76 km N (near Manoora), once Cobb & Co. staging post. **Visitor information:** 2 Lyndoch Rd; (08) 8522 6814. Web site www.gawler. sa.gov.au **See also:** Barossa Valley p. 248.

Goolwa
Pop. 3723

MAP REF. 297 I7, 301 C3, 303 L11

Goolwa is a rapidly growing holiday town on the last big bend of the Murray River, 12 km from its mouth near Lake Alexandrina. Once a key port in the golden days of the riverboats, the area has a strong tradition of shipbuilding, trade and fishing. Today the area is ideal for boating, surfing, fishing and aquatic sports, and popular with birdwatchers and photographers. **In town:** Historic buildings in B. F. Laurie Lane, off Cadell St: distinctive railway superintendent's house (1852), known as 'the round-roofed house'; RSL Club, in former stables of Goolwa Railway (1853). In Cadell St, display of first horse-drawn railway carriage used in SA between Goolwa and Port Elliot from 1854. Steam Ranger, steam-train rides between Goolwa and Victor Harbor. National Trust Museum, Porter St, in former blacksmith's shop dating from 1870s. Next door, in rebuilt cottage, Goolwa Print Room. Two hotels, the Goolwa in Cadell St and the Corio in Railway Pl., date from 1850s. Signal Point River Murray Interpretive Centre, The Wharf, interactive display of river and district before European settlement, and impact of local development. Self-guide walk, brochure available. South Coast Regional Arts Centre, wharf precinct, in restored original police station. Clydesdale wagon rides (weekends and school holidays); boat trips to The Coorong via Murray River (Oct.–June) depart from wharf. Armfield Slip, Admiral Tce, has working exhibition of boatbuilding. Market 1st and 3rd Sun. each month, Jaralde Park, The Wharf. Jan.: Milang to Goolwa Freshwater Sailing Classic. Mar.: Wooden Boat Festival (odd-numbered years). Nov.: Cocklefest. **In the area:** Excellent fishing. Bird sanctuary east of Goolwa, has swans, pelicans and other waterfowl, also bird hide. Nearby, the Barrages, desalination points that prevent salt water from reaching the Murray River. MV *Aroona*, MV *Spirit of the Coorong*, MV *Wetlands Explorer* and MV *Coorong Pirate* cruise to mouth of the Murray, The Coorong, the Barrages and the Lower Murray; details (08) 8555 2203. Milang, 33 km NE, on the shores of Australia's

Coonawarra wine country

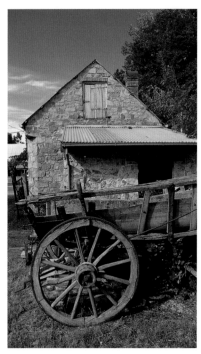

Rustic building typical of Hahndorf in the Adelaide Hills

largest lake, Lake Alexandrina, home to many water sports. On Hindmarsh Is., Captain Sturt Lookout and monument, location of first European sighting of mouth of Murray River. Scenic flights; airport 5 km N. At Currency Creek, 8 km N: Canoe Tree; Currency Creek Winery (with restaurant and fauna park); creekside park and walking trail. Middleton Winery, 11 km NE, tastings, sales and restaurant. **Visitor information:** Signal Point River Murray Interpretive Centre, Goolwa Wharf; (08) 8555 3488. Web site www.alexandrina.sa.gov.au **See also:** Fleurieu Peninsula p. 255.

Hahndorf   Pop. 1726

MAP REF. 296 D11, 297 I2, 301 C2, 303 L9

In the heart of the Adelaide Hills, Hahndorf is Australia's oldest surviving German settlement. Prussian Lutheran refugees, fleeing religious persecution in their homelands, settled the area in the late 1830s. Many of the early buildings have survived and the town has retained a distinctly Germanic look. A number of the local businesses and attractions have a German flavour. The surrounding countryside, with its rolling hills, historic villages, vineyards, gourmet produce farms and native bushland, is renowned as a touring destination. **In town:** In Main St: many historic buildings, some dating back to the 1840s and 1850s; German-style bakeries, delis, cafes and restaurants; Hahndorf's Smallgoods;

Hillstowe Wines for wine and cheese tastings (including local cheeses) art and craft shops; Hahndorf Academy, displays work of local artists; Antique Clock Museum, has 17th-century items; German Model Train Land, housed in historic butcher shop. *A Guide to Historic Hahndorf,* listing 42 historic properties, at information centre. In Heysen Rd, home of landscape artist Hans Heysen is open to the public; paintings on display. In Mount Barker Road, Beerenberg Strawberry Farm for fruit products, and berry-picking Nov.–May. Oct.: Heysen Festival. **In the area:** Many private gardens open seasonally (check dates). At Mount Barker, 6 km SE, many historic buildings in State's oldest town; gourmet outlets, including Springs Smoked Seafoods in Oborn Rd and Brezel Bakehouse in Victoria Cres.; steam-train rides to Strathalbyn, Goolwa and Victor Harbor; Mt Barker District Show held Apr. Nairne, 12 km E, quiet settlement with historic buildings. Mount Barker Summit, 15 km SE, panoramic views of surrounding countryside. Kanmantoo, 25 km SE, and Callington, 31 km SE, both via Nairne, are 1840s mining towns historically intact. Jupiter Creek Gold Fields, 12 km SW, features walking trails with interpretive signs across historic fields discovered 1852. To the west, Bridgewater, Aldgate, Stirling and Crafers are known for exquisite gardens, European-like streetscapes and historic buildings. Petaluma's Bridgewater Mill at Bridgewater, 6 km W, has wine tastings, sales and up-market restaurant for lunch in historic flour mill (1860). At Aldgate, 8 km W: art and craft shops; historic sites, including Aldgate Pump; excellent camellia garden at National Trust property Stangate House (open by appt); Autumn Leaves Festival held May. At Stirling, 10 km W, Hills Affare held Sept. and Mount Lofty Spring Bulb Festival in Apr. Warrawang Sanctuary, 10 km SW via Mylor, large native animal reserve for reintroduced and endangered species, offers dawn and evening walks. Mount Lofty Summit, 14 km NW, highest point of Mt Lofty Ranges: lookout with spectacular views across Adelaide; on-site restaurant and cafe. Cleland Wildlife Park, 6 km NW via Summit Road, has many native animals in superb natural setting within Cleland Conservation Park. Mt Lofty Botanic Gardens, 14 km NW via Piccadilly, Australia's largest botanic garden, features world-wide cool-climate garden species. Belair

National Park, 19 km W, oldest national park in the State: bushwalks, native fauna, picnic facilities; access to Old Government House (open Sun. and public holidays), built 1859 as governor's summer residence, set in historic garden. Wittunga Botanic Gardens, 21 km W, Shepherds Hill Rd, Blackwood, features large collection of native plants in lakeside setting. Old Apple Shed at Balhannah, 6 km N, for cherries and apples in season. At Oakbank, 7 km N: craft shops and historic buildings; Oakbank Easter Racing Carnival, major picnic race meeting. At Woodside, 11 km N, Woodside Horse and Trail Riding Centre offers scenic trail rides. Melba's Chocolate Factory and Heritage Park, 13 km N: chocolate-making and sales; craft studios with artisans at work. Mar: Hills Harvest Festival (several locations throughout district). **Visitor information:** 41 Main St; (08) 8388 1185. Web site www. visitadelaidehills.com.au   **See also:** Adelaide Hills p. 247.

Hawker   Pop. 319

MAP REF. 299 D10, 305 J9

This outback town is 369 km N of Adelaide. Once a railway town, it is now the centre for the Southern Flinders Ranges. **In town:** Museum at Hawker Motors, cnr Wilpena and Cradock rds. Historic buildings: post office (1882), Hawker Hotel (1882), both in Elder Tce; old railway station complex (1885), Leigh Creek Rd. Heritage walks through town, scenic flights and 4WD tours. May: Horseracing Carnival. Sept.: Art Exhibition. **In the area:** Entry points for Heysen Trail (walkers) and Mawson Trail (cyclists). Moralana Scenic Drive, 42 km N, joins roads to Wilpena and Leigh Creek. Opportunities for station holidays in surrounding area. Walking trail, scenic lookout at Jarvis Hill, 7 km SW. Rock paintings at Yourambulla Caves, 12 km S. Ruins at Kanyaka Homestead Historic Site, 28 km S, off main road to Quorn; nearby, Kanyaka Death Rock overlooks permanent waterhole, once an Aboriginal ceremonial ground. Ruins of Wilson Railway Station, Hookina and Wonoka. **Visitor information:** Hawker Motors, cnr Wilpena and Cradock rds; (08) 8648 4014. Web site www.hawker.mtx.net **See also:** Flinders Ranges & Outback p. 252; National Parks p. 282; Classic Tour p. 285.

Innamincka

Pop. 9

MAP REF. 307 Q7, 534 H10

This tiny settlement, 1027 km NE of Adelaide, is built around a hotel and trading post on the Strzelecki Track, and is on the banks of the Cooper Creek. *Motorists intending to travel along the track should ensure road conditions are suitable by phoning the Northern Roads Condition Hotline on 1300 361 033 before departure; also read the section on Outback Motoring (p. 599). There are no supplies or petrol between Lyndhurst and Innamincka.* **In town:** Rebuilt Australian Inland Mission hostel, now houses National Parks office. Boat and canoe hire. Aug.: Races. **In the area:** Picturesque Cullyamurra Waterhole on Cooper Creek, 16 km NE, has Aboriginal rock carvings and excellent fishing. Memorials to explorers Burke and Wills near Innamincka; famous 'Dig Tree' is best known, 71 km across border in Qld. Coongie Lakes, a haven for wildlife, 103 km NW (road conditions can vary considerably, 4WD recommended). **Visitor information:** South Tce; (08) 8675 9901. **See also:** Flinders Ranges & Outback p. 252.

Jamestown

Pop. 1430

MAP REF. 303 L3, 305 K13

Jamestown is a well-planned country town 205 km N of Adelaide. The surrounding country produces stud sheep and cattle, cereals, dairy produce and timber. **In town:** Self-guide town and cemetery walks, brochures available. Heritage murals, Ayr St. Railway Station Museum, Irvine St (check opening times). Parks along banks of Belalie Creek for picnics; banks floodlit at night. Easter: Bilby Hunt. Oct.: Agricultural Show. Dec.: Christmas Pageant. **In the area:** Scenic drive through Bundaleer Forest Reserve, 9 km S, has wildlife, walking trails; continue towards New Campbell Hill for panoramic views of plains, towards Mt Remarkable and The Bluff (self-guide drive and walk brochures available). Near Spalding, 34 km S: series of open waterways with picnic areas and trout fishing opportunities; Geralka Rural Farm, 49 km S, working commercial farm (tours). Appila Springs, scenic picnic spot 8 km from Appila, 24 km NW. **Visitor information:** Country Retreat Caravan Park, 103 Ayr St; (08) 8664 0077. Web site www.classiccountry.org.au/ jamestown.html **See also:** Clare Valley & the Mid-North p. 249.

Kadina

Pop. 3536

MAP REF. 302 I6

The largest town on Yorke Peninsula, Kadina is the chief commercial centre for this agriculturally rich region. The town's history includes the boom coppermining era during the 1800s and early 1900s, when Cornish miners flocked to the area. **In town:** Historic hotels: the Wombat, the Kadina, both in Taylor St; Royal Exchange, Digby St, with iron-lace balconies and shady verandahs. National Trust Kadina Heritage Museum, Matta Rd (access from Kadina–Moonta Rd or Russell St): Matta House (1863), former home of manager of Matta Matta Copper Mine; agricultural machinery; blacksmith's shop; printing museum; old Matta mine; the Kadina Story, a display of town history (check opening times). Banking and Currency Museum, Graves St, unique private museum (check opening times). Creative Arts Network, personalised learning experiences with local residents (available throughout region, contact information centre). Easter: Bowling Carnival. May: Kernewek Lowender, a Cornish festival held in conjunction with Wallaroo and Moonta (odd-numbered years); Mine Shafters B&S Ball. Aug.: Agricultural Show. **In the area:** Yorke Peninsula Field Days at Paskeville, 19 km SE, in Sept. (odd-numbered years). **Visitor information:** The National Dryland Farming Centre, 50 Yorke Rd; (08) 8821 2333, freecall 1800 654 991. Web site www.yorkepeninsula.com.au **See also:** Yorke Peninsula p. 250.

Kapunda

Pop. 2195

MAP REF. 296 E3, 303 L7

Kapunda is situated 80 km N of Adelaide on the edge of the Barossa Valley. Copper was discovered here in 1842 and Kapunda became Australia's first coppermining town. The population rose to 5000 and there were 16 hotels. A million pounds' worth of copper was dug out before the mines closed in 1878. **In town:** Historic Ford House, Main St, an 1860s general store with unusual vaulted iron roof, now B&B. In Hill St: Kapunda Museum (1870s); Bagot's Fortune, mine interpretation centre with mining history displays. Kapunda Gallery, cnr Main and Hill sts, a significant regional gallery. High School's main building on West

Tce, off Clare Rd, formerly residence of famous cattle king Sir Sidney Kidman. 'Map Kernow' (Sons of Cornwall), 8-m tall bronze statue at southern entrance to town, end of Main St, commemorates early miners, many of whom migrated from Cornwall in England. Kapunda Railway Station, Railway Tce, now B&B. Heritage trail and historic mine walking trail, maps available. Finishing point for Bicycle Federation of Australia trials held Aug.–Sept. Mar.: Celtic Music Festival. Nov.: Agricultural Show; Antique and Craft Fair. **In the area:** Pines Reserve, 6 km NW, nature reserve and wildlife. Historic local stone buildings at Tarlee, 16 km NW. Scholz Park Museum (open by appt) and heritage-listed railway station (check opening times) at Riverton, 30 km NW. Anlaby Station, 16 km NE, historic Dutton Homestead and gardens with fine coach collection (check opening times). Scenic drive 26 km NE through sheep, wheat and dairy country to Eudunda. **Visitor information:** Soldiers Memorial Hall, Hill St; (08) 8566 2902. Web site www.kaptour.mtx.net **See also:** Clare Valley & the Mid-North p. 249.

Keith

Pop. 1089

MAP REF. 301 G6, 303 P13

Keith is a farming town on the Dukes Hwy, 241 km SE of Adelaide, in the centre of the former Ninety Mile Desert (now Coonalpyn Downs). The area has been transformed from infertile pasture to productive farming by the use of modern farming methods. **In town:** National Trust-classified buildings in Heritage St: former Congregational Church (1910), with 11 locally made leadlight windows depicting the town's life and pioneering history; The Old Manse. Also in Heritage St, Keith Water Feature (water sculpture). Sept.: Market Day, local art and craft. **In the area:** Mount Rescue Conservation Park, 16 km N, a vast sandplain with heath, pink gums, Aboriginal campsites and burial grounds and an abundance of native wildlife. Old Settlers Cottage (1894), 2 km NE on Emu Flat Rd. Ngarkat Conservation Park, 25 km NE, has variety of flora and fauna. Mt Monster Conservation Park, 10 km S, for scenic views and diverse wildlife. **Visitor information:** 34 Hender St; (08) 8755 3347. **See also:** The Murray p. 253.

Kimba — Pop. 677

MAP REF. 302 F3, 304 E13

A small town on the Eyre Hwy, 155 km SW of Port Augusta, Kimba is a gateway to the outback. This is sheep- and wheat-growing country. **In town:** On Eyre Hwy: historical museum featuring Pioneer House (1908), school and blacksmith's shop; the Big Galah, 8 m high; locally mined and crafted jade (including rare black jade, mined here at world's only known site) at Kimba Halfway Across Australia Gem Shop. Pug 'n' Pine Gallery, High St, for local craft. Sept.: Agricultural Show. **In the area:** Sturt Desert Pea nursery on Eyre Hwy, 1 km W. Walking trail 1 km NE of town, meanders through 3 km of bushland to White's Knob Lookout (360° views). Lake Gilles Conservation Park, 20 km NE, habitat for mallee fowl. Caralue Bluff, 20 km SW, for rock climbing, good flora and fauna. At base of Darke Peak, 40 km SW, memorial to John Charles Darke, explorer who was speared to death in 1884; excellent views from summit. Pinkawillinie Conservation Park, 45 km W, habitat for small desert birds, emu and western grey kangaroo. Gawler Ranges, north-west, vast wilderness area; check road conditions and read section on Outback Motoring (p. 599). **Visitor information:** Kimba Halfway Across Australia Gem Shop, Eyre Hwy; (08) 8627 2766. Web site www.epta.com.au **See also:** Eyre Peninsula & Nullarbor p. 251.

Kingscote — Pop. 1529

MAP REF. 302 I12

The largest town on Kangaroo Island, 120 km SW of Adelaide, Kingscote was the first official European settlement in the State (1836). Travel to the island from the mainland is by vehicular ferry from Cape Jervis (45 min) or by air from Adelaide (30 min). **In town:** Hope Cottage, Centenary Ave, National Trust Folk Museum. St Alban's Church, Osmond St, has stained-glass windows and pioneer memorials. Town's cemetery, Seaview Rd, is oldest in State. Rock pool, for swimming. Penguin tours depart from Ozone Seafront Hotel, The Foreshore. Excellent fishing from jetty. Feb.: Racing Carnival; Street Fair. Oct.: Agricultural Show. **In the area:** At Parndana, 38 km SW, Kangaroo Island Easter Fair. Eucalyptus oil distillery,

'Larry Lobster' welcomes visitors to Kingston S.E.

20 km S on Willsons Rd, off South Coast Rd. Clifford's Honey Farm, 25 km S. Mt Thisby Lookout, 50 km S, for spectacular views. American River, a fishing village about 50 km E. At Penneshaw, on the north-east coast of Dudley Peninsula, where vehicular ferry arrives from Cape Jervis: Folk Museum in former old Penneshaw School; penguin tours, depart from Penguin Interpretive Centre; Art Exhibition held at Easter. Antechamber Bay, about 20 km SE of Penneshaw, excellent for bushwalking, fishing and swimming. At Emu Bay, 18 km NW: excellent swimming at tidal pool in town; Floraison (Flowering of the Vineyards Festival) in Nov. Island Pure, 12 km W at Cygnet River, a sheep-milk dairy. Gum Creek Marron Farm, 24 km W. At Stokes Bay, 45 km W, natural rock tunnel leads to rock pool (ideal for swimming). Flinders Chase National Park, 100 km W, sanctuary for some of Australia's rarest wildlife: Cape Borda Lighthouse in north-west of park; Remarkable Rocks and Admirals Arch in south-west (boardwalk for viewing New Zealand fur seals at Admirals Arch); camping and bushwalking tracks in park. Seal Bay Conservation Park, 58 km SW, large colony of Australian sea-lions, tours available. Further west (about 8 km past Seal Bay turnoff), Little Sahara, large sand dunes surrounded by bush. Murray Lagoon, en route to Seal Bay, well-known waterbird area. **Visitor information:** Kangaroo Island Visitor Information Centre, Howard Dr., Penneshaw; (08) 8553 1185. Web site www.tourkangarooisland.com.au **See also:** Kangaroo Island p. 256; Wildlife-Watching p. 280; National Parks p. 282.

Kingston S.E. — Pop. 1431

MAP REF. 301 F8

Located at the southern end of the Coorong National Park on Lacepede Bay, Kingston S.E. is a farming and fishing town and seaside resort. The shallow lakes and lagoons in the area are a haven for birdlife and a delight for naturalists and photographers. **In town:** Unusual sundial, on island in creek, adjacent to Apex Park, in East Tce. Aboriginal burial ground, Dowdy St. In Holland St: historic post office (1867); Power House engine, Lions Park. National Trust Pioneer Museum (1872), Cooke St. Cape Jaffa Lighthouse (built 1860s, dismantled and re-erected in 1970s), Marine Pde. Boat ramp, Maria Creek. Fresh lobsters in season (Oct.–Apr.). Giant 'Larry Lobster' at entrance to town, Princes Hwy. Jan.: Cape Jaffa Seafood and Wine Festival; Fishing Contest; Lobster Fest; Yachting Regatta. **In the area:** Butchers Gap Conservation Park, 6 km SW, has a variety of birdlife; walking trails and picnic areas. Scenic drive south-west to Cape Jaffa, a small fishing village popular with anglers and divers. The Granites, 18 km N, unique rock formations. Mt Scott Conservation Park, 20 km E, part of former coastal dune system. Jip Jip Conservation Park, 50 km NE, features prominent outcrop of unusually shaped granite boulders. **Visitor information:** The Big Lobster, Princes Hwy; (08) 8767 2555. **See also:** The South-East p. 254; Wildlife-Watching p. 280; National Parks p. 282.

Leigh Creek — Pop. 1006

MAP REF. 299 D3, 305 J4

Located in the Flinders Ranges, Leigh Creek is the second-largest town north of Port Augusta. The large open-cut coalfield consumed the original township, about 13 km N, and in 1982 residents moved to the current site. A tree-planting scheme transformed the new town into an attractive oasis. **In the area:** Viewing area for coal workings, 3 km from turn-off to coalfields, north on Hawker–Marree Hwy; free tours on Sat., late Mar.–late Oct., and school holidays. Copley Hotel, 6 km N. Lyndhurst (39 km N) and Marree (119 km N), respective end points of Strzelecki and Birdsville tracks. At Lyndhurst, unique gallery of sculptures by well-known talc-stone artist 'Talc Alf'. A further 5 km N of Lyndhurst are the colourful Ochre Cliffs, where

Aboriginal people used to dig for ochre (colours range from white to reds, yellows and browns). Aroona Dam, 4 km W, in steep-sided valley with coloured walls; picnic area near gorge. Gammon Ranges National Park, 64 km E, wilderness area. 'Almost ghost town' of Beltana 27 km S, historic reserve; Picnic Race Meeting and Gymkhana in Sept. Sliding Rock Mine ruins, 60 km S; access track rough in places. Lakes Eyre, Frome and Torrens, dry saltpans that occasionally fill with water; Desert Parks Pass required for Lake Eyre National Park (see National Parks for details). *As with all outback driving, care must be taken; check road conditions with Northern Roads Condition Hotline on 1300 361 033 before departure. Also read section on Outback Motoring (p. 599).* **Visitor information:** Leigh Creek Coalfield; (08) 8675 4320. **See also:** Flinders Ranges & Outback p. 252; National Parks p. 282; Classic Tour p. 285.

Loxton   Pop. 3310

MAP REF. 303 Q7

Known as the Garden City of the Riverland region, Loxton is 251 km NE of Adelaide. The surrounding irrigated land supports citrus, wine, dried-fruit, wool and wheat industries. The area was first named Loxtons Hut, after a boundary rider built a pine and pug hut here. The largest war-service settlement scheme in the State was carried out here after WW II. **In town:** Art galleries and craft shops feature local paintings and handcrafts. Heritage Walk, main street, brochures available. Loxton Historical Village, on riverfront, with over 30 re-created buildings (including Loxton's hut), and machinery and implements from late 1880s to mid-1900s. Nearby, pepper tree grown from seed brought by Loxton over 110 years ago. Nature trail along riverfront. Canoes for hire. Jan.: Apex Fisherama. Feb.: Mardi Gras. Sept.: Riverland Field Days. Oct.: Agricultural Show. Nov.: Loxton Lights Up (Christmas lights throughout town, self-guide tour map available). **In the area:** In Bookpurnong Rd, in Loxton North: Medea Cottage, fresh and pre-served local produce; Australian Vintage, wine-tasting, sales. Picnics on riverbank, map available. Lock 4, 14 km N, on Murray River. **Visitor information:** Riverland Information Centre, Book-purnong Tce; 1300 657 625. **See also:** The Murray p. 253.

Lyndoch   Pop. 1137

MAP REF. 296 E6, 300 C9, 303 L8

At the southern end of the Barossa Valley and an hour's drive from Adelaide, Lyndoch is one of the oldest towns in the State. Early industry was farm-oriented, and four flour mills operated. The Para River was used to operate a flour mill in the mid-1800s. Vineyards were established from the 1840s. **In town:** Stone mill wheel (1855), on display in Flebig Square. Self-guide historical walk, featuring buildings from mid-1800s, including many built from locally quarried hard ironstone; brochure available. Apr.: Barossa Vintage Festival (odd-numbered years). Sept.: Spring into the Barossa. Oct.: Barossa International Music Festival. **In the area:** Helicopter and balloon flights. Wineries, most open for tastings and cellar-door sales, include *to the north of town*: Kies Family Winery, Burge Family Winemakers, Charles Cimicky Wines, and Chateau Yaldara Estate (tours); *east of town*: Kellermeister Wines and Barossa Settlers; *south of town*: Twin Valley Estate; *west of town*: Wards Gateway Cellar and Tait Wines. *At Rowland Flat*, 5 km NE: Jenke Vineyard Cellars, Miranda Wines, Orlando Wines and Liebichwein. Goldfields Walk, starts 10 km SW near cnr Goldfields and Para Wirra rds, brochure available. Barossa Reservoir and Whispering Wall, 8 km SW, acoustic phenomenon allowing messages whispered at one end to be audible at the other end, 140 m away. At Kersbrook, 22 km S: historic buildings; trout farm. Lyndoch Lavender Farm, 6 km SE, over 30 varieties of lavender; shop, picnic/barbecue facilities (open Sept.–Feb.). **Visitor information:** Barossa Wine and Visitor Centre, 66 Murray St, Tanunda; (08) 8563 0600, freecall 1800 812 662. **See also:** Barossa Valley p. 248.

McLaren Vale   Pop. 2313

MAP REF. 296 A13, 297 F4, 298 E8, 301 B2, 303 K10

Centre of the McLaren winegrowing region, in which 53 wineries flourish, McLaren Vale is 42 km S of Adelaide. Serious winemaking commenced here in 1853 when Thomas Hardy bought Tintara Vineyards. Today, Hardy's is the largest winery in the area. **In town:** Historic buildings: Hotel McLaren and Congregational Church, both in Main Rd. Almond Train, Main Rd, variety of local almond produce housed in restored railway carriage. June: Sea and Vines Festival. Oct.: Continuous Picnic; Wine Bushing Festival. **In the area:** McLaren Vale walk, brochure available; many historic buildings are now restaurants, wineries, tearooms and galleries. Tourist Route 60, scenic drive through wine region; starts at information centre, brochure available. Most wineries open for tastings and cellar-door sales. At Hardy's Tintara Wines, on Main Rd, huge heritage-listed Moreton Bay fig tree in grounds and Dridans Fine Arts housed in former cellar. Salopian Inn, 1 km S, restaurant in historic building. McLaren Vale Olive Grove, 3 km N, has olive-growing, processing, bottling, sales and tours. Coriole Vineyards, 5 km NE, sells a range of fine oils and vinegars. At Old Noarlunga, 5 km NW: colonial buildings, walk brochures available; good swimming and fishing at nearby beaches, nude swimming at southern end of Maslin Beach and marked underwater trail along reef for divers and snorkellers at Port Noarlunga. At Hackham, 13 km NW, Lakeside Leisure Park. At Hallett Cove, 21 km NW, glacier tracks. **Visitor information:** Main Rd; (08) 8323 9944, freecall 1800 628 410. **See also:** Fleurieu Peninsula p. 255.

Maitland   Pop. 999

MAP REF. 302 I7

Maitland is in the heart of Yorke Peninsula and is the centre for this rich agricultural area. Wheat, barley, wool and beef cattle are the main primary industries. Parks surround the town centre and provide pleasant picnic spots. **In town:** St John's Anglican Church (1876), cnr Alice and Caroline sts, stained-glass depicting Biblical stories in Australian settings. Lions Bicycle Adventure Park, off Elizabeth St. Maitland National Trust Museum, in former school, cnr Gardiner and Kilkerran tces, displays local history (check times). Self-guide town heritage walk with interpretive signs, leaflet from District Council, Elizabeth St. Apr.: Agricultural Show. **In the area:** Coastal town of Balgowan, 15 km W, has safe, sandy beaches and is popular with anglers. **Visitor information:** Moonta Station Visitor Information Centre, Kadina Rd, Moonta; (08) 8825 1891. Web site www.classiccountry.org.au/maitland.html **See also:** Yorke Peninsula p. 250.

Murray River near Mannum

Mannum   Pop. 1966

MAP REF. 296 I9, 301 D1, 303 M9

Mannum, 82 km E of Adelaide, is one of the oldest towns on the Murray River. Wool, beef and cereals are produced in the region, and the town is the starting point for the Adelaide water-supply pipeline. Picturesque terraced banks overlook the river. The *Mary Ann*, the first paddle-steamer on the Murray, left Mannum in 1853 and the first steam car was built in town in 1894 by David Shearer. **In town:** Mary Ann Reserve, a popular recreation reserve riverbank; PS *River Murray Princess* is moored here between cruises. Historic Leonaville homestead (1883), River La., built by town's first private developer, Gottlieb Schuetze. PS *Marion* built in 1897, located in Arnold Park, Randell St. Twin ferries to eastern side of river and scenic upriver drive. Lookout, off Purnong Rd to east. River cruises available weekends in summer. Self-guide scenic and historic walks, brochures available. May: Houseboat Hirers' Open Days. **In the area:** Excellent scenic drive from Wongulla to Cambrai; begins 20 km N. Choni Cottage country collectables, 10 km NW on Palmer Rd. Kia Marina, 8 km NE, largest river marina in State (boats and houseboats for hire). Water sports at Walker Flat, 26 km NE. Scenic drive north-east to Purnong, runs parallel to Halidon Bird Sanctuary for 15 km. Mannum Waterfalls Reserve, 10 km S, for picnics and scenic walks. **Visitor information:** Arnold Park, Randell St; (08) 8569 1303. **See also:** The Murray p. 253.

Marree   Pop. 85

MAP REF. 304 I1, 306 I13

Marree is a tiny outback town 645 km N of Adelaide at the junction of the legendary Birdsville and Oodnadatta tracks. There are remnants of date palms planted by Afghan traders who drove their camel trains into the outback in the 1800s and played a significant role in opening up the outback. Desolate saltbush country surrounds the town. **In town:** Replica of early bush mosque. Mosaic sundial. Camel sculpture, made out of railway sleepers. June: Picnic Races. July: Australian Camel Cup. **In the area:** 2 km W from town centre, historic cemetery. *As with all outback driving, care must be taken when attempting the Birdsville and Oodnadatta tracks. These tracks are unsealed with sandy patches. Heavy rain in the area can cut access for several days. Motorists are advised to ring the Northern Roads Condition Hotline on 1300 361 033 for information before departure. Also read section on Outback Motoring (p. 599).* Daily road information available from information centre. On the Birdsville Track, fuel available only at Marree, Mungerannie Roadhouse (204 km N) and Birdsville (516 km N). On the Oodnadatta Track, fuel available only at Marree, William Creek (202 km NW), Oodnadatta (405 km NW) and Marla (617 km NW). Lake Eyre National Park, 90 km N, accessible via Muloorina Station; Desert Parks Pass required (available information centre; see section on National Parks p. 282). Ruins of railway sidings from original Ghan line to Alice Springs at Curdimurka Siding and Bore, about 90 km W; setting for Outback Ball in Oct. (even-numbered years). Wabma Kadarbu Mound Springs Conservation Park, 130 km W, features a series of mound springs, including Coward Springs, The Bubbler, Blanche Cup and Hamilton Hill (extinct); Desert Parks Pass required (available information centre; see section on National Parks p. 282); prolific birdlife at Coward Springs, an extensive pond formed by warm water bubbling to the surface; nearby old date palms and remnants of old plantation. **Visitor information:** Marree Outback Roadhouse and General Store, Oodnadatta Track; (08) 8675 8360. **See also:** Flinders Ranges & Outback p. 252.

Melrose   Pop. 205

MAP REF. 303 J2, 305 J12

Melrose, a quiet settlement at the foot of Mt Remarkable, 268 km N of Adelaide, is the oldest town in the Flinders Ranges. **In town:** In Stuart St: old police station and courthouse (1862), now National Trust Museum featuring colonial furniture and farm implements (2 p.m.–5 p.m. daily); Mt Remarkable Hotel (1857); Bluey's Blacksmith Shop (1865), now B&B and coffee shop; Serendipity Gallery. In Nott St: North Star Hotel (1854); Melrose Inn (Royal Exchange Hotel, 1857), National Trust property (not open to public). Ruins of Jacka's Brewery (1877), former flour mill. Self-guide historic walk, brochure available. Pleasant walks and picnic spots along creek. Scenic views from Monument and Melrose Mine, Joe's Rd. Further on, Cathedral Rock. **In the area:** Walking trail with superb views (5 hrs return) from town to top of Mt Remarkable (956 m); map available. Mt Remarkable National Park, 2 km W. Near Murray Town, 14 km S: scenic lookouts at Box Hill, Magnus Hill and Baroota Nob; scenic drive west through Port Germein Gorge; 3 km SW is Murratana sheep property specialising in breeding sheep with coloured wool (visitors welcome). Booleroo Steam Traction Preservation Society's Museum, at Booleroo Centre, 15 km SE (open by appt). **Visitor information:** Melrose Caravan Park, Joes Rd; (08) 8666 2060. Web site www.mtr.sa.gov.au/ **See also:** Flinders Ranges & Outback p. 252; National Parks p. 282.

Meningie
Pop. 918

MAP REF. 301 D4, 303 M12

Meningie is set on the edge of the freshwater Lake Albert and the northern tip of the vast saltpans of Coorong National Park, 159 km S of Adelaide. Fishing is a major industry. The area abounds with birdlife, including ibis, pelicans, cormorants, ducks and swans. Sailing, boating, water-skiing and swimming are popular. **In the area:** At The Coorong, south and west: inland waterways, islands, ocean beach and wildlife; 4WD tours. Camp Coorong, 12 km S, museum and cultural centre; bush tucker tours. Scenic drive west following Lake Albert, adjacent to Lake Alexandrina which is the largest permanent freshwater lake in the country (50 000 ha). Poltalloch homestead, 30 km NW, one of the oldest in the region; accommodation and tours. Further west, channel between lakes is crossed by ferry service at Narrung. **Visitor information:** Melaleuca Centre, 76 Princes Hwy; (08) 8575 1259. **See also:** The Murray p. 253; National Parks p. 282.

Millicent
Pop. 4717

MAP REF. 301 G11

A thriving commercial and industrial town 50 km from Mt Gambier, Millicent is in the middle of a huge tract of land reclaimed in the 1870s. Today rural and fishing industries contribute to the area's prosperity, with pine forests supporting a pulp mill, paper mill and sawmill. **In town:** On northern edge of town, gum trees surround a swimming lake and picnic area. Award-winning Living History Museum and Admella Gallery, housed in original primary school (1873), Mt Gambier Rd. **In the area:** Nangula Country Market, 7 km SE, 2nd Sun. each month (not Jan.). Tantanoola, 21 km SE, home of famous 'Tantanoola Tiger' (a Syrian wolf shot in the 1890s); 'tiger' now stuffed and displayed in the Tantanoola Tiger Hotel. Underground caves, 20 km SE in Tantanoola Caves Conservation Park, fascinating limestone formations. National Trust Woolshed (1863) at Glencoe, 29 km E. Scenic pine-forest drive to Mount Burr, 10 km NE. Millicent Wildlife Park and Nursery, 2 km N: native birds and animals, beautiful gardens, rare plants for sale. Lake McIntyre, 5 km N:

prolific birdlife, native fish and yabbies, walking trail, viewing platforms, bird hide, picnic/ barbecue facilities. Fresh farm flowers, 20 km N at Furner. Massive sand dune system and fascinating flora and fauna in Canunda National Park, 27 km W (accessed from Millicent and Southend); self-guide walks, leaflets available. **Visitor information:** 1 Mt Gambier Rd; (08) 8733 3205. **See also:** The South-East p. 254.

Minlaton
Pop. 733

MAP REF. 302 I9

Located 209 km W of Adelaide on the Yorke Peninsula, Minlaton was originally called Gum Flat because of the giant eucalypts in the area. Pioneer aviator Capt. Harry Butler, pilot of the *Red Devil*, a 1916 Bristol monoplane, was born here. **In town:** In Main St: *Red Devil* on display at Harry Butler Memorial; fauna park; National Trust Museum (check opening times); Harvest Corner Information and Craft, for local crafts. **In the area:** Gum Flat Homestead Gallery, 1 km E: pioneer homestead, local artwork. At Port Vincent, 25 km E: good swimming, yachting, water-skiing; Yacht Race in Jan. Gipsy Waggon holidays at Brentwood, 14 km SW. Scenic Port Rickaby and Bluff Beach, 16 km NW. **Visitor information:** Harvest Corner Information & Craft, 29 Main St; (08) 8853 2600. Web site www.classiccountry.org.au/ minlaton.html **See also:** Yorke Peninsula p. 250.

Mintaro
Pop. 80

MAP REF. 303 L5

The township nestles among rolling hills and rich agricultural land, 19 km SE of Clare. A Heritage Town, Mintaro is a timepiece of early colonial architecture. Many buildings display the fine slate for which the district is world-renowned; the quarry opened in 1854. **In town:** Early colonial buildings, 18 with heritage listings. Heritage walk, brochure available. Two historic cemeteries. **In the area:** Magnificent classical architecture of Martindale Hall (1880), 3 km SE; location for film *Picnic at Hanging Rock* (1975), now offers accommodation and dining. **Visitor information:** Town Hall, 229 Main North Rd, Clare; (08) 8842 2131. **See also:** Clare Valley & the Mid-North p. 249.

Moonta
Pop. 2898

MAP REF. 302 I6

The towns of Moonta, Kadina and Wallaroo form the corners of the 'Copper Coast' or 'Little Cornwall'. Moonta is a popular seaside town 163 km NW of Adelaide, with pleasant beaches and good fishing at Moonta Bay. A rich copper-ore deposit was discovered here in 1861 and soon thousands of miners, including many from Cornwall, flocked to the area. The mines were abandoned in the 1920s with the slump in copper prices and rising labour costs. **In town:** Stone buildings, charming Queen Square and picturesque town hall opposite the square in George St. All Saints Church (1873), cnr Blanche and Milne tces. Galleries and gift shops. Self-guide walks/drives in town and around mines, maps available. Twilight Market at Old Moonta Railway Station, Sat. evenings in Jan. May: Kernewek Lowender, prize-winning Cornish festival held in conjunction with Kadina and Wallaroo (odd-numbered years). Sept.: Agricultural Show. **In the area:** Moonta Mines, a State Heritage Area, 2 km SE, on Verran Tce: old primary school (1878), now Moonta Mines National Trust Museum, features mining artifacts and history of local Cornish miners; Cornish miner's cottage (1870) furnished in period style; pump house, shafts, tailings heaps, ruins of mines offices; Moonta Mines Railway tours through mines area (check opening times). Wheal Hughes Mine, 3 km N on Wallaroo Rd, tours 1 p.m. daily (book at information centre; subject to weather conditions and maintenance). Moonta Bay, 5 km W, excellent fishing; Moonta Wildlife Park. **Visitor information:** The National Dryland Farming Centre, 50 Yorke Rd, Kadina; (08) 8821 2333, freecall 1800 654 991. Web site www.yorkepeninsula.com.au **See also:** Yorke Peninsula p. 250.

Morgan
Pop. 492

MAP REF. 303 N6

Once one of the busiest river ports in the State, Morgan is on the Murray River, 164 km NE of Adelaide. **In town:** Antique shops, Railway Tce. Self-guide trail covers historic sites: the impressive wharves (1877), standing 12 m high, constructed for the riverboat industry; customs house and courthouse near railway station, reminders of town's thriving past. Picnic/barbecue facilities, with children's play area, near customs house. Dockyards

The picturesque Blue Lake, Mount Gambier

on Oval Rd (tours by appt). Port of Morgan Historic Museum in old railway buildings on riverfront, off High St (open by appt). PS *Mayflower* (1884), still operating; details from museum's caretaker. Houseboats for hire. **In the area:** Morgan Conservation Park, across river. Fossicking for fossils near township. White Dam Conservation Park, 9 km NW. On Renmark Ave: Engineering and Water Supply Pumping Station, 2 km E (tours by appt); Nor-West Bend private museum, 8 km E (open by appt); Riverland Camel Farm and Trail Ride, 13 km E (day and overnight trips). Free ferry across river, on road to Waikerie (operates 24 hours). **Visitor information:** Morgan Roadhouse, Fourth St; (08) 8540 2205. Web site www.riverland.net.au/~morgansa/ **See also:** The Murray p. 253.

Mount Gambier   Pop. 22 037

MAP REF. 301 H12

In 1800 Lieutenant James Grant sighted an extinct volcano and named it Mount Gambier. The city, 460 km SE of Adelaide, is in the centre of the largest softwood pine plantation in the Commonwealth and surrounded by rich farming, horti- culture, viticulture and dairy country. The Hentys built the first dwelling here in 1841. The white Mount Gambier stone used in most buildings, together with fine parks and gardens, make an attractive environment. **In town:** Historic buildings: town hall (1862),

Commercial St; Old Post Office (1865), Bay Rd; many old hotels. Heritage walks, leaflets available. Open caves: Cave Garden, Bay Rd; Umpherston Sinkhole, Jubilee Hwy East; Engelbrecht Cave, Jubilee Hwy (tours). Old Courthouse Law and Heritage Centre, Bay Rd, a National Trust museum. Lewis' Museum, Pick Ave. In Jubilee Hwy East: the Lady Nelson Visitor and Discovery Centre, has full-scale replica of Lady Nelson as part of centre's structure; Dimjalla Park, fun park. Riddoch Art Gallery, in complex of 19th century buildings, Commercial St East. Market, each Sat., Fletcher Jones Complex. Feb.: Country Music Festival. May: Generations in Jazz. Dec.: Carols by Candlelight. **In the area:** Christmas Lights drive, map available. On the outskirts of town: crater lakes, particu-larly Blue Lake (average depth 70 m), which changes from sombre winter blue to brilliant turquoise each Nov. then reverts at end of summer; scenic 5-km drive offers lookouts, wildlife reserve, picnic areas and boardwalks; Pumping Station at Blue Lake, daily tours down through pumping station to lake level. Timber mill tours; bookings essential. Blue Lake Papermill 2 km E, in Pollard Close, traditional paper-making (tours). Tarpeena Fairy Tale Park, 22 km N on Penola Rd. Glencoe Woolshed (1863), 23 km NW, National Trust building (open Sun. p.m. or by appt). Haig's Vineyard, 4 km S. Mount Schank, 17 km S, excel-lent views of surrounding district from

summit. Glenelg River cruises from Nelson (Vic.), 36 km SE; tours of spectac-ular Princess Margaret Rose Cave. Several gardens in area, details from information centre. **Visitor information:** Lady Nelson Visitor and Discovery Centre, Jubilee Hwy East; (08) 8724 9750. Web site www.mountgambiertourism.com.au **See also:** The South-East p. 254.

Murray Bridge   Pop. 12 831

MAP REF. 296 I12, 301 D2, 303 M10

Murray Bridge, which overlooks a broad sweep of the Murray River, is South Australia's largest river town. When settled in the 1850s it was a centre for the riverboat traders. Now water sports, river cruises and excellent accommodation make Murray Bridge a perfect holiday spot. The South Eastern Fwy provides access to Adelaide, 80 km away. **In town:** Captain's Cottage Museum, Thomas St. In Jervois Rd: Dundee's Wildlife Park; Puzzle Park, a funpark for adults as well as children. Heritage and Cultural Community Mural, 3rd St. Pomberuk Aboriginal Art Gallery, Adelaide Rd. Riverside reserves: Sturt Reserve, offering fishing, swim-ming, picnic and playground facilities; Hume Reserve, Hume Rd; Long Island Reserve, Long Island Rd. Sims Park, Lookout Dr., for views of town. Charter and regular cruises on MV *Barrangul* and PS *Captain Proud*; charter cruises on PS *Proud Mary*. Town and riverside walk. Sept.: International Pedal Prix, novelty bikes, endurance event. Oct.: 110 km Waterski Race. Nov.: Steam Rally Festival. **In the area:** Monarto Zoological Park, 10 km W off Old Princes Hwy, open-range zoo with many endangered species. Willow Point Winery, 10 km S on Jervois Rd. Riverglen Marina, 11 km S, has houseboats for hire. At the historic railway town of Tailem Bend, 25 km SE: excellent views across Murray River; children's play-ground featuring old steam locomotive; Old Tailem Town Pioneer Village, 5 km N; scenic drive via ferry across river to Jervois, then south-west to Wellington where river meets lake; restored courthouse (1864) at Wellington. Mypolonga, 14 km N, centre for sur-rounding citrus and stone-fruit orchard area and rich dairying country. Australia's largest clock, 8 km NW on Palmer Rd. At Avoca Dell, 5 km upstream: boating, water-skiing, mini-golf, popular picnic and caravan facilities. Thiele Reserve, east of river, popular for water-skiing. Other scenic riverside reserves are at Swanport, 5 km SE; White Sands, 10 km SE. Lookouts: White Hill, west on Princes Hwy; east at Swanport Bridge. **Visitor information:** Murray Bridge Information Centre, 3 South Tce; (08) 8539 1142. Web site www.rcmb.sa. gov.au **See also:** The Murray p. 253.

Naracoorte
Pop. 4674

MAP REF. 301 H9

Situated 330 km SE of Adelaide, Naracoorte dates from the 1840s. The area is renowned for its World Heritage-listed limestone caves. Beef cattle, sheep, grains and wine grapes are the main primary industries. **In town:** The Sheep's Back wool museum, craft gallery and information centre in former flour mill (1870), MacDonnell St. Naracoorte Museum and Snake Pit, Jenkins Tce, museum collection and live snakes (closed mid-July to end Aug.). Mini Jumbuk Factory, Ormerod St, has Visitor Centre and display gallery, including woollen products. Restored locomotive on display in Pioneer Park. Regional Art Gallery, Smith St. Jubilee Park, off Park Tce: nature park, walks, swimming lake. May: Swap Meeting; Young Riders Equestrian Event. Oct.: Agricultural Show. Dec.: Carols by Candlelight. **In the area:** At Naracoorte Caves Conservation Park, 12 km SE: World Heritage-listed Wonambi Fossil Centre, has life-like representations of large extinct animals in rainforest environment; Blanche Cave and Alexandra Cave, have spectacular stalagmites and stalactites; high-tech bat-viewing in interpretive centre; guided and self-guide cave tours and adventure tours. Tiny Train Park, 3 km S, mini-train rides and mini-golf. Wrattonbully wine district, 15 km E. Bool Lagoon Game Reserve, 17 km S, wetland area of international significance and haven for ibis and numerous water-bird species; boardwalks and bird hide. Coonawarra wine region, located 40 km S. Padthaway and Keppoch wine districts, about 40 km NW. Lucindale 26 km W, Lucindale Show in February. Bourne's Bird Museum, 27 km SW, huge display of mounted birds (check opening times). **Visitor information:** The Sheep's Back, MacDonnell St; (08) 8762 1518, freecall 1800 244 421. **See also:** The South-East p. 254; Wildlife-Watching p. 280; National Parks p. 282.

Nuriootpa
Pop. 3486

MAP REF. 296 F4, 300 G4, 303 M8

The Para River runs through Nuriootpa, its course marked by fine parks and picnic spots. The town is the commercial centre of the Barossa Valley. **In town:** Coulthard Reserve, off Penrice Rd. Pioneer settler's home, Coulthard House, Murray St (not open to public). Luhrs Pioneer German Cottage, Light Pass Rd. St Petri Church, First St. Apr.: Barossa Vintage Festival (odd-numbered years). May: Barossa Balloon Regatta. Sept.: Spring into the Barossa. Oct.: Barossa International Music Festival. **In the area:** Wineries, *south of town*: Elderton Wines, Hamilton's Ewell Vineyards, Yunbar Estate, Tarac Distillers (tastings), Penfolds Wines, Kaesler Wines; *west of town*: Branson Wines, Heritage Wines, Viking Wines, Gnadenfrei Estate Winery, Seppelt Wines (tours), Greenock Creek Cellars; *north-east of town*: The Willows Vineyard, Wolf Blass Wines; *south-east of town*: Barossa Cottage Wines; also other wineries in Barossa Valley; most wineries are open for tastings and cellar-door sales. Maggie Beer's Farm Shop, 5 km SW, sells gourmet farm produce and wine. **Visitor information:** Barossa Wine and Visitor Centre, 66 Murray St, Tanunda; (08) 8563 0600, freecall 1800 812 662. **See also:** Barossa Valley p. 248.

Oodnadatta
Pop. 160

MAP REF. 306 B6

A tiny but widely known outback town 1050 km NW of Adelaide, Oodnadatta is an old railway town with a well-preserved sandstone station (1890), now a museum. It is believed that the name Oodnadatta originated from an Aboriginal term meaning 'yellow blossom of the mulga'. Fuel and supplies available. May: Race Meeting and Gymkhana. **In the area:** Witjira National Park, gateway to Simpson Desert, 180 km N; hot thermal ponds at Dalhousie Springs; nearby, Dalhousie ruins (of early pastoral station); camping and accommodation at Mt Dare homestead; camping at Dalhousie Springs (permits from information centre). The Oodnadatta Track runs from Marree through Oodnadatta and joins the Stuart Hwy at Marla, 212 km W. Scenic drive to Painted Desert, 100 km SW. **Visitor information:** Pink Roadhouse, Ikaturka Tce; (08) 8670 7822, freecall 1800 802 074. **See also:** Flinders Ranges & Outback p. 252.

Penola
Pop. 1189

MAP REF. 226 A3, 301 I10

One of the oldest towns in the southeast of the State, Penola, 50 km N of Mount Gambier, has fine examples of 1850s slab- and hewn-timber cottages. Penola is noted for its association with Mary MacKillop, a Josephite nun, who in 1866 established here Australia's first school to cater for any child, regardless of income or social class. In 1994 she was beatified (the second-last step in the process of being declared a saint by the Vatican). Several Australian poets are also associated with Penola: Adam Lindsay Gordon, John Shaw Neilson and Will Ogilvie wrote poetry inspired by the landscape and lifestyle encountered here. **In town:** In Petticoat La.: heritage buildings and art and craft shops. Stone classroom in which Mary MacKillop taught, cnr Portland St and Petticoat La.; Mary MacKillop Interpretive Centre behind classroom. At information centre: details of bike trails and self-guide walk; John Riddoch Interpretive Centre featuring local history displays; Hydrocarbon Centre featuring hands-on and static displays of gas process. Jan.: Vigneron Cup. May: Penola Arts Festival. **In the area:** Yallum Park homestead (1880), 8 km W, historic homestead built by John Riddoch; founder of Coonawarra wine industry. Signposted woodland and wetland walk at Penola Conservation Park, 10 km W. Coonawarra region, 10 km N, more than 20 wineries; most open for tastings and sales. **Visitor information:** The John Riddoch Interpretive Centre, 27 Arthur St; (08) 8737 2855. **See also:** The South-East p. 254.

Peterborough
Pop. 1855

MAP REF. 303 L2, 305 L13

Peterborough is an old railway town 250 km N of Adelaide, surrounded by grain-growing and pastoral country. It is the principal town on the Port Pirie to Broken Hill railway line. **In town:** Steamtown, open daily: historic rolling stock, unique roundhouse and turntable; narrow-gauge steam-train trips during winter (check operation times). Rann's Museum, Moscow St, 19th-century exhibits including farm implements. The Gold Battery, end Tripney Ave, an ore-crushing machine (open by appt). Saint Cecilia, Callary St, gracious home (with splendid stained glass) once a bishop's residence, offering

First light at Port Augusta

accommodation, dining and murder-mystery nights. In Queen St: Ley's Museum, exhibition of antiques; Victoria Park, has constructed lake and islands. Guided bus tour of town. Self-guide drives and town walk, brochures available. Feb.: Rodeo. **In the area:** Terowie, 24 km SE, old railway town with several historic buildings, including Terowie Hotel (1874), Church of St Michael and St John (1877) and Pioneer Cottages (1882), brochure available. At Magnetic Hill, 8 km W of Black Rock, a vehicle with the engine turned off can roll uphill! **Visitor information:** Main St; (08) 8651 2708. **See also:** Clare Valley & the Mid-North p. 249.

Pinnaroo   Pop. 606

MAP REF. 110 A11, 230 A10, 301 I3, 303 R10

This little township on the Mallee Hwy is only 6 km from the Victorian border. **In town:** In Mallee Tourist and Heritage Centre, Railway Tce Sth: Australia's largest cereal collection (1300 varieties); Historical Museum; working printing museum; farm-machinery museum; Gum Family Collection of farm machinery. Animal park and aviary with native birds, South Tce. **In the area:** Walking trail in Karte Conservation Park, 30 km NW on Karte Rd. Peebinga Conservation Park, 42 km N on Loxton Rd. In Scorpion Springs Conservation Park, 28 km S, walking trail at Pine Hut Soak. Pertendi walking trail, 49 km S. Near Lameroo, 39 km W: Byrne pug and pine homestead (1898), Yappara Rd, contact information centre to gain entry; Baan Hill Reserve, 20 km SW, natural soakage

area surrounded by sandhills and scrub; Billiatt Conservation Park, 37 km N. **Visitor information:** Council Offices, Day St; (08) 8577 8002. **See also:** The Murray p. 253.

Port Augusta   Pop. 13 914

MAP REF. 299 A13, 304 I11

A thriving industrial city at the head of Spencer Gulf and in the shadow of the Flinders Ranges, Port Augusta is the most northerly port in South Australia, 308 km from Adelaide. It is a supply centre for the outback areas. Port Augusta is an important link on the Indian–Pacific railway and a stopover for the famous Ghan train to Alice Springs, which departs from Adelaide. It is also a popular stopping point for motorists en route to Flinders Ranges and the outback. The city has played a part in the State's development since the State Electricity Trust built major power stations here. Fuelled by coal from the huge open-cut mines at Leigh Creek, the stations generate more than a third of the State's electricity. **In town:** In Flinders Tce: multi-award-winning Wadlata Outback Centre, introduces sights and sounds of Flinders Ranges and the outback; Fountain Gallery, open during exhibitions. Homestead Park Pioneer Museum, Elsie St, has picnic areas, recreation of a blacksmith's shop, old steam train and crane, and rebuilt 130-year-old pine-log Yudnappinna homestead. Royal Flying Doctor Service Base, Vincent St, open weekdays. School of the Air, Power Cres., tours during school-term time. Curdnatta Art and Pottery Gallery

in town's original railway station, Commercial Rd (check opening times). Self-guide heritage walk, includes town hall (1887), Commercial Rd; courthouse (1884) with cells built of Kapunda marble, cnr Jervios St and Beauchamp's La.; St Augustine's Church (1882), Church St, with magnificent stained glass (brochure available). Australian Arid Lands Botanic Gardens, Stuart Hwy, northern outskirts of town. Northern Power Station, northern outskirts (tours Mon.–Fri., 11 a.m. and 1 p.m.). Scenic views and picnic facilities: McLellan Lookout, Whiting Pde, site of Matthew Flinders' landing in 1802; Water Tower Lookout (1882), Mitchell Tce. Matthew Flinders Lookout, end of McSporran Cres., provides excellent view of Gulf and Flinders Ranges. Mar.: Outback Surfboat Carnival. Apr.: Antique and Craft Fair. June: Cup Carnival (horseracing). **In the area:** Scenic drive north-east to splendid Pichi Richi Pass, historic Quorn, and Warren Gorge; see the same sights by train on Pichi Richi Railway, 33-km round trip operating from Quorn (Easter–Nov., check days of operation). Mt Remarkable National Park, 63 km SE, features rugged mountain terrain, magnificent gorges and abundant wildlife. Historic Melrose, 65 km SE, oldest town in Flinders Ranges. **Visitor information:** Wadlata Outback Centre, 41 Flinders Tce; (08) 8641 0793. Web site www.flinders.outback.on.net **See also:** Flinders Ranges & Outback p. 252; Wildlife-Watching p. 280; Classic Tour p. 285.

Port Broughton   Pop. 628

MAP REF. 303 J4

On the extreme north-west coast of Yorke Peninsula, Port Broughton is 169 km from Adelaide. Set on a protected inlet, the town is a major port for fishing boats and is noted for its deep-sea prawns. **In town:** Safe swimming beach along foreshore. Heritage Museum, Edmund St, has local historical displays. In Harvey St: Shandele porcelain dolls made and on display; Council Office Museum in old school building, has displays relating to history of local government in the area. Historical walking trail, brochure available. **In the area:** Fisherman's Bay, 10 km N, a popular fishing, boating and holiday spot. **Visitor information:** Council Offices, Bay St; (08) 8635 2107. Web site www.classiccountry.org.au/ ptbroughton.html   **See also:** Yorke Peninsula p. 250.

Port Elliot   Pop. 1427

MAP REF. 297 H8, 301 C3, 303 L11

Only 5 km NE of Victor Harbor, Port Elliot is a charming historic town with the main focus on its scenic Horseshoe Bay. The town was established in 1854, the same year Australia's first public horse-drawn railway operated between Goolwa and Port Elliot. **In town:** In The Strand: National Trust historical display at railway station (1911); council chambers (1879); police station (1853); St Jude's Church (1854); spectacular views from Freeman's Knob at end of The Strand. Port Elliot Art Pottery, Main Rd. Scheduled stop for steam-train rides on Steam Ranger, operating between Victor Harbor and Goolwa. Self-guide town walks, brochure available. Market 1st and 3rd Sat. each month, Primary School, North Tce. **In the area:** Crows Nest Lookout, 6 km N, excellent views of coast. North-east between town and Middleton, Basham Beach Regional Park has scenic coastal trails with interpretive signage. At Middleton, 6 km NE, Heritage Bakery; old flour mill, largest building in town; further 5 km, Middleton Winery. **Visitor information:** Dodd & Page Land Agents, 51 The Strand; (08) 8554 2029. **See also:** Fleurieu Peninsula p. 255.

Port Lincoln   Pop. 11 678

MAP REF. 302 D8

Port Lincoln, originally considered as a site for the State's capital, is set on attractive Boston Bay, which is three times the size of Sydney Harbour. The port, 250 km due west of Adelaide, was reached by Matthew Flinders in 1802 and settled by Europeans in 1839. With its sheltered waters, Mediterranean climate, scenic coastal roads and farming hinterland, Port Lincoln is a popular holiday destination. It is also the base for Australia's largest tuna fleet and tuna-farming industry, and an export centre for wheat, wool, fat lambs, live sheep, frozen fish, lobster, prawns, abalone and tuna. The indented coastline offers magnificent scenery, sheltered coves, steep cliff faces and impressive surf beaches. **In town:** Boston Bay for swimming, water-skiing, yachting and excellent fishing. Mill Cottage Museum (1867) and Settler's Cottage Museum, both in picturesque Flinders Park. Old Mill Lookout, Dorset Pl., offers views of town and bay. Lincoln Hotel (1840), Tasman Tce, oldest hotel on Eyre Peninsula. Axel Stenross

Maritime Museum, Lincoln Hwy, north end of town; nearby, First Landing site. Rose-Wal Memorial Shell Museum in grounds of Eyre Peninsula Old Folks Home, Flinders Hwy. Arteyrea Gallery, Washington St, community art centre. M. B. Kotz Collection of Stationary Engines, Baltimore St. Parnkalla Walking Trail, winds around edge of harbour, brochure available. Lincoln Cove, off Ravendale Rd, includes marina, leisure centre with waterslide, holiday charter boats and base for commercial fishing fleet. Yacht and boat charters for game-fishing, diving, day fishing and to view sea-lions, dolphins and birdlife around Sir Joseph Banks Group of islands and Dangerous Reef. Regular launch cruises of Boston Bay to visit commerical tuna farm. *Dangerous Reef Explorer* for group charter to Dangerous Reef, off Boston Island (home for large sea-lion colony), and Boston Bay. Apex Wheelhouse, original wheelhouse from tuna boat Boston Bay, adjacent to Kirton Point Caravan Park, Hindmarsh St. Jan.: Tunarama Festival (celebrates opening of tuna season). Feb.: Lincoln Week Yatching Regatta. **In the area:** Winter Hill Lookout, 5 km NW on Flinders Hwy. Glen-Forest Animal Park, 15 km NW, has native animals and bird-feeding (check opening times). Wildflowers in spring, 30 km NW near Wanilla. Boston Bay Winery, 6 km N on Lincoln Hwy; Delacolline Estate Winery, Whillas Rd, 1 km W, (both offer sales on weekends or by appt). At Poonindie, 20 km N, church (1850) with two chimneys. At Koppio, 38 km N: Koppio Smithy Museum (open Tues.–Sun. and school holidays) also houses fencing equipment museum; Glendarra Rose Garden (late Oct.–May); Tod Reservoir museum with heritage display, nearby picnic area. At Lincoln National Park, 20 km S: wildlife, network of walking trails; Flinders Monument on Stamford Hill for views; Flinders Tablet in Memory Cove, a plaque in memory of crew members lost in seas nearby during Flinders' 1802 voyage (gate key and permit from information centre). Whalers Way, a privately owned, scenic cliff-top tourist drive on southernmost tip of Eyre Peninsula: stunning coastal scenery from Flinders Lookout (permit from information centre). On road to Whalers Way: Constantia Designer Craftsmen, world-class furniture factory and showroom (guided tours); historic Mikkira sheep station (keys and permit

from information centre). For boating enthusiasts: Spilsby and Thistle islands (accommodation) and Boston Island; Thistle and Wedge islands (both privately owned), popular with bluewater sailors and anglers. **Visitor information:** 3 Adelaide Pl.; (08) 8683 3544. Web site www.portlincoln.net/touristinfo **See also:** Eyre Peninsula & Nullarbor p. 251.

Port MacDonnell   Pop. 662

MAP REF. 301 H13

Port MacDonnell, 28 km S of Mount Gambier, is a quiet fishing town that was once a thriving port. The rock-lobster fishing fleet here is the largest in the State. **In town:** Maritime Museum, Meylin St, features salvaged artifacts from shipwrecks and photographic history of town. Jan.: Bayside Festival. **In the area:** 'Dingley Dell' (1862, but restored), 2 km W, home of poet Adam Lindsay Gordon, now a museum. Opposite, start of Germein Reserve boardwalk, an 8-km-return walk through wetlands. Cape Northumberland Lighthouse, on coastline west of town. Devonshire teas at Ye Olde Post Office Tea Rooms at Allendale East, 6 km N. Walking track to summit of Mt Schank, 10 km N, crater of extinct volcano. Nearby Mt Schank Fish Farm sells fresh fish and yabbies. Heading east, good surf-fishing at Orwell Rocks. Sinkholes for experienced cave divers at Ewens Ponds, 7 km E, and Picaninnie Ponds conservation parks, 20 km E. **Visitor information:** District Council of Grant, 5 Charles St; (08) 8739 2576. **See also:** The South-East p. 254.

Port Pirie   Pop. 13 633

MAP REF. 303 J3, 304 I13

The major industrial and commerical centre of Port Pirie is located 227 km N of Adelaide on Spencer Gulf. The first European settlers came in 1845; wheat farms and market gardens were established around the region's sheep industry. Broken Hill Associated Smelters began smelting lead in 1889 and today the largest lead smelters in the world treat thousands of tonnes of concentrates annually from deposits at Broken Hill, NSW. Wheat and barley from the mid-north of the State are exported from here and there is a thriving fishing industry. The ocean is close by and swimming, water-skiing, fishing and yachting are

Quorn Railway Station, departure point for Pichi Richi Railway

popular sports on the river. **In town:** Regional Tourism and Arts Centre, Mary Elie St, features local and touring art exhibitions, craft shop and cafe. National Trust Museum Buildings, Ellen St, includes Victorian pavilion-style railway station. On waterfront: loading and discharging of Australian and overseas vessels. Northern Festival Centre in Memorial Park, off Gertrude St, venue for local and national performances. Self-guide walks, brochures available: National Trust walking tours; Journey Landscape, a 1.6-km nature trail representing changes in vegetation from Broken Hill to Port Pirie. Mary Elie St Market each Sun. Apr.: Regional Masters Games. Sept.: Blessing of the Fleet and associated festivals, celebrate role of Italians in establishing local fishing industry. Oct.: Festival of Country Music. Nov.: Cycling and Athletics Carnival. **In the area:** Weeroona Island, 13 km N, a good fishing, holiday area accessible by car. Port Germein, a beachside town 24 km N, with jetty said to be longest in Southern Hemisphere; Festival of the Crab held here in Jan. **Visitor information:** Regional Tourism and Arts Centre, 3 Mary Elie St; (08) 8633 0439, freecall 1800 000 424. Web site www.classiccountry.org.au/ptpirie.html **See also:** Yorke Peninsula p. 250.

Port Victoria   Pop. 311

MAP REF. 302 H7

A tiny township on the west coast of Yorke Peninsula, Port Victoria was once the main port for huge sailing ships exporting grain to England. **In town:** Geology trail along foreshore, booklet available from information centre explains coastline's ancient volcanic history. Swimming and jetty fishing, from original 1888 jetty at end of Main St. National Trust Maritime Museum, Main St (open Sun., public holidays, or by appt). **In the area:** Conservation

Islands are breeding areas for several bird species. Wardang Island, Aboriginal reserve, 10 km off coast; permission required from Point Pearce Community Council. Wardang Island Maritime Heritage Trail for scuba divers, includes visits to 8 wrecks; waterproof self-guide leaflet available. Near Goose Island, 1 km N Wardang Island, offshore reefs known for excellent fishing. **Visitor information:** Moonta Station Visitor Information Centre, old Moonta Railway Station, Kadina Rd, Moonta; (08) 8825 1891. Web site www.classiccountry. org.au/portvictoria.html **See also:** Yorke Peninsula p. 250.

Quorn   Pop. 1038

MAP REF. 299 B12, 304 I10

Nestled in a valley in the Flinders Ranges, 345 km N of Adelaide, Quorn was established as a railway town on the Great Northern Railway in 1878. Built by Chinese and British workers, the line was closed in 1957. Part of the line through Pichi Richi Pass has been restored as a tourist railway taking passengers on the scenic 33-km round trip. **In town:** Historic buildings; self-guide historic walk, leaflet available. In Railway Tce.: Quorn Mill (1878), originally a flour mill, now motel and restaurant; Quornucopia Gallery, large collection of Norman Lindsay paintings, and Bruse's Dining Hall; railway station, departure point for Pichi Richi Railway (Easter–Nov., check days of operation). Nairana Craft Centre, First St. Sept.: Agricultural Show. Oct.: Campdraft and Field Days. **In the area:** Colourful rocky outcrops of The Dutchmans Stern Conservation Park, 8 km W; walking trails in park. Junction Gallery, 16 km N on Yarrah Vale Rd. Warren Gorge, 23 km N, popular with climbers. Proby's Grave, 35 km N; Hugh Proby was the first settler at Kanyaka sheep station. Buckaringa scenic drive, 36 km N, through ranges north of town (signposted). Bruce,

22 km SE, features 1870s architecture. Scenic drive 10 km S to Devils Peak, Pichi Richi Pass, Mt Brown Conservation Park and picturesque Waukarie Creek, 16 km away; good walking trails in area. **Visitor information:** 3 Seventh St; (08) 8648 6419. Web site www.flinders-rangescouncil.sa.gov.au/tourism **See also:** Flinders Ranges & Outback p. 252; Classic Tour p. 285.

Renmark   Pop. 4366

MAP REF. 303 Q6

Renmark is at the heart of the oldest irrigation area in Australia, 260 km NE of Adelaide on the Sturt Hwy. In 1887 the Canadian Chaffey brothers were granted 250 000 acres (100 000 ha) to test their irrigation scheme. Today lush orchards and vineyards thrive here and there are canneries, wineries and fruit-juice factories. Wheat, sheep and dairy cattle are other local industries. **In town:** Historic Renmark Hotel, Murray Ave, community-owned and run. National Trust Museum 'Olivewood', former Chaffey homestead, cnr Renmark Ave (Sturt Hwy) and 21st St. Display of old hand-operated wine press, Renmark Ave. Chaffey original wood-burning irrigation pump on display outside Renmark Irrigation Trust Office (original Chaffey Bros. office), Murray Ave. PS *Industry* (1911), now floating museum, moored behind information centre; cruises available 1st Sun. of each month. Riverland Fruit Co-op packing shed, Renmark Ave, near 19th St, sales of local products (group tours). Zenith Art Gallery, Ral Ral Ave; Ozone Art Gallery, Ral Ral Ave. Big River Rambler cruises depart from Town Wharf, 2 p.m. daily. Houseboat hire. Renmarket, on Town Wharf, 1st Sat. each month. Mar.: Riverland Run, Rally and Rock. Oct.: Rose Festival. Dec.: Christmas Pageant. **In the area:** Self-guide tourist drive to historic sites and wineries (includes town walk), brochure available. Bookmark

Biosphere Reserve: conservation and ecological research; 900 000 hectares north and south of town, including Calperum Pastoral Lease and Chowilla Reserve. On Sturt Hwy: Renmano Winery, 5 km SW; unique collection of fauna, particularly reptiles, at Bredl's Wonder World of Wildlife, 7 km SW. Ruston's Roses, 4000 varieties, 7 km SW off Sturt Hwy (open Oct.–May). Angove's winery and distillery, Bookmark Ave, 5 km SW. On Loch 5 Rd: SA Water Corporation Loch 5 and Weir, 2 km SE; Margaret Dowling National Trust Park, 3 km SE, area of natural bushland. At Paringa, 4 km E: suspension bridge (1927); Bert Dix Memorial Park; the Black Stump, root system of river red gum estimated to be about 500 years old; houseboats for hire. Dunlop Big Tyre spans Sturt Hwy at Yamba Roadhouse, 16 km SE; also fruit fly inspection point (no fruit allowed into SA). Scenic drive 40 km E into Vic. to see spring blossoms at Lindsay Point Almond Park. Headings Lookout tower, 16 km NE, for excellent views of surrounding irrigated farmland and river cliffs. Murtho Forest Reserve, 19 km NE. Danggali Conservation Park, 60 km N: vast area of mallee scrub, bluebush and black oak woodland, and wildlife. **Visitor information:** Riverland Information Centre, 84 Murray Ave; (08) 8586 6704. **See also:** The Murray p. 253.

Robe
Pop. 816

MAP REF. 301 F9

A small, historic town on Guichen Bay, 336 km S of Adelaide, Robe is a fishing port and holiday centre. The rugged, windswept coast has many beautiful and secluded beaches. Lagoons and salt lakes surround the area and wildlife abounds. In the 1850s, Robe was a major wool port. During the gold rush, 16 500 Chinese disembarked here and travelled overland to the Victorian goldfields to avoid the Poll Tax. **In town:** National Trust buildings and art and craft, especially in Smillie and Victoria sts. Historic Interpretation Centre in Library building, Mundy Tce, has displays and leaflets on self-guide heritage walks/drives. Old Customs House (1863) in Royal Circus, includes museum, (check opening times). Karatta House, summer residence of Governor Sir James Fergusson in 1860s, off Christine Dr. (not open to public). Caledonian Inn (1858), Victoria St, accommodation and meals. Robe House, Hagen St: home of the Government resident 1847–1869, now B&B. Crayfish fleet anchors in Lake Butler

(Robe's harbour); fresh crays and fish Oct.–Apr. Jan.: Lions Regatta. Nov.: Robe Spring Village Fair, includes Blessing of the Fleet and Art and Craft Festival. **In the area:** Long Beach (17 km long), 2 km N. Yabbi Farm, 12 km N on Kingston Rd, yabbies for sale (or catch your own). Historic home Lakeside (1884), now offers accommodation and caravan park, 2 km SE on Main Rd. Water-skiing on adjacent Lake Fellmongery. Narraburra Woolshed, 14 km SE, sheepshearing and sheepdog demonstrations. Beacon Hill, 2 km S, panoramic views. Little Dip Conservation Park, 13 km S, features a complex moving sand-dune system, salt lakes, freshwater lakes and abundant wildlife. The Obelisk at Cape Dombey, 3 km W. **Visitor information:** Robe Library, Mundy Tce; (08) 8768 2465. Web site www.robe.sa.gov.au **See also:** The South-East p. 254.

Roxby Downs
Pop. 2446

MAP REF. 304 F4

A modern township built to accommodate employees of the Olympic Dam mining project, Roxby Downs is 85 km N of Pimba, which is just off Stuart Hwy, 568 km N of Adelaide. A road from Roxby Downs joins the Oodnadatta Track just south of Lake Eyre South, 125 km N of Roxby. **In town:** At information centre, Richardson Pl.: maps, history, photo gallery. **In the area:** Olympic Dam Mining Complex, 15 km N: over 2 million tonnes of ore mined annually to obtain refined copper, uranium oxide, gold and silver; surface tours operate mid-Mar.–mid-Nov. (bookings at Olympic Dam Tours; (08) 8671 8361). Heritage Centre and Missile Park, 90 km S at Woomera. **Visitor information:** Council Offices, Richardson Pl.; (08) 8671 0010. Web site www.roxby.net.au/~mucorodo./index.htm **See also:** Finders Ranges & Outback p. 252.

Stansbury
Pop. 524

MAP REF. 302 I9

Situated on the lower east coast of Yorke Peninsula and with scenic views of Gulf St Vincent, Stansbury was originally known as Oyster Bay because the bay was one of the best oyster beds in the State. A popular holiday destination, the bay is excellent for fishing and water sports, including diving and water-skiing. **In town:** School House Museum, in first Stansbury school (1878), North Tce. Jetty fishing. May: Sheepdog Trials. **In the area:** Coastal walking trail, brochures at

post office and stores. Lake Sundown, 15 km NW, one of many salt lakes in area; photographer's delight at sunset. Kleines Point Quarry, 5 km S, State's largest limestone quarry; a.m. tours of quarry including inspection of ship being loaded with limestone (bookings essential; (08) 8852 4104). **Visitor information:** Moonta Station Visitor Information Centre, Old Moonta Railway Station, Kadina Rd, Moonta; (08) 8825 1891. Web site www.classiccountry.org.au/stansbury.html **See also:** Yorke Peninsula p. 250.

Strathalbyn
Pop. 2962

MAP REF. 297 I4, 301 C3, 303 L10

An inland town with a Scottish heritage on the Angas River, Strathalbyn is 58 km S of Adelaide and a Heritage township. The Soldiers Memorial Gardens follow the river through town, offering shaded picnic grounds. **In town:** National Trust Museum, in old police station and courthouse, Rankine St. St Andrew's Church (1848), Alfred Pl. Old Provincial Gas Company (1868), South Tce. Antique and art and craft shops. May: Strathalbyn Settlers Celebration (even-numbered years). Aug.: Collectors, Hobbies and Antique Fair. Oct.: Glenbarr Scottish Festival; Agricultural Show. **In the area:** Lookout, 7 km SW, for views over town and district. Lakeside holiday town of Milang, 20 km SE, an old riverboat town; Port Milang Historical Railway Station, a local history museum. Langhorne Creek, 15 km E: centre for winegrowing district; museum; Vintage Affair held in May. Pottery at Paris Creek, near Meadows, 15 km NW. Iris gardens, 2 km W of Meadows (open Oct.–Mar.). Old gold diggings at Jupiter Creek Goldfields, 35 km NW. **Visitor information:** Old Railway Station, South Tce; (08) 8536 3212. **See also:** Fleurieu Peninsula p. 255.

Streaky Bay
Pop. 1101

MAP REF. 311 P12

Streaky Bay, 727 km NW of Adelaide, is a holiday town, fishing port and agricultural centre for the cereal-growing hinterland. Matthew Flinders, the explorer, named the bay for the streaking effect caused by seaweed. The town is almost surrounded by small bays and coves, sandy beaches and towering cliffs. Crayfish and many species of fish abound, and fishing from boat or jetty is good. **In town:** At information centre: fishing information and interesting shark replica. Powerhouse Restored Engine Centre, Alfred Tce, display of old working engines (open Tues. and Fri. or by appt). National Trust Museum in Old School House (1901), Montgomery Tce (check opening times). Hospital Cottage (1864), first building in Streaky Bay, now private residence. St Canutes Catholic Church (1912), Poochera Rd. Jan.: Family Fish Day Contest; Aquatic Carnival; Perlubie Sports Day. Apr.: Cup Race Meeting. Sept.: Agricultural Show. Nov.: Camel Cup Races. **In the area:** Magnificent coastal scenery and rugged cliffs; snorkelling and diving areas. Scenic drive via Cape Bauer and the Blowhole, 20 km NW, offers spectacular cliff-top views across the bight. Half-day tourist drive south-east along coast. Point Labatt Conservation Park, 55 km SE, has only permanent colony of Australian sea-lions on the mainland. Murphy's Haystacks, 40 km SE, 2 sculptural groups of ancient pink granite rocks (private property; entry by donation at gate). Port Kenny, 62 km SE on Venus Bay, offers excellent fishing. Further 14 km S, fishing village of Venus Bay; nearby, views from Needle Eye Lookout. Bairds Grave Monument, 25 km S. Felchillo Oasis, 20 km NE, incl. quandong (bush tucker) orchard and nursery, fauna park and example of alternative power generation. **Visitor information:** Streaky Bay Motel, 13–15 Alfred Tce; (08) 8626 1126. Web site www.epta.com.au **See also:** Eyre Peninsula & Nullarbor p. 251; Wildlife-Watching p. 280.

Swan Reach   Pop. 255

MAP REF. 303 N8

Swan Reach is a quiet little township on the Murray River, about 100 km E of Gawler. Citrus, grapes, almonds and Geraldton wax flowers are grown in the area. Picturesque river scenery and excellent fishing make the town a popular holiday destination. **In the area:** Murray River Educational Nature Tours, by appt; (08) 8570 2212. Swan Reach (11 km W) and Ridley (5 km S) conservation parks, abound with wildlife including wombats, emus and kangaroos. Punyelroo Caravan Park, 7 km S, offers fishing, boating and water-skiing. At Nildottie, nearby junction of Marne and Murray rivers, 14 km S, Ngaut Ngaut Aboriginal Conservation Park. Water sports at Walker Flat, 26 km S. Yookamurra Sanctuary, 21 km NW, a conservation project including eradication of feral animals and restocking with native animals (guided walks and

overnight accommodation, bookings essential). Murray Aquaculture Yabby Farm, 1.5 km E. **Visitor information:** Mannum Tourist Information Centre, Randall St, Mannum; (08) 8569 1303. **See also:** The Murray p. 253.

Tanunda   Pop. 3499

MAP REF. 296 F5, 300 E6, 303 L8

The town of Tanunda is the heart of the Barossa wine region. It was the focal point for early German settlement, growing out of the village of Langmeil, established 1843, part of which can be seen in the western areas of town. **In town:** Fine examples of Lutheran churches. Historical museum in former post and telegraph office (1865), Murray St, features collections specialising in German heritage. Barossa Wine and Visitor Centre, incorporates Wine Interpretation Centre, 66 Murray St. Story Book Cottage and Whacky Wood (for children), Oak St. Barossa Kiddypark, Menge St, family funpark with rides. For gourmet produce, Apex bakery in Elizabeth St and Tanunda's Nice Ice in Kavel Arcade. Award-winning Kev Rohrlach Collection, Barossa Valley Way, Tanunda Nth, displays range from pioneering heritage to satellites; Barossa Market held in grounds each Sun. Chateau Tanunda Estate Winery, Basedow Rd. The Woodcutters Haven, Buring Rd: rocking-horses, woodcarving items. Heritage Town Walk, brochure available. Feb.: Oompah Fest; Barossa Under the Stars; Tanunda Show and Essenfest. Apr.: Barossa Vintage Festival (odd-numbered years). Sept.: Spring into the Barossa. Oct.: Barossa International Music Festival; Brass Band Contest. **In the area:** Local wineries, *to the north*: Basedow Wines, Veritas Winery, Langmeil Winery, Richmond Grove Barossa Winery, Stanley Bros Winery, Peter Lehmann Wines, Chateau Dorrien Wines; *to the south*: Turkey Flat Vineyard, Glaetzer Wines, St Hallet Wines, Grant Burge Wines, Rockford Wines, Charles Melton Wines, Krondorf Wines. Bethany, first German settlement in Barossa, 4 km S, pretty village with creekside picnic area, pioneer cemetery, attractive streetscapes, winery (Bethany Wines) and walking trail along Rifle Range Rd. Norm's Coolie Sheep Dogs, south off Barossa Valley Way (performances 2 p.m. Mon., Wed., Sat.). The Keg Factory, makers of kegs, barrel furniture and wine racks, St Hallet Rd. At Kersbrook, 40 km S: historic buildings;

trout farm. **Visitor information:** Barossa Wine and Visitor Centre, 66 Murray St; (08) 8563 0600. Web site www.barossa-region.org **See also:** Barossa Valley p. 248.

Tumby Bay   Pop. 1151

MAP REF. 302 E7

Tumby Bay is a pretty coastal town 49 km N of Port Lincoln on the east coast of Eyre Peninsula. The town is known for its long crescent beach and white sand. **In town:** C. L. Alexander National Trust Museum, in old timber schoolroom on West Tce (open Fri. and Sat. p.m.). Police station (1871), Tumby Tce. For local art and craft: Rotunda Art Gallery, Tumby Tce; Briar Craft Shop, Wibberley Tce; Tumby Cottage Crafts, North Tce. Mangrove boardwalk, Berryman Cres., a 70-m walk, signs explain ecology of mangroves. **In the area:** Rock and surf fishing. At Lipson Cove, 10 km NE, visitors can walk to Lipson Island at low tide. Rugged, beautiful scenery and fishing at Ponta and Cowley's beaches, 15 km NE; catches include snapper, whiting and bream. At Port Neill, 42 km NE: grassed foreshore for picnics; safe swimming beach; Vic and Jill Fauser's Museum; Port Neill Lookout, 1 km N. Fishing, sea-lions, seals, dolphins and birdlife (including breeding colony for Cape Barren Geese) at Sir Joseph Banks Group of islands, south-east off coast; charter tours. Trinity Haven Scenic Drive leads south along coast. Island Lookout for good views, 3 km S. Shoalmarra, 5 km S, quandong bush tucker farm (open Tues. for tours or by appt). Fishing at Thuruna, 10 km S. At Cummins, 37 km NW, home to World Championship Kalamazoo Classic in Apr. **Visitor information:** Hales MiniMart, 1 Bratten Way; (08) 8688 2584. Web site www.tumbybay.aust.com **See also:** Eyre Peninsula & Nullarbor p. 251.

Victor Harbor   Pop. 7343

MAP REF. 297 G8, 301 B4, 303 L11

A popular coastal town and regional 'capital' of the Fleurieu Peninsula, Victor Harbor is 84 km S of Adelaide. Established in the early days of whaling and sealing (1830s), the town overlooks historic Encounter Bay, protected by Granite Island. **In town:** Historic buildings: Congregational Church (1869), Victoria St; Mount Breckan (1879), Renown Ave; Adare House (1852), The Drive; Old Customs House (1867), now National Trust Discovery Centre, Flinders Pde,

Horse-drawn tram, Victor Harbor

history of coast and whaling (check opening times); St Augustine's Church (1869), Burke St; Telegraph Station Art Gallery, in former telegraph station (1866); Old Goods Shed (1890), Railway Tce. SA Whale Centre, Railway Tce, has displays to aid conservation of the 25 species of whale and dolphin in southern Australian waters. Whale-watching, June–Oct. The Steam Ranger, a restored tourist railway service, operates between Victor Harbor and Goolwa, via Port Elliot, departs from Railway Tce, near causeway. Jan.: Granite Island Regatta; Regional Art Show. Easter: Craft Fair. Apr.: Triathlon. June: Whale Season Launch. Oct.: Folk and Music Festival. **In the area:** On Granite Island, joined to mainland by 630-m causeway (walk or take horse-drawn tram, which has operated since 1894); little (fairy) penguin rookeries (guided tours available at sunset); Fairy Penguin Interpretive Centre. The Bluff (Rosetta Head), facing Encounter Bay is a 500 million-year-old mass of granite, worth 100-m climb for views. Encounter Walkway, cliff-top and beach-side path leading in sections to the mouth of the Murray at Goolwa. Waitpinga Beach, 17 km SW, set within Newland Head Conservation Park, known for wild surf, coastal vegetation and wildlife. Spectacular Deep Creek Conservation Park, 50 km SW, features impressive flora and fauna, rugged cliffs and section of Heysen Walking Trail. Located alongside, Talisker Conservation Park, site of

historic silver-lead mine has old mine buildings and diggings. At tip of Fleurieu Peninsula, Cape Jervis, 70 km SW, offers panoramic views to Kangaroo Island. Hindmarsh Falls, 15 km NW, has pleasant walks and spectacular waterfalls. Spring Mount Conservation Park, 14 km NW. Inman Valley: Glacier Rock, 19 km NW, shows effect of glacial erosion (said to be the first recorded discovery of glaciation in Australia); Galloway Yabbie products. Hindmarsh and Inman rivers, north and west of town respectively: good fishing, peaceful picnic spots on-shore. Greenhills Adventure Park, 3.5 km N on banks of Hindmarsh River. Urimbirra Wildlife Park, 5 km N. Next door, Wild Rose Miniature Village. Opposite, Nangawooka Flora Reserve with more than 1200 species of Australian plants. **Visitor information:** Foreshore, adjacent to The Causeway (08) 8552 5738. **See also:** Fleurieu Peninsula p. 255; Wildlife-Watching p. 280.

Waikerie   Pop. 1798

MAP REF. 303 O6

Waikerie, the citrus centre of Australia, is surrounded by an oasis of irrigated orchards and vineyards in mallee-scrub country in the Riverland. Situated 170 km NE of Adelaide, the town has beautiful views of river gums and sandstone cliffs along the Murray River. There is abundant birdlife along the river and in the mallee scrub. **In town:** Waikerie

Citrus-packing House, Sturt Hwy, one of the largest in Australia. Rain Moth Gallery, Peake Tce. Lions Park, on riverfront, picnic/barbecue facilities. Harts Lagoon, Ramco Rd, a wetland area with bird hide. Houseboat hire. Mar.: Rotary Food Fair. Easter: Horse and Pony Club Easter Horse Show. May: Riverland Rock 'n' Roll Festival. Sept.: Riverland Field Days. **In the area:** On Sturt Hwy: clifftop lookout and walk, northern outskirts of town; The Orange Tree, 2 km E, fruit products and river-viewing platform. Area internationally acclaimed as a glider's paradise; joy rides and courses at Gliding Club, 4 km E off Sturt Hwy. Devlin's Pound, 11 km E, part of river where Devlin's ghost sighted. Holder Bend Reserve and Maize Island Conservation Park, 6 km NE via causeway. Waikerie Golf Course, 12 km W. Pooginook Conservation Park, across river then 20 km NE, birdwatching, no facilities, 4WD tracks only. Crystallised gypsum fossils in abundance at Broken Cliffs on northern side of river near Lock 2, 15 km NE on Taylorville Rd. At Blanchetown, 42 km W: first of Murray River's 6 SA locks; lookout at Blanchetown Bridge; floating restaurant. 11 km W of Blanchetown, Brookfield Conservation Park, home of southern hairy-nosed wombat. **Visitor information:** The Orange Tree, Sturt Hwy; (08) 8541 2332. **See also:** The Murray p. 253.

Wallaroo   Pop. 2516

MAP REF. 302 I6

Situated 154 km NW of Adelaide, Wallaroo is a key shipping port for Yorke Peninsula, exporting barley and wheat. Processing of rock phosphate is another major industry. The safe beaches and excellent fishing make the area a popular tourist destination. In 1859 vast copper-ore deposits were discovered. Thousands of Cornish miners arrived and the area boomed until the 1920s, when copper prices dropped and the industry slowly died out. The nearby towns of Moonta and Kadina form part of 'Little Cornwall', and there are many reminders of its colourful past. **In town:** At cemetery, Moonta Rd, grave of Caroline Carleton; author of 'Song of Australia'. National Trust Wallaroo Heritage and Nautical Museum, Jetty Rd, maritime exhibits in town's original post office (1865). Historical walks, brochure available at museum or town hall (guided tours Sun.). Historic buildings: old railway station, Owen Tce; in Jetty Rd, customs house

(1862), and Hughes chimney stack (1865), which contains over 300 000 bricks and is more than 7 square m at its base. Wallaroo–Kadina Tourist Train operates from Wallaroo railway station, John Tce (2nd Sun. each month and during school holidays). Jan.: New Year's Day Regatta. Apr.: Prawnfest (odd-numbered years). May: Kernewek Lowender, Cornish festival held in conjunction with Moonta and Kadina (odd-numbered years); Mine Shafters B&S Ball. **In the area:** Several charming old Cornish-style cottages in district. Bird Island, 10 km s, noted for crabbing. **Visitor information:** The National Dryland Farming Centre, 50 Yorke Rd, Kadina; (08) 8821 2333, freecall 1800 654 991. Web site www.yorkepeninsula.com.au **See also:** Yorke Peninsula p. 250.

Whyalla
Pop. 23 382

MAP REF. 302 I2, 304 H13

Whyalla, northern gateway to Eyre Peninsula, has grown from a small settlement, Hummock Hill (1901), to the largest provincial city in the State. It is known for its heavy industry, particularly the enormous iron and steel works, and ore mining in the Middleback Ranges. A shipyard operated here 1939–78. Whyalla is a modern city with safe beaches, good fishing and boating, and excellent recreational facilities. The area enjoys a sunny Mediterranean-type climate. **In town:** Whyalla Maritime Museum, Lincoln Hwy: 650-tonne corvette Whyalla, the largest permanently land-locked ship in Australia (entry includes guided tour of ship); collection of models, including 'OO' gauge model railway; Matthew Flinders Room. Next door, Tanderra Craft Village (check opening times). Mount Laura Homestead Museum (National Trust), includes Telecommunications Museum, Ekblom St (check opening times). Whyalla Art Gallery, Darling Tce. Foreshore area, includes safe beach, jetty for recreational fishing, landscaped picnic/barbecue area, and marina with boat-launching facilities. Hummock Hill Lookout, Queen Elizabeth Dr. Flinders Lookout, Farrel St. Ada Ryan Gardens, Cudmore Tce: mini-zoo, picnic facilities under shady trees. Park and wetlands with picnic/barbecue area, Broadbent Tce. Guided bus tour of steel works Mon., Wed., Sat. or by arrangement; book at information centre (for safety, visitors must wear long-sleeve top, trousers and closed footwear). Large, arid-lands wildlife

and reptile sanctuary, south-east on Lincoln Hwy, near airport (open sunrise to sunset). Whyalla Scenic Drive, brochure available. Easter: Australian Amateur Snapper Fishing Championship. Aug.: Agricultural Show. **In the area:** Cuttlefish spawning (May–Aug.) and temperate waters offer diverse marine ecosystem for divers to explore. Port Bonython, 34 km E. At Point Lowly, 36 km E: lighthouse (1882), oldest building in area (not open to public); scenic drive along Fitzgerald Bay to Point Douglas. Whyalla Conservation Park, 10 km N off Lincoln Hwy, incl. 30-min walking trail over Wild Dog Hill. **Visitor information:** Lincoln Hwy; (08) 8645 7900, freecall 1800 088 589. Web site www.whyalla.sa.gov.au **See also:** Eyre Peninsula & Nullarbor p. 251.

Willunga
Pop. 1622

MAP REF. 296 B13, 297 F4, 298 E11, 301 B3, 303 K10

A historic town, surveyed in 1839, Willunga was named from the Aboriginal word willa-unga, meaning 'the place of green trees'. The town is at the southern edge of the McLaren Vale winegrowing region and is also a major almond-growing centre. **In town:** The Willunga Walk, historic walk, brochures available. Historic pug cottages and fine examples of Colonial architecture. National Trust police station and courthouse (1855), High St. Anglican church, with Elizabethan bronze bell, St Andrews Tce. Quarry (1842), Delabole Rd, operated for 60 years, now National Trust site. Markets, 2nd Sat. each month, Scout Grounds, Aldinga Rd. Start of 52-km bicycle route to Port Noarlunga through vineyards and along coast. July: Almond Blossom Festival. **In the area:** Cowshed Gallery at Yundi, 9 km SE: Mt Magnificent Conservation Park, 12 km SE: western grey kangaroos in bushland; scenic walks; picnic areas and good views from the summit. At Mount Compass, 14 km S: gourmet farms and primary producers open for viewing and sales, including Polana Deer Farm, Ambersun Alpacas, Agon Berry Farm, Compass Pheasant, Deer and Marron Farm and Tooperang Rainbow Trout Farm; Cow Race held here each Feb. Kyeema Conservation Park, 14 km NE, for birdlife, good hiking and camping. **Visitor information:** McLaren Vale and Fleurieu Visitor Centre, Main Rd, McLaren Vale; (08) 8323 9944, freecall 1800 628 410. **See also:** Fleurieu Peninsula p. 255.

Wilmington
Pop. 261

MAP REF. 303 J1, 304 I11

A tiny settlement formerly known as Beautiful Valley, Wilmington is 292 km N of Adelaide in the Flinders Ranges. **In town:** In Main St: police station (1880), now a private residence; old coaching stables (1880) at rear of Wilmington Hotel (1879); early 20th-century billiard rooms (open by appt). Butter Factory (1898), adjacent to school, off Main St (now a private residence). Jan.: Rodeo. **In the area:** Views of Spencer Gulf at Hancocks Lookout, 8 km W, off road to Port Augusta; highest point of Horrocks Pass, named after explorer John Horrocks, who descended through the pass in 1846. Bruce, historic railway town, 35 km N: 1880s architecture, railway line used by Pichi Richi Railway Society. Mount Remarkable National Park, 13 km S, features clear mountain pools, dense vegetation and abundant wildlife; Mambray Creek and spectacular Alligator Gorge in park. Historic Melrose, 24 km S, oldest town in Flinders Ranges. Booleroo Steam and Traction Preservation Society's Museum (open by appt), Booleroo Centre, 48 km SE. Hammond, historic railway town, 26 km NE, 1870s architecture. At Carrieton, 56 km NE: historic buildings; Aboriginal carvings, further 9 km along Belton Rd; scenic drive to deserted Johnburgh. **Visitor information:** Wilmington General Store, Main St; (08) 8667 5155. **See also:** Flinders Ranges & Outback p. 252.

Wilpena
Pop. 20

MAP REF. 299 E8, 305 K7

Wilpena, 429 km N of Adelaide, consists of a resort and caravan/camping park near the entrance to Wilpena Pound. The pound, part of the Flinders Ranges National Park, is a vast natural amphitheatre surrounded by peaks that change colour with the light. The only entrance is through a narrow gorge and across Sliding Rock. In 1902 the Hill family (wheat farmers) built a homestead inside the pound, but abandoned their farm after a flood washed away the access road in 1914. **In the area:** Resort is powered by largest solar power system in Southern Hemisphere (tours). Organised tours, self-guide drives, 4WD tours, scenic flights, bushwalking and mountain climbing in surrounding countryside; brochures available. Numerous walking trails in

Wilpena Pound, including one to St Mary Peak, the highest point (1165 m). Aboriginal rock carvings and paintings at Arkaroo Rock on slopes of Rawnsley Bluff, 20 km s, and at Sacred Canyon, 19 km E. At Rawnsley Park station, 20 km s on Hawker Rd, demonstrations of sheep-drafting and shearing (Sept.–Oct.). Appealinna homestead (1851), 16 km N, off Blinman Rd, ruins of house built of flat rock from creek bed. Scenic drives: Stokes Hill Lookout, 12 km NE; Bunyeroo and Brachina gorges, Aroona Valley, 5 km NW; Moralana Scenic Drive, 25 km s; Wangarra Lookout, 10 km SW (also accessible by 12-km walking track). **Visitor information:** Wilpena Pound Tourist Resort; (08) 8648 0004. Web site www. wilpenapound.on.net **See also:** Flinders Ranges & Outback p. 252; Classic Tour p. 285.

Woomera Pop. 1349

MAP REF. 304 F6

Established in 1947 as a site for launching British experimental rockets, Woomera was a prohibited area until 1982. The town, 490 km NW of Adelaide, is still administered by the Defence Department. **In town:** Missile Park and Heritage Centre, cnr Dewrang and Banool sts, displays of rockets, aircraft and weapons. Old Guard Gate, Old Pimba Rd, opal sales. Breen Park picnic area, Girrahween Ave. **Visitor information:** Eldo Hotel, Kotara Cres.; (08) 8673 7867. **See also:** Flinders Ranges & Outback p. 252.

Wudinna Pop. 527

MAP REF. 302 C3, 304 B13

Wudinna is located on the Eyre Hwy, 571 km NW of Adelaide. The township is the gateway to the Gawler Ranges and a service centre for the Eyre Peninsula. The countryside surrounding Wudinna is often referred to as Granite Country because of the many unusually shaped outcrops. **In the area:** Airport: sealed strip, daily services to Adelaide. Mt Wudinna, thought to be second largest granite outcrop in Southern Hemisphere, 10 km NE: at summit (261 m), scenic views; at base, recreation area; 30-min return interpretive walking trail. Nearby, Turtle Rock, turtle-shaped ancient granite rock. Signposted tourist drives to all major rock formations in the area. Prolific wildlife and wildflowers in spring. At Minnipa, 37 km NW: Dryland Farming Research centre; Pildappa Rock (wave rock);

Tcharkuldu Rock. At Koongawa, 50 km E, Darke's Memorial on site where explorer John Charles Darke was speared to death in 1844. Ucontitchie Hill, 38 km SW, interesting geological feature. **Visitor information:** Council Offices, Burton Tce; (08) 8680 2002. Web site www.epta. com.au **See also:** Eyre Peninsula & Nullarbor p. 251.

Yankalilla Pop. 434

MAP REF. 297 D7, 301 B3, 303 K11

A growing settlement just inland from the west coast of Fleurieu Peninsula, Yankalilla is 35 km W of Victor Harbor. **In town:** In Main St: Uniting Church (1878); Bungala House and the Olde Peppertree Store, for gifts and pottery; Yankalilla Hotel, country-style counter meals; historical museum. Oct.: Agricultural Show. **In the area:** Seaside town of Normanville, 4 km W. Bay Tree Farm, 14 km SW on Cape Jervis Rd, has herbs, flowers, afternoon teas in farm setting. Paradise Wirrina Cove Resort, 10 km SW, family resort. Second Valley, 17 km SW, peaceful picnic spot with jetty for fishing. Cape Jervis, 35 km S, departure point for vehicular ferries to Kangaroo Island. Glacier Rock, a 500 million-year-old Cambrian quartzite, 22 km E. Steep hillsides and gullies, and western grey kangaroos at Myponga Conservation Park, 9 km NE. At Myponga, 14 km NE: historic

Innes National Park south-west of Yorketown

buildings; Myponga Reservoir, ideal barbecue/picnic setting and lookout; further 4 km NE, Begonia Farm (open Oct.–Apr.). **Visitor information:** 106 Main St; (08) 8558 2999. Web site www.yankalillabay.com **See also:** Fleurieu Peninsula p. 255.

Yorketown Pop. 692

MAP REF. 302 I9

The principal town at the southern end of Yorke Peninsula, Yorketown services the surrounding cereal-growing district. The landscape is dotted with numerous inland salt lakes, some of which are still mined. **In the area:** At Innes National Park, 77 km SW: rugged coastal scenery and peaceful hinterland; Inneston, historic mining town in park, managed as historic site by the Department for Environment, Heritage and Aboriginal Affairs; Browns Beach and Pondalowie Bay for surfing, fishing and diving; Yorke Surfing Classic each Oct. Many shipwrecks along coast including *The Ethel* (remains near Inneston). Surfing at Daly Head, 50 km W. South of Daly Head, blowhole. At Corny Point, on north-western tip of Peninsula, 55 km NW: lighthouse, lookout, camping, fishing. **Visitor information:** District Council of Yorketown, 15 Edithburgh Rd; (08) 8852 0200. Web site www.classic-country.org.au/ yorketown. html **See also:** Yorke Peninsula p. 250.

WILDLIFE-WATCHING

Pelicans are a common sight on the southern coastline

AROUND ADELAIDE

Victor Harbor, on the Fleurieu Peninsula just south of Adelaide, should be the first stop for keen whale-watchers. More than 25 whale and dolphin species swim off the South Australian coast, and the South Australian Whale Centre at Victor Harbor has an interpretive display explaining the life-cycles of these popular mammals. The centre's Whale Information Network tracks the movements of migratory whales and offers Statewide information on the best whale-watching localities. Southern right whales can be seen along the Fleurieu Peninsula coastline from June to October. Connected by causeway to Victor Harbor is Granite Island Recreation Park, a haven for little (fairy) penguins. There is an interpretive centre on the island as well as year-round penguin-viewing walks at sunset.

Kangaroo Island also has a healthy population of little (fairy) penguins; interpretive centres and guided tours operate at Penneshaw and Kingscote. Guided tours also operate at Seal Bay to see the 500-strong colony of Australian sea-lions, while Cape du Couedic in Flinders Chase National Park is the spot to encounter some of the thousands of New Zealand fur seals as they rest ashore after fishing excursions. The island is also home to about 240 bird species, and native animals including kangaroos, koalas, tammar, wallabies and the ever-elusive platypus.

IN THE SOUTH OF THE STATE

Bent-wing bats migrate each spring from south-eastern Australia to the Bat Cave in **Naracoorte Caves Conservation Park**, where they join the cave's resident bats. The Bat Cave Teleview Centre provides a unique view of the bats' activities. Infra-red cameras in the caves are connected to monitors in the centre, allowing visitors to view the tiny mammals without disturbing them. Each evening between November and February thousands of bats fly from the cave to feed on insects.

Bool Lagoon Game Reserve lies 17 kilometres south of Naracoorte. The lagoon is a vital habitat and essential drought refuge for many rare and endangered bird species. Its cycle of flooding and drying is perfect for the breeding patterns of waterbirds. In spring black swans crowd the lagoon. Take the Tea-tree Boardwalk into the heart of the lagoon, where ibis and spoonbills nest in the foliage. Bourne's Bird Museum, 10 kilometres west of Bool Lagoon, has a huge display of mounted birds for close-up viewing (closed Tuesdays and July–August).

Near the mouth of the Murray River is **Coorong National Park**, which curves 145 kilometres along the coast. Here, over 240 species of native birds live among the narrow saltwater lagoons, sand dunes, saltpans, claypans and bush. Take binoculars to view pelicans, crested terns and silver gulls. Pied oystercatchers feed along the beaches – their flattened bills allow them to dig up and open cockles. Flocks of tiny red-necked stints migrate to The Coorong from Siberia via Japan each year.

ALONG THE NORTHERN COASTLINE

Motorists heading north to make the Nullarbor crossing should consider taking the coastal route and stopping to meet the only permanent colony of Australian sea-lions on the mainland. On the east coast of the Eyre Peninsula, the islands off Tumby Bay, which are part of the **Sir Joseph Banks Group Conservation Park**, protect a sea mammal population of dolphins, sea-lions and seals. It is also Australia's largest breeding ground for Cape Barren Geese. Visitors to **Point Labatt Conservation Park**, south of Streaky Bay, can see these wonderful sea mammals resting and playing at remarkably close range.

Between June and October, Nullarbor travellers have the opportunity of viewing southern right whales from one of the best cliff-based whale-watching sites in the world. Twelve kilometres east of the Nullarbor Roadhouse on the Eyre Highway, a signposted turn-off extends from the

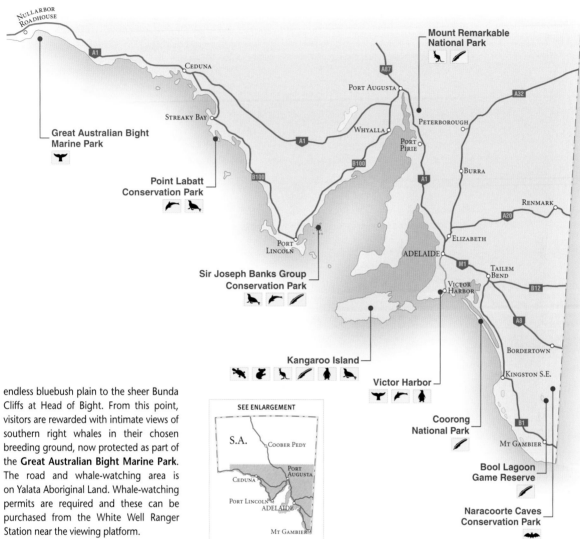

endless bluebush plain to the sheer Bunda Cliffs at Head of Bight. From this point, visitors are rewarded with intimate views of southern right whales in their chosen breeding ground, now protected as part of the **Great Australian Bight Marine Park**. The road and whale-watching area is on Yalata Aboriginal Land. Whale-watching permits are required and these can be purchased from the White Well Ranger Station near the viewing platform.

INLAND

Mount Remarkable National Park lies on the southern edge of the Flinders Ranges. Just outside the park there are red kangaroos in the plains surrounding Mambray Creek. Adelaide rosellas, little corellas and kookaburras are also residents, their riotous calls breaking the peace of the plains. Within the park, sugar gums and native pines in Mambray Creek Gorge offer shelter for euros. From a distance these may be confused with grey kangaroos, but euros are stockier and have darker paws, hindfeet and tail tips. Look also for the yellow-footed rock wallaby.

For a good overview of South Australian wildlife, visit the Cleland Wildlife Park at Mount Lofty, part of the larger Cleland Conservation Park just outside Adelaide. Here it is possible to view dingoes, wombats, kangaroos and wallabies; walk through the extensive aviaries; or join a guided night walk to spot nocturnal and endangered animals. For more information on wildlife-watching in national parks, contact The Environment Shop, 77 Grenfell St, Adelaide (GPO Box 1047, Adelaide SA 5001); (08) 8204 1910. Web site www.parksweb.sa.gov.au

WILDLIFE-WATCHING ETHICS

Do not disturb wildlife or wildlife habitats. Keep the impact of your presence to a minimum. Use available cover or hides wherever possible.

Do not feed wildlife, even in urban areas. (Note: supervised feeding is allowed at some locations)

Be careful not to introduce exotic plants and animals – leave your pets at home.

Stay on defined trails.

NATIONAL PARKS

Flinders Ranges National Park

AROUND ADELAIDE

Cleland Wildlife Park is located in the natural bushland of **Cleland Conservation Park**, on the slopes of Mount Lofty overlooking Adelaide. Here visitors are able to walk freely among the animals, which are housed in areas similar to their native habitat. For those wanting to spot nocturnal animals, rangers conduct guided night walks. Also within the park is the popular Waterfall Gully; its cascade is most impressive in winter. After walking the many trails in the area visitors can relax in the nearby bistro overlooking the wildlife enclosure.

Within Adelaide's southern suburbs is **Belair National Park**, established with great foresight in 1891. It now protects one of the last remaining pockets of native vegetation in the Adelaide Hills area. The park features a wide range of recreational facilities such as ovals, tennis courts, picnic shelters, barbecues and a playground. Visitors can also take one of the self-guide walks or join a tour of Old Government House.

IN THE SOUTH-EAST OF THE STATE

Coorong National Park, one of the State's finest, is 185 kilometres from Adelaide, south of the Murray River mouth. Named from the Aboriginal word *karangh*, meaning 'narrow neck', The Coorong is a series of saltwater lagoons fed by the Murray and separated from the sea by Younghusband Peninsula. The park contains wetlands of international importance. There are six island bird sanctuaries, which are prohibited to the public. These islands house rookeries of pelicans, crested terns and silver gulls. Around 240 species of birds have been recorded in The Coorong. You can take the pleasant drive along the coast road beside the waterway, stopping to camp or picnic. The ocean beach is a favourite haunt of anglers. At dusk, kangaroos and wombats can be seen feeding on the grassed open areas in the park.

Bool Lagoon Game Reserve is on the southern plains of South Australia, near Naracoorte. The lagoon's natural cycle of flooding and drying makes a perfect breeding ground for waterbirds. In spring, when the water is deepest, thousands of black swans crowd the lagoon. In summer and autumn, when the water is shallow, waterfowl and waders flock to feed on the rich plant life. Bool Lagoon is also the largest permanent ibis rookery in Australia. Dense thickets of paperbark and banks of reeds in the reserve's central reaches provide a safe breeding ground. Boardwalks allow access to wildlife without disturbing the environment.

The World Heritage-listed **Naracoorte Caves** are in a small conservation park in the south-east of the State. These impressive caves enclose a wonderland of stalagmites, stalactites, shawls, straws and other calcite formations. Four of the limestone caves, including Blanche Cave, the first to be discovered (1845), are open for inspection through guided or adventure tours. The Wonambi Fossil Centre, (08) 8762 2340, gives visitors the chance to see life-like representations of extinct animals, such as the giant browsing kangaroos, a hippopotamus-sized wombat and a marsupial lion, that roamed the area 200 000 years ago.

IN THE SOUTH-WEST OF THE STATE

Flinders Chase National Park, encompassing most of the western end of Kangaroo Island, protects pristine natural vegetation including mallee forests and stunted coastal plants. Bushwalkers can enjoy trails along creeks to secluded beaches, or follow the rugged coastline to observe the full force of the Southern Ocean. Lighthouses and keepers' cottages provide cultural interest. Visitors are provided with opportunities to see kangaroos, koalas, fur seals, echidnas and platypuses. **Seal Bay Conservation Park**, also on Kangaroo Island, allows visitors to see Australian sea-lion breeding colonies. The neighbouring **Cape Gantheaume Wilderness Protection Area** boasts a spectacular coastline of high cliffs and caves and is a popular area for experienced bushwalkers. Murray Lagoon, the largest wetland habitat on the island, is a haven for birdlife and birdwatchers alike. Camping is available in the adjacent Cape Gantheaume Conservation Park areas. More information is available from National Parks and Wildlife South Australia (NPWSA), 37 Dauncey St, Kingscote; (08) 8553 2381.

On the south-west tip of Yorke Peninsula is **Innes National Park**, where the ground is blanketed with wildflowers in spring and birdwatching is a favourite pastime. As well as native bushland and magnificent coastal scenery, there are many excellent fishing and surfing spots. Walking trails lead to the coast and to the historic ruins of Inneston (1913). This small settlement once housed miners who dug for gypsum, used for plaster and chalk; for many years nearly every schoolchild in Australia was taught with the aid of blackboard chalk mined here and shipped from Stenhouse Bay. Camping and accommodation are available.

The Eyre Peninsula, bordered to the north by the Eyre Highway, contains a number of parks. **Coffin Bay National Park** and **Lincoln National Park** feature wilderness areas and spectacular coastal scenery. Both parks provide excellent opportunities for bush camping, birdwatching and bushwalking. Coffin Bay National Park is 50 kilometres west of Port Lincoln and includes Coffin Bay Peninsula. The western coastline faces the Great Australian Bight while the eastern part has sheltered sandy beaches and islands. Inquire locally about safe swimming.

Lincoln National Park, a 15-kilometre drive south of Port Lincoln, occupies a large part of Jussieu Peninsula and is surrounded by small islands. At its northern tip, on Stamford Hill, the Flinders Monument commemorates exploration by Matthew Flinders in 1802. From this hill visitors can enjoy spectacular views of the surrounding area.

IN THE NORTH OF THE STATE

The Flinders Ranges, extending for 430 kilometres, contain three national parks. **Mount Remarkable National Park** lies in a rugged and dense area of the southern Flinders Ranges. Mount Remarkable itself rises to 960 metres, and provides spectacular views of the surrounding country. The rock is red quartzite and glows a beautiful red at sunset. Two creeks flow through the park, providing water for river red gums, white cypress pines and brilliant wildflowers in spring. Alligator Gorge, the weathered red cliffs of which are a photographer's delight, and Mambray Creek, have a number of well-marked walking trails.

The **Flinders Ranges National Park** is one of Australia's most popular national parks. The Wilpena section, in the south, comprises Wilpena Pound and the Wilpena Pound Range, covering 10 000 hectares. The Pound is one of the most extraordinary geological formations in Australia. Developed in the Cambrian period, it is a vast natural amphitheatre, ringed with sheer cliffs and jagged rocks. The Pound floor is flat and covered with trees and grassland. A homestead built by the Hill family in 1902, and abandoned after floods in 1914, stands as a reminder of the difficulties of farming in this environment. Rock paintings at Arkaroo Rock indicate that this was a significant area in Aboriginal mythology. Twenty-five kilometres north of Wilpena is the Oraparinna section of the park; this was a sheep station last century, at one time maintaining more than 20 000 sheep.

Further north the **Gammon Ranges National Park**, an arid, isolated region of rugged ranges and deep gorges, provides visitors with the experience of an extensive wilderness area. The mountains sparkle with exposed formations of quartz, fluorspar, hematites and ochres (fossicking is not permitted in geological sites). The Gammon Ranges are a sanctuary for many species of native fauna, including the western grey kangaroo, red kangaroo, euro rock-wallaby and the yellow-footed rock-wallaby. Nearby, the remote settlement of Arkaroola offers motel accommodation and a serviced camping ground.

Further north, in the State's arid lands, over 9 million hectares have been set aside to protect the unique desert environment. All parks and reserves in this vast desert area require a Desert Parks Pass; they include Lake Eyre National Park, Witjira National Park, Innamincka Regional Reserve, Simpson Desert Conservation Park and Regional Reserve, **Strzelecki Regional Reserve, Tallaringa Conservation Park, Wabma Kadarbu Mound Springs Conservation Park** and **Unnamed Conservation Park**. Passes can be obtained from The Environment Shop in Adelaide or NPWSA, 9 Mackay St, Port Augusta; (08) 8648 5300. The pass is valid for 12 months from the date of purchase. It enables visitors to enter the parks as many times as they wish and to camp for 5 nights at a time in any one location. The pass is supplied with the *Desert Parks South Australia Handbook*, which also includes detailed information and maps on each park and reserve.

Lake Eyre, the central feature of the park of the same name, is one of the world's greatest salinas or salt lakes and is 15 metres below sea level at its lowest point. Ironically, it is the hub of a huge internal drainage system while located in the driest part of the Australian continent. Vegetation is sparse, but after heavy rains, when the area floods, the ground is carpeted with colourful wildflowers, the lake teems with fish and birds flock to the area. Care needs to be taken when visiting this area; access to the park is by 4WD and campers must be fully self-sufficient.

Witjira National Park, 170 kilometres north of Oodnadatta, is an area of vast desert, gibber plains, sand dunes, saltpans and mound springs, upwellings of the Great Artesian Basin. Visitors may explore this extremely arid environment from the park's oasis and largest mound spring in Australia, Dalhousie Springs. Its pleasantly tepid waters are suitable for swimming.

The **Innamincka Regional Reserve** covers much of the flood-prone country around the Cooper and Strzelecki creeks up to the Queensland border. These arid wetlands, which comprise a series of semi-permanent overflow lakes, hold many surprises for birdwatchers.

The **Simpson Desert Conservation Park**, which is for the more adventurous park visitor, consists of spectacular red sand dunes, which in places can run parallel for hundreds of kilometres, as well as salt lakes, flood-out plains, hummock grasslands, gibber desert, gidgee woodland, tablelands and mesas. Worth visiting is an intruiging coolabah tree known as the Lone Gum, growing isolated and far from its natural habitat. Access to the park is by 4WD only.

IN THE WEST OF THE STATE

Situated along the Eyre Highway in the far west corner of the State, the **Nullarbor National Park** offers spectacular views of the Great Australian Bight. The park itself is entirely desert, with patches of mallee scrub and some ground cover of bluebush and saltbush; it is renowned for its unique desolate beauty. The Nullarbor Plain's substratum of limestone has been eroded to form one of the largest underwater cave systems in the world, popular with experienced potholers and cave divers. Access to the caves is available only through arrangement with NPWSA, 11 McKenzie St, Ceduna; (08) 8625 3144. The park is home to several nocturnal species, including a large population of southern hairy-nosed wombats.

The range of climatic zones enables visitors to spend time in these parks and reserves throughout the year; coastal parks are cool in summer and autumn, while mountain areas are ideal in winter and spring. In summer, however, many of the State's parks are very hot and have a high fire danger. If planning to visit during the peak fire season, check bushfire danger and fire restrictions. Contact National Parks and Wildlife, South Australia, (08) 8204 1910, for more details.

Many of South Australia's national parks charge camping and entrance fees. For information on camping restrictions, fees, annual and short-term passes, and other details relating to the State's national parks, contact The Environment Shop, 77 Grenfell St, Adelaide (GPO Box 1047, Adelaide SA 5001); (08) 8204 1910. Web site www.parks.sa.gov.au

The Great Australian Bight forms the southern boundary of the Nullarbor National Park

CLASSIC TOUR

OUTBACK ADVENTURE

Quorn to Blinman via Wilpena Pound and Arkaroola (702 km)

This journey through the Flinders and Gammon ranges provides a taste of the outback via well-maintained roads, enabling a conventional vehicle to be used. These rugged ranges to the north-east of Port Augusta have much to offer: extraordinary rock formations, Aboriginal art sites, a fascinating pastoral history and opportunities for bushwalking, camping and wildlife-watching. The tour will take at least a week to complete; those with less time could drive to Wilpena and return to Quorn in three or four days.

Before European settlement, the Flinders and Gammon ranges were occupied by the Wailpi, Kuyani, Jadliaura, Piladappa and Pangkala Aboriginal groups. The local ochre and stone was highly prized, making this area a centre for the great north–south trade routes. Today, the local Aboriginal people live and work in Nepabunna, Leigh Creek and Port Augusta. They identify themselves collectively as the Adnyamathanha, which means 'hills people'. This tour takes you past a number of Adnyamathanha art sites.

AN ADNYAMATHANHA CREATION STORY

Akurra is a giant water snake who has a beard, mane and very sharp fangs. He is the creator and keeper of all permanent waterholes and springs (awi). Akurra lived in the Gammon Ranges. One day he travelled to the plains looking for water. When he came across Lake Frome and Lake Callabonna, he drank them dry.

Because the water was salty Akurra became bloated and his trip back to the ranges was very slow. The heat from the sun warmed his bloated belly and made rumbling sounds that can still be heard over a great distance. As he went Akurra carved out the gorges in which creeks run and made waterholes and springs and finally Ikara (Wilpena Pound) and Ngarri Mudlanha (St Mary Peak).

*Reproduced from Flinders Ranges National Park: Yura Yarta *(Visitor Information, National Parks and Wildlife Service, South Australia, July 1998)*

1 Old railway town

The tour commences in **Quorn**, an old railway town built to service the wheatlands in the 1880s. The wheat failed, and the railway closed. Today, the 19th-century buildings make an attractive picture, with original awnings and ironwork balconies. If you are a railway enthusiast, time your visit to coincide with a trip on the restored steam train that runs along the narrow-gauge Pichi Richi Railway to Stirling North; phone ahead for operating times.

Pichi Richi Railway
Quorn Railway Station
Quorn
Phone: (08) 8395 2566

2 Rock wallabies

Leave Quorn via the road that leads to Port Augusta; just after the railway crossing, turn right onto the unsealed road which passes The Dutchmans Stern Conservation Park. You can visit this popular bushwalking area by taking the 2-kilometre detour, just over 6 kilometres from the turn-off. Otherwise, continue to the Warren Gorge turn-off, and take the short track down to a pebbly creek bed enclosed by towering cliffs. **Warren Gorge** is one of the prettiest gorges in the Flinders Ranges and an ideal

Kanyaka Homestead Historic Site

campsite. A gentle stream runs through the gorge for most of the year. If you are here at dawn or dusk you are most likely to catch a glimpse of the colony of endearing yellow-footed rock wallabies that inhabit the gorge.

3 The ruins of a dream

Return to the road and continue north, past stands of native pines and dry creekbeds lined with river red gums, towards **Kanyaka Homestead Historic Site**. You will pass the turn-offs to Buckaringa and Middle gorges, and Proby's Grave. Hugh Proby founded Kanyaka Station in 1851 at the age of 24; a year later he drowned while attempting to cross the flooded Willochra Creek. The property, which once employed 70 families, was completely abandoned by 1888, after years of drought and flood. Today you can see the sturdy remains of the homestead on your left, just 7 kilometres after joining the sealed Hawker Road. From the homestead you can drive a kilometre along the creekbed to see the remains of the once-substantial woolshed, a poignant reminder of the sheer scale of this pastoral operation – in 1864, some 40 000 sheep were shorn here.

4 Charcoal and ochre

Continue north along Hawker Road. Just past the ruins of Wilson Railway Station, turn left onto the unsealed road that leads to **Yourambulla Caves**, one of the Adnyamathanha art sites. There are two rock shelters, both about 30 minutes' walk from the car park (some ladder-climbing involved). As you make the ascent to the shelters, the expansive Willochra Plain opens out below. The largest shelter features mainly charcoal drawings and the other has yellow ochre paintings, including hand stencils.

5 Panoramic views

Continue on to the township of Hawker. The town centre, just off the main road, is a convenient stopping point for fuel and supplies. Like Quorn, this old railway town is now largely dependent on tourism for its survival.

From the main road, turn left along the unsealed road to **Jarvis Hill Lookout**. A marked 1-kilometre loop walk takes you from the car park to the summit of Jarvis Hill and provides panoramic views of the Flinders Ranges and the flat, arid landscape from which they emerge. These marvellous contortions of the earth's crust can be explained as the product of millions of years of geological activity, or in terms of the Adnyamathanha creation stories.

6 Dreamtime serpent

Return to the Hawker–Wilpena Road and continue north. You will pass several lookouts before reaching the turn-off to **Arkaroo Rock**. This important rock-art site, on the slopes of Rawnsley Bluff, just inside the boundary of the Flinders Ranges National Park, is

named after Akurra, the Adnyamathanha Dreamtime water snake. A 2-kilometre walking track leads to the sandstone rock where you will see snake lines, circles and representations of birds painted in charcoal and ochre.

7 Natural amphitheatre

Just north of the Arkaroo Rock turn-off is Rawnsley Bluff Lookout, offering great views of Rawnsley Bluff and the Elder Range. The country becomes increasingly timbered as you approach Wilpena, with rocky outcrops on the left and undulating hills on the right. Turn left at the Wilpena junction. Before you reach the camping and accommodation area, there is a Visitor Information Centre (camping permits can be obtained here) and general store. There is so much to see and do in the area that you should plan to stay at least a couple of nights.

To reach the famous dish-shaped formation known as **Wilpena Pound** you can either catch a shuttle bus from the Visitor Information Centre, or walk from the car park (45 minutes) to Pound Gap. From here, a walking trail (30 minutes) follows the creek to a restored hut built by the Hill family in 1902. The Hills came here to grow wheat and farm sheep and cattle, only to leave in 1914 after a drought-breaking flood washed away their access road. Before the arrival of the Hills, the area was used as a stock enclosure or 'pound'.

The walking track continues up Wangarra Hill for breathtaking views of the natural amphitheatre with its jagged rim. It is believed that the name 'Wilpena' derives from an Adnyamathanha word for 'cupped hand' or 'bent fingers', and, on viewing the pound, you will see how appropriate that description is. Native vegetation has regenerated and wattles and she-oaks flourish within the pound. At dawn and dusk you are likely to see euros (a type of kangaroo) on the slopes.

8 A special place

While you are staying at Wilpena, take a drive to **Sacred Canyon**, another Adnyamathanha art site. As you walk through this narrow, steep-walled canyon it is not hard to imagine the spiritual significance of the site. The walls have been engraved with images of animal tracks, human figures and waterholes; a rock shelter at the end of the gorge has been painted with ochre.

To reach Sacred Canyon, drive past the Visitor Information Centre to the Wilpena junction and turn left along the unsealed road. One kilometre after the distinctive Cazneaux Tree, immortalised by photographer Harold Cazneaux in 1937, a road branches off to the right and winds through native pines to Sacred Canyon car park. The canyon entrance is an easy 10-minute walk from here.

9 Sheltered oasis

Drive north from Wilpena on the Wilpena–Blinman Road (unsealed), then take the signposted turn-off to **Bunyeroo Gorge**. The roadside vegetation is varied and interesting: river red gums and coolibah grow along the creek beds, and native pines dominate the plains. In spring, the ubiquitous weed Salvation Jane (Paterson's Curse) adds its purple hues to the landscape. Kangaroos can be seen at dawn and dusk and there is a rich variety of birdlife. Emus, corellas, galahs, honeyeaters and wedge-tailed eagles are some of the species you might see as you drive along. Look out for reptiles too: geckos, blue-tongued lizards, bearded dragons and snakes.

Stop at Bunyeroo Valley Lookout for views across to Wilpena Pound and the vast horizontal layers of the Heysen Ranges. The road descends steeply to follow Bunyeroo Creek. The car park is at the head of Bunyeroo Gorge; continue along the creek on foot. As the water supply is permanent, the gorge is full of plant and animal life. Massive cliffs tower above the river red gums, providing shelter from the harsh environment.

The natural beauty of the Flinders Ranges

Bunyeroo Valley

10 Picturesque

Continue about 11 kilometres until you reach a crossroad. Turn right, then left after 500 metres to reach the road to **Aroona Valley**. Sir Hans Heysen painted some of his best-known landscapes while living in an old hut (recently restored) on various expeditions to this picturesque valley. He would explore the surrounding area on foot and set up his fold-away easel to paint the river red gums and multi-hued hillsides that so inspired him. The ruins of Aroona homestead, occupied from 1851 to 1862, are located on the nearby ridge, about 100 metres from the hut.

11 Geological trail

Retrace your steps to the cross-road and continue in a westerly direction to **Brachina Gorge**, one of Heysen's favourite subjects. The road is narrow and traverses the creek bed through the centre of the gorge. Magnificent gums grow beside the creek and the fresh green leaves are in stark contrast to the red sawtooth ridges. Roadside interpretive signs reveal the fascinating geological story of the gorge, layer by layer. Fossils at the western end of the gorge date as far back as 500–1000 million years.

12 Abandoned town

Head in a westerly direction to the Hawker–Leigh Creek Road (sealed). Turn right towards Parachilna and Leigh Creek. If you have time, take a detour at Parachilna to see the

spectacular scenery alongside the dirt road to Parachilna Gorge. Otherwise continue north past Red Range to Beltana Roadhouse. The old township of **Beltana** is off to the right.

Beltana was established to service the busy Sliding Rock copper mine (1871–77). It was also a focal point during the construction of the Trans Continental Railway in the 1880s; up until 1956, when the line was diverted, it was a railway town. In 1983, the Hawker–Leigh Creek Road was realigned to bypass

Beltana, resulting in the closure of the town's last business. It is now classified as a State Historic Site. Brochures for self-guide walks are available from the roadhouse. Residents still occupy some of the buildings, but the streets have a sense of eerie quiet, and the encroaching saltbush adds to the atmosphere of abandonment.

13 Open-cut coalmine

Return to the roadhouse and continue north to **Leigh Creek**, a modern township established to service the open-cut coalmine 22 kilometres north. The original town was built on the coalfield, but when the mine expanded in the 1970s the inhabitants were relocated to this new, purpose-built town.

A 2-kilometre train transports 9000 tonnes of coal from Leigh Creek to Port Augusta each day. You can see the workings of this massive mine on a 3-hour tour that departs each Saturday at 1 p.m., between late March and late October; inquire about tours during school holidays. Meet your tour bus at the tourist bay on the main road, 200 metres south of Leigh Creek (no bookings required).

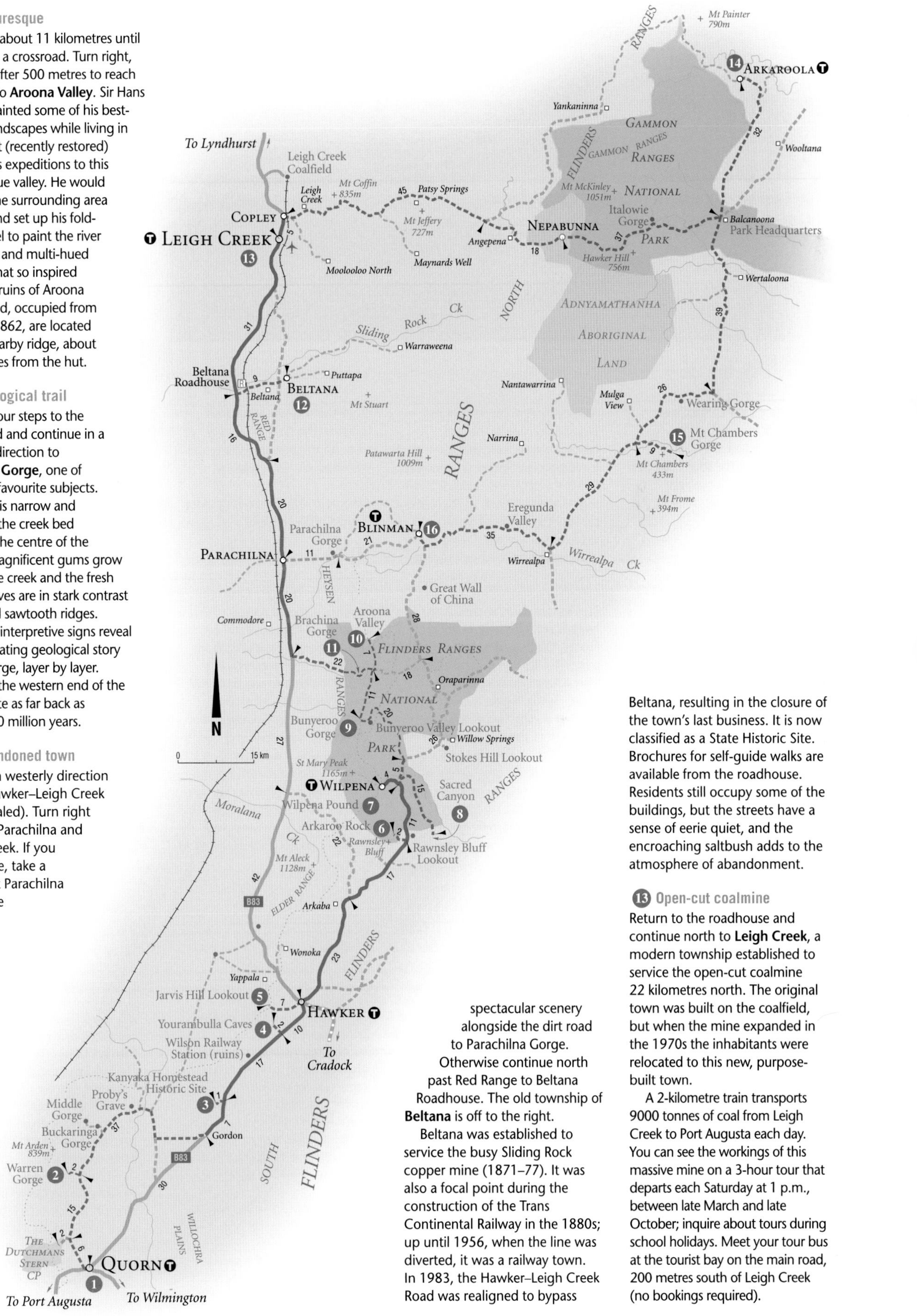

Ridgetop Tour

Before you leave Leigh Creek, remember to stock up on provisions, water and fuel. The next section of the tour – around 250 kilometres – is through rugged country, without facilities.

Leigh Creek Coalfield
Leigh Creek
Phone: (08) 8675 4320

14 Remote and rugged

Drive north to Copley, then turn right along the unsealed road towards Gammon Ranges National Park. The scenery becomes very wild and rugged. Acacias dominate the plains and there are native pines on some slopes, with porcupine grass on the higher ground and river red gums and melaleucas in the gorges.

After Nepabunna the road enters Gammon Ranges National Park and passes through pretty

Italowie Gorge. On reaching Balcanoona, where the park headquarters are located, turn left for Arkaroola Wilderness Sanctuary.

Most visitors stay at least two nights at **Arkaroola**, as there are plenty of activities and places to explore. For a breathtaking introduction to the geology and wildlife of this remote region, take the famous Ridgetop Tour. This 4-hour tour reaches dizzy heights and offers views of Lake Frome. Other guided tours include a bush tucker and bush medicine walk with an Adnyamathanha guide. Scenic flights provide another perspective of this magnificent terrain.

There are numerous walking trails, including some gentle walks through the nearby gorges. Dawn and dusk are the best times to sit quietly by a waterhole and watch as the animals come to drink.

Once the sun has gone down, you can view the clear desert sky through the powerful telescope at the Arkaroola Observatory.

Arkaroola Wilderness Sanctuary
Phone: 1800 676 042

15 Ancient engravings

Retrace your steps to Balcanoona then continue south. Once you leave the national park, the landscape flattens out and the road passes through pastoral stations and across several creeks. After 39 kilometres the road branches; take the right fork to Mount Chambers Gorge. En route, you will pass through Wearing Gorge – its cool shade is welcoming. A little further along on the left is the turn-off to **Mount Chambers Gorge**. Drive into the narrowing gorge; you will have to ford the creek several times and, unless there has

been rain, you should be able to reach the most spectacular part of the gorge, known as Main Bend, in a conventional vehicle. Be prepared to walk a little, though, if the track has deteriorated.

From here, walk north-east along the creekbed for about 500 metres to a gallery of Aboriginal engravings thought to be thousands of years old. A 45-minute walk leads from the gallery through the gorge to a waterhole called Three Sisters Waterhole. This beautiful pool, surrounded by river red gums, is surmounted by the rock formation that gives the place its name. As you walk along, keep an eye out for galahs, little corellas and wedge-tailed eagles. After rain, you might be treated to the gorgeous crimson of Sturt's desert pea in bloom.

16 Old copper town

Return to the main track and turn left, then right at Wirrealpa and on through the Eregunda Valley to **Blinman**. After rain, the valley is a tapestry of wildflowers and the birdlife is prolific.

At 610 metres above sea level, Blinman is South Australia's highest town. In 1869 this was a thriving coppermining town with a population of 1500. Since the mine closed in 1907 it has maintained a much quieter existence. The stories on the gravestones in Blinman cemetery give testimony to the harsh conditions of this once-thriving outback town. Just north-east of town is the Blinman Mine Historic Site. An interesting self-guide trail through the site takes about an hour to complete.

Kangaroo at waterhole

BE PREPARED

Beyond Wilpena, much of the tour is on unsealed roads. These roads are suitable for two-wheel drive vehicles but not all are safe for trailers or caravans. There are many creek crossings in the Flinders Ranges. Heavy rain can cut access and unsealed roads become treacherous after rain. Phone the Northern Roads Condition Hotline on 1300 361 033 before departure.

Wilpena and Arkaroola have camping and tourist accommodation and there are plenty of bush camps along the route, as well as farm-based accommodation and hotels/motels in larger centres. September and October are popular months, so remember to book ahead. Allow a leisurely pace, avoiding strenuous bushwalks, if you are taking this tour at the height of summer. Fire bans are enforced in the national parks from 1 November to 30 April, so campers should bring a portable gas stove (you may not gather firewood at any time).

The Flinders and Gammon ranges are popular bushwalking areas, but do not attempt long walks without preparing thoroughly: the terrain is difficult and water scarce.

To ensure you are prepared for outback driving, read the section on Outback Motoring on page 599.

Returning to Hawker and on to Adelaide

From Blinman, head south for Wilpena. You will pass the Great Wall of China on the left. It is a wall-like limestone ridge, but you won't confuse it with the real thing! Drive through the Flinders Ranges National Park, stopping at Stokes Hill Lookout for sweeping views of distant ranges. From Wilpena take the Hawker–Wilpena Road to Hawker.

From Hawker, you can drive to Adelaide via Quorn and Port Pirie (425 kilometres), or take a more scenic route, via Cradock, Orroroo, Jamestown and the towns of the Clare Valley wine region (376 kilometres).

SOUTH AUSTRALIA

LOCATION MAP

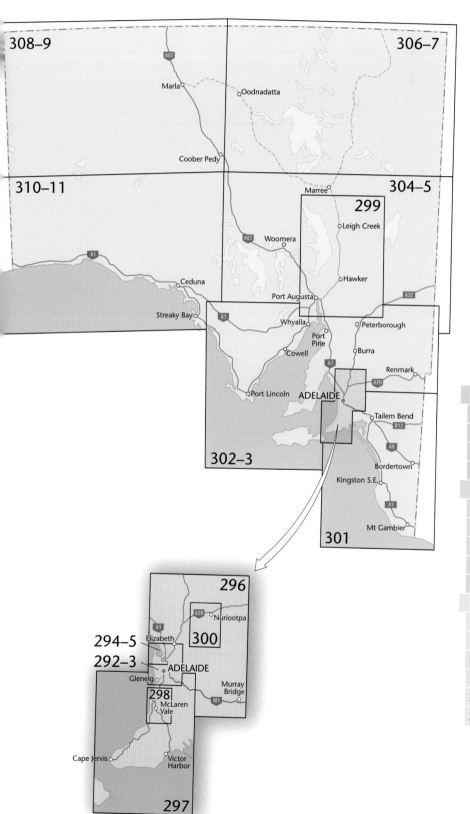

Adelaide and Suburbs

290	Central Adelaide
291	Adelaide Approach & Bypass Routes
292–3	Adelaide & Southern Suburbs
294–5	Northern Suburbs, Adelaide

Touring South Australia

296	Adelaide & Surrounds, North
297	Adelaide & Surrounds, South
298	McLaren Vale & Surrounds
299	Flinders Ranges
300	Barossa Valley

Complete State Coverage

301	South Eastern South Australia
302–3	South Central South Australia
304–5	Central South Australia
306–7	North Eastern South Australia
308–9	North Western South Australia
310–11	South Western South Australia

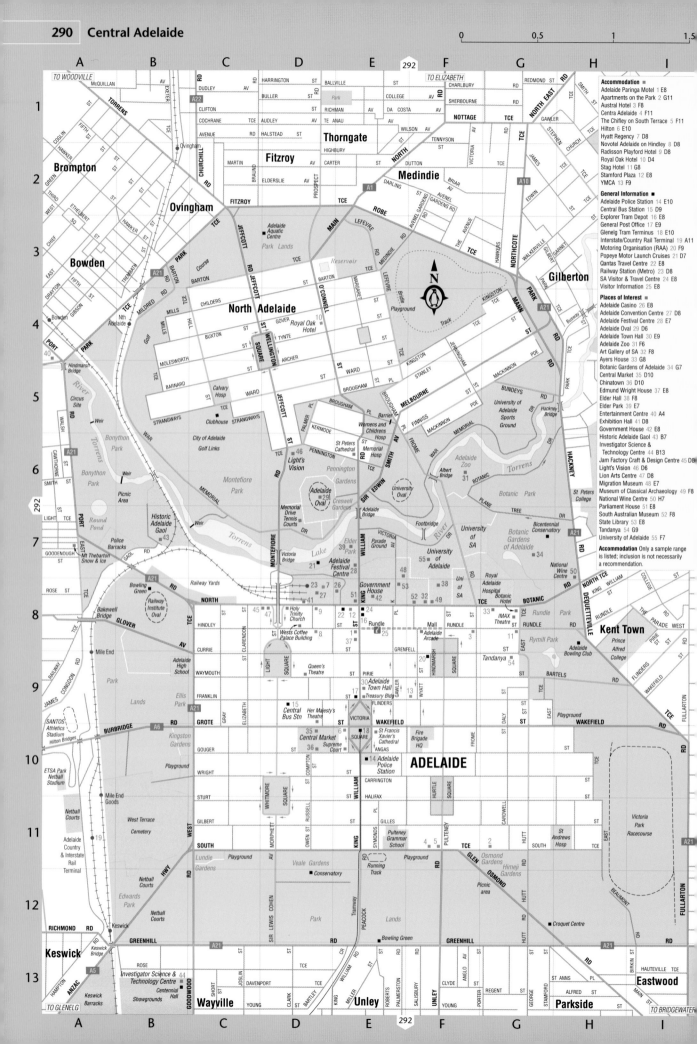

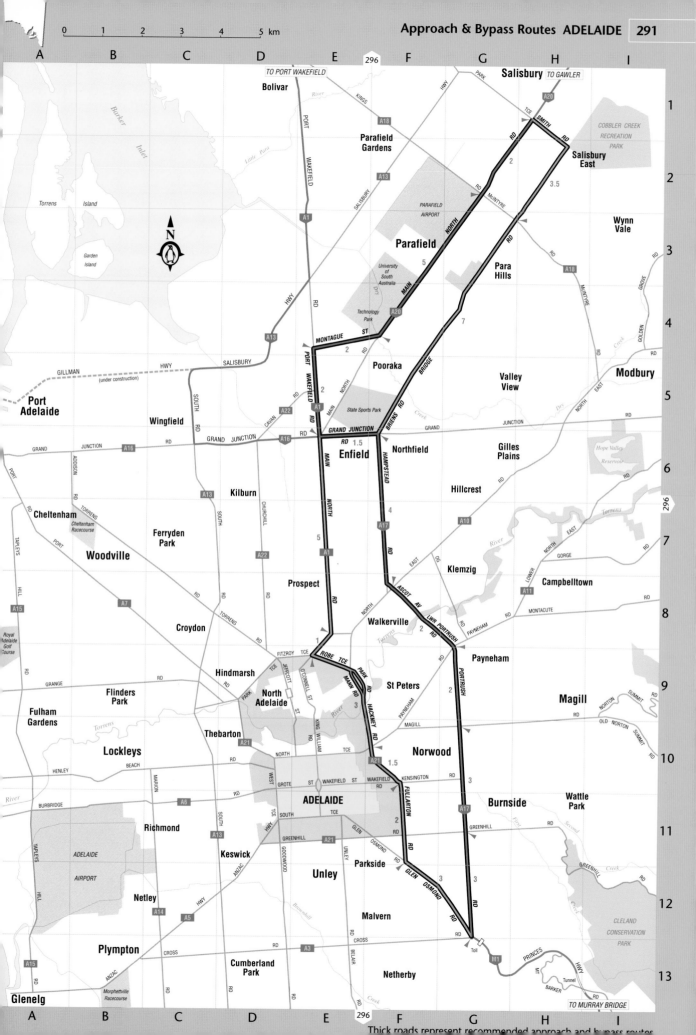

0 1 2 3 4 5 km

Thick roads represent recommended approach and bypass routes

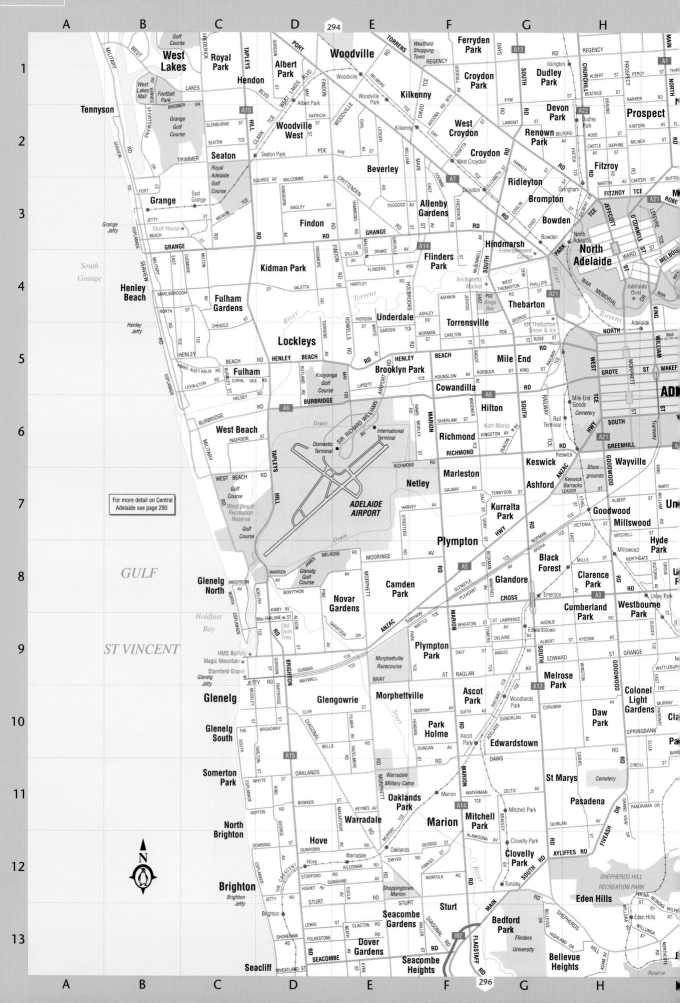

0 1 2 3 4 5 km

K L M N 295 O P Q R

Hampstead
Gardens
Manningham
Klemzig
EAST
Vale
Park
ASCOT
Marden
Felixstow
Royston
Park
St Peters
College
Park
Evandale
Maylands
Trinity
Gardens
Stepney
Paradise
Campbelltown
Newton
Rostrevor
Hectorville
Glynde
Payneham
Firle
St
Morris
Magill
Woodforde
Auldana
Teringie
Paradise
GORGE
Beulah
Park
Kensington
Gardens
Rosslyn Park
Skye
Norwood
Kensington
Rose
Park
Toorak
Gardens
Marryatville
Leabrook
Erindale
Wattle
Park
Stonyfell
Dulwich
Heathpool
Burnside
Linden
Park
Hazelwood
Park
Glenside
Beaumont
Frewville
Glenunga
St
Georges
Fullarton
Myrtle Bank
Netherby
Springfield
Glen Osmond
Mount
Osmond
Leawood
Gardens
Waterfall
Gully
Eagle on the Hill
Urrbrae
Castambul
BLACK
HILL
CONSERVATION
PARK
Montacute
Cherryville
Marble
Hill
Norton
Summit
Teringie
Greenhill
Ashton
Basket
Range
Uraidla
Summertown
Carey
Gully
ADELAIDE
HILLS
Piccadilly
Crafers
West
Crafers
Stirling
Bridgewater
Glenalta
BELAIR
NATIONAL
PARK
Upper Sturt
Aldgate
Strathalbyn
Hawthorndene
Heathfield

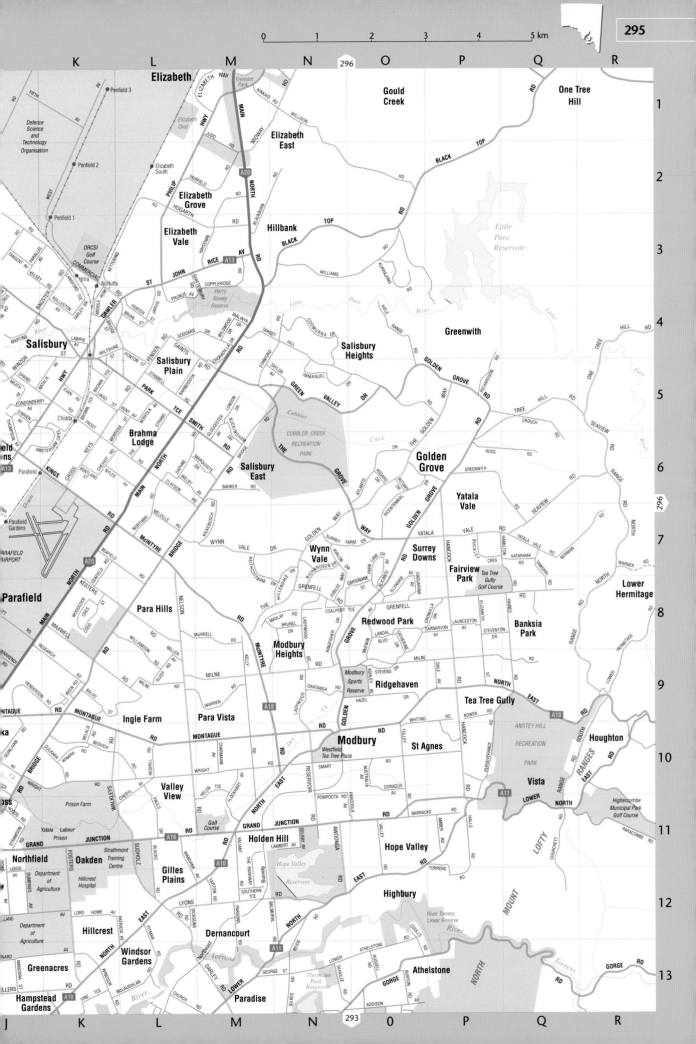

0 5 10 15 20 km

N

For more detail on the Barossa Valley see page 300

For more detail on Adelaide Suburbs see pages 292–5

TO BURRA

TO PORT WAKEFIELD

303

NORTH MOUNT LOFTY RANGES

BAROSSA VALLEY

BAROSSA WINE REGION

MOUNT LOFTY RANGES

ADELAIDE HILLS

Giles Corner · Alma · Owen · Pinery · Barabba · Hamley Bridge · Stockport · Linwood · Bethel · Tarlee · Hamilton · Allendale North · Bagot Well · Kooninderie · Neales Flat · Frankton · Brownlow

Kapunda · Kapunda Museum · St Kitts · Bald Hill · Koonunga · Dutton · Stonefield · Hansborough · Mt Rufus 547m

Mallala · Red Banks · Wasleys · Templers · Freeling · Fords · Greenock · Seppeltsfield · Nuriootpa · Moculta · Mt Karinya 444m · Truro · HWY A20

Roseworthy · Shea-Oak Log · Daveyston · Paterson Hill 300m · Tanunda · Angaston · Stockwell · Hawker Hill 442m

Two Wells · Lewiston · Kangaroo Flat · Concordia · Rosedale · Bethany · Rowland Flat · Keyneton · Towitta · Seda

Gawler · BAROSSA · Sandy Creek · Sandy Creek CP · Lyndoch · Kaiser Stuhl Conservation Park · Henschke Wines · Mons Hill 471m

Port Gawler · PORT GAWLER CONSERVATION PARK · Virginia · Angle Vale · Cockatoo Valley · Kies Hill · Williamstown · Eden Valley · Cambrai

SMITHFIELD · Whispering Wall · Para Wirra Recreation Park · Warren Reservoir · Mt Crawford 582m · Springton · Mt Colin

St Kilda · Waterloo Corner · Elizabeth · Little Para Reservoir · Bare Hill 344m · South Para Reservoir · Hale CP · WARREN CP · Karl Seppelt Grand Cru Estate · Cookes Hill 309m · Sanderston · Anga Valley

OUTER HARBOR · Barker Inlet · SALISBURY · A20 · GOLDEN GROVE · Kersbrook · Mt Gould 530m · Forreston · Mount Pleasant · Scotts Hill 473m · Millendella · Punthari

Largs Bay · PORT ADELAIDE · MODBURY · Houghton · Inglewood · Chain of Ponds · Mt Crawford Forest · Gumeracha · Birdwood · National Motor Museum · Tungkillo · Palmer · Apamurra

WEST LAKES · ENFIELD · Torrens · BLACK HILL CP · Castambul · MONTACUTE · Cudlee Creek · MOUNT CRAWFORD FOREST · Mt Torrens 453m · Fendlers Hill 473m · Murrays Hill 415m

HENLEY BEACH · MAGILL · MORIALTA CP · Norton Summit · Lobethal · Mount Torrens · Mannum · Reedy Creek

ADELAIDE · ADELAIDE AIRPORT · Ashton · Lenswood · Charleston · Mt Beavor 503m · Rockleigh · Caloote

GLENELG · MITCHAM · Crafers · Uraidla · Summertown · Forest Range · Woodside · Harrogate · Tepko · Pompoot

MARION · Stirling · Bridgewater · Cleland CP · Mt Lofty 727m · Aldgate · Oakbank · Balhannah · Brukunga · Whalleys Hill 357m

BRIGHTON · BELAIR NP · Mylor · Verdun · Hahndorf · Nairne · Kanmantoo · Monarto

HALLETT COVE · M2 · Sturt Gorge Recreation Park · Happy Valley Reservoir · Littlehampton · Shephards Hill 450m · Monarto South

PORT NOARLUNGA · MORPHETT VALE · Clarendon · SCOTT CREEK CP · Mount Barker · Echunga · Wistow · Callington · MURRAY BRIDGE · Swanport

HACKHAM · Kangarilla · Yaroona · Flaxley · Green Hills · MONARTO CONSERVATION PARK

MOANA · Old Noarlunga · McLaren Flat · Mt Panorama 359m · Meadows · Paris Creek · Macclesfield · Hartley · Woodchester

Port Willunga · Maslin Beach · McLaren Vale · KYEEMA CP · Prospect Hill · Bull Creek · Strathalbyn · Bletchley · Brinkley · FERRIES MCDONALD CONSERVATION PARK

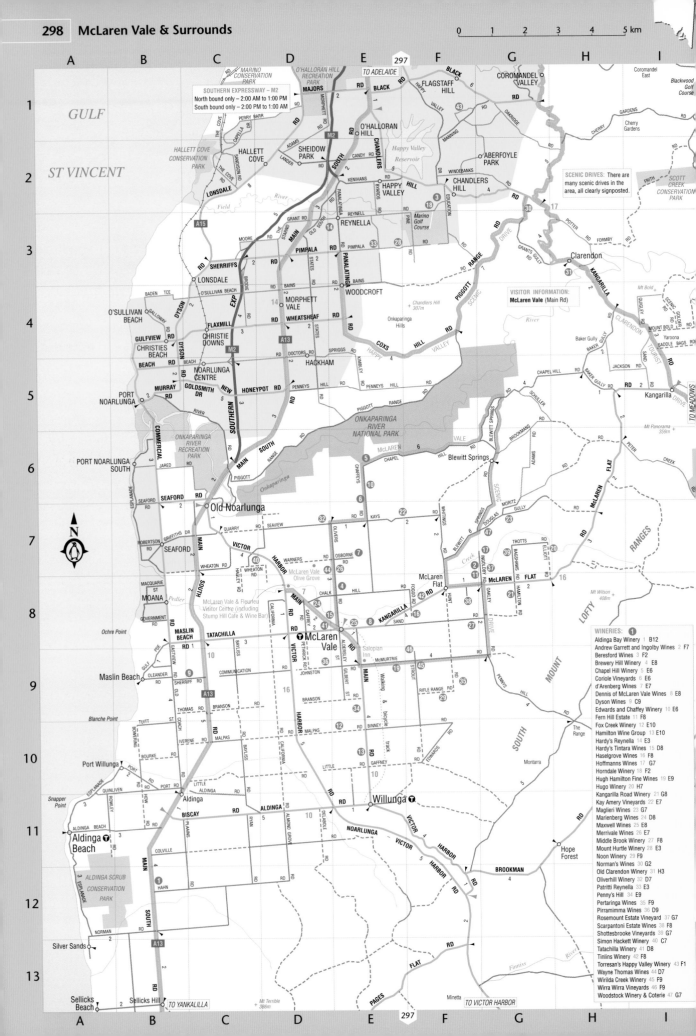

WINERIES:

Aldinga Bay Winery 1 B12
Andrew Garrett and Ingolby Wines 2 F7
Beresford Wines 3 F2
Brewery Hill Winery 4 E8
Chapel Hill Winery 5 E6
Coriole Vineyards 6 E6
d'Arenberg Wines 7 E7
Dennis of McLaren Vale Wines 8 E8
Dyson Wines 9 C9
Edwards and Chaffey Winery 10 E6
Fern Hill Estate 11 F8
Fox Creek Winery 12 E10
Hamilton Wine Group 13 E10
Hardy's Reynella 14 E3
Hardy's Tintara Wines 15 D8
Haselgrove Wines 16 F8
Hoffmanns Wines 17 G7
Horndale Winery 18 F2
Hugh Hamilton Fine Wines 19 E9
Hugo Winery 20 H7
Kangarilla Road Winery 21 G8
Kay Amery Vineyards 22 E7
Maglieri Wines 23 G7
Marienberg Wines 24 D8
Maxwell Wines 25 E8
Merrivale Wines 26 E7
Middle Brook Winery 27 F8
Mount Hurtle Winery 28 E3
Noon Winery 29 F9
Norman's Wines 30 G2
Old Clarendon Winery 31 H3
Oliverhill Winery 32 D7
Patritti Reynella 33 E3
Penny's Hill 34 E9
Pertaringa Wines 35 F9
Pirramimma Wines 36 D9
Rosemount Estate Vineyard 37 G7
Scarpantoni Estate Wines 38 F8
Shottesbrooke Vineyards 39 F9
Simon Hackett Winery 40 C7
Tatachilla Winery 41 D8
Tinlins Winery 42 F8
Torresan's Happy Valley Winery 43 F1
Wayne Thomas Wines 44 D7
Wirilda Creek Winery 45 F9
Wirra Wirra Vineyards 46 F9
Woodstock Winery & Coterie 47 G7

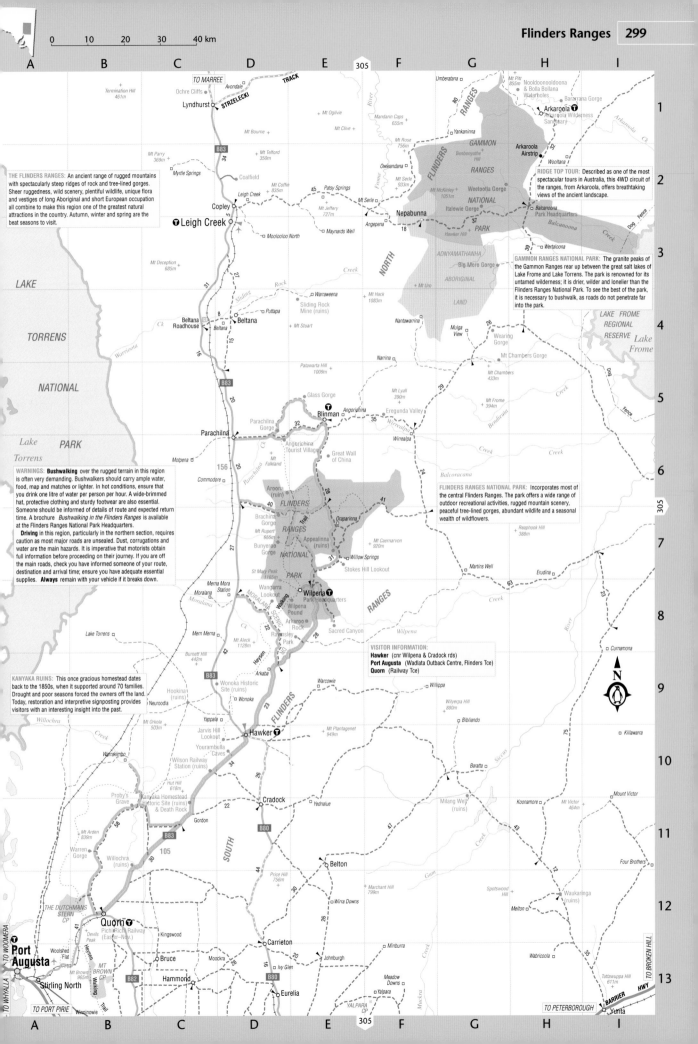

0   10   20   30   40 km

305

A   B   C   D   E   F   G   H   I

1

TO MAREE

TRACK

STRZELECKI

Termination Hill
461m

Avondale

Ochre Cliffs

Lyndhurst

Umberatana

Mt Pitt
855m   Nooldoonooldoona
& Bolla Bollana
Waterholes

Bararrana Gorge

Arkaroola   T

Arkaroola Wilderness
Sanctuary

Mt Bourne

Mt Ogilvie

River

Frome

80

RANGES

2

THE FLINDERS RANGES: An ancient range of rugged mountains with spectacularly steep ridges of rock and tree-lined gorges. Sheer ruggedness, wild scenery, plentiful wildlife, unique flora and vestiges of long Aboriginal and short European occupation all combine to make this region one of the greatest natural attractions in the country. Autumn, winter and spring are the best seasons to visit.

Mt Parry
369m

Myrtle Springs

Coalfield

B83
34

Mt Telford
350m

Mandarin Caps
655m

Mt Clive

Owieandana

Mt Rose
756m

Arkaroola
Airstrip

Wooltana

82

GAMMON

RANGES

Benbonyathe
Hill

Mt Serle
933m

Patsy Springs

45

Mt Coffin
835m

Mt McKinley
1051m

Weetootla Gorge

Italowie Gorge

NATIONAL

RIDGE TOP TOUR: Described as one of the most spectacular tours in Australia, this 4WD circuit of the ranges, from Arkaroola, offers breathtaking views of the ancient landscape.

Balcanoona
Park Headquarters

Balcanoona

Dog Fence

Leigh Creek

Copley

Mt Jeffery
727m

Mt Serle

Nepabunna

FLINDERS

Angepena

Hawker Hill

18

37

PARK

39

Wertaloona

Creek

3

T **Leigh Creek**

Moolooloo North

Maynards Well

Creek

NORTH

ADNYAMATHANHA

Big Moro Gorge

GAMMON RANGES NATIONAL PARK

GAMMON RANGES NATIONAL PARK: The granite peaks of the Gammon Ranges rear up between the great salt lakes of Lake Frome and Lake Torrens. The park is renowned for its untamed wilderness; it is drier, wilder and lonelier than the Flinders Ranges National Park. To see the best of the park, it is necessary to bushwalk, as roads do not penetrate far into the park.

4

LAKE

Mt Deception
685m

31

27

Sliding

Rock

Beltana
Roadhouse

Beltana

8

15

Puttapa

Sliding Rock
Mine (ruins)

Warraweena

Mt Hack
1083m

ABORIGINAL

Mt Uro

LAND

Nantawarrina

Mulga
View

26

Wearing
Gorge

LAKE FROME
REGIONAL

RESERVE   Lake
Frome

TORRENS

Warrioota

Ck

Beltana

Mt Stuart

Mt Chambers Gorge

Dog

29

Narrina

Mt Chambers
433m

Fence

5

NATIONAL

16

20

Patawarta Hill
1009m

Mt Lyall
390m

Eregunda Valley

Mt Frome
394m

35

Wirrealpa

Creek

Glass Gorge

Blinman   Angorichina

Bendieuta

6

Lake

PARK

Torrens

156

20

Parachilna

Parachilna
Gorge

32

Motpena

Commodore

Ck

Mt
Falkland

Angorichina
Tourist Village

Great Wall
of China

Balcoracana

Wirrealpa

24

Balcoracana

Creek

FLINDERS RANGES NATIONAL PARK: Incorporates most of the central Flinders Ranges. The park offers a wide range of outdoor recreational activities, rugged mountain scenery, peaceful tree-lined gorges, abundant wildlife and a seasonal wealth of wildflowers.

305

7

WARNINGS: Bushwalking over the rugged terrain in this region is often very demanding. Bushwalkers should carry ample water, food, map and matches or lighter. In hot conditions, ensure that you drink one litre of water per person per hour. A wide-brimmed hat, protective clothing and sturdy footwear are also essential. Someone should be informed of details of route and expected return time. A brochure *Bushwalking in the Flinders Ranges* is available at the Flinders Ranges National Park Headquarters.

Driving in this region, particularly in the northern section, requires caution as most major roads are unsealed. Dust, corrugations and water are the main hazards. It is imperative that motorists obtain full information before proceeding on their journey. If you are off the main roads, check you have informed someone of your route, destination and arrival time; ensure you have adequate essential supplies. **Always** remain with your vehicle if it breaks down.

Aroona
(ruin)

40

FLINDERS

28

Orapariinna

41

Reaphook Hill
388m

Brachina
Gorge

RANGES

Mt Rupert
665m

Appealinna
(ruins)

Mt Caernarvon
920m

Bunyeroo
Gorge

NATIONAL

31

Willow Springs

Martins Well

Erudina

63

29

8

St Mary Peak
1165m

Merna Mora
Station

Moralana

Wangarra
Lookout

PARK

Wilpena
Park Headquarters

Stokes Hill Lookout

Creek

Wilpena

Curnamona

Moralana

MORALANA

Wilpena
Pound

Arkaroo
Rock

Sacred Canyon

Mern Merna

SCENIC

Ravensley

Park

28

RANGES

Lake Torrens

Ck

Mt Aleck
1128m

22

Hergott

VISITOR INFORMATION:
Hawker (cnr Wilpena & Cradock rds)
Port Augusta (Wadlata Outback Centre, Flinders Tce)
Quorn (Railway Tce)

9

KANYAKA RUINS: This once gracious homestead dates back to the 1850s, when it supported around 70 families. Drought and poor seasons forced the owners off the land. Today, restoration and interpretive signposting provides visitors with an interesting insight into the past.

42

Burnett Hill
442m

Arkaba

Warcowie

Warcoona

Willippa

Wonoka Historic
Site (ruins)

Hookina
(ruins)

Wonoka

Neuroodla

Yappala

FLINDERS

23

Mt Plantagenet
949m

Wilyerpa Hill
880m

Bibliando

75

Killawarra

Willochra

Creek

Mt Orkola
503m

Jarvis Hill
Lookout

Yourambulla
Caves

34

Hawker   T

PARK

Baratta

Milang Well
(ruins)

Koonamore

Mt Victor
464m

Mount Victor

10

Wilson Railway
Station (ruins)

Hut Hill
618m

26

Proby's
Grave

Kanyaka Homestead
Historic Site (ruins)
& Death Rock

Gordon

22

Cradock

Yednalue

47

43

Milang

11

Mt Arden
839m

58

Warren
Gorge

Willochra
(ruins)

B83

30

105

SOUTH

B80

44

Price Hill
756m

Belton

Marchant Hill
799m

Gum

Spotswood
Hill

Waukaringa
(ruins)

Four Brothers

12

THE DUTCHMANS
STERN CP

41

Quorn   T

Pichi Richi Railway
(Easter–Nov.)

Kingswood

30

Wirra Downs

26

Johnburgh

Minburra

Siccus

Melton

Wabricoola

Tattiwuppa Hill
611m

13

**Port
Augusta**

Woolshed
Flat

Stirling North

Devils
Peak

Mt Brown
965m

MT
BROWN
CP

B82

Bruce

Hammond

Mockra

B80

16

20

Ivy Glen

Carrieton

Eurelia

Meadow
Downs

Yalpara

Mackay

YALPARA CP

Wabricoola

TO PETERBOROUGH

BARRIER

HWY

Yunta

TO WHYALLA

TO WOOMERA

TO PORT PIRIE

Winninowie

Hergott

Walking

Trail

305

TO BROKEN HILL

N

A   B   C   D   E   F   G   H   I

0 1 2 3 4 5 km

A B C D E 296 F G H I

N

Penguin

TO KAPUNDA

Koonunga

Belvidere 391 m

VISITOR INFORMATION:
Tanunda (Barossa Wine and Visitor Centre, 66 Murray St)

B81 **WALKING TRAILS:** The famous 1500-km Heysen Trail begins near Cape Jervis and ends in the Flinders Ranges. The Barossa section, which passes through vineyards, is particularly picturesque. Other trails have been organised in the region including one along Rifle Range Road (near Bethany F6); all are clearly marked.

HWY

Stockwell

TO BLANCHETOWN

TO BLACK

Freeling

NORTH MOUNT

Greenock

Daveyston

19 5

Nuriootpa

Light Pass

Luhrs Cottage Herman Cottage

Plush Corner

Paterson Hill 300m

16

Maranunga 14 44

35

Seppeltsfield 18

Penrice

Vintners Bar and Grill

Tappa Pass

Shea-Oak Log

STURT

A20

LOFTY

Maggie Beer Farm Shop

Dorrien

12

38

20

Nuraip 1

TO GAWLER

Kroemers Crossing

9 17

Kev Rohrlach Collection

Bethany Arts & Crafts

Angaston

Angas Park Fruit Co

Tanunda 43 30 31 39 48

Tanunda Pottery Shop

Vine Vale

34

RANGES

Gomersal

Crayford

Tanunda 3

BASEDOW

Barossa Kiddypark

MAGNOLIA

47

Historical Museum 10

41 BETHANY

Bethany

Mengler Hill Lookout

Rosedale

Story Book Cottage and Whacky Wood 13

RIFLE RANGE 33

Schreiberau

The Keg Factory

15 KRONDORF 32

8 23

4

Collingrove Homestead National Trust Property

TO EDEN VALLEY

11

37

7

Mooroooroo

B19

KAISER STUHL CONSERVATION PARK

Sandy Creek

BAROSSA 45

Warpoo

22

6

Rowland Flat 28

19 26 25

21

Lyndoch 24 VALLEY

2

TRIAL

Kaiserstuhl 599 m

SANDY CREEK CONSERVATION PARK

Pewsey Vale Peak 629 m

Pewsey Vale

BALMORAL

PIMPALA

Cockatoo Valley

WILLIAMSTOWN

Kies Hill 42

Lyndoch Lavender Farm

B31

Kies Hill

27

Goldfields Walk

Whispering Wall

Barossa Reservoir

FESTIVALS:
Barossa Vintage Festival: (Biennial, odd years): A week-long festival beginning Easter Monday to celebrate the grape harvest. Highlights include grape-picking, wine tasting, entertainment and processions.
Barossa Under the Stars: An annual event held in February, featuring an open air concert with internationally acclaimed artists performing in a natural amphitheatre.
Barossa International Music Festival: A 16-day festival of classical music held in October each year. It attracts musicians from around the country and overseas.

Williamstown

PARRA WIRRA RECREATION PARK

WIRRA

South Para Reservoir

Red Gum Flat

B31

HALE CONSERVATION PARK

WARREN

Warren Reservoir

B34

WARREN CONSERVATION PARK

MOUNT CRAWFORD FOREST

Mt Crawford 562 m

SPRINGTON

MOUNT CRAWFORD FOREST

MOUNT CRAWFORD FOREST

TO BIRDWOOD

WINERIES: 1
Barossa Cottage Wines 1 G5
Barossa Settlers 2 D9
Basedow Wines 3 F6
Bethany Wines 4 F7
Branson Wines 5 D4
Burge Family Winemakers 6 C8
Charles Cimicky Wines 7 C8
Charles Melton Wines 8 F7
Chateau Dorrien Wines 9 F5
Chateau Tanunda Estate 10 F6
Chateau Yaldara Estate 11 C8
Elderton Wines 12 G4
Glaetzer Wines 13 E6
Gnadenfrei Estate Winery 14 E4
Grant Burge Wines 15 E7
Greenock Creek Cellars 16 D4
Hamiltons Ewell Vineyards 17 G5
Heritage Wines 18 E4
Jenke Vineyard Cellars 19 D8
Kaesler Wines 20 G4
Kellermeister Wines 21 D8
Kies Family Winery 22 C8
Krondorf Wines 23 F7
Langmeil Winery 24 F5
Liebichwein 25 E8
Miranda Wines 26 D8
Mountadam Vineyard 27 G10
Orlando Wines 28 D8
Penfolds Wines 29 G4
Peter Lehmann Wines 30 F5
Richmond Grove Barossa Winery 31 F5
Rockford Wines 32 E7
St Hallett Wines 33 E7
Saltram Wine Estates 34 H5
Seppelt Wines 35 D4
Stanley Bros Winery 36 F5
Tait Wines 37 B8
Tarac 38 F4
Tarchalice Winery 39 G5
The Willows Vineyard 40 H3
Turkey Flat Vineyard 41 E6
Twin Valley Estate 42 D10
Veritas Winery 43 F5
Viking Wines 44 E4
Wards Gateway Cellar 45 B8
Wolf Blass Wines 46 H3
Yalumba Wines 47 I6
Yunbar Estate 48 G5

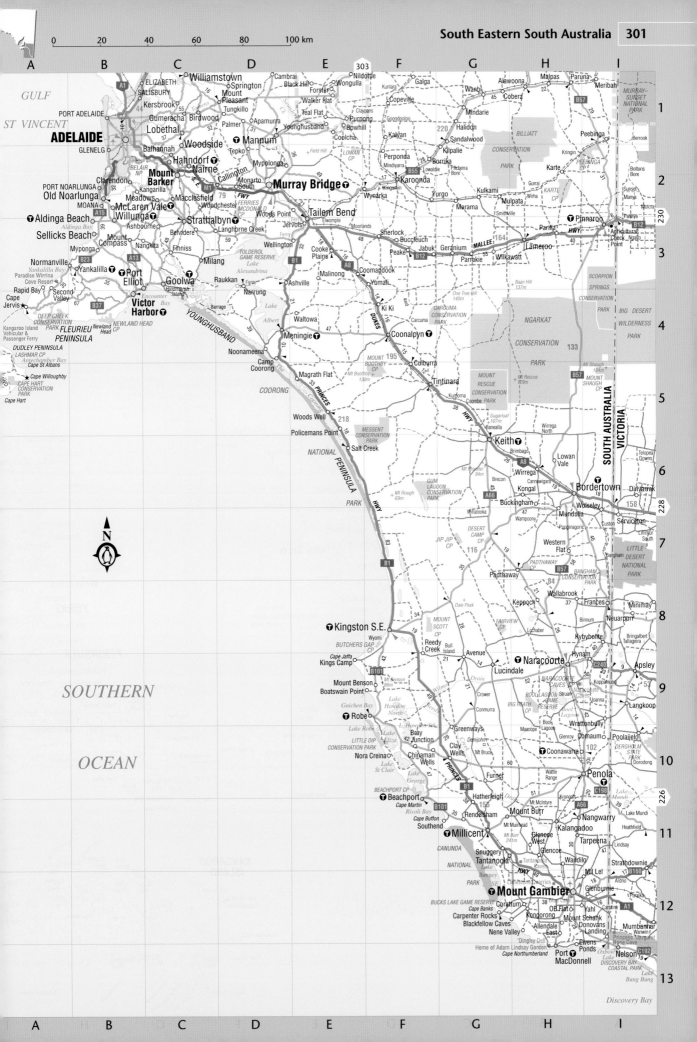

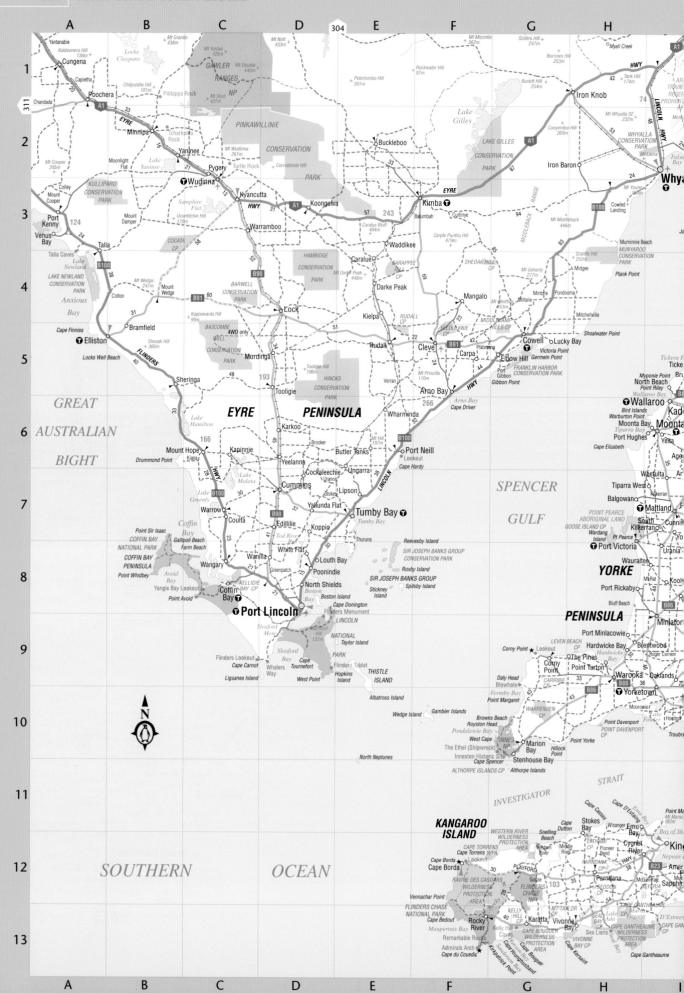

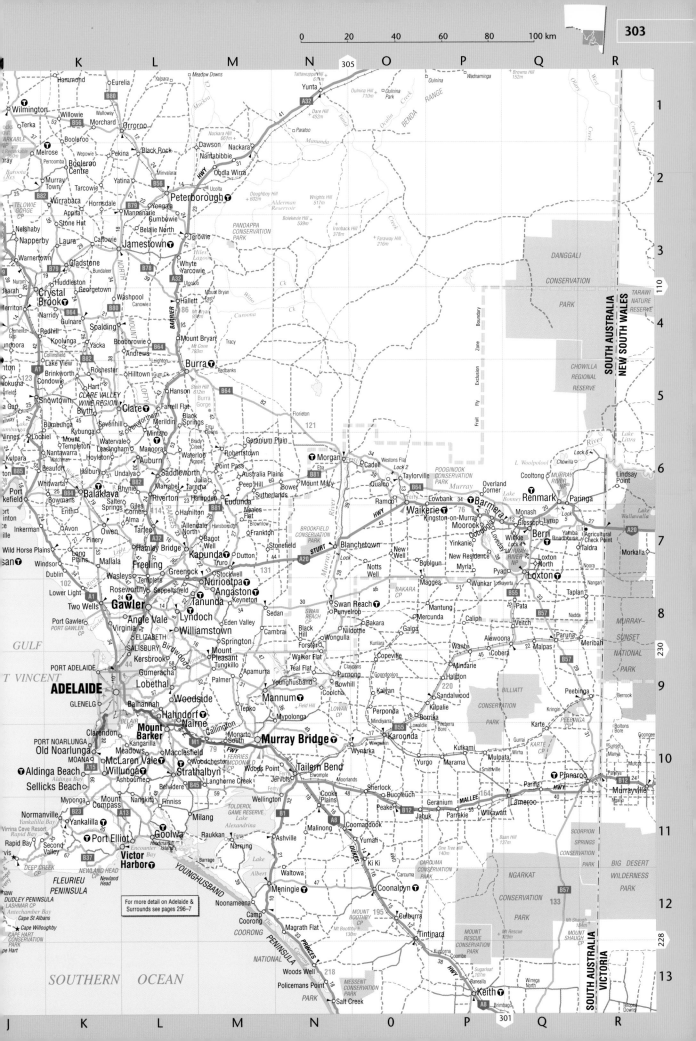

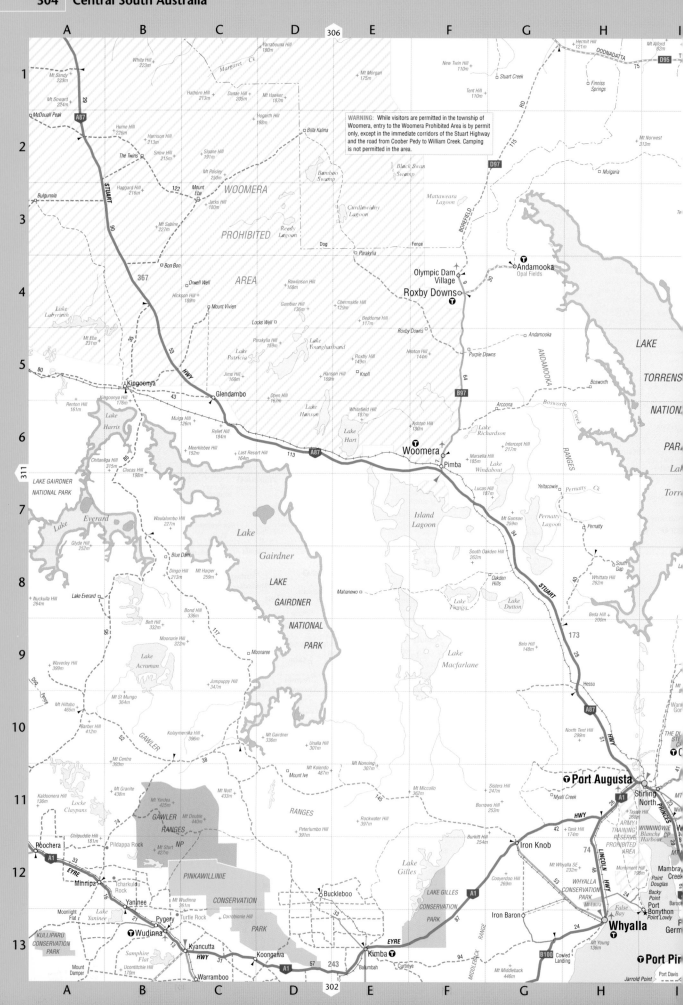

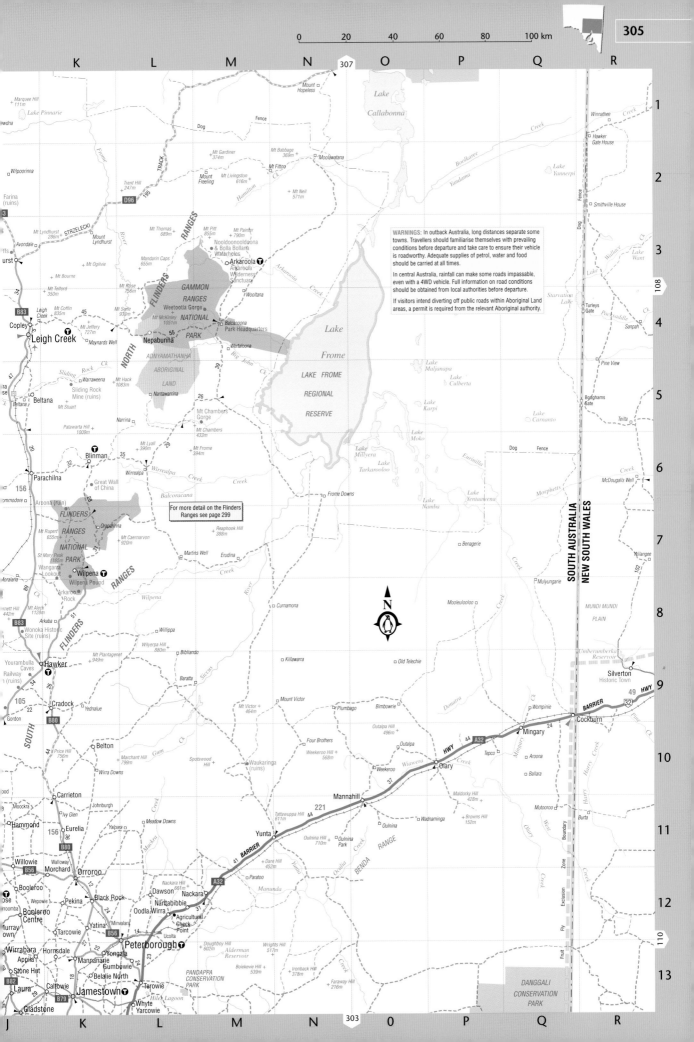

0   20   40   60   80   100 km

K   L   M   N   O   P   Q   R

1

Lake
Callabonna

Winnathee Creek

Mount
Hopeless

°Wilpoorinna

Lake Pinnaree

Marquee Hill
111m

Farina
(ruins)

Dog

Fence

Mt Gardiner
374m

Mount
Freeling

Mt Livingston
616m

Mt Babbage
369m

Mt Fitton

°Moolawatana

Boolkaree

Yandama

Creek

Hawker
Gate House

2

Trent Hill
247m

Hamilton

Mt Neil
571m

Fence

Dog

Smithville House

D96

STRZELECKI

Mt Lyndhurst
286m

RANGES

Mt Thomas
689m

Mt Pitt
855m

Mt Painter
790m

Nooldoonooldoona
& Bolla Bollana
Waterholes

WARNINGS: In outback Australia, long distances separate some
towns. Travellers should familiarise themselves with prevailing
conditions before departure and take care to ensure their vehicle
is roadworthy. Adequate supplies of petrol, water and food
should be carried at all times.

Lake
Wallace

Lake
Want

3

°urst

Mount
Lyndhurst

Mandarin Caps
655m

FLINDERS

GAMMON
RANGES

Arkaroola

Arkaroola
Wilderness
Sanctuary

Arkaroola

In central Australia, rainfall can make some roads impassable,
even with a 4WD vehicle. Full information on road conditions
should be obtained from local authorities before departure.

Starvation

108

B83

Mt Coffin
835m

Leigh
Creek

Mt Ogilvie

Mt Rose
756m

NATIONAL

Weetootla Gorge

Mt McKinley
1051m

Balcanoona
Park Headquarters

If visitors intend diverting off public roads within Aboriginal Land
areas, a permit is required from the relevant Aboriginal authority.

Lake

Turleys
Gate

Paddysuddle

4

Copley

Mt Telford
350m

Mt Bourne

NORTH

Mt Jeffery
727m

PARK

Nepabunna

Wirtaloona

Lake

Sanpah

Pine View

Leigh Creek

Maynards Well

°Wooltana

Frome

Lake
Maljanapa

Boughams
Gate

5

Beltana

Mt Hack
1083m

Mt Stuart

Sliding
Rock
Mine (ruins)

Warraweena

ADNYAMATHANHA

ABORIGINAL

LAND

Nantawarrina

Big

John

Ck

LAKE FROME

REGIONAL

RESERVE

Lake
Karpi

Lake
Culberta

Lake
Carnanto

Teilta

6

Parachilna

Blinman

Wirrealpa

Wirrealpa

Great Wall
of China

Balcoracana

Mt Chambers
Gorge

Mt Chambers
433m

Creek

Lake
Tarkarooloo

Lake
Moko

Lake
Millyera

Dog   Fence

Eurinilla

McDougalls Well

Creek

Morphetts

7

156

Arona (ruin)

Commodore

FLINDERS

Mt Rupert
655m

RANGES

Orapartina

NATIONAL

For more detail on the Flinders
Ranges see page 299

Mt Lyall
390m

Mt Frome
394m

Mt Caernarvon
920m

Reaphook Hill
388m

Frome Downs

Lake
Yentaawena

Lake
Namba

Benagerie

Willangee

102

8

St Mary Peak
1165m

PARK

Wilpena

Arkaroo
Rock

Mt Aleck
1128m

Wangarra
Lookout

Wilpena Pound

RANGES

Martins Well

Erudina

Creek

Wilpena

River

°Curnamona

N

°Mooleulooloo

°Mulyungarie

MUNDI MUNDI

PLAIN

9

Yourambulla
Caves
(ruins)

Railway

Hawker

Emmett Hill
442m

Arkaba

Wonoka Historic
Site (ruins)

FLINDERS

Mt Plantagenet
949m

Wilyerpa Hill
880m

Bibliando

°Killawarra

°Old Telechie

Domara

Umberumberka
Reservoir

Silverton
Historic Town

49   HWY

32

HWY

BARRIER

9

105

34

Cradock

Yednalue

Mount Victor

Mt Victor
464m

Plumbago

°Bimbowrie

Wompinie

Cockburn

10

22

Gordon

B80

Belton

Marchant Hill
799m

Spatswood

Four Brothers

Weekeroo Hill
568m

Outalpa Hill
496m

Outalpa

Tepco

HWY

A32

Mingary

24

Aroona

Ballara

Mingary

44

Carrieton

Johnburgh

Meadow Downs

Yalpara

Waukaringa
(ruins)

Weekeroo

Wiawera

Olary

Creek

37

°Mutooroo

Burta

11

Hammond

156

Eurelia

Ivy Glen

Wirra Downs

Mannahill

221

Oulnina Hill
710m

Oulnina
Park

RANGE

Maldorky Hill
428m

Browns Hill
152m

°Wadnaminga

West

Creek

36

B80

Willowie

Morchard

Walloway

Orroroo

Muckra

Yunta

41

BARRIER

Tattawuppa Hill
611m

A4

Dare Hill
452m

Yunta

BENDA

12

B56

Booleroo

Wepowie

Pekina

Black Rock

Dawson

Nackara Hill
661m

Nackara

Paratoo

Manunda

Oxalia

Creek

110

Booleroo
Centre

Narrtabibbie

Oodla Wirra

Agricultural
Check Point

Ucolta

A32

Tarcowie

B56

Minvalara

Yatina

Doughboy Hill
602m

Wrights Hill
517m

13

Wirrabara

Appila

Hornsdale

Mannanarie

Yongala

Gumbowie

Belalie North

Peterborough

PANDAPPA
CONSERVATION
PARK

Hiles Lagoon

Alderman
Reservoir

Boikerevie Hill
539m

Ironback Hill
378m

Faraway Hill
216m

DANGGALI
CONSERVATION
PARK

B82

Stone Hut

Laura

Caltowie

Jamestown

Gladstone

Whyte
Yarcowie

Terowie

B879

SOUTH AUSTRALIA
NEW SOUTH WALES

303

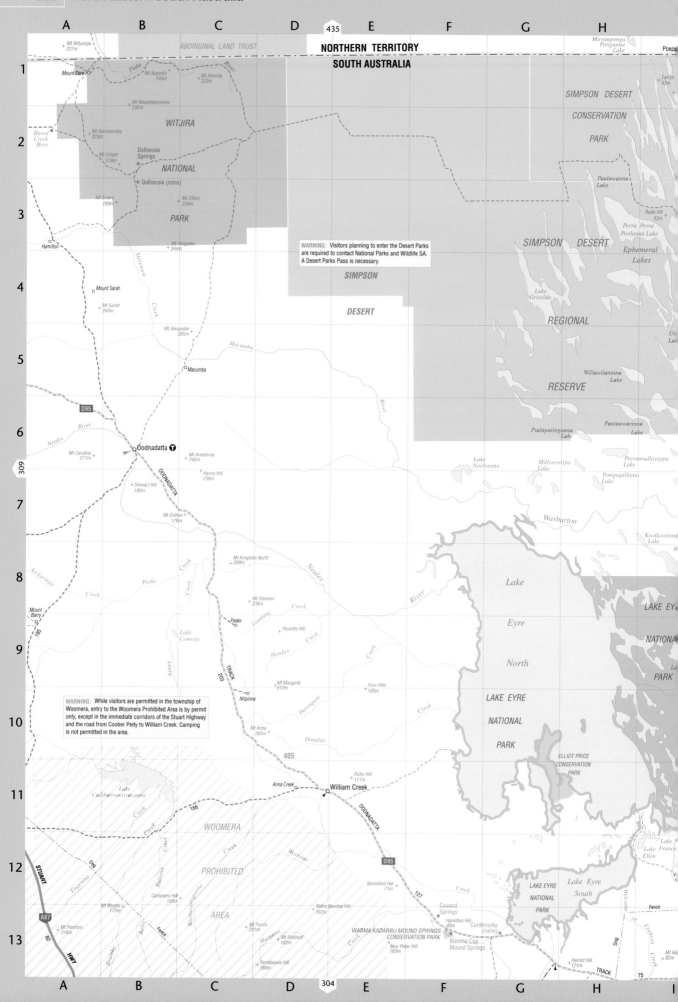

435

NORTHERN TERRITORY

SOUTH AUSTRALIA

WARNING: Visitors planning to enter the Desert Parks are required to contact National Parks and Wildlife SA. A Desert Parks Pass is necessary.

WARNING: While visitors are permitted in the township of Woomera, entry to the Woomera Prohibited Area is by permit only, except in the immediate corridors of the Stuart Highway and the road from Coober Pedy to William Creek. Camping is not permitted in the area.

ABORIGINAL LAND TRUST

WITJIRA

NATIONAL

PARK

SIMPSON DESERT CONSERVATION PARK

SIMPSON DESERT

SIMPSON

DESERT

Ephemeral Lakes

REGIONAL

RESERVE

Lake Eyre North

LAKE EYRE NATIONAL PARK

Lake Eyre South

LAKE EYRE NATIONAL PARK

WOOMERA

PROHIBITED

AREA

+ Mt Wilyunpa 227m

Mount Dare

Finke River

Mt Apperda 245m

Mt Alinerta 222m

Mt Weeahlakiminne 292m

Blood Creek Bore

Mt Hammersley 229m

Mt Crispe 279m

Dalhousie Springs

Dalhousie (ruins)

Mt Emery 289m

Mt Dillon 234m

Stevenson Creek

Hamilton

Mt Youngalee 244m

Mount Sarah

Mt Sarah 260m

Mt Alexander 285m

Macumba

Macumba

River

Neales River

D95

Mt Carulina 211m

Oodnadatta

Mt Areebinna 245m

Hanns Hill 238m

Stewart Hill 180m

Mt Dutton 176m

Mt Kingston North 209m

Neales River

OODNADATTA

Arckaringa Creek

Peake Creek

Creek

Mt Denison 238m

Ricketts Hill

Lambing Creek

Lake Noolyeana

Millyeewlpa Lake

Pompapillinna Lake

Peeramudlayeppa Lake

Mount Barry

Peake

Lake Conway

Hawker Creek

Aimee Creek

Creek

Mt Margaret 412m

Four Hills 105m

Creek

TRACK 203

Nilpinna

Davenport Creek

Lake Eyre

North

LAKE EYRE NATIONAL PARK

Mt Anna 265m

Douglas

405

ELLIOT PRICE CONSERVATION PARK

Lake Cadibarrawirracanna

Anna Creek

William Creek

Ruby Hill 111m

OODNADATTA

166

Creek

Warriner Creek

D95

127

Beresford Hill 71m

Coward Springs

Hamilton Hill 40m

Curdimurka (ruins)

STUART

Engenina Creek

Dog Fence

Mt Woods 170m

Campeera Hill 158m

Baluni Creek

Weltawilbinna Creek

A87

Mt Peorhyn 216m

82

HWY

Mt Purvis 201m

Margaret Creek

Mt Riddoch 182m

Yarrabouna Hill 180m

Bidna Boudna Hill 162m

New Peter Hill 163m

WABMA KADARBU MOUND SPRINGS CONSERVATION PARK

Blanche Cup Mound Springs

Hermit Hill 121m

TRACK

Mirranponga Ponguna Lake

Poepp

Larrys 63m

Poolowanna Lake

Beale Hill 53m

Perra Perra Poolanna Lake

Lake Griselda

Willawilaninna Lake

Pantoowarinna Lake

Pialopotingoona Lake

Warburton

Koolkootinna Lake

LAKE EYR

NATIONAL

PARK

Lake Francis

Lake Ellen

Lake Eyre South

Fence

Mt Ai 82m

75

309

198

304

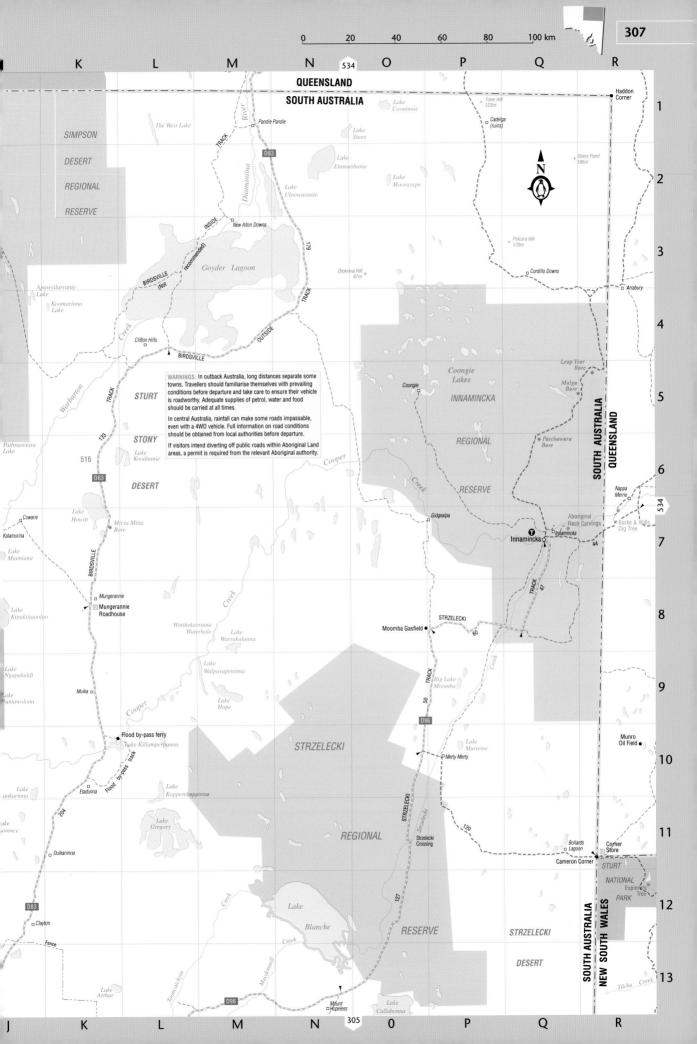

0   20   40   60   80   100 km

K   L   M   N   O   P   Q   R

QUEENSLAND

SOUTH AUSTRALIA

Haddon
Corner

1

SIMPSON

The West Lake

Pandie Pandie

Frew Hill
123m

Lake
Cooninnie

Cadelga
(ruins)

DESERT

Lake
Short

Stony Point
195m

2

REGIONAL

Lake
Etamunbanie

Lake
Mooraye pe

New Alton Downs

Pulcara Hill
170m

3

RESERVE

Goyder Lagoon

Dickinna Hill
87m

Cordillo Downs

Arrabury

4

Apawyilarranie
Lake

Koomarinna
Lake

Clifton Hills

BIRDSVILLE (Not recommended)

BIRDSVILLE

Leap Year
Bore

Mulga
Bore

Coongie
Lakes

5

Warburton

STURT

Coongie

INNAMINCKA

Patchawara
Bore

Pathraootara
Lake

STONY

Lake
Koodnanie

REGIONAL

Cooper

6

Nappa
Merrie

534

WARNINGS: In outback Australia, long distances separate some towns. Travellers should familiarise themselves with prevailing conditions before departure and take care to ensure their vehicle is roadworthy. Adequate supplies of petrol, water and food should be carried at all times.

In central Australia, rainfall can make some roads impassable, even with a 4WD vehicle. Full information on road conditions should be obtained from local authorities before departure.

If visitors intend diverting off public roads within Aboriginal Land areas, a permit is required from the relevant Aboriginal authority.

DESERT

Creek

RESERVE

Aboriginal
Rock Carvings

Burke & Wills
Dig Tree

Cowarie

Lake
Howitt

Gidgealpa

Innamincka

7

Kalamurina

Mirra Mitta
Bore

Lake
Miamiana

BIRDSVILLE

TRACK

STRZELECKI

Moomba Gasfield

8

Lake
Kittakittaooloo

Mungerannie

Mungerannie
Roadhouse

Winthekarrinna
Waterhole

Lake
Warrakalanna

Big Lake
Moomba

Lake
Ngapakaldi

Lake
Walpayapeninna

9

Lake
Puntawolona

Mulka

Cooper

Lake
Hope

Munro
Oil Field

10

Flood by-pass ferry

Lake Killamperpunna

Lake
Murteree

Merty Merty

STRZELECKI

Lake
ankarinna

Eladunna

Lake
Kopperekoppinna

REGIONAL

Bollards
Lagoon

Corner
Store

11

Dulkaninna

Lake
Gregory

Strzelecki
Crossing

Cameron Corner

STURT

12

Clayton

Fence

Lake
Blanche

RESERVE

STRZELECKI

NATIONAL

PARK

Explorers
Tree

SOUTH AUSTRALIA

NEW SOUTH WALES

DESERT

13

Lake
Arthur

Toonumbun

Macdonnell

Mount
Hopeless

Lake
Callabonna

Tilcha Creek

305

J   K   L   M   N   O   P   Q   R

A   B   C   D   434   E   F   G   H

NORTHERN TERRITORY

SOUTH AUSTRALIA

Surveyor Generals Corner

Mt Cockburn 1138m

Feltham Hill 863m

Alpara

Mt Woodward 1227m

Mt Hinckley 1018m

Kalka

MANN   RANGES

Mt Edwin 1193m

Mt Whinham 1231m

213

Mt Morris 1288m

Amata

Aylliffe Hill 1044m

63

Pipalyatjara

Aparawatatja

Kanypi

Mt Davies 1058m

Mt Cooperinna 1045m

Mt Caroline 1042m

Mt Davenport 1139m

MUSGRAVE

128

PITJANTJATJARA

ABORIGINAL

LAND

Mt Kintore 1070m

Mt Harriet 938m

Mt Crombie 835m

Mt Agnes 671m

Maryinna Hill (trig) 822m

Mt Lindsay 819m

Oonmooninna Hill 600m

Permano Hill 719m

408

Davies Hill

Mt Poondinna 678m

WARNINGS: In outback Australia, long distances separate some towns. Travellers should familiarise themselves with prevailing conditions before departure and take care to ensure their vehicle is roadworthy. Adequate supplies of petrol, water and food should be carried at all times.

In central Australia, rainfall can make some roads impassable, even with a 4WD vehicle. Full information on road conditions should be obtained from local authorities before departure.

If visitors intend diverting off public roads within Aboriginal Land areas, a permit is required from the relevant Aboriginal authority.

N

GREAT   VICTORIA   DESERT

UNNAMED
CONSERVATION
PARK

271

Vokes Hill Corner

Serpentine Lakes

MARALINGA

Nurrari Lakes

TJARUTJA

Wyola Lake

Halinor Lake

Lake Dey Dey

ABORIGINAL

Forrest Lakes

LAND

Lake Maurice

GREAT VICTORIA DESERT NATURE RESERVE

A   B   C   D   310   E   F   G   H

SOUTH AUSTRALIA
WESTERN AUSTRALIA

389

387

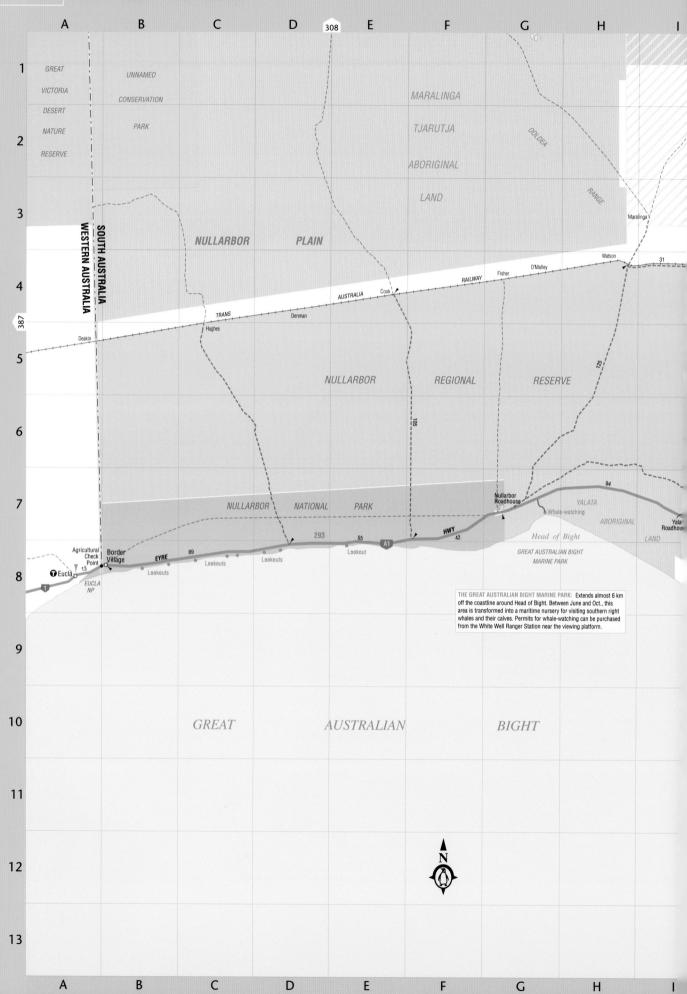

THE GREAT AUSTRALIAN BIGHT MARINE PARK: Extends almost 6 km off the coastline around Head of Bight. Between June and Oct., this area is transformed into a maritime nursery for visiting southern right whales and their calves. Permits for whale-watching can be purchased from the White Well Ranger Station near the viewing platform.

WESTERN AUSTRALIA

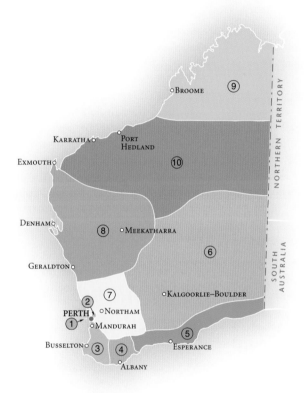

Western Australia, the nation's largest State, covers an area of 2 529 000 square kilometres. This is one third of the total area of the continent, yet its population of 1 805 400 (just 10 per cent of the national total) is concentrated around the capital city of Perth. In geographical terms, Western Australia is the country's most remote State: Perth is considerably closer to Singapore than it is to the cities of Australia's eastern seaboard.

Ancient landscapes

Western Australia occupies the world's most ancient landscape. A vast eroded plateau covers much of the State. In the far north lies The Kimberley, a remote, mythic land of strangely worn mountains, rock formations and gorges. A little to the south the majestic Hamersley Range, rich with deposits of iron ore, rises from red plains. Around Perth, river valleys, escarpments, vineyards and forests form a border to the outer suburbs. In the south-west, giant jarrah and karri forests cover much of the landscape, while to the south-east, the treeless Nullarbor Plain lies across the world's largest limestone slab.

Trackless deserts and arid plains separate Western Australia from the rest of the continent. This natural border has created a zone of biological isolation that has produced unique native flora. Wildflowers carpet the deserts, plains and valleys in spring; some 75 per cent of the 11 000 or so species found in Western Australia are found nowhere else in the world.

Francois Peron National Park on Shark Bay

The 12 500-kilometre coastline starts in the Timor Sea, stretches out along the Indian Ocean, and sweeps east to meet the Southern Ocean. Its far north section is one of the most remote coastal areas in the world. Around the tropical resort town of Broome are long sandy, beautiful beaches. Further south is the World Heritage-listed Shark Bay, with its prolific population of dolphins, dugongs and turtles and its strange stromatolites, said to represent life in its most ancient form. Along the entire coast, hundreds of surf beaches, coves, inlets, harbours, headlands, cliffs, islands and offshore reefs provide opportunities for every kind of water recreation.

Early history

The first inhabitants of what is now called Western Australia were Aboriginal peoples of many different language groups who domiciled according to the availability of resources. They occupied four distinct geographical and cultural zones and had a total population of between 40 000 and 80 000. The earliest confirmed archaeological site, a camp on the Swan River, dates back 39 500 years. Unconfirmed estimates of the age of The Kimberley's rock art, however, suggest a human presence dating back as far as 80 000 years.

The Exchange Hotel, one of 92 hotels in Kalgoorlie's heyday

Dutch seafarers made many sightings of the west coast of Australia after Dirk Hartog approached it in 1616, invariably describing the land as sterile, forbidding and inhospitable. The British sent a small party of soldiers and convicts to King George Sound in 1826 to discourage French interest. When Captain James Stirling had convinced the British government that the country of the Swan River was not inferior to the plains of Lombardy, Captain Fremantle claimed Western Australia for the British Crown on 2 May 1829.

The colony did not prove as lush and fertile as Stirling had believed. Most of the new settlers soon ran out of money and the white colony struggled for the next sixty years. Wool provided much-needed income as the settlers occupied the grasslands to the north and east. Between 1850 and 1868 the British government sent out 9718 convicts for public works.

Politics of isolation

Western Australia remained a Crown colony for longer than the other Australian colonies. Representative government arrived in 1890 with a Legislative Assembly and, three years later, an elected Legislative Council. Since the 1920s, government has been shared fairly evenly between the Labor and Coalition parties. The present Labor government was elected in 2001.

Western Australia joined the Commonwealth at Federation in 1901. For several decades many Western Australians remained unconvinced, in 1933 voting by 2:1 to secede. However, the House of Commons ruled that secession could not be demanded by a State. The threat of Japanese invasion in 1942 silenced most of the secessionists.

Wealth and wonder

The great gold discoveries around Coolgardie and Kalgoorlie in the 1890s attracted the immigrants and capital that transformed Western Australia from a remote pastoral backwater into one of the world's great producers of gold, iron ore, nickel, diamonds, mineral sands and natural gas.

Despite the pronounced urbanisation of its population, Western Australia has always relied on primary industry, principally wheat, sheep, beef and, controversially, hardwood from the great southern forests. Tourism is the latest industry to thrive on the State's natural resources. Each year, increasing numbers of visitors experience the unspoilt beauty, compelling vastness and ancient mysteries of this landscape.

Modern exploration

Travellers to the south of the State can enjoy the temperate Mediterranean-style climate year-round. Those planning to visit the tropical north should go during the dry season (May to October), while outback adventurers should avoid the summer.

In most parts of the State, long distances separate towns. Travellers intending to explore remote areas should familiarise themselves with prevailing conditions, ensure that their vehicles are roadworthy and carry adequate supplies of water, food and petrol.

For more information on Western Australia, see Tourist Bureaus on p. 591.

PERTH

Perth skyline from South Perth

WITH a Mediterranean-type climate and magnificent coastal river setting, Perth is ideal for an outdoor lifestyle. Visitors to this city will find clean surf beaches, tranquil forests and well-kept parklands – all within easy reach of the city centre.

VISITOR INFORMATION
Western Australian Visitor Centre (WATC)
cnr Forrest Pl. & Wellington St, Perth
(08) 9483 1111;
freecall 1300 361 351
www.westernaustralia.net

Perth is a cosmopolitan city with a population of almost 1.4 million. The Swan River winds through the suburbs, widening to lake size near the city centre. The 404-hectare Kings Park contrasts dramatically with Perth's modern skyline, and the serene blue hills of the Darling Range form a more distant backdrop.

EXPLORING PERTH
The city centre is compact and easy to explore. A free, regular bus service known as CAT (Central Area Transit) System operates around central Perth; the blue CAT runs in a north–south loop and the red CAT operates in an east–west loop. You can also travel free with Transperth bus or train within the Free Transit Zone

GETTING AROUND

Airport shuttle bus
Airport Express Passenger Service
1800 999 819; Feature Tours (08) 9479 4131

Motoring organisation
Royal Automobile Club of Western Australia
(RAC) (08) 9421 4000; 13 1111

Car rental
Avis 13 6333; Budget 13 2727;
Hertz 13 3039; Thrifty 1300 367 227

Public transport
Transperth 13 6213

'Tram' tours
Perth Tram Co. (08) 9322 2006;
Trams West (08) 9339 8719

Taxis
Silvertop 13 1008; Swan 13 1330

Swan River boat cruises
Captain Cook (08) 9325 3341;
Boat Torque Cruises (08) 9221 5844

Bicycle hire
Bikewest (08) 9216 8000

in the city centre. Transperth produces a handy *Tourist Guide and Map*, which shows the Free Transit Zone.

A good way to discover the city is on the Perth Tram Co. tours, which operate daily. These replicas of the city's first trams extend east to Burswood International Resort Casino and west to the University of Western Australia. You can break your journey at any point. On weekdays, Trams West operates a 'tram' tour (the vehicle is actually a bus) around the streets of historic Subiaco and out to Lake Monger.

EXPLORING THE SWAN RIVER

The Swan River foreshores, on both the city side and around South Perth, provide pleasant walking and cycling trails; obtain a Bikewest *Touring Perth and Kings Park by Bike* map for details. Bicycles can be hired just off Riverside Drive near the Causeway, at the Barrack Street Jetty and at Kings Park.

If you are touring by car, the circuit route around the Swan River foreshore is a must. Follow the Canning Highway along the southern side of the river, then cross over at Stirling Bridge and return via the Stirling Highway.

Ferries and cruise boats depart regularly from the Barrack Street Jetty to various destinations, including Fremantle, South Perth and the Swan Valley wine region. Dinner cruises are a popular way to see the city light up at night.

CITY CENTRE

The centre of Perth is a well-balanced mixture: elegant colonial buildings sit comfortably alongside the steel and glass giants from the heady days of the 1980s; old-fashioned friendliness mingles with a sharp-edged competitiveness.

Most of Perth's shops and arcades are in the blocks bounded by St Georges Terrace and William, Wellington and Barrack streets, centering around **Hay Street Mall**, **Murray Street Mall** and **Forrest Place**. Perth's shopping and business area is linked by malls, overpasses and underground walkways. **London Court**, an arcade with the appearance of a quaint Elizabethan street, runs from Hay Street Mall to St Georges Terrace. At the Hay Street Mall entrance, knights joust above a replica of Big Ben every 15 minutes, while St George and the Dragon

PERTH BY AREA

CITY CENTRE
NORTHBRIDGE
EAST OF THE CITY CENTRE
KINGS PARK AND FORESHORE
WESTERN SUBURBS
OCEAN BEACHES
SOUTH OF THE SWAN

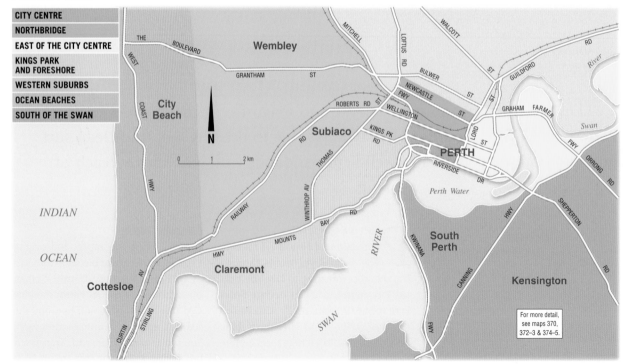

Perth Town Hall clocktower

do battle above the clock over the St Georges Terrace entrance.

Looking in a westerly direction along St Georges Terrace, the older buildings are largely overshadowed by modern office buildings; however, you can see the cast-iron verandahs of the **Bank West** building (formerly the Palace Hotel, 1895), the decorative brickwork of the **Cloisters** (1859) and the gothic-style **Old Perth Boys' School** (1846). At the end of St Georges Terrace, not far from the perspex skirt of the modern **QV1 Building**, is **Barracks Archway**. The central arch is all that remains of the Pensioners' Barracks, a structure that originally had two wings, with 120 rooms. This building housed the British soldiers who guarded the convicts in the mid-1800s. Across the road (the other side of the Mitchell Freeway) is Western Australia's **Parliament House**. Weekday tours are available; bookings essential.

For a stroll through the oldest part of Perth, start at the **Central Government Building** near the north-east corner of St Georges Terrace and Barrack Street. Perth was founded here with a tree-felling ceremony in 1829. Convicts and hired labour commenced work on the Central Government Building in 1874. At one stage, it housed the General Post Office, and a plaque on the building's east corner marks the point from which all distances in the State are measured.

Cross St Georges Terrace and walk through the **Stirling Gardens** to Perth's oldest surviving building, the **Old Court House**. Built in 1836, it is now home to the Frances Burt Law Museum. Walk through the **Supreme Court Gardens** towards the new Barrack Square development and its centre-piece, the **Swan Bells**. This striking bell-tower is possibly one of the largest musical instruments in the world and houses the historic bells of St Martin-in-the-Fields, Buckingham Palace's parish church.

Back on St Georges Terrace, look out for Perth's Tudor-style **Government House** (1859). Across the road, on the Pier Street corner, you will see the **Deanery** (1859) and **St George's Cathedral** (1879); this Anglican church

NOT TO BE MISSED IN PERTH

	Map Ref.
Ferry Trip Past the exclusive waterside suburbs to Fremantle	370 D8
Kings Park Bushland reserve with good views of city	370 A7
Lake Monger To see black swans and other waterbirds	372 F1
Northbridge For its lively arts precinct	370 C4
Ocean Beaches To surf, swim or relax by the sparkling sea	372 & 374
Perth Mint Lift a gold bar and watch a gold pourer at work	370 F7
Perth Zoo Beautiful butterflies and animals of the night	370 C12

TOP EVENTS

Hopman Cup (Jan.)
Prestigious international tennis event

Perth International Arts Festival (Jan.–Feb.)
Exciting programme of great diversity

Kings Park Wildflower Festival (Sept.)
Australia's premier native plant and wildflower exhibition

Rally Australia (Nov.)
Four days of action-packed, world-class motor sport

For further details visit the web site
www.westernaustralia.net/whats_on/index.shtml

CLIMATE **PERTH**

	J	F	M	A	M	J	J	A	S	O	N	D
Max. °C	30	31	29	25	21	19	18	18	20	22	25	27
Min. °C	18	19	17	14	12	10	9	9	10	12	14	17
Rain mm	8	12	19	45	123	184	173	136	80	54	21	14
Raindays	3	3	4	8	14	17	18	17	14	11	6	4

PERTH ON FOOT

Guntrips Walking Tours
2-hour guided walks around city and Kings Park; bookings essential

Heritage Walk
2-hour guided walk of central business district; bookings essential

Perth Heritage Trails
Self-guide heritage trails

Perth Walking Tours
2-hour guided heritage walks; bookings essential

For further information and bookings, contact WATC

SPORT

Spectator

*The famous **WACA** cricket ground is the venue for national and international cricket and Australian Football League (AFL) matches. The night games held Fridays and Saturdays draw huge crowds, particularly when Perth's two AFL teams, the West Coast Eagles and Fremantle Dockers, battle it out. Night harness racing can be seen near the WACA at **Gloucester Park**, and other racing is held at the **Ascot** and **Belmont Park** racecourses. The **Perth Entertainment Centre** in the heart of the city is the place to see the popular Perth Wildcats basketball team, which plays to capacity crowds.*

Participator

*Sailing, windsurfing and other water-related activities are Perth's grandest obsession, and yachts, kayaks and dinghies can be hired on the popular **Swan River** foreshore. Golf courses are plentiful around Perth, and the 18-hole **Burswood Park**, only three minutes from the city centre, has a day/night driving range and instruction available. Tennis enthusiasts will enjoy the facilities at the nearby **State Tennis Centre of Western Australia**, where professional coaching is at hand and a cafe and licensed bar sustain competitors.*

HISTORY

Perth was founded by Captain James Stirling in 1829, three years after a British party from Sydney landed at King George Sound (Albany) to abate fears of French colonisation. The progress of the isolated Swan River settlement, made up of free settlers, was slow. It was not until the first shipment of convicts arrived in 1850 that the colony found its feet. The convicts were soon put to work building roads, bridges and fine public buildings, and in 1856 Perth was proclaimed a city. Gold discoveries in the State in the 1880s gave Perth another boost and, more recently, the huge diamond finds in The Kimberley and the reopening of goldmines in the Kalgoorlie region have stimulated new growth.

Swan Bells, the centrepiece of Barrack Square

features a rich jarrah ceiling, perhaps the finest in Perth.

Continue along Pier Street to the National Trust-classified Murray Street Precinct, which includes the **Former Government Printer's Office**, the **Old Fire Brigade Building** which now houses a fire museum, and **Kirkman House** (with its massive fig tree). This harmonious group of buildings is a legacy of the wealth of the gold era. At the eastern end of Murray Street, in Victoria Square, is the Gothic-style **St Mary's Cathedral** (1863).

To complete your historic ramble, return along Murray Street and turn left into Barrack Street. The decorative **Perth Town Hall** (1867) with its distinctive clocktower is on the corner of Hay and Barrack streets.

NORTHBRIDGE

The inner-city suburb of **Northbridge** is connected to the city centre via an extensive walkway that crosses Perth Railway Station and leads directly to the **Perth Cultural Centre** complex. The **Art Gallery of Western Australia**, home to a fine display of Western Australian art, is located here. So, too, is the **Perth Institute of Contemporary Arts (PICA)** where you can sample the latest in visual and performance art. On weekends, the **Galleria Art and Craft Markets** create a colourful atmosphere in the Cultural Centre Mall. Across the mall is the excellent **Western Australian Museum**, which includes the original Perth Gaol (1856) and an 1860s cottage.

On Friday and Saturday nights, the streets west of the Perth Cultural Centre provide popular places to eat, drink and go nightclubbing. Many of the restaurants and bars open out into the streets to take advantage of the mild Perth evenings.

EAST OF THE CITY CENTRE

Towards the eastern end of Hay Street is the **Perth Mint** (1899) with its imposing facade built from Rottnest Island limestone – one of the best examples of Perth gold-boom architecture. Here, visitors can see the world's largest collection of natural gold specimens and watch gold being poured.

Queens Gardens, at the corner of Hay and Plain streets, is on the site of the former brickworks, source of the lovely mellow bricks used in many of Perth's colonial buildings. In 1899 the clay pits were transformed into ornamental lily ponds and garden beds.

Those interested in cricket will want to pay homage to the **Western Australian Cricket Association (WACA) Oval**, in Nelson Crescent. Every Tuesday at 10 a.m. regular tours are conducted around the museum and the 'Wacca' ground; phone (08) 9265 7222.

Across the Swan are the beautifully landscaped gardens of **Burswood Park**, an adventurous blend of native and exotic plants. The Atrium Lobby in the **Burswood International Resort Casino** is one of the city's modern architectural highlights. This 47-metre high pyramid of shimmering glass contains a tropical garden and waterfall.

KINGS PARK AND FORESHORE

Just minutes from the city centre, **Kings Park** is one of Perth's major attractions. Within this huge natural bushland reserve there are landscaped gardens and walkways, lakes, children's playgrounds and a war memorial. During spring, the **Botanic Gardens** on Mount Eliza Bluff are ablaze with wildflowers.

Drive along the river past Kings Park to the suburb of Crawley and the **University of Western Australia**, with its Mediterranean-style buildings and landscaped gardens. Within the university grounds you will find the Brendt Museum of Anthropology and the Lawrence Wilson Art Gallery. Nearby, the grassy Matilda Bay shoreline has shady spots and views back up the river and towards the city. The **Royal Perth Yacht Club** is located near Pelican Point.

Continuing along the river foreshore towards the ocean, you will pass through the exclusive water-front suburbs – **Nedlands, Dalkeith, Claremont, Peppermint Grove** and **Mosman Park** – with their charming village-style shopping areas, fashionable galleries and foreshore restaurants. **Claremont Museum**, once the Freshwater School (1862), has an interesting social history display.

WESTERN SUBURBS

Just west of the city on the edge of Kings Park is the popular shopping, cafe and market area **Subiaco**, one of Perth's oldest suburbs.

In West Perth at the City West shopping complex are the **Scitech Discovery Centre**, which features a hands-on science and technology display, and the massive screen of the **Omni Theatre**. Just north of West Perth in Leederville is **Lake Monger**, the best place in Perth to see Western Australia's famous black swans.

OCEAN BEACHES

Swimming and surfing are part of the joy of Perth and several beautiful Indian Ocean beaches – including Cottesloe, Swanbourne (a nude bathing beach), City, Floreat, Scarborough, Trigg and North beaches – are close to the city.

A drive along the foreshore to **Cottesloe** is full of surprises: the distinctive Norfolk Island pines, the colonial splendour of the **Indiana Tea House** and the Spanish-style **Cottesloe Civic Centre** with its magnificent gardens.

Further north at **Scarborough**, you will find wonderful weekend stalls at the **Scarborough Fair Markets**, adjacent to the five-star **Rendezvous Observation City**. Hillarys Boat Harbour at **Sorrento Quay** features recreational facilities, a marine retail village and a world-class oceanarium, **Underwater World**. Ferries depart daily from here for Rottnest Island and there are whale-watching tours from September to November. Near Hillarys Boat Harbour is **Marmion Marine Park**, offering fishing, snorkelling, diving and Little Island, a wildlife reserve where visitors can watch sea-lions and whales.

SOUTH OF THE SWAN

There are a host of interesting attractions south of the Swan River. South Perth is home to **Perth Zoo**, with its magnificent garden environment, butterfly house and Australian animal exhibits. The trip can be combined with a visit to the **Old Mill**, on the South Perth foreshore. This picturesque whitewashed windmill, built in 1838, now houses an interesting collection of early colonial artifacts.

On the other side of Canning River is **Wireless Hill Park**, a natural bushland area with beautiful spring wildflowers. Three lookout towers

SHOPPING	Map Ref.
Department Stores Myer and Aherns are the two major ones	370 D5, D6
King Street High fashion, galleries and cafes with style	370 C6
London Court Mock-Tudor arcade with souvenir and jewellery stores	370 D6
Squares & Malls Hay Street Mall; Murray Street Mall; Forrest Place	370 D5, D6
Suburban Village-Style Shopping Strips Claremont (Bay View Terrace)	372 D6
Cottesloe (Napoleon Street, off Leake Street)	372 C7
Subiaco (Rokeby Road)	372 F3

MARKETS	Map Ref.
Canning Vale Sunday Markets, Canning Vale Huge undercover flea market	373 K12
Galleria Art and Craft Markets, Perth Cultural Centre, Northbridge Handcrafted items (Sat. & Sun.)	370 D5
Scarborough Fair Markets, Scarborough Beach Specialty stalls and a food hall (Sat. & Sun.)	374 B10
Station Street Markets, Subiaco Eclectic array of goods and live entertainment (Sat. & Sun.)	372 F2
Subiaco Pavilion Markets, Subiaco Art and craft stalls in restored warehouse adjacent to station (Thurs.–Sun.)	372 F3

ENTERTAINMENT

It is worth timing your visit to experience a performance in His Majesty's Theatre, Australia's only remaining Edwardian theatre. Other major venues include the Perth Concert Hall in St Georges Terrace, the Perth Entertainment Centre off Wellington Street and the splendid Art Deco Regal Theatre in Subiaco. For avant-garde theatre, try the small performance venues in Northbridge. Burswood International Resort Casino is another lively night-time destination. Alternatively, why not make the most of Perth's glorious weather and check out the outdoor theatre and cinema venues during summer.

For entertainment details check the West Australian newspaper on Thursdays or pick up a free copy of the X-Press gig guide.

RESTAURANTS AND CAFES   Map Ref.

One of the highlights of Perth is the opportunity to taste seafood straight from the clear waters of the Indian Ocean, accompanied by a superb range of fresh fruit and vegetables, and complemented by quality Western Australian wines or locally brewed beers.

Barrack Street Jetty   370 D7
Brunch or dinner by the river

King Street (in the city centre)   370 C6
International cafe-style fare

Leederville (along Oxford Street)   372 G2
The inner-city alternative

Northbridge   370 C4
Italian and Asian cuisine at reasonable prices

Northern Foreshore   372
Quality seafood and glorious views

South Perth   370 C12
Bright modern cafes overlooking the river

Subiaco   372 F3
Street cafes, stylish pubs and fine restaurants

GALLERIES AND MUSEUMS   Map Ref.

Art Gallery of Western Australia   370 E5
Collection of Australian and international works

Artist in Residence Gallery   370 A7
An Aboriginal art gallery where you can watch the current resident artist at work

Craftwest   370 C5
Craft by leading Western Australian artists

Creative Native   370 C5
Aboriginal art and craft, traditional and modern

Perth Institute of Contemporary Arts (PICA)   370 D5
Vibrant contemporary art and performance space

Western Australian Museum   370 E4
Comprehensive collection including some of Perth's oldest buildings

'Tram' tours through Kings Park

provide views of the Swan River and the city skyline. The **Telecommunications Museum** is housed in the original Wireless Station and is open weekends. Further south, black swans and other waterbirds can be seen at **Bibra Lake** in the suburb of the same name. Also at Bibra Lake is the State's biggest theme park, **Adventure World**, which is open October to April and offers among its attractions a wildlife park, animal circus, rides and Australia's largest swimming pool.

Bannister Road, in the south-east suburb of Canning Vale, is the location of Western Australia's biggest undercover marketplace, the **Canning Vale Sunday Markets**. Nearby in Baile Road you will find the **Swan Brewery**, renowned for its Swan and Emu beers. Tours of this state-of-the-art brewery are available; bookings essential, phone (08) 9350 0222.

Closer to the coast, in Spearwood, there are two other attractions: **Cables Water Ski Park**, a water-ski fun park, and the **Stock Road Markets**, held under cover at weekends.

Perth is a modern capital in a splendid natural setting. Renowned for its outdoor and easy going lifestyle, this compact city offers a host of urban pleasures.

DAY TOURS FROM PERTH

Rottnest Island
Just off the coast of Perth, the low-key island resort of Rottnest makes for a perfect day tour. Access is via ferry from Fremantle, Perth and Hillarys Boat Harbour. No private cars are permitted; island transport is by foot, bike or bus. Visitors to Rottnest divide their time between the beach and the scenic and historic attractions of the island. *For more details see region coverage, p. 324.*

Darling Range
Follow the Great Eastern Highway for a tour of the Darling Range and its 80 000 hectares of escarpment and jarrah forest in the Hills Forest area. Highlights include a scenic drive through the John Forrest National Park and a visit to the huge, forest-fringed Mundaring Weir. *For more details see region coverage, p. 325.*

Swan Valley
Swan Valley is best known as a premier winegrowing district, with vineyards along the scenic Swan River. Other attractions include historic Guildford, the Victorian mansion Woodbridge House in West Midland, the wildflower fields of Walyunga National Park, and Whiteman Park – an Australian theme park. *For more details see region coverage, p. 325.*

Yanchep National Park
Yanchep, on the coast north of Perth, has long been one of the city's favourite recreation areas. Hire a rowing-boat to explore Loch McNess, or take a guided tour of Crystal Caves, where stalactites hang above the inky waters of an underground pool. *For more details see region coverage, p. 330.*

FREMANTLE

Blessing of the Fleet takes place annually in October

VISITOR INFORMATION

Fremantle Visitor Information Centre
Fremantle Town Hall
cnr William and Adelaide sts
(08) 9431 7878
www.freofocus.com.au

GETTING AROUND

Car rental
Avis 13 6333; Budget 13 2727;
Hertz 13 3039

Public transport
Transperth 13 6213

Taxis
Swan 13 1330; Silvertop 13 1008

Scooter hire
Scootabout (08) 9336 3471

Bicycle hire
Fleet Cycles 0414 398 179

Tourist tram
Fremantle tram (departs from Fremantle
Town Hall) (08) 9339 8719

Although now linked to Perth by suburbs, Fremantle ('Freo' to the locals) has a feel that is quite different, in both its architecture and its atmosphere. It stands at the mouth of the Swan River, 19 kilometres south-west of Perth, and was the site of the first European settlement in Western Australia.

Today Fremantle is a major port and fishing centre with a well-preserved nineteenth-century port streetscape. It is also a place to stay, to unwind, and to watch the world go by. You can visit historic buildings, shop at the famous market, take a tram ride, or rest at a cafe and wait for the arrival of the 'Fremantle doctor', the cool, refreshing, afternoon wind that blows in from the ocean. Fremantle combines the bustle of a port with the relaxed feeling of a holiday destination.

European settlers first arrived in 1829, and Fremantle grew slowly, its existence dependent on whaling and fishing. Its population was boosted with the arrival of British convicts in 1850. They constructed the forbidding Fremantle Prison, now open to the public, and

the imposing lunatic asylum, now the Fremantle Arts Centre and History Museum. Many heritage houses, terraces and cast-iron balconies have survived from this era.

Fremantle was at the centre of the world stage in 1987 when it hosted the America's Cup series of yacht races, in defence of the cup won by *Australia II* – a Fremantle yacht – in 1983. Preparations for this huge event included the restoration of many old buildings in Fremantle, and the boost to its tourist economy has lasted to the present.

EXPLORING FREMANTLE

The centre of Fremantle is compact, so exploring on foot is an option, although the Fremantle Arts Centre and History Museum are outside the city centre. If you are driving, there are a number of carparks along the foreshore on Marine Terrace and the Esplanade, and in the city centre, as well as metered street parking.

For train travellers to Fremantle, the station is close to the city centre and the

GETTING TO FREMANTLE FROM PERTH

By car
A drive of 20 to 30 minutes, either via Stirling Hwy on north bank of Swan River, or via Canning Hwy on south bank.

By train
A 30-minute journey from Perth Railway Station, Wellington St. Trains depart every 15 minutes on weekdays, less frequently at weekends.

By bus
Many buses and routes link both cities. Timetables and route details from Wellington St Bus Station in Perth, Transperth, or Fremantle Town Hall.

By ferry
Various ferry operators travel twice daily between Perth and Fremantle, departing Barrack Street Jetty, Perth.

Combined travel packages
Two packages, Tourist Trifecta organised by Perth Tram and Tourist Quartet organised by Fremantle Trams, combine ferry travel and train tours. The Quartet package includes bus or train back to Perth.

wharves. If you arrive by ferry, you can catch the tourist 'tram' into town. The replica tram (actually a bus) is a great way to see Fremantle. It departs from the Town Hall hourly (10 a.m.–4 p.m.), passes the popular sights and has a commentary. For the more energetic, bicycle and scooter hire are available.

HISTORIC CENTRE

To explore the historic centre, start at the **Fremantle Town Hall** in Kings Square, on the corner of William and Adelaide streets. The **Fremantle Tourist Bureau** is here, so you can pick up information on the city's attractions before you set out. The town hall, built in 1887, has a clock tower. Nearby in Adelaide Street is **St John's Anglican Church** with its stone bell-tower.

From the town hall, walk along High Street towards the sea, past the shops, and turn right into Henry Street, which ends at Phillimore Street. On Phillimore

Street are three imposing buildings: the Georgian-style **Old Customs House**, built in 1853, one of the oldest buildings in Fremantle; the **Old Fremantle Fire Station** (now a restaurant) and, alongside, the **Chamber of Commerce**, with stained-glass panels around its door. Turn left along Cliff Street and go past the lavish, Victorian-era **Lionel Samson Building** on your way to the Western Australian Maritime Museum at the far end.

Between 1851 and 1862 convicts built the Commissariat store, which now houses the **Western Australian Maritime Museum**. Its most popular exhibit is the reconstructed stern of the *Batavia*, wrecked off the Western Australian coast in 1629, which looms above the visitor. The Batavia room contains a stone portico that was being transported to Java when the wreck occurred.

From the Western Australian Maritime Museum stroll along Marine

Terrace to Fremantle's **Old Courthouse** (1883), on the corner of Mouat Street and Marine Terrace and now part of the University of Notre Dame. The **Esplanade Hotel Fremantle**, overlooking The Esplanade Reserve on Marine Terrace, is a grand old hotel with a lovely wooden verandah reminiscent of the 1890s gold-rush era. Head back to Collie Street to visit **Artisans of the Sea**, where there is a pearling industry heritage display and award-winning Kailis Broome pearl jewellery. Turn left onto Pakenham Street and second on the right is Bannister Street. Here you will find the **Bannister Street Craft Workshops**, where a co-operative of artisans create, display and sell their work.

At the end of Bannister Street, turn right into Market Street and along **South Terrace**, the cappuccino strip, an ideal place to take a break at a cafe or restaurant. The **Sail and Anchor Hotel** was Western Australia's first pub brewery and serves specialty beers – it even has a banana beer!

In this strip you will also find the **Fremantle Markets** in a gorgeously restored Victorian building. It is one of Fremantle's most popular attractions, and contains a diversity of stalls: produce, books, clothes, pottery and crafts. The markets are open Friday to Sunday.

From the markets walk up Henderson Street to the **Fremantle Police Station and Courthouse**, a limestone building dating from the 1890s. Nearby are the **Warders' Quarters**, a row of cottages built by convicts in 1851.

HARBOURSIDE

At the port of Fremantle the industrial activities are across the river on the northern side, but there are plenty of boats on this side of the Swan in the Harbourside area. Furthest south is **Success Boat Harbour**, home to the yachts of the Fremantle Sailing Club. Alongside is **Fishing Boat Harbour**, where the 500-strong fishing fleet moors. Restaurants line the wharves here, giving you a chance to sample the deliciously fresh catch, particularly lobster. West of this is **Challenger Harbour**, built for the America's Cup.

FREMANTLE BY AREA

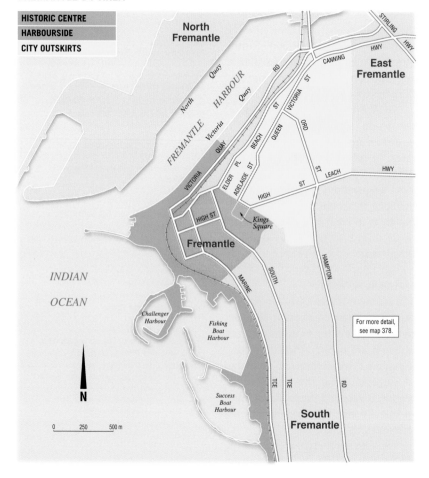

HISTORIC CENTRE
HARBOURSIDE
CITY OUTSKIRTS

North
Fremantle

East
Fremantle

For more detail, see map 378.

INDIAN
OCEAN

Kings
Square

Fremantle

Challenger
Harbour
Fishing
Boat
Harbour

Success
Boat
Harbour

South
Fremantle

N

0   250   500 m

The Old Customs House

**NOT TO BE MISSED
IN FREMANTLE**   Map Ref.

**Fremantle Arts Centre
and History Museum**   378 G5
For an insight into Fremantle's history

Fremantle Prison   378 G8
Huge, forbidding and full of history

Round House   378 C8
Western Australia's oldest public building

Western Australian Maritime Museum 378 D8
Home of the *Batavia* wreck

TOP EVENTS

Sardine Festival (Jan.)
*Taste freshly caught sardines from the waters
of Fremantle*

Blessing of the Fleet (Oct.)
Traditional Italian blessing of the fishing fleet

Festival Fremantle (Nov.)
*Streets come to life with food, music, theatre,
dance, and exhibitions*

*For further details visit the web site
www.fremantle.wa.gov.au*

Continue north to the end of Bathers Beach, to the area known as Arthur Head. Dominating the hill here, behind a limestone-retaining wall, is the **Round House**. The Round House actually has twelve sides, constructed around a central yard, and is the oldest building in the State, built in 1830 as a gaol. At 1 p.m. daily, the Round House's signal station fires a cannon – the time gun – and a time ball is activated. There are Fremantle Heritage Guides on site daily, between 10 a.m. and 5 p.m. November to April, and between 10.30 a.m. and 3.30 p.m. May to October.

From here it is a short stroll past the shipyards to the river and the sheds that line **Victoria Quay**. **A Shed** houses a cafe; and **E Shed** a market (open Friday to Sunday) and more cafes. Also on the riverfront is the towering Fremantle **Port Authority** building; at 1.30 p.m. on weekdays you can catch the guided tour to the Observation Deck for a great view.

The *Leeuwin*, a traditional square-rigger and the largest tall ship in Australia, has a berth at Victoria Quay. It takes people on weekend, day and half-day cruises, as part of the crew.

CITY OUTSKIRTS

The first convicts arrived in Fremantle in 1850 and were immediately set to work to build a prison. The limestone used in construction was quarried on site. Huge, forbidding and full of history, the **Fremantle Prison** was in use until 1991. Now, visitors can experience the atmosphere on a guided tour. The entrance is in The Terrace, and can be reached via steps and a walkway around Fremantle Oval from Parry Street.

Hampton Road (later Ord Street), at the far side of the prison, takes you to **Samson House** (1888), on the corner of Ellen Street. This mansion has been restored to elegance and is open on Sunday afternoons (1 p.m. to 5 p.m.).

Further along Ord Street is the magnificent limestone **Fremantle Arts Centre and History Museum**. Also built by convicts, it was the old female lunatic asylum. With its steeply pitched roofs and Gothic arcades it is a striking building. It offers contemporary art exhibitions, an interesting display on the history of Fremantle, a ghost walk and a garden area with a cafe.

Close by, in Burt Street, the **Army Museum of Western Australia** is open Saturday and Sunday afternoons, while the **World of Energy**, with its fascinating interactive displays, is in Quarry Street on the way back to town from the Fremantle Arts Centre and History Museum.

From Fremantle's Victoria Quay you can catch a ferry to Rottnest Island, a favourite beach spot for Western Australians. With its relaxed, almost Mediterranean atmosphere, its architecture, its working port and fishing-boat harbour, its renowned markets and its cafe-lined South Terrace, Fremantle attracts large numbers of visitors and locals, particularly at weekends: it is the playground for Perth.

ROTTNEST ISLAND

In 1696 Dutch explorer Willem de Vlamingh declared Rottnest Island a 'terrestrial paradise', although he named it Rotte-nest (Rats' nest) for the rat-like beasts he encountered. The island, 11 km long and 5 km wide, lies in azure waters 18 km west of Perth. Although about half a million people visit annually it remains unspoiled, with sandy coves and bays, interesting flora and fauna, and land and underwater heritage sites. Daytrips are popular, as are longer stays in the low-key accommodation on offer. Ferries and an air taxi service operate from the mainland. No private cars are permitted; explore the island by foot, bike, bus or train.

TOP EVENTS

Jan.–
Mar. *Rottnest Island Celebrates Summer*

Feb. *Rottnest Island Channel Swim*

Oct. *Marathon and Fun Run*

Nov. *Surf Assault*

Dec. *Rottnest Swim Thru*

EXPERIENCE IT!

❶ *Fish the recreational waters of Rottnest for species such as flathead, tailor, moon wrasse, marlin and tuna*

❷ *Watch for humpback whales off Cape Vlamingh in the winter months*

❸ *Enjoy a late-afternoon drink in the beer garden at the Rottnest Hotel*

VISITOR INFORMATION

Rottnest Island
Visitor Information Centre
Settlement: (08) 9372 9752
www.rottnest.wa.gov.au

FOCUS ON

Island heritage

Known as Wadjemup to the Nyungar people, Rottnest was unoccupied when Europeans arrived, although there is evidence of occupation around 7000 years ago, when the island was linked to the mainland. Europeans settled on the island in 1831. From 1838 to 1903 it was used as a prison for Aboriginal people. During WW I it became an internment camp and in 1917 it was declared an A-class reserve. Many heritage sites are well preserved and Rottnest has an early streetscape, Settlement's Vincent Way. Other interesting sites are the prison buildings of Settlement, Rottnest Lighthouse (1859) at Wadjemup Hill and Oliver Hill Gun Battery (1930s).

CLIMATE

	J	F	M	A	M	J	J	A	S	O	N	D
Max. °C	26	27	25	23	20	18	17	17	18	20	22	24
Min. °C	18	19	18	16	14	13	12	12	13	15	17
Rain mm	7	13	14	37	106	156	149	104	61	39	17	10
Raindays	2	2	4	8	15	18	20	18	14	11	6	3

The Basin

An outer reef surrounds Rottnest, protecting the clear waters and creating calm conditions for family swimming. The Basin provides one of a number of beautiful sandy beaches on the eastern end of the island. It is within easy walking distance of the Settlement area, and has basic facilities.

Underwater heritage

Heritage-listed wrecks around Rottnest include the *City of York*, wrecked in 1899 after the captain failed to identify a lighthouse flare correctly and set course for the rocks. Waterproof maps of the island's 15 sites are available. Scuba and snorkelling tours are popular, as are tours aboard the glass-bottomed *Underwater Explorer*.

West End

The 'West End' of Rottnest can be reached on an 11-km bike ride along a sealed road, or on a bus tour. There are stunning ocean views from Cape Vlamingh and a 1-km heritage trail that affords sightings of wedge-tailed shearwaters, fairy terns, quokkas and bottle-nosed dolphins.

Map: ROTTNEST ISLAND — INDIAN OCEAN, North Point, Charlotte Point, The Basin, Bathurst Point, SETTLEMENT, Thomson Bay, Ferry, Wadjemup Hill, Oliver Hill, Rocky Bay, South Point, Strickland Bay, Salmon Bay, Porpoise Bay, Salmon Point, Parker Point, Cape Vlamingh (West End)

Quokka country

The quokka is a native marsupial found primarily on Rottnest. It is nocturnal, furry and grows to hare size. There are about 10 000 quokkas on the island. Find the interpretive signs about 1 km south of Settlement (heading towards Kingstown Barracks) and good viewing spots around the salt lakes.

Rottnest Museum

Built by Aboriginal prisoners in 1857 as the island granary, this heritage building now houses a series of fascinating displays charting the cultural, environmental and maritime history of the island.

DARLING RANGE & SWAN VALLEY

Barely half an hour from the centre of Perth are two distinct country landscapes, perfect for scenic touring, picnicking, walking and wildflower-watching. To the north-east is the wine district of Swan Valley, offering cellar-door tastings, restaurants and cafes, galleries, native landscapes including Walyunga National Park (a good spot for wildflowers), and charming B&B accommodation. Directly east is the Darling Range incorporating the Hills Forest (an 80 000-ha stretch of unique Western Australian jarrah forest), where visitors can choose from national parks, historic towns, lakes and weirs, scenic drives with spectacular views, and a superb botanic garden.

For more detail see maps 375 & 376. For descriptions of ❶ towns see Towns from A to Z (p. 335).

TOP EVENTS

Apr. Mundaring Hills Festival (Mundaring)

Aug. Avon Descent (along Avon/Swan River)

Oct. Spring in the Valley (wine festival, throughout Swan Valley)

Nov. Arts Festival (Darlington, near Mundaring)

EXPERIENCE IT!

❶ **Travel** the one-way Zig Zag Scenic Drive for views and wildflowers, via Kalamunda

❷ **Picnic** in Walyunga National Park and enjoy wildflowers in spring

❸ **See** the Lesmurdie Brook drop 50 m over Darling Escarpment, in Lesmurdie Falls National Park

VISITOR INFORMATION

Mundaring Tourist Association
Mundaring: (08) 9295 0202
Swan Valley Tourist Information Centre
Guildford: (08) 9279 9859
www.mundaringtourism.com.au

FOCUS ON

Heritage sites

In historic Guildford you can enjoy two heritage sites. Pause at the Rose and Crown Hotel (1841), the oldest trading hotel in the State. If you time your visit for Sunday afternoon you can roam among yesteryear's farm tools, fashions and household items at the Old Courthouse, Gaol and Museum. At nearby West Midland and overlooking the Swan River is the National Trust's Woodbridge House (1855), a fine example of Victorian architecture. Just south of Upper Swan, in a charming setting on the western bank of the river, is the State's oldest church, the 1830s All Saints Church.

CLIMATE GUILDFORD

	J	F	M	A	M	J	J	A	S	O	N	D
Max. °C	32	32	30	27	22	19	18	19	21	23	27	30
Min. °C	17	17	15	13	10	8	7	8	9	10	13	15
Rain mm	8	10	17	43	122	177	172	139	86	56	20	13
Raindays	2	2	4	7	14	17	19	17	14	11	6	4

Whiteman Park

This recreation park offers Australian experiences that include bushwalking, camel-riding, whip-cracking and sheep-shearing. Bush music and Aboriginal cultural displays are offered on regular Australiana theme days, and visitors can tour the native landscape of the park aboard a vintage tram or horse-drawn cart.

Swan Valley wineries

There are nearly 30 wineries in the Valley, with some of Australia's finest vineyards in West Swan Road. The climate favours full-bodied whites: labels you will come across include Houghton (pictured), Evans and Tate, and Sandalford. For a treat that offers scenery as well as wine-tasting, take the Swan River wineries cruise.

Araluen Botanic Park

Tall forest trees (jarrah, eucalypt and marri) frame the rock pools, waterfalls and European-style terraces of these beautiful 59-ha gardens. Established in the 1930s by the Young Australia League, the gardens have picturesque walking trails, picnic and barbecue areas and, in spring, magnificent tulip displays.

John Forrest National Park

Located in the Hills Forest area, John Forrest was declared a national park in 1947. A drive through the park has vantage points with heart-stopping views across Perth and the coastal plain. A popular walk is the Heritage Trail on the western edge, past waterfalls and an old rail tunnel.

Mundaring Weir

The rolling lawns and bushclad surrounds of the weir reserve make it ideal for picnics. Drop into the C. Y. O'Connor Museum (named for the man who met the challenge of supplying water to the goldfields) and the Hills Forest Activity Centre, where visitors can sign up for activities including bushcraft.

THE SOUTH-WEST

Western Australia's south-west corner, with a climate comfortable enough to allow year-round visits, is about three-and-a-half hours' drive from Perth. Mandurah, at the beginning of a stretch of low, sandy inlets and lakes, is the first of a number of seaside resorts. The rocky Limestone Coast beyond Cape Naturaliste, broken by good surf beaches, ends at Cape Leeuwin where the Indian and Southern oceans meet. The State's premier winegrowing region, at Margaret River, is a few kilometres inland. The old-growth jarrah and karri forests on the low plateau 30 km from the coast are one of the south-west's unique features.

TOP EVENTS

Jan.	Summerfest (Busselton)
Feb.	Amberley Semillon and Seafood Weekend (Amberley Estate, near Yallingup)
Feb.	Crab Festival (Mandurah)
Feb.–Mar.	Leeuwin Estate Concert (Leeuwin Estate, near Margaret River)
Mar.	Margaret River Masters (surfing competition, Margaret River)
June	15 000 Motocross (Manjimup)
Aug.	Tulip Festival (Balingup, near Donnybrook)
Nov.	Wine Festival (Australind, even-numbered years)
Nov.	Spring Festival (Rockingham)

EXPERIENCE IT!

❶ **Climb** the spiral ladder to the top of the 61-m karri Gloucester Tree in Gloucester National Park

❷ **Cruise** to see dolphins in Koombana Bay at Bunbury

❸ **Visit** the restored 1859 homestead Wonnerup House, 10 km east of Busselton

VISITOR INFORMATION
Mandurah: (08) 9550 3999
Margaret River: (08) 9757 2911
www.margaretriverwa.com

FOCUS ON

Old-growth forests
Western Australia's only forests are in the cool, well-watered south-west. Jarrah, a beautifully grained, deep-red hardwood, flourishes between Dwellingup and Collie. Forests of karri, one of the world's tallest trees, reaching 90 m in a hundred years, are found in the wetter areas, from Manjimup to Walpole. Pemberton is the focus of a struggle over logging between the timber industry and conservationists that has become a State and Federal political issue. Dwellingup's Forest Heritage Centre shows both sides of the controversy and features the forest (at treetop level, from the Canopy Walk) and the furniture made from forest timbers, in the workshops below.

CLIMATE BUSSELTON

	J	F	M	A	M	J	J	A	S	O	N	D
Max. °C	29	28	26	23	19	17	16	17	18	20	24	27
Min. °C	14	14	13	11	9	8	8	8	8	9	11	13
Rain mm	10	11	22	42	118	175	167	117	75	52	24	13
Raindays	3	2	4	8	15	19	22	19	16	13	7	4

Peel Coast
The coastal towns south of Rockingham offer swimming, boating, fishing and crabbing. The Yalgorup National Park protects ten coastal lakes, with views over ocean and dunes at high points. From Preston Beach, a walking track crosses tuart and peppermint woodlands to Lake Pollard, where black swans gather from October to March.

Limestone Coast
Protected by the Leeuwin–Naturaliste National Park, the Limestone Coast offers a splendid stretch of rocky headlands, wild beaches and limestone caves. Walking, surfing at Yallingup beach, scuba-diving, and whale-watching and salmon fishing from September to December, are other attractions.

For more detail see maps 376, 377, 379, 380 & 384. For descriptions of ❶ towns see Towns from A to Z (p. 335). For touring details see Classic Tour (p. 366).

Blackwood Valley
The Blackwood River meanders for 500 km through wheat-belt plains and forested valleys to its broad estuary at Augusta. Secluded spots along the river between Nannup and Alexandra Bridge offer tranquil camping, fishing, swimming and canoeing. The Sheoak Walk is a 1-hour loop through the forest close to Nannup.

Margaret River wine styles
The region's reputation for premium wines rests principally on cabernet sauvignon and chardonnay grown on grey-brown, gravelly-sandy soils. Try the cabernet from Vasse Felix, Moss Wood and Cullen and the chardonnays from Leeuwin Estate, Voyager Estate (pictured) and Ashbrook.

Pemberton
At tiny Pemberton you can take the tramway (pictured) through the heart of the great karri and marri forests, and visit the virgin forests in Warren and Beedelup national parks. You can also sample the marron – freshwater cray – grown in local hatcheries, and tour the 28 or so wineries.

GREAT SOUTHERN

The Great Southern region begins at Katanning and Kojonup, small towns at the southern extremity of the wheat belt. The road south crosses sheep country, with views of the jagged peaks of the blue and purple Stirling Range. A stop at Mount Barker offers a chance to taste the intensely floral rieslings grown in the region's burgeoning winegrowing area. Albany, on panoramic King George Sound, is the centre of the region. This comfortable, historic town, with its range of accommodation and restaurants, is the ideal base for exploring the rugged coast east to Bremer Bay and west to the surfing beaches near the secluded riverside town of Denmark.

TOP EVENTS

Mar. *Wine Summer Festival (Porongurup, near Mount Barker)*

Easter *Brave New Works (new performance art, Denmark)*

Aug. *Prophet Mohammad's Birthday (Katanning)*

Aug. *Strauss Festival (Albany)*

Sept. *Country and Wildflower Festival (Kojonup)*

Oct. *Great Southern Wine Festival (Albany)*

Oct. *Wildflower Weekend (Porongurup, near Mount Barker)*

Nov. *Art Show (Cranbrook)*

Dec. *Vintage Blues Festival (Albany)*

EXPERIENCE IT!

❶ **Surf** the mighty Southern Ocean at Denmark's Ocean Beach

❷ **See** southern right whales with their newborn calves around Bremer Bay, from August to November

❸ **Eat** at The Old Farm (the State's oldest farm), Strawberry Hill, 2 km west of Albany's centre

VISITOR INFORMATION

Albany: (08) 9841 1088;
1800 644 088
www.albanytourist.com.au

FOCUS ON

Albany heritage

Albany, the oldest white settlement in Western Australia, was officially founded on 21 January 1827 by a party of 21 soldiers and 23 convicts who had arrived on the *Amity* a month earlier. Albany's magnificent harbour, commanding the sea lanes between Europe and Asia and eastern Australia, became a whaling station and later a coaling port for steamships. Museums now occupy three historic buildings, and a full-size replica of the *Amity* stands next to one, the Residency Museum. Stirling Terrace has some evocative Victorian shopfronts while Princess Royal Fortress on Mount Adelaide has restored buildings, gun emplacements and fine views.

CLIMATE ALBANY

	J	F	M	A	M	J	J	A	S	O	N	D
Max. °C	25	25	24	22	19	17	16	16	17	19	21	24
Min. °C	14	14	13	12	10	8	8	7	8	9	11	12
Rain mm	27	24	28	63	102	103	124	106	82	78	48	25
Raindays	8	9	11	14	18	19	21	21	18	15	13	10

Frontier and flowers
The Old Military Barracks in Kojonup, now a museum, was built in 1845 to protect travel on the road between Perth and Albany. Gardens are also a feature of the town with many residents taking part in the Australian Open Garden Scheme. The surrounding countryside is lush with wildflowers in spring.

For more detail see maps 380–1 & 386. For descriptions of ❶ towns see Towns from A to Z (p. 335).

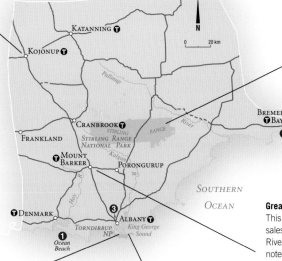

Stirling Range National Park
This park has stunning mountain scenery. From a distance the range changes colour, depending on the weather, season and time of day. The spectacular jagged peaks, including the great Bluff Knoll, are popular with walkers and climbers.

Torndirrup National Park
The Southern Ocean has sculpted The Blowholes, The Gap, and Natural Bridge in this park just 15 minutes from Albany on a sealed road. Granite outcrops and cliffs alternate with dunes, and sandy heath supports peppermint, banksia and karri. Whales can be seen from the cliffs from August to November.

Great Southern wineries
This region has over 30 wineries, most open for sales. The dozen that extend from the Frankland River east through Mount Barker to Porongurup are noted for aromatic rieslings grown on well-drained, gravelly-sandy soils. The region's unwooded chardonnay, shiraz and light reds are also popular.

Albany Whaleworld
The bloody realities of whaling are displayed at the old Cheynes Beach Whaling Station on Frenchman Bay, 25 km south-east of Albany. Visitors can explore *Cheynes IV*, a restored whalechaser, and relive the sights and sounds of the hunt. Recorded songs of whales at sea provide background music.

ESPERANCE & NULLARBOR

This is a coastline of rare and remote beauty. The beaches of Esperance are among the most spectacular in Australia, famed for their white sand, brilliant turquoise waters, and views across a network of offshore islands. To the north-east, beyond the desert beaches, underwater caves, sheer fossil-encrusted cliffs and drifting dunes lies the vast Nullarbor Plain. While Esperance is a large and well-serviced holiday centre, the Nullarbor is remote touring country. Advance bookings should be made for the limited accommodation en route, and travellers should observe basic outback travel precautions such as ensuring adequate fuel and water supplies.

TOP EVENTS

Jan.   Summer Festival (Hopetoun)
Feb.   Offshore Angling Classic (Esperance)
May   Golf Classic (Eucla)
Sept.   Wildflower Show (Ravensthorpe)
Sept.   Wildflower Show (Esperance)
Oct.   Agricultural Show (Esperance)
Oct.–   Festival of the Wind
Nov.   (Esperance, even-numbered years)
Nov.   Border Dash (Border Village to Eucla)

EXPERIENCE IT!

❶ **Visit** the Esperance Municipal Museum to see debris from NASA's spaceship Skylab

❷ **See** the many species of orchids in spring in remote Cape Arid National Park

❸ **Ride** a camel and eat bush tucker at Eremia Camel Farm near Ravensthorpe

CLIMATE ESPERANCE

	J	F	M	A	M	J	J	A	S	O	N	D
Max. °C	26	26	25	23	20	18	17	18	19	21	23	25
Min. °C	16	16	15	13	11	9	8	9	10	11	13	14
Rain mm	22	27	31	43	76	82	98	84	58	50	36	17
Raindays	6	6	8	11	14	16	17	17	14	12	10	7

VISITOR INFORMATION

Esperance: (08) 9071 2330;
1300 664 455
Eucla: (08) 9039 3468

FOCUS ON

The Nullarbor

The Nullarbor is one of the country's premier touring experiences. It is a 250 000-sq-km, treeless limestone slab. Initially part of the seabed, it has been partly formed by deposits of marine fossils. The terrain is riddled with sinkholes, caverns and caves, the largest of which is the 6-km-long Cocklebiddy Cave (just north-west of the town of Cocklebiddy), one of the longest underwater caves in the world. Although it can seem featureless, the country is far from monotonous, particularly where the highway veers to the coast for a view of dramatic cliffs and the wild Southern Ocean, and perhaps a lucky sighting of migrating southern right whales.

Great Ocean Drive

A 39-km circuit drive explores the coast west of Esperance. Attractions include Australia's first wind farm; sheltered swimming at Twilight Cove; and Pink Lake, rendered lipstick-coloured by algae. There are coastal lookouts and sightings of southern right whales from June to November.

Cape Le Grand National Park

Swimming beaches, sheltered coves, heathlands, sandplains and the Whistling Rock are all features of this park, 56 km east of Esperance. There are easy walking trails and two camping areas. Good scenic spots include Lucky Bay (where you can launch a boat), Thistle Cove and Hellfire Bay.

Eucla

This isolated outpost was established in 1877 as a telegraph station. Coastal dunes partially obscure the ruins (pictured), 4 km from town. On the beach, a lonely jetty stretches out into startlingly blue waters. In Eucla National Park, under mallee scrub and heathland, lies the 45-m-high chamber of Koonalda Cave.

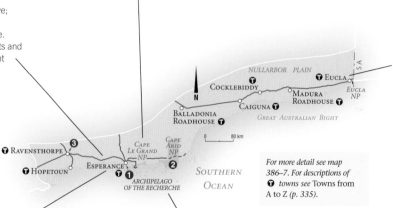

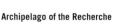

For more detail see map 386–7. For descriptions of ❶ towns see Towns from A to Z (p. 335).

Coastal delights

Esperance is a water-sports paradise. Wave-sail at Observatory and Fourth beaches; windsurf on the harbour; dive or snorkel around the islands. Fishing charters tour the islands for sampson fish, queen snapper and red snapper, while land-based anglers can cast a line from Tanker Jetty.

Archipelago of the Recherche

This offshore nature reserve of 105 granite islands and 1500 islets runs 250 km along the Esperance coast. Boat tours, available from Esperance, may include sightings of fur seals, sea lions, dolphins and, in season, southern right whales. Visitors can stay overnight in safari huts or camp on Woody Island.

THE GOLDFIELDS

Western Australia's historic Goldfields region occupies a landscape of alluvial flats and saltplains broken by rocky outcrops and a surprising diversity of native vegetation – around 100 species of eucalypt as well as brilliant displays of wildflowers in spring. Gold continues to be mined here, while sheep stations the size of small nations produce fine wool. The area's main attractions are its fascinating heritage and the opportunity to tour Western Australia's vast outback, where April to October is the best time to visit. Those planning to explore beyond the main centres should observe basic outback safety precautions.

TOP EVENTS

Apr. Nullarbor Muster
(Rawlinna, via Kalgoorlie)

Aug. Gwalia Market Day
(Gwalia, near Leonora)

Sept. Kalgoorlie Cup (Kalgoorlie)

Sept. Spring Festival (Kalgoorlie)

Sept. Balzano Barrow Race (Kalgoorlie)

Sept. Fishing in the Desert (Kambalda)

Sept. Coolgardie Day (Coolgardie)

Sept.– Metal Detecting Championships and
Oct. Fun Day (Coolgardie)

Oct. Art Prize (Leonora)

Dec. St Barbara's Festival (Kalgoorlie)

EXPERIENCE IT!

❶ **Drive** to Kambalda's Red Hill Lookout for the view of Lake Lefroy

❷ **Experience** the Ngaanyatjarraku people's art and culture at the Tjulyuru Cultural and Civic Centre, Warburton

❸ **Board** the Loopline Tourist Railway, Kalgoorlie, for a circuit of the Golden Mile

VISITOR INFORMATION

Kalgoorlie–Boulder: (08) 9021 1966
Norseman: (08) 9039 1071
www.kalgoorlieandwagoldfields.com.au

FOCUS ON

Goldfields history

The discovery of gold in the region in 1892 secured the economic success of Western Australia. Since then, goldmines from Norseman to Laverton have yielded well over 1000 tonnes. A railway from Perth in 1896 and a water pipeline in 1903 helped Kalgoorlie and Boulder to sustain a population of 30 000, the liquor requirements of which were met by 93 hotels. By 1900 surface gold was exhausted and big companies went underground. Exhausted mines have left a belt of ghost towns north of Kalgoorlie, while nickel mining since the 1960s has allowed towns such as Kambalda and Leonora to survive.

CLIMATE KALGOORLIE–BOULDER

	J	F	M	A	M	J	J	A	S	O	N	D
Max. °C	34	32	30	25	20	18	17	18	22	26	29	32
Min. °C	18	18	16	12	8	6	5	5	8	11	14	17
Rain mm	22	28	19	19	28	31	26	20	15	16	18	15
Raindays	3	4	4	5	7	8	9	7	5	4	4	3

For more detail see maps 386–7 & 389. For descriptions of ❶ towns see Towns from A to Z (p. 335).

North of Kalgoorlie

Menzies has 230 people and several intact old buildings; Kookynie has retained its spacious 1894 Grand Hotel. Gwalia, almost a ghost town, has a museum, a restored State Hotel and tin houses preserved in their lived-in state (pictured). Laverton, 100 km east, has historic buildings saved by the nickel industry.

Kalgoorlie–Boulder

Kalgoorlie–Boulder produces half Australia's gold; the adjacent Golden Mile is the world's richest square mile of gold-bearing ore. Visitors to Hannans North Historic Mining Reserve can sample the rigours of mining in the 1800s. Don't miss the gold vault at the Museum of the Goldfields.

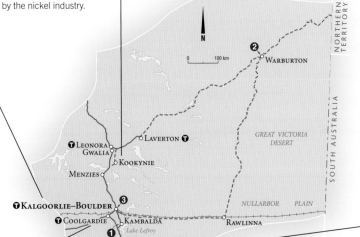

Norseman, gateway to the West

The Eyre Highway across the Nullarbor ends at Norseman, once the centre of the second richest goldfield in Western Australia; some mines still operate here. The Historical Collection has displays of memorabilia and geological specimens. Beacon Hill Lookout offers views of the town and surrounding salt lakes.

Coolgardie

Historical street markers are a good introduction to this first town in the eastern goldfields, with its splendid, historic public buildings. Examples include The Marble Bar Hotel now the RSL (pictured), and the 1898 Warden's Court. The latter, an architectural treasure, houses the comprehensive Goldfields Exhibition museum and the Tourist Bureau.

Peak Charles National Park

South-west of Norseman, granite mountains rise in wave-cut platforms to a height of 651 m. A track, suitable only for experienced walkers and climbers in favourable weather, leads from the carpark up to the south ridge for views across saltpans, sand plains and dry woodlands to Peak Eleanora.

THE HEARTLANDS

Western Australia's wheat belt dominates in this region: a vast golden landscape of historic towns, windmills and broad-verandahed homesteads. A string of surf beaches extends north from Perth. Major lobster ports are also attractive holiday centres, and a number of national parks protect spectacular landscapes, including one of the State's must-see features – The Pinnacles. Inland lie pockets of forested country with something English about them, while Spanish Colonial is the main style of one of Australia's most unusual towns. Each spring, from the coast to the wheat fields, wildflowers provide a common theme for this otherwise diverse region.

TOP EVENTS

Jan. State Gliding Championships (Narrogin)

Mar. Autumn Alternative Agricultural Show (Pingelly)

Aug. Daffodil Festival (York)

Aug. Avon River Festival (Northam)

Sept. Jazz Weekend (York)

Oct. Bush Races Weekend (at Jilakin Rock, near Kulin)

Oct. Spring Festival (Narrogin)

Oct. Multicultural Festival (Northam)

Nov. Marine Expo and Blessing of the Fleet (Jurien Bay)

EXPERIENCE IT!

❶ **Go** rowing on Loch McNess at the heart of Yanchep National Park

❷ **Drive** through pretty Chittering Valley, near Gingin, to see wildflowers and visit the wineries

❸ **Observe** rare wildlife in natural surroundings at Dryandra Woodland, north-west of Narrogin

VISITOR INFORMATION

Northam: (08) 9622 2100
York: (08) 9641 1301
www.heartlands.com.au

FOCUS ON

Wildflowers

There are over 9000 named species and 2000 unnamed species of wildflowers in Western Australia, giving the State one of the richest floras in the world. Most wildflowers occur in the south-west of the State and about 75 per cent of the species are unique to this region. Flowering begins in August and continues through spring and early summer. The Heartlands is one of the best and most accessible places to see wildlflower displays. Top spots include: Lesueur and Badgingarra national parks near Jurien Bay, the Chittering Valley near Gingin, and the sand plains around Southern Cross.

CLIMATE NORTHAM

	J	F	M	A	M	J	J	A	S	O	N	D
Max. °C	34	34	31	26	21	18	17	18	20	24	28	32
Min. °C	17	17	15	12	9	7	5	6	7	9	12	15
Rain mm	10	13	19	23	57	83	84	62	37	25	12	9
Raindays	2	2	3	6	11	15	16	14	11	7	4	2

New Norcia
This town, Spanish Colonial in style, was built in 1846 by Benedictine monks who aimed to establish a mission for the local indigenous population. It remains Australia's only monastic town. Visitors can tour the buildings (pictured) and visit the fascinating Museum and Art Gallery.

Central wheat belt
This is an area of endless horizon, dusty golden paddocks and brilliant wildflower clusters in spring. Attractions include Kellerberrin Hill, the third-largest monolith in Australia, and Meckering where a 1968 earthquake has left an impressive fault line.

The Pinnacles Desert
Thousands of limestone pillars, the eroded remnants of what was once a thick bed of limestone, create this weirdly beautiful landscape in what is now Nambung National Park. Other park attractions include a beautiful coastline with superb beaches where visitors can fish, swim, snorkel, walk or picnic.

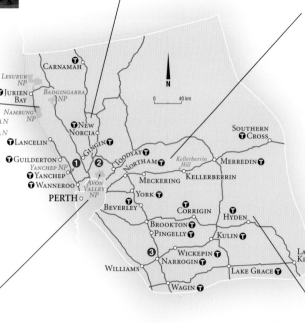

For more detail see maps 376, 384 & 386. For descriptions of ❶ towns see Towns from A to Z (p. 335).

Avon Valley
In the 1860s bushranger Moondyne Joe hid in the forests, caves and wildflower fields of this lush valley. Now Avon Valley National Park preserves much of the landscape. In the valley's heart, and marking the start of the wheat belt, are the historic towns of Northam and York.

Wave Rock and Mulka's Cave
Wave Rock, east of Hyden, is a 2.7 billion-year-old piece of granite, 15 m high and 100 m long. It looks like a giant wave frozen at the moment of breaking and has vertical bands of colour caused by algal growth. To the north is Mulka's Cave, featuring Aboriginal rock art.

OUTBACK COAST & MID-WEST

The ancient landforms of Western Australia's interior meet the startlingly blue waters of the Indian Ocean in this vast area known for the richness and rarity of its natural features. Reefs, eroded cliffs and gorges, ancient rocks, life forms billions of years old, sea mammals, diverse flora, and stretches of red outback are all to be found. A series of towns (mostly coastal) offer good holiday facilities as well as glimpses of Western Australia's pioneer and maritime history. Much of this country is remote; for those planning to explore beyond the main tourist routes, safety precautions for outback travelling are essential.

TOP EVENTS

Mar.	Sport Fishing Classic (Kalbarri)
Mar.	Sea Jazz Spectacular (Geraldton)
June	Batavia Celebrations (Geraldton)
Aug.	Wildflower Show (Mullewa)
Aug.	Festival (Carnarvon)
Oct.	Airing of the Quilts (Northampton)
Oct.	Octoberfest (Exmouth)
Oct.	Sunshine Festival (Geraldton)
Nov.	Blessing of the Fleet (Kalbarri)

EXPERIENCE IT!

❶ **Visit** Peron Homestead in Francois Peron National Park, once part of a sheep station

❷ **Dive** around the Houtman Abrolhos Islands, a group of more than 100 coral islands

❸ **Stay** at Wooleen Station, near Murchison, in the shearers' quarters or the National Trust-listed homestead

VISITOR INFORMATION

Carnarvon: (08) 9941 1146
Geraldton: (08) 9921 3999
www.outbackcoast.com

FOCUS ON

Shark Bay

World Heritage-listed Shark Bay is a sunny paradise of shallow azure waters, bays and inlets, blessed with a great complement of unusual and interesting natural features. It supports the world's most diverse and abundant examples of stromatolites – sedimentary rocks made up of layers of 3.5 billion-year-old fossilised blue-green algae. It has 12 species of seagrass, the world's greatest collection. It also boasts an extraordinary marine population: 10 000 or so dugongs (ten per cent of the world's population); humpback whales resting on their long migrations; green and loggerhead turtles; and, most famously, a large pod of dolphins.

Reef to range

Ningaloo Marine Park protects Western Australia's largest reef. Along the coast is Cape Range National Park, where beach campsites are ideal for visitors wanting to explore the corals and fish of the stunning underwater landscape, as well as the gorges and rivers of the landscape beyond the coast.

CLIMATE CARNARVON

	J	F	M	A	M	J	J	A	S	O	N	D
Max. °C	31	33	31	29	26	23	22	23	24	26	27	29
Min. °C	22	23	22	19	15	12	11	12	14	16	19	21
Rain mm	12	21	16	14	38	48	47	19	6	6	4	2
Raindays	2	3	2	3	5	7	7	5	3	2	1	1

Kalbarri National Park

Kalbarri is best known for its 80 km of gorges, carved out by the Murchison River. Water sports are popular on the river's lower reaches. The park is also one of the world's richest wildflower areas. Dolphins, whale sharks and whales frequent the coastal waters and fishing is excellent.

Mount Augustus National Park

Mount Augustus, or Burringurrah as it is known by the Watjarri people, rests on an ancient piece of granite twice the size of Uluṟu. The park also features Aboriginal art sites and walking trails. Camping is available nearby. Travellers in 2WD vehicles should check road conditions before departure.

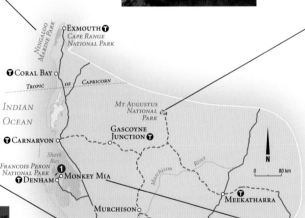

For more detail see maps 385 & 386. For descriptions of ⊕ towns see Towns from A to Z (p. 335).

Geraldton

This large town is a suitable base for exploring the Batavia Coast's swimming and surfing beaches. In town, Mahomets Beach is one of Australia's top windsurfing destinations. The town has a good regional gallery, and a number of impressive buildings including a Byzantine-style cathedral (pictured) built in the early 1900s.

Monkey Mia

About 400 bottlenose dolphins live around Monkey Mia in the Shark Bay World Heritage Area. Each morning, several dolphins drift into the shallows to be hand-fed with fish, which they occasionally offer back. The world's largest population of dugongs lives here. Take a dugong-watching cruise to see them.

THE KIMBERLEY

The Kimberley, bigger than Germany, has a population of just 25 000 people. It is one of Australia's true frontiers, with an ancient, reddened landscape of rivers and gorges, a wild inhabited coastline, and the signature beehive shapes of the Bungle Bungles. At the time of white colonisation there were around two dozen Aboriginal language groups. Early white explorers were enchanted by the romantic grandeur of The Kimberley and appalled by the distances, hardships and dangers. Visitors today will find the grandeur largely untouched and travelling conditions highly variable. While the coastal town of Broome is becoming increasingly well known as a resort destination, there are large tracts of this region that are completely inaccessible by road – or accessible by 4WD only – and offering only the most basic of facilities. Travellers should familiarise themselves with prevailing conditions and carry adequate supplies.

CLIMATE HALLS CREEK

	J	F	M	A	M	J	J	A	S	O	N	D
Max. °C	37	36	36	34	30	27	27	30	34	37	38	38
Min. °C	24	24	23	20	17	14	13	15	19	23	25	25
Rain mm	153	137	74	22	13	5	6	2	4	17	37	77
Raindays	13	13	8	3	2	1	1	1	1	3	6	11

FOCUS ON

Aboriginal art

The Kimberley is one of Australia's most important regions for Aboriginal rock art and is renowned for two styles – the Bradshaw and the Wandjina. The Bradshaw 'figures' as they are known, are painted in red ochre. According to one Aboriginal legend, birds drew the figures using their beaks. One rock-face frieze shows figures dancing and swaying; another depicts figures elaborately decorated with headdresses, tassels, skirts and epaulets. Significant Bradshaw sites have been found on the Drysdale River. The more recent Wandjina figures, named for ancestor spirits from the sky and sea who brought rain and fertility, are in solid red or black, outlined in red ochre, and sometimes on a white background. Wandjina figures are typically human-like, with pallid faces and wide, staring eyes and, for reasons of religious belief, no mouth. Good examples of Wandjina art have been found near Kalumburu on the King Edward River and at the burial site known as Panda-Goornnya on the Drysdale River.

TOP EVENTS

Easter *Dragon Boat Regatta (Broome)*

May *Ord Valley Muster (Kununurra)*

May *King Tide Day (festival celebrating highest tide in Australia, Derby)*

June *Dam to Dam Dinghy Race (Kununurra)*

June *Moonrise Rock Festival (Derby)*

June *Mowanjum Festival (indigenous art and culture, Derby)*

June– July *Race Round (horseracing week, Broome)*

Aug. *Rodeo (Kununurra)*

Aug. *Opera Under the Stars (Broome)*

Aug.– Sept. *Shinju Matsuri (Festival of the Pearl, Broome)*

Sept. *Munumburra Music Festival (Wyndham)*

Sept. *Night Rodeo (Kununurra)*

Nov. *Mango Festival (Broome)*

EXPERIENCE IT!

❶ *Take a scenic flight from Derby over the Buccaneer Archipelago, with a swim and refreshments at Cape Leveque*

❷ *Inspect 130-million-year-old dinosaur footprints at Gantheaume Point near Broome*

❸ *Stay at El Questro Station, Australia's most luxurious outback resort, and enjoy the hot springs*

❹ *Ride a camel along the magnificent Cable Beach in Broome*

❺ *Fly from Kununurra to a camp on the remote Mitchell Plateau and see rainforest, waterfalls, birdlife and Aboriginal art*

VISITOR INFORMATION
Broome: (08) 9192 2222
Kununurra: (08) 9168 1177

Gibb River Road

This unsealed road, starting at Derby and running 649 km through The Kimberley, provides a true outback adventure. River crossings, passable only during the Dry, offer scenic campsites. Along the way are spectacular gorges, and swimming spots with waterlilies. Read the *Gibb River Road Guide* before commencing your journey.

Dampier Peninsula

The 200-km unsealed Broome–Cape Leveque route traverses open eucalypt country and Aboriginal Reserve land. Within the reserve land are a church at Beagle Bay with an unusual mother-of-pearl altar (pictured) and a church at Lombadina–Djarindjin. See unique pindan vegetation in Point Coulomb Nature Reserve and perhaps humpback whales from Cape Leveque Lighthouse.

Port of pearls

Broome has a balmy winter climate, the white, palm-fringed Cable Beach, and a multicultural heritage. In Chinatown there are Chinese merchants, pearl dealers, and restaurants serving a variety of cuisines. The history of pearling is told at the old customs house, the pearling luggers display, and the Japanese Cemetery (pictured).

Cruising the Wandjina Coast
This coastline is a succession of capes, gulfs, bays and mangrove swamps, and rivers emptying onto mudflats. There are 3000 islands and countless reefs. A good way to see the 11-m tide running over Montgomery Reef and into the bays and estuaries is on a cruise from Broome.

Lake Argyle and Kununurra
Lake Argyle was formed in the 1960s as part of the Ord River Scheme, the success of which is evident in the lush crops of the area (pictured). The lake is so large that it has developed its own ecosystems. By taking a boat cruise you can experience the magnificent scenery and abundant wildlife of the area. Start from Kununurra, which has excellent tourist facilities.

For more detail see map 390–1. For descriptions of ❶ towns see Towns from A to Z (p. 335).

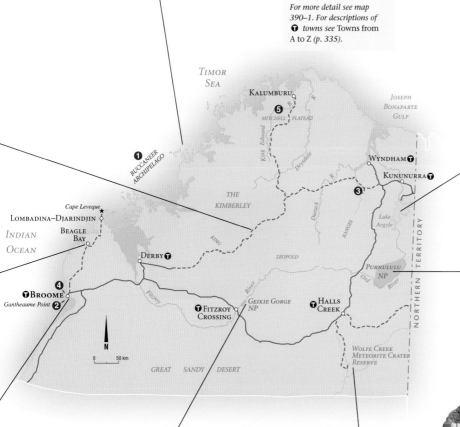

Purnululu National Park
A rough 50-km track off the Great Northern Highway leads to the spectacular Bungle Bungle Range in Purnululu National Park on the Ord River. A fantastic landscape of huge black-and-orange sandstone domes is intersected by narrow, palm-lined gorges where pools reflect sunlight off sheer walls.

Geikie Gorge
North-east of Fitzroy Crossing the Fitzroy River cuts through the Geikie Range to create a 7-km gorge with sheer walls bleached by annual flooding. The riverbanks are inhabited by freshwater crocodiles, fruit bats and many bird species. The only way to see the gorge is by boat – during the Dry.

Wolfe Creek Meteorite Crater
Two hours by unsealed road south of Halls Creek, and across some inhospitable country, is the world's second largest meteorite crater. It is 850 m across and was probably formed by a meteorite, weighing at least several thousand tons, crashing to earth a million years ago.

THE PILBARA

This region's centrepiece is the vivid, ochre-hued Hamersley Range, which stretches 300 km through this mineral-rich area. In the 1860s pastoralists settled in the western Pilbara and established Roebourne and Cossack. Iron-ore discovery in the 1960s saw the establishment of modern towns such as Tom Price and Newman, which today provide comfortable bases for touring the area's magnificent landscapes, including the gorges and waterfalls of Karijini National Park. The Pilbara coast from Exmouth Gulf to Eighty Mile Beach is a place of vast tidal flats broken by mangroves. Coral reefs and offshore islands offer swimming, boating and beachcombing.

TOP EVENTS

June   Pilbara Pursuit Jetboat Classic (Karratha)

June   Black Rock Stakes (wheelbarrow race, Port Hedland)

Aug.   FeNaCLNG Festival (Annual Show, Karratha)

Aug.   Game-fishing Classic (Dampier, near Karratha)

Aug.   Campdraft and Rodeo (Newman)

Aug.   Spinifex Spree (Port Hedland)

Aug.   Royal Show (Roebourne)

Aug.   Roebourne Cup and Ball (Roebourne)

Aug.   Nameless Festival (Tom Price)

EXPERIENCE IT!

❶ **Swim** in the Chinderwarriner Pool in Millstream–Chichester National Park, 150 km south of Roebourne

❷ **Take** Karratha's 3-hour Jaburara Heritage Trail to Aboriginal rock carvings and artifact scatters

❸ **Follow** the 52-km Emma Withnell Heritage Trail around Roebourne, Cossack and Point Samson's historic sites

VISITOR INFORMATION

Karratha: (08) 9144 4600
Tom Price: (08) 9188 1112
www.pilbara.com

FOCUS ON

Hamersley Range resources

One of the world's richest deposits of iron ore was discovered in 1962 in the Hamersley, spearheading the Hamersley Iron Project. Towns with swimming pools, gardens and golf courses sprang up in this landscape of mulga scrub, spinifex and red mountains. Visitors can inspect open-cut mines at Tom Price. At Dampier and Port Hedland there are iron-ore shipping ports; the latter boasts the largest iron-ore export tonnage in Australia. Offshore from Karratha is the massive North West Shelf Gas Project; a visitors' centre on Burrup Peninsula explains the project.

CLIMATE ROEBOURNE

	J	F	M	A	M	J	J	A	S	O	N	D
Max. °C	39	38	38	35	30	27	27	29	32	35	38	39
Min. °C	26	26	25	22	18	15	14	15	17	20	23	25
Rain mm	59	67	63	30	29	30	14	5	1	1	1	10
Raindays	3	5	3	1	3	3	2	1	0	0	0	1

Pilbara islands

Dampier Archipelago's nearest islands are 20 minutes by boat from Dampier. The islands' cliffs and sand plains are the focus for bushwalkers and birdwatchers, while pristine beaches offer swimming and fishing. Turtles and seabirds nest on the islands, and dolphins and humpbacked whales can be seen offshore.

Cossack

This first port in the north-west was built between 1870 and 1898 and is now a ghost town. Many buildings have been restored including Galbraiths Store (pictured). The old post office houses a gallery and the courthouse a museum, while police barracks offer budget accommodation.

For more detail see maps 385, 388–9 & 390. For descriptions of ❼ towns see Towns from A to Z (p. 335).

Karijini National Park

Karijini is the name given to this area by the original inhabitants, the Banjima. It is renowned for extraordinary gorges, multicoloured walls and hidden pools and waterfalls. Brilliant wildflowers carpet the rust-red hills in spring. Camping is available inside the park.

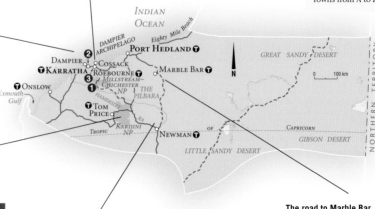

The Newman waterholes

Kalgans Pool, Eagle Rock Falls, Punda Pool and Weeli Wolli Spring are waterhole areas north-west of Newman. Some have spectacular gorges, others feature waterfalls and river-gum scenery. Wanna Munna is an interesting rock-art site. All these areas can be reached from Newman within 90 minutes, but most are accessible by 4WD only.

The road to Marble Bar

Australia's hottest town was named for a unique bar of red jasper. Marble Bar is a mining and pastoral centre in the eastern Pilbara, and popular with tourists. The 184-km route from Port Hedland, sealed for about two thirds of the journey, crosses a landscape of gorges, spinifex and red and purple rocks.

WESTERN AUSTRALIA
TOWNS FROM A TO Z

Albany
Pop. 20 493

MAP REF. 381 N12, 384 H13, 386 F12

Picturesque Albany is the State's oldest town. On the edge of King George Sound and the magnificent Princess Royal Harbour, the town is 408 km S of Perth. Albany dates from 1826, when a military post was established to give the British a foothold in the west. Whaling was important in the 1840s; in the 1850s Albany became a coaling station for steamers from England. As WA's most important holiday centre, it offers a wealth of history and coastal, rural and mountain scenery. Its harbours, weirs and estuaries provide excellent fishing. **In town:** Colonial Buildings Historic Walk, brochure available. Old Post Office-Intercolonial Communications Museum, cnr Stirling Tce and Spencer St. Victorian shopfronts in Stirling Tce. In Residency Rd: Residency Museum (1850s), originally home of Resident Magistrates, now houses historical and environmental exhibits; Old Gaol and Museum (1851) has two gaols in one. Vancouver Arts Centre, Vancouver St. House of Gems, Frenchman Bay Rd. The Old Farm (1836), Middleton Rd, Strawberry Hill, site of first Government farm in WA. Faithfully restored Patrick Taylor Cottage (1832), Duke St, has extensive collection of period costumes and household goods. Princess Royal Fortress (commissioned 1893), off Forts Rd, on Mt Adelaide, Albany's first federal fortress. Mt Adelaide Forts Heritage Trails, starting cnr Apex Dr. and Forts Rd; self-guide leaflets available. Old Railway Station, Proudlove Pde, end of 963-km Bibbulmun Track between Kalamunda and Albany. On Princess Royal Dr.: the *Amity*, full-scale replica of brig that brought Major Lockyer and convicts to establish Albany in 1826. Desert Mounted Corp Memorial statue, on Apex Dr. near top of Mt Clarence; spectacular view here and at John Barnesby Memorial Lookout, on Melville Dr., at Mt Melville. Southern right whale-watching cruises, daily from town jetty (Aug.–Nov.). Aug.: Strauss Festival. Oct.: Great Southern

Lighthouse at Albany

Wine Festival. Dec.: Vintage Blues Festival. **In the area:** Fishing at: Jimmy Newhill's Harbour, 20 km S; Frenchman Bay, 25 km SE; Emu Point, 8 km NE; Oyster Harbour, 15 km NE. *To the north:* Deer-O-Dome deer farm (6 km); Mt Romance Sandalwood Oil Company (12 km); Porongurup National Park (37 km), has huge granite peaks and easy walking tracks to splendid views; Stirling Range National Park (80 km) for climbing and bushwalking, breathtaking scenery, brilliant spring wildflowers, some unique to area. *To the west towards Denmark:* West Cape Howe National Park (30 km) for walking, fishing, swimming and hang-gliding, and has excellent lookout; Torbay Head is southernmost point in WA. Care should be taken when exploring the coast; king waves can be dangerous, rushing in unexpectedly, with loss of life. *To the south:* Torndirrup National Park (17 km) for spectacular coastal views, The Gap and Natural Bridge, and The Blowholes; whale-watching from cliffs, Aug.–Nov. *To the south-east:* On Vancouver Peninsula: Point Possession Heritage Trail with views, interpretive plaques; brochures available. Also on peninsula is Camp Quaranup (20 km), site of old quarantine station, historical walk south on Geake Point. Albany Whaleworld at the old Cheynes Beach Whaling Station (25 km)

which ceased operation in 1978; in its heyday the Station's chasers took up to 850 whales per season. *To the east:* Two Peoples Bay Marron Farm (20 km); Nanarup (20 km) and Little Beach (40 km) have sheltered waters; Willowie Game Park (30 km); Two Peoples Bay Nature Reserve (40 km), noted for the noisy scrub-bird (*Atrichornis clamosus*), thought to be extinct, rediscovered 1961. **Visitor information:** Old Railway Station, Proudlove Pde; (08) 9841 1088, freecall 1800 644 088. Web site www.albanytourist.com.au **See also:** Great Southern p. 327; National Parks p. 362; Wildlife-Watching p. 364.

Augusta
Pop. 1087

MAP REF. 377 C13, 379 D13, 384 B11, 386 B11

The town of Augusta overlooks the mouth of the Blackwood River, the waters of Flinders Bay and rolling, heavily wooded countryside. Augusta is one of the oldest settlements in WA and a popular holiday town. Jarrah, karri and pine forests supply the district's 100-year-old timber industry. **In town:** In Blackwood Ave: Augusta Historical Museum; Lumen Christi Catholic Church. Crafters Croft, Ellis St, for art and craft. Sept.–Oct.: Spring Flower Show. **In the area:** Picturesque coastline; excellent swimming and surfing; fishing in river and ocean. Marron (freshwater crayfish) in season, fishing licence required, available post office, Blackwood Ave. Augusta–Busselton Heritage Trail; pamphlet available. Cruises on Blackwood River and Hardy Inlet. Views from Hillview Lookout and golf course, 6 km NW. Jewel Cave has colourful limestone formations, and Moondyne Cave has guided adventure tours; both 8 km NW. At Karridale, 14 km NW, Alan Fox Glass Studio. Alexandra Bridge, 10 km N, picnic spot with towering jarrah trees and beautiful wildflowers in spring. Boranup Maze, 18 km N. Boranup Lookout, 19 km N: fine views of Leeuwin–Naturaliste National Park; picnic spot. Winery at Hamelin Bay, 18 km NE. The Landing Place, 3 km S, where first European settlers landed in area. Whale Rescue Memorial, 4 km S, commemorating the 1986 rescue of pilot whales beached here. Matthew Flinders Memorial, 5 km S. Cape Leeuwin, 8 km SW, most southwesterly point of Australia and where Indian and Southern oceans meet; at cape, limestone lighthouse (1895) and old water wheel. **Visitor information:** 70 Blackwood Ave; (08) 9758 0166. Web site www.margaretriverwa.com **See also:** The South-West p. 326.

Australind
Pop. 5694

MAP REF. 377 G4, 384 C8, 386 C10

This popular holiday town is 11 km NE of Bunbury on the Leschenault Estuary. Fishing, crabbing, swimming and boating on the estuary and the Collie River are the main attractions. **In town:** In Paris Rd: Henton Cottage (1841), now real estate agency; restored Church of St Nicholas (1842), thought to be smallest church in WA. Featured Wood Gallery, Piggot Dr. (off Paris Rd), traditional wood furniture and craft (open Thurs.–Mon.). Pioneer Memorial, on Old Coast Rd. Scenic 2-km drive along Cathedral Ave, a shaded avenue of paperbark trees. Mar.: Ocean Festival. Nov.: Wine Festival (even-numbered years). **In the area:** Leschenault Inlet Fishing Groyne, built along old pipeline, 1 km S; excellent fishing spot. Australind–Bunbury Tourist Drive: coastal scenery, good crabbing and picnic spots; brochure available. Cemetery, 2 km N, has pioneer graves and beautiful wildflowers in season. Pleasant beach towns to the north: Binningup (26 km) and Myalup (30 km).

Visitor information: Henton Cottage, Paris Rd; (08) 9796 0102. **See also:** The South-West p. 326.

Balladonia Roadhouse
Pop. 10

MAP REF. 387 L8

Balladonia is on the Eyre Hwy, 191 km E of Norseman. At this point the road crosses undulating dryland forest through the Fraser Range. Visitors can see claypans and stone fences built in the 1800s. **In town:** At Roadhouse, Cultural Heritage Museum, includes display on crashlanding of Skylab debris near town in 1979. **In the area:** Arid desert woodland, one of the world's oldest landscapes, seashells millions of years old. Wildflowers in spring. Balladonia Station homestead (1886), 22 km E behind old telegraph station, has gallery of paintings depicting local history (open by appt). Newmans Rocks, 50 km W on Eyre Hwy, rocky outcrops and granite sheets. **Visitor information:** Roadhouse, Eyre Hwy; (08) 9039 3453. **See also:** Esperance & Nullarbor p. 328.

Beverley
Pop. 787

MAP REF. 384 F4, 386 D8

On the Avon River, 130 km E of Perth, is the town of Beverley. **In town:** Picnic spots beside Avon River. In Vincent St: Aeronautical Museum, shows development of WA aviation and includes biplane built in 1929 by local aircraft designer Selby Ford; Courthouse (1897) designed by architect George Temple Poole (check opening times, Shire Council). In Hunt Rd: Dead Finish (1872), one of oldest buildings in town (open Sun. or by appt); Barry Ferguson's Garage, has display of old hand-operated machinery. St Mary's Anglican Church (1890), John St, fine stained-glass windows. Aug.: Agricultural Show. Sept.: Duck Race (with plastic ducks). **In the area:** The Avon Ascent, self-guide drive tour of the Avon Valley; leaflet available. Magnificent view from Seaton Ross Hill, Top Beverley Rd, on northern outskirts of town. Restored St Paul's Church (consecrated 1862), opposite original town site, 5 km NW. Beverley Gliding Club, 2 km W, dual-seat glider flights over town and valley (Fri.–Sun., bookings essential). Avondale Discovery Farm, 6 km NW, has range of historic farm implements, an agricultural museum and Clydesdale horses; Harvest Festival each Nov. Restored church, St John's in the Wilderness (consecrated 1895), 27 km SW. County Peak

lookout, 35 km SE, offers bushwalking, picnic area and spectacular views from summit. **Visitor information:** Aeronautical Museum, 139 Vincent St; (08) 9646 1555. Web site www.beverleywa.com **See also:** The Heartlands p. 330.

Boyup Brook
Pop. 553

MAP REF. 380 E2, 384 E9, 386 D11

Near the junction of Boyup Creek and the Blackwood River, Boyup Brook is a centre for the district's sheep, dairy-farming and timber industries. Blackboys, granite boulders, pools, cottages and farms are some of the features. **In town:** Pioneers Museum, Jayes Rd (check opening times). Sandy Chambers Art Studio, Gibbs St, for artworks; aviaries and camels outside. Stagline Woollen Clothing, Henderson St. Old Flax Mill, on Blackwood River off Barron St, now caravan park. Haddleton Flora Reserve, Arthur River Rd. Carnaby Collection of beetles and butterflies at information centre. Bicentennial Walk Trail, historical walk; leaflet available. Feb.: WA Country Music Awards. May: Autumn Art Affair. Oct.: Blackwood Marathon (running, canoeing, horseriding, cycling, swimming to Bridgetown); Spring Garden Expo. **In the area:** Visits to farms (wheat, sheep, pig, Angora goat, deer); Boyup Brook Flora Drives, leaflet available. Glacial rock formations at Glacier Hill, 18 km S. Blackwood Crest winery at Kulikup, 40 km E. Gregory Tree blazed by explorer Captain Gregory in 1845, 15 km NE. School and teacher's house (1900) at Dinninup, 18 km NE. At Wilga, 22 km NW, vintage engines and old timber mill. Stormboy Jumpers, 20 km W on Jayes Rd, for local woollen goods (open by appt). Scotts Brook Winery at Mayanup, 14 km SE, tastings and sales (open by appt). Norlup Homestead, 27 km SE, off Norlup Rd (open by appt). **Visitor information:** cnr Bridge and Able sts; (08) 9765 1444. Web site www.avon.net.au/tourism/beverley/index.htm **See also:** The South-West p. 326.

Bremer Bay
Pop. 221

MAP REF. 386 G11

Bremer Bay, a popular holiday destination 181 km NE of Albany, was named in honour of the captain of HMS *Tamar*, Sir Gordon Bremer. The town was built around the Old Telegraph Station at the mouth of Wellstead Estuary (named after John Wellstead, an 1850s white settler).

Camel riding on Cable Beach, near Broome

In town: Fishing, boating, surfing, scuba diving, water-skiing, whale-watching (Aug.–Nov.) and bay cruises. Rammed-earth buildings, including hotel/motel, Franton Way; church in John St, over-looking estuary. Wellstead Homestead, Wellstead Rd, has historic vehicles and heirlooms, Ann Crawford Gallery (tours by appt). **In the area:** At Fitzgerald River National Park, 17 km N: abundant wildflowers (June–Nov.); Quaalup Homestead, built by John Wellstead (1858), restored as museum, also offers meals, self-guide park walks; at Point Ann, 45 km NE, whale-watching (Aug.–Nov.). At Fishery Beach, 6 km W, good boat-launching facilities. At Peppermint Grove, 3 km S: first residence in area, built by John Wellstead (1850), now Peppermint Grove Museum with historic farm equipment and vintage cars and motorbikes. **Visitor information:** BP Roadhouse, 5 Gnombup Tce; (08) 9837 4093. Web site www.sage. alphawest.net.au/~bremertc/index.html **See also:** Great Southern p. 327.

Bridgetown   Pop. 2123

MAP REF. 380 C3, 384 D10, 386 D11

Bridgetown is in pretty, undulating country in the south-west corner of WA. Here the Blackwood River is well stocked with trout. The first European settlers arrived in 1857 and planted apple trees. **In town:** In Hampton St: Bridgetown Pottery; Brierley Jigsaw Gallery (at information centre); Gentle Era craft shop; St Paul's Church (1911), with paintings by local artists; Memorial Park, a peaceful picnic area. Bridgedale (1862),

on South Western Hwy near bridge and overlooking river, constructed of local clay and timber by first European settler John Blechynden; restored by National Trust. Also on South Western Hwy, Blackwood River Park: picnics; river walks. Markets, fortnightly on Sun., at Blackwood River Park. Sept.: Blackwood Classic (powerboat event). Oct.: Blackwood Marathon (running, canoeing, swimming, horseriding and cycling the 58.3-km course between Boyup Brook and Bridgetown). Nov.: Blues at Bridgetown; Festival of Country Gardens. **In the area:** Wildflowers and apple blossom in spring. Geegelup Heritage Trail (52 km) retraces history of agriculture, mining and timber. Scenic drives through green hills, orchards and valleys into noted karri and jarrah timber country. Fine views: Sutton's Lookout, off Phillips St; Hester Hill, 5 km N. Greenbushes Historical Park, at Green-bushes, 18 km N: displays of tin-mining industry; Gwalia Mine Site Lookout. Bushwalking and picnicking at Bridgetown Jarrah Park, 15 km W and at Karri Gully, a further 5 km W. **Visitor information:** 154 Hampton St; (08) 9761 1740, freecall 1800 777 140. **See also:** The South-West p. 326.

Brookton   Pop. 526

MAP REF. 384 F5, 386 D8

An attractive town 137 km SE of Perth near the Avon River, in fertile farming country, Brookton was founded in 1884 when the Great Southern Railway line opened. **In town:** In Robinson Rd: Old Railway Station, houses information

centre; Old Police Station Museum (inquire at information centre); St Mark's Anglican Church (1895). Lions Picnic Park, off Corrigin Rd, on bank of Avon River, at eastern entrance to town. Mar.: Old Time Motor Show (even-numbered years). Easter: King of the Hill (off-road car racing). **In the area:** Brookton Pioneer Heritage Trail, incl. places significant to Nyongah Aboriginal people; brochure available. Nine Acre Rock, 12 km E on Brookton–Kweda Rd, large granite outcrop; nearby, remnants of pioneer Jack Hansen's home. Christmas Tree Well Picnic Area, 60 km E. Yenyening Lakes Nature Reserve, 35 km NE: salt lake; picnic area; water-skiing and sailing (if adequate water); profusion of wildflowers in spring. Boyagin Rock, 18 km SW: picnic area; scenic views; rare flora and fauna. **Visitor information:** Old Railway Station, Robinson Rd; (08) 9642 1316. **See also:** The Heartlands p. 330.

Broome   Pop. 11 368

MAP REF. 390 G9

Broome enjoys wide beaches, turquoise water and a warm, sunny climate. Closer to Bali than to Perth, and with a major airport, the town is lively and cos-mopolitan. The discovery of pearling grounds off the coast in the 1880s led to the foundation of the Broome town-ship in 1883. By 1910 Broome was the world's leading pearling centre. The industry suffered when world markets collapsed in 1914 but stabilised in the 1970s as cultured-pearl farming devel-oped. With increasing tourism, Broome is again rapidly expanding. **In town:**

Self-guide heritage trail (2 km) introduces buildings and places of interest incl.: Chinatown, with Pearl Emporium, a reminder of Broome's early multicultural mix; Historical Society Museum, in Old Customs House, Saville St; Library, Haas St. In Hamersley St: Captain Gregory's House, now art gallery (access through Matso's Store); Bedford Park, relics of Broome's history; Courthouse (former Cable House). Crocodile Park, Cable Beach Rd. Shell House, Guy St, contains one of largest shell collections in Australia. Sun Pictures, Carnarvon St, opened 1916 and believed to be oldest operating outdoor cinema in the world. In Dampier Tce, restored original pearl luggers; former divers conduct maritime history tours daily. On Port Dr.: Chinese Cemetery; Japanese Cemetery (graves of early Japanese pearl divers). Pioneer Cemetery in Lions Pioneer Park. Market, each Sat. at Courthouse. Easter: Dragon Boat Regatta. Apr.: Pentathlon. June–July: Race Round (horseracing week). Aug.: Opera Under the Stars. Aug.–Sept.: Shinju Matsuri (Festival of the Pearl, recalls Broome's heyday). Oct.: National Indigenous Art Awards. Nov.: Mango Festival. **In the area:** Beaches ideal for swimming and shell-collecting; good fishing all year. Staircase to the Moon: natural phenomenon, visible at most full moons during dry season (Apr.–Oct., dates and times from information centre); markets often held on town beach, Robinson St, at these times. Hovercraft *Spirit of Broome* visits local beaches. Safaris, cruises, scenic flights, short tours. Floatplane scenic flights over Buccaneer Archipelago. Charter boats: 6- to 10-day Kimberley expeditions to coral reefs, Rowley Shoals, Prince Regent River and waterfalls at Kings Cascades. Day tours to: former Lombadina Mission, 200 km NE; Cape Leveque, 220 km NE. Cable Beach, 3 km NW, is 22 km long, named after underwater cable linking Broome to Java; camel rides. At Gantheaume Point, 5 km SW, giant dinosaur tracks believed to be 130 million years old; seen 30 m from cliff base at very low tide. At Roebuck Bay, 18 km E: Buccaneer Rock, at entrance to Dampier Creek, landmark to Capt. William Dampier and HMAS *Roebuck*; Broome Bird Observatory. Willie Creek Pearl Farm, 35 km N, tours available. **Visitor information:** cnr Bagot St and Broome Rd; (08) 9192 2222. Web site www. ebroome.com/tourism **See also:** The Kimberley p. 332.

Bunbury
Pop. 24 945

MAP REF. 377 F4, 384 C8, 386 C10

Bunbury, known as 'Harbour City', is the major port, and commercial and regional centre for the south-west. Situated 185 km S of Perth on the Leschenault Estuary, at the junction of the Preston and Collie rivers, the town enjoys a warm temperate climate, beautiful beaches and the Darling Range in the distance. Originally called Port Leschenault, Bunbury was settled by Europeans in 1838, and the Koombana Bay whalers provided a market for pioneers. Today the port is the main outlet for the timber industry, mineral sands and produce of the fertile hinterland. **In town:** 12-km heritage trail from old railway station, Wellington St. King Cottage (1880), Forrest Ave, an historical museum with displays of domestic life in early 20th century (check times). Tree-lined pathways lead to Boulter's Heights Lookout, Haig Cres., for views of city and surrounds. Basaltic rock, on foreshore, at end of Clifton St (off Ocean Dr.); formed by volcanic lava flow 150 million years ago. Lighthouse, at end of Ocean Dr., painted in black-and-white check, has lookout at base. Marlston Hill Lookout, Apex Dr., original lighthouse site and whale-spotting point for early whaling fleet. Lighthouse Beach pathway follows coastline to original harbour breakwater. Harbour City Markets, cnr Victoria and Carey sts, open daily. Rose Hotel (1865), cnr Stephens and Victoria sts, grand heritage building with period furnishings. Paisley Centre (1887), Arthur St, originally the Bunbury Boys School, attended by 3 early WA premiers (not open to public). Centenary Gardens, cnr Wittenoom and Prinsep sts in city centre, a peaceful picnic spot. Estuary foreshore has picnic/barbecue facilities, playground and boat ramp. Miniature railway, Forrest Park, Blair St (3rd Sun. each month). Excellent beaches; surf club at Ocean Beach. Drive along breakwater to Koombana Bay, modern harbour facilities, popular for water-skiing and boating; in Koombana Dr., Dolphin Discovery Centre, offers chance to wade or swim with dolphins under ranger guidance; opposite, beginning of mangrove cave and shipwreck trail (with interpretive signage) through the southernmost mangrove colony in WA. Good deep-sea fishing and fishing for bream, flounder, tailor and whiting in bay. Succulent blue manna crabs in estuary (in season).

Variety of birdlife in bush near waters of inlet. Big Swamp Wildlife Park, Prince Phillip Dr., displays over 100 species of native birds, mammals and reptiles. Historic jetty in outer harbour, busy international trading hub from the 1860s– 1960s, currently under restoration. Tours of city sights; night bush tours; dolphin cruises. Mar.: Show. **In the area:** South West Museum, 12 km S. Killerby Wines, 17 km S. At Capel, 27 km S, Capel Vale Wines. Restored St Mark's (1842), 5 km SE at Picton, second oldest church in WA, retains some original timber structure. Wansborough Wines, 27 km SE, open weekends; nearby, Joshua Creek Fruit Wines, tastings Sat., Sun., public holidays. King Tree Winery, 35 km SE, open p.m. Bunbury–Australind Tourist Drive along Old Coast Rd; coastal scenery, good crabbing and picnic spots; brochure available. **Visitor information:** Old Railway Station, Carmody Pl.; (08) 9721 7922, freecall 1300 656 202. Web site www. justsouth.com.au **See also:** The SouthWest p. 326.

Busselton
Pop. 10 642

MAP REF. 377 D7, 379 F3, 384 B9, 386 C10

First settled by Europeans in the 1830s, and one of the oldest towns in WA, Busselton is a seaside holiday destination at the centre of a large rural district. It is situated 228 km S of Perth, on the shores of Geographe Bay and the picturesque Vasse River. Inland are jarrah forests, logged by the local timber industry, as well as dairy and beef cattle farms, and vineyards. Fishing is important, particularly crayfish and salmon in season. **In town:** Prospect Villa (1855), Pries Ave, now a B&B. Opposite, Ballarat Engine, first steam locomotive in WA. St Mary's (1844), Peel Tce, oldest stone church in State. Villa Carlotta (1897), Adelaide St, boarding-school for 50 years, now guest house. Jetty, on beachfront near Queen St, longest timber jetty (2 km) in the Southern Hemisphere; partially destroyed by Cyclone Alby in 1978, still popular with anglers; small train runs along jetty. Offshore museum. Nearby on beachfront: Nautical Lady Entertainment Centre with giant water slide, Jetty Point tower and nautical museum. Old Courthouse, Queen St, restored gaol cells, arts complex, tearooms. In Peel St: Old Butter Factory Museum, on riverbank, displays old butter- and cheese-making equipment; Vasse River Parkland, with barbecue/ picnic facilities. In Layman Rd, restored

Coastline near Carnarvon

old school and teacher's house, built of local timber. Archery Park and Minigolf, Bussell Hwy. Geographe Bay has good sheltered beaches for swimming, diving, fishing, boating and dolphin-watching. Western coast ideal for surfing. Jan.: Australia Day Yacht Regatta; Beach Festival; Summerfest. Mar.: Naturaliste Bluewater Classic (fishing). Apr.: Heritage Festival Day. **In the area:** Numerous vineyards and wineries. Scenic drive west, excellent views of rugged coast. Wildflower, scenic, canoe and 4WD tours; diving and deep-sea fishing cruises; whale-watching cruises and flights (Oct.–Dec.). Wonnerup House (1859), 10 km E, a National Trust Museum and fine example of colonial Australian architecture furnished in period style. Augusta–Busselton Heritage Trail, pamphlets available. Bunyip Craft Centre,15 km E at Ludlow. Whistle Stop, a miniature railway on Vasse Hwy, 11 km SE. Tuart Forest National Park, 12 km NE, only natural tuart forest in the world; forest walks and picnic sites in magnificent setting. **Visitor information:** 38 Peel Tce; (08) 9752 1288. Web site www.downsouth.com.au **See also:** The South-West p. 326; Classic Tour p. 366.

Caiguna   Pop. 10

MAP REF. 387 N8

Caiguna is the first stop for petrol and food after the long drive from Balladonia Roadhouse, 182 km W. This section of the Eyre Hwy is one of the longest straight stretches of sealed road in Australia. **In the area:** South of town, Nuytsland Nature Reserve, scenic area bounded by sheer cliffs fronting the Southern Ocean. **Visitor information:** John Eyre Motel; (08) 9039 3459. **See also:** Esperance & Nullarbor p. 328.

Carnamah   Pop. 338

MAP REF. 386 C5

Carnamah is a small, typically Australian country town, 290 km N of Perth. Wheat and sheep are the local industries. **In town:** Historical Society Museum, McPherson St, displays old farm machinery. Mar.: Wimbledon of the Wheatbelt. Sept.: Agricultural Show. **In the area:** McPherson Homestead (1880), 1 km E, grounds open to the public, house open by appt. Tathra National Park, 50 km SW, renowned for variety of wildflowers in spring. Lake Indoon, 61 km SW, for water-skiing. At Three Springs, 23 km NW, open-cut talc mine tours. Cockatoo Canyon, 36 km W of Three Springs, bush reserve popular with wildflower enthusiasts. **Visitor information:** Shire Offices, McPherson St; (08) 9951 1055. **See also:** The Heartlands p. 330.

Carnarvon   Pop. 6357

MAP REF. 385 B8

Carnarvon, at the mouth of the Gascoyne River, 904 km N of Perth, is the commercial centre of the Gascoyne region. The district was seen in 1616 by Dutch navigator Dirk Hartog. Another explorer, Willem de Vlamingh, landed at Shark Bay in 1697. By the 1880s Europeans had settled in the region. Today, sheep, beef cattle and fishing are important industries and the Gascoyne River irrigates extensive tropical fruit and vegetable plantations. The USA National Aeronautics and Space Administration (NASA) operated nearby at Browns Range 1964–74. Carnarvon has warm winters and looks tropical when the bougainvilleas and hibiscus bloom. **In town:** The main street (c. 1880s) was 40 m wide to enable camel trains to turn; it is now divided by trees and gardens. Jubilee Hall (1887), Francis St. Pioneer Park, Olivia Tce. Tropical Bird Park, Angelo St. Rotary Park, North West Coastal Hwy. Heritage walk trail, 20 historic landmarks around town; map available. Courtyard markets at civic centre, Robinson St, 1st Sat. each month. May: Fremantle–Carnarvon Yacht Race (even-numbered years). June: Carnafin (fishing competition). Aug.: Festival; Gascoyne Showcase Gala Concert. Dec.: Mainstreet Party. **In the area:** Excellent fishing for snapper or groper, game-fishing for marlin or sailfish; charter boat available. On Babbage Island, connected to township by causeway: Carnarvon Maritime Heritage Precinct incorporating museum at old lighthouse keeper's cottage; travel by steam train from One Mile Jetty to town bridge and return; prawning factory at old whaling station, tours in season, usually mid-Apr.–late-Oct.; Pelican Point, near southernmost tip of the island, for picnics, swimming and fishing. Westoby Banana Plantation, 5 km E, tours available (closed Tues.). Mammoth 29-m diameter reflector ('The Big Dish'), 8 km E, part of old NASA station, views of town and plantations from base. Rocky Pool, 55 km E along Gascoyne Rd, picnic area and deep billabong ideal for swimming. Munro's Banana Plantation, 10 km N via hwy and South River Rd, has fruit and vegetables for sale in season (tours Sun.– Fri.). Bibbawarra artesian bore, 16 km N, where hot water surfaces at 65°C; picnic area nearby. Bibbawarrah Trough adjacent to bore, 180 m long, believed to be the longest in the Southern Hemisphere. Miaboolya Beach, 22 km N, has good fishing, crabbing and swimming. Blowholes, 73 km N, 20 m high; about 1 km S, a superb sheltered beach with oysters on rocks, *but beware of king waves and tides, which can cause loss of life.* Cairn commemorating loss of HMAS *Sydney* in 1941, 80 km N (via blowholes). A further 20 km N, Cape Cuvier, natural port with 60-m cliff where ships can be seen loading salt and gypsum. **Visitor information:** 11 Robinson St; (08) 9941 1146. Web site www.outbackcoast.com **See also:** Outback Coast & Mid-West p. 331.

Cocklebiddy
Pop. 9

MAP REF. 387 O8

This tiny settlement is on the Eyre Hwy, between Madura and Caiguna, 310 km from the SA border. **In the area:** Cocklebiddy Cave, just north-west, for adventure caving (directions at information centre). South of town, track leads to escarpment for views of Southern Ocean; from here 4WD necessary to reach both Eyre Bird Observatory and Post Office Historical Society Museum in old telegraph station building (tours available, 24-hr notice required, contact information centre). Whale-watching at Eyre Bird Observatory (Aug.–Oct.). **Visitor information:** Wedgetail Inn; (08) 9039 3462. **See also:** Esperance & Nullarbor p. 328.

Collie
Pop. 7194

MAP REF. 384 D8, 386 C10

Collie, the centre of the State's only coal-producing region, has been important in WA's development. In dense jarrah

Wildflowers in the Stirling Range, near Cranbrook

forest, 202 km S of Perth near the winding Collie River, the town has an abundance of parks and gardens. There are fine views on the Coalfields Rd approach. **In town:** Central Precinct Historic Walk, brochure available. In Throssell St: Collie Mosaic Footpath; tourist coal mine, guided tours daily; Coalfields Museum, in old Roads Board buildings, displays coal-industry and area history; Steam Locomotive Museum; old police station (1926); post office (1898); art gallery, at Shire Office, has local art. Courthouse (1913), cnr Wittenoon and Pendleton sts. Impressive Norman-style All Saints' Anglican Church (1915), Venn St. Soldiers Park, on banks of Collie River, Steer St, has shady trees and lawns. Suspension bridge, River Ave. Minninup Pool, off Mungalup Rd, in bushland; wildflowers in season. Market at Westrail Reserve, Forrest St, 1st Sun. each month (except winter). Aug.: Collie–Donnybrook Cycle Race. **In the area:** Tours of Bunnings Timber Mill, 2 km E. Collie River Scenic Drive, offers views of jarrah forest and wildflowers in season, brochures available. The recently-declared Wellington National Park incorporating Wellington Dam and Honeymoon Pool, 18 km W, in heart of Collie River Irrigation Scheme: fishing; bushwalking; grassy picnic spots on shore. Beautiful picnic area surrounds Harris Dam, 14 km N. Muja Power Station, 24 km SE; tours available. (*Muja* is the Aboriginal word for the bright yellow Christmas tree that grows in area.) Glen Mervyn Dam,

18 km S, offers canoeing, marroning and water-skiing. **Visitor information:** 156 Throssell St; (08) 9734 2051. Web site www.collierivervalley.org.au **See also:** The South-West p. 326.

Coolgardie
Pop. 1258

MAP REF. 386 I6

The old goldmining town of Coolgardie is 550 km E of Perth and 39 km SW of Kalgoorlie–Boulder. After alluvial gold was found in 1892, Coolgardie grew in 10 years to a town of 15 000 people, 23 hotels, 6 banks and 2 stock exchanges. The main street was wide enough for camel trains to turn and splendid buildings were erected. The gold soon petered out and by 1985 there were only 700 people; however, with tourism the population is increasing. **In town:** Markers documenting points of historical interest; index to markers is in Bayley St, next to information centre. Historic buildings in Bayley St: Warden's Court (1898), houses Goldfields Exhibition Museum; post office (1898); old gaol; Denver City Hotel (1898), with handsome verandahs; Ben Prior's Open-air Museum, displays incl. wagons, horse- and camel-drawn vehicles; The Marble Bar Hotel, now RSL. Railway Station (1896), Woodward St, now a museum: transport exhibition; display of famous Varischetti mine rescue. Warden Finnerty's house (1895), McKenzie St, striking example of early Australian architecture and furnishings. Adjacent, C. Y. O'Connor Dedication, a fountain and water course in memory of O'Connor, who masterminded the Coolgardie Water Scheme. St Anthony's Convent, Lindsay St, now boarding-school. Gaol Tree, Hunt St, used for restraining prisoners in early gold-rush days. Lions Bicentennial Lookout, near southern end of Hunt St. Lindsay's Pit Lookout, over open-cut goldmine, Ford St. Sept.: Coolgardie Day. Sept.–Oct.: Metal Detecting Championships and Fun Day. **In the area:** Pioneer Cemetery, 1 km W, evokes harsh early days of gold rush. Coolgardie Camel Farm, 4 km W. Kurrawang Emu Farm, 20 km NE. Burra Rock, 55 km S, originally called Woodline Dam (built 1890s to supply water for mining-industry locomotives), popular picnic area. Goldfields Woodlands National Park, 60 km SW. **Visitor information:** 62 Bayley St; (08) 9026 6090. Web site www. kalgoorlieandwagoldfields.com.au **See also:** The Goldfields p. 329.

Coral Bay
Pop. 936

MAP REF. 385 B5

The Ningaloo Reef system approaches the shore at Coral Bay, 150 km S of Exmouth. Unspoilt white beaches offer good swimming, snorkelling, boating and fishing. **In the area:** Ningaloo Marine Park, just off beach; reef comprises 220 species of coral and supports 500 varieties of fish. Good views of reef from coral-viewing vessels. Diving equipment for hire. Coastal 4WD track to secluded beaches, for the adventurous; map available. Marine wildlife-watching tours: whale sharks (Mar.–June), humpback whales (June– Nov.) and manta rays (all year). Numerous shipwreck sites at Pt Cloates, 8 km N. **Visitor information:** Coastal Adventure Tours, Coral Bay Arcade, Robinson St; (08) 9948 5190. Web site www.gta.asn.au **See also:** Outback Coast & Mid-West p. 331.

Corrigin
Pop. 703

MAP REF. 384 H5, 386 E8

Rich farming country surrounds Corrigin, 230 km SE of Perth. **In town:** In Kunjin St: pioneer museum; miniature railway. RSL monument, Gayfer St, is a Turkish mountain gun from Gallipoli. Art and craft shop, Walton St. Sept.: Agricultural Show. **In the area:** Lookout, 3 km W, on signposted Wildflower Scenic Drive. Dog cemetery, 5 km W. Kunjin Farm, 18 km W, for emus and alpacas. Yealering Lake, 40 km SW and Gorge Rock, 20 km SE, for picnics. **Visitor information:** Shire Offices, 9 Lynch St; (08) 9063 2203. **See also:** The Heartlands p. 330.

Cranbrook
Pop. 283

MAP REF. 381 L6, 384 H11, 386 E11

In the 1800s sandalwood for incense was exported from Cranbrook to China. Today this attractive town, near the Stirling Range foothills, 320 km SE of Perth, is a sheep and cereal-growing centre. **In town:** Station House Museum (1889), Gathorne St, restored and furnished 1930s-style. Wildflower Walk, 300 m, to Stirling Gateway on Salt River Rd; orchids in spring. Sept.: Wildflower Display. Nov.: Art Show. **In the area:** Wildflower Drive and Frankland Heritage Trail, brochures available. Sukey Hill Lookout, 5 km E off Salt River Rd, expansive views of farmland, salt lakes and Stirling Range. Stirling Range National Park, 10 km SE:

almost 1000 species of flowering plants (100 unique to the area), best time for wildflowers is Aug.–Nov.; spectacular mountain peaks, good climbing and walking; accommodation at Stirling Range Retreats. Quality table wines produced in Frankland River region, 50 km W; Alkoomi, Frankland Estate and Marribrook wineries open to public. Also in region, largest plantings of olive trees in the State. Big Poorarecup Lagoon (known locally as Lake Poorarecup), 40 km SW, for swimming and water-skiing; picnic facilities and camping on foreshore of lagoon. **Visitor information:** Shire Offices, 17 Gathorne St; (08) 9826 1008 or (08) 9826 1118. **See also:** Great Southern p. 327.

Cue
Pop. 241

MAP REF. 385 H13, 386 E1, 388 B13

Cue, 650 km NE of Perth on the Great Northern Hwy, was a boom town and centre for the Murchison goldfields. **In town:** National Trust-classified buildings in Austin St: bandstand built over well; impressive government offices. Former Masonic Lodge (1899), Dowley St, built largely of corrugated iron. **In the area:** Gem-fossicking; heritage trail, incl. old hospital ruins. Day Dawn, 5 km W, original town site on gold reef; town disappeared when reef died out in 1930s, mine manager's house is last remaining building; new open-cut mine nearby. Big Bell, 30 km W, large mine opened in 1989 (access restricted). Walga Rock, 50 km W, a monolith 1.5 km long and 5 km around base with largest gallery of Aboriginal rock paintings in WA. Spectacular variety of wildflowers. **Visitor information:** Apr.–Oct. only: Robinson St, (08) 9963 1216. **See also:** Outback Coast & Mid-West p. 331.

Denham
Pop. 1140

MAP REF. 385 B10

Two peninsulas form the geographical feature of Shark Bay, 833 km from Perth. Denham is the most westerly town in Australia and the centre for the Shark Bay region. Dirk Hartog, the Dutch navigator, landed on an island at the bay's entrance in 1616. The town was named after Capt. Denham, who surveyed the region in 1858. Pearling developed as the main industry and the population was a mixture of Malays, Chinese and Europeans. Once Shark Bay was known for its fishing, but today it is a World Heritage Area and is renowned for the

wild dolphins which come inshore nearby at Monkey Mia. It also protects dugongs, humpback whales, green and loggerhead turtles and diverse seagrass species. **In town:** Shark Bay Fisheries, Dampier Rd (check opening times). Stone on which Capt. Denham carved his name is in Pioneer Park, Hughes St. **In the area:** At Monkey Mia, 26 km NE: wild dolphins come inshore to be fed (local centre and rangers provide information); daily dugong-watching cruises. Aquaria, aquatic wildlife park, 25 km NE on Monkey Mia Rd. Shark Bay Heritage Trail; coastal scenery. Catamarans MV *Hartog Explorer* and *Sea Eagle* offer cruises. Safaris and coach tours. Boat trips (weekends), also charter flights, to historic Dirk Hartog Island (homestead and backpacker accommodation on island). Francois Peron National Park, 7 km N, incl. Peron Homestead with its 'hot tub' of artesian water. Eagle Bluff, 20 km S, habitat of sea eagle. Nanga Bay Resort, 50 km S, huge sheep station: motel units; restaurant; tourist facilities; sailboard and dinghy hire on beach. Shell Beach, 50 km S, 110 km of unique Australian coastline comprised of countless tiny shells. Striking scenery at Zuytdorp Cliffs, 160 km S and extending further south to Kalbarri (4WD access only). On shores of Hamelin Pool, 100 km SE: historic displays in Flint Cliff Telegraph Station and Post Office Museum (1894); remarkable stromatolites (sedimentary rocks formed of fossilised blue-green algae) in nature reserve. Spectacular coastal scenery at Steep Point, westernmost point on mainland (260 km W by road, 4WD only). **Visitor information:** 71 Knight Tce; (08) 9948 1253. Web site www.outbackcoast.com **See also:** Outback Coast & Mid-West p. 331; Wildlife-Watching p. 364.

Denmark
Pop. 1978

MAP REF. 381 K12, 384 G13, 386 E12

This beautiful century-old former timber town, 54 km W of Albany, is at the foot of Mt Shadforth, overlooking the tranquil Denmark River and Wilson Inlet. The town offers excellent fishing, sandy white beaches, and scenic drives through farming country and karri forests. **In town:** Kurrabup Aboriginal Art Gallery, McLeod Rd. In Mitchell St: Historical Museum; Cottage Industries Shop. Denmark Gallery, Strickland St. Art, craft and antiques at Old Butter Factory,

Elephant Rocks at William Bay, south-west of Denmark

North St. Pentland Alpaca Stud and Tourist Farm, Scotsdale Rd. Jassi Skincraft, Glenrowan Rd, off Mt Shadforth Scenic Drive. Mt Shadforth Lookout, top of Mohr Dr., for magnificent views. Berridge and Thornton parks, both along riverbank in Holling Rd, offer shaded picnic areas. Michael Cartwright Art Gallery, McNabb Rd. Craft market with entertainment, on riverbank in Dec., Jan. and Easter (check dates at information centre). Jan.: Pantomime (in Berridge Park). Easter: Brave New Works (new performance art); Market Day. **In the area:** Brochures available for Mt Shadforth and Scotsdale scenic drives, featuring wineries, galleries, lookouts and forest walks; Mokare and Wilson Inlet Heritage Trail (walk); tours of wineries, forest and wildflowers; cruises of Denmark River and Wilson Inlet; pony trekking. Wineries incl.: Howard Parks Wines, 2 km N; Matilda's Meadow Winery and Restaurant, 4 km N; Misty Creek Wines and Restaurant, 5 km W; Tinglewood Wines, 8 km W; Karriview Wines, 11 km W; Mariner's Rest Wines, 13 km W. Eden Gate Blueberry Farm, 25 km E, spray-free fruit and blueberry wines. Whale-watching (on cliff) at Lowlands Beach, 28 km E (July–Oct.), also fishing and swimming. Jonathan Hook Ceramics, Lantzke Rd, 5 km NW. The Edge Gallery and Coffee House, 14 km NW. Bridgart's Orchard, 9 km W, for fresh fruit and preserves. Kurrabup Aboriginal Art Gallery, 18 km W. Bartholomew's Meadery, 20 km W, features honey,

honey wines, other bee products and live beehive display. Parry's Beach, 25 km W, for fishing (salmon in season). Spiral Studio Pottery, 32 km W. Majestic Merino Wool Craft Shop, 38 km W. Aqua Blue Marron Farm, 40 km W. Lookout at top of Monkey Rock, 10 km SW. Lights Beach, 13 km SW, with back beach, swimming and fishing. At William Bay National Park, 17 km SW: Greens Pool, natural sea pool, ideal for fishing, swimming and snorkelling; waterfall enters ocean at Madfish Bay, spectacular coastal views. West Cape Howe National Park, 30 km SW, for walking, fishing and swimming, incl. WA's most southerly point (Torbay Head). Ocean Beach, 8 km S, for good surfing. **Visitor information:** 60 Strickland St; (08) 9848 2055. **See also:** Great Southern p. 327.

Derby   Pop. 3236

MAP REF. 382 B9, 391 J7

Derby is an administrative centre for several Aboriginal communities and a hinterland rich in pastoral and mineral wealth. Near King Sound, 223 km NE of Broome, the town is an ideal base for exploring the outback regions of The Kimberley. Roads have been greatly improved, incl. the Gibb River Rd, spanning the 649 km from Derby to the junction of the Great Northern Hwy between Wyndham and Kununurra. However, as rain closes some roads in the area Nov.–Mar., check conditions before setting out on any excursion.

In town: In Loch St: Botanic Gardens; Old Derby Gaol; Wharfinger House Museum, with photographic display. In Clarendon St: Kimberley School of the Air; Royal Flying Doctor Service. Ngunga Craft Shop, Stanley St. Derby Wharf, to see the extraordinary difference in level between high and low tides. Market, Clarendon St, every Sat. May–Sept. May: Willare Cascade (powerboat race on Fitzroy River); King Tide Day (festival celebrating higest tide in Australia). June: Races; Moonrise Rock Festival; Garden Competition; Mowanjum Festival (indigenous art and culture). July: Boab Festival (rodeo, mardi gras, mud football, Stockmen and Bushies Weekend); Cup Day. Aug.: Flower and Produce Show. Dec.: Boxing Day Sports. **In the area:** Charter boats to various locations, incl. Buccaneer Archipelago and Walcott Inlet. Charter flights also over the Buccaneer Archipelgo or Kimberley coast, King Leopold Ranges, Cockatoo and Koolan islands and horizontal, reversible waterfall. Crabbing tours (just out of town). Pigeon Heritage Trail, from Derby to Windjana Gorge and Tunnel Creek National Park. Prison Tree, 7 km S, boab tree reputedly used as an early prison. Close by, Myall's Bore, a 120-m-long cattle trough. Fitzroy River empties into King Sound, 48 km S. Camel tours from Udialla Bush Camp, 110 km SW (bookings essential, at information centre). Tours to: spectacular Windjana Gorge, 145 km E in Windjana Gorge

National Park; remarkable Tunnel Creek in Tunnel Creek National Park, 184 km E, where flying foxes can be seen late in the year if you wade through tunnel with torch; also Pigeon's Cave, hideout of 1890s Aboriginal outlaw. King Leopold Ranges, 200 km E. Sir John Gorge, 350 km E (4WD access only). Lennard Gorge, 190 km NE (4WD access only). Adcock Gorge, 270 km NE, rock pools and falls early in year. Barnett River Gorge, 340 km NE (4WD recommended). Mitchell Plateau, 580 km NE via Gibb River Rd and Kalumburu Rd, features Wandjina rock-art and spectacular Mitchell Falls, King Edward River and Surveyor's Pool; in this remote region, visitors must be entirely self-sufficient *(read section on Outback Motoring p. 599 before departure)*. **Visitor information:** 2 Clarendon St; (08) 9191 1426. Web site www.derbytourism.com **See also:** The Kimberley p. 332.

Dongara
Pop. 1874

MAP REF. 386 B4

Dongara and nearby Port Denison are coastal towns, 359 km N of Perth. Dongara has beaches, reef-enclosed bays and an abundance of rock lobster. There is good fishing around Port Denison. **In town:** Historic buildings in Waldeck St: Anglican rectory (1882) and church (1884); old police station (1870); Royal Steam Flour Mill (1894). Russ Cottage (1870), Point Leander Dr. Main street, Moreton Tce, shaded by 90-year-old Moreton Bay fig trees. In cemetery, Dodd St, headstones date from 1874. Heritage Trail, Old Mill to historic Priory Lodge, brochure available. Easter: Horse Races. Easter Sat.: Craft market at old police station. Nov.: Blessing of the Fleet. **In the area:** Fisherman's Lookout, near Leander Point, Port Denison, for views of harbour. At Eneabba, 81 km SE, RGC Mineral Sands: open-cut, hydrolic and dredge mining, with advanced revegetation scheme; tours Wed., public and school holidays. Western Flora Caravan Park, 60 km S, noted for spring wildflowers in bushland and river setting. Holiday towns south-west of Eneabba: Leeman, 38 km, Green Head, 51 km. Ellendale Bluffs and Pool, 28 km NW, permanent waterhole at base of steep rock face. **Visitor information:** Dongara Library, 7 Waldeck St; (08) 9927 1404. **See also:** Outback Coast & Mid-West p. 331.

Donnybrook
Pop. 1635

MAP REF. 377 H6, 384 C8, 386 C10

The township of Donnybrook, the home of Granny Smith and Lady Williams apples, is in the oldest apple-growing area in WA, 210 km S of Perth. Gold was found here in 1897, but mined for only 4 years. Donnybrook stone has been used in construction State-wide. **In town:** On South Western Hwy: Anchor and Hope Inn (1865), once staging post for mail coaches, now a restaurant; Cadenza Gallery, wood-turning products. Arboretum, junction Irishtown Rd and South Western Hwy. Easter: Apple Festival Ball. **In the area:** Old Goldfields Orchard and Cider Factory, 5 km S. Scenic drives, maps available. Glen Mervyn Dam, 30 km NE, picnic/barbecue facilities. Cedar Shed Pottery, 10 km SE. Old Stables Pottery, 25 km SE; nearby, Blackwood Inn, old staging post, now restaurant and accommodation. At Balingup, 30 km SE: art and craft outlets, incl. Old Cheese Factory; Tinderbox, herbs and herbal remedies; Birdwood Park Fruit Winery; Small Farm Field Day each Apr.; Tulip Festival each Aug.; further 2 km SE, Golden Valley Tree Park. At Boyanup, 12 km NW, Boyanup Transport Museum. **Visitor information:** Stationmaster's Cottage, South Western Hwy; (08) 9731 1720. **See also:** The South-West p. 326.

Dunsborough
Pop. 1154

MAP REF. 377 C7, 379 C2, 384 B9, 386 B10

Dunsborough is a quiet town on Geographe Bay, west of Busselton, popular for its beaches. **In town:** For local art, Dunsborough Gallery, Naturaliste Tce. Rivendell Gardens, Wildwood Rd, has winery, cottage gardens, cafe. Market at Dunsborough Hall, cnr Gibney St and Gifford Rd, 2nd Sat. each month. Lions Market, Lions Park, some Sat. (check dates). Nov.: Margaret River Wine Festival. **In the area:** Whale-watching boat charters Sept.–Dec.; scuba diving, snorkelling and canoeing; wildflowers; craft; and tours of wineries. Scenic coastline to NW of town: Meelup, 5 km; Eagle Bay, 8 km; Bunker Bay, 12 km; Sugar Loaf Rock, 13 km. At Cape Naturaliste, 13 km NW: Lighthouse and Museum; whale-watching platform (best time Sept.–Dec.); several walking tracks with spectacular views of coastline. Wreck of HMAS *Swan*, off Point Picquet, just south of Eagle Bay, submerged Dec. 1997; dive site, tour bookings and permits at information

centre. Wise Winery, 6 km NW. Bannamah Wildlife Park; Country Life, farm with animals and hayrides; both 1 km W on Cowes Rd. Torpedo Rock, 10 km W. Several wineries in the south-west. Quindalup Fauna Park, 4 km E. **Visitor information:** Seymour Blvd; (08) 9755 3299. Web site www.capeweb.com.au/escape **See also:** The South-West p. 326.

Dwellingup
Pop. 399

MAP REF. 376 D11, 384 D6, 386 C9

This small town, 24 km SE of Pinjarra and 109 km SE of Perth, was rebuilt after the 1961 bushfire. The impressive jarrah forests nearby supply the local timber mill. Bauxite is mined in the area. **In town:** In Marrinup St: Community Hotel, last community hotel in WA; at information centre, photographic exhibition depicting 1961 bushfire and local lifestyles. Forest Heritage Centre, Acacia Rd, has timber-related exhibits, tree-tops walk, forest trails and wood products. Forest Ranger Tour, steam-train ride to Perth and return (May–Oct., check dates). Etmilyn Forest Tramway, old-style steam train, goes from railway station into jarrah forest (check times). Feb.: Log Chop Day. Aug.: Forest Heritage Festival. **In the area:** Lane–Poole Reserve, 10 km S in jarrah forest, with Baden Powell Pool, a popular recreational area. Loop walk, starts 3 km SW and passes scenic Marrinup Falls. Oakly Dam and Falls, 7 km SW. **Visitor information:** Marrinup St; (08) 9538 1108. **See also:** The South-West p. 326.

Esperance
Pop. 8647

MAP REF. 387 J10

Wide sandy beaches, a scenic coastline and the Archipelago of Recherche are attractions near Esperance, on the south coast of WA. The town, 720 km from Perth via Wagin, is the port and service centre for the agricultural and pastoral hinterland. In 1863 the first permanent European settlers arrived. The town boomed in the 1890s as a goldfields port. From the 1950s the heath plains were converted into pasture and farms. **In town:** Municipal Museum, James St, has old machinery, furniture, farm equipment; also display of Skylab, which fell to earth over Esperance in 1979. Mermaid Marine Leather, Wood St, produces and sells fashion leathers from discarded fish skins. Charter boats and dive instruction at Esperance Diving and Fishing, The Esplanade. Fishing and seal-watching from Tanker Jetty. 10-km waterfront walk and bicycle path. Wave-sailing at Observatory and Fourth beaches. Beach-fishing excursions and horseriding. Feb.: Offshore Angling Classic. Sept.: Wildflower Show. Oct.: Agricultural Show. Oct.–Nov.: Festival of the Wind (even-numbered years). **In the area:** Great Ocean Dr., 39-km loop road along spectacular coastline; passes windfarms, supplier of 30 per cent of town's electricity, Salmon Beach (5 km W) and Ten Mile Lagoon (16 km W); map available. Whale-watching (June–Nov.) as southern right whales visit bays and protected waters to calve. Rotary Lookout or Wireless Hill, 2 km W, for views of bay, town and Archipelago of Recherche. Pink Lake, 5 km W, a pink salt-water lake. Twilight Cove, 12 km W, for sheltered swimming. Views of bay and islands from Observatory Point and Lookout, 17 km W. Monjingup Lake Reserve, 20 km W. Dalyup River Wines, 42 km W (open weekends and public holidays). Archipelago of Recherche (Bay of Isles), 105 small unspoiled islands providing haven for seals and sea lions. Daily cruises (3 hrs 30 min) around Cull, Button, Charlie, Woody and other islands; landing permitted only on Woody Island. Full-day cruises to Woody Island, developed as tourist attraction (camping facilities, accommodation in safari huts and visitor's centre). Cape Le Grand National Park, 56 km E, has spectacular coastline, attractive beaches (Lucky Bay, Hellfire Bay, Thistle Cove), coastal and bush walks (brochures available) and displays of wildflowers in spring; also Whistling Rock ('whistles' under certain wind conditions), and magnificent view from Frenchmans Peak. Cape Arid National Park, 120 km E: many orchid species in spring; fishing; camping; 4WD routes. Helms Arboretum, 15 km N. Telegraph Farm, 21 km N on South Coast Hwy, has proteas, deer, buffalo and native animals (farm tours). Speddingup Wildflower Sanctuary, 35 km N, guided walks through magnificent wildflowers in season. **Visitor information:** Museum Village, Dempster St; (08) 9071 2330, freecall 1300 664 455. **See also:** Esperance & Nullarbor p. 328.

Eucla Pop. 30

MAP REF. 310 A8, 387 R7

Eucla is 13 km from the WA–SA border, on the Eyre Hwy. There is a border quarantine checkpoint for westbound travellers; they should ensure they are not carrying fruit, vegetables, honey, used fruit and produce containers, plants or seeds. **In town:** Local history museum at information centre. May: Golf Classic. **In the area:** Cross on escarpment, 5 km S, dedicated to Eyre Hwy travellers; illuminated at night. Bureau of Meteorology Weather Station, 1 km E (open to public 9.30 a.m.–1.30 p.m. daily). At Border Village, 13 km E, Border Dash race to Eucla each Nov. Highway westward from Eucla descends to coastal plain via Eucla Pass; midway down Pass (about 200 m) is Eucla National Park featuring Koonalda Cave, with 45-m-high chamber. Also at this point is a track left to sand-covered ruins of old telegraph station and former town site, 4 km S. **Visitor information:** Eucla Motel; (08) 9039 3468. **See also:** Esperance & Nullarbor p. 328.

Exmouth Pop. 3058

MAP REF. 385 C3

One of the newest towns in Australia, Exmouth was founded in 1967 as a support town for the Harold E. Holt US Naval Communications Station, the main source of local employment. Excellent year-round fishing and nearby beaches have made Exmouth a major tourist destination. The town is on the north-eastern side of North West Cape, the nearest point in Australia to the continental shelf, so there is abundant marine life. In March 1999 Exmouth was hit by Cyclone Vance. **In town:** Ningaloo Impressions Gallery and Studio, Eurayle St. Sun. mall market (Apr.–Sept.). May: Golf Classic. July: Arts Quest. Oct.: Octoberfest. Oct.–Nov.: Gamex (world-class game-fishing). **In the area:** Turtle-nesting Nov.–Jan.; coral-spawning Mar.–Apr.; boat cruises and air flights to see whale sharks Mar.–June; humpback whales can be seen Aug.–Nov. from lighthouse, 17 km N, and from whale-watching boat tours; snorkellers can swim with manta rays located by cruise boats. Swimming, snorkelling, fishing; fishing-boat charter; coral-viewing boat cruises; safari tours of cape, national parks and naval base; dive courses and dive trips. In Cape Range National Park, south of town: Shothole Canyon, a spectacular gorge accessed via Shothole Canyon Rd; Charles Knife Canyon, accessed via Charles Knife Rd (spectacular views); Yardie Creek Gorge, with deep-blue water and multi-coloured rock; Milyering Visitor Centre, 52 km SW; beach campsites; abundant wildlife, picnic spots, scenic lookouts and walking trails. Ningaloo Marine Park, 14 km W of cape, largest fringing coral reef in Australia; 500 fish species identified and 220 reef-building coral species. Views from Vlaming Head Lighthouse, 17 km N. Wreck of SS *Mildura*, 100 m offshore. **Visitor information:** Murat Rd; (08) 9949 1176; freecall 1800 287 328. Web site www.outbackcoast.com **See also:** Outback Coast & Mid-West p. 331; Wildlife-Watching p. 364.

Fitzroy Crossing Pop. 1147

MAP REF. 382 G11, 391 L9

Fitzroy Crossing is 254 km inland from Derby where the Great Northern Hwy crosses the Fitzroy River. The town has grown as a result of Aboriginal settlement, mining by Western Metals at Cadjebut (80 km SE), and an increase in visitors to the nearby Geikie Gorge National Park. Apr.: Garnduwa Amboorny Wiran Festival (song, dance and sport). July: Rodeo. Sept.: Junction Races. Nov.: Fishing Competition; Night Rodeo. **In the area:** Check road conditions before setting out on any excursions Dec.–Mar. as area is prone to flooding. Scenic flights, bookings essential. Picturesque waterholes surrounding town support abundance of fish and other wildlife. Magnificent Geikie Gorge, 18 km NE in Geikie Gorge National Park: wildlife, incl. sawfish, barramundi, stingrays (adapted to fresh water) and freshwater crocodiles; cruises, incl. Aboriginal Heritage Cruise (May–Nov.). Tunnel Creek National Park, 110 km NW: creek tunnel through mountain range; 4WD access only; tours. Windjana Gorge National Park, 145 km NW: rock pools supporting variety of fish and birdlife; walking trails; 4WD access only; tours to Windjana Gorge. Landor Station, 210 km E, holds horse races each Sept. **Visitor information:** cnr Great Northern Hwy and Flynn Dr.; (08) 9191 5355. **See also:** The Kimberley p.332; National Parks p. 362.

Gascoyne Junction Pop. 38

MAP REF. 385 D8

Located 170 km E of Carnarvon, at the junction of the Gascoyne and Lyons rivers, this town is the administration centre for the area. **In town:** Old Roads Board Museum, memorabilia of area (check times). The old-fashioned pub is a good rest stop. **In the area:** Scenic Kennedy Range National Park, 60 km N. Mt Augustus National Park, 294 km NE: Mt Augustus (Burringurrah), rests on world's largest rock, 1.65 billion years old, twice the size of Ulu<u>r</u>u; Aboriginal art sites; walks and drives; brochures available. **Visitor information:** Junction Hotel; (08) 9943 0504. **See also:** Outback Coast & Mid-West p. 331.

Geraldton   Pop. 25 243

MAP REF. 386 A3

The port and administration centre for the mid-west area, Geraldton is 424 km N of Perth on Champion Bay. A year-round sunny climate and a mild winter make it a popular holiday destination. The flourishing city has interesting museums, white, sandy beaches and good fishing. Mahomets Beach attracts windsurfers from all over the country. The area has rich agricultural land, magnificent spring wildflowers and picturesque countryside. The Houtman Abrolhos Islands, a group of over 100 coral islands named in the 16th century, lie 64 km off the coast and are used as a base for diving and rock-lobster fishing. **In town:** Heritage trail, brochure available. In Cathedral Ave: Queens Park Theatre, surrounded by gardens; St Francis Xavier Cathedral, designed by Mons. John C. Hawes, architect of fine buildings in area. On Marine Tce: Sir John Forrest Memorial; Geraldton Museum (incl. maritime display building), features relics from shipwrecks. Art Gallery, cnr Durlacher St and Chapman Rd. Old Gaol Craft Centre, Bill Sewell Complex, Chapman Rd. Lookout and wishing-well on Waverley Heights, Brede St. Point Moore Lighthouse (1878), Willcock Dr. Excellent fishing from town's breakwater. At Fisherman's Wharf, watch hauls of lobster being unloaded in season (Nov.–June). Lobster factory tours. Jan.: Windsurfing Classic. Mar.: Sea Jazz Spectacular. June: Batavia Celebrations. Oct.: Sunshine Festival. **In the area:** For good fishing: Sunset Beach, 6 km N; Drummond Cove, 10 km N; mouth of Greenough River, 10 km S. Banks of Greenough River: picnics; Greenough River Walk, starts at river mouth; safe swimming for children; daily river cruises; market here 3rd Sun. each month. Greenough, 24 km S: restored by National Trust to 1880s appearance; guided tours. Mill's Park Lookout, 15 km NE on Waggrakine Cutting, offers

Jetty ruins at Eucla

excellent views over Moresby Range and coastal plain towards Geraldton. Chapman Valley, 35 km NE, a farming district noted for its spectacular spring wildflowers; Chapman Valley Wines, tastings daily. **Visitor information:** Bill Sewell Complex, cnr Bayley St and Chapman Rd; (08) 9921 3999. Web site www.geraldtontourist.com.au **See also:** Outback Coast & Mid-West p. 331.

Gingin   Pop. 549

MAP REF. 384 C2, 386 C7

Situated 83 km N of Perth and 30 km from the coast, Gingin is mainly a centre for mixed farming, horticulture, and cattle and sheep breeding. As a daytrip from Perth it offers alternative return trips along the coast or inland via the scenic Chittering Valley, where there are wildflowers in spring. The town is built around a loop of Gingin Brook, which flows strongly all year. **In town:** Fine examples of Australian architecture in village-like atmosphere. In Weld St: St Luke's Anglican Church (1860s), Granville (1871), Uniting Church (1868), and Dewar's House (1886). In Brockman St: Philbey's Cottage (1906), now a real estate agency. Uniforms of the World Museum, Brook St (closed Mon.). Adjacent to Granville Scenic Park, Weld St, Jim Gordon V. C. Trail, a delightful 30-min. walk along Gingin Brook. Apr.: Gingin Expo (horticulture

and primary production). May: British Car Day. **In the area:** A number of small wineries; details from information centre. Gingin Cemetery, northern outskirts of town on Dewar Rd, has prolific display of kangaroo paws in spring. Neergabby Pottery, 25 km W. At Bullsbrook, 42 km S: The Maze; Bullsbrook Antiques and Cottage Crafts. Golden Grove Citrus Orchard and Observatory at Lower Chittering, 30 km SE. Colamber Bird Park, just east of town on Mooliabeenie Rd. At Bindoon, 29 km E: Neroni Wines; Chittering Valley Estate; Kay Road Art and Craft Gallery. **Visitor information:** Shire Offices, 7 Brockman St; (08) 9575 2211. Web site www.iinet.net.au/~ginginwa **See also:** The Heartlands p. 330.

Guilderton   Pop. 174

MAP REF. 384 B2, 386 C7

Located at the mouth of the Moore River, 94 km N of Perth, Guilderton is a popular daytrip from Perth and a holiday destination. There is excellent fishing in both river and sea, and safe swimming for children. Dutch relics have been found here, possibly from the wreck of the *Vergulde Draeck* (Gilt Dragon) in 1656. **In town:** Cruises on Moore River, depart Edward St. **In the area:** Seabird, 20 km N, a small but growing fishing village with a safe beach. **Visitor information:** Caravan Park, 2 Dewar St; (08) 9577 1021. **See also:** The Heartlands p. 330.

Halls Creek
Pop. 1263

MAP REF. 383 N11, 391 P9

In the heart of The Kimberley, 2832 km from Perth, at the edge of the Great Sandy Desert, is Halls Creek, site of WA's first gold find in 1885. In 3 years 10 000 men came to The Kimberley goldfields, then gradually drifted away, leaving 2000 on the diggings. Today beef cattle is the main industry. **In town:** Russian Jack Memorial, Thomas St, tribute to miner who pushed his sick friend in a wheelbarrow from Halls Creek to Wyndham for medical help. **In the area:** Aboriginal dreamtime places, brochures available from Kimberley Language Resource Centre, Terone St. Scenic flights to Purnululu National Park; bookings essential, at information centre. China Wall, 6 km E, a natural quartz formation. Prospecting at Old Halls Creek, 16 km E; mud-brick ruins of original settlement; caravan park. Caroline Pool, 10 km E, near old town site off Duncan Rd, for swimming and picnicking (best Oct.–May). Fishing, swimming and picnicking at Palm Springs (41 km E), and Sawpit Gorge (43 km E), both on Black Elvire River. Canning Stock Route, old route to take cattle to southern goldfields, begins 80 km E (Heritage Trail follows part of this route). Purnululu National Park, 160 km NE, has spectacular Bungle Bungle rock formations. Wolfe Creek Meteorite Crater, 148 km S, almost 1 km wide, and 49 m deep; second largest meteorite crater in world. **Visitor information:** Great Northern Hwy; (08) 9168 6262. **See also:** The Kimberley p. 332.

Harvey
Pop. 2570

MAP REF. 377 H2, 384 C7, 386 C10

The thriving town of Harvey, 139 km S of Perth, is set in some prime agricultural country. Bordered by the Darling Range and the Indian Ocean, the fertile plains are perfect for dairying. The irrigation storage dams and recreation areas are popular with tourists. **In town:** Historical Society Museum, in old railway station (1914), Harvey St (open 2 p.m.–4 p.m. Sun.). Information centre has local industry displays. Stirling Cottage, behind information centre, replica of 1880s home of May Gibbs (author of *Snugglepot and Cuddlepie*). Internment Camp Memorial Shrine, South Western Hwy, built by prisoners of war in 1940s; key from information centre. Mar.: Harvest Festival. Sept.: Spring Markets. Oct.: Agricultural Show. **In the area:** Weir, 3 km E, off Weir Rd; Weir Walk, a 1-km trail alongside Harvey River. Scenic drive around north-west side of Stirling Dam (venue for world canoe championships), 17 km E, leads to Harvey Falls and Trout Ladder. Logue Brook Dam, 15 km NE, for swimming, water-skiing and trout fishing. Hoffmans Mill, 25 km NE, has picnic and camping facilities. At Yarloop, 15 km N: historic steam-age Workshops Museum; heritage trail, details from museum. Myalup and Binningup beaches, 25 km W off Old Coast Rd, are wide and sandy, ideal for swimming, fishing and boating. **Visitor information:** South West Hwy; (08) 9729 1122. **See also:** The South-West p. 326.

Hopetoun
Pop. 319

MAP REF. 386 H11

Hopetoun is a peaceful holiday town overlooking the Southern Ocean. Located 49 km S of Ravensthorpe, the town offers rugged, beautiful coastal scenery and year-round wildflowers. Once called Mary Ann Harbour, Hopetoun has a colourful history. **In town:** White, sandy beaches, sheltered bays, excellent fishing. Chatterbox Crafts, Veal St, for local art and craft, and visitor information. Jan.: Summer Festival. **In the area:** Scenic drives, brochures available. Lookout at Table Hill, 1 km N: views over town and ocean; has cairn to explorer John Eyre. Dunn's Swamp, 5 km N: picnics; bushwalking; birdwatching. Lookout at No Tree Hill, 27 km NW, offers views across to Eyre Range. Fitzgerald River National Park, 10 km W: incl. the Barrens, a series of rugged mountains, undulating sandplains and steep narrow gorges; East Mt Barren Footpath, walk to summit (2–3 hrs return); Hamersley Inlet, a scenic picnic and camping spot. *Take care fishing from rocks – king waves can roll in unexpectedly and take lives.* **Visitor information:** Chatterbox Crafts, Veal St; (08) 9838 3100. Web site www.comswest.net.au/~hopetel **See also:** Esperance & Nullarbor p. 328; National Parks p. 362.

Hyden
Pop. 150

MAP REF. 386 F8

Hyden is 351 km E of Perth, in the semi-arid eastern wheat area of WA. **In the area:** Fascinating rock formations, especially Wave Rock, 4 km E, a 2700-million-year-old granite outcrop rising 15 m, like a giant wave about to break. At Wave Rock: Wildlife Park; coffee shop; caravan park with cabins; Pioneer Town, with collection of Australiana; lacework (from 1600s) at information centre; 1 km E of centre, salt lakes for swimming and picnics, good reflections of rock. Other rock formations within walking distance of Wave Rock: Hippos Yawn; The Breakers; The Falls. Scenic flights from airfield, 5 km E, bookings essential. Aboriginal rock paintings at Mulka's Cave, 18 km N of Wave Rock. Nearby, The Humps, another unusual granite formation. **Visitor information:** Wave Rock Visitors Centre, Wave Rock Rd, 4 km E of town; (08) 9880 5182. Web site www.promaco. com.au/mapping/hyden **See also:** The Heartlands p. 330.

Jurien Bay
Pop. 636

MAP REF. 386 B6

Located 266 km N of Perth on a sheltered bay, Jurien Bay is a lobster-fishing centre. The town is also a holiday destination because of its magnificent safe swimming beaches, excellent climate and reputation as an angler's paradise. Jurien Bay boat harbour, a 17-ha inland marina, has excellent boating facilities. **In town:** Tours of rock-lobster processing factory, Roberts Rd, in fishing season. Nov.: Marine Expo and Blessing of the Fleet (start of rock-lobster season). **In the area:** Spectacular sand dunes along coast. Cockleshell Gully, 31 km N, has great diversity of flora and fauna. Stockyard Gully National Park, 50 km N (4WD access only), has walk through 300-m Stockyard Gully Tunnel along winding underground creek (torch necessary, tours available). Lesueur National Park, 25 km E, noted for variety of spring wildflowers. At Badgingarra National Park, 61 km E: 2-km walking trail through heathlands; spring wildflowers; Badgingarra Shears Competition each Aug. At Cervantes, 55 km S, Slalom Carnival (windsurfing) held in Dec. At nearby Nambung National Park: The Pinnacles, thousands of spectacular calcified spires, 1–4 m high and around 30 000 years old, scattered over 400 ha of multicoloured desert sand (coach tours daily); superb beaches; check road conditions before leaving Jurien Bay if taking coastal track (main signposted route further inland recommended). **Visitor information:** Shire Offices, Bashford St; (08) 9652 1020. Web site www.promaco.com.au/mapping.twcc **See also:** The Heartlands p. 330.

Kalbarri

Pop. 1788

MAP REF. 385 C13, 386 A2

This popular holiday town is between Geraldton and Carnarvon, 591 km N of Perth. The town offers a picturesque Murchison River estuary setting, a year-round sunny climate, the spectacular gorges of Kalbarri National Park, excellent fishing and the brilliance of more than 500 wildflower species. **In town:** In Grey St: Recollections, a doll and marine museum; Gemstone Mine. In Porter St: Kalbarri Entertainment Centre; bicycle hire available. Pelican feeding on foreshore (8.45 a.m.). Mar.: Cycle Races and Triathlon; Sport Fishing Classic. Nov.: Blessing of the Fleet. **In the area:** Majestic coastal gorges and precipitous red cliffs dropping to Indian Ocean. *River Queen* ferry cruises; camel safaris; coach, 4WD, and abseiling adventure tours; canoe safaris; joy flights. Kalbarri Big River Ranch, 3 km E, for horseriding. At Kalbarri National Park, a large area of magnificent virgin bushland surrounding town: Meanarra Lookout, 7 km E; spectacular Murchison River gorges, 30 km E; coastal views from Hawks Head Lookout and Ross Graham Lookout, both 39 km E; abundance of wildlife and native flora; no camping. Rainbow Jungle and Tropical Bird Park, 3.5 km S. Red Bluff, 4 km S, for swimming, fishing and rock-climbing. Cairn at Wittecarra Creek, 4 km S, site of first permanent landing of Europeans in Australia. Views from the Loop and Z Bend lookouts, 30 km NE. **Visitor information:** Grey St; (08) 9937 1104, freecall 1800 639 468. Web site www.wn.com.au/kalbarrionline **See also:** Outback Coast & Mid-West p. 331; National Parks p. 362.

Kalgoorlie–Boulder

Pop. 28 087

MAP REF. 386 I6

At the heart of WA's largest goldmining area is the city of Kalgoorlie–Boulder, 597 km E of Perth and located on the Golden Mile, reputed to be the richest square mile in the world. Over 1300 tonnes of gold have been mined from this small area. Paddy Hannan found gold in 1893 and by 1902 the population was 30 000, with 93 hotels. Fortunes were made overnight; impressive stone buildings and wide streets are reminders of this golden era. The tent camp on the Golden Mile near the Great Boulder Mine became the town of Boulder. Tree plantings date from the late 1800s; many of the 50 species are eucalypts from the surrounding woodlands. Determination and the brilliant scheme of engineer C. Y. O'Connor saved the area from a crippling shortage of water. A pipeline completed in 1903 carried water 563 km from a reservoir near Perth. Goldmining continues today in a climate of fluctuating gold prices. The Kalgoorlie–Boulder region is also important for high-quality wool. **In town:** Heritage walk along Hannan and Burt sts, brochures available. Fine examples of early Australian architecture in Hannan St: Exchange, Palace and Australia hotels; Government buildings; Kalgoorlie Post Office; distinctive Kalgoorlie Town Hall (1908), featuring original statue of Paddy Hannan, impressive staircase, and paintings by local artists. Also in Hannan St: Museum of the Goldfields, incorporating the British Arms Hotel (1899), with display recalling heyday of gold-rush; replica statue of Hannan; Desert Art Shop. Goldfields Aboriginal Art Gallery, Dugan St. Paddy Hannan's Tree, Outridge Tce, marks site of first gold find in Kalgoorlie. School of Mines Mineral Museum, Egan St, incl. world-class display of most minerals found in WA. In Cassidy St, Goldfields Arts Centre has regular exhibitions. At Hannans North Historic Mining Reserve, Broad Arrow Rd, underground and surface tours, gold-pouring demonstrations. Super Pit Lookout, off Eastern Bypass Rd. In Burt St: Boulder Town Hall (1908), has unique Goatcher curtain and miners' monument; Goldfields War Museum has personal war memorabilia and outdoor armoured vehicle display. Picturesque Cornwall Hotel (1898), Chesapeake St. Royal Flying Doctor Service Base, at airport (off Gatacre St): serves one of largest areas in Australia; tours weekdays; scenic flights over goldfields and Golden Mile Super Pit Lookout. Hammond Park, Lyall St, a wildlife sanctuary with lake and model of Bavarian castle. Karlkurla Bushland Park, off Riverina Way in Hannans; guided tours Apr.–Oct. Mt Charlotte Reservoir and Lookout, off Sutherland St; reservoir is storage for Kalgoorlie's vital fresh-water supply. The Loopline, a tourist railway line around the Golden Mile; timetable at information centre. Sept.: Kalgoorlie Cup; Spring Festival; Balzano Barrow Race. Dec.: St Barbara's Festival. **In the area:** Carpet of wildflowers in season. City is an ideal base for visiting old gold-mining towns in district (all within a day's drive, all active, tours July–Oct.): Coolgardie, 37 km SW; Broad Arrow, 38 km N; Ora Banda, 54 km NW; Kookynie, 200 km N; Leonora and Gwalia, 235 km N. Scenic flights, and bush tours including Aboriginal tours with local Wongi people; WA's only legal Bush Two-up (a gambling game), 7 km N of Kalgoorlie–Boulder on eastern side of road to Menzies. Rowles Lagoon, 34 km NW, excellent for water sports. Kurrawang Emu Farm, 18 km W, also features Aboriginal artifacts (closed Sun., tours available). At Kambalda, 55 km S: Red Hill Lookout; Lake Lefroy; Fishing in the Desert competition each Sept. Rawlinna, 350 km E, hosts Nullarbor Muster each Apr. **Visitor information:** 250 Hannan St; (08) 9021 1966. Web site www.kalgoorlieandwagoldfields.com.au **See also:** The Goldfields p. 329.

Karratha

Pop. 10 057

MAP REF. 385 G1

This modern town was established on Nickol Bay in 1968 as a result of expansion of the Hamersley Iron Project. The town grew further when Woodside Petroleum developed the immense offshore gas reserve on the North West Shelf, and Karratha now has the best facilities in The Pilbara. Karratha's winter temperatures make it a good place to escape the cold. **In town:** Excellent views from TV Hill lookout, Millstream Rd. June: Pilbara Pursuit Jetboat Classic. Aug.: FeNaCLNG Festival (annual show). **In the area:** Scenic flights, day tours and safari tours of Pilbara outback. Jaburara Heritage Trail, 3-hr walk, features Aboriginal rock carvings and artifact scatters. At Dampier, 22 km N: Hamersley Iron deepwater port (tours Mon.–Fri.); salt-harvest ponds near port; water sports and boat hire; boat access to Dampier Archipelago for bushwalking, swimming, fishing and wildlife-watching; Game-fishing Classic held Aug. Near Dampier: North West Shelf Gas Project Visitors Centre (8 km NW on Burrup Peninsula), and Aboriginal rock carvings nearby. Chichester Range Camel Trail and Millstream–Chichester National Park, 124 km S. **Visitor information:** 4548 Karratha Rd; (08) 9144 4600. Web site www.pilbara.com **See also:** The Pilbara p. 334.

Boab tree near Kununurra

Katanning Pop. 4035

MAP REF. 381 L1, 384 H9, 386 E10

A thriving town 186 km N of Albany, Katanning's well-planned streets have some impressive Federation buildings. The countryside is given over to grain-growing and pastoral activities, and is noted for its fine merino sheep. **In town:** Self-guide scenic and heritage walks, brochure available. Old Mill Museum (1889), cnr Clive St and Austral Tce, features outstanding display of vintage roller flour-milling process. Majestic Kobeelya mansion (1902), Brownie St, a country retreat now owned by Baptist Church (open by appt). All Ages Playground, Clive St, has miniature steam railway. Old Winery ruins, Andrews Rd, being restored. In Dore St, largest country-based sheep-selling facility in WA; regular sales on Wed. throughout year; ram sale in Aug. Metro Meats meatworks, Wagin Rd (tours by appt, contact Metro Meats or information centre). Market at Blyth's Tree Farm, Prosser St (Sun. a.m., check dates). Feb.: Triathlon. Aug.: Prophet Mohammad's Birthday. Dec.: Caboodle. **In the area:** Katanning–Piesse Heritage Trail, a 20-km drive/walk trail. Lakes surrounding town are excellent for swimming, boating and water-skiing. **Visitor information:** Flour Mill, cnr Austral Tce and Clive St; (08) 9821 2634. **See also:** Great Southern p. 327.

Kojonup Pop. 1035

MAP REF. 381 J2, 384 G9, 386 E11

Situated on the Albany Hwy, 154 km NW of Albany, Kojonup takes its name from the Aboriginal word *kodja*, meaning 'stone axe'. In 1837, when surveying the road from Albany to the Swan River settlement, Alfred Hillman was guided to the Kojonup Spring by local Aboriginal people. Later, a military outpost there marked the beginning of the town. **In town:** In Spring St: Kojonup Spring and picnic area; Military Barracks (1845), Barracks Pl., houses Kojonup Pioneer Museum (open Sun. p.m. or by appt). Elverd's Cottage (1851), Soldier Rd, has display of pioneers' tools and implements. On Albany Hwy: Sundial in Hillman Park; Kojonup Brook Walk, a walk alongside stream and featuring swing bridge. Walsh's Cattle Complex, Broomehill Rd, has regular cattle sales. At Farrar Reserve, Blackwood Rd, wildflower display in spring. Myrtle Benn Memorial Flora and Fauna Sanctuary, Tunney Rd. Heritage Harness Display, Railway Shed, Benn Pde (next to information centre). Feb.: Rodeo. Sept.: Country and Wildflower Festival. Oct.: Agricultural Show. **In the area:** Variety of flora (incl. more than 60 orchid species) and fauna (especially birds). Outlets for local jarrah furniture, hand-turned grass-tree articles, woollen jumpers. Proandra Flowers, 20 km W, a protea farm. Lake Towerrining, 40 km NW,

ideal for boating, onshore camping. Australian Bush Heritage Funds Reserve at Cherry Tree Pool, 16 km N: walk through *Eucalyptus wandoo*; wildflowers. **Visitor information:** Albany Hwy; (08) 9831 1686. Web site www.promaco.com.au/kojonup **See also:** Great Southern p. 327.

Kulin Pop. 360

MAP REF. 384 I6, 386 F9

A centre for the sheep and grain farms of the district, Kulin is 283 km SE of Perth. *Eucalyptus macrocarpa* is a spectacular feature of the local flora. **In town:** Kulin Herbarium, specialising in wildflowers from local area, tours by appt. On Kondinin–Wickepin Rd, Cooperative Bulk Handling Facility (huge grain-storage bins); tours, bookings essential. Sept.: Charity Rally (for pre-1977 cars). **In the area:** Several species of native orchids. Wildflower walks/drives; brochure available. Jilakin Rock and Lake, 15 km E: salt lake with salt plants; wildflowers in spring; Kulin Bush Races Weekend held here in Oct. Buckley's Breakaway (pit with coloured hollows caused by granite decomposing to kaolin), 58 km E; also unusual coloured rock formations and wildflowers in area. Hopkins Nature Reserve, 20 km NE, an important flora conservation area. Historic Kondinin Cottage, 32 km NW at Kondinin, National Trust-classified mudbrick settler's cottage: goods for sale; afternoon teas. **Visitor information:** Kulin Woolshed, Johnston St; (08) 9880 1275 or Shire Offices, Johnston St; (08) 9880 1204. Web site www.kulin.com.au **See also:** The Heartlands p. 330.

Kununurra Pop. 4884

MAP REF. 383 P2, 391 Q5

Kununurra is situated alongside Lake Kununurra on the Ord River. Adjacent is the magnificent Mirima National Park. The town supports several industries, incl. agriculture and mining, and is the major site for the Argyle Diamond Mine (the largest producing diamond mine in the world) and the Ord River Irrigation Area. **In town:** Sales of pink diamonds from the Argyle Diamond Mine, and other gems, at various outlets. Diversion Gallery, River Fig Ave, for fine Kimberley artworks. May: Ord Valley Muster. June: Dam to Dam Dinghy Race; Mardi Gras. July: Agricultural Show. Aug.: Rodeo. Sept.: Night Rodeo. Oct.: Apex Barra Bash. **In the area:** Kununurra is starting point for tours and flights to: remarkably coloured and shaped Bungle Bungles in Purnululu National Park to the south; Argyle Diamond Mine in the south-west (access via tour only); Mitchell Plateau and Kalumburu in the north-west Kimberley. Minibus tours of local attractions, charter flights and bush camping. Good fishing; barramundi a prized catch. Mirima National Park, 2 km E (no camping). 2 km N: Warringarri Aboriginal Arts; Kelly's Knob Lookout, for views of surrounding irrigated land. Barra Barra Banana Farm, 9 km N, tastings and sales (daily May–Oct.). Top Rockz Gallery, 10 km N, exhibits gemstones and precious metals (open May–Sept.). Melon Farm, 12 km N. Ivanhoe Crossing, 12 km N, for fishing. Middle Springs, 30 km N; Black Rock Falls, 32 km N, flows only in the Wet. Cruises on Lake Kununurra and upstream into the Everglades and gorges for teeming birdlife. El Questro Station, 100 km SW: Aboriginal rock art; rugged scenery; hot springs; fishing and boating; camping and accommodation; Barrafest Competition in Oct. Sleeping Buddha (Elephant Rock), 10 km S. Zebra Rock Gallery, 16 km S. Scenic Lake Argyle, 72 km S in Carr Boyd Range, largest body of fresh water in Australia, created by Ord River Dam, which transformed mountain peaks into islands. Argyle Homestead Museum, lake cruises, caravan park and accommodation at Lake Argyle Tourist Village. **Visitor information:** Coolibah Dr.; (08) 9168 1177. **See also:** The Kimberley p. 332; National Parks p. 362.

Lake Grace   Pop. 575

MAP REF. 386 F9

A pleasant town with good facilities, situated 252 km N of Albany in the peaceful countryside of the central south wheat belt, Lake Grace derives its name from the shallow lake just west of the settlement. **In town:** In Stubbs St: mural depicting pioneer women, in Lake Grace Plaza; restored Inland Mission hospital, last in WA; old railway buildings. **In the area:** Roe Heritage Trail, retraces part of J. S. Roe's explorations in 1848. Lookout, 5 km W. **Visitor information:** Shire Council; (08) 9865 1105. **See also:** The Heartlands p. 330.

Lake King   Pop. 29

MAP REF. 386 G9

With a tavern and several stores, Lake King is a crossroads stopping-place for visitors travelling across arid country and through Frank Hann National Park to Norseman. **In the area:** Colourful wildflowers in season, 5 km W. Lake King, 5 km W, a saltwater lake. At Pallarup, 15 km S: pioneer well; Lake Pallarup. Mt Madden cairn and lookout, 25 km SE, also picnic area. Frank Hann National Park, 32 km E, good representation of inland sand plain heath flora. Park is traversed by Lake King–Norseman Rd, a formed gravel road; check road conditions before departure. *Note: No visitor facilities or supplies available between Lake King and Norseman.* **Visitor information:** Lake King Agencies, 13 Ravensthorpe Rd; (08) 9874 4015. **See also:** The Heartlands p. 330.

Lancelin   Pop. 597

MAP REF. 384 B1, 386 B7

This little fishing town on the shores of Lancelin Bay is 127 km N of Perth. A natural breakwater extends from Edward Island to Lancelin Island, providing a safe harbour and a perfect breeding ground for fish. There are rock lobsters on the offshore reefs outside the bay. Stretches of white sandy beach provide ideal swimming for children. Lancelin is becoming known as the sailboard mecca of WA: each Dec. large numbers of visiting windsurfers take part in the Ledge Point Ocean Race. Jan.: Ledge to Lancelin Windsurfing Race. Easter: Dune Buggy Championships. Sept.: Lily Festival and Market Day. **In the area:** Large off-road area for dune buggies at northern end of town. Whalewatching Oct.–Mar. Ledge Point, 15 km S, a community built around fishing industry; good beach fishing. Dive trail to 14 shipwrecks (c. 1760), map available. Eco cruise around islands. Self-guide wildflower drives, maps available. Track (4WD only) leads 76 km N to Nambung National Park; check road conditions at information centre before setting out; map available; alternative bitumen-road route is 166 km. **Visitor information:** 102 Gingin Rd; (08) 9655 1100. **See also:** The Heartlands p. 330.

Laverton   Pop. 644

MAP REF. 387 J3

Laverton, officially gazetted in 1900 and situated 360 km NE of Kalgoorlie on the edge of the Great Victoria Desert, is surrounded by numerous old mine workings and modern mines, including new nickel and gold projects. With an annual rainfall of around 200 mm, summers are hot and dry; Apr.–Oct. is the recommended time to travel. **In town:** Historic buildings in Craiggie St: Courthouse; Old Police Station and Gaol; Railway Station. **In the area:** Wildflowers Aug.–Sept. Windarra Heritage Trail, 28 km NW on Old Windarra Minesite Rd, incl. rehabilitated mine site and has interpretive plaques along route. Great Victoria Desert escorted 4WD tours (Apr.–Nov.), bookings at information centre. Empress Springs, 305 km NE near Tjukayirla Roadhouse; site discovered by explorer David Carnegie in 1896. At Warburton, 565 km NE, Tjulyuru Cultural and Civic Centre shows art and culture of the Ngaanyatjarraku people. From Laverton to Uluṟu via Outback Hwy (1200 km), all roads are unsealed but regularly maintained. The following points should be noted:

• Permit required to travel through Aboriginal Reserves and Communities; obtained from Aboriginal Affairs Department, Perth, or the Central Land Council in Alice Springs.
• Water is scarce.
• Supplies at Laverton. Fuel, supplies and accommodation at Tjukayirla Roadhouse (305 km NE), Warburton, and Warakurna Roadhouse.
• Credit card facilities are not necessarily available at desert stops.
• Check road conditions before departure, at the Laverton Police Station or Laverton Shire Offices. Roads can be closed due to heavy rain.

Visitor information: Shire Offices, MacPherson Pl.; (08) 9031 1202. Web site www.kalgoorlieandwagoldfields.com.au **See also:** The Goldfields p. 329.

Leonora   Pop. 1143

MAP REF. 386 I3

Leonora, 243 km N of Kalgoorlie, has wide streets and verandahed shopfronts. The town is the busy railhead for the north-eastern goldfields, with mining of gold, copper and nickel at Laverton, 120 km NE, and Leinster, 134 km NW. Most of the surrounding country is flat mulga scrub, but there are brilliant wildflowers in Aug. and early Sept. after good rains. Oct.: Art Prize. **In the area:** 3 major gold producers, incl. famous Sons of Gwalia. At Gwalia, 2 km S: renovated State Hotel (1903), fine example of former prosperity; old mine offices now house a museum depicting miners' lifestyle; old houses restored to show conditions in which early miners lived; 1-km heritage trail; Market Day in Aug. Small goldmining town of Menzies, 110 km S, has historical cemetery. Kookynie, 92 km SE, a small town with old mine workings; Grand Hotel offers warm welcome. Malcolm, 20 km E; good picnic spot alongside Malcolm Dam. **Visitor information:** Gwalia Historical Township and Museum; (08) 9037 7210 or Shire Offices, Tower St; (08) 9037 6044. Web site www.leonora.wa.gov.au **See also:** The Goldfields p. 329.

Madura Roadhouse Pop. 15

MAP REF. 387 P8

The Hampton Tablelands form a backdrop to Madura, 195 km from the WA–SA border, on the Eyre Hwy. The settlement dates from 1876 when horses for the British Imperial Army were bred here. Now it is surrounded by private sheep stations. **In the area:** Blowholes at The Pass, 1 km N. Spectacular views from escarpment lookout, 1 km W on hwy. **Visitor information:** Madura Pass Oasis Motel and Roadhouse; (08) 9039 3464. **See also:** Esperance & Nullarbor p. 328.

Mandurah Pop. 35 945

MAP REF. 376 B9, 384 C5, 386 C9

This popular holiday destination is on the coast, 74 km S of Perth. The Murray, Serpentine and Harvey rivers meet here, forming the vast inland waterway of Peel Inlet and the Harvey Estuary. This river junction was once a meeting site for Aboriginal groups who travelled here to barter; the town's name is derived from the Aboriginal word *Mandjar*, meaning trading place. Today the river and the Indian Ocean offer excellent yachting, boating, swimming, water-skiing and fishing. **In town:** Heritage Art and Historic Heritage walks, brochures available. Hall's Cottage (1832), Leighton Rd, a small whitewashed cottage (open Sun. p.m.). Christ Church (1870), cnr Pinjarra Rd and Sholl St, features hand-carved furniture. Community Museum, in old school building (1898), Pinjarra Rd (open Tues. and Sun.). Peel Discovery Centre, Mandurah Tce, interactive exhibition of the history and natural wonders of the region. Old Mandurah Traffic Bridge, cnr Mandurah Tce and Pinjarra Rd, excellent crabbing and fishing. Parrots in Bellawood Park, Furnissdale Rd. Estuary cruises depart information centre. Boat hire. Dolphins sometimes seen in estuary.

Waters also attract abundance of birdlife. King Carnival Amusement Park, in Hall Park (weekends and school holidays, a.m.). Jan.: Festival. Feb.: Crab Festival. **In the area:** At Halls Head, 3 km E: Peel Pottery and good beaches just over Old Mandurah Traffic Bridge. Mandurah Wreck Trail for divers; brochure available. Bavarian Castle Fun Park, Old Coast Rd, 2 km S. Further south, Dawesville Channel between inland waterways and ocean; good fishing from bridge. Erskine Conservation Park, 5 km S, features 1-km nature trail with boardwalk over wetlands. Bouvard Gallery at Melros, 15 km SW, sculptures depicting Australian folklore. In Yalgorup National Park, 45 km S: lakes incl. Clifton and Preston, long, narrow lakes parallel to coast; at Lake Pollard, black swans in summer. Wineries at Cape Bouvard, Mt John Rd (22 km S); Peel Estate and Baldivis Estate Winery, Fletcher Rd, Baldivis (20 km N). At Karnup, 12 km N, Linga Longa Park and Marapana Wildlife World, wildlife and recreation parks. Houseboat hire at South Yunderup, 12 km SE. Western Rosella Bird Park, 5 km E, has native birds in natural settings. Also 5 km E, Murray Mandurah Markets, weekends and Mon. public holidays. **Visitor information:** 75 Mandurah Tce; (08) 9550 3999. **See also:** The South-West p. 326.

Manjimup Pop. 4390

MAP REF. 380 D6, 384 D10, 386 D11

Fertile agricultural country and magnificent karri forests surround Manjimup, 307 km S of Perth. This is the commercial centre of the State's south-west and one of its most diversified horticultural regions. Fruit and vegetables are grown for the local and Asian markets; the area is well-known for its apples. Timber is the main industry, while wine, wool and dairy food are growing in importance. **In town:** Manjimup Regional Timber Park, cnr Edward and Rose sts: information centre; Blacksmith's Shop; Timber Museum with original sawmill steam loco; Age of Steam Museum; Historic Hamlet; Fire Tower Lookout; gallery and tearooms; picnic/barbecue facilities; timber tours. June: 15 000 Motocross. Nov.: Horticultural and Forestry Expo. **In the area:** Wildflowers Sept.–Nov. Abseiling, rock-climbing, bushcraft, horseriding adventures, horse-drawn picnic excursions, forest discovery tours and safari tours. Diamond Tree Fire Lookout, 9 km S, a 52-m-high karri tree in

use 1941–74 (can be climbed by visitors); nearby, children's adventure trail and picnic/ barbecue area. Swimming at Fonty's Pool, 10 km S, originally dammed in 1925 for irrigation; picnicking in landscaped surrounds. Collect walnuts and chestnuts in season (Apr.–May) at Fontanini's Nut Farm, next to Fonty's Pool. Tours of Bunnings Diamond Woodchip Mill, 12 km S. Black George's Winery and Alpaca Centre, 12 km S on South Western Hwy, features historic cottage, alpaca stud and wine-tasting. Nyamup, 20 km SE, old mill town redeveloped as a tourist village. Southern Wildflowers farm, 33 km SE at Quinninup. King Jarrah, 4 km E, a 47-m-high tree estimated to be 300–400 years old; heritage trail begins here. Perup Forest Ecology Centre, 50 km E, night spotlight walks to see rare, endangered and common native animals. Pioneer cairn, 9 km NE. Pioneer cemetery, 10 km NE. The 19-km round trip to Dingup, north-east of Manjimup, passes through farmland and forest; at Dingup, church (1896) and historic house (1870). Curragundi Wildlife Park, 2 km N (closed Tues.). One Tree Bridge, 22 km W, a karri tree felled in 1904 to cross Donnelly River; pleasant walk along river's edge to the Four Aces (four magnificent karri trees, 300–400 years old). Donnelly River Holiday Village, 28 km W, features horseriding and abundant wildlife. **Visitor information:** cnr Rose and Edward sts; (08) 9771 1831. **See also:** The South-West p. 326.

Marble Bar Pop. 318

MAP REF. 388 D2

Known as the hottest town in Australia because of its consistently high temperatures, Marble Bar lies 184 km SE of Port Hedland (approx. 60 km of road is unsealed). This typical WA outback town is named for the unique bar of red jasper that crosses the Coongan River, 4 km W of town. Alluvial gold was discovered at Marble Bar in 1891, and in 1931 at Comet Mine. Today the major industries are goldmining and pastoral production. **In town:** Government buildings (1895), General St, built using locally quarried stone. State Battery site (1910), Newman–Tabba Rd (not open to public). **In the area:** Beautiful scenery, especially in winter and after rain when spinifex country is transformed by flowering plants; rugged ranges, rolling plains, steep gorges and deep rock pools.

White sandy beaches are a feature of the Margaret River region

Jasper deposit at Marble Bar Pool, 4 km W. Nearby, Chinaman's Pool, an ideal picnic spot. Flying Fox Lookout, 6 km SW, spectacular when river is running. Corunna WW II RAAF Base, 40 km SE. Old goldmines at Nullagine, 111 km SE. Good swimming at Coppin's Gap, 68 km NE and Kitty's Gap, further 6 km. **Visitor information:** Marble Bar Travellers' Stop, Lot 232, Halse Rd; (08) 9176 1166. Web site www.pilbara.com **See also:** The Pilbara p. 334.

Margaret River   Pop. 2846

MAP REF. 377 C10, 379 C7, 384 A10, 386 B11

This pretty township is on the Margaret River near the coast, 280 km SW of Perth. The area is noted for its world-class wines, magnificent coastal scenery, excellent surfing beaches and spectacular cave formations. **In town:** Historic steam train in Rotary Park, Bussell Hwy; starting point for heritage walks, brochures available. On Bussell Hwy: Old Settlement Historical Museum; Margaret River Gallery; Margaret River Pottery. Melting Pot Glass Studio, Boodjidup Rd. Grange on Farrelly (1885), Farrelly St, inn and restaurant, formerly homestead. Mar.–Apr.: Margaret River Masters (surfing competition). **In the area:** Wineries incl. Cowaramup (10 km N)

and Willyabrup (20 km N); regional wine directory available. Leeuwin Estate Winery, 8 km S, has restaurant with contemporary Australian paintings and picnic/barbecue facilities; venue for Leeuwin Estate Concert each Feb.–Mar. Eagles Heritage, 5 km S, has large collection of birds of prey. Bellview Shell Museum, 6 km S at Witchcliffe. Boranup Gallery, 20 km S on Caves Rd, Boranup. Boranup Eco Walks, guided bushwalks through Leeuwin–Naturaliste National Park. Trout fishing and marron delicacies at Margaret River Marron Farm, 9 km SE. Pioneer Settlers Memorial, 14 km SE. The Berry Farm and Winery, 15 km SE. Cheese outlets on Bussell Hwy: Fonti's and Margaret River Cheese Factory, 4 km N. At Cowaramup, 10 km N: Margaret River Regional Wine Centre; Utopiary Studio for art and craft (closed Tues.); Cowaramup Pottery. Ellensbrook Homestead (1857), a National Trust property, 15 km NW. Prevelly, on coast 8 km W; Greek Chapel at Prevelly Park. Mammoth Cave, 21 km SW, features fossil remains of prehistoric animals; 4 km on is Lake Cave and CaveWorks, with dynamic working cave model, and boardwalk offering spectacular views of collapsed cavern. Other coastal areas incl. Gracetown, 15 km NW; Redgate, 10 km S; Hamelin Bay, 34 km S.

Augusta–Busselton, Margaret River and Hamelin Bay heritage trails, brochures available. Adventure tours offering abseiling, caving, dolphin-watching and canoeing; details from information centre. **Visitor information:** cnr Tunbridge Rd and Bussell Hwy; (08) 9757 2911. Web site www.margaretriver.wa.com **See also:** The South-West p. 326.

Meekatharra   Pop. 1270

MAP REF. 385 I11, 388 C12

Meekatharra lies 768 km NE of Perth on the Great Northern Hwy. Gold, copper and other minerals are mined in the area, and there are huge sheep and cattle stations. Meekatharra was once important as the railhead for cattle that had travelled overland from northern areas. **In town:** In Main St: State Battery relics; Royal Flying Doctor Service base (open 9 a.m.–2 p.m. Mon.–Fri.). School of the Air, High St (open to public during school terms 8 a.m.–10.30 a.m.). Old Courthouse, Darlot St. **In the area:** Old goldmining towns, relics of mining equipment, mine shafts; several mines, incl. Peak Hill (no access), have reopened. Peace Gorge (The Granites), 5 km N. Bilyuin Pool, 88 km NW, for swimming (no water in summer). Mt Gould, 156 km NW; nearby, restored police

Wheatfields near Merredin

station. Mt Augustus National Park, 360 km NW: Mt Augustus, a sandstone and quartz massif that rises out of arid shrubland; good walks and drives. **Visitor information:** Shire Offices, 54 Main St; (08) 9981 1002. Web site www.meekashire.wa.gov.au **See also:** Outback Coast & Mid-West p. 331.

Merredin

Pop. 2911

MAP REF. 384 I2, 386 F7

A main junction on the Kalgoorlie–Perth railway line, this important wheat centre is 259 km E of Perth. Merredin grew up as a shanty town as miners stopped on their way to the goldfields. Now, forty per cent of the State's wheat is grown within a 100-km radius of the town. **In town:** Cummins Theatre (1926), Bates St, oldest theatre outside Perth. Military Museum, East Barrack St: WW II collection; departure point for Merredin Peak Heritage Trail (self-guide drive or walk, brochure available) featuring wildflowers in season, and historical and geological sites. Old Railway Station Museum, Great Eastern Hwy. CBH wheat storage and transfer depot, Gamenya Ave, is largest horizontal storage depot in Southern Hemisphere, capacity 220 000 tonnes. Oct.: Vintage Car Festival (odd-numbered years). **In the area:** Pumping Station No. 4 (1902), 3 km W, designed by C. Y. O'Connor, a fine example of early industrial architecture; station closed

1960 to make way for electrically driven stations. Lookout over Edna May Goldmine, 32 km E at Westonia. At Kellerberrin, 55 km W: folk museum; scenic lookout at top of Kellerberrin Hill; Durakoppin Wildlife Sanctuary, 27 km N of Kellerberrin, and Gardner Flora Reserve, 35 km SW. Totadgin Dam Reserve, 16 km SW of Merredin; Totadgin Rock has wave formation similar to Wave Rock. At Bruce Rock, 50 km SW: museum, craft centre and Australia's smallest bank. Good views from summit of Kokerbin Rock, 90 km SW. Picnics and bushwalking near Hunts Dam, 5 km N. Lake Chandler, 45 km N. Mangowine Homestead, 40 km NW at Nungarin, a National Trust property. Museum, 140 km NW at Koorda; several wildlife reserves in vicinity. **Visitor information:** Barrack St; (08) 9041 1666. **See also:** The Heartlands p. 330.

Mingenew

Pop. 313

MAP REF. 386 B4

The little town of Mingenew is in the wheat district of the mid-west, 378 km N of Perth. **In town:** In Main St: Mingenew Hotel, a restored colonial building (c. 1900); Old Railway Station with local art and craft (check times). Heritage-listed Schools Inn B&B (c. 1900), William St. Museum, Victoria St, in original school building, displays pioneer relics (check times). Views of surrounding wheat-growing area from Mingenew

Hill lookout and Pioneer Memorial, off Mingenew–Mullewa Rd. Sept.: Lions Expo (incl. wildflower display). **In the area:** Wildflower walks, incl. spider orchids; brochure available. Picnic spots at Depot Hill, 15 km W. At Coalseam Conservation Park, 32 km NE, the State's first coal shafts; Irwin Gorge, riverbed rocks for rockhunters and wildflowers in spring. **Visitor information:** Schools Inn B&B, 26 William St; (08) 9928 1149. **See also:** Outback Coast & Mid-West p. 331.

Morawa

Pop. 692

MAP REF. 386 C4

Renowned for its grain harvests, Morawa is in the mid-west, 362 km N of Perth. The area has an abundance of wildflowers in spring. **In town:** In Prater St: Historical Museum (open by appt); St David's Anglican Church. Tiny Catholic church, Davis St, claimed to be smallest in world; part of Mons. Hawes Heritage Trail. **In the area:** Wildflower and historical walks and drives, brochures available. Gliding flights and lessons, book at information centre. Koolanooka Mine Site and Lookout, 19 km E. Koolanooka Springs Reserve, 24 km E, ideal for picnics. Bilya Rock Reserve, 5 km W, with 20-min walk around rock. **Visitor information:** Shire Council, Prater St; (08) 9971 1204. **See also:** Outback Coast & Mid-West p. 331.

Mount Barker

Pop. 1648

MAP REF. 381 M9, 384 H12, 386 E12

Situated in the Great Southern district of WA, Mount Barker is 360 km from Perth with the Stirling Range to the north and the Porongurups to the east. The area was visited by Europeans in 1829 and white settlers arrived in the 1830s. Vineyards were first established here in the late 1960s. Today, Mount Barker is a major wine-producing area. **In town:** On Albany Hwy: historic police station and gaol (1868), now museum (open Sat., Sun. and school holidays); Old Station House Craft Shop. Plantagenet Cottage Craft, Mt Barker Rd. Banksia Farm, western end of town (cnr Pearce and Marmion sts). Shire Art Gallery, Lowood Rd, exhibitions incl. work of local artists. Heritage trail, 30-km drive through town and surrounds; map available. Mar.: Machinery Field Day. **In the area:** Self-guide scenic and historical St Werburghs Way Tourist Drive, map available. About 10 wineries, details from information centre. Lookout on summit of Mt Barker,

5 km SW, pinpointed by 168-m-high television tower, has excellent views of Stirling Range across to Albany. St Werburgh's Chapel (1872), 12 km SW, a small privately owned mud-walled chapel overlooking Hay River Valley. Craft at Narrikup Country Store, 16 km S. At Porongurup, 24 km E: Porongurup National Park, features granite peaks, karri forests and seasonal wildflowers; Wine Summer Festival each Mar.; Wildflower Weekend each Oct. Tall peaks, picturesque plains and over 1000 species of native flora at Stirling Range National Park, 80 km NE. Historic town of Kendenup, 16 km N, location of WA's first gold find. **Visitor information:** 57 Lowood Rd; (08) 9851 1163. Web site www.comswest.net.au/~mtbarkwa **See also:** Great Southern p. 327.

Mount Magnet   Pop. 747

MAP REF. 386 E2

The goldmining town of Mount Magnet, a stopping-place for motorists driving north to Port Hedland, is in a pastoral farming area 562 km from Perth on the Great Northern Hwy. There are spectacular wildflowers in the area in spring. **In town:** Heritage walk, 1.4 km, brochure available. Pastoral Museum, Hepburn St, has pioneering and mining artifacts. **In the area:** Tourist drive (37 km) incl. views of old open-cut goldmine from lookout, and takes in The Granites and various ghost towns; map available. Fossicking for gemstones, *but take care as there are dangerous old mine shafts in the area.* The Granites, 7 km N, has Aboriginal rock art and picnic spot nearby. Ghost town of Lennonville, 11 km N. Near Sandstone, 166 km E: The Brewery, a historic constructed cave formerly used for beer storage; London Bridge, a rock formation. **Visitor information:** Hepburn St; (08) 9963 4172. **See also:** Outback Coast & Mid-West p. 331.

Mullewa   Pop. 591

MAP REF. 386 B3

Gateway to the Murchison goldfields, Mullewa is 99 km NE of Geraldton. **In town:** Kembla Zoo, Stock Rd. In Maitland Rd: Our Lady of Mount Carmel Church; Monsignor John C. Hawes Priesthouse Museum. Water Supply Reserve, Lovers La., features native plants. Aug.: Wildflower Show; Agricultural Show. **In the area:** Mons.

Hawes Heritage Trail (drive then walk), begins at signboard in Jose St and extends through the Mid-West and Murchison. Waterfalls after heavy rain, 5 km N near airport. Tallering Peak and Gorge, 58 km N, has spectacular wildflowers in spring. At Wooleen Station, near Murchison, 202 km N, accommodation in shearers' quarters or National Trust-listed homestead. Bindoo Hill Glacier Bed, 40 km NW. Tenindewa Pioneer Well (1900s), a stone-lined well, 18 km W. Butterabby grave site, 18 km S, burial-place of Aboriginial people hanged there after clash with European settlers. St Mary's Agricultural School, 40 km SE near Tardun. Tallering Station, 40 km NE: gallery featuring Aboriginal and other local art and craft; accommodation; camping (open Apr.–Oct.). **Visitor information:** Jose St; (08) 9961 1505 (May–Nov.) or Shire Offices, cnr Padbury and Thomas sts; (08) 9961 1007. **See also:** Outback Coast & Mid-West p. 331.

Mundaring   Pop. 1912

MAP REF. 376 E4, 386 C8

Mundaring is situated on the Great Eastern Hwy, 34 km E of Perth. The picturesque Mundaring Weir is the water source for the goldfields 500 km to the east. The original dam was opened in 1903. The hilly bush setting makes the weir a popular picnic spot. **In town:** Fred Jacoby Park, Mundaring Weir Rd, has picnic/barbecue facilities. Sculpture Park, Jacoby St, with sculptures by WA artists. Arts Centre, Great Eastern Hwy, has program of varied exhibitions. Apr.: Mundaring Hills Festival. **In the area:** Several heritage trails, incl. Farming Heritage Trail and John Forrest Heritage Trail. Lake Leschenaultia, 12 km NW: swimming; canoeing; walks; camping; picnic/barbecue facilities; miniature scenic railway on shore. Walyunga National Park, 30 km NW: beautiful bushland and wildflowers; Avon Descent, a major white-water canoeing event, here each Aug. Old Mahogany Inn (1842), 3 km W, WA's oldest residential inn. Mount Olive Stained Glass Studio, 6 km W. John Forrest National Park, 6 km W, on high point of Darling Range: views; picnic spot beside natural pool at Rocky Pool. Quatre Sessions Heritage Rose Garden, 9 km W, one of State's largest private collections. At Darlington, 10 km W: Darling Estate Winery, Nelson Rd (open Thurs.–Sun.); Arts Festival held each Nov. At Mundaring Weir, 8 km S: C. Y. O'Connor Museum

(1880s), housed in former pumphouse, depicts the mammoth project of connecting the weir to the goldfields; features models of pipeline. Nearby, Hills Forest Activity Centre offers activities such as abseiling and bushcraft, and performances by Aboriginal dance groups and bush bands (details at information centre). Kalamunda National Park, 23 km S, has walking trails through jarrah forest, incl. first section of the 963-km Bibbulmun Track. History Village, nearby at Kalamunda, a collection of historic buildings (open Sat.–Thurs.). A further 6 km S, Lesmurdie Falls National Park: spectacular falls drop over Darling Escarpment; good views of Perth and Rottnest Island. Carosa Vineyard, 7 km E at Mount Helena (open Sat. and Sun.). **Visitor information:** The Old School, 7225 Great Eastern Hwy; (08) 9295 0202. Web site www.mundaring tourism.com.au **See also:** Darling Range & Swan Valley p. 325.

Nannup   Pop. 521

MAP REF. 377 G10, 380 A4, 384 C10, 386 C11

Nannup is in the Blackwood Valley, 290 km S of Perth. The countryside is lush, rolling pasture alongside jarrah and pine forests. **In town:** Heritage trail (2.5 km) and river walk, brochures available. In Brockman St: Old Police Station (1922), now information centre and surrounded by Blythe Family Gardens; Arboretum (planted 1926). In Warren Rd: Bunnings Timber Mill, largest jarrah sawmill in State (tours Mon., Wed. and Fri.); Nannup Temptations and Crafty Creations, for jarrah goods; Old Templemore Antique Shop, converted historic house, specialises in antique tools; Gemstone Museum (closed Wed.). Blackwood Winery. Market 2nd Sat. each month, Warren Rd. Mar.: Music Festival. Aug.: Flower and Garden Month. **In the area:** Self-guide wildflower (in spring), waterfall (in winter) and forest walks; scenic drives through jarrah forest and pine plantations, including 40-km Blackwood Scenic Drive; brochures available. Blackwood River for camping, swimming, canoeing and trout fishing. Hillbrook tulip farm, 1 km S (open July–Sept.). Carlotta Crustaceans marron farm, 14 km S off Vasse Hwy. Donnelly River Wines, 45 km S. Barrabup Pool, 10 km W, largest of a number of pools, ideal for swimming and fishing. Tathra, 14 km NE, fruit winery and restaurant.

Visitor information: 4 Brockman St; (08) 9756 1211. Web site richie.comp. west.net.au/~nannuptb **See also:** The South-West p. 326.

Narrogin   Pop. 4491

MAP REF. 384 G6, 386 E9

The centre of prosperous agricultural country, Narrogin is 192 km SE of Perth on the Great Southern Hwy. Sheep, pigs and cereal farms are the major industries. The town's name is derived from an Aboriginal word *gnarojin*, meaning waterhole. **In town:** In Egerton St: History Hall, with local history collection; Courthouse Museum (1894), originally a school, later district courthouse (open Mon.–Sat. or by appt). Foxes Lair, Williams Rd, 45 ha of bushland. Lions Lookout, Kipling St, for excellent views. In Federal St: Gallery (open Feb.–Nov.); Restoration Group Museum, displays cars, stationary engines and other machinery (check times). Gnarojin Park, in town centre next to Narrogin Brook: picnic/barbecue facilities; pathway marked with 100 locally designed commemorative tiles relating local history, brochure available. Jan.: State Gliding Championships. Oct.: Spring Festival; Agricultural Show; Orchid Show. **In the area:** Heritage trail, brochure available. Yilliminning and Birdwhistle rocks, 11 km E, unusual rock formations. Dryandra Woodland, 30 km NW, features walking trails and fauna incl. numbats and mallee fowl; 'Sounds of Dryandra' (tune into 100 FM for information at signposted 'radio stops'), features information on Aboriginal culture and local wildlife; map available. **Visitor information:** cnr Earl and Egerton sts; (08) 9881 2064. **See also:** The Heartlands p. 330.

New Norcia   Pop. 75

MAP REF. 384 D1, 386 C6

In 1846 Spanish Benedictine monks established a mission at New Norcia, 132 km N of Perth in the secluded Moore Valley, in an attempt to help the local Aboriginal population. The handsome Spanish-inspired buildings come as a surprise, surrounded by farms and bushland. New Norcia still operates as a monastery and is Australia's only monastic town. Visitors may join the monks at daily prayers. **In town:** Self-guide heritage trail (2 km), incl. inspection of oldest operating flour mill in WA (1879)

(mill has interpretive display), abbey church, cemetery, hotel (1927), Bishops Well, Rosendo Salvado Statue; or guided 2-hr tour of town; guide booklet available. Benedictine community's Museum and Art Gallery, Great Northern Hwy, has priceless religious art, both Australian and European, and Spanish artifacts (many the gifts of Queen Isabella of Spain); museum displays history of monks' involvement with indigenous population; shop sells local food products, incl. olive oil pressed at the monastery. Group accommodation for up to 250 in old convent and college buildings (advance bookings required). Daily tours of monastery, incl. interiors. Salvado Restaurant, in Roadhouse, Great Northern Hwy, style resembles monastery refectory. **In the area:** At Mogumber, 24 km SW, one of State's highest timber and concrete bridges. Historic hotel at Bolgart, 49 km SE. Former Wyening Mission, 50 km SE, a historic site (open by appt, inquire at information centre). Piawaning, 31 km NE, has magnificent stand of eucalypts north of town. **Visitor information:** Museum and Art Gallery, Great Northern Hwy; (08) 9654 8056. Web site www.newnorcia.wa.edu.au **See also:** The Heartlands p. 330.

Newman   Pop. 4790

MAP REF. 388 D6

This town was built by Mt Newman Mining Co. for employees involved in the extraction of iron ore. Mt Newman ships its ore from Port Hedland; a 426-km railway connects the towns. In 1981 the town became part of the local shire. **In town:** Mt Whaleback Mine, largest iron ore open-cut mine in world, tours depart from information centre Mon.– Sat. At information centre: BHP Iron Ore Silver Jubilee Museum and Gallery, mining museum. Radio Hill Lookout, off Newman Dr., good views over town; walking trail and climb from museum to lookout. Aug.: Camp Draft and Rodeo; Fortescue Festival. **In the area:** Opthalmia Dam, 15 km N, for swimming; picnic/barbecue facilities. Good views from Mt Newman, 20 km NW. Kalgans Pool, 51 km NW (daytrip, 4WD access only). Eagle Rock Falls, 69 km NW, has permanent pools and picnic spots nearby (road to falls requires 4WD). Aboriginal rock carvings, rock pools and waterholes at Punda (4WD only, 75 km NW), Wanna Munna (70 km W), and Weeli Wolli (90 km W).

Visitor information: cnr Fortescue Ave and Newman Dr.; (08) 9175 2888. Web site www.pilbara.com **See also:** The Pilbara p. 334.

Norseman   Pop. 1516

MAP REF. 387 J8

Norseman, 195 km S of Kalgoorlie, is the last large town on the Eyre Hwy for travellers heading east towards SA. Gold put Norseman on the map in the early 1890s with one of the richest quartz reefs in Australia. The town is steeped in goldmining history, reflected in its colossal tailings dumps. The area is popular with amateur prospectors and gemstone collectors; gemstone fossicking permits are available from information centre. **In town:** Historical Collection, Battery Rd, incl. mining tools and household items. Heritage Mining Park, Prinsep St, open-plan park with displays, stream and picnic facilities. Post office (1896), cnr Prinsep and Ramsay sts. Heritage trail (33 km), follows Cobb & Co. route, incl. a graduated descent into the old Iron Duke Mine site. In Roberts St: statue commemorating horse called Norseman, who allegedly pawed the ground and unearthed a nugget of gold, thus starting a gold rush in area; Dollykissangel, toy museum. Beacon Hill Lookout, Mines Rd, offers good views of surrounding salt lakes (spectacular at sunrise and sunset). **In the area:** Dundas Rocks, 22 km S, over 2 million years old; excellent picnic area and old Dundas town site nearby. Bromus Dam, 32 km S, freshwater dam with picnic area nearby. In Peak Charles National Park, 50 km S then 40 km W off hwy: Peak Charles; good-weather track for experienced walkers and climbers to Peak Eleanora; magnificent views. Gemstone leases on Eyre Hwy and off Kalgoorlie Hwy. Mt Jimberlana, 5 km E of town, walking trail to summit and views. Buldania Rocks, 28 km E, has picnic area and beautiful spring wildflowers. To south-west, Frank Hann National Park, 50 km E of Lake King township, traversed by Lake King–Norseman Rd; check road conditions before departure; no visitor facilities or supplies between Norseman and Lake King. Cave Hill Nature Reserve, 55 km N, then 50 km W (on unsealed road, exercise care, especially when wet): spectacular granite outcrops, caves, waterholes, wildlife. **Visitor information:** 68 Roberts St; (08) 9039 1071. Web site www.kalgoorlieandwagoldfields.com.au **See also:** The Goldfields p. 329.

Northam
Pop. 6300

MAP REF. 376 H2, 384 E3, 386 D7

The regional centre of the fertile Avon Valley at the junction of the Avon and Mortlock rivers, Northam is on the Great Eastern Hwy 99 km E of Perth. Settled in 1836, it is now an important supply point for the eastern wheat belt and a major railway centre. **In town:** In Wellington St: Old police station (1866); courthouse (1896); town hall (1897); Avon Valley Arts Society Gallery. Flour Mill (1871), Newcastle St. In Fitzgerald St: Old Railway Station Museum (open Sun.); Shamrock Hotel (1886), fully renovated. At information centre, Heaton Ave, WW II migrant exhibition. Footbridge over Avon River, adjacent to information centre, one of the longest swing bridges in Australia. White swans and much native birdlife can be seen between Peel Tce bridge and weir. Morby Cottage (1836), Old York Rd, Northam's first house, built by the pioneer Morrells (open Sun.). National Trust-classified Sir James Mitchell House (1905), cnr Duke and Hawes sts. Northam–Katrine Heritage Trail, history of early settlers in town, brochure available. Aug.: Avon Descent (white-water classic); Avon River Festival. Oct.: Multicultural Festival. **In the area:** Muresk University of Technology, 10 km S, former early farming property. At Meckering, 35 km E, huge fault line resulting from 1968 earthquake. Hot-air ballooning Apr.–Nov., Northam Airfield, 2 km NE. Aronbrook Valley Winery at Clackline, 19 km NE, open for tastings (by appt). At Dowerin, 70 km NE: museum; craft centre; Hagbooms Lake; Field Days here in Aug. Avonlea Alpaca Tourist Farm, 12 km NW (check opening times). **Visitor information:** Minson Ave; (08) 9622 2100. **See also:** The Heartlands p. 330.

Northampton
Pop. 842

MAP REF. 386 A3

Northampton is a heritage-listed town nestled in the valley of Nokarena Brook, 51 km N of Geraldton. Inland there is picturesque country with vivid wildflowers in spring. The drive west leads to the coast, with beaches for swimming and fishing. **In town:** Heritage Walk, brochure available. In Hampton Rd: Chiverton House Museum (open Thurs.–Mon.); Old Convent, now heritage

Karri forest near Northcliffe

accommodation, and Church of Our Lady in Ara Coeli, designed by Mons. Hawes. Gwalla church site and cemetery, Gwalla St. Miners' cottages (1860s), Brook St. Market at Kings Park, cnr Essex St and Hampton Rd, 1st Sat. each month. Sept.: Agricultural Show. Oct.: Airing of the Quilts (quilts hung in main street, raffle and judging). **In the area:** Wildflower tours in spring. Alma School House (1915), 12 km N. Near coast at Gregory, 47 km NW: Lynton Station, incl. ruins of labour-hiring depot for convicts (in use 1853–56); Lynton House, (not open to public), a squat building with slits for windows, probably erected as protection from hostile Aboriginal people; Sanford House (1853). Hutt Lagoon, near Gregory, appears pink in midday sun. At Horrocks Beach, 20 km W, pleasant bays, sandy beaches, good fishing and surfing. **Visitor information:** Hampton Rd; (08) 9934 1488. **See also:** Outback Coast & Mid-West p. 331.

Northcliffe
Pop. 239

MAP REF. 380 C9, 384 D12, 386 D12

Magnificent virgin karri forests surround the little township of Northcliffe, 31 km S of Pemberton in the State's south-west corner. Unique flora and fauna is found here. **In town:** In Wheatley Coast Rd: Pioneer Museum, has historical relics and photographs; at information centre, large rock and mineral collection, Aboriginal Interpretation Room, and photographic folio of native flora and birds; Northcliffe Art and Craft. South West Timber Trekking Company, off Wheatley Coast Rd, offers horseriding along forest tracks. Mountain-bike hire, contact information centre. Oct.: Mountain-bike Championship. **In the area:** Pemberton Tramway, tramcars based on 1907 Fremantle trams operate daily in summer through tall-forest country between Northcliffe and Pemberton; depart from information centre. Adjacent to town, Forest Park has Hollow Butt Karri and Twin Karri walking trails, and picnic areas. Warren River, 8 km N, trout fishing and sandy beaches. Petrene Estate Vineyard, 2 km E, has sales. Mt Chudalup, 10 km S, a giant granite outcrop with walking trail to summit for views. Point D'Entrecasteaux, 27 km S; cliffs popular with rock climbers. Windy Harbour and Salmon Beach, 27 km S. Bibbulmun Track links the 3 national parks: D'Entrecasteaux (5 km S), Warren (20 km NW) and Shannon (30 km E). The Great Forest Trees Drive (48 km) through

Shannon National Park, east of town; picnic spots and signposted walks in park, brochure available. Boorara Tree (once a fire lookout) and Lane–Poole Falls, 18 km SE. **Visitor information:** Wheatley Coast Rd; (08) 9776 7203. **See also:** The South-West p. 326.

Onslow
Pop. 588

MAP REF. 385 D3

Onslow, on the north-west coast, is the base for off-shore gas and oil fields. The town, originally at the Ashburton River mouth,was moved to Beadon Bay in 1925 after cyclones caused the river to silt up. Onslow was a bustling pearling centre and in the 1890s gold was discovered. During WW II, submarines refuelled here, and the town was bombed twice. In 1952 it was the mainland base for Britain's nuclear experiments at Montebello Islands. **In town:** Ian Blain Memorial Walkway, a signposted scenic walk; map available. Heritage trail, brochure available. Goods Shed Museum, Second Ave, items of historical interest. Karijini Aboriginal Corporation, Third Ave, art gallery. **In the area:** Remains of old town site, 48 km SW, brochure available. Excellent fishing; boat charters to Mackerel and Montebello islands June–Sept. Native fauna, including emus, red kangaroos, sand goannas and a variety of birdlife. Sturt's desert pea and Ashburton pea are among the many spring wildflowers. Termite mounds, 10 km S on Onslow Access Rd, with interpretive display. **Visitor information:** Second Ave; (08) 9184 6644 or Shire Offices, Second Ave; (08) 9184 6001. Web site www.pilbara.com **See also:** The Pilbara p. 334.

Pemberton
Pop. 994

MAP REF. 380 C7, 384 D11, 386 C11

Pemberton, 335 km S of Perth, is in a quiet valley surrounded by karri forests with some of the tallest hardwood trees in the world and, in spring, brilliant flowering plants. It is a centre for high-quality woodcraft. **In town:** Craft outlets incl. Peter Kovacsy Studio, in Jamieson St; Fine Woodcraft Gallery, Dickinson St. In Brockman St: Karri Visitors Centre, incl. museum with collection of historic photographs and forestry equipment, and Karri Forest Discovery Centre; Pemberton Sawmill (tours Mon.–Fri.). Pemberton Tramway, tramcars based on 1907 Fremantle trams, operate daily through tall-forest country between Pemberton and Northcliffe; depart from railway station, Railway Cres.; steam train Easter–Nov., runs weekends and holidays. On Pump Hill Rd: Forest Park and Pool, offers walking trails and picnic spots; Trout and Marron Hatchery, supplies WA rivers and dams, tours available. **In the area:** Forest Industry tours into logging and regrowth areas; walking trails; scenic bus tours; 4WD adventure tours; horseriding; fishing in rivers (inland fishing licence required for trout and marron); self-guide forest drives. About 28 wineries; many offer tours, tastings and sales, incl. Warren Vineyard, Conte Rd; Gloucester Ridge, Burma Rd; Mountford Wines, Bamess Rd; Salitage, Vasse Hwy. Moon's Crossing, 18 km SE, for picnics (4WD access in winter). In Gloucester National Park, 1 km S: The Cascades for picnics, bushwalking and fishing; Gloucester Tree, signposted off Brockman St, tallest fire lookout in world (over 61 m high with 153 rungs spiralling upwards), open for climbing during daylight. Brockman Saw Pit, 13 km S, restored to show timber-sawing in 1860s. King Trout Farm, 8 km SW. Warren National Park, 9 km SW: some of the best accessible virgin karri forest; Marianne North Tree (subject of painting by artist); Dave Evans Bicentennial Tree, lookout tree with picnic facilities and walking tracks nearby. Eagle Springs marron farm, 18 km W. Nearby, Beedelup National Park: falls; suspension bridge; magnificent wildflowers in spring; giant karri tree with a hole cut through it. Donnelly River Wines, 35 km NW. Lavender and Berry Farm, 4 km N, off Vasse Hwy. Big Brook Dam and Arboretum, 7 km N. Founders Forest, 10 km N on Smiths Rd, has karri re-growth trees over 120 years old. Rosebank Cottage Crafts, 4 km NE, off Vasse Hwy. Piano Gully Vineyard, 24 km NE, off South Western Hwy. **Visitor information:** Karri Visitors Centre, Brockman St; (08) 9776 1133, freecall 1800 671 133. Web site www.pembertontourist.com.au **See also:** The South-West p. 326.

Perenjori
Pop. 600

MAP REF. 386 C4

Located on the Wubin–Mullewa Rd, 352 km NE of Perth, Perenjori is on the fringes of the Murchison goldfields and the great sheep stations of the west. **In town:** Historical Museum and Tourist Bureau, Fowler St (open July–Oct., closed Sun.). Historic Catholic Church, Carnamah Rd, designed by Mons. Hawes. Aug.: Bush Bouquet Craft Festival. Sept.: Agricultural Show. **In the area:** Wildflowers in season (July–Sept.), especially near Wubin, 85 km S. Numerous scenic drives, brochures available. Perenjori–Rothsay Heritage Trail (180 km), recalls early goldmining days. Many gemstones for fossickers in this mineral-rich region. Goldmines in surrounding area (4WD access only); *take care as unfenced pits make the area dangerous.* Aboriginal Stones at Damperwah Soak, 40 km NE (4WD access only). Salt lakes with variety of waterbirds, incl. Mongers Lake (lookout near lake), 50 km NE. **Visitor information:** Fowler St (July–Oct.); (08) 9973 1105. **See also:** Outback Coast & Mid-West p. 331.

Pingelly
Pop. 756

MAP REF. 384 F5, 386 D9

On the Great Southern Hwy, 154 km SE of Perth, Pingelly is part of the central southern farming district. The cutting of sandalwood was once a local industry, but today sheep and wheat are the major produce. **In town:** In Parade St: Community Craft Centre; Courthouse Museum. Apex Lookout, Stone St, for fine views of town and country. Mar.: Autumn Alternative Agricultural Show. Aug.: Art and Tulip Festival. **In the area:** At Moorumbine, 10 km E: Heritage Trail, 1-hr walk; historic St Patrick's Church (1873). Tuttanning Flora and Fauna Reserve, 21 km E. Pingelly Heights Observatory, 4 km SE. **Visitor information:** Shire Offices, 17 Queen St; (08) 9887 1066. **See also:** The Heartlands p. 330.

Pinjarra
Pop. 1892

MAP REF. 376 C10, 384 C6, 386 C9

A pleasant drive 84 km S of Perth along the shaded South Western Hwy brings the visitor to Pinjarra, which has a picturesque setting on the Murray River. The Alcoa Refinery, north-east of town on the South Western Hwy, is the largest alumina refinery in Australia. **In town:** Pinjarrah Heritage Trail, 30-min river walk featuring historic sites and buildings. In Henry St: St John's Church (1862), made of mud bricks; Heritage Rose Garden, incl. war memorial; Liveringa (1874), early home of McLarty family; Old School (1896); Teacher's House. Edenvale (1888), George St, house built by McLarty family, now restored:

information centre; arts and crafts; tearoom. Suspension bridge across the Murray River, picnic facilities on either side. **In the area:** Hotham Valley Tourist Railway, steam-train rides Pinjarra–Dwellingup each Wed. May–Oct. Alcoa Scarp Lookout, 14 km E, for good views of coastal plain, surrounding farming area and Alcoa Refinery. Athlone Angora Stud and Goat Farm, 16 km E. Alcoa Refinery, 4 km NE (bus tours Wed.). At North Dandalup, 10 km NE, Whittakers Mill, for bushwalking, camping and barbecues. North Dandalup Dam, 16 km N then 6 km E: coastal views from lookout; recreation lake and picnic area. Award-winning Tumbulgum Farm, 38 km N at Mundijong, features native and farm animals, Aboriginal culture, farm shows and WA products sales. Old Blythewood (1860s), 4 km S, a former post office, coaching inn and family home (check opening times). Lake Navarino Forest Resort and Waroona Dam, 33 km S, for water sports, fishing, walking and horseriding. **Visitor information:** Edenvale, George St; (08) 9531 1438. **See also:** The South-West p. 326.

Port Hedland

Pop. 12 846

MAP REF. 388 C1, 390 B13

Port Hedland's remarkable growth has been due to the iron ore boom, starting in the early 1960s. The town was named after Capt. Peter Hedland, who reached the harbour in 1863. Today Port Hedland handles the largest iron ore export tonnage of any Australian port. Iron ore from some of the world's biggest mines is loaded on to huge ore carriers. The 2.6-km-long trains operated by BHP Iron Ore arrive 9 times daily. Salt production is another major industry, with about 2 million tonnes exported per annum. **In town:** Self-guide historic town walk/drive, brochure available. Town tour Mon., Wed., Fri., numbers permitting. Observation Tower, at information centre, Wedge St. Lions Park, cnr Athol and Darlots sts, has pioneer relics. BHP industrial tours (Mon.–Fri.); book at information centre. Don Rhodes Mining Museum, Wilson St. At Two Mile Ridge, opp. fire brigade in Wilson St, Aboriginal carvings in limestone ridge (key from Aboriginal Affairs, open Mon.–Fri.). Historic St Matthew's Church (1917), Edgar St, view by appt. Old Port Hedland cemetery, Stevens St, has graves of early gold prospectors and Japanese pearl divers. Markets, Wedge St, 2nd Fri. each

month (evenings). June: Black Rock Stakes (wheelbarrow race, stalls and street party). Aug.: Spinifex Spree. **In the area:** Stairway to the Moon, a natural wonder, when full moon rises over shoreline at low tide; best alongside caravan park at Cooke Point. Picnic, fish and swim at Pretty Pool, next to Cooke Point Caravan Park. *Poisonous stone fish frequent coast, especially Nov.–Mar.; make local inquiries before swimming in sea.* At Cargill Salt, 8 km S, giant cone-shaped mounds of salt awaiting export. At airport, 15 km S: Royal Flying Doctor Service Base, open to public 9 a.m.–1.p.m. Mon.–Fri.; School of the Air, visitors welcome, a.m. only. Whale-watching trips June–Oct.; scenic harbour and sunset cruises. Excellent fishing; charter boat hire. Birdlife is abundant; watch for bustards, eagles, herons, cockatoos, galahs, ibises, pelicans and a variety of parrots. **Visitor information:** 13 Wedge St; (08) 9173 1711. Web site www.pilbara.com **See also:** The Pilbara p. 334.

Ravensthorpe

Pop. 354

MAP REF. 386 H10

Ravensthorpe, situated 533 km SE of Perth, is the centre of the Phillips River Goldfield. Copper mining reached a peak in the late 1960s; the last copper mine shut in 1972. Many old mine shafts

can be seen around the district. Wheat, sheep and mixed farming are the local industries. **In town:** Historic buildings: Anglican Church, Dunn St; Old Mine Manager's House, Carlisle St. In Morgans St: Dance Cottage (museum); Palace Hotel; restored Commercial Hotel (now Community Centre). Also in Morgans St, Rangeview Park features local plant species. Sept.: Wildflower Show, features over 700 local species. **In the area:** Scenic drives, brochures available. Rock-collecting, check locally to avoid trespass. Ravensthorpe Range, 3 km N, and Mt Desmond, 10 km SE, for views. WA Time Meridian at first rest bay west of town. Eremia Camel Farm, 2 km SE, offers rides and bush tucker. Old copper smelter, 3 km SE. Fitzgerald River National Park, 46 km S, now Biosphere Reserve for UNESCO. **Visitor information:** Morgans St; (08) 9838 1277. Web site www.wn.com.au/ourstate/goldfields.htm **See also:** Esperance & Nullarbor p. 328.

Rockingham

Pop. 49 917

MAP REF. 376 B7, 384 C4, 386 C8

At the southern end of Cockburn Sound, 47 km S of Perth, Rockingham is a coastal city and seaside destination. Established in 1872 as a timber port, the harbour fell into disuse with the opening of the Fremantle inner harbour in 1897. Today

Cargill Salt near Port Hedland

its magnificent golden beaches and protected waters are Rockingham's main attraction. **In town:** Museum, Kent St, features local history exhibits. In Civic Blvd.: Art Gallery; Art and Craft Centre. The Granary, Rockingham Rd, northern outskirts of town, displays history of WA's grain industry (tours by appt). At nearby Kwinana Beach: hull of wrecked SS *Kwinana*; jetskiing (jetskis for hire). Lookout and WW II coastal battery at Cape Peron, Point Peron Rd. Mersey Point Jetty at Shoalwater, departure point for cruises and island tours. Markets Sun., Flinders La. Nov.: Spring Festival. Dec.: Christmas Regatta; Cockburn Yachting Regatta. **In the area:** Penguin Island, has a colony of little (fairy) penguins; Penguin Experience Island Discovery Centre (open Sept.–May). Three Island Tour to Penguin, Seal and Bird islands. Garden Island, home to HMAS *Stirling*, naval base; access by private boat during the day (causeway link to mainland closed to public). Offshore reefs and wrecks, popular with dive enthusiasts; diving excursions and cruises available. Shoalwater Bay Islands Marine Park, extends from just south of Garden Island to Becher Point; cruises of park, incl. swim-with-dolphins tours (Oct.–May). Near Lake Richmond, 4 km SW, walks, freshwater flora and fauna, and domed thrombalites (unlayered stromatolites). Sloan's Cottage (1911), 2 km W at Leda, restored pioneer cottage (open Mon.–Fri.). Marapana Wildlife World, 15 km S, drive-through deer and wildlife park. Wineries: Baldivis Estate, 15 km SE; Peel Estate, 17 km SE. Scenic drive 48 km SE to Serpentine Dam, WA's major water conservation area; brilliant wildflowers in spring; gardens; bushland; nearby, Serpentine Falls. WA Water Ski Park, at Baldivis, 5 km E, constructed water-ski complex. Self-guide Nature Reserve Environmental Walk, nearby at Karnup; brochure available. Tumblegum Farm, 29 km E at Mundijong: Aboriginal culture; native and farm animals; farm shows; WA product sales. Old Rockingham and Rockingham–Jarrahdale heritage trails. **Visitor information:** 43 Kent St; (08) 9592 3464. **See also:** The South-West p. 326.

Roebourne
Pop. 958

MAP REF. 385 G1, 388 A2

Named after John Septimus Roe, the State's first surveyor-general, Roebourne was established in 1864 and is the oldest town on the north-west coast. It was developed as the north-west's capital. As the centre for the early mining and pastoral industries in The Pilbara, it was connected, by tramway, to the pearling port of Cossack, and later to Point Samson, for the transport of passengers and goods. **In town:** Old stone buildings (some National Trust-classified): police station, Queen St; post office (1887), Sholl St; in Hampton St, hospital (1887) and courthouse (1887); Holy Trinity Church (1894), Withnell St; in Roe St, Union Bank (1889) and Victoria Hotel (1866), last of town's five original pubs; Old Roebourne Gaol (1886), Queen St, now information centre and museum. Good views from Mt Welcome, Fisher Dr. Aug.: Royal Show; Roebourne Cup and Ball. **In the area:** Emma Withnell Heritage Trail (52 km), historical drive taking in Roebourne, Cossack and Point Samson; brochure available. Wickham, 12 km N, Robe River Iron Associates company town: processes and exports Pannawonica iron ore; tour of plant, port (at Cape Lambert) and historic Cossack departs from information centre, bookings essential. Wickham Expo here in May. Cossack (once called Tien Tsin), 14 km N: first port in the north-west; ghost town, but almost completely restored; historic buildings (open Apr.–Christmas); interesting cemetery; boat hire; Cossack Art Awards held July. Point Samson, 19 km N: good swimming, fishing and skindiving; fishing trawlers moored here; boat ramp; boat hire and fishing charter; offshore game-fishing. Fishing at Cleaverville, 25 km N. In Millstream–Chichester National Park, 150 km S: safe swimming in Chinderwarriner Pool; walking trails; old homestead now information centre. **Visitor information:** Old Gaol, Queen St; (08) 9182 1060. Web site www.pilbara. com **See also:** The Pilbara p. 334.

Southern Cross
Pop. 1147

MAP REF. 386 G7

A small, flourishing town on the Great Eastern Hwy, 368 km E of Perth, Southern Cross is the centre of a prosperous agricultural and pastoral region and a significant gold-producing area. The town's wide streets allowed camel trains to turn, and were named after stars and constellations. **In town:** First courthouse in eastern goldfields (1893), Antares St, now a history museum. Other historic buildings: post office (1891), Antares St; Railway Tavern (1890s), Spica St. Restored Palace Hotel (1912), Orion St. Sept.: Agricultural Show. **In the area:** Wildflowers on sand plains in spring. Goldmining activities at Marvel Loch (35 km S), and Bullfinch (36 km N). Hunt's Soak, 7 km N, a picnic area. Koolyanobbing, 52 km N, built for miners extracting iron ore; mining of the rich iron ore recommenced in 1994 following closure in 1983. Interesting rock formations with ideal picnic areas at Frog Rock (30 km S), and Baladjie Rock (50 km NW). **Visitor information:** Great Eastern Hwy; (08) 9049 1001. **See also:** The Heartlands p. 330.

Tom Price
Pop. 3872

MAP REF. 385 H4, 388 B5

The huge iron-ore deposit now known as Mt Tom Price was discovered in 1962, after which the Hamersley Iron Project was established. A mine, 2 towns (Dampier and Tom Price) and a railway between the towns all followed. Today the town is an oasis in the dry countryside. The nearby Karijini National Park, and a chance to tour an open-cut mining operation make the town a popular stopping-place. Aug.: Nameless Festival. **In the area:** Hamersley Iron open-cut iron ore mine, tours departing from information centre, Central Rd. In Karijini National Park, 50 km E: Dales Gorge, with permanent waterfalls; Kalamina Gorge and Pool, the most accessible gorge; Joffre, Hancock, Weano and Red gorges join below Oxer Lookout; Hamersley Gorge, with permanent pools for swimming and coloured folds in rock; trail with interpretive signs on Aboriginal heritage and flora and fauna winds up to Mt Bruce; camping. *To the north-east is Wittenoom, an old asbestos mining town. While the mine was closed in 1966, there is still a health risk from microscopic asbestos fibres present in the abandoned mine tailings in and around Wittenoom. If disturbed and inhaled, blue asbestos dust may cause cancer. The Ashburton Shire Council advocates avoidance of the Wittenoom area.* Kings Lake, 2 km W, constructed lake; nearby, park with picnic/barbecue facilities. Good views of district around Tom Price from Mt Nameless Lookout, 6 km W, via walking trail or 4WD track. Aboriginal carvings, 10 km S. **Visitor information:** Central Rd; (08) 9188 1112. Web site www.pilbara.com **See also:** The Pilbara p. 334.

Toodyay
Pop. 674

MAP REF. 376 G1, 384 E2, 386 D7

The National Trust-classified town of Toodyay is nestled in the Avon Valley, 85 km NE of Perth, and surrounded by picturesque farming country and virgin bushland. **In town:** Many historic buildings in or near Stirling Tce, particularly Stirling House (1908), now tearooms, and Toodyay Antiques; Connor's Mill (1870s), now housing information centre, displays a steam-driven flour mill, still in working order. In Clinton St: Old Newcastle Gaol Museum (1865), where infamous bushranger Moondyne Joe was imprisoned; police stables (1870), opposite, convict-built with random rubble stone. Duidgee Park, Harper Rd, popular picnic spot on riverbank, has miniature railway and walking track. Pelham Reserve Lookout, Duke St. Market, Stirling Tce, each Sat. May: Moondyne (colonial and convict) Festival. **In the area:** Windmill Hill Cutting, 6 km SE, deepest railway cutting in Australia. Coorinja Winery, 4 km S, dates from 1870 (open Mon.– Sat.). Hoddywell Archery and Caravan Park, 8 km S. Emu farm, 15 km SW, one of the oldest in Australia. Enchantmentland, 4 km W on Beaufort Rd: dioramic nursery-rhyme display in 2-acre garden; Australiana; dolls' houses and gifts. Trout farm, 12 km SW, offers fishing and sales. Avon Valley National Park, 25 km SW; spectacular scenery; seasonal wildflowers; wildlife-watching; Avon Descent, a whitewater canoe race, held here in Aug. Cartref Park, 16 km NW, 2 ha of English gardens and landscaped native plants with prolific birdlife. **Visitor information:** Connor's Mill, Stirling Tce; (08) 9574 2435. **See also:** The Heartlands p. 330.

Wagin
Pop. 1337

MAP REF. 384 G8, 386 E10

The prosperous countryside around Wagin supports grain crops, and pastures for sheep, cattle and emu. Located 177 km E of Bunbury, Wagin is an important railway-junction town. **In town:** Wagin Historical Village, Kitchener St, has huge collection of early pioneer artifacts set in 20 authentic old buildings. Heritage trails through historical village or fine Victorian buildings and shopfronts in Tudhoe and Tudor sts. Giant Ram (7 m high), Arthur River Rd,

Valley of the Giants Tree Top Walk, near Walpole

in park with ponds and waterfalls. Regular horse-trotting meets at Trotting Grounds, Kitchener St. Mar.: Woolorama, attended by sheep farmers nation-wide, attracts more than 28 000 people. June: Foundation Day. **In the area:** Corralyn Emu Farm, 4 km N. Mt Latham, 6 km W, for bushwalking and summit views. Puntapin, 6 km SE, a rock formation used as water catchment; wildflowers abound in spring. Lake Norring (intermittent), 13 km SE, for swimming, sailing and water-skiing. Lake Dumbleyung, 18 km E, where Donald Campbell established new world water-speed record in 1964; swimming, boating, birdwatching. At Dumbleyung, 40 km E, signposted bush trails. At Kukerin, 79 km E, Tracmach Vintage Fair Sept.–Oct. Wheatbelt Wildflower Drive, includes Tarin Rock Nature Reserve. **Visitor information:** Shire Offices,

Arthur Rd; (08) 9861 1177 or Wagin Historical Village, Showgrounds, Kitchener St; (08) 9861 1232. **See also:** The Heartlands p. 330.

Walpole
Pop. 337

MAP REF. 380 G12, 384 F13, 386 D12

The forest meets the sea at Walpole. Trees in the surrounding Walpole–Nornalup National Park include karri, jarrah and the giant red tingle. The region is known for its wildflowers in season as well as its wildlife. **In town:** Pioneer Cottage in Pioneer Park, South Coast Hwy, opened 1987 to commemorate district pioneers; cottage follows design of early pioneer homes. Daily ferry trips on Nornalup Inlet, depart jetty off Boronia Ave. Houseboat hire, Boronia Ave. Oct.: Wildflower Week. **In the area:** Coalmine Beach Heritage Trail; Knoll Drive, 3 km E.

At Walpole–Nornalup National Park: Valley of the Giants, 16 km E, famous for its Tree Top Walk, 38 m above the forest floor, and a boardwalk through a grove of veteran tingle trees known as the Ancient Empire. Giant Tingle Tree, off Hilltop Rd, 8 km SE. Peaceful Bay, 28 km SE. Circular Pool, on Frankland River, 11 km NE. Thurlby Herb Farm, 13 km N, features herb gardens, herbal produce, tearooms. Mt Frankland National Park, 29 km N. Fernhook Falls, 32 km NW. For bushwalkers, Nuyts Wilderness area, 7 km W, and other walking trails. Ocean, river and inlet for anglers. **Visitor information:** Pioneer Cottage, Pioneer Park; (08) 9840 1111. **See also:** The South-West p. 326; National Parks p. 362.

Wanneroo
Pop. 9864

MAP REF. 376 B3, 386 C8

A short drive from Perth, the district around Wanneroo stretches along 50 km of varied coastline. **In town:** Botanic Golf, Burns Beach Rd, tee off in a botanical garden. **In the area:** On West Coast Dr. at Hillarys Boat Harbour: Underwater World, with submerged tunnel, touch pool and Microworld display; whale-watching tours (Sept.–Nov.). In Prindiville Dr., 8 km S: Gumnut Factory, craft outlet and Gumnut Land Model Village Railway; Wanneroo Weekend Markets, Wangara, 8 km S, huge market in carnival-like atmosphere Sat. and Sun. In Wanneroo Rd, Conti Estate Wine Cellars. Cameleer Park Camel Farm, 10 km NE, has camel rides. Carabooda Estate Wines, 20 km N. **Visitor information:** Sunset Rent a car, 206 West Coast Hwy, Scarborough; (08) 9245 3279. **See also:** The Heartlands p. 330.

Wickepin
Pop. 249

MAP REF. 384 G6, 386 E9

This town dates from the 1890s, when the first European settlers arrived. It is set in farming country, 214 km SE of Perth. Albert Facey's autobiography *A Fortunate Life* details much of Wickepin's pioneering lifestyle. **In town:** Good examples of Edwardian architecture in Wogolin Rd. Nov.: Art and Craft Show (even-numbered years). **In the area:** Wildflowers in spring. Albert Facey Heritage Trail, brochure available from Wickepin Shire Council. Toolibin Lake Reserve, 20 km S, has wide variety of waterfowl. Malyalling Rock, 15 km NE,

unusual rock formation. Tiny town of Yealering, and Yealering Lake, 30 km NE. Sewell's Rock Nature Reserve, 44 km NE via Yealering, ideal for picnics and nature walks. **Visitor information:** Newsagency and Milkbar, 28 Wogolin Rd; (08) 9888 1070. **See also:** The Heartlands p. 330.

Wyndham
Pop. 868

MAP REF. 383 N1, 391 P4

Wyndham is the most northerly town and safe port harbour in WA. There are 2 main areas: the original Wyndham Port, on Cambridge Gulf, and Wyndham ('Three Mile'), on the Great Northern Hwy, the residential and shopping area. The meatworks, Wyndham's main industry, closed in 1985. Today Wyndham services nearby Aboriginal communities, the pastoral industry, mining exploration and tourism. Wyndham Port handles live cattle shipment to South-East Asia and stores and exports raw sugar and molasses produced at Kununurra. **In town:** Wyndham Heritage Walk, short walk from Museum to Port, brochure available. Historic buildings in Port Town historic precinct, main street (O'Donnell St): old Shire Hall, now Boab Art and Craft Gallery; Durack's Wool Store; courthouse, now historic museum; Anthon's Landing. Warriu Park Aboriginal Monument, in town centre. Port display next to Marine and Harbours offices, near wharf. Crocodile-spotting from wharf. Daily feeding of crocodiles, alligators and komodo dragons at Zoological Gardens and Crocodile Park, Barytes Rd, Wyndham Port. Wyndham Caravan Park, off Great Northern Hwy, has huge boab tree, 1500–2000 years old. Aug.: Races (horseracing). Sept.: Munumburra Music Festival. **In the area:** Self-guide drive, brochure available. To south-west on King River Rd: Aboriginal rock paintings (18 km); Prison Tree, boab tree 2000–4000 years old, once used by local police as a lock-up, (22 km); check road conditions before departure. Horse treks from Diggers Rest Station, 33 km W. Five Rivers Lookout, 5 km N atop Bastion Range, for spectacular views of Kimberley landscape, mountain ranges, Cambridge Gulf, Wyndham Port and rivers. Afghan cemetery, 1 km E. Parry CK Rd, begins 14 km SE: 4WD route to Kununurra, via Ord River and Ivanhoe Crossing; camping and fishing en route. Abundant wildlife at Marglu Billabong,

15 km SE, part of Parry Lagoons Nature Reserve, 70 sq km of wetlands. The Grotto, 36 km E (2 km off road), a rock-edged waterhole, estimated to be 100 m deep, offering a cool, shaded oasis and safe year-round swimming. Sealed road leading to Wyndham passes through splendid gorge country. El Questro Station, 100 km S: vast cattle station, incl. Emma Gorge (1.6-km walking track from parking area to gorge), swimming; numerous touring and accommodation options. **Visitor information:** Kimberley Motors, 6 Great Northern Hwy; (08) 9161 1281. **See also:** The Kimberley p. 332.

Yalgoo
Pop. 80

MAP REF. 386 D3

Yalgoo lies 216 km E of Geraldton along an excellent road through typical Australian outback country. Alluvial gold was discovered here in the 1890s. Traces of gold are still found in the district, which encourages fossicking by locals and visitors. **In town:** Courthouse Museum, Gibbons St. Restored Dominican Convent Chapel (1922), Henty St. **In the area:** Abundant native wildlife in the area and prolific wildflowers in season (July–Sept.). Joker's Tunnel, 12 km SE on Paynes Find Rd, carved through solid rock by early prospectors, named for Joker mining syndicate. Chinaman Rock, 43 km N on Cue Rd, interesting granite outcrop. **Visitor information:** Shire Offices, 15 Shamrock St; (08) 9962 8042. **See also:** Outback Coast & Mid-West p. 331.

Yallingup
Pop. 175

MAP REF. 377 B7, 379 C2, 384 A9, 386 B10

Yallingup is known for its excellent whale-watching and salmon fishing (Sept.–Dec.), surf and magnificent limestone caves. **In town:** Caves House Hotel, off Caves Rd, built by government as holiday hotel in 1903. Early visitors arrived from Busselton via horse and buggy along dirt road, a journey of 2 hours. Hotel was rebuilt 1938 after a fire; now has award-winning accommodation and restaurant. Dec.: Classic Longboard Surfing Competition. **In the area:** At Yallingup Beach, scuba-diving, canoeing, whale-watching, and salmon-fishing Sept.–Dec. Leeuwin–Naturaliste National Park, protects most of Limestone Coast, stretches north to Cape Naturaliste and south to Cape Leeuwin. Ngilgi (Yallingup) Caves, 2 km E. Shearing Shed, Wildwood Rd, 10 km SE, has shearing demonstrations and wool shop (check opening times). Rivendell Gardens, 10 km SE, cellar-door sales. Canal Rocks and Smith's Beach, 5 km SW, offer fishing, surfing and swimming. Gunyulgup Gallery and Yallingup Gallery, both 9 km SW. Wineries in the surrounding region incl.: Hunts Foxhaven Estate, 3 km S; Wildwood Winery, 5 km S; Cape Clairault Wines, 10 km S; Willyabrup Valley district, 20 km S; Happ's Vineyard and Pottery, 8 km SE; Abbey Vale Vineyards, 11 km SE; further 8 km, Bootleg Brewery; Amberley Estate Winery, 5 km E, Semillon and Seafood weekend here in Feb. **Visitor information:** Seymour Blvd, Dunsborough; (08) 9755 3299. **See also:** The South-West p. 326.

Yanchep   Pop. 1790

MAP REF. 376 A1, 384 C2, 386 C7

Yanchep is a quiet beachside holiday spot, only 51 km N of Perth. **In the area:** In Yanchep National Park, 5 km E, covering 2842 ha of natural bushland: Gloucester Lodge Museum has displays of local history incl. park history (check opening times); historic Yanchep Inn for refreshments; koala-viewing area; Yonderup and Crystal caves, featuring magnificent limestone formations; launch cruises on freshwater Loch McNess (Sun.), rowing-boats for hire; walking trail through Loch McNess wetland. Aboriginal cultural tours through park and Balga Mia Village; bookings essential, at information centre. Wild Kingdom, 3 km NE, a wildlife park and zoo. Marina at Two Rocks, 6 km NW. Caraboda Estate Wines, 10 km S. Wreck of *Alkimos*, south of Yanchep, said to be guarded by ghost. Picturesque Gnangara Lake, 30 km SE, with picnic facilities around the shore. **Visitor information:** Information Office, Yanchep National Park; (08) 9561 1004. Web site www.calm.wa.gov.au **See also:** The Heartlands p. 330; National Parks p. 362.

York   Pop. 1923

MAP REF. 376 I4, 384 F3, 386 D8

First settled by Europeans in 1831, York is on the banks of the Avon River in the fertile Avon Valley, 97 km from Perth. The town has a wealth of historic buildings, carefully preserved. **In town:** Heritage trails, booklet available. In Avon Tce: Old Gaol and Courthouse, and Police Station, built of local stone in 1895; Settlers' House (1850), restored 2-storey mud-brick building, now offering old-world accommodation; Castle Hotel, Imperial Inn and The York, fine examples of early coaching inns; Romanesque Town Hall (1911); Mill Gallery, featuring recycled jarrah craftwork; Loder Antiques; York Motor Museum, one of Australia's best collections of veteran, classic and racing cars (and some bicycles and motorcycles); Talking Points Antique Toy Train Museum, open Sun. and by appt; Sandalwood Yards and Tipperary School, old sandalwood storage area and now site of relocated school (1874). Avon Valley Historical Rose Garden, Osnaberg Rd, roses in season. In Brook St: Old York Hospital, with original shingle roof; Residency Museum (1843), displaying colonial furniture and early photographs. Old-world costumes at The Needle and I, cnr Georgiana and Macarthy sts (appt only). Fine churches: Holy Trinity (consecrated 1858), Suburban Rd; St Patrick's Church (1886), South St; Uniting Church (1888), Grey St. In Low St: Suspension Bridge (originally 1906) across river; picnic/barbecue facilities at Avon Park; market also in Avon Park (check times). Aug.: Daffodil Festival; Agricultural Show. Sept.: Jazz Weekend. Oct.: Flying 50s (car rally). **In the area:** Mt Brown Lookout, 3 km SE; follow signs from Castle Hotel to Pioneer Dr. and then to Mt Brown. Miniature Village, 3 km S on Great Southern Hwy. Picnic area overlooking river at Gwanbygine Park, 10 km S. Near Quairading, 64 km E, Toapin Weir and panoramic views from Mt Stirling. **Visitor information:** 81 Avon Tce; (08) 9641 1301. Web site www.yorkwa.com.au **See also:** The Heartlands p. 330.

Town Hall, York

NATIONAL PARKS

Munjina Gorge in Karijini National Park

AROUND PERTH

At **Nambung National Park**, 230 kilometres north of Perth on the coast, unusual rock formations are to be found. Here a moonscape of coloured quartz is studded with limestone pillars ranging in size from stony 'twigs' to 4-metre-high columns. This is the unique Pinnacles Desert, a favourite subject for photographers. **Yanchep National Park**, about 50 kilometres north of Perth on a belt of coastal limestone, has forests of massive tuart trees, underground limestone caves and spring wildflowers.

Some 80 kilometres north-east of Perth is **Avon Valley National Park**; its popular attractions are upland forests and river valleys, as well as wildflowers in season. Bald Hill, the highest point, provides panoramic views of the Avon River. After winter rains, a tributary of the Avon, Emu Spring Brook, spills 30 metres down in a spectacular waterfall.

A cluster of national parks to the east of Perth includes **John Forrest National Park**; Western Australia's first national park. It features granite outcrops, dams and waterfalls, creeks and rock pools. Other nearby national parks are **Kalamunda, Greenmount, Gooseberry Hill** and **Lesmurdie Falls**, all within 20 to 25 kilometres of Perth. The Bibbulmun Track, a walking trail that links the forests, east of Perth, to the area once occupied by the Bibbulmun people of the south-west, begins its 950-kilometre route in Kalamunda National Park.

Proclaimed as the State's first flora and fauna reserve in 1894, **Serpentine National Park** is about 60 kilometres south of Perth and a firm favourite of day trippers who picnic at the falls area in the park. Jarrah and marri forests, and wildflowers in spring, are some of the park's attractions.

IN THE SOUTH OF THE STATE

Leeuwin–Naturaliste National Park extends along the rugged south-west coast. There are over 100 limestone caves in the area, some containing fossils of marsupials, no longer found on the mainland. The park is home to rare ospreys and rufous bristlebirds, as well as the more common sea birds. Whales can occasionally be seen offshore.

Along the lower south-west coast of the State is **Walpole–Nornalup National Park**. A network of roads and walking tracks, through forests of karri and tingle, attracts bushwalkers and birdwatchers. Here visitors can follow the Tree Top Walk through the Valley of the Giants. Inlets rich in fish create a haven for anglers and boating enthusiasts.

About 100 kilometres east is **West Cape Howe National Park**, the spectacular coastline of which includes the gabbro cliffs of West Cape Howe and the granite of Torbay Heads, fronting the cold waters of the Southern Ocean. Extensive coastal heath, swamps, lakes and karri forest cover the inland area, and the park is popular with outdoor enthusiasts.

The South Western Highway bisects **Shannon National Park**, 358 kilometres south of Perth. In the park is the former timber-milling town site of Shannon, now a camping area. The rest of the park is towering karri and jarrah forests, surrounding the Shannon River. Visitors can take the Great Forest Trees Drive (48 km) through the forest and tune into 100 FM at the signposted 'radio stops'; self-guide books are available from the Department of Conservation and Land Management.

Stirling Range National Park, 450 kilometres south-east of Perth, is one of Australia's outstanding reserves. Surrounded by a flat, sandy plain, the Stirling Range rises abruptly to over 1000 metres, its jagged peaks veiled in swirling mists. The cool, humid environment created by these low clouds contributes to the survival of 1000 flowering plant species, some unique to this area. There is camping at the Stirling Range Retreats.

Brilliant displays of wildflowers are also a feature of the nearby **Porongurup National Park**, where the granite domes of the Porongurup Ranges are clothed in a forest of karri trees.

Spectacular coastal scenery is the main attraction of the **Torndirrup National Park**, 460 kilometres south of Perth. Also on the south coast is

Cape Le Grand National Park; its magnificent bays and beaches are protected by granite headlands. Also near Esperance, **Stokes National Park** hugs the coastline around Stokes Inlet and features long sandy beaches and rocky headlands backed by sand dunes and low hills. Stokes Inlet and its associated lakes support a rich variety of wildlife. Inland from Stokes lies **Peak Charles National Park**. A walk to the ridge of this ancient granite peak allows sweeping views of its companion, Peak Eleanora, and the dry sand plain heaths and salt-lake systems of the surrounding country.

One of the loveliest sections of the south coast of Western Australia is **Fitzgerald River National Park**, a World Biosphere Reserve, through which the rugged Barren Range stretches from west to east. The park's 330 000 hectares comprise gently undulating sand plains, river valleys, precipitous cliff edges, narrow gorges, and beaches for swimming and rock-fishing. The park contains many rare species of flora and fauna.

IN THE NORTH OF THE STATE

North of Geraldton lies **Kalbarri National Park**. Here, the lower reaches of the Murchison River wind through spectacular gorges to the Indian Ocean. Sea cliffs in layers of multi-coloured sandstone loom over the crashing white foam at Red Bluff.

Cape Range National Park, near Exmouth, is cut by deep gorges but remains arid for most of the year. Vegetation is sparse, except around the creek and after cyclonic storms have flooded the area. Yardie Creek, the only permanent water in the area, is a landlocked river that occasionally breaks through the sandbar and meets the sea. River tours operate regularly from March to December.

In the Pilbara, 1400 kilometres north of Perth, is **Karijini National Park**. It is in the Hamersley Range and part of a massive block of weathered rock over 450 kilometres long. Within this huge, spectacular park are many well-known gorges, including Dales Gorge, its strata in horizontal stripes of blue, mauve, red and brown dating back almost 2000 million years. A trail in the park winds up to Mt Bruce, the State's second highest point. Interpretive displays along the trail provide an insight into the Aboriginal heritage, as well as the flora and fauna, of the area. Further north, still in The Pilbara, **Millstream–Chichester National Park** encompasses almost 200 000 hectares of clay tablelands and sediment-capped basalt ranges. At Millstream, on the Fortescue River, natural freshwater springs have created an oasis featuring waterlilies, Millstream palms and paperbarks. In contrast, there are the Chichester Ranges: rolling hills, hummocks of spinifex, white-barked snappy gums on the uplands, and pale coolibahs along the usually dry watercourses.

In the far north of the State are the national parks of The Kimberley. **Geikie Gorge**, the largest, is 20 kilometres north-east of Fitzroy Crossing and has an area of 3136 hectares. The multi-coloured cliffs are reflected in the waters of the Fitzroy River, which flows through the gorge. The area is too rugged for extensive walking, but organised boat trips go up the river through the gorge, enabling visitors to see one of Australia's most beautiful waterways.

Other national parks nearby are **Windjana Gorge** and **Tunnel Creek**, both north-west of Geikie Gorge.

Tunnel Creek is a permanent watercourse that flows underground for 750 metres. It is possible to walk through the high, wide tunnel to a small river beach beyond; some deep wading may be necessary, and carry a torch.

South of Lake Argyle is the spectacular **Purnululu National Park**, with its tiger-striped, beehive-shaped domes, deep gullies and unique palms. Access is by 4WD vehicle only. The park is closed from October to May.

Mirima National Park, east of Kununurra, is typical of The Kimberley: banded sandstone outcrops, boab trees, red soil dotted with eucalypts, and black kites circling overhead. Aboriginal rock paintings are also a feature.

Further west, on the remote Mitchell Plateau is the **Mitchell River National Park**, incorporating the stunning Mitchell Falls. The abundance of bird and mammal species in the area is interesting to scientists investigating biodiversity in the Kimberley.

For further information on Western Australia's national parks and for details of visitor fees that apply to some parks, contact the Department of Conservation and Land Management, Technology Park, Western Precinct, 17 Dick Perry Ave, Kensington (Locked Bag 104, Bentley Delivery Centre, WA 6983); (08) 9334 0333. Web site www.calm.wa.gov.au

WILDLIFE-WATCHING

Dolphins at Monkey Mia, near Denham

IN PERTH

Swan Estuary Marine Park is a haven for migratory birds each spring. Sections of Perth's picturesque waterway have been set aside, including Alfred Cove, Pelican Point and Milyu. Between August and November the birds touch down on the estuary mudflats, and they stay until late March. Some of the smallest visitors are red-necked stints, which arrive from breeding grounds in Arctic Siberia, weighing only 30–40 grams.

Perth also has some rather unusual wildlife-watching locations. Only 4 kilometres north of Perth city centre visitors to Lake Monger can stand among a variety of birdlife including dozens of black swans, attracted by a constructed breeding island at the western end of the lake. Golfers at **Joondalup public golf course** in the city's northern outskirts look out for western grey kangaroos when teeing off. Kangaroos are quite common on local golf courses.

AROUND PERTH

Rottnest Island, a short ferry ride from the port of Fremantle, is a 'must-see' for wildlife-watchers. The island was named after its marsupial quokkas were mistaken for rats by the early Dutch explorer Vlamingh. Dusk and dawn are the best times to glimpse these animals, though sharp-eyed tour-bus drivers can often find them through the day. Good quokka spotting locations are around the bakery at Settlement and at Watsons Glade near the road to Jeannies Lookout (eastern arm). Humpback whales can also be spotted off Cape Vlamingh during the winter months.

The turquoise waters surrounding the island provide memorable experiences. At Pocillopora Reef off the south of the island is a not-to-be-missed underwater snorkelling trail. The reef, named after its beautiful pink coral, is alive with marine life. Snorkellers can fin through coral landscapes, following illustrated underwater plaques that explain the reef's plants and animals. Each stopping point has handles for snorkellers while they read –

fortunately there is one breath's worth of information per plaque.

Off the coast of Rockingham to the south, visitors to **Penguin Island** can see a breeding colony of about a thousand little (fairy) penguins and may catch sight of dolphins and sea lions, in the surrounding waters of Shoalwater Marine Park, where marine life is abundant.

Perth-based wildlife-watchers have several good mainland parks and reserves within a short drive. **Avon Valley National Park** has a healthy population of echidnas; their long trench-like diggings can be seen throughout the park. Late afternoon is a good time to see the park's western grey kangaroos as they move into the open after having spent their day in thick bushland. Euros are also present, although these sure-footed kangaroos prefer the steeper rocky country.

John Forrest National Park, just east of Perth, is good for birdwatching. Unusually named and brilliantly coloured 'twenty eight' parrots can be seen in the woodlands, along with less common red-capped parrots. Rufous and golden whistlers are noisy residents, and New Holland honeyeaters enjoy the spring wildflower season. Also, keep an eye out for racehorse goannas on the park's roads and tracks.

IN THE NORTH OF THE STATE

A classic wildlife experience is interacting with bottlenose dolphins at **Shark Bay**, north of Perth. They often swim into the shallows at Monkey Mia to make contact with humans and receive offerings of fish. The best time to meet these marine mammals is between 8 a.m. and 1 p.m., when they are fed under the supervision of park rangers. The dolphins may feel more sociable on some days than others. Part of the attraction of Monkey Mia is that the dolphins set the day's agenda and visitors respond, rather than forcing the animals to perform on cue.

Shark Bay supports a variety of marine life besides dolphins; sea turtles, school sharks, manta rays and dugongs flourish in the area. At Eagle Bluff,

20 kilometres south of Denham, school sharks and turtles can sometimes be seen in the clear green waters below. Boat tours leave from Monkey Mia to view the dugongs or 'sea cows' which graze among the seagrass beds. Dugongs feature unusual flattened snouts designed to shovel through the sand in search of the choicest plants. A catamaran also leaves from Denham to spot a variety of marine life, including the giant yet harmless manta rays.

Further north again is Ningaloo Reef, Western Australia's largest coral reef and one of its most spectacular features. The great diversity of marine life is protected by **Ningaloo Marine Park**. March to late May are the best months to view the park's most famous visitors, the whale sharks. These are huge but docile fish with beautifully mottled backs and flattened heads. They swim with their mouths open to filter the tiny marine organisms on which they feed. While the complete life cycle of the world's largest fish is a mystery, it is now believed their arrival corresponds with the recently discovered phenomenon of mass coral-spawning at Ningaloo (March to April). The spawning results in an abundance of food for the sharks. Fortunately for whale shark-watchers, when the fish arrive they cruise slowly just under the surface and can be seen from boat cruises and air flights from Exmouth.

August to November is a good time for humpback whale-watching cruises at Ningaloo as the whales travel to their Antarctic feeding grounds and north-west shelf breeding area. Humpbacks are the show-ponies of the whale world. It is hard to believe how active these huge mammals are until you see 30 tonnes of whale launching itself from the water or splashing its mighty tail – humpbacks are anything but shy. Cruises leave regularly from Exmouth during the whale season.

Another reason to visit at this time is the arrival of large schools of manta rays. They are more elusive than humpbacks, though once a school is located, snorkellers on tour boats out of Exmouth can swim among these harmless plankton-feeders.

Extending to the shores of Ningaloo Marine Park is **Cape Range National Park**, and within this park is a rich tidal inlet called Mangrove Bay. The bay is home to some of the park's 125 bird species, particularly waders such as ibis and heron, which emerge onto the exposed flats at low tide. A bird hide provides a discreet viewpoint, and a stroll along the boardwalk gives a fascinating perspective on inlet life. There is also a fauna hide at Mangrove Bay, built alongside a waterhole that is a magnet for wildlife. Keep an eye out here for emus, euros and flocks of galahs. Also in the park is Yardie Creek Gorge, where regular cruises operate. Bring binoculars to spot ospreys and herons nesting on the cliff-faces, and the numerous black-footed rock wallabies.

ON THE SOUTH-WEST COAST

Southern right whales spend time off the southern coast around **Albany** each year from August to November. Albany's association with whales has not always been a friendly one, with commercial whaling ceasing only in 1978. Whale numbers are now on the increase, and Whaleworld near Albany provides a good introduction to the behaviour and life cycles of these magnificent marine mammals.

Whale-watching cruises depart daily from Albany's wharf in season. For land-based spotters there is the platform at Point Ann in Fitzgerald River National Park. If whales are about, Point Ann offers the best chance to see one. With luck you may see a mother whale with her calf.

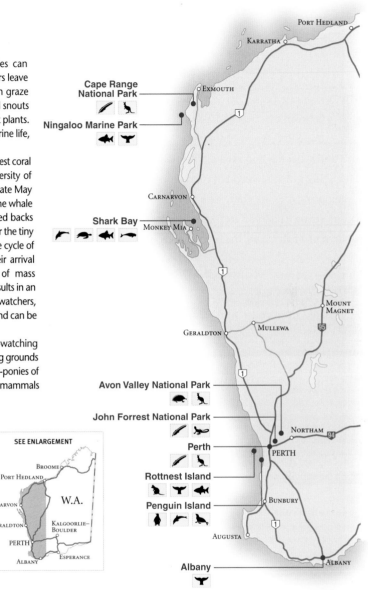

WILDLIFE-WATCHING ETHICS

Do not disturb wildlife or wildlife habitats. Keep the impact of your presence to a minimum. Use available cover or hides wherever possible.

Do not feed wildlife, even in urban areas.
(Note: supervised feeding is allowed at some locations)

Be careful not to introduce exotic plants and animals – definitely no pets.

Stay on defined trails.

For more information on wildlife-watching in national parks and reserves contact the Department of Conservation and Land Management, Technology Park, Western Precinct, 17 Dick Perry Ave, Kensington (Locked Bag 104, Bentley Delivery Centre, WA 6983); (08) 9334 0333. Web site address www.calm.wa.gov.au

CLASSIC TOUR

CAPE TO CAPE

Busselton to Cape Leeuwin via Cape Naturaliste (188 km)

Travelling from Cape Naturaliste to Cape Leeuwin takes you on a route that runs between the coast and a picturesque landscape of forest, farmland and wineries, and through Leeuwin–Naturaliste National Park. A limestone ridge stretches from cape to cape, and water has hollowed out vast caverns underground. A visit to one or more of these caves is sure to be a highlight of your tour. Allow at least two days to take in the sights between Busselton and Augusta; those with a special interest in either caves or wineries should allow at least one extra day. If you are touring between June and December, you may also be treated to the sight of whales along the coast.

1 The longest jetty

The tour starts in **Busselton**, located on the shore of magnificent Geographe Bay, 228 kilometres south of Perth. The sea here is generally placid, in contrast to the wilder coastline between the capes. Dolphins swimming in the bay may be sighted from the picturesque 2-kilometre wooden jetty, the longest in Australia. When the jetty was built in 1865, it serviced the American whaling ships; later, it was extended to take a railway line for the loading of timber. Today, a small tourist train chugs along the jetty on the hour between 10 a.m. and 4 p.m.

Humpback whale

2 To the lighthouse

From Busselton, head west along the Bussell Highway, then turn right onto Caves Road and on to the popular holiday town of Dunsborough. Skirt the town centre and turn right onto Cape Naturaliste Road, which leads to the lighthouse. Peppermint and banksia trees shade the road, gradually giving way to cycads, grass trees and coastal heath. Between mid-September and the end of October the heath is a carpet of pinks, reds and purples.

Cape Naturaliste Lighthouse (1906), which was the last staffed lighthouse in Western Australia, is now automated. Visitors can climb the steep steps to the top of the tower where the prismatic lens is in constant rotation. At the entrance to the lighthouse grounds there is a small, interesting display on the history and technology of lighthouses.

If you are here in season, the easy 800-metre stroll to the whale-watching platform is a must. Humpbacks often swim close to shore as they round the cape on their annual migration from the Antarctic to The Kimberley coast in the north of the State (April to June), returning south from October to December. Southern right whales sometimes venture this far north to calve in the shallow waters (June to September).

For those who wish to explore the natural wonders of the cape, there is a network of well-marked walking trails. The wild seas and lunar landscape of the western headland are in stark contrast to the scenic coastline and sheltered waters of Bunker Bay to the east.

Cape Naturaliste Lighthouse
Phone: (08) 9755 3955
Open: 9.30 a.m.–3.30 p.m. daily; extended hours in summer and school holidays

3 Surf and salmon

Drive back along Cape Naturaliste Road, then turn left onto Eagle Bay Road. The road winds along the rocky coastline, offering extended vistas of Geographe Bay, and eventually rejoins Cape Naturaliste Road. At Dunsborough, turn onto Caves Road. Just past Ngilgi Cave, there is a road on the right that leads to the internationally renowned Yallingup surf beach. The beaches from here to the south have powerful surf and fearful names, such as Guillotines, Gallows and Suicides. This section of coast is also excellent fishing territory.

Return to Caves Road, head south for a short distance and turn right onto the road leading to **Canal Rocks**. This canal-like rock formation, which extends for many metres out into the surf, was caused by an ancient fault.

The fault line is best viewed from the Rotary Lookout on the cliff. For a close encounter with the ocean, you can follow the boardwalk, which has been built out across the rocks, but beware, the waves can be dangerous. Between May and June, Canal Rocks attracts large numbers of enthusiastic anglers. At this time of year huge schools of Australian salmon swim north on their annual spawning run.

4 The moon's bathing place

Rejoin Caves Road and continue south through the heart of the Margaret River wine region. The scenery is a patchwork of emerald-green pasture and vineyards; enticing cellar-door and B&B signs line the road.

Six kilometres after you have passed the turn-off to Gracetown, turn right onto Ellensbrook Road which leads to **Ellensbrook** (1857). This wattle and daub homestead was the first home of the Bussell family, after whom Busselton was named. The homestead, which is set by a bubbling brook, was the hub of a beef and dairy cattle lease that stretched 30 kilometres along the coast. A signposted 1.3-kilometre circuit walk winds past Meekadarribee Waterfall and Grotto. At the grotto there is an enchanting storybook display outlining an Aboriginal legend that describes the grotto as 'the moon's bathing place'.

Ellensbrook

Ellensbrook Road, off Caves Road
Margaret River
Phone: (08) 9321 6088
Open: weekends; walking trail open daily

Wine barrels

⑤ Wild and free

Return to Caves Road and head south through wine country before turning left along Wallcliffe Road to Margaret River. Here there is a wide range of accommodation in and around the town, making it an ideal base for touring the region's wineries and caves.

At Margaret River, take the Bussell Highway to the southern outskirts of town and turn right along Boodjidup Road to reach **Eagles Heritage**, a rehabilitation centre for injured birds of prey. Here you can see about 20 of the 24 Australian raptor species, depending on releases into the wild, and there are free-flight displays of these magnificent birds at 11 a.m. and 1.30 p.m. daily. A 1-kilometre walk winds around the park, through the magnificent bushland setting.

As you continue along Boodjidup Road towards Caves Road, you will pass the turn-off to two of the area's leading wineries, Voyager Estate and Leeuwin Estate, both of which are open for tastings and cellar-door sales.

Eagles Heritage

Boodjidup Road
Margaret River
Phone: (08) 9757 2960
Open: 10 a.m.–5 p.m. daily

⑥ Underground wonders

From Boodjidup Road turn left onto Caves Road, which winds through farmland for about 4 kilometres until it reaches a section of Leeuwin-Naturaliste National Park. Two caves are nearby: Mammoth Cave to the left, about a kilometre on, and Lake Cave

on the right after another 2 kilometres. Frances Bussell is credited with the discovery of Lake Cave; she came across the crater-like entrance while searching for lost cattle in 1851. At the mouth of Lake Cave is **CaveWorks**, a fascinating interpretive centre with a dynamic working cave model.

CaveWorks

Off Caves Road
Phone: (08) 9757 7411
Open: 9 a.m.–5 p.m. daily

⑦ Karri forests to Hamelin Bay

Rejoin Caves Road and, 3 kilometres south of CaveWorks, turn right onto Boranup Drive, an unsealed road that winds through karri forest for 14 kilometres before meeting up again with Caves Road. Take care after heavy rain and watch for oncoming traffic.

The forest here is regenerating from extensive logging, which took place between 1890 and 1910. In the late 19th century, Maurice Coleman Davies created a vast business empire from these giant trees. Today, the largest trees in the forest are around 50 metres tall and wildflowers carpet the ground in spring. Boranup Lookout, at the southern end of this scenic

WINERIES

The Margaret River wine region has been compared favourably with the French Bordeaux district. The first vines were planted as recently as 1967, at Vasse Felix, but more wineries soon followed. Over 15% of Australia's premium wines are now produced in the area.

Many wineries are open to the public for tasting and cellar-door sales, while others have restaurants and tours of their premises. A good starting point is the Margaret River Regional Wine Centre in Cowaramup (open Mondays–Saturdays 10 a.m.–8 p.m., Sundays 12 noon–6 p.m.). Here you can pick up information about all the wineries and taste the local produce.

There are now more than forty wineries in the Margaret River region, many of which are marked on the road map on page 379. Amberley Estate, Leeuwin Estate, Vasse Felix, Cape Mentelle, Brookland Valley Vineyard and Voyager Estate are just some of the wineries with fine reputations and facilities for visitors. There are more unusual ones too: Seventy Organic Wines grows organic grapes for its vintages, while The Berry Farm has a range of fruit wines, from sparkling strawberry to pink plum port, as well as a selection of vinegars and jams. Bootleg Brewery is a must for those who enjoy their beer.

Hamelin Bay

CAVES

As you travel from cape to cape you are passing over an extensive network of limestone caves, five of which are regularly open to the public:

Ngilgi Cave – the largest cave in the area; 'adventure' caving; self-guide tours with access to a guide in the main chamber
Mammoth Cave – contains the remains of an extinct wombat-like creature; self-guide tour with CD headset
Lake Cave – features a reflective lake-like stream; guided tours
Jewel Cave – includes the largest straw stalactite in any tourist cave; guided tours
Moondyne Cave – guided 'adventure' caving with helmets, lamps and overalls

The CaveWorks entrance fee includes admission to one of either Jewel, Lake, Mammoth or Moondyne caves; phone CaveWorks for opening hours and tour details; (08) 9757 7411. Contact Ngilgi Cave directly for details; (08) 9755 2152.

drive, provides panoramic views of the coast and the Leeuwin–Naturaliste ridge.

After rejoining Caves Road, continue south before turning right to **Hamelin Bay**. At the end of the road is a windswept beach with crumbling limestone cliffs. The skeleton of an old jetty is all that remains of what was once a focal point in international trade.

At the height of Davies' timber empire, massive amounts of jarrah and karri were transported from Hamelin Bay to London, Sydney and South Africa. The port's exposure to the treacherous north-west winds resulted in 11 wrecks. There is now a wreck trail for experienced divers just offshore, and the

beach is popular for fishing and swimming. Watch out for stingrays around the old jetty.

8 Historical themes

Return to Caves Road and continue south, past the entrance to Jewel and Moondyne caves, to join the Bussell Highway on the outskirts of **Augusta**. Along with Busselton, Augusta is one of the oldest settlements in the State. The Augusta Historical Museum explores a number of interesting themes: the life of the early pastoralists, the timber and whaling industries, and the story of the 'group settlers' – English migrants who cleared the land for farming in the 1920s.

For superb views of Augusta's riverside setting, the karri forests and the coast, make a short detour west from the centre of town along Hillview Road (10-km return).

Jewel Cave

Cape Leeuwin Lighthouse

Augusta Historical Museum
Blackwood Avenue
Augusta
Phone: (08) 9758 1948
(Leeuwin Souvenirs)
Open: 10 a.m.–12 noon daily;
also 2 p.m.–4 p.m. Sept.–Apr.
and school holidays

9 A view of two oceans

From Augusta continue south to the tip of Cape Leeuwin; the Bussell Highway becomes Blackwood Avenue in Augusta, then Leeuwin Road.

Cape Leeuwin was named by Captain Matthew Flinders in 1801 when he set out from this point to charter the entire east coast. Stop at the Matthew Flinders Memorial at the Groper Bay turn-off, particularly if you are travelling between July and September, when you may sight whales offshore.

Continue towards **Cape Leeuwin Lighthouse**; just before you reach it you will see on the right the unusual sight of a wooden waterwheel apparently turning to stone. It once supplied water to the keepers from an underground spring. Minerals from the spring have precipitated onto the wood, resulting in a limestone coating that is gradually covering the structure.

The Cape Leeuwin Lighthouse, the final destination on your cape to cape tour, is located on Western Australia's south-western tip. Commissioned by Davies in 1895, the limestone tower overlooks both the Indian and Southern oceans. You can climb to the top for even more spectacular views of the two oceans, but be prepared for blustery conditions.

Cape Leeuwin Lighthouse
Phone: (08) 9758 1920
Open: 9 a.m.–4 p.m. daily

Continuing on, or returning to Perth

To return to Perth from Cape Leeuwin, drive north along the Bussell Highway, through Augusta, Margaret River, Busselton and Bunbury (143 kilometres).

Alternatively, drive north from Augusta to Karridale. Turn right along the Brockman Highway, over Alexandra Bridge and on to Nannup. From there, continue across the Great Australian Bight to South Australia or follow the Balingup Road through Donnybrook and on to Bunbury and Perth (370 kilometres).

WESTERN AUSTRALIA
LOCATION MAP

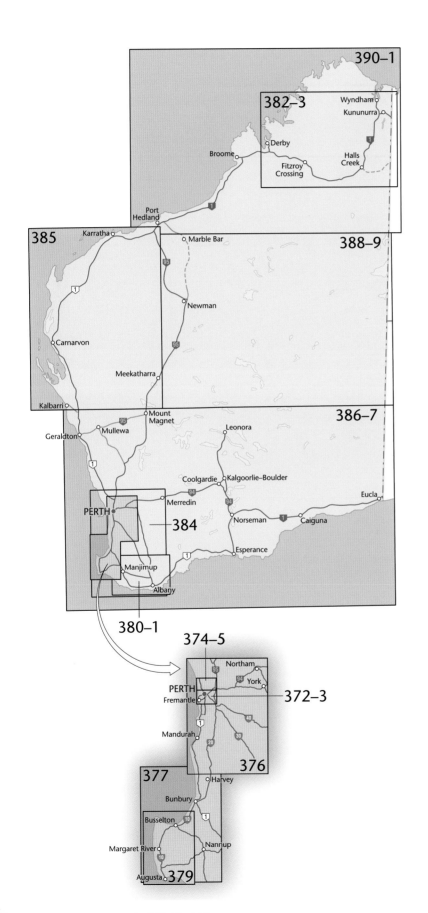

390–1

382–3
Wyndham
Kununurra
Derby
Broome
Fitzroy
Crossing
Halls
Creek

385
Karratha
Port
Hedland
Marble Bar
388–9
Newman
Carnarvon
Meekatharra
Kalbarri
Mount
Magnet
386–7
Geraldton
Mullewa
Leonora
Coolgardie
Kalgoorlie–Boulder
Eucla
Merredin
PERTH
384
Norseman
Caiguna
Esperance
Manjimup
Albany

380–1

374–5
Northam
PERTH
York
Fremantle
372–3
Mandurah
376
377
Harvey
Bunbury
Busselton
Margaret River
Nannup
Augusta
379

Perth and Suburbs	
370	Central Perth
371	Perth Approach & Bypass Routes
372–3	Perth & Southern Suburbs
374–5	Northern Suburbs, Perth
Touring Western Australia	
376	Perth & Surrounds
377	The South-West
378	Fremantle
379	Margaret River & Surrounds
380–1	The South Coast
382–3	The Kimberley
Complete State Coverage	
384	South Western Western Australia
385	Central Western Western Australia
386–7	Southern Western Australia
388–9	Central Western Australia
390–1	Northern Western Australia

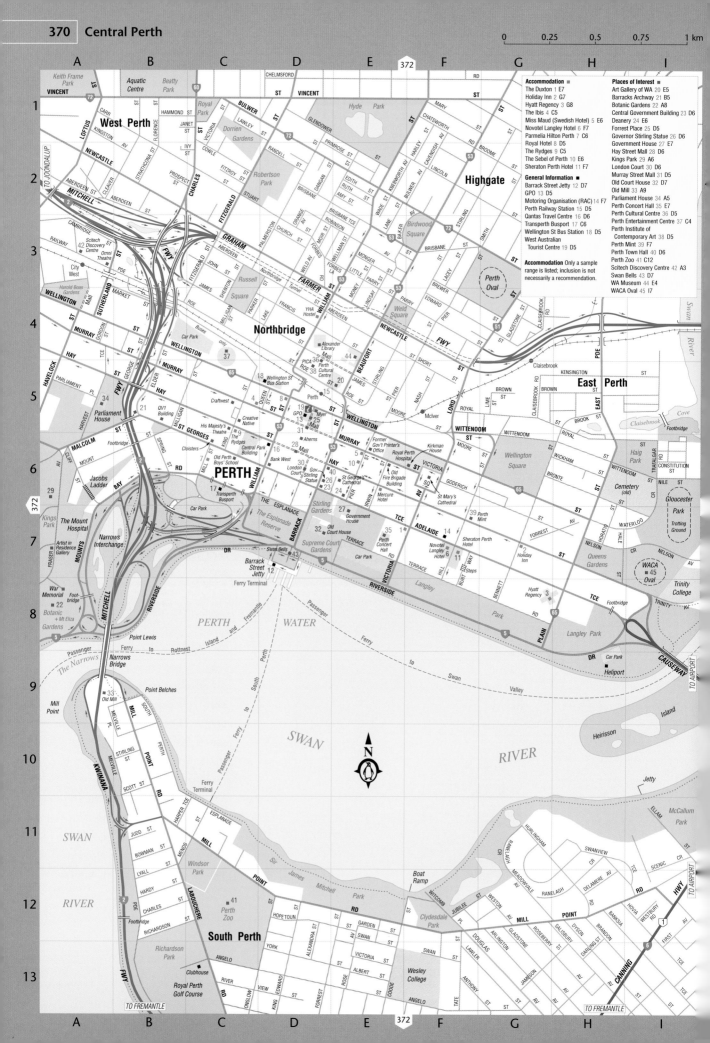

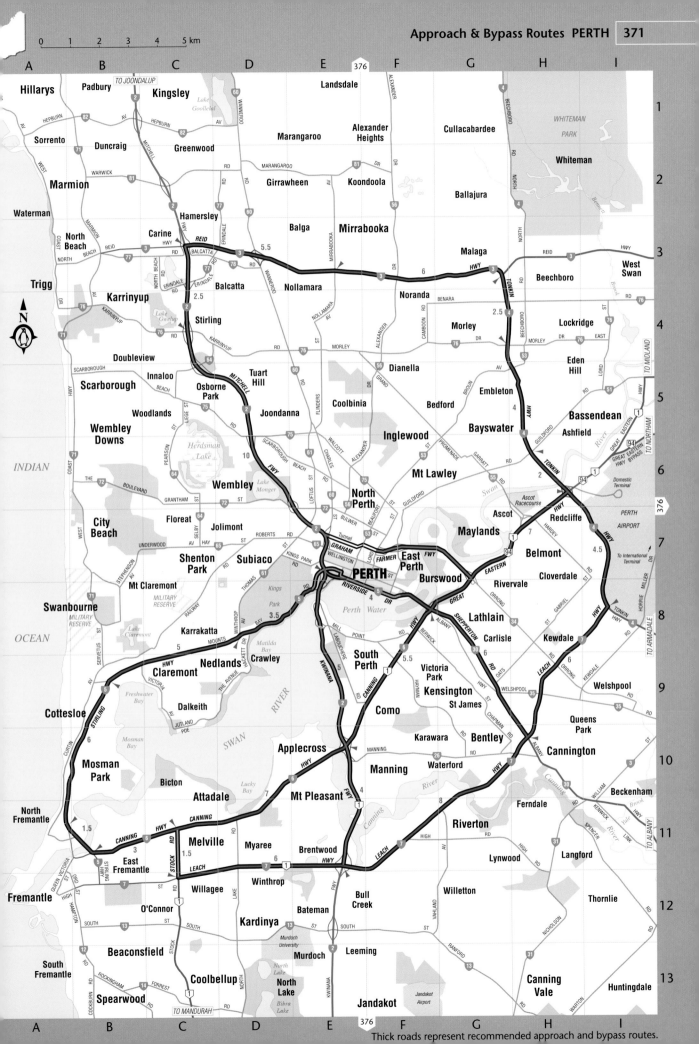

Thick roads represent recommended approach and bypass routes.

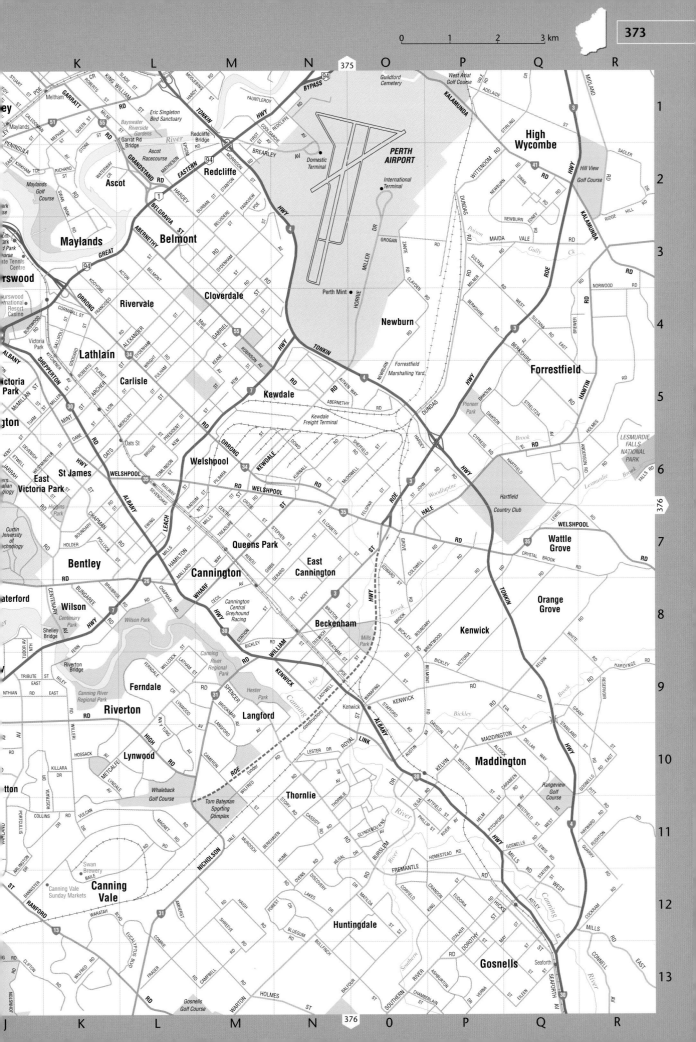

Grid columns: A B C D E F G H
Grid rows: 1 2 3 4 5 6 7 8 9 10 11 12 13

Suburbs and localities

Mullaloo
Beldon
Edgewater
Gnangara
Craigie
Kallaroo
Wangara
Woodvale
Hillarys
Padbury
Kingsley
Landsdale
Sorrento
Duncraig
Greenwood
Marangaroo
Alexander Heights
Marmion
Warwick
Girrawheen
Koondool
Waterman
Carine
Hamersley
Balga
Mirra
North Beach
Karrinyup
Gwelup
Westminster
Trigg
Balcatta
Nollamara
Scarborough
Doubleview
Stirling
Yokine
Innaloo
Tuart Hill
Osborne Park
Joondanna
Menora
Wembley Downs
Woodlands
Coolbinia
Churchlands
Glendalough
Mt Hawthorn
Leederville
North Perth
Wembley
Floreat
City Beach

Parks and reserves

Lake Joondalup
Nanovich Park
Lakelands Golf Course
Badgerup Lake
Gnangara Lake
Wanneroo Water Board Reserve
Yellagonga Regional Park
Walluburnup Swamp
Beenyup Swamp
Pinaroo Valley Memorial Park
Lake Goollelal
Kingsway Reserve
Marangaroo Golf Course
Reservoir
Hillarys Boat Harbour
Sorrento Quay
Underwater World
Sorrento Beach
Star Swamp Reserve
Charles Riley Reserve
Hamersley Golf Course
Lake Karrinyup Golf Course
Careniup Swamp
Mt Yokine Reservoir
North Beach
Millington Reserve
Lake Gwelup
Dianella
Trigg Beach
West Australian Golf Course
Scarborough Beach
Rendezvous Observation City
Scarborough Fair Markets (Sat. & Sun.)
Brighton Beach
Jackadder Lake
Woodrow
Yokine Reserve
Mount Lawley Golf Course
Herdsman Lake
Jon Sanders
Edith Cowan University
Wembley Golf Complex
Bold Park
Floreat Beach
Lake Monger
Lake Monger Reserve
Leederville
Hyde Park
City Beach

MARMION MARINE PARK
INDIAN OCEAN

Major roads

OCEAN REEF RD
MARMION AV
MITCHELL FWY
WHITFORDS AV
HEPBURN AV
WARWICK RD
BEACH RD
REID HWY
BALCATTA RD
KARRINYUP RD
SCARBOROUGH BEACH RD
WANNEROO RD
MORLEY DR
POWIS
ANZAC
CAMBRIDGE ST
GRANTHAM ST
VINCENT ST
NEWCASTLE ST
WEST COAST DR
THE BOULEVARD
OCEANIC DR

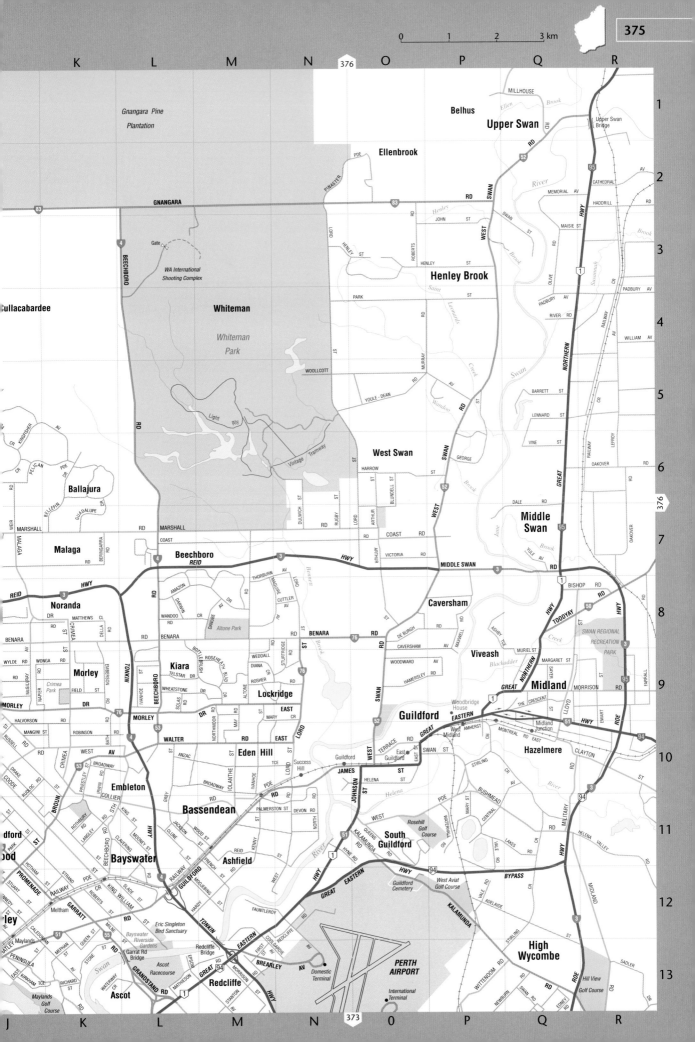

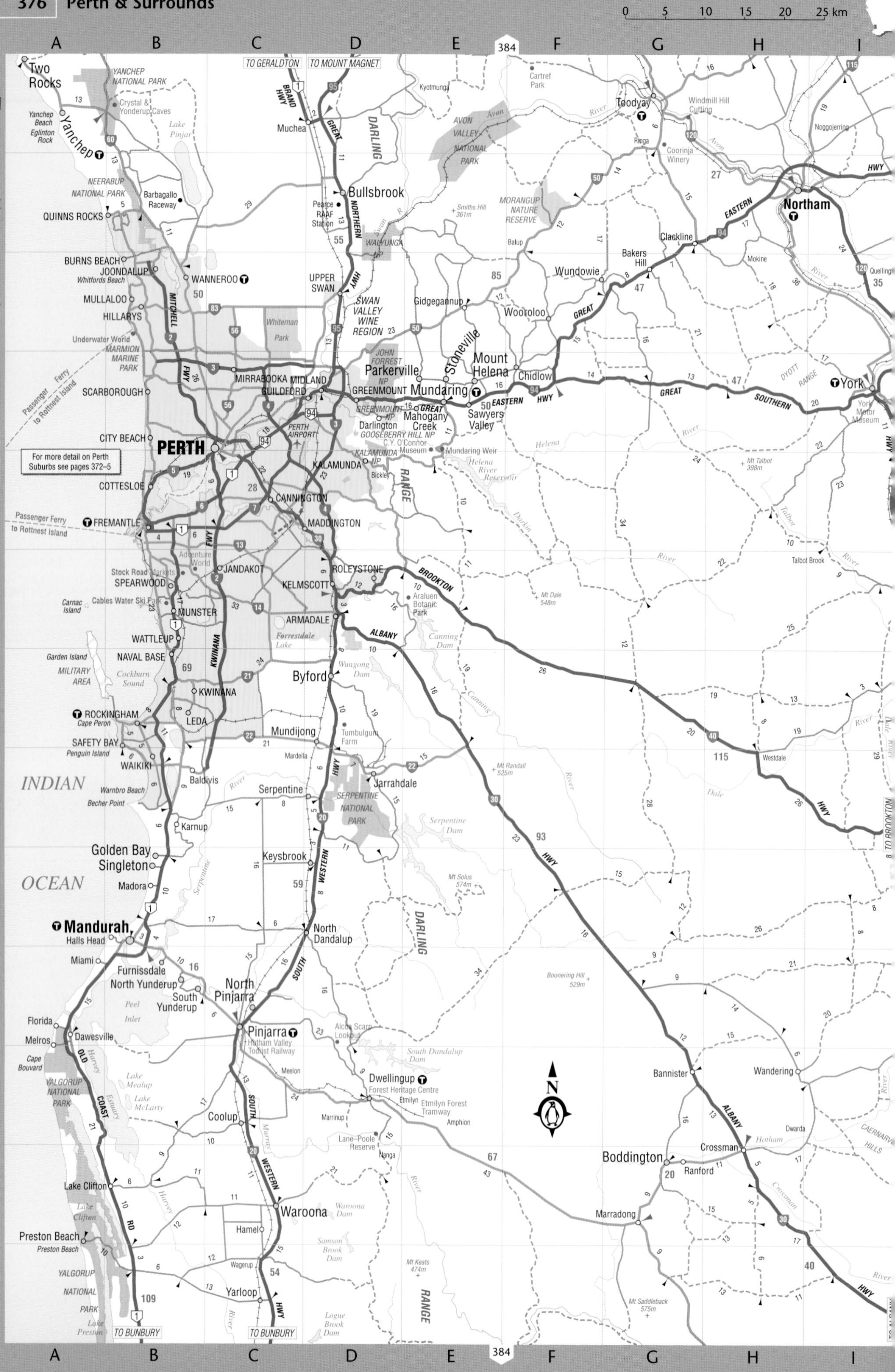

0 5 10 15 20 25 km

A B C D E 384 F G H I

1
Two Rocks
YANCHEP NATIONAL PARK
TO GERALDTON
TO MOUNT MAGNET
BRAND HWY
GREAT NORTHERN HWY
DARLING
Kyotmung
Cartref Park
Toodyay
Windmill Hill Cutting
Noggojerring
Yanchep Beach
Eglinton Rock
Yanchep
13
60
Crystal & Yonderup Caves
Lake Pinjar
Muchea
River
Ringa
Coorinja Winery
120
Avon

2
NEERABUP NATIONAL PARK
Barbagallo Raceway
QUINNS ROCKS
Bullsbrook
Pearce RAAF Station
AVON VALLEY NATIONAL PARK
Smiths Hill 361m
MORANGUP NATURE RESERVE
Balup
Clackline
Northam
EASTERN HWY
Mokine
Quellington
35
50
27
15
94

3
BURNS BEACH
JOONDALUP
Whitfords Beach
MULLALOO
HILLARYS
WANNEROO
MITCHELL FWY
Whiteman Park
UPPER SWAN
SWAN VALLEY WINE REGION
Gidgegannup
Woorooloo
Wundowie
Bakers Hill
GREAT
47
50
83
56
55
23

4
Underwater World
MARMION MARINE PARK
SCARBOROUGH
CITY BEACH
MIRRABOOKA MIDLAND GUILDFORD
JOHN FORREST NP
Parkerville
Stoneville
Mount Helena
Chidlow
GREENMOUNT NP
GREENMOUNT
Mahogany Creek
Sawyers Valley
GOOSEBERRY HILL NP
C.Y. O'Connor Museum
Mundaring Weir
York
York Motor Museum
EASTERN HWY
GREAT SOUTHERN
DYOTT RANGE
Mt Talbot 398m
26
56
18
94
16
14
47
20
24
22
23

5
Passenger Ferry to Rottnest Island
PERTH
COTTESLOE
PERTH AIRPORT
KALAMUNDA
CANNINGTON
Bickley
KALAMUNDA NP
Helena River Reservoir
RANGE
Darling
Talbot Brook
River
For more detail on Perth Suburbs see pages 372–5
9 19
22
28
34
22
10
23

6
Passenger Ferry to Rottnest Island
FREMANTLE
Adventure World
Stock Road Markets
SPEARWOOD
Cables Water Ski Park
MUNSTER
JANDAKOT
KELMSCOTT
MADDINGTON
ROLEYSTONE
Araluen Botanic Park
BROOKTON
Mt Dale 548m
Carnac Island
ARMADALE
Forrestdale Lake
ALBANY
Canning Dam
26
33
14
30
16
10
12
25
13

7
Garden Island
MILITARY AREA
NAVAL BASE
KWINANA
KWINANA FWY
LEDA
ROCKINGHAM
Cape Peron
Byford
Wungong Dam
Canning River
River
20
40
19
13
69
21
24
16
115

8
INDIAN
Cockburn Sound
SAFETY BAY
Penguin Island
WAIKIKI
Baldivis
Warnbro Beach
Becher Point
Mundijong
Mardella
Tumbulgum Farm
SERPENTINE NATIONAL PARK
Jarrahdale
Serpentine
Serpentine Dam
Mt Randall 525m
Westdale
River
Dale
22
15
8
30
23
28
29

9
OCEAN
Golden Bay
Singleton
Madora
Karnup
Serpentine
Keysbrook
WESTERN HWY
DARLING
Mt Solus 574m
93
59
17
16
11
15
20

10
Mandurah
Halls Head
Miami
Furnissdale
North Yunderup
South Yunderup
North Pinjarra
North Dandalup
SOUTH
Boonering Hill 529m
River
15
16
17
10
34
26
21
20
14

11
Florida
Melros
Cape Bouvard
Dawesville
OLD COAST
YALGORUP NATIONAL PARK
Peel Inlet
Lake Mealup
Lake McLarty
Pinjarra
Hotham Valley Tourist Railway
Meelon
Alcoa Scarp Lookout
South Dandalup Dam
Dwellingup
Forest Heritage Centre
Etmilyn
Etmilyn Forest Tramway
Amphion
Bannister
Wandering
Crossman
Hotham
Dwarda
CARNARVON HILLS
ALBANY HWY
16
13
9
12
17
20

12
Lake Clifton
Coolup
Marrinup
Lane-Poole Reserve
Nanga
WESTERN HWY
Mt Keats 474m
Boddington
Ranford
Marradong
River
67
43
20
5
15
11

13
Preston Beach
Preston Beach
YALGORUP NATIONAL PARK
Lake Preston
TO BUNBURY
Yarloop
Hamel
Waroona
Wagerup
SOUTH WESTERN HWY
Waroona Dam
Samson Brook Dam
Logue Brook Dam
RANGE
Mt Keats 474m
Mt Saddleback 575m
TO BUNBURY
109
54
40
30

N

A B C D 384 E F G H I

0 5 10 15 20 25 km

A B C D E F G H I

INDIAN OCEAN

N

TO PERTH
TO PERTH
376

YALGORUP NATIONAL PARK
Lake Preston
OLD
109
COAST
Wagerup
13
Yarloop
Logue Brook Dam
15
HWY
1
23
18
T Harvey
Harvey Weir
19
Myalup
3
Wokalup
Warawarrup
Stirling Dam
Binningup
2
11
Benger
SOUTH
Beela
Worsley Aluminium Refinery
10
19
20
40
WESTERN
Leschenault
Brunswick
13
Brunswick Junction
19
107
Worsley
Leschenault Inlet
9
Roelands
T Australind
12
Burekup
WELLINGTON NATIONAL PARK
Koombana Bay
Eaton
21
Waterloo
T Bunbury
4
7
Picton
11
Wellington Dam
3
Gelorup
Dardanup
19
River
HWY
10
Bunbury Speedway
9
1
10
5
Stratham
14
Boyanup
15
63
Lowden
16
Peppermint Grove Beach
51
9
18
Capel
River
Donnybrook
384
Cape Naturaliste
Lighthouse & Museum
TUART FOREST NP
SOUTH
18
Eagle Bay
Point Picquet
Sugarloaf Rock
Meelup
13
Geographe Bay
Wonnerup
Ludlow
7
18
13
WESTERN
Newlands
17
Grimwade
Dunsborough
Wonnerup Beach
TUART FOREST NP
10
Ludlow
Kirup
T Yallingup
Quindalup
BUSSELL
8
Busselton
BUSSELL
20
Abba
1
Mullalyup
6
15
Canal Rocks
2
Vasse
Yunderup
104
Ruabon
Tutunup
River
Balingup
Cape Clairault
Marybrook
16
41
HWY
Carbunup River
River
Yoongarillup
VASSE
19
58
Jarrahwood
HWY
LEEUWIN–
Quinnup
Jindong
River
NATURALISTE
Yelverton
Acton Park
14
Metricup
49
14
RANGE
104
NATIONAL
19
WHICHER
24
PARK
Willyabrup
Chapman Hill
16
Blackwood
41
Cowaramup Point
4
9
Cowaramup
13
Treeton
River
Gracetown
13
Bramley
THE RAPIDS CONSERVATION PARK
12
HWY
For more detail on Margaret River & Surrounds see page 379
Margaret
Mowen
23
Whinstone Hills
Cape Mentelle
Margaret River
27
Mt Yates,
Heritage Trail
21
T Nannup
23
10
Rosa Glen
Pioneer Settlers Memorial
HWY
Prevelly
4
Eagles Heritage
13
18
BUSSELL
Witchcliffe
Augusta-Busselton
19
River
45
Cape Freycinet
HWY
Blackwood
Sues Bridge
BLACKWOOD CONSERVATION PARK
10
LEEUWIN–
27
Warner Glen Bridge
9
VASSE
NATURALISTE
18
BROCKMAN
HWY
The Four Aces
NATIONAL
Boranup Hill
Alexandra Bridge
10
89
13
22
10
PARK
North Point
Nillup
12
Boranup
BROCKMAN
18
12
One Tree Bridge
Boranup Lookout
Karridale
11
21
Hamelin Bay
East Hill
17
Hamelin Island
BUSSELL
5
7
Hamelin Bay
2
Kudardup
HWY
Foul Bay
15
10
SCOTT NATIONAL PARK
Scott
River
Cape Hamelin
Hillview Lookout & Golf Course
Hardy Inlet
15
LEEUWIN–
17
NATURALISTE
Augusta
NATIONAL
Green Hill
NATURE RESERVE
Gingilup Swamps
HWY
PARK
Flinders Bay
D'ENTRECASTEAUX NATIONAL PARK
Lake Jasper
Lighthouse
Cape Leeuwin
Matthew Flinders Memorial
Seal Island
Flinders Bay
Lake Quitjup
TO PEMBERTON
BEEDELUP NP
384

1 2 3 4 5 6 7 8 9 10 11 12 13

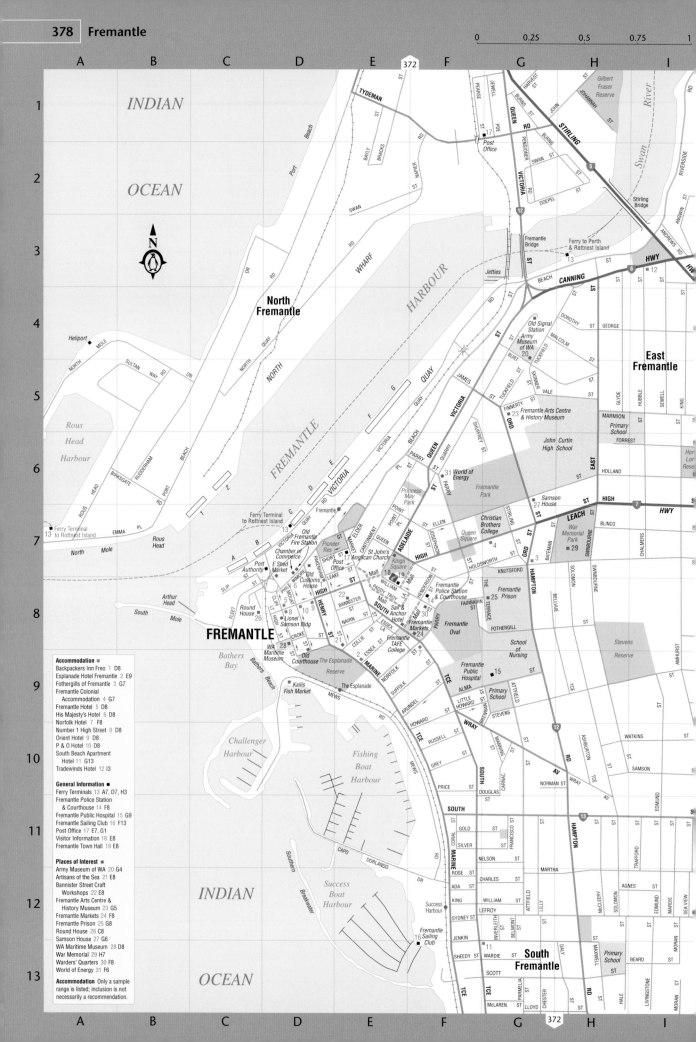

Accommodation ■
Backpackers Inn Freo 1 D8
Esplanade Hotel Fremantle 2 E9
Fothergills of Fremantle 3 G7
Fremantle Colonial
  Accommodation 4 G7
Fremantle Hotel 5 D8
His Majesty's Hotel 6 D8
Norfolk Hotel 7 F8
Number 1 High Street 8 D8
Orient Hotel 9 D8
P & O Hotel 10 D8
South Beach Apartment
  Hotel 11 G13
Tradewinds Hotel 12 I3

General Information ■
Ferry Terminals 13 A7, D7, H3
Fremantle Police Station
  & Courthouse 14 F8
Fremantle Public Hospital 15 G9
Fremantle Sailing Club 16 F13
Post Office 17 E7, G1
Visitor Information 18 E8
Fremantle Town Hall 19 E8

Places of Interest ■
Army Museum of WA 20 G4
Artisans of the Sea 21 E8
Bannister Street Craft
  Workshops 22 E8
Fremantle Arts Centre &
  History Museum 23 G5
Fremantle Markets 24 F8
Fremantle Prison 25 G8
Round House 26 C8
Samson House 27 G6
WA Maritime Museum 28 D8
War Memorial 29 H7
Warders' Quarters 30 F8
World of Energy 31 F6

Accommodation Only a sample
range is listed; inclusion is not
necessarily a recommendation.

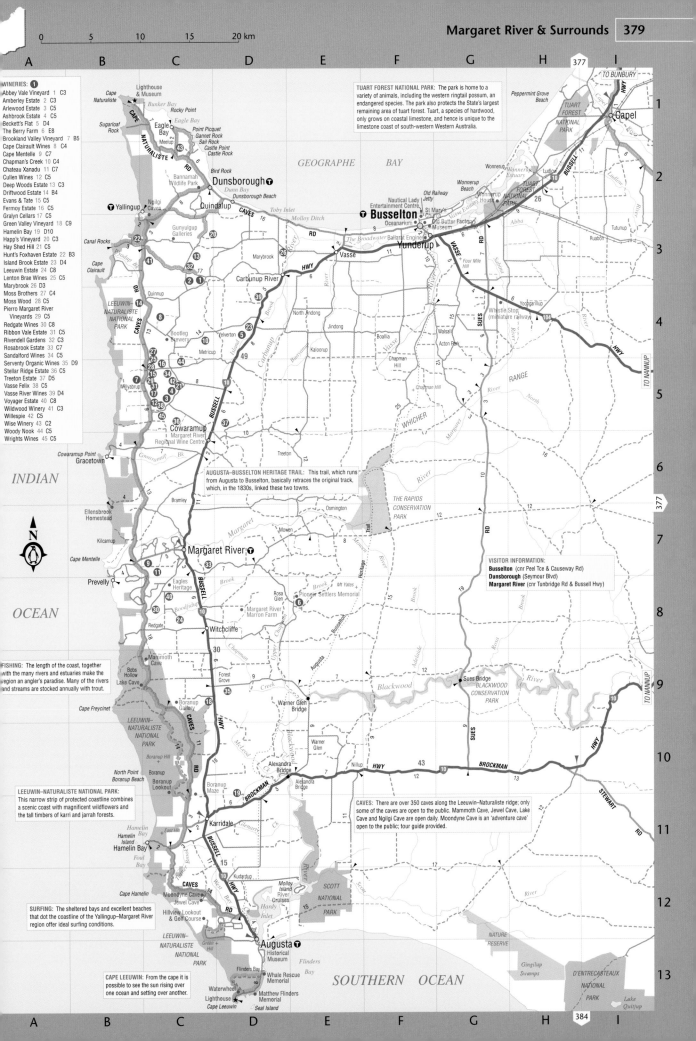

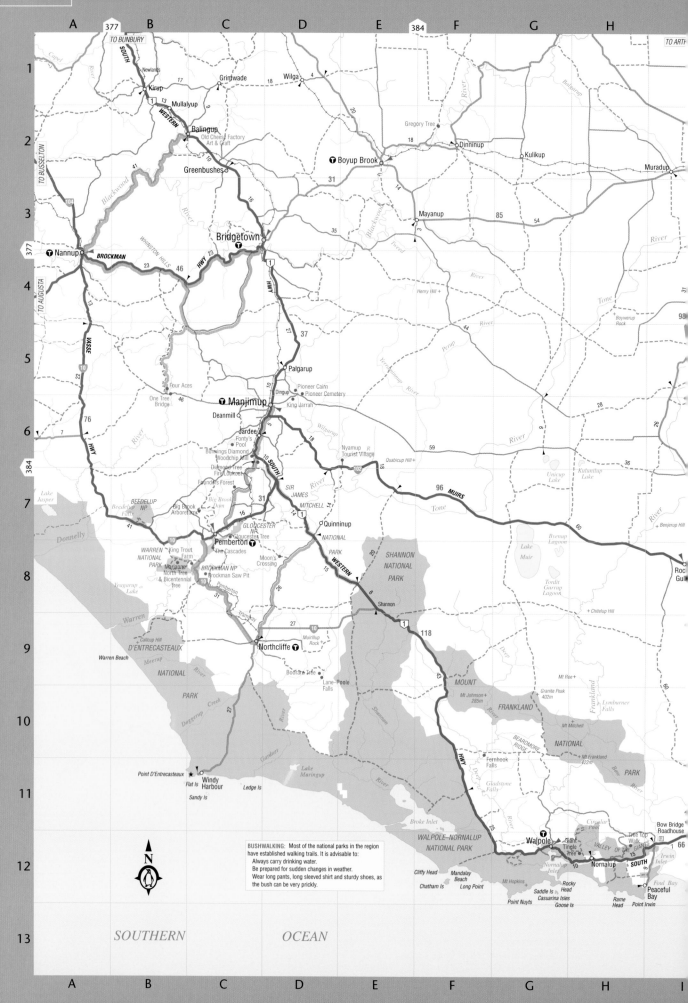

A map of the South Coast region. Grid columns A–H (top and bottom), rows 1–13.

TO BUNBURY

377

TO BUSSELTON

TO AUGUSTA

377

384

Newlands
Kirup
Mullalyup
17
1
13
WESTERN
SOUTH
6
Balingup
Old Cheese Factory Art & Craft
Greenbushes
41
10
Grinwade
18
Wilga
4
20
Gregory Tree
18
Dinninup
Kulikup
Muradup
31
14
Boyup Brook
85
54
River
Mayanup
3
35
Henry Hill +
44
River
Boywerup Rock
98
Tone
River

Nannup
BROCKMAN
23
46
HWY
23
16
Bridgetown
1
HWY
27
37
13
VASSE
22
104
Blackwood River
WHINSTON HILLS
Palgarup
10
Dingup
Pioneer Cairn
Pioneer Cemetery
King Jarrah
River
Perup
Yerkiminnup
28
26
HWY
76
7
Four Aces
One Tree Bridge
46
Manjimup
Deanmill
Jardee
Fonty's Pool
Bunnings Diamond Woodchip Mill
Diamond Tree Fire Lookout
Founders Forest
5
10 SOUTH
18
Wilgarup
Nyamup Tourist Village
102
Quabicup Hill +
59
36
Unicup Lake
Kulunilup Lake
96 MUIRS
9
26
River

BEEDELUP NP
Beedelup Falls
41
Big Brook Arboretum
Big Brook Dam
16
31
GLOUCESTER NR
Gloucester Tree
Pemberton
King Trout Farm
The Cascades
14
1
SIR JAMES MITCHELL
12
Quinninup
NATIONAL
18
Tone River
Lake Muir
Rvenup Lagoon
60
River
Benjerup Hill

WARREN NATIONAL PARK
Marianne North Tree & Bicentennial Tree
Brockman Saw Pit
10
BROCKMAN NP
Pemberton
Founders Forest
Moon's Crossing
15
PARK
WESTERN
20
6
SHANNON NATIONAL PARK
Shannon
Tordit Gurrup Lagoon
+ Chitelup Hill
Rocky Gull

D'ENTRECASTEAUX
Callcup Hill
Warren Beach
31
Tram Way
27
Muirillup Rock
10
Northcliffe
1
118
43
MOUNT
Mt Johnson + 285m
Granite Peak 402m
FRANKLAND
Mt Roe +
Mt Mitchell
Lymburner Falls
60
River

NATIONAL
River
Creek
Yeagarup Lake
Meerup River
Warren
Degerup Creek
27
Boodarie Tree
Lane-Poole Falls
River
Gardner River
Lake Maringup
Shannon River
Deep River
Fernhook Falls
NATIONAL
+ Mt Frankland 422m
BEARDMORE RIDGE
Gladstone Falls
PARK

Point D'Entrecasteaux
Flat Is
Windy Harbour
Sandy Is
Ledge Is
25
Broke Inlet
WALPOLE-NORNALUP NATIONAL PARK
Walpole
Giant Tingle Tree
Nornalup Inlet
10
Nornalup
Tree Top Walk
VALLEY OF THE GIANTS
Circular Pool
Bow Bridge Roadhouse
66
1
SOUTH
15
Irwin Bay

BUSHWALKING: Most of the national parks in the region have established walking trails. It is advisable to:
Always carry drinking water.
Be prepared for sudden changes in weather.
Wear long pants, long sleeved shirt and sturdy shoes, as the bush can be very prickly.

N

Penguin

Cliffy Head
Chatham Is
Mandalay Beach
Long Point
Mt Hopkins +
Saddle Is
Casuarina Isles
Goose Is
Rame Head
Point Nuyts
Point Irwin
Peaceful Bay
Foul Bay

SOUTHERN   OCEAN

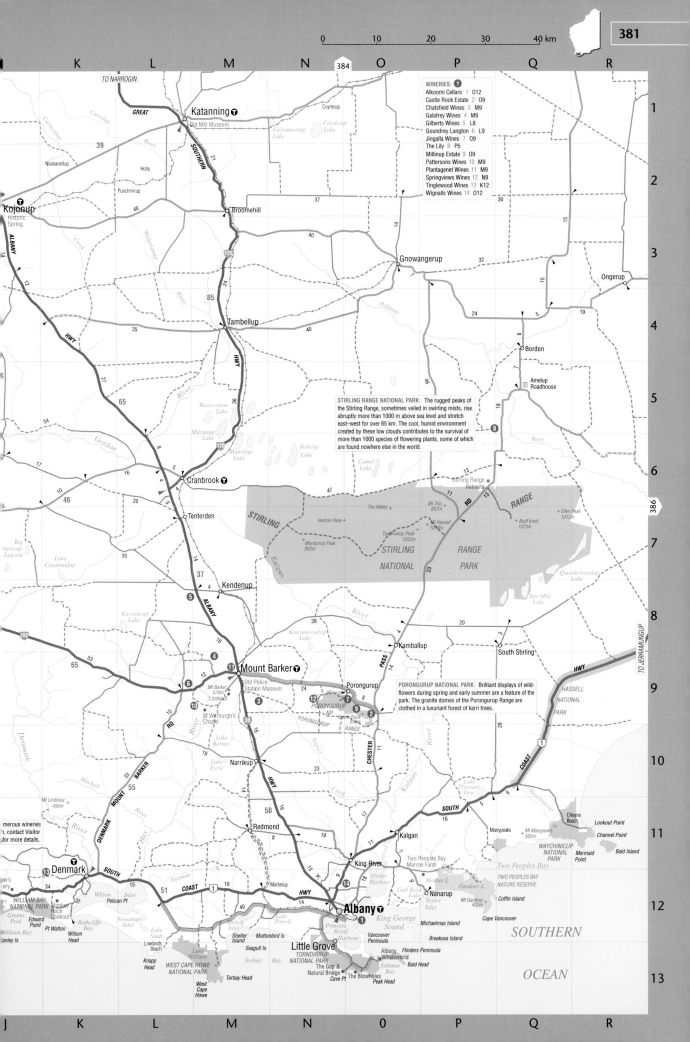

WINERIES: 1
Alkoomi Cellars 1 O12
Castle Rock Estate 2 O9
Chatsfield Wines 3 M9
Galafrey Wines 4 M9
Gilberts Wines 5 L8
Goundrey Langton 6 L9
Jingalla Wines 7 O9
The Lily 8 P5
Millinup Estate 9 O9
Pattersons Wines 10 M9
Plantagenet Wines 11 M9
Springviews Wines 12 N9
Tinglewood Wines 13 K12
Wignalls Wines 14 O12

STIRLING RANGE NATIONAL PARK: The rugged peaks of the Stirling Range, sometimes veiled in swirling mists, rise abruptly more than 1000 m above sea level and stretch east–west for over 65 km. The cool, humid environment created by these low clouds contributes to the survival of more than 1000 species of flowering plants, some of which are found nowhere else in the world.

PORONGURUP NATIONAL PARK: Brilliant displays of wildflowers during spring and early summer are a feature of the park. The granite domes of the Porongurup Range are clothed in a luxuriant forest of karri trees.

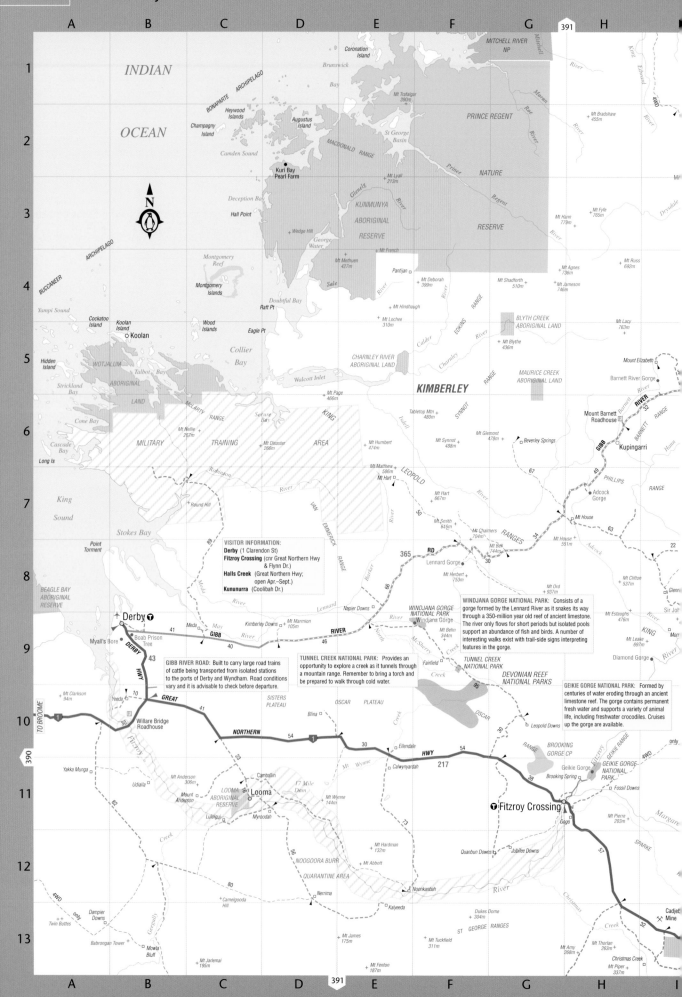

INDIAN

OCEAN

BONAPARTE ARCHIPELAGO

Coronation Island

Brunswick Bay

MITCHELL RIVER NP

Heywood Islands

Champagny Island

Augustus Island

Camden Sound

St George Basin

PRINCE REGENT

Mt Trafalgar 390m

Mt Bradshaw 455m

Kuri Bay Pearl Farm

Mt Lyall 213m

NATURE

Deception Bay

KUNMUNYA

Mt Hann 779m

Mt Fyfe 765m

Hall Point

ABORIGINAL

RESERVE

Mt Russ 692m

ARCHIPELAGO

Wedge Hill

George Water

Mt French

Mt Agnes 736m

BUCCANEER

Montgomery Reef

Mt Methuen 427m

Pantijan

Mt Deborah 399m

Mt Shadforth 510m

Mt Jameson 746m

Yampi Sound

Montgomery Islands

Doubtful Bay

Raft Pt

Sale

Mt Hindhaugh

RANGE

BLYTH CREEK ABORIGINAL LAND

Mt Lacy 763m

Cockatoo Island

Koolan Island

Wood Islands

Eagle Pt

Mt Lochee 310m

EDKINS

Mt Blythe 436m

Mount Elizabeth

Hidden Island

Koolan

Collier Bay

CHARNLEY RIVER ABORIGINAL LAND

Charnley

MAURICE CREEK ABORIGINAL LAND

Barnett River Gorge

WOTJALUM

Talbot Bay

Walcott Inlet

KIMBERLEY

RANGE

Strickland Bay

ABORIGINAL

Mt Page 466m

Tabletop Mtn 480m

SYMNOT

Mount Barnett Roadhouse

RIVER

Cone Bay

LAND

McLARTY RANGE

Secure Bay

KING

Idaill

Mt Glemont 478m

Beverley Springs

GIBB

Kupingarri

Cascade Bay

Mt Nellie 267m

Mt Disaster 266m

Mt Humbert 474m

Mt Synnot 488m

Phillips RANGE

Long Is

MILITARY

TRAINING

AREA

Mt Matthew 586m

Mt Hart

LEOPOLD

Adcock Gorge

King Sound

Robinson

Mt Hart 667m

Mt House

RANGE

Point Torment

Round Hill

VAN

EMMERICK

River

50

Mt Smith 616m

RANGES

Mt House 551m

22

Stokes Bay

RANGE

365

RD

Mt Chalmers 704m

Mt Bell 744m

Mt House 937m

Mt Clifton 537m

VISITOR INFORMATION:
Derby (1 Clarendon St)
Fitzroy Crossing (cnr Great Northern Hwy & Flynn Dr.)
Halls Creek (Great Northern Hwy; open Apr.–Sept.)
Kununurra (Coolibah Dr.)

Butler

66

Lennard Gorge

30

Mt Herbert 753m

Mt Ord 937m

Mt Estaughs 476m

KING

BEAGLE BAY ABORIGINAL RESERVE

Medu

Lennard

Napier Downs

River

North

WINDJANA GORGE NATIONAL PARK

Windjana Gorge

Mt Behn 344m

McSherry

Mt Leake 697m

Sir Jol

Derby

Meda

Kimberley Downs

Mt Marmion 105m

RIVER

46

Morr

Diamond Gorge

Boab Prison Tree

41

GIBB

WINDJANA GORGE NATIONAL PARK: Consists of a gorge formed by the Lennard River as it snakes its way through a 350-million year old reef of ancient limestone. The river only flows for short periods but isolated pools support an abundance of fish and birds. A number of interesting walks exist with trail-side signs interpreting features in the gorge.

Myall's Bore

DERBY

40

May

River

Fairfield

TUNNEL CREEK NATIONAL PARK

DEVONIAN REEF NATIONAL PARKS

43

HWY

GIBB RIVER ROAD: Built to carry large road trains of cattle being transported from isolated stations to the ports of Derby and Wyndham. Road conditions vary and it is advisable to check before departure.

TUNNEL CREEK NATIONAL PARK: Provides an opportunity to explore a creek as it tunnels through a mountain range. Remember to bring a torch and be prepared to walk through cold water.

Creek

95

GEIKIE GORGE NATIONAL PARK: Formed by centuries of water eroding through an ancient limestone reef. The gorge contains permanent fresh water and supports a variety of animal life, including freshwater crocodiles. Cruises up the gorge are available.

TO BROOME

1

Mt Clarkson 94m

Yeeda

10

GREAT

41

SISTERS PLATEAU

OSCAR PLATEAU

OSCAR

30

Leopold Downs

GEIKIE RANGE

RANGE

only

4WD

Willare Bridge Roadhouse

30

NORTHERN

54

Blina

Creek

BROOKING GORGE CP

GEIKIE GORGE NATIONAL PARK

390

Fitzroy

Ellendale

HWY

54

Geikie Gorge

Yakka Munga

23

Mt Anderson 306m

Camballin

Mt Wynne

30

Calwynyardah

217

RANGE

BROOKING

38

Brooking Spring

Fossil Downs

Udialla

Mount Anderson

LOOMA ABORIGINAL RESERVE

Looma

17 Mile Dam

Mt Wynne 144m

Gogo

Fitzroy Crossing

Mt Pierre 203m

82

Lulligui

Myroodah

73

Quanbun Downs

Jubilee Downs

57

Margare

Creek

56

NOOGOORA BURR

Mt Hardman 132m

Mt Abbott

River

SPARKE

4WD only

Dampier Downs

80

QUARANTINE AREA

Nerrima

Noonkanbah

Dukes Dome 304m

Christmas

32

Cadjet Mine

Twin Buttes

Kalyeeda

ST GEORGE RANGES

Mt Amy 268m

Mt Thorlan 263m

Babrongan Tower

Mowla Bluff

Mt Jarlemai 195m

Mt James 175m

Mt Fenton 187m

Mt Tuckfield 311m

Mt Piper 337m

Christmas Creek

390

391

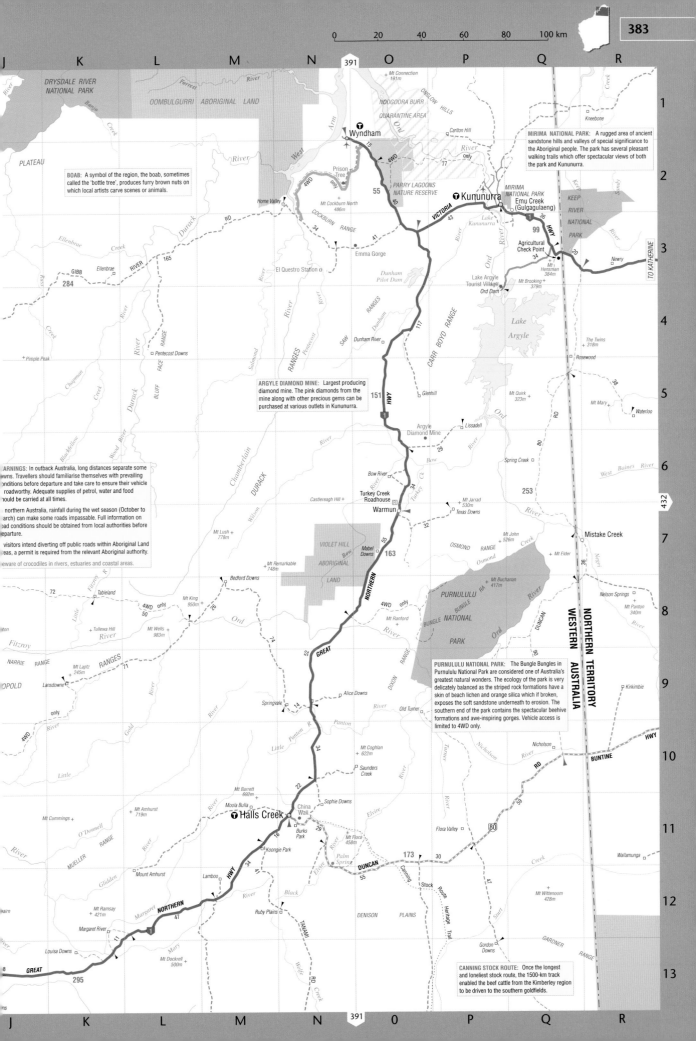

0   20   40   60   80 km

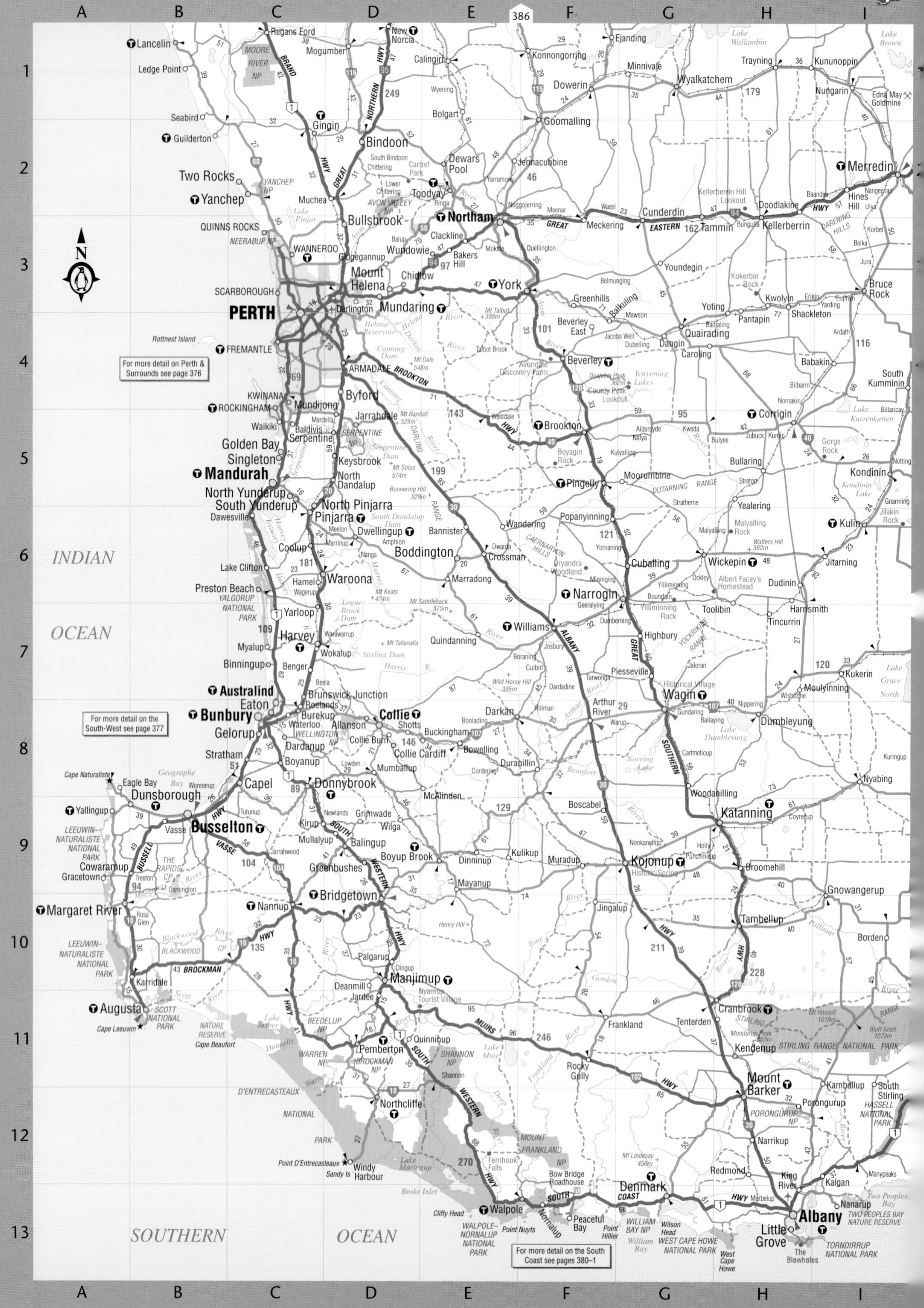

A   B   C   D   E   F   G   H   I

INDIAN

OCEAN

N

For more detail on Perth & Surrounds see page 376

For more detail on the South-West see page 377

For more detail on the South Coast see pages 380–1

1

Lancelin
Ledge Point
Regans Ford
Mogumber
New Norcia
Calingiri
Konnongorring
Ejanding
Trayning
Kununoppin
MOORE RIVER NP
Wyalkatchem
Minnivale
Dowerin
Nungarin
Edna May Goldmine

2

Seabird
Guilderton
Two Rocks
Yanchep
Gingin
Muchea
Bindoon
South Bindoon
Chittering
Dewars Pool
Toodyay
Jennacubbine
Yarramony
Goomalling
Bolgart
Wyening
Merredin
Hines Hill
Nangeenan
YANCHEP NP
Lower Chittering
Cartref Park
Ringa

3

QUINNS ROCKS
WANNEROO
Bullsbrook
Gidgegannup
Balun
Wundowie
Clackline
Bakers Hill
Northam
Noggojerring
Meenar
Waeel
Cunderin
Doodlakine
Kellerberrin
Korbel
Belka
Jura
Bruce Rock
SCARBOROUGH
NEERABUP NP
Mount Helena
Chidlow
Meckering
GREAT EASTERN
Tammin
Bungulla
DARLING HILLS
Belka

4

PERTH
FREMANTLE
Darlington
Mundaring
York
Greenhills
Belmunging
Beverley East
Jacobs Well
Dangin
Caroling
Quairading
Ardath
Babakin
South Kummimin
Rottnest Island
Helena Reservoir
Talbot Brook
Avondale Discovery Farm
Quairading

5

KWINANA
ROCKINGHAM
Waikiki
Baldivis
Serpentine
Byford
Jarrahdale
Brookton
Boyagin Rock
Aldersyde
Nalya
Kweda
Bulyee
Bullaring
Corrigin
Kondinin Lake
Notting
Golden Bay
Singleton
Keysbrook
North Dandalup
Mt Solus 574m
SERPENTINE NP
Serpentine Dam

6

MANDURAH
North Yunderup
South Yunderup
Dawesville
Pinjarra
North Pinjarra
Dwellingup
Bannister
Wandering
Crossman
Pingelly
Moorumbine
Popanyinning
Yealering
Kulin
Coolup
Marrinup
Boddington
Marradong
Cuballing
Wickepin
Jitarning
INDIAN OCEAN
Lake Clifton
Hamel
Nanga
Dryandra Woodland
Minnigin

7

OCEAN
Waroona
Yarloop
Harvey
Myalup
Benger
Warawarrup
Quindanning
Williams
Narrogin
Highbury
Toolibin
Harrismith
Tincurrin
Logue Brook Dam
Stirling Dam
Culbin
Boraning
Josbury
Piesseville
Kukerin
Moulyinning
Binningup
Wokalup

8

Australind
Bunbury
Eaton
Brunswick Junction
Roelands
Burekup
Collie
Shotts
Darkan
Arthur River
Wagin
Dumbleyung
Lake Dumbleyung
Nyabing
Gelorup
Stratham
Waterloo
Allanson
Collie Burn
Collie Cardiff
Bowelling
Buckingham
Dardadine
Woodanilling
Kuringup
Dardanup
Boyanup
Mumballup
Durabillin
Cordering
Beaufort
Norring Lake

9

Eagle Bay
Dunsborough
Vasse
Busselton
Capel
Donnybrook
McAlinden
Boscabel
Katanning
Nyabing
Yallingup
Cowaramup
Gracetown
Kirup
Newlands
Grimwade
Wilga
Mullalyup
Balingup
Boyup Brook
Dinninup
Kulikup
Muradup
Kojonup
Broomehill
Gnowangerup
LEEUWIN-NATURALISTE NATIONAL PARK
Jarrahwood
Greenbushes
Mayanup

10

Margaret River
Nannup
Bridgetown
Palgarup
Jingalup
Tambellup
Borden
Rosa Glen
BLACKWOOD
BROCKMAN
Dingup
Manjimup
Frankland
LEEUWIN-NATURALISTE NATIONAL PARK

11

Karridale
Augusta
Cape Leeuwin
SCOTT NATIONAL PARK
Deanmill
Jardee
Pemberton
Quinninup
Nyamup
Tourist Village
Rocky Gully
Cranbrook
Kendenup
Mount Barker
Kamballup
South Stirling
WARREN NP
BEEDELUP NP
SHANNON NP
Lake Muir
STIRLING RANGE NATIONAL PARK

12

D'ENTRECASTEAUX
NATIONAL
PARK
Northcliffe
Shannon
MOUNT FRANKLAND NP
Narrikup
Porongurup
PORONGURUP NP
HASSELL NATIONAL PARK
Redmond
King River
Manypeaks
Kalgan

13

SOUTHERN   **OCEAN**
Point D'Entrecasteaux
Sandy Is
Windy Harbour
Broke Inlet
Walpole
Cliffy Head
Point Nuyts
WALPOLE-NORNALUP NATIONAL PARK
Peaceful Bay
Point Hillier
Bow Bridge Roadhouse
Fernhook Falls
Denmark
COAST
WILLIAM BAY NP
Wilson Head
WEST CAPE HOWE NATIONAL PARK
West Cape Howe
The Blowholes
Albany
Little Grove
Nanarup
Two Peoples Bay
TWO PEOPLES BAY NATURE RESERVE
TORNDIRRUP NATIONAL PARK

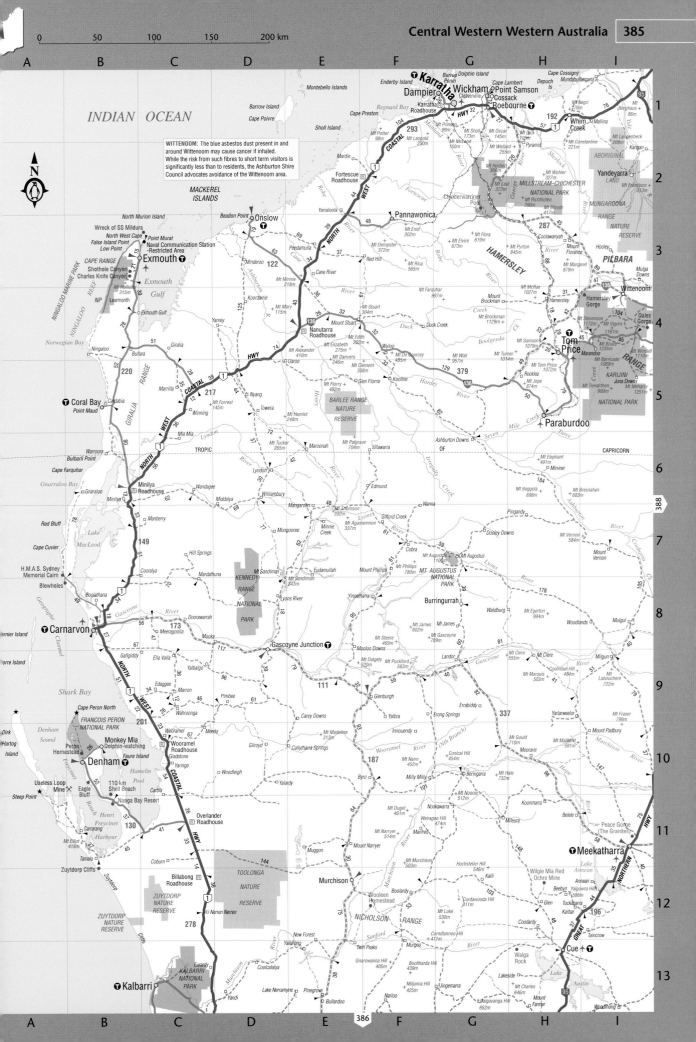

388

INDIAN OCEAN

WITTENOOM: The blue asbestos dust present in and around Wittenoom may cause cancer if inhaled. While the risk from such fibres to short term visitors is significantly less than to residents, the Ashburton Shire Council advocates avoidance of the Wittenoom area.

MACKEREL ISLANDS

Montebello Islands

Barrow Island
Cape Poivre

Karratha
Wickham Point Samson
Dampier Cossack
Roebourne

PILBARA

Exmouth

Onslow

Pannawonica

HAMERSLEY

Wittenoom

Tom Price

KARIJINI NATIONAL PARK

Coral Bay

Paraburdoo

TROPIC OF CAPRICORN

Carnarvon

Gascoyne Junction

Burringurrah

MT AUGUSTUS NATIONAL PARK

Denham
Monkey Mia

Meekatharra

Murchison

Kalbarri

Cue

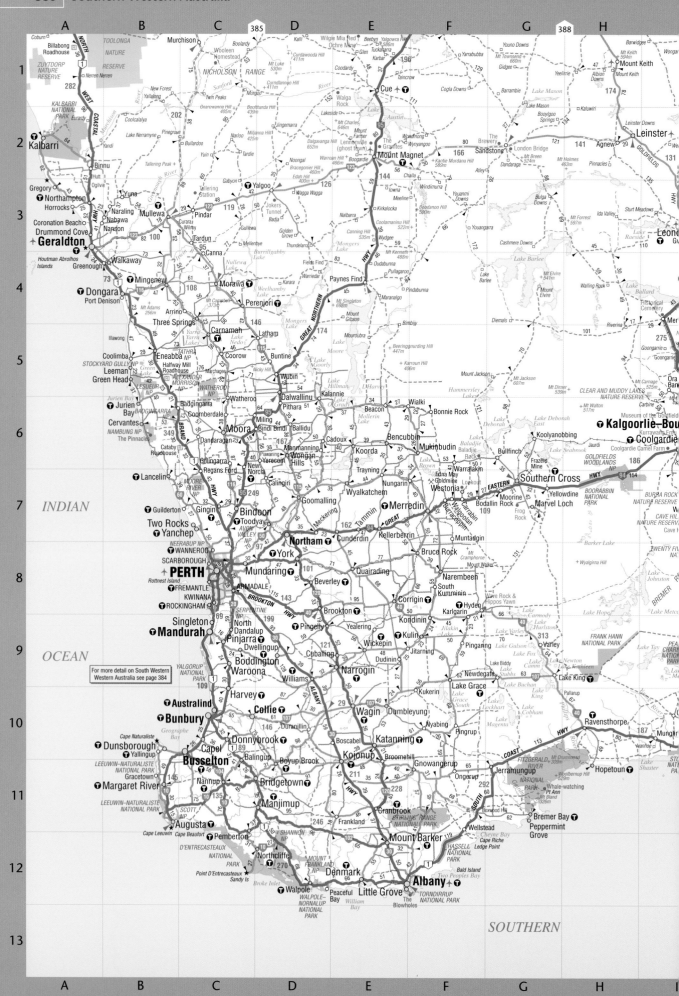

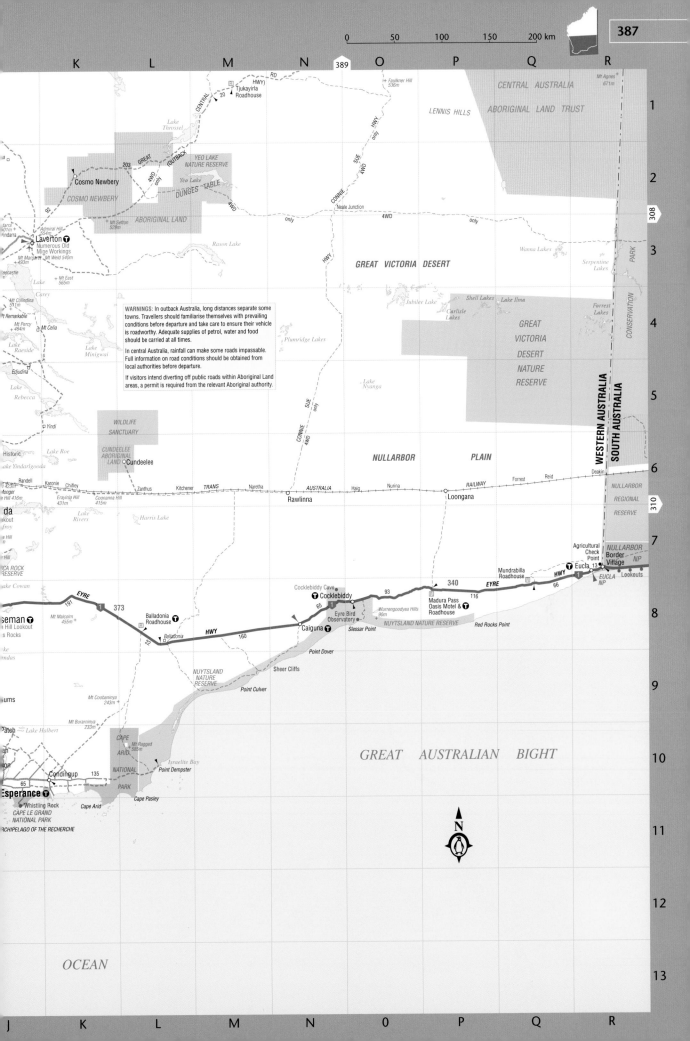

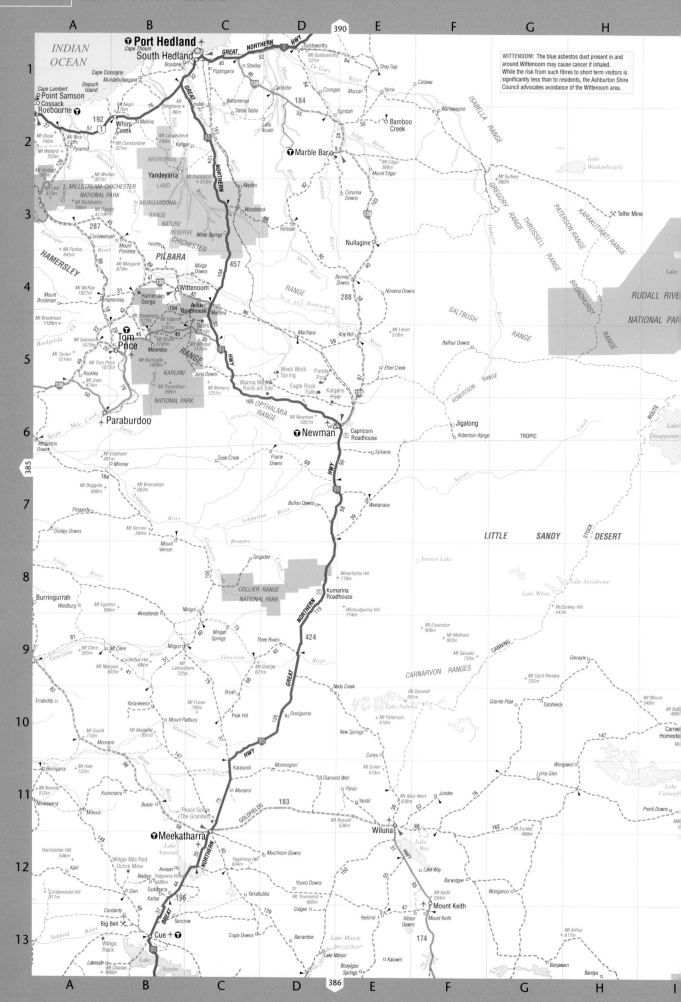

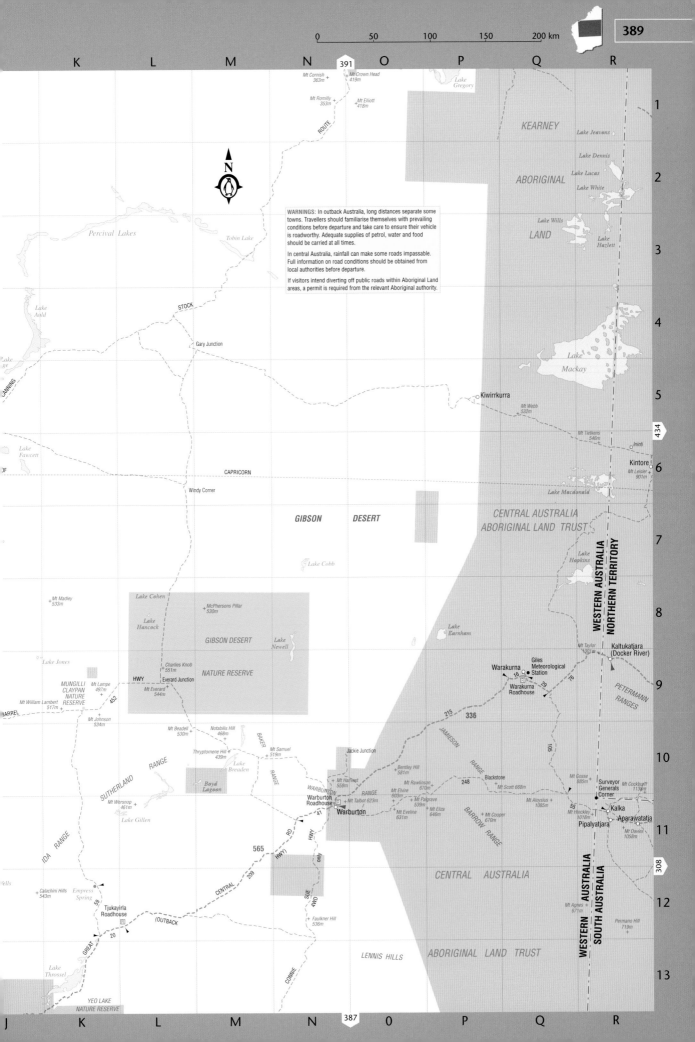

INDIAN OCEAN

N

Cape Leveque
One Arm Point
Thomas Bay
Cygnet Bay
Lombadina–Djarindjin
LOMBADINA
ABORIGINAL
RESERVE
Pender Bay
75
Beagle Bay
Beagle
Bay
BEAGLE BAY
ABORIGINAL
RESERVE
*Lake
Paterson*
Cape Baskerville
Carnot Bay
DAMPIER
PENINSULA
*Country
Downs*
Cape Bertholet
Fraser
River
POINT COULOMB
NATURE RESERVE
Coulomb Point
James Price Point
122
4WD only
Cape Boileau
145
Roebuck
Roadhouse
115
NORTHERN
Waterbank
BROOME
HWY
Cable Beach
34
Lake Eda
Taylory
Lagoon
Broome
Roebuck
Ungani Lakes
Gantheaume Point
30
Plains
Roebuck Bay
Thangoo
Cape Villaret
153
Gourdon Bay
Cape Latouche Treville
GREAT
Port Smith
4WD only
False Cape Bossut
La Grange Bay
Bidyadanga
Cape Bossut
Frazier Downs
Admiral Bay
Cape Frezier
Cape Jaubert
Desault Bay
Cape Missiessy
Nita Downs
286
Anna Plains
Mt Phire
90m
Beach
103
GREAT SANDY DESERT
Mile
Mandora
Wallal Downs
HWY
Eighty
Sandfire
139
NORTHERN
Roadhouse
281
Pardoo
Station
50
GREAT
Pardoo
Roadhouse
Port Hedland
De Grey
South Hedland
Goldsworthy
Cape Thouin
1
Mt Goldsworthy
131m
84
52
Boodarie
40
Strelley
De Grey River
Shay Gap
Cape Cossigny
52
46
Pippingarra
Callawa
Mundabullangara
Coongan
Muccan
Yarrie
Depuch Island
385
388
Cartindie

A B C D E F G H

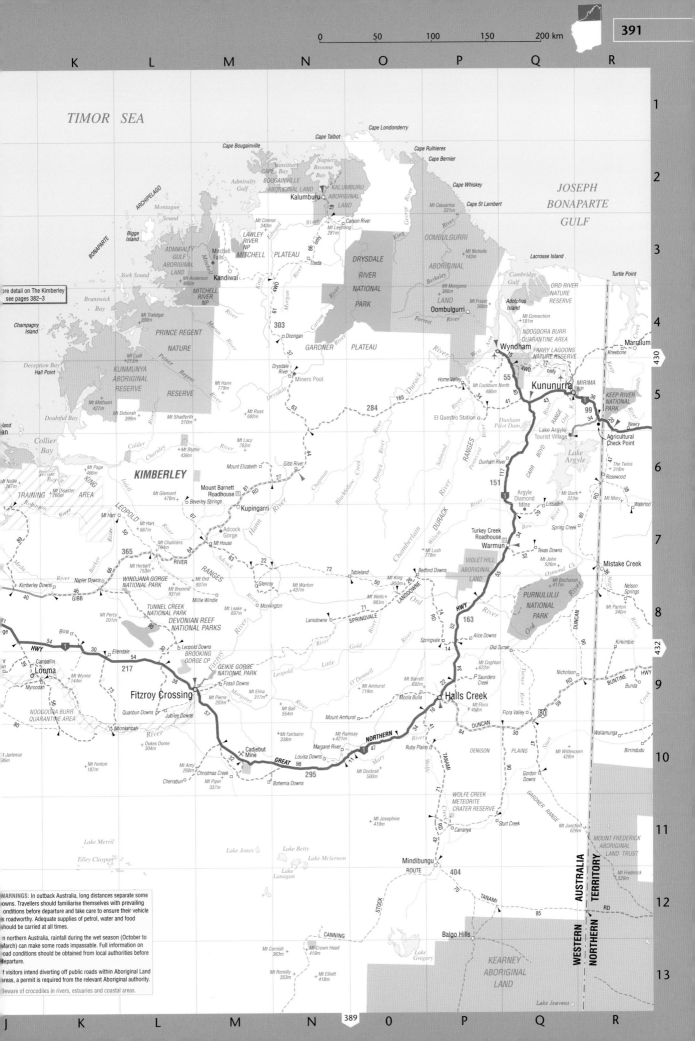

NORTHERN TERRITORY

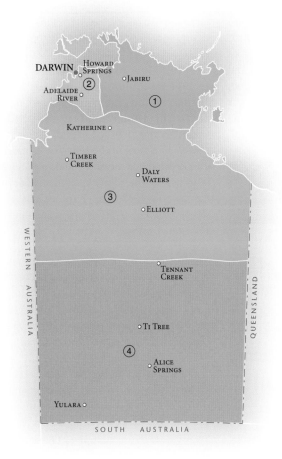

The Northern Territory lies midway across the continent. Its Top End includes the steamy tropics to the far north and its southern extremity reaches into Australia's desert heart. It is a frontier of sometimes extraordinary remoteness where vast tracks of land are unsettled, where climate dominates even urban life and where some of the country's most remarkable natural landscapes are to be found.

Floodplains to desert plains

The Timor Sea, the Arafura Sea and the Gulf of Carpentaria, scattered with islands, front the Northern Territory's tropical coastline. Flood plains, mudflats and mangroves dominate the coast, and some of Australia's most significant wetland areas are found just east of Darwin. Rivers near the coast, ranging from the big tidal waterways of the west to the small crystal flows in the east, support big populations of barramundi and other freshwater species.

The western border of the Territory abuts Western Australia's Kimberley region and shares much of its ancient, rugged character. South from the coast the land rises gently to the low, sandstone Barkly Tableland, where millions of hectares of tussock grassland are watered for cattle pasture by artesian

Ghost gum, Central Australia

bores during the dry season. Much of the interior tableland is desert or semi-arid. Viewed from above, it is a landscape wrinkled with the shapes of ancient landforms such as the MacDonnell Ranges.

Lands and landscapes

Some 50 per cent of the Territory's area is Aboriginal land or land under claim. This includes most of the offshore islands, the north-east corner of Arnhem Land, a section of the west coast and a piece of the eastern half of the Territory stretching from Timber Creek to the South Australian border.

The Territory's most distinctive landscapes are protected by national parks, some in remote regions. Two of the parks are World Heritage areas. The first, Kakadu in the tropical north, is a wonderland of diversity and contains one of the world's oldest and largest Aboriginal rock-art galleries. The second, Uluṟu–Kata Tjuṯa, which lies in The Red Centre, is home to Uluṟu, the monolith that has become Australia's most recognised natural symbol.

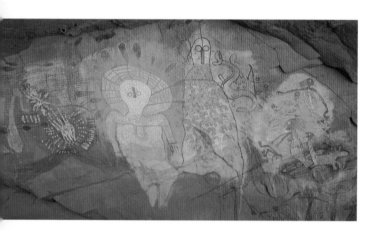

Aboriginal rock art, Northern Territory

First peoples

Archaeological evidence points to a human presence in Australia that goes back at least 50 000 and possibly 80 000 years. At the time of white settlement there was an estimated population in the Territory area of 35 000 Aboriginal people living in 126 tribal groups, broken down into family groups of about twenty. As in other parts of Australia, the Aboriginal people made good use of the available resources and were able to cope with the climatic extremes.

A faltering foothold

A Dutch ship, the *Arnhem*, sighted the Territory coast in 1623. The British, concerned about Dutch interest in northern Australia, established three settlements on the coast between 1824 and 1849. All three struggled against environment and remoteness, and failed.

In 1863 the Northern Territory became part of South Australia. Palmerston, renamed Darwin in 1911, was selected as the main town in 1869. A telegraph line linking Adelaide to Palmerston and the overseas cable was completed in 1872. A gold rush at Pine Creek in 1874 attracted prospectors and in the 1880s pastoralists began to settle on the Barkly Tableland to raise cattle for live export to Asia.

The Territory's post-colonial history has been one of the most turbulent in Australia. Apart from the struggle to maintain settlement in one of the world's most forbidding landscapes, the Territory was bombed extensively by the Japanese in the 1940s and has faced three major cyclones. Cyclone Tracy effectively destroyed the capital Darwin in 1974.

Governing the Never Never

In 1911 South Australia surrendered the Northern Territory to the Commonwealth. An administrator then ran the Territory until a partly elected Legislative Council was established in 1947. From 1922, voters elected a member of the House of Representatives in Canberra but that member could vote only on matters relating to the Territory. Aboriginal adults were given the vote in 1962. The Territory was granted full self-government in 1978, but a referendum in October 1998 voted against its becoming a State.

Territorians

The Territory has a population of 192 000, the lowest of any State or Territory. Darwin has around 90 000 people and Alice Springs 26 000. Around 20 per cent of the population claim an overseas birthplace, mainly the United Kingdom and New Zealand but increasingly the Philippines, East Timor and Indonesia.

Nearly a quarter of all Territorians, around 47 000 people, identify as Aboriginal people. Historically, the remoteness of Arnhem Land and the deserts kept Europeans at bay, although missionaries did penetrate some remote regions. The Territory's indigenous communities retain their language and culture to a far greater degree than elsewhere in Australia.

Visitors by the million

The Territory's main industries are mining, beef cattle, pearl farming, fishing, crocodile farming and tourism. One and a quarter million visitors, nearly half from overseas, arrive each year to experience the Territory's unique natural and cultural features. Activities tend to be based around the two main centres 1500 kilometres apart: Darwin in the tropical north and Alice Springs in the desert centre. The peak time to visit is May to October, during the Top End's dry season and the Centre's pleasantly warm winter.

For more information on the Northern Territory, see Tourist Bureaus on p. 591.

DARWIN

A famous Fannie Bay sunset

DARWIN looms larger in the imagination than the size of its population might warrant. Its climate, hot and dry, then hot and humid, has always presented an enormous challenge to settlers. The site of Australia's worst natural disaster and of its worst wartime disaster; it is the country's furthest outpost.

VISITOR INFORMATION
Tourism Top End
cnr Mitchell and Knuckey sts, Darwin
(08) 8936 2499
www.ntholidays.com

Twice rebuilt, Darwin has a spacious, ordered feel thanks to the wide streets, newish, low buildings and expansive, manicured lawns. But it is also a city with a magnificent tropical chaos as streets give way to mangrove estuaries, brightly coloured foliage and huge ocean tides.

Darwin is about the size of a large provincial town (population around 90 000), with all the facilities you would expect of a capital city, such as major cultural and social institutions, great restaurants, international hotels and a range of leisure activities. Culturally and ethnically it is Australia's most diverse city. The mix includes: southern

DARWIN BY AREA

| CITY CENTRE |
| THE ESPLANADE |
| STATE SQUARE |
| WHARF PRECINCT |
| NORTH OF THE CITY CENTRE |
| SUBURBS |

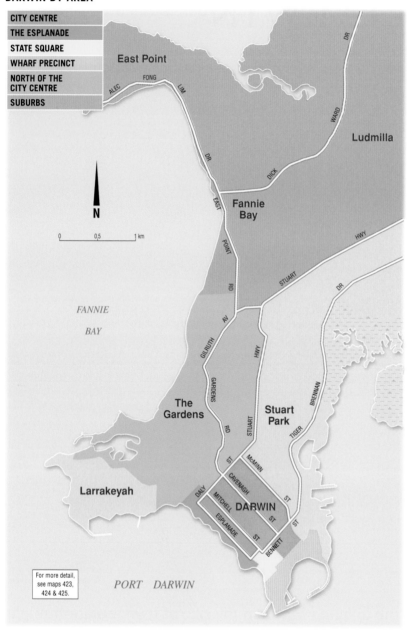

East Point

Ludmilla

Fannie Bay

FANNIE

BAY

The Gardens

Stuart Park

Larrakeyah

DARWIN

PORT DARWIN

For more detail, see maps 423, 424 & 425.

dry and still. The period from October to mid-December is known locally as 'the build-up': humidity increases dramatically and the sky is heavy with storm clouds. This is a dreaded time of random madness, as residents wait for the monsoonal downpours to start. When the thunderclouds finally break, the surrounding landscape turns a lush tropical green and the local wildlife population expands.

EXPLORING DARWIN

Darwin is a very easy city to negotiate either by car or on foot. The streets are well signed and traffic is light even at peak times. The **Tour Tub** is a service that provides a bus tour of the city's top sights. It departs daily from the north end of Smith Street Mall and extends as far north as East Point, and south to the Darwin Wharf Precinct. The service completes a loop every hour, and you can get on and off as you please. The extensive network of paths around town, along with the benefit of a fairly flat terrain, makes Darwin a terrific place to explore by bicycle. A tour of the harbour is a must. Cullen Bay Marina is the departure point for cruises around Fannie Bay, Stokes Hill Wharf and Frances Bay, and for ferry trips to Mandorah on the Cox Peninsula. The Darwin Bus Service provides a vital link between the city centre and outlying suburbs; the main terminal is on Harry Chan Avenue. If you are planning to hire a car, it is important to check the stipulations for driving on unsealed roads, particularly if you are travelling beyond Darwin.

CITY CENTRE

Start your exploration of Darwin in **Smith Street Mall**, the city's retail heart. Within this pleasant area of plazas, modern shops and giant tropical trees is the **Victoria Hotel**, built in the 1890s. Still a fully operational hotel and popular with visitors and locals alike, it now has a small shopping complex.

Walk south down Smith Street, beyond the mall, to the corner of Harry

transients on northern assignments; tourists from as far away as Europe on extended stays; Aboriginal communities to whom the site of Darwin once belonged; the stayers, the settlers who have lived through successive disasters (and who have kept coming back); and the large immigrant communities, most hailing from nearby South-East Asia and China.

The climate of the Top End is legendary. The temperatures sit for most of the year in the low thirties. Between May and October the air is

Sailing is a popular weekend activity

Chan Avenue and **Brown's Mart**, now home to the Darwin Theatre Company. It was built in 1883, making it Darwin's oldest surviving commercial structure. Visitors with thespian aspirations can participate in the workshops held regularly. Opposite, lie the ruins of the **Palmerston (Darwin) Town Hall**, which was built in 1883 and survived a devastating cyclone in 1897 and the bombings of World War II, before being destroyed by Cyclone Tracy in 1974.

Continue south along Smith Street, towards the harbour, to **Christ Church Cathedral**. The original church was built in 1902. It served as the Garrison Church during the war, was hit by Japanese fire in 1942 and was destroyed by Cyclone Tracy in 1974. The new porch, which serves as a memorial to the victims of the cyclone, and an incredible altar that was hewn from a jarrah log believed to be more than 400 years old. Behind the church, in the back courtyard of Darwin City Council's Civic Centre, you will find the **'Tree of Knowledge'**, an ancient spreading banyan tree (Aboriginal name, *duramunkamani*), bearing an inscription that says it has served as a meeting place for 'travellers, wise old-timers and free-thinking young people'.

Walk back towards the city, passing the Magistrates Court and along Bennett Street, before turning into Woods Street to visit the **Chinese Temple**. Rebuilt in 1978 from the remains of the original temple constructed in 1887, it serves to mark the long history and cultural impact of the Asian population in Darwin. Visitors are welcome, but remember that the temple is still used for religious purposes.

THE ESPLANADE

The Esplanade runs north–south along the western foreshore of the city centre. Large international hotels and some lovely old tropical-style houses are perfectly positioned to catch those incomparable Darwin sunsets. **Bicentennial Park** fronts the foreshore. It has extensive walking trails, brilliant views from the

GETTING AROUND

Airport shuttle bus
Darwin Airport Shuttle 1800 358 945
Territory Shuttle (08) 8928 1155

Motoring organisation
Automobile Association of the Northern Territory (AANT) (08) 8981 3837

Car rental
Avis 13 6333; Britz Camperdown Rentals 1800 331 454; Budget 1300 362 848; Hertz 13 3039

Public transport
Darwin Bus Service (DPS) (08) 8924 7666

Bus tours
Tour Tub (08) 8981 5233

Taxis
Darwin Radio Taxis 13 1008

Boat cruises
City of Darwin Cruises 0417 855 829; Darwin Pearl Lugger Cruises (08) 8942 3131; Spirit of Darwin (08) 8981 3711

Bicycle hire
Chilli's Backpackers (08) 8941 9722; Melaleuca Lodge 1800 623 543

CLIMATE **DARWIN**

	J	F	M	A	M	J	J	A	S	O	N	D
Max. °C	32	31	32	33	32	31	30	31	32	33	33	33
Min. °C	25	25	24	24	22	20	19	21	23	25	25	25
Rain mm	406	349	311	97	21	1	1	7	19	74	143	232
Raindays	21	20	19	9	2	0	1	1	2	7	12	16

DARWIN ON FOOT

Casuarina Coastal Reserve
Marked walking trail along this beautiful coastal stretch

Darwin Botanic Gardens
Self-guide walks through different environments; pamphlets available from information centre at Geranium Street entrance to gardens

The 'Discovering Darwin' series
Eight self-guide walks, including wharf precinct, Esplanade, city centre, northern suburbs, East Point and Fannie Bay

Historic walk
Excellent self-guide walk in the official visitor's guide, Darwin and the Top End Today

For further information contact
Tourism Top End

Parliament House in State Square

TOP EVENTS

Touring Car Championships (May)
V8 Supercars in a three-day contest

Royal Darwin Show (July)
Three-day premier event

International Guitar Festival
(July, odd-numbered years)
Internationally renowned artists perform

Darwin Rodeo and Country Music Concert
(July or Aug.)
Three days of yee-ha, Top End style

Darwin Cup Carnival (Aug.)
The city's premier horserace

Darwin Beer Can Regatta (Aug.)
'Darwin-style' boat race with a difference

Darwin Fringe Festival (Aug.–Sept.)
Three weeks of cultural activities in
tropical venues

National Aboriginal Art Award (Aug. or Sept.)
Acknowledges the finest indigenous art

Festival of Darwin (Sept.)
A feast of visual and performing arts

For further details visit the web site
www.ntholidays.com

HISTORY

Darwin's history is one of survival against the odds of isolation and climate. The area, first reached in 1839 by the ship the Beagle, *was named Port Darwin after the evolutionist, Charles Darwin. The first township, Palmerston, was established at the mouth of the Adelaide River and was wiped out by a disastrous wet season in 1865. Settlement then moved to the present site but the city's growth was hampered by environmental conditions and remoteness. Revitalisation came during World War II with the influx of servicemen and women and the completion of the Stuart Highway; however, the city was emptied as residents fled the Japanese bombers in 1942–43. Rebuilding was a slow process, but the residents returned and gradually the town took shape. On Christmas Eve 1974 came Cyclone Tracy, Australia's worst natural disaster. For two decades now the city has prospered from tourism and mineral wealth.*

many lookout points and a series of memorial sites, many commemorating World War II, as well as a steady population of joggers, power walkers and late afternoon strollers. Start your exploration at the southern end. In the park, near the corner of the Esplanade and Herbert Street is an Anzac War Memorial. Also a great sunset-viewing spot. Further north, along the Esplanade, is **Old Admiralty House**, built in 1937 to a design by Beni Burnett, whose work set a benchmark for housing in the Top End for at least two decades. Across Knuckey Street is **Lyons Cottage** (B.A.T. House), which is run by the Museum and Art Gallery of the Northern Territory. It was built in 1925 to house staff from the British and Australian Telegraph Company. It now operates as a museum with exhibits on the history of the city. At the northern end of the Esplanade, off Doctors Gully Road, is **Aquascene**. Visitors gather here to hand-feed the hundreds of fish of many different species, which turn up at high tide, in time for breakfast or dinner.

STATE SQUARE

This grassy pocket perched on the sea cliffs is the Territory's place of governance. **Parliament House** dominates the square. Opened in 1994, it is a huge white structure drawing inspiration from the architecture of the warm climes, namely Asia and the Middle East. The building, which also houses the **Northern Territory Library**, opens to the public daily, with tours on Saturdays; bookings essential. Also in State Square is the **Supreme Court** (entrance off Mitchell Street), which was built in 1990 and features a foyer with an extraordinary floor mosaic designed by the Aboriginal artist Nora Napaltijari. **Liberty Square**, the grassy apex between these buildings, was the site of a popular uprising against the tyrannical Administrator in 1918, an event that is second only to the Eureka Stockade in terms of the history of Australia's insurrections. The **Overland Telegraph Memorial**, located near the southern corner of Liberty Square between Parliament House and the Supreme Court, marks the centenary of other key events in Darwin's history: the completion of the Overland Telegraph line between Adelaide and Darwin, and the laying of the overseas cable to Java, Indonesia. Across the Esplanade are the lush tropical gardens of **Government House**. Built in 1883, the elegant gabled colonial residence is Darwin's oldest building. It is open to the public once a year.

At the south-east end of the Esplanade, on the corner of Smith Street, is the **Old Police Station and Courthouse**, dating back to 1884. It was built for the South Australian Government in the days when the Territory was administered by South Australia. Nowadays the building is used as the office of the Northern Territory Administrator.

WHARF PRECINCT

Stokes Hill Wharf, which stretches out into the harbour immediately below the city centre, was once the main port for the city and, with some revamping, has become a popular leisure area. There are food outlets, a pearl store, and a bar and restaurant. A facility for servicing cruise ships is also located here. The potential of this magnificent site has not been fully realised, but there are plans afoot for future development of the precinct.

Start your exploration of the Wharf Precinct at **Survivors Lookout** on the southern side of the Esplanade. The lookout marks the spot where the battles of World War II were witnessed and reported by teams of journalists and photographers. A set of steps leads down to Hughes Avenue, then to Kitchener Drive where you will find the **World War II Oil Storage Tunnels**. This network of five concrete tunnels was built to store oil for the navy after the above-ground storage tanks were bombed by the Japanese. One tunnel is open to the public and features photographs and stories of the tumultuous war years. Continue down Kitchener Drive to the entrance to Stokes Hill Wharf. Here you will find the **Indo Pacific Marine**, where local coral ecosystems have been expertly re-created in a series of self-maintaining exhibits. In the same building is the **Australian Pearling Exhibition**, which features exhibits on the history and science of this important Territory industry, and some superb examples of the produce. To the north is the outdoor **Deckchair Cinema** which, during the rain-free period of May to October, offers alternative films beneath a tropical starlit sky.

NORTH OF THE CITY CENTRE

The **Cullen Bay Marina** is to the immediate north-west of the city and is

Government House

NOT TO BE MISSED IN DARWIN

	Map Ref.
Aquascene Hand-feed Darwin's many fish species	423 B7
Bicentennial Park Take a stroll on the Esplanade at sunset	423 C8
Crocodylus Park For a safe encounter with these prehistoric monster reptiles	426 D2
Cullen Bay Marina Wonderful views and waterfront dining; departure point for sunset cruises	424 B10
Darwin Botanic Gardens Lush tropical gardens	423 D1
Deckchair Cinema Dry-season screenings of alternative films under the stars (May–Oct.)	423 I9
Harbour Cruise Explore the beautiful Darwin coastline	424 B10
Mindil Beach Sunset Market Exotic foods, arts and crafts, a tropical sunset and great music (in the dry season, May–Oct.)	423 B1
Museum & Art Gallery of the Northern Territory Features one of the most significant Aboriginal collections in the country, and the Cyclone Tracy Exhibition	424 D7
Parliament House Darwin's most imposing modern building; free guided tour, Sat. 10 a.m. and 12 noon.	423 F10

SHOPPING

*Darwin's shopping is particularly varied. The main shopping precincts are the city centre (**Smith Street Mall and Knuckey Street**) and **Casuarina Shopping Square** in the northern suburbs. A highlight of Darwin shopping is the fine selection of Top End Aboriginal and Torres Strait Islander art and craftwork, ranging from traditional items such as baskets and boomerangs to modern garments with indigenous designs.*

*There are a few markets around town, including the **Mindil Beach Sunset Market** (Thurs. evenings May to Oct.; Sun. evenings June to Sept.) and the **Parap Market** (Sat., 8 a.m.–2 p.m.), noted for its stalls of tropical fruit and Asian food. Other markets include the **Palmerston Night Markets** (Fri. evenings: outdoors in Frances Mall Apr. to Oct.; inside Palmerston Shopping Centre Nov. to Mar.); **Rapid Creek Markets** (Sun. mornings); and **Nightcliff Markets** (Sun. 8 a.m.–2 p.m.).*

Darwin's international casino, near Mindil Beach

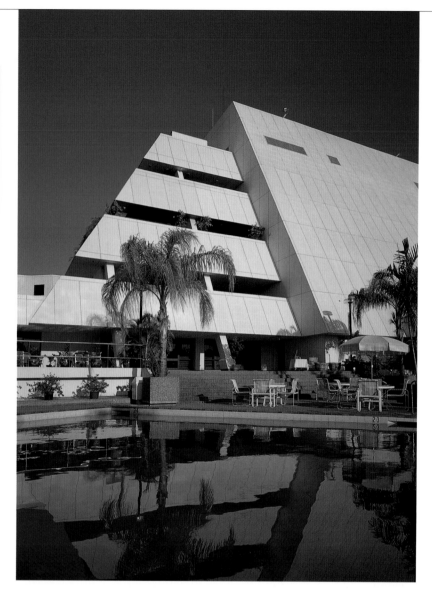

SPORT

Spectator

*Evening sporting matches are popular in Darwin, when the temperature has cooled. The city has facilities for all the major ball sports, the main centre being the popular **Marrara Sporting Complex** near the airport. There is a motor-sports complex at **Hidden Valley** and a racecourse at **Fannie Bay**.*

Participator

*There are three public golf courses, at **Marrara**, **Gardens Park** and **Palmerston**. Swimming pools are located at **Parap**, **Casuarina**, **Nightcliff** and **Palmerston**. Swimming in the sea is not recommended because box jellyfish and saltwater crocodiles, both dangerous, are found in the waters off Darwin. Sailing and other water sports are very popular in Darwin – just don't fall in. Fishing is huge in the Top End, and yes, you can hook a barra in the Darwin vicinity. There are some great game-fishing opportunities in the outer harbour area. To get you on your way, obtain a free copy of the locally produced Fishing Territory. Contact Tourism Top End for information about boat hire, charter and experienced guides.*

RESTAURANTS AND CAFES

*Popular dining precincts include **Cullen Bay Marina**, **Stokes Hill Wharf** and **Mitchell Street** in the city. The quality and variety of food available at restaurants is generally excellent given the size of the city. The diverse multicultural population guarantees excellent opportunities for ethnic dining. And in the dry season (May–Oct.), don't forget the **Mindil Beach Sunset Market** for superb ethnic food at affordable prices. There is a good section on dining out in the local visitors' guide, Darwin and the Top End Today, available from Tourism Top End.*

GALLERIES AND MUSEUMS	Map Ref.
Australian Aviation Heritage Centre Exhibits include a massive B52 bomber and a Wessex helicopter	425 I12
Australian Pearling Exhibition Story of pearling in northern Australia	423 I11
East Point Military Museum Artillery, warplanes and WW II history	424 B2
Fannie Bay Gaol Museum Discover the history of Darwin from 1883 to 1979	424 D5
Indo Pacific Marine Explore the wonders of the tropical ocean floor	423 I11
Museum & Art Gallery of the Northern Territory Excellent Aboriginal and regional art collections and Cyclone Tracy Exhibition	424 D7

the departure point for harbour cruises and ferries. It is also establishing itself as a leisure precinct, with restaurants, cafes, apartments, small shops and a pleasant boardwalk area. Just east of the marina is the Myilly Point Heritage Precinct, a small group of pre-World War II houses constructed for senior public servants. One of these is **Burnett House** (named after the architect Beni Burnett) now headquarters for the National Trust. As you head north along Gilruth Avenue, the streets and buildings give way to sprawling parkland, of which the **Darwin Botanic Gardens** are a part. The gardens, which occupy 42 hectares of land, date back to a vegetable patch established in the 1870s by a German settler. These days the gardens boast a superb tropical collection, with some 1500 species in all. There are impressive orchid and palm collections, and a self-guide Aboriginal plant-use trail.

Also accessed from Gilruth Avenue is Mindil Beach, home of the **Mindil Beach Sunset Market** – the penultimate Darwin experience. The exotic smells of food from many cultures, carried on the warm air of the early evening, seem to draw together the grand themes of life at the Top End. Live entertainment, a variety of art and craft stalls and spectacular beach fireworks add the final touches to the spectacle. The market operates Thursday nights between May and October, and Sunday nights from June to September. **Mindil Beach** is a lovely 2-kilometre stretch of white sand where people stroll, play and picnic. The water is incredibly inviting, but off-limits at least from September to April when the box jellyfish come in. The locals say, 'Don't swim in the sea during the months where there's an "r" in the spelling' – but always check the local situation, as the jellyfish can appear outside the season and saltwater crocodiles are also found in Darwin waters. **MGM Grand Darwin**, located near the shore of Mindil Beach, is a large complex offering luxury accommodation, restaurants and discos; it also houses Darwin's international casino.

Follow Gilruth Avenue into East Point Road, then turn into Conacher Street to reach the **Museum and Art Gallery of the Northern Territory**, set on the cliff top overlooking Fannie Bay. Within the modern building the collection focuses on the life, history and culture of the Territory. The collection of Aboriginal paintings and artifacts held here is regarded as one of the best in the world. The complex also features a Cyclone Tracy gallery, which captures the experience and aftermath of Australia's worst natural disaster, and the 'Sweet and Sour' exhibit, recognising the contribution of Chinese families to Darwin's history. Next door to the gallery is **Territory Craft**, which houses a variety of exhibitions year-round.

SUBURBS

Heading north away from the city along East Point Road is the **Fannie Bay Gaol Museum**, housed in what was Darwin's prison between 1883 and 1979. The displays relate to the region's history, and include remnants of prison history such as old cells and gallows. There are some lovely beaches and picnic spots in the area.

Continue along East Point Road into Alec Fong Lim Drive to reach **East Point Reserve**, with its walking and cycling paths, and picnic areas. It features a saltwater man-made lake, Lake Alexander, which offers crocodile-free swimming and windsurfing, and access to mangrove swamps, a dominant ecosystem in the Darwin area. The lookout at Dudley Point provides sensational views across Fannie Bay towards central Darwin. The **East Point Military Museum**, at the western end of East Point Reserve, features artillery, war planes, archival footage of the Japanese bombings and an impressive photographic collection. Outside the museum are the gun turrets that were erected during World War II to protect the northern coastline from the Japanese onslaught.

Military history is also on display at the **Australian Aviation Heritage Centre**, located north-east of Darwin along the Stuart Highway in Winnellie. This museum houses an impressive list of exhibits including a massive B52 bomber (one of only two outside the US) and the wreckage of a Zero fighter shot down over Darwin in 1942.

Crocodylus Park is at the end of McMillans Road not far from the airport. The park is a research centre as well as a public education forum featuring a museum, crocodile-feeding displays and a variety of wildlife. Further north past the airport is the **Casuarina Coastal Reserve**, where there is a long white sandy beach backing onto dunes, mangrove and monsoon vine thickets, and patches of rainforest. A walking and cycling track runs along the reserve to Nightcliff. Sites of interest include World War II artillery observation posts and a registered Aboriginal Sacred Site, Old Man Rock (*Dariba Nunngalinya*).

Darwin has a relaxed and tropical atmosphere all its own and, despite the extremes of climate, distance and isolation, exerts a perverse attraction on both its inhabitants and visitors to this 'last frontier'.

CITY BY NIGHT

*Darwin is a live-it-up place, and boasts increasingly varied night-time activities. There are plenty of clubs, pubs and theme bars, and, of course, the **MGM Grand Casino**, with its special offering of jazz on the lawns on certain Sundays (check details with MGM). For more jazz, go to **Cullen Bay Marina** for Jazz on the Lawn, every Sunday. The **Deckchair Cinema** is popular with night owls, while **Mitchell Street** – a lively quarter with theme pubs, bars and cafes – is the spot to go for a nightcap. Try the Blush wine bar there. The Darwin Theatre Company has an excellent reputation and performances can be seen at **Brown's Mart**, or the **Darwin Entertainment Centre** – also the venue for interstate and international performances. Friday's edition of the* Northern Territory News *publishes a roundup of what's on in the 'Gig Guide'.*

DAY TOURS FROM DARWIN

Howard Springs and Darwin Crocodile Farm
Howard Springs on Stuart Highway is a nature reserve with a spring-fed, crocodile-free pool for swimming. Further south is Darwin Crocodile Farm, with a population of 7000 freshwater and saltwater crocodiles. There are tours, feeding displays and products for sale.

Territory Wildlife Park
This award-winning park on Cox Peninsula Road showcases Top End flora and fauna. Many exhibits are connected by a 4-km walk or shuttle-train route. Nearby is Berry Springs for picnics and crocodile-free swimming.

Window on the Wetlands
Located on the Adelaide River, this interpretive centre has displays on the ecology of the Top End's wetlands, and wonderful views. Nearby, a river cruise gives an up-close view of the environment and a chance to spot crocodiles.

Mary River
Much of this important wetland area is in Mary River National Park. Most accessible is Mary River Crossing on Arnhem Highway, just over 100 km east of Darwin. Picnic and boat-launch facilities make this spot popular with anglers. To the north are 4WD tracks to other places to fish.

Litchfield National Park
Two hours' drive south of the capital, this park offers a sample of the Territory's superb natural landscapes. Best known are the magnificent waterfalls, which drop into inviting pools (check the signs before swimming). There are walks, views and picnic areas.

For more details on all of the above see region coverage, p. 404.

KAKADU & ARNHEM LAND

The ancient Arnhem Land escarpment meanders 500 km north to south, separating Kakadu National Park in the west from Arnhem Land in the east. World Heritage-listed Kakadu is of enormous cultural and environmental significance. The main access is via the sealed Arnhem Highway from Darwin. Some park areas are 4WD only. Facilities are excellent and park accommodation ranges from resort-style to camping. To the east is Aboriginal-owned Arnhem Land, traditional home to a number of language groups: this is one of Australia's most remote and least traversed regions. Within Arnhem Land Aboriginal Land, general access is limited to Cobourg Peninsula in the north-west and, on Gove Peninsula in the east, Nhulunbuy Town Lease and Buku-Larrnggay Mulka (the Aboriginal art museum at Yirrkala). Visitors can go to other areas on tours with Aboriginal guides, however. Permits are needed for the approaches by road to both peninsulas. During the Wet (November to April) some areas of the region may be inaccessible by road.

TOP EVENTS

July   *National Aboriginal and Islander Day of Celebration (Nhulunbuy)*

Aug.   *Wind Festival (Jabiru)*

EXPERIENCE IT!

❶ **Walk** to Sunset Lookout at Ubirr for spectacular escarpment views at sunset

❷ **Fish** for barramundi in one of the many beautiful billabongs

❸ **Go** by boat to Cobourg Peninsula's Victoria Settlement, the ruins of a British garrison set up in 1838 to defend the north

❹ **Take** an Aboriginal-guided cultural tour of the East Alligator River, via Border Store

❺ **Enjoy** a vast and beautiful landscape on a scenic flight from Jabiru

VISITOR INFORMATION

Tourism Top End
Darwin: (08) 8936 2499
www.ntholidays.com

Bowali Visitor Centre
Kakadu: (08) 8938 1121

CLIMATE JABIRU

	J	F	M	A	M	J	J	A	S	O	N	D
Max. °C	34	33	33	34	33	31	32	34	36	37	36	35
Min. °C	25	24	24	24	22	19	18	19	21	24	25	25
Rain mm	347	332	318	66	11	1	3	4	9	27	158	211
Raindays	22	21	20	7	2	0	0	0	1	3	12	16

FOCUS ON

Natural and cultural Kakadu

Kakadu is one of only a few World Heritage sites worldwide that are listed for both their natural value and their cultural value. A place of enormous natural beauty and grand landscapes, it contains most habitats of northern Australia, including monsoonal rainforest, tidal estuary and floodplain, and riverine floodplain and woodland. It is one of the most biologically diverse areas of the country, home to 50 or more mammal species, 280 bird species, 123 reptile species, 52 freshwater fish species and 1600 plant species. Culturally, Kakadu's credentials are just as impressive. Because of its rich resources, Kakadu was one of the continent's most intensely populated areas before European settlement. With an estimated 5000 rock-art sites, it has the world's oldest and largest rock-art collection. As well as being aesthetically invaluable, some of the work records important events over the millennia, such as the presence and extinction of the thylacine and the contact between Aboriginal people and Macassan traders.

Walks at South Alligator River
Towards the end of the Dry, thousands of waterbirds, including jabirus (pictured), congregate to feed in the Mamukala Wetlands. A short nature trail through the wetlands starts just east of the Arnhem Highway crossing of South Alligator River. In contrast, the Gungarre Monsoon Rainforest Walk (west of the river) passes through a closed forest environment.

Bowali Visitor Centre
Dynamic displays in Kakadu National Park's main visitor centre tell the story of Kakadu from indigenous and non-indigenous perspectives. An excellent first stop on any tour of the area, Bowali has a theatrette that shows audio-visuals of the park's highlights. Park headquarters is on the same site.

Yellow Water
Yellow Water (Ngurrungurrudjba) is a spectacular wetlands area with prolific birdlife, particularly in the dry season. Boat tours give visitors a close-up view of the birdlife and the Territory's crocodiles; the sunrise and sunset tours are particularly rewarding. Tours depart from Gagudju Lodge, Cooinda.

Cobourg Peninsula
Custodianship of this peninsula, protected by Gurig National Park, is shared by four Iwaidja clan groups. Visitors can fish, and explore the remote and beautiful landscape. Access is by 4WD through Arnhem Land, or by charter flight. Contact the Territory's Parks and Wildlife Commission for permits and campsite bookings.

Ubirr
Ubirr, on the Arnhem Land escarpment, houses one major rock-art gallery and some 36 smaller sites nearby. The paintings are predominantly in the X-ray style, although there are also Mimi paintings (depictions of delicate spirit figures), believed to be older. A circuit walk takes in the main sites.

Gove Peninsula
The Gove Peninsula is the traditional home of the Yolngu people, who have freehold title of the area. This remote paradise with its islands and cays, reefs and beaches is a frontier for anglers. Access is via charter flight, or by 4WD through Arnhem Land. Contact the Northern Land Council for permits.

For more detail see maps 427 & 430–1. For descriptions of 🚩 *towns see* Towns from A to Z *(p. 408).*

Ranger Uranium Mine
Uranium was discovered in the region in 1953. The Ranger mine opened in 1981 and the nearby township of Jabiru was established to accommodate mine workers. Tours of the mine are run in the Dry (May to October).

Map labels:
GURIG NATIONAL PARK
COBOURG PENINSULA
VAN DIEMEN GULF
ARAFURA SEA
BORDER STORE
Ubirr
KAKADU
JABIRU
NATIONAL
ARNHEM
LAND
PLATEAU
PARK
NHULUNBUY
YIRRKALA
GOVE PENINSULA
GULF OF CARPENTARIA
N
0   40 km

Jim Jim and Twin Falls
Jim Jim Falls (Barrkmalam) and Twin Falls (Gungkurdul) are reached via a 4WD track, 60 and 70 km respectively off the Kakadu Hwy. Both falls are best seen early in the Dry. Jim Jim, a 215-m drop, has a sand-fringed pool for year-round swimming. Twin Falls (pictured) has grand rock formations.

Nourlangie Rock
Nourlangie on the Arnhem Land escarpment is one of Kakadu's main Aboriginal rock-art areas. On the Nourlangie Art Site Walk visitors see a variety of styles, including prime examples of Kakadu X-ray art, which shows the anatomy of humans and animals in rich detail. Enjoy splendid views as you walk.

AROUND DARWIN

The attractions within easy reach of Darwin provide an introduction to the natural wealth of the Territory and offer a glimpse of the local culture as well. Litchfield National Park showcases some extraordinary geological features, the wetlands of the Adelaide and Mary rivers teem with birdlife, and the Territory Wildlife Park offers up-close encounters with the creatures of northern Australia. During the Wet (November to April) some areas of the region may be inaccessible by road.

TOP EVENTS

May	Gold Rush Festival (Pine Creek)
May	Races (horseracing, Pine Creek)
June	Bush Race Meeting (horseracing, Adelaide River)
June	Show (rodeo, country music, crafts, Adelaide River)
June	Rodeo (Pine Creek)
June/ July	International Skydiving and Parachuting Championships (Batchelor)

EXPERIENCE IT!

❶ Swim in the crocodile-free, spring-fed natural pool at Howard Springs Nature Park.

❷ Take a 4WD tour to The Lost City, a landscape of sandstone block formations in Litchfield National Park.

❸ Visit Fogg Dam at sunrise or sunset to see the Top End's prolific wildlife in natural surroundings

VISITOR INFORMATION
Tourism Top End
Darwin: (08) 8936 2499
www.ntholidays.com

FOCUS ON

Crocodiles

Crocodiles are both compelling and deadly creatures. Of the two types in northern Australia the most dangerous is the estuarine crocodile ('saltie'). This well-camouflaged reptile is found out at sea, along the coastline, in tidal rivers and creeks, and in rivers up to 100 km from the coast. Never go swimming where 'salties' have been seen. The freshwater crocodile ('freshie') inhabits rivers and lagoons; it is smaller, but can still inflict a serious wound. Both types nest and sun themselves near the water's edge. Always seek local advice before swimming, camping or boating. View these reptiles safely at Darwin Crocodile Farm, 40 km south of the city and Crocodylus Park, an education and research centre in Darwin's north-eastern suburbs.

Tiwi Islands

Bathurst and Melville islands form the Tiwi Islands, 80 km offshore from Darwin. They belong to the Tiwi people, whose unique culture results from their historic isolation. The spectacular landscape offers escarpments, lakes, waterfalls, pristine beaches and forests. One- and two-day Tiwi-led tours are run during the Dry.

CLIMATE **ADELAIDE RIVER**												
	J	F	M	A	M	J	J	A	S	O	N	D
Max. °C	32	31	32	33	32	31	30	31	33	33	33	33
Min. °C	25	25	25	24	22	20	19	21	23	25	25	25
Rain mm	429	353	322	103	21	1	1	6	16	73	141	250
Raindays	21	20	19	9	2	1	1	1	2	7	12	16

Territory Wildlife Park
This award-winning park shows Northern Australia's native fauna and flora. Features include aviaries, raptor displays (pictured), an aquarium tunnel and a large nocturnal house. Nearby, Berry Springs Nature Park features a spring-fed pool – safe for swimming – in natural bushland.

Adelaide River wetlands

Central to this wetland area is Window on the Wetlands Visitor Centre, which provides an overview of the ecology of wetlands as well as stunning views across floodplains. For waterlilies in bloom, visit mid-year.

Mary River wetlands

Monsoon and paperbark forests fringe the billabongs and riverbanks of this magnificent wetland. Visitors in 2WD vehicles can picnic and fish at Mary River Crossing on Arnhem Highway. Those with 4WDs can head further north to the famed fishing spots of Corroboree Billabong, North Rockhole and Shady Camp.

Litchfield National Park
Litchfield, 2 hours from Darwin, has waterfalls, gorges, pockets of rainforest, giant termite mounds, walks and campsites. Enjoy the scenic pools at the bottom of the park's waterfalls; most offer crocodile-free swimming, but read the signs before you take the plunge.

TIMOR SEA
TIWI ISLANDS
Bathurst Island
Melville Island
VAN DIEMEN GULF
BEAGLE GULF
DARWIN
❶ HOWARD SPRINGS
NOONAMAH
❸
MARY RIVER NP
❷ BATCHELOR
MARY RIVER CROSSING
MARY RIVER NP
ADELAIDE RIVER
LITCHFIELD NATIONAL PARK
N
0   30 km
PINE CREEK

For more detail see maps 426 & 430. For descriptions of ❶ towns see Towns from A to Z (p. 408).

GULF TO GULF

Lying between the major tourist areas of the Red Centre and Top End are places where visitors can experience the natural riches of the Territory away from crowds. Some of these places are well known, particularly the world-famous gorges of Nitmiluk National Park. Other attractions are scarcely on the map: the rugged national parks of the far west; the string of remote barramundi fishing destinations along the east and west coasts; and a number of 4WD destinations. Long distances separate towns in these areas; travellers should familiarise themselves with prevailing conditions and carry adequate supplies.

TOP EVENTS

Easter *Fishing Classic (Borroloola)*

Apr.– *Fishing competitions*
May *(Timber Creek)*

May *Back to the Never Never Festival (Mataranka)*

May *Art Show (Mataranka)*

June *Burunga Sport and Cultural Festival (Katherine)*

June *Katherine Cup (horseracing, Katherine)*

June *Canoe Marathon (Katherine)*

Aug.– *Flying Fox Festival*
Sept. *(Katherine)*

Sept. *Races (horseracing, Timber Creek)*

EXPERIENCE IT!

1 *Explore Cutta Cutta Caves, a 2-km-long underground limestone formation, south-east of Katherine*

2 *Fly, via Cape Crawford, to Lost City, an eerie landscape of pillars rising out of the plain*

3 *Try bush tucker and learn traditional crafts at Manyallaluk Aboriginal community*

VISITOR INFORMATION

Katherine: (08) 8972 2650

Tourism Top End
Darwin: (08) 8936 2499
www.ntholidays.com

FOCUS ON

Barramundi fishing

Barrumundi, Australia's premier native sports fish, is nowhere as prolific or accessible to anglers as it is in the Northern Territory. There is good barra fishing along both east and west coasts. The rugged west features tropical wetlands and a network of waterways. Popular spots include Daly River (known for the size of its barramundi and its fishing lodges), Nitmiluk (Katherine Gorge), and Victoria River via Timber Creek. The numerous eastern rivers are smaller, with minimal tides but very clear water. Top spots here are Borroloola on McArthur River and Roper Bar on Roper River.

CLIMATE KATHERINE

	J	F	M	A	M	J	J	A	S	O	N	D
Max. °C	35	34	35	34	32	30	30	33	35	38	38	37
Min. °C	24	24	23	20	17	14	13	16	20	24	25	24
Rain mm	235	213	161	33	6	2	1	1	6	29	87	197
Raindays	15	13	10	2	1	0	0	0	1	3	7	12

Nitmiluk National Park

The traditional home of the Jawoyn people, this park is world-renowned for its 13 stunning gorges, carved from red sandstone over 20 million years. Visitors can navigate the gorges in canoes, take a boat tour with a Jawoyn guide, swim in the pools or explore the 100-km network of walking tracks.

Keep River National Park

This remote park includes the traditional land of the Miriwoong and Kadjerong peoples and contains many important art sites, including the accessible Nganalam site. A major attraction is the park's rugged sandstone formations, similar to those of Purnululu National Park's Bungle Bungles. There are designated camping areas and good walks.

Gregory National Park

Forming a transitional zone between the tropics and the Central Australian desert, Gregory's two sectors offer a rugged, remote landscape of sandstone escarpments, limestone gorges, billabongs and woodlands. There are 4WD scenic routes, walking tracks and interesting Aboriginal and European heritage sites.

Never Never country

Jeannie Gunn wrote *We of the Never Never* (1908) after living at Elsey Station. Now you can visit Mataranka Homestead, a faithful replica of Gunn's home. Nearby in Elsey National Park visitors can enjoy the Mataranka thermal pool (pictured), which pumps out 20 million litres of water daily.

Eastern frontiers

The area adjoining the Gulf of Carpentaria is popular with 4WD travellers seeking new frontiers. The main settlement, Borroloola, is central for barramundi anglers and offers access to the waters around Barranyi (North Island) National Park.

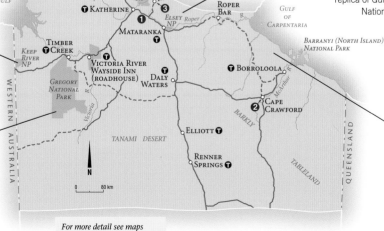

JOSEPH BONAPARTE GULF
NITMILUK NP
MANYALLALUK
KATHERINE
ELSEY NP · Roper
ROPER BAR
GULF OF CARPENTARIA
MATARANKA
BARRANYI (NORTH ISLAND) NATIONAL PARK
TIMBER CREEK
KEEP RIVER NP
VICTORIA RIVER WAYSIDE INN (ROADHOUSE)
DALY WATERS
GREGORY NATIONAL PARK
BORROLOOLA
WESTERN AUSTRALIA
Victoria
CAPE CRAWFORD
BARKLY
ELLIOTT
TANAMI DESERT
RENNER SPRINGS
TABLELAND
QUEENSLAND

N
0   80 km

For more detail see maps 430–1 & 432–3. For descriptions of ⊙ towns see Towns from A to Z (p. 408).

THE RED CENTRE

This is Australia's geographical, scenic and mythic heart. With its spectacular landforms, deserts, blue skies and monumental sense of scale, it has become a powerful symbol of the ancient grandeur of the Australian continent. For many thousands of years the region has been home to Aboriginal people from numerous groups – including the Arrernte and the Anangu – who named, mapped and inscribed with spiritual meaning almost every one of the landforms, from the massive Uluru to ancient riverbeds and obelisks. The Europeans colonised the area in the 1870s with the building of the Overland Telegraph Line. Tourism began in the 1940s and has flourished since the 1970s; facilities range from excellent at Alice Springs and Yulara to non-existent at some of the far-flung attractions. The best time to visit is during the winter months; the summer is very hot. Visitors intending to explore beyond the beaten track need to be fully self-sufficient.

TOP EVENTS

Jan.	Lasseter's Indoor Challenge (Alice Springs)
Apr.	Country Music Festival (Alice Springs)
Apr.– May	Racing Carnival (horseracing, Alice Springs)
May	Bangtail Muster (Alice Springs)
May	Cup Day (horseracing, Tennant Creek)
May	Go-Kart Grand Prix (Tennant Creek)
June	Finke Desert Race (vehicle-racing, Alice Springs)
July	Camel Cup (Alice Springs)
July	Show (Alice Springs)
July	Show (Tennant Creek)
Aug.	Rodeo (Alice Springs)
Aug.	Henley-on-Todd Regatta (Alice Springs)
Sept.	Desert Harmony Festival (Tennant Creek)
Oct.	Masters Games (mature-age athletics, Alice Springs, even-numbered years)
Nov.	Corkwood Festival (Alice Springs)

VISITOR INFORMATION

Central Australian Tourism Industry Association
Alice Springs: (08) 8952 5800
www.centralaustraliantourism.com

CLIMATE ALICE SPRINGS

	J	F	M	A	M	J	J	A	S	O	N	D
Max. °C	36	35	32	28	23	20	19	22	27	31	33	35
Min. °C	21	21	17	13	8	5	4	6	10	15	18	20
Rain mm	36	42	37	14	17	15	16	12	9	21	26	37
Raindays	5	5	3	2	3	3	3	2	2	5	6	5

Kings Canyon
Spectacular Kings Canyon features sandstone walls rising to 100 m. A 6-km-return trail scales the side of the canyon and leads past beehive formations to the Garden of Eden. The surrounding Watarrka National Park, traditional land of the Luritja people, includes lush relic vegetation and classic red sand dunes.

Kata Tjuta
Uluru's sister rock formation Kata Tjuta, meaning 'many heads' comprises 36 magnificently rounded and coloured dome-like shapes covering about 35 sq km. The 3-hour Valley of the Winds walk winds through the crevices and gorges of the rock system.

FOCUS ON

The story of Uluru

Uluru lies in the territory of the Anangu people. European explorer William Gosse named it Ayers Rock in 1873. Along with The Olgas (now Kata Tjuta) and surrounding land it became a national park in 1958. In 1985 it was returned to its traditional owners and was gazetted as Uluru. The rock is Australia's most identifiable natural icon. It is a massive, red, rounded monolith rising 348 m above the plain and 863 m above sea level, and reaching 6 km below the earth's surface. Uluru's circumference measures 9.4 km. It has no joints so, despite its valleys, fissures and caves it is a true monolith. Uluru attracts tourists because of its size and singularity. For the Anangu, however, the rock is not a single spiritual object but a thing of many parts: along with Kata Tjuta, it is the physical evidence of the deeds, actions, journeys and artifacts of the Tjukurpa, the ancestral beings of creation times.

Exploring Uluru
The Anangu prefer tourists not to climb Uluru. There are four guided walks: a 9.5-km walk around the base; the Mala walk to art sites; the Liru walk explaining the use of bush materials; and the Kuniya walk, during which creation stories are told. Pictured here are quandong fruit.

West MacDonnell Ranges
The traditional home of the Arrernte people, these ranges offer extraordinarily diverse flora (about 600 species, 75 of them rare) and some of Australia's best gorge scenery. Sites to visit include Simpsons Gap, Ellery Creek Big Hole, Serpentine Gorge and Ormiston Gorge. All are accessible in a 2WD vehicle. For walkers, there is the Larapinta Trail.

Devils Marbles
This collection of huge, precarious-looking spherical boulders lies in clusters in a shallow valley. The area is protected as an Aboriginal site. According to legend, the Marbles are the Rainbow Serpent's eggs.

EXPERIENCE IT!
❶ *Taste* the wines at Chateau Hornsby, Northern Territory's only winery
❷ *Inspect* the ruins at Arltunga Historical Reserve, site of Central Australia's first gold rush in 1887
❸ *Discover* the cultural and environmental history of Uluru–Kata Tjuta National Park at its award-winning Cultural Centre
❹ *Swim* in the refreshingly cold waters of Trephina Gorge
❺ *Take* a 4WD trip to Tnorala (Gosse Bluff), a massive crater formed when a comet crashed to earth over 130 million years ago

For more detail see maps 428–9, 432–3 & 434–5. For descriptions of ❂ towns see Towns from A to Z (p. 408). For touring details see Classic Tour (p. 415).

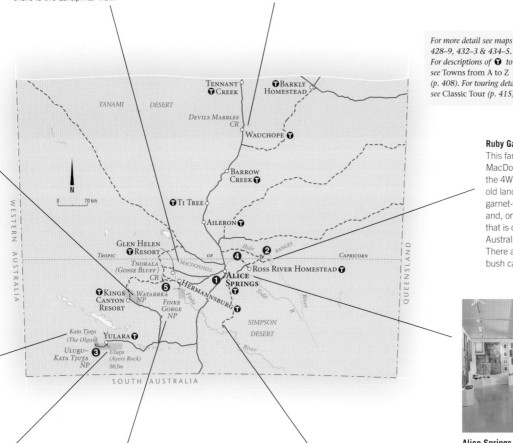

Ruby Gap Nature Park
This far-flung park in the East MacDonnell Ranges is well worth the 4WD trip. Its 850 million-year-old landscape includes the garnet-strewn gorge at Glen Annie and, on the Hale River, another that is often considered to be Australia's most beautiful gorge. There are no facilities, although bush camping is permitted.

Alice Springs
Australia's best-known country town was originally a waterhole, named for a telegraph official's wife. Alice Springs today is a lively, well-serviced centre with around 400 000 visitors each year. Attractions include the Museum of Central Australia, Araluen Galleries (pictured) and the Telegraph Station Historical Reserve.

Finke Gorge National Park
This park is 4WD access only. Its unique feature is Palm Valley, a 10 000-year-old oasis where 3000 red fan palms cluster in a valley. The Finke River, which has carved out Finke Gorge, has maintained its course for over 100 million years and is possibly the world's oldest river.

Simpson Desert and Chambers Pillar
The world's largest sand-dune desert was formed around 18 000 years ago after the continent's central lakes had dried up. Much of the desert is impossibly remote; however, this northern section is accessible by 4WD. The main attraction is Chambers Pillar, a sandstone obelisk towering 50 m above the plain.

NORTHERN TERRITORY
TOWNS FROM A TO Z

Alice Springs from Anzac Hill

Adelaide River   Pop. 279

MAP REF. 426 E8, 430 E7

A small settlement in pleasant country, 112 km SE of Darwin on the Stuart Hwy, Adelaide River was the location for 30 000 Australian and American soldiers during WW II. **In town:** Charlie the Buffalo (of *Crocodile Dundee* fame) at Adelaide River Inn, Stuart Hwy. June: Bush Race Meeting; Show (rodeo, country music and crafts). **In the area:** War Cemetery, just north of town, has graves of 434 servicemen. Historic Mount Bundy Station, 3 km NE, offers rural experience, fishing, walking, swimming and a wide range of accommodation. Robin Falls, 15 km S, flow most of the year. At Daly River, 114 km SW: roadside inn; good fishing; local Aboriginal art and craft; native flora and fauna; Merrepen Arts Festival here in June. **Visitor information:** Tourism Top End, cnr Mitchell and Knuckey sts, Darwin; (08) 8936 2499. **See also:** Around Darwin p. 404.

Aileron   Pop. 10

MAP REF. 434 I6

A popular rest stop on the Stuart Hwy, Aileron is 133 km N of Alice Springs. **In town:** At Roadhouse: Aboriginal art,

native wildlife, Sunday roast lunch, playground, picnic/barbecue facilities. **In the area:** Ryans Well Historical Reserve, 7 km SE. **Visitor information:** Roadhouse, Stuart Hwy; (08) 8956 9703. **See also:** The Red Centre p. 406.

Alice Springs   Pop. 22 488

MAP REF. 429 N4, 435 J8

Alice Springs, at the heart of the Red Centre and almost 1500 km from the nearest capital city, is en route to many attractions including Uluṟu (Ayers Rock). More than 350 000 visitors a year pass through this well-maintained town in the scenic MacDonnell Ranges. The area has a strong beef-cattle industry, and more recent industries include cut-flowers, camel meat and date-growing. The Todd River, which runs through town, is dry except after heavy rains; for the Henley-on-Todd Regatta held every Oct. the boats are carried, or wheeled. Between May and Sept. days are warm and nights can be cold. For the rest of the year daytime temperatures rise to the high 30s but nights are milder. Rains, usually brief, can come at any time of year. Alice Springs' pioneering history began when the town site was seen by William Whitfield Mills in 1871, when surveying for the Overland Telegraph

Line. He named the river after the SA Superintendent of Telegraphs, Sir Charles Todd, and a nearby waterhole Alice Springs after Lady Todd. The first European settlement was at the repeater station, built for transmitting messages across the continent. In 1860 John McDouall Stuart had passed about 50 km W of the site. He named Central Mt Sturt after Captain Sturt, who had commanded an earlier expedition; however, the SA Government renamed the mountain in Stuart's honour. Pastoralist John Ross also helped to look for a route for the telegraph line. Until 1880 the repeater station was the only reason for a few Europeans being in this remote area, then the Government sent surveyors north seeking sites for railheads. The township of Stuart, 3.2 km from the telegraph station, was gazetted in 1880 but the railway remained unbuilt. Supplies came by camel train from Port Augusta. Even the discovery of gold at Arltunga, 113 km NE, did little to develop Stuart. The Federal Government took control of NT from SA in 1911; the township then developed slowly. The Australian Inland Mission stationed Sister Jane Finlayson there in 1916 and local need led to the establishment of Adelaide House nursing hostel in 1926. The railway was completed in 1929 and the service became known as *The Ghan*, after the

Afghan camel drivers. Soon there was confusion between Stuart and Alice Springs, only 3 km apart, so the name Stuart was dropped. **In town:** In Todd Mall: Flynn Memorial Church, in memory of founder of Royal Flying Doctor Service; Adelaide House, originally hospital now museum housing pedal-radio equipment used by Flynn, and other memorabilia; Sounds of Starlight Theatre, musical journey through Central Australia, Apr.–Nov. (check times); various outlets for Aboriginal art and artifacts. Aboriginal Art and Culture Centre, Todd St. Royal Flying Doctor Service base, Stuart Tce (tours daily). In Hartley St: Panorama 'Guth', a 360° landscape painting of Central Australia; National Pioneer Women's Hall of Fame, Old Courthouse Building; Minerals House, featuring geological and mineral displays (open Mon.–Fri.). Old Stuart Gaol, Parsons St. Museum of Central Australia, cnr Larapinta Dr and Memorial Ave. Technology, Transport and Communications Museum, Memorial Dr. Araluen Galleries, Larapinta Dr., for visual arts; magnificent stained-glass window by local artist Wenten Rubuntja. *At the northern end of town:* Anzac Hill, Wills Tce, for excellent views of town; School of the Air, Head St. *At the western end of town:* Alice Springs Desert Park, Larapinta Dr.: desert animals and plants and information about their traditional use by Aboriginal people; film and interactive displays. *Across the river:* Lasseter's Casino, Barrett Dr.; Olive Pink Botanic Gardens, cnr Barrett Dr., Australia's only arid-zone botanic garden. Self-guide town walks, brochure available. Market at Todd Mall, 2nd Sun. Mar.–Dec., and Thurs. evenings in summer. Jan.: Lasseter's Indoor Challenge (several competitions incl. backgammon, bridge and scrabble). Apr.–May: Racing Carnival; Country Music Festival. May: Bangtail Muster. June: Finke Desert Race (car and motorbike racing). July: Camel Cup; Show (cooking, crafts and camels). Aug.: Rodeo; Henley-on-Todd Regatta. Oct.: Masters Games (mature-age athletic carnival, even-numbered years). Nov.: Corkwood Festival (art, craft, music and dance). **In the area:** Great variety of tours covering scenic attractions, Aboriginal culture and specialist interests; by bus or coach, train, limousine, 4WD safari, Harley-Davidson motorcycle, camel, horse, aircraft, helicopter or hot-air balloon. *To the north:* Alice Springs Telegraph Station Historical Reserve (3 km), with original stone buildings and equipment,

historical display, guided tours, bushwalking and wildlife. *To the north-east:* Arltunga Historical Reserve (117 km), site of Central Australia's first gold rush in 1887; at Gemtree (135 km), Mud Tank zircon field offers prospecting for zircons, guided fossicking tours and your gems cut at the caravan park. *To the east:* Pitchi Richi Sanctuary (2 km), an open-air museum displaying William Ricketts' clay sculptures; Frontier Camel Farm (7 km) features camel rides, reptile house and museum displays highlighting importance of camels and Afghans to the area; nearby, Mecca Date Gardens, Australia's first commercial date farm; Chateau Hornsby, NT's only commercial winery (10 km), Emily Gap (13 km), Jessie Gap (18 km) and Ruby Gap (154 km) nature parks. *To the south:* Old Timers' Museum (5 km), features exhibits dating from the 1890s; Transport Heritage Centre (10 km), has re-creation of a 1930s railway siding and display showing ingenuity in overcoming outback hardships; Ghan Preservation Society rail museum at MacDonnell Siding (10 km), features the *Old Ghan* which runs on 23.5 km of private line between MacDonnell Siding and Ewaninga; Ewaninga Rock Carvings Conservation Reserve (35 km SE), an Aboriginal cultural site with rock engravings; Chambers Pillar Historical Reserve (149 km), incl. 50-m high rock pillar which served as a landmark feature for the Centre's early pioneers and explorers. *To the south-west:* Camel Outback Safaris (93 km), offers camel and trail rides; Henbury Meteorites Conservation Reserve (147 km). *To the west:* Grave site of Rev. John Flynn (5 km); Simpsons

Gap (25 km), also linked to Alice Springs by sealed bicycle path; Standley Chasm (50 km). Ellery Creek Big Hole (93 km); Serpentine Gorge (104 km); Ochre Pits (119 km), natural quarry once mined by Aborigines; Ormiston Gorge (132 km); Glen Helen Gorge (133 km); the nearby Glen Helen Resort, used as a base by many to explore the area; Hermannsburg (125 km); Palm Valley, in Finke Gorge National Park (140 km, 4WD access only); Redbank Gorge (170 km, 4WD access only); Tnorala (Gosse Bluff) meteor crater (210 km, 4WD access only, permit required, note permit for Mereenie Loop allows access to Tnorala); most of these are in West MacDonnell National Park, as is Larapinta Trail, a well-marked walking track through the West MacDonnell Ranges. Mereenie Loop links Alice Springs, Kings Canyon, and Uluṟu (Ayers Rock) and Kata Tjuṯa (The Olgas) via the West MacDonnell Ranges and Glen Helen; permit required because section of the route passes through Aboriginal Land. **Visitor information:** Central Australian Tourism Industry Association, Gregory Tce (south end of Todd Mall); (08) 8952 5800, freecall 1800 645 199. Web site www.central australiantourism.com **See also:** The Red Centre p. 406; Classic Tour p. 415.

Barkly Homestead   Pop. 15

MAP REF. 433 N11

Barkly Homestead is a comfortable fuel or accommodation stop at the junction of Barkly and Tablelands hwys, 187 km E from the junction of Stuart and Barkly hwys. **See also:** The Red Centre p. 406.

Mereenie Loop links Alice Springs with major attractions

Barrow Creek
Pop. 10

MAP REF. 435 J4

Located on the Stuart Hwy, 285 km N of Alice Springs, Barrow Creek was originally a telegraph station and a rest stop for cattle-droving on the North–South Stock Route. **In town:** Old Telegraph Station (1872). Barrow Creek Hotel (1932). **Visitor information:** Barrow Creek Hotel; (08) 8956 9753. **See also:** The Red Centre p. 406.

Batchelor
Pop. 645

MAP REF. 426 D7, 430 E7

The former town for Rum Jungle, Australia's first uranium mine (now closed), Batchelor is the gateway to Litchfield National Park. **In town:** Coomalie Cultural Centre, Batchelor College, cnr Awilla Rd and Nurudina St, has display of Aboriginal works and culture. Mini replica of Karlstein Castle of Bohemia, Rum Jungle Rd. Scenic flights, parachuting and gliding, at airport. June (sometimes July): International Skydiving and Parachuting Championships. **In the area:** Lake Bennett Wilderness Resort, Chinner Rd, 18 km NE: fishing, abseiling, swimming, windsurfing, boat hire, walks, restaurant, range of accommodation. Rum Jungle Lake, 10 km W, for swimming. Litchfield National Park, 40 km W, a wilderness area with rivers, spectacular waterfalls (Wangi, Sandy Creek, Florence and Tolmer), sandstone block formations, magnetic termite mounds, pockets of scenic rainforest, secluded waterholes, fauna, bushwalks and camping grounds. **Visitor information:** Tarkarri Rd; (08) 8976 0444. **See also:** Around Darwin p. 404; National Parks p. 418.

Borroloola
Pop. 551

MAP REF. 431 O13, 433 O3

A small settlement on the McArthur River and once one of the larger and more colourful frontier towns, Borroloola is now popular with fishing and 4WD enthusiasts. Although the town is in Aboriginal land, no permit is required to visit it. **In town:** Museum in old police station (1886), Robinson Rd. Fishing charters. Scenic flights over town and the islands of the Sir Edward Pellew group. Easter: Fishing Classic. Aug.: Agricultural Show; Rodeo. **In the area:** Cape Crawford, 110 km SW: base for seeing Bukalara Rock Formations (60 km E), mass of chasms winding through ancient sandstone formations (in very remote area, guide recommended); and Lost City, accessible only by helicopter, visitors must be accompanied by a guide. Limmen Bight Fishing Camp, 250 km NW: range of accommodation; check wet-season road access. Excellent angling around Barranyi (North Island) National Park, offshore 70 km NE. **Visitor information:** Lot 384, Robinson Rd; (08) 8975 8799. **See also:** Gulf to Gulf p. 405.

Daly Waters
Pop. 20

MAP REF. 432 I3

Situated 4 km N of the junction of Stuart and Carpentaria hwys, Daly Waters became the first international refuelling stop for Qantas in 1935. **In town:** Historic hotel (1930), Stuart St. Sept.: Rodeo. **In the area:** Airport museum, 1 km NE, off Stuart Hwy at Old Daly Waters aerodrome. Tree, 1 km N, reputedly marked with letter 'S' by explorer John McDouall Stuart. Other stopping-places on Stuart Hwy: Dunmarra, 44 km S and 8 km S of Buchanan Hwy turnoff; Larrimah, 93 km N, historic WW II sites. **Visitor information:** Daly Waters Hotel, Stuart St; (08) 8975 9927. **See also:** Gulf to Gulf p. 405.

Elliott
Pop. 432

MAP REF. 433 J6

Elliott, on the Stuart Hwy 254 km N of Tennant Creek, was named after Captain Elliott, the officer in charge of a camp for troops during WW II. The town is a green, shady spot with good facilities. **In town:** Site of WW II camp on southern outskirts of town. **In the area:** At Newcastle Waters, an old droving town 24 km NW: bronze statue 'The Drover'; historic buildings; no services. **Visitor information:** Elliott Hotel, Stuart Hwy; (08) 8969 2069. **See also:** Gulf to Gulf p. 405.

Glen Helen Resort
Pop. 5

MAP REF. 428 I5, 434 H8

On Namatjira Drive, 132 km W of Alice Springs, this small homestead-style resort is an excellent base for exploring the superb scenery of West MacDonnell National Park. **In the area:** At Glen Helen Gorge, 300 m E, walk along Finke River bed, between towering cliffs. Helicopter flights to surrounding areas incl. Mt Sonder. In West MacDonnell National Park: Ormiston Gorge, 12 km NE, the 'jewel of the MacDonnell Ranges'; Ochre Pits, 21 km E, natural ochre quarry once mined by Aborigines for painting and ceremonial decoration; Serpentine Gorge, 35 km E, narrow winding gorge with beautiful scenery, wildlife and walking trails; Ellery Creek Big Hole, 45 km E, large waterhole with high red cliffs and sandy creek fringed with river red gums; further east towards Alice Springs are Standley Chasm and Simpsons Gap; Redbank Gorge, 24 km NW, 4WD access only. Larapinta Walking Trail winds through West MacDonnell Ranges; it extends 80 km and can be walked in total (registration necessary) or in part (some sections are overnight walks). Mereenie Loop links Glen Helen Resort to Kings Canyon Resort in far south west; permit required. **Visitor information:** Glen Helen Homestead, Namatjira Dr.; (08) 8956 7489. **See also:** The Red Centre p. 406; National Parks p. 418.

Hermannsburg
Pop. 462

MAP REF. 428 I6, 434 H9

This Aboriginal community, 125 km W of Alice Springs, occupies the site of a former mission station established by German Lutherans in 1877. For many years it was the home of artist Albert Namatjira. The Arrernte Aboriginal community have owned freehold title to the land since 1982: visitors to town are restricted to the shop, petrol station and historic precinct. **In town:** Historic precinct: Strehlow's House (1897), now Kata-Anga Tea Rooms, known for their apple strudel; old manse (1888), now a gallery housing watercolours by Aboriginal artists of the Hermannsburg school (guided tours); remains of mission station, incl. schoolhouse (1896) and tannery (1941); museum in the Old Colonists House (1885), displays historic items from missionary era. **In the area:** Monument to Albert Namatjira on Larapinta Dr., 2 km E. Cultural tours and camping at Wallace Rockhole Aboriginal community, 46 km SE. Finke Gorge National Park, 20 km S (4WD access only), features red fan palms (*Livistona mariae*) in Palm Valley, and amazing rock formations: 'amphitheatre', 'sphinx' and 'battleship'. Tnorala (Gosse Bluff) meteorite crater, 35 km W; Mereenie Loop Pass required for access. **Visitor information:** CATIA, Gregory Tce (south end of Todd Mall); (08) 8952 5800, freecall 1800 645 199. Web site www.centralaustralian tourism.com **See also:** The Red Centre p. 406; Classic Tour p. 415.

Jabiru Pop. 1696

MAP REF. 427 P4, 430 H6

A mining town within the Kakadu National Park, 280 km from Darwin on the Arnhem Hwy, Jabiru's services are designed for minimal effect on the surrounding World Heritage-listed National Park. **In town:** Gagudju Crocodile Hotel, Flinders St, a 250-m crocodile-shaped building; design was approved by the Gagudju people, to whom the crocodile is a totem. Frontier Kakadu Lodge and Caravan Park, Jabiru Dr., laid out in traditional Aboriginal circular motif. Jabiru Olympic Swimming Pool, Civic Dr., largest in NT; nearby, 9-hole golf course. Aug.: Wind Festival. **In the area:** 4WD roads are usually accessible only in the Dry (May–Oct.). Fishing and safari tours. At airport, 6 km E, scenic flights over unique Kakadu territory: see inaccessible sandstone formations standing 300 m above vast flood plains; seasonal waterfalls; wetland wilderness; remote beaches and ancient Aboriginal rock-art sites. Tourist walk (1.5 km) west from town centre through bush to Bowali Visitor Centre. Nourlangie Rock, 34 km S, has significant Aboriginal rock art around its base. Yellow Water near Cooinda, 55 km SE, a billabong with prolific flora and fauna; waterbirds best seen by boat cruise (departs near Gagudju Lodge, Cooinda). Nearby, Warradjan Aboriginal Cultural Centre built in shape of a Warradjan (pig-nosed turtle): offers fascinating insight into Aboriginal culture in Kakadu region; Aboriginal craft gallery. Further south, Jim Jim Falls and Twin Falls (both 4WD access only), after rains (Nov.–Apr.) the two largest falls in park. Ranger Uranium Mine, 6 km E, daily tours May–Oct. Ubirr, 40 km N, section of Arnhem escarpment and renowned Aboriginal rock-art site in Kakadu National Park, with galleries featuring a range of styles; ranger-guided walks and tours, during the Dry only. From Ubirr, exceptional sunset views across East Alligator River flood plains; from Border Store, just south of Ubirr, Aboriginal-guided tours of river. Further north-east at Oenpelli, Injalak Art and Craft Centre (permit required, visitors welcome). Near South Alligator River crossing, 40 km W along Arnhem Hwy: Mamukala Wetlands Walk; Gungarre Monsoon Rainforest Walk. **Visitor information:** 6 Tasman Plaza; (08) 8979 2548. **See also:** Kakadu & Arnhem Land p. 402; National Parks p. 418; Wildlife-Watching p. 420.

Historic mission buildings, Hermannsburg

Katherine Pop. 7979

MAP REF. 430 G10

Katherine is on the southern side of the Katherine River, 310 km SE of Darwin. The river was named after a daughter of one of the sponsors of John McDouall Stuart. Stuart first saw it in 1862. The town's economic mainstays are the Mt Todd goldmine, tourism, and the Tindal RAAF airbase, 28 km SE. In some of NT's best agricultural and grazing country, Katherine is the centre of scientific experiments designed to improve the beef-cattle industry. **In town:** Katherine Museum, Gorge Rd (check opening times). Railway Station Museum, Railway Tce, has displays of history of railways in the area (check opening times); old steam engine adj. to museum. School of the Air, Giles St (open weekdays Apr.–Oct., check visiting times). O'Keefe House, Riverbank Dr., one of the oldest houses in town. Self-guide Pioneer Walk around town. NT Rare Rocks, Zimmin Dr., rock and gem displays. Katherine Orchid Nursery, Stutterd St, 25 000 orchids (open Wed.–Sat.). Self-guide Arts and Crafts Trail, brochure available. Market, Warburton St, each Sat. (Apr.–Sept.). Tick Markets, Lindsay St, 1st Sat. each month (Apr.– Sept.). June: Burunga Sport and Cultural Festival; Katherine Cup; Canoe Marathon. July: Agricultural Show. Aug.–Sept.: Flying Fox Festival (community festival, theatre and music). **In the area:** Heli tours, scenic flights, 4WD safaris, barramundi fishing tours, horse trail-rides. Nitmiluk Gorge in Nitmiluk National Park, 29 km NE, has ancient rock walls dotted with caves; Aboriginal paintings thousands of years old on both faces of the gorge above the floodline. Numerous reptile and amphibian species; kangaroos and wallabies in higher reaches. Self-guide walk, brochure available. The best way to see the gorge is by flat-bottomed boat; hire a canoe and camp in the gorge overnight, or take a guided tour; daily cruises (book at information centre); no private motorboats allowed in gorge May–Oct. Weather is hot (yet countryside is at its best) Nov.–Mar.; in the remaining months humidity is low, days warm and nights cool. Also in park, Edith Falls, 62 km N; surrounding area ideal for bushwalking, picnicking and camping. Springvale Homestead (1878), 8 km W on Shadforth Rd: oldest remaining homestead in NT, built by Alfred Giles; market each Sun. (Apr.–Sept.). Flora River Nature Park, 86 km SW, for interesting mineral formations, pools and cascades along river, and camping. Natural hot springs, 3 km S on Victoria Hwy, on banks of Katherine River. Cutta Cutta Caves Nature Park, 27 km SE (cave tours daily). Elsey National Park near Mataranka Homestead, 112 km SE, features thermal pool believed to have therapeutic powers. Old Gallon Licensed Store (1847) (now private residence), 2 km E on Giles St, marks original site of township. Manyallaluk Aboriginal Community, 100 km NE: camping; Aboriginal cultural tours; bookings essential (08) 8975 4727. **Visitor information:** cnr Lindsay St

The spectacular Kings Canyon

and Stuart Hwy; (08) 8972 2650. Web site www.ntholidays.com **See also:** Gulf to Gulf p. 405.

Kings Canyon Resort
Pop. 50

MAP REF. 434 F9

Kings Canyon, an enormous natural amphitheatre with 100-m sheer rock faces, is the main feature of Watarrka National Park, 333 km SW of Alice Springs. Kings Canyon Resort, in park, is a base from which to explore the region. Aboriginal tours and scenic helicopter flights. **In the area:** 6-km circuit Rim Walk of Kings Canyon, features boardwalk through prehistoric cycads in lush Garden of Eden; unusual rock formations, particularly The Lost City; views across canyon. From same starting point, Kings Creek Walk, 1 hr return, up centre of canyon. Giles Walk, 13 km, from Kings Canyon, for experienced walkers. Also in park, Carmichael Crag (3 km N), displays majestic colours, particularly at sunset. Mereenie Loop to Glen Helen Resort (permit required). **Visitor information:** Kings Canyon Resort, Luritja Rd; (08) 8956 7442. **See also:** The Red Centre p. 406.

Mataranka
Pop. 667

MAP REF. 430 I11

This small town is 106 km SE of Katherine. **In town:** Self-drive Discovery Trail of town and surrounding area, brochure at information centre. On Stuart Hwy: Stockyard Gallery, for NT artists' works

incl. leather sculpture; Territory Manor, daily feeding of barramundi, 9.30 a.m. and 1 p.m.; Museum of the Never Never, outdoor displays of railway history, Overland Telegraph and bush workshop; giant termite mound. May: Back to the Never Never Festival; Art Show. Aug.: Rodeo. **In the area:** Elsey National Park, 5 km E: thermal pools, Mataranka and nearby Bitter Springs, in lush tropical forest, popular for swimming; walking tracks through pockets of rainforest; wildlife observation points; camping area; barramundi fishing on Roper River; canoe hire; departure point for walking trail to Mataranka Falls at Twelve Mile Yards. Mataranka Homestead Tourist Resort, near thermal pool: replica of Elsey Homestead; camping. Elsey Cemetery, 20 km S, graves of outback pioneers immortalised by Jeannie Gunn (lived at Elsey Station homestead 1902–03, wrote the book *We of the Never Never*); nearby, cairn marking site of original homestead. **Visitor information:** Stockyard Gallery, Roper Tce; (08) 8975 4530. **See also:** Gulf to Gulf p. 405.

Nhulunbuy
Pop. 3695

MAP REF. 431 P5

Nhulunbuy is on the north-eastern tip of Arnhem Land, on the Gove Peninsula. The whole peninsula is held freehold by the Yolngu people. *Intending visitors must obtain a permit from the Northern Land Council (contact (08) 8920 5100) beforehand; rules apply. Allow 2 weeks for processing.* Originally a service town for

the bauxite-mining industry, Nhulunbuy is now the administrative centre for the Arnhem Region as well. Access is by a year-round daily jet air service from Darwin or Cairns, or, with permit, by 4WD through Arnhem Land. Local car hire. *A recreation permit is required for travel outside the Nhulunbuy Town Lease (contact (08) 8987 3992).* **In town:** Gayngaru (Town Lagoon) self-guide nature walk. July: National Aboriginal and Islander Day of Celebration. **In the area:** At Nambara Arts and Crafts, Melville Bay Rd, 15 km NW: traditional and contemporary Aboriginal art and craft. Buku-Larrnggay Mulka, at Yirrkala Community, Melville Bay Rd 20 km SE: renowned community-based Aboriginal art museum; no permit required for museum visit. Stunning beaches with tropical-blue water, accessible by permit (fee applies). Boat charters for game-, reef- and barramundi-fishing. Also water sports, birdwatching, croc-spotting, Yolngu guides, guided 4WD, and bauxite mine tour (Fri.). **Visitor information:** Westall St; (08) 8987 1777. **See also:** Kakadu & Arnhem Land p. 402.

Noonamah
Pop. 8

MAP REF. 426 E4, 430 E6

Noonamah is on the Stuart Hwy, 43 km S of Darwin. **In the area:** Over 7000 crocodiles at Darwin Crocodile Farm, just north of town; feeding displays and tours. Howard Springs Nature Park, 23 km NW: safe swimming; bird-watching; picnicking. On Cox Peninsula Rd: Berry Springs Nature Park, 14 km SW, safe swimming in spring-fed pool in monsoon forest; alongside, Territory Wildlife Park, has native fauna in 400-ha bushland setting viewed via walking trails or motorised open train; 4 km W of wildlife park, Lakes Resort, has watersports, waterski and jetski hire, and accommodation. South of Lakes Resort on Pipeline Rd, Southport Siding Exotic Fruit Farm: orchard tours; sales; wildlife. Majestic Orchids, orchid-growing area, 24 km SW. Tumbling Waters Deer Park, 26 km SW. Manton Dam, 25 km S: water sports; picnicking. Fogg Dam, 41 km NE, prolific wildlife, best at sunrise or sunset. Further east, Adelaide River wetland area, incl. Window on the Wetlands Visitor Centre and cruises. On Arnhem Hwy 45 km E of Fogg Dam turnoff, fishing at Mary River crossing; 4WD tracks north to prime fishing spots. **Visitor information:** Noonamah Tavern; (08) 8988 1054. **See also:** Around Darwin p. 404.

Pine Creek
Pop. 521

MAP REF. 426 I13, 430 F8

Pine Creek, on the Stuart Hwy, 90 km NW of Katherine, experienced a brief gold rush in the 1870s after a discovery by workers building the Overland Telegraph Line. Today the town benefits from the reopened goldmine, one of the largest opencut goldmines in NT. **In town:** Numerous historic buildings; trail brochure available. Miners Park, Main Tce, has historic mining machinery. Railway Station museum and historic steam train used in film *We of the Never Never,* off Main Tce (check opening times). Museum and Library, Railway Tce, has display on Overland Telegraph. Mine Lookout, off Moule St. At Gun Alley Gold Mining, Gun Alley, restored steam ore crusher, gold-panning tours. Bird Park, tropical birds in lush garden setting. Old Timers Rock Hut, Jenson St, has rock and mineral display. May: Gold Rush Festival (incl. didgeridoo competition); Races. June: Rodeo. **In the area:** Gold fossicking (licence required). Copperfield Recreation Reserve at Copperfield Dam, 6 km SW, foreshore has ideal picnic areas. Umbrawarra Gorge, 22 km SW: good swimming, rock-climbing and walking. Bonrook Lodge and station, 6 km SE, wild horse sanctuary. Edith Falls, 67 km SE in north-western end of Nitmiluk National Park, for swimming and bushwalking in area. The Rock Hole, 65 km NE via Kakadu Hwy, a secluded waterhole (4WD access only). Gunlom (Waterfall Creek), 113 km NE via Kakadu Hwy, beautiful falls and permanent waterhole in Kakadu National Park. Tjuwaliyn (Douglas) Hot Springs Nature Park, 64 km NW, off Stuart Hwy; camping available. Butterfly Gorge Nature Park, 113 km NW, named for butterflies that settle in its rock crevices (4WD access only). **Visitor information:** Diggers Rest Motel, 32 Main Tce; (08) 8976 1442. **See also:** Around Darwin p. 404.

Renner Springs
Pop. 11

MAP REF. 433 J8

A roadside stop on the Stuart Hwy, 160 km N of Tennant Creek, Renner Springs was named after Frederick Renner, doctor to workers on the Overland Telegraph. Dr Renner discovered springs when he observed bird flocks gathering there. The source of the springs is unknown. Fuel, supplies and meals at Renner Springs Desert Inn. Picnic/barbecue facilities. **See also:** Gulf to Gulf p. 405.

Ross River Homestead
Pop. 30

MAP REF. 429 P4, 435 K8

At Ross River is ranch-style Ross River Homestead, with cabins, backpacker accommodation, camping and caravan park, 83 km E of Alice Springs. The homestead offers outback activities incl. boomerang-throwing and whip-cracking with billy tea and damper as refreshment; feeding kangaroos; horse and camel treks; overnight safaris. **In the area:** Trephina Gorge Nature Park, 17 km NW: scenic walks; swimming; camping; picnic facilities. N'Dhala Gorge Nature Park (4WD access only), 11 km SW: Aboriginal rock engravings; walking tracks; ancient fossil deposits. Corroboree Rock Conservation Reserve, 33 km SW, has signposted walk explaining significance of rock to Eastern Arrernte people. Arltunga Historical Reserve (4WD access only), 45 km NE: old goldmining town with stone ruins, scattered workings and gravestones; restored police station and gaol; visitor centre displays local history. Nearby, gold panning and metal-detecting in declared fossicking area; fossicking permits at Arltunga Hotel. Further east, Ruby Gap Gorge (4WD access only) on the intermittent Hale River. **Visitor information:** Ross River Homestead, Ross Hwy; (08) 8956 9711, freecall 1800 241 711. **See also:** The Red Centre p. 406.

Tennant Creek
Pop. 3856

MAP REF. 433 K10

According to legend, the town of Tennant Creek was founded when a beer wagon broke down at the site. The town is 506 km N of Alice Springs, on the Stuart Hwy. Gold and copper deposits account for its development as a centre for the Barkly Tableland. **In town:** National Trust Museum in historic Tuxworth Fullwood House, Schmidt St: photographic collection; displays of early mine buildings and equipment; open May–Sept. (check times). Travellers Rest Area in Purkiss Reserve, Ambrose St, has picnic area and swimming pool nearby. Scenic drives; heritage walk; leaflets available. May: Cup Day (horseracing); Go-Kart Grand Prix. July: Show (cooking, crafts and camels). Sept.: Desert Harmony Festival (arts and culture). **In the area:** Tours of goldmining areas, incl. night tour of early goldmine. Gold-fossicking.

Trephina Gorge Nature Park, near Ross River

Gregory National Park, west of Timber Creek

Battery Hill, 1.5 km E on Peko Rd: one of three 10-stamp batteries still operational in Australia; modern underground mine with working machinery; displays and films; nature walk. Past the Battery, Ben Allen Lookout offers views of town and area. Juno Horse Centre, 10 km E: horseriding; cattle drives. Nobles Nob, 16 km E, once richest open-cut goldmine in world. Mary Ann Dam, 5 km NE, for water sports. Restored telegraph station (1875), 12 km N. Three Ways Roadhouse, junction of Stuart and Barkly hwys, 25 km N; nearby, John Flynn Memorial. Attack Creek Historical Reserve, 73 km N; memorial marks encounter between John McDouall Stuart and local Aboriginal people. The Pebbles, 16 km NW, miniatures of Devil's Marbles (huge 'balancing rocks' found 106 km S). **Visitor information:** Battery Hill Mining Centre, Peko Rd; (08) 8962 3388. Web site www.centralaustraliantourism. com **See also:** The Red Centre p. 406.

Ti Tree   Pop. 50

MAP REF. 434 I5

A rest stop on the Stuart Hwy, Ti Tree is 192 km N of Alice Springs. **In town:** Opposite Roadhouse, Gallereaterie, features local Aboriginal art (exhibitions and sales), also eating-house. Ti Tree Park, with picnic area and playground. **In the area:** Central Mt Stuart Historical Reserve, 18 km N, incl. monument at base of mountain marking the spot as the centre of Australia. **Visitor information:** Roadhouse, Stuart Hwy; (08) 8956 9741. **See also:** The Red Centre p. 406.

Timber Creek   Pop. 556

MAP REF. 430 D13, 432 D2

Timber Creek is 285 km SW of Katherine on the Victoria Hwy. **In town:** National Trust Museum, off hwy, has displays of historical artifacts (open Apr.–Aug.). Boat and fishing tours, cruises, scenic flights. Office for Parks and Wildlife Commission of the Northern Territory, Victoria Hwy, provides information for travellers to Gregory and Keep River national parks. Apr.–May: Fishing competitions. May: Rodeo. Sept.: Timber Creek Races (horseracing). **In the area:** Gregory National Park, 15 km W and 92 km E (2 sectors) features Limestone Gorge, Aboriginal and European heritage sites and boab trees. Keep River National Park, 175 km W, features rugged scenery, Aboriginal rock art and wildlife; most trails 4WD only. For both parks, check with Parks and Wildlife Commission for access details. Jasper Gorge, 48 km SW, a scenic gorge with permanent waterhole. **Visitor information:** Timber Creek Tourist Park, Victoria Hwy; (08) 8975 0722. **See also:** Gulf to Gulf p. 405; National Parks p. 418.

Victoria River Roadhouse
Pop. 6

MAP REF. 430 E12, 432 E2

Victoria River is a rest stop located where the Victoria Hwy crosses the mighty Victoria River. Victoria River Roadhouse complex: boat tours, fishing trips (both from roadhouse); range of accommodation. Scenic bushwalks in area, particularly Joe's Creek Walk, 10 km W. **Visitor information:** Roadhouse, Victoria Hwy; (08) 8975 0744. **See also:** Gulf to Gulf p. 405.

Wauchope   Pop. 7

MAP REF. 433 K13, 435 K2

Wauchope is on the Stuart Hwy, 114 km S of Tennant Creek. The historic hotel once served the old Wolfram Mines. **In the area:** Devils Marbles, 8 km N, large, precariously balanced granite boulders. Wycliffe Well (1872), 17 km S, opposite Wycliffe Well Roadhouse. Davenport Range National Park, 118 km E: Aboriginal heritage and waterhole ecology; isolated area, high clearance or 4WD access only, advise travel; (08) 8964 1959 or Wauchope Hotel. **Visitor information:** Wauchope Hotel, Stuart Hwy; (08) 8964 1963. **See also:** The Red Centre p. 406.

Yulara   Pop. 1200

MAP REF. 428 B12, 434 E11

Situated on the outskirts of Uluru–Kata Tjuta National Park, this town is the location for the world-class Ayers Rock Resort. The resort offers full visitor facilities and air-conditioned accommodation in all price brackets; advance bookings essential. **In town:** Information Centre has displays of geology, history, flora and fauna of the region; also spectacular photographic collection. Tours incl. Uluru Experience Night Sky Show, which offers night-sky viewing and narration of Aboriginal and European interpretations of the night sky; book tours at information centre or reception in accommodation areas. **In the area:** On approach road to Uluru, Uluru–Kata Tjuta Cultural Centre, designed in shape of two snakes, has displays and sales of Aboriginal culture and arts. Uluru (Ayers Rock), 20 km SE, Australia's famous sandstone monolith: Aboriginal rock-art sites; spectacular sunrises and sunsets; guided walks and tours around base of Uluru, highlighting the monolith's Aboriginal significance. Kata Tjuta (The Olgas), 50 km W, the Centre's other famous landmark: Valley of the Winds walk; good views; flora and fauna. **Visitor information:** Visitors Centre; (08) 8957 7888. **See also:** The Red Centre p. 406; National Parks p. 418.

CLASSIC TOUR

DREAMTIME TRAIL
Alice Springs to Glen Helen Gorge (187 km)

This tour from Alice Springs into the West MacDonnell Ranges is a journey into the Dreamtime landscape of the Arrernte Aboriginal people. Here, amid some of the most spectacular gorge scenery in Australia, you will also discover a wealth of flora and fauna. Although the two-wheel drive version of the tour could be completed in a single day, this would leave little time to explore the natural highlights on offer. Ideally, allow for an overnight stop at Glen Helen Resort or stay at one or more of the camping areas along the tour. Relax, watch the sunset and take in the grandeur of the star-filled outback sky.

1 The lore of the land

The outback town of Alice Springs, starting point for your tour, holds remarkable sway in the popular imagination. If possible, spend a few days here to get a feel for the area, its history and its people.

Many of the geographic features you will see on this tour are important and sacred places for the Arrernte people, having strong associations with various ancestral beings. While in Alice Springs, visit the **Aboriginal Art and Culture Centre** for an insight into the customs, history and art of the Pwerte Marnte Marnte (Southern Arrernte) people.

Aboriginal Art and Culture Centre
86 Todd Street
Alice Springs
Phone: (08) 8952 3408
Open: 9 a.m.–6 p.m. daily

2 The colours of the outback

From Alice Springs head west along Larapinta Drive. Two kilometres along on your left is **Araluen Galleries** in the Alice Springs Cultural Precinct which houses a permanent collection of works by Albert Namatjira and other artists from the Hermannsburg school of landscape painters. These paintings capture the vibrant colours of the country: the subtle blue and purple hues of the ranges contrasting with the rich orange of the rocks and the stark, white trunks of the ghost gums. Each year in late September and early November, the Araluen Galleries presents The Desert Mob Art Show, featuring recent works by Central Australian artists.

Thorny devil, a creature of the desert

The stained-glass windows in the foyer of the centre are also a feature, telling the Honey Ant Dreaming story.

Araluen Galleries
Alice Springs Cultural Precinct
Larapinta Drive
Alice Springs
Phone: (08) 8951 1120
Open: 10 a.m.–5 p.m. daily

3 Animals of the desert

The next stop, also on the left, is at the **Alice Springs Desert Park**, 4 kilometres further along Larapinta Drive. The Desert Park provides an excellent introduction to the plants, animals and habitats you are likely to see along this tour. A 1.6-kilometre path winds through three arid zone habitats: Desert Rivers, Sand Country and Woodlands. The nocturnal house provides a rare opportunity to see many of the animals that would otherwise remain hidden, living underground or emerging only at night. If possible, time your visit to include the Birds of Prey exhibition, daily at 10 a.m. and 3.30 p.m. in the Nature Theatre. You need to allow three hours to fully explore the Desert Park.

Alice Springs Desert Park
Larapinta Drive
Alice Springs
Phone: (08) 8951 8788
Open: 7.30 a.m.–6 p.m. daily

4 Into the ranges

The outback beckons, so continue west on Larapinta Drive. Just 300 metres along on the left is a sign for John Flynn's Grave. Flynn,

BE PREPARED
Before setting out, ensure you have plenty of fuel; petrol (leaded and unleaded) and diesel are available only at Glen Helen Resort and Hermannsburg. While a limited amount of drinking water is available throughout West MacDonnell National Park and kiosk facilities are available at Standley Chasm and Glen Helen Resort, you are strongly advised to carry sufficient water for your party.

To ensure that you are prepared for outback driving, read the section on Outback Motoring on page 599.

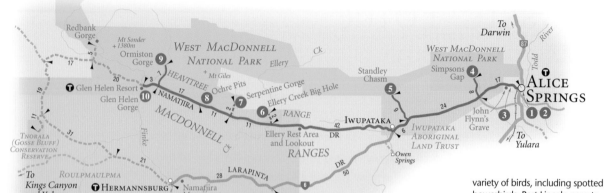

the founder of the Royal Flying Doctor Service, was buried here, in the foothills of Mt Gillen. Continue west for 10 kilometres, then turn right to visit **Simpsons Gap**.

The gap is located within West MacDonnell National Park. A short walk from the car park along a sandy creek bed lined with huge river red gums leads to a small waterhole. The creek has cut an impressive gap through the ridge, leaving red cliffs towering several hundred metres above the waterhole. Aboriginal legend associates this place with the Perentie (Goanna) Dreaming. A resident population of about 20 black-footed rock wallabies can often be seen on the boulder-strewn eastern slope of the Gap. Swimming is not permitted here but there are plenty of opportunities to enjoy a refreshing dip further along the tour.

Simpsons Gap
Larapinta Drive
Open: 5 a.m.–8 p.m. daily

5 **A midday marvel**
Return to Larapinta Drive and continue west until you reach the turn-off on the right to **Standley Chasm**. The chasm, located on Iwupataka Aboriginal land, is part of the Termite Ancestress Dreaming. A 20-minute walk, past cycads and ferns that flourish in this protected environment, brings you to a narrow cleft in the range. The chasm is spectacular at midday when the sun transforms it into a glowing red corridor. Dingoes and rock wallabies are frequent visitors.

Standley Chasm
Larapinta Drive
Open: 8 a.m.–6 p.m. daily

6 **Birds at the Big Hole**
Return to Larapinta Drive and continue west until the road branches. Take the right branch, Namatjira Drive, and after 32 kilometres, stop at the lookout on the left (Ellery Rest Area and Lookout) and enjoy the great views to the south. A further 10 kilometres along, take the turn-off to **Ellery Creek Big Hole**. As you follow the gravel road to the waterhole, look at the rocks around you. What were once horizontal layers are now vertical, displaying the fascinating geological history of the area.

A short walk from the car park brings you to this beautiful waterhole, surrounded by river red gums and backed by red cliffs on which the rare MacDonnell Ranges cycad grows. The pool is a popular swimming and picnic spot. The permanent water also attracts a variety of birds, including spotted bowerbirds, Port Lincoln parrots, white-plumed honeyeaters, pied butcherbirds and white-faced herons. The Dolomite Walk, a 3-kilometre loop, starts near the waterhole on the west of the creek.

7 **Carpet Snake Dreaming**
Return to Namatjira Drive and continue west. After 11 kilometres, turn right to **Serpentine Gorge**. The gorge winds through the rocks just like a snake, thus it is no surprise that it is part of the local Carpet Snake Dreaming. It is possible to swim at the first waterhole but not at the higher ones: these are protected habitats for rare plants and animals, including the Centralian flannel-flower. Found only around here, it has a white flower and seems to grow straight out of the cliff walls.

When the water level is low, you can walk along the creek to the gorge (1-hour return). There is also a steep climb to a lookout on the east of the gorge from the first pool (30-minute return) which rewards you with spectacular views of Serpentine Gorge and the mountains to the south.

The colours of the West MacDonnell Ranges

8 Red and yellow paints

Return to Namatjira Drive and continue west for another 11 kilometres before turning right to go to the **Ochre Pits**. Ochre plays an important part in traditional Aboriginal life. It can be mixed with water or animal fat to produce a paste or paint and is used to decorate the body during ceremonies and to heal various ailments. Rock paintings are also produced using ochre.

Follow the path 300 metres along the creek to the deposit. The exposed ochre pit represents 700 million years of geological history. Ranging from deep red through to bright yellow and pure white, the colourful layers are caused by the presence of iron oxide in varying quantities. The white ochre has little or no iron oxide and a high level of kaolin, a white clay mineral. The Arrernte bushtrack (3-hour return) commences at the end of the Ochre Pits and leads to Inarlanga Pass, a remote and spectacular gorge; signs along the track explain local Aboriginal land management and customs.

9 Emu Dreaming

Return to Namatjira Drive, continue west for another 17 kilometres, then take the turn-off on the right to **Ormiston Gorge**. The cliffs in this gorge are the highest you will see; their breathtaking scale dwarfs the visitor. Ormiston Gorge is part of the local Emu Dreaming, and the waterhole is sacred. There is a

Standley Chasm

visitor centre here; check the information board for ranger-conducted activities.

Two walks start at the gorge. The Ghost Gum Walk (1 hour) is memorable for the startling white tree trunks against the red cliffs. This walk takes you along the creek and up on to the ridge behind the gorge. The other walk takes you into Ormiston Pound, a bowl in the mountains formed by erosion. This is a longer walk (4 hours), but you will be rewarded with wonderful views over the pound and the gorge. It is a loop and, for maximum scenic enjoyment, an anti-clockwise direction is recommended.

If you are planning an overnight stop, Ormiston Gorge is welcoming, with a camping area, toilets, solar-heated showers and gas barbecues.

10 Finally, the Finke

Return to Namatjira Drive and continue west to Glen Helen Resort. At **Glen Helen Gorge**, about 700 metres from the resort and car park, the Finke River has cut through layers of sandstone to produce a rather unusual formation. The permanent waterhole in the gorge is one of the few along the Finke River system. Surrounded by reeds, the waterhole is a haven for ducks, herons and waders; ospreys, jabirus and crakes are occasional visitors. Swimming is allowed. There are no marked trails, but you can climb over the ridge to the south side of the waterhole, and then walk to the next ridge to see the Organ Pipes. This unusual geological formation consists of a series of vertically uplifted sandstone columns that look just like the pipes of an organ.

Returning to Alice Springs

If you are travelling in a two-wheel drive vehicle, retrace your journey along Namatjira Drive and Larapinta Drive.

Four-wheel drive parties have a longer option (265 km), returning to Alice Springs via Redbank Gorge, Tnorala (Gosse Bluff) Conservation Reserve and Hermannsburg. You must pick up a Meerenie Tour Pass to enter Tnorala (Gosse Bluff) Conservation Reserve; these are available at visitor information centres in Alice Springs and at Glen Helen Resort.

Before leaving Glen Helen Resort, check road conditions for the unsealed section of Namatjira Drive. After 20 kilometres take the turn-off on the right to Redbank Gorge, to see the narrow chasm formed by the icy waters of Redbank Creek. Further west is Tnorala (Gosse Bluff) Conservation Reserve. Tnorala is a spectacular crater, kilometres across, produced by a comet impact 130 million years ago. From Tnorala, return to Alice Springs via Hermannsburg – site of a historic Lutheran missionary settlement where Albert Namatjira painted – and Larapinta Drive.

A popular extension of the four-wheel drive return option is to turn south from Hermannsburg to Finke Gorge National Park, where you will find a shady camping area with toilets and solar showers. The rough four-wheel drive track along the creek bed is impassable after rain. Finke Gorge features spectacular outcrops of sandstone that have been weathered into extraordinary shapes. Within the gorge is an area known as Palm Valley, where palm-like cycads and rare red fan palms create a prehistoric atmosphere.

Ghost gums, a feature of the West MacDonnell Ranges

NATIONAL PARKS

Palm Valley in Finke Gorge National Park

AT THE TOP END

The splendid **Kakadu National Park** is leased by the traditional Aboriginal owners to the Federal Director of National Parks. Here the visitor can see Aboriginal rock art and the magnificent scenery of the Arnhem Land escarpment, go bushwalking or take a boat cruise through wetlands. Access is by sealed road from Darwin. Some areas within the park are 4WD only.

Litchfield National Park is 100 kilometres south of Darwin. Waterfalls cascade from the sandstone plateau of Tabletop Range and create beautiful pools for year-round swimming. Monsoonal rainforests contrast with treeless black-soil plains where magnetic termite mounds dot the landscape. Tjaynera Falls (Sandy Creek), and The Lost City with its fascinating sandstone formation, are on 4WD tracks. Swimming, photography, wildlife observation and bushwalking are all popular activities. On the way to this park, do not miss the Territory Wildlife Park, where you can see native fauna in a bush setting; the nocturnal house, aquarium and huge walk-through aviary are popular attractions.

Gurig National Park, on the Cobourg Peninsula, is Aboriginal land managed by agreement with the Parks and Wildlife Commission of the Northern Territory. Because the approach route is also through Aboriginal land, a permit is necessary. The park can be reached by 4WD, but road access is May–October only. This isolated park is rich in Aboriginal

culture as well as containing lonely ruins of early European attempts at settlement.

Located 29 kilometres north-east of Katherine is **Nitmiluk National Park**. This fascinating river gorge, with its Aboriginal rock paintings, can be seen from a walking track, canoe or tour boat. In the dry season (May–October), anglers catch barramundi and other fish in the gorge's deep pools. **Elsey National Park**, 112 kilometres south-east of Katherine, is alongside the Roper River. The park includes Mataranka Hot Springs, a swimming area believed to have therapeutic powers.

On the Victoria Highway south-west of Katherine is **Flora River Nature Park**, home of the Wardaman people and interesting for its riverine forest. Further along the highway are **Gregory** and **Keep River** national parks. Both feature tropical and semi-arid plant life, spectacular range and gorge scenery, significant Aboriginal sites and evidence of early European pastoral history. Boat tours on the Victoria River in Gregory National Park can be arranged at Victoria River Roadhouse and Timber Creek.

IN CENTRAL AUSTRALIA

South of Tennant Creek is **Devils Marbles Conservation Reserve**. The large spherical boulders were formed by the weathering of granite outcrops on a wide quartz plain. Devils Marbles are particularly attractive at sunset, when they glow a deep red. There is a short self-guide walk, or visitors can take longer walks in easy terrain. Further east is **Davenport Range National Park** which features a permanent waterhole ecology. This isolated park is accessible by four-wheel drive or high clearance vehicles only and visitors should take reasonable precautions for travelling in a remote area.

The best known park in the Centre is World Heritage-listed **Uluru–Kata Tjuta National Park**, which contains the monolith Uluru (Ayers Rock) and Kata Tjuta (The Olgas). The area is of vital cultural and religious significance to Anangu (the traditional Aboriginal owners), whose ancestors have lived in the area for at least 30 000 years.

Anangu encourage visitors to seek alternatives to climbing Uluru, out of respect for its sacred status. A good choice is the 9.5-kilometre circuit walk or guided coach tour around the rock base to see significant traditional sites, such as the Mutitjulu Rock shelter, containing Aboriginal paintings, and Kantju Gorge. Walks are conducted by Aboriginal guides. Visitors who decide to climb the rock should be aware that the journey to the 348-metre summit is strictly for those with a good head for heights. It should not be attempted by anyone who is unfit or unwell, or in hot weather; casualties are common.

Further west, the great domes of Kata Tjuta are separated by deep clefts, many of which support an abundance of wildlife such as euros, very much at home in this rocky country. The name Kata Tjuta means 'many heads'. There are several walks, such as Valley of the Winds and Olga Gorge, which take from one to four hours. Keep to the marked tracks and carry plenty of water.

In the **West MacDonnell National Park** lie the MacDonnell Ranges, the land of the Arrernte Aboriginal people. The park is a paradise for photographers and artists. There are spectacular gorges offering crimson and ochre rock walls bordering deep blue pools, and slopes covered with spring wildflowers. Close to Alice Springs is Simpsons Gap, only 25 kilometres west. There are several walking tracks, as well as seasonal ranger-guided tours, through rocky gaps and along steep-sided ridges overlooking huge gums and timbered creek flats. A bicycle path linking Alice Springs to Simpsons Gap provides a different way to see this part of the MacDonnell Ranges. Other well-known scenic spots include Ormiston Gorge and Pound, where fish bury themselves in the mud as a string of waterholes shrink to puddles, then wait for the rains. The deepest part of Ormiston Creek is a magnificent permanent pool the Arrernte link to the Emu Dreaming story (Kwartetweme). At the far end of the gorge, the walls are curtained by a variety of ferns and plants, including the lovely Sturt's desert rose and the relic *Macrozamia* or cycad.

Finke Gorge National Park, a scenic wilderness straddling the Finke River (possibly the oldest river in the world), includes the picturesque Palm Valley. This valley is a refuge for cycads and the rare red fan palm, *Livistona mariae*, estimated to be about 5000 years old. The park is particularly rugged and visitors who do not join tours are advised to use a 4WD.

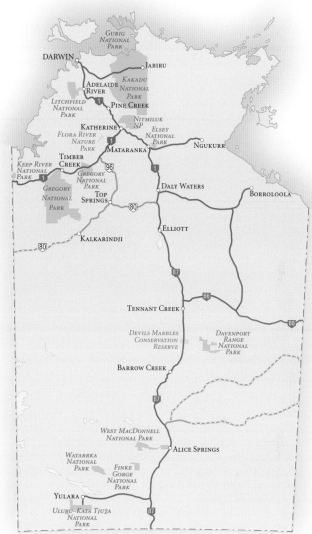

Between Finke Gorge and Uluru lies **Watarrka National Park**, including the amazing Kings Canyon. Waterholes, rock formations and wildlife provide excellent photographic and bushwalking opportunities.

Note: In national parks, reserves and other areas, it is essential to heed local advice on the dangers of swimming. Both saltwater and freshwater crocodiles are found throughout waterways in the Top End. The saltwater crocodile is particularly dangerous and can be found in both salt water (including the sea) and fresh water. Heed local warning advice and warning signs. In the Centre, daytime heat can be extreme, especially in summer. Avoid walking in the heat of the day and always carry plenty of water.

For more information about Kakadu and Uluru, contact Parks Australia, 7th Floor, TCG Centre, 80 Mitchell St, Darwin NT 0800 (postal address GPO Box 1260, Darwin NT 0801); (08) 8946 4300. For information about the Territory's other parks and reserves, contact the Parks and Wildlife Commission of the Northern Territory, PO Box 496, Palmerston NT 0830; (08) 8999 5511. Web site www.nt.gov. au/paw

WILDLIFE-WATCHING

Water monitors can be spotted in Elsey National Park

AROUND DARWIN

A visit to the Darwin area would be incomplete without some wildlife-spotting. While the region is best known for its crocodiles and birdlife, fish are the drawcard at Aquascene in **Doctors Gully** on the edge of Darwin's city centre. Hundreds of milkfish, batfish, catfish and other species come to these shallow waters for a free meal each high tide. These wild fish can be hand-fed as you wade among them.

Visitors in search of crocodiles and birdlife might be tempted to head straight for Kakadu, but those who stop along the way will have some wonderful wildlife-watching experiences. **Fogg Dam** was constructed east of Darwin in the 1950s for an ill-fated rice-growing scheme, and was an unexpected gift to the Territory's bird population. It is now a peaceful conservation reserve with bird-viewing platforms and boardwalks through paperbark swamps and rainforest. You are likely to encounter comb-crested jacanas as they step nimbly over waterlilies, as well as pairs of green pygmy-geese among the reeds. Harmless water pythons and wallabies are often seen in the evenings. Nearby on the Arnhem Highway is the Window on the Wetlands Visitor Centre, which offers an overview of the area's ecology.

Further east is **Mary River National Park**, a fascinating mix of salt and freshwater habitats. There is no shortage of saltwater crocodiles here, and a river cruise is the best way to see them. A close-up view of these oversized reptiles explains why there are no 'swim-with-the-croc' tours. Boat tours operate regularly through both the fresh-water and salt-water sections. For birdwatchers, the Mary River floodplains are also home to a large population of sea eagles and egrets. Pelicans, jabirus, jacanas, spoonbills and kingfishers are often seen as well.

AT THE TOP END

Kakadu National Park is world-renowned for its ecological and cultural significance. It is the temporary or permanent home to one-third of Australian bird species so it makes good sense to begin with a bird checklist. This can be obtained from the Bowali Visitor Centre.

Two of the best birdwatching sites within the park are Mamukala and Yellow Water (Ngurrungurrudjba). Between August and October, towards the end of the dry season, these and other billabongs become welcome oases for Kakadu's birds. Large flocks of magpie geese, plumed whistling-ducks and many other waterbirds crowd in as the surrounding country dries out. The opportunity to see this wonderful parade of birds should not be missed. Bring your binoculars to the bird hide at Mamukala, or enjoy the spectacle from the raised croc-proof boardwalk at Yellow Water. Regular boat cruises through Yellow Water provide an opportunity to spot saltwater crocodiles as well as birds.

Campers may see brown bandicoots at night and wallabies and wallaroos in the park's open grassy areas. Northern short-necked turtles may rest on logs at the water's edge, and many kinds of monitor lizards can be spotted around billabongs and on road verges.

Near Mataranka on the Stuart Highway is **Elsey National Park**, known for its rejuvenating thermal pools. When the sun is high overhead the pools are the best place to be – time your wildlife-spotting for the early morning and late afternoon. At these cooler times of day the animals are at their most active. Wallabies and goannas can be seen, as well as water monitors and occasional freshwater crocodiles along the river – treat the latter with the same respect as their notorious saltwater cousins. Evening is a good time to glimpse a possum or flying fox in the trees.

IN CENTRAL AUSTRALIA

Much of Central Australia's wildlife is right at your feet. Larger animals are less common, though insects and lizards flourish in the harsh desert environment. Their tiny tracks criss-cross the sand and tell a fascinating tale of the previous night's adventures and activities.

In **Uluṟu–Kata Tjuṯa National Park** birds are always a welcome sight against the deep-blue skies. Cockatoos, ringneck parrots and budgerigars keep an eye out for birds of prey such as kestrels and whistling kites. Honeyeaters are at home in the park, as are flocks of tiny zebra finches.

For a close-up view of Central Australian wildlife the Alice Springs Desert Park should not be missed. This park showcases a range of common and rare Central Australian plants and animals. In its desert nocturnal house tiny mammals, bats and birds go about their business, oblivious of curious visitors. Visitors to the Top End should consider a visit to the Territory Wildlife Park just south of Darwin. Features of this expansive park include eleven aviaries with different habitats and a walk-through tunnel in which barramundi and turtles swim overhead. For more information on wildlife-watching in national parks and reserves, contact the Parks and Wildlife Commission of the Northern Territory, PO Box 496, Palmerston NT 0830; (08) 8999 5511. Web site www.nt.gov. au/paw

The jacana, a resident of the Top End wetlands

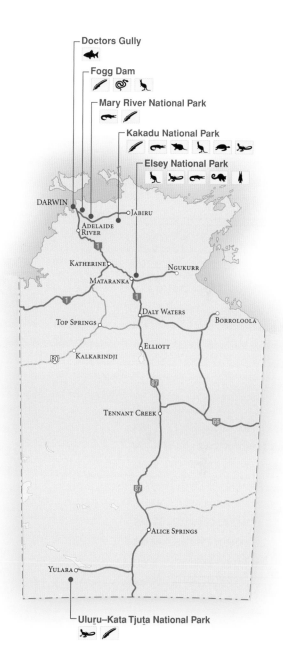

WILDLIFE-WATCHING ETHICS

Do not disturb wildlife or wildlife habitats. Keep the impact of your presence to a minimum. Use available cover or hides wherever possible.

Do not feed wildlife, even in urban areas. (Note: supervised feeding is allowed at some locations)

Be careful not to introduce exotic plants and animals – definitely no pets.

Stay on defined trails.

Northern Territory

Location Map

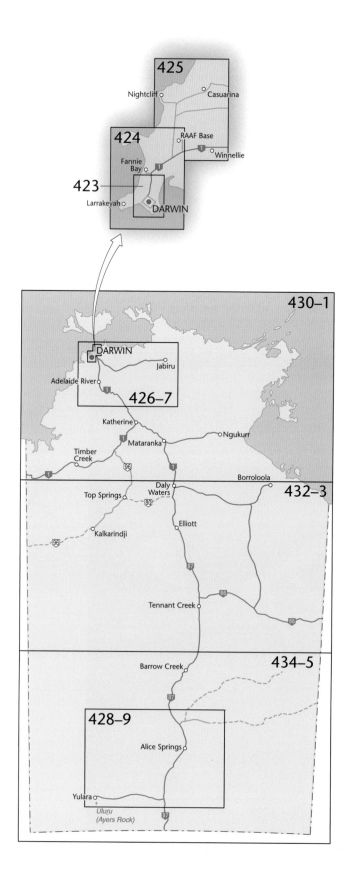

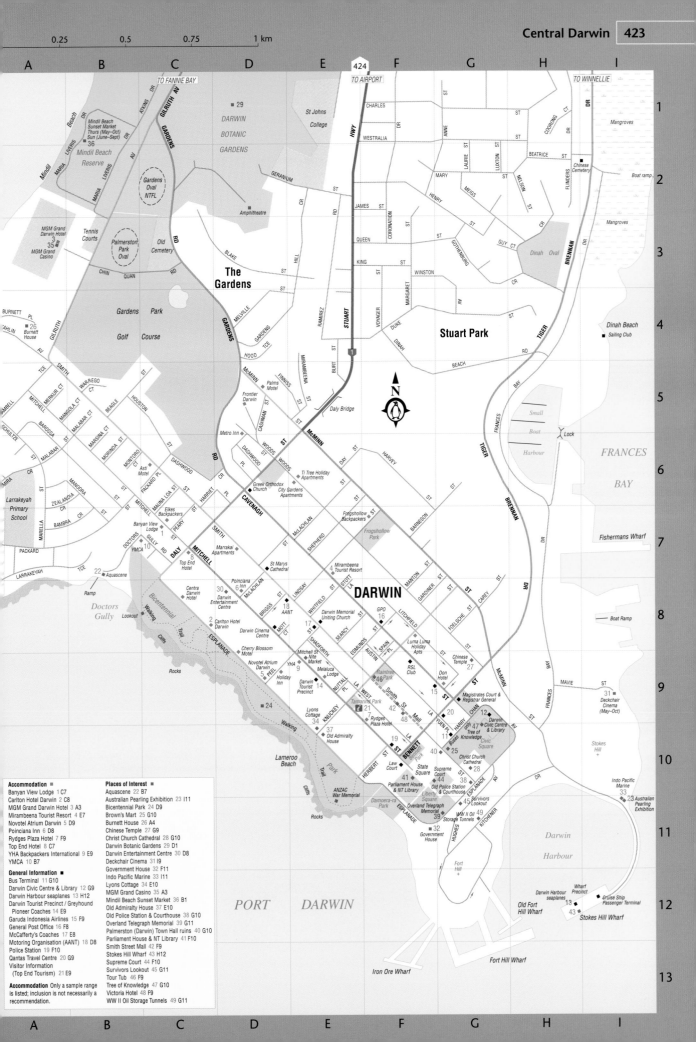

0.25 0.5 0.75 1 km

Accommodation ■
Banyan View Lodge 1 C7
Carlton Hotel Darwin 2 C8
MGM Grand Darwin Hotel 3 A3
Mirambeena Tourist Resort 4 E7
Novotel Atrium Darwin 5 D9
Poinciana Inn 6 D8
Rydges Plaza Hotel 7 F9
Top End Hotel 8 C7
YHA Backpackers International 9 E9
YMCA 10 B7

General Information ■
Bus Terminal 11 G10
Darwin Civic Centre & Library 12 G9
Darwin Harbour seaplanes 13 H12
Darwin Tourist Precinct / Greyhound
   Pioneer Coaches 14 E9
Garuda Indonesia Airlines 15 F9
General Post Office 16 F8
McCafferty's Coaches 17 E8
Motoring Organisation (AANT) 18 D8
Police Station 19 F10
Qantas Travel Centre 20 G9
Visitor Information
   (Top End Tourism) 21 E9

Accommodation Only a sample range
is listed; inclusion is not necessarily a
recommendation.

Places of Interest ■
Aquascene 22 B7
Australian Pearling Exhibition 23 I11
Bicentennial Park 24 D9
Brown's Mart 25 G10
Burnett House 26 A4
Chinese Temple 27 G9
Christ Church Cathedral 28 G10
Darwin Botanic Gardens 29 D1
Darwin Entertainment Centre 30 D8
Deckchair Cinema 31 I9
Government House 32 F11
Indo Pacific Marine 33 I11
Lyons Cottage 34 E10
MGM Grand Casino 35 A3
Mindil Beach Sunset Market 36 B1
Old Admiralty House 37 E10
Old Police Station & Courthouse 38 G10
Overland Telegraph Memorial 39 G11
Palmerston (Darwin) Town Hall ruins 40 G10
Parliament House & NT Library 41 F10
Smith Street Mall 42 F9
Stokes Hill Wharf 43 H12
Supreme Court 44 F10
Survivors Lookout 45 G11
Tour Tub 46 F9
Tree of Knowledge 47 G10
Victoria Hotel 48 F9
WW II Oil Storage Tunnels 49 G11

0   0.25   0,5   0.75   1 km

425

DARWIN AIRPORT

Ludmilla

TOTEM RD

BAGOT RD

WARD DR

DICK DR

FITZER ST
HARVEY ST
TUDAWALI ST

NADPUR ST

BAGOT ABORIGINAL COMMUNITY

NEMARLUK ST
CARDO ST

BENWERRIN

CAMARA

RAAF Base

BUKATILLA
CAREELA ST
CURRINGA
CURRINGA
GANDARRA

COGRABIN
DAMALA
COORABIDA

COORABIDA
BELLARA

BILLEROY

GANDARRA

The Narrows

NARROWS
FLEMING ST
WILMOT ST
WELLS AV
Dwyer Park

SNELL ST
REICHARDT ST
STEEL ST
CATO ST
COONAWARRA

BISHOP ST

BRENNAN DR

TIGER BRENNAN DR

Bayview Haven

Mangroves

Mangroves

Mangroves

CHARLES DARWIN NATIONAL PARK

Rocks

East Point

East Point Military Museum

East Point Reserve

Mangroves

Boat Ramp

Lake Alexander

Dudley Point
Lookout

FANNIE BAY

Bayview
GEORGE
PHILIP ST
BANYAN ST
WARATAH
HINKLER CR
KURINGAL CT

Waratah Sports Club

Ross Smith Memorial
Fannie Bay Gaol Museum

Trailer Boat Club
Boat Ramp
Sailing Club

Vesteys Beach

Boat Ramp

Fannie Bay

Water-ski Club
Boat Ramp

Museum and Art Gallery of the Northern Territory

Bullocky Point
Rocks

Darwin High School

The Gardens

Mindil Beach Sunset Market

Mindil Beach

Gardens Oval NTFL

Darwin Botanic Gardens

Old Cemetery

Amphitheatre

MGM Grand Darwin
Tennis Courts

Myilly Point
Park
Rocks

Burnett House

Darwin Harbour Cruises

Cullen Bay Marina

Passenger Ferry
Ferries to Mandorah
Lock

Emery Point

Larrakeyah

LARRAKEYAH ARMY BASE

Elliott Point

Patrol Boat Harbour

Doctors Gully

Aquascene Ramp

Lyons Cottage

Old Admiralty House
Lameroo Beach

Parliament House

Government House

Iron Ore Wharf

Fort Hill Wharf

Stokes Hill Wharf

PORT DARWIN

Parap
Parap Market (Saturday)

ROSS ST
SMITH ST
PARSONS
CLANCY
GILBERT ST
LUDMILLA
BREMER
WELLS
PLAYFORD

Fannie Bay Racecourse

Richardson Park (Rugby League)

Ludmilla Primary School

Olympic Pool

Primary School
URQUHART

Darwin Bowling Club

GOYDER RD

Sacred Heart College

St Johns College

Darwin Botanic Gardens

GERANIUM

WESTRALIA

Stuart Park

Chinese Cemetery
Boat Ramp

Primary School

Dinah Oval

Dinah Beach

Small Boat Harbour
Lock

Fishermans Wharf

DARWIN

Daly Bridge

Deckchair Cinema

FRANCES BAY

Stokes Hill

Indo Pacific Marine and Australian Pearling Exhibition

Darwin Harbour

Fort Hill

For more detail on Central Darwin see page 423

STUART HWY
TIGER BRENNAN DR
WOOLNER RD

Bayview Haven

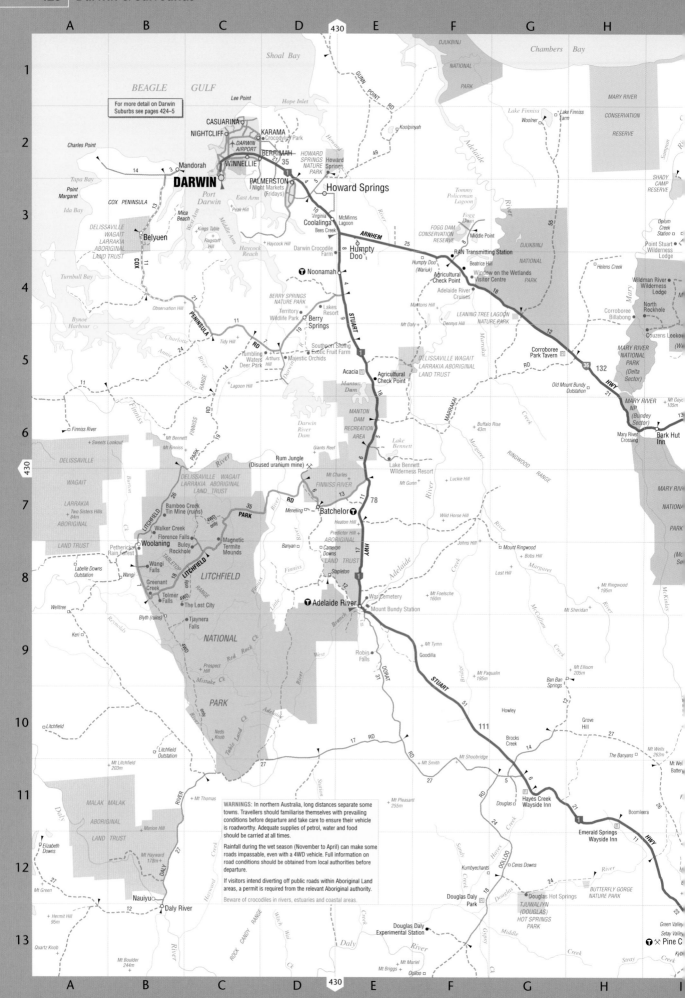

WARNINGS: In northern Australia, long distances separate some towns. Travellers should familiarise themselves with prevailing conditions before departure and take care to ensure their vehicle is roadworthy. Adequate supplies of petrol, water and food should be carried at all times.

Rainfall during the wet season (November to April) can make some roads impassable, even with a 4WD vehicle. Full information on road conditions should be obtained from local authorities before departure.

If visitors intend diverting off public roads within Aboriginal Land areas, a permit is required from the relevant Aboriginal authority.

Beware of crocodiles in rivers, estuaries and coastal areas.

0 10 20 30 40 km

J K L M N O P Q R

Oenpelli

Oenpelli Hill (Injalak)

Cannon Hill (Ngamarr-kanangka)

Ubirr Art Site Walk & Sunset Lookout
Border Store

Cahills Crossing

East Alligator Ranger Station

ARNHEM

LAND

Mayamarleprard Waterhole

Mt Howship 368m

POINT STUART COASTAL RESERVE

CARMOR PLAIN

Finke Bay

WIM CREEK CONSERVATION RESERVE

KAKADU

CULALY PLAIN

MAGELA PLAIN (MARNANJ)

Nardaba

Munmarlary (Manmularri)

MAGELA PLAIN

JABILUKA MINERAL LEASE

Road impassable in wet

Mudginberri

RANGER PROJECT AREA

ABORIGINAL

LAND

TRUST

Four Mile Hole

BOGGY PLAIN (NANJBAGU)

HWY 80

Boat Ramp

Dawumba Hill

Cashew Plantation

Two Mile Hole

Gungarre Monsoon Rainforest Walk

Mamukala Wetlands Walk

Frontier Kakadu Village

Bowali Visitor Centre & Park Headquarters

Jabiru

Gagudju Crocodile Hotel

Ranger Uranium Mine

Mt Brockman 289m

Northern Park Entrance Station

Chirracarwoo Lagoon

Nourlangie Billabongs

Ilagadjarr Wetlands Walk

Nangaluwar Art Site

Baboalba Springs (Gubara)

ARNHEM

Red Lilly Billabong

58

Nourlangie Rock

KOONGARRA MINERAL LEASE

Yellow Water (Ngurrungurrudjba) Boardwalk

Warradjan Aboriginal Cultural Centre

11

Mt Cahill 154m

Mirral Lookout

Nourlangie Art Site Walk

Alligator Billabong

Cooinda

10

Gagudju Lodge Cooinda

Mardugal Billabong Walk

Jim-Jim Billabong

Namarrgon

ARNHEM LAND

OLD

JIM

Spring Peak

9

Mt Basedow 220m

Sandy Billabong

Table Top 465m

Kunkamoula Billabong (Gunkumulu)

Mundogie Hill

Dird Djahdjam Hill 247m

NATIONAL

Adder Creek

430

RD

Craig Ck

Long Billabong

PLATEAU

ARNHEM

21

Gungural Recreation Area

Jim Jim Falls Plunge Pool Walk

Jim Jim Falls (Barrkmalam)

Mine

Coirwong

Maguk Plunge Pool Walk

Twin Falls (Gungkurdul)

LAND

Goodparla (ruins)

15

18

ABORIGINAL

Waterfall Creek Falls

Halfway Peak 217m

Mary River

22

Gunlom Lookout Walk

Road impassable in wet

LAND

Bukbukluk Lookout

151

Old Goodparla (ruins)

13

27

Yirmikmik Walking Tracks

18

TRUST

Saunders

27

Southern Entrance & Ranger Station

11

Mt Callanan 318m

Gimbat

Gimbat Recreation Area

Mt Evelyn 365m

HWY

Mary River Roadhouse

Coronation Hill (Guratba) 300m

Fisher

36

Moline Goldmine

Big Sunday (Niiyanjurrung) 338m

21

Mt Gardiner 264m

Coronet Hill 320m

PARK

Ngartluk Hill 364m

Cullen Hill 216m

McCarthy Hill

Ranford Hill

Aston Hill

Two Sisters 260m

MANYALLALUK ABORIGINAL LAND TRUST

Ngartluk Billabongs

J K L M N O P Q R

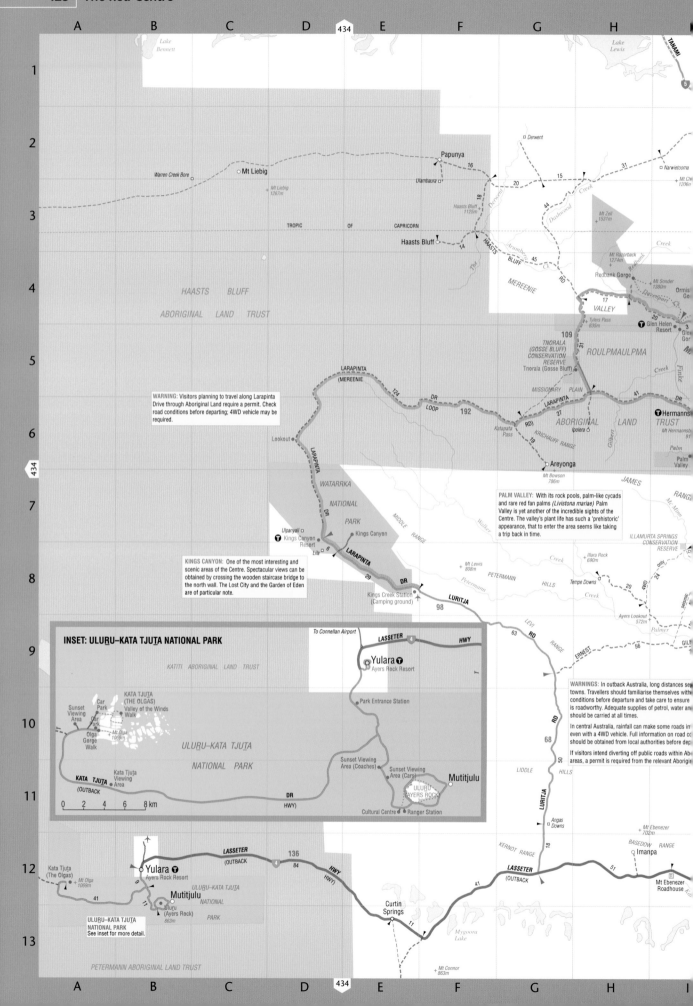

WARNING: Visitors planning to travel along Larapinta Drive through Aboriginal Land require a permit. Check road conditions before departing; 4WD vehicle may be required.

PALM VALLEY: With its rock pools, palm-like cycads and rare red fan palms *(Livistona mariae)* Palm Valley is yet another of the incredible sights of the Centre. The valley's plant life has such a 'prehistoric' appearance, that to enter the area seems like taking a trip back in time.

KINGS CANYON: One of the most interesting and scenic areas of the Centre. Spectacular views can be obtained by crossing the wooden staircase bridge to the north wall. The Lost City and the Garden of Eden are of particular note.

WARNINGS: In outback Australia, long distances se[...] towns. Travellers should familiarise themselves with [...] conditions before departure and take care to ensure [...] is roadworthy. Adequate supplies of petrol, water an[...] should be carried at all times.

In central Australia, rainfall can make some roads im[...] even with a 4WD vehicle. Full information on road co[...] should be obtained from local authorities before dep[...]

If visitors intend diverting off public roads within Ab[...] areas, a permit is required from the relevant Aborigi[...]

INSET: ULURU–KATA TJUTA NATIONAL PARK

ULURU–KATA TJUTA NATIONAL PARK
See inset for more detail.

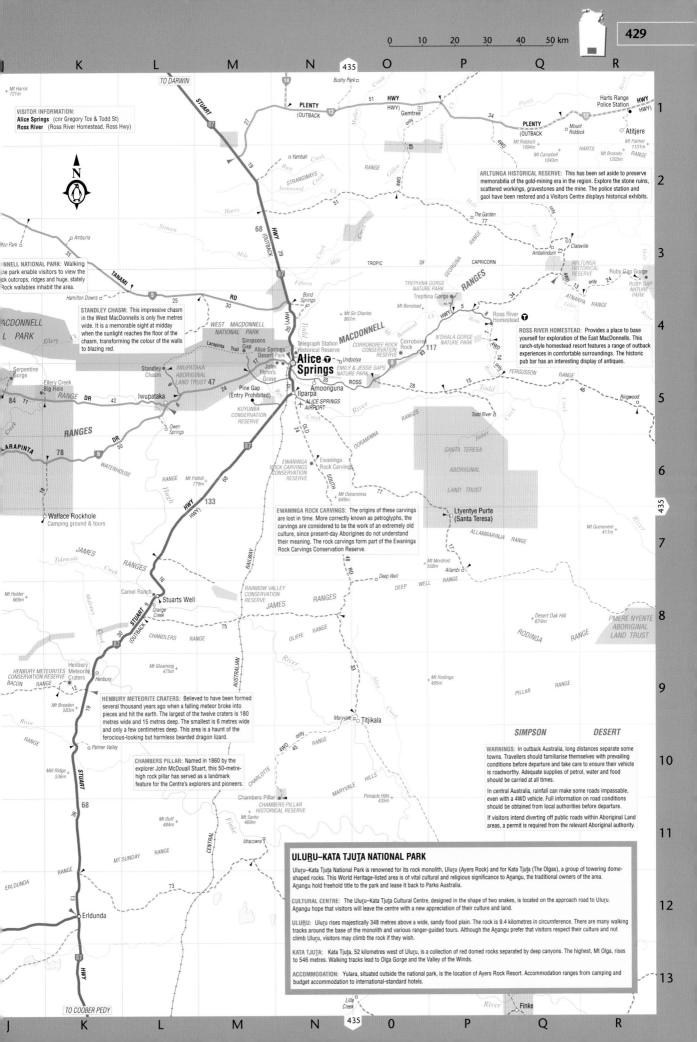

0 10 20 30 40 50 km

VISITOR INFORMATION:
Alice Springs (cnr Gregory Tce & Todd St)
Ross River (Ross River Homestead, Ross Hwy)

ARLTUNGA HISTORICAL RESERVE: This has been set aside to preserve memorabilia of the gold-mining era in the region. Explore the stone ruins, scattered workings, gravestones and the mine. The police station and gaol have been restored and a Visitors Centre displays historical exhibits.

STANDLEY CHASM: This impressive chasm in the West MacDonnells is only five metres wide. It is a memorable sight at midday when the sunlight reaches the floor of the chasm, transforming the colour of the walls to blazing red.

NNELL NATIONAL PARK: Walking he park enable visitors to view the ck outcrops, ridges and huge, stately Rock wallabies inhabit the area.

ROSS RIVER HOMESTEAD: Provides a place to base yourself for exploration of the East MacDonnells. This ranch-style homestead resort features a range of outback experiences in comfortable surroundings. The historic pub bar has an interesting display of antiques.

EWANINGA ROCK CARVINGS: The origins of these carvings are lost in time. More correctly known as petroglyphs, the carvings are considered to be the work of an extremely old culture, since present-day Aborigines do not understand their meaning. The rock carvings form part of the Ewaninga Rock Carvings Conservation Reserve.

HENBURY METEORITE CRATERS: Believed to have been formed several thousand years ago when a falling meteor broke into pieces and hit the earth. The largest of the twelve craters is 180 metres wide and 15 metres deep. The smallest is 6 metres wide and only a few centimetres deep. This area is a haunt of the ferocious-looking but harmless bearded dragon lizard.

CHAMBERS PILLAR: Named in 1860 by the explorer John McDouall Stuart, this 50-metre-high rock pillar has served as a landmark feature for the Centre's explorers and pioneers.

WARNINGS: In outback Australia, long distances separate some towns. Travellers should familiarise themselves with prevailing conditions before departure and take care to ensure their vehicle is roadworthy. Adequate supplies of petrol, water and food should be carried at all times.

In central Australia, rainfall can make some roads impassable, even with a 4WD vehicle. Full information on road conditions should be obtained from local authorities before departure.

If visitors intend diverting off public roads within Aboriginal Land areas, a permit is required from the relevant Aboriginal authority.

ULURU–KATA TJUTA NATIONAL PARK

Uluru–Kata Tjuta National Park is renowned for its rock monolith, Uluru (Ayers Rock) and for Kata Tjuta (The Olgas), a group of towering dome-shaped rocks. This World Heritage-listed area is of vital cultural and religious significance to Anangu, the traditional owners of the area. Anangu hold freehold title to the park and lease it back to Parks Australia.

CULTURAL CENTRE: The Uluru–Kata Tjuta Cultural Centre, designed in the shape of two snakes, is located on the approach road to Uluru. Anangu hope that visitors will leave the centre with a new appreciation of their culture and land.

ULURU: Uluru rises majestically 348 metres above a wide, sandy flood plain. The rock is 9.4 kilometres in circumference. There are many walking tracks around the base of the monolith and various ranger-guided tours. Although the Anangu prefer that visitors respect their culture and not climb Uluru, visitors may climb the rock if they wish.

KATA TJUTA: Kata Tjuta, 52 kilometres west of Uluru, is a collection of red domed rocks separated by deep canyons. The highest, Mt Olga, rises to 546 metres. Walking tracks lead to Olga Gorge and the Valley of the Winds.

ACCOMMODATION: Yulara, situated outside the national park, is the location of Ayers Rock Resort. Accommodation ranges from camping and budget accommodation to international-standard hotels.

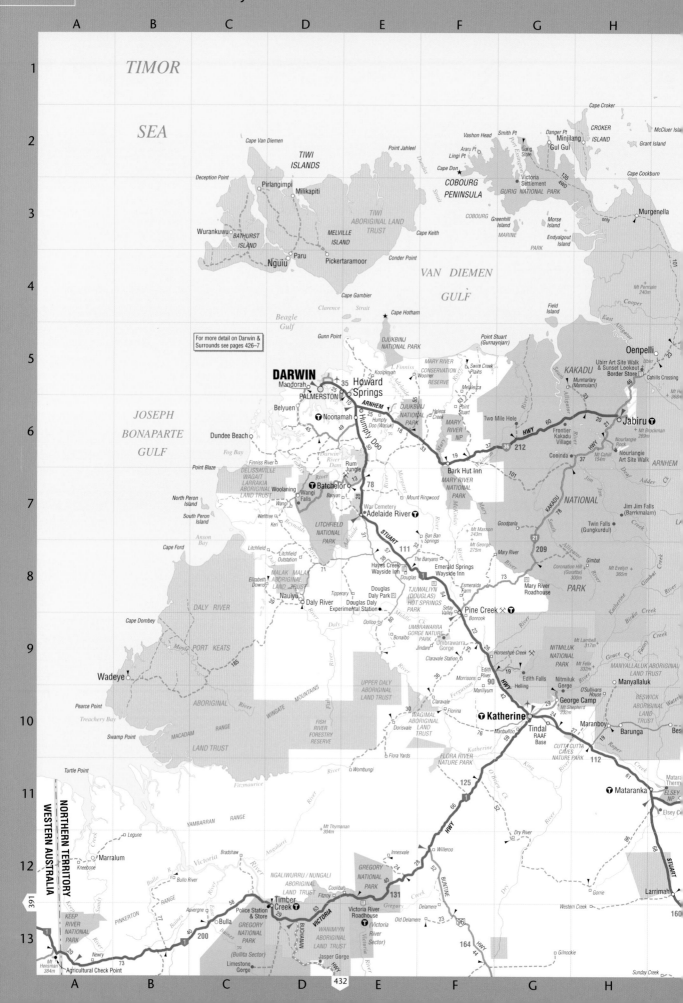

0   50   100   150 km

K   L   M   N   O   P   Q   R

ARAFURA   **SEA**

N

1

★ Cape Wessel

2

WESSEL ISLANDS

Marchinbar Island

3

NDS

Braithwaite Point

Drysdale Island

Guluwuru Island

4

ELCHO ISLAND

Cape Stewart

Mooroongga Is

HOWARD ISLAND

Point Napier

Point Wilberforce

▲ Maningrida

Ji-Marda

○ Milingimbi

☆ Galiwinku

Bremer Island

5

66

35

Castlereagh Bay

Gapuwiyak Landing Ground

○ Rorruwuy

Gunyangara ○

Nhulunbuy ⊕

81

Ngangalala ○

Arnhem Bay

79 ✈ Yirrkala

Buku-Larrnggay Mulka
(Aboriginal Art Museum)

○ Ramingining

□ Old Arafura

Gapuwiyak ○

GOVE

Cape Arnhem

ARNHEM LAND

Manmoyi ○

Mirrngadja Village

PENINSULA

Gurrumuru ○

6

112

River

Gulbuwangay

○ Garrthalala

ABORIGINAL

Gayder

ARNHEM   160

Maduurga

FREDERICK

HILLS

172

Birany Birany ○

Point Alexander

MITCHELL

CENTRAL

RANGE

RD

River

Cape Grey

7

LAND

Creek

Koolatong

Cape Shield

Arnie

PARSONS

RANGE

BATH

RANGE

Walker

○ Baniyala

83

Wilton

776

Isle Woodah

8

Bulman ○

+ Mt Marumba

TRUST

Vaughton

Harris

River

River

Creek

Cape Barrow

Milyakburra ○ ★

★

○ Alyangula

116

RD

Mountain Valley

○ Mainoru

DOWNERS

Phelp

Creek

Bickerton Island

Angurugu ○

✈ **GROOTE**
EYLANDT

Umbakumba ○

CARPENTARIA

9

Mt Furner 188m

RANGE

COLLERA

Numbulwar ▼

Tasman Point

Cape Beatrice

156

Lake Allen

10

River

MTNS

RD

HWY

63

Roper Bar

198

Roper Bar Store

24

○ Ngukurr

91

St Vidgeon (ruins)

River

Port Roper

PORT

ROPER

RD

Limmen
Bight

44

○ Maria Island

47

□ Roper Valley

39

WARNINGS: In northern Australia, long distances separate some
towns. Travellers should familiarise themselves with prevailing
conditions before departure and take care to ensure their vehicle
is roadworthy. Adequate supplies of petrol, water and food
should be carried at all times.

11

Mt Harriet 187m

MARRA ABORIGINAL
LAND TRUST

Towns

Rainfall during the wet season (November to April) can make some
roads impassable, even with a 4WD vehicle. Full information on road
conditions should be obtained from local authorities before departure.

Miniyeri ○

HODGSON
DOWNS
LEASE

NATHAN

208

□ Limmen Bight River Fishing Camp

If visitors intend diverting off public roads within Aboriginal Land
areas, a permit is required from the relevant Aboriginal authority.

Beware of crocodiles in rivers, estuaries and coastal areas.

12

96

Maryfield (ruins)

ALAWA
ABORIGINAL

River

Nathan River

RIVER

West Island

North Island

SIR EDWARD PELLEW GROUP

BARRANYI (NORTH ISLAND)
NATIONAL PARK

○ Hodgson River

LAND

Rosie

Creek

Bing Bong

SW Is

Centre Island

Vanderlin Island

18

Nutwood Downs

TRUST

River

Cox

○ Lorella Springs

RD

WADA
WADALLA
LEASE

King Ash Bay

13

Hodgson

○ Minamia

River

Limmen Bight

Batten

Creek

Garawa ○

NARWINBI
ABORIGINAL LAND

○ Manangoora

⊕ Borroloola

26

Wandangula ○

28

Mara ○

J   K   L   M   N   O   P   Q   R

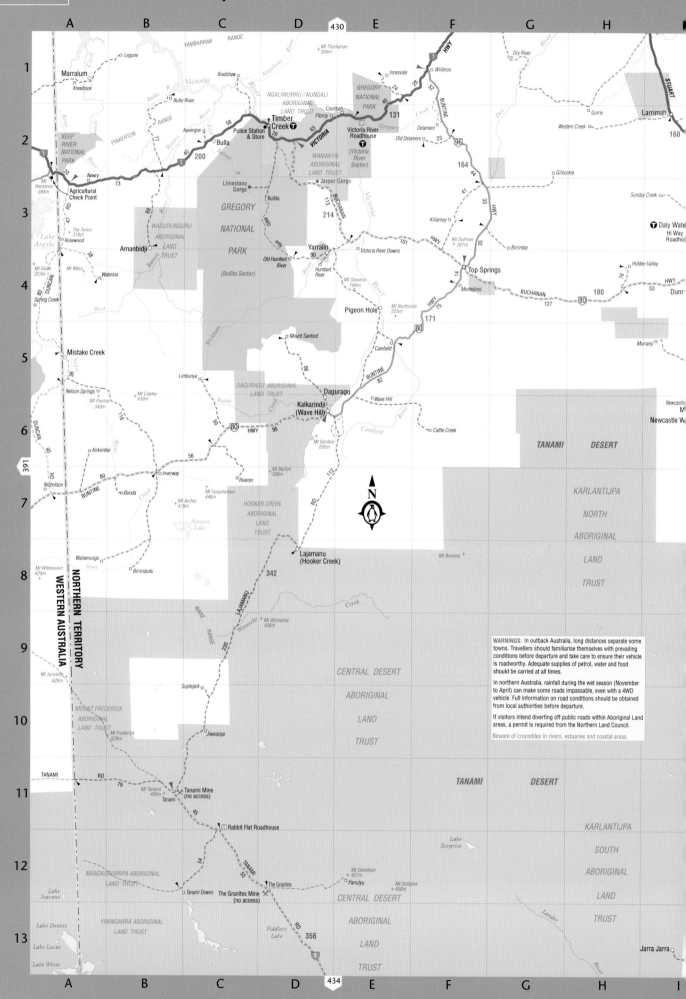

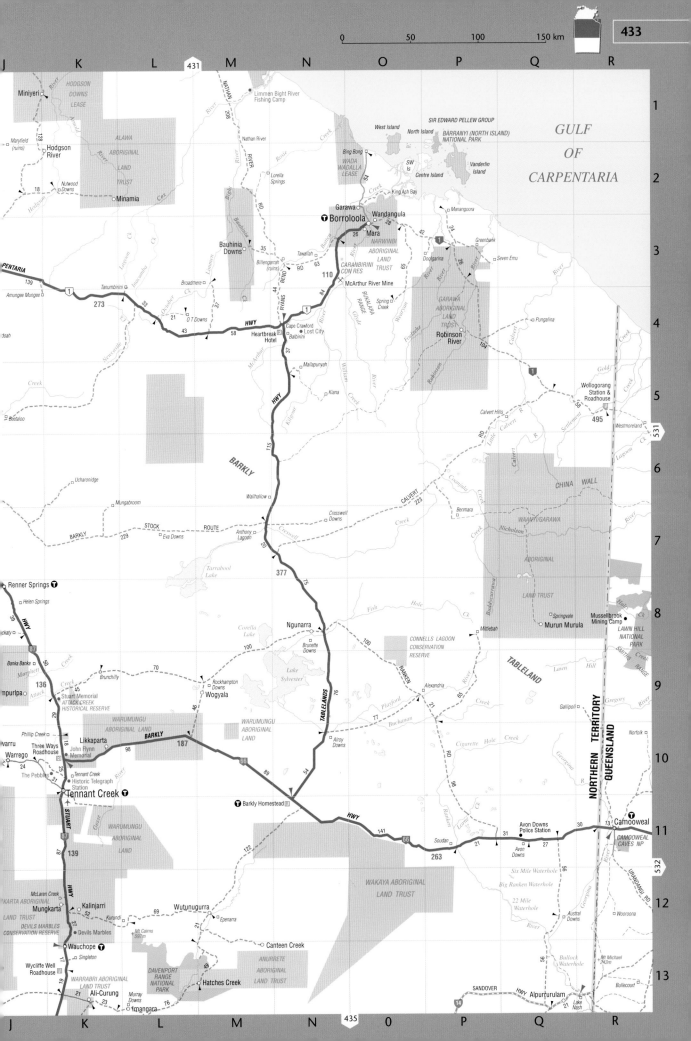

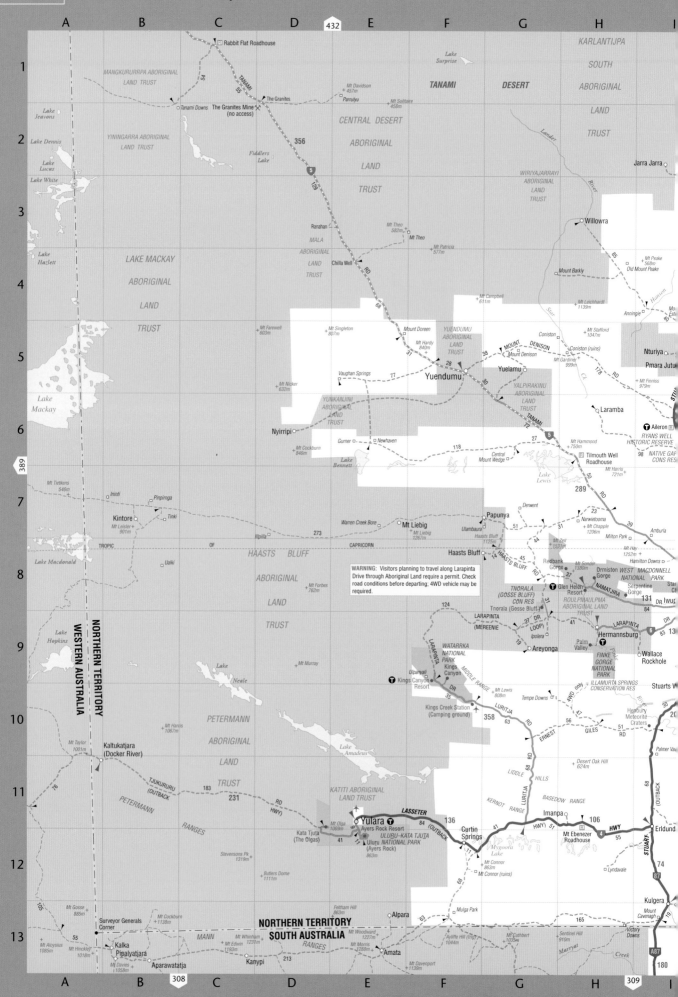

432

A | B | C | D | E | F | G | H

KARLANTIJPA

1

MANGKURURRPA ABORIGINAL
LAND TRUST

Rabbit Flat Roadhouse

SOUTH

Lake
Surprise

Lake
Jeavons

TANAMI

54

TANAMI   DESERT

ABORIGINAL

Lake Dennis

YININGARRA ABORIGINAL
LAND TRUST

2

Tanami Downs

The Granites Mine
(no access)

The Granites

55

Mt Davidson
+457m

Parrulyu

CENTRAL   DESERT

Mt Solitaire
458m

356

Lander

LAND

Lake Lucus

Fiddlers
Lake

ABORIGINAL

River

TRUST

Jarra Jarra

Lake White

129

LAND

WIRIYAJARRAY
ABORIGINAL
LAND
TRUST

3

Ranahan

MALA
ABORIGINAL
LAND
TRUST

Mt Theo
582m

Mt Theo

Willowra

85

Lake Hazlett

TRUST

Mt Patricia
577m

Mt Peake
+568m
Old Mount Peake

Chilla Well

LAKE MACKAY

RD

Mount Barkly

4

ABORIGINAL

68

Mt Campbell
+611m

Mt Leichhardt
1139m

Anningie

Hanson

Mo
Este
40

LAND

Mt Farewell
603m

Mt Singleton
+807m

Mount Doreen

YUENDUMU
ABORIGINAL
LAND
TRUST

Star

Coniston

Mt Stafford
+1047m

Nturiya

5

TRUST

Vaughan Springs

31

Mt Hardy
840m

MOUNT

DENISON

Coniston (ruins)

Mount Denison

38

178

Pmara Jutu

389

Mt Nicker
+632m

77

28

Yuendumu

Yuelamu

Mt Gardiner
999m

Mt Finniss
979m

30

YALPIRAKINU
ABORIGINAL
LAND
TRUST

Laramba

ST

6

Nyirripi

YUNKANJINI
ABORIGINAL
LAND
TRUST

Gurner

Newhaven

27

TANAMI

Aileron

RYANS WELL
HISTORIC RESERVE

Mt Cockburn
846m

118

Mt Hammond
+750m

5

T2

Lake
Bennett

Central
Mount Wedge

50

98

NATIVE GAP
CONS RES

Lake
Lewis

289

Mt Harris
+721m

RD

7

Mt Tietkens
546m

Ininti

Pinpirnga

Tinki

Derwent

Narwietooma

23

39

Kintore

Mt Leisler
901m

Warren Creek Bore

273

Mt Liebig

Papunya

51

31

Mt Chapple
1206m

Milton Park

Amburla

Illpilla

Mt Liebig
1267m

Ulambaura

44

Mt Zeil
1531m

Mt Hay
1252m

Hamilton Downs

TROPIC

OF

CAPRICORN

Haasts Bluff
1125m

Redbank
Gorge

Mt Sonder
1380m

Ormiston
Gorge

WEST MACDONNELL
NATIONAL
PARK

Lake Macdonald

Ualki

Mt Forbes
+762m

HAASTS   BLUFF

Haasts Bluff

14

45

HAASTS BLUFF RD

37

Serpentine
Gorge

Star
C

8

ABORIGINAL

WARNING: Visitors planning to travel along Larapinta
Drive through Aboriginal Land require a permit. Check
road conditions before departing; 4WD vehicle may be
required.

TNORALA
(GOSSE BLUFF)
CON RES

31

Glen Helen
Resort

NAMATJIRA

131

Iwup

LAND

124

Tnorala (Gosse Bluff)

LARAPINTA
(MEREENIE)

27

DR

41

ROULPMAULPMA
ABORIGINAL
LAND
TRUST

84

DR

83

DR

Lake
Hopkins

TRUST

Ipolera

LOOP)

19

Ulpanvali

Areyonga

LARAPINTA

Hermannsburg

6

9

WATARRKA
NATIONAL
PARK

Mt Murray

Kings
Canyon

Palm
Valley

FINKE
GORGE
NATIONAL
PARK

Wallace
Rockhole

Kings Canyon
Resort

LARAPINTA

Lake
Neale

DR

MIDDLE RANGE

ILLAMURTA SPRINGS
CONSERVATION RES

Stuarts W

35

Mt Lewis
808m

Tempe Downs

4WD only

Hermary
Meteorite
Craters

30

20

10

PETERMANN

Mt Harris
1067m

358

63

LURITJA

56

47

GILES

RD

51

Palmer Val

Mt Taylor
1001m

Kings Creek Station
(Camping ground)

68

ERNEST

RD

ABORIGINAL

Kaltukatjara
(Docker River)

LIDDLE

HILLS

Desert Oak Hill
+624m

68

NORTHERN TERRITORY

WESTERN AUSTRALIA

Lake
Amadeus

LAND

LURITJA

BASEDOW
RANGE

Palmer Vai

11

78

TJUKURURU
(OUTBACK

183

231

TRUST

RD

KATITI ABORIGINAL
LAND TRUST

LASSETER

KERNOT

RANGE

Imanpa

106

HWY

(OUTBACK

Erldund

PETERMANN

HWY)

Mt Olga
1069m

Yulara

136

84

(OUTBACK

Mt Connor
+863m

41

HWY) 51

Mt Ebenezer
Roadhouse

4

55

RANGES

Kata Tjuta
(The Olgas)

41

Ayers Rock Resort

ULURU–KATA TJUTA

Uluru NATIONAL
PARK
(Ayers Rock)
863m

Curtin
Springs

Mygoora
Lake

STUART

87

12

Stevensons Pk
1319m

NATIONAL PARK

68

Mt Connor (ruins)

74

Butlers Dome
1111m

Lyndavale

Kulgera

105

Mt Gosse
885m

Feltham Hill
863m

Mount
Cavenagh

19

NORTHERN TERRITORY
SOUTH AUSTRALIA

Mt Cockburn
+1138m

Alpara

Mulga Park

165

Victory
Downs

A87

13

Mt Aloysius
1085m

55

Surveyor Generals
Corner

MANN

Mt Whinham
1231m

RANGES

Mt Woodward
1227m

Ayltte Hill (high)
1044m

Mt Cuthbert

Sentinel Hill
910m

Kalka
Pipalyatjara

Mt Hinckley
1018m

Mt Davies
+1058m

Aparawatatja

Kanypi

213

Amata

Mt Morris
+1288m

Mt Davenport
1139m

Marryat

Creek

180

308

309

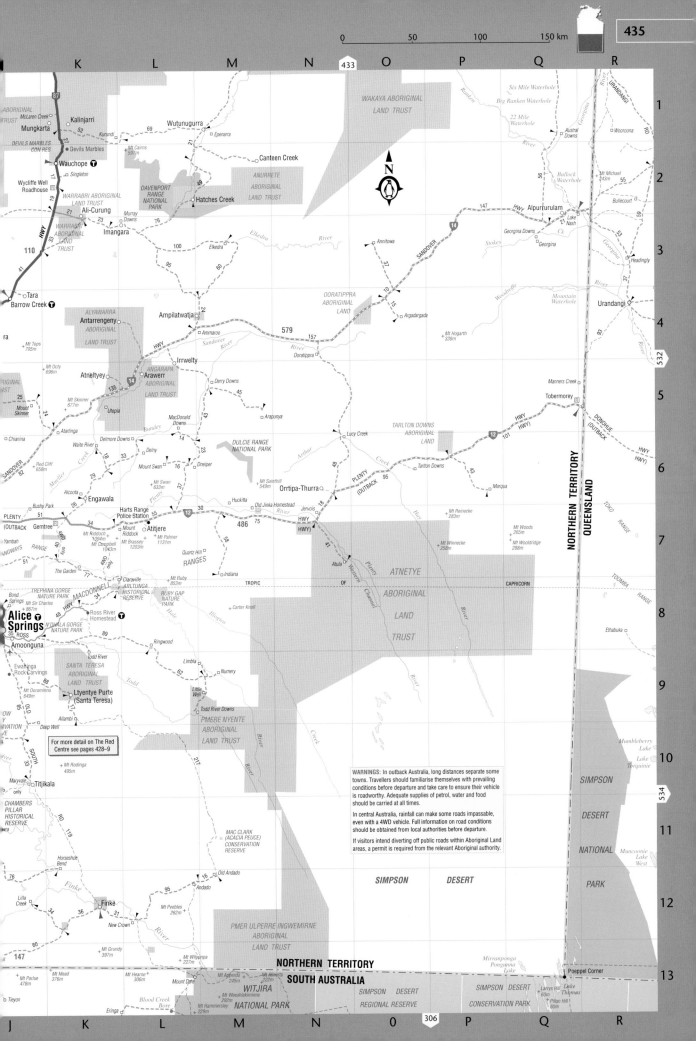

0   50   100   150 km

K   L   M   N   O   P   Q   R

1

2

3

4

5

6

7

8

9

10

11

12

13

ABORIGINAL
TRUST
McLaren Creek
Mungkarta   Kalinjarri
52   Kurundi   69   Wutunugurra
DEVILS MARBLES   21   Epenarra
CON RES   Devils Marbles   21
Wauchope
Wycliffe Well   Singleton   Canteen Creek
Roadhouse   DAVENPORT
RANGE   49   ANURRETE
WARRABRI ABORIGINAL   NATIONAL   Hatches Creek   ABORIGINAL
LAND TRUST   PARK   LAND TRUST
Ali-Curung
Murray   76
Imangara   Downs   100   Elkedra
WARRABRI   95   Elkedra   River
ABORIGINAL   60
LAND   24
TRUST   Ammaroo   579   157
Tara   Sandover   River
Barrow Creek   HWY   Ooratippra
Mt Tops   Ampilatwatja   River   Ooratippra
705m   Antarrengeny
ALYAWARRA   Irrwelty   ANGARAPA   Derry Downs
ABORIGINAL   Atneltyey   Arawerr   ABORIGINAL   45
LAND TRUST   LAND TRUST
Mt Octy   135   14   Arapunya
696m
25   Mt Skinner   Utopia   MacDonald
677m   Downs   23
Mount   24   Bundey   14   DULCIE RANGE
Skinner   Delmore Downs   Delny   NATIONAL PARK   Lucy Creek
Chianina   18   Mount Swan   16   Dneiper   TARLTON DOWNS
Red Cliff   33   29   Mt Swan   Huckitta   ABORIGINAL
658m   Alcoota   633m   Old Jinka Homestead   LAND
SANDOVER   26   Engawala   37   Orrtipa-Thurra   River   Jervois
82   Mueller   Creek   Plenty   30   486   75   HWY   PLENTY   95
Bushy Park   Harts Range   12   (OUTBACK
PLENTY   51   34   Police Station   55   HWY
(OUTBACK   Gemtree   Mt Riddoch   58
Yambah   Mount   1094m   Mt Palmer   Indiana
RANGE   Riddock   Mt Campbell   1131m   Atula
4WD   1043m   Mt Brassey
only   1203m   Quartz Hill
The Garden   RANGES   Mt Ruby   TROPIC   OF   CAPRICORN
853m   Carter Knoll
TREPHINA GORGE   Claraville   RUBY GAP
NATURE PARK   ARLTUNGA   NATURE   ATNETYE
Bond   HISTORICAL   PARK
Springs   Mt Sir Charles   RESERVE   ABORIGINAL
Alice   867m   Ross River
Springs   N'DHALA GORGE   Homestead   Hale   Illogwa   LAND
ROSS   NATURE PARK   89
Amoonguna   Ringwood   TRUST
Ewaninga   SANTA TERESA   Todd River
Rock Carvings   ABORIGINAL   Limbla
Mt Ooraminna   LAND TRUST   62   Numery
649m
Ltyentye Purte   Little
(Santa Teresa)   Well
Allambi
OLD   85   Deep Well   Todd River Downs
33   PMERE NYENTE
For more detail on The Red   ABORIGINAL
Centre see pages 428-9   LAND TRUST
Maryvale   Mt Rodinga
495m
Titjikala
CHAMBERS
PILLAR
HISTORICAL
RESERVE   119
Horseshoe
Bend   MAC CLARK
(ACACIA PEUCE)
CONSERVATION
RESERVE
76   16   Old Andado
Finke   95   Andado
Lilla   River   Finke
Creek   34   36   31   New Crown
Mt Peebles
262m
60   Mt Grundy   New Crown
397m   Mt Wilyunpa
227m
147   NORTHERN TERRITORY
SOUTH AUSTRALIA
Mt Parlue   Mt Mead   Mt Hearne   Mt Dare   Mt Aperdila   Mt Almerta   WITJIRA
478m   376m   306m   245m   222m
Tieyon   WITJIRA   SIMPSON   DESERT
Eringa   NATIONAL PARK   Mt Hammersley   REGIONAL RESERVE   CONSERVATION PARK
Blood Creek   229m
Bore

87

110

17

33

41

HWY

Six Mile Waterhole
Ranken   Big Ranken Waterhole
22 Mile
Waterhole
WAKAYA ABORIGINAL
LAND TRUST   River
Bullock
Waterhole
56   Austral
Downs   Mt Michael   55
147   HWY   Alpurrurulam   243m
14   Lake   Bullecourt
Annitowa   Nash   53   59
Georgina Downs   21
37   SANDOVER   Stokes   Georgina   Headingly
10   Argadargada   37
15   Woodroffe   Mountain
Mt Hogarth   Waterhole   Urandangi
338m   River   89
Manners Creek   532
Tobermorey
TARLTON DOWNS   HWY   101   DONOHUE
ABORIGINAL   12   HWY)   (OUTBACK
LAND   HWY
43   Marqua   HWY
Mt Reinecke
283m   TOKO
Mt Woods   RANGE
265m
Mt Winnecke   Mt Wooldridge
258m   288m
TOOMBA
RANGE
Ethabuka
Mumbleberry
Lake
Lake
Torquinie
SIMPSON
534
DESERT
Muncoonie
Lake West
NATIONAL   Muncoonie
Lake West
SIMPSON   DESERT   PARK
Mirramponga
Ponguna
Lake   Poeppel Corner
Larrya Hill   63m
Lake   Pitlari Hill
Thomas   60m

NORTHERN TERRITORY
QUEENSLAND

URANDANGI

RD

Wooroona

306

WARNINGS: In outback Australia, long distances separate some
towns. Travellers should familiarise themselves with prevailing
conditions before departure and take care to ensure their vehicle
is roadworthy. Adequate supplies of petrol, water and food
should be carried at all times.

In central Australia, rainfall can make some roads impassable,
even with a 4WD vehicle. Full information on road conditions
should be obtained from local authorities before departure.

If visitors intend diverting off public roads within Aboriginal Land
areas, a permit is required from the relevant Aboriginal authority.

QUEENSLAND

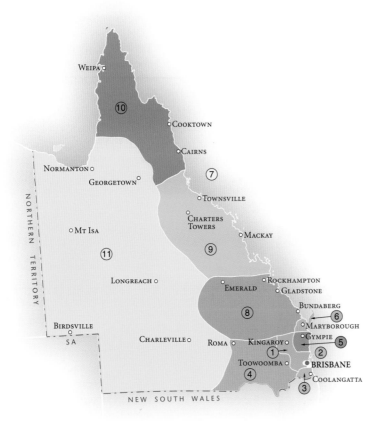

Queensland is Australia's second-largest State, covering 1 727 200 square kilometres in the continent's north-east corner. Of its 3 500 000 residents, 54 per cent live outside the capital Brisbane, making Queensland Australia's most decentralised State. World-famous natural features have earned Queensland a reputation as a premier holiday destination with both interstate and international tourists.

Natural wonders

Queensland's east coast is a narrow strip of beaches, headlands, lagoons, estuaries and mangrove swamps between the Pacific Ocean and the Great Dividing Range. Offshore, the islands and coral reefs of the Great Barrier Reef form one of the great wonders of the natural world – a marine playground without peer. Ancient rainforests cover the Great Dividing Range and west of the range, tableland country with rich volcanic soil supports some of Australia's most productive agricultural regions. Inland lie the vast plains of the Gulf and Channel country. Meandering rivers, dry for much of the year, empty into the mangrove swamps and tidal flats of the Gulf and wind towards the interior of Australia in a maze of channels. Run-off from tropical rains on the western slopes of the Great Dividing Range over millions of years has seeped under the plains to create the Great Artesian Basin.

Two-thirds of Queensland is in the tropics. The north-east coast is subject to monsoon conditions during the Wet, which runs from November to April. The subtropical south-east coast has warm, humid summers tempered by sea breezes, while summers on the plains are hot and dry. Queensland – from the outback to the tropics – is best visited from

View from South Molle Island near the Great Barrier Reef

May to October, when the climate is pleasantly mild and dry.

Early Days

The first inhabitants of what is now the State of Queensland were the Aboriginal people, spread across six geographical and cultural regions each containing several different language groups. About 5000 Torres Strait Islander people, ethnically and culturally distinct from the mainland Aboriginal people, inhabited some of the many islands between Cape York and Papua New Guinea.

The Dutchman Willem Jansz was the first known European to sight Australia when he sailed the *Duyfken* down the west coast of Cape York Peninsula in March 1606. The British established a penal settlement at Moreton Bay in 1824. The district was opened to 'free settlers' in 1842 and they quickly

Imperial Hotel in the old goldmining town of Ravenswood

occupied the Brisbane River valley, the Darling Downs, and the Burnett country to the north. These areas became the colony of Queensland in 1859 and Queensland achieved statehood as part of the Commonwealth of Australia in 1901.

Troubled times

White settlement was not to the benefit of the indigenous population. Conflict between the Aboriginal people and settlers was brutal in central and northern Queensland. Massacres at Hornet Bank in 1857 and near Emerald in 1861 resulted in indiscriminate reprisals led by the notorious Native Police. Legislation in 1897 confined Queensland's Aboriginal people to mission stations and government reserves. Government protectors could remove Aboriginal children from their families without right of appeal.

Sunshine democracy

On the colony's separation in 1859, the constitution of Queensland was similar to that of New South Wales: an elected Legislative Assembly and an appointed Legislative Council. The world's first Labor government held office in Queensland for seven days in December 1899. The Labor Party governed Queensland from 1915 to 1957, except for the period from 1929 to 1932. Labor abolished the Legislative Council in 1922, the only Australian State to do so. The Country– Liberal coalition, first elected 1957, was voted out in 1989 following corruption allegations and inquiries. A minority Labor government was elected in November 1999; Labor recorded a landslide victory in February 2001.

Capital and cultural wealth

Queensland occupies one of Australia's richest pockets of land in terms of resources. Sheep, cattle and sugar farming were established in the first half of the 19th century and have remained strong industries. The rich volcanic soils of the Darling Downs tableland have provided the State with huge crops of wheat, oil, fruit, tobacco, cotton and most recently wine. Tropical fruit orchards are found along the coast. The discovery of gold and copper in 1867 set off the first Queensland mining boom. Production of coal, gold, copper, silver, lead, zinc, bauxite, mineral sands and natural gas currently contributes over six billion dollars to the State's income.

The value of this extraordinary land has also been an issue for Queensland's indigenous people, many of whom have maintained strong spiritual and cultural connections with their traditional lands. Much of Cape York Peninsula has been subject to native title claims during the last decade and thousands of square kilometres along the west coast have been returned to traditional owners. Australia's two most significant land rights claims, Mabo (1992) and Wik (1996), were Queensland claims.

Welcoming the world

Tourism now accounts for about 10 per cent of Queensland's gross product. About 30 per cent of all overseas visitors to Australia specify Queensland as their main destination. The often unique natural scenery, an ancient culture's artifacts, an easy pace and affordable facilities are attracting increasing numbers of visitors from around the world. Eco-tourists, backpackers, jetsetters and old-fashioned sun-and-surf-lovers are just some of the types of people drawn to the self proclaimed sunshine state.

For more information on Queensland, see Tourist Bureaus on p. 591.

BRISBANE

Story Bridge and the Brisbane city skyline

THE city of Brisbane straddles the lazy curves of the Brisbane River. Moreton and Stradbroke islands create a barrier to the Pacific Ocean, providing the city with a vast body of calm water at its foreshore. Inland, a hilly subtropical terrain provides breathing space and a beautiful backdrop for the city.

VISITOR INFORMATION

Brisbane Visitor Information Centre
Queen St Mall
(07) 3006 6290
www.brisbanetourism.com.au

Redcliffe Visitor Information
Pelican Park, Hornibrook Esplanade
(07) 3284 3500;
1800 659 500

The mixture of old and new, so much a feature of the Australian city, is nowhere as pronounced as it is in Brisbane. Gold-hued sandstone buildings from colonial times sit among the classic 'Queenslanders' on stilts, and the gleaming metal and glass giants of the past decade; masses of tropical foliage provide a visual link, as does the shimmering subtropical light. The streetscapes, full of odd shapes hailing from a dozen different periods, achieve a certain harmony. With a population of more than 1.6 million, this busy city offers a modern and extensive public transport system, a wide selection of restaurants, quality cultural institutions and a strong historical heritage.

GETTING AROUND

Airport shuttle bus
Coachtrans Airport Shuttle Service
(07) 3860 6999

Airtrain Citylink
Rail link from airport to city and Gold Coast
(07) 3211 2855

Motoring organisation
Royal Automobile Club of Queensland (RACQ)
13 1905

Car rental
Avis 13 6333; Budget 1300 362 848;
Hertz 13 3039; Thrifty 1300 367 227

Public transport
TransInfo (bus, ferry, rail) 13 1230

Bus tours
City Sights and City Nights Tourist trips aboard
open-air tram replicas around the city and
suburban sights 13 1230

Brisbane River trips
Club Crocodile River Queens (07) 3221 1300;
Mirimar Cruises (07) 3221 0300

Taxis
Black & White Cabs 13 1008;
Yellow Cabs 13 1924

EXPLORING BRISBANE

Brisbane has very little traffic congestion and has well-signed, well-maintained roads – yet it is not an easy city for the first-time visitor to negotiate. The city's phenomenal growth in recent times has resulted in a criss-crossing network of major motorways on the doorstep of the city centre and, in the city centre itself, there is a large number of one-way streets. The Brisbane River twists its way through the city and suburbs, resulting in a complex road system. An up-to-date road map, and some careful route planning at the beginning of each day, is a good idea.

Brisbane city centre is small and, with its wide streets, parks, good weather and lovely scenery, is a terrific place for strolling. The public transport system, made up of bus, rail and ferry networks, is comprehensive and efficient, with a couple of excellent bus routes designed specifically for visitors. A boat trip on the Brisbane River is a must: plenty of tours are available to riverside tourist attractions, and there is an excellent commuter ferry service that stops at several points in the city and South Bank area. The Moreton Bay islands are reached by car ferry from a number of spots along the coastline.

CITY CENTRE

Despite the fact that it is the commercial and retail heart of Brisbane, the city centre – with its open spaces, overhanging Moreton Bay fig trees and plenty of outdoor activity – retains the buoyant holiday spirit that pervades the entire State.

A good way to explore the city centre is to start at **Queen Street Mall** and move in a roughly clockwise direction around the city. The mall, located between Edward and George streets, is an exceptional example of the best civic planning. It is strictly pedestrian only, although a bus station is conveniently located beneath the mall. There are more than 1500 shops, including department stores, as well as

BRISBANE BY AREA

CITY CENTRE
CITY FORESHORE
SOUTH BANK
INNER NORTH-EAST
WEST OF THE CITY
ALONG THE COAST
(see inset below)

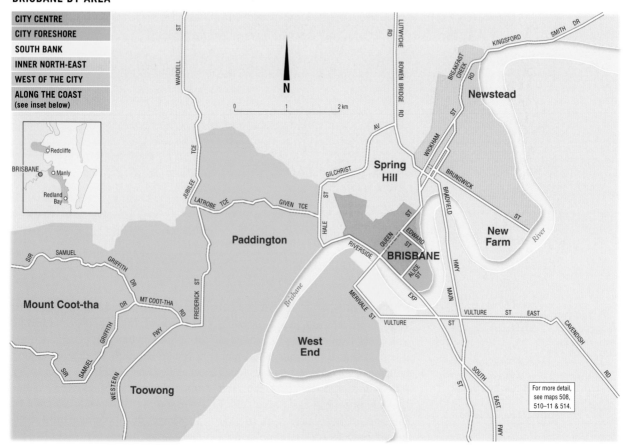

Brisbane City Hall clock tower

buskers, cinemas, theatres, nightspots and restaurants.

Around the middle of the mall turn left into Albert Street (there is an excellent visitor information booth on the corner of Albert and Queen streets) to reach **King George Square**, the location of the impressive **Brisbane City Hall**. Erected between 1920 and 1930, the sandstone building with its classic columns, soaring clock tower and splendid interiors is fairly typical of the grand Greek Revival style that dominated public structures in Australia in the earlier years of the 20th century. Visitors can wander around the superb marbled public rooms of the ground and first floors and take a lift up the tower for some fine city views.

A side trip from here is a visit to the **Old Windmill** in Wickham Terrace, just beyond the boundary of the city centre. Walk along Ann Street on the northern side of the Brisbane City Hall to Edward Street and turn left. Follow Edward Street to Turbot Street then head up Jacobs Ladder, a long set of steps lying straight ahead and running alongside **King Edward Park**. At the top, turn left along Wickham Terrace to reach the Old Windmill. Built in 1828 by convicts to grind flour and maize, the building has been used for a variety of purposes since 1861. Brisbane's oldest structure no longer has its original sails and treadmill, but the interpretive board re-creates the fascinating history of the site.

Nearby on Roma Street are the **Roma Street Parklands**, a new development on the former site of Brisbane's rail yards. It features an activity precinct, restaurants and shops as well as a tropical rainforest, lake and boardwalks.

Return along Roma Street and turn left into Ann Street. Past Wharf Street you will find **St John's Cathedral** (consecrated 1910), a Gothic-style church with an exterior built in Brisbane porphyry stone. This cathedral is commonly described as one of the finest churches in the Southern Hemisphere. Adjacent to St John's Cathedral is the **Deanery**, built in 1850 and formerly the residence of Queensland's first governor, Sir George

	NOT TO BE MISSED IN BRISBANE	Map Ref.

Brisbane City Hall — 508 D6
Architectural landmark of the city centre

Fortitude Valley — 508 H1
A lively inner-city neighbourhood encompassing Brisbane's Chinatown and Brunswick Street Mall

Lone Pine Koala Sanctuary — 510 C12
Visit the world's largest koala sanctuary

Manly — 511 N7
Enjoy a day by the calm waters of Moreton Bay

Mount Coot-tha Forest Park — 510 B8
Take in the sensational views and wander through Mt Coot-tha Botanic Gardens

Newstead House — 510 G6
A classic 19th-century Australian homestead on the banks of the river

Queensland Cultural Centre — 508 B7
The State's top cultural institutions at South Bank

South Bank Parklands — 508 D9
Home to over 16 hectares of parklands and inland beach

CLIMATE **BRISBANE**

	J	F	M	A	M	J	J	A	S	O	N	D
Max. °C	29	29	28	27	24	21	21	22	24	26	27	29
Min. °C	21	21	20	17	14	11	10	10	13	16	18	20
Rain mm	169	177	152	86	84	82	66	45	34	102	95	123
Raindays	14	14	15	11	10	8	7	7	7	10	10	11

South Bank

Bowen. From the eastern side of this cathedral complex, turn right into Adelaide Street and head south to **Anzac Square**, yet another of the generous, grassy enclaves that are so much a part of the Brisbane cityscape.

Walk through Anzac Square, then through **Post Office Square**, to reach the **General Post Office** on Queen Street. Built between 1871 and 1879, it stands on the site of the Female Factory Prison and is admired for the restrained elegance of its design. Take the walkway through the Post Office to Elizabeth Street and **St Stephen's Cathedral**. The cathedral is a magnificent twin-spired Gothic Revival structure designed by the prominent colonial architect Benjamin Backhouse and completed in 1874. Next door is the more modest **Old St Stephen's Church**, a simple building in the Gothic idiom, which served as the original cathedral; it was dedicated in 1850 and stands today as Brisbane's oldest surviving church.

Continue south along Elizabeth Street to George Street, and turn left. Between Charlotte and Mary streets is the Old Government Printing Office facade, which has an interesting inscription. Immediately behind you will find **Sciencentre**, an interactive science museum with around 170 hands-on displays demonstrating something of the science of having a good time – a great stop for the children. Cut down Stephens Lane to William Street where you will find the **Commissariat Stores** along to the left. This solid stone landmark, built in 1829, is an excellent example of an early colonial building constructed by convicts. Used for many purposes in the past, including a period as a migrant hostel, today it houses the offices of the Royal Historical Society of Queensland, incorporating a small museum.

Head north-west along William Street past the Conrad International Hotel, housed in the historic Executive Building, then turn right into Queen Street. In the first block lies the old Treasury Building, now the **Conrad International Treasury Casino**. Built between 1885 and 1928, it is an impressive Italian Renaissance building with concessions to the climate: a series of deep verandahs intended as cooling spaces for the rooms beyond.

CITY FORESHORE

While the south-west foreshore of central Brisbane is dominated by the Riverside Expressway, the eastern riverbank is easily accessible. In recent years this one-time wharf and warehouse precinct has been redeveloped and is one of the city's most attractive and vibrant areas. At its northern end near the intersection of Queen and Eagle streets is **Customs House** (1889). This stately old building features an entrance of Corinthian columns and a majestic copper dome; inside there is an excellent gallery and restaurant. Look north-east from Customs House and you can't miss **Story Bridge**. This Brisbane landmark is the largest steel cantilever bridge in Australia. Just south of Customs House is the **Riverside Centre**, an office complex with restaurants and cafes fronting the river. Further south is **Eagle Street Pier**, a popular gathering spot with restaurants, bars and cafes; this is the place to be on a Friday night. On Sundays it is the site for Brisbane's liveliest street market, the **Riverside Markets**.

The **City Botanic Gardens** spread across a prime city spot, claiming absolute frontage on the south-eastern bend of this section of the Brisbane River. Ornamental plantings, lawns and glittering ponds make this one of the most pleasant places in Brisbane. Occupying 20 hectares of land, it also features a mangrove boardwalk along the bank of the river, which enables visitors to observe the fascinating marine life in the tidal mangrove reserves and the variety of resident birdlife.

Old Government House (1862), home to the National Trust of Queensland, is a graceful sandstone building on the south-western edge of the gardens. Nearby on the corner of Alice and George streets is the French-Renaissance-style **Parliament House** (1868). This is a grand public building in the best colonial traditions, fringed with beautiful mature palms. Guided tours (excluding Saturday) provide a glimpse into the world of Queensland politics.

SOUTH BANK

Across Victoria Bridge is **South Bank**, Brisbane's major leisure precinct incorporating an extensive area of parkland and the city's major cultural institutions.

The **South Bank Parklands** were developed on the World Expo '88 site and cover 16 hectares of river frontage. The landscaping represents Australian environments from lagoons to beaches and rainforest, and includes **The Arbour**, a flower-covered walkway winding the full length of the precinct. It is a great place to ride bikes, walk or have a barbecue. As well, there are weekly markets, around 20 cafes and restaurants, and plenty of live entertainment, from buskers and free street entertainment to international acts in the 2600-seat **South Bank Piazza**.

Near the Victoria Bridge end of the parklands is the Rainforest Walk, where you can encounter the beautiful subtropical vegetation for which Queensland is famed. Follow the Riverside Promenade to reach **Pauls Breaka Beach**. As far as the kids are concerned, this is the drawcard of the area. Where else but in the Sunshine State would you find a palm-fringed, sandy beach, patrolled by lifesavers, slap-bang in the middle of a big city?

Just outside the south-eastern corner of the parklands is the **Queensland Maritime Museum**, offering an overview of Queensland's maritime history dating back to the Dutch landing at Cape York in 1606. In the Exhibition Hall there is an impressive collection of nautical models, re-created cabins, shipwreck relics and archives, while outside in the old South Brisbane dry dock the World War II frigate HMAS *Diamantina* can be explored from stern to bow. A vital link between the southern end of South Bank and the City Botanic Gardens is provided by a 450-metre pedestrian and cycle bridge, thought to be one of the world's longest.

There are plenty of shops and restaurants behind the parklands. Grey Street has been recently redeveloped as a grand, tree-lined boulevard. Here, you will find the latest entertainment addition, the **IMAX Theatre**, housing a giant cinema screen for 2- and 3-D releases. The screen has been crafted especially for this new format, which is known for its stunning image clarity. Heading north-west along Grey Street, you will pass the **Brisbane Convention**

Tropical Dome, Mount Coot-tha Botanic Gardens

and Exhibition Centre on the left, a 7.5-hectare complex that houses the 4000-seat Great Hall, a ballroom, and exhibition halls used for regular trade and retail exhibitions.

Towards the northern end of South Bank, on both sides of Melbourne Street, are the buildings of the **Queensland Cultural Centre**. The various theatres of the **Queensland Performing Arts Complex** are located on the south side. There is the intimate Cremorne Theatre (seating 350), used for works at the experimental end of the scale; the newly built 850-seat Optus Playhouse, which features the work of the Queensland Theatre Company, as well as other local and international groups; the Lyric Theatre (seating 2000) where you can expect everything from

performances by Opera Queensland to the latest blockbuster musical; and the 2000-seat Concert Hall where there are regular performances by Queensland's two orchestras, as well as performances by classical and pop artists from overseas. Guided tours are available Monday to Friday.

Across Melbourne Street is the **Queensland Museum**, housed in a large modern building, the entrance of which is overseen by two giant whales. In addition to the extensive natural-history collection, including the 'endangered species' exhibit, there are excellent local social-history displays, and some hair-raising interactive displays for the kids, such as a 'virtual' trip back 220 million years. The **Queensland Art Gallery**, part of the same complex, features an internal water feature called the Water Mall. The gallery exhibits art from around the world, with an emphasis on Aboriginal and contemporary Asian works. The **State Library of Queensland** has been archiving and preserving books, images, prints, maps and other material charting the history and culture of Queensland since 1896. There are some excellent collections including the James Hardy Library, with its preserve of fine Australian art and rare books. The reference section is enormous and widely used for both academic and general purposes.

INNER NORTH-EAST

The suburb of **Fortitude Valley** lies on the city's north-east border. It can be easily reached on foot or by train, while drivers can make the short trip along Wickham Street. Known as 'the Valley', the area was settled in 1849 by 256 'free settlers', who arrived in Moreton Bay aboard the *Fortitude*; it retains a good degree of its 19th-century heritage. Post-war it became somewhat seedy and notorious as a stomping ground for bohemians; these days it manages to hang on to an element of this despite rising property prices. It contains the best of the cheaper restaurants in Brisbane, great nightspots and the city's most eclectic shopping opportunities. The **Brunswick Street Mall** hosts a lively art, craft and anything-goes kind of market on Saturdays along with a busy cafe society. Look out for **McWhirter's Apartments**, on the corner of Wickham Street and Brunswick Street Mall, a landmark dating from 1912, with an Art Deco corner facade that was added in 1930. **Chinatown** in Duncan Street was built from the ground up in the 1980s, and is the place to find Chinese cinemas, restaurants, imported goods and traditional herbalists.

Brunswick Street leads to the adjacent suburb of **New Farm**. This was the site of early attempts to feed the colony, before it became a residential area. Take a stroll around the streets to see excellent examples of domestic architecture, ranging from grand Victorian to Spanish

Mission. The suburb has housed a significant migrant population since World War II and there are some good ethnic shops and restaurants around Brunswick Street. **New Farm Park** is nestled on the river bend at the end of Brunswick Street. Established in 1912, it offers a garden oasis filled with both tropical and traditional species. There are thousands of rose bushes in what is regarded as one of the most significant rose gardens in the Southern Hemisphere, as well as sprawling Moreton Bay fig, poinciana and jacaranda trees. Next to the park is the **Brisbane Powerhouse**, an exciting new centre for live arts including contemporary theatre, dance, art and music. On the second Saturday of each month, people from all over Brisbane flock here to buy fresh seasonal produce at the Farmers' Markets.

Breakfast Creek Road, heading north, leads to **Miegunyah** (1886), in Jordan Terrace, Bowen Hills. Built in the traditional Queensland style with substantial verandahs and ironwork, the house has been refurbished in original style. It is home to the Queensland Women's Historical Association and serves as a memorial to the State's pioneering women (open Wednesdays, weekends, or by appointment). A further half-kilometre along Breakfast Creek Road is **Newstead House** in Newstead Park. This is Brisbane's oldest house, an elegant residence overlooking the river. Patrick Leslie, the first white settler on the Darling Downs, built it in 1846. The house has been beautifully restored and, with its spacious verandahs, formal gardens and lawns down to the river, it offers an image of the quintessential Australian homestead. **Breakfast Creek Hotel**, just across the creek in Albion, is a historic pub renowned for its steak and beer.

WEST OF THE CITY

Lying just behind South Bank, the **South Brisbane/West End** area has gained a reputation as a great place to go, be seen and enjoy the interesting range of European and Asian cafes, restaurants, and bars.

SHOPPING

The **Queen Street Mall**, between Edward and George streets, is the heart of Brisbane and its major shopping precinct. The inner-city suburbs of **Fortitude Valley**, **Milton** and **Paddington** offer individual-style outlets selling fashion, collectibles and books.

MARKETS   Map Ref.

Open-air markets are a way of life in these subtropical climes, offering clothes, crafts, various new-age therapies, food and fun activities for the kids.

Riverside Markets, City   508 F6
Brisbane's largest open-air market at Eagle Street Pier (Sun.)

Brunswick Street Mall Market, Fortitude Valley   508 H2
Open-air street market (Sat.)

Farmers' Markets, Brisbane Powerhouse, New Farm   510 H8
Fresh produce from south-east Queensland (second Sat. of every month)

Lantern Village Market, South Bank Parklands   508 D10
Shoppers can browse through picturesque lantern-lit stalls (Fri. evening)

Craft Village, South Bank Parklands   508 D10
Brightly-coloured canopies filled with arts and handicrafts (Sat. & Sun.)

Summit of Mount Coot-tha

SPORT

Spectator

Brisbane's famous 'Gabba' ground at Woolloongabba hosts international and State cricket games, and is the home ground for the Brisbane Lions AFL football team. Rugby Union is an important sport in this State, and well-attended matches are played at the Ballymore Stadium at Herston. The ANZ Stadium in Nathan and the Suncorp Stadium in Lang Park, Milton, host the matches of Rugby League giants, the Brisbane Broncos. The Brisbane Convention and Exhibition Centre at South Bank is home for the National Basketball League team, the Brisbane Bullets. There are horseracing venues at Doomben and Eagle Farm. Albion Park Paceway is the venue for trotting and greyhound racing.

Participator

Golfers should try the riverside Indooroopilly course (members only on Saturdays) or the Brisbane and Victoria Park public courses. Swimmers can lap at Sleeman Sports Complex in Chandler, originally built for the 1982 Commonwealth Games. The best jogging spots are at Kangaroo Point Cliffs, South Bank Parklands Boardwalk and New Farm Park.

On the western city side of the river, **Red Hill**, **Paddington** and **Toowong** are among the inner suburbs that can lay claim to a marvellously eclectic range of local domestic architecture. Most notable alongside the Victorian and Edwardian houses are the Queenslanders, the traditional galvanised-iron-roofed timber houses on stumps, frequently surrounded by colourful subtropical trees and shrubbery. A relaxing day could easily be spent in Paddington, just shopping, browsing and eating. **Caxton Street**, at the Petrie Terrace end of Paddington, has nightclubs, interesting cafes, some good restaurants and hosts a popular wine and seafood festival each May. **Given** and **Latrobe terraces**, further west, are where many of the city's historic public buildings and sites are to be found. The Paddington brochure published by Brisbane City Council provides some fascinating insights on the history of the area. The **Toowong Cemetery** contains about a hundred thousand graves, some dating back to 1875; headstones tell the story of the trials, tribulations and triumphs of Queensland's early settlers.

The **Lone Pine Koala Sanctuary** at Fig Tree Pocket, some 11 kilometres south-west of the city, can be reached via the *Mirimar* cruise that leaves North Quay. This is the world's largest koala sanctuary and also houses more than 100 other species of Australian animals and birds. Visitors can cuddle a koala, feed the kangaroos, wallabies and emus, and see wombats, Tasmanian devils, possums and cockatoos in their natural environment.

Just 8 kilometres due west of the city along Milton Road is **Mount Coot-tha Forest Park**, with its extraordinary views from **Mount Coot-tha Lookout** over Greater Brisbane, Moreton Bay, and the green hills and folds of the landscape. There are some attractive picnic and barbecue spots in the reserve, including those at **Simpson Falls and J C Slaughter Falls**. The scenic Sir Samuel Griffith Drive links all the major sights. On the way, in the foothills, lies the **Mount Coot-tha Botanic Gardens**, comprising 52 hectares of land housing some 20 000 plant species from around the world. Features include a **Tropical Dome**, which hothouses a superb display of tropical plants, the supremely elegant **Japanese Garden** and the **Australian Plant Community** area, which groups plants according to ecosystems, covering everything from tropical rainforests to melaleuca wetlands. The gardens contain the largest planetarium in Australia, the **Thomas Brisbane Planetarium**, which features various public programs including projections of the night skies, and all related phenomena, on the ceiling of the domed theatre.

ALONG THE COAST

Brisbane, somewhat surprisingly for the capital of the surf and sun State, is set well back from the coast and, even when you get to the coast, you will find a glassy sheet of calm water instead of the crashing surf of the Pacific Ocean.

Redcliffe rests on the northern border of Greater Brisbane, 28 kilometres north-east of the city via Gympie Road. The Redcliffe Peninsula juts out into the bay and boasts beautiful sandy beaches. Swimming is generally safe and the fishing is rewarding. From the top of the volcanic red cliffs, there are excellent views of the islands across Moreton Bay. Within the town there are a number of interesting historic sites; ask at the town's information centre for a heritage trail brochure. Ferries leave from Scarborough at Redcliffe for Bulwer on Moreton Island.

Inland from Redcliffe, off the Bruce Highway at Kallangur, is the **Alma Park Zoo**. Set in subtropical surrounds and landscaped gardens, the zoo features exotic animals as well as hands-on contact with Australian wildlife. Visitors can hold koalas, feed kangaroos in a walk-through enclosure, and view wombats, dingoes and goannas. There is an interesting range of tropical monkeys and a walk-through deer enclosure.

The **Wynnum–Manly** area is 15 kilometres east of the city. There are some lovely beaches here, offering good swimming and fishing, and plenty of places to unwrap a picnic. The adjoining suburbs have a history dating back to

the 1860s and boast some interesting historic sights best explored on foot. The Brisbane City Council's local Heritage Trail brochure includes information on the old fort and quarantine area located here at the mouth of the Brisbane River. Charters and hire boats are available locally for interested anglers; most of this activity is centred around Manly Boat Harbour. Tours to the island of **St Helena** depart from here. The island, about two-thirds of which is national park, served as a penal settlement between 1867 and 1932, and prison life is recalled in the grim structures that remain.

Further south, **Cleveland** is the centre of the Redland Bay district. There is an exceptional historic house in the area: **Ormiston House** (1862), the former home of the founder of the sugar industry in Queensland (open Sunday, March to November). Cleveland is the departure point for passenger and vehicular ferries to North Stradbroke Island.

Continue down the coast to the peaceful holiday village of **Redland Bay**, known for its markets, gardens and annual Strawberry Festival in September. Boats can be hired right along this section of the coastline, so you can set off to do your own fishing and explore the peaceful waters of Moreton Bay.

Although Brisbane is Australia's third largest city and an international tourist destination, it has a relaxed atmosphere compared with its large southern counterparts. Its languid pace, riverside setting, subtropical vegetation and warm, sunny climate make for a welcoming environment.

DAY TOURS FROM BRISBANE

Mount Glorious
The sleepy settlement of Mount Glorious lies to the north-west of Brisbane in Brisbane Forest Park, a 28 500-hectare reserve of subtropical forests and hills. Mount Glorious is a base for a number of walking tracks. Nearby Wivenhoe Lookout offers extraordinary views of the surrounding country. *For more details see region coverage, p. 448.*

Daisy Hill State Forest
Close to Brisbane's south-eastern suburbs is Daisy Hill State Forest, best known for its large colony of koalas. The Daisy Hill Koala Centre has a variety of displays and, from a tower, visitors can see wild koalas in the treetops. *For more details see region coverage, p. 448.*

Bribie Island
Bribie is the most accessible of the Moreton Bay islands, connected as it is to the mainland by bridge at Caboolture. Fishing, boating and crabbing are among the most popular activities. For a quiet picnic and a walk, visit Buckleys Hole Conservation Park at the southern end. *For more details see region coverage, p. 449.*

Moreton Island
This large sand island is almost completely protected by national park. It is reached by vehicular or passenger ferry from Scarborough or the Brisbane River. Vehicle access is 4WD only, but guided tours are available. Walking, swimming, fishing and dolphin-watching are popular activities. *For more details see region coverage, p. 449.*

North Stradbroke Island
Stradbroke is the most developed of the Moreton Bay islands, although there are plenty of places to get away from it all. Visit Blue Lake National Park at the centre of the island for freshwater swimming and walking (access by 4WD or 45-minute walk), or enjoy ocean views along the North Gorge Headlands Walk. Island access is via car or vehicular ferry from Cleveland. *For more details see region coverage, p. 449.*

The Gold Coast
The Gold Coast, an hour's drive from Brisbane, is Australia's busiest holiday region with beautiful surf beaches and huge family theme parks. All activities on offer, from deep-sea fishing and golf to dining and shopping, are of international-resort standard. *For more details see region coverage, p. 450.*

Gold Coast Hinterland
The 'green behind the gold' as it is called, offers a peaceful retreat from the bustle of the coast. The most popular spot is Lamington National Park, part of a World Heritage area and Queensland's most visited park. It preserves a beautiful rainforest environment and a large wildlife population with many bird species. *For more details see region coverage, p. 450.*

BRISBANE HINTERLAND

This region offers a number of easily reached attractions. The heavily forested hills of the D'Aguilar Ranges create a subtropical haven just 20 minutes west of the city; the main access point is the hamlet of Mount Glorious, in Brisbane Forest Park. Also to the west is the heritage city of Ipswich. Further north-west, the diverse crops and heritage villages in the area known as South Burnett offer pleasant rural touring while the native landscape, including stands of rare pine rainforest, is preserved in Bunya Mountains National Park. Scattered throughout the region are attractions that include animals – perfect for families.

TOP EVENTS

Mar. Peanut and Harvest Festival (Kingaroy, odd-numbered years)

Mar. Pine Rivers Heritage Festival (Strathpine)

Apr. Food and Wine Fest (Kingaroy)

Apr. Great Horse Ride (Kilkivan, near Murgon)

May Pumpkin Festival (Goomeri, near Murgon)

Aug. Camp Oven Bush Poets Festival (Strathpine)

Oct. Potato Carnival (Gatton)

Oct. Bjelke-Petersen Dam Fishing Competition (Murgon)

Oct. Pioneer Festival (Nanango)

EXPERIENCE IT!

❶ **Tour** the rail workshops in Ipswich, where Queensland's first train line was launched in 1864

❷ **Take** a balloon flight from Laidley, over orchards and market gardens

❸ **Drive** the Mount Glorious–Samford Road, one of the State's most scenic routes

VISITOR INFORMATION

Brisbane Tourism
Brisbane: (07) 3006 6290
www.brisbanetourism.com.au
South Burnett Visitor Information Centre
Kingaroy: (07) 4162 3199
www.southburnett.com.au

FOCUS ON

Animal antics

The Walk-about Creek Wildlife Centre, in Brisbane Forest Park, features a freshwater creek environment populated with water dragons, frogs, platypuses, pythons and fish. The Australian Woolshed, just past Samford, re-creates life on a sheep station. Shearing demonstrations, ram shows and cattle-dog demonstrations are staged daily, while native animals roam freely. Daisy Hill State Forest is a pocket of eucalypt forest and acacia scrub 25 km south of Brisbane, where visitors can scan the canopy for koalas from a treetop tower. The Daisy Hill Koala Centre in the central picnic area has information about koalas and their habitats.

CLIMATE MOUNT GLORIOUS

	J	F	M	A	M	J	J	A	S	O	N	D
Max.°C	25	24	24	21	18	16	15	17	20	22	24	25
Min. °C	18	17	17	15	12	10	9	9	11	14	15	17
Rain mm	238	252	222	129	126	84	86	56	57	114	123	167
Raindays	15	16	16	12	11	8	8	7	7	10	11	13

South Burnett

This comfortable slice of rural Queensland invites you to the historic timber towns of Blackbutt and Yarraman or to wineries along the scenic Barambah Wine Trail. Go to the Nanango or Kilkivan areas to fossick for gold, or to Kingaroy, a prosperous agricultural centre. Accommodation includes B&Bs and farmstays.

Booubyjan Homestead

Two Irish brothers, the Clements, took up this run near Goomeri in 1847, replacing sheep with cattle in the 1880s. The property is still owned by the family. The homestead, open daily, provides a glimpse of pioneering life and the changes wrought by five generations of continuous occupation.

Bunya Mountains

This isolated spur of the Great Dividing Range is a cool, moist region of waterfalls, green and scarlet king parrots and the remaining stands of bunya pine (pictured), a species much depleted by early timber-getters. Walk the easy 4-km Scenic Circuit from the Dandabah camping area, through rainforest to Pine Gorge Lookout.

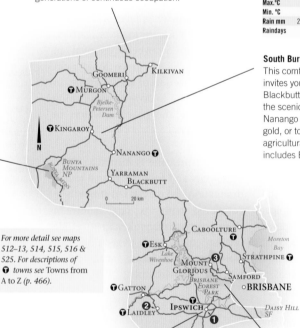

For more detail see maps 512–13, 514, 515, 516 & 525. For descriptions of ❶ towns see Towns from A to Z (p. 466).

Ipswich

Ipswich, Queensland's oldest provincial city, was established in 1827 as a convict outstation, but soon thrived as a river port. Its early wealth and confidence is reflected in its 19th-century buildings, which include grand public edifices, several of the State's oldest churches and some impressive mansions. A self-guide walk is available.

Brisbane Forest Park

Few cities have on their doorstep the diverse, pristine rainforest, towering trees, cascading waterfalls, deep pools, mountain streams and incredible wildlife (pictured) offered by the Brisbane Forest Park. The small settlement of Mount Glorious is a base for forest walking tracks. Wivenhoe Lookout, 10 km further on, has superb views west to Lake Wivenhoe.

BRISBANE ISLANDS

The calm blue waters of Moreton Bay encircle the mouth of the Brisbane River and extend along the Brisbane coastline and beyond. There are over 350 islands in this touring region, including the sizeable islands of Moreton, North Stradbroke, St Helena and Bribie. Despite some development, these islands have managed to retain an aura of wilderness, with endless white beaches, creeks, lakes, pockets of eucalpyt forest, wildflowers and wildlife. All, with the exception of St Helena, are major holiday destinations with a range of accommodation and facilities. They offer surfing, snorkelling, diving, fishing, bushwalking and scenic touring.

TOP EVENTS

Aug. *Fishing Classic (North Stradbroke Island, biggest fishing competition in Australia)*

Sept. *River Festival (celebrates Brisbane River and Bay area)*

Sept. *Festival in Ruins (celebrates history and ecology of St Helena Island)*

Sept.– Oct. *Festival (including mullet throwing competition, Bribie Island)*

EXPERIENCE IT!

❶ Swim *in the beautiful freshwater Blue Lake on North Stradbroke Island*

❷ Walk *to Queensland's oldest operating lighthouse (1857) at the tip of Cape Moreton*

❸ Go *crabbing in Pumicestone Channel off Bribie Island*

Bribie Island

Bribie is connected to the mainland at Caboolture by bridge. Magnificent birdlife and wildflowers are the main attractions, while fishing, boating and crabbing are popular activities. Woorim, in the southeast, is an old-fashioned resort with great surfing beaches. Nearby, Buckleys Hole Conservation Park is a good picnic spot for daytrippers, and has walking tracks to the beach and through various vegetation types.

St Helena Island

This low sandy island, 8 km from the mouth of the Brisbane River, was used as a prison from 1867 to 1932, during which time it was dubbed 'the hell-hole of the South Pacific'. Historic ruins remain and are protected in the island's national park. Tours of the island depart from the Brisbane suburbs of Manly and Breakfast Creek.

VISITOR INFORMATION

Brisbane Tourism
Brisbane: (07) 3006 6290
www.brisbanetourism.com.au

FOCUS ON

Marine life

Moreton Bay supports a marine population that includes dolphins, whales, dugongs and turtles. Visitors to Moreton Island can see dolphins at the Tangalooma Wild Dolphin Resort, where a care program has been developed, or at several spots along the western shore. Migrating humpback whales can be seen between June and November from Cape Moreton and from North Gorge Headland on North Stradbroke Island. Pumicestone Channel, between Bribie and the mainland, is a haven for turtles, dolphins and dugongs. Diving and snorkelling are available on all three islands, allowing visitors to explore the crystal waters and rich underwater life of this magnificent bay.

CLIMATE MORETON ISLAND

	J	F	M	A	M	J	J	A	S	O	N	D
Max.°C	33	32	32	32	31	30	30	31	32	34	35	34
Min.°C	23	23	23	21	19	18	17	16	18	20	21	23
Rain mm	326	331	287	115	22	10	8	4	5	17	65	198
Raindays	20	20	19	11	6	4	4	2	2	2	5	12

Moreton Island

Almost all this large sand island is national park. Its 280-m Mt Tempest is probably the world's highest stable sandhill; on the east coast is an unbroken 36-km surf beach, with calmer beaches on the west coast (pictured). Get to the island by passenger or vehicular ferry from Scarborough or the Brisbane River. A 4WD and a permit are required for self-drive touring; or you can take a guided tour.

For more detail see maps 511, 516 & 517. For descriptions of ❶ towns see Towns from A to Z (p. 466).

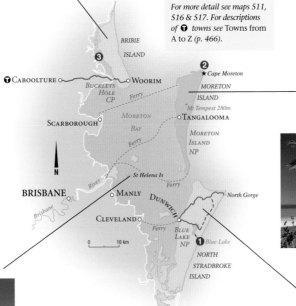

North Stradbroke Island

'Straddie' is a coastal and bushland paradise, with contained pockets of development. Blue Lake National Park is an ecologically significant wetland; access is by 4WD or a 45-minute walk. Other island walking trails include the popular North Gorge Headland Walk. Travel to North Stradbroke by vehicular ferry from Cleveland to Dunwich, the site of a 19th-century quarantine and penal centre.

GOLD COAST & HINTERLAND

Some 4 million visitors arrive each year to holiday along the Gold Coast's 70 km of coastline, which includes no less than 35 famously beautiful beaches stretching from South Stradbroke Island to the New South Wales border. Shopping, restaurants, nightlife, family entertainment, high-rise hotels, golf, fishing, sailing, surfing and unbelievably good weather – around 300 days of sunshine per year – are the trademark features of what has become Australia's biggest and busiest holiday destination. To the west lies the Gold Coast hinterland, another kind of world altogether. Here a superb natural landscape of tropical rainforests, unusual rock formations and cascading waterfalls – much of it protected by national park – offers visitors opportunities for such nature-based activities as bushwalking, camping, and wildlife-watching.

CLIMATE COOLANGATTA

	J	F	M	A	M	J	J	A	S	O	N	D
Max.°C	28	28	27	25	23	21	20	21	22	24	26	26
Min. °C	20	20	19	17	13	11	9	10	12	15	17	19
Rain mm	184	181	213	114	124	122	96	103	49	108	137	166
Raindays	14	15	16	14	10	9	7	9	9	11	11	13

TOP EVENTS

Jan. New Age of Aquarius Expo (Southport)

Jan. Australian Open Beach Volleyball (Surfers Paradise)

Mar. Somerset Celebration of Literature (Mudgeeraba)

Apr. Rathdowney Heritage Festival (Beaudesert)

May– June Gold Coast Cup Outrigger Canoe Ultra Marathon (Coolangatta)

June Wintersun Festival (Coolangatta)

June Philippine Festival (Bundall, near Surfers Paradise)

June Gold Coast City Marathon (Runaway Bay, near Main Beach)

June Country and Horse Festival (Beaudesert)

Aug. Australian Arena Polo Championships (Nerang)

Aug.– Sept. Gold Coast Show (Southport)

Sept. Springfest (Palm Beach)

Oct. Gold Coast Tropicarnival (Surfers Paradise)

Oct. Honda Indy 300 (Surfers Paradise)

Nov. Australian Music Week (Surfers Paradise)

EXPERIENCE IT!

❶ **Try** your luck at the popular Conrad Jupiters Casino at Broadbeach

❷ **Learn** to water-ski at Cable Ski World, Runaway Bay

❸ **Stroll** across the treetops on the rainforest canopy walk at Green Mountains in Lamington National Park

❹ **Board** a charter to fish for mackerel, tuna, bonito and snapper, just offshore at Surfers Paradise

❺ **Take** a scenic flight from Broadbeach, aboard a Tiger Moth plane

VISITOR INFORMATION

Gold Coast Tourism Bureau
Coolangatta: (07) 5536 7765
Surfers Paradise: (07) 5538 4419
www.goldcoasttourism.com.au

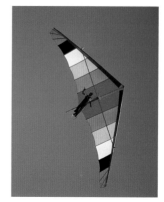

Tamborine Mountain
This 552-m plateau lies on the Darlington Range, a spur of the McPherson Range. It is a picturesque and popular spot for hang-gliders (pictured). Tamborine National Park comprises seventeen small areas including Witches Falls, the first national park area in the State. Visitors will also find villages full of galleries, cafes, antique stores and craft shops, and a couple of splendid gardens.

FOCUS ON

Theme parks and family attractions

The Gold Coast theme parks have become, since the 1980s, one of the region's most popular attractions. Warner Bros Movie World, south of Oxenford, is based on the legendary Hollywood movie set. It is a fully operational film set as well as a theme park. Nearby is Wet 'n' Wild Water World, Australia's largest aquatic park. At Coomera to the north is Dreamworld, which includes Tiger Island, the Tower of Terror and the Giant Drop. Sea World, north of Main Beach, is the region's oldest 'world', having begun in the 1950s as a water show on the Nerang River. Today it is the largest marine park in the Southern Hemisphere, offering performances by dolphins, seals, sea-lions and penguins, among others. At Surfers Paradise, Ripleys Believe it or Not Museum exhibits oddities that stretch credibility. Other attractions in the region include the David Fleay Wildlife Park at West Burleigh, Currumbin Wildlife Sanctuary and, further south, Tropical Fruit World (in NSW).

Lamington National Park
Part of a World Heritage area, this popular park preserves a wonderland of rainforest and volcanic ridges, criss-crossed by 160 km of walking tracks. Visitors will experience rich plant and animal life. The main picnic, camping and walking areas are at Binna Burra and Green Mountains, sites of the award-winning Binna Burra Lodge and O'Reilly's Rainforest Guest House.

Warner Bros Movie World
This popular theme park, south of Oxenford, offers visitors the chance to 'meet' their favourite Hollywood characters and see the business of movie-making up close. Studio tours, stunt shows and Looney Tune characters are a few of the many features. Rides include the Batman, Lethal Weapon, Wild West Adventure and the Road Runner Rollercoaster (for the toddlers).

Golf at Sanctuary Cove
With 40 courses, the Gold Coast is one of the Southern Hemisphere's great golfing destinations. Sanctuary Cove boasts two championship courses: the exclusive Pines, one of the toughest; and the immaculate Palms, designed around groves of cabbage palms. Pick up a golfing guide from the Gold Coast Tourism Bureau.

For more detail see maps 517 & 518. For descriptions of ❉ towns see Towns from A to Z (p. 466).

South Stradbroke Island
South Stradbroke, separated from North Stradbroke by the popular fishing channel Jumpinpin, is a peaceful alternative to the Gold Coast. Access is by launch from Runaway Bay. Cars are not permitted; visitors walk or cycle. There are two resorts, a camping ground, a range of leisure activities, and beautiful beaches.

The Broadwater
This calm expanse, fringed by waterfront houses and protected by the long finger of South Stradbroke Island, is popular for boating and fishing. Land-based anglers can try the breakwalls inside the Broadwater entrance. Here visitors can hire boats to explore this waterway, as well as its tributaries and the Nerang River.

Surfers Paradise
Surfers Paradise is the Gold Coast's signature settlement. The first big hotel was built here in the 1930s among a clutch of shacks along one of the State's most beautiful beaches. Since then the area has become an international holiday metropolis attracting every kind of visitor, from backpacker to jetsetter.

Springbrook National Park
Volcanic gorges and forests of 4000-year-old beech trees are among the attractions of this magnificent park on the State border. Other highlights include the spectacular Purlingbrook Falls (pictured), and Natural Bridge (in the park's remote western section), an unusual-looking rock arch spanning a mountain creek.

Standout beaches
The Gold Coast is a surfers' mecca. The southern beaches are the best, including Currumbin (pictured), and Kirra Point (in Coolangatta) said to have one of the 10 best breaks in the world. Greenmount Beach (also in Coolangatta) is great for families, as is Tallebudgera (north of Palm Beach), offering both estuary and ocean swimming.

DARLING DOWNS

The Darling Downs, beginning 100 km west of Brisbane, is a huge agricultural district spread across 72 000 sq km of undulating plains, 900 m above sea level. The region's rich black volcanic soil yields grapes, oil seeds and wheat, as well as some of the country's most magnificent gardens, particularly around the large city of Toowoomba. Throughout the countryside, English-style plantings of elms, plane trees and poplars, along with lush tropical growth, fringe green pastures, neat grainfields and historic towns. National parks preserve a native landscape of eucalypt forests and granite outcrops, and provide opportunities for camping and walking.

TOP EVENTS

Feb. Melon Festival
(Chinchilla, odd-numbered years)

Mar. Cotton Week (Dalby)

Easter Easter in the Country (Roma)

Apr. National Rock Swap Festival (Warwick)

June– Aug. Brass Monkey Season (winter festival, Stanthorpe and Warwick)

Sept. Carnival of Flowers (Toowoomba)

Oct. Festival of the Horse (Toowoomba)

Oct. Granite Belt Spring Wine Festival (Stanthorpe)

Oct. Australia's Famous Rose and Rodeo Festival (Warwick)

EXPERIENCE IT!

❶ **Enjoy** magnificent views of the Lockyer Valley from Toowoomba's Picnic Point

❷ **Visit** Queen Mary Falls in the southern part of Main Range National Park

❸ **Take** the Warwick City Walk Tour to see the town's historic architecture

CLIMATE TOOWOOMBA

	J	F	M	A	M	J	J	A	S	O	N	D
Max.°C	28	27	26	23	20	17	16	18	21	24	26	28
Min. °C	17	17	15	12	9	6	5	6	9	12	14	16
Rain mm	135	122	95	63	60	58	54	40	48	73	89	120
Raindays	12	11	11	8	8	8	7	6	7	8	10	11

For more detail see map 524–5. For descriptions of ❶ towns see Towns from A to Z (p. 466).

VISITOR INFORMATION

Stanthorpe: (07) 4681 2057
www.qldsoutherndowns.org.au
Toowoomba: (07) 4639 3797;
1800 331 155

FOCUS ON

Gardens of the Downs

The climate and soils of the Darling Downs have created one of Australia's great gardening districts. Toowoomba has 150 public parks and gardens, including the Japanese Garden, the Wetlands of the World Park, the Scented Garden – for visually impaired people – and the 6-ha mountainside Boyce Gardens (Monday to Friday), with 700 species of trees, shrubs and perennials. Warwick is known for its roses, particularly the red 'City of Warwick', best seen in Leslie Park. There are superb private gardens throughout the region. Some open daily, some seasonally and some as part of the Open Garden Scheme; check with the information centre for details.

Jondaryan Woolshed

This 1859 woolshed on historic Jondaryan Station, 45 km north-west of Toowoomba, is the centrepiece of a complex of old farm buildings. Blacksmithing and shearing demonstrations are held daily. The shearers' quarters is now a youth hostel, featuring iron beds and a cooking and dining area with a sawdust-covered floor.

Granite Belt wineries

Queensland's only significant wine region is on an 800-m plateau in the Great Dividing Range around Ballandean and Stanthorpe. About 28 boutique wineries, most with tastings and sales, grow major grape varieties on the well-drained granite soils, favouring soft, low-tannin reds made from shiraz and merlot grapes.

The Toowoomba Japanese garden

A thousand visitors a week stroll the 3 km of paths at Ju Raku En, a Japanese garden at the University of Southern Queensland. Opened in 1989, it showcases the harmony and beauty of ancient Japanese garden design with its lake, willowy beeches, islands, bridges, stream and pavilion.

Allora

This evocative town lies just off the highway between Toowoomba and Warwick. Victorian verandahed shopfronts and three old timber hotels line the main street. St David's Anglican Church (1888), is one of Queensland's finest timber churches. Glengallan Homestead, north of town, was built in 1867, during pastoralism's golden age.

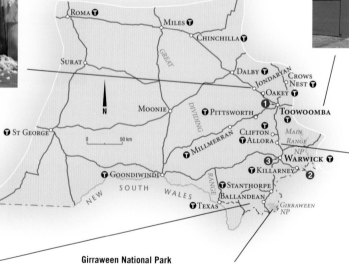

Girraween National Park

This 11 700-ha national park is on the edge of the New England Tableland. Granite outcrops and strangely balanced boulders sit among eucalypt forest and heath that comes alive with colour in spring. There are walking tracks, and camping and picnic facilities at Bald Rock Creek and Castle Rock.

SUNSHINE COAST

Beautiful beaches, bathed by the blue South Pacific and fringed by native bush, stretch from Rainbow Beach southward to the tip of Bribie Island to form the Sunshine Coast. The weather is near perfect, with winter temperatures around 25ºC. Well-serviced holiday towns cater to all interests from golf and fishing to fine dining and cafe-squatting. Inland lie the forested folds and ridges of the hinterland, where visitors can enjoy hillside villages, waterfalls, walks, scenic drives, superb views and a couple of trademark Queensland holiday attractions. In the south of this area, the Glass House Mountains loom above the surrounding plains.

TOP EVENTS

Jan.	Ginger Flower Festival (Yandina)
Easter	Easter Festival (Tin Can Bay)
Apr.	Sunshine Coast Festival of the Sea
June	William Landsborough Day (Landsborough)
Aug.	National Country Music Muster (Gympie)
Sept.–Oct.	Jazz Festival (Noosa Heads)
Oct.	Gold Rush Festival (Gympie)
Oct.	Nambour Yarn Festival (Mapleton, near Nambour)
Oct.–Nov.	Triathlon Multi Sport Festival (Noosa Heads)

EXPERIENCE IT!

❶ **Glide** along Noosa River in a gondola at sunset, with champagne and music

❷ **Experience** the transparent tunnel at the UnderWater World complex at Mooloolaba

❸ **Fish** for bream, flathead, whiting and dart in the surf along Rainbow Beach

VISITOR INFORMATION

Caloundra: (07) 5491 0202; 1800 644 969

Cooloola area: (07) 5483 5554

Maroochydore: (07) 5479 1566; 1800 882 032

Noosa Heads: (07) 5447 4988; 1800 448 833

www.sunshinecoast.org

FOCUS ON

Tropical produce

The Sunshine Coast hinterland, with its subtropical climate and volcanic soils, is renowned for its produce. Nambour's Big Pineapple symbolises the importance of food as a tourist attraction in the region. Visitors can take a train, trolley and boat through a plantation growing pineapples and other fruit, macadamia nuts, spices and flowers. Yandina's Ginger Factory, the world's largest, sells ginger products including ginger ice-cream. For freshly picked local fruit and vegetables, visit the Saturday morning markets at Eumundi, north of Yandina. The Superbee Honey Factory, south of Buderim, has beekeeping demonstrations and 28 varieties of honey for tasting.

The coloured sands of Teewah

Located in the Cooloola section of Great Sandy National Park, the coloured sands rise in 40 000-year-old, 200-m-high multicoloured cliffs. It is thought that oxidisation or the dye of vegetation decay has caused the colouring; Aboriginal legend attributes it to the slaying of a rainbow serpent.

Mountain villages

The 70-km scenic drive here is one of Queensland's best. Starting on the Bruce Highway near Landsborough, it passes the antiques shops, B&Bs, galleries and cafes of the pretty mountain villages of Maleny, Montville, Flaxton and Mapleton, offering beautiful coastal and mountain views as well. The drive ends near the town of Nambour.

CLIMATE NAMBOUR

	J	F	M	A	M	J	J	A	S	O	N	D
Max.ºC	30	29	28	26	24	22	21	22	25	27	28	29
Min. ºC	19	20	18	15	12	9	8	8	10	14	16	18
Rain mm	242	262	236	149	143	91	92	53	48	105	141	176
Raindays	16	18	18	13	13	9	9	8	9	12	12	13

Noosa Heads

Noosa Heads offers luxury hotels, top restaurants, hip bars and stylish boutiques. The town is flanked by ocean on one side and an estuary on the other, and is overlooked by the headland of Noosa National Park with its pandanus-fringed beaches.

Map showing: Tin Can Bay, Rainbow Beach ❸, Great Sandy National Park, Noosa R, Cooloola Coast, South Pacific Ocean, Gympie, Pomona, Tewantin, Noosa Heads ❶, Noosa National Park, Eumundi, Kenilworth, Nambour, Yandina, Mapleton, Flaxton, Buderim, Montville, Maroochydore, Mooloolaba ❷, Maleny, Landsborough, Caloundra, Glass House Mountains NP, Glass House Mountains, Bribie Island, Conondale National Park. N, 0 10 km

Southern coastal

The towns of Caloundra, Mooloolaba and Maroochydore make a pleasant daytrip from Brisbane, as well as being good spots for a family holiday. The area offers patrolled surfing beaches, protected lakes and rivers for boating and fishing, holiday flats and caravan parks, boat hire, and a range of child-friendly attractions.

Glass House Mountains

These 20-million-year-old crags, the giant cores of extinct volcanoes, mark the southern entrance to the Sunshine Coast. Glasshouse Mountains Road leads to sealed and unsealed drives through the mountains, with some spectacular lookouts along the way. There are walking trails, picnic grounds and challenges aplenty for rock-climbers.

For more detail see maps 516, 519 & 525. For descriptions of ❶ towns see Towns from A to Z (p. 466). For touring details see Classic Tour (p. 504).

FRASER ISLAND & COAST

This region has two of Queensland's signature attractions: Hervey Bay, a large resort town with the best whale-watching in Australia, and offshore, the nature-based holiday destination of Fraser Island. Offering spectacular white beaches and coloured sand cliffs, and dunes, creeks, lakes, wildflower heathland and rainforest, Fraser is reached by vehicular barge from Hervey Bay or Rainbow Beach further south; a 4WD is essential. Hervey Bay offers a range of accommodation and other facilities, Fraser a narrower choice. The heritage town of Maryborough and the calm waters of Great Sandy Strait are among the region's other attractions.

TOP EVENTS

Feb. Yagubi Festival (multicultural festival, Hervey Bay)

Easter Amateur Fishing Classic (Burrum Heads)

Apr. Gladstone–Hervey Bay Blue Water Classic (Hervey Bay)

May Best of Brass (Maryborough)

Aug. Whale Festival (Hervey Bay)

Sept. Heritage City Festival (Maryborough)

Oct. Masters Games (Maryborough)

Oct. Seafood Festival (Hervey Bay)

EXPERIENCE IT!

① **Visit** the Thursday heritage market in Maryborough

② **Catch** the July–October run of tailor on the northern half of Fraser Island's Seventy Five Mile Beach

③ **Swim** in the dazzling sand-bottomed Lake McKenzie on Fraser Island

CLIMATE MARYBOROUGH

	J	F	M	A	M	J	J	A	S	O	N	D
Max.°C	31	30	29	27	25	22	22	23	26	28	29	31
Min. °C	21	21	19	17	13	10	9	9	12	15	18	20
Rain mm	166	173	159	90	80	67	54	40	43	75	85	128
Raindays	13	14	14	12	11	8	7	6	6	8	9	11

VISITOR INFORMATION

Hervey Bay: (07) 4124 4050; 1800 811 728

Maryborough: (07) 4121 4111

www.frasercoast.org

FOCUS ON

Fraser Island

World Heritage-listed in 1992, this is the world's largest sand island, covering 184 000 ha. It has dunes that reach 240 m in height, and about 40 dune lakes, approximately half the number in the world. Fraser supports an extraordinary diversity in rainforest, wildflower heath, mangroves, 350 bird species and a large population of dingoes, said to be the purest strain in Australia. The island was home to the Badtjala Aboriginal people for some 5000 years, during which time it was known as K'gari. The *Stirling Castle* was wrecked here 1836, and Europeans named the island after Eliza Fraser, the captain's wife.

Whale-watching

Each year around 2000 humpback whales migrate from the Antarctic to Australia's eastern subtropical coast. On their return, between August and October, up to 400 rest and regroup in Hervey Bay. For an up-close view, visitors can take a whale tour from Urangan Boat Harbour.

Hervey Bay

This once sleepy settlement is now a booming resort town of over 43 000 people. The bay itself is a large, calm body of water warmed by tropical currents. The area's protected beaches are perfect for family swimming. Other popular activities include sailing, diving, windsurfing, fishing, kayaking and skydiving.

Great Sandy Strait

This narrow strait between the mainland and Fraser Island makes for good boating; houseboats and other vessels are for hire. Drop into the Kingfisher Bay Resort and Village on Fraser Island. Look out for dugongs, the world's only plant-eating marine mammals, and fish in the estuary of Mary River, around River Heads.

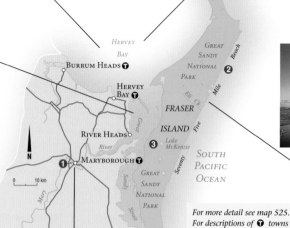

Fraser Island's east coast

Fraser Island's surf coast takes in the beautiful Seventy Five Mile Beach; The Cathedrals, 15-m sheer cliffs composed of different coloured sands; the wreck of the *Maheno* (pictured), a trans-Tasman luxury liner; and Eli Creek, a freshwater creek filtered through the dunes, where visitors can float beneath the pandanus trees.

For more detail see map 525. For descriptions of ❶ towns see Towns from A to Z (p. 466).

Maryborough Heritage Walk and Drive

A European settlement since 1847, Maryborough is one of Queensland's oldest and best-preserved provincial cities. A self-guide brochure leads visitors through tree-lined streets past heritage sites and well-restored Queenslander-style houses, and along the historic streetscape of Wharf Street (pictured).

GREAT BARRIER REEF

The reef is Australia's most prized and visited natural destination. Extending over 2000 km along the coast of Queensland, this breathtakingly beautiful marine environment features tropical islands, aquamarine waters, rare and brilliantly coloured corals, sea grass beds, fish, sea-going mammals and birds. It is considered to be one of the world's great destinations for diving, sailing and a large number of other activities including fishing, swimming, walking, windsurfing, kayaking and even horseriding. Only 22 of the reef's 900 islands cater for tourists. Some islands support large resorts with every level of accommodation, whilst others are completely protected by national park and offer camping only. Day trips from the mainland are a popular way of seeing the reef for those with limited time.

For more detail see maps 521, 523, 525, 527 & 529. For descriptions of ❶ towns see Towns from A to Z (p. 466).

VISITOR INFORMATION

Great Barrier Reef Central Reservations Office
Milton: (07) 3876 4644
www.great-barrier-reef.com

Southern Reef Islands
Bundaberg: (07) 4152 9289
www.bdtdb.com.au

Gladstone: (07) 4972 4000
www.gladstoneregion.org.au

Rockhampton: (07) 4922 5339

Whitsunday Islands
Proserpine: (07) 4946 6673;
1800 801 252
www.whitsundayinformation.com.au

Tropical North Islands
Cairns: (07) 4051 3588
www.tnq.org.au

Queensland National Parks and Wildlife Service offices
Airlie Beach: (07) 4946 7022
Cairns: (07) 4053 4533
Gladstone: (07) 4971 6500
Ingham: (07) 4077 2822
www.env.qld.gov.au

ISLAND ACCESS

TROPICAL NORTH ISLANDS

MAGNETIC ISLAND *8 km NE of Townsville*
From Townsville, by vehicular ferry, catamaran or water taxi.

ORPHEUS ISLAND *80 km N of Townsville*
From Townsville or Cairns, by sea plane.

HINCHINBROOK ISLAND *5 km E of Cardwell*
From Cardwell, by launch.

BEDARRA ISLAND *35 km SE of Cardwell*
From Dunk Island, by launch.

DUNK ISLAND *5 km SE of Mission Beach*
From Cairns, by plane. From Clump Point near Mission Beach, by launch. From Wongaling Beach and South Mission Beach, by water taxi.

FITZROY ISLAND *30 km SE of Cairns*
From Cairns, by catamaran.

GREEN ISLAND *27 km NE of Cairns*
From Cairns, by catamaran, sea plane or helicopter.

LIZARD ISLAND *93 km NE of Cooktown*
From Cairns or Cooktown, by plane or sea plane.

WHITSUNDAY ISLANDS

BRAMPTON ISLAND *32 km NE of Mackay*
From Mackay, by light plane or launch, or from Hamilton Island by plane.

LINDEMAN ISLAND *67 km N of Mackay*
From Airlie Beach or Shute Harbour, by light plane or boat. From Mackay by plane, or Hamilton Island by boat or plane.

HAMILTON ISLAND *16 km SE of Shute Harbour*
Direct flight from Sydney, Brisbane and Melbourne; connections to all major cities. From Shute Harbour, Whitsunday Coast, by launch.

LONG ISLAND *9 km from Shute Harbour*
From Shute Harbour or Hamilton Island, by launch or helicopter. From Whitsunday Airport by sea plane.

SOUTH MOLLE ISLAND *8 km from Shute Harbour*
From Shute Harbour, Whitsunday coast or Hamilton Island, by launch.

DAYDREAM ISLAND *5 km from Shute Harbour*
From Shute Harbour or Hamilton Island, by launch or helicopter.

WHITSUNDAY ISLAND *25 km E of Shute Harbour*
From Shute Harbour or Able Point Marina, Airlie Beach, by boat.

HOOK ISLAND *20 km NE of Shute Harbour*
From Shute Harbour or Able Point Marina, Airlie Beach, by launch.

HAYMAN ISLAND *25 km NE of Shute Harbour*
Direct flight to Hamilton Island from Sydney and Brisbane (connections to all major cities), then by launch to Hayman Island. From Airlie Beach, by water taxi.

SOUTHERN REEF ISLANDS

LADY ELLIOT ISLAND *80 km NE of Bundaberg*
From Bundaberg or Hervey Bay, by plane.

LADY MUSGRAVE ISLAND *105 km N of Bundaberg*
From Bundaberg, by sea plane, catamaran or trimaran. From Seventeen Seventy, by catamaran.

HERON ISLAND *72 km NE of Gladstone*
From Gladstone, by catamaran or charter helicopter.

NORTH WEST ISLAND *75 km NE of Gladstone*
From Gladstone, by charter boat.

GREAT KEPPEL ISLAND *48 km NE of Rockhampton*
From Rockhampton, by light plane. From Yeppoon by launch.

COOKTOWN

TROPICAL NORTH ISLANDS

CAIRNS

TOWNSVILLE

SHUTE HARBOUR — WHITSUNDAY ISLANDS

MACKAY

SOUTHERN REEF ISLANDS

ROCKHAMPTON

GLADSTONE

BUNDABERG

TROPICAL NORTH ISLANDS

CLIMATE FITZROY ISLAND

	J	F	M	A	M	J	J	A	S	O	N	D
Max. °C	31	30	29	28	26	24	24	25	27	29	30	31
Min. °C	12	12	10	8	7	5	4	5	6	7	9	10
Rain (mm)	27	25	31	60	89	100	106	103	86	68	40	35
Raindays	6	5	7	11	15	18	17	18	15	13	9	7

Lizard Island
Game-fishing, excellent reef surrounds, snorkelling and diving, and national park walks. Small, luxurious resort with bungalow-style lodgings (max. 80 people) or camping (max. 20 people); camping permits from Cairns parks office.

Fitzroy Island
Low-key destination with national park, white coral beaches and magnificent flora and fauna. Bushwalking, diving and snorkelling. Hostel-style and cabin accommodation (max. 160 people) and camping (max. 60 people).

Green Island
True coral cay covered with thick tropical vegetation. Glass-bottomed boats for reef viewing and underwater observatory. Popular day-trip destination with small resort (max. 90 people).

Bedarra Island
Island of untouched tropical beauty, off-limits to day visitors and children under 15. Bushwalking, snorkelling, fishing, swimming, windsurfing, sailing and tennis. Exclusive resort (max. 30 people).

Dunk Island
National park with walking tracks through rainforest and prolific birdlife, butterflies and wild orchids. Parasailing, water-skiing, sailing, clay target shooting and horseriding. Resort accommodation (max. 360 people) and camping (max. 30 people).

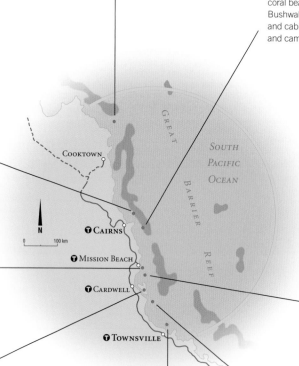

Hinchinbrook Island
National park with wonderland of mountains, tropical vegetation, waterfalls and sandy beaches. Snorkelling, swimming, fishing and bushwalking. Small, low-key resort (max. 45 people).

Orpheus Island
Small island surrounded by coral reefs and protected by national park. Birdwatching, water sports, glass-bottomed boats, island walks and fishing. 5-star resort (max. 74 people) or bush camping (max. 54 people); camping permits from Ingham parks office.

Magnetic Island
National park and beautiful beaches. Horseriding, bushwalking, snorkelling, parasailing, swimming, fishing, sea kayaking and reef excursions. Permanent population and range of accommodation from budget to deluxe.

WHITSUNDAY ISLANDS

CLIMATE **HAMILTON ISLAND**

	J	F	M	A	M	J	J	A	S	O	N	D
Max. °C	30	30	29	27	25	23	22	23	25	28	29	30
Min. °C	25	25	24	23	21	19	18	18	20	22	23	24
Rain (mm)	13	322	262	242	159	100	80	59	23	52	89	215
Raindays	15	18	19	19	18	12	10	11	7	8	8	13

Daydream Island
Small island of volcanic rock, coral and dense tropical foliage. 'Kids Club', tennis, outdoor cinema, water sports centre, snorkelling, diving and reef and island trips. Luxurious resort (max. 900 people).

Long Island
Part of Conway National Park. Walking tracks leading to scenic lookouts. Water sports, fishing and resort activities. Three resorts: Club Crocodile (max. 400 people), Palm Bay (max. 60 people) and Whitsunday Wilderness Lodge (max. 16 people).

Brampton Island
National park, wildlife sanctuary and fine golden beaches. Snorkelling trail, bushwalking, sea-plane trips and water-sports. Resort-style accommodation (max. 280 people).

Hayman Island
Close to the outer reef. Fishing, sightseeing trips, scenic flights, diving, water sports, 'Kids Club' and whale-watching excursions. Luxury resort (max. 450 people).

Hook Island
Small low-key wilderness resort with cabins and campsites (max. 140 people). Snorkelling, scuba diving, fishing, reef trips, coral submarine trips and fish-feeding.

South Molle Island
Small, lightly timbered island. Numerous inlets and splendid views of Whitsunday Passage. Golf, bushwalking, snorkelling, scuba diving, windsurfing and sailing. Medium-size resort (max. 520 people).

Whitsunday Island
Entire island is uninhabited national park. Beautiful 7-km white silica beach and complex mangrove system. Camping only (max. 40 people); details from Airlie Beach parks office.

Hamilton Island
Large island with wide range of facilities and activities. Shops, marina and fauna park. Windsurfing, sailing, fishing, scuba diving, parasailing, helicopter rides, tennis, squash, and reef and inter-island trips. Resort (max. 1500 people).

Lindeman Island
Secluded beaches, national park, and prolific birds and butterflies. Golf course, full range of water sports and other island activities. Club Med resort (max. 460 people).

SHUTE HARBOUR
AIRLIE BEACH
MACKAY

N
0   100 km

SOUTHERN REEF ISLANDS

CLIMATE **LADY ELLIOT ISLAND**

	J	F	M	A	M	J	J	A	S	O	N	D
Max. °C	29	29	28	27	24	22	21	22	24	25	27	28
Min. °C	24	24	23	22	20	18	17	17	19	20	22	23
Rain (mm)	27	174	133	106	120	93	99	58	38	59	71	86
Raindays	13	15	15	15	15	12	10	9	8	9	8	10

North West Island
Second largest coral cay on reef. Superb bird- and turtle-watching opportunities. Camping only (max. 150 people); permit details from Gladstone parks office.

Heron Island
Small coral cay, entirely national park. Turtle-nesting site, birdwatching and prolific flora. Diving, snorkelling, reef and ecology walks. Resort-style accommodation (max. 250 people).

Great Keppel Island
White, sandy beaches and unspoiled tropical island scenery. Tennis, water-skiing, diving, snorkelling, fishing, sea kayaking, golf, parasailing, coral viewing and island cruises. 'Kids Club' during holidays. Camping, cabins and lodge-style accommodation (max. 650 people).

Lady Musgrave Island
Coral cay with navigable lagoon. Glass-bottomed boats, floating pontoon, semi-submersible submarine, prolific birdlife and turtle-nesting site. Camping only (max. 50 people); permit details from Gladstone parks office.

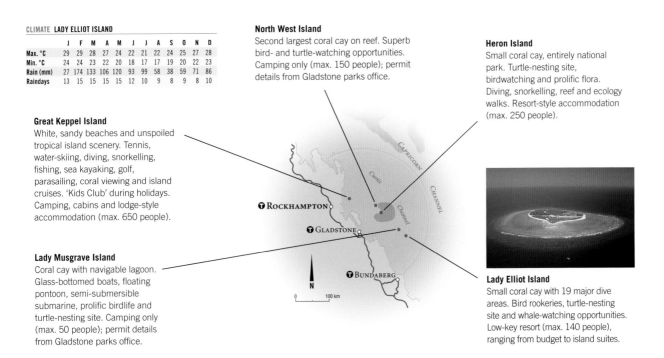

Lady Elliot Island
Small coral cay with 19 major dive areas. Bird rookeries, turtle-nesting site and whale-watching opportunities. Low-key resort (max. 140 people), ranging from budget to island suites.

ROCKHAMPTON
GLADSTONE
BUNDABERG
CAPRICORN
CHANNEL
Curtis Channel

N
0   100 km

CAPRICORN

Spanning the Tropic of Capricorn, this highly productive region combines mining, industry, agriculture and cattle-raising with tourism. Offshore lie the southernmost islands of the Great Barrier Reef. The coastline is relatively untouched by commercial development. Remote beaches and river estuaries with unspoilt coastal bushland are found in the national parks of the Discovery Coast south of Gladstone. Inland, the eroded sandstone plateaus of the Great Dividing Range rise abruptly from the plains, most notably in the Carnarvon and Blackdown Tableland national parks. Most of Queensland's coal exports come from open-cut mines around Blackwater. Mining also occurs in gemfields west of Emerald. The area has three big towns: Bundaberg is a centre for sugarcane, subtropical fruits and vegetables; Gladstone is a major port and industrial centre; and Rockhampton is a cattle town, servicing properties in the Fitzroy River valley and to the west.

EXPERIENCE IT!

❶ *Visit* the Aboriginal Dreamtime Cultural Centre, north of Rockhampton, and learn about the Darumbal people, the original inhabitants of the Fitzroy River area

❷ *Savour* a mud crab sandwich at Miriam Vale's Shell Roadhouse

❸ *Watch* crocodiles feeding and baby crocs hatching at the Koorana Crocodile Farm, Keppel Sands

❹ *Canoe,* fish, ski, sail or swim in the vast, calm Lake Awoonga

❺ *See* the 25-million-year-old Mystery Craters, north-east of Gin Gin

VISITOR INFORMATION

Bundaberg: (07) 4152 9289;
1800 060 499
www.bdtdb.com.au

Gladstone: (07) 4972 4000
www.gladstoneregion.org.au

Rockhampton: (07) 4922 5339
www.rockhampton-qld.gov.au

The gemfields
Some of the world's richest sapphire fields are found around the tiny, ramshackle settlements of Anakie, Sapphire, Rubyvale and Willows Gemfields, some 50 km west of Emerald. The same area yields zircons, amethysts, rubies and topaz. Fossicking licences can be bought on the gemfields for a small fee. If you don't find what you're after, the area also has plenty of gemstone outlets.

Blackdown Tableland National Park
This undulating 800-m high sandstone plateau of open forest, heath, waterfalls and gorges lies 50 km south-east of Blackwater. There is a camping ground at Mimosa Creek, a gorge with swimming holes at Rainbow Falls, and a number of scenic trails. Visit Sunset Lookout for superb sunrise and sunset views.

CLIMATE ROCKHAMPTON												
	J	**F**	**M**	**A**	**M**	**J**	**J**	**A**	**S**	**O**	**N**	**D**
Max.°C	32	31	30	29	26	23	23	25	27	30	31	32
Min. °C	22	22	21	18	14	11	9	11	14	17	19	21
Rain mm	136	141	103	47	52	35	31	29	24	48	68	105
Raindays	11	12	10	7	7	5	5	4	4	7	8	10

FOCUS ON

Discovery Coast
Seventeen Seventy, a small town on a narrow, hilly peninsula above an estuary, was named to mark Captain Cook's landing at Bustard Bay on 24 May 1770. The main access is from Miriam Vale on the Bruce Highway (about 60 km on a partly sealed road). Today's visitors come for the views from the headland north across the bay, and for fishing, mud crabbing and boating. Agnes Water, a few kilometres south, has Queensland's northernmost surfing beach; rolling surf and a balmy climate attract visitors all year round. Eurimbula National Park, just across Round Hill Inlet from Seventeen Seventy, has dunes, mangroves, salt marshes and eucalypt forests. From Agnes Water an 8-km track south to Deepwater National Park is suitable for 4WD vehicles only. The long beaches of this park, broken by the estuaries of freshwater creeks, form a breeding ground for loggerhead turtles.

Carnarvon National Park
The towering sandstone cliffs rise abruptly from the plain in Carnarvon National Park, 250 km south of Emerald. The Art Gallery and Cathedral Cave, major Aboriginal art sites, contain countless stencils and engravings. The signature attraction is Carnarvon Gorge, a twisting sandstone chasm with lush eucalypt forest. Camping (pre-book with the ranger), cabins and tours are all available.

Mount Morgan
This goldmining town south of Rockhampton has hardly changed in a century. Take the town heritage tour, or visit the goldmines and the caves excavated for brick clay. The cemetery, containing graves of Chinese workers and other nationals, tells the town's history, as do the Railway Station and the Historical Museum.

Australia's beef capital
Over two million cattle graze in the Fitzroy River valley and the lovely country west of Rockhampton (pictured). The town has many heritage buildings, a good regional art gallery and historic botanic gardens. Large numbers of barramundi are found in the Fitzroy River, often in the section close to town.

Capricorn Coast
Thirteen beaches stretch out along Keppel Bay, taking in Yeppoon (pictured), Emu Park and Keppel Sands. Picturesque bays are framed by rocky headlands, pockets of rainforest, peaceful estuarine waters and wetlands – some of the natural features that have helped make sunny Capricorn Coast a popular resort area.

For more detail see maps 524–5 & 526–7. For descriptions of ❶ towns see Towns from A to Z (p. 466).

TOP EVENTS

Easter	Harbour Festival (Gladstone, includes finish of Brisbane–Gladstone Yacht Race)
May	Seventeen Seventy Commemorative Festival (Gladstone)
June	Country and Western Muster (Biloela)
June	Orange Festival (Gayndah, odd-numbered years)
June	Rocky Rush Rodeo (Rockhampton)
July	Multicultural Food and Wine Festival (Childers)
Aug.	Gemfest (Emerald)
Sept.	Music Spectacular (Emerald)
Sept.	Pineapple Festival (Yeppoon)
Sept.	Bundy in Bloom Festival (Bundaberg)
Oct.	Octoberfest (Yeppoon)
Oct.	Seafood Festival (Gladstone)
Oct.	Barra Bounty (Rockhampton)
Dec.	Summer Solstice Light Spectacular (Rockhampton)
Dec.–Jan.	Bent Wing Bat Flight Emergence (Rockhampton)

Industrial powerhouse
Gladstone has Queensland's biggest power station, the world's largest alumina plant (pictured) and aluminium refinery, Australia's biggest cement plant and Queensland's largest multi-cargo port. Tours of the major industries are available. The town is built around a magnificent deep-water harbour, which, despite the industry, retains much of its natural beauty.

Mon Repos turtle rookery
Mon Repos Conservation Park, 15 km north-east of Bundaberg, is one of Australia's most important turtle rookeries. Sea turtles lay eggs in the sand from November to January and the young emerge and make for the sea from mid-January to March. In season there is an on-site interpretative centre and supervised viewing.

Rum town
On the southern coast of the Capricorn region is Bundaberg, home of 'Bundy' rum. The rum distillery (pictured) runs daily tours. In the Botanical Gardens are the Hinkler House Memorial and Fairymead House Sugar museums, and steam train rides on Sundays. Around the town are sugar plantations, avocado orchards and market gardens.

THE MID-TROPICS

Gold, cattle and sugar spearheaded the settlement of this area and established the towns of Mackay and Townsville in the 1860s. Today cattle and sugar remain key industries. Much of the coast – stretches of sandy shoreline, warm tropical waters, bush-covered headlands and large pockets of rainforest – remains intact despite development, and the district provides a great holiday alternative to some of Queensland's busier coastal areas. Accessible from several coastal points is the Great Barrier Reef and its islands. Inland, on the edge of the Outback, are a couple of the State's best-preserved historic towns.

TOP EVENTS

Jan.	Goldfield Ashes Cricket Carnival (Charters Towers)
Mar.	Greek Festival (Townsville)
May	Australian–Italian Festival (Ingham)
May	Country Music Festival (Charters Towers)
July	Australian Festival of Chamber Music (Townsville)
July	Troy Dunn International Bull Riding (Mackay)
July	Camp Draft (Nebo, near Mackay)
Aug.	Sarina Annual (Agricultural Show, Sarina)
Aug.	Gold Festival (Clermont)

EXPERIENCE IT!

❶ Tour the Fairleigh Sugar Mill near Mackay, July–October

❷ Swim, saunter and savour the atmosphere at The Strand waterfront development, Townsville

❸ Dive to the wreck of the SS Yongala, 16 km off Cape Bowling Green

Marine attractions

At Reef HQ in Townsville, touch-tanks and underwater viewing-tunnels reveal some of the Great Barrier Reef's ecological mysteries. Next door, the Museum of Tropical Queensland features a full-scale reproduction of the bow of the HMS *Pandora* (pictured), a British vessel wrecked on the reef in 1791.

VISITOR INFORMATION

Mackay: (07) 4952 2677
www.mackayregion.com

Townsville: (07) 4721 3660;
1800 801 902.
www.townsvilleonline.com.au

FOCUS ON

Heritage

This region preserves some interesting pockets of heritage. Ravenswood, east of Charters Towers, is now almost a ghost town. It flourished in the second half of the 19th century as a centre for the surrounding goldfields and many of its buildings from this period are in a near-original state. West of Mackay is Greenmount Historic Homestead – now a museum – built in 1915 on the Cook family's grazing property. Bowen, established in the 1860s, is North Queensland's oldest town. History here is recorded in 22 murals detailing the stories, personalities and events of the town.

CLIMATE MACKAY

	J	F	M	A	M	J	J	A	S	O	N	D
Max.°C	30	29	28	27	24	22	21	22	25	27	29	30
Min. °C	23	23	22	20	17	14	13	14	16	20	22	23
Rain mm	293	311	303	134	104	59	47	30	15	38	87	175
Raindays	16	17	17	15	13	7	7	6	5	7	9	12

Wallaman Falls

In Lumholz National Park, part of the Wet Tropics World Heritage area, Wallaman Falls has a 305-m sheer drop, the longest in Australia. Most of the park, named for a 19th-century Norwegian explorer, is trackless wilderness. The 1-hour drive from Ingham is mostly on unsealed road. Camp near the falls.

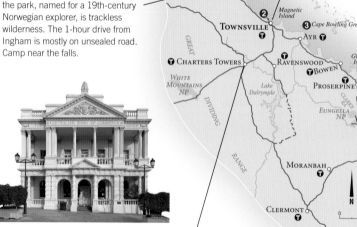

Charters Towers

Charters Towers was Queensland's second largest city during the 1870s gold rush; then, it was known as 'The World' because of its size and cosmopolitan population. Today it is a showpiece of the original, with many beautifully preserved buildings including the Bank of Commerce (pictured), now restored as the New World Theatre Complex. The surrounding cattle country provides a scenic backdrop to this major settlement.

For more detail see maps 520, 521, 526–7 & 529. For descriptions of ❶ towns see Towns from A to Z (p. 466).

Cape Hillsborough and the Hibiscus Coast

Steep rainforest-clad hills plunge to rocky headlands linked by white sandy beaches in this lovely and surprisingly peaceful district north of Mackay. Wildlife, walking trails and camping are among the features of Cape Hillsborough National Park.

Eungella National Park

This national park, spanning the Clarke Ranges, preserves 50 000 ha of rainforest, gorges, clear pools and tumbling falls. Much of the park remains wilderness, accessible only to experienced walkers. There are easier walking tracks around Broken River and Fern Flat in the south-west, and limited camping at Fern Flat.

THE FAR NORTH

The Far North is a region of ancient rainforest, remote islands and a coastline that fronts the world's most spectacular reef. National parks, some of which are part of the World Heritage Wet Tropics, protect the superb beauty and natural value of the landscape and offer extensive opportunities for camping, fishing, walking and 4WD touring. Cape York is a vast undeveloped region with a population of just 10 000. On the west coast lie the frontier mining town of Weipa and several Aboriginal communities. At the northern tip, via often impassable roads, is the town of Bamaga, and beyond, the Torres Strait Islands. Some of the country's finest Aboriginal rock art is found near Laura, and the region generally is richly inscribed with the heritage of its original occupants. To the south, the coast between Innisfail and Mossman is the Riviera of tropical Australia. The 'capital' of the tropics, Cairns, is a major destination for tourists from around the world.

Daintree National Park

TOP EVENTS

May	*Village Carnivale (Port Douglas)*
May	*Races, Concert and Rodeo (Chillagoe)*
May	*Folk Festival (Kuranda)*
June	*Endeavour Festival (Cooktown)*
June	*Yuletide (Yungaburra)*
July	*Jazz Festival (Yungaburra)*
July	*Agricultural Show (Cairns)*
July	*Polocrosse Carnival (Cooktown)*
July	*Harvest Festival (Innisfail)*
July	*Laura–Cape York Aboriginal Dance Festival (Cooktown, odd-numbered years)*
July	*Rodeo (Mareeba)*
Sept.	*Air Show (Mareeba)*
Oct.	*Reef Festival and Hook, Wine and Sinker Festival (Cairns)*
Oct.	*Country Music Festival (Mareeba)*
Oct.	*Folk Festival (Yungaburra)*

VISITOR INFORMATION

Tourism Tropical North Queensland
Cairns: (07) 4051 3588
www.tnq.org.au

Cotton trees are found along this coast, and flower for most of the year

FOCUS ON

Tropical rainforests

The World Heritage Wet Tropics area covers 894 000 ha along the eastern escarpment of the Great Dividing Range between Townsville and Cooktown, and features rainforest, mountains, gorges, fast-flowing rivers and numerous waterfalls. The rainforest here is one of the most biologically diverse and ancient environments on Earth. It represents the major stages in Earth's evolutionary history and has the world's greatest concentration of primitive flowering plants or 'green dinosaurs', as they are known. Australia's largest area of rainforest wilderness is in the Daintree River valley just north of Mossman. At Cape Tribulation two World Heritage areas come together: rainforest and reef along the coast. Queensland's tropical rainforests can be seen on short walks, or on hikes lasting days; on sealed roads or 4WD treks along rutted tracks that cross creek fords; from scenic railways and cableways; and by boat or raft on forest rivers.

Whitewater rafting on the Tully River

EXPERIENCE IT!

❶ **Ride** *a raft on the white water of the Tully River (via Tully in The Mid-Tropics touring region), which descends from the Atherton Tableland through rainforest gorges*

❷ **Marvel** *at The Boulders (west of Babinda), rounded by fast-flowing river waters*

❸ **Climb** *Mount Bartle Frere, Queensland's highest mountain, on a 12-hour walk through Wooroonooran National Park*

❹ **Enjoy** *more than 200 species of palms at the Flecker Botanic Gardens in Cairns, established in 1886*

❺ **Shop** *for arts, crafts, fashions and food at the Kuranda country markets, the largest in the region*

CLIMATE CAIRNS

	J	F	M	A	M	J	J	A	S	O	N	D
Max.°C	31	31	30	29	28	26	26	27	28	29	31	31
Min.°C	24	24	23	22	20	18	17	18	19	21	22	23
Rain mm	413	435	442	191	94	49	28	27	36	38	90	175
Raindays	18	19	20	17	14	10	9	8	8	8	10	13

Weipa

The world's largest bauxite deposits are found around Weipa on the west coast of Cape York. In 1961 Comalco built a modern mining town with all facilities on the site of an Aboriginal mission station and reserve. The company offers tours of its mining operations. The fishing in the rivers and the waters of the Gulf is excellent.

Torres Strait Islands

Australia's only non-Aboriginal indigenous people come from this group of around 100 islands off the northern tip of Cape York. The commercial centre is Thursday Island, reached by ferry from Seisia, or ship or plane from Cairns. The Torres Strait Islander people are of Melanesian descent and include among their number the late Eddie Mabo, famous for his successful 1992 land claim in Australia's High Court.

Tropical cuisine

A menu at a restaurant in the exclusive holiday town of Port Douglas might offer Gulf bug tempura skewered on lemongrass accompanied by a Tableland salad of greens, mango slices, coconut slivers and wasabi mayonnaise, and with a tropical-fruit ice-cream for dessert. Chefs trained in the culinary styles of the east and west are using the abundant local produce to create a true regional cuisine.

Chillagoe Caves

This outstanding cave system is in a limestone belt extending north to the Palmer River. Vine thickets, towering above-ground structures, bat colonies and richly decorative stalactites and stalagmites create an unforgettable natural environment. There are regular tours of some caves, and visitors can wander through others without a guide.

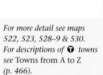

For more detail see maps 522, 523, 528–9 & 530. For descriptions of ⓣ towns see Towns from A to Z (p. 466).

Atherton Tableland

This 900-m-high tableland south-west of Cairns is a productive farming district, thanks to its high rainfall and rich volcanic soil. The historic town of Yungaburra is listed with the National Trust. Nearby is the remarkable Curtain Fig Tree, a strangler fig that has subsumed its host, sending down a curtain of roots. Volcanic lakes and spectacular waterfalls, including Millaa Millaa Falls (pictured) and Zillie Falls, are among the other scenic attractions.

Undara Lava Tubes

These lava tubes are set in a beautiful national park expanse of savannah woodland and fringed with pockets of rainforest. Formed 190 000 years ago, Undara (an Aboriginal word for 'long') includes a 160-km lava tunnel, the longest on Earth. Accommodation, including camping, is available at Lava Lodge, also the starting point for tours of the area.

Lakefield National Park

Lakefield is Queensland's second-largest national park. A near-wilderness of grassland, woodland, swamp and mangroves is cut by three major rivers and their tributaries. Access for conventional vehicles is via the township of Laura (during the Dry). Camping areas are at Hann and Kalpowar crossings. Visit the Old Laura Homestead, fish for barramundi and watch the wildlife.

Aboriginal rock art

The Split Rock and Gu Gu Yalangi rock-art sites, south of Laura, are a sample of what the Laura and Cooktown region has to offer, namely one of the largest collections of prehistoric rock art in the world. The most distinctive works are the Quinkan figures, stick-like figures representing spirits that might emerge suddenly from rock crevices. Tours are available through the local Ang-Gnarra community.

Cooktown

Captain Cook beached the *Endeavour* near the site of Cooktown in 1770. The town was built a century later when gold was discovered on the Palmer River to the south-west. Cooktown has botanic gardens dating from the 1880s, two museums, and a cemetery with hundreds of Chinese graves. Cruises along the river and out to the reef to experience the amazing marine life are available.

Scenic routes to Kuranda

Kuranda, an Aboriginal word for 'village in the rainforest', can be reached from Cairns via a couple of spectacularly scenic routes. A 19th-century steam-train carries visitors 34 km up steep slopes, through rainforest, along Barron Gorge and past Barron Falls. The Skyrail Rainforest Cableway (pictured) is a gondola cableway, passing through and above the rainforest canopy.

Cairns

Cairns, located on the edge of two extraordinary natural environments, the reef and the rainforest, is an ideal base for activities ranging from big-game fishing to diving, walking and 4WD touring. A casino (pictured), five-star hotels, excellent restaurants and pulsating nightclubs cater for the most sophisticated travellers, while cafes, backpacker lodges and a lively atmosphere attract the backpacker crowd.

FOCUS ON

Aboriginal Cape York

Before white people arrived, the Aboriginal people of Cape York were divided into two main groups, East Cape and West Cape, with many language and cultural groups within these broad divisions. The distinctive art of the East Cape Aboriginal people survives in the rock-art galleries around Laura, some of the most extensive and unusual in Australia. Laura is also home to the Laura Dance Festival, staged biennially by the Ang-Gnarra community. Cairns, along with nearby Kuranda, is home to a range of Aboriginal galleries, tours and cultural centres. The Aboriginal groups of West Cape, an area that proved largely resistant to European expansion, maintained sizeable reserves around Mapoon and Aurukun. Native title legislation since the 1950s has handed much of the West Cape back to its Aboriginal owners. There are a couple of camping and fishing areas around Mapoon. Visitors wishing to gain access need a permit; contact the Mapoon Community, (07) 4090 9124.

Daintree National Park

The Mossman Gorge section of this World Heritage park takes visitors into the rainforest's green shady heart via an easy 2.7-km walk to the Mossman River. The Cape Tribulation section is a rich mix of coastal rainforest, mangroves, swamp and heath. There is camping at Noah Beach. From here, walking trails lead to spectacular reef and rainforest scenery.

OUTBACK & GULF COUNTRY

This is a remote, sparsely populated and – in parts – stunningly beautiful region extending west from the slopes of the Great Dividing Range. In the north, savannah grasslands give way to the lagoons and mangrove-lined estuaries of the Gulf of Carpentaria coastline. From the north to the centre, the low rise of fossil-strewn landforms punctuate the vastness of the surrounding plains. In the Channel Country of the south-west, dry waterholes and salt pans dominate the landscape, except when floodwaters from the north bring brilliant life to the country in the form of native flowers and grasses and flocks of birds. Many of the stories and legends of Australia's pioneering days were born here, and the themes of mateship, egalitarianism and a fair go are celebrated in the region's museums and monuments. Distances are vast and temperatures extreme: those intending to travel beyond sealed roads should plan their trips with care.

EXPERIENCE IT!

❶ *Drop* in on Minmi, Australia's best-preserved dinosaur, at Kronosaurus Korner Fossil Centre in Richmond

❷ *Visit* the Burke and Wills Cairn, site of the explorers' most northerly camp, on the Normanton–Burketown Road

❸ *Travel* from Boulia by 4WD to see billabongs, coolibahs and waterbirds in Diamantina National Park

❹ *Experience* the Gulf country's birdlife, aboard a river cruise via Karumba

❺ *Trace* the history of Australia's famous medical service at the Royal Flying Doctor Service Museum in Cloncurry

VISITOR INFORMATION

Gulf Savannah Tourist Organisation
Cairns: (07) 4031 1631
www.gulf-savannah.com.au

The Outback Queensland Tourism Authority
Mount Isa: (07) 4743 7966
www.outbackholidays.tq.com.au

Lawn Hill National Park
Lawn Hill Gorge, about 205 km from Burketown, is this remote park's main attraction. The gorge area protects an oasis of lush rainforest. Canoeing, swimming and walking are the main activities and there are two accessible Aboriginal art sites. Campsite bookings should be made 6 to 8 weeks ahead.

Riversleigh fossil fields
The fossils in this World Heritage-listed part of Lawn Hill National Park record the evolution of mammals over 20 million years as the vegetation changed from rainforest to semi-arid grassland. Tours run from Mount Isa, where there is an interpretive centre featuring displays of local fossil discoveries (pictured), and Adels Grove near the park entrance.

Mount Isa
This is Queensland's largest inland town. The mine, dating from 1924 and with 4600 km of tunnels, produces lead, silver, copper and zinc. Take a 3-hour hard-hat mine tour (adults only), inspect the National Trust-owned early-settler tent house, or visit the Riversleigh Fossils Centre and Mount Isa Tourist Information.

CLIMATE NORMANTON

	J	F	M	A	M	J	J	A	S	O	N	D
Max.°C	35	34	34	34	32	29	29	31	34	36	37	36
Min. °C	25	25	24	22	19	16	15	17	20	23	25	25
Rain mm	260	249	158	31	8	9	3	2	3	10	44	143
Raindays	14	14	9	2	1	1	1	0	0	1	4	9

FOCUS ON

Fishing the Gulf
The Gulf is one of Australia's true fishing frontiers. Anglers can fish the rivers – the Nicholson, Albert, Flinders, Norman and Gilbert – the coastal beaches, and the offshore waters and reefs of the Gulf via island resorts. Karumba, on the Norman River estuary, is a popular base for both river and offshore anglers. Sweers Island, in the Wellesley group, has a fishing resort offering access to thousands of hectares of reef where coral trout, parrotfish, sweetlip and sea perch (and in winter, pelagics such as mackerel and tuna) are plentiful. Mornington Island is home to the Birri Fishing Resort, offering crabbing, and sport and bottom fishing, all with professional masters. You can also stay at Escott Barramundi Lodge, on the Nicholson River, via Burketown. Fishing charters take you along the nearby lagoons and rivers, where you can catch barramundi, catfish and mangrove jack.

Channel Country
Monsoon rains in the tropical north flood the hundreds of inland river channels that meander through Queensland's south-west corner. Here cattle graze on huge semi-desert pastoral holdings. Spectacular red sandhills (pictured) are found in the area, particularly in Simpson Desert National Park in the far west beyond Birdsville, Queensland's most isolated settlement.

Tourist train

Every Wednesday the *Gulflander* leaves Normanton for the 153-km journey through the Gulf to the historic goldmining town of Croydon. With stops at points of interest along the line, the trip takes 4 hours. Travellers can explore Croydon with a local guide and return to Normanton on Thursday.

TOP EVENTS

May	Gregory River Canoe Races (Gregory, near Burketown)
May	Dirt and Dust Triathlon (Julia Creek)
May	Outback Muster and Drovers Reunion (Longreach)
June	Waltzing Matilda Festival (Winton)
July	Black Stump Camel Races (Blackall)
July	Drovers Reunion Festival (Camooweal)
July	Great Matilda Camel Races and Festival (Charleville)
July	Desert Sands Camel Race and Festival (Boulia)
Aug.	'Surf' Carnival (inland Iron Man contest, Kynuna)
Aug.	Isa Rodeo (Mount Isa)
Aug.	World Lizard Races (Cunnamulla)
Aug.	World Lizard Races (Eulo)
Sept.	Outback Festival (Winton, odd-numbered years)
Sept.	Birdsville Races (Birdsville)
Oct.	Lake Moondarra Fishing Classic (Mount Isa)

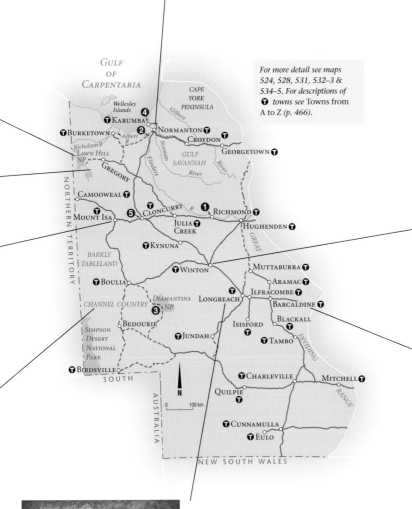

For more detail see maps 524, 528, 531, 532–3 & 534–5. For descriptions of ⊕ towns *see* Towns from A to Z (p. 466).

Waltzing Matilda country

Winton, the railhead town for sheep and cattle from the Channel Country, is the birthplace of 'Waltzing Matilda', Australia's favourite ballad. The song was penned at nearby Dagworth Station by bush poet Banjo Paterson and performed in the area in 1895. Winton's Waltzing Matilda Centre charts the song's history.

Barcaldine

The 'Garden City of the West' was the first Australian town to tap the waters of the Great Artesian Basin, an event commemorated by the town's giant windmill. The Australian Workers Heritage Centre recollects the 1891 shearers' strike and the Australian Workers Party, forerunner of the Australian Labor Party.

Australian Stockman's Hall of Fame

This impressive institution is just east of Longreach on the Matilda Highway. Imaginative displays show the development of white settlement in the Outback, including the contribution of women and Aboriginal people. Don't miss the nearby Qantas Founders Outback Museum, which tells the story of the English-speaking world's oldest airline.

QUEENSLAND

TOWNS FROM A TO Z

Airlie Beach, on the beautiful Whitsunday coast

Airlie Beach
Pop. 3029

MAP REF. 527 K3

Airlie Beach is the centre of the thriving Whitsunday coast. The town overlooks the Whitsunday Passage and from here and Shute Harbour, passengers can travel to the outer reef and reef-fringed islands. Airlie is a holiday town offering a beach, marina, major resorts with all facilities, top-grade accommodation and a range of visitor activities and services. **In town:** Vic Hislop's Shark Show, 13 Waterson Rd. Dive schools. Community market each Sat. on foreshore. Aug.: Triathlon. Sept.: Whitsunday Fun Race. **In the area:** Neighbouring Shute Harbour and islands of Whitsunday Passage. Sea or air access to Lindeman. Sea access to Hook, Whitsunday and Hayman islands. Fishing trips to nearby coastal wetlands and crocodile safaris. Conway National Park, 5 km S, renowned for its natural beauty and habitat of the Proserpine rock wallaby and many species of butterfly. **Visitor information:** Tourism Whitsundays, Shop 3/6 The Esplanade; (07) 4946 6673, freecall 1800 801 252. Web site www. whitsundayinformation.com.au **See also:** Great Barrier Reef p. 455; The Mid-Tropics p. 460; Wildlife-Watching p. 501.

Allora
Pop. 998

MAP REF. 525 N10

North of Warwick just off the Toowoomba road, this picturesque town is in a prime agricultural area. **In town:** Allora Historical Museum, Drayton St (open Sun. p.m. or by appt). St David's Anglican Church, in Church St, one of Queensland's finest timber churches. June: Apex Auction. **In the area:** National Trust-classified Talgai Homestead (c. 1860), 6 km W, offers meals and accommodation. Glengallan Homestead (1867), 15 km N on New England Hwy, heritage-listed relic of colonial pastoral life (check times). Goomburra State Forest, 35 km E in western foothills of Great Dividing Range. **Visitor information:** 49 Albion St (New England Hwy), Warwick; (07) 4661 3401. Web site www.qldsoutherndowns.org.au **See also:** Darling Downs p. 452.

Aramac
Pop. 342

MAP REF. 526 C10, 533 Q10

This small pastoral town is 67 km N of Barcaldine. Originally called Marathon, it was renamed by explorer William Landsborough as an acronym of 19th-century Qld Premier Sir Robert Ramsay Mackenzie (RRMac). **In town:** White Bull replica, Gordon St, commemorating Captain Starlight's arrest for cattle-stealing. Tramway Museum, McWhannell St, has old rail motor and historical exhibits. May: Ballyneety Rodeo. **In the area:** Grey Rock, 35 km E, large sandstone rock with engraved names from early 1900s to present. Lake Dunn, 68 km NE, for swimming, fishing and birdwatching (follow signs to 'The Lake' rather than to adjacent Lake Dunn property). **Visitor information:** Post Office, Gordon St; (07) 4651 3147. Web site www.outbackholidays.tq.com.au **See also:** Outback & Gulf Country p. 464.

Atherton
Pop. 5693

MAP REF. 521 B1, 523 C12, 529 M7

Atherton is the agricultural hub of the Atherton Tableland. 100 km SW of Cairns on the Kennedy Hwy, the town is in a patchwork of dense rainforest that abounds in birdlife. The fertile basalt soil, undulating terrain and abundant rainfall have made the region the centre of dairy, sugar and grain-growing industries. The area between Atherton, Kairi and Tolga grows tomatoes, avocados, potatoes, peanuts, maize and other grains. **In town:** Chinese Joss House and Old Post Office Gallery, Herberton Rd. Fascinating Facets and the Crystal Caves mineral museum, Main St, has constructed underground tunnels and chambers, and displays of minerals and gemstones. **In the area:** Picturesque Atherton Tableland: rainforest-fringed volcanic crater lakes; spectacular waterfalls; fertile farmlands. Bushwalking at a number of locations incl. Hallorans Hill, 1 km E; Baldy Mountain, 3 km SW; Wongabel State Forest, 8 km SE. At Tolga, 5 km N: woodworks, peanut factory and craft. At Herberton, 19 km SW: Foster's Winery; Historical Village with more than 30 restored buildings. Steam-train journeys with 1927 locomotive, from Atherton to Herberton and return, along steepest track in Qld; departs Wed. and weekends (closed Feb.) from Platypus Park,

Herberton Rd. Mt Hypipamee National Park, 26 km s, includes sheer-sided explosion crater 140 m deep, and variety of wildlife. Lake Tinaroo, 15 km NE, for fishing, water-skiing and sailing; houseboat hire; Danbulla Forest Drive, 28 km scenic drive around lake. **Visitor information:** Old Post Office Gallery, 86 Herberton Rd; (07) 4091 4222. Web site www.athertontableland.com **See also:** The Far North p. 461; National Parks p. 498; Wildlife-Watching p. 501.

Ayr   Pop. 8697

MAP REF. 521 I10, 526 H1, 529 Q13

This busy town on the north side of the Burdekin delta is surrounded by irrigated sugarcane fields, the most productive in Australia. The Burdekin River Irrigation Scheme is the State's largest land and water conservation scheme, and makes Ayr the largest mango-producing area in Australia. **In town:** Ayr Nature Display, Wilmington St, fine collection of emu-egg carvings, butterflies and beetles. Burdekin Cultural Complex, Queen St, includes 530-seat theatre, library and activities centre; distinctive 'Living Lagoon' in theatre forecourt. ESA markets, Plantation Creek Park, Bruce Hwy, 3rd Sun. each month. Sept.: Water Festival. Nov.: Home Hill Harvest Festival. **In the area:** Alva Beach, 18 km N, for beach walks, birdwatching, swimming and fishing; market 1st Sun. each month. At Cape Bowling Green, 20 km N: Australian Institute of Marine Science; wreck of SS *Yongala*, 16 km off coast, for divers. Hutchings Lagoon, 5 km NW, for watersports and picnics. Lions Diorama, 10 km s, shows agricultural achievements of Burdekin region. At Charlie's Hill, 24 km s, WW II historic site. Good views from Mt Inkerman, 30 km s. Scenic drives in area, brochures available. **Visitor information:** 161 Queen St; (07) 4783 9897 or Tourist Hut, Plantation Creek Park, Bruce Hwy; (07) 4783 5988. **See also:** The Mid-Tropics p. 460.

Babinda   Pop. 1228

MAP REF. 521 D1, 523 H13, 529 N7

A small sugar town, 57 km s of Cairns, Babinda is adjacent to Wooroonooran National Park. In the park are the State's 2 highest mountains, Mt Bartle Frere (1622 m) and Mt Bellenden Ker (1582 m), and Josephine Falls. **In town:** Deeral Cooperative, Nelson Rd, makes footwear and Aboriginal artifacts. **In the area:** The

Boulders, 10 km w, offers excellent bushwalking along Babinda Creek below Mt Bartle Frere. Deeral, 14 km N, departure point for cruises through rainforest and the saltwater-crocodile haunts of the Mulgrave and Russell rivers. **Visitor information:** Bruce Hwy and Munro Street; (07) 4067 1008. Web site www.tnq.org.au **See also:** The Far North p. 461; National Parks p. 498.

Barcaldine   Pop. 1592

MAP REF. 526 C11, 533 Q11

Barcaldine is a pastoral and rail town, 108 km E of Longreach. A good supply of artesian water ensures its status as Garden City of the West; all the streets are named after trees. **In town:** Mad Mick's Hoppers and Huts Funny Farm, cnr Pine and Bauhinia sts, features 8 settlers' buildings (including woolskin buyer's residence housing large doll collection, and Cobb & Co. office, now studio and art gallery), old shearing sheds with plant and press, and hand-reared wildlife. Historical Folk Museum, cnr Gidyea and Beech sts. 'Tree of Knowledge', ghost gum in Oak St, the meeting-place for 1891 shearers' strike, which resulted in the formation of the Australian Labor Party. Australian Workers Heritage Centre, Ash St, features buildings containing tributes to Australia's workers in landscaped oasis. National Trust-classified buildings: Masonic Lodge, Beech St; Anglican Church, Elm St; Shire Hall, Ash St. Mini steam-train rides last Sun. each month (Mar.–Oct.). Easter: Easter in the Outback. **In the area:** Barcaldine Outback Zoo, 1 km w: native and exotic birds, reptiles and small and large animals. Botanical walk, 9 km s, through varied bushland. Red Mountain scenic drive from Richmond Hills station, 55 km E. **Visitor information:** Oak St; (07) 4651 1724. Web site www.outbackholidays.tq.com.au **See also:** Outback & Gulf Country p. 464.

Beaudesert   Pop. 3734

MAP REF. 517 D11, 525 P10

Beaudesert is a major market town on the Mt Lindesay Hwy, 64 km sw of Brisbane and 60 km from the NSW border. The district is noted for dairying, beef cattle, horse-breeding and fruit- and vegetable-growing. Country markets are an attraction; details from information centre. **In town:** Historical Museum, Brisbane St. Apr.: Rathdowney Heritage Festival; Carp Fishing Competition.

June.: Country and Horse Festival. Sept.: Agricultural Show. Oct.: Rodeo. **In the area:** Woollahra Farmworld, 8 km N at Gleneagle. Unique flora and good views at Tamborine Mountain, 35 km E. Nearby, dig for your own thunder eggs at Cedar Creek Lodge. Bigriggen Park, 30 km sw and Darlington Park, 12 km s, both recreation areas with picnic/barbecue facilities. At Lamington National Park, 40 km s: subtropical rainforest; canopy walk at O'Reillys Plateau; resorts; excellent graded walking tracks. At Tamrookum, 24 km sw, fine example of a timber church; tours by appt. Mt Barney National Park, 55 km sw, camping (permit required, apply to ranger). **Visitor information:** 54 Brisbane St; (07) 5541 3740. Web site www.goldcoasttourism.com.au **See also:** Gold Coast & Hinterland p. 450; National Parks p. 498.

Biggenden   Pop. 686

MAP REF. 525 N4

This agricultural centre 100 km SE of Bundaberg, is near Mt Walsh National Park and The Bluff. Oct.: Rose Festival (odd-numbered years). **In the area:** Mt Walsh National Park, 8 km s, wilderness park popular with experienced bushwalkers. Coalstoun Lakes National Park, 20 km sw, protects 2 volcanic crater lakes. Coongara Rock (4WD access only), 20 km s, a volcanic core surrounded by rainforest. Mt Woowoonga, 10 km NW, forestry reserve with bushwalking and picnic/barbecue facilities. Chowey Bridge (1905), 20 km NW, concrete arch railway bridge (one of two surviving in Aust.); picnic facilities nearby. Silver Bell Novelty Farm, 2 km N on Old Coach Rd, has buildings and collections; open by appt. **Visitor information:** Weekdays, Shire Council, Edward St; (07) 4127 1440, weekends and holidays, Bundaberg Regional Visitor Information Centre; (07) 4152 2333, freecall 1800 060 499. Web site www.bdtdb.com.au **See also:** Capricorn p. 458.

Biloela   Pop. 5161

MAP REF. 525 K1, 527 N13

This thriving town (Aboriginal for 'white cockatoo') in the fertile Callide Valley is at the crossroads of the Burnett and Dawson hwys, 142 km s of Rockhampton. Underground water irrigates lucerne, cotton, sorghum, wheat and sunflower crops. **In town:** Greycliffe Homestead,

The hotel at Birdsville provides a resting place for travellers

Gladstone Rd, open by appt. The Silo, Primary Industries Exhibition, Dawson Hwy: theme park; hi-tech farming techniques; scenes of rural life; 3 markets each year (check dates). Bus tours of town weekdays. June: Country and Western Muster. **In the area:** Callide Dam, 5 km NE, for boating, fishing and swimming. Nearby, Callide power station, tours. Lyle Semgreen Gems at Jambin, 32 km NW, open by appt. Baralaba Historical Village, 100 km NW. Mt Scoria, 14 km S, solidified volcano core. Thangool, 10 km SE, renowned for its race days. **Visitor information:** Callide St; (07) 4992 2405. **See also:** Capricorn p. 458.

Birdsville
Pop. 100

MAP REF. 534 E5

The historical Birdsville Track goes from here into and across SA. In the 1870s the first European settlers arrived in Birdsville, nearly 2000 km by road west of Brisbane, and by 1900 it had 3 hotels, several stores, a customs office and a cordial factory. When the toll on cattle crossing the border was abolished after Federation in 1901, prosperity declined. **In town:** Museum, McDonald St, features Australiana, domestic artifacts and working farm equipment. In Adelaide St: ruins of Royal Hotel (1883), reminder of Birdsville's boom days; Birdsville Hotel (1884), a hive of activity during Birdsville Races (first Fri. and Sat. in Sept.) as population swells to about 6500. Birdsville Hotel is an important overnight stop for tourists travelling down the Track, west across the Simpson Desert (4WD country), north to Mount Isa or east to Brisbane. *Travel in this area can be hazardous, especially in the hotter months (approx. Oct.–Mar.). Supplies of food and water should always be carried, as well as at least 2 spare tyres, and petrol, oil and spare parts. Motorists are advised to ring the Northern Roads Condition Hotline on (08) 11633 for information before departing down the Track, and to advise police if heading west to the Simpson Desert National Park; motorists should also read section on Outback Motoring (p. 599). There is no hotel or fuel at Betoota, 164 km E, but fuel is available at Windorah.* The famous Flynn of the Inland founded the first Australian Inland Mission at Birdsville; there is still a well-equipped medical clinic in Adelaide St. Birdsville's water comes almost at boiling point from a 1219-m-deep artesian bore; a cooling pond brings it to a safe temperature. Electricity is supplied by 2 diesel generators. Sept.: Races. **In the area:** Waddi trees and Dingo Cave Lookout, 14 km N. Big Red, a huge sand dune, 35 km W. **Visitor information:** Wirrarri Centre, Billabong Blvd; (07) 4656 3300. **See also:** Outback & Gulf Country p. 464.

Blackall
Pop. 1432

MAP REF. 524 A1, 526 D13, 533 R13, 535 R1

Centre of some of the most productive sheep and cattle country in central Qld, Blackall has many sheep and cattle studs in its vicinity. In 1892 the legendary Jackie Howe set the record of shearing 321 sheep with blade shears in less than 8 hours, at Alice Downs Station, 25 km N. Blackall sank the first artesian bore in Qld in 1885. **In town:** Jackie Howe statue, junction of Short and Shamrock sts. Also in Shamrock St: petrified tree stump, millions of years old; Major Mitchell Memorial clock. In Thistle St is a replica of the Black Stump, reference point used when area was surveyed in 1886. Self-guide historical walk; property tours to see shearing. July: Black Stump Camel Races. **In the area:** Steam-driven Blackall Wool Scour (1906), 4 km N on Clematis St; guided tours daily or by appt. Idalia National Park, 100 km SW, renowned as habitat of the yellow-footed rock wallaby. **Visitor information:** Short St; (07) 4657 4637. Web site: www.outbackholidays. tq.com.au **See also:** Outback & Gulf Country p. 464.

Blackwater
Pop. 5931

MAP REF. 527 K11

This major coal-mining town is 190 km W of Rockhampton on the Capricorn Hwy. The name comes from the discolouration of the local waterholes by ti-trees. Coal mined in the area is railed to Gladstone. The town's population is multinational and it displays what is claimed to be the most varied collection of flags this side of the United Nations. Cattle rearing is the traditional industry. **In town:** In town park, Capricorn Hwy: Japanese garden provided by sister town in Japan; also a Leichhardt 'Dig Tree'. **In the area:** Utah Coal Mine, 35 km S, tours available; bookings necessary. Expedition Range (732 m), 139 km SW near Springsure, discovered by Ludwig Leichhardt. At Comet, 30 km W, Show and Camp Draft each Sept. Blackdown Tableland National Park, 50 km SE: swimming at Rainbow Falls gorge; Sunset Lookout; walking trails; picnic/barbecue facilities at Horseshoe Lookout; camping at Mimosa Creek. **Visitor information:** Clermont St, Emerald; (07) 4982 4142. **See also:** Capricorn p. 458.

Boonah
Pop. 2234

MAP REF. 517 A11, 525 P10

Eighty-six km SW of Brisbane between Warwick and Ipswich, Boonah is the main town in the Fassifern district, a highly productive agricultural and pastoral area. Its location was noted as a 'beautiful vale' by 19th-century explorers. **In town:** Art Gallery, Highbury St, leadlight and other displays. Skydiving, gliding, and ultralight tours; details from information centre. Boonah Country Markets, Springleigh Park, Sat. each fortnight. May: Country Show. **In the area:** Kalbar, 10 km N, holds Autofest in Sept. At Templin, 5 km W,

Historical Village; open Sun.–Thurs. Moogerah Peaks National Park, 12 km W. Lake Moogerah, 20 km SW, for water sports. Main Range National Park, 35 km W, part of the Scenic Rim, a ring of mountains and national parks around Brisbane offering scenic drives (brochure available), bushwalking, trail-riding, rock-climbing, skydiving, water sports, picnic spots, recreation facilities, camping and accommodation; Cunninghams Gap Lookout in park has good views, with walking tracks from lookout. **Visitor information:** Boonah–Fassifern Rd; (07) 5463 2233. Web site www.boonah.net **See also:** Gold Coast & Hinterland p. 450.

Boulia   Pop. 243

MAP REF. 532 F9

Near the Burke River, 360 km W of Winton, 295 km S of Mt Isa and 242 km E of the NT border, Boulia is the capital of the Channel Country. **In town:** In Pituri St, town's oldest house, Stone Cottage (1880s), now a museum displaying Aboriginal artifacts and historic relics of region. In Herbert St: Min Min Centre has display on 'Min Min' light; the Red Stump, warning travellers of dangers of Simpson Desert; artificial 'Min Min' light. Tree, near Boulia State School, last known corroboree tree of Pitta Pitta community. Varied birdlife around river. Easter: Rodeo and Races. July: Desert Sands Camel Race (and festival). **In the area:** Mysterious Min Min light, first sighted near ruins of Min Min Hotel (130 km E). Cawnpore Hills, 108 km E, good views from summit. Ruins of police barracks, 19 km NE. The Burke and Wills tree, 110 km NE on the west bank of the Burke River. Diamantina National Park, 150 km SE. *Travel by road in wet season can be difficult. Read Outback Motoring (p. 599).* **Visitor information:** Herbert St; (07) 4746 3386. Web site www.outbackholidays.tq.com.au **See also:** Outback & Gulf Country p. 464.

Bowen   Pop. 8985

MAP REF. 527 J2

Situated halfway between Mackay and Townsville, Bowen was named after the State's first Governor. The town was established in 1861 at Port Denison and was the first European settlement in north Qld. It boasts an average of 8 hours sunshine daily. Bowen region is known for its tomatoes, and its mangoes (in season Nov.–Jan.). **In town:** Signposted Golden Arrow tourist drive starts at Salt Works,

Don St. 22 historical murals in central city area. Historical Museum, Gordon St. Aug.: Art, Craft and Orchid Expo. Oct.: Coral Coast Festival. **In the area:** Excellent small bays within 7 km of town (Rose and Horseshoe bays connected by walking track) for fishing, snorkelling and swimming. Collinsville coal mines, 82 km SW. **Visitor information:** Bruce Hwy, Mt Gordon; (07) 4786 4494. Web site www.townsvilleonline. com.au **See also:** The Mid-Tropics p. 460.

Buderim   Pop. 12 458

MAP REF. 516 G4, 519 G9, 525 Q7

Buderim is just inland from the Sunshine Coast, high on the fertile red soil of Buderim Mountain. It is a popular residential and retirement area. **In town:** Several galleries in Main St. In Burnett St, Buderim Festive Markets, in Old Ginger Factory (open daily; entertainment on weekends). Restored pioneer timber cottage (1876), Ballinger Rd, one of Buderim's earliest houses, retaining many original furnishings. Historical town walk, brochure from pioneer cottage. **In the area:** Buderim Forest Park, Quorn Close (just north of town), features waterfalls and walking tracks; wheelchair access to lower end, entry from Lindsay Rd. Rainforest walks at Foote Sanctuary, north-eastern end of town. Self-guide Tanawha–Forest Glen Tourist Drive includes: Superbee Honey Factory; Forest Glen Sanctuary (deer and native fauna); Bellingham Maze, largest hedge maze in Australia (includes aviary) and Enchanted Lair. **Visitor information:** Old Post Office, Burnett St; (07) 5477 0944. Web site www.sunshinecoast.org **See also:** Sunshine Coast p. 453.

Bundaberg   Pop. 41 025

MAP REF. 525 O2

Bundaberg, on the Burnett River 368 km N of Brisbane, is the southernmost access point to the Great Barrier Reef, and an important provincial city in the centre of the fertile Burnett River plains. The district is known for its sugar, timber, beef, tomatoes and avocados. Raw sugar is exported from a storage and bulk facility at Port Bundaberg, 16 km NE. Sidelines include the world-famous Bundaberg Rum, refined sugar, and the manufacture and export of advanced Austoft cane-harvester equipment. Bundaberg is a city of parks and botanical gardens; its wide streets lined with fig, poinciana and bauhinia trees make a brilliant spring and summer display. Bundaberg has been home to distinguished solo aviator Bert Hinkler; singer Gladys Moncrieff; cricketer Don Tallon; and rugby league star Mal Meninga. **In town:** Historic city walks, brochures available. Alexandra Park and Zoo on river bank, Quay St: free zoo, historic band rotunda, cactus garden and children's playground. Whaling Wall, Bourbong St, a 6-storey-high whale mural. In East Bundaberg: Bundaberg Rum Distillery, Avenue St, offers daily tours; Baldwin Swamp Conservation Park, Steindl St, has boardwalks and pathways, waterlily lagoons, abundant birdlife and native fauna; Schmeider's Cooperage and Craft Centre, Alexandra St, has demonstrations of barrel-making. Across the river in North Bundaberg: Botanical Gardens (Mt Perry Rd) include the Hinkler House Memorial Museum (aviation history), railway (steam-train rides Sun. around lakes), Bundaberg Historical Museum, and Fairymead

The remote Channel Country around Boulia

House Sugar Museum; Tropical Wines (unique tropical-fruit wine) and Sunny Soft Drinks also in Mt Perry Rd. Shalom College Markets, Fitzgerald St, West Bundaberg, each Sun. West School Craft Markets, George St, West Bundaberg, 2nd Sun. each month. Easter: Country Music Roundup. Sept.: Bundy in Bloom Festival. Oct.: Arts Festival. **In the area:** Diving opportunities and dive schools. Coastal and hinterland self-drive tours, brochures available. Boat tours to see migrating humpback whales, mid-Aug.–mid-Oct. Cane fires, sugarcane harvesting season (July–Nov.). Fishing at Burnett Heads (15 km NE), Elliott Heads (18 km SE) and Moore Park (21 km NW). Popular surf beach at Bargara, 13 km NE; nearby, Neilson Park and Kelly's beaches. Hummock Lookout, 7 km NE, for views over city, canefields and coast. Mon Repos Conservation Park, 15 km NE, largest and most accessible mainland loggerhead turtle rookery in Australia; giant sea turtles come ashore to lay their eggs Nov.–Jan., and babies hatch mid-Jan.–Mar.; interpretive centre and viewing in season. In 1912 Bert Hinkler, as engineering apprentice, flew 9 m high in his home-made glider off Mon Repos Beach, starting his career in aviation. Meadowvale Nature Park, 10 km W, features rainforest and walkway to Splitters Creek. Sharon Gorge, 12 km SW, features rainforest and walkway to Burnett River. Unexplained mystery, 25 km SW: 35 intriguing craters said to be 25 million years old. Avocado Grove, 10 km S, subtropical gardens. Near Childers, 45 km S, Isis Central Sugar Mill (tours July–Nov.). Sea or air access to Lady Musgrave Island. Air access to Lady Elliot Island. **Visitor information:** 186 Bourbong St; (07) 4152 9289,

freecall 1800 060 499. Web site www.bundaberg.qld.gov.au **See also:** Great Barrier Reef p. 455; Capricorn p. 458; Wildlife-Watching p. 501.

Burketown   Pop. 220

MAP REF. 531 E8

The centre of rich beef country, Burketown is 229 km W of Normanton and provides boat access to the Gulf of Carpentaria. The town is near the Albert River and on the dividing line between the wetlands to the north and the Gulf Savannah grass plains to the south. In Sept. and Oct. visitors can see Morning Glory, a tube-like cloud formation that rolls across the sky. **In town:** 100-year-old bore, which issues 68°C water. Burketown Hotel (1860s), originally customs house, oldest building in the Gulf. Burketown to Normanton telegraph line. Original post office. Easter: World Barramundi Championships. May: Camp Draft and Gymkhana. June: Agricultural Show. **In the area:** Original Gulf meatworks just north of town. Cemetery, 2 km N, for insights into town's historic past. Fishing in Albert River. Nicholson River wetlands, 17 km W, breeding grounds for crocodiles, and variety of fish and birdlife. Escott Barramundi Lodge, 17 km W, on operating cattle station; camping and accommodation. Lawn Hill National Park, 205 km SW: rare vegetation; World Heritage-listed Riversleigh Fossil Site; 2 accessible Aboriginal art sites; canoeing, swimming and walking; book campsites 6–8 weeks ahead; near entrance to park is Adels Grove, remains of exotic garden planted by French botanist Albert De Lestang in 1930s. Leichhardt Falls, 71 km SE: picturesque area, walks and flowing falls in rainy months. Landsborough Tree,

5 km E, blazed by explorer in 1862 when searching for Burke and Wills. At Gregory, 207 km S, Canoe Races in May. **Visitor information:** Bowen St; (07) 4745 5177. Web site www.gulf-savannah.com.au **See also:** Outback & Gulf Country p. 464; National Parks p. 498.

Burrum Heads   Pop. 834

MAP REF. 525 P3

This pleasant holiday resort, at the mouth of the Burrum River and on the foreshore of Hervey Bay, 45 km N of Maryborough, offers excellent fishing and beaches. **In town:** Easter: Amateur Fishing Classic. **In the area:** Fishing villages of Buxton and Walkers Point on north side of Burrum River. Magnificent ocean beach at Woodgate, 90 km N (5 km N by boat). Nearby, Burrum Coast National Park, accessible from Woodgate, features walking tracks (including boardwalk), prolific birdlife, picnic spots and camping areas. **Visitor information:** Hervey Bay Visitors Centre, 353 The Esplanade, Hervey Bay; (07) 4124 4050. Web site www.fraser-coast.org **See also:** Fraser Island & Coast p. 454; National Parks p. 498.

Caboolture   Pop. 17 571

MAP REF. 516 F8, 517 C1, 525 P8

Just off the Bruce Hwy, 46 km N of Brisbane, Caboolture is a commercial centre surrounded by subtropical fruit farms. **In town:** Market at showground, Beerburrum Rd, each Sun. June: Show; Medieval Tournament. July: St Peter's and St Columban's Arts and Cultural Expo. Aug.: Air Show (odd-numbered years). Dec.: Rodeo. **In the area:** Fishing towns: Donnybrook and Toorbul (20 and

View from Hummock Lookout near Bundaberg

22 km NE); Beachmere (13 km SE). Caboolture Historical Village, faithfully restored; 2 km N on Beerburrum Rd. Distinctive forested volcanic plugs in Glass House Mountains National Park, 22 km N. At Woodford, 22 km NW, Folk Festival each Dec. Abbey Museum, 9 km E, just off road to Bribie Island, traces growth of Western civilisation. War Plane Museum, 2 km E, restored fighter planes. Bribie Island, 23 km E: family daytrips; picnic areas; safe swimming; fishing; walking tracks; Festival here Sept.–Oct. **Visitor information:** 55 King St; (07) 5495 3122. **See also:** Brisbane Hinterland p. 448; National Parks p. 498.

Caloundra on the Sunshine Coast

Cairns   Pop. 92 273

MAP REF. 522, 523 F8, 529 N6

This modern, colourful city is the capital of the tropical north. The cosmopolitan Esplanade traces the bay foreshore, and parks and gardens abound with tropical colour. Cairns' location is superb: the Great Barrier Reef to the east, the mountain rainforests and plains of the Atherton Tableland to the west, and palm-fringed beaches to the north and south. Cairns is a great black-marlin fishing location and offers access to the Great Barrier Reef for anglers, snorkellers, scuba-divers and visitors wishing to see the coral from glass-bottomed boats. **In town:** National Trust-classified Regional Gallery, cnr Shields and Abbott sts. Cairns Museum, cnr Lake and Shields sts, displays of Aboriginal, gold-rush, timber and sugarcane history. The McLeod Street Pioneer Cemetery honours local pioneers. Game-fishing boats moor at Marlin Marina, Marlin Jetty and Trinity Wharf, end of Spence St. The Reef Hotel Casino complex, Wharf St. Wetland areas incl. the Esplanade; opportunities for birdwatching. Flecker Botanic Gardens, Collins Ave: plants used by Aboriginal people; exotic trees and shrubs; over 200 species of palms. Walking track links gardens to Centenary Lakes Parkland. Tanks Centre, near Botanic Gardens, multi-purpose centre in revamped WW II oil storage tanks. Jack Barnes Bicentennial Mangrove Boardwalk, Airport Ave. Rainforest walk to top of Mt Whitfield, in park opposite airport. Royal Flying Doctor Service Visitor Centre, Junction St, Edge Hill. Bulk sugar terminal, Cook St, Portsmith, south of city centre, has guided tours during crushing season (June–Dec.). Dive schools. Markets: Rusty's Bazaar, Grafton

and Sheridan sts, Fri. p.m., Sat. and Sun. a.m.; at the Pier, Sat. and Sun. July: Agricultural Show. Oct.: Reef Festival and Hook, Wine and Sinker Festival. **In the area:** Skyrail Rainforest Cableway, gondola ride with boardwalk stops through rainforest to Kuranda; departs Caravonica Lakes Station, Smithfield, 11 km NE (return via Scenic Railway, or vice versa). Award-winning Tjapukai Aboriginal Cultural Park, adjacent to Caravonica Lakes Station, performances daily. Cairns beaches, 26 km of spectacular coastline, extend from Machans Beach (10 km N) north to Ellis Beach. Holloways Beach, 11 km N, popular seaside spot. Australian Woolshed at Smithfield, 13 km N: daily ram shows, spinning, shearing, working sheepdog demonstrations. Wild World and Outback Opal Mine, 22 km NW. Freshwater Connection historical complex, 34 km NW, departure point for 100-year-old Kuranda Scenic Railway trip through Barron Gorge to rainforest village of Kuranda. Bushwalking, hiking, whitewater rafting and camping in Barron and Freshwater valleys, north and south of Cairns; attractions incl. Crystal Cascades, Barron Gorge hydro-electric power station and Copperlode Dam (Lake Morris). Reef and islands can be explored by private charters, daily cruises and by air (seaplane and helicopter). Longer cruises to resort islands and reef on *Coral Princess* and *Kangaroo Explorer*. Sea access to Green and Fitzroy islands and Frankland Islands. Air access to Green, Orpheus, Dunk and Lizard islands. Access to wilderness areas of Atherton Tableland, Daintree, Cape Tribulation, Cape York and Gulf Savannah regions. Safaris (4WD) to

Cape York and Gulf Savannah. **Visitor information:** Tourism Tropical North Queensland, 51 The Esplanade; (07) 4051 3588. Web site www.cairns. gov.au **See also:** Great Barrier Reef p. 455; The Far North p. 461; National Parks p. 498.

Caloundra   Pop. 28 329

MAP REF. 516 H6, 519 I13, 525 Q7

This popular holiday spot on the Sunshine Coast is 95 km N of Brisbane, via a turn-off from the Bruce Hwy. The main beaches are Kings, Shelly, Moffat, Dicky, Golden and Bulcock. The main shipping channel to Brisbane is just offshore. Pumicestone Channel (State Marine Park) to the south, between Bribie Island and the mainland, has sheltered waters for fishing, boating, water-skiing and sailboarding. **In town:** Queensland Air Museum at airport, Pathfinder Dr. Scenic flights available from airport. Market at Caloundra Hospital grounds, West Tce, each Sun. May: Glass House Mountains Discovery Day (family entertainment). Aug.: Art and Craft Show. **In the area:** Scenic drives: north along coastal strip; west to Blackall Range; south-west to Glass House Mountains National Park. Wreck of SS *Dicky* (1893), Dicky Beach, 3 km N. Currimundi Lake Conservation Park, 4 km N. Pt Cartwright Lookout, 15 km N. Opals Down Under and House of Herbs, Bruce Hwy, 15 km NW. Aussie World incorporating Ettamogah Pub, Bruce Hwy, 16 km NW. **Visitor information:** 7 Caloundra Rd; (07) 5491 0202, freecall 1800 644 969. Web site www. caloundra. qld.gov.au **See also:** Sunshine Coast p. 453; National Parks p. 498.

Civic Club, relic of Charters Towers' golden past

Camooweal   Pop. 258

MAP REF. 433 R11, 532 B2

On the Barkly Hwy, 188 km NW of Mount Isa, Camooweal is the last Qld town before crossing the NT border, 13 km W. **In town:** On Barkly Hwy: Shire Hall (1922–23), The Drovers Store, Barkly Tableland Heritage Centre, and Freckleton's Store (1901); all National Trust-classified. Ellen Finlay Park, Morrison St, has shady trees ideal for picnics. July: Drovers Reunion Festival. **In the area:** Cemetery, 1 km E on hwy, headstones tell local history. Caves in Camooweal Caves National Park, 25 km S; challenge to experienced pot-holers. **Visitor information:** Post Office, Barkly St; (07) 4748 2110. Web site www.outbackholidays.tq.com.au **See also:** Outback & Gulf Country p. 464.

Cardwell   Pop. 1421

MAP REF. 521 D5, 529 N10

From Cardwell, 52 km N of Ingham, there are beautiful views of Rockingham Bay and the Great Barrier Reef islands in the region. Excellent fishing and snorkelling. The Channel is a sheltered area for house-boats. **In town:** Museum (part of library), Victoria St. At Port Hinchinbrook, 1 km S on Bruce Hwy: departure point for cruises to nearby islands including Hinchinbrook Island (camping, early booking essential, 4-day walk available); houseboat and yacht hire, contact information centre. National Parks Office, Victoria St, information about local national parks and Great Barrier Reef Marine Park. Market on

Cardwell Esplanade, 1st Sat. each month. June: Coral Sea Memorial. **In the area:** Scenic drives in Cardwell Forest (spectacular coastal scenery), and Kirrama Range, 9–10 km N, on Kennedy Rd. Murray Falls in State Forest Park, 42 km NW; also camping and picnic areas. Blencoe Falls, 71 km E. Camping and boat hire on Goold and Garden islands. **Visitor information:** Bruce Hwy, Tully; (07) 4068 2288. Web site www.speak.com.au/cardwell **See also:** Great Barrier Reef p. 455; The Mid-Tropics p. 460.

Charleville   Pop. 3327

MAP REF. 524 B6

Charleville marks the terminus of the Westlander rail service and is at the centre of a rich sheep and cattle district. The Warrego River was explored by Edmund Kennedy in 1847, and in 1862 William Landsborough camped nearby when searching for Burke and Wills. By the late 1890s Charleville had its own brewery, 10 hotels and 500 regis-tered bullock teams. Cobb & Co. had a coach-building factory here in 1893. The last coach on Australian roads ran to Surat in 1923. A monument 19 km NW of the town marks the spot where Ross and Keith Smith landed with engine trouble on the first London–Sydney flight in 1919. Amy Johnson also landed here in 1920. Qantas started flights from Charleville in 1922. The town is the heart of Mulga Country; the mulga provide shade, and during drought are cut for sheep fodder. **In town:** Self-guide heritage

walk (brochures available), and guided tours (available most days, check with information centre). In Alfred St: Historic House Museum in restored Qld National Bank building (1880), features 5-m-long 'vortex gun' used in unsuccessful rain-making experiments in 1902; Cobb & Co. coach and craft shop. Outback Queensland Skywatch at Meteorological Bureau at airport, Sturt St, features galac-tic theatre and telescope garden; guided 'Tour of the Night Sky'. Parks and Wildlife Service Centre, Park St: captive breeding programme, rare yellow-footed rock wallabies, bilbies; open Mon.–Fri; bilby tours 4 nights per week Apr.–Oct. (check times). Royal Flying Doctor Service Base and Visitors Centre, Old Cunnamulla Rd. Market, Historic House Museum, 1st Sun. each month. May: Show. July: Great Matilda Camel Races (and festival). **In the area:** Scenic and nature lovers' self-guide drives, brochures available. **Visitor information:** Cunnamulla Rd; (07) 4654 3057. Web site www.outback holidays.tq.com.au **See also:** Outback & Gulf Country p. 464.

Charters Towers   Pop. 8893

MAP REF. 521 E12, 526 E2

Charters Towers is situated in the Burdekin basin, 132 km SW of Townsville, on both the Flinders Hwy and the rail line to Mount Isa. At the height of the gold rush, it was Queensland's second largest city. With a cosmopolitan population of 30 000 it was commonly referred to as 'The World'. On 25 December 1871 an Aboriginal boy, Jupiter, made the first gold strike while looking for lost horses. He brought gold-laden quartz to his employer, Hugh Mosman, who rode to Ravenswood to register the claim, and the gold rush was on. Between 1872 and 1916, Charters Towers produced ore worth 25 million pounds. Today mining and cattle-raising are the main industries in the area; several large goldmines are operating, the result of another gold boom. The town is also an important centre for education. **In town:** Much classic Australian architecture with verandahs and lacework, particularly facades in Mosman and Gill sts. In Mosman St: Zara Clark Museum, for local history; Stock Exchange (1887), now home to National Trust and Mining Museum; Bank of Commerce (1891) now restored as New World Theatre complex (tours daily). Guided town walks, daily from information centre. Historic homes: Ay-Ot Lookout (1886), Hodgkinson St; Pfeiffer House (1880), Paull St. Civic Club (1900), Ryan St, remarkably preserved interior with original furnishings including 2 full-sized snooker tables. Venus Gold Battery, Millchester Rd, guided tours. Rotary Lookout, Fraser St. Showgrounds Markets, cnr Mary and Show sts, 2nd Sun. each month. National Trust Markets, Stock Exchange, 1st and 3rd Sun. each month. Jan.: Goldfield Ashes Cricket Carnival. Easter: Rodeo. Apr.–May: Towers Bonza Bash (festival including music and bush poets). May: Country Music Festival. June: Annual Vintage Car Restorers' Swap Meet. **In the area:** Guided bus tours (daily, check times). Towers Hill, 1.5 km W along Mosman St, has old mine shafts and ammunition bunkers from WW II. Mt Leyshon goldmine, 30 km S, tours Wed. Great Basalt Wall, part of the Great Basalt Wall National Park, 80 km NW, 4-million-year-old solidified lava wall extending 100 km. **Visitor information:** Mosman St; (07) 4752 0314. Web site www.charterstowers.qld.gov.au **See also:** The Mid-Tropics p. 460.

Childers
Pop. 1483

MAP REF. 525 O3

Childers is a picturesque sugar town, 53 km S of Bundaberg. Much of it was destroyed by fire in 1902; today it is a National Trust town. **In town:** Historic Childers, self-guide town walk taking in historic buildings, including Old Butcher's Shop (1896), North St, and Grand and Federal hotels, Churchill St. Also in Churchill St: Gaydon's Building (1894), now Pharmaceutical Museum, art gallery and tourist centre. Royal Hotel, Randall St. Historic Complex, Taylor St, includes school, cottage and locomotive. May: Agricultural Show. July: Multicultural Food and Wine Festival. **In the area:** Burrum Coast National Park, 40 km E. Isis Central Sugar Mill, Cordalba, 10 km N; tours July–Nov. **Visitor information:** 90 Churchill St; (07) 4126 1994. Web site www.bdtdb. com.au **See also:** Capricorn p. 458.

Chillagoe
Pop. 250

MAP REF. 529 K7

Chillagoe, once a thriving town where copper, silver, lead, gold and wolfram were mined, is now a small outback town where tourism, marble mines and the Red Dome goldmine have returned the town to some of its former glory. **In town:** Guided historical walking tours of town and Smelters Reserve. Local museum, Hill St: history of town, incl. display of relics from old mining days. May: Races, Concert and Rodeo. **In the area:** 4WD self-guide adventure trek, mud maps and clues provided. Full- and half-day tag-along tours: Aboriginal culture, history, geology, marble quarries. Rugged limestone outcrops and magnificent caves in Chillagoe–Mungana Caves National Park, 7 km S: cave system, originally an ancient coral reef, is studied by scientists world-wide; guided tours. At Mungana, 16 km W, Aboriginal rock paintings and historic cemetery. **Visitor information:** 7 Hill St; (07) 4094 7109. Web site www.athertontableland.com **See also:** The Far North p. 461.

Chinchilla
Pop. 3247

MAP REF. 525 K7

Chinchilla is a prosperous town in the western Darling Downs, 295 km NW of Brisbane on the Warrego Hwy. Ludwig Leichhardt named the area in 1844 after *jinchilla*, the local Aboriginal name for cypress pines. Grain-growing is the traditional industry, as well as cattle, sheep, pigs, timber and, more recently, grapes, cotton and watermelons. **In town:** Historical Museum, Villiers St, features working steam engines, sawmill and slab cottage (1880s). Newman's Collection of Petrified Wood, Boyd St. Market, Warrego Hwy, Easter Saturday. Feb.: Melon Festival (odd-numbered years). May: Rotary May Day Carnival. July: Polocrosse Carnival. Oct.: Heritage Day. **In the area:** Fishing on Charley's Creek and Condamine River. Guided tours of surrounding area. Cactoblastis Memorial Hall, at Boonarga, 8 km E, dedicated to the insect introduced to eradicate the prickly pear cactus. Fossicking for petrified wood, treefern and agate at 3 district properties. **Visitor information:** Chinchilla St; (07) 4668 9564. **See also:** Darling Downs p. 452; National Parks p. 498.

Clermont
Pop. 2388

MAP REF. 526 H9

Clermont, named after the French town, is the centre of a fertile region which breeds cattle and sheep, and grows wheat, sorghum, cotton, safflower and sunflower as well as hardwood timber. The township, 274 km SW of Mackay, was established over 130 years ago after the discovery of gold. At first the settlement was at Hoods Lagoon, but it was moved after a major flood in 1916 in which 60 people died. Remnants of the gold rushes can still be seen. **In town:** Scenic and historical drive, tape from information centre. Hoods Lagoon, Lime St on northern edge of town: Mary MacKillop Grotto; boardwalk and walking track; birdlife. Also on northern outskirts, cemetery with historic mass grave. Aug.: Gold Festival. **In the area:** Fossicking for gold. Clermont and District Historical Museum, 4 km NW on road to Charters Towers. Blair Athol open-cut mine, 23 km NW, largest seam of steaming coal in the world; mine tours (Tues. and Fri.); wildlife sanctuary at mine. Copperfield Store museum, 7 km S, in original shop from coppermining era. Copperfield Chimney, 8 km SW, chimney from coppermining days. Copperfield Cemetery, 10 km SW, 19th-century graves of copper miners; monument to those who died in the district. Theresa Creek Dam, 17 km SW: water-skiing and fishing, picnic areas and bushwalks nearby. **Visitor information:** Capella St; (07) 4983 1406. **See also:** The Mid-Tropics p. 460.

Clifton
Pop. 833

MAP REF. 525 N10

Located between Toowoomba and Warwick, Clifton is the centre of a rich grain-growing and dairying area. **In town:** Historic buildings: Club Hotel (1889), King St; Church of St James and St John (1890s), cnr Tooth St and Meara Pl. Museum in old butter factory, King St: early implements and farm life; open by appt. Alister Clark Rose Garden, Edward St, largest Qld collection of these roses. Oct.: Rose and Iris Show. **In the area:** Peanut factory, 5 km E, tours. Arthur Hoey Davis (Steele Rudd), author of *On Our Selection*, grew up at Greenmount East, 25 km N. At Nobby, 8 km N: burial site of Sister Kenny, renowned for her unorthodox method of treating poliomyelitis; Sister Kenny Memorial and Museum. Rudd's Pub (1893), where Arthur Hoey Davis used to write, has museum in dining room. Tourist drive through 'Steele Rudd country'. At Leyburn, 30 km W, Historic Race Car Sprints in Aug. **Visitor information:** Shire Offices, 70 King St; (07) 4697 4222. Web site www.clifton.qld.gov.au **See also:** Darling Downs p. 452.

Chinese shrine, Cooktown

Cloncurry   Pop. 2459

MAP REF. 532 G4

Cloncurry is an important mining town, 118 km E of Mount Isa in the Gulf Savannah region, with an interesting history and on the brink of another mining boom. In 1861 John McKinlay, leading a search for Burke and Wills, reported traces of copper. Six years later, pastoralist Ernest Henry discovered the first copper lodes. A rail link to Townsville was built in 1908. During WW I, Cloncurry was the centre of a copper boom and in 1916 it was the largest source of copper in Australia, with 4 smelters operating. Copper prices slumped post-war and a pastoral industry took its place. In 1920 a new Qantas air service linked Cloncurry to Winton. In 1928 the town became the first base for the famous Royal Flying Doctor Service (RFDS). In 1979 a rare type of pure 22-carat gold, was discovered and is now used for making jewellery. The region is mainly cattle country, and Cloncurry is a major railhead for transporting stock. **In town:** John Flynn Place, Daintree St, includes Fred McKay Art Gallery and RFDS Museum, cultural centre, outdoor theatre and Cloncurry Gardens. Cloncurry–Mary Kathleen Memorial Park, McIlwraith St: 4 buildings from abandoned uranium mining town of Mary Kathleen; historic items including Robert O'Hara Burke's water bottle; comprehensive rock, mineral and gem collection. Cloister of Plaques (RFDS memorial), Uhr St. In Schaeffe St: Post Office (1885); Courthouse (1898). Afghan Cemetery, Henry St. Chinese Cemetery, Flinders Hwy. In Sir Hudson Fyshe Dr.: old Qantas hangar at aerodrome; cattleholding yards. Market, at Florence Park, Scarr St, 1st Sat. each month. June: Agricultural Show. July: Stockman's Challenge and Campdraft (incl. Night Rodeo); Country Music and Bush Poets Festival. Aug.: Merry Muster Rodeo. **In the area:** Rotary Lookout, 2 km W near Normanton Rd turn-off, Mt Isa Hwy. Burke and Wills cairn near Corella River, 43 km W. Great Australia Copper Mine, 2 km S (tours). Kuridala ghost town, 88 km S; amethyst fossicking a further 8 km, signposted. Ernest Henry Copper and Gold Mine, 29 km NE (tours, inquire at information centre). Ruins of Mount Cuthbert, goldmining town, 10 km from Kajabbi (77 km NW); at Kajabbi, Yabby Races in May. **Visitor information:** Mary Kathleen Memorial Museum & Park, McIlwraith St; (07) 4742 1361. Web site www.outbackholidays.tq.com.au **See also:** Outback & Gulf Country p. 464.

Cooktown   Pop. 1411

MAP REF. 529 L3

Captain James Cook beached the *Endeavour* here in 1770 for repairs, after running aground on the Great Barrier Reef. Gold was discovered at Palmer River in 1873 and by 1877 Cooktown was a gold-rush port with 37 hotels and a transient population of some 18 000 a year, including 6000 Chinese. Cooktown today has 3 hotels and the main industry is tourism. Located 342 km NW of Cairns, it is the departure point for Cape York Peninsula. The district is good agriculturally and the town is also supported by prawning and fishing. **In town:** Cooktown Wharf, dates from 1880s, excellent fishing location. Historic cemetery, Boundary Rd, with grave of tutor, early immigrant and heroine Mary Watson; nearby, Chinese Shrine to the many who died on the goldfields. Grassy Hill, Hope St, offers views across the reef, township and hinterland. James Cook Historical Museum, Helen St: collection tracing town's white-settler history; anchor from the *Endeavour*. Cooktown Museum, cnr Helen and Walker sts: maritime history of area; shell collection. Cooktown Botanic Gardens, Walker St. Markets at Endeavour Lions Park, every 2nd Sat. June: Endeavour Festival (long weekend), with re-enactment of Cook's landing. July: Laura–Cape York Aboriginal Dance Festival (odd-numbered years). July: Polocrosse Carnival. **In the area:** Snorkelling and diving tours to Outer Reef; fishing charters; river cruises. Walking trails to Cherry Tree Bay and Finch Bay start at Botanic Gardens; brochures on other local walks available. Bicentennial National Trail (5000 km) for walkers and horseriders, runs from Cooktown to Healesville in Vic. Endeavour River National Park, just north of town. Black Mountain, 28 km S. Spectacular white silica Elim Beach, 65 km N; Coloured Sands 400 m along beach (Aboriginal Land, permit required), check road conditions. Lakefield National Park, 146 km NW: river, lagoon and swamp habitat for a variety of wildlife, crucial for crocodile conservation; camping at Hann and Kalpowar crossings; access via Laura for conventional vehicles during the Dry. Beautiful sandstone escarpments at Split Rock and Gu Gu Yalangi rock-art sites, 12 km S of Laura (134 km W of Cooktown), perhaps the largest Aboriginal art site in Australia; guided tours of hundreds of cave paintings. Old Laura Homestead, 27 km N of Laura. Offshore, Lizard Island, 90 km NE, offers resort, national park and secluded beaches; access by air. **Visitor information:** 101 Charlotte St; (07) 4069 5446, freecall 1800 001 770. Web site www.tnq.org.au **See also:** Great Barrier Reef p. 455; The Far North p. 461; National Parks p. 498.

Coolangatta   Pop. 6618

MAP REF. 517 H13, 518 I11, 525 Q11

Coolangatta is the most southerly of Qld's coastal towns, with its twin town of Tweed Heads across the border in NSW. **In town:** May–June: Gold Coast Cup Outrigger Canoe Marathon. June: Wintersun Festival. **In the area:** Excellent surfing beaches. Scenic drive, brochure available. Coolangatta Airport, Bilinga, services Gold Coast for domestic flights, charters, joy flights and tandem skydiving. Captain

Cook Memorial Lighthouse, North Head. Tom Beaston Outlook (Razorback Lookout), behind Tweed Heads, for excellent views. **Visitor information:** Gold Coast Tourism Bureau, Shop 14B, Coolangatta Pl., cnr Griffith and Warner sts; (07) 5536 7765. Web site www. goldcoasttourism.com.au **See also:** Gold Coast & Hinterland p. 450.

Crows Nest   Pop. 1214

MAP REF. 525 N8

This small town, 44 km N of Toowoomba, was named after Jimmy Crow, a Kabi-Kabi Aboriginal who made his home in a hollow tree near the present police station; memorial in Centenary Park. **In town:** John French VC Memorial Library, William St. In Thallon St: Carbethon Folk Museum and Pioneer Village; Salts Antiques, open weekends. Oct.: Crows Nest Day (children's worm races, fun run, painting competitions). **In the area:** Walking and bike tracks to Toowoomba, map available. Crows Nest National Park, 6 km E (look for sign to Valley of Diamonds): walking tracks to falls, picnic and camping facilities. Ravensbourne National Park, 25 km SE, has red cedars and picnic areas. **Visitor information:** Toowoomba Information Centre, cnr James and Kitchener sts, Toowoomba; (07) 4639 3797, freecall 1800 331 155. **See also:** Darling Downs p. 452.

Croydon   Pop. 223

MAP REF. 528 F10

This Gulf town, 559 km SW of Cairns, is the eastern terminus for the *Gulflander* train service, which leaves each Thurs. for Normanton. In town, many original buildings (1887–97), classified by National Trust and Australian Heritage Commission, have been restored to the splendour of goldmining days. **In town:** In Samwell St: Old Police Precinct incl. gaol (housing Tourist and Family History Information Centre), Hospital Museum; courthouse with original furniture and historical documents; Town Hall with murals; Outdoor Museum, featuring a display of mining machinery from the age of steam; gas lamps on footpath. Hospital Ward (now a meeting place), Brown St. General Store and Museum, Sircom St. Self-guide and guided town walks. June: Rodeo. Aug.: Camp Draft. Sept.: Poddy Dodger Music Festival week. **In the area:** Working Mine Museum including battery stamper,

1 km N. Old cemetery, 1 km W, has historic graves. Lake Belmore, 5 km N, one of many sites for birdwatching. **Visitor information:** Samwell St; (07) 4745 6125. Web site www.gulf-savannah. com.au **See also:** Outback & Gulf Country p. 464.

Cunnamulla   Pop. 1461

MAP REF. 524 A10, 535 R10

Cunnamulla is near the Warrego River, 118 km N of the NSW border. It is the biggest wool-loading station on the Qld railway network, with 2 million sheep in the area, plus beef cattle. Explorers Sir Thomas Mitchell and Edmund Kennedy were the first European visitors in 1846 and 1847 respectively. By 1879 the town had regular Cobb & Co. services. In 1880 Joseph Wells held up the local bank but could not find his escape horse. Locals bailed him up in a tree (known as 'The Robber's Tree', now a landmark in Stockyard St). **In town:** Bicentennial Museum, John St, has Historical Society display. Yupunyah Tree planted by Princess Anne, cnr Louise and Stockyard sts. Lost Generation Arts and Crafts, Stockyard St, has local Aboriginal art. Centenary Park, Jane St, has picnic/ barbecue facilities. Outback Botanic Gardens and Herbarium, on Matilda Hwy on eastern outskirts of town. Apr.: Races. Aug.: World Lizard Races. **In the area:** Wildflowers in spring; varied wetland birdlife, particularly black swans, brolgas, pelicans and eagles. At Noorama, 110 km SE, race meetings (horseracing) each Apr. At Yowah, 162 km W, Opal Festival in July. **Visitor information:** Centenary Park; (07) 4655 2481. Web site www. outbackholidays.tq.com.au **See also:** Outback & Gulf Country p. 464.

Currumbin   Pop. 2696

MAP REF. 517 H12, 518 G10, 525 Q11

Situated at the mouth of the Currumbin Creek, this Gold Coast town has many attractions. **In town:** Currumbin Wildlife Sanctuary, 20-ha reserve owned by National Trust: free-ranging animals in open areas; lorikeet feeding (twice daily); walk-through rainforest aviary with pools and waterfalls; rides through sanctuary on miniature railway. Opposite, World of Bees: live displays; walk with bees; honeymaking; products for sale. **In the area:** At Palm Beach, 2 km N, Spring Fest in Sept.; at Tallebudgera, just north, estuary and ocean swimming. Scenic drive, brochure available. David Fleay Wildlife Park, 8 km NW on West Burleigh Rd: Qld's native animals in natural settings; croc-feeding (summer); Aboriginal culture. Olson's Bird Gardens, 9 km SW in Currumbin Valley, has large landscaped aviaries in subtropical setting. Section of Springbrook National Park, 22 km SW at end of Currumbin Creek Rd, scenic rainforest area ideal for bushwalking and picnicking. **Visitor information:** Shop 14B, Coolangatta Pl., cnr Griffith and Warner sts, Coolangatta; (07) 5536 7765. **See also:** Gold Coast & Hinterland p. 450; National Parks p. 498; Wildlife-Watching p. 501.

Daintree   Pop. 200

MAP REF. 523 A1, 529 M5

This unspoilt township, 119 km NW of Cairns, lies in the heart of the Daintree River catchment basin surrounded by the McDowall Ranges. The area has abundant native plant life, birds and tropical butterflies. Australia's prehistoric reptile, the saltwater crocodile, can be seen in the mangrove-lined creeks

Saltwater crocodile, a resident of the Daintree River

and tributaries of the Daintree River. **In town:** Daintree Timber Museum. Local art and craft. River cruises; vehicular ferry, one of last cable ferries in Australia. **In the area:** Wonga-Belle Orchid Gardens, 17 km SE, 3.5 ha of lush gardens. Daintree Rainforest Environmental Centre, 11 km N via ferry, has boardwalk through rainforest. Cape Tribulation, 35 km NE, where rainforest meets reef: features crystal-clear creeks; forests festooned with creepers and vines; palm trees; orchids; butterflies; cassowaries; Dubuji Boardwalk (1.2 km); Kulki Boardwalk and Lookout. Bloomfield Falls, 85 km N, via Cape Tribulation. **Visitor information:** Port Douglas Daintree Tourism Association, 40 Macrossan St, Port Douglas; (07) 4099 4588. Web site www.tnq.org.au **See also:** The Far North p. 461.

Dalby   Pop. 9517

MAP REF. 525 M8

Dalby, 83 km NW of Toowoomba on the Darling Downs, is at the crossroads of the Warrego, Bunya and Moonie hwys. It is the centre of Australia's richest grain- and cotton-growing area. Cattle, pigs, sheep and coal add wealth to the district. **In town:** Pioneer Park Museum, Black St: historic buildings; household and agricultural items; craft shop. Obelisk in Edward St marks spot where explorer Henry Dennis camped in 1841. Cairn in Myall Creek picnic area, Marble St, pays homage to the cactoblastis, the Argentinian caterpillar which eradicated prickly pear in the 1920s. Cultural and Administration Centre, Drayton St, includes theatre, cinema, art gallery and restaurant. Self-guide heritage walk and self-guide drive, brochures available. Walkway along banks of Myall Creek; varied birdlife. Mar.: Cotton Week. **In the area:** Lake Broadwater Conservation Park, 29 km SW: boating and water-skiing on lake when full; 3-km walk; tower for birdwatching; picnic/barbecue facilities; camping. Historic Jimbour House, 29 km N, grounds open daily except in wet weather. Rimfire Vineyards and Winery, 47 km NE, tastings daily. Bunya Mountains National Park, 60 km NE, walking tracks and waterfalls. **Visitor information:** Thomas Jack Park, cnr Drayton and Condamine sts; (07) 4662 1066. Web site www.dalby town.com **See also:** Darling Downs p. 452; National Parks p. 498.

Emerald   Pop. 9345

MAP REF. 526 I11

An attractive town 270 km W of Rockhampton at the junction of the Capricorn and Gregory hwys, Emerald is the hub of the Central Highlands. The largest sapphire fields in the Southern Hemisphere are nearby. As well as the cattle industry, grain, oilseeds and soybeans, cotton and citrus fruit are important. **In town:** Shady Moreton Bay fig trees line Clermont and Egerton sts. National Trust-classified railway station (1901), Clermont St. Pioneer Cottage and Museum, Harris St. Pastoral College, Capricorn Hwy. Easter: Sunflower Festival. June: Wheelbarrow Derby (odd-numbered years). Aug.: Gemfest. Sept.: Music Spectacular. **In the area:** Day tours of local cattle stations, and farm stays. Fossicking for gems, licence required. At Rubyvale, 60 km NW: Miner's Heritage Walk-in Mine, tours of underground sapphire mine and gem-cutting displays; Bobby Dazzler Walk-in Mine, also has museum and shop; various gem outlets; 4WD tours of Tomahawk Creek gemfields and other local gemfields. At Capella, 51 km NW: Capella Pioneer Village, includes Peak Downs Homestead (1869), first settlement in area; Capella Pioneer Village Arts and Crafts Fair in Apr. Lake Maraboon/Fairbairn Dam, 19 km S, for fishing and water sports. At Springsure, 66 km S: Aboriginal Yumba–Brin Crypt in Cemetery Reserve; historic schoolhouse, storehouse and slab homestead at Old Rainworth Historical Complex, also a commemoration of 1861 Wills Massacre of Aboriginals, the worst in nation's history, which occurred 30 km NW. Carnarvon National Park, 250 km S: 2 major Aboriginal art sites; dramatic Carnarvon Gorge; camping; ranger tours. **Visitor information:** Clermont St; (07) 4982 4142. **See also:** Capricorn p. 458; National Parks p. 498.

Esk   Pop. 953

MAP REF. 516 B10, 525 O8

Esk, in the Upper Brisbane Valley, is 99 km NW of Brisbane. The valley is renowned for its beautiful lakes and dams. **In town:** Numerous antique and local craft shops. Market, Old Hay Barn, Ipswich St, each Sat. July: Picnic Races. **In the area:** Lakes and dams: Lake Somerset (25 km NE); Lake Wivenhoe (25 km E), source of Brisbane's main water supply; Atkinson Dam (30 km S); all popular swimming, fishing and

boating spots. Lake Wivenhoe is State's main centre for championship rowing. At Coominya, 22 km SE: historic Bellevue Homestead; Watermelon Festival in Jan. Boss Camel Races in Sept. Clydesdale Bush Carnival in Oct., 44 km SE near Lowood. Further north, fine grazing country; progeny of a small herd of deer presented to the State by Queen Victoria in 1873 still roam. Caboonbah Homestead (1890), 19 km NE, headquarters of Brisbane Valley Historical Society; closed Thurs. **Visitor information:** Shire Offices, 2 Redbank St; (07) 5424 1200. **See also:** Brisbane Hinterland p. 448.

Eulo   Pop. 42

MAP REF. 535 Q11

Once the centre for opal mining in the area, Eulo is on the banks of the Paroo River, 68 km W of Cunnamulla. **In town:** In Leo St: Eulo Queen Hotel, owes its name to Isobel Robinson who ran the hotel and virtually reigned over the opal fields at the turn of the 20th century; WW II air-raid shelter, in grounds of General Store. Eulo Date Farm, western outskirts of town (open Aug.–Sept.). Destructo Cockroach Monument, commemorates death of a champion racing cockroach. Aug.: World Lizard Races. **In the area:** At Yowah, 87 km NW: visitors' fossicking area; tours of Fossickers' Paradise open-cut mine; views from The Bluff; Craft Day in June; Opal Festival in July (includes international opal jewellery competition). Mud Springs, 7 km W, natural pressure valve to artesian basin, currently inactive. Lake Bindegolly, in Lake Bindegolly National Park, 100 km W, for birdwatching. Thargomindah, 130 km W; mud map at information centre for Burke and Wills 'Dig' Tree site. Noccundra waterhole on Wilson River, 260 km W, has good fishing. Currawinya National Park, 60 km SW, for birdwatching and fishing. **Visitor information:** Centenary Park, Cunnamulla; (07) 4655 2481. Web site www. outbackholidays.tq.com.au **See also:** Outback & Gulf Country p. 464.

Gatton   Pop. 5328

MAP REF. 525 O9

First settled by Europeans in the 1840s, this agricultural town in the Lockyer Valley is midway between Ipswich and Toowoomba, and 90 km W of Brisbane via the Warrego Hwy. Small-crop farming and vegetable production are the main industries. **In town:** May: Clydesdale and Heavy Horse Field Days. Oct.: Potato Carnival. **In the area:** Agricultural College (University of Queensland), 5 km E, opened 1897. Helidon, 16 km W, noted for its sandstone, used in many Brisbane buildings, and for its spa water. Grantham, 8 km SW, known for fresh fruit and vegetables; many roadside stalls offer local produce. Tourist drive (82-km circuit) through surrounding countryside, includes visits to farms. **Visitor information:** Lake Apex Dr.; (07) 5462 3430. **See also:** Brisbane Hinterland p. 448.

Gayndah
Pop. 1781

MAP REF. 525 N4

Gayndah is one of Qld's oldest towns, founded 1849. It is near the Burnett River, 147 km W of Maryborough, in a significant citrus-growing area. **In town:** Original school (1863), still in use. Historical Museum, Simon St, incl. Ban Ban Springs Homestead and Ideraway Homestead (both 1850s). June: Orange Festival (odd-numbered years). **In the area:** Several 1890s homesteads. Claude Warton Weir Recreation Area, 3 km W, for fishing and picnics. Natural springs at Ban Ban Springs, 26 km S, a popular picnic area. **Visitor information:** Historical Museum, 3 Simon St; (07) 4161 2226. **See also:** Capricorn p. 458.

Georgetown
Pop. 298

MAP REF. 528 I10

Georgetown is on the Gulf Developmental Rd to Croydon and Normanton. It was once one of many small gold-mining towns on the Etheridge Goldfield. The area is now noted for its gemstones, especially agate and gold nuggets. **In town:** Jan. and Dec.: Turf Club Races. May: Camp Draft. Oct.: Bushman's Ball. **In the area:** From Forsayth, 40 km S, train trip on *Savannahlander* to Cairns, departs Friday. Cobbold Gorge, 75 km S: boat tours on river through gorge; camping. Gemfields at Agate Creek, 95 km S, and O'Briens Creek, 129 km NE. Tallaroo hot springs, 55 km E; tours of surrounding property. Undara Volcanic National Park, 129 km E: birdlife; unique lava tubes, access only with guide; nearby Undara Lava Lodge has camping/caravan facilities and accommodation in converted railway carriages. **Visitor information:** Etheridge Shire Offices, St George St; (07) 4062 1233. Web site www.gulf-savannah.com.au **See also:** Outback & Gulf Country p. 464.

Unique geological formations at Undara Volcanic National Park near Georgetown

Gin Gin
Pop. 958

MAP REF. 525 N2

Some of Qld's oldest cattle properties are in the area around this pastoral town on the Bruce Hwy, 51 km SW of Bundaberg. The district is known as Wild Scotchman Country, after James McPherson, Qld's only authentic bushranger. **In town:** Historical Society Museum Complex, Mulgrave St: The Residence, former police sergeant's house now displaying pioneering memorabilia; 'The Bunyip', old sugar-cane locomotive, part of historic railway display. March: Wild Scotchman Festival. June: Mount Perry Mountain Cup (mountain-bike race). **In the area:** Mystery Craters, 27 km NE on the Bundaberg Rd, 35 craters about 25 million years old. Lake Monduran, 24 km NW, held back by Fred Haigh Dam (Qld's second largest), for boating and picnics. Boolboonda Tunnel, 27 km W, longest non-supported tunnel in Southern Hemisphere; now part of scenic tourist drive; brochure available. Goodnight Scrub National Park, 25 km SW: dense hoop pine forest; bottle trees; historic Kalliwa Hut; good views. **Visitor information:** Mulgrave St; (07) 4157 3060. Web site www.bdtdb.com.au **See also:** Capricorn p. 458.

Gladstone
Pop. 26 415

MAP REF. 527 P12

Matthew Flinders discovered Port Curtis, Gladstone's deep-water harbour, in 1802, but it did not develop until the 1960s. As an outlet for central Qld's mineral and agricultural wealth, Gladstone, 546 km NW of Brisbane, is a prosperous seaboard city; its harbour is one of Australia's busiest. The world's largest single alumina refinery is at Parsons Point, where bauxite from Weipa on the Gulf of Carpentaria is processed annually into alumina. A large power station in Gladstone supplies power to the refinery and smelter and feeds into the State's electricity grid. Chemical processing is a new regional industry. Gladstone is close to the southern section of the Great Barrier Reef and Heron Island, and is known for its mud crabs and prawns. **In town:** In Goondoon St: historic Kullaroo House (1911); Radar Hill Lookout. Gladstone Regional Art Gallery and Museum, cnr Goondoon and Bramston sts. Potter's Place, Dawson Hwy, art and craft. In Glenlyon Rd: Tondoon Botanic Gardens, has only native species (tours weekends); next to gardens, Gecko Valley Vineyard (tastings and sales); Reg Tana Park, incl. Railway Dam. Barney Point Beach and Friend Park, Barney St. Waterfall, end Auckland

St, floodlit at night. Auckland Hill Lookout, Harbour Tce, has views of harbour and islands. Round Hill Lookout, Boles St, West Gladstone. Auckland Inlet offers anchorage alongside James Cook Park. Marina, Marina Dr., departure point for daily Barrier Reef dive and fishing trips and harbour cruises. Easter: Harbour Festival (incl. finish of Brisbane–Gladstone Yacht Race). May: Seventeen Seventy Commemorative Festival. Aug.: Multicultural Festival. Oct.: Seafood festival. **In the area:** Tours of major industries; bookings at information centre. Curtis Island, north of town in Gladstone Harbour, is a family recreation area. Sea or air access to Heron Island: charter boat to North West Island. Nearby towns of Boyne Island and Tannum Sands are linked by bridge. Boyne Island has beautiful foreshore parks and beaches; Boyne Aluminium Smelter on island has information centre and guided tours; Boyne–Tannum Hookup Fishing Competition in June. Tannum Sands offers sandy beaches with year-round swimming; Gladstone Triathlon here in Oct. Various national parks in region, maps available. Spectacular views from Mt Larcom summit, 33 km W. Port Curtis Historical Village, 26 km SW at Calliope River; major art and craft markets on selected Sundays. Lake Awoonga, 30 km S: picnic and camping areas; water-based recreation; walking trail; wildlife; Catfish Festival each Jan. Many Peaks, historic town, 80 km SE. **Visitor information:** Ferry Terminal, Bryan Jordan Dr.; (07) 4972 4000. Web site www.gladstoneregion.org.au **See also:** Great Barrier Reef p. 455; Capricorn p. 458; National Parks p. 498.

Goondiwindi
Pop. 4374

MAP REF. 106 H2, 525 K11

This country town at the junction of 6 highways is beside the picturesque MacIntyre River, which explorer Allan Cunningham reached in 1827 and which forms the State border. The Aboriginal word *goonawinna* means 'resting place of the birds'. The district's thriving economy is based on cotton, wheat, beef and wool, and a growing manufacturing sector. **In town:** Statue of famous racehorse Gunsynd, the 'Goondiwindi Grey', in Apex Park, MacIntyre St. Customs House Museum, opposite park. Historic Victoria Hotel, Marshall St. Tours of Bulk Grains depot and cotton gin (by appt, in season).

Walking track along riverbank, brochure available. Markets, in Town Park, Marshall St, 2nd Sun. each month. Feb.: Hell of the West Triathlon. Sept.: Rodeo. Oct.: Spring Festival (coincides with flowering of jacarandas and silky oaks). **In the area:** Botanic Gardens of Western Woodlands (25 ha), access from Brennans Rd, 1 km W. **Visitor information:** McLean St; (07) 4671 2653. Web site www.qldsoutherndowns.org.au **See also:** Darling Downs p. 452.

Gordonvale
Pop. 3682

MAP REF. 523 F10, 529 N7

This town is 24 km S of Cairns. **In town:** Mulgrave Sugar Mill, Gordon St, tours June–Nov. **In the area:** Gillies Hwy, with 295 bends, leads west to Atherton. Goldsborough Valley State Forest, 6 km W (15 km off Gillies Hwy), for walking, swimming, canoeing and picnicking. Wooroonooran National Park, 10 km S, spectacular views from summit of Walsh's Pyramid. Orchid Valley Nursery and Gardens, 15 km SW, tropical gardens and coffee shop; tours. **Visitor information:** Babinda Information Centre, cnr Bruce Hwy and Munro St, Babinda; (07) 4067 1008. **See also:** The Far North p. 461; National Parks p. 498.

Gympie
Pop. 10 813

MAP REF. 525 P6

James Nash discovered gold here in 1867. The field proved extremely rich: 4 million ounces had been found by the time the gold petered out in the 1920s. By then dairying and agriculture were well established. On the banks of the Mary River and 162 km N of Brisbane via the Bruce Hwy, Gympie, attractive with jacarandas, silky oaks, cassias, poincianas and flame trees, is the major city servicing the Cooloola region. **In town:** Woodworks, Forestry and Timber Museum, Fraser Rd. Self-guide heritage walk. Gold-panning in Deep Creek, Counter St. Market, Gympie South State School, 2nd and 4th Sun. each month. May: Show. June: Race the Rattler (people race the steam train). Aug.: National Country Music Muster. Oct.: Gold Rush Festival. **In the area:** Historical and scenic drives, maps available. Gold Mining Museum, Brisbane Rd, 5 km S; nearby, cottage of Andrew Fisher, first Queenslander to become Prime Minister (1908). Cooloola Rocks and Minerals, Bruce Hwy, 15 km S. Amamoor State Forest Park, 30 km S,

picnics and rainforest walk. Mothar Mountain, 20 km SE, rock pools and excellent views. Imbil Forest Drive through scenic pine-forest plantations south of town. Mary Valley Scenic Way runs south between Gympie and Maleny, via Kenilworth. Mary Valley Heritage Railway operates between Gympie and Imbil. **Visitor information:** Cooloola Region Information Centre, Bruce Hwy, (near Lake Alford); (03) 5483 5554, freecall 1800 444 222. Web site www.cooloola.org.au **See also:** Sunshine Coast p. 453.

Hervey Bay
Pop. 32 054

MAP REF. 525 P3

Hervey (pronounced 'Harvey') Bay is the large area of water between Maryborough and Bundaberg that is protected by Fraser Island. It is also the name of a thriving city that comprises the seaside spots along its southern shore, some 34 km NE of Maryborough. The climate is ideal, and during winter there is an influx of visitors. Hervey Bay is promoted as 'Australia's family aquatic playground': there is no surf, swimming is safe even for children. Fishing is the main recreation; boats may be hired. **In town:** In Pialba: M. K. Model Railways, Old Maryborough Rd; Nature World Wildlife Park, Maryborough Rd, features koalas, other marsupials, lorikeets, crocodiles and other reptiles. In Scarness: Hervey Bay Historical Society Museum, Zephyr St, recalls pioneer days. In Torquay: Golf 'n' Games, Cypress St, with 18-hole mini-golf and 120-m water-slide. At Urangan: memorial at Dayman Park commemorates landing by Matthew Flinders in 1799 and the Z-Force commandos who trained there on the *Krait* in WW II; 1-km long pier, off The Esplanade, used by anglers; Neptune's Reefworld, Pulgul St, has performing seals; Vic Hislop's Shark Show, The Esplanade. Humpback whales visit Hervey Bay early Aug.–mid-Oct.; viewing cruises available. Sun. markets at Urangan and Nikenbah. Feb.: Yagubi Festival (multicultural festival). Apr.: Gladstone–Hervey Bay Blue Water Classic. Aug.: Whale Festival. Oct.: Seafood Festival. **In the area:** World Heritage-listed Fraser Island to the east: Great Sandy National Park has rainforest, sand cliffs and dunes, clear creeks and lakes (swimming in Lake MacKenzie); resort at Kingfisher Bay; access from Hervey Bay; 4WD essential; tours available. Air access to Lady Elliot Island.

Nina Peak on Hinchinbrook Island, near Ingham

Hervey Bay Marine Park, 40 km N. Quiet seaside resorts at Toogoom and Burrum Heads, 15 km NW. Historic Brooklyn House at Howard, 33 km W. **Visitor information:** 353 The Esplanade; (07) 4124 4050. Web site www.frasercoast.org **See also:** Fraser Island & Coast p. 454; National Parks p. 498; Wildlife-Watching p. 501.

Hughenden   Pop. 1444

MAP REF. 526 A4, 533 O4

The first recorded Europeans to pass this spot on the Flinders River were members of Frederick Walker's 1861 expedition to find the explorers Burke and Wills. Two years later Ernest Henry selected a cattle station here, and Hughenden came into existence. The town is on the Townsville–Mount Isa rail line and the Flinders Hwy, 243 km SW of Charters Towers. The major regional industries are beef cattle and merino wool. **In town:** Historic coolibah tree, Stansfield St East, on east bank of Station Creek: blazed by Walker in 1861, and again by William Landsborough in 1862 when he was also searching for the Burke and Wills expedition. Dinosaur Display Centre, Gray St, houses 7-m replica of *Muttaburrasaurus langdoni*. Apr.: Country Music Festival. Aug.: Dinosaur Festival (even-numbered years). Oct.: Night Rodeo. **In the area:** At Prairie, 44 km E on Flinders Hwy: mini-museum; historical relics at Cobb & Co. Yards. Torrens Creek, 88 km E: Exchange Hotel, home of 'dinosaur steaks'; WW II airstrip. Porcupine Gorge National Park,

63 km N, features 'mini Grand Canyon'. Gemstone fossicking at Chudleigh Park, 138 km N. **Visitor information:** 37 Gray St; (07) 4741 1021. Web site www. outbackholidays.tq.com. au **See also:** Outback & Gulf Country p. 464.

Ilfracombe   Pop. 198

MAP REF. 526 A11, 533 P11

This town, 27 km E of Longreach on the Matilda Hwy, was developed in 1891 as a transport nucleus for the large Wellshot Station. The first Qld motorised mail service departed from Ilfracombe in 1910. **In town:** Langenbaker House, Mitchell St, an early settler's house. Transport Heritage Museum (several sites along highway) incl.: historic Oakhampton Cottage, has local craft display; Folk Museum; Damien Curr's Back to the Bush Show (daily); extensive range of early machinery; historic Wellshot Hotel; Hilton's Bottle Display. Easter: Easter in the Outback. **Visitor information:** Shire Offices, Devon St; (07) 4658 2233. Web site ilfracombe.outbackqld.net.au **See also:** Outback & Gulf Country p. 464.

Ingham   Pop. 5012

MAP REF. 521 E6, 529 N11

A major sugar and sightseeing town near the waterways of the Hinchinbrook Channel, Ingham is on the Bruce Hwy, 109 km NW of Townsville. The town has a strong Italian and Spanish Basque cultural background. **In town:** Macknade Mill, Halifax Rd, oldest sugar mill still

operating on original site. Victoria Sugar Mill, Forrest Beach Rd, largest in Southern Hemisphere; guided tours in crushing season (July–Nov.). Botanic Gardens, Palm Tce. Raintree market, Herbert St, 3rd Sun. each month; Conroy Hall Markets, McIlwraith St, 2nd Sat. each month. May: Australian–Italian Festival. Oct.: Maraka Festival. **In the area:** Cemetery, 5 km E, has interesting Italian mausoleums. Forrest Beach, 17 km SE, 16 km of sandy beach overlooking Palm Islands; stinger net swimming enclosures installed in summer. Taylors Beach, 23 km NE, popular family seaside spot. Hinchinbrook and Orpheus resort islands offshore. Lucinda, 27 km NE on banks of Herbert River, excellent base for fishing holidays. Lumholtz National Park, 51 km NW: 305-m Wallaman Falls; spectacular scenery; walking track; camping, swimming and picnic spots. Broadwater State Forest Park, 45 km W, in the Herbert River Valley; popular camping and picnic area, incl. 1.6-km rainforest walk. Mt Fox, extinct volcano, 65 km SW. Jourama Falls in Paluma Range National Park, 25 km S; 1.5-km walk to lookout. Spectacular view from McClellands Lookout, 48 km S off Bruce Hwy. **Visitor information:** Hinchinbrook Visitors Centre, cnr Bruce Hwy & Lannercost St; (07) 4776 5211. Web site www.ace-comp.com.au/hinchinbrook **See also:** Great Barrier Reef p. 455; The Mid-Tropics p. 460; National Parks p. 498.

Innisfail   Pop. 8987

MAP REF. 521 D2, 529 N8

Innisfail is a prosperous, colourful town on the banks of the North and South Johnstone rivers, 88 km SE of Cairns. Sugar has been grown here since the early 1880s and this is celebrated with a Harvest Festival in July. The area also produces bananas, pawpaws and other tropical fruit, and beef cattle. The town has a prawn and reef fishing fleet. **In town:** Local history museum, Edith St. Chinese Joss House, Owen St. Cane Cutter Monument, Fitzgerald Espl. Warrina Lakes and Botanical Gardens, Charles St. Historic town walk, brochure available. Lovely parks with riverside picnic facilities. Market, ANZAC Memorial Park, 3rd Sat. each month. July: Agricultural Show; Harvest Festival. **In the area:** Flying Fish Point and Ella Bay, 5 km NE, swimming and camping. Johnstone River Crocodile Farm, 8 km NE. Eubenangee Swamp National Park, 29 km NE via Miriwinni, birdwatching. Bramston Beach, palm-fringed shoreline, 39 km NE.

Qld's highest peak Mt Bartle Frere (1622 m), 25 km NW in Wooroonooran National Park; track to summit; Josephine Falls at base. Johnstone River Gorge, 18 km W via Palmerston Hwy, has walking tracks to several waterfalls. Crawfords Lookout, 38 km W, off the Palmerston Hwy, spectacular views of Johnstone River. Australian Sugar Museum at Mourilyan, 7 km S. Etty Bay, 15 km S, beach and picnic area. Innisfail is an excellent base for exploration of quieter lagoons and islands (incl. Dunk) of Great Barrier Reef. Scenic drives, brochure available. **Visitor information:** Cassowary Coast Development Bureau, 1 Edith St; (07) 4061 7422. Web site www.gspeak.com.au/Innisfail **See also:** The Far North p. 461; National Parks p. 498.

Ipswich
Pop. 66 048

MAP REF. 515 C8, 517 B7, 525 P9

In 1827 a convict settlement was established alongside the Bremer River to quarry limestone. In 1842 the settlement (Limestone) opened to 'free settlers' and in 1843 it was renamed Ipswich. As well as being a major industrial centre with railways, coalmining, sawmills and foundries, Ipswich is known for its cultural and sporting activities. Australia's largest RAAF base is in the suburb of Amberley. **In town:** Numerous heritage buildings, incl. Uniting Church (1858), Ellenborough St; St Paul's Anglican Church (1859), Brisbane St; St Mary's Catholic Church (1904), Elizabeth St; Claremont (1858), Milford St; Gooloowan (1864), Quarry St; Ginn Cottage, Ginn St; Ipswich Grammar School (1863), Burnett St. Global Arts Link, cnr Limestone St and D'Arcy Doyle Pl., interactive art gallery and social history museum. Queens Park Nature Centre, Goleby Ave, native flora and fauna. Historic Rail Workshops, North St, North Ipswich: tours; original dining hall for refreshments. Self-guide historic walk, brochure available. Showground market, Warwick Rd, each Sun. Redbank Woollen Mills markets, each Sat. and Sun. June: Winternationals Drag Racing Championship. July: Ipswich Cup and Race Meeting. **In the area:** North-east: College's Crossing (7 km), Mt Crosby (12 km) and Lake Manchester (22 km) – all popular picnic spots (swimming at College's Crossing only). At Willowbank, 15 km W: Queensland Raceway, Champions Way, hosts V8 Supercar

Series. At Rosewood, 20 km W: St Brigid's Church, largest wooden church in South Pacific (tours by appt); steam-train rides, 4 km N of Rosewood, last Sun. each month. Swanbank Power Station, 12 km SE: tours by appt; steam trains run by Qld Pioneer Steam Railway Co-op, 1st Sun. each month, bookings essential. Restored historic homestead Wolston House at Wacol, 16 km E. **Visitor information:** cnr Brisbane St and D'Arcy Doyle Pl.; (07) 3281 0555. Web site www.ipswichtourism.com.au **See also:** Brisbane Hinterland p. 448.

Isisford
Pop. 150

MAP REF. 526 A13, 533 P13, 535 O1

Established in 1877 by hawkers William and James Whitman, Isisford is 116 km S of Longreach. First called Wittown, the town was renamed in 1880 to recall the nearby Barcoo River ford and Isis Downs Station. **In town:** Bicentennial Museum, Centenary Dr. **In the area:** Huge (largest in Australia) semicircular prefabricated shearing shed (1913), at Isis Downs Station, 20 km E; visits by appt. Oma Waterhole, 16 km W, popular spot for fishing and water sports. **Visitor information:** Shire Offices, St Mary St; (07) 4658 8900. Web site www.outbackholidays.tq.com.au **See also:** Outback & Gulf Country p. 464.

Julia Creek
Pop. 519

MAP REF. 533 J4

Located on the Flinders Hwy, Julia Creek is 134 km E of Cloncurry. A sealed road runs north-west to Normanton in the Gulf Savannah. The town is an important cattle-trucking and sale centre. **In town:** In Burke St: Duncan McIntyre Museum; Dunnart Craft Store, local art and craft. May: Julia Creek Dirt and Dust Triathlon; Campdraft (cattle drafting competition with horseriders). **In the area:** Punch Bowl, 40 km NE, waterhole picnic area. Saxby Roundup each June at Taldora Station, an isolated area 230 km N; access via Julia Creek. **Visitor information:** Shire Offices, 29 Burke St; (07) 4746 7166. Web site www.outbackholidays.tq.com.au **See also:** Outback & Gulf Country p. 464.

Jundah
Pop. 100

MAP REF. 535 M2

Jundah (Aboriginal for 'women'), 217 km SW of Longreach, was gazetted as a town in 1880. For 20 years the area was

important for opal mining, but lack of water caused the mines to close. **In town:** Barcoo Historical Museum, Perkins St. Oct.: Race Carnival. **In the area:** Jundah Opal Fields, 27 km NW. Welford National Park, 20 km S. At Windorah, 95 km S, International Yabby Racer in Sept. **Visitor information:** Barcoo Shire Council, Dickson St; (07) 4658 6133. Web site www.outbackholidays.tq.com.au **See also:** Outback & Gulf Country p. 464.

Karumba
Pop. 1043

MAP REF. 528 B8, 531 H8

Karumba, 71 km NW of Normanton, is at the mouth of the Norman River and is the easiest access point for the Gulf of Carpentaria. It is the centre for the Gulf's prawning industry. A barramundi fishing industry and live-cattle industry also operate. **In town:** Slipway once used by the Sydney-to-England Empire Flying Boats Service. Karumba Point, boat hire and accommodation. Barra Restocking Ponds, Riverview Dr.: barramundi display, feeding 4.45 p.m. daily. May: Karumba Kapers (fair). Dec.: Fishermen's Ball. **In the area:** Flat wetlands extending 30 km inland; habitat of saltwater crocodiles and several species of birds, including brolgas and cranes. Charter vessels for fishing and exploration of the Gulf and Norman River. *The Ferryman*, cruises on Norman River. Old cemetery, 2 km NW, on road to Karumba Point, a small settlement 6 km NW. Fishing resorts on Mornington and Sweers islands to the north-west. **Visitor information:** Shire Offices, Haig St, Normanton; (07) 4745 1166. Web site www.gulf-savannah.com.au **See also:** Outback & Gulf Country p. 464.

Kenilworth
Pop. 285

MAP REF. 525 P7

West of the Blackall Range, through the Obi Obi Valley, is Kenilworth, known for its Kenilworth Country Foods hand-crafted cheeses. This enterprise began when the local cheese factory closed and 6 employees started the venture. **In town:** Kenilworth Museum, Alexandra St, has machinery, dairy display and audiovisuals (open Sun.). Lasting Impressions Gallery of Fine Art, Elizabeth St. **In the area:** Kenilworth Bluff, 6 km N, steep walking track to lookout point. Little Yabba Creek, 8 km S, good picnic spot where bellbirds are often heard. Lake Borumba, 32 km NW, for picnics and water sports;

fishing competition each Mar. Nearby, Imbil Forest Drive through scenic forests and farmlands to Gympie. **Visitor information:** Maroochy Tourist Information Centre, cnr Sixth Ave and Aerodrome Rd, Maroochydore; (07) 5479 1566. Web site www.sunshinecoast.org **See also:** Sunshine Coast p. 453.

Killarney
Pop. 832

MAP REF. 107 N1, 525 O11

This attractive small town is on the banks of the Condamine River, 33 km SE of Warwick, and very close to the NSW border. **In town:** Feb.: Agricultural Show. Nov.: Rodeo. **In the area:** Noteworthy mountain scenery. Dagg's and Brown's waterfalls, 4 km S. Cherrabah Homestead Resort, 7 km S, offers horseriding, golf, sailing and excellent bushwalking. Carrs Lookout, 33 km E. Queen Mary Falls in Main Range National Park, 15 km E; native birds fed daily at kiosk. **Visitor information:** 49 Albion St (New England Hwy), Warwick; (07) 4661 3401. Web site www.qldsoutherndowns.org.au **See also:** Darling Downs p. 452; National Parks p. 498.

Kingaroy
Pop. 7013

MAP REF. 525 N6

This prosperous agricultural town is known for its peanuts and navy beans and is the home of Sir Johannes (Joh) Bjelke-Petersen, a former Premier of Qld. Maize, wheat, stonefruit, grapes, and soy and navy beans are also grown, and specialised agricultural equipment is manufactured. Kingaroy is 210 km NW of Brisbane, and its giant peanut silos are a landmark. **In town:** In Haly St: Kingaroy Bicentennial Heritage Museum; information centre, with videos on peanut and navy-bean industries. Mar.: Peanut and Harvest Festival (odd-numbered years). Apr.: Food and Wine Fest. **In the area:** Scenic drives, brochure available. A number of wineries open daily for sales. Mt Wooroolin scenic lookout, 3 km W. Bunya Mountains National Park, 56 km SW: last stands of bunya pine; bird-watching; rainforest walk to Pine Gorge Lookout. **Visitor information:** South Burnett Visitor Information Centre, 128 Haly St (opp. silos); (07) 4162 3199. Web site www.southburnett.com.au **See also:** Brisbane Hinterland p. 448; National Parks p. 498.

The Scenic Railway between Kuranda and Cairns

Kuranda
Pop. 666

MAP REF. 523 E7, 529 M6

This village is in the rainforest at the top of the Macalister Range. **In town:** Railway station with platforms adorned by lush ferns and orchids. Skyrail Rainforest Cableway, spectacular gondola ride through World Heritage–classified rainforest to Cairns; return via 100-year-old Kuranda Scenic Railway (34 km); or vice versa. In Rod Veivers Dr.: The Incredible Birdworld, spectacular tree-lined paths and endangered birds; Australian Butterfly Sanctuary, over 2000 butterflies in forest setting; guided tours. In Coondoo St: Wildlife Noctarium, native wildlife in re-created nocturnal rainforest environment; Windmill Gallery. The Aviary, Thongon St, colourful native birds in walk-through enclosures surrounded by rainforest. River Esplanade Walk along Barron River, also Jungle Walk and Forest Walk. Markets, Rod Veivers Dr., daily. May: Folk Festival. **In the area:** River cruises depart from riverbank below railway station; also guided rainforest walks. Wrights Lookout, 7 km SE in Barron Gorge National Park, views of the Barron Falls, spectacular after heavy rain. Mini-golf, 2 km E. Rainforestation Nature Park, 35 km E: rainforest tours in amphibious army duck; Pamagirri Aboriginal Dancers and Dream-time Walk; Koala and Wildlife Park. **Visitor information:** Therwine St; (07) 4093 9311. Web site www.kuranda.org **See also:** The Far North p. 461; National Parks p. 498.

Kynuna
Pop. 18

MAP REF. 533 J6

On the Matilda Hwy, 164 km NW of Winton, Kynuna was established in the 1860s and was a staging post for Cobb & Co. coaches. **In town:** Famous Blue Heeler Hotel, with illuminated blue heeler statue on roof. Waltzing Matilda Exhibition, open during tourist season, in tent opposite road-house. Aug.: 'Surf' Carnival (inland version of Iron Man contest). Nov.: Rodeo. **In the area:** Combo Waterhole, 24 km SE on western side of old Winton–Kynuna Rd, scene of the events described in 'Waltzing Matilda', Banjo Paterson's song. Walkabout Creek Hotel at McKinlay, 74 km NW, location for film *Crocodile Dundee.* **Visitor information:** Roadhouse and Caravan Park, Matilda Hwy; (07) 4746 8683. Web site www.outbackholidays. tq.com.au **See also:** Outback & Gulf Country p. 464.

Laidley
Pop. 2329

MAP REF. 525 O9

Laidley, 87 km from Brisbane, off the Warrego Hwy, is between Ipswich and Gatton, in the Lockyer Valley. It is the principal town in an area of the Greater Brisbane Region regarded as 'Queensland's country garden'. **In town:** Das Neumann Haus (1893), William St: local history museum; information centre; art and craft; cafe. Country markets each Fri., and last Sat. each month. Apr.: Rodeo and Heritage Day. Sept.: Chelsea Flower Show. **In the area:** Laidley Pioneer Village, 1 km s, features original buildings from old township. Adjacent, Narda Lagoon: flora and fauna sanctuary; suspension footbridge over lagoon; picnic/ barbecue facilities. Lake Dyer, 1 km w: fishing; short-stay camping; picnic/barbecue facilities. Lake Clarendon, 17 km NW, birdwatching and picnicking. Self-guide historic and scenic walks and drives; leaflets available. **Visitor information:** Lockyer Valley Tourist Information Centre, Warrego Hwy, Hatton Vale; (07) 5465 7642. Web site www.laidley.qld.gov.au **See also:** Brisbane Hinterland p. 448.

Landsborough   Pop. 1343

MAP REF. 516 G6, 519 E13, 525 P7

Landsborough is just north of the magnificent Glass House Mountains National Park. **In town:** In Maleny St: Excellent local history museum; De Maine Pottery. June: William Landsborough Day (festival to commemorate explorer); Bronco Branding Festival. **In the area:** 70-km scenic Blackall Range drive to Nambour. Queensland Reptile and Fauna Park, 4 km S. Dularcha National Park, 1 km NE; *Dularcha* is an Aboriginal word describing blackbutt eucalyptus country. Big Kart Track, 5 km N, unsealed road suitable for conventional vehicles (except after heavy rain). **Visitor information:** Historical Museum, Maleny Rd; (07) 5494 1755. Web site www.sunshinecoast.org **See also:** Sunshine Coast p. 453.

Longreach   Pop. 3766

MAP REF. 526 A11, 533 O11

On the Thomson River, Longreach is some 700 km by road or rail west of Rockhampton. The area supports 800 000 sheep and 20 000 beef cattle. It is the most important town in central west Qld. In 1870 Harry Redford (Captain Starlight), with 4 mates, rounded up 1000 cattle and drove them 2400 km into SA over wild unmapped country before selling them. He was arrested and tried; the jury acquitted him, probably because his daring was admired. These events were the basis for Rolf Boldrewood's novel *Robbery Under Arms*. In 1992, Longreach Airport became the first base for Qantas (Queensland And Northern Territory Aerial Service), after moving from its birthplace a year earlier at Winton. The hangar used then became Australia's first aircraft factory and the first of 6 DH-50 biplanes was assembled in 1926. The world's first Flying Surgeon Service started from Longreach in 1959. **In town:** Broad streets and several historic buildings. In Galah St: Uniting Church (1892), built for Grazier's Association; courthouse (1892). Post office (1902), cnr Duck and Eagle sts. Railway station (1916), Sir Hudson Fysh Dr. Powerhouse Museum, Swan St, displays of old machinery; open Mar.–Oct. Arts and Crafts, Ibis St; open p.m. Mar.–Oct. On Matilda Hwy: Australian Stockman's Hall of Fame and Outback Heritage Centre, featuring exhibition hall, theatre with audiovisuals, library and resource centre; nearby, Banjo's Outback Theatre and Pioneer Shearing Shed (open Mar.–Oct.); Botanical Gardens, has walking and cycling trails; School of Distance Education (tours weekdays during term); Longreach Pastoral College (tours); Qantas Founders Outback Museum at airport. Qantas Park, Eagle St, replica of original Qantas booking office, now houses information centre. Pamela's Doll Display and Syd's Outback Collection Corner, Quail St. Cobb & Co. coach rides around town. *Yellowbelly Express* and Billabong Boat Cruises, for Thomson River cruises. Easter: Easter in the Outback. May: Outback Muster and Drovers Reunion. July: Diamond Shears (Australia's premier shearing competition). **In the area:** Quarter-horse stud at Longway Station, 14 km N (group tours). Oakley Station, 17 km N, sheep and cattle station (tours). Folk Museum at Ilfracombe, 27 km E. Toobrac Station, 107 km SW, 100-year-old homestead; accommodation and camping. **Visitor information:** Qantas Park, Eagle St; (07) 4658 3555. Web site www.longreach.qld.gov.au **See also:** Outback & Gulf Country p. 464.

Mackay   Pop. 44 880

MAP REF. 527 L5

Mackay produces one-third of the nation's sugar crop. Five mills operate, and the bulk-sugar loading terminal is the world's largest. Sugar was first grown here in 1866. Mackay became a major port in 1939 when a breakwater

Sugar cane harvest in the Mackay region

Australian Stockman's Hall of Fame and Outback Heritage Centre, Longreach

was built, making it one of Australia's largest artificial harbours. The nearby Hay Point coal-loading terminals handle the output from the central Qld coalfields. Mackay's economy also depends on beef cattle, dairying, timber, grain, seafood and tropical fruit. Tourism is a growth industry, with sea or air access to Brampton Island, and sea access to Lindeman Island and the Great Barrier Reef. **In town:** Self-guide heritage walk of historic buildings incl.: Commonwealth (1880) and National (1939) banks, town hall (1912), courthouse (1838), police station (1885), Ambassador Hotel (1937) and customs house (1902). Queens Park and Orchid House, Goldsmith St. Entertainment Centre, Gordon St. Replica of old Richmond sugar mill, Nebo Rd, houses information centre. Just north of town, lookouts at Mt Bassett Weather Station, Mt Pleasant Reservoir, Eimeo and Lamberts Beach. Numerous beaches: Harbour, Town, Blacks, Bucasia, Illawong, Lamberts and Shoal Point. Cruises, fishing charters and scenic flights. Two Sat. markets: Harbour Rd; Showgrounds, Milton St. City Heat Markets, Victoria St, Sun. July: Festival of the Arts; Troy Dunn International Bull Riding. Sept.: Sugartime Festival. **In the area:** Discovery and eco-tours to national parks, coal mines and Whitsundays. Farleigh Sugar Mill, 15 km N; tours during crushing season (July–Oct.).

That Sapphire Place, 20 km N, sapphire display and gem-cutting demonstrations. Cape Hillsborough National Park, 40 km N. Polstone Sugar Cane Farm, 15 km W; tours July–Oct. Greenmount Historic Homestead, 20 km W, near Walkerston. Kinchant Dam, 20 km W of Walkerston. Stoney Creek Cottage, 32 km W, trail rides and accommodation. At Mirani, 33 km W, museum in Victoria St. Eungella National Park, 79 km W: platypuses, Ulysses butterflies, nocturnal wildlife; rainforest discovery self-guide trail; limited camping at Fern Flat. Nebo, 93 km SW of Mackay on Peak Downs Hwy: Nebo Museum; Camp Draft in July. Orchidways, orchid farm on Homebush Rd, 25 km S (closed Thurs.). At Homebush, 25 km S: art and craft gallery; self-drive tour through historic area, brochure available. **Visitor information:** The Mill, 320 Nebo Rd; (07) 4952 2677. Web site www.mackayregion.com **See also:** Great Barrier Reef p. 455; The Mid-Tropics p. 460; National Parks p. 498; Wildlife-Watching p. 501.

Main Beach
Pop. part of Gold Coast

MAP REF. 517 G11, 518 F5, 525 Q10

Towards the northern end of the Gold Coast strip, Main Beach is packed with attractions. **In the area:** The Broadwater immediately north, for

boating and fishing; boat hire. Scenic drive, brochure available. At Main Beach on The Spit: Sea World, noteworthy marine park; Marina Mirage and Mariner's Cove, tourist complexes with specialty shops, restaurants, outdoor cafes and weekend entertainment. At Southport, 2 km N: New Age of Aquarius Expo in Jan.; Gold Coast Triathlon in May; Gold Coast Show Aug.–Sept. At Sanctuary Cove, 18 km N: championship golf courses; houseboat hire and cruises. Tropical Fruit World, 6 km NW at Labrador. At Runaway Bay, 9 km NW: Cable SkiWorld; Gold Coast City Marathon in June. South Stradbroke Island to the east: 2 resorts; camping; fine beaches; launch access from Runaway Bay (no cars permitted). **Visitor information:** Gold Coast Tourism Bureau, Cavill Walk, Surfers Paradise; (07) 5538 4419 or 1300 130 001. Web site www.goldcoasttourism.com.au **See also:** Gold Coast & Hinterland p. 450.

Maleny
Pop. 880

MAP REF. 516 E5, 519 B11, 525 P7

A steep road climbs from the coast west to Maleny, in the Blackall Range, 50 km SW of Maroochydore. The surrounding area is excellent dairy country, although farmland is increasingly being sold for residential development. The town is popular with alternative lifestylers and has a number of co-operative stores

Step back in time at Brennan & Geraghty's Store, Maryborough

and cafes. From McCarthys Lookout, south-east of town, there is a fine view of the Glass House Mountains to the south. **In town:** Art and craft galleries. **In the area:** 28-km scenic drive (one of the best in south-east Qld), north-east from Maleny through Montville and Flaxton to Mapleton: views of Sunshine Coast, Moreton Island, Bribie Island and nearby pineapple and sugarcane fields; museums; antique shops; fruit stalls; tea rooms and tourist attractions; drive can be extended to Nambour. Montville, 7 km NE: main street lined with cafes, gift shops, potteries and art and craft galleries. At Flaxton, 3 km further N: miniature English village; Flower Gardens Winery has working potter and tearooms; Flaxton Winery, excellent coastal views. Flaxton Barn, 2 km further N, has model railway and tearooms. Kondalilla and Mapleton Falls national parks, between Montville and Mapleton. Howells Knob, 4 km W, lookout with 360° views. Mary Cairncross Park, 7 km SE, rainforest walks. McCarthys Lookout, 5 km SE, spectacular views. **Visitor information:** Sunshine Coast Information, cnr Sixth Ave and Aerodrome Rd, Maroochydore; (07) 5479 1566. Web site www. sunshinecoast.org **See also:** Sunshine Coast p. 453.

Mareeba   Pop. 6874

MAP REF. 523 C9, 529 M7

Tobacco is still grown here, along with mango, tea-tree oil, coffee and sugarcane crops. Farms in the Mareeba–Dimbulah area are irrigated from Lake Tinaroo. Mining and cattle are also important. **In town:** Self-guide historical walk, brochure available. In Mason St, Bicentennial Lakes, a park with plantings to encourage wildlife. In Centenary Park, Byrnes St: Mareeba Heritage Museum, has local history exhibits incl. rail ambulance and old dairy shed; Mareeba Art Society Gallery; markets, 2nd Sat. each month. July: Rodeo. Sept.: Air Show. Oct.: Country Music Festival (even-numbered years). **In the area:** Horseriding at Pinevale Ranch, 10 km E. The Coffee Works, Mason St, 2 km S (tours). Aviation and Military Museum, 5 km S on Kennedy Hwy, has the Beck Collection (military hardware). Granite Gorge, 12 km SW, off Chewko Rd. Paddy's Green Plantation (North Queensland Gold coffee), 9 km W on Mareeba–Dimbulah road. Tryconnell Historic Gold Mine, 76 km W (tours). Wetlands Project, 22 km N at end of Fabis Rd, extends for 5000 ha and backs onto Hann Tablelands. **Visitor information:** Heritage Museum, Centenary Park,

345 Byrnes St; (07) 4092 5674. Web site www.tnq.org.au **See also:** The Far North p. 461.

Maroochydore   Pop. 28 509

MAP REF. 516 H4, 519 H9, 525 Q7

A popular beach resort, Maroochydore, 106 km N of Brisbane, is the business centre of the Sunshine Coast. **In town:** Good surfing beaches. Maroochy River, with pelicans and swans, offers safe swimming. Cotton Tree, at river mouth, popular camping area. Replica of Captain Cook's ship *Endeavour*, David Low Way. **In the area:** Cruises up Maroochy River to Dunethin Rock through sugarcane fields. Nostalgia Town, 7 km NW, emphasises humour in history. Bli Bli Castle, 10 km NW, a 'medieval' castle with dungeon torture chamber and doll museum. **Visitor information:** cnr Sixth Ave and Aerodrome Rd; (07) 5479 1566, freecall 1800 882 032. Web site www.maroochytourism.com **See also:** Sunshine Coast p. 453.

Maryborough   Pop. 21 286

MAP REF. 525 P4

Maryborough is an attractive city on the banks of the Mary River, 3 hours' drive north of Brisbane. The Maryborough region was first explored by Europeans in 1842. A village and port soon grew to handle the wool being produced inland. Maryborough is a heritage city; visitors can see excellent early architecture. The climate is dry subtropical with warm moist summers and mild winters. **In town:** Colonial architecture: St Paul's bell tower (1887), Lennox St, with one of the last sets of pealing bells in Qld; Brennan & Geraghty's Store, property of National Trust. Also in Lennox Street at Central Railway Station, *Mary Ann*, replica of Qld's first steam engine; rides in Queens Park last Sun. of month. Bond Store Museum, Wharf St, has historical displays. In Ferry St: Croydon Foundry Office Museum. Old's Engine House, North St, collection of engine models, tours Thurs. Pioneer gravesites and original township site in Alice St, Baddow; historic time gun outside city hall, Kent St. Several parks: in Sussex St, Queen's Park, unusual domed fernery and waterfall; in Kent St, Elizabeth Park, rose gardens; on cnr Cheapside and Alice sts, Anzac Park; Ululah Lagoon, off Lions Dr., a scenic waterbird sanctuary where black swans, wild geese, ducks and waterhens may be hand-fed.

Maryborough Heritage Walk and Drive, brochure available. Heritage City Market, Adelaide and Ellena sts, each Thurs. May: Best of Brass. Sept.: Heritage City Festival. Oct.: Maryborough Masters Games. **In the area:** Pioneer museum at Brooweena, 49 km W on Biggenden Rd. Teddington Weir, 15 km S. Tuan Forest, 24 km SE. **Visitor information:** BP South, Bruce Hwy; (07) 4121 4111. Web site www.maryborough.qld.gov.au **See also:** Fraser Island & Coast p. 454.

Miles
Pop. 1187

MAP REF. 525 K7

Ludwig Leichhardt passed through this district, 337 km NW of Brisbane, on 3 expeditions. He named the place Dogwood Crossing. In 1878 the western railway line reached Dogwood Crossing, and Cobb & Co. continued the journey to Roma. The town was renamed Miles after a local member of parliament. The area is good sheep country, but today the emphasis is on cattle and wheat; tall silos dominate the surroundings. After the spring rains the wildflowers are magnificent. **In town:** Historical village, Warrego Hwy: 'pioneer settlement' with all types of early buildings, a war museum, and vehicles and implements. Sept.: Back to the Bush (incl. Wildflower Festival). **In the area:** Myall Park Botanical Gardens at Glenmorgan, 134 km SW. Wildflower drive in Sept., brochure available. **Visitor information:** Historical Village, Murilla St; (07) 4627 1492. **See also:** Darling Downs p. 452.

Millaa Millaa
Pop. 324

MAP REF. 521 B2, 529 M8

Located 73 km inland from Innisfail, Millaa Millaa is central to many spectacular waterfalls, and other Atherton Tableland attractions. The town's main industry is dairying. **In town:** Eacham Historical Society Museum, Main St. **In the area:** Millaa Millaa Falls, Zillie Falls and Ellinjaa Falls – all seen from 15-km Waterfalls Circuit road (mostly sealed) that leaves and rejoins Palmerston Hwy east of town; also nearby, Souita, Papina and Mungalli falls. World Heritage-listed Wooroonooran National Park, 20 km SE: rainforest walks; Nandroya, Walicher and Tchupala falls; Crawfords Lookout. Millstream Falls, 40 km SW. Millaa Millaa Lookout to west of town for excellent 360° views of district. At Ravenshoe, 26 km SW: woodcraft; heritage steam-train ride to nearby Tumoulin and

return, times from information centre. In Undara Volcanic National Park, 150 km SW: lava tubes and tunnel (access only with guide); camping, accommodation and tours at nearby Lava Lodge. **Visitor information:** Millaa Millaa Tourist Park, Malanda Rd; (07) 4097 2290. Web site www.eachamshire.qld.gov.au **See also:** The Far North p. 461; National Parks p. 498.

Millmerran
Pop. 1054

MAP REF. 525 M10

The farms around this town on the Condamine River produce eggs, cotton, grain, vegetables, cattle and wool. **In town:** Historical Society Museum, Charlotte St. Oct.: Camp Oven Festival. **In the area:** Ned's Corner, 27 km N, offers camp-oven meals, Australiana, yarns and poetry (open by appt). **Visitor information:** Toowoomba Information Centre, cnr James & Kitchener sts, Toowoomba; (07) 4638 7555. **See also:** Darling Downs p. 452.

Miriam Vale
Pop. 421

MAP REF. 525 M1, 527 Q13

Situated on the Bruce Hwy, 150 km N of Bundaberg, this town is renowned for its mud-crab sandwiches. The hinterland is ideal for bushwalking, four-wheel driving and horseriding. **In the area:** Twin towns of Agnes Water, 57 km NE (the most northerly surfing beach in Qld), and Seventeen Seventy, 63 km NE. Captain Cook, while on his voyage of discovery in Australian waters, made his first landing in Qld at the town of Seventeen Seventy; commemorative Festival held each May. Sea access from Seventeen Seventy to Lady Musgrave Island. Estuary and beaches provide ideal recreation; fishing is excellent. Nearby, Eurimbula and Deepwater national parks; 4WD necessary. **Visitor information:** Discovery Coast Information Centre, Bruce Hwy; (07) 4974 5428. Web site www.gladstoneregion.org.au **See also:** Capricorn p. 458; National Parks p. 498.

Mission Beach
Pop. 1013

MAP REF. 521 D3, 529 N9

This quiet 14-km-long beach with magnificent golden sand, close to Tully, is fringed by coconut palms and World Heritage-listed wet tropical rainforest. The Great Barrier Reef is closest to shore here. Day cruises and sailing trips to Beaver Cay

and Dunk and surrounding islands depart from Clump Point jetty. A cairn at South Mission Beach Esplanade commemorates the ill-fated 1848 Cape York expedition of Edmund Kennedy. Artists, potters, sculptors, jewellers, tapestry artists and cane weavers have settled in the area. **In town:** Next to information centre, Porters Promenade, woodcarving exhibition and rainforest arboretum. Markets: Porters Promenade, 1st Sat. and 3rd Sun. each month; Monster Markets, Recreation Centre, Cassowary Dr., last Sun. each month (Easter–Nov.). June: Mudfest (3-day music and cultural festival). Aug.: Banana Festival. Oct.: Aquatic Festival. **In the area:** Art and craft galleries. Boat, catamaran and jetski hire, tandem parachuting, game and island reef fishing. Water taxi to Dunk Island, departs Wongaling Beach and South Mission Beach. Spectacular walking trails to Bicton Hill and Cuttens Lookout, from base of Bicton Hill, off Mission Beach, to Bingil Bay Rd. Guided and self-guide rainforest walks; scenic drives; calm-water, guided canoe and kayak trips; game-fishing; croc-spotting tours on Hull River. **Visitor information:** Porters Promenade; (07) 4068 7099. Web site www.gspeak.com.au/missionb **See also:** Great Barrier Reef p. 455; The Mid-Tropics p. 460.

Mitchell
Pop. 967

MAP REF. 524 F6

Mitchell, on the banks of the Maranoa River and 600 km W of Brisbane, lies on the Warrego Hwy between Roma and Charleville. The town was named after Sir Thomas Mitchell, explorer and Surveyor-General of NSW, who visited the region in 1846. **In town:** Kenniff Courthouse and Visitor Information Centre, Cambridge St: bushranger exhibition; art and craft; video of local points of interest; landscaped courthouse grounds incorporating community mosaic, operating artesian windmill and small billabong. Also in Cambridge St: Great Artesian Spa has artesian waters of ideal temperature, in garden surroundings; Nalingu Aboriginal Corporation for guided tours of local area. **In the area:** *Read section on Outback Motoring (p. 599).* This region was stronghold of turn-of-century bushrangers, the Kenniff brothers; monument 7 km S at the site of their last stand. Daytrips to the Mount Moffatt section of the Carnarvon National Park, 256 km N: camping; walking tracks; 2 major Aboriginal art sites; views of impressive sandstone rock formations. Bird sanctuary and picnic/ barbecue facilities near Neil Turner Weir, 3.5 km NW. Maranoa River Nature Walk (1.8-km circuit) begins at Fishermans Rest, 1.7 km W. **Visitor information:** 6 Cambridge St; (07) 4623 1073. Web site www.maranoa.org.au **See also:** Outback & Gulf Country p. 464.

Monto

Pop. 1339

MAP REF. 525 M2

Monto, on the Burnett Hwy, 250 km inland from Bundaberg, is the centre of a rich dairying, beef cattle and agricultural district. **In town:** Monto History Centre, cnr Kelvin and Lister sts, local history displays and videos. June: Dairy Festival (even-numbered years). **In the area:** Cania Gorge National Park, 25 km NW. The Bonnie View Collection, 2 km S, incl. over 1000 dolls. Wuruma Dam, 50 km S: swimming, sailing, waterskiing. Wattle Dale Ostrich Farm, 28 km SW. **Visitor information:** Three Moon Motel, Burnett Hwy; (07) 4166 1777. Web site www.bdtdb.com.au **See also:** Capricorn p. 458; National Parks p. 498.

Mooloolaba

Pop. part of Maroochydore

MAP REF. 516 H4, 519 H9, 525 Q7

Because of its excellent beach, restaurants and nightlife, Mooloolaba is popular with both families and young people. The Mooloolaba Esplanade, offering beachside resort shopping, rises to the bluff at Alexandra Headland. From the headland there are sweeping views to the Maroochy River and Mudjimba Island, with Mt Coolum as an impressive backdrop. Alexandra Headland beach is popular for surfing. One of the safest anchorages on the eastern coast is at Mooloolaba Harbour. **In town:** UnderWater World complex, includes 80-m transparent tunnel for viewing 3 marine environments; the Wharf, and many restaurants and specialty shops. Harbour, finishing point for the annual Sydney-to-Mooloolaba Yacht Race in Apr., and base for Sunshine Coast's main prawning and fishing fleet. Yachting and game-fishing trips to nearby offshore reefs. Paraflying off Mooloolaba Beach. Apr.: Triathlon Festival. **Visitor information:** Mooloolaba International, Shop 18; (07) 5444 5755. Web site www.maroochy tourism.com **See also:** Sunshine Coast p. 453.

Moranbah

Pop. 6508

MAP REF. 526 I7

Just off the Peak Downs Hwy, 182 km SW of Mackay, this modern mining town established in 1971 services the huge open-cut coal mines of the expanding Bowen Coal Basin. Coking coal is railed to the Hay Point export terminal just south of Mackay. **In town:** Tours to BHP's Peak Downs Mine leave Town Square each Thurs. 10 a.m. (book at information centre). May: May Day Union Parade and Fireworks. **Visitor information:** Library, Town Square; (07) 4941 7221. **See also:** The Mid-Tropics p. 460.

Mossman

Pop. 1917

MAP REF. 523 B3, 529 M5

Mossman, 82 km NW of Cairns on the Captain Cook Hwy, is surrounded by green mountains and fields of sugarcane. **In town:** Markets, Front St, each Sat. **In the area:** Mt Demi (1159 m) towers over town. Popular beaches: Cooya Beach, Newell and Wonga. Mossman Gorge, 9 km W: short walk through rainforest to picturesque cascades; regular guided walks by Kuku Yulanji people whose ancestors were original inhabitants; part of Daintree National Park, largest tract of tropical rainforest in Australia. Hartleys Creek Wildlife Reserve, 35 km S, features crocodiles and other native fauna. Karnak Rainforest Sanctuary, 9 km N. Tropical fruit and restaurant in rainforest setting at High Falls Farm, Miallo, 15 km N. **Visitor information:** Port Douglas Daintree Tourism Association, 40 Macrossan St, Port Douglas; (07) 4099 4588. Web site www.pddt.com.au **See also:** The Far North p. 461; National Parks p. 498.

Mount Isa

Pop. 21 751

MAP REF. 532 E4

In 1923, John Campbell Miles discovered a rich silver-lead deposit here. Today the city of Mount Isa is the most important industrial, commercial and administrative centre in north-west Qld, an oasis of civilisation in Outback spinifex and cattle country. Mount Isa Mines operates one of the world's largest silver-lead mines; copper and zinc are also mined and processed. Ore trains run 900 km E to Townsville for shipment. Mount Isa hosts the world's third-largest rodeo, attracting rough-riders from all over Qld and almost doubling the town's population. **In town:** Surface and underground mine tours, advance bookings essential. Lead smelter stack, Australia's tallest free-standing structure (265 m). Riversleigh Fossils Centre and Mount Isa Tourist Information, Centenary Park, Marian St, features displays of ancient fossils found in the Riversleigh area, some dating back 20 million years. John Middlin Mining Display and Visitors Centre, Church St. Frank Aston Underground Museum, Shackleton St. National Trust Tent House, Fourth Ave. In Marian St: Kalkadoon Tribal Centre and Cultural Keeping Place; clock tower with ashes of John Campbell Miles. Mount Isa Potters Gallery, Alma St. Royal Flying Doctor Service Base and Visitors Centre, Barkly Hwy. School of Distance Education, Kalkadoon High School, Abel Smith Pde; open schooldays, tours a.m. City Lookout, Hilary St. Donaldson Memorial Lookout and walking track, off Marian St. Sat. market, West St; Sun. market, Camooweal St. Aug.: Rodeo. Oct.: Lake Moondarra Fishing Classic. **In the area:** Tours of World Heritage-listed Riversleigh Fossil Site, 267 km NW, an extension of Lawn Hill National Park, 332 km NW. Artificial Lake Moondarra, 20 km N; wildlife sanctuary; swimming; water sports; picnic/barbecue facilities. Gunpowder Resort, 127 km N, offers activities ranging from bull-catching to water-skiing. West Leichhardt Station, 30 km NE, 113 400-ha cattle property; inquire at information centre for day or overnight visits. Lake Julius and surrounds, 99 km NE: Aboriginal cave paintings; fishing; water-skiing; nature trails; abandoned goldmine. Air-charter flights to excellent barramundi fishing grounds near Birri Fishing Lodge at Birri Beach on Mornington Island and Sweers Island in Gulf of Carpentaria. Mount Frosty, 53 km E, old limestone mine and swimming-hole (not recommended for children as hole is some 9 m deep with no shallow areas); popular area for fossickers; Burke and Wills memorial cairn near Corella River, 74 km E. Malbon Vale Station, 43 km S, 172 000-ha cattle property; inquire at information centre for day or overnight visits. **Visitor information:** Riversleigh Fossils Centre, Centenary Park, Marian St; (07) 4749 1555. Web site www. riversleigh.qld.gov.au **See also:** Outback & Gulf Country p. 464; National Parks p. 498.

Mount Morgan   Pop. 2487

MAP REF. 527 N11

Located 38 km SW of Rockhampton, the crater of the Mount Morgan open-cut gold, silver and copper mine is the largest excavation in the Southern Hemisphere. In the mine's heyday, around 1910, the town had 14 000 people. **In town:** Town heritage tour. Historical Museum, Morgan St. Courthouse and other historic buildings have National Trust classifications. At Railway Station, Burnett Hwy: tearooms; rail museum; restored 1904 steam engine operates Sun.; fettler's trolley-rides along 4-km track operate Mon.–Fri. Tours of mines and brick-clay caves. May: Golden Mount Festival. **In the area:** The Big Dam, 2.7 km N via William St, for good boating and fishing. At Wowan, 40 km SW, Scrub Turkey Museum in old butter factory. **Visitor information:** Railway Station, Burnett Hwy; (07) 4938 2312. **See also:** Capricorn p. 458.

Mourilyan   Pop. 484

MAP REF. 521 D2, 529 N8

Mourilyan, 8 km S of Innisfail, is the bulk-sugar outlet for the Innisfail area. **In town:** Australian Sugar Museum, Bruce Hwy. **In the area:** South-west on Old Bruce Hwy: tours of South Johnstone Sugar Mill (8 km) in season (July–Oct.); National Trust-classified Paronella Park (14 km), ruins of Spanish-style castle set in rainforest; suspension bridge, waterfall, and picnic and camping areas nearby. Etty Bay, 9 km E: quiet tropical beach, caravan and camping facilities. **Visitor information:** Cassowary Coast Development Bureau, 1 Edith St; (07) 4061 7422. **See also:** The Far North p. 461.

Mundubbera   Pop. 1238

MAP REF. 525 M4

Mundubbera, 2 km off the Burnett Hwy and 398 km NW of Brisbane, is the main citrus-growing area for the State but also has dairies, piggeries, broad-acre farming and a timber mill. **In town:** Jones Weir, Bauer St. **In the area:** Golden Mile Orchard, 5 km S, open Apr.–Sept. (tours of packing sheds). Auburn River National Park, 40 km SW. Peanut, maize and bean crops on Gurgeena and Binjour plateaus, to north-east. Rare *Neoceratodus* (lungfish) found in Burnett River. **Visitor information:** Big Mandarin Information Centre,

Mossman Gorge, near the town of Mossman

Mundubbera–Durong Rd; (07) 4165 4549. Web site www.bdtdb.com.au **See also:** Capricorn p. 458; National Parks p. 498.

Murgon   Pop. 2088

MAP REF. 525 N6

Murgon, known as the beef capital of the Burnett, is one of the most attractive towns in southern Qld. Settlement dates from 1853 and the name comes from an Aboriginal word for 'lily pond'. Beef, dairying, pigs and mixed crops are the main industries; a wine industry is developing. The town is 96 km inland from Gympie and 46 km N of Kingaroy. **In town:** Queensland Dairy Museum, Gayndah Rd. Adjacent, relocated Trinity homestead, one of district's original buildings. Oct.: Bjelke-Petersen Dam Fishing Competition. **In the area:** Several wineries, follow Barambah Wine Trail by car or bus tour to Barambah Ridge, Rodericks, Bridgeman Downs, Clovely Estate; tastings and sales. Cherbourg Emu Farm at Cherbourg Aboriginal Community, 5 km SW: walk-through enclosures, educational displays; sales of emu products and Aboriginal artifacts. Bjelke-Petersen Dam, 15 km SE, for water sports and fishing. Scenic drives, brochures available. Nature walk and views in Jack Smith Scrub Conservation Park, 15 km NE; self-guide walks in Boat Mountain Conservation Park, adjacent. Goomeri, 19 km NE, known as 'clock town': unique memorial clock in town centre; Pumpkin Festival in May. Booubyjan Homestead (1847), 24 km N of Goomeri, open daily. Part of Bicentennial National Trail (5000-km

trail for walkers and horseriders) runs through Kilkivan, 44 km NE. Also at Kilkivan: gold-fossicking; Great Horse Ride in April. **Visitor information:** CBD Park; (07) 4168 3864. Web site www.murgon.qld.gov.au **See also:** Brisbane Hinterland p. 448.

Muttaburra   Pop. 92

MAP REF. 526 B9, 533 P9

Muttaburra, 119 km N of Longreach, was developed in the late 1870s. The name comes from an Aboriginal word meaning 'meeting of the waters'. **In town:** Dr Arratta Memorial Museum, in old hospital, Sword St; tours by appt. Behind museum, site of 1891 Shearers' Strike. Replica of dinosaur, Bruford St. June: Landsborough Flock Ewe Show. **In the area:** Many fossil remains, as it was formerly part of an inland sea. The name *Muttaburrasaurus* was given to a previously unknown dinosaur, the fossilised bones of which were discovered in 1963 in a creek close to Thomson River. Fishing and water-skiing in Thomson River, 6 km S, bush camping on riverbanks. Agate fossicking, 5 km W. **Visitor information:** Post Office/General Store, Sword St; (07) 4658 7147. Web site www.outbackholidays.tq.com.au **See also:** Outback & Gulf Country p. 464.

Nambour   Pop. 12 205

MAP REF. 516 F4, 519 E8, 525 P7

Nambour is a busy provincial town, 106 km N of Brisbane, just off the Bruce Hwy. Development began in the 1860s, and sugar has been the main crop since the 1890s. Small locomotives pulling

The Big Pineapple complex, south of Nambour

trucks of sugar-cane across the main street to Moreton Central Mill during the crushing season (July–Oct.). Pineapples and other tropical fruit are grown extensively. *Nambour* is the Aboriginal name for the local red-flowering tea-tree. **In the area:** Spectacular Glass House Mountains to south. Blackall Range scenic drive (70 km) to Landsborough. The Big Pineapple complex and Macadamia Nut Factory, 7 km S. Forest Glen Sanctuary (deer and native wildlife) and Superbee Honey Factory, 10 km further S on Tanawha–Forest Glen Tourist Dr. Mapleton, 13 km W, has a Yarn Festival (storytelling) in Oct. **Visitor information:** 5 Coronation Ave; (07) 5476 1933. Web site www.sunshine coast.org **See also:** Sunshine Coast p. 453; National Parks p. 498.

Nanango   Pop. 2711

MAP REF. 525 N7

Gold was mined here 1850–1900, but the area, 24 km SE of Kingaroy, now produces beef cattle, beans and grain, while grape-growing is expanding. The 1400-megawatt Tarong Power Station

and Meandu Coal Mine, 16 km SW, are also important. **In town:** Ringsfield Museum (1908), former house, then a maternity hospital from 1912; restored 1993 (check times, also by appt). Market, 1st Sat. each month. Oct.: Pioneer Festival. **In the area:** Forest drives, permit and maps from Forestry Dept, Yarraman, 21 km S. Historic timber towns: Yarraman, and Blackbutt, 20 km E of Yarraman. Berlin's Gem and Historical Museum, 17 km SW. Coomba Falls, near Maidenwell, 28 km SW. Bunya Mountains National Park, 70 km SW. Seven Mile Diggings, 11 km SE, gold- and gem-fossicking. Tipperary Flat, 2 km E: park with replica of old goldmining camp, picnic facilities. **Visitor information:** cnr Henry & Drayton sts; (07) 4171 6871. Web site www.southburnett.com.au **See also:** Brisbane Hinterland p. 448; National Parks p. 498.

Nerang   Pop. 14 467

MAP REF. 517 G11, 518 C5, 525 Q10

This town in the Gold Coast hinterland is 10 km W of Southport. **In town:** Aug.: Australian Arena Polo Championships.

In the area: Scenic drive, brochure available. At Carrara, 5 km SE, weekend market. At Mudgeeraba, 12 km S, Somerset Celebration of Literature in Mar. Hinze Dam on Advancetown Lake, 8 km SW: sailing; bass-fishing. Spectacular scenery in Numinbah Valley area, 15 km SW near Beechmont. Towards Springbrook, 42 km SW: Wunburra Lookout on Springbrook Plateau; Best of All View, off Repeater Station Rd; Purlingbrook Falls in Springbrook National Park. Natural Bridge section of Springbrook National Park, 38 km SW: popular picnic spot, walking tracks through scenic rainforest, lookout nearby, glow-worms in cave under bridge. Lamington National Park (World Heritage Area), 35 km SW: rainforest; walking tracks, picnic areas, camping and lodges at Binna Burra and O'Reilly's Plateau; canopy walk at latter. Paradise Country, 2 km W, small working farm. Historic River Mill (1910), 10 km W, arrowroot mill. South of Oxenford, 12 km N: Wet'n'Wild Water World; Warner Bros Movie World. North of Oxenford near Coomera, Dreamworld theme park. Near Mount Tamborine village, 20 km NW: lookout with spectacular views to Gold Coast and north to South Stradbroke Island; Tamborine National Park; other picturesque villages; splendid gardens. **Visitor information:** Cavill Walk, Surfers Paradise; (07) 5538 4419. Web site www.goldcoasttourism. com.au **See also:** Gold Coast & Hinterland p. 450; National Parks p. 498.

Noosa Heads   Pop. 17 776

MAP REF. 516 H1, 519 H1, 525 Q6

Noosa Heads (commonly known as Noosa) is a coastal resort set on Laguna Bay on the Sunshine Coast. The relaxed lifestyle, the weather and safe year-round swimming make this a popular holiday destination. Development is low-rise and the beautiful natural setting is an added attraction. Walking distance from the cosmopolitan Hastings Street is Noosa National Park, 454 ha of protected coves, surfing beaches and seascapes. **In town:** In Hastings St: numerous restaurants, shops and galleries. Noosa Main Beach for safe family swimming. Aug.: Half Marathon. Sept.: Jazz Festival. Oct.: Beach Car Classic; Triathlon Multi Sport Festival. **In the area:** In Noosa National Park, 1 km E, walks through rainforest and heathland. Sunshine Beach, 3 km SE, popular for surfing. Laguna Lookout, on Noosa Hill, for views of Noosa River and lakes. Noosaville, 5 km N, family-style resort with Noosa River as focal point; departure point for river cruises. At Tewantin, 7 km N: Noosa Regional Gallery, Big Shell and House of Bottles. Cooloola section of Great Sandy National Park, 14 km N, separated from Sunshine Coast by Noosa River (accessible via ferry from Tewantin): bushwalking, camel riding, horseriding, surfing; Teewah Coloured Sands, multicoloured sand cliffs; shipwrecked freighter *Cherry Venture* (accessible via 4WD or inland by conventional vehicle); beach access to departure point of Fraser Island ferry. Lakes Cooroibah and Cootharaba, 27 km N, ideal for boating, sailing and windsurfing (accessible by car or boat from Noosaville). At Lake Cootharaba: sleepy lakeside town of Boreen Point; 2-km walk from Teewah Landing to North Shore beaches; Kinaba Information Centre; boardwalks into surrounding wetlands. Noosa River extends over 40 km north into Great Sandy National Park: cruises to Everglades, waters known for their reflections; Harry's Hut, relic of timber-cutting days. Eumundi, 24 km SW, known for market held each Sat. a.m. Volcanic gems at Thunder Egg Farm, 29 km SW. **Visitor information:** Hastings St roundabout, Noosa Heads; (07) 5447 4988, freecall 1800 448 833. Web site www.tourismnoosa.com.au **See also:** Sunshine Coast p. 453; National Parks p. 498.

Normanton Pop. 1328

MAP REF. 528 C8, 531 I8

Normanton, 153 km W of Croydon, is the central town of the Gulf Savannah, and is on a high ridge on the edge of the savannah grasslands extending west and wetlands extending north. The town is also the terminus of the historic Normanton-to-Croydon railway, and the award-winning *Gulflander* tourist train, which leaves for Croydon on Wednesdays and returns Thursdays. **In town:** Penitentiary, Haig St. Restored Bank of NSW building, Little Brown St. Disused town well, Landsborough St. In Shire Office Gardens, Haig St: life-size replica of Krys the Savannah King, 8.6-metre saltwater crocodile. Self-guide scenic walk and drive, brochure available. Giant barramundi, outside Gulfland Motel, Landsborough St. Apr.: Barra Classic. June: Rodeo and Campdraft. **In the area:** Fishing and

camping at Walkers Creek, 32 km NW, and Norman River at Glenore, 25 km SE. Lakes on outskirts of Normanton attract jabirus, brolgas, herons and other birds. Shady Lagoon, 18 km E, for bush camping, birdwatching and wildlife. Dorunda Station, 197 km NE, cattle station offering barramundi and saratoga fishing in lake and rivers, and accommodation. Kowanyama Aboriginal Community, 359 km NE: excellent barramundi fishing, guest house, camping; Aboriginal Land, permit to visit required from Kowanyama Community Council. Burke and Wills Cairn, 40 km SW on Burketown Rd. Bang Bang Jump Up rock formation, 106 km SW: a solitary hill on the surrounding flat plains, road goes over top, excellent views. **Visitor information:** Shire Offices, Landsborough St; (07) 4745 1166. Web site www.gulf-savannah.com.au **See also:** Outback & Gulf Country p. 464.

Oakey Pop. 3396

MAP REF. 525 N9

On the Warrego Hwy, 29 km NW of Toowoomba, Oakey is the base for Australian Army Aviation. The town is surrounded by beautiful rolling hills and dark soil plains. **In town:** Bronze statue of racehorse Bernborough in front of Community Centre, Campbell St. Oakey Historical Museum, Warrego Hwy. Flypast Museum of Australian Army Flying, at army base via Kelvinaugh Rd, has large collection of original and replica aircraft (some in flying condition), and aviation memorabilia. **In the area:** Acland Coal Mine Museum, 18 km N; open Mar.–Jan., Sat.–Wed. or by appt. Jondaryan Woolshed (1859), off Warrego Hwy, 22 km NW: memorial to pioneers of wool industry; huge woolshed and other buildings; shearing demonstrations; sheepdogs; billy tea and damper; sales of goods at wool store; Australian heritage festival at Woolshed in Aug. **Visitor information:** Library, 64 Campbell St; (07) 4691 2306. **See also:** Darling Downs p. 452.

Palm Cove Pop. 2800

MAP REF. 523 E7, 529 M6

Serene Palm Cove, 27 km NW of Cairns, offers a selection of accommodation with splendid boutiques, art galleries and souvenir shops – on a tropical beach. Dive and cruise bookings to the Great Barrier Reef. Pick-up services for day tours to

the Atherton Tableland and surrounding areas. There is also convenient access to Mossman and Port Douglas. **In the area:** On Captain Cook Hwy at Clifton Beach, 3 km S: Wild World, features exotic range of flora and fauna; Outback Opal Mine, simulated mine with displays of Australia's most famous stone. Bungee tower in rainforest, McGregor Rd, Smithfield, 14 km S. Hartley's Crocodile Farm, 15 km N: hundreds of crocodiles, including 'Charlie', there since 1934; native fauna; snake shows and pat-the-animal. Rex Lookout, 17 km N, for stunning coastal views. **Visitor information:** 36 Aplin St; (07) 4051 4048. Web site www.tnq. org.au **See also:** Great Barrier Reef p. 455; The Far North p. 461.

Pittsworth Pop. 2323

MAP REF. 525 N9

Pittsworth is a typical Darling Downs town, situated 46 km SW of Toowoomba on the road to Millmerran. It is the centre of a rich grain and dairying district and cotton is grown with irrigation. The jacarandas and silky oaks are spectacular in late spring. **In town:** Some buildings listed by National Trust: Folk Museum; Pioneer Way, incl. pioneer cottage; blacksmith's shop; early school. Private gardens open at certain times (check with information centre). Jan. (Australia Day): Crimson Flash Shield (foot race). **Visitor information:** Sunkist Cafe, Yandilla St; (07) 4693 1246. Web site www.pittsworth.qld.gov.au **See also:** Darling Downs p. 452.

Pomona Pop. 967

MAP REF. 516 E1, 519 B1, 525 P6

This small farming centre is in the northern hinterland of the Sunshine Coast, 33 km S of Gympie. Mt Cooroora (439 m) dominates the town. **In town:** Majestic Theatre, cinema museum and location for annual film festival. July: King of the Mountain (race attracting mountain runners world-wide). Sept: Country Show. **In the area:** Water sports at Lake Cootharaba, 19 km NE, a large, shallow saltwater lake on Noosa River near where Mrs Eliza Fraser spent time with Aborigines after wreck of *Stirling Castle* on Fraser Island in 1836. **Visitor information:** Noosa Information Centre, Hastings St roundabout, Noosa Heads; (07) 5447 4988, freecall 1800 448 833. **See also:** Sunshine Coast p. 453.

Four Mile Beach, Port Douglas

Port Douglas
Pop. 3641

MAP REF. 523 C4, 529 M5

Port Douglas is 73 km NW of Cairns along one of the most scenic coastal drives in Australia. Once a small village, it has become an international tourist destination. The town, off the main highway, is surrounded by lush vegetation and pristine rainforests. Its tropical mountain setting, along with its proximity to the Great Barrier Reef, makes the town an ideal holiday destination. **In town:** Numerous restaurants offering a variety of cuisine. Ben Cropp's Shipwreck Museum and Courthouse Museum, Anzac Park, Macrossan St. Rainforest Habitat, Port Douglas Rd; wildlife sanctuary with tree-top walk, flora and fauna in natural setting. Flagstaff Hill, end Murphy St, commands excellent views of Four Mile Beach and Low Isles. Dive schools. Market, Anzac Park, each Sun. May: Village Carnivale. **In the area:** Tours incl.: horse trail-riding; rainforest tours; 4WD safaris; coach tours to Mossman Gorge, Daintree National Park, Cape Tribulation, Kuranda and Cooktown; reef tours to Outer Barrier Reef and Low Isles; *Lady Douglas* paddle-wheel cruise. **Visitor information:** Port Douglas Daintree Tourism Association, 40 Macrossan St; (07) 4099 4588. Web site www.tnq.org.au **See also:** Great Barrier Reef p. 455; The Far North p. 461; National Parks p. 498.

Proserpine
Pop. 3247

MAP REF. 527 J3

A sugar town, Proserpine is close to Airlie Beach, Shute Harbour and the islands of Whitsunday Passage. **In town:** Proserpine Historical Museum, Main St (check times). Oct.: Harvest Festival (incl. World Championship Cane Cutting). **In the area:** Conway National Park, 28 km E, views across islands of Whitsunday Passage. Lake Proserpine at Peter Faust Dam, 20 km W, offers boat hire, water-skiing, fishing and swimming; nearby, Cedar Creek Falls. **Visitor information:** Shop 3/6 The Esplanade, Airlie Beach; (07) 4946 6673. Web site www. whitsundays. com.au **See also:** Great Barrier Reef p. 455; The Mid-Tropics p. 460.

Quilpie
Pop. 730

MAP REF. 535 O7

Quilpie, 200 km W of Charleville, was established as a rail centre for the area's large sheep and cattle properties, but is better known as a boulder opal town. It takes its name from the Aboriginal word *quilpeta*, meaning 'stone curlew'. *Travellers heading west to Birdsville should note that there is no hotel or fuel at Betoota – extra fuel should therefore be carried from Windorah. Read section on Outback Motoring (p. 599).* **In town:** cuseum and gallery at information centre, Brolga St; historical and modern exhibitions. Sales of opals

at town outlets. Altar, font and lectern of St Finbarr's Catholic Church, Buln Buln St, made from opal-bearing rock. June: Boulder Opal Expo. June and Aug.: Diggers Races. Late Aug.: Kangaranga Doo. Sept.: Agricultural Show. **In the area:** Opal workings just outside town. Lake Houdraman, 6 km NE on river road to Adavale, popular recreation area. Baldy Top, large geological formation 3 km S, allowing spectacular views. At Toompine Roadhouse, 76 km S, historic hotel and cemetery; designated opal-fossicking areas nearby. Guided tours of opal fields, 75 km W (no general access). Eromanga, 103 km W, reputedly the furthest town from the sea in Australia: Royal Hotel, once Cobb & Co. staging post; Easter Rodeo; Race Day in May. **Visitor information:** Brolga St; (07) 4656 2166. Web site www.outbackholidays. tq.com.au **See also:** Outback & Gulf Country p. 464.

Ravenswood
Pop. 300

MAP REF. 521 G12, 526 G2

Ravenswood, 'not quite a ghost town', is 85 km E of Charters Towers via Mingela. A century ago it was the classic gold-rush town. Visitors will find interesting old workings and perhaps a little gold. **In town:** Several restored historic buildings in town, incl. Courthouse Museum and Craft Shop, Imperial Hotel, other shops and the ambulance centre. Thrice-weekly gold-panning (check times). May: Back to Ravenswood Festival. Oct.: Halloween Ball. **In the area:** Burdekin Falls Dam, 80 km SE, recreational area. Rodeo each May at Mingela, 38 km NW. **Visitor information:** Charters Towers Visitor Information Centre, 74 Mosman St, Charters Towers; (07) 4752 0314. Web site www. charterstowers.qld.gov.au **See also:** The Mid-Tropics p. 460.

Richmond
Pop. 733

MAP REF. 533 M4

This small town on the Flinders River, 500 km SW of Townsville, serves the surrounding sheep and cattle properties. The town's main street is lined with beautiful bougainvilleas. **In town:** In Goldring St: restored Cobb & Co. coach; Richmond Hotel, known as Mud Hut Hotel, historic flagstone and adobe building; Gidgee Wheel Arts and Craft. Kronosaurus Korner Fossil Centre, cnr Goldring St and Flinders Hwy, exhibits of excellent vertebrae fossils, all found in

Richmond Shire. St Johns Church, Crawford St, has silky-oak fittings and lead-light windows. Sandalwood Mill, Simpson St. Pioneer Cemetery, Flinders Hwy, on western edge of town. **In the area:** The area is rich in fossils. **Visitor information:** Kronosaurus Korner Richmond Fossil Centre, Flinders Hwy; (07) 4741 3429. Web site www.outbackholidays.tq.com.au **See also:** Outback & Gulf Country p. 464.

Rockhampton   Pop. 57 770

MAP REF. 527 N11

Rockhampton is called the beef capital of Australia, with some 2.5 million cattle in the region. Gold was discovered at Canoona, 60 km NW of Rockhampton, in 1858; however, cattle became the major industry. Rockhampton straddles the Tropic of Capricorn. It is a prosperous city on the banks of the Fitzroy River and has considerable architectural charm. Many of the original stone buildings and churches remain, set off by flowering bauhinia and brilliant bougainvilleas. **In town:** In Quay St, Australia's longest National Trust-classified street, with over 20 classified buildings: ANZ Bank (1864) and Customs House (1901). Cruises on Fitzroy River, departing Quay St wharf, cover history of river and district. Heritage walk around city centre. Scattered around the city are carefully preserved old Queensland houses. Botanic Gardens on Athelstane

Range, via Spencer St, has fine tropical displays, orchid and fern house, a Japanese-style garden, monkeys, koala park and walk-in aviary. Kershaw Gardens, Bruce Hwy, features Australian native flora Braille Trail. Fitzroy River Barrage, Savage St: separates tidal saltwater from upstream freshwater; opportunities for barramundi fishing. Capricorn Spire (14 m) at Curtis Park, Gladstone Rd, marks the line of Tropic of Capricorn. Rockhampton City Art Gallery, Victoria Pde: changing exhibitions, chamber music recital 2nd Sun. each month. Rocky markets, Denison St, Sat. and Sun. June: National Rodeo Finals. Oct.: Barra Bounty. Nov.–Jan.: Bent Wing Bat Flight Emergence. Dec.–Jan.: Summer Solstice Light Spectacular. **In the area:** Air access to Great Keppel Island. Natural events: bent-wing bats exodus, late Nov.–late Jan; summer solstice light spectacular, early Dec.–mid-Jan. Capricorn Scenic Loop tourist drive, brochure available. Old Glenmore historic homestead, 8 km N, has displays and historic buildings. Dreamtime Cultural Centre, 7 km N on Bruce Hwy, features culture of the Darumbal language group. St Christopher's Chapel, 20 km N, on Emu Park Rd, built by American servicemen. Rockhampton Heritage Village, Parkhurst, 9 km N: heritage buildings with hall of clocks and pioneering tools, also steam engine; open daily, working displays weekends only. Olsen's

Capricorn Caverns and Cammoo Caves, both limestone cave systems, 23 km N; tours daily; Carols in the Caverns, in Olsen's Capricorn Caverns, each Dec. Mt Hay Gemstone Tourist Park, 40 km W on Capricorn Hwy, thunder-egg fossicking. Drive to lookout at top of Mt Archer, 6 km E. **Visitor information:** Customs House, 208 Quay St; (07) 4922 5339, freecall 1800 676 701. Web site www.rockhampton. qld.gov.au **See also:** Great Barrier Reef p. 455; Capricorn p. 458.

Roma   Pop. 5744

MAP REF. 524 H6

Roma, first surveyed in 1862, is 267 km W of Dalby at the junction of the Warrego and the Carnarvon hwys. It was named after the wife of Qld's first Governor. The Mt Abundance cattle station was established in 1847 and sheep and cattle became the area's economic mainstay. The historic trial of Captain Starlight was held in Roma in 1872. In 1863 Samuel Symons Bassett brought vine cuttings to Roma and Qld's first wine-making enterprise began. Australia's first natural gas strike was at Hospital Hill in 1900 (tourist drive, brochure available), and this gas was used, in 1906, to light the town. Roma has supplied Brisbane with gas since 1969, but a major pipeline now brings gas from far western Qld to supplement the Roma area's depleting reserves. **In town:** Oil rig,

Carnarvon Gorge in Carnarvon National Park near Roma

Shute Harbour at sunset

named Big Rig by locals, at eastern entrance to town on Warrego Hwy; adjacent, Big Rig Research Centre records early oil exploration in area. Romavilla Winery, Injune Rd. Roma–Bungil Cultural Centre, cnr Bungil and Injune rds, includes three-dimensional mural by local artists. Roma Bottle Trees, in Heroes' Ave, planted to commemorate local soldiers who died in WW I; adjacent park has picnic facilities. Markets at Big Rig site, 2nd and 4th Sun. each month. Easter: Easter in the Country. **In the area:** Largest inland cattle market in Australia, 4 km E on Warrego Hwy. Meadowbank Museum, 15 km W on Warrego Hwy. Carnarvon National Park, 244 km NW: Carnarvon Gorge, Aboriginal cave paintings, varied scenery and walks; guided tours; accommodation. **Visitor information:** Big Rig Visitor Information Centre, 2 Riggers Rd; (07) 4622 4355, freecall 1800 222 399. Web site www.the bigrig.com.au **See also:** Darling Downs p. 452; National Parks p. 498.

St George
Pop. 2463

MAP REF. 524 G10

Situated at a major road junction, St George is in the centre of a rich grape, peanut and cotton-growing district. It is on the Balonne River, 118 km NW of Mungindi on the Carnarvon Hwy, and 289 km SW of Dalby on the Moonie Hwy. It is often referred to as the inland fishing capital of Qld. As St George has a rainfall of only 500 mm a year, extensive irrigation is carried out by means of a dam and 3 weirs. Cotton-growing and harvesting is completely mechanised. Wheat, barley, oats and sunflowers are also irrigated, and sheep and cattle are raised. **In town:** Riversands Vineyards, Whytes Rd. Carved, illuminated emu eggs displayed at Balonne Sports store, Victoria St. Easter: St George's Day. May: Country Show; Wool and Craft Show. Oct.: Regional Fishing Competition. **In the area:** Boolba Wool and Craft Show, variety of events, held in May at Boolba, 50 km W. Rosehill Aviaries, 64 km W, one of Australia's largest private collections of Australian parrots. At Bollon, 112 km W: large koala population in trees along Wallan Creek; Heritage and craft centre, George St, local history exhibits. Pastoral township, Dirranbandi, 97 km SW near the NSW border: Railway Park, Railway St; Cubbie Station, 33 km further west, largest privately owned cotton property in State, tours available. Culgoa Floodplain National Park, 130 km SW of Dirranbandi: floodplain and mulga country; birdlife; 4WD access only; campers must be self-sufficent. Cotton Ginnery, 20 km S; open by appt Mar.–July. Historic hotel (1863) at Nindigully, 44 km SE, motorbike riders arrive each June for Nindigully 5-hour Enduro. Thallon, 76 km SE: swimming and fishing at Barney's Beach on Moonie River; nearby historic Bullamon homestead (1860), mentioned in Steele Rudd's 'Memoirs of Corporal Keeley', has original shingle roof and canvas ceilings, tours by appt. Further 3 km, restored vintage tractor collection, open by appt. Ancient rock well, 37 km E, hand hewn by Aborigines possibly thousands of years ago. E. J. Beardmore Dam, 21 km N, for fishing and water sports; scenic picnic spots in surrounding parklands. **Visitor information:** The Terrace (cnr Roe St); (07) 4625 4996 and Kamarooka Caravan Park, 56 Victoria St; (07) 4625 3120. **See also:** Darling Downs p. 452.

Sarina
Pop. 3201

MAP REF. 527 L6

In the sugar belt, Sarina lies 36 km S of Mackay on the Bruce Hwy. The area has many fine beaches, incl. Sarina Beach, Campwin Beach, Grasstree, Salonika, Half Tide, and, to the south, Armstrong Beach. Sarina produces molasses and ethyl alcohol as by-products of the sugar industry. The CSR Plane Creek Central Sugar Mill and Distillery on Bruce Hwy produces fertiliser for local sugarcane crops. **In town:** In Broad St: rose gardens; Sarina Surprise pictorial quilt at library, 3.5 m x 2.5 m depiction of town's buildings, landmarks, industries and lifestyle. In Railway Sq.: palm and rose gardens; old courthouse (1901), houses Sarina Tourist Art and Craft Centre, with local art and craft and local industry information. Flea market, Broad St, last Thurs. each month. Beach markets, last Sun. each month. May: Mud Trials (buggy-racing on a mud track). June: Fishing Classic. July: Visual Arts Festival. Aug.: Sarina Annual Show. Sept.: Grasstree Beach Bike Races. **In the area:** Cape Palmerston National Park, 78 km SE, 4WD access only. Viewing gallery at Hay Point and Dalrymple Bay coal terminal complex, 12 km N. **Visitor information:** Lot 3, Bruce Hwy; (07) 4956 2251. **See also:** The Mid-Tropics p. 460.

Shute Harbour
Pop. 200

MAP REF. 527 K3

Shute Harbour, 36 km NE of Proserpine, has one of the largest marine passenger terminals in Australia, second only to Sydney's Circular Quay. **In town:** Sea or air access to Long, Daydream and Lindeman islands. Sea access to

Whitsunday, Hook, South Molle and Hamilton islands. Boom-net riding daily. Sea plane ride to Hardy's Lagoon on the outer Great Barrier Reef for snorkelling among the coral. Day trips to the pontoon at Hardy Reef for swimming, scuba diving and snorkelling. Sail and power vessels, varying sizes and classes, for hire. Lions Lookout, Whitsunday Dr., for spectacular views. June: Hamilton Island Cup (outrigger canoes). Aug.: Hamilton Island Race Week (sailing). Sept.: Hamilton Island Beach Volleyball Pro Tour. **In the area:** Conway National Park, 15 km S. Great Barrier Reef and 74 tropical islands in the Whitsunday group. **Visitor information:** Tourism Whitsundays, Shop 3/6 The Esplanade, Airlie Beach; (07) 4946 6673, freecall 1800 801 252. Web site www.whitsundays. com.au **See also:** Great Barrier Reef p. 455; The Mid-Tropics p. 460.

Stanthorpe Pop. 4154

MAP REF. 107 M2, 525 N12

The main town in the Granite Belt and in the mountain ranges along the border between Qld and NSW, Stanthorpe, 221 km SW of Brisbane, came into being after the discovery of tin at Quartpot Creek in 1872. Silver and lead were discovered in 1880 but the minerals boom did not last. The area has produced excellent wool but is best known for its apples, pears, plums, peaches and grapes. Stanthorpe is 915 m above sea level and is often the coolest part of the State. Spring is particularly beautiful with fruit trees and wattles in bloom. There are 90 varieties of wild orchids found in the area. **In town:** Museum, High St. Art Gallery and Library Complex, Weeroona Park, Marsh St. Market in the Mountains, cnr Marsh and Lock sts, 2nd Sun. each month. Feb.: Apple and Grape Harvest Festival (even-numbered years); Rodeo. May: Opera at Sunset. June–Aug.: Brass Monkey Season (winter festival). Oct.: Granite Belt Spring Wine Festival; Australian Small Winemakers Show. **In the area:** Heritage trail, towns in area, brochure available. Mt Marlay, 1 km E, for excellent views. Granite Belt wineries, most open for tastings and sales: Old Caves, just north of town; Stanthorpe Wine Centre, 9 km N; Castle Glen at The Summit, 10 km N; Heritage Wines at Cottonvale, 12 km N; Inigo Wines, Stone Ridge, Felsberg, Mountview, Kominos and the Bramble

Patch berry gardens and winery, near Glen Aplin, 11 km SW; Rumbalara at Fletcher, 14 km SW; Ballandean Estate, Golden Grove, Winewood, Bungawarra and Robinson's Family Winery, near Ballandean, 21 km SW; Bald Mountain at Wallangarra, 30 km S. Summertime Jazz on the Rocks in Jan. at Ballandean and Ballandean Estate. Sundown Observatory at Ballandean: astronomy displays; open nightly, check with information centre. Sundown National Park, 79 km SW: wilderness area; camping on Severn River in south-west of park. Girraween National Park, 32 km S, for camping, bushwalking, rock-climbing and spectacular wildflowers in spring. Storm King Dam, 26 km SE, for canoeing and water-skiing. Falls in Boonoo Boonoo National Park (NSW), 60 km SE. **Visitor information:** 26 Leslie Pde; (07) 4681 2057. Web site www. qldsoutherndowns.org.au **See also:** Darling Downs p. 452; National Parks p. 498.

Strathpine Pop. 10 108

MAP REF. 514 A10, 516 F11, 517 D3

Strathpine is north of Brisbane in the Pine Rivers region, a peaceful district that includes the forested areas and national parks closest to Brisbane. Taking advantage of this rural setting so close to the city are a number of art and craft industries. **In town:** Mar.: Pine Rivers Heritage Festival. Aug.: Camp Oven Bush Poets Festival. **In the area:** Self-guide scenic mountain walks, brochures available. Alma Park Zoo at Dakabin, 14 km N: native and exotic animals; Friendship Farm for children. Lakeside Racing Circuit, 14 km N, venue for major events. Osprey House, environmental centre, Dohles Rocks Rd, 18 km N. Sun. market at North Pine Country Park, 6 km NW. Australian Woolshed at Ferny Hills, 16 km SW: demonstrations of shearing, spinning and working sheepdogs; bush dances with bush band. Brisbane Forest Park, via Ferny Hills: pristine rainforest; walking tracks from settlement of Mount Glorious; Wivenhoe Lookout, 10 km NW of Mount Glorious. Mount Glorious–Samford Rd is scenic route. **Visitor information:** Pine Rivers Tourism Centre, Daisy Cottage, cnr Gympie and South Pine rds; (07) 3205 4793. Web site www.brisbane hinterland.com **See also:** Brisbane Hinterland p. 448; National Parks p. 498.

Surfers Paradise
Pop. part of Gold Coast

MAP REF. 517 G11, 518 F5, 525 Q10

Surfers Paradise is one of Australia's most popular holiday destinations. With its sunny subtropical climate, world-famous surf beaches, international standard accommodation, festive atmosphere and exciting attractions, Surfers Paradise appeals to a wide range of holidaymakers. **In town:** Attractions include: mall at Cavill Ave, regular free entertainment, Hard Rock Cafe, Ripleys Believe It or Not Museum; Orchid Avenue, just off Cavill Ave, European designer fashions and outdoor cafes; beach volleyball area near Cavill Ave; beachfront art and craft markets, each Fri. evening; KP Go Karting, Ferny Ave; Flycoaster and Bungee Rocket thrill rides, Cypress Ave; Gold Coast City Art Gallery and Arts Centre, and riverside Evandale sculpture walk, Bundall Rd. Fishing charters. Jan.: Honda Magic Millions Racing Carnival; Australian Open Beach Volleyball. Aug.–Sept.: Gold Coast Show. Oct.: Honda Indy 300; Gold Coast Tropicarnival; UNICEF's Universal Children's Day. Nov.: Australian Music Week. **In the area:** At Broadbeach, 4 km S: Conrad Jupiters Casino; scenic flights. Philipine Festival in June at Bundall, 4 km W. **Visitor information:** Gold Coast Tourism Bureau, Cavill Walk; (07) 5538 4419. Web site www.goldcoasttourism. com.au **See also:** Gold Coast & Hinterland p. 450.

Tambo Pop. 378

MAP REF. 524 B2

Tambo, 101 km SE of Blackall on the Matilda Hwy, was established in the mid-1860s to service surrounding pastoral properties. Explorer Thomas Mitchell first saw the Barcoo River from the town site, in 1846. **In town:** Self-guide heritage walk; Coolibah Walk, nature walk along Barcoo River, brochures available. Arthur St: in Shire Hall, Tambo Teddies Workshop, produces all-wool teddy bears; courthouse (1888), now library. Apr.: Stockshow. Sept.: Spring Festival. **In the area:** Wilderness Way 320-km self-guide drive, incl. historic sites, Aboriginal rock art, and Salvator Rosa section of Carnarvon National Park, 130 km E, birdwatching (camping permitted). Contact information centre for drive brochures and information about road conditions.

Toowoomba countryside

Visitor information: Arthur St; (07) 4654 6082. Web site www.outback holidays.tq.com.au **See also:** Outback & Gulf Country p. 464; National Parks p. 498.

Taroom Pop. 662

MAP REF. 525 J4

Taroom is on the banks of the Dawson River almost 300 km w of Maryborough. Cattle-raising is the main local industry. **Of interest:** Coolibah tree in main street, marked 'L. L.' by explorer Ludwig Leichhardt on his 1844 trip from Jimbour House near Dalby to Port Essington (north of Darwin). Museum, Kelman St, features old telephone-exchange equipment, farm machinery and items of local history; by appt only. May: Agricultural Show. Aug.: Leichhardt Festival. **In the area:** Scenic and historic tourist drives, brochure available. Rare Livistona palms near Leichhardt Hwy, 15 km n. Lake Murphy, 30 km n, pristine lake with birdlife, picnics, camping. Glebe Weir, 40 km n, off Leichhardt Hwy, water-skiing and fishing. **Visitor information:** Shire Offices, Yaldwyn St; (07) 4622 6113. **See also:** Capricorn p. 458.

Texas Pop. 772

MAP REF. 107 K3, 525 M12

Texas lies alongside the Dumaresq River and the Qld–NSW border, 55 km s of Inglewood. **In town:** Historical Museum in old police station (1893), Fleming St, open Sat. or by appt. Old Texas, on river off Schwenke St, remains of original town. July: Agricultural Show. Nov.: Roundup (even-numbered years). **In the area:** Beacon Lookout, 3 km SE, on Stanthorpe Rd. Good fishing along the river and in Glenlyon Dam, 45 km SE. Whyalla Feedlot, eastern side of Texas–Yelarbon Rd, largest cattle feedlot in Australia. Cunningham Weir, 31 km w off Texas–Yelarbon Rd, site where Allan Cunningham crossed the Dumaresq River in 1827. Coolmunda Reservoir, 75 km n: boating, pelicans and swans. **Visitor information:** Ridgways, 40 High St; (07) 4653 1245. Web site www. qldsoutherndowns.org.au **See also:** Darling Downs p. 452.

Theodore Pop. 508

MAP REF. 525 J2

Grain and cotton are the main crops on the irrigated land around this town on the Leichhardt Hwy, 220 km n of Miles. Timber-milling and cattle-grazing are also significant and you can see the huge draglines operating at the coal mines. Theodore was named after Edward Theodore, Qld Premier 1919–25, and designed by Walter Burley Griffin. **In town:** Theodore Hotel, The Boulevard, only cooperative hotel in Qld. Dawson Folk Museum, Second Ave, open by appt. **In the area:** Irrigation area: birdwatching, cotton-picking (Mar.–May). Fishing on Theodore Weir, southern outskirts of town. Isla Gorge National Park, 35 km sw. Cracow, 49 km SE, where gold was produced from famous Golden Plateau mine 1932–76. **Visitor information:** The Boulevard; (07) 4993 1900. **See also:** Capricorn p. 458.

Tin Can Bay Pop. 1779

MAP REF. 525 P5

Half an hour's drive north-east of Gympie takes travellers to Tin Can Bay and nearby Rainbow Beach. These two hamlets are popular fishing, prawning and crabbing areas; the quiet waters of Tin Can Bay are ideal for boating and fishing, while Rainbow Beach has good surfing. **In town:** Boat and yacht hire. Market, Gympie Rd, 3rd Sat. each month. Easter: Festival. June: Seafood and Leisure Festival. Dec.: Robert Pryde Memorial Surf Classic. **In the area:** Fishing Classic at Rainbow Beach, 41 km E, each July. Road south from Rainbow Beach (4WD) leads to the coloured sands and beaches of Cooloola section of Great Sandy National Park. At Inskip Point, 53 km NE: camping access along Point; vehicular ferry to Fraser Island. At Carlo Point, 3 km E: cruising, fishing, swimming, houseboats and yachts for hire. **Visitor information:** 4 Gympie Rd; (07) 5486 4140. Web site www.sunshinecoast.org **See also:** Sunshine Coast p. 453; National Parks p. 498.

Toowoomba Pop. 83 350

MAP REF. 525 N9

This city has a distinctive charm and graciousness in its wide, tree-lined streets, colonial architecture and 150 parks and gardens. Toowoomba is 127 km w of Brisbane, on the rim of the Great Dividing Range. It began in 1849 as a village near an important staging post, and was known as The Swamp. Aborigines pronounced the name 'T'wamp-bah'; this became 'Toowoomba'. Today it is the commercial centre for the fertile Darling Downs, with butter and cheese factories, sawmills, flour mills, tanneries, engineering and railway workshops, a modern iron foundry, and clothing and shoe factories. It has an active cultural and artistic life. **In town:** Self-guide Russell St heritage walk, brochure available. Cobb & Co. Museum, Lindsay St, traces history of horse-drawn vehicles. St Patrick's Cathedral (1880s), James St. St Luke's Anglican Church (1897), cnr Herries and Ruthven sts. Parks and gardens include: Lake Annand, MacKenzie St, for birdlovers; Scented Garden within Laurel Bank Park, cnr Herries and West sts; Botanic Gardens and adjacent Queens Park, Lindsay St; Waterbird Habitat, MacKenzie St; Boyce Gardens, North St; Japanese Garden at the University of Southern Queensland, Baker St. Wetlands of the World Park, cnr Stenner and Alderly sts. Royal Bull's Head Inn (1847), Brisbane St, fully restored by National Trust. Toowoomba Art Gallery in Ruthven St, brochure available. Antique and craft shops. Tourist drive with floral markers, brochure available. Markets: Eat Street Market, Margaret St, 1st Sun. each month; Queens Park, Margaret St, 3rd Sun. each month. Sept.: Carnival of Flowers. Oct.: Festival of the Horse. **In the area:** Walking and bike tracks, 'Fitch's Feats' brochure available. Scenic drives, brochure available: 48-km circuit to Spring Bluff (old railway station at Spring Bluff, approx. 16 km N of city, has superb gardens) and Murphys Creek, approx. 25 km N; 100-km circuit to Heifer Creek, known as Valley of the Sun, provides spectacular scenery; 255-km circuit takes in Bernborough Centre, historic Jondaryan Woolshed (daily shearing demonstrations), Cecil Plains Cotton Ginnery, Millmerran Museum and Pittsworth Folk Museum. Picnic Point, 5 km E, offers views of Lockyer Valley, mountains and waterfall. At Highfields, 12 km N: Orchid Park, Danish Flower Art, Pioneer Village. At Cabarlah, 19 km N: Black Forest Hill Cuckoo Clock Centre, Country Markets last Sun. each month. **Visitor information:** cnr James & Kitchener sts; (07) 4639 3797, freecall 1800 331 155. Web site www.toowoomba.qld.gov.au **See also:** Darling Downs p. 452.

Townsville   Pop. 75 990

MAP REF. 520, 521 G9, 529 P12

In 1864 sea captain Robert Towns commissioned James Melton Black to establish a settlement on Cleveland Bay to service the new inland cattle industry. Today, including its twin city of Thuringowa, Townsville is Australia's largest tropical city. There are many historic buildings, particularly around Cleveland Bay. The city's port handles minerals from Mount Isa and Cloncurry; beef and wool from the western plains; sugar and timber from the coastal region; and its own

Townsville Harbour

manufacturing and processing industries. Townsville is the administrative, commercial, education and manufacturing capital of northern Qld. It is becoming a renowned centre for research into marine life and is the headquarters for the Great Barrier Reef Marine Park Authority. **In town:** The Strand has tropical parks, waterfall and overhanging bougainvillea gardens. At the end of The Strand: rockpool for year-round swimming; Jezzine Military Museum. Jupiters Townsville Hotel and Casino, Sir Leslie Thiess Dr. Flinders St East: historic buildings; Reef HQ, features aquarium with touch-tank and walk-through transparent underwater viewing-tunnel; Imax Dome Theatre; Museum of Tropical Queensland, featuring artifacts from shipwreck of HMAS *Pandora*; ferry terminal for Magnetic Island and day cruises to the Great Barrier Reef. Billabong Sanctuary, Bruce Hwy, features koala feeding and crocodile shows. Perc Tucker Regional Art Gallery, Flinders Mall. Queen's Gardens, cnr Paxton and Gregory sts. Botanic Gardens, Anderson Park, Kings Rd. Castle Hill Lookout, off Stanley St. Townsville Town Common Conservation Park, Pallarenda Rd, a coastline park with prolific birdlife. Maritime Museum, Palmer St, South Townsville. Dive schools. Cotters Market in Flinders Mall each Sun. Mar.: Greek Festival. July: Australian Festival of Chamber Music. **In the area:** Cruises to Cairns via resort islands and reef on luxury catamaran *Coral Princess*; reef day-trips and dive cruises; day sailing around Magnetic Island; extended cruises to the Whitsundays; daily air connections to Orpheus Island; day outback tours, rainforest and whitewater rafting tours. Bowling Green Bay National Park, 25 km S, off Bruce Hwy. Pangola Park, 32 km S. Near Giru, 50 km SE: waterfalls, bushwalks, swimming; picnic and camping facilities. Australian Institute of Marine Science, 30 km E at Cape Ferguson, tours (bookings required). Offshore, Magnetic Island, resident population of more than 2000; two-thirds of island is national park featuring beaches, walks and wildlife. **Visitor information:** 303 Flinders Mall; (07) 4721 3660, freecall 1800 801 902. Web site www.townsvilleonline.com.au **See also:** Great Barrier Reef p. 455; The Mid-Tropics p. 460.

Cape York, the northernmost region in Queensland

Tully   Pop. 2509

MAP REF. 521 D3, 529 N9

Situated at the foot of Mt Tyson, Tully receives one of the highest annual rainfalls in Australia, around 4200 mm. Major industries are sugarcane, bananas, tropical fruit, cattle and timber. **In town:** Tully Sugar Mill tours (June–Nov.), bookings essential. Market, 2nd Sat. each month. July: Show. Nov.: Rodeo. **In the area:** Reef and island cruising. Whitewater rafting and kayaking on Tully River, beginning at Tully Gorge (44 km W); also superb scenery and swimming in the top reaches of the river. Fishing and beautiful Googorra Beach at Tully Heads, 22 km SE. Alligators Nest, 10 km S; beautiful rainforest, swimming in stream. Spectacular rainforests at Murray Falls (40 km SW) and Tully River Gorge (44 km W). **Visitor information:** Bruce Hwy; (07) 4068 2288. Web site www.townsvilleonline.com.au **See also:** The Mid-Tropics p. 460.

Warwick   Pop. 10 947

MAP REF. 107 M1, 525 N11

An attractive city in the Southern Downs, Warwick is 158 km SW of Brisbane on the Cunningham Hwy and 86 km S of Toowoomba on the New England Hwy. The area was explored by Allan Cunningham in 1827; in 1840

the Leslie brothers established a sheep station at Canning Downs. The NSW government asked Patrick Leslie to select a town site, and in 1849 Warwick was established. The railway from Ipswich was opened in 1871 and the town became a city in 1936. Warwick is alongside the willow-shaded Condamine River, and calls itself 'the Rose and Rodeo City'. The surrounding rich pastures support famous horse and cattle studs and produce fine wool and grain. Fruit, vegetables and timber grow well, and the area is noted for its dairy products and bacon. **In town:** Self-guide walk around historic buildings, map available. Pringle Cottage (1870), Dragon St, houses large historic photo collection, vehicles and machinery. Jubilee Gardens, cnr Alice and Helene sts, and Leslie Park, cnr Palmerin and Fitzroy sts, feature displays of roses. Warwick Regional Art Gallery, Albion St. Apr.: National Rock Swap Festival. June–Aug.: Brass Monkey Season (winter festival). Oct.: Australia's Famous Rose and Rodeo Festival. **In the area:** Heritage and cultural 80-km drive, brochure available. Leslie Dam, 15 km W, for water sports. Sheep and emu farm at Mirambeena, 15 km E, along Yangan Rd and right at Wiedmans Rd. **Visitor information:** 49 Albion St (New England Hwy); (07) 4661 3401. Web site www.qldsoutherndowns.org.au **See also:** Darling Downs p. 452.

Weipa   Pop. 2200

MAP REF. 530 B7

Located on the west coast of Cape York, the town of Weipa, built 1961 on the site of a mission station and Aboriginal reserve, is the home of the world's largest bauxite mine. The town provides a full range of services for travellers. **In town:** Guided tours of bauxite mine provide excellent coverage of whole mining process at Weipa. **In the area:** Number of fishing and camping areas near the town, developed for the well-equipped visitor; camping also at Mapoon, 85 km N (Aboriginal Land, access permit required). **Visitor information:** Tourism Tropical North Queensland, 51 The Esplanade, Cairns; (07) 4051 3588. Web site www.tnq.org.au **See also:** The Far North p. 461.

Winton   Pop. 1142

MAP REF. 533 M8

Banjo Paterson wrote Australia's most famous song, 'Waltzing Matilda', on Dagworth Station near Winton in 1895. Combo Waterhole was then part of Dagworth, and the ballad had its first public airing in Winton. The town is 177 km NW of Longreach on the Matilda Hwy. A major sheep area, Winton is also a trucking centre for the giant road trains bringing cattle from the Channel Country to the railhead. In 1920 the first office of Qantas was registered in Winton. The town's water supply comes out of deep artesian bores at a temperature of 83°C. **In town:** In Elderslie St: Historic Royal Theatre, open-air movie theatre and museum, one of the oldest still operating in Australia; swagman statue near swimming pool; Gift and Gem Shop with 'Opal Walk' inside. Also in Elderslie St, Waltzing Matilda Centre: displays based on the famous song; Qantilda Museum, highlights Winton's role in the birth of Qantas and displays a 9000-item heritage collection; opal mining display; outback art gallery. Arno's Wall, Vindex St, opposite Shire Offices, ongoing concrete-wall creation containing 'every item imaginable'. Easter: Easter in the Outback. June: Waltzing Matilda Festival. Sept.: Outback Festival (odd-numbered years). **In the area:** Bladensburg National Park, 2 km S, self-drive tour of park. Skull Hole, 40 km S, has Aboriginal paintings and bora ceremonial grounds. Opalton, 115 km S, remains of historic town; working gemfields nearby. Carisbrooke

Station, 85 km SW, a working sheep station; Aboriginal cave paintings and scenic drives in surrounds; day tours and accommodation. Lark Quarry Conservation Park, 110 km SW, features preserved tracks of dinosaur 'stampede'. Combo Waterhole Conservation Park, 150 km NW via Matilda Hwy. **Visitor information:** Waltzing Matilda Centre, Elderslie St; (07) 4657 1466. Web site www.matildacentre.com.au **See also:** Outback & Gulf Country p. 464.

Yandina
Pop. 931

MAP REF. 519 E6

Yandina lies 9 km N of Nambour and is the home of The Ginger Factory, the largest such factory in the world, located in Pioneer Rd. Visitors can see Gingertown, watch ginger cooking demonstrations, watch ginger being processed and ride on the historic Queensland Cane Train through the landscaped gardens. Bunya Park, a small wildlife sanctuary, is in the factory grounds. **In town:** Opposite Ginger Factory, Nutworks Macadamia Processors: see processing of macadamia nuts; tastings. Carinya, historic homestead on Bruce Hwy at northern edge of town. Jan.: Ginger Flower Festival. **In the area:** Wappa Dam, just west of town. At Eumundi, 10 km N: Country Fair selling fresh produce each Wed.; widely known markets each Sat. a.m., selling goods ranging from local fruit and vegetables to art and craft; impressive old Imperial Hotel near markets. **Visitor information:** Sunshine Coast Information, cnr Aerodrome Rd and Sixth Ave, Maroochydore; (07) 5479 1566, freecall 1800 882 032. **See also:** Sunshine Coast p. 453.

Yeppoon
Pop. 8810

MAP REF. 527 O10

This popular coastal resort, 40 km NE of Rockhampton, lies on the shores of Keppel Bay. Yeppoon and the beaches to its south – Cooee Bay, Roslyn Bay, Causeway Lake, Emu Park and Keppel Sands – are known as the Capricorn Coast. Great Keppel Island Resort is 13 km offshore. Market, 1st Sun. each month. Fig Tree Markets, next to information centre, 3rd Sun. each month. Jan.: Australia Day Celebrations. Feb.: Surf Lifesaving Championships. Aug.: Ozfest, with World Cooeeing Competition. Sept.: Pineapple Festival. Oct.: Octoberfest. **In the area:** Scenic

drives and adventure tours. Wetland Tour at Capricorn International Resort, 9 km N. Cooberrie Park, 15 km N, a noted flora and fauna reserve. Further 17 km N, Byfield State Forest, home of extremely rare Byfield fern, boardwalk along Waterpark Creek; rainforest cabins nearby. Keppel Bay Marina at Rosslyn Bay Harbour, 7 km S, bareboat and fishing charters; sea access to Great Keppel Island and nearby underwater observatory. Blow Hole at Double Head, 7 km S. At Emu Park, 19 km S: 'singing ship' memorial to Captain Cook (sea breezes cause hidden organ pipes to make sounds); Service of Remembrance (memorial to American troops) each July; Octoberfest each Oct. Koorana Crocodile Farm, 38 km SW, off Emu Park–Rockhampton Rd at Keppel Sands. **Visitor information:** Capricorn Coast Tourist Information Centre, Scenic Hwy; (07) 4939 4888, freecall 1800 675 785. **See also:** Great Barrier Reef p. 455; Capricorn p. 458.

Yungaburra
Pop. 985

MAP REF. 521 B1, 523 D12, 529 M7

On the edge of the Atherton Tableland, 13 km E of Atherton, the town is known for its National Trust Historic Precinct listing. **In town:** Self-guide Historic Precinct Buildings Walk. Lake Eacham Hotel, Cedar St. Platypus-viewing platform at

Peterson Creek, on Gillies Hwy, best times sunrise and sunset. The Chalet Rainforest Gallery, Gillies Hwy: murals, timber art and Rainforest Folk (dolls). Artists Galleries, cnr Gillies Hwy and Cedar St. Various gem and craft shops. Widely known produce and craft markets, on Gillies Hwy, 4th Sat. each month. June: Yuletide. July: Jazz Festival. Oct.: Folk Festival. **In the area:** Curtain Fig Tree, 2.5 km SW, spectacular example of strangler fig, with aerial roots in curtain-like formation. The Seven Sisters, 7 volcanic cinder cones, 2 km N. Tinaburra, 3 km N on the shores of Lake Tinaroo. Views of lake from Tinaroo Falls dam outlet, 23 km N. Spectacular views over Gillies Range from Heales Outlook Lookout, 16 km NE. In Crater Lakes National Park, 2 volcanic lakes: Lake Eacham (5 km E) has circuit track through rainforest; Lake Barrine (10 km NE), has cruises. At Malanda, 20 km S: 19th-century Majestic Theatre; market, 3rd Sat. each month; Agricultural Show in June. Malanda Falls Conservation Park, on the edge of town, signposted rainforest walks and the Jungle Interpretive Centre. McHugh Road Lookout, 20 km S of Malanda. **Visitor information:** Nick's Swiss-Italian Restaurant, Gillies Hwy; (07) 4095 3330. Web site www.eachamshire.qld.gov.au **See also:** The Far North p. 461; National Parks p. 498.

Water activities at Great Keppel Island near Yeppoon

NATIONAL PARKS

Spectacular Coomera Falls in Lamington National Park

IN THE SOUTH-EAST OF THE STATE

Around Brisbane, the crescent of national parks, or Scenic Rim, includes **Main Range, Mount Barney, Lamington** and **Springbrook** national parks, which form part of a World Heritage-listed area. These offer panoramic views, extensive walking tracks, picnic facilities and a range of recreational opportunities. Lamington attracts thousands of visitors to its cool rainforest, rich in elkhorn and staghorn ferns and over 700 other plant species, including orchids.

Tamborine National Park, in the Gold Coast hinterland, attracts many day visitors from Brisbane and the Gold Coast to its rainforests, waterfalls and scenic lookouts. **Girraween National Park**, the 'Place of Flowers', south of Stanthorpe and close to the New South Wales border, offers visitors excellent floral displays. This area is a photographer's paradise, while the park's massive granite outcrops provide a challenge for walkers.

Offshore in Moreton Bay, **Moreton Island National Park** is predominantly a wilderness area with vast tracts of sand dunes including Mt Tempest (280 m), which is probably the tallest permanent sand dune in the world. On the leeward side at Tangalooma Wild Dolphin Resort, wild dolphins make regular visits to be fed by resort guests.

Bunya Mountains National Park, 250 kilometres north-west of Brisbane, was established to preserve the largest remaining bunya pine rainforest in the world. It was here that Aboriginal people gathered about every third year to feast on bunya nuts. There is camping available and excellent graded tracks for walking. Further east lie the **Glass House Mountains**, eroded volcanic plugs that rise suddenly from the landscape. First sighted by Captain Cook in 1770, seven of these mountains – Coonoorwin, Tibrogargan, Ngungun, Miketeebumulgrai, Coochin, Elimbah and Beerwah – are in the national park.

Noosa National Park, 140 kilometres north of Brisbane, offers the visitor a wide variety of coastal scenery. Walking tracks lead to lookouts from which can be seen such unusual rock formations as Hell's Gates and Boiling Pot. Located further north, off Hervey Bay, is the world's largest sand island, Fraser Island. The northern third of the island is part of **Great Sandy National Park**. This and its Cooloola section on the mainland are largely 4WD territory; the Cooloola section offers excellent boating opportunities, particularly on the Noosa River.

Launches and charter vessels from several central Queensland ports will take visitors to Heron, Masthead, North West and Lady Musgrave

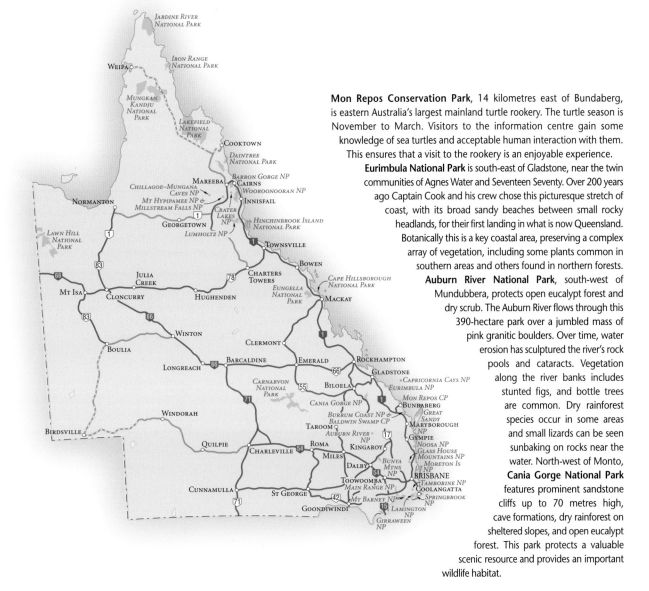

Map labels:
JARDINE RIVER NATIONAL PARK
IRON RANGE NATIONAL PARK
WEIPA
MUNGKAN KANDJU NATIONAL PARK
LAKEFIELD NATIONAL PARK
COOKTOWN
DAINTREE NATIONAL PARK
BARRON GORGE NP
MAREEBA
CAIRNS
CHILLAGOE–MUNGANA CAVES NP
WOOROONOONAN NP
MT HYPIPAMEE NP & MILLSTREAM FALLS NP
INNISFAIL
NORMANTON
CRATER LAKES NP
GEORGETOWN
HINCHINBROOK ISLAND NATIONAL PARK
LUMHOLTZ NP
LAWN HILL NATIONAL PARK
TOWNSVILLE
BOWEN
JULIA CREEK
CHARTERS TOWERS
CAPE HILLSBOROUGH NATIONAL PARK
MT ISA
CLONCURRY
HUGHENDEN
EUNGELLA NATIONAL PARK
MACKAY
WINTON
CLERMONT
BOULIA
BARCALDINE
EMERALD
ROCKHAMPTON
LONGREACH
GLADSTONE
CARNARVON NATIONAL PARK
BILOELA
CAPRICORNIA CAYS NP
EURIMBULA NP
WINDORAH
CANIA GORGE NP
MON REPOS CP
BUNDABERG
BURRUM COAST NP
BALDWIN SWAMP CP
GREAT SANDY NP
BIRDSVILLE
TAROOM
MARYBOROUGH
AUBURN RIVER NP
GYMPIE
QUILPIE
ROMA
KINGAROY
NOOSA NP
GLASS HOUSE MOUNTAINS NP
CHARLEVILLE
MILES
MORETON IS NP
DALBY
BUNYA MTNS NP
BRISBANE
TAMBORINE NP
COOLANGATTA
CUNNAMULLA
ST GEORGE
TOOWOOMBA
MAIN RANGE NP
SPRINGBROOK NP
MT BARNEY NP
LAMINGTON NP
GOONDIWINDI
GIRRAWEEN NP

Mon Repos Conservation Park, 14 kilometres east of Bundaberg, is eastern Australia's largest mainland turtle rookery. The turtle season is November to March. Visitors to the information centre gain some knowledge of sea turtles and acceptable human interaction with them. This ensures that a visit to the rookery is an enjoyable experience.

Eurimbula National Park is south-east of Gladstone, near the twin communities of Agnes Water and Seventeen Seventy. Over 200 years ago Captain Cook and his crew chose this picturesque stretch of coast, with its broad sandy beaches between small rocky headlands, for their first landing in what is now Queensland. Botanically this is a key coastal area, preserving a complex array of vegetation, including some plants common in southern areas and others found in northern forests.

Auburn River National Park, south-west of Mundubbera, protects open eucalypt forest and dry scrub. The Auburn River flows through this 390-hectare park over a jumbled mass of pink granitic boulders. Over time, water erosion has sculptured the river's rock pools and cataracts. Vegetation along the river banks includes stunted figs, and bottle trees are common. Dry rainforest species occur in some areas and small lizards can be seen sunbaking on rocks near the water. North-west of Monto, **Cania Gorge National Park** features prominent sandstone cliffs up to 70 metres high, cave formations, dry rainforest on sheltered slopes, and open eucalypt forest. This park protects a valuable scenic resource and provides an important wildlife habitat.

islands, all rich in coral and marine life and a paradise for snorkellers and scuba divers. The Southern Reef islands are outstanding rookeries of the loggerhead and green turtles, and the summer nesting-grounds for thousands of wedge-tailed shearwaters and white-capped noddies. Lady Musgrave Island section of **Capricornia Cays National Park** is a charming coral cay reached from Bundaberg and Seventeen Seventy. Around the cay's edge, exposed to wind and salt spray, grows a vegetation fringe of casuarina and pandanus, which protects the shady pisonia forest on the inner part of the island. The sheltered lagoon is popular for sailing, snorkelling and reef-viewing in glass-bottomed boats.

Coastal parks around Bundaberg include Burrum Coast National Park and Baldwin Swamp and Mon Repos conservation parks. **Burrum Coast National Park**, south of Bundaberg, covers 22 500 hectares of essential wildlife habitat; plant communities in the park include mangroves lining the Gregory and Burrum rivers, wallum heathland, eucalypt and angophora forests, tea-tree swamps and small pockets of palm forest. Roads in the park are gravel or sand, and 4WD vehicles are recommended, although at times conventional vehicle access is possible. Only 3 kilometres east of Bundaberg and covering 40 hectares is the Baldwin Wetlands, containing the **Baldwin Swamp Conservation Park**. Walking tracks and a boardwalk allow observation of the park's wildlife.

IN THE NORTH-EAST OF THE STATE

Queensland's central and northern coastal islands range from large, steep continental types to coral cays, many of them lying between the mainland and the outer Great Barrier Reef. Several national park islands have been developed for tourism; these include **Hinchinbrook**, one of the world's largest national park islands with 39 900 hectares of wilderness and quiet beaches. More than 90 per cent of the 100 islands in the Whitsunday Group are national parks and six also have resorts. Sail-yourself yachts are a novel way to visit some of the more isolated spots.

Eungella National Park, 83 kilometres west of Mackay, is the Aboriginal 'Land of the Clouds'. It is one of Queensland's most majestic parks, and the freshness under the canopy of rainforest makes it a perfect destination for a day trip. Camping is available at Fern Flat. **Cape Hillsborough National Park**, 50 kilometres north-west of Mackay, combines the beauty of an island with the accessibility of the mainland. Wildlife includes kangaroos, wallabies, possums, echidnas and numerous bird species.

Within a several-hundred-kilometre radius of Cairns are scores of national parks catering for all tastes. About 50 kilometres from Cairns is the Atherton Tableland, on which lie several national parks. Here visitors can follow walking tracks through spectacular rainforest at **Mount Hypipamee**, or visit the 65-metre-wide **Millstream Falls**, or the famous crater lakes of Eacham and Barrine in **Crater Lakes National Park**.

A north Queensland visit would not be complete without a train trip to Kuranda via **Barron Gorge National Park** and a return gondola ride on the Skyrail Rainforest Cableway, or a visit to the **Wooroonooran**, **Lumholtz** and **Daintree** national parks. This relatively undeveloped mountainous country, with its scenic waterfalls and lush rainforest, should not be missed. **Chillagoe–Mungana Caves National Park**, three hours' drive from Cairns, is dominated by weird limestone outcrops, castle-like pinnacles that house a wonderland of colourful caves. Guided tours are conducted daily. Once Queensland's leading mineral producing area, it is still popular with fossickers.

Today Cape York Peninsula is a magnet for tourists, even though the only aim of thousands of visitors may be simply to stand at its tip. The peninsula's vast and monotonous country is interspersed with surprising pockets of forest, broad vegetation-fringed rivers and occasional waterfalls – all home to a wide variety of wildlife. **Jardine River**, **Mungkan Kandju** and **Iron Range** national parks are destinations for keen and experienced wilderness explorers. However, a growing number of visitors divert to **Lakefield**. Its fringing rainforest, paperbark woodland, open grassy plains, swamps and coastal mudflats leading to mangroves along Princess Charlotte Bay all offer a variety of attractions. Basic campsites are located along many watercourses.

CENTRAL QUEENSLAND

One of the most breathtakingly beautiful scenic reserves in Australia is **Carnarvon National Park**, 720 kilometres by road north-west of Brisbane. The Carnarvon Gorge section of this park, a dramatic, twisting chasm gouged from soft sandstone cliffs, is a popular destination for campers. Formed walking tracks lead through forests of eucalypt,

she-oaks, tall cabbage palms, and relict macrozamia palms. Two major Aboriginal art sites, the Art Gallery and Cathedral Cave, contain rock stencils and engravings of great significance. Limits on campsite visitor numbers protect the ecology of the park (bookings essential; remove your own rubbish).

IN THE NORTH-WEST OF THE STATE

In the remote north-west of Queensland, **Lawn Hill National Park** is an oasis on the edge of the Barkly Tableland. The road into the park is very rough in places, so 4WD travel is recommended, especially for caravanners. Lawn Hill Gorge has colourful cliffs rising 60 metres to the surrounding plateau. On the gorge walls are Aboriginal rock paintings, and middens also remain. Visitors can see these from the boardwalk and viewing platforms. The creek has permanent water and offers a habitat for tropical vegetation, including cabbage tree palms and Leichhardt pines. The water attracts various bird species, and reptiles including freshwater crocodiles, tortoises and water monitors. There are several walking tracks in the park. World Heritage-listed Riversleigh Fossil Field, site of unique fossil finds of previously unknown animals, is an extension of the park.

For more information about Queensland's national parks, including the requirement for camping permits, contact the Naturally Queensland Information Centre, 160 Ann St, Brisbane (PO Box 155, Brisbane Albert St 4002); (07) 3227 8186. Web site www.env.qld.gov.au

Hinchinbrook Island, one of the world's largest national park islands

WILDLIFE-WATCHING

The cobalt-blue Ulysses butterfly

AROUND BRISBANE

Do not let the busy cityscape and bustling seaside shopping plazas fool you – there are many wildlife-watching opportunities in and around Brisbane.

Some favourite wildlife-watching destinations in the hinterland area include Daisy Hill State Forest and Brisbane Forest Park. **Daisy Hill State Forest**, a bushy pocket on the outskirts of Brisbane's southern suburbs, supports a variety of animals, including a colony of koalas. The Daisy Hill Koala Centre in the park provides a wealth of information on these animals and their habitats. Visitors can climb the treetop tower to scan the surrounding canopy for wild koalas. **Brisbane Forest Park**, which abuts the eastern suburbs of the city, features Walk-about Creek Wildlife Centre, a simulated creek environment with perspex windows. Brisbane Forest Park is also home to a colourful array of forest birdlife and nocturnal animals such as possums and gliders; inquire on (07) 3300 4855 for guided spotlight tours.

Wildlife-watching opportunities are also numerous along the coast. In particular, the waters around **Moreton Island**, only 35 km east of Brisbane, are a haven for a variety of marine mammals including dolphins, whales, dugongs and turtles.

Dolphins can be seen frolicking in the warm shallow waters surrounding Moreton Island on the bay and surf sides. The Tangalooma Wild Dolphin Resort has developed a wild dolphin care and hand-feeding programme. A diet chart has been developed and care is taken to feed the dolphins only one third of their daily food needs. Resort guests may participate, but are asked not to touch or handle the dolphins in any way, although it is not uncommon for the animals to give a friendly nudge as they approach humans.

Humpback whales can also be spotted passing the island between June and November. Cape Moreton is the best vantage point. Commercial whale-watch cruises operate in season. There is some irony in this new attraction, given that Tangalooma was a whaling station from 1952 to 1962, when an estimated 600 whales were slaughtered per year.

Another marine mammal common to these waters is the dugong, which grazes on the seagrass beds fringing the island's western shores. These elusive creatures can sometimes be seen surfacing for air near the shores of the island. Turtles are often seen swimming in the waters around Cape Moreton.

With its variety of habitat types, ranging from inter-tidal wetlands to swamps, heathlands and open forests, Moreton Island also supports nearly one hundred species of sea and shore birds, as well as over eighty

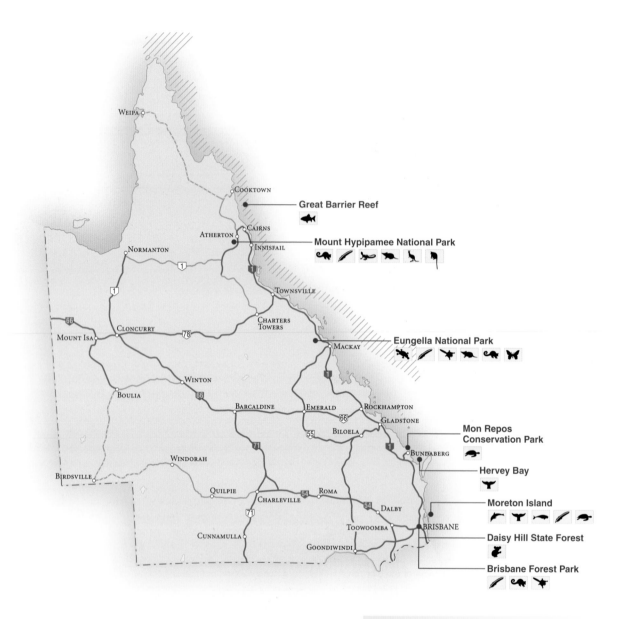

species of land birds. Prime birdwatching sites include Mirrapool and the tidal flats on the south-western side of the island, where thousands of migratory birds feed and roost from September to April. Here the birds rest before their long journey back to the Northern Hemisphere. At all sites, visitors can help by driving slowly and not congregating in a large group when birdwatching.

IN THE GREAT BARRIER REEF

The **Great Barrier Reef** brims with life: iridescent blue starfish; pink sponge baubles; bright green turtle weed; fragile needle coral; brain coral; mushroom coral; slender yellow trumpet fish; vivid parrot fish with beak-like jaws; schools of delicate blue pillars; butterfly fish and angel fish... This maze of coral reefs and coral cays, extending over 2000 kilometres along the Queensland coast, supports the most diverse collection of marine life to be found anywhere in the world.

The Great Barrier Reef can be viewed on one of the many day cruises operating from mainland ports, including Cairns, Port Douglas, Townsville, Airlie Beach and Mission Beach. The cruise companies offer a variety of packages and generally include expert guides and the use of snorkelling equipment. Alternatively, you might choose to base yourself on one of the islands on or near the reef. If you go reef walking, remember to walk gently, following marked trails where available. Take care not to break the fragile

---

WILDLIFE-WATCHING ETHICS

Do not disturb wildlife or wildlife habitats. Keep the impact of your presence to a minimum. Use available cover or hides wherever possible.

Do not feed wildlife, even in urban areas.
(Note: supervised feeding is allowed at some locations)

Be careful not to introduce exotic plants and animals – definitely no pets.

Stay on defined trails.

coral, wear strong-soled shoes for your own protection and keep an eye on the tides. Enjoy nature's display, but refrain from collecting or disturbing the marine life. Watch out for dangerous creatures, including stonefish, sea urchins and cone shells.

IN THE MACKAY REGION

Eighty kilometres west of Mackay, in the enchanting rainforest setting of **Eungella National Park**, there runs a clear mountain stream which is home to one of nature's great mysteries, the platypus. This egg-laying mammal with webbed feet, a flat paddle-like tail and a duck-shaped bill is frequently

A humpback whale tail-slaps as it passes the Queensland coast

spotted swimming below the special viewing platform on the banks of the Broken River.

Platypuses are generally sighted at dusk and in the early morning. It is important to keep quiet because they have sensitive hearing and are easily disturbed. Concentric rings on the water surface indicate that platypuses are active below. They feed on creatures such as insect larvae and freshwater shrimps found at the bottom of pools and creeks. The platypuses store their food in their cheeks and can be seen returning to the surface at intervals to chew and swallow.

As darkness closes in, the forest floor and treetops rustle with nocturnal life. An evening walk by torchlight will reveal a large number of busy animals, including birds such as tawny frogmouths, curlews and boobook owls, as well as gliders, bandicoots and brushtail possums.

Eungella is also known as the southernmost location of the spectacular cobalt-blue Ulysses butterfly, often sighted in the wind tunnels created by gullies and roads. The Ulysses grubs feed on the euodia trees in the park. It is not unusual to see the magical 'flashing of the blue' on a visit to Eungella, but do not expect to see these butterflies in large numbers.

ON THE FRASER COAST

Whale-watching is fast becoming a not-to-be-missed activity for visitors to Queensland's coastal destinations, from Stradbroke Island to the Whitsundays. Every year humpback whales leave the cold Antarctic waters in April and migrate along Australia's eastern shoreline, past Fraser Island and on to their breeding grounds in the Great Barrier Reef.

An estimated 400 humpback whales travel through **Hervey Bay** (between Fraser Island and the mainland) between August and October each season, making this one of the prime whale-watching spots in Queensland. The humpbacks provide great entertainment for their human audience. To see a 30–40 tonne whale exhale then arch its expansive back and roll forward, tail in air, is to bear witness to one of nature's greatest spectacles. Other antics include the 'spy hop', 'pec-slapping' and 'tail-slapping'. Numerous whale-watching cruises operate in the area. Contact the Maryborough Information Centre for information and bookings; (07) 4121 4111.

Mon Repos Conservation Park near Bundaberg features the largest mainland turtle rookery in eastern Australia. It is the hatching ground for loggerhead, green and Australian flatback turtles that nest between November and January. Hatchlings emerge from mid-January to March. A ranger is present during the turtle season to provide information and ensure visitors do not disturb the turtles. Visitor numbers are strictly limited to minimise the impact on breeding. Successful breeding here is critical to the survival of the turtles, particularly the endangered loggerhead species.

The best time of day to view nesting turtles is after dark, near high tide, whereas hatchlings are best viewed between 8 p.m. and midnight. It is recommended that you phone the Mon Repos Information Centre on (07) 4159 1652 to check times. Remember that turtles are wild marine animals, so there are occasions when they choose not to arrive.

During nesting time, visitors watch as the large female loggerheads haul themselves onto the beach and scoop a nest in the sand with their rear flippers, then fill it with eggs. Later in the season, young turtles provide another great spectacle as they emerge from the sand and scurry into the sea.

ON THE ATHERTON TABLELAND

Seven species of possum inhabit the dense rainforest surrounding an extinct volcanic crater in **Mount Hypipamee National Park**. This small pocket of dense vegetation, surrounded by farmland on the Atherton Tableland in northern Queensland, really comes alive at night. Day visitors can expect to see the usual gang of brush turkeys scavenging for scraps around the main picnic area; honeyeaters are also commonly seen here. During daylight hours, most of the possums are asleep in their dens, but careful observation may reveal a green ringtail possum snoozing on a branch. Visitors who stay until dusk and wait quietly as the sun sets, will enjoy a more exciting wildlife-watching experience. Leaves rustle on the forest floor; geckoes, bandicoots and pademelons start to emerge.

Most of the possum species at Mount Hypipamee can be seen by torchlight in the short distance between the main picnic area and the road leading into the park. The most common is the coppery brushtail. Other species include the green ringtail possum with green-tinged fur, and the lemuroid ringtail possum, which leaps through the air from branch to branch.

Another nocturnal mammal, the Lumholtz's tree kangaroo, is often found here and in other pockets of forest on the Atherton Tableland. These animals spend the day asleep in a crouched sitting position in the crown of a tree or on a branch. As evening approaches, they unfold their powerful limbs and display their remarkable climbing skills. Tree kangaroos are the only kangaroos that can move their hind legs independently of each other, making them able to 'walk' as well as hop.

For a good introduction to Queensland's wildlife visit David Fleay Wildlife Park on the Gold Coast; features include the Nocturnal House and 'Creature Feature' wildlife demonstrations. For more information on wildlife-watching in Queensland's national parks, contact the Environmental Protection Agency's Naturally Queensland Information Centre, 160 Ann St, Brisbane (PO Box 155, Brisbane Albert St 4002); (07) 3227 8186. Web site www.env.qld.gov.au

CLASSIC TOUR

HINTERLAND ESCAPE

Noosa Heads to Landsborough via the Glass House Mountains (150 km)

This journey into the Blackall Range and the Glass House Mountains is a delightful diversion from the beaches and popular resorts of Queensland's Sunshine Coast. The Blackall Range forms an impressive natural backdrop to the coast, rising almost 400 metres above the plain. From the ridge, there are expansive views over rolling hills down to the Pacific Ocean and south to the distinctive profile of the Glass House Mountains. The range features a string of charming mountain villages where you can browse through galleries, meet the local artisans and enjoy a leisurely lunch. As a grand finale, you will descend from the range and drive into the Glass House Mountains before returning to the coast. This tour can be completed in a day, but there are plenty of B&Bs and guesthouses en route if you want to make the most of your hinterland experience.

1 Noosa lifestyle

Your tour commences at **Noosa Heads**, a fashionable resort set on lovely Laguna Bay at the mouth of the Noosa River, just 140 kilometres north of Brisbane. Here you can browse through a diverse range of shops, sample the offerings of some of Australia's most innovative chefs and relax on the beautiful beaches.

The nearby headland is part of Noosa National Park, where a network of walking tracks leads through rainforest and coastal heathland to sandy beaches and dramatic cliff-top vantage points. Laguna Lookout, at the end of Viewland Drive (just off the main road into Noosa Heads) provides sweeping coastal views to the north and views of Noosa River to the west, especially beautiful at sunset. For another perspective on the waterscape, take a cruise up the Noosa River, through the inland lakes system to the reflective tannin-coloured waters of The Everglades.

2 Marvellous market

To begin your hinterland escape, drive through Noosaville and turn left onto Eumundi–Noosa Road. The road meanders inland through forest and open farmland to the historic 19th-century timber town of **Eumundi**. On Saturday mornings this is the setting for one of Australia's most colourful markets. Aim to arrive as early as possible – breakfast at the

Noosa Heads

Eumundi Market is a real treat. Taste the fine locally grown produce, browse through the clothing and crafts, relax in the shade and be entertained by the buskers.

3 Ginger galore

Continue through Eumundi, travelling south for several kilometres before crossing the Bruce Highway to join Bunya Road. On reaching Yandina, turn left from the centre of town and follow the signs to **The Ginger Factory**, one of Queensland's most visited attractions. Ginger is a major local crop, and The Ginger Factory has combined its operations with a range of interesting experiences. You can see how ginger is processed, watch cooking

demonstrations, purchase jams and other treats from the Ginger Shoppe, ride the historic Queensland Cane Train and visit Bunya Park, a wildlife sanctuary that is part of this complex.

The Ginger Factory
50 Pioneer Road
Yandina
Phone: (07) 5446 7096
Open: daily 9 a.m.–5 p.m.

4 Climbing the escarpment

Return to the centre of Yandina and continue south along Nambour Road, running parallel to the Bruce Highway. As you enter the outskirts of Nambour, turn right onto National Park Road which becomes Nambour–Mapleton Road.

Leaving Nambour behind, the road winds up the eastern escarpment of the Blackall Range. Just before you reach Mapleton, take time to stop at the Dulong Lookout situated at the top of the climb; to reach the lookout take the short signposted road to the left. The views are exhilarating: rolling green hills to the east and dense forest to the north.

From the centre of Mapleton, follow the Obi Obi Road to **Mapleton Falls National Park**, containing a mixture of forest types on the sheltered western escarpment. The falls plunge a dramatic 120 metres into the valley below. Peregrine Lookout, on the edge of the falls, is a 10-minute walk downhill from the car park.

5 Cascades

Return to Mapleton and turn right along the Montville–Mapleton Road. The road follows the ridge of the Blackall Range, providing magnificent views to the east and west as you drive along. Some of the finest views towards the coast are from Flaxton Gardens, on your left – there is a pottery workshop, winery and restaurant in the grounds.

Shortly after Flaxton, take the signposted turn-off to **Kondalilla National Park**. Here, the clear mountain waters cascade over mossy boulders and flow into a rock pool at the top of Kondalilla Falls. The park is also noted for its abundant wildlife: because of the remarkable diversity of vegetation, there are over 100 bird species in an area of only 327 hectares.

Take the Picnic Creek Circuit (1-hour return) through tall open forest to view the falls from above, or continue along the longer Kondalilla Falls Circuit through the rainforest to the base of the falls. If you take either of these walks, be warned that the uphill return is very steep.

6 Mountain village

Return to the main road and continue to **Montville**, the picturesque artistic centre of the Blackall Range. Settled by citrus growers in 1887, it has an English-style village green as its centrepiece. A signposted heritage trail starts at the Village Hall. Take time to browse through the pottery, art and craft galleries that line the streets. Montville is an ideal spot to stop for lunch: there are many cafes and restaurants to choose from.

If you prefer a picnic, turn right on Western Avenue and take the signposted road to Lake Baroon, which branches off to the left. At the foot of a very steep incline lies Baroon Pocket Dam, an attractive and accessible picnic spot: tables are set among the pine trees on the lake foreshore.

7 Unlimited vistas

Travelling south along the ridge from Montville towards Maleny, you will be treated to **12 kilometres of spectacular views** in all directions. Gerrard Lookout, situated on the left side of the road, is an absolute must. Standing here, at 375 metres above sea level, you can see the entire stretch

of the Sunshine Coast – from the high-rise outline of Caloundra in the south to the natural beauty of the coastline around Noosa Heads in the north. Balmoral Lookout, a few kilometres further on the right, offers an entirely different perspective. Here you can see north across farmland to the nearby Lake Baroon, and westward to the forests around Kenilworth and the mountainous country beyond.

Montville

Glass House Mountains

8 Looking south

When you reach the Landsborough–Maleny Road, turn right towards Maleny (as signposted). Maleny is one of the larger settlements in the Blackall Range, a service centre for the surrounding farmland and also catering for tourists. At the end of the commercial centre of town, turn left down the Maleny–Stanley River Road, then left into Mountain View Road at the T-intersection.

Almost immediately after turning onto Mountain View Road, stop at McCarthys Lookout (on the right) for your first breathtaking **overview of the Glass House Mountains**; an illustrated sign identifies each of the 13 peaks, eight of which belong to Glass House Mountains National Park. These uncompromising formations, the eroded remnants of ancient volcanoes, rise abruptly from the plain. Captain James Cook gave the mountains their unusual name when he sailed past in 1770: viewed from the coast, they resembled the glass furnaces of his native Yorkshire.

Continue along Mountain View Road, heading east along the ridge. Mary Cairncross Park, on your left, is the legacy of 19th-century environmentalist Mary Cairncross. The park has a fascinating natural history centre that provides an introduction to the varied plant and animal life of the hinterland. There is a lookout and picnic area nearby and an easy 40-minute nature walk through the rainforest.

Mountain View Road rejoins the Landsborough–Maleny Road for the winding descent to Landsborough. Instead of continuing into the centre of town, turn right onto Old Gympie Road, immediately before the railway line, to commence your drive through the Glass House Mountains.

9 Glass House Mountains loop

Proceeding south, just after crossing Kilcoy–Beerwah Road, you are confronted with the twin peaks of Coochin Hills on the left. This is your first **close-up view of the Glass House Mountains**. Further on, the tall and pointy shaft of rock known as Mount Coonowrin (Crook-neck), rises up on your right.

Once these peaks are behind you, watch out for a signposted turn-off to the Glass House Mountains Lookout. Here you can take in 360-degree views of the peaks, all of which are shown on a podium located at the lookout. Just to the north is Mount Beerwah, the tallest of the mountains, rising abruptly to 556 metres.

Return to the Old Gympie Road and turn left; retrace your steps for about 1 kilometre, then turn right into Marshs Road which becomes Barrs Road. The road skirts the base of Mount Tibrogargan before joining Glasshouse Mountains Road. Turn left to the township of Glass House Mountains. For more details on walks and picnic spots in the district, drop into the visitor information centre in the main street. Those seeking a challenge can inquire about the 700-metre trail to the summit of Mount Ngungun, west of town. Access to the track is via Coonowrin and Fullertons roads. If you intend to make the ascent, allow two hours (return) and be aware that the track is steep in places, often passing close to the cliff-line.

Continue along the Glasshouse Mountains Road, through Beerwah to return to Landsborough. En route you will pass the Queensland Reptile and Fauna Park, one of many great family attractions in the area.

Returning to the coast

(See map on p. 505 for return route shown in pink.)
Continue along the Glasshouse Mountains Road until it joins the Bruce Highway. From this point, Brisbane is 82 kilometres south along the highway and Caloundra is 13 kilometres east (straight ahead) on the Caloundra Road.

To return to Noosa Heads (50 kilometres), head north along the Bruce Highway, passing Aussie World and Ettamogah Pub on the left. At the junction of the Bruce Highway and the Sunshine Motorway follow the Tanawha–Forest Glen Tourist Drive 25 signs to the left. After 1.5 kilometres, you have the option of turning right to Buderim or continuing along the tourist drive to visit the many family attractions in the area (see below).

From Buderim, head north down Buderim Mountain Road to meet David Low Way on the Maroochy River. Follow this road through the outskirts of Bli Bli to the coast. The beaches of the South Pacific Ocean and the Coral Sea unfold as you travel north. Point Perry Lookout on the southern end of Coolum Beach offers expansive views extending northwards to Noosa Heads, past Peregian, Marcus, Castaways and Sunshine beaches, all easily accessible and worth a visit.

FAMILY ATTRACTIONS

Superbee Honey Factory *– honey-tastings, bee-handling demonstrations, fairytale houses and tropical gardens.*
Bellingham Maze *– find your way out of Australia's largest hedge maze.*
Forest Glen Sanctuary *– deer and Australian marsupials in a bushland setting; feed the animals and pose for a photo with a furry companion.*
The Big Pineapple *– one of Queensland's best-known icons; board the Sugar Cane Train for a journey through the tropical plantation; take a ride on the Nutmobile to the Macadamia Nut Factory.*
UnderWater World *– seal shows, coral displays, brilliant tropical fish and monsters of the deep; definitely worth a visit (located on the coast at Mooloolaba).*

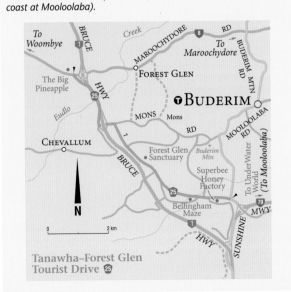

Tanawha–Forest Glen Tourist Drive 25

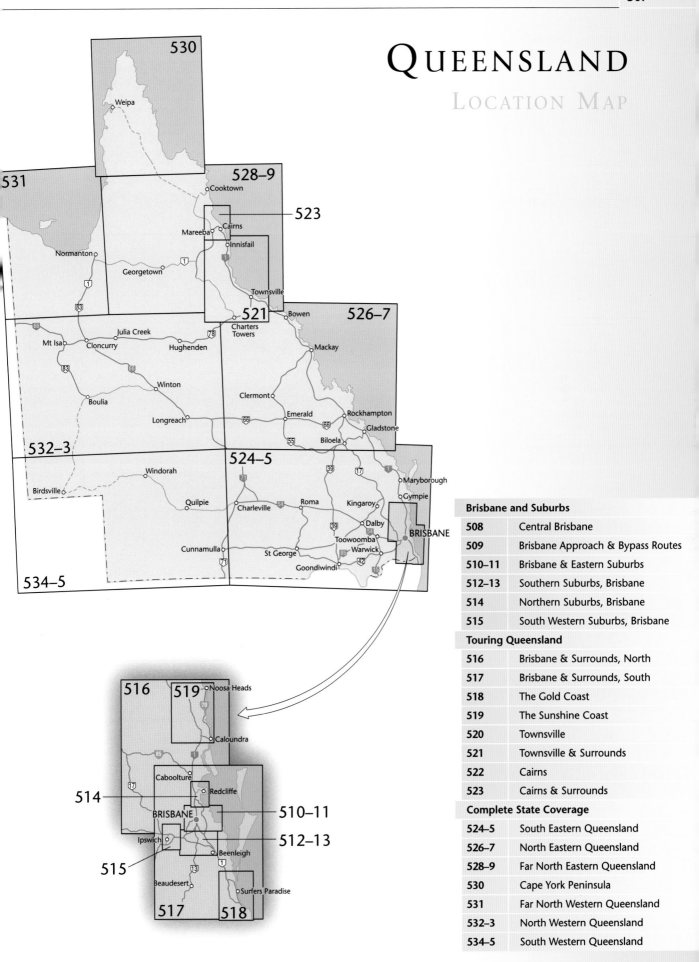

QUEENSLAND
LOCATION MAP

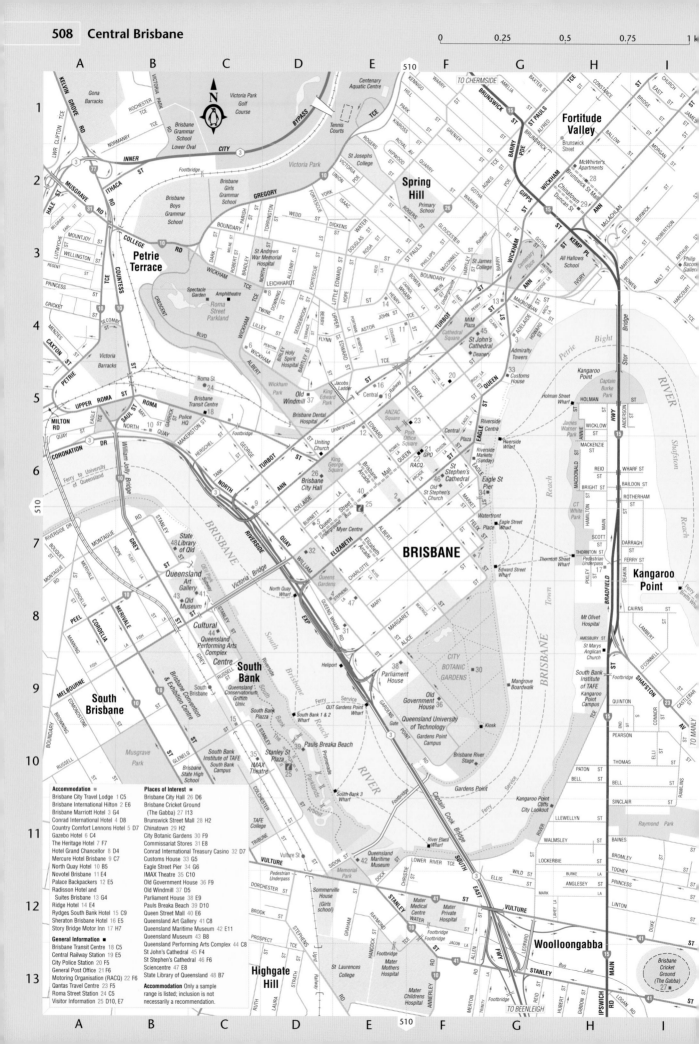

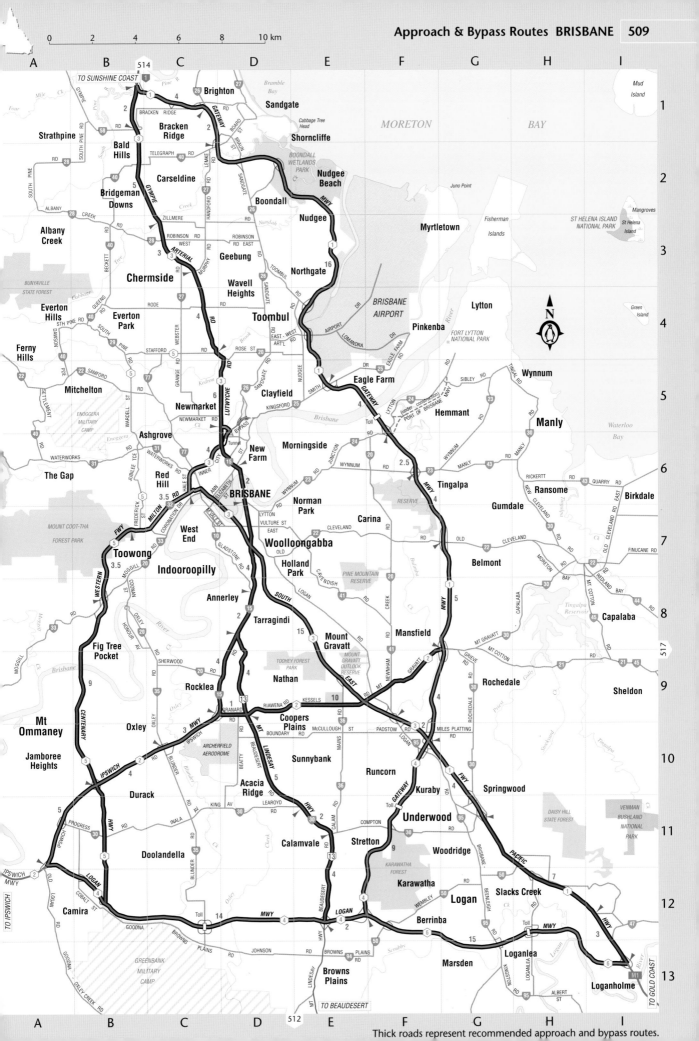

Thick roads represent recommended approach and bypass routes.

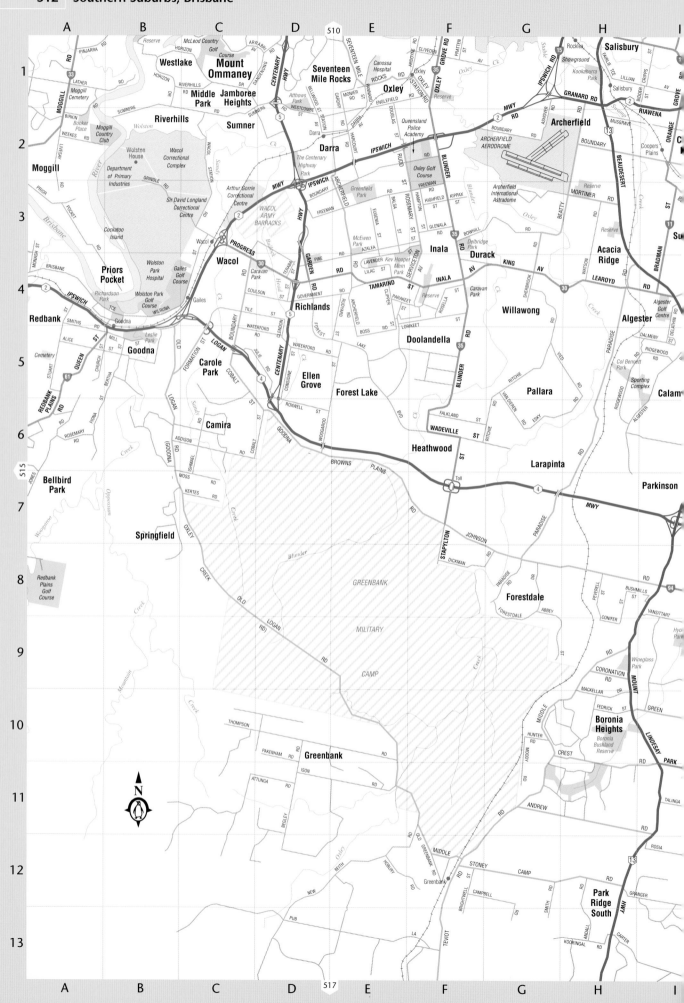

0   1   2   3   4   5 km

Deception Bay

FRESHWATER NATIONAL PARK

Deception   Bay

Cemetery

Rothwell

Redcliffe Aerodrome

Nathan Road Wetlands Reserve

Scarborough Harbour

Castlereagh Point

Scarborough Point

Scarborough

Osbourne Point

Talobilla Park

Kippa-Ring

Redcliffe Showgrounds

Redcliffe

Redcliffe Point

Alma Park Zoo

Mango Hill Golf Course

Mango Hill

Dakabin

Pine Rivers Golf Course

Brickworks

Kallangur

Redcliffe Paceway

Kroll Gardens

Clontarf

Margate

Redcliffe Golf Course

Scotts Point

Woody Point

Woody Point

Hays Inlet

John Oxley Reserve

Griffin

Petrie

Sweeney Res

Murrumba Downs

Clontarf Point

Fresh Water

Bramble Bay

MORETON

Brighton Park

Decker Park

Brighton

Lawnton Showground

Robert G. Akers Sporting Reserve

Tinchi Tamba Wetlands Reserve

Pine   River

BAY

Bray Park

Strathpine

Canterbury Park

Pine Rivers Park

North Point College

Deagon Wetlands

Sandgate

Moora Park

Bald Hills Rec Reserve

Recreation Res

Racecourse

Shorncliffe

Cabbage Tree Head

Brendale

SOUTH

Carrs Island

Bald Hills

Bracken Ridge

Sandgate Golf Course

Deagon

Golf Course

Fitzgibbon

Taigum

Brisbane Entertainment Centre

Boondall Wetlands Park

Nudgee Beach Reserve

Nudgee Beach

Nudgee Beach

Bridgeman Downs

Wolter Park

Pinaroo Lawn Cem

Carseldine

Boondall

North Boondall

Albany Creek Road Reserve

Qld Uni of Tech Carseldine Campus

Carseldine

Memorial Park

O'Callaghan Park

Zillmere

Recreation Reserve

Nudgee

BRISBANE AIRPORT

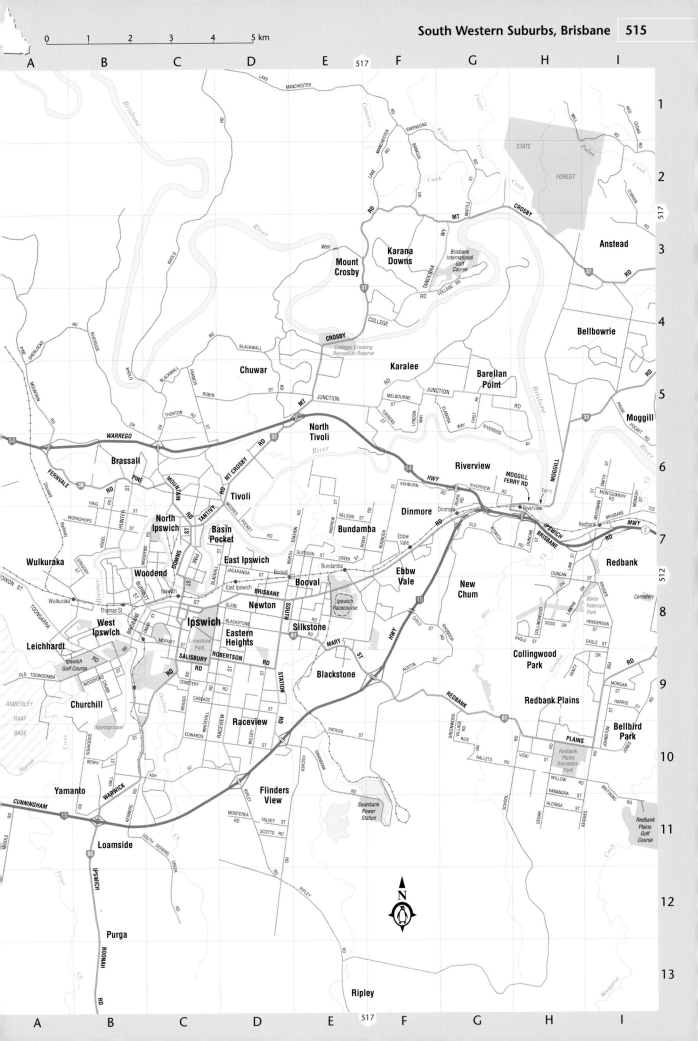

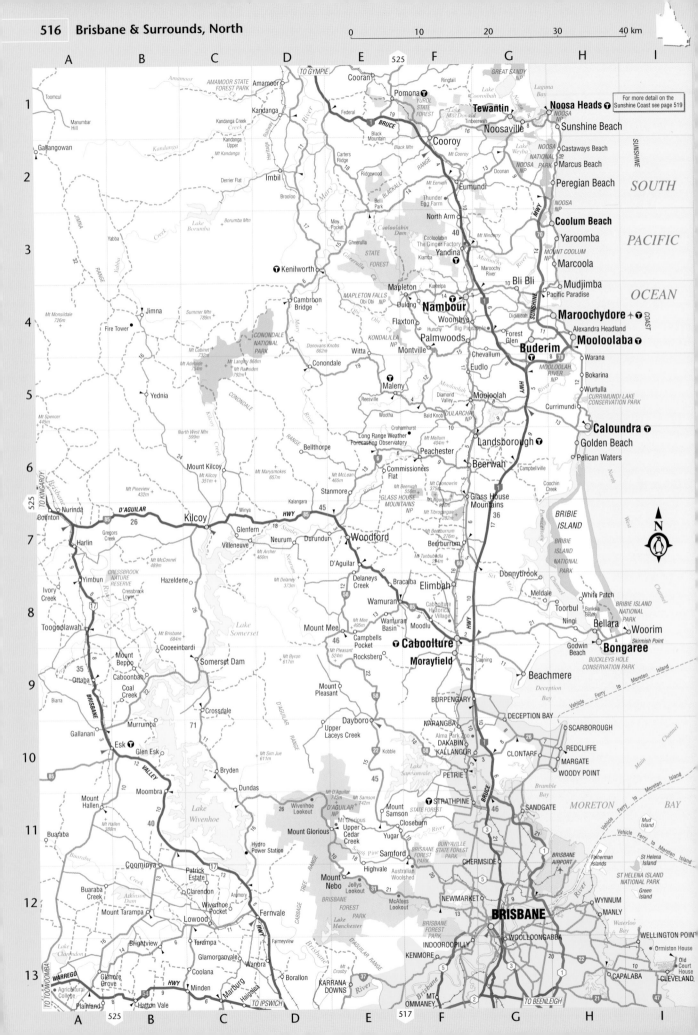

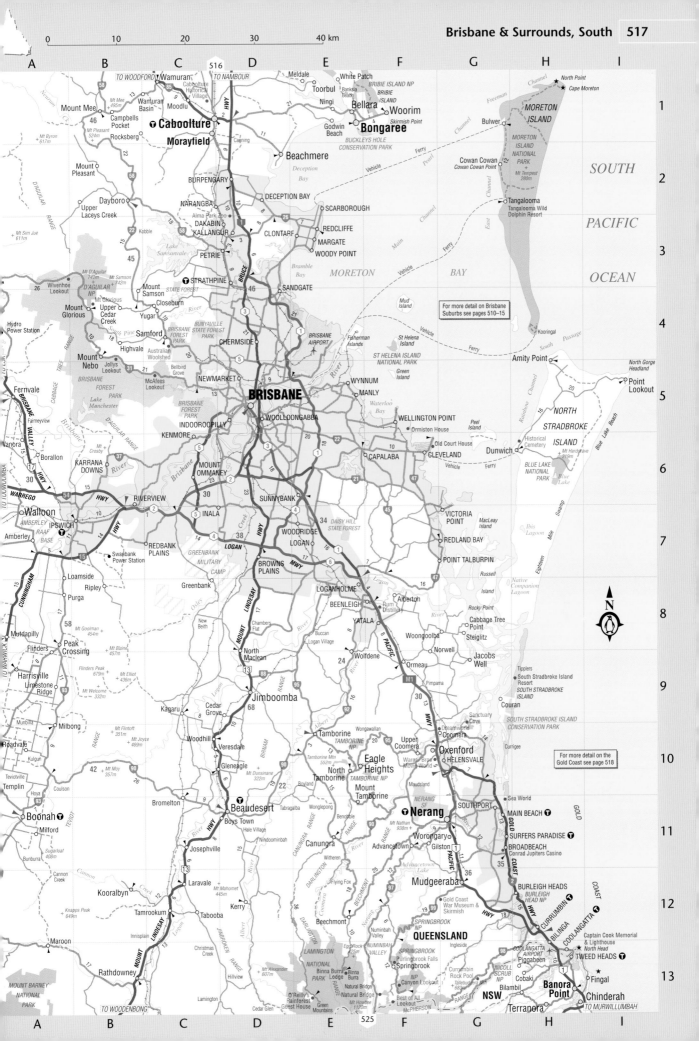

0 2 4 6 8 10 km

DREAMWORLD: A family-oriented entertainment complex set amid landscaped gardens & natural bushland. It features various exciting rides, a computerised animated koala theatre, a water playground, specialty shops and restaurants.

WARNER BROS MOVIE WORLD: Based on the world-famous Hollywood movie set, it is a theme park as part of a fully operational movie studio.

WET 'N' WILD WATER WORLD: An amazing variety of waterslides and pools set in a landscaped barbecue and picnic area.

SANCTUARY COVE: Exclusive residential resort with waterfront shopping village, marina, golf courses, tennis complex and Hyatt Regency Hotel.

SOUTH STRADBROKE ISLAND: Cruises leave from Southport for this largely uninhabited island.

SEA WORLD: A popular family-oriented theme park featuring dolphin and sea-lion performances, shark-feeding demonstrations, a walk-through aquarium, water-ski shows and many exciting rides.

VISITOR INFORMATION:
Coolangatta (Gold Coast Tourism Bureau, cnr Griffith and Warner sts)
Surfers Paradise (Gold Coast Tourism Bureau, Cavill Ave)

ADVANCETOWN LAKE: Sailing (no power boats), picnic and barbecue facilities, scenic drives and the Hinze Dam.

WAR MUSEUM: Indoor and outdoor displays of army memorabilia, military equipment and games.

DAVID FLEAY WILDLIFE PARK: Wildlife park run by the Queensland Parks & Wildlife Service to display and breed many of Queensland's rarer animals. Visit the nocturnal house to see the bilbies.

CURRUMBIN WILDLIFE SANCTUARY: Australian fauna, including waterbirds, koalas and kangaroos. Visitors can feed the brightly coloured lorikeets twice daily.

PURLINGBROOK FALLS: One of the most spectacular falls in the hinterland. Resorts such as Binna Burra and O'Reillys are in nearby Lamington National Park.

OLSON'S BIRD GARDENS: Exotic pheasants, colourful parrots and tiny finches are displayed in huge walk-through landscaped aviaries.

SOUTH

PACIFIC

OCEAN

QUEENSLAND

NEW SOUTH WALES

SOUTH STRADBROKE ISLAND

SPRINGBROOK NATIONAL PARK

NERANG STATE FOREST

Selected place names: SANCTUARY COVE, SANTA BARBARA, COOMERA, Oxenford, Upper Coomera, Helensvale, BOYKAMBIL, SOUTHPORT, PARADISE POINT, HOLLYWELL, COOMBABAH, RUNAWAY BAY, BIGGERA WATERS, LABRADOR, Gaven, Ernest, Molendinar, ASHMORE, SOUTHPORT, MAIN BEACH, SURFERS PARADISE, BUNDALL, BENOWA, BROADBEACH WATERS, BROADBEACH, Nerang, Worongary, Carrara, Advancetown, Gilston, Merrimac, CLEAR ISLAND WATERS, MERMAID WATERS, MERMAID BEACH, Mudgeeraba, Robina, Stephens, MIAMI, BURLEIGH WATERS, BURLEIGH HEADS, WEST BURLEIGH, ANDREWS, PALM BEACH, CURRUMBIN, ELANORA, CURRUMBIN WATERS, TUGUN, BILINGA, COOLANGATTA, TWEED HEADS, Springbrook, Piggabeen, Cobaki, Bilambil, Terranora, BANORA POINT, Chinderah

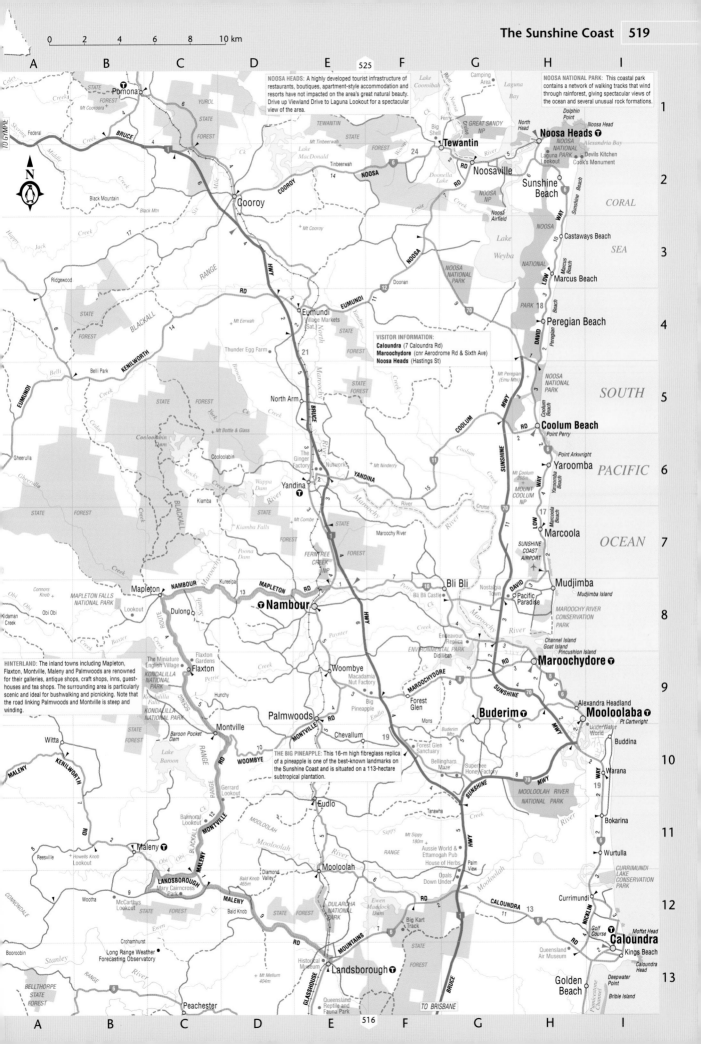

0 2 4 6 8 10 km

A B C D E F G H I

525

NOOSA HEADS: A highly developed tourist infrastructure of restaurants, boutiques, apartment-style accommodation and resorts have not impacted on the area's great natural beauty. Drive up Viewland Drive to Laguna Lookout for a spectacular view of the area.

NOOSA NATIONAL PARK: This coastal park contains a network of walking tracks that wind through rainforest, giving spectacular views of the ocean and several unusual rock formations.

VISITOR INFORMATION:
Caloundra (7 Caloundra Rd)
Maroochydore (cnr Aerodrome Rd & Sixth Ave)
Noosa Heads (Hastings St)

HINTERLAND: The inland towns including Mapleton, Flaxton, Montville, Maleny and Palmwoods are renowned for their galleries, antique shops, craft shops, inns, guesthouses and tea shops. The surrounding area is particularly scenic and ideal for bushwalking and picnicking. Note that the road linking Palmwoods and Montville is steep and winding.

THE BIG PINEAPPLE: This 16-m high fibreglass replica of a pineapple is one of the best-known landmarks on the Sunshine Coast and is situated on a 113-hectare subtropical plantation.

Pomona, Cooroy, Eumundi, Tewantin, Noosaville, Noosa Heads, Sunshine Beach, Castaways Beach, Marcus Beach, Peregian Beach, Coolum Beach, Yaroomba, Marcoola, Mudjimba, Nambour, Mapleton, Flaxton, Woombye, Palmwoods, Montville, Maleny, Landsborough, Buderim, Maroochydore, Mooloolaba, Caloundra, Golden Beach

CORAL SEA, SOUTH PACIFIC OCEAN

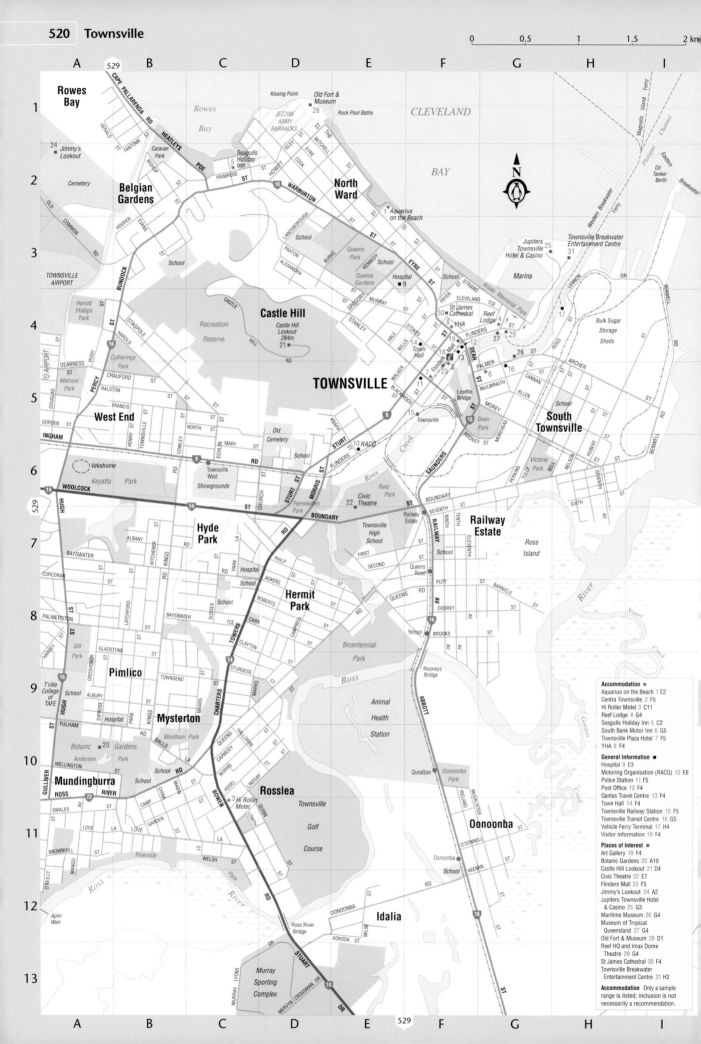

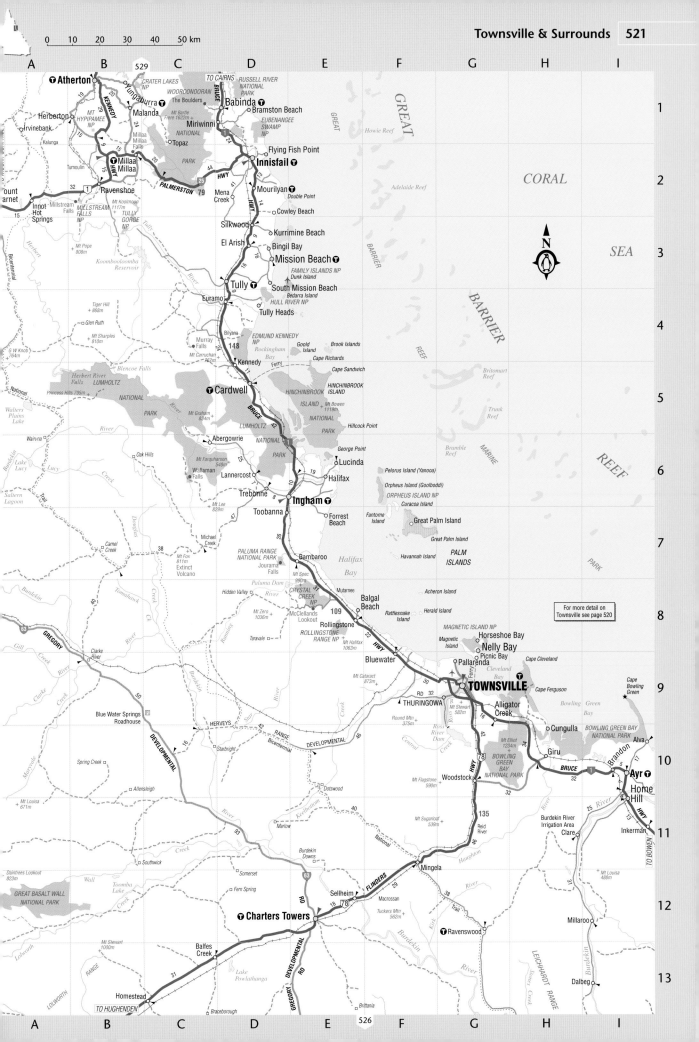

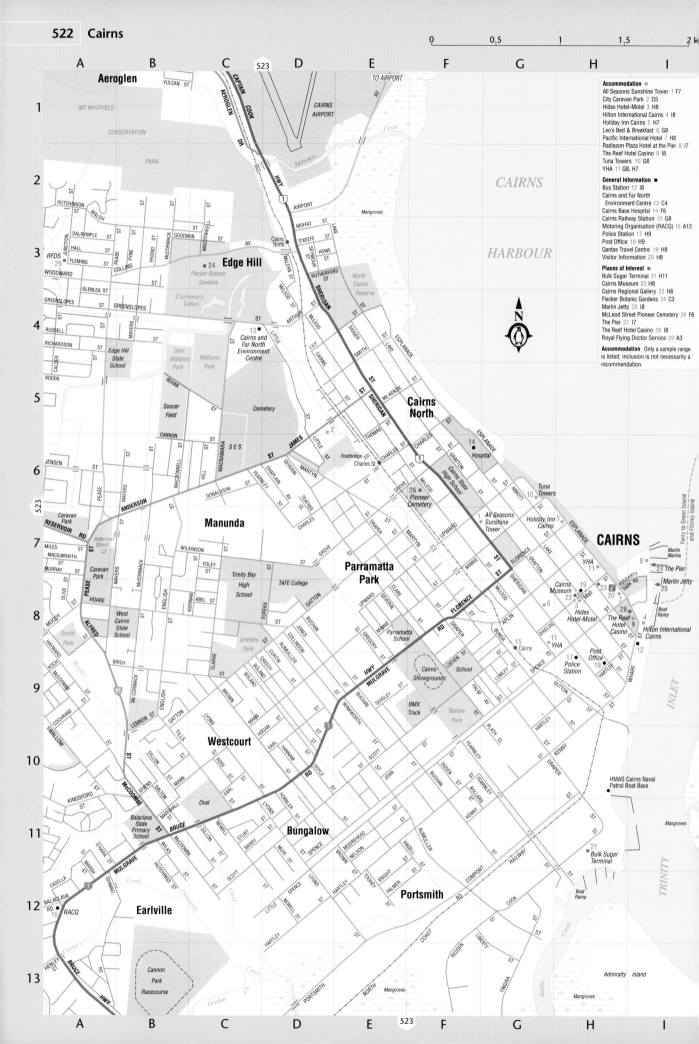

Aeroglen

CAIRNS
AIRPORT

Edge Hill

Cairns
North

CAIRNS
HARBOUR

Manunda

Parramatta
Park

CAIRNS

Westcourt

Bungalow

Portsmith

Earlville

TRINITY
INLET

Admiralty Island

Accommodation ■
All Seasons Sunshine Tower 1 F7
City Caravan Park 2 D5
Hides Hotel-Motel 3 H8
Hilton International Cairns 4 I8
Holiday Inn Cairns 5 H7
Leo's Bed & Breakfast 6 G8
Pacific International Hotel 7 H8
Radisson Plaza Hotel at the Pier 8 I7
The Reef Hotel Casino 9 I8
Tuna Towers 10 G6
YHA 11 G8, H7

General Information ■
Bus Station 12 I8
Cairns and Far North
 Environment Centre 13 C4
Cairns Base Hospital 14 F6
Cairns Railway Station 15 G8
Motoring Organisation (RACQ) 16 A12
Police Station 17 H9
Post Office 18 H9
Qantas Travel Centre 19 H8
Visitor Information 20 H8

Places of Interest ■
Bulk Sugar Terminal 21 H11
Cairns Museum 22 H8
Cairns Regional Gallery 23 H8
Flecker Botanic Gardens 24 C3
Marlin Jetty 25 I8
McLeod Street Pioneer Cemetery 26 F6
The Pier 27 I7
The Reef Hotel Casino 28 I8
Royal Flying Doctor Service 29 A3

Accommodation Only a sample range
is listed; inclusion is not necessarily a
recommendation.

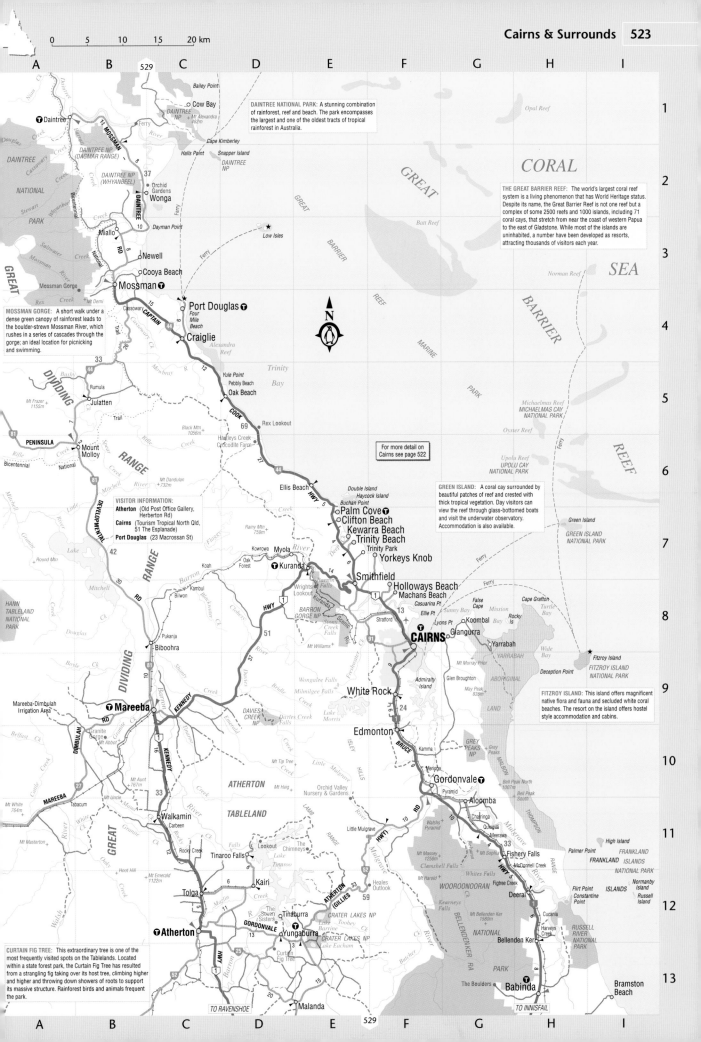

0   5   10   15   20 km

A B C D E F G H I

DAINTREE NATIONAL PARK: A stunning combination of rainforest, reef and beach. The park encompasses the largest and one of the oldest tracts of tropical rainforest in Australia.

CORAL

THE GREAT BARRIER REEF: The world's largest coral reef system is a living phenomenon that has World Heritage status. Despite its name, the Great Barrier Reef is not one reef but a complex of some 2500 reefs and 1000 islands, including 71 coral cays, that stretch from near the coast of western Papua to the east of Gladstone. While most of the islands are uninhabited, a number have been developed as resorts, attracting thousands of visitors each year.

SEA

MOSSMAN GORGE: A short walk under a dense green canopy of rainforest leads to the boulder-strewn Mossman River, which rushes in a series of cascades through the gorge; an ideal location for picnicking and swimming.

For more detail on Cairns see page 522

GREEN ISLAND: A coral cay surrounded by beautiful patches of reef and crested with thick tropical vegetation. Day visitors can view the reef through glass-bottomed boats and visit the underwater observatory. Accommodation is also available.

VISITOR INFORMATION:
Atherton (Old Post Office Gallery, Herberton Rd)
Cairns (Tourism Tropical North Qld, 51 The Esplanade)
Port Douglas (23 Macrossan St)

FITZROY ISLAND: This island offers magnificent native flora and fauna and secluded white coral beaches. The resort on the island offers hostel style accommodation and cabins.

CURTAIN FIG TREE: This extraordinary tree is one of the most frequently visited spots on the Tablelands. Located within a state forest park, the Curtain Fig Tree has resulted from a strangling fig taking over its host tree, climbing higher and higher and throwing down showers of roots to support its massive structure. Rainforest birds and animals frequent the park.

Daintree — Cow Bay — Mossman — Port Douglas — Craiglie — Mount Molloy — Palm Cove — Clifton Beach — Kewarra Beach — Trinity Beach — Yorkeys Knob — Kuranda — Smithfield — Holloways Beach — Machans Beach — CAIRNS — Giangurra — White Rock — Mareeba — Edmonton — Gordonvale — Aloomba — Walkamin — Tinaroo Falls — Kairi — Tolga — Atherton — Tinaburra — Yungaburra — Malanda — Fishery Falls — Deeral — Bellenden Ker — Babinda — Bramston Beach

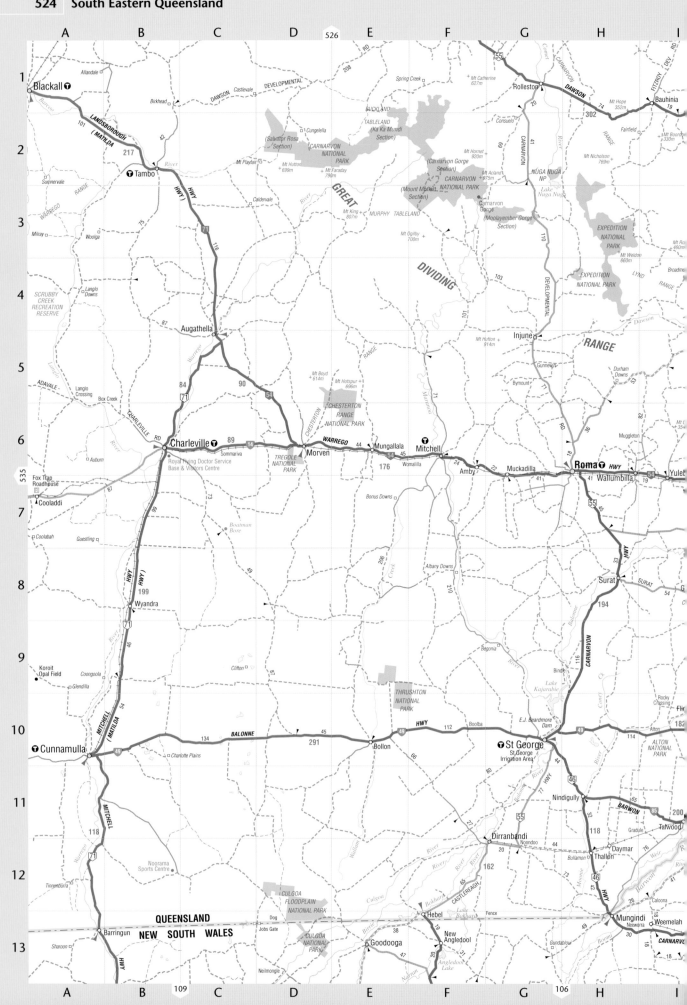

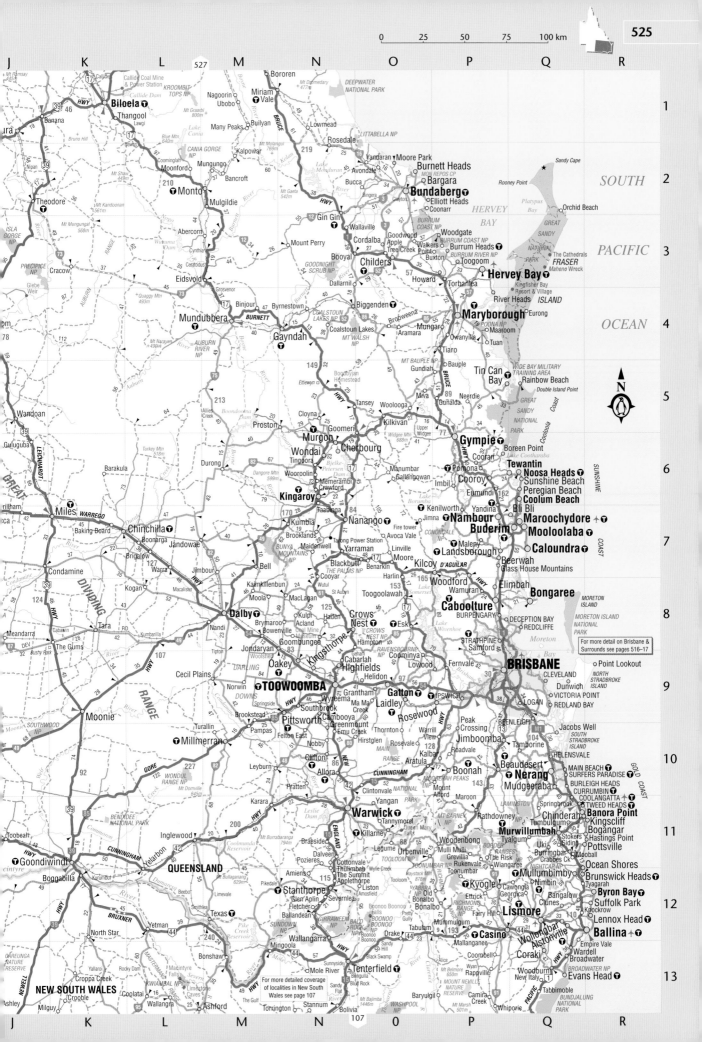

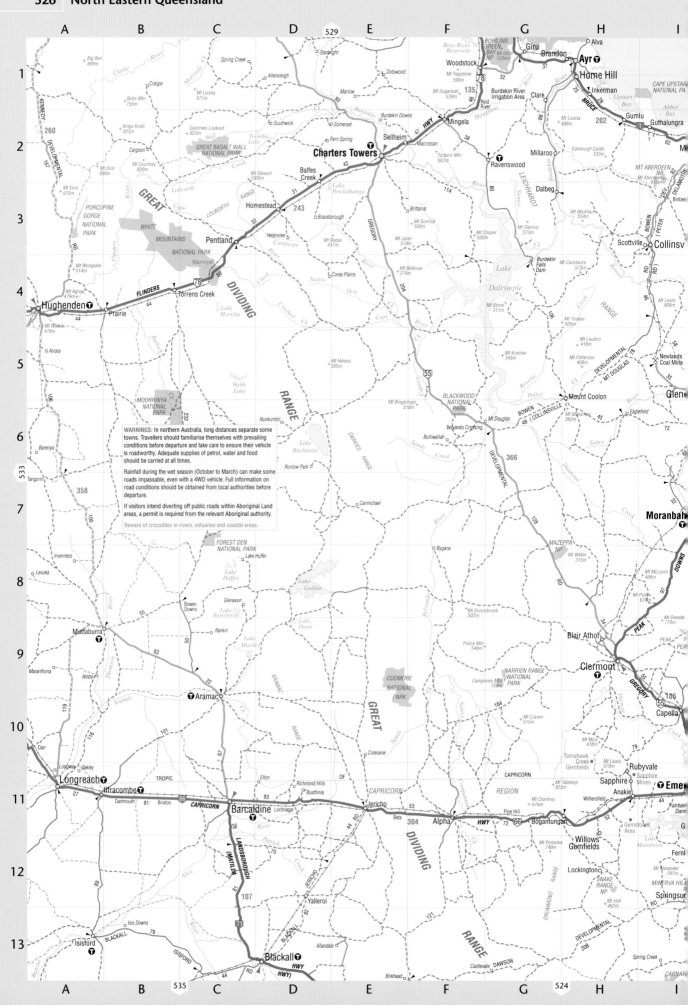

0   25   50   75   100 km

J   K   L   M   N   O   P   Q   R

CORAL   SOUTH   1

GREAT   SEA   PACIFIC

Gloucester Island
GLOUCESTER ISLAND NP
Dingo
Beach
Earlando
THE WHITSUNDAYS
Hayman Island   2
Hook Island
Airlie   North Molle Is
Beach   Daydream Is
Cannonvale   South Molle Is
WHITSUNDAY ISLANDS NP
Whitsunday Island
serpine   Shute
Harbour   Hamilton Island   OCEAN   3
CONWAY   Long Island
NP   Lindeman
Island
Shaw Island
184   Midge Point   Repulse
Bay   SMITH ISLANDS
oomsbury   Elaroo   NATIONAL PARK
Mt Crompton
792m   BARRIER   4
Yalboroo   SOUTH CUMBERLAND ISLANDS
Seaforth Ball Bay   Brampton Island   NATIONAL PARK
BRUCE   Calen   Hibiscus Coast   Keswick Is
Seaforth Cape Hillsborough   Scawfell Island
EUNGELLA   Mount   CAPE HILLSBOROUGH   St Bees
NP   Jissa   JUKES NP   Island
Kuttabul Shoal Point
Bucasia Eimeo   REEF
Eungella   Walkerston Slade Point
Finch   Mackay
Hatton   Bakers Creek
HOMEVALE   Elton   Hector
NATIONAL   Homebush Half Tide   MARINE   5
PARK   Grasstree
il Creek   Homevale   Campwin Beach
Sarina   Sarina Beach
Armstrong Beach
50
Fort Cooper   Blue Mtn   Koumala   CAPE PALMERSTON
528m   625m   NATIONAL PARK
Nebo   Mt White Ilbilbie   Middle Island   6
594m
273   29
pabella   Mt Scott   NORTHUMBERLAND   REEF
852m   South Island
Orange   Carmila   WEST HILL NP
530m   Flaggy Rock   ISLES
DIPPERU   26
NATIONAL   Saltbush Park   7
PARK   White Bluff Mtn Clairview   Quail Island
520m   Stanage
oxendean   334
480m
Broad   Mt Price
St Lawrence   Sound   164m
Townshend Is   8
sart   Bar Mtn   Mt Edward
308m   +171m
Mt Joss   BRUCE   Mt Westall
421m   560m
Mt Buffalo   Mt Phillip
518m   Ogmore   393m   Mt Wellington
Glenprairie   528m   MILITARY
Mt Magoo   Mt Mulgrave   TRAINING   9
575m   655m   AREA
iddlemount   Mt Bora   Marlborough
350m   Double Mtn
Junee   747m
Mt Gardiner   Clifton
Oaky Creek   450m   HWY   BYFIELD
Mine   Royles   Kunwarara   NATIONAL
Arizona   Merimal   PARK
orie   Fairhill   Apis Creek   Glen   51
Burkan   Geddes
Ensham   Yaamba   Farnborough   Great Keppel Island   10
Mine   Telson   Mikan   Yeppoon
South Yaamba   The Caves   Mulambin
Round Mtn   Ridgelands   Kinka Beach
446m   Parkhurst   KEPPEL BAY ISLANDS
FOLEYVALE   Emu Park   NATIONAL PARK
ABORIGINAL   Tungamull   Keppel Sands
COMMUNITY   ROCKHAMPTON   Joskeleigh
Dalma   Gracemere
Kabra   TROPIC   OF   CAPRICORN 11
Sorrel Hills   Wycarbah   Midgee   North West
Comet   CAPRICORN   Bluff   Stanwell   Island
Blackwater   Westwood   Bouldercombe   Port
Blackwater   Dingo   Gogango   Alma   CAPRICORNIA CAYS
Mine   Wallaroo   Bajool   Mt Barker   NATIONAL PARK
Mt Battery   161m   CURTIS
486m   Mount   Raglan   ISLAND
BLACKDOWN   Morgan   BRUCE   Southend
TABLELAND   Mt Wheal   Ambrose   12
South   NATIONAL   606m   Dululu   107   Mt Larcom
Blackwater   PARK   145   Mount Larcom   Gladstone
Mine   Mt Success   Wowan   Yarwun
490m   Cedric Mtn   Boyne Island
Mt Dawson   699m   Tannum Sands
317m   Lancefield   Benaraby   EURIMBULA NP
Rannes   Mt Redshirt   Calliope   Lady Musgrave Island
597m   Turkey   Bustard
Baralaba   102   Beach   Bay
Goovigen   66   CASTLE   Seventeen Seventy
TOWER   Agnes Water
DAWSON   Jamblin   Argoon   Barmundu   Bororen   13
Biloela   Calide Coal Mine   Mt Dromedary
Rolleston   HWY   & Power Station   KROOMBIT TOPS   477m   DEEPWATER
Banana   Calide Dam   NATIONAL PARK   Miriam Vale   NATIONAL PARK
Thangool   Nagoorin   PARK
Mt Graarbi   Ubobo
800m

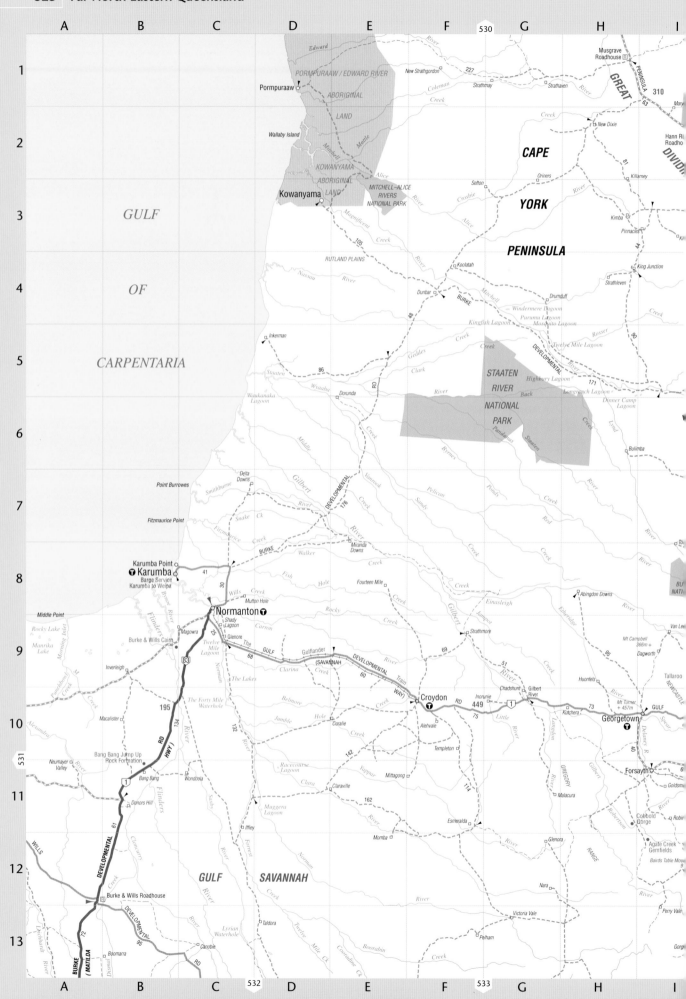

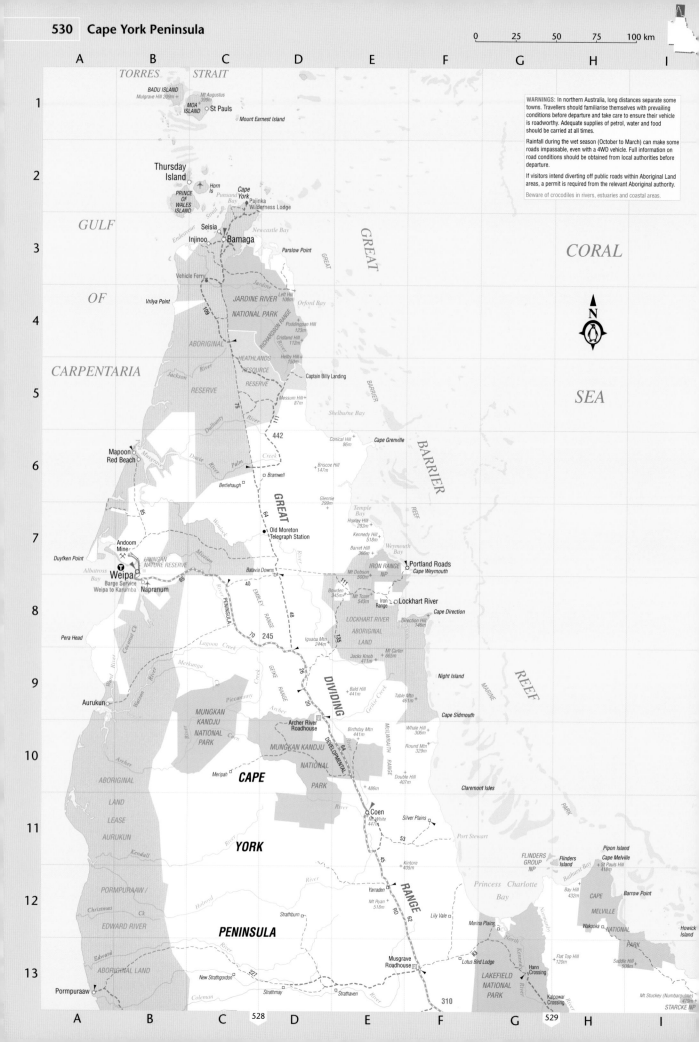

0 25 50 75 100 km

A B C D E F G H I

1

TORRES STRAIT

BADU ISLAND
Mulgrave Hill 209m +

Mt Augustus
399m
MOA
ISLAND
St Pauls

Mount Earnest Island

2

Thursday
Island

GULF

Horn
Is
Cape
York
Pajinka
Wilderness Lodge

Punsand Bay

PRINCE
OF
WALES
ISLAND

3

Seisia
Injinoo
Bamaga

Newcastle Bay

Parslow Point

Endeavour Strait

CORAL

OF

Vehicle Ferry

Vrilya Point

JARDINE RIVER

Orford Bay

4

N

NATIONAL PARK

Left Hill
108m

109

RICHARDSON RANGE

Puddingpan Hill
123m

Cridland Hill
112m

Helby Hill
150m

CARPENTARIA

ABORIGINAL

HEATHLANDS

Jackson
River

RESOURCE

Captain Billy Landing

5

RESERVE

75

Messum Hill
87m

Dulhunty
River

111

Shelburne Bay

SEA

BARRIER

6

Mapoon
Red Beach

Dacie
River

442

Palm
Creek

Conical Hill
86m

Cape Grenville

Bramwell

Briscoe Hill
147m

Bertiehaugh

64

GREAT

Glennie
299m

Temple
Bay

Huxley Hill
283m

BARRIER

7

85

Andoom
Mine

UNINGAN
NATURE RESERVE

Old Moreton
Telegraph Station

Kennedy Hill
518m

Weymouth
Bay

REEF

Duyfken Point

Weipa

Batavia Downs

Barret Hill
366m

IRON RANGE
NP

Portland Roads
Cape Weymouth

Albatross
Bay

Barge Service
Weipa to Karumba

Napranum

85

40

111

Mt Dobson
500m

8

PENINSULA

EMBLEY RANGE

48

Bowden
345m

Mt Tozer
543m

Iron
Range

Lockhart River

Cape Direction

Pera Head

70

245

Iguana Mtn
244m

135

LOCKHART RIVER

Direction Hill
146m

Lagoon
Creek

ABORIGINAL

Jacks Knob
411m

Mt Carter
665m

LAND

9

Aurukun

Merkanga

Archer

GENKE RANGE

26

20

DIVIDING

Bald Hill
441m

Grakie Creek

Table Mtn
461m

Night Island

MARINE

Cape Sidmouth

REEF

MUNGKAN
KANDJU
NATIONAL
PARK

Archer River
Roadhouse

Birthday Mtn
441m

McILWRAITH RANGE

Whale Hill
306m

10

Archer

MUNGKAN KANDJU

64

Round Mtn
329m

Claremont Isles

Meripah

NATIONAL

Double Hill
407m

ABORIGINAL

CAPE

PARK

486m

11

LAND

River

Coen

Mt White
447m

Silver Plains

Port Stewart

FLINDERS
GROUP
NP

Flinders
Island

Pipon Island
Cape Melville
St Pauls Hill
418m

LEASE

YORK

53

AURUKUN

45

Kintore
405m

Bathurst Bay

Bay Hill
432m

Barrow Point

Kendall

RANGE

Yarraden

*Princess Charlotte
Bay*

*CAPE
MELVILLE*

12

PORMPURAAW /

Christmas
Ck

Mt Ryan
518m

RD

82

Lily Vale

Marina Plains

Wakooka

NATIONAL

Howick
Island

EDWARD RIVER

Strathburn

PENINSULA

Holroyd
River

New Strathgordon

227

Strathmay

Musgrave
Roadhouse

83

Lotus Bird Lodge

Hann
Crossing

PARK

Flat Top Hill
120m

Saddle Hill
508m

13

ABORIGINAL LAND

Edward

Pormpuraaw

Coleman
River

Strathaven

310

*LAKEFIELD
NATIONAL
PARK*

Kalpowar
Crossing

Mt Stuckey (Numbargulan)
478m

STARCKE NP

A B C D E F G H I

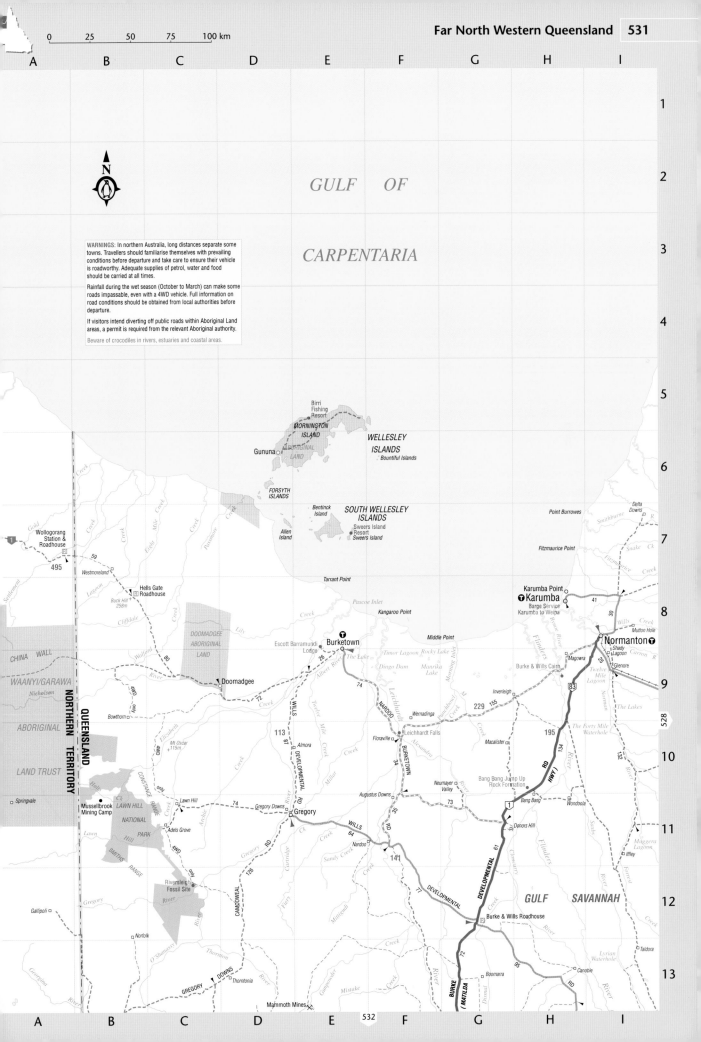

A B C D E F G H I

0 25 50 75 100 km

N

GULF OF

CARPENTARIA

WARNINGS: In northern Australia, long distances separate some towns. Travellers should familiarise themselves with prevailing conditions before departure and take care to ensure their vehicle is roadworthy. Adequate supplies of petrol, water and food should be carried at all times.

Rainfall during the wet season (October to March) can make some roads impassable, even with a 4WD vehicle. Full information on road conditions should be obtained from local authorities before departure.

If visitors intend diverting off public roads within Aboriginal Land areas, a permit is required from the relevant Aboriginal authority.

Beware of crocodiles in rivers, estuaries and coastal areas.

Birri Fishing Resort

MORNINGTON ISLAND

WELLESLEY ISLANDS

Gununa

ABORIGINAL LAND

Bountiful Islands

FORSYTH ISLANDS

Bentinck Island

SOUTH WELLESLEY ISLANDS

Allen Island

Sweers Island Resort
Sweers Island

Point Burrowes

Delta Downs

Smithburne

Fitzmaurice Point

Snake Ck

Wollogorang Station & Roadhouse

59

495

Westmoreland

Hells Gate Roadhouse

Buck Hill 258m

CHINA WALL

WAANYI/GARAWA

Nicholson

ABORIGINAL

LAND TRUST

Springvale

Musselbrook Mining Camp

LAWN HILL NATIONAL PARK

Adels Grove

Riversleigh Fossil Site

Gallipoli

Norfolk

NORTHERN TERRITORY

QUEENSLAND

Tarrant Point

Pascoe Inlet

Kangaroo Point

Karumba Point

Karumba
Barge Service
Karumba to Weipa

41

30

Wills Ck

Mutton Hole

Normanton

Shady Lagoon

Glenore

Middle Point

Escott Barramundi Lodge

Burketown

The Lake

26

Timor Lagoon

Rocky Lake

Dingo Dam

Manrika Lake

Burke & Wills Cairn

Magowra

Twelve Mile Lagoon

Doomadgee

74

72

Bowthorn

113

87

Mt Oscar 115m

Almora

Floraville

Leichhardt Falls

Wernadinga

229 155

Inverleigh

The Forty Mile Waterhole

195

134

The Lakes

132

Augustus Downs

Neumayer Valley

Bang Bang Jump Up Rock Formation

Bang Bang

Wondoola

Lawn Hill

Gregory Downs

Gregory

74

Nardoo

64

WILLS RD

Sandy Creek

141

35

73

Donors Hill

Iffley

Muggera Lagoon

77

DEVELOPMENTAL

61

GULF SAVANNAH

Burke & Wills Roadhouse

72

95

Boomarra

Canoble

Taldora

Lyrian Waterhole

Mammoth Mines

Thornton

Thorntonia

528

532

A B C D E F G H I

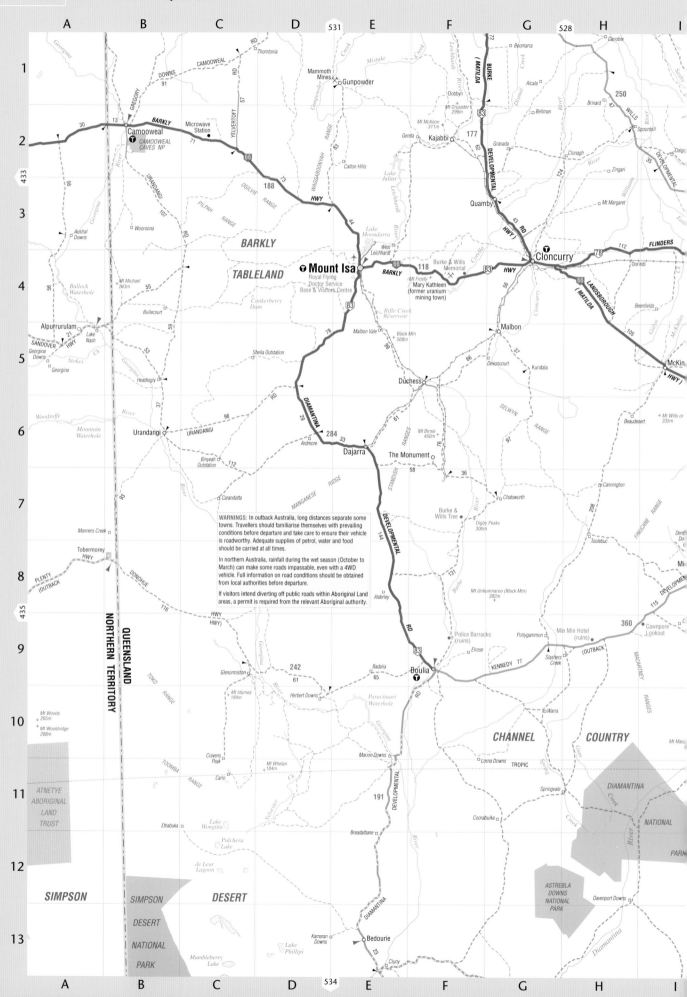

WARNINGS: In outback Australia, long distances separate some towns. Travellers should familiarise themselves with prevailing conditions before departure and take care to ensure their vehicle is roadworthy. Adequate supplies of petrol, water and food should be carried at all times.

In northern Australia, rainfall during the wet season (October to March) can make some roads impassable, even with a 4WD vehicle. Full information on road conditions should be obtained from local authorities before departure.

If visitors intend diverting off public roads within Aboriginal Land areas, a permit is required from the relevant Aboriginal authority.

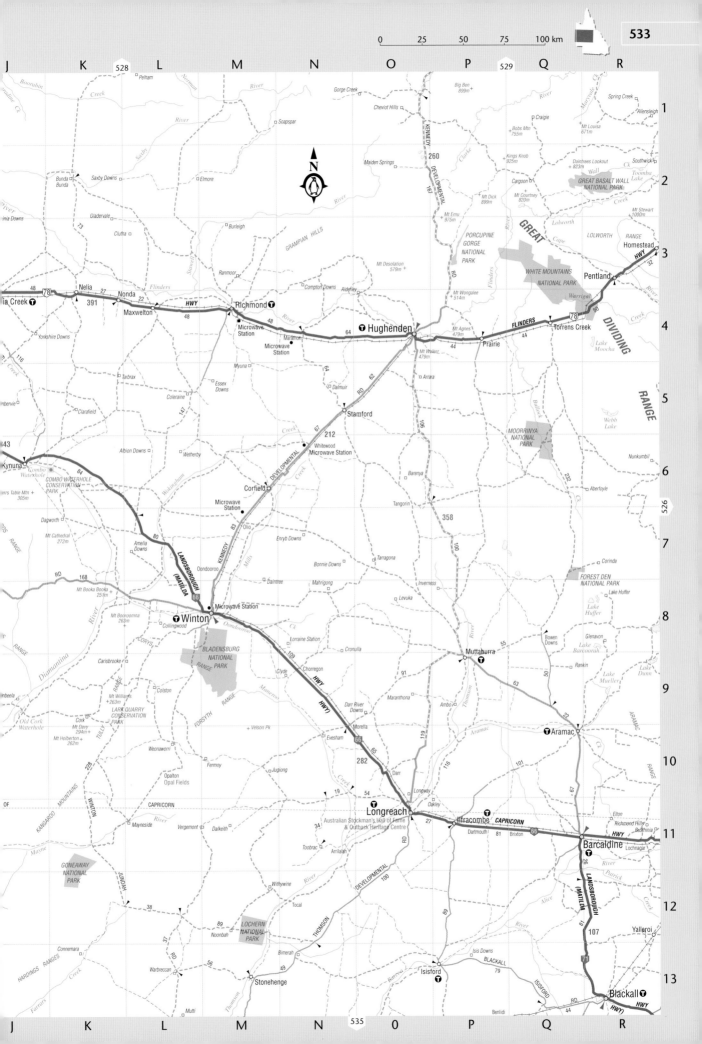

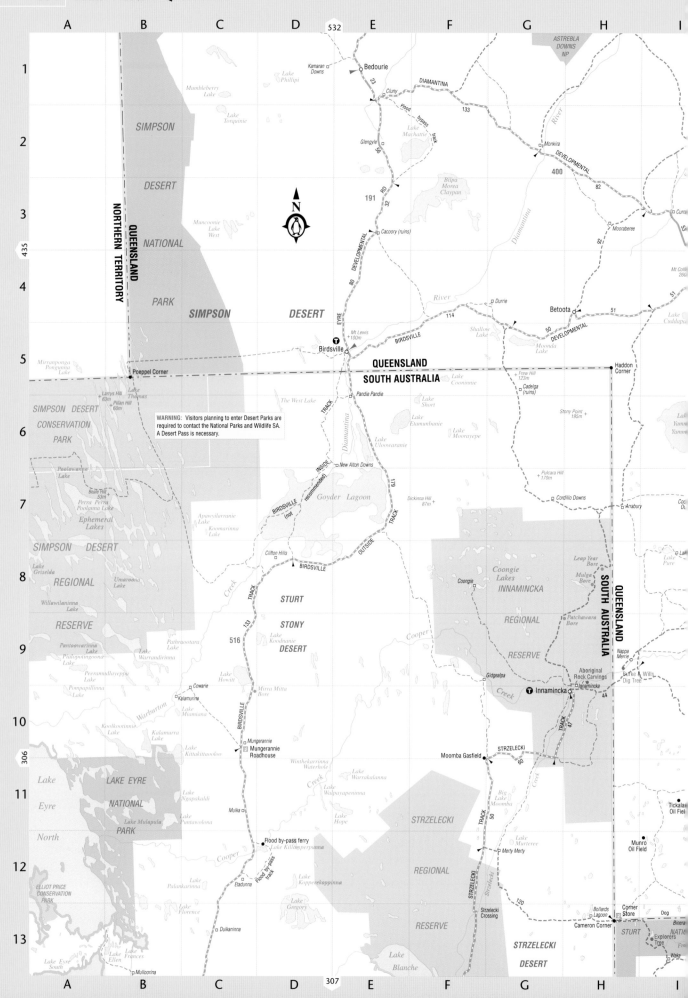

WARNING: Visitors planning to enter Desert Parks are required to contact the National Parks and Wildlife SA. A Desert Pass is necessary.

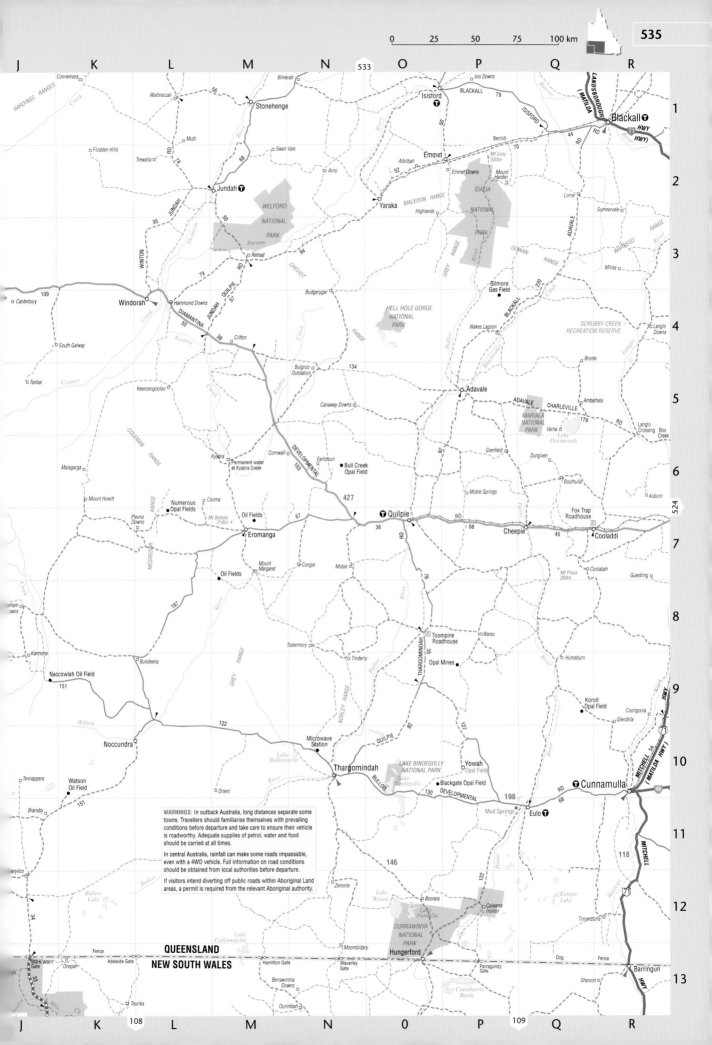

0 25 50 75 100 km

J K L M N O 533 P Q R

1
Connemara
HARDINGS RANGES
Creek
Warbreccan
Stonehenge
Bimerah
Isisford
BLACKALL
79
Isis Downs
LANDSBOROUGH (MATILDA
Blackall
HWY (MATILDA HWY)

2
Mutti
Flodden Hills
Trewalla
74
Jundah
56
Swan Vale
Arno
Benlidi
ISISFORD RD
44
Emmet
50
Albilbah
Yaraka
52
Emmet Downs
Mt Grey 533m
Mount Harden
IDALIA
NATIONAL
Lorne
70
Sumnervale
WARREGO RANGE

3
95
WINTON
JUNDAH RD
50
WELFORD NATIONAL PARK
Retreat
94
Barcoo
CHEVIOT
Highlands
MACEDON RANGE
GREY RANGE
River
PARK
GOWAN RANGE
ADAVALE RD
Gilmore Gas Field
220
SCRUBBY CREEK RECREATION RESERVE
Milray

4
109
Canterbury
Windorah
Hammond Downs
DIAMANTINA
JUNDAH QUILPIE RD
57
79
38
Clifton
Kyabra
Creek
Budgerygar
HELL HOLE GORGE NATIONAL PARK
Bulloo
Wakes Lagoon
BLACKALL
Blackwater
Bronte
Langlo
Langlo Downs

5
South Galway
Tanbar
Cooper
Creek
Keeroongooloo
COLEMAN RANGE
Kvabra
50
Bulgroo Outstation
134
Canaway Downs
DEVELOPMENTAL
103
Adavale
ADAVALE
CHARLEVILLE RD
MARIALA NATIONAL PARK
Varna
179
Lake Dartmouth
Langlo Crossing
Box Creek
Ambathala

6
Malagarga
Mount Howitt
Numerous Opal Fields
Cooma
Kyabra
Permanent water at Kyabra Creek
Cornwall
Earlstoun
Bull Creek Opal Field
97
Moble Springs
Grenfield
Dungiven
Boothulla
Auburn
524

7
Plevna Downs
Mt Befallie 216m
Oil Fields
67
427
36
Quilpie
RD
68
Cheepie
45
Cooladdi
MCGREGOR RANGE
Eromanga
Fox Trap Roadhouse

8
Mount Margaret
Oil Fields
167
Congie
Moble
Mt Prara 309m
Coolabah
Guestling
River
RIVER
76

9
Naccowlah Oil Field
151
GREY RANGE
Bundeena
Karmoha
Tobermory
NORLEY RANGE
Tinderry
THARGOMINDAH
Toompine Roadhouse
35
Opal Mines
Wareo
Humeburn
Koroit Opal Field
Coongoola
Glendilla
MITCHELL (MATILDA) HWY
HWY

10
Noccundra
122
Wilson River
Lake Bullawarra
Microwave Station
Thargomindah
82
QUILPIE RD
Lake Bindegolly
LAKE BINDEGOLLY NATIONAL PARK
Blackgate Opal Field
127
Yowah Opal Field
198
Cunnamulla
MITCHELL 54

11
Tennappera
Watson Oil Field
151
Orient
BULLOO
River
130
DEVELOPMENTAL
RD
68
Eulo
Mud Springs
118
MITCHELL

12
aryilco
Bulloo
River
Bulloo Lake
146
Zenonie
122
Lake Wyara
Lake Numilla
Boorara
CURRAWINYA NATIONAL PARK
Caiwarro (ruins)
122
Kungie Lake
Tinnenburra

13
34
Warri Warri Gate
Onepah
Adelaide Gate
QUEENSLAND
NEW SOUTH WALES
Fence
Lake Callamulcha
Hamilton Gate
Moombidary
Waverley Gate
Hungerford
Parraguundy Gate
Dog
Fence
Barringun
HWY

33
Teurika
Berrawinnia Downs
Ourimbah
Cattaburra Basin
Sharoon

WARNINGS: In outback Australia, long distances separate some towns. Travellers should familiarise themselves with prevailing conditions before departure and take care to ensure their vehicle is roadworthy. Adequate supplies of petrol, water and food should be carried at all times.

In central Australia, rainfall can make some roads impassable, even with a 4WD vehicle. Full information on road conditions should be obtained from local authorities before departure.

If visitors intend diverting off public roads within Aboriginal Land areas, a permit is required from the relevant Aboriginal authority.

J K 108 L M N O P 109 Q R

TASMANIA

KING
ISLAND ⑥

FLINDERS
ISLAND

⑥

SMITHTON

BURNIE
DEVONPORT   BRIDPORT

④   ST HELENS

LAUNCESTON

③

QUEENSTOWN   MIENA   ②

SWANSEA

⑤

① RICHMOND

HOBART

PORT
ARTHUR

T asmania's
beauty has won
more hearts than
it can claim square kilometres.
The State of Tasmania includes the Bass Strait islands
to the north, and Macquarie Island, 800 nautical miles
to the south (subantarctic and not a general tourist
destination). This total area is less than one per cent of
the Australian landmass. The main island of the State,
commonly referred to as Tasmania, offers a multitude
of attractions in an area that is a mere 296 kilometres
north to south and 315 kilometres east to west.

Wild and rustic

In recent times, Tasmania has become known as one
of the world's great wilderness destinations. The south-
west and a section of the Central Plateau form one
Tasmanian Wilderness World Heritage Area (the other
is Macquarie Island, declared 1997). This is landscape
of dolomite mountains, glacial lakes, trackless rainforest and ancient Aboriginal art sites. The north-west,
parts of the east coast, the Bass Strait islands, and
a number of areas around Hobart, including

Bruny Island, are renowned for their wild and largely
untouched coastal beauty.

Different, but equally attractive, is Tasmania's rural
scenery. A decentralised population, good rainfall,
short distances and a strong agricultural economy have
translated historically into the establishment of numerous small rural settlements laid out in a pattern more
European than Australian. Georgian and Victorian villages, freestone cottages, hedges, bridges, fields of hops
and poppies and neatly tended orchards and vineyards
dominate the Midlands south of Launceston, and the
Derwent and Huon valleys north-west and south of
Hobart respectively.

The locals

Tasmania's population of 471 900 is the smallest
of the Australian States. Overseas immigration to
Tasmania has, for economic reasons, always been
low, contributing only 0.05 per cent to its population

The Styx River, near Bushy Park, in Tasmania's south-east

increase in recent years. Tasmania has fewer residents born overseas than other States and so is less ethnically and culturally diverse.

Aboriginal people (Palawa) migrated to Tasmania about 35 000 years ago. They numbered between 4000 and 10 000 on the eve of white settlement. Divided into nine groups, they led a nomadic life, moving from place to place with the seasonal changes in the supply of shellfish, seals, birds, marsupials, and fruit and nuts.

The 1996 census counted 13 873 Aboriginal and Torres Strait Islander people in Tasmania. Many claim descent from the Palawa women who were kidnapped by white Bass Strait sealers or who formed unions with white settlers and convicts in remote districts. Tasmania's indigenous people are endeavouring to strengthen their ethnic and cultural identity through language and cultural projects, and through land management assisted by the return of 12 significant sites under legislation passed in 1995.

Early colonial building on Maria Island

A dark past

Abel Tasman sighted and named Van Diemen's Land in 1642. French and British explorers followed from 1772. In 1803 the British government, concerned at growing French interest in Van Diemen's Land, established a settlement on the River Derwent. The colony soon acquired a reputation for violence and lawlessness, plagued by escaped convicts who had become bushrangers, and seeing the presence of the indigenous inhabitants as a problem.

White settlers drove the Palawa from their hunting grounds. Following the Black War of the 1820s, the government rounded up the few survivors and sent them to Flinders Island. After 13 years,

only 47 of the original 133 sent there had survived, with most succumbing to disease and despair. The remaining few were later transfered to Oyster Bay near Hobart, where the last of the group, Truganini, died in 1876.

For fifty years Van Diemen's Land was a penal colony, and an infamously brutal one at that. Despite this, some semblance of normal society took root: houses were built, communities born, and whaling, sealing, shipbuilding and wool-growing industries established.

In 1825 Van Diemen's Land was separated from New South Wales and given its own nominated Legislative Council. A campaign by prominent residents resulted in no more convicts being sent to the colony after 1852. In 1856 the British government changed the colony's name to Tasmania and elections were held for a Legislative Assembly and Legislative Council. Unlike the other States, Tasmanian elections are now based on the Hare-Clark system. The present Labor government, elected in 1998, is the first in 16 years to command a Lower House majority.

Niche markets

Two-thirds of Tasmania is too rugged and wet for farming or grazing; however, agriculture occupies 2 100 000 hectares of land in the north, Midlands and south-east. Unable to compete with the large-scale farming of the mainland, Tasmania has developed boutique agricultural and aqua-cultural industries producing high-quality gourmet fare. Cool-climate wines, lobster, abalone, oysters and Tasmanian salmon, apples, berries and other fruit, and quality dairy products are now being exported beyond Australia. Many visitors to Tasmania come to eat and drink their way around the island.

Tourism is Tasmania's fastest growing industry, with over half a million visitors now arriving each year. Tasmania is a niche rather than a mass tourist destination. It offers clean air and water, a choice of accessible or remote wilderness, beaches, historic sites and villages, quality food, distinctive cool-climate wines, and numerous fishing opportunities.

Tasmania's busy holiday period is December to March and bookings should be made well in advance. Travel options include a heavily subsided car ferry from Melbourne or the fly/drive packages, which are popular with travellers from further afield.

For more information on Tasmania, see Tourist Bureaus on p. 591.

HOBART

Victoria Dock

H OBART, Australia's second oldest and most southerly city, is situated on the broad estuary of the River Derwent under the spell of majestic Mount Wellington. A strong maritime flavour and sense of the past give Hobart an almost European air.

VISITOR INFORMATION
Tasmanian Travel & Information Centre
cnr Elizabeth & Davey sts, Hobart
(03) 6230 8233
www.discovertasmania.com.au

This feeling is heightened in winter, when Mount Wellington is often snow-capped and daytime temperatures drop to a crisp average maximum of 12°C. However, it is also very much an Australian city, sur+rounded as it is by bushland and boasting prime examples of distinctive colonial architecture.

Hobart's population of just over 194 000 spreads on both sides of the graceful Tasman Bridge and extends into the foothills of Mount Wellington. The city centre is probably the most historically intact in Australia. Whole areas appear today as they would have when Hobart was a seafaring town in the 19th century. Houses, churches and

GETTING AROUND

Airport shuttle bus
Tasmania's Own Redline Coach Services
1300 360 000

Motoring organisation
Royal Automobile Club of Tasmania (RACT)
13 2722

Car rental
Avis 13 6333; Budget 1300 362 848;
Hertz 13 3039; Thrifty 1800 030 730

Public transport
Metropolitan Transport Trust 13 2201

Taxis
Silvertop Taxis 13 1008; Yellow Cabs 13 2227

River Derwent cruises
The Cruise Company (03) 6234 9294
Captain Fells Ferries (03) 6223 5893

warehouses were built with social and commercial urgency rather than with forethought. The result is a small, compact city without the usual distinction between residential, business and retail precincts. It is a short stroll from the cottages of Battery Point to the grandeur of Parliament House, from the vibrant seafront to the bustle of the city centre.

EXPLORING HOBART

Motorists will discover that the traffic flows freely throughout Hobart. Be warned though, many of the city streets are one way. Metered street parking is readily available and the Hobart City Council operates several multi-storey car parks at modest rates. Alternatively, there is public transport. Metro Tasmania operates a bus service that runs frequently during business hours, with a limited evening/weekend timetable. Much of Hobart's city centre can be covered on foot – for those who are not put off by the undulating streets. Walking is certainly the best way to appreciate the rich historical experience of the waterfront and Battery Point.

River cruises offer an opportunity to extend your acquaintance with this waterside city. Ferries and cruise boats leave regularly from Franklin Wharf and Brooke Street Pier at Sullivans Cove. The Cruise Company's *Derwent Explorer* cruise to the Cadbury Schweppes Chocolate Factory is a year-round favourite. During summer, sailing vessels run charter tours as far afield as Port Arthur and Bruny Island. There are also a number of coach tours, including a daily tour of the city and suburbs.

QUEENS DOMAIN

The parklands of Queens Domain, on the western side of the Tasman Bridge, form a gentle interlude between the river and the city centre. To visit the **Royal Tasmanian Botanical Gardens**, turn off the Tasman Highway, near the Gothic-style **Government House**. The beautifully landscaped botanical gardens, contained within convict-built walls, are set on the side of a hill overlooking the river and include the **Botanical Discovery Centre**, which has an Interpretation Gallery, a new Plant House and a restaurant. A recent addition to the centre is the Drombrovskis Gallery, which houses 150 photographs by the late Peter Drombrovskis, one of Australia's most influential wilderness photographers. Beyond the rather English confines of the gardens, the **Queens Domain** features tracts of remnant bushland, sports fields and the **Tattersall's Hobart Aquatic Centre** which has an Olympic-size swimming pool and excellent facilities for children. The fields in front of Government House give the Domain a friendly, rural feel, unusual for an area

HOBART BY AREA

- QUEENS DOMAIN
- INNER CITY – NORTH
- ALONG THE WATERFRONT
- BATTERY POINT
- INNER CITY – SOUTH
- CENTRAL SHOPPING AREA
- SOUTHERN SUBURBS & BEYOND
- NORTHERN SUBURBS & BEYOND
- EAST OF THE DERWENT

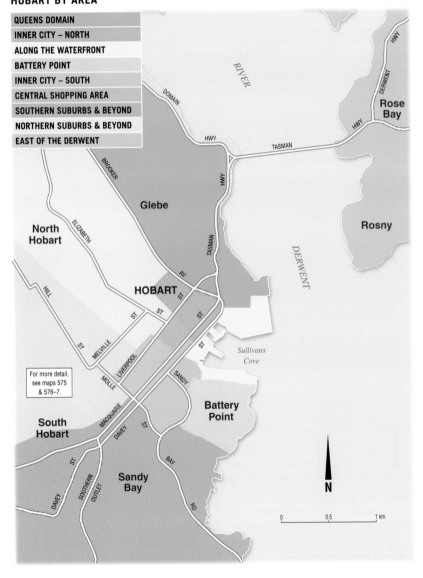

Shot Tower near Taroona

so close to the central business district – it is not uncommon to see cows grazing here. On the other side of the highway, open lawns extend up to the **Cenotaph** and down towards a shipyard area. From here, a cycle path follows the old railway line to Hobart's northern suburbs. Bicycles and rollerblades are available for hire on weekends and public holidays.

INNER CITY – NORTH

Just off the Tasman Highway near the main waterfront precinct is the **Gasworks Shopping Village**, home to Australia's only commercial whisky distillery (open daily for tours). To explore Hobart's historic inner-city buildings, continue along Davey Street past the **Federation Concert Hall** and Hotel Grand Chancellor, then right into Argyle Street. On the corner of Macquarie and Argyle streets is the **Tasmanian Museum and Art Gallery**, notable for its magnificent collection of colonial landscape paintings. Within the museum complex is the Bond Store, central Hobart's oldest building, completed in 1808. Near the intersection of Argyle and Macquarie streets, facing the Italianate columns of the **Town Hall**, is **Ingle Hall**. This fine Georgian-style 1814 building is the oldest residential building still standing in the centre of Hobart. Turn right into Macquarie Street and continue to Market Place. On the corner you will see the **Hope and Anchor Tavern**, reputedly Australia's oldest licensed hotel (1807).

Return to Ingle Hall. From there continue along Argyle Street and turn right into Brisbane Street. The convict-built **Penitentiary Chapel and Criminal Courts** are located on the corner of Brisbane and Campbell streets. Visitors can view the tunnels, courtrooms and solitary confinement cells inside these buildings; ghost tours operate most evenings. Returning to the waterfront via Campbell Street, look out for the tiny **Theatre Royal** (1837) on the left, opposite the Royal Hobart Hospital. The theatre's charming Georgian interior is still in use, making it Australia's oldest operating venue.

NOT TO BE MISSED IN HOBART

	Map Ref.
Antarctic Adventure Explore the world's most isolated continent	575 G9
Battery Point Former mariners' village	575 G9
Cadbury Schweppes Chocolate Factory A chocolate-lover's dream come true	576 D1
Cascade Brewery Australia's oldest brewery	576 E9
Constitution Dock Historic hub of Hobart's busy waterfront	575 G7
Mount Wellington Superb views of the city and its river setting	576 B9
Royal Tasmanian Botanical Gardens The State's horticultural jewel	575 G2
Runnymede Georgian-style house with lovely gardens	576 F6
Salamanca Place Setting for the bustling Saturday market	575 G8
Theatre Royal Australia's oldest theatre still in operation	575 F6

HOBART ON FOOT

Battery Point
National Trust guided walk;
leaves Franklin Square each Sat. morning;
bookings essential

Battery Point & Sullivans Cove
Self-guide walk; brochure available

Battery Point Lamplight Walking Tours
Historical walk; bookings essential

Hobart Rivulet Tour
Underground walk; bookings essential

'In Her Stride'
Women's history walk; bookings essential

For further information and bookings, contact
*the **Tasmanian Travel & Information Centre***

CLIMATE **HOBART**

	J	F	M	A	M	J	J	A	S	O	N	D
Max. °C	22	22	21	18	15	13	12	13	15	17	19	20
Min. °C	12	12	11	9	6	5	4	5	6	7	9	11
Rain mm	37	38	40	49	41	29	49	49	42	48	48	59
Raindays	9	8	10	11	13	11	13	15	14	13	14	13

Salamanca Market

TOP EVENTS

Antique Fair *(New Year period)*
The State's largest antique fair,
held over 5 days at City Hall

Hobart Cup Carnival *(Jan.)*
Tasmania's premier racing carnival

Sailing South *(Jan.)*
One of the largest sailing events in Australia

People in the Parks *(Jan.–Mar.)*
Enjoy a variety of activities from jazz
to kite-flying

Royal Hobart Regatta *(Feb.)*
Family regatta and fireworks display

Australian Wooden Boat Festival *(Feb.)*
Hobart's waterfront at its colourful best

10 Days on the Island *(Mar.–Apr.)*
Local and international arts, music,
dance, film and theatre

Working Craft Fair *(July)*
Over a hundred exhibitors display their craft at
the Derwent Entertainment Centre

Tulip Festival of Tasmania *(Sept.)*
Hobart welcomes spring

Point to Pinnacle Road Run and Walk *(Nov.)*
A 22-km journey to the summit of
Mount Wellington

Sydney and Melbourne to Hobart
yacht races *(Dec.)*
Party time at Constitution Dock

Taste of Tasmania *(Dec.)*
The very best of Tasmanian food and wine

Summer Festival *(Dec.–Feb.)*
Hobart buzzes with colour, music
and entertainment

For further details visit the web site
www.tourism.tas.gov.au/wha/eve

RESTAURANTS AND CAFES

Eating out is an integral part of experiencing Hobart. Increasingly, this city and its surrounding countryside are attracting gourmet travellers keen to sample the innovative menus, fine seasonal produce and distinctive local wines. The local seafood is hard to beat – whether it is masterfully presented in one of the many waterfront restaurants or unwrapped and eaten with gusto on the edge of a pier. **Battery Point** *and the suburb of* **North Hobart** *are home to some of Hobart's most highly praised restaurants and cafes. For more information, refer to* A Guide to Tasmania's Restaurants, *a free publication produced by the Restaurant and Caterers Association of Tasmania, available from the Tasmanian Travel & Information Centre.*

Adjacent to the theatre is the one-time red-light district of **Wapping**, which is being redeveloped as a tourist and residential precinct.

ALONG THE WATERFRONT

Hobart's waterfront retains much of its early character and it is easy to imagine the whaling days when this was a brawling seaport known to sailors around the world. The **Maritime Museum of Tasmania**, on the corner of Davey and Argyle streets, has relics and documents from this period, as well as various displays relating to shipbuilding and early exploration. Today, foreign ships tie up almost in the centre of town and battered whaling boats are now replaced by trawlers and yachts moored at the docks along Franklin Wharf. At **Victoria Dock** and **Constitution Dock**, you can buy fresh seafood from the moored punts that line the dock, or dine at the renowned Mures Fish Centre, a two-storey restaurant and cafe complex. Shortly after Christmas every year, Constitution Dock is the setting for one of Australia's greatest parties, when the crews from the boats competing in the

Sydney to Hobart Yacht Race celebrate the end of their long and challenging haul. The **Elizabeth Street Pier** has been developed as apartment accommodation and a restaurant complex. **Franklin Wharf** and **Brooke Street Pier** are the main departure points for ferries and cruise boats.

Salamanca Place, situated at the southern end of the waterfront, displays the finest row of early merchant warehouses in Australia. Built between 1835 and 1840, the warehouses are now home to quality art and craft galleries, as well as an increasing number of cafes and restaurants. On Saturdays, a bustling market attracts shoppers and buskers, and the politically active voice their concerns amid the general cacophony.

Salamanca Square, just off Salamanca Place, is a residential and tourist development built in a disused quarry. It features **Antarctic Adventure**, an interpretative centre celebrating Australia's relationship with the great southern continent. The centre's hands-on exhibits range from the rather gimmicky Blizzard simulator ride, to evocative accounts of researchers based in the inhospitable Antarctic environment.

BATTERY POINT

The steep **Kellys Steps**, wedged between two old warehouses in Salamanca Place, lead to the heart of Battery Point. This delightful part of Hobart was once a lively mariners' village with fishermen's cottages, shops, churches, a village green and a riot of pubs. Today, Battery Point has many inviting restaurants and tea-rooms, and several antique shops to explore, but it is still mainly a residential area. Most of the houses are tiny dormer-windowed fishermen's cottages, with a few grander houses such as **Narryna** and **Lenna**. Narryna now houses the **Van Diemen's Land Folk Museum**, with its interesting collection of colonial relics, and the lavish Italianate Lenna is a boutique hotel.

A stroll around the narrow, hilly streets of Battery Point reveals enchanting glimpses of the harbour, yachts and mountains at every turn. On top of the hill in De Witt Street (off Hampden Road) is **St George's Anglican Church**, built in the 1830s and 1840s. The church's octagonal tower, based on the Temple of Winds in Athens, is floodlit each night until 10.30 p.m. One of the highlights of Battery Point is **Arthur Circus**, where fifteen immaculately preserved Georgian cottages are built around the former village green. Pubs such as Knopwood's Retreat and the Shipright's Arms add to the feeling that time has stood still.

Battery Point got its name from a battery of guns set up on the hill in front of a small guardhouse in 1818. This soon became a **signalling station** and is now the oldest building in Battery Point. To see this building, return to Salamanca Place via Princes Park, where there is a fascinating interpretive board explaining the history of the site.

INNER CITY – SOUTH

Towards the city end of Salamanca Place, behind a square of old European trees, is Tasmania's **Parliament House**.

Originally used as a customs house, the building was designed by the colonial architect John Lee Archer and constructed by convicts between 1835 and 1840. Visitors may ask to see the Legislative Council Chamber; the ceiling has been painstakingly repainted in its original ornate pastel patterns and the benches refurbished in plush red velvet.

St David's Park, on the corner of Salamanca Place and Davey Street, is an ideal place to rest. The park was Hobart's first colonial burial ground – the pioneer gravestones, which date from 1804, make fascinating reading. Opposite the park in Davey Street is the **Royal Tennis Court**, built in 1875. The unusual walled court still operates as a venue for the ancient game of Royal Tennis; there is a small display on the outside wall and visitors are welcome to go inside and watch Royal Tennis being played.

Hobart has a wealth of beautiful Georgian buildings, mostly concentrated around Macquarie and Davey streets. More than ninety of them have a National Trust classification. Built around 1846, the **Anglesea Barracks**, off Davey Street, is the oldest military establishment in Australia still used by the defence forces. The buildings are remarkable for their simple Georgian elegance; guided tours are available on Tuesday mornings.

Those with an interest in rare books and antiques will want to visit the **State Library/Allport Library** and **Museum of Fine Arts** on the corner of Murray and Bathurst streets. Also in Murray Street is **St David's Cathedral**, Hobart's first purpose-built church, consecrated in 1824.

CENTRAL SHOPPING AREA

The main shopping area of Hobart is centred around the **Elizabeth Street Mall**, between Collins and Liverpool streets. This is where you will find Myer and Harris Scarfe, Hobart's main department stores, as well as bookshops, bushwalking stores and other specialty shops. The **Cat and Fiddle Arcade**, an under-cover shopping area located

SHOPPING	Map Ref.
Battery Point An antique shop around every corner	575 G9
Central Shopping Area Department stores and specialty shops	575 F7
Salamanca Market (Sat.) Local art, craft and food produce	575 G8
Salamanca Place Quality art and craft in historic warehouses	575 G8

GALLERIES AND MUSEUMS	Map Ref.
Maritime Museum of Tasmania Treasure chest of seafaring relics	575 G7
State Library/Allport Library & Museum of Fine Arts Rare books and fine antiques	575 E7
Tasmanian Museum & Art Gallery Colonial paintings, Aboriginal history and the convict experience	575 G7
Van Diemen's Land Folk Museum (Narryna) Colonial collection in historic townhouse	575 F9

HISTORY

Hobart, Australia's second oldest city, was established in 1803 in response to fears held by the Governor of New South Wales of possible French colonisation. Convicts constituted the majority of the European settlers in the early 19th century and their forced labour built many of the beautiful old buildings that can be seen today. The small colony flourished and Hobart's deepwater harbour soon became a thriving seaport, particularly as a base for the whaling and sealing ships operating in the Southern Ocean. Hobart retains more of its historic heritage than any other Australian capital, as it has not developed as rapidly this century as the mainland capitals. This, combined with the care taken to preserve historic buildings, has resulted in the survival of a wealth of colonial Georgian buildings and precincts.

ENTERTAINMENT

To tune in to the best and the latest, do what the locals do and consult the Mercury *newspaper on Thursdays and Saturdays. It is worth planning your visit to coincide with a performance at the* **Theatre Royal***, the oldest operating theatre in Australia. Otherwise, you might like to venture into one of the cosy historic pubs bearing seafaring names. No description of Hobart's after-dark attractions would be complete without mention of the city's favourite modern landmark,* **Wrest Point Hotel-Casino***. The casino, Australia's first when it opened in 1973, continues to be popular with residents and visitors alike. The* **Derwent Entertainment Centre** *is a busy venue for circuses, concerts and other live entertainment. As well, it houses trade and public exhibitions. Call Ticketmaster, (03) 6273 0233, for bookings and times. A new home for the Tasmanian Symphony Orchestra is the* **Federation Concert Hall***, part of the Hotel Grand Chancellor waterfront complex.*

SPORT

Spectator

Bellerive Oval *is the venue for cricket, including interstate Sheffield Shield matches and One Day International Series competition. Tasmanian Football League games can be seen at the* **North Hobart Football Oval***, including the grand final in late September. The Hobart Cup horserace is at* **Elwick** *in January, and racing can also be seen regularly at the Elphin track.*

Hobart is well known as the destination port for the Sydney to Hobart and Melbourne to Hobart yacht races held around New Year. Watch the winners cross the line and join the celebrations on **Constitution Dock***.*

Participator

Golfers are well catered for in Tasmania, with more golf courses per head of population than any other State. There are several courses close to Hobart, including the 18-hole **Rosny Park***, which is open to the public. Those keen to cycle around the city can hire a bike from Cycling Adventures Tasmania in* **Salamanca Square***, which also conducts guided rides in and around Hobart. Several cruise companies operate boating tours along the sheltered waters of the* **River Derwent***. They offer half-day, full-day and overnight tours, some on old-fashioned yachts and square riggers. For those wanting to take a dip in warmer waters, the climate-controlled Hobart Aquatic Centre in the* **Queens Domain** *has a 50 metre pool, dive pool, toddlers pool and water slide.*

between the mall and Murray Street, is named after the charmingly kitsch animated mural that performs on the hour. Outside in the mall, shoppers and city workers relax and enjoy the lunchtime street entertainment.

SOUTHERN SUBURBS & BEYOND

Just south of the city centre, under the towering bluff of Battery Point, is the suburb of **Sandy Bay**. Sailing is one of Tasmania's most popular sports and the prestigious Royal Yacht Club of Tasmania has its headquarters here. Nearby is the distinctive tower of **Wrest Point Hotel-Casino**, Australia's first casino. For inspiring views of the Derwent estuary, head for the **Mount Nelson Signal Station Lookout** or the convict-built **Shot Tower** just past Taroona. Lower Sandy Bay is also home to the unusual **Tudor Court Model Village**.

A visit to Hobart would not be complete without a drive to the summit of **Mount Wellington**, which rises 1270 metres above the city. The enclosed lookout point commands panoramic views of the D'Entrecasteaux Channel to the south and the Derwent Valley to the north. The summit itself has the qualities of an alpine wilderness, remarkable for a location

that is just 20 kilometres from the city centre. Be prepared for gusty winds and a considerable drop in temperature, even in summer.

Cascade Brewery, in the foothills of Mount Wellington, makes an interesting return stop. Over 150 years old, the brewery offers tours on weekdays. The ruins of the historic **Female Factory** – a workhouse prison for female convicts where they made soap, took in Hobart's washing, spun wool and made blankets – are nearby in Degraves Street at the base of the Cascade Gardens. One of the five prison yards is now occupied by Island Produce Confectionery. The confectionery factory is open weekdays and Saturdays; inquire about guided tours of the factory and historic site. Bookings are essential for the confectionery and brewery tours, and closed footwear must be worn.

NORTHERN SUBURBS & BEYOND

North Hobart, only a few minutes from the centre of the city, is the gourmand's suburb. A concentration of excellent restaurants and delicatessens have proliferated here to the delight of both residents and visitors. Slightly further north, in the suburb of New Town, is **Runnymede**, a Georgian-style National Trust homestead. Beautifully restored

Battery Point

The Hotel Grand Chancellor and the Federation Concert Hall

and set in a lovely garden, it commands views over New Town Bay and Risdon Cove, where Hobart's first European settlement began.

The **Tasmanian Transport Museum**, built around the relocated New Town railway station, is just off the Brooker Highway in the suburb of Glenorchy. The museum, which is open on weekend and public holiday afternoons, has a wide range of rolling stock in various stages of restoration. It is also the departure point for Classic Rail Tours (bookings through the RACT).

Moorilla Estate Winery is located at Berriedale in a scenic riverside setting. The Vineyard Restaurant is open Tuesday to Sunday; tours and cellar-door sales are available daily. From here it is only a five-minute drive to one of Hobart's premier attractions, the **Cadbury Schweppes Chocolate Factory** at Claremont. Tours operate on weekdays, except on public holidays and during some school holidays; book early to avoid disappointment and remember to wear closed footwear. The aroma of chocolate and toffee inside the factory is truly memorable. Free samples are offered during the tour and participants are able to purchase chocolate at bargain prices in the factory shop. If all that chocolate leads to thoughts of Switzerland, Claremont is also home to **Alpenrail**, an indoor Swiss model village and railway.

EAST OF THE DERWENT

Across the Tasman Bridge in Bellerive are the ruins of the **fort at Bellerive Bluff**, built to guard Hobart against a feared Russian invasion late last century. Bellerive is also the home of Tasmanian cricket; the seaside cricket ground features regularly on televised test matches. To reach some of Hobart's best beaches, take the South Arm Highway to the western shores of Frederick Henry Bay. **Seven Mile Beach**, **Lauderdale** and **Cremorne** are popular for swimming and beachside strolls, and the wild ocean beach at **Clifton** is ideal for surfing.

Four kilometres north-west of Lauderdale is **Rokeby** (1809), which produced the first wheat grown in Tasmania and the first export apples. Rokeby's historic cemetery contains graves of many First Fleeters. St Matthew's Church (1843) contains some chancel chairs that were carved from wood from a ship in Nelson's fleet; the church's organ, brought from England in 1825, is still in use.

Hobart offers the visitor an impressive State capital, rich in history and with a wide variety of natural attractions only minutes away.

DAY TOURS FROM HOBART

Richmond
This small settlement just north of Hobart is probably Australia's best-preserved Georgian Colonial village and is one of Tasmania's most visited attractions. Highlights include: the convict-built Richmond Bridge, Australia's oldest bridge; the gaol, which pre-dates Port Arthur; and galleries and cafes housed in historic shopfronts and cottages. *For more details see region coverage, p. 546.*

Tasman Peninsula
The stunning setting of Port Arthur – lawns, gardens, cliffs – and the beauty of the buttery sandstone buildings belie the site's tragic history. Other sites on the peninsula include the spectacular rock formations around Eaglehawk Neck. *For more details see Classic Tour, p. 567 and region coverage, p. 546.*

Derwent Valley
The Derwent Valley, with its neat agricultural landscape and historic buildings forms one of the loveliest and most 'English-looking' rural areas of Australia. Visit the trout hatchery of Salmon Ponds, the National Trust-classified New Norfolk, and the nearby hop museum at Oast House. *For more details see region coverage, p. 546.*

D'Entrecasteaux Channel
The beauty and intricacy of Tasmania's south-east coastline can be experienced on a leisurely drive south from Hobart. There are stunning water views, particularly at Tinderbox (via Kingston) and Verona Sands at the Huon River entrance. At Kettering a car ferry goes to remote Bruny Island. *For more details see region coverage, p. 546.*

Huon Valley
The Huon Valley is the centre of the island's recently revitalised apple-growing industry. The signposted Huon Trail follows the valley between rows of apple trees and a backdrop of forested mountains. In the far south at Hastings, visitors can tour a dolomite cave and swim in a thermal pool. *For more details see region coverage, p. 546.*

THE SOUTH-EAST

Rivers, sea and mountains dominate the landscape of this extraordinarily rich and interesting region, one of Australia's most scenic touring destinations. The coastline fronting the Tasman Sea is a long, ragged and spectacularly beautiful strip of peninsulas, islands, inlets and channels. Imposing mountains shadow the coast in scenes more reminiscent of the seasides of Europe than those of Australia where the coastal plain is typically broad. Two major rivers, the Huon and Derwent, rise in the high country and meander through heavily pastured valleys. A leisurely pace of development over the last 200 years has kept much of the natural landscape intact. It has also ensured the preservation of many colonial sites, from the poignant sandstone ruins of Port Arthur to the elegant houses, public buildings, pubs and bridges of the small towns that dot the countryside.

CLIMATE **NEW NORFOLK**

	J	F	M	A	M	J	J	A	S	O	N	D
Max. °C	24	24	21	18	14	11	11	13	15	17	19	21
Min. °C	11	11	10	7	5	3	2	3	5	6	8	10
Rain mm	40	35	39	48	45	49	48	47	49	55	47	50
Raindays	8	7	9	10	11	12	13	14	13	14	12	11

FOCUS ON

The convict system

Reminders of Australia's convict years, long gone in other places, are a feature of Tasmania's south-east. The island was colonised in 1803 as a penal settlement and over the next 50 years 52 227 males and 12 595 females, 46 per cent of the entire Australian convict consignment, were transported to its remote shores. Many prisoners worked on public buildings and other infrastructure until the early 1820s, after which most were assigned to private settlers. Re-offending convicts from other prison colonies were sent to Port Arthur on the Tasman Peninsula from 1830 and, in the following years, a penal settlement for re-convicted criminals was built there. Transportation to Tasmania ended in 1852 after a bitter public campaign. Other convict sites on the Tasman Peninsula include the Coal Mines Historic Site (north of Port Arthur) and Eaglehawk Neck, while the fruits of convict labour can be seen in many early structures, such as those in the heritage town of Richmond.

TOP EVENTS

Jan.	*Huon Valley Folk and Music Festival (Cygnet)*
Feb.	*Royal Hobart Regatta*
Feb.	*Country Music Festival (Richmond)*
Mar.	*Hop Harvest Festival (New Norfolk)*
Mar.	*International Highland Spin-In (wool-spinning competition, Bothwell)*
Oct.	*Village Fair (Richmond)*
Oct.	*Spring in the Valley (incl. open gardens, New Norfolk)*
Oct.	*Olie Bollen (Dutch community festival, Kingston)*
Nov.	*Agricultural Show (Brighton, near Pontville)*
Nov.	*Huon Agricultural Show (Huonville)*
Dec.	*Boxing Day Woodchop (Port Arthur)*

VISITOR INFORMATION

Tasmanian Travel and Information Centre
Hobart: (03) 6230 8233
www.discovertasmania.com.au

Derwent Valley

In the rolling country around New Norfolk rows of poplars mark the old hop fields. The Oast House at New Norfolk is a hop industry museum. Hops are still grown at Bushy Park, Glenora and Westerway, where shingled barns and waterwheels recall farming life over a century ago.

Mount Field National Park

Tasmania's oldest national park, 80 km north-west of Hobart, is a wilderness for beginners and daytrippers. The 40-m Russell Falls (pictured) is a wheelchair-friendly 15 minutes from the car park. Other trails wind through moorland, past lakes, and vistas of mountain and forest.

D'Entrecasteaux Channel

Between the Hartz Mountains and this deep-blue channel lies a world's-end coast of tiny towns in sheltered coves. The famous apple orchards are now complemented by boutique fruit and berry farms, salmon and wine. Woodbridge Hotel dining room, overlooking the channel, serves superb food based on local produce.

Trout fishing

This region's lakes and rivers boast some of Australia's best freshwater fishing. A favourite among trout anglers is Ouse River, which joins the Derwent north of Hamilton. Other spots include Clyde, Jordan and Coal rivers east of the Derwent, and Tyenna, Styx and Plenty rivers west of the Derwent.

Bothwell

In the 1820s Scottish immigrants settled the valley of the Clyde River, an area on the fringe of the central plateau that reminded them of their homeland. Bothwell has 53 National Trust-classified buildings, a hotel built in 1821, Australia's oldest golf course and good trout fishing.

Richmond

This historic town 26 km from Hobart has 50 National Trust-classified 19th-century buildings. Some, like the courthouse and old post office, date from the 1820s. Convict-built Richmond Bridge (1823–25), is Australia's oldest bridge. Old Richmond Gaol (1825) retains its original cells and has displays on the convict system.

For more detail see maps 577, 578–9 & 583.
For descriptions of ☺ towns see Towns from A to Z *(p. 553).*

For more detail see maps 577, 578–9 & 583.

For descriptions of ☺ towns see Towns from A to Z *(p. 553).*

EXPERIENCE IT!

❶ *Enjoy* the views in Hartz Mountains National Park, a window onto Tasmania's trackless wildernesses

❷ *Visit* Devils Kitchen, Tasman Blowhole and Tasmans Arch, dramatic rock formations on Tasman Peninsula

❸ *Swim* in the thermal pool and take an underground cave tour at Hastings Caves

❹ *Learn* about rainbow and mountain trout and Australian salmon at Salmon Ponds and Museum of Trout Fishing

❺ *Paddle* a sea-kayak in the D'Entrecasteaux Channel (from Kettering)

Southern Tasmanian Wine Route

Tasmania's first vineyard was established at New Town in 1821. The modern industry began in 1958 when Claudio Alcorso set up the acclaimed Moorilla Estate on the Derwent. There are now about 18 boutique wineries fanning out from Hobart. Start with a map from information centres in the area.

Tasmanian Devil Park

As well as other native creatures, at this park you can see the Tasmanian devil, a fierce-looking black furry creature the size of a small dog. The park also has interesting displays on the thylacine (Tasmanian tiger), a large marsupial regarded as extinct although unconfirmed sightings are still reported.

Bruny Island

Bruny Island was home to the Nuenonne people, of whom Truganini, Tasmania's most famous Aboriginal, was one. Ferries run from Kettering. In the north are farms and holiday shacks; the south is part national park. Visitors can fish, swim, bushwalk and see penguins at The Neck Reserve (pictured) on the isthmus.

Port Arthur Historic Site

Port Arthur is Tasmania's most popular tourist attraction and one of Australia's most significant historic sites. Imposing sandstone prison buildings are set in 40 ha of spectacular landscaping. There are ghost tours and summer boat trips to Isle of the Dead, final resting-place for convicts and prison personnel alike.

THE EAST COAST

The East Coast is Tasmania's premier seaside destination for good reason. It boasts a mild sunny climate, some of Australia's most exquisite coastal scenery, historic sites, gourmet produce, and national park landscapes of peaks, gorges, waterfalls and forests. Many visitors come for a week or two, staying in one of a number of lovely low-key fishing and holiday villages; others choose to explore the coast in a leisurely manner, stopping off for a night here and there as the mood strikes them. There are many activities to enjoy, including diving and fishing in the rich marine environment directly offshore.

TOP EVENTS

Mar. *Fingal Valley Festival (Fingal)*

Mar. *Tasmanian Game-Fishing Classic (St Helens)*

Easter *Jazz in the Vineyard (Freycinet Vineyard, near Bicheno)*

June *Suncoast Jazz Festival (St Helens)*

Nov. *Fun Fish (bream fishing competition, Swansea)*

Dec. *Craft Fair (Cranbrook, near Swansea)*

EXPERIENCE IT!

❶ **Explore** the history of the East Coast in St Helens History Room

❷ **See** Aboriginal middens in the Bay of Fires Conservation Area

❸ **Meet** wombats, devils and birds at the East Coast Birdlife and Animal Park near Bicheno

Mount William National Park

This fairly remote park, created in 1973, protects Tasmania's Forester kangaroo. Many bird species also enjoy a haven here. The view from Mount William takes in the sandy beaches and coastal heath of Tasmania's north-east corner and extends north to the Furneaux Group islands and south to St Marys.

East Coast fishing

The fishing is excellent along this coast, and particularly around St Helens, which is the base for those planning to fish the East Australian Current for tuna, marlin and shark. For land-based and inshore anglers there is the long, narrow estuary of Georges Bay.

For more detail see maps 579, 583 & 585. For descriptions of ❶ towns see Towns from A to Z (p. 533).

VISITOR INFORMATION

Gateway Tasmania Travel Centre
Launceston: (03) 6336 3133;
1800 651 827
www.discovertasmania.com.au

FOCUS ON

East Coast Gourmet Trail

This region's indigenous Paredarerme people based their diet on shellfish. Fishing remains a vital industry. Visitors can taste and buy oysters at Freycinet Marine Farm near Coles Bay, or cray, oysters and scallops from Wardlaw's Cray Store at Chain of Lagoons, south of St Marys. The area is also known for its dairy produce – try the cheddar at Pyengana Dairy Company in the tiny river town of Pyengana. Kate's Berry Farm near Swansea is a gourmet institution, specialising in fresh berries and berry produce. At Swansea Wine and Wool Centre visitors can taste the pinots and chardonnays of the small local industry.

CLIMATE BICHENO

	J	F	M	A	M	J	J	A	S	O	N	D
Max. °C	21	21	20	19	16	14	14	14	16	17	18	20
Min. °C	13	13	12	10	8	7	6	6	7	8	10	11
Rain mm	55	59	56	61	58	61	55	49	45	55	58	73
Raindays	8	8	8	9	9	9	9	9	8	10	10	10

Underwater wonders

The underwater landscape of the East Coast is an unsung wonder. Offshore from Bicheno is Governor Island Marine Reserve. Here, beneath clear waters, granite outcrops create underwater cliffs, caves and deep fissures, which provide a home for diverse marine communities. Glass-bottomed boat and diving tours are available.

Maria Island

Maria Island, 20 km long and 13 km at its widest, combines history and natural beauty. A ferry from Louisville Point, 6 km north of Orford, goes thrice daily to Darlington, a restored penal settlement that operated 1825–51. The island, now national park, allows no private cars.

Freycinet Peninsula

This long, narrow paradise features forests, cliffs, beaches and trails. The beautiful Peninsula Walking Track ends at Wineglass Bay (pictured), regarded by many as one of the world's best beaches. Coles Bay, which now has an upmarket resort, is a peaceful base from which to explore the area.

MIDLANDS & THE NORTH

The undulating Midland plains run south from Launceston, along the island's spine. This fertile region was developed in the 19th century by new arrivals who planted crops and grazed livestock. Colonial gentry built elegant mansions, such as Entally House, Woolmers, Brickendon and Clarendon, in an effort to re-create rural England. These days small-scale wine and gourmet food production captures something of the style of those early years, as do original buildings in towns like Westbury, Ross and Oatlands. Natural landscapes that have survived development are preserved in national parks and offer walking, skiing and, Tasmania's great recreation, trout fishing.

TOP EVENTS

Feb. Launceston Cup (horseracing)

Feb. Festivale (food and wine, Launceston)

Feb. Village Fair and National Penny Farthing Championships (Evandale)

Mar. A Night in the Gorge (Launceston)

Easter Three Peaks Yacht Race (Beauty Point to Hobart)

Apr. Car Rally (Targa)

May Agfest (Carrick)

Nov. Craft Festival (Deloraine)

Dec. Gold Festival (Beaconsfield)

EXPERIENCE IT!

❶ Taste leatherwood honey, unique to Tasmania, at Stephen's Honey Factory at Mole Creek

❷ Take a scenic cruise from Launceston along the Tamar River

❸ Stroll through lavender fields at Bridestowe Estate Lavender Farm near Nabowla (December–January)

A stroll through Launceston
Begin at Princes Square, a serene old park surrounded by Georgian churches. Walk north up John Street to one of Australia's oldest synagogues, and then to the Town Hall and some imposing Victorian bank buildings. Continue past a restored Georgian warehouse to the elegant Customs House facing the river.

VISITOR INFORMATION
Gateway Tasmania Travel
Launceston: (03) 6336 3133;
1800 651 827
www.discovertasmania.com.au

FOCUS ON

Tasmanian Wine Route
Northern Tasmania's 13 wineries are distributed between the west bank of the Tamar River, Pipers Brook and Lilydale. Pipers Brook Vineyard, started in 1974 and now a listed company, is the largest and best-known producer in the region. Cool-climate varieties ripen well in northern Tasmania and the local riesling, pinot noir and sparkling wines are gaining international recognition. Cabernet sauvignon, pinot gris, sauvignon blanc, chardonnay and gewurtztraminer are also grown. The superb quality of the wine is due to the dry, warm autumn. Start by picking up a Tasmanian Wine Route brochure at a visitor information centre.

CLIMATE LAUNCESTON

	J	F	M	A	M	J	J	A	S	O	N	D
Max. °C	23	23	21	17	14	11	11	12	14	16	19	21
Min. °C	10	10	9	7	5	3	2	3	4	6	7	9
Rain mm	40	43	43	58	63	61	81	80	65	63	51	53
Raindays	8	7	9	11	13	13	16	16	13	13	11	10

Woolmers Estate
Regarded as Australia's most significant colonial property, Woolmers (near Longford) has buildings, antique cars, photographs, art and furniture that reflect the life of six generations of one family, from 1817 to the present day.

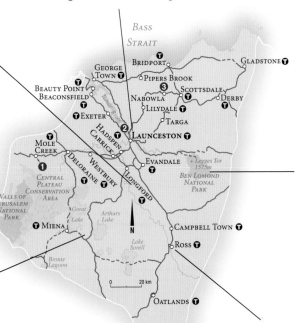

For more detail see maps 580–1, 583 & 584–5. For descriptions of ❶ towns see Towns from A to Z (p. 553).

Ben Lomond National Park
Tasmania's best snow skiing is to be found on Ben Lomond Range, a plateau rising to over 1575 m. The scenery is magnificent, especially the view from Legges Tor, Tasmania's second highest peak. The park offers easy bushwalking and is ablaze with wildflowers in spring and early summer.

Trout fishing in the Central Highlands
Great Lake, Arthurs Lake, Lake Sorrell and Bronte Lagoon are renowned for their stocks of brown trout. January and February are the peak months for trout fishing.

Ross
This tiny village (founded 1812) boasts the decoratively carved Ross Bridge (pictured), a fine example of convict building skill. The remains of Ross Female Factory, a prison for female convicts and their children, is nearby. Other points of interest include the barracks, the Uniting and Anglican churches and the Scotch Thistle Inn.

THE NORTH-WEST

This region is a delight for bushwalkers as well as for more traditional holiday-makers. Along the north coast, a scenic road intersected by regional centres and holiday villages skirts the mountains that meet the waters of Bass Strait. The undulating country near the coast is a patchwork of farms producing vegetables, dairy products, honey and flowers. Further south are the dolomite peaks and still lakes of Cradle Mountain–Lake St Clair National Park, a World Heritage Area. On the west coast, the Arthur and Pieman rivers tumble through gorges and rainforest to a coastline of rolling breakers, dangerous headlands and rich Aboriginal sites.

TOP EVENTS

Feb.	*Grande Fiesta Ng Filipino (Latrobe)*
Feb.	*Miners and Axemen Festival (Rosebery)*
Feb.	*Tasmazia Lavender Harvest Festival (near Sheffield)*
Mar.	*Taste the Harvest (Devonport)*
Mar.	*Splash of Colour Festival (Penguin)*
Mar.	*Ripcurl West Coast Classic (near Marrawah)*
Mar.	*Norwest Country Music Awards (Burnie)*
July	*North West Festival of Fire (Burnie)*
Oct.	*Taste of Ulverstone*

EXPERIENCE IT!

❶ **See** rock engravings at Tiagarra Aboriginal Centre on Devonport's Mersey Bluff

❷ **Cruise** the Pieman River from Corinna

❸ **Taste** Mount Roland Cheese in Latrobe

VISITOR INFORMATION

Burnie: (03) 6434 6111
Devonport: (03) 6424 4466
www.devonport.tco.asn.au/tourist.htm

FOCUS ON

Wilderness walks

An unforgettable way of seeing the lakes, tarns, buttongrass heaths, wildflowers, woodland and rainforest of Tasmanian alpine wilderness is by walking the 85-km Overland Track, one of Australia's most awe-inspiring treks. It runs the length of Cradle Mountain–Lake St Clair National Park and passes Mount Ossa, Tasmania's highest mountain. Each year about 5000 people attempt the 5 to 8-day walk. There are 12 unattended huts for overnight stays. These quickly fill up; be prepared to camp. In the park's northern half are shorter trail options, all of them through majestic landscapes. Summer is the best walking season in this area.

The Nut

Historic Stanley is dominated by the 152-m-high volcanic Circular Head (known as The Nut). A steep stairway and a chairlift go to the clifftop, where a 40-minute circuit walk offers views of coast and ocean.

CLIMATE WARATAH

	J	F	M	A	M	J	J	A	S	O	N	D
Max. °C	17	18	16	12	10	8	7	8	10	12	14	16
Min. °C	6	7	6	4	3	1	1	1	2	3	4	5
Rain mm	110	96	123	175	215	229	251	252	225	204	169	142
Raindays	16	14	18	21	23	23	25	25	24	23	20	18

The fresh air of Woolnorth

The Van Diemen's Land Company, which was granted tracts of north-west Tasmania in the 1820s, still owns this sheep, cattle and plantation-timber property. Tours from Smithton include lunch and a visit to spectacular Cape Grim where the air is the world's cleanest.

Arthur–Pieman Conservation Area

This reserve is reached via the scenic but controversial Western Explorer Road. This 3.5-hour route, steep sections of which are sealed, links Corinna and Arthur River. The conservation area was home to the Peerapper Aboriginal people, whose legacy is seen in middens and other archeological sites; access is limited.

For more detail see maps 580 & 584. For descriptions of ❶ towns see Towns from A to Z (p. 553).

Bass Highway

The spectacular scenery on the Ulverstone to Stanley section of this highway recalls Victoria's Great Ocean Road. The route's highlights include: the little (fairy) penguins at the village of Penguin; the Lactos Cheese Tasting Centre in Burnie; and the colourful fields of Table Cape Tulip Farm near Wynyard.

Cradle Mountain–Lake St Clair National Park

This glaciated landscape – rare in Australia – is part of the island's Wilderness World Heritage Area. Cradle Mountain (pictured) and Lake St Clair, in the north and south respectively, are both easily accessible.

SOUTH-WEST WILDERNESS

Tasmania's south-west is one of the planet's great wildernesses, an almost uninhabited landscape of fretted mountains, glacial lakes, majestic rivers, waterfalls, gorges, virgin temperate rainforest and 1000-year-old trees. In the valleys and along the coast are rock-art galleries and middens, representing some of Earth's best-preserved Ice Age sites. The region attracts nature lovers and adventurers from far afield. The Franklin River is one of the world's great whitewater destinations, and the network of wilderness tracks challenge the most experienced walkers. For the less adventurous there are shorter day walks, and guided extended walks on the coast.

TOP EVENTS
Jan. Mount Lyell Picnic (Strahan)
Mar. Piners' Festival (Strahan)
Oct. Robert Sticht Festival (Queenstown)

EXPERIENCE IT!
1 *Go* fishing or horseriding along the 36-km Ocean Beach near Strahan, Tasmania's longest beach

2 *Board* Queenstown's chairlift for views across the extraordinary surrounding landscape

3 *Take* a self-guide tour of National Trust-classified Zeehan, once a large mining town

CLIMATE STRATHGORDON

	J	F	M	A	M	J	J	A	S	O	N	D
Max. °C	19	20	17	14	12	9	9	10	12	13	16	17
Min. °C	10	10	9	7	5	4	3	3	4	5	7	8
Rain mm	150	114	150	214	247	203	270	278	261	247	191	195
Raindays	17	14	18	21	22	21	25	25	24	23	20	20

The Wilderness Railway
One of Tasmania's most recent tourist attractions is a restored 1896 rack-and-pinion railway, which travels a scenic 35 km across rivers and through forests. The journey begins at Queenstown, known for its landscape of bare multicoloured hills and gullies, and finishes at Strahan.

VISITOR INFORMATION
Strahan: (03) 6471 7622
www.strahan.tco.asn.au

FOCUS ON

Preserving the wilderness
The 1972 flooding of Lake Pedder for the Gordon River hydro-electric scheme sparked a campaign to preserve the south-west wilderness from further inroads. Despite the region's 1982 World Heritage listing, the Tasmanian government pressed on. Conservationists blockaded a proposed dam site from December 1982 until the election of a new Federal Labor government in March 1983. Arrests and clashes with police made headlines and earned the movement support from mainstream Australia. Finally, Federal legislation to stop the project survived a High Court challenge. The historical and ecological significance of the south-west wilderness is imaginatively presented at Strahan Visitors Centre.

Macquarie Harbour and Strahan
Strahan (pictured) is a charming holiday town offering a huge range of outdoor activities. Originally a timber-milling town, today Strahan has a population of artists and craftspeople. Macquarie Harbour is best explored by boat; stop off at Sarah Island, which once housed the most intractable of the colony's convicts.

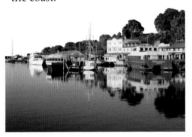

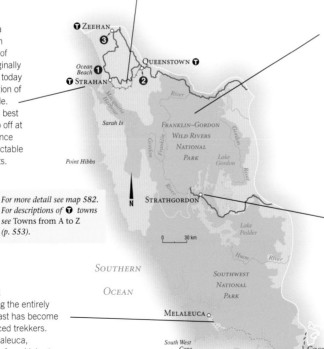

For more detail see map 582. For descriptions of ❶ towns see Towns from A to Z (p. 553).

The South Coast Track
This 10-day walk along the entirely uninhabited south coast has become a mecca for experienced trekkers. The walk starts at Melaleuca, reached by light plane from Hobart. From here walkers head east across a landscape of mountain ranges, rivers, swampy plains and wild beaches to reach Cockle Creek.

Franklin–Gordon Wild Rivers National Park
One way to visit this grand wilderness is by boat from Strahan. Cruises run up the Gordon to Heritage Landing, where there is a short walk to a 2000-year-old Huon pine, a species unique to Tasmania. Guided rafting trips south along the Franklin River begin near Lyell Highway.

Strathgordon and hydro-electricity
Strathgordon is the place to see Tasmania's massive hydro-electricity industry at work. Sights along Gordon River Road include the huge lakes Pedder and Gordon; Gordon Dam; and the underground Gordon Power Station, the biggest in Australia. Bushwalkers can enter Southwest National Park (pictured) via the Creepy Crawly Nature Trail.

BASS STRAIT ISLANDS

These islands, known for their produce, fauna and windswept beauty, are the remains of the land bridge between Tasmania and mainland Australia. They offer low-key holidays where the most energetic activity might be a coastal stroll, although more active experiences (game-fishing, diving and fossicking) are on offer. King and Flinders are the main islands. King, with 1700 residents, gets about 13 000 visitors a year, who mostly fly from Melbourne. Flinders (in the Furneaux Group of 53 islands) has 900 residents and welcomes 6000 or so visitors a year, most of whom fly in from Launceston or Melbourne.

TOP EVENTS

Jan.	*King Island Racing Cup (Currie)*
Mar.	*Wybalenna Festival (Flinders Island)*
Mar.	*Agricultural Show (King Island)*
Mar.	*Imperial 20 (footrace, King Island)*
June	*Pheasant Season (King Island)*
Sept.	*Wind Festival (arts and crafts, Flinders Island)*
Oct.	*Agricultural Show (Flinders Island)*
Nov.	*Golf Open (King Island)*

EXPERIENCE IT!

❶ **Fossick** for the elusive 'Killiecrankie diamond', a type of topaz, on Flinders Island

❷ **See** the Australian fur seals at Reid Rocks, a short boat ride from King Island

❸ **Enjoy** the view across to Victoria from Wickham Lighthouse (1861), tallest lighthouse in the Southern Hemisphere

VISITOR INFORMATION

Tasmanian Travel and Information Centre
Hobart: (07) 6230 8233
Flinders Island Visitor Information
Whitemark: (03) 6359 2380
www.focusonflinders.com.au
www.kingisland.net.au

FOCUS ON

Fishing

The Bass Strait islands offer superb coastal fishing. On Flinders Island, Australian salmon, flathead, gummy shark, silver trevally, pike and squid can be caught from rocks and beaches. From Lady Barron, Emita and Killiecrankie several charter boats take anglers offshore for catches of all the above as well as snapper, yellowtail kingfish, trumpeter and various kinds of tuna. On King Island there is excellent fishing for Australian salmon, flathead and whiting from the beaches along the east coast. South of Currie is British Admiral Reef, where boat anglers can try for morwong, warehou, yellowtail kingfish and squid.

King Island produce

The Bass Strait islands have, in recent years, developed a strong reputation for quality food exports. The name King Island is synonymous with rich cheeses and creams made from unpasteurised milk. The matchless double brie and camembert can be sampled at the King Island Dairy, north of Currie.

Furneaux Group boat tour

The Furneaux Group of islands, charted in 1798 by Matthew Flinders, became a base for sealers (called Straitsmen), many of whom were ex-convicts. Apart from Flinders, the only inhabited island is Cape Barren, where residents mostly fish and farm. Boat tours of the islands leave from Lady Barron on Flinders.

CLIMATE CURRIE

	J	F	M	A	M	J	J	A	S	O	N	D
Max. °C	20	21	20	17	15	14	13	13	14	16	17	19
Min. °C	13	13	13	11	10	9	8	8	8	9	10	11
Rain mm	36	39	48	68	99	102	124	115	84	75	60	52
Raindays	11	10	14	17	21	22	24	24	21	19	15	13

Wybalenna Historic Site

Wybalenna ('black man's home'), was set up on Flinders Island in 1834 to house 133 Aboriginal people, survivors of Tasmania's pre-European population of over 4000. It is one of the most important historic sites in Tasmania. Nearby is a National Trust-restored church and cemetery (pictured).

For more detail see maps 582 (inset), 583 (inset) & 585.

Diving at wrecks

In the storm-lashed waters around King Island lie over 60 shipwrecks. The best known is the *Cataraqui* which sank in 1845 with the loss of 399 immigrants and crew, making it Australia's worst peacetime disaster. A number of wrecks around the island are accessible to scuba divers; diving tours are available.

Strzelecki National Park

The granite Strzelecki Range occupies the south-west corner of Flinders Island. On a clear day, the highlight of this largely undeveloped park is a 5-hour-return walk to the summit of Strzelecki Peaks (pictured).

TASMANIA
TOWNS FROM A TO Z

Beaconsfield Pop. 1014

MAP REF. 581 J5, 585 K7

Impressive brick ruins with Romanesque arches dominate this quiet town on the West Tamar Hwy, 46 km NE of Launceston. Formerly a thriving gold township (called Cabbage Tree Hill), the ruins are of Tasmanian Gold Mine pithead buildings dating back to 1904. When the mine closed in 1914 after water seepage, the worth of ore from the reef totalled 6 million dollars. Now the mine shaft of the recently reopened Beaconsfield Gold Mine towers overhead. **In town:** Grubb Shaft Gold and Heritage Museum in old mine building, West St, features working models, relics and interactive displays. Restored miner's cottage and original Flowery Gully School opposite museum. Van Diemen's Gallery, Weld St, art and craft. Dec.: Gold Festival. **In the area:** York Town monument at site of first European settlement in northern Tasmania, 9 km N on Kelso–Greens Beach Rd. At Rowella, 15 km E, Holm Oak Vineyards. Auld Kirk (1843), convict-built church at Sidmouth, 13 km SE; nearby, Batman Bridge, its A-frame reaching 100 m above Tamar River. **Visitor information:** Tamar Visitor Centre, cnr Main & Winkleigh rds, Exeter; (03) 6394 4454, freecall 1800 637 989. Web site www.wtc.tas.gov.au **See also:** Midlands & the North p. 549.

Beauty Point Pop. 1194

MAP REF. 581 K5, 585 K6

This popular fishing and yachting centre on the West Tamar Hwy, 48 km NW of Launceston, is the oldest deepwater port in the area. Originally constructed to serve the Beaconsfield goldmine, the port facilities today serve the Australian Maritime College. Commercial cargo is loaded at Bell Bay across the river. **In town:** Seahorse World, a seahorse aquaculture farm: visitor centre; aquarium; guided tours. Nearby Sandy Beach for safe swimming. Easter: Three Peaks Yacht Race (to Hobart). **In the area:** Holiday towns: Kelso, 15 km NW, dates back to early York Town settlement; Greens Beach, 20 km NW, at mouth of Tamar River. Narawntapu National Park, 25 km NW: coastline views; walks ranging from 10 min to the 5-hr trail from Badger Head to Bakers Beach. Marion's Vineyard on Foreshore Dr., Deviot, 21 km SE. **Visitor information:** Tamar Visitor Centre, Main Rd, Exeter; (03) 6394 4454, freecall 1800 637 898. **See also:** Midlands & the North p. 549; National Parks p. 572.

Bicheno Pop. 700

MAP REF. 583 Q2, 585 Q12

A sealing and whaling town from about 1803, and later a coalmining port (1854), Bicheno's main industry today is crayfishing. Situated 195 km NE of Hobart, this small fishing port on the east coast is popular for holidays. It has a mild climate, sandy beaches nearby and a picturesque setting. Visitors can fish in the surf, off rocks, offshore and in the estuary. Licensed seafood restaurants and a range of accommodation add to Bicheno's appeal. **In town:** Dive Centre, Tasman Hwy, offers diving instruction and charters. Foreshore walkway, from Redbill Point north of town, south to Blowhole. Lookouts at top of twin hills: Whalers Lookout,

Wineglass Bay near Bicheno

off Foster St, and National Park Lookout, off Morrison St; rock orchids, unique to east coast, spectacular in Oct. and Nov. Grave of Aboriginal heroine Waubedebar, in Lions Park, Burgess St. Mountain-bike hire from information centre. Historic tours. Seafood outlets with lobsters in season. **In the area:** Fishing and scuba diving charters, and glass-bottomed boat rides to see underwater life in Governor Island Marine Reserve. Little (fairy) penguin colony, 6 km N; nightly guided tours in season. East Coast Birdlife and Animal Park, 8 km N, exhibits Tasmanian devils and other native fauna. Adjacent is Denison River Trail Rides, for beach and forest horserides. Douglas Apsley Vineyard, 11 km N. Lookout in Douglas–Apsley National Park, 14 km NW. Wardlaw's Cray Store, 27 km N (Nov.–May). Freycinet Vineyard and the adjacent Springbrook Vineyard, 18 km SW on Tasman Hwy; Jazz in the Vineyard festival at Freycinet Vineyard, Easter Sun. Scenic flights from Belarine Aviation, Coles Bay Rd, 20 km S. Freycinet National Park, 40 km S, for coastal scenery and wildlife watching. **Visitor information:** Bicheno Penguin Tours, Tasman Hwy; (03) 6375 1333.

See also: The East Coast p. 548; National Parks p. 572.

Boat Harbour   Pop. 109

MAP REF. 584 F5

The clear water and rocky points of this attractive village make it ideal for diving and spear-fishing. Situated on the north-west coast, 31 km W of Burnie, it adjoins one of the State's richest agricultural areas. **In town:** Shannondoah Cottage, Bass Hwy: local craft; lunches; Devonshire teas. **In the area:** Boat Harbour Beach, 3 km N: safe swimming; marine life in pools at low tide; fishing; water-skiing; bushwalking. Mallavale Farm, 3 km NW: local art and craft; tearooms; coastal views. Sisters Beach, 8 km NW, good fishing and swimming. Nearby, Birdland Native Gardens. Rocky Cape National Park, 19 km NW: Aboriginal caves; coastal walks; brochures at Wynyard information centre. **Visitor information:** Seaside Garden Motel, The Esplanade; (03) 6445 1111. **See also:** The North-West p. 550.

Bothwell   Pop. 356

MAP REF. 583 K5

Peaceful Bothwell in the beautiful Clyde River valley, 74 km NW of Hobart, has been proclaimed an historic village. It has 53 buildings classified or registered by the National Trust. Surveyed in 1824 and named by Lieutenant-Governor Arthur after the Scottish town, it is now the centre of sheep and cattle country. It is claimed that Australia's first golf was played at the nearby homestead of Ratho in the 1830s. This course is open to visitors with golf-club membership elsewhere. **In town:** Bothwell Grange (c. 1836), Alexander St, guesthouse with tea-rooms and art gallery. Australasian Golf Museum, Market Pl. On Patrick St: Expressions of Interest Art Gallery features leading Tasmanian artists; Lamont Weaving Studio, home of Tasmanian tartan, has demonstrations and sales. St Luke's Church (1830), Dennistoun Rd. In High St: Georgian brick Slate Cottage (1836), restored and furnished heritage-style; Old Bootmaker's Shop, tours by appt. Self-guide walking trail, brochure available. Mar.: International Highland Spin-In (wool-spinning competition). **In the area:** Good trout fishing. **Visitor information:** Australasian Golf Museum, Market Pl.; (03) 6259 4033. Web site www.bothwell.tco.asn.au/about.html **See also:** The South-East p. 546.

Bridgewater   Pop. 4250

MAP REF. 578 H4, 583 L7

This town, 19 km N of Hobart, is at the main northern crossing of the River Derwent. The 1830s causeway was built by 200 convicts, who barrowed 2 million tonnes of stone and clay from a nearby quarry. The original bridge was opened in 1849; the present one dates from 1946. **In the area:** At Granton, 1 km S across bridge: Old Watch House (1838), now a petrol station, was built by convicts to guard the causeway and has the smallest cell in Australia (50 cm square, 2 m high); Black Snake Inn (1833), also convict-built. Risdon Cove Historic Site, 15 km SE, site of original Hobart town settlement. **Visitor information:** Council Offices, Tivoli Rd, Gagebrook; (03) 6263 0333. **See also:** The South-East p. 546.

Bridport   Pop. 1234

MAP REF. 581 R2, 585 N6

Bridport is a popular holiday and fishing town on the north-east coast, 85 km NE of Launceston. **In town:** Fine beaches, excellent fishing in rivers, lakes and sea. Wildflower Reserve on western outskirts, best months Sept.–Oct. Scenic walking path, brochure available. **In the area:** Bowood Homestead (1838), 8 km W; gardens open by appt. Views from Waterhouse Point and Ranson's Beach. Winegrowing area around Pipers Brook, 18 km SW; Tasmanian Wine Route, brochure available. **Visitor information:** Bridport '2000 Plus' Information Shop, Main St, 10 a.m.–4 p.m.; (03) 6356 0280. Web site www.bridport.tco.asn.au **See also:** Midlands & the North p. 549.

Bruny Island   Pop. 581

MAP REF. 578 H12, 583 M11

Almost two islands, separated by an isthmus, Bruny was named after the French Admiral Bruni D'Entrecasteaux, who surveyed the channel between the island and the mainland in 1792; the Aboriginal name for the island was Lunawannaaloona. Abel Tasman saw the island in 1642 but did not land. Other 18th-century European visitors incl. Furneaux (1773), James Cook (1777) and William Bligh (1788, 1792). Tasmania's first apple trees are said to have been planted here by a Bligh expedition botanist. **In the area:** Ferry 10 times daily from mainland Kettering. Nature tours of the island, incl. wildlife and temperate rainforest. Cape Queen Elizabeth Walk, 3 hrs return. Morella Island Retreat, hothouse, cafe, gumtree maze. On the isthmus between North and South Bruny: memorial to Truganini, Tasmania's most famous Aboriginal (died 1876); lookout with coastal views; boardwalk; little (fairy) penguins and short-tailed shearwaters (muttonbirds). On South Bruny: Bligh Museum, exhibits island's recorded history; Captain Cook's Landing Place, has model of Cook's ship; Mavista Falls, in scenic reserve; lookouts at Adventure and Cloudy bays; lighthouse (1836) at Cape Bruny, second oldest in Australia; walking tracks to Mt Mangana and Mt Bruny; boat tours from Adventure Bay. On North Bruny: Dennes Point beach, D'Entre-casteaux Channel, has picnic/barbecue facilities; at Variety Bay, remains of convict-built church on private property near airstrip, conducted tours; at Barnes Bay, vault of white settler William Lawrence. Fishing, camel tours. **Visitor information:** Bruny D'Entrecasteaux Visitor Centre, 81 Ferry Rd, Kettering; (03) 6267 4494. Web site www.bruny.tco.asn.au/visitor.html **See also:** The South-East p. 546.

Buckland   Pop. 228

MAP REF. 579 M2, 583 N7

A 14th-century stained-glass window depicting John the Baptist's life is in the Church of St John the Baptist (1846) in this tiny township, 64 km NE of Hobart. History links the window with England's Battle Abbey. Oliver Cromwell sacked the abbey in the 17th century, but the window was hidden for safety; two centuries later the Marquis of Salisbury gave it to Rev. T. H. Fox, Buckland's first rector. It is now in the east wall of the church on the Tasman Hwy. The original figure-work is intact. Also of interest is Ye Olde Buckland Inn, Kent St, 19th-century tavern and restaurant. **Visitor information:** Ye Olde Buckland Inn, Kent St; (03) 6257 5114. **See also:** The East Coast p. 548.

Burnie   Pop. 16 007

MAP REF. 584 G6

The rapid expansion of Burnie, now Tasmania's fourth largest city, is based on one of the State's largest enterprises, Australian Paper. Situated on the banks of Emu Bay, 148 km NW of Launceston, Burnie has a deepwater port, which serves the west coast mining centres. Other industries incl. the production of mining equipment, and dried milk, chocolate products and cheese. **In town:** Lactos Cheese Tasting and Sales Centre, Old Surrey Rd. Free guided tours of Amcor paper mill, (Mon.–Fri.), Marine Tce (book at information centre). Pioneer Village Museum, at information centre, incl. reconstruction of small shops (c. 1900). Burnie Inn, town's oldest building, re-erected as a cafe in Burnie Park. Glen Osborne, Aileen Cres., historic building, now B&B. Market, Spring St (opp. railway), 1st and 3rd Sat. each month. Scenic and heritage town walk, brochure available. Jan: New Year's Day Athletic Carnival. Mar.: Norwest Country Music Awards. July: North West Festival of Fire. Oct.: Skilled Burnie 10 (footrace); Rhododendron Festival. **In the area:** Views from Round Hill, 5 km E. Fern Glade, off Old Surrey Rd, 5 km W, for riverside walks and picnics. Emu Valley Rhododendron Gardens, off Cascade Rd, 6 km S. Annsleigh Gardens, 9 km S on Mount Rd, closed in winter. Guide Falls near Ridgley, 17 km S; Guide Falls Alpaca Farm, 1 km further on. Upper Natone Forest Reserve, 20 km S, for picnics. Scenic drive northwest via Somerset, then inland through Elliott to Yolla. Scenic Hellyer Gorge State Reserve, 23 km S of Yolla on Murchison Hwy. **Visitor information:** Tasmanian Travel and Information Centre, Civic Centre Plaza, off Little Alexander St; (03) 6434 6111. **See also:** The North-West p. 550.

Campbell Town   Pop. 816
MAP REF. 583 M2, 585 N12

Campbell Town, 66 km SE of Launceston on the Midland Hwy, has strong links with the wool industry; Saxon merinos were introduced to the Macquarie Valley west of town in the early 1820s. Timber and stud beef are also important primary industries. The town and Elizabeth River were named by Governor Macquarie for his wife, Elizabeth Campbell. **In town:** Self-guide heritage walks, brochure available. National Trust-classified buildings in King St are Wesleyan Chapel (1846), no longer operational, and St Michael's Church (1857); in Bridge St is Balmoral Cottage (1840s); in High St are Fox Hunters Return (1830s), now colonial accommodation, St Luke's Church (1839), The Grange (1847), Campbell Town Inn (1840), convict-built Red Bridge (1837) and Kean's Brewery (1840), now an antique outlet. Also in High St: memorial to Harold Gatty, first round-the-world flight navigator; displays at

Picturesque farmland near Deloraine

Heritage Highway Museum; market at Town Hall, 4th Sun. each month. June: Agricultural Show (oldest in Australia). **In the area:** Trout fishing, particularly in Lake Leake, 30 km SE. Evansville Game Park, 30 km E. **Visitor information:** Heritage Highway Museum and Visitor Centre, 103 High St; (03) 6381 1353. **See also:** Midlands & the North p. 549.

Coles Bay   Pop. 120
MAP REF. 583 Q4, 585 Q13

This beautiful unspoiled bay, 42 km S of Bicheno on the Freycinet Peninsula, is a good base for visits to Freycinet National Park. **In the area:** At Freycinet National Park: pleasant beaches, clear waters and heathland; swimming, game-fishing and bushwalking, incl. scenic Peninsula Walking Track to Wineglass Bay; abundant birdlife; wildflowers, incl. 60 varieties of ground orchid; rock-climbing on The Hazards, spectacular granite peaks rising to 620 m, and nearby cliffs; water-skiing, scuba-diving, canoeing, sailing; charter boat trips to Schouten Island. Freycinet Marine Farm, 9 km N, oysters (5 p.m.–6 p.m.) and tours; (03) 6257 0140. **Visitor information:** Freycinet National Park Ranger; (03) 6257 0107. **See also:** The East Coast p. 548; National Parks p. 572.

Cygnet   Pop. 851
MAP REF. 578 F10, 583 K10

The centre of a fruit-growing district 52 km SW of Hobart, the town was originally named Port de Cygne Noir (Black Swan Port) by the French Admiral Bruni D'Entrecasteaux because of the number of swans in the bay. **In town:**

Art and craft shops. Cygnet Guest House, Mary St: woodcraft; art gallery; Devonshire tea; B&B. Jan.: Huon Valley Folk and Music Festival. **In the area:** Boating, fishing, bushwalking, gem-fossicking, wineries, small berry-fruit farms. Magnificent wattle, apple and pear blossom Sept.–Oct. Nine Pin Point Marine Nature Reserve, 18 km S, near Verona Sands. Good beaches and boat-launching facilities at Randalls Bay, 14 km S; also at nearby Verona Sands, and Egg and Bacon Bay 15 km S. Panorama Vineyard, 9 km N. Unique Lymington lace agate sometimes found at Drip Beach, Lymington, 7.5 km SW. Lymington Geological (car) Trail; brochure available. Pelverata Falls 20 km N on Sandfly Rd. The Deepings, woodturners' workshop and sales, 10 km E at Nicholls Rivulet. Talune Wildlife Park and Koala Gardens, 6 km SE at Gardners Bay: good picnic/barbecue facilities; sells own cider and fruit wine. Hartzview Wine Centre, 10 km SE. **Visitor information:** Talune Wildlife Park, 1106 Gardners Bay; (03) 6295 1775. Web site www.southcom.com.au/~wombat **See also:** The South-East p. 546.

Deloraine   Pop. 2168
MAP REF. 580 I11, 585 J9

With Bass Strait (north) and the Great Western Tiers (south), Deloraine is an ideal base for exploring northern Tasmania. The surrounding countryside is used mainly for dairying and mixed farming. **In town:** Deloraine Folk Museum, 98 Emu Bay Road. Gallery 9, West Barrack St. 'Yarns', large multi-panelled artwork in silk, Community Complex, Alveston Dr., open Mon.–Wed. or by appt. Walk along riverbank, through parkland. Markets at showgrounds,

Lake Hwy, 1st Sat. each month. Easter: Grand National Steeplechase. Nov.: Craft Festival. **In the area:** Elizabeth Town, 10 km NW: Ashgrove Farm, English-style cheese; Christmas Hills Raspberry Farm. Lobster Falls, 15 km W, 2-hr return walk from roadside; Westmoreland Falls, further 10 km SW at Caveside. Trowunna Wildlife Park, 18 km W on Mole Creek Rd, has nocturnal enclosure. Montana Falls, 9 km SW, small but pretty; 5–10 min walk. Meander Falls in Meander Forest Reserve, 22 km SW, 5-hr return walk from carpark (not accessible after heavy snow); other walking tracks in reserve. Quamby Bluff, 20 km S, solitary mountain behind town; walking track to summit (6-hr return, medium difficulty) starts near Lake Hwy. Liffey Falls, 29 km S, 45-min-return walk from carpark. Brochures available for all walks. Scenic drive south to Central Highlands area via Golden Valley, to Great Lake, one of the largest high-water lakes in Australia; check road conditions, (03) 6259 8163. Dry's Bluff, 40 km SE, part of Great Western Tiers. Excellent trout fishing on lake and in Mersey and Meander rivers. **Visitor information:** Deloraine Folk Museum, 98 Emu Bay Rd; (03) 6362 3471. Web site www.meandervalley.com **See also:** Midlands & the North p. 549.

Derby   Pop. 200

MAP REF. 585 O7

Derby is a former mining town on the Tasman Hwy, 34 km E of Scottsdale in the north-east. Although tin is still worked in the area, there has been a gradual swing to rural production. **In town:** In Main St: Derby Tin Mine Museum, in old school (1897), has history displays, gemstones, minerals and tin panning; reconstructed Shanty Town has original local shop and office buildings and two cells from old Derby gaol; woodcraft at Classic Crafts and The Gallery; Bank House Antiques and Craft, in old bank. Oct.: Derby River Derby. **In the area:** At Moorina, 8 km NE: gemstone-fossicking park on Tasman Hwy; cemetery has graves of Chinese miners. At former tin-mining town of Branxholm, 12 km SW, Y. Woodcrafts (wood-turning). Near Ringarooma, 24 km SW, Ralph Falls; lookouts at Mathinna Hill and Mt Victoria; scenic drives. Ringarooma Agricultural Show in Oct. **Visitor information:** Derby Tin Mine Centre, Main Rd; (03) 6354 2262. **See also:** Midlands & the North p. 549.

Lighthouse on Mersey Bluff, Devonport

Devonport   Pop. 22 299

MAP REF. 580 E5, 584 I6

Devonport is a busy port for agricultural and industrial exports and terminal for the vehicular ferry *Spirit of Tasmania* which crosses Bass Strait from Melbourne. The town has its own airport and is an ideal base for seeing northern Tasmania. **In town:** Tiagarra, Tasmanian Aboriginal Culture and Art Centre, Bluff Rd, Mersey Bluff; 1-km circuit walk to Aboriginal rock engravings. Devonport Gallery and Arts Centre in historic church, Stewart St. Devonport Maritime Museum and Historical Society, Victoria Pde; model ships and history room. National Trust-classified Home Hill, Middle Rd, home of former Prime Minister Joseph Lyons and Dame Enid Lyons (check times). Scenic flights. Jan.: Devonport Cup. Feb.: St George Triathlon. Mar.: Taste the Harvest Festival; Apex Regatta. Oct.: Classic Challenge Motorsport Event. Dec.: Melbourne–Devonport Yacht Race. **In the area:** Tasmanian Trail, 477-km Dover–Devonport trail for walkers, horseriders and mountain-bikers. Walking and cycling track from town to Don, 7 km W, via Mersey Bluff lighthouse, for excellent views. At Don: Don River Railway and Museum; vintage trains (Mon.–Sat.), steam trains (Sun., public holidays). Braddon's Lookout, further 9 km W near Forth, has panoramic view of coastline. At Eugenana, 10 km S: Tasmanian Arboretum (45 ha); walking tracks; picnic area. **Visitor information:** Tasmanian

Travel and Information Centre, 92 Formby Rd; (03) 6424 4466. Web site www.devonport.tco.asn.au/tourist.htm **See also:** The North-West p. 550.

Dover   Pop. 481

MAP REF. 578 E12, 583 K11

This attractive fishing port, south-west of Hobart, was once a convict station. The Commandant's Office remains but underground cells, near the wharf, can no longer be seen. From late 1850s large sawmills produced first-class timber. The main industries today are fruit-growing, fishing and Atlantic salmon fish-farming. Quaint cottages and English trees give the town an old-world atmosphere. The three bay islands are called Faith, Hope and Charity. **In town:** Charter fishing trips, Atlantic salmon cruises, and twilight and adventure cruises on *Olive May*, depart end Jetty Rd. **In the area:** Attractive scenery and unspoiled beaches, ideal for bushwalking and swimming. To the west, start of Tasmanian Trail: 477-km Dover–Devonport trail for walkers, mountain-bikers and horseriders; booklet available. Several old graves on Faith Island. **Visitor information:** Forest and Heritage Centre, Church St, Geeveston; (03) 6297 1836. **See also:** The South-East p. 546.

Dunalley   Pop. 286

MAP REF. 579 M6, 583 N9

This small fishing village borders the isthmus connecting the Forestier Peninsula to the rest of Tasmania. The Denison Canal, spanned by a swing bridge, provides access to the east coast for small vessels. **In town:** Tasman Memorial, Imlay St, marks first landing by Europeans in 1642; actual landing occurred to the north-east, near Cape Paul Lamanon. **In the area:** The Denison Canal, built in the early 20th century, provides a short-cut for fishing vessels travelling between Hobart and the east coast of Tasmania; a swing bridge spans the canal. Extensive display of memorabilia at Copping Colonial and Convict Collection, 11 km N. **Visitor information:** Dunalley Hotel, 210 Arthur Hwy; (03) 6253 5101. **See also:** The South-East p. 546.

Eaglehawk Neck   Pop. 209

MAP REF. 579 N8, 583 O9

In convict days this isthmus separating the Tasman and Forestier peninsulas was guarded by a line of ferocious, tethered dogs. Soldiers and police also stood guard to ensure that no convicts escaped from the notorious convict settlement at Port Arthur. Few prisoners escaped by sea. The town today is a pleasant fishing destination. A charter tuna-fishing fleet operates from Pirates Bay. **In town:** Museum in restored historic Officers' Quarters, off Arthur Hwy, features story of Port Arthur escapee Martin Cash. Dogline marked by bronze dog sculpture; access by short walking track. **In the area:** Tessellated Pavement, 1 km N and Pirates Bay Lookout, 1.5 km N; halfway between is Eaglehawk Dive Centre, lessons and charters. Coastal rock formations in Tasman National Park, 4 km E, off Arthur Hwy: Tasmans Arch, Devils Kitchen and Tasman Blowhole. Tasmanian Devil Park and World Tiger Snake Centre, 12 km S. South along coast from Waterfall Bay to Munro Bight: water sports; picnics in Tasman National Park; coastal walking track from Waterfall Bay to Fortescue Bay. Good sailing in Eaglehawk Bay. Port Arthur Historic Site, 21 km SW. **Visitor information:** Officers' Mess, off Arthur Hwy; (03) 6250 3635. **See also:** The South-East p. 546; National Parks p. 572.

Evandale

Pop. 1033

MAP REF. 581 P12, 585 M9

This little township, 20 km from Launceston and 4 km from the airport, has been proclaimed an historic village. Founded 1829, some of its buildings date from 1809. Originally Morven, it was renamed in 1836 in honour of Tasmania's first Surveyor-General, G. W. Evans. There are unspoiled streetscapes and many buildings of historical and architectural significance. **In town:** Antique and craft outlets. Self-guide heritage walk from Tourism and History Centre, High St; brochure available. Also in High St: Solomon House (1836), now cafe and accommodation; St Andrew's Anglican (1871) and Uniting (1839) churches; Blenheim (1840s), now workshop (antiques and sales of stained glass). Clarendon Arms Hotel, Russell St, has mural depicting local history. Cornwall Cottage, Scone St, unusual bicycles for hire. Market, each Sun. a.m. at Falls Park, Russell St. Feb.: Village Fair and National Penny Farthing Championships. Nov.: Railex (model-train exhibition). **In the area:** Clarendon (1838), 8 km S near Nile, grand Georgian mansion in extensive formal gardens. Symmons Plains Raceway, 10 km S, venue for national and State

Touring Car Championships (usually in Mar.), track open for public use; (03) 6249 4683. At Deddington, 24 km SE, chapel (1840) on private land, designed by artist John Glover; Glover's grave beside chapel. Trout fishing in South Esk and North Esk rivers. **Visitor information:** Tourism and History Centre, 18 High St; (03) 6391 8128. **See also:** Midlands & the North p. 549.

Exeter

Pop. 382

MAP REF. 581 L7, 585 L7

Exeter, once a busy shipyard town 24 km NW of Launceston, now serves a large fruit-growing and wine-producing area. **In town:** In Main St: outdoor go-kart track, Tatana Karts; historic Exeter Bakery, wood-fired oven; Kerrisons Orchard, fruit sales. **In the area:** Four wineries with cellar-door sales in West Tamar area; Wine Centre in Tamar Court Brasserie, Main Rd, tastings and sales of local wines; Tasmanian Wine Route, brochure available. Mini golf at Crazy Putt Golf, 5 km E at Gravelly Beach. Walking track (5 km return) from Paper Beach, 9 km E, to Supply River. Near mouth of Supply River, 10 km N off Gravelly Beach Rd, ruins of first water-driven flour mill in Tasmania, built 1825. At Robigana, 10 km N, Artisan Gallery. Notley Fern Gorge at Notley Hills, 11 km SW, 10-ha rainforest reserve with picnic/barbecue areas. On Rosevears Dr., just south of Exeter: historic Rosevears Hotel, first licensed 1831; Waterbird Haven, wetlands habitat with treetop hide; Clever Hands Crafts; monument to John Batman's locally built ship *Rebecca*, in which he crossed Bass Strait to Yarra River; St Matthias Vineyard; Strathlynn Wine Centre. 5 km SE in State reserve, Brady's Lookout, a rocky outcrop used by notorious bushranger Matthew Brady. Grindelwald Swiss Village, 10 km SE, a resort in Swiss-architectural style. **Visitor information:** Tamar Visitor Centre, Main Rd; (03) 6394 4454, freecall 1800 637 898. **See also:** Midlands & the North p. 549.

Fingal

Pop. 379

MAP REF. 583 P1, 585 P10

In the Esk Valley, 21 km inland from St Marys on the South Esk River, Fingal is the headquarters of the State's coal industry. The first payable gold in Tasmania was found in 1852 at The Nook, near Fingal. **In town:** Historic buildings: St Joseph's Church, Grey St; Masonic Lodge, Brown St. In Talbot St: St Peter's Church;

Holder Bros. General Store (1859); Fingal Hotel (licensed 1844); Fingal History Room, by appt only. On eastern outskirts, view coal-washing process at Cornwell Coal Company washery. Mar.: Fingal Valley Festival (incorporating World Coal Shovelling Championships and Roof Bolting Championships). **In the area:** In Evercreech Forest Reserve, 30 km N on road to Mathinna, large white gums, incl. 89-m specimen; also picnic/barbecue area and walking tracks. Mathinna Falls, 36 km N near Mathinna; picnic/barbecue area nearby. At Avoca, 27 km SW, historic buildings; town in foothills of Ben Lomond Range. **Visitor information:** Old Tasmanian Hotel Community Centre, Main Rd; (03) 6374 2344. **See also:** The East Coast p. 548.

Geeveston

Pop. 778

MAP REF. 578 D10, 583 J10

This timber town is the gateway to Tasmania's south-west World Heritage Area. **In town:** In Church St: Forest and Heritage Centre, complex featuring interpretive 'forest room' and Hartz Gallery (quality woodcrafts and exhibitions); The Bears Went Over the Mountain, shop selling traditional teddy bears. **In the area:** Apple blossom late Sept.–early Oct. Scenic drives and walks through Arve Valley, west of town, incl. Arve Road Forest Dr.: Arve River Picnic Area (10 km W); Big Tree Lookout (15 km W), world's tallest flowering species, *Eucalyptus regnans*, Tasmanian Swamp Gum; Keoghs Creek Walk (15 km W); West Creek Lookout (20 km W) over fern gully, leatherwood and swamp gums; Tahune Forest Reserve (27 km W), camping, fishing, rafting, short walks among Huon pines, Tahune Forest AirWalk on riverbank, Visitor Centre. Hartz Mountains National Park, 23 km SW off Arve Rd: birdwatching; waratah and other wildflowers spring and summer; short walks to waterfalls, glacial tarns, Waratah Lookout; self-guide brochure available. At Port Huon, 4 km NE, river cruises visit salmon farms. **Visitor information:** Forest and Heritage Centre, Church St; (03) 6297 1836. **See also:** The South-East p. 546.

George Town

Pop. 4522

MAP REF. 581 K4, 585 K6

Situated at the mouth of the Tamar River, George Town (Australia's third settled

Entally House, near Hadspen

town, after Sydney and Hobart) was settled by Europeans in 1811 and named for King George III. Today it is a commercial centre, mainly for the Comalco plant at Bell Bay and other industrial developments, and the terminal for the vehicular ferry *Devil Cat* (George Town to Melbourne Dec.–Apr.), bookings essential; 13 2010. **In town:** Self-guide Discovery Trail of region, brochure available. Monument on Esplanade commemorates landing in 1804 when HMS *Buffalo* ran aground during a storm. The Grove (c. 1838), cnr Elizabeth and Cimitiere sts, Devonshire teas and lunches. Market at Community Hall, Macquarie St, 2nd Sat. each month. **In the area:** At Bell Bay, 6 km S: Comalco and BHP Temco plants; tours. At Hillwood, 24 km SE, apple orchards and Hillwood Strawberry Farm, Fruit Wine and Cheese Centre. Lookout from Mt George, 1 km E. Lefroy, 10 km E, former goldmining settlement with ruins, old diggings, cemetery. Wineries in Pipers Brook region to the east; tastings, sales; Tasmanian Wine Route, brochure available. Historic maritime village Low Head, 5 km N, has surf and river beaches; Maritime Museum in Australia's oldest continuously used pilot station, opened 1803; nearby, lighthouse and little (fairy) penguin colony, guided tours at dusk. Cruises to fur seal colony at mouth of Tamar River and at Tenth Island to the north-east. **Visitor information:** cnr Victoria St & Main Rd; (03) 6382 1700. **See also:** Midlands & the North p. 549; Wildlife-Watching p. 570.

Gladstone
Pop. 200

MAP REF. 585 P6

Gladstone is a small service centre for surrounding dairy, sheep and cattle farms. The district was once a thriving tin

and goldmining area with a colourful history. Now many once substantial townships nearby are ghost towns or nearly so. **In town:** Chinese graves at Gladstone Cemetery, eastern outskirts of town. **In the area:** Geological formations south-west in area between Gladstone and South Mount Cameron. At South Mount Cameron, 8 km S, Blue Lake, a disused tin mine filled with brilliant blue water coloured by pyrites. At Mt William National Park, 25 km E: extensive views from Mt William; prolific flora and fauna, excellent beaches, historic lighthouse at Eddystone Point (35 km E). **Visitor information:** Gladstone Hotel, Chaffey St; (03) 6357 2143. **See also:** Midlands & the North p. 549.

Hadspen
Pop. 1730

MAP REF. 581 N11, 585 L9

The township of Hadspen, settled by Europeans in the early 1820s, has many historic buildings, some offering accommodation and/or meals. **In town:** Row of Georgian buildings, Main Rd: Red Feather Inn (c. 1844); old coaching station; Hadspen Gaol (c. 1840); Church of the Good Shepherd – construction began 1858, funded by Thomas Reibey, who withdrew support after a dispute with the bishop; completed 1961, almost 50 years after Reibey's death. **In the area:** Entally House (1819), 1 km W on banks of South Esk River, one of Tasmania's most famous historic homes; Regency furniture and fine silverware. At Carrick, 10 km SW: Georgian and Victorian buildings; Agfest held May. **Visitor information:** Gateway Tasmanian Travel Centre, cnr St John and Paterson sts, Launceston; (03) 6336 3133. Web site www.gatewaytas.com.au **See also:** Midlands & the North p. 549.

Hamilton
Pop. 150

MAP REF. 578 D1, 583 J6

A National Trust-classified historic town in a rural setting, Hamilton has retained many of its colonial buildings. **In town:** Old School House (1858), Lyell Hwy; B&B accommodation and antique shop in grounds. Glen Clyde House (c. 1840), Grace St, tearooms and craft gallery with works of over 100 craftspeople. Jackson's Emporium (1856), local products, wines. **In the area:** Guided tours of farming and industry. Meadowbank Lake, 10 km NW, a popular venue for picnics, boating, water-skiing and trout fishing. **Visitor information:** Council Offices, Tarleton St; (03) 6286 3202. **See also:** The South-East p. 546.

Hastings
Pop. 20

MAP REF. 578 D13, 583 J12

This tiny town, about 100 km SW of Hobart on the Huon Hwy, has dolomite caves, local gemstones and a nearby scenic railway. **In the area:** Hastings Forest Tour, self-drive, cassette guide available, begins off Hastings Rd and leads north-west to Esperance River. Hastings Caves, 13 km NW: tours of illuminated Newdegate Cave; swimming in thermal pool; streamside walks; picnic/barbecue facilities. Lune River, 3 km S: Lunaris, gemstone display and shop; glow-worm cave adventure tours (bookings essential, (03) 6298 3163). 2 km further S, Ida Bay Scenic Railway, originally built to carry dolomite, now carries passengers 7 km to Deep Hole Bay. Cockle Creek, 41 km S, in Southwest National Park at the start of 10-day South Coast walking track, offers fishing, boating, bushwalking. Southport, 6 km SE, a fishing port in sealing and whaling days, offers good fishing, swimming, surfing, bushwalking. **Visitor information:** Forest and Heritage Centre, Church St, Geeveston; (03) 6297 1836. **See also:** The South-East p. 546.

Huonville
Pop. 1718

MAP REF. 578 F8, 583 K9

Huonville is the centre of the apple-producing district and is the largest town in the region. As well as apples, available year-round, the Huon Valley grows cherries, blueberries, strawberries, and raspberries, which in season can be bought from roadside stalls and at pick-your-own farms. The prized Huon pine was discovered in this district.

In town: Fishing for trout and salmon in Huon River and tributaries; fish punt on foreshore. Horseback Wilderness Tours, Sale St. Pedal boat and aqua-bike hire, Esplanade. Nov.: Huon Agricultural Show (biggest one-day agricultural show in State). **In the area:** Huon River jet boat rides over rapids to Glen Huon. Scenic drives, brochures available. Doran's Jam Factory and the Apple and Heritage Museum at Grove, 6 km NE. Antique Motor Museum near Ranelagh, 5 km NW. Snowy Range Trout Fishery, Little Denison River, 25 km NW. Appleheads and Model Village at Glen Huon, 8 km W, features apples carved to resemble heads. At wooden-boatbuilding town of Franklin, 8 km SW: Franklin Tea Gardens beside river has cottage gardens, crafts and curios; Franklin Lodge, one of the State's most established colonial accommodation places. River cruises to salmon farms at Plenty depart Port Huon, 18 km SW. **Visitor information:** Huon River Jet Boats, Esplanade; (03) 6264 1838. **See also:** The South-East p. 546.

Kettering   Pop. 314

MAP REF. 578 H9, 583 L10

This town on the Channel Hwy south of Hobart serves a large fruit-growing district. **In town:** Bruny Island ferry: 10 daily trips from Ferry Rd terminal; extra services during holidays. Oyster Cove Inn and marina, Ferry Rd. Boats for hire; skippered cruises and fishing charters available. Roaring 40s Ocean Kayaking, Ferry Rd, for sea-kayak lessons, rentals and tours. **In the area:** Bruny Island. Channel Historical and Folk Museum, 5 km N, open Nov.–Apr. Nearby, Coningham, 6 km N, for good swimming and boating. At Snug, 8 km N: Mother's Favourites, for seafood; holiday cottages; pleasant walks in Snug Falls Track area. Woodbridge Hill Handweaving Studio, 4 km S on Woodbridge Hill Rd. Monument to French explorer Admiral Bruni D'Entrecasteaux, 21 km S at Gordon. **Visitor information:** Bruny D'Entrecasteaux Visitor Centre, Ferry Rd; (03) 6267 4494. **See also:** The South-East p. 546.

Kingston   Pop. 5588

MAP REF. 578 H7, 583 L9

Kingston, 12 km S of Hobart, is the administrative centre for the D'Entrecasteaux Channel and Bruny Island districts.

In town: Foyer display in Federal Government's Antarctic research headquarters, southern outskirts on Channel Hwy; open Mon.–Fri. Market every Sun., Coles carpark. Oct.: Olie Bollen (Dutch community) Festival. **In the area:** Boronia Hill Flora Trail (2 km) follows ridgeline between Kingston and Blackmans Bay through remnant bush. Scenic drives south through Blackmans Bay, Tinderbox and Howden; magnificent views of Droughty Point, South Arm Peninsula, Storm Bay and Bruny Island from Piersons Point. At Margate, 3 km S, 1950s passenger train (non-operational); tearooms in buffet car; adjacent antique sales and Sun. market. Small blowhole at Blackmans Bay, 7 km S at reserve on Blowhole Rd; spectacular in stormy weather. At Tinderbox, 11 km S, underwater snorkel trail in Tinderbox Marine Reserve. Shot Tower, 7 km NE near Taroona; wonderful views of Derwent estuary from top. **Visitor information:** Tasmanian Travel and Information Centre, 20 Davey St, Hobart; (03) 6230 8233. **See also:** The South-East p. 546.

Latrobe   Pop. 2765

MAP REF. 580 E6, 584 I7

This historic township (gazetted 1851), situated on the Mersey River 9 km SE of Devonport, was once a busy shipyard town. **In town:** Buildings and shopfronts dating from 1840s, some National Trust-classified; self-guide walk, leaflet available. Court House Museum, Gilbert St, for local history, incl. prints and artifacts; open Fri. and Sun. Bells Parade Reserve, off Gilbert St along riverbank, has sculpture and picnic areas. Also on Bells Pde: Australian Axeman's Hall of Fame, commemorating the history of woodchopping and bush skills; Sherwood Hall, an historic timber structure. Sheean Memorial Walk, Gilbert St, 3-km-return walk commemorates local soldiers and WW II hero. Mount Roland Cheese, Speedway Dr. (weekdays). Markets, every Sun. at Gilbert and James sts. Jan.: Henley-on-the-Mersey Australia Day Regatta. Feb.: Grande Fiesta Ng Filipino. Dec.: Wheel & Gift (athletics, cycling and woodchopping carnival). **In the area:** Myrtle Hole, 3 km S, for picnics and water sports. Henry Somerset Orchard Reserve, 7 km S, has platypus, native orchids and other rare flora. **Visitor information:** Shop 1, 70 Gilbert St; (03) 6426 2693. **See also:** The North-West p. 550.

Launceston   Pop. 67 701

MAP REF. 581 O10, 585 L8

Although Tasmania's second-largest city and a busy tourist centre, Launceston retains a relaxed atmosphere. Nestled in hilly country where the Tamar, North Esk and South Esk rivers meet, Launceston is also at the junction of three main highways and has direct air links with Melbourne and Hobart. It is sometimes referred to as the Garden City because of its parks and gardens. **In town:** Yorktown Square, The Avenue, Quadrant Mall, Civic Square, and Princes Square with its magnificent baroque-style fountain and fine surrounding buildings. Main shopping area is around the Mall. Old Umbrella Shop, George St, unique 1860s shop preserved by National Trust. Penny Royal World, Paterson St, collection of buildings originally near Cressy, and moved stone by stone to Launceston; incl. tavern, museum, working watermill, corn mill, windmill, Mole Hill Fantasy (mole diorama), accommodation, restaurants; linked by restored tramway to Penny Royal Gunpowder Mill at old Cataract quarry site; boat trips on artificial lake, paddlesteamer cruise on *Lady Stelfox* along the Tamar River and nearby Cataract Gorge. This spectacular gorge is one of Launceston's outstanding natural attractions. Historic Kings Bridge (1867) spans the Tamar River at the gorge entrance. Cataract Cliff Grounds Reserve, on north side of gorge, a formal park with lawns, European trees, peacocks and restaurant. Area linked to swimming pool and kiosk on south side by chairlift and suspension bridge. Walks on both sides of gorge. Ritchies Mill Arts Centre, Paterson St; art and craft. National Automobile Museum, Cimitiere St. Parks incl. 5-ha City Park with Monkey Island and conservatory (nearby Design Centre of Tasmania displays contemporary art and craft), end of Cameron St; Royal Park, formal civic park on South Esk River; Zig Zag Reserve, leading to Cataract Gorge area. At Queen Victoria Museum and Art Gallery, in Royal Park off Wellington St, displays of: Aboriginal and convict relics; Tasmania's mineral wealth; flora and fauna; early china and glassware; colonial and modern art. At Queen Victoria Museum and Art Gallery–Inveresk, on the northern outskirts of town, Invermay Rd, displays of: colonial and contemporary art; Aboriginal shell necklaces; and Asian and Pacific collections. Boags Brewery, William St, guided or self-guide tours, brochures available. Feb.: Country Music Festival; Launceston Cup

Wildflowers on the Central Plateau near Miena

(State's biggest race day); Festivale (food and wine). Mar.: A Night in the Gorge. Sept.: Garden Festival. Oct.: Royal National Show; Tasmanian Poetry Festival. Nov.: Tamar River Festival. **In the area:** Trevallyn Dam, 6 km W, good picnic spot. Nearby, Australia's only cable hang-gliding simulator. Launceston Lakes Trout Fishery, 17 km W, has fly-fishing lessons. Punchbowl Reserve and Rhododendron Gardens, 5 km SW, has native and European fauna in natural surroundings. Alpine Village in Ben Lomond National Park, 60 km SE; open during ski season; good views from Legges Tor; easy bushwalking; spring and summer wildflowers. Launceston Federal Country Club Casino, 7 km SW. Waverley Woollen Mills, 5 km E, offers tours that incl. historic collection of plant machinery used to create the wool industry for which Launceston earned its national reputation. St Matthias' Church, Windermere, 15 km N. Tasmanian Wine Route, Pipers Brook andTamar Valley regions, north of the city; brochure available. Three National Trust historic houses: Entally House, 18 km SW at Hadspen; Franklin House, 6 km S; Clarendon 28 km SE, near Nile. Regular flights to Flinders Island, 175 km NW in Bass Strait. **Visitor information:** Gateway Tasmania Travel Centre, cnr St John and Paterson sts; (03) 6336 3133, freecall 1800 651 827. **See also:** Midlands & the North p. 549.

Lilydale   Pop. 343

MAP REF. 581 P6, 585 M7

Situated at the foot of Mt Arthur, 27 km from Launceston, the town of Lilydale has many bush tracks and picnic spots. **In the area:** Tasmanian Wine Route (brochure available): incl. Clover Hill Vineyards, 12 km N; Brook Eden Vineyard, 15 km N; Providence Vineyards, 4 km W. Lilydale Falls Reserve, 3 km N, has two oak trees grown from Windsor Great Park acorns, planted on coronation day of British King George IV in 1937. At Lalla, 4 km W: Walker Rhododendron Reserve; Appleshed Tea House for local art and craft. Ash tree plantation at Hollybank Forest Reserve, Underwood, 5 km S, picnic/barbecue areas. Scenic walks to top of Mt Arthur (1187 m), 20 km SE. **Visitor information:** Gateway Tasmania Travel Centre, cnr St John and Paterson sts, Launceston; (03) 6336 3133, freecall 1800 651 827. **See also:** Midlands & the North p. 549.

Longford   Pop. 2829

MAP REF. 581 N13, 585 L9

Longford, 22 km S of Launceston, was established 1813 when former settlers of Norfolk Island were given land grants in the area. Its previous names were Norfolk Plains and Latour. Now classified as an historic town, it serves a rich agricultural district. Australian artist Tom Roberts spent his last few years here and was buried in the area. **In town:** Historic buildings, incl. some convict-built and many now converted to self-contained colonial cottage and B&B accommodation. In Wellington St: Christ Church (1839), has outstanding stained-glass window and pioneer gravestones; 'Car in window' and Grand Prix memorabilia at Country Club Hotel. Tom Roberts Gallery in Marlborough St, has old prints, books and information. Walking track along South Esk River; Heritage and Headstones Tour. The Village Green, cnr Wellington and Archer sts, originally the town market, now a picnic/barbecue spot. Jan.: Longford Cup. Mar.: Blessing of the Harvest Festival; Brickendon and Woolmers Hunt. **In the area:** Brickendon, 2 km S, a homestead built by William Archer (1824), still owned by descendants; now a working farm and historic farm village. Woolmers Estate (c. 1817), 5 km S, 6-generation Archer family 'museum': colonial cottages; tea rooms; guided tours of main house and gardens. Cressy, 10 km S, renowned for its fly-fishing at Brumbys Creek, especially in Nov. when mayflies hatch. At Perth, 5 km NE, historic buildings: Eskleigh, Jolly Farmer Inn, Old Crown Inn and Leather Bottell Inn. Perth Market, every Sun. a.m., in Old School. Bowthorpe Farm and Gardens, 11 km N, pastoral estate set on South Esk River: Georgian farmhouse; cottage garden; tearooms. **Visitor information:** Brickendon Historic Farming Village, Woolmers La; (03) 6391 1251. Web site www.longford. tco.asn.au **See also:** Midlands & the North p. 549.

Miena   Pop. 46

MAP REF. 583 J2, 585 J12

This small settlement, on the shores of Great Lake in Tasmania's Central Plateau, has been popular with anglers since brown trout were released into the lake in 1870. The surrounding region, also known as the Lake Country, is an important supplier of hydro-electric power. Be prepared when travelling in this relatively remote region, as snow and freezing weather are a possibility, even in summer; road closures may occur. **In the area:** Excellent trout fishing at many lakes, incl. Great Lake (one of Australia's largest freshwater lakes), Little Pine Lagoon (9 km SW) and Arthurs Lake (23 km E). At Liawenee, 10 km N, Inland Fisheries Commission hosts annual stripping of ova from spawning trout in May. West of Liawenee, hundreds of isolated lakes and tarns for fly-fishing (4WD recommended for several lakes; some accessible only to experienced bushwalkers). Walls of Jerusalem National Park, access via Liawenee or Bass Highway in the north, for experienced bushwalkers only (no daytrippers). At Steppes, 27 km SE: old Steppes homestead, by appt; Circle of Life bronze sculptures by Steven Walker, each representing an aspect of region's history and character; rodeo each May. At Waddamana: 33 km S, Power Museum incl. history of hydro-electricity in Tasmania and display of early electrical appliances. Boat service from Cynthia Bay on Lake St Clair, 63 km W, provides access to north of lake and to renowned 85-km Overland Track, which passes through the spectacular Cradle Mountain–Lake St Clair National Park. **Visitor information:** Great Lake Hotel, Great Lake Hwy; (03) 6259 8163. **See also:** Midlands & the North p. 549; National Parks p. 572.

Mole Creek Pop. 256

MAP REF. 580 E12, 584 I9

This town, 74 km S of Devonport, and nestled at the foot of the Great Western Tiers, serves an important farming and forestry district. It was named after the creek which 'burrows' underground. The unique honey from the leatherwood tree, which grows only in the west-coast rainforests of Tasmania, is processed here. Each summer, apiarists transport hives to the nearby leatherwood forests. **In town:** Stephen's Honey Factory, Pioneer Dr., for extraction and processing of honey; open Mon.–Fri. **In the area:** Guided tours of fine limestone caves in Mole Creek Karst National Park: Marakoopa Cave, 8 km W, has glow-worm display; smaller but still spectacular King Solomons Cave 16 km W. Wild Cave Tours, full- or half-day tours of undeveloped caves. Walls of Jerusalem National Park, 45 km SW, treks for experienced bushwalkers only (no daytrippers). Devils Gullet, 40 km SE, a natural lookout above Fisher River Valley, in World Heritage Area; reached by 30-min-return walking track. Trowunna Wildlife Park, 4 km E. Spectacular Alum Cliffs Gorge, 3 km NE, 30 min return. **Visitor information:** Mole Creek Guest House, 100 Pioneer Dr.; (03) 6363 1399. Web site www.deloraine.tasonline.org/tourism/molecrk.htm **See also:** Midlands & the North p. 549.

New Norfolk Pop. 5286

MAP REF. 578 F4, 583 K8

Colonial buildings among English trees and oast houses in hop fields give this National Trust-classified historic town a look similar to that of Kent in England. Located on the River Derwent, 33 km NW of Hobart, the town was called New Norfolk because European settlers from the abandoned Norfolk Island settlement were granted land here. Although the district produces most of the hops used by Australian breweries, the chief industry today is paper manufacture. **In town:** River walk from Esplanade to Tynwald Park Wetlands Conservation Area. At Historical Centre in Council Chambers, Circle St: genealogical and other records;

also self-guide historic walk leaflets. Scenic lookouts: Peppermint Hill, off Blair St; Pulpit Rock and Four Winds Display Gardens, off Rocks Rd. Old Colony Inn (1835), Montague St, now museum with large antique dolls' house and original kitchen. On Lyell Hwy: Oast House, Tynwald Park, with hop museum, Hop House Cafe, and art gallery; Bush Inn Hotel (1815), has one of the oldest licences in Commonwealth. Jet boat rides on Derwent River rapids leave from near Bush Inn Hotel. St Matthew's Church (1823), Bathurst St, reputedly oldest church in Tasmania; craft centre in adjoining close. Sat. market, Stephen St. Mar.: Hop Harvest Festival. Oct.: Spring in the Valley (incl. open gardens). **In the area:** Tours of Australian Newsprint Mill, 5 km E at Boyer; 24-hrs notice required. Salmon Ponds, 11 km NW at Plenty: first brown and rainbow trout in Southern Hemisphere bred here 1864; restaurant; Museum of Trout Fishing. Meadowbank Vineyard, 20 km NW. Mt Field National Park, 40 km NW: impressive Russell Falls; Lady Barron Falls; various walks. Trout fishing in Lake Pedder, 96 km W. Tour of Gordon Power Station from Gordon Dam, 156 km W, bookings essential; (03) 6280 1166. Along Gordon River Rd: lookouts to lakes Gordon and Pedder; Creepy Crawly Nature Trail into Southwest National Park. **Visitor information:** Derwent Valley Council, Circle St; (03) 6261 0700 (Mon.–Fri.). **See also:** The South-East p. 546; National Parks p. 572.

Oatlands Pop. 539

MAP REF. 583 M5

This National Trust-classified historic town on the shores of Lake Dulverton, 84 km N of Hobart, attracts both anglers and lovers of history. It was designated a garrison town by Governor Macquarie in 1821 and surveyed in 1832. Many of the unique sandstone buildings were constructed in the 1830s and most residents live in historic houses. **In town:** Convict-built courthouse (1829), Campbell St. St Peter's Church (c. 1838), William St, has wide range of tapestries; contact information centre. Callington Flour Mill (1836), Mill La. Lake Dulverton Wildlife Sanctuary, Esplanade. Historic self-guide walks around town and on lake foreshore; brochures available. Fielding's Ghost Tours. **In the area:** Convict-built mud walls, 13 km S on Jericho Rd. Trout fishing in Lake Sorell, 29 km NW, and adjoining

Lake Crescent. Guided garden tours in spring, brochures available, bookings essential; (03) 6230 8233. **Visitor information:** Central Tasmanian Tourism Centre, 85 High St; (03) 6254 1212. **See also:** Midlands & the North p. 549.

Penguin Pop. 3030

MAP REF. 580 A4, 584 H6

The Dial Range rises over this quiet town, named after the nearby colonies of little (fairy) penguins. **In town:** In Main St: St Stephen's Church and Uniting Church, both National Trust-classified; Percy Studio, glass engravers and artists; much-photographed Big Penguin. Hiscutt Park, off Crescent St, has Dutch windmill and tulips in season. Miniature Railway on foreshore, 2nd and 4th Sun. each month. Penguin colony on eastern outskirts, tours by appt (Sept.–Apr.). Penguin Roadside Gardens, on Old Coast Rd to Ulverstone, tended by community volunteers. Old School Market, King Edward St, 2nd and 4th Sun. each month. Mar.: Splash of Colour Festival. **In the area** Mt Montgomery, 5 km S, magnificent view from summit. Mason's Fuchsia Fantasy, 20 km E on Lillico Rd, 1200 varieties; open Mon.–Fri. p.m. and Sat. Ferndene Gorge Nature Reserve, 6 km S: scenic picnic spot; good walking tracks. Pioneer Park, 10 km SW at Riana: gardens; walks; picnic facilities. Pindari Holiday Farm, 15 km SW: wildlife park; restaurant; accommodation; check opening times; (03) 6437 6171. Scenic drive south-east to Ulverstone via Coast Road. **Visitor information:** Main St; (03) 6437 1421. **See also:** The North-West p. 550.

Pontville Pop. 1424

MAP REF. 578 H3, 583 L7

Much of the freestone used in Tasmania's old buildings was quarried near this National Trust-classified historic town. On the Midland Hwy, 27 km N of Hobart, Pontville was founded in 1830 and many early buildings remain. **In town:** Historic buildings on or adjacent to Midland Hwy incl.: St Mark's Church (1841); The Sheiling (built 1819, restored 1953), behind church; old post office; Crown Inn; and 'The Row', thought to have been built in 1824 as soldiers' quarters, now restored. **In the area:** Towns nearby with historic buildings: Bagdad, 8 km N; Kempton, 11 km further N; Broadmarsh, 10 km W; Tea Tree, 7 km E. Brighton, 3 km S, an important military post;

Agricultural Show held Nov. Bonorong Park Wildlife Centre, 5 km S. **Visitor information:** Brighton Council Offices, Tivoli Rd, Gagebrook; (03) 6268 7000. **See also:** The South-East p. 546.

Port Arthur Pop. 190

MAP REF. 579 N10, 583 N10

This historic settlement on the scenic Tasman Peninsula was one of Australia's most infamous penal settlements from the 1830s to the 1870s. Visitors still sense the incredible hardship endured by the convict population. **In town:** Port Arthur Historic Site: stabilised and restored ruins of the convict settlement, period houses, museum; self-guide and guided walks, incl. nightly ghost tours; scenic flights; Convict Trail drive, brochure available. Huon pine cross and plaque on the waterfront commemorate victims of tragic massacre in 1996. The Visitor Centre: interpretation gallery, giftshop, cafe, restaurant, ghost tour bookings. Dec.: Boxing Day Wood-chop. **In the area:** Daily cruises on harbour and (summer) to Isle of the Dead (1949 convict, military and civil graves). Historic and nature walk to nearby Stewarts Bay, brochure available. Steam-train rides at Bush Mill Steam Railway and Settlement, 1km N. Coal Mines Historic Site, 30 km NW, Tasmania's first operational mine. Palmers Lookout, 3 km S, views of harbour and coastline. Remarkable Cave, 6 km S on coast in Tasman National Park. Sea-kayaking tours. **Visitor information:** The Visitor Centre, Port Arthur Historic Site, Arthur Hwy; (03) 6250 2539, freecall 1800 659 101. **See also:** The South-East p. 546; National Parks p. 572.

Port Sorell Pop. 1818

MAP REF. 580 G5, 585 J6

Sheltered by hills, this holiday town on the Rubicon River estuary, 18 km E of Devonport, enjoys a mild climate. Named after Governor Sorell and established 1822, it is the oldest township on the north-west coast. Many of its oldest buildings were destroyed by bushfires early this century. **In town:** River and sea-fishing, swimming, boating and bushwalking. Views from Watch House Hill, off Meredith St, once site of old gaol, now a bowling green. Narawntapu National Park across estuary, with numerous isolated beaches, sand dunes and grasslands covered in wildflowers.

Jan.–Feb.: Latrobe–Port Sorell Summer Festival. **In the area:** Walking track from Port Sorell (beach end of Rice St) to Hawley Beach (6 km return); excellent views of Narawntapu National Park and coastline. At Hawley Beach: safe swimming, good fishing; historic Hawley House (1878) offers meals and accommodation. **Visitor information:** Shop 1, 70 Gilbert St, Latrobe; (03) 6426 2693. **See also:** The North-West p. 550; National Parks p. 572.

Queenstown Pop. 2631

MAP REF. 582 E3, 584 E12

The discovery of gold and mineral resources in the Mt Lyell field in the 1880s led to the rapid emergence of Queenstown, a town carved out of the mountains that tower starkly around it. Mining was continuous in Queenstown 1893–1994, and the field produced over 670 000 tonnes of copper, 510 000 kg of silver and 20 000 kg of gold. Copper Mines of Tasmania resumed mining for copper, silver and gold at the end of 1995; tours of the mine are available. The town has modern facilities, but its wide streets, remaining historic buildings and unique setting give it an old-mining-town flavour. In certain lights, multi-coloured boulders on the bare hillsides surrounding the town reflect the sun's rays and turn to amazing shades of pink and gold. **In town:** Spion Kop Lookout, off Bowes St in town centre. Famed gravel football oval, Bachelor St. Penghana, former mine manager's residence (c. 1898), off Preston St. Guided tours of Mt Lyell Mine depart from information centre; surface tours by minibus (1 hr 15 min) and underground mine tours (3 hrs 30 min). Galley Museum, cnr Sticht and Driffield sts, displays history of west coast, photographs and memorabilia. Chairlift, from Penghana Rd to old silica and limestone quarries; magnificent views, particularly at sunset. The Wilderness Railway, restored 1896 rack-and-pinion railway, train departs from town, travels 35-km river and forest track to Strahan. Oct.: Robert Sticht Festival (celebration of history of Queenstown, triathlon, slag-shovelling, home-brew beer-tastings). **In the area:** Spectacular views from Lyell Hwy as it climbs steeply out of town. Original Iron Blow goldmine (1883), off Lyell Hwy at Gormanston, 6 km E. Ghost town of Linda, 9 km E. Mt Jukes Rd lookout, 7 km S; road leads past old mining

settlement of Lynchford, and Crotty Dam. Lake Burbury, offers excellent brown and rainbow trout fishing. Lake Margaret, 12 km N. Lyell Tours, offers 4WD day or half-day tours south to Bird River rainforest area and Mt McCall. **Visitor information:** Mt Lyell Mine Tour Office, 1 Driffield St; (03) 6471 2388 or Strahan Visitors Centre; (03) 6471 7622. **See also:** South-West Wilderness p. 551.

Richmond Pop. 768

MAP REF. 579 J4, 583 M7

Richmond, 26 km from Hobart, is one of the most important historic towns in Tasmania. The much-photographed Richmond Bridge is the oldest surviving freestone bridge in Australia (1823–25). Many town buildings were constructed in the 1830s or earlier. The bridge and other structures were built by convicts under appalling conditions. Legend has it that the ghost of an over-seer murdered by convicts still haunts the bridge. **In town:** Self-guide leaflet of town and area available. Old Richmond Gaol (1825), Bathurst St, one of Australia's best-preserved convict prisons; guided tours. St John's (1837), St John's Circle, oldest Catholic church in Australia still in use. St Luke's Church (1834–36), Torrens St, has fine timber ceiling. General store and former post office (1832), Bridge St, oldest postal building in Australia. Also in Bridge St: galleries featuring local art and craft, incl. Saddler's Court (c. 1848) and Peppercorn Gallery (c. 1850); restored Bridge Inn, one of town's oldest buildings, housing complex of shops incl. courtyard Bakery Cafe; Richmond Arms Hotel (1888); Old Hobart Town, a model of Hobart in early 1800s; Toy Museum; The Maze; Village Store (1836), one of oldest general stores still operating in Tasmania. Prospect House (1830s), Georgian mansion, off Hobart Rd, supposedly haunted by ghost of Mrs Buscombe; offers meals and colonial accommodation. Feb.: Country Music Festival. Oct.: Village Fair. **In the area:** Scenic drive north through Campania (8 km) and Colebrook (19 km). Stoney Vineyard, 6 km N, on Colebrook Rd. Crosswinds Vineyard, 10 km NW. Southern Tasmanian Wine Route, brochure available. **Visitor information:** Old Hobart Town, 21a Bridge St; (03) 6260 2502. Web site www.richmondvillage.com.au **See also:** The South-East p. 546.

Ross
Pop. 275

MAP REF. 583 M3, 585 N12

One of the oldest and most beautiful bridges in Australia spans the Macquarie River at this National Trust-classified historic township. The bridge, completed 1836, was designed by colonial architect John Lee Archer and built by convicts. The convict stonemason Daniel Herbert received a free pardon in recognition of his 186 fine bridge carvings. Herbert's grave is in the old burial ground in Park St. Ross was established in 1812 as a military post for the protection of travellers who stopped there to change coaches. Today it is still an important stopping-place on the Midland Hwy between Launceston and Hobart and has a range of accommodation incl. self-contained colonial cottages. The district is known for its superfine wool. **In town:** Self-guide and guided walks; brochures available. Off Bond St: Female Factory Historic Site, the most archaelogically intact female convict site in Australia; Overseer's Cottage has historical display and model of Female Factory, a prison workhouse 1847–54. In Church St: Heritage and Wool Museum at information centre, has fascinating displays highlighting the area's links with wool industry; avenue of English elms complements historic sandstone buildings, incl. Scotch Thistle Inn and Coach House, former coaching stop; old Ross General Store and Tea Room, now selling Tasmanian crafts and Devonshire teas; Uniting Church (1885), prominent on hill overlooking town; Orderly Rooms, original headquarters of 50th Ordinance Corps in early 1830s, moved two doors south in 1836 to present Memorial Library, Billiard and Recreation Room. In Bridge St, old barracks building, restored by local National Trust; street leads to Ross Bridge (floodlit at night). The four corners of the intersection of Church and Bridge sts at the centre of town are said to represent temptation (hotel), recreation (Town Hall), salvation (church) and damnation (gaol, now a residence). Apr.: Festival of the Arts. **In the area:** World-class fly-fishing for brown trout in Macquarie River. Some of the State's best trout-fishing lakes – Sorell, Crescent, Tooms and Leake – are within an hour's drive of town. **Visitor information:** Tasmanian Wool Centre, Church St; (03) 6381 5466. Web site www.taswoolcentre.com.au **See also:** Midlands & the North p. 549.

St Helens
Pop. 1280

MAP REF. 585 Q8

This popular resort on the shores of Georges Bay is renowned for its crayfish and scalefish. Three fish-processing plants handle the catch of the fishing fleet based in its harbour. **In town:** St Helens History Room, Cecilia St: mining history; information on 4WD tours and rainforest walks. Bay beaches ideal for swimming, coastal beaches for surfing. Charter boats for deep-sea fishing and dinghy hire for bay-fishing, Tasman Hwy. Excellent fishing for bream and trout on Scamander River. Many local restaurants specialise in fish dishes. Mar.: Tasmanian Game-Fishing Classic. June: Suncoast Jazz Festival. **In the area:** Bushwalks and tours (20 min to 5 hrs) to view birdlife and wildflowers. Binalong Bay, 11 km NE, has good surf- and rock-fishing. Beaumaris, 12 km S, good beaches and lagoons. Scamander, holiday town 17 km S: sea- and river-fishing; good swimming; walks and drives in forest plantations south of town. 10 km W of Scamander, Trout Creek Reserve has fishing landing stage and picnic/barbecue facilities. At Pyengana, 28 km W: St Columba Falls; Pyengana Dairy Company; Healey's Cheese Factory; the 'Pub in the Paddock', hotel in middle of empty paddock. Bay of Fires Conservation Area, 9 km N: Aboriginal middens; lagoons; good beach-fishing; camping. Mt William National Park, 35 km N: native fauna; rare flora; sheltered bays and beaches. **Visitor information:** St Helens History Room, 61 Cecilia St; (03) 6376 1744. **See also:** The East Coast p. 548.

St Marys
Pop. 588

MAP REF. 585 Q10

The chief town of the Break O'Day Plains, St Marys is situated in the Eastern highlands at the head of the Fingal Valley. Access is through picturesque passes or the valley. **In town:** Rivulet Park: platypus, Tasmanian native hens and picnic/barbecue facilities. Public golf course. **In the area:** Convict-built St Marys Pass (1842–45), 1.5 km N; Grey Mare's Trail to St Marys Waterfall at top, 10 min return. St Patricks ('Paddys') Head, 1.5 km E, named by Capt. Furneaux in 1773: challenging walk (1 hr 40 min return) to top for excellent coastal views. South Sister, 3 km NW, spectacular views of Fingal Valley from hilltop; more views to south through Elephant Pass, 4 km S, sole habitat of blind velvet worm. Small coastal township of Falmouth, 14 km NE, historic early settlement, with several convict-built structures, fine beaches, rocky headlands and good fishing. Wardlaw's Cray Store, 19 km S (Nov.–May). **Visitor information:** Library, 31 Main St (Mon., Wed., Fri.); (03) 6372 2114 or St Marys Coach House Restaurant, 34 Main St; (03) 6372 2529. **See also:** The East Coast p. 548.

Scottsdale
Pop. 1922

MAP REF. 585 N7

Scottsdale, the major town in Tasmania's north-east, serves some of the richest agricultural and forestry country on the island. The town's main industries are food processing, specialising in the deep-freezing of locally grown potatoes, and timber. **In town:** Settlers Museum and Gift Shop, King St, which operated as a theatre 1924–72, has photos and an old tools collection. Materials Research Laboratory (MRL), George St, makes dried food; tours on request. Nov.: Agricultural Show. **In the area:** Cuckoo Falls at Tonganah, 8 km SE. Bridestowe Estate Lavender Farm near Nabowla, 13 km W: sales of lavender products; tours in flowering season, Dec.–Jan. Views of township and surrounding countryside from Sideling Lookout, 16 km W. Golconda, 20 km W, holds Tasmanian Circus Festival each Feb. South Springfield Forest Park, 20 km S. Mt Maurice Forest Reserve, 30 km S. At Targa, 34 km SW, 7-day car rally held Apr. **Visitor information:** Lyric Lunchbox, 27 King St; (03) 6352 3235. **See also:** Midlands & the North p. 549.

Sheffield
Pop. 1016

MAP REF. 580 D9, 584 I8

Sheffield, 30 km S of Devonport, is located in the foothills of Mt Roland, in one of the most scenic areas of the State. The town's economy is based on farming. **In town:** On buildings, 36 murals depict area's history; video about murals at Diversity, Main St. Kentish Museum, Main St, has exhibits on local history and hydroelectricity. Mural House, High St, unusual interior murals. Red Water Creek Steam and Heritage Society runs steam train 1st weekend of month (departs cnr Spring and Main sts) and daily around New Year. Claude Road Hall markets, 3rd weekend in Mar., June, Sept. and Dec. Mar.: Mt Roland Folklore Festival. Sept.: Spring Flower Festival; Daffodil Day. **In the area:** Lakes and dams of Mersey-Forth Power Development Scheme, 10 km W. Lake

Barrington, part of scheme, a major recreation area and international rowing venue, 14 km SW. At entrance to venue is Tasmazia, world's largest maze complex: lavender farm, model village, Honey Boutique, restaurant and Pancake Parlour; Tasmazia Lavender Harvest Festival each Feb. Lake Barrington Estate Vineyard, 10 km W, for tastings and sales. Devil's Gate Dam, 13 km NW, with semi-circular dam wall; spectacular scenery from viewing areas; power station. Stoodley Forest Reserve, 7 km NE, between Sheffield and Railton; walking tracks and picnic/barbecue areas. Cradle Mountain–Lake St Clair National Park, 61 km SW: bushwalking, incl. famed Overland Track; spectacular rainforest and mountain scenery; rich flora and fauna. **Visitor information:** 5 Pioneer Cres.; (03) 6491 1036. **See also:** The North-West p. 550; National Parks p. 572.

Smithton
Pop. 3313

MAP REF. 584 C4

This substantial town is the administrative centre of Circular Head, which is renowned for its unique blackwood swamp forests and was the first European settlement in the far north-west. Smithton services the most productive dairying and vegetable-growing area in the State, and is also the centre of one of Tasmania's most significant forestry areas, with several large sawmills. Fishing is another major industry. **In town:** Lookout tower, Tier Hill, end of Massey St. Western Esplanade Community Park, centre of town overlooking the mouth of Duck River: fishing; walking; picnic spot. **In the area:** Forestry Tasmania reserves in district offer a range of recreational activities. Duck River and Duck Bay, 2 km N, for fishing and boating. Lacrum Tasmanian Dairy Farm, 6 km W at Mella: milking demonstrations during summer; afternoon teas; cheese-tastings and sales. Nearby, Wombat Tarn: picnic/barbecue area; lookout; bushwalks; playground. Further west, at island's north-west extremity: spectacular Cape Grim; Woolworth, sheep, cattle and timber property; coach day tour from Smithton takes in both. Near Marrawah, 51 km SW, excellent surfing and wavesailing; Rip Curl West Coast Classic each Mar. Sumac Lookout, 4 km S on Sumac Rd, for views over Arthur River and surrounding eucalypt forest. Allendale Gardens, 13 km S at Edith Creek: rainforest walks; Devonshire teas. At Arthur River, 70 km SW, river cruises (Aug.–mid-June); nearby at Gardiner Point is The Edge of the World

landmark. **Visitor information:** Council Offices, Goldie St; (03) 6452 1265. **See also:** The North-West p. 550.

Sorell
Pop. 3199

MAP REF. 579 K5, 583 M8

Named after Governor Sorell, this town is 23 km NE of Hobart. Founded 1821, it was important in early colonial history for providing most of the State's grain (1816–60). It also supplied grain to the colony of NSW for over 20 years. The area is still an important agricultural district, specialising in sheep-farming and forestry. **In town:** In Somerville St, historic Blue Bell Inn. Pioneer Park, Parsonage Pl., has picnic/barbecue facilities. Orielton Lagoon, internationally significant bird sanctuary, on western shore of town. Market at Memorial Hall, Cole St, 2nd and 4th Sun. each month, Mon. if long weekend. Nov.: Bushranger Festival. **In the area:** Orani Vineyard, 3 km E; Bream Creek Vineyard, 22 km E; Southern Tasmanian Wine Route, brochure available. Sorell Fruit Farm, 2 km E, off Arthur Highway. Popular beach areas around Dodges Ferry and Carlton, 18 km S. **Visitor information:** Council Offices, 12 Somerville St; (03) 6265 2201. **See also:** The South-East p. 546; Wildlife-Watching p. 570.

Stanley
Pop. 543

MAP REF. 584 D3

This quaint village, steeped in history, nestles under an ancient outcrop called The Nut, which rises to 152 m sheer on three sides. Stanley was the site for the headquarters of the Van Diemen's Land (VDL) Company, set up 1825 to establish a high-quality merino wool industry. Its wharf then handled whalers and sailing ships; today these are replaced by a strong fleet of cray and other fishing boats, but little else has changed. The birthplace of Australia's only Tasmanian prime minister, the Hon. J. A. (Joe) Lyons, Stanley has been declared an historic town. **In town:** Historic buildings in wharf area: bluestone bond store, Wharf Rd; former VDL Co. store, in Marine Park, designed by colonial architect John Lee Archer, who lived in township. Archer's own home, now Poet's Cottage, Alexander Tce, at base of The Nut; not open to public. Also in Alexander Tce, Lyons Cottage, birthplace of J. A. Lyons. In Church St: still-licensed Union Hotel (1849), with cellars and narrow stairways; Commercial Hotel (1842), now

private residence; Stanley Craft Centre for fine Tasmanian craft; Discovery Centre Folk Museum. Touchwood, quality craft and woodwork, in Main St. Chairlift, from Browns Rd to top of The Nut (152 m); 40-min circuit walk along cliffs for spectacular coastal views. Significant graves in burial ground on Browns Rd, dating from 1828, incl. those of John Lee Archer and explorer Henry Hellyer. Evening tours to small colonies of little (fairy) penguins near wharf and cemetery, and on Scenic Dr. Seal cruises. Dec.: Agricultural Show. **In the area:** Highfield Historic Site (1835), headquarters of VDL Co., 2 km N on Scenic Dr.: homestead, chapel, schoolhouse, barn, stables, workers' cottages and remains of barracks nearby; two arched gates remain of former deer park. Dip Falls, 40 km SE off hwy, via Mawbanna; nearby, Big Tree (giant eucalypt) and picnic area. Pelletising plant of Savage River Mines, Port Latta, 20 km SE, where ore is moved by conveyor to jetty for loading onto bulk-ore ships. **Visitor information:** The Nut Chairlift, Browns Rd; (03) 6458 1286. **See also:** The North-West p. 550.

Strahan
Pop. 701

MAP REF. 582 D3, 584 D12

This pretty little port on Macquarie Harbour, on Tasmania's forbidding west coast, is best known as the departure point for cruises to the Franklin–Gordon Wild Rivers National Park. Originally a Huon pine timber-milling town, its growth was

A jetty at Strahan

boosted by the copper boom at the Mt Lyell Mine. When the Strahan–Zeehan railway opened in 1892 it became a busy port. Today it is a popular holiday town with a variety of accommodation, incl. holiday units and cabins. It is also used as a base by crayfish, abalone and shark-fishing operators, but the harbour is limited by the formidable bar at Hells Gates, its mouth. **In town:** At Strahan Visitors Centre: excellent historical display of Tasmania's south-west, from Aboriginal times to present, incl. the fight to save the Franklin River from being dammed; audio-visual slide show; nightly performance of 'The Ship That Never Was' in amphitheatre. Adjacent: Morrison's Mill, one of four remaining Huon pine sawmills in Tasmania; woodturning, art and craft at Strahan Woodworks. Tuts Whittle Wonders, Reid St, has carvings from forest wood. Ormiston House, The Esplanade, one of Strahan's first houses, for morning or afternoon tea in splendid setting. Views of township and harbour from Water Tower Hill. Mineral and gemstone display, Innes St. The Wilderness Railway, 35-km Queenstown–Strahan train ride on rack-and-pinion line. Jan.: Mt Lyell Picnic. Mar.: Piners' Festival. **In the area:** Ocean Beach, 6 km W, Tasmania's longest beach (36 km): horseriding; beach-fishing; short-tailed shearwater (muttonbird) rookeries (Oct.–Mar.). King River Forest Drive passes through Teepookana Forest Reserve, 16 km SE, brochure available. At the reserve: Huon pines; walking tracks; historic iron bridge; 10-m viewing platform for bird's-eye view of forest. At Henty Dunes, 12 km N on Strahan–Zeehan Hwy: spectacular vast sand dunes; lagoon; picnic/barbecue areas; tours. Contact information centre for details of and bookings for: cruises upstream along the Gordon River to Heritage Landing and Sarah Island (Settlement Island), and across Macquarie Harbour to Hells Gates; guided tours of convict settlement ruins on Sarah Island; helicopter flights around Strahan; seaplane flights over Gordon River and Frenchmans Cap, landing at Sir John's Falls; jet boat rides; yacht charters overnight to Gordon River and evening or fishing cruises; hovercraft for joyrides and charter; 4WD tours, incl. fishing tour, Huon pine forestry tour, Henty Dunes tour; horse trail-rides; rafting tours along Franklin River; sea kayaks, canoes, motorbikes and bicycles for hire. **Visitor information:** The Esplanade; (03) 6471 7622. Web site www.strahan.tco. asn.au **See also:** South-West Wilderness p. 551; National Parks p. 572.

Swansea   Pop. 495

MAP REF. 583 P4, 585 P13

Swansea is a small town of historic interest on scenic Great Oyster Bay, in the centre of Tasmania's east coast. **In town:** Self-guide leaflet on town and area available. Original council chambers (c. 1860), Noyes St, still in use. At information centre: The Swansea Bark Mill and Yesteryear Museum (c. 1885); restored wattlebark mill machinery; Swansea Wine and Wool Centre, outlet for Tasmanian wines; tearooms. In Franklin St: Morris' General Store (1838), run by Morris family for over 100 years; Community Centre (c. 1860), has museum with unusually large slate billiard table made for 1880 World Exhibition. Colonial accommodation (some self-contained cottages, some B&B) in and around town. Waterloo Point, at edge of golf course near town centre: 1-km walking track for seeing short-tailed shearwaters (muttonbirds) at dusk; Aboriginal middens; views across bay to Freycinet Peninsula. Coswell Beach, 1 km S along coast from Waterloo Point, for seeing little (fairy) penguin at dusk. Nov.: Swansea Fun Fish (Australia's premiere bream fishing event). **In the area:** Guided garden tours in spring, bookings essential; (03) 6230 8233. Kate's Berry Farm, 2 km S: fresh berries, ice-cream and fruit wines. Splendid views from Duncombes Lookout, 3 km S. Spikey Beach, 7 km S, with picnic area and excellent rock-fishing. Kabuki, Japanese restaurant on clifftop, 12 km S. Mayfield Beach, 14 km S: safe swimming; fishing; walking track from camping area to Three Arch Bridge. Meetus and Lost falls, 50 km NW. At Cranbrook, 15 km N: Craft Fair in Dec.; Springvale, Coombend, Freycinet and Craigie Knowe vineyards for cellar-door sales (weekends and holidays). **Visitor information:** Swansea Bark Mill & East Coast Museum, 96 Tasman Hwy; (03) 6257 8382. **See also:** The East Coast p. 548.

Triabunna   Pop. 766

MAP REF. 579 O1, 583 O6

When Maria Island was a penal settlement, Triabunna, 86 km NE of Hobart, was a garrison town and whaling base. Today it is a centre for the scallop and abalone industries, with a major export wood-chipping mill just south of the town. **In town:** On Esplanade: Tasmanian Seafarers' Memorial, commemorating all seafarers lost in Tasmanian waters; Bicentennial Park, with picnic/barbecue areas;

Pioneer Park, featuring historic farm machinery. Girraween Gardens and Tearooms, Henry St. **In the area:** Daily ferry from Eastcoaster Resort at Louisville Point, 7 km S, to Maria Island. On Maria Island: Painted Cliffs, extensive fossil deposits. Historic penal settlement of Darlington in Maria Island National Park; buildings incl. Coffee Palace (1888), housing old photographs and newspapers, mess room (1845) and chapel (1847); dormitory-style accommodation and camping; walking trails across island (good map essential, check weather conditions, no food available on island). At Orford, 7 km SW of Triabunna, walk along Old Convict Rd following Prosser River. Thumbs Lookout, 9 km SW, overlooks Maria Island. Local beaches for swimming, water-skiing and fishing. **Visitor information:** cnr Charles St and Esplanade West; (03) 6257 4090. **See also:** The East Coast p. 548; Wildlife-Watching p. 570; National Parks p. 572.

Ulverstone   Pop. 9792

MAP REF. 580 C5, 584 H6

Situated 19 km W of Devonport, near the mouth of the Leven River, Ulverstone is a well-equipped tourist centre, established as a town in 1852. Dairying, furniture-making and poultry- and vegetable-farming are the area's main industries. **In town:** Shrine of Remembrance Clock Tower (1953), Reibey St. History Museum, Main St. On Beach Rd: Riverside Anzac Park, with playground and picnic/barbecue areas; Fairway Park, a wildfowl reserve, with giant water slide. Footpath, inscribed with excerpts of 75-year history of Royal Australian Navy, leads from town centre to HMAS *Shropshire* Naval Memorial Park in Dial St. Antique and art and craft shops. Legion Park, on Esplanade in West Ulverstone, has magnificent coastal setting. Boer War Memorial in Tobruk Park, Hobbs Pde; Queens Gardens in Kings Pde. Weeda Copper, Eastland Dr., for handmade local copperware. Lookout at eastern end of Upper Maud St. Apex House Market, Grove St, 1st and 3rd Sun. each month. Feb.: Twilight Rodeo. Oct.: Taste of Ulverstone. Dec.: Christmas Mardi Gras. **In the area:** Extensive beaches east and west of town, safe swimming for children. Good fishing on beach, river and estuary. Miniature railway, 2 km E; check opening times. At Leith, 12 km E, little (fairy) penguins at dusk. Goat Island Sanctuary, 5 km W; walking access to island at low tide only. At Gunns Plains, 24 km SW: Gallery 321, Raymond Rd, for art, craft, light refreshments. Near Gunns Plains: Gunns Plains Hop Farm, basket-weaving workshop in Mar.; limestone caves featuring underground river and glow-worms (guided tours). Scenic views at Preston Falls, 19 km S. Castra Falls, 30 km S. Walking tracks to viewing platform with spectacular views at Leven Canyon, 41 km S; beyond, west of South Nietta, Winterbrook Walk and Falls in rainforest. **Visitor information:** Car Park La. (behind post office); (03) 6425 2839. **See also:** The North-West p. 550.

Waratah
Pop. 230

MAP REF. 584 E8

This picturesque little settlement, set in mountain heathland 100 km N of Queenstown, was the site of the first mining boom in Tasmania. In 1900 it had a population of 2000 and Mount Bischoff was the richest tin mine in the world. The deposits were discovered in 1871 by James 'Philosopher' Smith, a colourful local character, and the mine closed in 1947, with dividends totalling 200 pounds for every one pound of original investment. **In town:** Self-drive tour of town, brochure available. In Smith St: Waratah Waterfall; Waratah Museum and Gift Shop, for early photographs and artifacts; adjacent, Philosopher Smith's Hut, replica of miner's hut; Atheneum Hall (c. 1887), has portrait of Smith; St James' Anglican Church (1880), first church in Tasmania to be lit by hydro-power. Near Lake Waratah, Rhododendron Garden: picnic/barbecue areas; camping. Feb.: Axemen's Carnival. **In the area:** Walks and drive to old mining sites, brochure available. Trout fishing in rivers and lakes. At the fascinating former goldmining town of Corinna, 66 km SW, cruises on Pieman River, bookings essential; (03) 6446 1170. **Visitor information:** Fossey River Information Bay, 8 km S on Murchison Hwy or Council Offices, Smith St; (03) 6439 7100. **See also:** The North-West p. 550.

Westbury
Pop. 1280

MAP REF. 581 K11, 585 K9

A village green, said to be unique in Australia, gives this town a decidedly English air. Situated on the Bass Hwy, 35 km SW of Launceston, Westbury was surveyed in 1823 and laid out in 1828; it has several fine old colonial buildings. **In town:** Self-guide leaflet on town and

area available. On the Village Green, King St: White House (c. 1841), comprising extensive colonial museum (featuring superb antique dolls' house), house, bakery, coach-house, courtyard and stable complex (open Tues.–Sun., Sept.–June); former police barracks (c. 1832), now an RSL Club; St Andrews Church; antique shop and colonial accommodation. On Bass Hwy: Hedge maze, open Oct.–June; Pearn's Steam World, a large collection of working steam traction engines. Tractor Shed, Veterans Row, a museum of old tractors and farm machinery; also scale-model tractor exhibition. Culzean in William St, on the northern edge of town, an open garden Sept.–May. Market, 2nd Sun. each month at St Andrews Church. Mar.: St Patrick's Day Festival. Nov.: Steam Spectacular. **In the area:** At Hagley, 5 km E, St Mary's Anglican Church, fine east window donated by Lady Dry, wife of Sir Richard Dry, first Tasmanian-born premier. Heidi Farm Cheese, 7 km W, tastings and sales. Trout fishing at Brushy Lagoon, 15 km NW, and Four Springs Creek, 15 km NE. **Visitor information:** Clarke's Antiques and Gingerbread Cottages, 52 William St; (03) 6393 1140. **See also:** Midlands & the North p. 549.

Wynyard
Pop. 4509

MAP REF. 584 F5

This small centre at the mouth of the Inglis River, west of Burnie, has become a well-developed tourist centre, offering a range of accommodation and easy access to many attractions and activities. There are daily flights between nearby Burnie–Wynyard airport, King Island and Melbourne. The Waratah–Wynyard region is a prosperous dairying and mixed-farming district and the town has a large, modern dairy factory. **In town:** Gutteridge Gardens, riverside gardens in heart of town. Tasmanian tiger (thylacine) interpretive sculpture, at information centre. Table Cape Tulip Farm, open in season. Oct.: Tulip Festival. **In the area:** Scenic walks and drives in Wynyard and surrounding districts, brochures available; network of nature walks, incl. boardwalk along Inglis River. Scenic flights over coast and wilderness. Excellent sea-fishing and fly-fishing for trout. Oldest marsupial fossil in Australia found at Fossil Bluff, 3 km N; displayed at the Tasmanian Museum and Art Gallery in Hobart. Table Cape Lookout, 5 km N, for coastal and inland views. Renowned Lapoinya Rhododendron Gardens, 20 km W,

Australia's largest collection of rhododendrons and exotic shrubs, in bushland setting. **Visitor information:** cnr Hogg and Goldie sts; (03) 6442 4143. **See also:** The North-West p. 550.

Zeehan
Pop. 1116

MAP REF. 582 D1, 584 D11

Named after one of Abel Tasman's ships, this former mining town, 36 km NW of Queenstown, is now a National Trust-classified historic town. Silver-lead deposits were discovered here in 1882. By 1901, Zeehan had 26 hotels and a population of 11 000, making it Tasmania's third largest town. Just 7 years later mining began to decline and Zeehan became almost a ghost town. In the boom period between 1893 and 1908, ore worth 8 million dollars had been recovered. Now the town is benefiting from the reopening of the Renison Bell tin mine. **In town:** Self-guide scenic drives in town and surrounding area, brochures available. Many boom buildings in Main St, incl. Gaiety Theatre at Grand Hotel; ANZ Bank; St Luke's Church; post office and courthouse. Also in Main St: 4 old miners' cottages available as accommodation; West Coast Pioneers Memorial Museum, in School of Mines building (1894), has mineral, historical and geological collections. Adjacent to museum, display of steam locomotives and rail carriages used on west coast. Frank Long Memorial Park, Dodd St; Long discovered silver-lead deposit here. Pioneer cemetery, on southern outskirts of town. **In the area:** Old mine workings at Dundas, 13 km E. Montezuma Falls, highest waterfall in State, 17 km NE; accessible by 4WD or walking track. Surface tours of zinc mine, 22 km NE at Rosebery. At Tullah, further 12 km NE: picturesque lake; historical Wee Georgie Wood Railway (check operating times); Tullah Challenge held Nov. Corinna, 48 km NW, once a bustling goldmining town, now a base for gold-panning, trout fishing, bushwalking; *Fatman* car ferry crosses Pieman River to Western Explorer Road, the 98-km (3.5-hr) partly sealed link to Arthur River via the Arthur Pieman Conservation Area. Fishing and boating on Lake Pieman, 50 km NW. Trial Harbour, 20 km W, popular fishing area. Unsealed road sections to both areas often in poor condition; check before departure. Trout fishing on Henty River, 25 km S. **Visitor information:** West Coast Pioneers' Memorial Museum, Main Rd; (03) 6471 6225. **See also:** South-West Wilderness p. 551.

CLASSIC TOUR

PENINSULA TRAIL

Hobart to Coal Mines Historic Site via Port Arthur (148 km)

This two or three day tour to the Forestier and Tasman peninsulas is an ideal introduction to Tasmania's fascinating past and extraordinary natural heritage. The ruins of Port Arthur convict settlement are undoubtedly the highlight, but the sombre beauty of the coastline is just as evocative. While it is possible to visit Port Arthur as a day trip from Hobart, this tour offers a much richer experience – from the quiet eccentricity of Copping and Doo Town, to the grandeur of the eastern cliffs and the isolation of the western dunes.

1 Another time

The tour commences in Hobart. Follow the Tasman Highway (A3) past the airport and along the narrow causeway that extends for kilometres across the shallows of Pitt Water to Sorell. On a windy day, waves break at the roadside and the air is filled with seaspray.

At Sorell take the Arthur Highway (A9) which winds through open farmland to the tiny settlement of **Copping**, home to a truly eccentric museum, the Copping Colonial and Convict Collection. The collection is a marvellously overcrowded jumble of artifacts and features rather eerie-looking figures, cleverly positioned throughout the display, which come to life at the push of a button – lights flicker, wheels turn and bellows fill with air.

Copping Colonial and
Convict Collection
Arthur Hwy
Copping
Phone: (03) 6253 5373
Open: 9 a.m.–5 p.m. daily (summer);
9 a.m.–1 p.m. daily (winter)

2 Prepare to slow down

From Copping, continue to **Dunalley**, a quiet fishing village situated on a narrow isthmus which marks the start of the Forestier Peninsula. In the early 20th century, bullock teams and a small locomotive engine were used to build a canal through the isthmus. This shortcut for fishing vessels travelling between Hobart and the east coast of Tasmania is still in use. You may have to stop at the swing bridge while a boat chugs through the entrance.

Pirates Bay

3 Nature's mosaic

Follow the highway until you reach the signposted turn-off to Pirates Bay Drive. After 700 metres, pull in at Pirates Bay Lookout. On a fine day you can expect to see across the bay, past the eastern side of Eaglehawk Neck to the massive coastal cliffs of the Tasman Peninsula. This vantage point offers a scenic overview of the next section of the tour, where the interplay between land and sea is at its most dramatic.

Pirates Bay Drive descends through eucalypt forest to the Art Deco-style Lufra Hotel. Below the hotel is one of the most interesting rock formations on this section of the coast, the **Tessellated Pavement**, a mudstone platform on the edge of the sea. A gentle, 300-metre walking track leads down to this seemingly man-made mosaic of square rock 'tiles', reminiscent of the ruins of a forgotten civilisation. The tiled appearance, known as jointing, is the product of fluctuating moisture levels and the smoothing action of the sea. The best time to view the pavement is at low tide, when the surface is exposed.

4 The Neck

Pirates Bay Drive rejoins the highway just before **Eaglehawk Neck**, a narrow strip of land less than 100 metres wide, which connects the Forestier and Tasman peninsulas.

For the convicts at nearby Port Arthur penal settlement, Eaglehawk Neck was a formidable natural barrier between servitude and freedom. Those daring or desperate enough to make the dash for freedom had to evade military guards and ferocious dogs spread in a line across this narrow strip of land. To discourage sea escapes, dogs were also kept on pontoons in the bay. This, combined with a rumour that the surrounding waters were shark-infested, ensured that few convicts tried their luck as 'bolters'. Even fewer were successful. At Eaglehawk Neck Historic Site, the Dogline, reached by walking track from the Officers' Quarters, is marked by a bronze dog sculpture.

The Officers' Quarters is the only building left from the period of military occupation. Believed to be the oldest wooden military building in Australia, it is well worth a visit. The historical display inside provides vivid accounts of the relationship between this wild landscape and the people who lived there. One of the most interesting stories is the connection between the site and the Pydairrerme Aborigines, a band of the East Coast Oyster Bay tribe.

Officers' Quarters
Eaglehawk Neck Historic Site
Off Arthur Hwy
Eaglehawk Neck
Phone: (03) 6250 3635
Open: daily (inquire at Officers' Mess)

5 Confronting the elements

Just south of Eaglehawk Neck, a signposted turn-off leads to tiny Doo Town, where all the house names incorporate the name 'Doo'. Here, the road branches off to three dramatic rock features: the **Tasman Blowhole**, **Tasmans Arch** and **Devils Kitchen**.

Constantly pounding wave action has caused the cliff-line to collapse and erode in places, resulting in a series of impressive formations. The confrontation between land and sea is a dynamic spectacle as water blasts through fissures in the cliff-face, floods rock pools and creates random spray patterns.

If you are seeking a more contemplative experience away from the inevitable summer crowds, follow the walking track from Devils Kitchen to Waterfall Bay (2 hours return). This cliff-side track passes through banksia forest and heathland and offers marvellous views of the coastline. Take care, as some of the lookout points are unfenced. For those interested in bushwalking there are many other wonderful opportunities on the peninsula, including the strenuous but truly spectacular overnight hikes to Cape Pillar and Cape Raoul.

6 Devils and snakes

Return to Eaglehawk Neck and continue south along the highway as it skirts the gentle western shores of the peninsula. Just after the township of Taranna is the **Tasmanian Devil Park**, where injured and orphaned native animals are nursed. Tasmanian devils are permanent residents here and are best seen at feeding times: 10 a.m. and 11 a.m daily. Other guests may include quolls, rare golden possums, eagles and owls. Another feature of the centre is the Tasman Bird Trail, which winds for 1.5 kilometres, past a lovely natural brook and through open shrubland to the shore of nearby Norfolk Bay. This is a great place to spot eagles, falcons, honeyeaters and a range of seabirds. Binoculars and bird identification notes are available for hire at the centre.

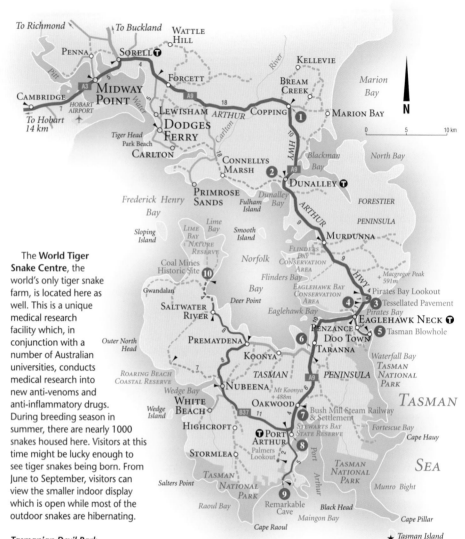

The **World Tiger Snake Centre**, the world's only tiger snake farm, is located here as well. This is a unique medical research facility which, in conjunction with a number of Australian universities, conducts medical research into new anti-venoms and anti-inflammatory drugs. During breeding season in summer, there are nearly 1000 snakes housed here. Visitors at this time might be lucky enough to see tiger snakes being born. From June to September, visitors can view the smaller indoor display which is open while most of the outdoor snakes are hibernating.

Tasmanian Devil Park
Arthur Hwy
Taranna
Phone: (03) 6250 3230
Open: 9 a.m.–5 p.m. daily
World Tiger Snake Centre
Arthur Hwy
Taranna
Phone: (03) 6250 3230
Open: 9 a.m.–5 p.m. daily

7 Life at the mill

Continue along the highway and, a short distance after the township of Oakwood, you will find the **Bush Mill Steam Railway and Settlement**.

The Bush Mill depicts the life of timber cutters on the peninsula in the late 1800s. Buildings on the reconstructed mill site include a rough slab hut, bark shelters, a mill manager's cottage and a general store. The steam-powered sawmill, imaginative sound and light displays and blacksmith demonstrations bring this era back to life. A miniature K-class Garratt locomotive, built in the mill's own workshops, takes visitors on a 4-kilometre narrow-gauge railway journey through picturesque bushland.

Bush Mill Steam Railway and Settlement
Arthur Hwy
Port Arthur
Phone: (03) 6250 2221
Open: 9 a.m.–4 p.m. daily;
until 5 p.m. in summer

Bush Mill Steam Railway

8 Convict heritage

Further along the highway is the entrance to the **Port Arthur Historic Site**, the most poignant symbol of Tasmania's days as a penal colony. Its sandstone walls once resounded with the blows of the convict chisel; they now stand testament to the incredible hardships and human tragedy of early convict life. It is still possible, particularly in bleak weather, for the ruins to impart some of the atmosphere of hopelessness and misery that existed here about 160 years ago. The prison settlement was established in 1830, and was home to around 12 000 convicts before the cell doors closed for the last time in 1877.

Today the historic site encompasses 40 hectares, including the separate prison with its cell blocks and chapel, the asylum, the commandant's house and the port area. Hourly guided walks are conducted on a daily basis. In summer, visitors can take a harbour cruise to the Isle of the Dead, where hundreds of convicts, civilians and military personnel are buried. Scenic flights operate when weather permits. Your entry ticket entitles you to two days at Port Arthur. As there is a range of accommodation near the site, and given the concentration of attractions nearby, this would make an ideal overnight stop. The lamplight ghost tours of the historic site are an added bonus for those who decide to break their journey here, and the self-guide nature trail to Stewarts Bay would make a pleasant early-morning walk.

Port Arthur sunset

The Visitor Centre
Port Arthur Historic Site
Off Arthur Hwy
Port Arthur
Phone: (03) 6251 2300,
freecall 1800 659 101
Open: 8.30 a.m.–dusk, daily

9 Remarkable places

Just 400 metres along the highway after the Port Arthur Historic Site is a signposted turn-off to Palmers Lookout and Remarkable Cave. To visit Palmers Lookout, take the turn-off and then the unsealed road almost immediately to the right. Carefully tended flower beds and a collection of gnomes mark the entrance to this charming picnic spot. The view from the lookout is superb – from here you can see the point at which the sheltered waters of Port Arthur enter the open sea.

Palmers Lookout

Return to the sealed road to continue to **Remarkable Cave**, a majestic rock formation. After parking at the car park, you will need to descend a long, steep set of steps to reach the viewing platform. Remarkable Cave is located in a deep gully, the base of which is lined with perfectly tumbled rocks. Between the gully and the ocean is a cliff about 30 metres thick. Ocean water thunders through a tunnel in the cliff and rushes over the rocks at irregular intervals.

10 The beauty and the terror

Return to the Arthur Highway and continue to the coastal settlement of Nubeena. The road passes through forest, open farmland and a very pretty valley, before reaching the sea at Wedge Bay. There is an interesting diversion just after Nubeena: take a left turn and drive along a winding, unsealed road past the Atlantic salmon ponds to the wild, grassy sand dunes of Roaring Beach Coastal Reserve. If you venture down this road after rain, take special care at the bends. From Nubeena, the road rises through the hills to the centre of the peninsula. During winter and spring, the rolling pasture is emerald green and the blue sea in the distance makes a brilliant backdrop. At Premaydena, turn left and continue past farmland to Saltwater River. A further 4 kilometres along a largely unsealed road is the **Coal Mines Historic Site**. Tasmania's first mine was established here following the discovery of coal in 1833. By 1839 there were 150 convicts working the site, along with 29 officers.

Repeat offenders 'of the worst class' from Port Arthur were sent to the mines. Conditions underground were appalling. Bathed in dirt and perspiration, convicts toiled relentlessly in damp, dark and stifling tunnels. The most intractable of the inmates were denied the light of day, housed underground in punishment cells. In 1848 the coal mines were closed, for both moral and financial reasons.

Ruins of the settlement have been stabilised, and a walking trail joins the various buildings. The remains of the convict barracks, chapel and officers' quarters are still evident, along with the commissariat store and main shaft. On a sunny day it is hard to imagine the hardship that was life for some in this once-isolated settlement.

Returning to Hobart

From the Coal Mines Historic Site return to Premaydena and turn left to go through Koonya and on to the Arthur Highway to return to Hobart. If you are reluctant to leave the coast at Dunalley, take the coastal route back via Dodges Ferry. It will not take much longer and you will be rewarded with lingering views of turquoise seas and beaches fringed with she-oaks.

WILDLIFE-WATCHING

Bennett's wallabies can be seen at many locations across the State

IN AND AROUND HOBART

Hobart is one of the most accessible places in Australia to view wild peregrine falcons. Visitors who venture down to the Tasman Bridge at dusk in winter might be lucky enough to see these birds of prey in action. Peregrines swoop down on the flocks of starlings returning to roost under the bridge. Keep your binoculars ready to see the peregrines catch their prey in mid-air.

For a more tranquil bird-watching experience, visit Orielton Lagoon at **Sorell**, north-east of Hobart. This wetland area is protected by the international Ramsar Convention because of its significance as a habitat for migratory birds. Birds seen wading here at low tide have travelled many thousands of kilometres along the East Asian–Australasian Flyway from as far afield as Siberia. Waders, such as plovers and oystercatchers, feed on the mud flats as the tide is falling and when the tide is almost high they seek a safe roosting place. Tide times are published in the *Mercury* newspaper; Sorell's low tide is 2.5 hours later than Hobart's. There are a number of access points to the lagoon: from the Sorell Causeway, from Henry Street on the east side of the lagoon, and from Shark Point Road. You will need patience, a good field guide, binoculars and, after rain, a pair of gumboots.

ON THE EAST COAST

Maria Island National Park, a short ferry ride from Louisville on the east coast, is a natural showcase for Tasmania's unique bird species. It is the only national park where all of the State's 11 endemic species can be spotted. These include the yellow wattlebird, Tasmanian thornbill, yellow-throated honeyeater and the dusky robin. This range of birdlife is the result of incredibly diverse habitats on this small island, ranging from ocean, wetland, cleared-grazing and dry sclerophyll forest, to moist gully environments.

The grasslands of Darlington at the northern end of the island are active with wildlife at all times of the day. Thriving in the absence of foxes and dingoes (Tasmania has neither), Bennett's wallabies and pademelons

---

THE THYLACINE (TASMANIAN TIGER)

Along with its smaller relative the Tasmanian devil, the thylacine (Tasmanian tiger) would have to be one the State's best-known native animals. This is despite the fact that the last recorded thylacine was captured in 1933 and died in 1936. Like a mythical beast, the thylacine has lived on in the popular imagination, sustained by well-publicised but unsubstantiated sightings.

Referred to as the Tasmanian tiger because of the stripes on its back and rump, this lean-bodied marsupial with a large head and short legs is more like a dog in overall appearance.

In recent years, most reported sightings of the thylacine have occurred in the north of the State. However, if you are keen to come face-to-face with this mysterious creature, your best opportunity is to visit the life-size hologram at Lake St Clair Park Centre in Cradle Mountain–Lake St Clair National Park.

(also a type of wallaby) graze here, as does Tasmania's only kangaroo, the Forester kangaroo. Flocks of Cape Barren geese regularly graze and breed in this area; they mate in autumn and lay eggs in grassland tussocks. The fluffy goslings develop rapidly in winter and are ready to fly by late spring.

Freycinet Peninsula, roughly midway between Hobart and Launceston, offers a range of wildlife-watching opportunities. Bennett's wallabies and pademelons tend to congregate in the Freycinet National Park carpark throughout the day and in the grassland by the beaches at dusk. Nocturnal mammals include Tasmanian devils, brushtail possums and common wombats.

Freycinet Sea Charters operate regular wildlife cruises featuring seasonal sightings of bottlenose and common dolphins, Australian fur seals, white-bellied sea-eagles and southern right and humpback whales.

Moulting Lagoon Game Reserve, located at the beginning of Freycinet Peninsula, is another wetland of international significance protected by the

Ramsar Convention.
Birds commonly
seen here include the
migratory waders, as
well as black swans,
wild ducks, egrets,
cormorants, pelicans
and birds of prey.

IN THE NORTH-EAST OF THE STATE

Mount William National Park was originally established as a national park in order to protect its substantial Forester kangaroo population. Forester Kangaroo Drive passes through the pasture area in the northern section of the park, where Bennett's wallabies can also be seen, especially at dawn or dusk. As darkness falls, a whole cast of nocturnal wildlife appears. Eastern quolls (probably extinct on the mainland), common wombats, possums and pademelons are just some of the characters you might expect to see.

Narawntapu National Park, which has the advantage of being slightly closer to the main ports of Devonport and Launceston, has a similar array of wildlife. The north-eastern parks are probably the best places in the State to view the icon of Tasmanian wildlife, the Tasmanian devil. This squat little meat-eater, renowned for its spine-chilling screeches, is active after dark, when it roams in search of carcasses.

Birdwatching is a popular activity in these two north-eastern parks. Gulls, oystercatchers, terns, hooded plovers, pelicans and albatrosses can all be sighted along the coastline. Musselroe Point and Campsite 4 in Mount William National Park and the bird hide behind Bakers Beach in Narawntapu National Park are prime birdwatching locations.

Also in the north-east is George Town, the jumping-off point for cruises to see the Australian fur seal colony at **Tenth Island**. The fur seals, with their endearing whiskered faces, can be seen year-round. As the boat approaches, the playful pups swim towards it and dive underneath, while the large bull seals look on from the rocks about 100 metres away. Pelicans, black swans and dolphins are a common sight en route to Tenth Island.

At **Low Head** near George Town, little (fairy) penguins can be viewed at dusk during the breeding period (July to April). Access is by tour only; inquire at the George Town information centre for cruise and tour details; (03) 6382 1700.

IN THE WEST OF THE STATE

Cradle Mountain–Lake St Clair National Park is one of the State's most popular wildlife-watching destinations. Visitors are guaranteed to see a range of nocturnal marsupials such as Bennett's wallabies, pademelons, wombats and possums around the camping and accommodation areas, especially in the evenings. Platypuses live in the lakes and streams but are far more elusive. Tasmanian devils are generally spotted at night on the edges of roadways, ripping apart the carcasses of animals killed by cars.

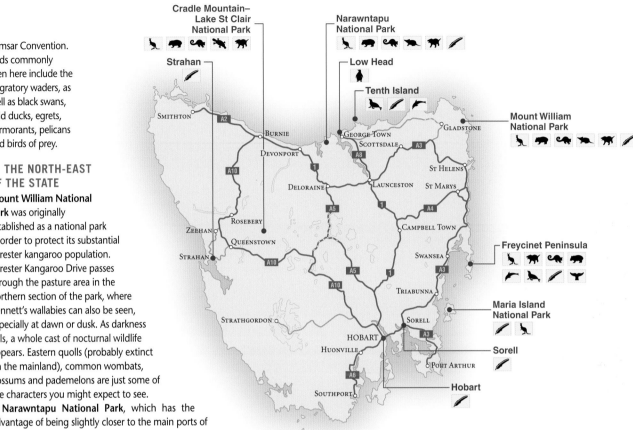

WILDLIFE-WATCHING ETHICS

Do not disturb wildlife or wildlife habitats. Keep the impact of your presence to a minimum. Use available cover or hides wherever possible.

Do not feed wildlife, even in urban areas. (Note: supervised feeding is allowed at some locations)

Be careful not to introduce exotic plants and animals – definitely no pets.

Stay on defined trails.

Strahan is probably best-known as the jumping-off point for cruises along the Gordon River. Many visitors, however, have discovered another attraction during the summer months. Every year in late September, the first of thousands of short-tailed shearwaters (muttonbirds) reach their rookeries on Ocean Beach, having travelled 15 000 kilometres from the Arctic region. Throughout summer, the sky fills with shearwaters every evening as they return with food for their young.

For more information on wildlife-watching in Tasmania's national parks, contact the Parks and Wildlife Service, 134 Macquarie Street, Hobart (GPO Box 44A, Hobart 7001); (03) 6233 6191. Web site www.parks.tas.gov.au

NATIONAL PARKS

Spectacular view from Mount Olympus in Cradle Mountain–Lake St Clair National Park

NEAR HOBART

Mount Field National Park, 80 kilometres north-west of Hobart, offers a diversity of activities ranging from picnicking to overnight bush-walking. It also has the only developed skiing area in southern Tasmania. There are several waterfalls in the park, the best-known being Russell Falls. The 15-minute walk to these falls is suitable for wheelchairs. Here water plunges in two stages into a forested valley where tree ferns filter sunlight and create a lovely mosaic effect. The forest includes large myrtles, giant 250-year-old gum trees, sassafras, huge tree ferns, the unique horizontal scrub and a variety of mosses, ferns, lichens and fungi. There are many walks, including the Tall Trees Walk and a gentle circuit walk that takes in Russell, Horseshoe and Lady Barron falls. The drive to Lake Dobson enables visitors to enjoy the Tasmanian high country with its snow gums, alpine moorlands and glacial lakes.

A one-and-a-half-hour drive from Hobart, through Geeveston to the south-west, brings visitors to the popular bushwalking area of **Hartz Mountains National Park**. Most of the area is over 600 metres in altitude, while Hartz Peak is 1255 metres. There are basic facilities for the day visitor, but no camping facilities.

South Bruny National Park, on South Bruny Island, is one of Tasmania's newer parks. It takes in spectacular and varied coastal scenery, including the rugged cliffs of Fluted Cape and Tasman Head. Sea birds and marine mammals can be seen, including little (fairy) penguins, albatrosses, Australian fur seals and dolphins.

Proclaimed in 1999, **Tasman National Park** covers 9346 hectares south-east of Hobart on the Forestier and Tasman peninsulas. This park offers magnificent coastal scenery including unusual rock formations. Day trippers can visit Eaglehawk Neck and nearby Tasman Blowhole, Tasmans Arch, Waterfall Bay and Remarkable Cave. The park also contains rare plants (including three rare species of *Euphrasia*) and provides opportunities to see raptors, seals, penguins, dolphins and whales. Camping is available at Fortescue Bay.

IN THE SOUTH-WEST OF THE STATE

Tasmania's largest national park is **Southwest National Park**, which has 618 010 hectares of mainly remote wilderness country. Here there are dolerite- and quartzite-capped mountains, sharp ridges and steep glacial valleys. The dense forests are made up of eucalypts, myrtles, sassafras and leatherwood, often covered with mosses, ferns and lichens, and tangled with pink-flowered climbing heath and bauera. The Creepy Crawly Nature Trail is an ideal introduction to the temperate rainforest environment. Climbers will find a challenge in Federation Peak, Mount Anne and Precipitous Bluff; anglers can fish for trout at lakes Pedder and Gordon. A specially built bird hide at remote Melaleuca can be used in summer to observe the rare and endangered orange-bellied parrot.

The 446 000-hectare **Franklin–Gordon Wild Rivers National Park** forms the central portion of Tasmania's World Heritage Area. The Franklin River attracts wilderness adventurers world-wide to test its challenging rapids. Cruise boats navigate the more placid lower Gordon River past stands of 2000-year-old Huon pine. The Lyell Highway, the road link between Hobart and the west coast, runs through the park. Excellent short walks lead off the highway to rainforests, waterfalls and spectacular lookouts. For experienced bushwalkers, the 4 to 5 day Frenchmans Cap track offers majestic scenery.

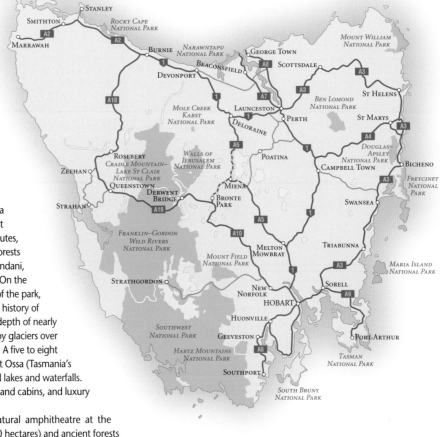

IN THE CENTRAL NORTH OF THE STATE

Covering some of Tasmania's highest country is **Cradle Mountain–Lake St Clair National Park**. There is a visitor centre and accommodation near the northern park entrance at Cradle Mountain; a nature walk winds through the nearby rainforest. Cradle Mountain has a variety of bushwalks and is the starting point for one of Australia's best-known walking routes, the 85-kilometre Overland Track, through forests of deciduous beech, Tasmanian 'myrtle', pandani, King Billy pine and a wealth of wildflowers. On the shores of Lake St Clair at the southern end of the park, there is a visitor centre with displays on the history of the area. The tranquil Lake St Clair, with a depth of nearly 200 metres, occupies a basin gouged out by glaciers over the last 20 000 years. Cruises operate daily. A five to eight day trek traverses the park, taking in Mount Ossa (Tasmania's highest mountain) and a range of highland lakes and waterfalls. At Lake St Clair there are several campsites and cabins, and luxury accommodation nearby.

Steep, jagged mountains create a natural amphitheatre at the **Walls of Jerusalem National Park** (51 800 hectares) and ancient forests of pencil pines ring tiny glacially formed lakes, making the park very popular with bushwalkers. The park is not accessible for day trips.

IN THE NORTH OF THE STATE

The central north coastal strip of **Narawntapu National Park** is a refuge for a wide variety of birds, as well as wombats, kangaroos and wallabies. Its islands off Port Sorell provide an important breeding area for little (fairy) penguins, and the tidal and mud flats are ideal feeding grounds for migratory seabirds. On the unspoiled beaches, white sands come to life with thousands of soldier crabs.

Further west, **Rocky Cape National Park** (3064 hectares) encompasses rugged coastline with small sheltered beaches backed by heath-covered hills. It is known for its rock shelters used for over 8000 years by Tasmanian Aboriginal people.

In the north central region, **Mole Creek Karst National Park** is located in the forested hills below the impressive Western Tiers. Underground streams have made caves with splendid calcite formations. Guided tours of King Solomons and Marakoopa caves are available.

IN THE EAST OF THE STATE

Many of Tasmania's national parks are important wildlife reserves. The 18 439-hectare **Mount William National Park**, is a sanctuary for native creatures, including the Forester kangaroo (Tasmania's only kangaroo), pademelon, Tasmanian devil and the Australian grayling in Ansons River. At Lookout Point, thousands of colourful rock orchids cover the granite rocks, and wildflowers carpet the park in spring. The rush lily (vanilla plant) and smoke-bush, both rare, have their habitat here. Sheltered bays and beaches complete this little-known but beautiful park.

Fifty kilometres south-east of Launceston is **Ben Lomond National Park**, one of Tasmania's two main ski fields offering downhill and cross-country skiing, with an alpine village, ski-tows, ski hire, tavern with accommodation, and a public shelter.

A short distance north of Freycinet National Park is **Douglas–Apsley National Park** (16 080 hectares). Proclaimed in 1990, this park contains the State's last large dry sclerophyll forest and can be traversed along a 3-day north–south walking track. Lightly forested ridges contrast with patches of rainforest and river gorges, while waterfalls and spectacular coastal views add to the grandeur of the area.

Freycinet National Park offers wide stretches of white sand, rocky headlands, granite peaks, quiet beaches and small coves, and an excellent choice of short and long walking tracks. Freycinet National Park also includes Schouten Island, separated from the Freycinet Peninsula by a kilometre-wide passage, and reached only by boat. Near the park is Coles Bay, a fishing and swimming destination with delightful coastal scenery and a range of accommodation.

Maria Island, off the east coast, is well worth a visit. You can get there by light aircraft or passenger ferry from Louisville. On arrival you step into another world, for no tourist vehicles are permitted. This island national park embraces magnificently coloured sandstone cliffs and is a refuge for over 80 species of birds. Forester kangaroos and Cape Barren geese roam freely in this unspoiled landscape. Its intriguing history and historic buildings date back to the convict era which began in 1825.

All parks are accessible year-round. An entry fee applies in all national parks. Some tourists believe the highland parks are best in summer and autumn, when the weather is more reliable, the wildflowers bloom and flowering trees and shrubs attract birdlife. Bushwalking is popular; however in the highland parks there can be sudden storms and snowfalls, even in summer. Be prepared for unexpected changes in the weather. For further information on Tasmania's national parks, contact the Parks and Wildlife Service, 134 Macquarie Street, Hobart (GPO Box 44A, Hobart 7001); (03) 6233 6191. Web site www.parks.tas.gov.au

TASMANIA
LOCATION MAP

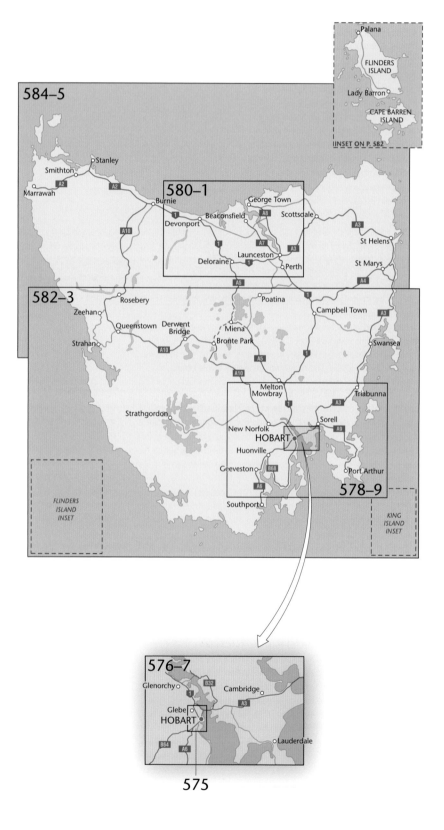

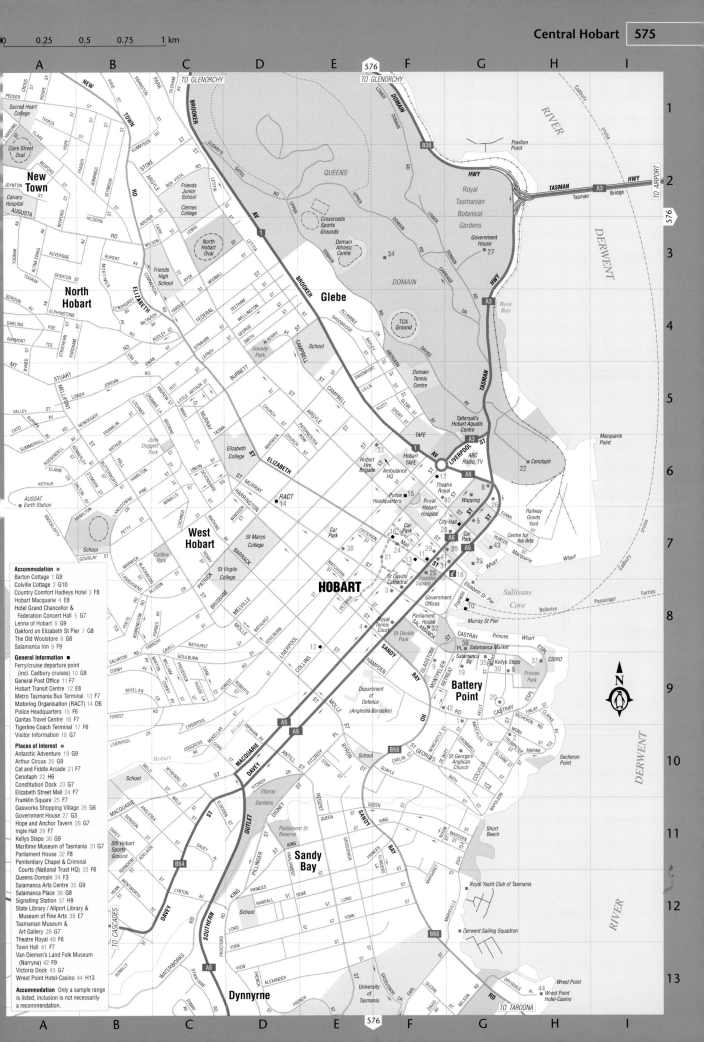

0   0.25   0.5   0.75   1 km

New Town

North Hobart

West Hobart

Glebe

HOBART

Battery Point

Sandy Bay

Dynnyrne

QUEENS DOMAIN

Royal Tasmanian Botanical Gardens

RIVER DERWENT

Accommodation ■
Barton Cottage 1 G9
Colville Cottage 2 G10
Country Comfort Hadleys Hotel 3 F8
Hobart Macquarie 4 E8
Hotel Grand Chancellor &
    Federation Concert Hall 5 G7
Lenna of Hobart 6 G9
Oakford on Elizabeth St Pier 7 G8
The Old Woolstore 8 G6
Salamanca Inn 9 F9

General Information ■
Ferry/cruise departure point
    (incl. Cadbury cruises) 10 G8
General Post Office 11 F7
Hobart Transit Centre 12 E8
Metro Tasmania Bus Terminal 13 F7
Motoring Organisation (RACT) 14 D6
Police Headquarters 15 F6
Qantas Travel Centre 16 F7
Tigerline Coach Terminal 17 F6
Visitor Information 18 G7

Places of Interest ■
Antarctic Adventure 19 G9
Arthur Circus 20 G9
Cat and Fiddle Arcade 21 F7
Cenotaph 22 H6
Constitution Dock 23 G7
Elizabeth Street Mall 24 F7
Franklin Square 25 F7
Gasworks Shopping Village 26 G6
Government House 27 G3
Hope and Anchor Tavern 28 G7
Ingle Hall 29 F7
Kellys Steps 30 G9
Maritime Museum of Tasmania 31 G7
Parliament House 32 F8
Penitentiary Chapel & Criminal
    Courts (National Trust HQ) 33 F6
Queens Domain 34 F3
Salamanca Arts Centre 35 G9
Salamanca Place 36 G8
Signalling Station 37 H9
State Library / Allport Library &
    Museum of Fine Arts 38 E7
Tasmanian Museum &
    Art Gallery 39 G7
Theatre Royal 40 F6
Town Hall 41 F7
Van Diemen's Land Folk Museum
    (Narryna) 42 F9
Victoria Dock 43 G7
Wrest Point Hotel-Casino 44 H13

Accommodation Only a sample range
is listed; inclusion is not necessarily
a recommendation.

TO GLENORCHY

TO CASCADES

TO TAROONA

University of Tasmania

Wrest Point
Hotel-Casino

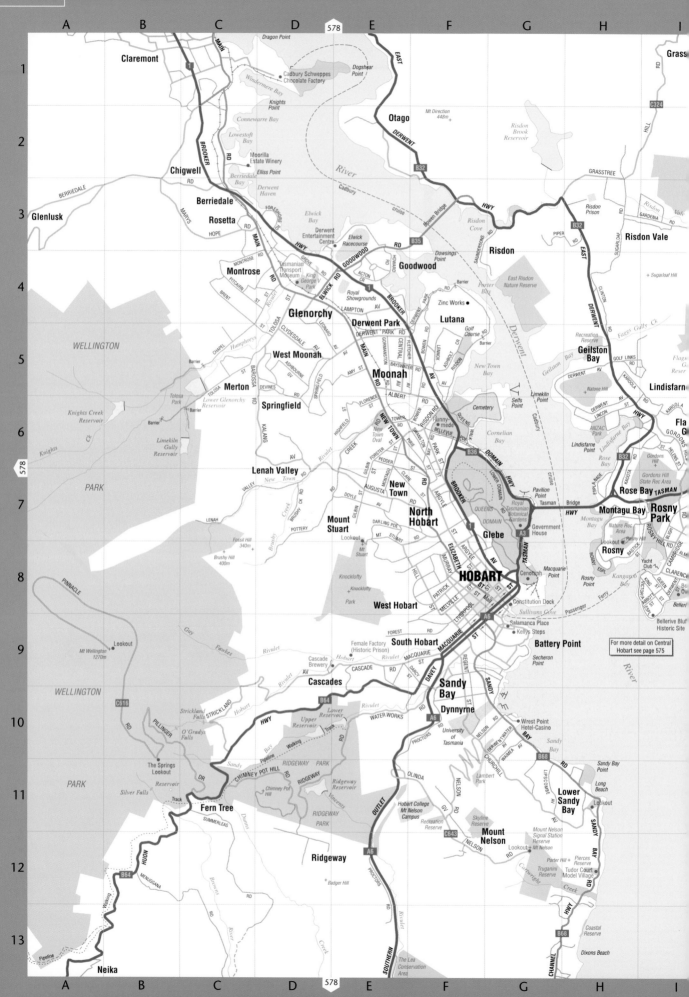

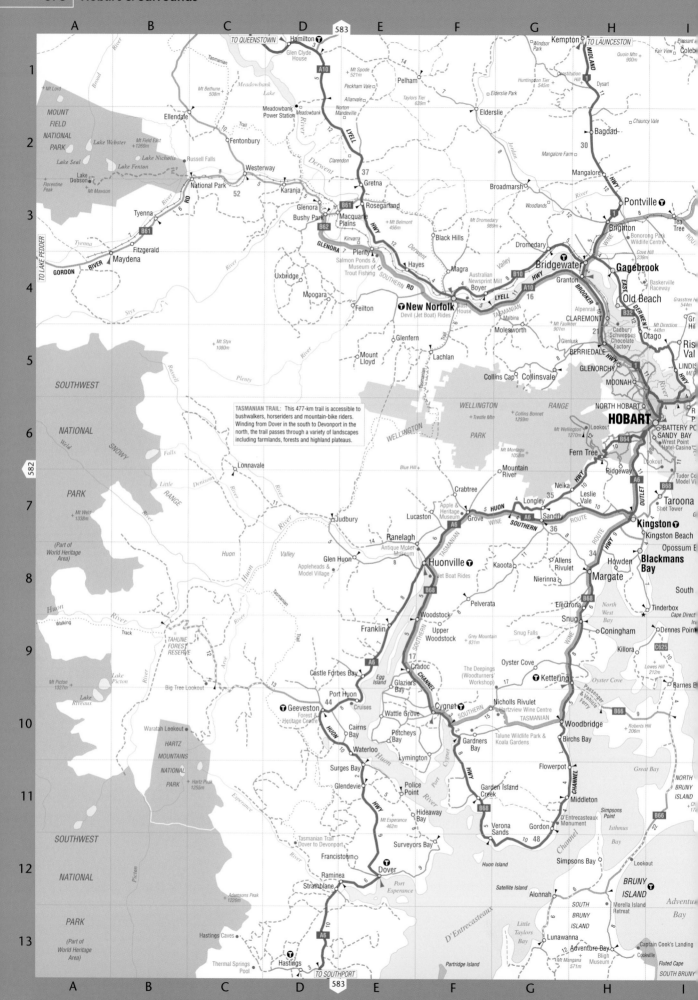

TASMANIAN TRAIL: This 477-km trail is accessible to bushwalkers, horseriders and mountain-bike riders. Winding from Dover in the south to Devonport in the north, the trail passes through a variety of landscapes including farmlands, forests and highland plateaus.

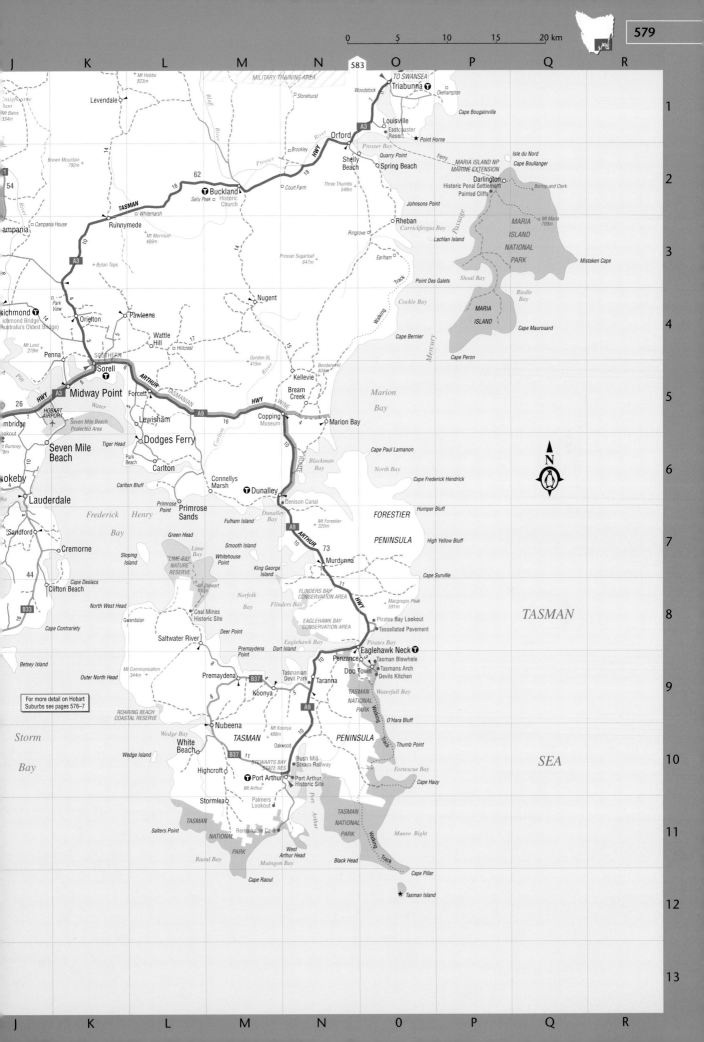

0   5   10   15   20 km

583

J   K   L   M   N   O   P   Q   R

MILITARY TRAINING AREA

Triaglbourne Dam

Mt Bains
334m

Levendale

+ Mt Hobbs
823m

Stonehurst

TO SWANSEA
Triabunna ⊤
Woodstock

Okehampton

Cape Bougainville

Brown Mountain
792m

Bluff River

A3

Louisville
Eastcoaster
Resort
★ Point Horne

ampania

Campania House

TASMAN

Runnymede

62

18

Buckland ⊤
Historic
Church

Sally Peak

Whitemarsh

Prosser River

HWY

18

Orford
Prosser Bay
Shelly
Beach

Quarry Point
Spring Beach

Ferry

MARIA ISLAND NP
MARINE EXTENSION

Isle du Nord
Cape Boullanger

54

Brockley

Court Farm

Three Thumbs
549m

Darlington
Historic Penal Settlement
Painted Cliffs

Bishop and Clerk

A3

10

Mt Morrison
469m

+ Byron Tops

14

Prosser Sugarloaf
647m

Rheban
Carrickfergus Bay

Lachlan Island
Johnsons Point

Mt Maria
709m

MARIA
ISLAND
NATIONAL
PARK

richmond
Richmond Bridge
(Australia's Oldest Bridge)

Park
View

Orielton

Pawleena

Nugent

14

Ringrove

Earlham

Point Des Galets

Shoal Bay

Mistaken Cape

4

Mt Lord
279m

Penna

Wattle
Hill

17

Hillcrest

SOUTHERN

15

Gordon SL
415m

Kellevie

Benders Hill
404m

Walking

Cape Bernier

MARIA
ISLAND

Cape Maurouard

Sorell ⊤

ARTHUR

Bream
Creek

HWY

Copping
Museum

4

Marion Bay

Marion
Bay

Cape Peron

Midway Point

A3
HWY

Forcett

TASMANIAN

A9

16

Carlton River

WINE

Cockle Bay

Cape Paul Lamanon

5

26

HOBART
AIRPORT

Lewisham

Dodges Ferry

10

Blackman
Bay

North Bay

Cape Frederick Hendrick

6

Seven Mile
Beach
Protected Area

Tiger Head

Park
Beach

Carlton

ROUTE

Seven Mile
Beach

Rumney

Carlton Bluff

Connellys
Marsh

Dunalley ⊤

Denison Canal

Humper Bluff

okeby

Lauderdale

Frederick
Bay

Henry

Primrose
Point

Primrose
Sands

Fulham Island

Dunalley
Bay

Mt Forestier
320m

FORESTIER

PENINSULA

High Yellow Bluff

7

Sandford

Cremorne

Green Head

Lime
Bay

Smooth Island

Whitehouse
Point

A9

ARTHUR

73

Murdunna

Cape Surville

TASMAN

8

44

Cape Deslacs

Clifton Beach

B33

16

Cape Contrariety

Sloping
Island

LIME BAY
NATURE
RESERVE

Mt Stewart
130m

King George
Island

Norfolk
Bay

Flinders Bay

11

FLINDERS BAY
CONSERVATION AREA

Macgregor Peak
591m

HWY

EAGLEHAWK BAY
CONSERVATION AREA

Pirates Bay Lookout
Tessellated Pavement

North West Head

Gwandalan

Coal Mines
Historic Site

Deer Point

Pirates Bay

Eaglehawk Neck ⊤

9

Betsey Island

Outer North Head

Mt Communication
344m

Saltwater River

Premaydena
Point

Dart Island

Eaglehawk Bay

Penzance
Doo Town

Tasman Blowhole
Tasmans Arch
Devils Kitchen

Premaydena

B37

Tasmanian
Devil Park

10

Taranna

Waterfall Bay

TASMAN

NATIONAL

O'Hara Bluff

Thumb Point

Koonya

5

A9

For more detail on Hobart
Suburbs see pages 576-7

ROARING BEACH
COASTAL RESERVE

8

Nubeena

TASMAN

Mt Koonya
488m

Oakwood

10

PENINSULA

Walking

Track

SEA

10

Storm

Bay

Wedge Bay

White
Beach

Wedge Island

B37

11

STEWARTS BAY
STATE RES

Bush Mill
Steam Railway

Fortescue Bay

Highcroft

Mt Arthur

Port Arthur ⊤
Port Arthur
Historic Site

Cape Hauy

Palmers
Lookout

TASMAN

NATIONAL

11

Stormlea

TASMAN
NATIONAL
PARK

Salters Point

Remarkable Cave

West
Arthur Head

PARK

Walking

Track

Munro Bight

Raoul Bay

Maingon Bay

Black Head

Cape Pillar

12

Cape Raoul

★ Tasman Island

13

J   K   L   M   N   O   P   Q   R

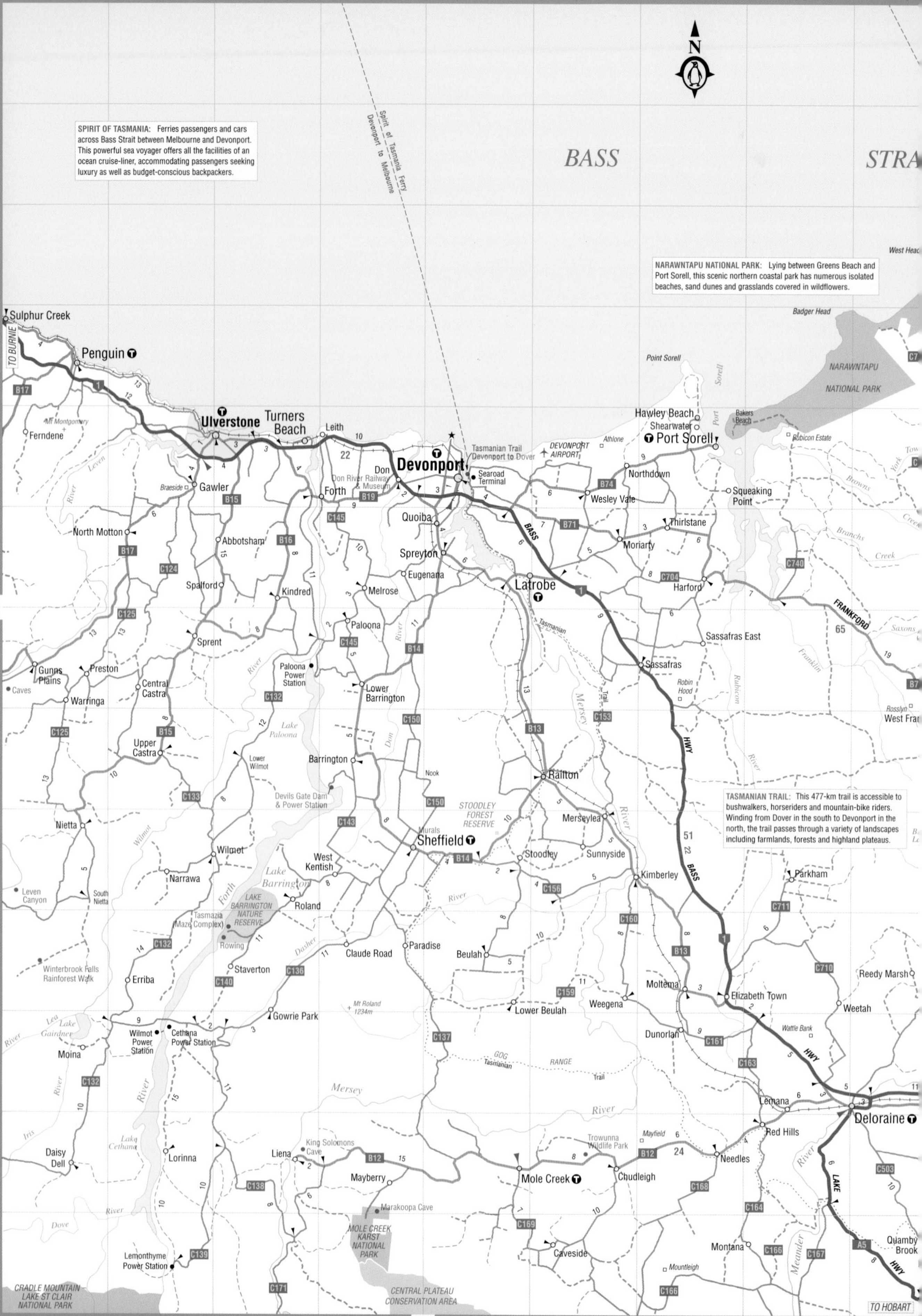

A B C D E F G H I

BASS **STRA**

N

SPIRIT OF TASMANIA: Ferries passengers and cars across Bass Strait between Melbourne and Devonport. This powerful sea voyager offers all the facilities of an ocean cruise-liner, accommodating passengers seeking luxury as well as budget-conscious backpackers.

Spirit of Tasmania Ferry Devonport to Melbourne

West Head

NARAWNTAPU NATIONAL PARK: Lying between Greens Beach and Port Sorell, this scenic northern coastal park has numerous isolated beaches, sand dunes and grasslands covered in wildflowers.

Badger Head

Sulphur Creek
Penguin
TO BURNIE
B17
Ferndene
Mt Montgomery
Ulverstone
Turners Beach
Leith
Point Sorell
NARAWNTAPU NATIONAL PARK
Hawley Beach
Shearwater
Port Sorell
Bakers Beach
Robicon Estate
C7

Devonport
Tasmanian Trail Devonport to Dover
DEVONPORT AIRPORT
Athlone
Don
Don River Railway Museum
Searoad Terminal
Northdown
Squeaking Point
B19
Forth
B74
Wesley Vale
North Motton
Gawler
B15
Quoiba
Thirlstane
Moriarty
C704
Harford
C740
Abbotsham
B16
Spreyton
Eugenana
Spalford
Braeside
C124
Kindred
Melrose
Latrobe
Sassafras East
FRANKFORD
65
Saxons
Sprent
C125
Paloona
B14
BASS
HWY
Sassafras
Robin Hood
Franklin
West Fran
B7
Gunns Plains
Preston
Central Castra
Paloona Power Station
C145
Lower Barrington
C150
B13
C153
Rosslyn
West Fran
Caves
Warringa
Upper Castra
B15
C132
Barrington
Lower Wilmot
Nook
Railton
Merseylea
TASMANIAN TRAIL: This 477-km trail is accessible to bushwalkers, horseriders and mountain-bike riders. Winding from Dover in the south to Devonport in the north, the trail passes through a variety of landscapes including farmlands, forests and highland plateaus.
Nietta
C133
Devils Gate Dam & Power Station
C143
STOODLEY FOREST RESERVE
C150
Murals
Sheffield
B14
Stoodley
Sunnyside
Kimberley
Parkham
Wilmot
West Kentish
C156
C160
C711
Narrawa
Lake Barrington
LAKE BARRINGTON NATURE RESERVE
Roland
Paradise
Beulah
B13
C710
Reedy Marsh
South Nietta
Leven Canyon
Tasmazia (Maze Complex)
Rowing
Claude Road
Moltema
Elizabeth Town
Weetah
Winterbrook Falls Rainforest Walk
Erriba
C132
C140
Staverton
C136
Gowrie Park
C159
Weegena
Lower Beulah
Dunorlan
C161
Wattle Bank
Moina
Wilmot Power Station
Cethana Power Station
Mt Roland 1234m
C137
GOG RANGE
Tasmanian Trail
C163
Lemana
Red Hills
Deloraine
Daisy Dell
Lorinna
Lake Cethana
Liena
King Solomons Cave
B12
Mayberry
Trowunna Wildlife Park
Mayfield
B12
Needles
LAKE HWY
C503
Lemonthyme Power Station
C139
Marakoopa Cave
MOLE CREEK KARST NATIONAL PARK
C169
Mole Creek
Chudleigh
C168
C164
Montana
C166
C167
Quamby Brook
A5 HWY
CRADLE MOUNTAIN LAKE ST CLAIR NATIONAL PARK
C171
Caveside
Mountleigh
C166
Meander River
TO HOBART
CENTRAL PLATEAU CONSERVATION AREA

A B C D E F G H

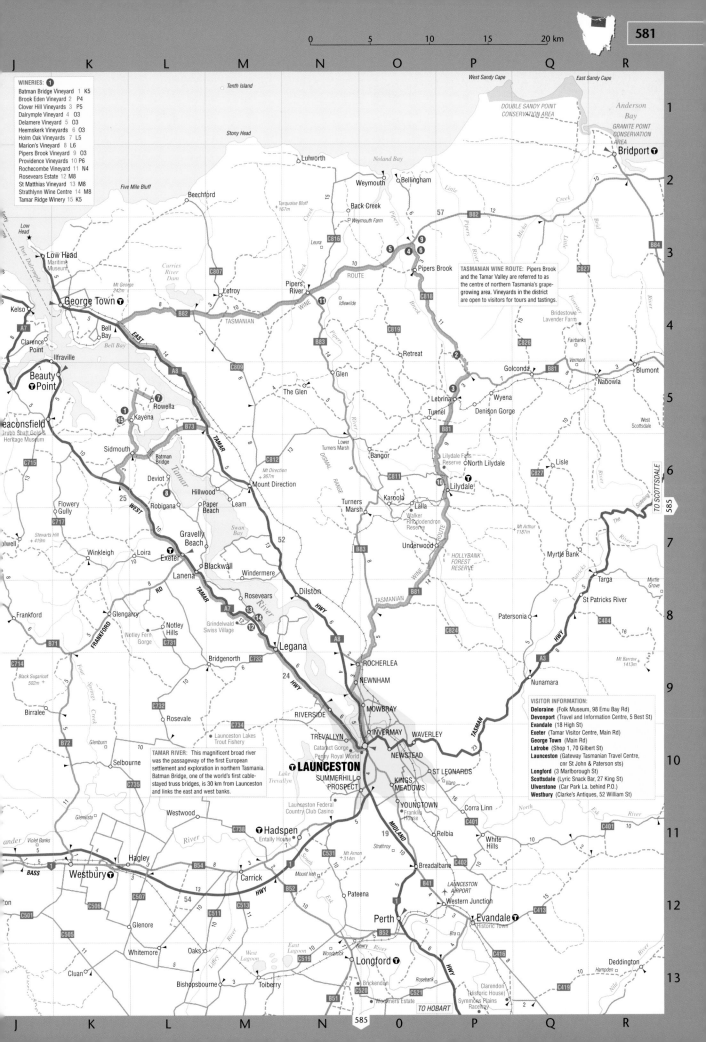

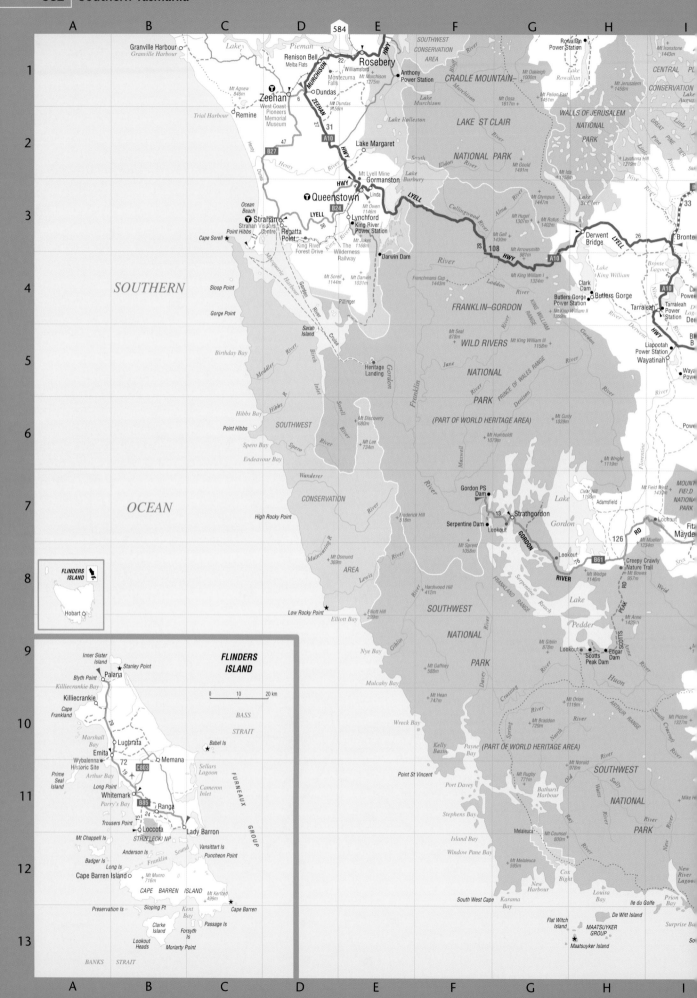

MAKING THE MOST OF YOUR TRIP

PLANNING AHEAD

There is much of Australia to see and many ways to see it. Today, even the most remote sections of this vast continent are accessible, particularly in 4WD vehicles designed for use on bush tracks and unmade roads.

For some, exploring Australia will mean touring the sealed highways and staying in motels, B&Bs and farmstays. Others will tow their accommodation behind them in the form of a caravan or camper trailer, and probably, as a result, stay mainly on sealed roads. Still others will opt for a mobile home with sleeping and cooking facilities, and yet another group, perhaps the true adventurers, will load a tent into the back of a 4WD and go bush. In all cases, some careful planning will greatly enhance the journey.

ADVANCE INFORMATION

Try to gather as much information as possible as far ahead of your planned departure as you can. Remember, the planning is half the fun. Research will confirm, or perhaps deny, your original choice of destination; it will also reveal ways and means, and problems where they exist. However, always bear in mind that although information sources are extensive, there is nothing like local on-the-spot knowledge.

The first places to obtain information are: State tourist bureaus and motoring organisations (see: Useful Information p. 591). They are excellent sources for travel brochures, regional maps and accommodation guides, and they usually have up-to-date knowledge of local conditions. For details of specific areas, these organisations can put you in touch with the appropriate tourist authority.

Travel agencies, airline travel centres and the main railway booking offices in each State can help if you are planning a fly/drive holiday, or intend to combine rail and motor travel.

HOW FAR AHEAD TO START

It can be a major disappointment to decide on a certain destination and then discover that motels, caravan parks and camping grounds in the area are booked out. In some regions at certain times of the year – Christmas, Easter, and school holiday periods – accommodation can be booked out a year in advance. When booking accommodation, always remember to allow enough time to travel comfortably to your destination. Your trip will lose a great deal of its charm if you have to rush from one point to the next (see: Itineraries p. 590).

While all popular destinations are likely to be busy at holiday peak times, some will be booked out around the time of special events: Melbourne at Melbourne Cup time, for example (see: Top Events in the capital city and touring region pages).

If you wish to go to a favourite hotel or try a special type of accommodation – a farmstay, a houseboat or B&B – book well ahead. And remember, a number of national parks require advance notice for camping permits.

WHEN TO GO

With a few exceptions you can travel Australia at any time of the year. The exceptions include parts of the Far North between November and April, that is, in the Wet, or tropical monsoon season (this applies particularly if you plan to use bush tracks and unmade roads, many of which are impassable for months). Tropical cyclones are random summer hazards between November and April. In the New South Wales and Victorian high country, from about May to August, many roads will be snow-bound. The Red Centre is not especially inviting in midsummer, when daytime temperatures can reach 45°C.

Great Ocean Road, Victoria, one of Australia's touring highlights

Otherwise, remember the holiday peaks. If you can avoid travelling during major holiday periods, do so.

WHICH WAY TO GO

If you flinch at the thought of driving seemingly endless kilometres, you should consider an alternative: both fly/drive packages and motor-rail facilities eliminate time-consuming travel and allow for concentration on areas of interest. Cost them against the expenses involved in using your own car for the entire trip.

Fly/drive Contact a travel agent or airline travel centre for advice and information on fly/drive packages.

Motor-rail For information on this easy way of covering long distances, contact the railway companies (see below). Inquire about discount fares; a reduction in rail fare is available on some interstate services if travel is booked and paid for in advance.

Great Southern Railway

Indian Pacific
Perth–Sydney–Perth
Crosses the continent from ocean to ocean; over the Blue Mountains and across the Nullarbor Plain. Two services a week each way: leaves Sydney Mon. and Thurs., leaves Perth Fri. and Mon.; 70 hours.
Perth–Adelaide–Perth
Two services a week each way: leaves

Adelaide Tues. and Fri., leaves Perth Mon. and Fri.; 43 hours. This service connects with *The Overland* to Melbourne.
The Overland
Melbourne–Adelaide–Melbourne
Daily, except Tues. Wed. & Sat., each way (overnight); 11 hours.
The Ghan
Sydney–Alice Springs–Sydney
Melbourne–Alice Springs–Melbourne
Adelaide–Alice Springs–Adelaide
A classic and adventurous journey. Travel in luxury across the outback, one service a week from Melbourne and Sydney, twice weekly from Adelaide in both directions; 45 hours, 35 hours and 18 hours respectively.

For all bookings and inquiries:
Great Southern Railway
Keswick Rail Passenger Terminal
PO Box 445
Marleston Business Centre, SA 5033
13 2147
www.gsr.com.au

Queensland Rail

The Queenslander
Brisbane–Townsville–Cairns–
Townsville–Brisbane
Operates March–December, one service a week each way: leaves Brisbane Sun., leaves Cairns Tues.; 31 hours.
Spirit of the Outback
Brisbane–Longreach–Brisbane
Two services a week each way: leaves Brisbane Tues. and Fri., leaves Longreach Thurs. and Sun.; 24 hours.

For all bookings and inquiries:
Queensland Rail
Ground Floor, 305 Edward St,
Brisbane 4001
(07) 3235 1323; Reservation Centre
13 2232
www.traveltrain.qr.com.au

Heritage Train Company

Great South Pacific Express
Timetables vary from month to month. Up-to-date times are listed on the website.
Sydney–Brisbane–Cairns/Kuranda–
Brisbane–Sydney
Includes side trip to Great Barrier Reef and Kuranda Skyrail. Generally, once a month each way.
Sydney–Brisbane–Sydney
Generally, two services a month each way: leaves Sydney Thurs.; leaves Brisbane Mon.; 22 hours.
Brisbane–Cairns/Kuranda–Brisbane
Two services a month each way: leaves Brisbane Mon., leaves Kuranda Wed.; 48 hours.

For all bookings and inquiries:
Heritage Train Company
33 Park Rd, Milton 4064
(07) 3247 6595; freecall 1800 000 395
www.orient-expresstrains.com

For information on passenger services contact the following State railway offices:
New South Wales
Countrylink Travel Centre
11–31 York St, Sydney 2000
13 2232
Victoria
V/Line Reservations and Information
Level 2, Transport House
589 Collins St, Melbourne 3000
13 6196
Western Australia
Westrail Centre
West Pde, East Perth 6000
(08) 9326 2222, 13 1053 (WA only)

OTHER TOURING POSSIBILITIES

Ferries to Tasmania *The Spirit of Tasmania I* and *II* passenger and car ferries make daily voyages across Bass Strait between Melbourne and Devonport. Bookings: TT Line Tasmania, 13 2010; or through your local Tasmanian Travel and Information Centre or travel agent.

Campervan rental Available in all States and most cities and major towns, the campervans are fully equipped and vary

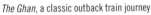
The Ghan, a classic outback train journey

in size and level of luxury. Costs vary accordingly, depending also on the season. There are often restrictions on where you can take a campervan, so check first.

Escorted group trips If you are interested in a full-on adventure tour, but are intimidated by the thought of doing it alone, motoring organisations and many private tour operators provide escorted group trips into more remote areas such as Cape York. These tag-along tours save you the worry of navigation and planning (except for preparing your vehicle) and also provide expert help and backup in case of a mechanical breakdown.

Other ideas You could leave your vehicle behind and tour in a 4WD coach, take a camel trek or try a canoe adventure – or travel almost any way you choose. Check with your travel agent or tourist bureau (**see:** Useful Information p. 591).

WHERE TO STAY
State motoring organisations, tourist bureaus and booksellers all have accommodation guides; some include information on camping and caravan parks. Travel agents and airline travel centres can also provide information.

Resorts, hotels and motels Contact the relevant State tourist bureau, motoring organisation (**see:** Useful Information p. 591), your travel agent or airline travel centre for details and bookings. Major motel chains, such as Best Western, Budget Motel Chain, Golden Chain and Flag Choice Hotels, cover most areas. Accommodation brochures are available from central booking offices.

Self-contained holiday units, cottages and apartments If you are planning a stay in a city or at any holiday destination for a length of time, this provides a sensible family alternative to motel or hotel accommodation. The relevant tourist bureau (**see:** Useful Information p. 591) will provide you with the details.

House-swapping This is yet another possibility for a lengthy stay. This can be arranged through home exchange organisations (see Accommodation Inquiry Services in the *Yellow Pages* telephone book). In addition, advertisements for those seeking a house-swapping holiday often appear in the classified sections of the newspapers. Make sure you are totally satisfied with the arrangements made concerning your commitments and that you are happy with the people with whom you are dealing. Also check that your householder's insurance covers you in such circumstances (**see:** Insurance p. 590).

Farmstays Such accommodation varies from spartan to luxurious and, in some cases, guests are invited to take part in farm life. State associations (**see:** Useful Information p. 591) or tourist authorities will provide details.

Bed and breakfast accommodation Contact Bed & Breakfast Australia (**see:** Useful Information p. 591) for information on B&B accommodation in homestay or farmstay environments throughout Australia.

Guesthouses This form of accommodation is currently making something of a comeback. Standards vary greatly – some guesthouses are magnificently renovated with modern amenities and excellent restaurants, while others are budget-style with shared bathrooms but plenty of charm.

Backpacker accommodation This type of accommodation is provided at budget rates in a communal environment and is becoming very popular, particularly among younger travellers. Note, however, that the accommodation offered is not always suitable for children. To obtain information on the range of accommodation available, contact VIP Backpackers Resorts of Australia (**see:** Useful Information p. 591). There are also over 100 youth hostels throughout Australia open to members and (for an additional fee) non-members. YHA accommodation is used by all age groups and rooms range from large dormitories to private rooms. For information, contact Australian YHA (**see:** Useful Information p. 591).

Floating accommodation If you are into staying afloat, consider hiring a houseboat on the Hawkesbury River or Eildon Weir, taking a paddlewheeler cruise on the Murray, or even chartering a yacht to cruise in the Whitsundays. Obtain details from your travel agent or the relevent State tourist bureau (**see:** Useful Information p. 591).

DIVIDING UP THE DOLLARS
Very few people can afford the 'money-no-object' approach to holidays, no matter what the length of stay. You will need principally to consider accommodation, food, fuel and entertainment, although emergency funds should not be forgotten. Travel insurance is a wise precaution (**see:** Insurance p. 590).

Accommodation Accommodation costs can be estimated when you book, but you might simply average the figure. If you do, estimate high rather than low.

Food This is a matter of personal choice: you may eat out every night or prepare all or some of your meals yourself. Allow for the unexpected, and for the

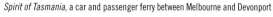
Spirit of Tasmania, a car and passenger ferry between Melbourne and Devonport

Exploring Victoria's rugged mountain terrain

higher cost of food and meals in popular holiday destinations or in remote areas. Remember to budget for snacks and treats, especially if you are travelling with children.

Fuel Once you know your vehicle's fuel consumption you can work out your fuel costs in advance. The usual method is based on litres per 100 kilometres. If your vehicle uses 16 litres per 100 kilometres and your journey distance works out at 5000 kilometres, you will use 50 times 16 litres of fuel, or 800 litres. Allow for rises in the cost of petrol and remember that fuel is more expensive in remote areas.

Entertainment and other costs When budgeting, allow for such 'budget biters' as admission charges, postcards, camera film, chemist's items, bridge/ferry tolls and car repairs. Remember also that accommodation, travel and rental charges rise during peak periods.

Carrying large amounts of cash with you is not a good idea, hence credit cards, EFTPOS and automatic teller machines are good alternatives (except in remote areas where some of these facilities may not be available). It is advisable to carry more than one card in case a card is 'eaten' by an ATM, or damaged.

CAR MAINTENANCE COURSES

If you plan to tour in remote areas, you should acquire basic mechanical knowledge and skills. In general you should have a broad understanding of the technology of your vehicle and know how much roadside repair is possible in the event of a breakdown (**see:** Breakdowns p. 602). You should also have some specific knowledge; for example how to change a tyre on the vehicle you will be using; and whether you can use jumper leads to start your car and if so, how it is done. Car care and basic car-maintenance courses are run by Adult Education centres, TAFE Colleges and motoring organisations in all States. Test your knowledge by reading through the Tools and Spare Parts list (p. 603) and Troubleshooting (p. 604).

INSURANCE

The benefits of a comprehensive insurance policy on your vehicle, caravan or trailer are obvious. As well as cover against loss or damage due to accident, theft and vandalism, your personal effects are covered against loss or damage when they are in the insured vehicle. Additional policies will cover such eventualities as, for example, the cost of temporary accommodation should your caravan become uninhabitable. Short-term travel insurance is available from several companies to cover loss of luggage or cancellation of accommodation bookings, etc. Information and advice can be obtained from the various motoring organisations (**see:** Useful Information p. 591), insurance companies and travel agents.

ITINERARIES

Some people make itineraries and stick to them; others do not. At the very least, a rough schedule to ensure a good mixture of travel and sightseeing time is essential. Build some flexibility into your plans. You never know what might detain you: the weather (frequent rest breaks are necessary in extreme heat), or children, who have a low tolerance for long periods without a break (**see:** Child's Play p. 607).

CLOTHING

Be strict with yourself and the family when you are packing and travel as lightly as you can. It is better to spend an hour at a laundromat than overburden your vehicle with clothing you probably will not wear.

Essentials are a warm jumper or jacket, even in summer; sensible, comfortable, closed shoes; and a wide-brimmed hat to protect yourself from the sun at all times. Carry items like swimwear, towels, spare socks and jumpers in a bag that can be kept within easy reach. Gumboots are a handy item also.

FIRST-AID KIT

A first-aid kit is essential. Include band-aids, bandages, headache tablets, extra blockout, insect repellent and a soothing lotion for bites. Eye drops are a good idea, as is a thermometer and a pressure bandage. Kits are available from various suppliers including St John Ambulance Australia, which also conducts basic courses in first aid. As carsickness is often a problem on long journeys, particularly with young children, include medication to counter this. Your chemist or a doctor will advise you.

USEFUL EXTRAS

Depending on the length and nature of your tour, some items are valuable, some essential (**see:** Tools and Spare Parts p. 603). Carry picnic and barbecue equipment, tissues, toilet paper and a container or plastic bag for rubbish (if there are no bins take it with you). Rugs or blankets are a necessary extra, as is a large sheet of plastic, which can be used as an emergency windscreen. Having a mobile phone may be useful if you are travelling within signal range; check the coverage before departure. If you are going to the outback, a necessary item is some type of shade cover, such as a tarpaulin, in case of an emergency stop (**see:** Outback Motoring p. 599).

USEFUL INFORMATION

TOURIST BUREAUS

New South Wales
New South Wales Visitor Information Line
13 2077
Sydney Visitor Centre
Sailors' Home, 106 George St,
The Rocks 2000
(02) 9255 1788
www.sydneyvisitorcentre.com
www.visitnsw.com.au

Australian Capital Territory
Canberra Visitors Centre
330 Northbourne Ave, Dickson 2602
(02) 6205 0044,
1800 100 660 (bookings)
www.canberratourism.com.au

Victoria
Melbourne Visitor Information Centre
Melbourne Town Hall
cnr Swanston and Little Collins sts,
Melbourne 3000
13 2842
www.visitvictoria.com

South Australia
South Australian Travel Centre
18 King William St, Adelaide 5000
(08) 8303 2099, 1300 655 276
www.tourism.sa.gov.au

Western Australia
WA Visitor Centre
cnr Forrest Pl. and Wellington St, Perth 6000
(08) 9483 1111, 1300 361 351
www.westernaustralia.net

Northern Territory
Northern Territory Tourist Commission
13 3068
www.ntholidays.com.au

Tourism Top End
cnr Mitchell and Knuckey sts, Darwin 0800
(08) 8936 2499, 1300 138 886
www.tourismtopend.com.au

Central Australian Tourism Industry Association
60 Gregory Tce,
Alice Springs 0870
(08) 8952 5800, 1800 645 199
www.centralaustraliantourism.com

Queensland
Tourism Queensland
Level 10, 30 Makerston St,
Brisbane 4000
13 8833
www.queensland-holidays.com.au

Tasmania
Tasmanian Travel and Information Centre
cnr Elizabeth and Davey sts, Hobart 7000
(03) 6230 8233
www.discovertasmania.com.au

MOTORING ORGANISATIONS

New South Wales
National Roads & Motorists'
Association (NRMA)
74–76 King St, Sydney 2000
13 2132

Australian Capital Territory
National Roads & Motorists'
Association (NRMA)
92 Northbourne Ave, Canberra 2601
13 2132

Victoria
Royal Automobile Club of Victoria (RACV)
422 Little Collins St, Melbourne 3000
13 1955

South Australia
Royal Automobile Association of SA (RAA)
41 Hindmarsh Sq., Adelaide 5000
(08) 8202 4600

Western Australia
Royal Automobile Club of WA (RAC)
228 Adelaide Tce, Perth 6000
13 1111 (WA only)

Northern Territory
Automobile Association of NT (AANT)
AANT Building
79–81 Smith St, Darwin 0800
(08) 8981 3837

Queensland
Royal Automobile Club of Queensland (RACQ)
300 St Pauls Tce, Fortitude Valley 4006
13 1905

Tasmania
Royal Automobile Club of Tasmania (RACT)
cnr Patrick and Murray sts, Hobart 7000
(03) 6232 6300, 13 2722 (Tasmania only)

For Motorcyclists
Motorcycle Riders' Association of Australia
22 Ross St, South Melbourne 3205
(03) 9699 1811; Fax: (03) 9699 1833
www.mraa.org.au

ACCOMMODATION

Bed & Breakfast Australia
29 Burlington Rd Homebush 2140
(02) 9763 5833; Fax: (02) 9763 1677
www.bedandbreakfast.com.au

Farmstays
Australia-wide/New South Wales
Australian Farm Host Holidays Pty Ltd
Suite 87, 24 Buchanan St,
Balmain 2041
(02) 9810 0800; Fax: (02) 9810 3233
www.australiafarmhost.com.au

Victoria
Farm & Country Tourism Victoria
Level M2, 525 Collins St, Melbourne 3000
(03) 9614 0892; Fax: (03) 9620 3577
www.factv.com

South Australia
SA Farm and Country Holidays Inc.
3 Devon St, South Brighton 5048
(08) 8296 3617

Queensland
Australian Holidays
1/130 Bundall Rd, Bundall 4217
1800 351 572; Fax: (07) 5574 1533

VIP Backpackers Resorts of Australia
3/41 Steel Pl., Morningside 4170
(07) 3395 6111

Australian YHA
422 Kent St, Sydney 2000
(02) 9261 1111
www.yha.com.au

VEHICLE STANDARDS AUTHORITIES

New South Wales
Vehicle Registration Branch
Roads and Traffic Authority
Centennial Plaza, 260 Elizabeth St,
Surry Hills 2010
13 2213, 1800 624 384
www.rta.nsw.gov.au

Australian Capital Territory
Road User Services
Department of Urban Services
13–15 Challis St, Dickson 2602
(02) 6207 7000
www.urbanservices.act.gov.au

Victoria
Road Safety Department, VicRoads
60 Denmark St, Kew 3101
(03) 9854 2666
www.vicroads.vic.gov.au

South Australia
Vehicles Unit, Transport SA
EDS Bldg, 108 North Tce, Adelaide 5000
13 1084
www.transport.sa.gov.au

Western Australia
Department of Transport
441 Murray St, Perth 6000
13 1156 (WA only), (08) 9216 8000
www.transport.wa.gov.au

Northern Territory
Motor Vehicle Registry
Department of Transport and Infrastructure
GPO Box 2520, Darwin 0801
(08) 8999 5511
www.nt.gov.au/dtw/

Queensland
Queensland Transport
GPO Box 673, Fortitude Valley 4006
13 2380 (Qld only), (07) 3834 2011
www.transport.qld.gov.au

Tasmania
Transport Division
Department of Infrastructure,
Energy and Resources
10 Murray St, Hobart 7000
1300 135 513; Fax: (03) 6233 5223
www.transport.tas.gov.au

EMERGENCY (for all States)
Police, ambulance and fire brigade,
dial 000. If using a mobile, dial 112.

OTHER INFORMATION

PETS

Leaving them behind

- Pet care services (see *Yellow Pages* telephone book): provide care of pets in their own environment. They will also care for plants and property, etc.
- Dog boarding kennels and catteries (see *Yellow Pages*): provide care and accommodation. Some have pickup and delivery services.
- Animal welfare organisations and veterinary surgeons (see *Yellow Pages*): for advice and information.

Taking them with you

- Make sure, in advance, that the accommodation or mode of travel permits animals. Many caravan parks and most national parks do not admit pets.
- During the trip, carry additional water and stop at regular intervals for toileting and exercise.
- Do not leave an animal unattended in a vehicle for any length of time; always provide fresh air.
- Allow sufficient room in the vehicle to comfortably accommodate the animal.
- Do not transport an animal in a moving caravan.
- Consider purchasing a dog harness for your vehicle to protect yourself and the animal in case of sudden braking.
- See *Holidaying with Dogs*, published by Life. Be In It, for more suggestions.

BEFORE DEPARTURE

- Cancel newspapers, mail deliveries.
- Make arrangements for the garden to be watered and lawns mowed. Board out your indoor plants or place them in the sink, surround with damp peat and water thoroughly. Encasing each pot in a sealed polythene bag also helps retain moisture.
- If you have a pet, arrange for its safekeeping well in advance.
- Arrange for a neighbour to keep an eye on the house. Alternatively, consult a professional home security service (see *Yellow Pages*).

- Valuable items, such as jewellery, are best left for safekeeping at a bank safe deposit.
- Turn the electricity off at the mains and leave the fridge door open. If you have equipment that must operate in your absence, for example a stocked freezer, leave power on and remove plugs from all other power points. Make sure that everything else that should be turned off is off.
- Check that all windows and doors are locked; then check again.
- Always leave a contact address with a friend or neighbour.

CARRYING A CAMERA

You probably will want to preserve the highlights of your trip on film. Check the following points:

- If you have recently bought a camera, take at least one test film before departure so that you know how the equipment reacts to different light conditions.
- As weather conditions may vary, it is a good idea to carry film with a range of speeds. If you are not an expert, talk to your local dealer about the varieties of film available.
- Before you leave, have a good supply of film, fresh batteries and a lens brush. Other useful accessories are a close-up lens, lens hood, filters and a tripod.
- Keep your equipment in a plastic bag inside a camera bag to protect it from water, heat, sand and dust. It can get very hot in a closed car, so always keep the camera in the shade. The best place is on the floor, on the side opposite the exhaust pipe. Make sure, however, that the bag cannot rattle around.
- High temperatures and humidity can damage colour film. Store your film in the coolest spot available and do not break the watertight vapour seal until just before use. Once the film is used, remove from the camera and mark with an E for 'exposed'.
- When using the camera in bright conditions, even with automatic

exposure, it may be necessary to allow one stop or half of a stop down to compensate for the brilliance of the light. If in doubt, consult the instruction sheet included with the film.
- Check that your personal property insurance covers the loss of cameras and photographic equipment while travelling (**see:** Insurance p. 590).

TIME ZONES

Australia has 4 time zones:

- Eastern Standard Time (EST), in Queensland, Australian Capital Territory, New South Wales, Victoria and Tasmania. (Note: Broken Hill, in central western New South Wales, operates on CST, half an hour behind the rest of New South Wales.)
- Central Standard Time (CST is half an hour behind EST), in South Australia and Northern Territory.
- Western Standard Time (WST is 2 hours behind EST), in Western Australia.
- Central Western Time (CWT is 45 minutes ahead of WST), a local time zone operating from 3 km east of Caiguna in Western Australia to the South Australian border.

Daylight saving is adopted by some States in summer. In New South Wales, Victoria, Tasmania, Australian Capital Territory and South Australia, clocks are put forward 1 hour at the beginning of summer (the last Sunday in October, except in Tasmania, where the clocks are adjusted on the first Sunday in October). Northern Territory, Western Australia and Queensland do not have daylight saving.

QUARANTINE REGULATIONS

Throughout Australia, State quarantine regulations prohibit the transport by travellers of certain plants and foods, and even soil, across designated borders. Further information is available from offices of agricultural departments in all States.

Aboriginal Land

Tnorala (Gosse Bluff), on Aboriginal land west of Alice Springs

Aboriginal land is privately owned. In some parts of Australia, Commonwealth and State laws do not permit people to enter Aboriginal land unless they have been issued with a permit.

Like other landowners in Australia, Aboriginal people have the legal right to grant or refuse permission to people wishing to enter or travel through their land. The permit system is also designed to help protect the privacy of Aboriginal communities, preserve Aboriginal culture, safeguard the natural environment and promote visitor safety. Unauthorised entry to Aboriginal land can result in fines of up to $1000.

Typically, there are three kinds of permits applicable to travel through Aboriginal land: transit, entry, or extended entry permits. A transit permit allows travel through Aboriginal land on designated roads, but camping and off-road access are prohibited. An entry permit allows entry to a designated area of Aboriginal land or an Aboriginal community for a specific purpose and period of time. An extended entry permit allows entry for an extended period up to one year (usually for work purposes).

It should be noted that, as a general rule, land councils have been asked by traditional owners not to issue entry permits for unaccompanied tourist travel. This does not affect visitors travelling on organised tours on to Aboriginal land where tour bookings include the necessary permit.

If there is a likelihood of a need to enter Aboriginal land for any reason, including fuel, travellers should seek permits from the relevant land councils. When making an application for entry to any Aboriginal land, applicants must state the reason for entry, dates and duration of intended stay, names of persons travelling, vehicle details, and itinerary and routes to be used while on these lands. Permits can be issued only after consultation and approval of traditional owners and relevant Aboriginal communities. Processing entry permit applications can take up to four weeks, while transit permits are normally processed within a few days.

All public roads that cross Aboriginal land are exempt from the permit requirements; the exemption covers the immediate road corridor only. If travellers are unsure about the status of roads on which they are driving, they should seek advice from the land councils before departure. Some towns within Aboriginal land are also exempt from the provisions.

The relevant land councils, to whom applications for permits and any inquiries must be directed, are:

Northern Territory
Alice Springs & Tennant Creek regions
Central Land Council
31–33 Stuart Hwy
Alice Springs NT 0871
(08) 8951 6211
Web site www.clc.org.au

Darwin, Nhulunbuy & Katherine regions
Northern Land Council
9 Rowling St
Casuarina NT 0810
(08) 8920 5100
Web site www.nlc.org.au

Melville & Bathurst islands
Tiwi Land Council
Unit 5, 3 Bishop St
Stuart Park NT 0820
(08) 8981 4898

Western Australia
Aboriginal Lands Trust
Level 1, 197 St Georges Tce
Perth WA 6850
(08) 9235 8000
Web site www.aad.wa.gov.au

Queensland
Queensland Aboriginal Coordinating Council
17 Aplin St
Cairns QLD 4870
(07) 4044 2999
Web site www.accq.org.au

South Australia
Anangu Pitjantjatjaraku Yankuytjatjara Land Council
PMB Umuwa
via Alice Springs NT 0872
(08) 8950 1511

Have a Good Trip

CHECKING THE CAR

All the care that you devote to your own comfort can be for nothing if you do not make sure that the car checks out too.

For a one-, two- or three-day tour, you could simply fuel up, check the tyre pressures, clean all the windows and head off; if you maintain your vehicle at all times in reasonable condition – as indeed you should – probably little further preparation is required. However, a vacation of a week or more, or journey involving long-distance driving, will need more thorough preparation. If you plan to travel through remote areas, for example, you should first check that your vehicle is able to handle off-road conditions. The service department of your State motoring organisations (**see:** Useful Information p. 591) will give advice and will make a preliminary inspection of your vehicle.

Regardless of the length of your tour, you should check the wheel brace, jack and under-vehicle jacking points, in case you have to change a tyre.

Unless you are able to service your vehicle yourself, this preparation should be left to your mechanic. To avoid breakdowns and to confirm the reliability of safety-related items, ask the mechanic to include a check of the fuel supply, electrics, brakes, tyres and certain ancillary equipment, as follows.

Fuel supply Check fuel pump for flow. Check carburettor for wear and potential blockages or check condition of electronic or mechanical fuel injection. When the tank is almost empty, remove the drain plug and drain the tank to check that the remaining fuel is perfectly clean. Check fuel-supply lines for cracks and poor connections, and make sure no fuel line is exposed to damage by rocks or low-clearance projections.

Electrics Check battery output and condition (including terminals), alternator/generator output and condition, spark plugs, condenser, coil, distributor and all terminals and cables. If the vehicle is fitted with electronic ignition it should be carefully checked in the prescribed manner.

Lights Check all lights, not just to see that they work, but to make sure that they are aligned correctly and are likely to continue working. It can be extremely dark at night in outback Australia.

Brakes Check wear of pads and/or linings, check discs for runout and drums for scoring. Brake dust should be cleaned off. Check brake lines and hoses for cracks and wear. Make sure brake lines are not liable to be damaged by rocks or low projections. Check parking brake for adjustment and cable stretch.

Tyres Check for uneven or excessive wear. Check walls for cracks and stone or kerb fractures. Check pressures. Include spare (or spares) in all checks. Make sure that the spare wheel matches those on the car, and uses the same kind of wheel nuts.

Windscreen-wiper blades Check for wear and proper contact, and check washers for direction and effectiveness. Include rear wiper and washer, where fitted.

Windscreen glass Check for cracks and replace if necessary.

Seat mountings and adjustments Check.

Lubricant levels Check (including brake and clutch fluid) and either top up or drain and refill.

Wheel bearings Check for play and adjust or replace.

Universal and constant velocity joints Check and replace if necessary.

Dust and water sealing A pre-run test in appropriate conditions will reveal any problems. What you do not need is dust, exhaust fumes or water inside the vehicle.

Roof-rack Check mounts and welds for weaknesses and cracks.

Seatbelts Check for tears or sun-hardening. Replace if necessary. Also check inertia reels.

Radiator water level and condition Check; drain and flush if necessary. Check

Location of engine parts required for checking fluid levels

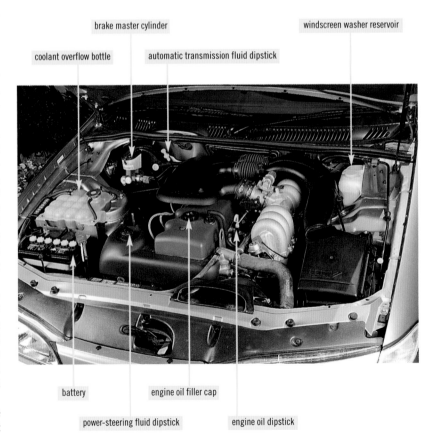

brake master cylinder

windscreen washer reservoir

coolant overflow bottle

automatic transmission fluid dipstick

battery

engine oil filler cap

power-steering fluid dipstick

engine oil dipstick

radiator for leaks and radiator pressure cap for pressure release accuracy. Check water-pump operation. Check radiator and heater hoses for cracks and general condition, and replace if necessary. Check hose clamps.

Fanbelt Check for tension and fraying.

All this should be done as near as practicable to your departure date. Allow time for unexpected work or part replacement, and for a return to the garage if a particular problem persists. Note: *Nothing should be overlooked – lives may be at stake.*

PACKING THE CAR

First and most important, you should limit the items carried in the passenger compartment to include only the necessities. In a sedan this is not difficult. You have a boot, and that is where most items should be carried; but in a station wagon it is much more difficult and some planning is required. Loose items in the passenger compartment get under your feet (especially hazardous for the driver), interfere with your comfort and become dangerous projectiles if you have a collision. So for your station wagon, buy or rig up a safety net, which can be fitted behind the rear seat to separate you from the objects that could otherwise harm you.

This rule applies also to food and drink. Empty bottles and cartons should be stowed out of the way in a rubbish bag until you are able to dispose of them properly.

In order to provide extra space, many drivers fix a roof-rack to their vehicle. This is not recommended. Laden roof-racks upset the balance of the vehicle by changing its centre of gravity, making it top-heavy. They disturb the air flow, which can destabilise the vehicle, and they certainly increase fuel consumption by interfering with the aerodynamics. In some circumstances they can snag on overhanging limbs of trees.

If you must use a roof-rack, carry as little on it as possible and keep the maximum loading height as low as you can. Protect the load by wrapping it in a tarpaulin or groundsheet and, if possible, create a sharp (aerofoil) leading edge on the load to improve air flow.

A good alternative to a roof-rack is a small, strong, lightweight trailer, but there are times when towing will be a disadvantage, so you need to consider the terrain.

If you are towing a caravan, some items can be carried inside the van on the floor, preferably strapped down (anything loose will be flung about) and located over the axle (or axles). In some States, caravans must be fitted with a fire extinguisher. And remember, no people or animals are to be transported in a towed caravan.

Once your vehicle is loaded, and preferably with the passengers aboard, check the tyre pressures (yes, even as you leave home on day one). The additional load will mean higher pressures are needed. The tyre placard or owner's handbook can be used as a guideline. The tyre will bag if it is under-inflated and destabilise the car. It also will offer a baggy sidewall to rocks and stones, encouraging wall fractures and potential blowouts. Laden-tyre pressure requirements vary with tyre size and design, but the pressure is important. If in any doubt contact the tyre manufacturer.

WHEN TO SET OFF

There is evidence to suggest that people drive best during the hours in which they are accustomed to being awake, and probably at work. As drowsiness is deadly in drivers, this is worth noting. Leaving home, for example at 1 a.m., might avoid the heat of the day and beat the traffic to a large extent, but somewhere between 3 and 5 a.m. you are likely to find yourself wanting to doze off again.

Plan to share long-distance driving as much as possible. Depart around or just before sunrise and stop no later than sundown. Allow regular stops, not just to stretch your legs but to take nourishment as well. Food helps keep the energy levels up. You might care to leave later if you are travelling east, to avoid the rising sun shining in your eyes, and finish earlier if you are travelling west, for the converse reason.

LEAVING HOME

Everyone knows the feeling that usually comes when you are a good distance from home: did I lock all the windows, turn off the electricity at the meter, cancel the newspaper and mail delivery? Usually all is well, but it is reassuring to double-check everything before you leave (**see:** Before Departure p. 592).

An early start at Bright, Victoria

BETTER DRIVING

In skilful driving, the two most important ingredients are concentration and smoothness.

Concentration Find a comfortable position and stay comfortable; discomfort destroys concentration. Lack of concentration is the biggest single cause of road accidents.

Wear the right clothes: loose-fitting, cool or warm as appropriate, but capable of being changed (not while you are driving!) as temperatures change. Lightweight shoes are better than boots. Wear good quality antiglare sunglasses. Sit comfortably: neither too close to the steering wheel and cramped, nor too far back and stretching; and be sure you can reach the foot controls through the entire length of their movement. Drive with both hands all the time. No one can control a car properly with one hand. Driving gloves are recommended. Make all seat, belt and rear-view mirror adjustments before you drive off (particularly if you share the driving with someone who is not your size).

Concentration means *no distractions*. It is probably unrealistic to suggest that no conversation takes place while you are driving, but do not allow conversations to interfere with your concentration. Aim to keep the children quiet and amused (**see:** Child's Play p. 607). If an important issue needs to be resolved, first stop the car and then sort it out.

Smoothness Smoothness is vital for the vehicle's safe, effective operation, but unfortunately many people are not smooth drivers. A vehicle in motion is a tonne or so of iron, steel and plastic sitting atop a set of springs. It is inherently unstable and prone to influences such as pitch and roll. This is difficult enough to control in normal motion, but worse when the driver exaggerates these instabilities by stabbing at the brakes, jerking the steering wheel and crashing the gears. Two things derive from being a smooth driver. The first is passenger comfort; on a long trip, everyone will arrive much fresher and more relaxed if the driver has provided a smooth and therefore pleasant journey. The second is increased safety; the vehicle will react better to smooth driving than it will to ham-fisted driving. Smooth driving

Take extra care on icy roads

brings even further benefits: less wear and tear and lower fuel consumption.

However, to define better driving as a combination of concentration and smoothness only would not be wholly accurate. There are other factors:

Know your vehicle Understand its breaking capacities, especially in emergencies – some cars move around a lot, or become directionally unstable under harsh braking. Be aware of its useable power and its limitations. And drive well within the cornering and road-holding limits of the vehicle's suspension and tyre combination.

Drive defensively It is worth assuming that a proportion of road users are inattentive or devoid of skill. It is remarkable how your driving awareness is increased by such an attitude.

Do not be impatient Advance planning should have provided you with ample time for the day's journey.

Do not drive with an incapacitating illness or injury Something as simple as a bruised elbow might restrict rapid arm movement when you most need it.

DRIVING EMERGENCIES
Of course, the best way to handle emergencies is to avoid them. However, to suggest that one problem or another will never occur is unrealistic. A course in defensive driving is an advantage; contact your local motoring organisation to obtain more information (**see:** Useful Information p. 591).

Skidding The possibility of skidding worries most drivers, as well it should. There are a number of causes of a skid, some of them composite. Essentially, skidding occurs when the tyres lose their grip on the road.

The most common form is a front-wheel (or sometimes all-wheel) skid caused by over-braking. When the wheels stop rolling, the vehicle will no longer react to steering input. If you avoid jumping on the brake pedal (that is, drive smoothly) you will avoid this type of skid. However if you do skid, quickly ease just sufficient pressure off the brake pedal to allow the wheels to roll again. The steering will come back, which at least will allow you to take avoiding action as well as to slow down.

A rear-wheel skid also may occur as a result of harsh braking, usually while turning at the same time (for example if corner entry speed is too high, or braking too harsh). In slippery conditions the tail of the car may also fishtail because you have entered a corner too fast or, in rear-wheel drive vehicles, because too much power has been applied too soon, causing the rear tyres to break traction. A rear-wheel skid of any kind requires some reverse steering, often only briefly. It is not enough to advise turning the steering in the direction of the skid: the question is, by how much? Turn the steering wheels to point them in the direction you wish to travel and, at the same time, try to recognise what you did to cause the skid in the first place. If it was because of excessive acceleration, back off a little and re-apply the accelerator more gently. If it was because you entered the corner too fast or because of your braking (or both at the same time), ease the brakes and let your corrective steering realign the car and then, smoothly, increase the power again by gently applying the accelerator.

Skids can be complex and difficult to control. Over-correction is common, with the result that the vehicle swings into another skid in the opposite direction. It is important not to panic, and to be smooth in your reaction. Easy to say – not so easy to do!

Aquaplaning This is a form of skidding where the tyres roll a layer of water up in front of the vehicle and then ride on to it, breaking contact with the road surface. What you sense is a sudden loss of driving 'feel'. Slow down, very smoothly, until the tyres come off the layer of water

and then proceed more carefully. Watch out for deep puddles: they are the danger.

Driving in snow, ice and mud also produces adhesion problems. Once again, smooth, steady progress, while 'feeling' the vehicle and staying on top of its movements, is the only answer.

Icy roads For a visit to the snow, your vehicle should be fitted with chains. If it is not and the car's back wheels begin to spin wildly on packed and rutted snow or ice:
• Stop the car.
• Look for and remove any obstructions under the car.
• Pack loose gravel, sticks or vegetation under the driving wheels.
• Remember that on a level surface a gentle push sometimes will get the car moving again.

Because it cannot be seen, ice can be more dangerous than snow.

Foggy conditions When driving in fog:
• Switch on dipped headlights, or fog-lights if your car is fitted with them.
• Use front and back demisters.
• If visibility is reduced to such an extent that driving becomes an ordeal, pull as far off the road as you can, switch on your emergency lights and wait until the fog lifts and you feel able to continue.

The advice in this section applies equally to driving in the cities and in the outback. The techniques are the same; only the conditions vary (**see:** Outback Motoring p. 599, for more detail on driving in the outback).

SAFE DRIVING

BASIC TRAFFIC LAWS

In December 1999, Australia's State and Territory governments introduced uniform national road rules. Changes to existing legislation in each State and Territory were implemented in March 2000. A number of rules that involve linemarking, signage and other physical changes will be phased in over several years as part of regular maintenance work.

It is important to note that some rules will still vary to suit local conditions. One example is the undefined speed limit outside some town areas in the Northern Territory. Another is the unique hook turn in the centre of Melbourne, necessitated by the concentration of trams – at specified intersections a vehicle making a right-hand turn must move to the far left of the intersection and wait until the traffic clears and the traffic lights change to green on the road that the vehicle is entering before completing the turn. Overtaking on the right of a tram is forbidden and no vehicle may pass a stationary tram at a recognised tram stop.

For more information on road rules and State/Territory differences, contact your local motoring organisation (**see:** Useful Information p. 591) or access the National Road Transport Commission website, www.nrtc.gov.au.

IN CASE OF ACCIDENT

In all States of Australia, any accident in which someone is injured or killed must be reported to

police at once, or within 24 hours. In Western Australia, all car accidents must be reported if damage exceeds $1000, if drugs or alcohol are involved, or if there is any dispute.

It is highly advisable to report to the nearest police station any accident that involves substantial property damage, especially if you are unable to report to the property owner. Police may or may not decide to attend the scene, but they at least will have your report on record, which may well be useful should there be legal proceedings or insurance claims.

When involved in an accident, you *must* produce your driver's licence to police upon request. If you do not have it with you, you may be liable for an on-the-spot fine.

It is advisable to obtain the insurance details of the other parties involved in the accident. You should also exchange names, addresses, and vehicle registration details. Do not volunteer any other information. In particular, do not discuss the accident. Should court action result, you may find something said in the stress of the aftermath of the accident used against you. Above all, do not admit you are at fault in any way.

You are not obliged to make a statement to police. If you are disturbed and upset, wait until you can think clearly.

An accident that involves damage to persons or property should be reported to your insurance company as soon as possible.

POSITIONING

Positioning is vital on any road.
• Try to stagger the position of your car in the line of traffic so that you can see well ahead.

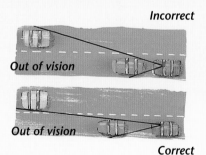

Incorrect

Out of vision

Out of vision

Correct

• When turning right on a two-lane highway, do not angle the car; keep it square to the other traffic so that cars can pass on the left.

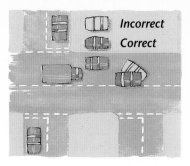

Incorrect

Correct

TOWING

Towing your accommodation behind you will provide the advantage of low-budget touring and flexibility with stopovers. It can be a disadvantage also, in that it may restrict access to some areas. You can, however, use the caravan for most sections of your journey and park it in a safe place while you go off in the car and explore the more difficult tracks.

Obtain advice If you are new to towing, the first thing you must do is contact the local vehicle standards authority (**see:** Useful Information p. 591) for advice on your towing hitch and information on towing regulations. It is very important that the rig (that is, car plus caravan, boat or trailer) is balanced and the weight over the tow ball is not excessive. An adjustable height hitch with spring bars is best.

Touring near the Hamersley Range in Western Australia

Learn to reverse Once you have decided on the hitch and you have learned how to hook up and unhook, you must learn to reverse the rig. Find a wide open area, an empty car park for example, and practise. Get the feel of the rig and become proficient at reversing before you depart.

Allow for added length On the road, remember to make allowances for the added overall length and give yourself extra space for turning and extra distance for overtaking. The added weight will obviously affect the towing vehicle's performance with regard to acceleration and braking: both will be slower.

Know the speed limit High-speed towing of vans and trailers can cause major difficulties, magnifying driving problems substantially. Contact the local vehicle standards authority for information on speed limits (**see:** Useful Information p. 591).

Avoid trailer sway Crosswinds can be a problem when towing a caravan; the van's slab sides act like sails. The combination of high speed and crosswinds can cause trailer sway, a dangerous characteristic that dramatically destabilises both towing vehicle and caravan. You probably will feel it happening before you see it, but

checking in the rear-view mirrors will confirm it. Should the trailer begin to move about, ease back on your speed, braking if necessary, but very gently. Harsh or sudden braking will compound the problem. When the caravan stabilises, resume speed, perhaps very gradually if you are continuing in a crosswind area.

Fit good-quality towing mirrors on your vehicle It is very important that your rear view down both sides of the trailer or caravan is not obscured.

Be courteous If, because of the relative slowness of your progress, you observe in the rear-view mirror a line of vehicles banking up behind you, be courteous and pull over when and where you can, to allow vehicles to overtake.

Locate load correctly The carrying of goods and equipment in a caravan has been mentioned, but it is worth repeating that such items should be located as much as possible over and just to the front of the caravan axle (or axles); never behind, as this will lift the front of the caravan and the tow ball.

Check the rig Before setting off and every day of the trip, whatever the vehicle, always check and double-

check that the hitch is secure, that the safety chains are correctly fitted, and that the electrical connections are working so that indicator lights function at the rear of the towed vehicle.

Allow extra time Remember to allow extra time for rest breaks and sightseeing during each day's travel; it is important to remain alert.

CHECKLIST
When towing anything:
- Contact the local vehicle standards authority (**see:** Useful Information p. 591) for advice and details on national towing regulations.
- Check the hitch for security. The law in most States demands that tow bars are fitted with safety chains.
- Check that the tail and stop lights, marker lights and signal lights are working.
- Remember to check the air pressure in the caravan or trailer tyres.
- If towing a boat, check the lashings.
- Check that caravan doors, windows and roof vents are closed before departure.
- If the caravan or trailer is fitted with separate brakes, check these as soon as you start to move.

Outback Motoring

Australia's size and remoteness deter many people from exploring it. However, properly set up and equipped, and armed with common sense and a little background knowledge, every intending traveller can explore the country's huge open spaces.

If you intend travelling in the outback, planning ahead is vital, for it is possible to travel in some sections of the Australian outback and not see another vehicle or person for several days. The Canning Stock Route is a good example.

It is possible to travel in some areas of the outback in a 2WD vehicle, but it is safer and much more practical to use a 4WD vehicle suited to off-road conditions. Remember that, if you rent a vehicle, there may be restrictions on insurance if you drive on unclassified roads; seek advice from the car rental company before you make any plans.

Your vehicle should be fitted with air conditioning to counteract high inland daytime temperatures and to allow you to drive with all the windows closed through dusty areas. You should be able to carry out small running repairs and must carry an owner's manual for the vehicle, tools and spare parts (**see**: Tools and Spare Parts p. 603).

DRIVING CONDITIONS

Outback driving conditions vary greatly. The deserts are usually dry; conditions change after rain. Many parts of the tropics are accessible only in the dry season (May to October), and even then there are streams to ford and washaways to contend with.

Pre-reading road conditions is vital. Always be on the alert. Recognising that a patch of different colour may represent a change in surface is an example. Sand can give way to rock; rock may lead to mud; hard surfaces become bulldust with little warning.

Bulldust Bulldust is a fine, talc-like dust that can cause damage if sucked into engines or when it accumulates around greasy engine components. Even more dangerous is the badly damaged road surface below the deceptively smooth dust. Take caution. Drive slowly through bulldust patches to avoid raising the dust, damaging your undercarriage and chocking your air filter.

Soft sand and mud These are best negotiated at the highest reasonable speed, in the highest possible gear and in 4WD. However, examine the road surface first. Never enter deep mud or mud covered with water without first establishing the depth of either or both.

Deep sand Requires low tyre pressures. Carry a tyre pressure gauge and drop pressures to about 10 psi. Reinflate when on gravel or bitumen roads again, because the soft tyres will perform very badly and may blow out as a result of stone fractures on hard surfaces. Whether driving on beach or desert sand, do not overload the vehicle and especially do not load up the roof rack – this can alter the centre of gravity of the vehicle and be extremely dangerous.

Crossing a creek or stream Stop to check the track across for clear passage and water depth. If the water level is above tyre height, look for an alternative route. If the water is deep but fordable, cover the front of the vehicle with a tarpaulin and remove the fanbelt to stop water being sprayed over the engine electrics. Drive through in low range second gear or high range first gear, and clear the opposite embankment before stopping again. If it has rained, beware of flash flooding.

Dips Dips are common on outback roads and can break suspension components if you enter too fast. To cross a dip, brake on entry to drop the vehicle's nose, and hold the brake on until just before the bottom of the depression. Then accelerate again to lift the nose, and therefore the suspension, as you exit. This will prevent the springs from bottoming out and will also give maximum clearance.

Cattle grids These are often neglected, with broken approaches and exits. If a grid appears to be in disrepair, stop and check first, before attempting to cross.

Road trains These multi-trailered, long trucks are difficult and often dangerous to overtake, particularly on dusty roads. Wait for a chance to get the front of your vehicle out to a position where the road-train driver can see you in the rearview mirror, but even then do not try to overtake until the driver has signalled acknowledgement that you are there. Sometimes it is prudent to stop and take a break, rather than try to overtake a road train. If you meet an oncoming road train, pull over and stop until it has passed.

Animals There are vast areas of unfenced property in the outback where stock roam free. A bullock or a large kangaroo can seriously damage your vehicle. Be especially wary around sunrise and sunset when animals are more active. A bull-bar or roo-bar provides limited protection at low speeds only, especially against larger animals. Driver concentration should be at as high a level as in city peak hours.

SURVIVING IN THE OUTBACK

In the event of being stranded in a remote area, you should be equipped to wait at that spot until you are found. Always carry a week's supply of spare water, a minimum of 28 litres per head. Keep it for an emergency. Emergency supplies of dry biscuits and canned food will keep hunger at bay, but body evaporation and thirst is the vital factor. Do not drink radiator coolant. Often it is not water but a chemical compound, and even if it is water, usually it has been treated with chemicals.

Do not try to walk out of a remote area. You are going to survive only if you wait by the car. Before entering a remote area, check with police or a local authority and tell them where and when you are going, and when you expect to arrive. When you reach your destination, telephone and advise of your arrival. This is important, as failure to do so causes unneccessary and expensive searches.

If stranded, set up some type of shelter and, in the heat of the day, remain in its shade as motionless as possible.

DIRECTION-FINDING

Clever electronic hand-held navigation devices, using the Global Positioning System (GPS), are now available from bushwalking shops, boating stores and outdoor centres. These can be used with or without a map and are much more sophisticated and accurate than a compass. The GPS is a navigation system developed and maintained by the United States Department of Defence. A GPS receiver determines the user's position by collecting distance/time measurements from satellites via an antenna. A GPS unit can also be used to store your current position, to navigate to your destination and to display and track the course travelled.

If you cannot read a map or use a compass, or if you have no navigational device with you,

it is vital to have some means of orientating yourself if you are lost.

A simple method of finding north is to use a conventional wristwatch. Place the 12 on the watch in line with the sun and bisect the angle between it and the hour hand. This will give a fairly accurate indication of north. Remember to take daylight saving into consideration. Also be aware that this method of direction-finding does not apply north of the Tropic of Capricorn during the summer months.

At night, the Southern Cross can be used to determine south.

When exploring a side track off the main road, be sure to make a rough sketch of the route you are following, noting all turnoffs and distances between them (using the speedometer), together

with any prominent landmarks. When you return, reconcile your return route with the sketch, point by point.

HOW TO OBTAIN WATER

Even less than 24 hours without water can be fatal in outback heat.
- It is essential to conserve body moisture. Take advantage of any shade that can be found.
- **DO NOT LEAVE your vehicle**. It may be the only effective shade available.
- Ration your drinking water. Do not drink your car's radiator coolant – it often contains chemicals.

Although a river or creek bed may be dry, there is often an underground water source. A hole dug about a metre deep may produce a useful soak.

Making an Arizona Still
Where there is vegetation, it is possible to extract water from it using an Arizona Still.
- Before the heat of the day, dig a hole about one metre across and a little more than half a metre deep.
- Put a vessel of some kind in the hole's centre to collect the water.
- Surround the vessel with cut vegetation. (Fleshy plants hold more moisture than drier saltbush.)
- Cover the hole with a plastic sheet held down by closely packed rocks, so that the hole is sealed off.

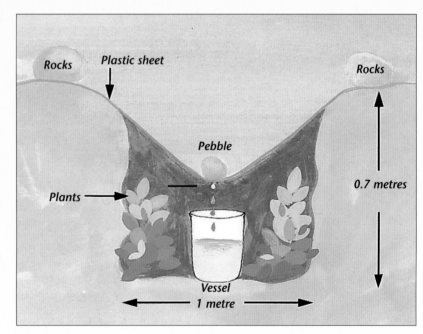

- Put a small stone in the centre of the sheet, directly above the collection vessel.

The sun's heat will evaporate moisture from the plants. This moisture will condense on the inside of the plastic, run down and drip off into

the vessel. In uninterrupted sunlight, about one litre of water should be collected about every six hours. The Still takes about three hours to start producing and it will become less efficient as the ground moisture dries out. A new hole will need to be dug at intervals.

OUTBACK ADVICE

CRITICAL RULES FOR OUTBACK MOTORING

- Check intended routes carefully.
- Check the best time of year to travel.
- Check that your vehicle is suited to outback conditions.
- Keep your load to a minimum.
- Check ahead for local road conditions, weather forecasts and fuel availability.
- Advise someone of your route, destination and arrival time.
- Ensure that you have essential supplies: water, food, fuel, spare parts.
- Carry detailed maps.
- Carry an extra supply of food and water in case of emergency; four to five litres of water per person per day in hot areas.
- Always remain with your vehicle if it breaks down.

Warning
When driving on desert roads, remember:
- There is no water, except after rains.
- Unmade roads can be extremely hazardous, especially when wet.
- Traffic is almost non-existent, except on main roads.

OUTBACK ADVICE SERVICE
The Royal Flying Doctor Service of Australia (RFDS) provides emergency outback assistance. RFDS bases provide advice on outback safety, communications and emergency procedures. It highly recommends travellers carry a radio transceiver set with an emergency call button in case of accident or sickness. These bases can advise travellers as to where such equipment can be hired or purchased. Note that mobile phones are ineffective in many areas; they cannot be relied upon for communication in remote parts of Australia.

New South Wales
Broken Hill: Broken Hill Airport 2880
(08) 8080 1777 (base)
(08) 8088 1188 (emergency assistance)

South Australia
Port Augusta: 4 Vincent St 5700
(08) 8642 2044

Western Australia
Emergency assistance for all of WA:
1800 625 800
Derby: Loch St 6728
(08) 9191 1211
Jandakot: 3 Eagle Dr., Jandakot Airport 6164 (08) 9417 6301
Kalgoorlie: Kalgoorlie–Boulder Airport 6430
(08) 9093 7500

Northern Territory
Alice Springs: Stuart Tce 0870
(08) 8952 1033 (base)
(08) 8952 2200 (emergency assistance)
(08) 8952 5733 (after hours emergency assistance)

Queensland
Cairns: 1 Junction St 4870
(07) 4053 1952 (base)
(07) 4053 5419 (emergency assistance)

Charleville: Old Cunnamulla Rd 4470
(07) 4654 1233 (base)
(07) 4654 1443 (emergency assistance)
Mount Isa: 11 Barkly Highway 4825
(07) 4743 2800 (base)
(07) 4743 2802 (emergency assistance)
Rockhampton: Unit 3,
83 Bolsover St 4700
(07) 4921 2221 (base)
(07) 4931 7198 (emergency)
Townsville: Gypsy Moth Crt 4810
(07) 4775 3111 (base)
(07) 4727 4870 (after hours)

For general information on the Royal Flying Doctor Service, contact: The Australian Council of the Royal Flying Doctor Service of Australia, Level 5, 15–17 Young St, Sydney 2000; (02) 9241 2411. Web site www.flyingdoctor.net

SHARING THE OUTBACK
As you travel the outback, you share the land with its traditional Aboriginal owners, pastoralists, other tourists – and nature itself. In order to preserve the outback for others:
- Respect Aboriginal lands and sacred and cultural sites; heritage buildings; and pioneer relics.
- Protect native flora and fauna; take photographs not specimens.
- Follow restrictions on the use of firearms. These restrictions protect wildlife and stock.
- Carry your own fuel source (for example a portable gas stove), to avoid lighting fires in fire-sensitive areas.
- When lighting a campfire (if you must), keep it small and use any fallen wood sparingly. Never leave a fire unattended; extinguish completely before you leave.
- Do not drive off-road.
- Do not camp immediately adjacent to water sources (for example on riverbanks or by dams). Allow access for stock and native animals.
- Do not bury your rubbish; carry out everything you take in.
- Dispose of faecal waste by burial.
- Leave gates as you find them: open or shut.
- Do not ignore signs warning of dangers or entry restrictions. These are there for your protection.

Sign beside the Eyre Highway in South Australia

BREAKDOWNS

There are many causes of motor vehicle breakdown, but fortunately modern vehicle technology has vastly reduced the possibility of being stuck by the roadside. Breakdowns that do occur can sometimes be cured with a roadside 'fix'; but this is often less possible with today's computer-driven vehicles. Inexpert or makeshift repairs may lead to further complications and a bigger repair bill.

Proper vehicle preparation and maintenance should at least reduce the possibility of roadside breakdowns and, on long journeys, the regular vehicle-service schedule should be maintained.

In areas where you have access to service through a motoring organisation, it is better to leave even slightly complicated repairs to the specialist. Remember to carry your membership card, which entitles you to assistance in other States (**see:** Useful Information p. 591). Most car rental companies list their recognised repair organisations in the manual supplied with the car. Before you drive the car, you should check that these details are provided. If your rental vehicle cannot be repaired immediately, you should request an exchange vehicle.

If you plan to journey into remote areas, it is a good idea to first take a basic course in vehicle maintenance (**see:** Car Maintenance Courses p. 590). As well, you should carry a range of tools and spare parts (**see:** Tools and Spare Parts p. 603).

MODERN VEHICLES
Most modern vehicles are fitted with electronic engine-management systems, or with electronic ignition and fuel injection. Generally these are more reliable than older systems and usually, in case of partial failure of the system, they have a 'limp home' mode, which enables travelling a limited distance at limited speed. However, total failure of such a system is difficult or impossible to remedy at the roadside without expert knowledge and equipment. This means that travel into remote areas is rendered much safer by travelling with at least one other vehicle, and by

Roadside repairs in northern Queensland

installing or hiring an appropriate long-range radio transmitter, receiver and aerial (**see:** Outback Advice p. 601).

EARLIER-MODEL VEHICLES
For those who drive earlier-model vehicles with less complex electrical and fuel systems, the troubleshooting flow charts are designed to be of assistance (**see:** Troubleshooting p. 604). But first, always remember to:

Watch warning gauges These have been installed to warn you that things may be going wrong. A flickering battery warning light will suggest all is not well with the generator/alternator charge rate, and this should be attended to promptly. A fluctuating temperature gauge *may* suggest the onset of a problem with the cooling system. Act on the warning at the earliest opportunity.

Make a daily check of fluid levels Check fuel, water and oil (including spare supplies); also tyre pressures, and fanbelt tension and condition. Make a regular check of brake-fluid and battery-acid levels, and pressure of spare tyre.

If the vehicle develops an unexplained sound, move to the side of the road as soon as possible. Park on flat ground if you can. You may have to spend some time under the bonnet, so look for shade or shelter. Try to locate the source of the sound. If it is coming from the engine, do nothing and seek help.

WHEN THE ENGINE STOPS
When the engine either splutters to a stop, constantly misfires or stops suddenly but was otherwise running smoothly, the problem is probably in one of two areas: fuel supply or electrics. Use the Troubleshooting flow charts (p. 604) to establish where the problem lies. If the problem is within the drive-train – the gearbox, drive-shaft or differential – once again, seek help.

TOOLS AND SPARE PARTS

Remote-area travelling requires a sound knowledge of the basics of breakdown repairs (**see:** Breakdowns p. 602). This means carrying emergency tools, spare parts and spare fuel, and the *vehicle owner's manual*. The following is a guide to what may be appropriate for your vehicle:

TOOLS

- Set of screwdrivers (blade and Phillips head)
- Small set of socket spanners
- Set of open-end/ring combination spanners
- Small and medium adjustable wrenches
- Small ballpein (engineer's) hammer
- Pliers and wire-cutters
- Hand drill and bits
- Workshop scissors
- Aerosol puncture repair can
- Tyre pump
- Puncture repair kit
- Tyre-pressure gauge
- Wheel brace
- Jack with supplementary wide base for sand or mud (block of wood, approximately the size of an A4 sheet of paper and 3 cm thick)
- Jumper leads (capacitor-type if for EFL engine)
- Hydrometer
- Small spade
- Vice grips
- Good quality tow-rope
- Heavy duty torch, spare batteries and globe
- Pocket knife
- Fire extinguisher(s)

SPARE PARTS

- Epoxy resin bonding 'goo' (for repair of punctured fuel tank)
- Plastic insulating tape
- Spare radiator and heater hoses
- Engine accessory belts (fan, alternator, power steering, etc.)
- Roll of cloth adhesive tape
- 1 metre fuel line (reinforced plastic)
- Insulated electric wire
- Spare electrical connections (range)
- Spare hose-clips (range)
- Distributor cap
- Set of high tension leads
- Condenser (where appropriate)
- Rotor
- Set of spark plugs
- Can of dewatering spray
- Set of points
- Spare fuel, air and oil filters
- Fuel pump kit, water pump kit
- Small-diameter plastic tubing
- Range of spare light globes and fuses

Be prepared when travelling in remote areas

- Nuts, bolts, washers, split pins
- Lubricants: automatic transmission and power-steering fluid
- Radiator sealant
- Tube of hand cleaner, clean rags

FUEL

- Spare fuel (40 litres minimum) in steel jerry cans. Do not use non-approved plastic containers; some plastics react with fuel. Also check fuel range, and the distance between refuelling points.
- At least one spare wheel (slightly over-inflated to allow for some air loss). If travelling in remote areas, consider additional tyres/tubes.

TROUBLESHOOTING (for earlier-model vehicles)

ENGINE WILL NOT TURN OVER

1 Check battery for charge.

2 If battery is flat...
recharge or replace, or tow-start (if manual transmission vehicle) until next service opportunity. If automatic, check handbook. Most autos cannot be tow- or clutch-started.

3 If battery is OK...
check if battery terminals and straps are loose, broken or dirty. If so, clean, repair or replace.

4 If terminals are OK...
check for jammed starter motor. For manual vehicle, put in top gear and rock back and forth to try to free pinion. An indication that starter may be jammed is an audible click when you try to start the engine and it will not turn over. With an automatic vehicle, try to turn engine back and forth with a spanner on crankshaft pulley to free pinion. Put gearbox into 'N' first.

5 If starter motor is free...
it is possible a solenoid has failed. Unless you are an auto electrician and carry a spare, seek help.

STARTER MOTOR WHIRRS BUT WILL NOT TURN ENGINE

Very likely, you have stripped a starter ring-gear, which means major repair work. But check to see that the starter motor is fully bolted to its mounting bracket, and tighten if not.

ENGINE TURNS OVER BUT WILL NOT FIRE, OR FIRES BUT WILL NOT RUN CLEANLY, OR MISFIRES REGULARLY, OR RUNS AND STOPS

Problem may be electrics or fuel supply. If unsure, begin with electrics.

Electrics

1 Check that spark is getting to spark plugs
Remove high tension (HT) lead from No. 1 plug and remove No. 1 plug. Re-attach HT lead to plug and hold plug body with pliers 1 mm from cylinder-head bolt or similar and turn engine over. Spark plug should produce strong blue spark at regular intervals.

2 If there is a problem with the electrics...
the simplest and fastest way to deal with an

Check fluid levels regularly to avoid a breakdown

electrical problem is to replace parts, either at once or progressively, with spares (**see:** Tools and Spare Parts p. 603). Replace coil and all HT leads and try engine. If problem persists, remove distributor cap and replace condenser and points. Re-set points and fit new rotor and distributor cap. Engine should start and run cleanly.

3 If you carry no spare parts...
you can still confirm electrics as the problem by a process of elimination. If there is no spark at the spark plugs, the problem has to be between battery and plug. Check that the low tension lead at side of distributor is connected properly and tightly mounted. If so, remove distributor cap and check for cracks. If there is a crack, repair with an epoxy glue/filler until it can be replaced. Check that condenser is tightly mounted and its LT wire is connected. Check that points open and close properly by turning engine over by hand slowly and watching

for a spark between points. Points may be burned or deeply pitted. If so, remove points and use nail-file to clean up faces, then replace and re-set. If, however, you have established an electrical problem and you have no spares, seek assistance.

4 If you have a spark at the plugs...
most likely you have a fuel-supply problem.

Fuel supply

1 Check fuel tank for fuel
Despite gauge reading, it is possible that the gauge is faulty.

2 If fuel is OK...
check accelerator cable connection and for free operation, and check choke cable and operation. For vehicle with automatic choke, remove air-cleaner carrier and element, and look down choke tube. If choke butterfly is not fully open, open it and check to see if it stays

open. If it closes again, engine is flooding, and may not run for that reason. A faulty auto choke cannot be repaired at the roadside.

3 If accelerator and choke cables are operating correctly...
do not replace air cleaner; remove fuel line to carburettor and turn engine over. Fuel should flow freely. If so, check it is not contaminated by pumping small amount into clear glass or plastic container and examine for water and/or dirt.

4 If water or dirt are apparent...
check and replace fuel filter and remove and check fuel pump. Examine glass for contamination. If none or very little, replace fuel line to carburettor and try engine again.

5 If there is substantial contamination...
it may be coming from fuel tank. Tank will need to be drained and perhaps flushed. Drained fuel should be saved and strained back. If you are travelling a long way before next fuel stop, be careful not to waste fuel.

6 If there is no fuel at fuel line and no apparent blockage...
fuel pump has failed for some reason. If you

are carrying a spare, replace pump. If not, seek mechanical assistance.

7 If fuel is clean and running freely...
blockage may be inside carburettor. Carefully remove top and then main jet and float. Clear main jet and clean out float bowl. Be careful not to interfere with float level. Replace parts and try engine again.

OVERHEATING IN A WATER-COOLED ENGINE

Occurs when coolant level falls or circulation is interrupted. Dash gauge gives warning, but vehicle will also lose power.

1 Stop vehicle
Do not remove radiator cap. Check hoses and hose connections for signs of leakage, or steam if system is boiling. Any identified leak can be cured temporarily with spare hoses or by binding with cloth tape.

2 If there is no sign of leakage...
after about 10 minutes, and holding radiator cap with a thick cloth, slowly remove cap, letting out steam under pressure at same time. Top up radiator while engine is running

and car's heater is on hot setting. Do not add cold water until engine is running.

3 Check again for leaks

4 If there is a slow drip from radiator core...
fix with an internal chemical sealant or externally with an epoxy filler or adhesive.

5 If no leak is apparent...
check fanbelt for tension. It may be slipping and not driving water pump. If so, tighten by releasing bolts on generator/alternator and increasing tension and re-tightening.

6 If you cannot account for overheating by any of the preceding...
you may have a failed water pump, a blocked system, a failed pressure cap or a combination of all three. Seek help as soon as possible, but you may drive on if you can continue topping up.

Back on the road again

WARNING!

FLOOD

In some remote areas, floods can occur without warning. Do not camp in dry river beds or close to the edges of creeks or streams. Always exercise extreme caution when approaching flooded roads or bridges.

If you are caught in a flash flood there is a good chance you will lose some possessions – and perhaps the car. However, your life is more important than both, so get out of the car and onto high ground and worry about the car and possessions later. If the car is washed away, it is not likely to travel far before being stopped by a tree or rock or stranded in shallow water.

If you cannot keep your feet after leaving the car, swim or float *with* fast-running water, not against it, and look out for a projecting embankment or overhanging limb to help you climb to higher ground.

When the flood has passed you may be able to retrieve the vehicle, dry it out on higher ground and continue.

BUSHFIRE

If you have to travel on days of critical fire danger (that is, total fire ban days), make sure you carry some wool blankets (not cotton or synthetic) and a filled water container. If you are trapped as a bushfire approaches:

- Do not panic.
- Stop the car in the nearest cleared area.
- Wind up all the windows.
- Turn on the hazard lights to warn any other traffic.
- DO NOT GET OUT OF YOUR CAR. The temperature may become unbearably hot, but it is still safer to stay in the car.
- Lie on the car floor, below window level, to avoid radiant heat.
- Cover yourself and your passengers with the blankets.
- Drink the water to avoid dehydration, and counteract heatstroke by wetting the skin and head.

The car will not explode or catch fire, and a fast-moving wildfire will pass quickly overhead.

ANIMALS

Although some species of Australia's unique wildlife are immensely appealing, some species are extremely dangerous.

Marine life

- **Box jellyfish (or marine stingers).** These are found in the coastal waters of Queensland and northern Australia in the summer months (October–May) and sometimes outside this period. A sting from

Exercise extreme caution when crossing water

their many long tentacles can be lethal, and for that reason swimming on coastal beaches north of Rockhampton is prohibited in the main stinger season. Outside this season, always check with the locals. Walking or paddling in a few centimetres of water is just as dangerous as swimming.

- **Stonefish.** Among Australia's several species of poisonous stinging fish, the stonefish, found all around the northern coastline, is particularly dangerous. Walking gently in the water, wearing sandshoes and not turning over coral and rocks will reduce the likelihood of a sting.

- **Blue-ringed octopuses.** Common in rock pools in all Australian States, their bite can paralyse in 15 minutes resulting in death. Do not handle in any circumstances and warn children of the potential hazard. Unless provoked, the distinctive blue rings of this dangerous octopus may not be evident.

- **Sharks.** Sharks are common in Australian waters. Do not swim where sharks have been seen or are known to congregate. Do not swim near dogs or other domestic pets. Do not swim at dusk or after dark, or at locations where water becomes abruptly deeper. Avoid areas of low visibility and turbid water.

- **Saltwater and freshwater crocodiles.** These are found throughout northern Australia. The saltwater crocodile is particularly dangerous and may be found in both salt water (including the sea) and fresh water. The freshwater crocodile is less dangerous but will bite, thus caution is necessary for both species. Neither species is easy to see in the water. Both species rest and sun themselves near the water's edge

on banks and beaches. Heed local warning signs and do not swim or paddle in fresh or salt water or allow children or animals near the water's edge. People standing in or near water while feeding or cleaning fish are particularly vulnerable, as are shore-based anglers and small-boat operators.

SNAKES

As a rule, snakes are timid and generally do not attack unless threatened. However, several species are highly venomous.

SPIDERS

Funnel-web spiders and red-back spiders. The bite from both species can be deadly. The funnel-web is found in southern and eastern States. The red-back is found in all of the Australian States.

INSECTS

Wasps, **bees**, **ants** (particularly bull-ants), **scorpions**, **centipedes** and **mosquitoes**. These insects are found throughout Australia. Their sting or bite normally is not harmful, except to those people who are allergy-prone, but it may cause pain and discomfort. Mosquitoes are of more serious concern in areas affected by Ross River virus. **Ticks** are a serious health threat, especially for children. When located, a tick should be removed promptly with tweezers, keeping the tick's body intact – do not compress it.

Study Australia's wildlife and learn to identify dangerous species. Remember that some plant species are poisonous. In a new area, check with local authorities for dangerous species.

CHILD'S PLAY

Parents may dread a long car trip when children are likely to become bored and irritable. A little planning will ease the strain on all concerned.

DOS AND DON'TS

In advance, make a list of 'dos' and 'don'ts'. Explain that the rules are safety measures. Reinforce this message on departure. For example:

DO NOT unbuckle seat belts or restraints while the car is moving.

DO NOT play with door handles or locks. (Set the child-proof locks on rear doors.)

DO keep head, arms and hands inside the car – never lean out.

DO NOT fight or yell while the car is in motion. This distracts the driver and may cause an accident.

HANDY HINTS

- A long car trip can be tiring. Make sure the children are cool and comfortable. Organise sun screens for rear windows. A security blanket or favourite soft toy may save the day if a small child is upset or sleepy.
- Pack moist towelettes or a damp face cloth in a small bag.

- Stock your first-aid kit with junior paracetamol, sunblock, insect repellent and any medication taken by your children. Bring a mosquito net to cover your baby's bassinette outdoors.
- Make up a 'busy box' for the back seat. Fill with note-pads, crayons and activity books. Include favourite storybooks.
- Pack tapes of stories and songs for 'quiet times' and as soothers.
- Take some games suitable for delays, and also for evenings and rainy days. Encourage older children to keep a diary. Include a rubber ball and skipping rope for stops and outdoor play.
- Use a tray or clipboard to support books or colouring-in.
- Stop the car every hour or so (preferably at a park or playground), so that the children can let off steam.
- If children feel sick, stop the car and let them out for some fresh air. Offer a sip of water before continuing the trip.
- Make regular toilet stops. Do not delay until they get desperate.

- Pack food and drink for the trip: eating little and often is the ideal. Pack snacks in individual lunch boxes. Sultanas, nuts (for older children only), bananas, grapes, cheese cubes and celery and carrot sticks are good for snacks. For lunches, pack easy-to-eat meals: chicken drumsticks, or bite-size rolls of cold meat with crackers, or small sandwiches with manageable fillings.
- Buy drinks in small cartons and have a supply of straws. If you carry drinks in a flask, take training cups for young children. For older children take plastic cups with straws and tight-fitting lids.
- Have plastic bags for waste.

CHILD RESTRAINTS

The law in each State and Territory is very specific on child restraints in cars. It is important to check with the motoring organisations of the States in which you are travelling (**see:** Useful Information p. 591). Under certain ages and weights, children in passenger cars must be in the rear seat in an approved child restraint.

SAFETY

SAFE SWIMMING, SURFING

- Swim or surf only at those beaches patrolled by lifesavers.
- Never swim alone.
- Read and obey all warning signs.
- Swim or surf within the area indicated by the red-and-yellow flags. The sign 'Danger – closed to bathing' indicates the beach is unsafe; do not swim or surf in this area.
- Do not enter the water directly after a meal or under the influence of alcohol or drugs.
- If you are caught in a rip or strong current and you are a strong swimmer, swim across it to safer waters. Otherwise, float and raise one arm as a distress signal until help arrives; do not panic.
- If seized with a cramp, keep the affected part perfectly still, float and raise one arm until help arrives.
- Don't run and dive in the water, even if you have checked for hazards earlier – conditions can change.

SAFE BOATING

- Tell someone where you are going.
- Check the weather forecast.
- Carry adequate equipment.
- Carry adequate clothing (including sunscreen, long-sleeved clothing, hat and sunglasses).
- Carry effective life jackets.
- Carry enough fuel and water.
- Ensure engine reliability.
- Guard against fire.
- Do not overload the craft.
- Know the boating rules and local regulations; also distress signals.
- Watch the weather.
- Do not drink alcohol while boating.

SAFE SKIING

Skiing is fun, but like any sport, there is the risk of injury. It is also strenuous. If possible, train beforehand, and avoid overdoing it on the slopes. All ski resorts have instructors if you need to take lessons.

- Choose slopes that suit your ability.
- Wear clothing suited to the conditions.
- Check equipment before setting out.
- Avoid skiing alone; if you must, then tell someone where you are going.
- If lost, stay where you are; only retrace your tracks if they are very clear.

Cross-country skiing requires careful planning:

- Tell someone in authority of your intended ski route.
- Travel in a group.
- Take plenty of food and adequate equipment for your survival.
- Protect yourself against sunburn.
- Watch the weather.
- Be alert for signs of exposure (hypothermia): tiredness, reluctance to carry on, clumsiness, loss of judgement and collapse.

INTER-CITY ROUTE MAPS

The following inter-city route maps will help you plan your route between major cities. They include distances between towns, location of roadside rest areas and information on road conditions. The map below provides an overview of the routes covered.

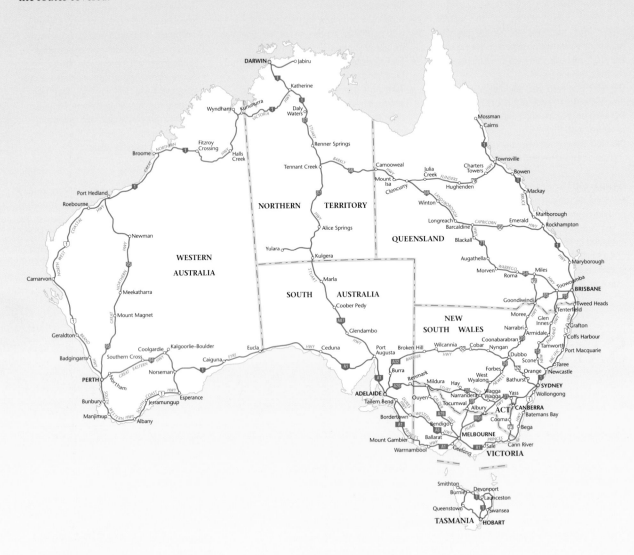

PAGE	ROUTE	DISTANCE	TRAVELLING TIME
609	Sydney–Melbourne via Hume Hwy/Fwy 31 M31	873 km	12 hrs
	Sydney–Melbourne via Princes Hwy/Fwy 1 A1 M1	1040 km	15 hrs
	Sydney–Brisbane via New England Hwy 1 15	1001 km	14 hrs
	Melbourne–Adelaide via Western & Dukes hwys M8 A8 M1	732 km	8 hrs
	Melbourne–Adelaide via Princes Hwy M1 A1 M1	906 km	11 hrs
610	Melbourne–Brisbane via Newell Hwy M31 A39 39 B5 54	1671 km	20 hrs
	Adelaide–Darwin via Stuart Hwy A1 A87 87 1	3037 km	31 hrs
	Adelaide–Perth via Eyre & Great Eastern hwys A1 1 94	2716 km	32 hrs
	Adelaide–Sydney via Sturt & Hume hwys A20 20 31	1415 km	19 hrs
	Perth–Darwin via Great Northern Hwy 95 1	4043 km	46 hrs
611	Sydney–Brisbane via Pacific Hwy 1 1	984 km	14 hrs
	Brisbane–Darwin via Warrego Hwy 54 71 66 87 1	3406 km	39 hrs
	Brisbane–Cairns via Bruce Hwy 1	1699 km	20 hrs
	Hobart–Launceston via Midland Hwy 1	200 km	3 hrs
	Hobart–Devonport via Midland & Bass hwys 1 B52	286 km	4 hrs

SYDNEY–MELBOURNE
via HUME HIGHWAY/ FREEWAY

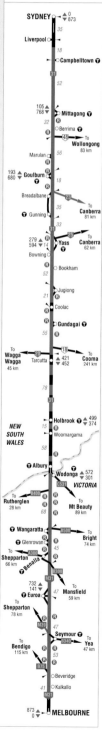

SYDNEY–MELBOURNE
via PRINCES HIGHWAY

SYDNEY–BRISBANE
via NEW ENGLAND HIGHWAY

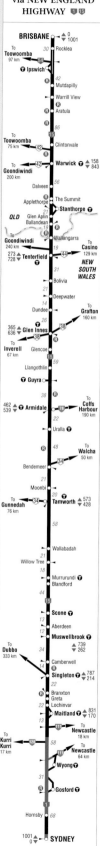

MELBOURNE–ADELAIDE
via WESTERN & DUKES HIGHWAYS

MELBOURNE–ADELAIDE
via PRINCES HIGHWAY

MELBOURNE –BRISBANE
via HUME, NEWELL GORE & WARREGO HIGHWAYS

DARWIN– ADELAIDE
via STUART HIGHWAY

ADELAIDE– PERTH
via EYRE & GREAT EASTERN HIGHWAYS

ADELAIDE– SYDNEY
via STURT & HUME HIGHWAYS

PERTH– DARWIN
via GREAT NORTHERN, VICTORIA & STUART HIGHWAYS

SYDNEY–BRISBANE
via PACIFIC HIGHWAY

BRISBANE–DARWIN
via WARREGO, LANDSBOROUGH, BARKLY & STUART HIGHWAYS

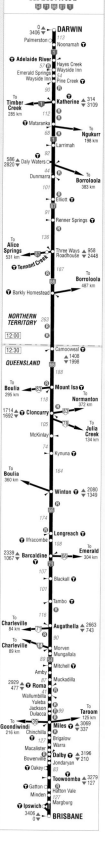

BRISBANE–CAIRNS
via BRUCE HIGHWAY

HOBART–LAUNCESTON
via MIDLAND HIGHWAY

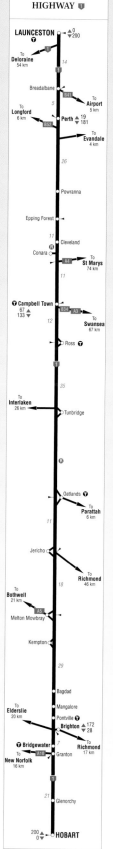

HOBART–DEVONPORT
via MIDLAND & BASS HIGHWAYS

Index of Place Names

This index includes all towns, localities, roadhouses and national parks shown on the maps and mentioned in the text. In addition, it includes major places of interest, landforms and water features.

Place names are followed by a map page number and grid reference, and/or the text page number on which that place name occurs. A page number set in **bold** type indicates the main text entry for that place name. For example:
Bairnsdale Vic. 225 P4, 234 F13, 154, **159**
Bairnsdale – Place name
Vic. – State
225 P4, 234 F13 – Bairnsdale appears on these map pages

154 – Bairnsdale is mentioned on this page
159 – Main entry for Bairnsdale

The alphabetical order followed in the index is that of 'word-by-word', where all entries under one word are grouped together. Where a place name consists of more than one word, the order is governed by the first and then the second word. For example:
Green Point
Greenbank
Greens Beach
Greenwood
Greg Greg
Gregory

Names beginning with Mc are indexed as Mac and those beginning with St, as Saint.

The following abbreviations and contractions are used in the index:
ACT – Australian Capital Territory
JBT – Jervis Bay Territory
NSW – New South Wales
NT – Northern Territory
Qld – Queensland
SA – South Australia
St – Saint
Tas. – Tasmania
Vic. – Victoria
WA – Western Australia

Coolabah NSW 109 P8
Coolac NSW 103 B4, 104 D11
Cooladdi Qld 524 A7, 535 R7
Coolah NSW 104 H1, 106 G13
Coolah Tops National Park NSW 104 I1,
106 H13, 55
Coolalie NSW 103 E3, 104 F11
Coolalinga NT 426 D3
Coolamon NSW 104 B11, 111 Q9
Coolana Qld 516 C13
Coolangatta NSW 99 F12, 36
Coolangatta Qld 107 Q1, 517 H13,
518 I11, 525 Q11, 66, 450, 451, **474**
Coolaroo Vic. 204 F1
Coolatai NSW 107 J4, 525 L13
Coolbellup WA 372 E12
Coolbinia WA 374 H11
Coolcha SA 301 E1, 303 N9
Coolgardie WA 386 I6, 314, 329, **340**,
347
Coolimba WA 386 B5
Coolongolook NSW 105 O2
Cooloolabin Qld 516 F3, 519 C6
Cooltong SA 303 Q6
Coolum Beach Qld 516 H3, 519 H5,
525 Q6
Coolup WA 376 C11, 384 C6
Cooma NSW 100 A2, 103 E9, 126 G11,
235 M3, 29, **41**
Cooma Vic. 232 G6
Cooma West NSW 103 E9, 126 F11,
235 M3
Coomalbidgup WA 386 I10
Coomandook SA 301 E3, 303 N11
Coomba NSW 105 P2
Coombabah Qld 518 E2
Coombah Roadhouse NSW 110 C3
Coombe SA 301 G5, 303 P13
Coombell NSW 107 P3, 525 P13
Coomberdale WA 386 C6
Coombogolong NSW 106 B8
Coomera Qld 517 G10, 518 C1, 450
Coominglah Qld 525 L2
Coominya Qld 516 B11, 525 O9, 476
Coomoora Vic. 210 E2, 221 N9
Coonabarabran NSW 106 F11, 21, **41**
Coonalpyn SA 301 F4, 303 O12, **262**
Coonamble NSW 106 C10, **42**
Coonarr Qld 525 O2
Coonawarra SA 226 A2, 228 A13,
301 H10, 254, **262**, 271
Coonerang NSW 100 A4, 126 G13
Coongie Lakes SA 307 P5, 252
Coongulla Vic. 225 L5
Coongulmerang Vic. 225 O4, 234 E13
Coonong NSW 111 O10
Coonooer Bridge Vic. 229 M8
Cooper Creek SA 307 N6, 252
Coopernook NSW 95 D12, 105 P1,
107 O13
Coopers Creek Vic. 225 K5
Coopers Plains Qld 512 I2
Cooplacurripa NSW 107 M12
Coopracambra National Park Vic.
100 A13, 103 E12, 235 N10, 163
Coorabakh National Park NSW 95 C11,
63
Coorabie SA 311 K9
Cooran Qld 516 E1, 525 P6
Cooranbong NSW 97 F12, 105 M5
Coorong National Park SA 301 D5,
303 M12, 237, 253, 263, 266, 269,
280, 282

Coorow WA 386 C5
Cooroy Qld 516 F2, 519 D2, 525 P6
Coorparoo Qld 510 H10
Cootamundra NSW 103 B3, 104 D10,
27, **42**
Cooya Beach Qld 523 B3, 529 M5, 486
Cooyal NSW 104 H3
Cooyar Qld 525 N7
Copacabana NSW 94 H7
Cope Cope Vic. 229 L7
Copeland NSW 105 N1, 46
Copeville SA 301 F1, 303 O9
Copi Hollow NSW 108 E13, 55
Copley SA 299 D2, 305 J4, 288
Copmanhurst NSW 107 O5
Coppabella Qld 527 J7
Copping Tas. 579 N5, 583 N8, 556, 567
Cora Lynn Vic. 211 N9, 224 G6
Corack Vic. 229 K6
Corack East Vic. 229 K6
Coradgery NSW 104 C4
Coragulac Vic. 210 A10, 216 I6, 227 N8
Coraki NSW 107 Q3, 525 Q13
Coral Bank Vic. 223 M3, 233 Q7,
234 C5
Coral Bay WA 385 B5, **341**
Coral Sea 527 N1, 530 H3
Coralville NSW 95 E12, 105 P1, 107 O13
Coram Vic. 216 I8
Coramba NSW 107 P8
Corang NSW 103 G5, 104 I12, 127 N2
Corattum SA 301 H12
Cordalba Qld 525 O3, 473
Cordering WA 384 E8
Coree South NSW 111 M11
Coreen NSW 111 O12, 233 M2
Corfield Qld 533 M6
Corinda Qld 510 D12
Corindhap Vic. 210 C7, 217 J1, 227 O5
Corindi NSW 107 P7, 70
Corinella Vic. 211 M12, 224 F8
Corinna Tas. 584 C9, 550, 566
Corio Vic. 210 F8, 217 O4, 224 A6,
227 R7
Corlette NSW 97 H2
Cornella Vic. 232 E8
Corner Store Qld 108 A1, 307 R11,
534 H13
Cornubia Qld 513 Q8
Cornwall Tas. 585 Q10
Corny Point SA 302 G9, 279
Corobimilla NSW 111 O9
Coromandel East SA 298 I1
Coromandel Valley SA 298 G1
Coromby Vic. 228 I8
Coronation Beach WA 386 A3
Coronet Bay Vic. 211 M12, 224 F8
Corop Vic. 232 F6
Cororooke Vic. 210 A11, 216 I6, 227 N8
Corowa NSW 111 O13, 233 M3, 30, **42**
Corra Linn Tas. 581 P11, 585 M9
Corrigin WA 384 H5, 386 E8, **341**
Corrimal NSW 91 M13, 98 F3, 99 H5,
105 K9
Corringle NSW 104 B7, 111 R5
Corringle Vic. 235 J13
Corroboree Park Tavern NT 426 G5
Corryong Vic. 103 B8, 234 G2, 152, 153,
166, 181
Corunna NSW 100 H3, 127 M12
Cosgrove Vic. 233 J5
Cosmo Newbery WA 387 K2
Cossack WA 385 G1, 388 A1, 334, 358

Costerfield Vic. 232 F9
Cottan–Bimbang National Park NSW
107 M12
Cottesloe WA 372 B6, 376 B5, 319
Cottles Bridge Vic. 211 L4, 224 E2,
232 H13
Cottonvale Qld 107 M2, 525 N11, 493
Couangalt Vic. 210 H4
Cougal NSW 107 P1
Coulson Qld 517 A10
Coulta SA 302 C7
Countegany NSW 100 C1, 126 I11
Courada NSW 106 H7
Couran Qld 517 G9
Couridjah NSW 91 J12
Couta Rocks Tas. 584 B6
Coutts Crossing NSW 107 P6
Cow Bay Qld 523 C1, 529 M5
Cow Flat NSW 90 B6
Cowabbie West NSW 104 A10, 111 Q8
Cowan NSW 87 J1, 91 N5, 94 D12
Cowan Cowan Qld 517 G2
Cowandilla SA 292 F5
Cowangie Vic. 110 B10, 230 C10
Cowaramup WA 377 C9, 379 C6,
384 B9, 351, 367
Cowell SA 302 G5, **262**
Cowes Vic. 211 L12, 213 O11, 224 E9,
156, 166, 196
Cowled Landing SA 302 H3, 304 G13
Cowley Beach Qld 521 D2, 529 N8
Cowleys Creek Vic. 216 E9
Cowper NSW 107 P5
Cowra NSW 104 F8, 21, **42**
Cowwarr Vic. 225 L6
Coyrecup WA 381 N1, 384 H9
Crabbes Creek NSW 107 Q2, 525 Q11
Crabtree Tas. 578 F7, 583 K9
Crace ACT 124 G4
Cracow Qld 525 K3
Cradle Mountain Tas. 584 G10, 550,
573
Cradle Mountain–Lake St Clair
National Park Tas. 580 A13, 582 F1,
584 F10, 550, 561, 564, 570, 571, 573
Cradle Valley Tas. 584 G9
Cradoc Tas. 578 E9, 583 K10
Cradock SA 299 D11, 305 K9
Crafers SA 293 O11, 296 C10, 297 H1,
264
Crafers West SA 293 N11
Craigie NSW 103 E12, 235 M8
Craigie Vic. 221 J6
Craigie WA 374 B2
Craigieburn Vic. 211 J4, 224 C2,
232 F13
Craiglie Qld 523 C4, 529 M5
Cramenton Vic. 230 H7
Cramps Tas. 583 J2, 585 K11
Cranbourne Vic. 209 H8, 211 L9,
224 E6, 174
Cranbourne South Vic. 209 G11,
211 L9, 213 O1, 224 E6
Cranbrook Tas. 583 P3, 585 P12, 548,
565
Cranbrook WA 381 L6, 384 H11,
386 E11, 327, **341**
Crater Lakes National Park Qld 521 C1,
523 E12, 497, 499
Craven NSW 105 N2
Cravensville Vic. 103 A9, 234 F4, 187
Crawford Qld 525 N6
Crawley WA 372 F5, 319

Crayfish Creek Tas. 584 E4
Crayford SA 300 E6
Creek Junction Vic. 233 K9
Creek View Vic. 232 E7
Creighton Vic. 232 I8
Creighton Creek Vic. 232 I9
Cremorne NSW 85 N8
Cremorne Tas. 579 K7, 583 M9, 545
Cremorne Point NSW 85 N8
Crescent Head NSW 95 H4, 107 P11,
17, 52
Cressbrook Lower Qld 516 B8
Cressy Tas. 583 L1, 585 L10, 560
Cressy Vic. 210 B8, 217 J3, 227 N6
Crestmead Qld 513 K10
Creswick Vic. 210 C3, 221 K9, 227 O2,
229 O13, 232 A12, 148, **166**
Crib Point Vic. 211 L11, 213 N8,
224 E8
Croajingolong National Park Vic.
103 F13, 235 M13, 154, 163, 176, 194,
197
Crohamhurst Qld 516 E6, 519 B12
Cromer NSW 85 P1, 87 N11
Cronulla NSW 89 M12, 91 N10, 11
Crooble NSW 106 H4, 525 K13
Crooked River Vic. 225 N2, 233 Q13,
234 C10
Crookwell NSW 103 F2, 104 H10, 23, **43**
Croppa Creek NSW 106 I4, 525 K13
Crossdale Qld 516 C9
Crossley Vic. 226 H9
Crossman WA 376 H12, 384 E6
Crossover Vic. 211 P9, 224 H6
Crow Mountain NSW 107 J8
Crowdy Bay National Park NSW
95 F11, 105 P1, 107 O13, 17, 53, 63
Crowdy Head NSW 95 F12
Crower SA 301 G9
Crowlands Vic. 220 D6, 227 L1,
229 L12
Crows Nest NSW 82 B2, 85 M7
Crows Nest Qld 525 N8, 475
Crows Nest National Park Qld 525 O8,
475
Crowther NSW 103 C1, 104 E9
Croxton East Vic. 226 G5
Croydon NSW 84 H11, 89 J1
Croydon Qld 528 F10, 465, **475**
Croydon SA 292 F2
Croydon Vic. 207 L2, 211 L6
Croydon Hills Vic. 205 R8, 207 L1
Croydon Park NSW 84 H11, 89 J2
Croydon Park SA 292 F1
Crymelon Vic. 228 H6
Cryon NSW 106 D7
Crystal Brook SA 303 J4, **262**
Crystal Creek National Park Qld
521 E8, 529 O12
Cuballing WA 384 G6, 386 E9
Cubbaroo NSW 106 E7, 68
Cucania Qld 523 H12
Cuckoo Tas. 585 N7
Cudal NSW 104 F6
Cuddell NSW 111 O9
Cudgee Vic. 216 B7, 226 I9, 189
Cudgen NSW 107 Q1
Cudgewa Vic. 103 A8, 234 G2
Cudgewa North Vic. 103 B8, 234 G2
Cudlee Creek SA 296 D9
Cudmirrah NSW 103 I5, 127 Q3
Cudmirrah National Park NSW 105 J12,
127 P2

Cudmore National Park Qld 526 E9
Cue WA 385 H13, 386 E1, 388 B13, **341**
Culbin WA 384 F7
Culburra NSW 99 G13, 105 K11, 60
Culburra SA 301 F5, 303 O12
Culcairn NSW 111 Q12, 233 Q1, **43**
Culfearne Vic. 229 P2, 231 Q13, 232 B1
Culgoa Vic. 110 G12, 229 L3, 231 L13
Culgoa Floodplain National Park Qld 109 Q1, 524 D12, 492
Culgoa National Park NSW 109 Q2, 524 D13
Culla Vic. 226 D2, 228 E13
Cullacabardee WA 375 J4
Cullen Bay Marina NT 424 B10, 399, 400, 401
Cullen Bullen NSW 90 F3, 104 I6
Cullendulla NSW 103 H7, 127 O6
Culler NSW 103 F3, 104 G11
Culloden Vic. 225 N4, 234 D13
Cullulleraine Vic. 110 C7, 230 D4
Cumberland Park SA 292 H8
Cumborah NSW 106 B6
Cummins SA 302 D7, 251, 276
Cumnock NSW 104 F4
Cundare Vic. 210 A9, 216 I4
Cundeelee WA 387 L6
Cunderdin WA 384 G3, 386 E7
Cundletown NSW 95 D13
Cungena SA 302 A1, 311 Q11
Cungulla Qld 521 H10, 529 Q13
Cunjurong NSW 127 Q3
Cunliffe SA 302 I6
Cunnamulla Qld 524 A10, 535 R10, 465, **475**
Cunningar NSW 103 C3, 104 E10
Cunningham SA 302 I7
Cunninyeuk NSW 110 H10, 231 O10
Cuprona Tas. 584 G6
Curara WA 386 C3
Curban NSW 106 D12
Curdie Vale Vic. 216 D9, 227 J10
Curl Curl NSW 85 Q4, 87 O13
Curlewis NSW 106 H11
Curlwaa NSW 110 D6, 230 F2
Currabubula NSW 107 J11
Currajong Qld 520 A6
Curramulka SA 302 I8
Currarong NSW 105 K12
Currawang NSW 103 F4, 104 H11
Currawarna NSW 104 A12, 111 Q10
Currawinya National Park Qld 109 J1, 535 O12, 476
Currency Creek SA 297 H7, 264
Currie Tas. 583 Q12, 552
Currigee Qld 517 G10, 518 E2
Currimundi Qld 516 H5, 519 I12
Currowan Corner Upper NSW 103 H6, 104 I13, 127 M5
Currumbin Qld 517 H12, 518 G10, 525 Q11, 451, **475**
Currumbin Waters Qld 518 G10
Curtin ACT 124 E12, 125 C3
Curtin Springs NT 428 E13, 434 F12
Curtinye SA 302 F3, 304 E13
Curtis Island Qld 527 P11, 478
Curtis Island National Park Qld 527 P11
Curyo Vic. 110 F13, 229 J4
Custon SA 228 A7, 301 I7
Cuttabri NSW 106 F8, 68
Cygnet Tas. 578 F10, 583 K10, 546, **555**

Cygnet River SA 302 I12, 266
Cynthia Qld 525 L3

D'Aguilar Qld 516 E7
D'Aguilar National Park Qld 516 D11, 517 B4
D'Entrecasteaux Channel Tas. 578 F13, 583 K12, 544, 545, 546, 547, 554, 559
D'Entrecasteaux National Park WA 377 F13, 379 H13, 380 B9, 384 C12, 386 C12, 355
Daceyville NSW 89 P4
Dadswells Bridge Vic. 228 I11
Daguragu NT 432 D6
Dahlen Vic. 228 G9
Dahwilly NSW 111 K11
Daintree Qld 523 A1, 529 M5, 471, **475**
Daintree National Park Qld 523 A2, 529 M4, 529 M4, 463, 486, 490, 500
Daisy Dell Tas. 580 A12, 584 H9
Daisy Hill Qld 513 O6
Daisy Hill Vic. 221 J6, 227 O1, 229 O12
Daisy Hill State Forest Qld 513 O5, 517 E7, 447, 448, 501
Dajarra Qld 532 E6
Dakabin Qld 514 A5, 516 F10, 517 D3, 493
Dalbeg Qld 521 I13, 526 G3
Dalby Qld 525 M8, 452, **476**
Dales Gorge WA 385 I4, 388 C4, 337, 358, 363
Dalgety NSW 101 I12, 103 D10, 126 E13, 235 L5, 36
Dalhousie Springs SA 306 B2, 271, 284
Dalkeith WA 372 E7, 319
Dallarnil Qld 525 N3
Dalma Qld 527 N11
Dalmalee Vic. 228 G5
Dalmeny NSW 100 I2, 103 H8, 127 N11, 235 R2
Dalmorton NSW 107 N6
Dalton NSW 103 E3, 104 G11
Dalveen Qld 107 M2, 525 N11
Dalwallinu WA 386 D5
Daly River NT 426 B13, 430 D8, 408
Daly Waters NT 432 I3, **410**
Dalyston Vic. 211 N13, 224 F9
Dalyup WA 387 J10, 344
Dampier WA 385 G1, 334, 347, 358
Dandaloo NSW 104 C2
Dandaragan WA 386 C6
Dandenong Vic. 207 J13, 209 E1, 211 L8, 224 E5
Dandenong Ranges Vic. 207 O5, 132, 141, **151**, 169, 180
Dandenong Ranges National Park Vic. 207 O5, 211 L6, 214 A11, 224 E4, 180, 193
Dandenong South Vic. 209 F3
Dandongadale Vic. 222 I6, 233 N8, 234 A6
Dangar Island NSW 94 E10
Dangarfield NSW 105 L2
Dangarsleigh NSW 107 L9
Dangin WA 384 G4
Danyo Vic. 230 C10
Dapto NSW 99 G7
Darby Falls NSW 103 D1, 104 F8
Darbyshire Vic. 234 E2
Dardadine WA 384 F7
Dardanup WA 377 G5, 384 C8
Dareton NSW 110 D6, 230 F2, 68
Dargo Vic. 225 O2, 233 R13, 234 D11, 160

Dargo High Plains Vic. 223 N11, 233 Q11, 171
Dark Corner NSW 90 E3, 104 I6
Darkan WA 384 E8
Darke Peak SA 302 E4
Darkwood NSW 107 O8
Darley Vic. 210 G5, 221 Q13
Darling Downs Qld 525 M9, 438, 445, 452, 494
Darling Harbour NSW 81 B10, 4, 8
Darling Point NSW 85 O10, 11
Darling Range WA 376 D3, 384 D5, 320, 325, 346, 353
Darling River NSW 108 F12, 110 D5, 31, 37, 55, 68
Darlinghurst NSW 81 H10, 85 N10
Darlington Tas. 579 P2, 583 P7, 548, 565, 570
Darlington Vic. 216 E3, 227 K7, 167
Darlington WA 376 D4, 384 D3, 325, 353
Darlington Point NSW 111 N8
Darnick NSW 110 H2
Darnum Vic. 211 Q10, 224 I7, 189
Daroobalgie NSW 104 D6
Darr Qld 526 A10, 533 O10
Darra Qld 512 D2
Darraweit Guim Vic. 211 J3, 224 C1, 232 F12
Darriman Vic. 225 M9
Dart Dart Vic. 228 G7
Dartmoor Vic. 226 C6
Dartmouth Qld 526 B11, 533 P11
Dartmouth Vic. 103 A10, 223 R2, 234 E5, 187
Darwin NT 423, 424 E11, 426 C2, 430 D5, 394, **395–401**, 404, 418, 420, 421
Darwin Crocodile Farm NT 426 D4
Dattuck Vic. 228 H2, 230 H12
Davenport Range National Park NT 433 L13, 435 L2, 414, 419
Daveyston SA 296 E4, 300 C4
Davidson NSW 85 M1, 87 K11
Davies Creek National Park Qld 523 D9
Davis Creek NSW 105 L2
Davistown NSW 94 G7
Daw Park SA 292 H10
Dawes Qld 525 L2
Dawes Point NSW 81 D2, 82 D12
Dawesville WA 376 A10, 384 C6
Dawson SA 303 M2, 305 L12
Dawson Vic. 225 L5
Dawsons Hill NSW 105 L2
Dayboro Qld 516 E10, 517 B2
Daydream Island Qld 527 K3, 455, 457, 492
Daylesford Vic. 210 E2, 221 N9, 227 Q2, 229 Q13, 232 B12, 141, 150, 166
Daymar Qld 106 E2, 524 H12
Daysdale NSW 111 O12, 233 M1
Daytrap Vic. 231 J10
Daytrap Corner Vic. 231 J10
Dead Horse Gap NSW 101 C13, 126 A13, 28
Deagon Qld 514 E11
Deakin ACT 122 A13, 124 F12, 125 E2, 119
Deakin WA 310 A5, 387 R6
Dean Vic. 210 D3, 221 L10, 227 P3, 232 B12
Deanmill WA 380 C6, 384 D10
Deans Marsh Vic. 210 D12, 217 L8, 227 O9, 175

Deception Bay Qld 514 D2, 516 G10, 517 D2, 525 P8
Deddick Vic. 103 C11, 235 J8
Deddington Tas. 581 R13, 585 N10, 557
Dederang Vic. 223 M1, 233 Q6, 234 C4
Dee Lagoon Tas. 582 I4
Dee Why NSW 85 Q2, 87 O12, 91 O7
Deep Creek Vic. 103 A11, 234 F7
Deep Lead Vic. 229 J11
Deepwater NSW 107 M5, 46
Deepwater National Park Qld 525 N1, 527 Q13, 458, 485
Deer Park Vic. 208 G3
Deeral Qld 523 H12, 529 N7, 467
Delacombe Vic. 219 A10
Delahey Vic. 208 G1
Delamere SA 297 C8
Delaneys Creek Qld 516 E7
Delatite Vic. 211 R1, 222 D11, 233 L11
Delburn Vic. 211 R11, 225 J8
Delegate NSW 103 E11, 235 M8, 37, 181
Delegate River Vic. 103 D11, 235 L8
Dellicknora Vic. 103 D12, 235 K8
Deloraine Tas. 580 I11, 585 J9, 549, **555**
Delta Qld 526 I2
Delungra NSW 107 J6
Delvine Vic. 225 O5
Denham WA 385 B10, 341, 365
Denicull Creek Vic. 220 A9
Deniliquin NSW 111 L11, 30, **43**
Denison Vic. 225 M5
Denison Gorge Tas. 581 P5
Denistone NSW 84 G5
Denman NSW 102 H7, 105 K3
Denman SA 310 D4
Denmark WA 381 K12, 384 G13, 386 E12, 327, **341**
Dennes Point Tas. 578 I9, 583 L10
Dennington Vic. 216 A7, 226 H9
Denver Vic. 210 F2, 221 O8, 227 Q2, 229 Q13, 232 C11
Depot Beach NSW 127 O6
Deptford Vic. 103 A13, 225 Q3, 234 F12
Derby Tas. 585 O7, **556**
Derby Vic. 229 P9, 232 B8
Derby WA 382 B9, 391 J7, 332, **342**
Dereel Vic. 210 C6, 217 K1, 227 O5
Dergholm Vic. 226 B3
Dering Vic. 230 G11
Deringulla NSW 106 F12
Dernancourt SA 295 M12
Derrier Flat Qld 516 C2
Derrinal Vic. 232 E9
Derrinallum Vic. 216 F2, 227 L6, **167**
Derriwong NSW 104 B5, 111 R3
Derwent Bridge Tas. 582 H3, 584 H13
Derwent Park Tas. 576 E5
Derwent Valley Tas. 578 E3, 537, 544, 545, 546
Detention River Tas. 584 E4
Detpa Vic. 228 F5
Deua National Park NSW 103 G7, 127 K8, 235 P1, 56
Devenish Vic. 233 K5
Devils Kitchen Tas. 579 O9, 547, 567, 568
Devils Marbles NT 433 K12, 435 K2
Devils Marbles Conservation Reserve NT 433 J12, 407, 414, 418
Deviot Tas. 581 L6, 585 L7, 553
Devlins Bridge Vic. 211 M3
Devon Meadows Vic. 213 P2

Krowera Vic. 211 O12
Ku-ring-gai Chase National Park NSW 86 H8, 87 N3, 91 O6, 94 F11, 105 L7, 13, 16, 46, 74
Kudardup WA 377 C12, 379 D12
Kuitpo SA 296 C13, 297 G4
Kuitpo Colony SA 297 H5
Kukerin WA 384 I7, 386 F10, 359
Kulgera NT 434 I13
Kulgun Qld 517 A10
Kulikup WA 380 G2, 384 E9, 336
Kulin WA 384 I6, 386 F10, 330, 348
Kulkami SA 301 G2, 303 P10
Kulkyne Vic. 230 H6
Kulnine Vic. 230 D3
Kulnine East Vic. 110 C7, 230 D3
Kulnura NSW 91 O2, 94 A2, 105 L5, 71
Kulpara SA 303 J6
Kulpi Qld 525 N8
Kulwin Vic. 230 I9
Kulyalling WA 384 F5
Kumarina Roadhouse WA 388 D8
Kumarl WA 387 J9
Kumbarilla Qld 525 L8
Kumbatine National Park NSW 107 O11
Kumbia Qld 525 N7
Kumorna SA 301 G5, 303 P13
Kunama NSW 103 B6
Kunat Vic. 229 N1, 231 N12
Kundabung NSW 95 G5, 107 O11, 52
Kungala NSW 107 P7
Kunghur NSW 107 P2
Kunjin WA 384 H5
Kunlara SA 301 F1, 303 O8
Kununoppin WA 384 H1
Kununurra WA 383 P2, 391 Q5, 332, 333, 348, 360, 363
Kunwarara Qld 527 N9
Kupingarri WA 382 H6, 391 M7
Kuraby Qld 513 L4
Kuranda Qld 523 E7, 529 M6, 461, 463, 471, 481, 490
Kuranda Scenic Railway Qld 523 E8, 471, 481
Kureelpa Qld 516 F4, 519 D8
Kuridala Qld 532 G5, 474
Kuringup WA 384 I8
Kurmond NSW 91 K5
Kurnbrunin Vic. 228 E4
Kurnell NSW 89 P9, 91 O10, 11, 74
Kurnwill Vic. 110 B8, 230 C5
Kurraca Vic. 229 N8
Kurraca West Vic. 229 N8
Kurrajong NSW 91 K5
Kurrajong Heights NSW 91 J5, 105 K6, 62
Kurralta Park SA 292 G7
Kurri Kurri NSW 97 C9, 105 M4
Kurrimine Beach Qld 521 D3, 529 N9
Kurting Vic. 229 O8, 232 A7
Kurumbul Qld 106 I2, 525 K12
Kuttabul Qld 527 K5
Kweda WA 384 G5
Kwiambal National Park NSW 107 J4, 50
Kwinana WA 376 B7, 384 C4, 386 C8
Kwolyin WA 384 H3
Kyabram Vic. 232 G5, 174
Kyalite NSW 110 H9, 231 N8
Kyancutta SA 302 C3, 304 C13
Kybeyan NSW 100 C3
Kybunga SA 303 K5

Kybybolite SA 228 A10, 301 I8
Kydra NSW 100 B4
Kyeamba NSW 103 A6, 104 C13, 111 R11
Kyeemagh NSW 89 M5
Kyndalyn Vic. 110 F9, 231 K7
Kyneton Vic. 210 G1, 221 Q8, 227 R1, 229 R12, 232 D11, 150, 174
Kynuna Qld 533 J6, 465, 481
Kyogle NSW 107 P2, 525 P12, 52
Kyotmunga WA 376 E1
Kyup Vic. 226 F4
Kyvalley Vic. 232 G5
Kywong NSW 111 P10

La Perouse NSW 89 P8, 91 O10, 11, 74
Laanecoorie Vic. 221 L3, 229 P10, 232 A9, 168
Laang Vic. 216 C7, 227 J9
Labertouche Vic. 211 O9, 224 G6, 189
Labrador Qld 518 E4, 483
Lachlan Tas. 578 F5, 583 K8
Lacmalac NSW 126 B2
Lady Barron Tas. 582 B11, 585 R1, 552
Lady Bay Tas. 583 K12
Lady Elliot Island Qld 455, 457, 470, 478
Lady Julia Percy Island Vic. 226 F9, 182
Lady Musgrave Island Qld 527 R12, 455, 457, 470, 485, 498
Ladys Pass Vic. 232 E9
Ladysmith NSW 103 A5, 104 C12, 111 R10
Laen Vic. 229 J7
Laen North Vic. 229 J7
Laggan NSW 103 F2, 104 H9, 43
Lah Vic. 228 H5
Laharum Vic. 228 H11, 145
Laheys Creek NSW 104 G2
Laidley Qld 525 O9, 448, 481
Lajamanu (Hooker Creek) NT 432 D8
Lake Alexandrina SA 301 D3, 253, 269
Lake Argyle WA 383 Q4, 391 Q6, 333, 349, 363
Lake Barrine National Park *see* Crater Lakes National Park
Lake Barrington Tas. 580 C9, 584 H8, 563
Lake Bathurst NSW 103 F4, 104 H11
Lake Biddy WA 386 G9
Lake Bindegolly National Park Qld 535 O10, 476
Lake Boga Vic. 110 H11, 229 N1, 231 N11, 173, 187
Lake Bolac Vic. 227 J5, 174
Lake Boort Vic. 229 N5, 162
Lake Buloke Vic. 229 K7
Lake Burley Griffin ACT 122 C7, 123 E4, 124 F10, 125 D1, 113, 114, 115, 119
Lake Cave WA 379 B9, 367, 368
Lake Cargelligo NSW 111 O4, 52
Lake Cathie NSW 95 G9, 107 O12, 61
Lake Charm Vic. 110 H12, 229 O2, 231 O13, 232 A1
Lake Clifton WA 376 B12, 384 C6
Lake Condah Vic. 226 E7
Lake Conjola NSW 103 I5, 105 J12, 127 Q3
Lake Cowal NSW 104 B7, 111 R5
Lake Eildon Vic. 211 P1, 233 K10, 152, 158, 176, 177, 195

Lake Eildon National Park Vic. 211 P1, 222 A11, 224 H1, 233 K11, 152, 158, 168, 195
Lake Eppalock Vic. 221 R3, 232 D9, 172
Lake Eyre SA 306 G8, 237, 252, 267, 275, 284
Lake Eyre National Park SA 306 G10, 534 B11, 252, 267, 268, 284
Lake Gairdner National Park SA 304 D8, 311 R7
Lake George NSW 23, 47
Lake Gilles Conservation Park SA 302 F2, 266
Lake Goldsmith Vic. 220 F11, 160
Lake Gordon Tas. 582 G7
Lake Grace WA 386 F9, 349
Lake Hindmarsh Vic. 228 E5, 173, 184
Lake Hume Vic. 111 Q13, 233 Q3, 30, 32
Lake Jindabyne NSW 29
Lake King WA 386 G9, 349, 354
Lake Leake Tas. 583 O3, 585 O12, 555, 563
Lake Macquarie NSW 97 G11, 14, 15, 59
Lake Margaret Tas. 582 E2, 584 E11, 562
Lake Marmal Vic. 229 N6
Lake Meering Vic. 229 O4
Lake Monger WA 372 F1, 374 F12, 316, 317, 319, 340, 364
Lake Mountain Vic. 211 P4, 224 H2, 233 K13, 151, 177
Lake Mulwala NSW 30
Lake Mundi Vic. 226 B4, 301 I11
Lake Munmorah NSW 91 R1, 97 H12, 105 M5
Lake Pedder Tas. 582 H8, 551, 561, 572
Lake Poomaho NSW 110 H10, 231 N9
Lake Powell Junction Vic. 231 K6
Lake Rowan Vic. 233 K5
Lake St Clair Tas. 582 H3, 584 H12, 550, 560, 573
Lake Tabourie NSW 103 H6, 127 P5
Lake Torrens National Park SA 299 A3, 304 I5
Lake Tyers Vic. 234 H13, 175
Lake View SA 303 K4
Lakefield National Park Qld 529 J1, 530 E13, 463, 474, 500
Lakeland Qld 529 K4
Lakemba NSW 84 G13, 88 I3
Lakes Entrance Vic. 225 R5, 234 H13, 154, 174
Lakesland NSW 91 J12, 99 D2
Lal Lal Vic. 210 D5, 221 M13, 227 P4
Lalbert Vic. 110 G12, 229 M2, 231 M13
Lalbert Road Vic. 229 M1, 231 M12
Lalla Tas. 581 O6, 585 M7, 560
Lallat Vic. 229 J9
Lallat North Vic. 229 J8
Lalor Vic. 205 J2
Lameroo SA 301 H3, 303 Q11, 272
Lamington Qld 517 C13
Lamington National Park Qld 107 P1, 517 E13, 525 P11, 447, 450, 467, 488, 498
Lamplough Vic. 210 A1, 220 H6, 227 M1, 229 N12
Lancaster Vic. 232 G5
Lancefield Vic. 210 I2, 232 E11, 191
Lancelin WA 384 B1, 386 B7, 349
Landsborough Qld 516 G6, 519 E13, 525 P7, 453, 482, 488, 506

Landsborough Vic. 220 D5, 229 L11
Landsdale WA 374 H3
Lane Cove NSW 85 K6, 91 N8
Lane Cove National Park NSW 84 G2, 85 J4, 86 E12, 91 N7, 74
Lanena Tas. 581 L7, 585 L7
Lang Lang Vic. 211 N10, 224 F7
Langford WA 373 M9
Langhorne Creek SA 301 D3, 303 M10, 255, 275
Langi Kal Kal Vic. 210 A3, 220 H9, 227 N2, 229 N13
Langi Logan Vic. 220 B9, 227 K2, 229 K13
Langkoop Vic. 226 B1, 228 B12, 301 I9
Langley Vic. 210 G1, 221 Q7, 227 R1, 229 R12, 232 D11
Langlo Crossing Qld 524 A5, 535 R5
Langloh Tas. 583 J6
Langsborough Vic. 225 L10
Langtree NSW 111 M5
Langville Vic. 229 O4, 232 A2
Langwarrin Vic. 209 D11, 213 N1
Langwarrin South Vic. 209 E12
Lankeys Creek NSW 103 A7, 111 R12
Lannercost Qld 521 D6, 529 N11
Lansdowne NSW 84 B12, 88 D2, 95 D12, 105 P1, 107 N13
Lansvale NSW 84 A11, 88 C1
Lapoinya Tas. 584 E5, 566
Lapstone NSW 93 R9
Lara Vic. 210 G8, 217 P3, 224 A5, 227 R7, 142, 196
Lara Lake Vic. 210 F8, 217 O3
Laramba NT 434 H6
Larapinta Qld 512 G6
Laravale Qld 517 C12
Largs Bay SA 294 A10
Largs North SA 294 B9
Larpent Vic. 210 A11, 216 I7, 227 N9
Larrakeyah NT 424 B10
Larras Lee NSW 104 F5
Larrimah NT 430 I12, 432 I2, 410
Lascelles Vic. 110 E12, 228 I2, 230 I12
Latham ACT 124 B5
Latham WA 386 D5
Lathlain WA 373 K4
Latimers Crossing Qld 518 B6
Latrobe Tas. 580 E6, 584 I7, 550, 559
Lauderdale Tas. 577 O10, 579 J6, 583 M9, 545
Laughtondale NSW 91 M4
Launceston Tas. 581 O10, 585 L8, 537, 549, 559
Launching Place Vic. 211 N6, 214 E9, 224 F4
Laura Qld 529 K3, 461, 463
Laura SA 303 K3, 305 J13, 262
Laurel Hill NSW 103 B7
Laurieton NSW 95 F10, 107 O12, 53
Lauriston Vic. 210 F1, 221 P8, 227 R1, 229 R12, 232 C11
Lavers Hill Vic. 216 H11, 227 M11, 158, 200
Laverton Vic. 208 F10
Laverton WA 387 J3, 329, 349
Lawgi Qld 525 L1
Lawler Vic. 229 J7
Lawley River National Park WA 391 M3
Lawloit Vic. 228 D7
Lawn Hill National Park Qld 433 R8, 531 B11, 464, 470, 486, 500
Lawrence NSW 107 P5, 54

Marchagee WA 386 C5
Marcoola Qld 516 H3, 519 H7
Marcus Beach Qld 516 H2, 519 H3
Marcus Hill Vic. 210 H10, 217 Q6, 224 B7
Mardella WA 376 C8, 384 C5
Marden SA 293 K2
Mareeba Qld 523 C9, 529 M7, 461, **484**
Marengo NSW 107 N7
Marengo Vic. 217 J12, 227 N12
Margaret River WA 377 C10, 379 C7, 384 A10, 386 B11, 326, **351**, 366, 367
Margate Qld 514 H6, 516 H10, 517 E3
Margate Tas. 578 H8, 583 L9, 559
Margooya Vic. 231 J7
Maria Island Tas. 579 P4, 583 P7, 548, 565, 573
Maria Island National Park Tas. 579 Q3, 583 P7, 565, 570
Mariala National Park Qld 535 Q5
Marian Qld 527 K5
Maribyrnong Vic. 204 E7
Marion SA 292 F11, 296 B10, 297 F1
Marion Bay SA 302 G10
Marion Bay Tas. 579 N5, 583 O8
Markdale NSW 103 E2, 104 G9
Markwell NSW 105 O2
Markwood Vic. 222 G1, 233 N6, 234 A4
Marla SA 309 N5, 271
Marlbed Vic. 229 K4
Marlborough Qld 527 M9
Marlee NSW 95 A12, 105 O1, 107 N13
Marleston SA 292 F7
Marlinja NT 432 I6
Marlo Vic. 235 J13, 154, 181
Marma Vic. 228 I9
Marmion WA 374 B6
Marmor Qld 527 O11
Marnoo Vic. 229 K9
Marnoo West Vic. 220 A1, 229 J9
Marong Vic. 221 N2, 229 Q9, 232 B8
Maroochy River Qld 516 G3, 519 F7
Maroochydore Qld 516 H4, 519 H9, 525 Q7, 453, **484**
Maroon Qld 107 O1, 517 A13, 525 P11
Maroona Vic. 220 A10, 227 J3
Maroota NSW 91 M4
Maroubra NSW 89 Q5, 91 O9
Marp Vic. 226 B6
Marrabel SA 303 L6
Marradong WA 376 G12, 384 E6
Marralum NT 391 R4, 430 A12, 432 A1
Marramarra National Park NSW 86 E1, 91 N5, 94 A11, 105 L6
Marrangaroo NSW 90 F4
Marrar NSW 104 B11, 111 R9
Marrara NT 425 H8, 400
Marrawah Tas. 584 B4, 550, 564
Marraweeny Vic. 233 J8
Marree SA 304 I1, 306 I13, 252, 266, **268**
Marrickville NSW 85 J13, 89 L3, 91 N9
Marrinup WA 376 D11, 384 D6, 343
Marryatville SA 293 K5
Marsden NSW 104 B7, 111 R5
Marsden Qld 513 L9
Marsden Park NSW 91 L7
Marshall Vic. 210 F10, 217 O5, 224 A7, 227 R8
Marshdale NSW 97 B1
Martindale NSW 102 H9, 105 K3
Martins Creek NSW 97 B4
Martins Creek Vic. 103 C13, 235 K10
Martinsville NSW 97 E12

Marulan NSW 103 G3, 104 I11
Marulan South NSW 103 H4, 104 I11
Marungi Vic. 232 I4
Marvel Loch WA 386 G7, 358
Mary River Crossing NT 426 H6, 404
Mary River National Park NT 426 I4, 430 F7, 401, 420
Mary River Roadhouse NT 427 L11, 430 G8
Maryborough Qld 525 P4, 454, **484**
Maryborough Vic. 221 J5, 229 O11, 148, **177**
Marybrook WA 377 C7, 379 D3
Maryfarms Qld 529 L5
Maryknoll Vic. 211 N8
Marysville Vic. 211 O4, 214 I3, 224 G2, 233 J13, 151, **177**, 189, 192
Maryvale NSW 104 F3
Maryville NSW 96 A2
Mascot NSW 85 L13, 89 N3
Maslin Beach SA 296 A13, 297 E4, 298 B9, 257, 267
Massey Vic. 229 K6
Masthead Island Qld 498
Matakana NSW 111 N3
Mataranka NT 430 I11, 405, 411, **412**, 418, 420
Matcham NSW 91 P4, 94 G5, 64
Matheson NSW 107 L6
Mathiesons Vic. 232 F7
Mathinna Tas. 585 P9, 557
Mathoura NSW 111 K12, 232 F2, 43, 168
Matlock Vic. 211 R5, 225 J3
Matong NSW 104 A11, 111 Q9
Matraville NSW 89 Q6
Maude NSW 111 J8, 231 R5, 49
Maude Vic. 210 E7, 217 N2, 227 Q6
Maudsland Qld 517 F10, 518 A4
Mawbanna Tas. 584 E5, 564
Mawson ACT 125 D6
Mawson WA 384 G4
Maxwelton Qld 533 L4
May Reef Vic. 229 R8, 232 D7
Mayanup WA 380 F3, 384 E9, 336
Mayberry Tas. 580 D12, 584 I9
Maydena Tas. 578 A4, 582 I7
Mayfield Tas. 583 P4, 585 P13
Maylands SA 293 K3
Maylands WA 373 K3
Mayne Qld 510 G6
Mayrung NSW 111 L11
Mays Hill NSW 84 B7
Maytown Qld 529 J4
Mazeppa National Park Qld 526 G7
Mead Vic. 229 Q3, 232 B2
Meadow Creek Vic. 222 G3, 233 N7
Meadow Flat NSW 90 E4
Meadowbank NSW 84 G6
Meadows SA 296 D13, 297 H3, 301 C2, 303 L10, 275
Meandarra Qld 525 J8
Meander Tas. 585 J10
Meandu Creek Qld 488
Meatian Vic. 229 M2, 231 M12
Meckering WA 384 F3, 386 D7, 330, 355
Medindie SA 290 E2, 292 I3
Medindie Gardens SA 293 J2
Medlow Bath NSW 90 H6, 92 C7, 22, 36
Medowie NSW 97 F4
Meeandah Qld 511 J5
Meekatharra WA 385 I11, 388 C11, **351**

Meelon WA 376 C11, 384 D6
Meelup WA 377 B6, 379 C2, 343
Meenar WA 384 F2
Meeniyan Vic. 224 I10, 175
Meerawa Qld 523 G11
Meerlieu Vic. 225 O5
Meerschaum Vale NSW 107 Q3
Megalong NSW 90 H7, 92 B9, 36
Megan NSW 107 O8
Melaleuca Tas. 582 G11, 551, 572
Melba ACT 124 C4
Melba Flats Tas. 582 D1, 584 D10
Melba Gully State Park Vic. 216 H11, 227 L11, 158, 194, 199, 200
Melbourne Vic. 202, 211 J6, 224 D4, 130, **131–41**, 193, 196
Meldale Qld 516 G8, 517 E1
Mella Tas. 584 C4, 564
Mellis Vic. 228 I6
Melros WA 376 A10, 350
Melrose NSW 104 A4, 111 Q2
Melrose SA 303 J2, 305 J12, **268**, 272, 278
Melrose Tas. 580 D6, 584 I7
Melrose Park NSW 84 G7
Melrose Park SA 292 G9
Melton SA 303 J6
Melton Vic. 210 H5, 221 R13, 224 B3, 159
Melton Mowbray Tas. 583 L6
Melton South Vic. 210 H5
Melville WA 372 E9
Melville Forest Vic. 226 F3
Melville Island NT 430 D3, 404
Memana Tas. 582 B10
Memerambi Qld 525 N6
Mena Creek Qld 521 D2, 529 N8
Mena Park Vic. 210 A4, 220 G11
Menai NSW 88 F9
Menangle NSW 91 K11, 99 F2, 39
Menangle Park NSW 91 K11, 99 F1
Mendooran NSW 104 G1, 106 E13
Mengha Tas. 584 D4
Menindee NSW 108 E13, 110 E1, 31, 55
Meningie SA 301 D4, 303 M12, 269
Menora WA 374 H11
Mentone Vic. 206 D12
Menzies WA 386 I4, 329, 347, 350
Menzies Creek Vic. 207 Q9, 211 M7, 214 B12, 169
Mepunga East Vic. 216 C8, 227 J10
Mepunga West Vic. 216 B8, 226 I10
Merah North NSW 106 F7
Merbein Vic. 110 D7, 230 G3
Merbein South Vic. 110 D7, 230 F3
Merbein West Vic. 110 D7, 230 F3
Mercunda SA 303 O8
Merebene NSW 106 E9
Meredith Vic. 210 E6, 217 M1, 227 P5
Merewether NSW 96 A11, 97 G8
Meribah SA 110 A9, 230 A6, 301 I1, 303 R8
Merildin SA 303 L5
Merimal Qld 527 N10
Merimbula NSW 100 F9, 103 G11, 235 Q7, 26, **55**
Merinda Qld 526 I2
Meringa Qld 523 F10
Meringo NSW 103 H8, 127 N9
Meringur Vic. 110 B8, 230 C4
Meringur North Vic. 110 B7, 230 C4
Merino Vic. 226 D5

Mermaid Beach Qld 518 F7
Mermaid Waters Qld 518 E7
Mernda Vic. 211 K4, 224 D2, 232 G13
Merredin WA 384 I2, 386 F7, **352**
Merriang Vic. 222 I2, 233 O7, 234 A5
Merriang Vic. 211 K3, 224 D2, 232 G13
Merriang South Vic. 222 I3
Merricks Vic. 211 K12, 213 L9, 155, 169
Merricks North Vic. 213 K8
Merrigum Vic. 232 G6
Merrijig Vic. 222 E11, 233 M10, 177
Merrimac Qld 518 D7
Merrinee Vic. 110 C8, 230 E4
Merrinee North Vic. 230 E4
Merriton SA 303 J4
Merriwa NSW 105 J2, **55**
Merriwagga NSW 111 M5
Merrygoen NSW 104 G1, 106 F13
Merrylands NSW 84 B8, 91 M8
Merrywinbone NSW 106 D6
Merseylea Tas. 580 F9, 584 I8
Merton Tas. 576 C5
Merton Vic. 233 J10
Metcalfe Vic. 221 Q6, 229 R11, 232 D10, 174
Methul NSW 104 A10, 111 Q8
Metricup WA 377 C8, 379 C4
Metung Vic. 225 R5, 234 G13, 154, 160, 175
Meunna Tas. 584 E6
Mia Mia Vic. 221 R5, 232 D10
Miallo Qld 523 B3, 529 M5, 486
Miami Qld 518 F8
Miami WA 376 A10
Miandetta NSW 109 Q10
Michael Creek Qld 521 C7, 529 N11
Michelago NSW 103 E7, 123 F10, 126 G6
Mickleham Vic. 211 J4, 224 C2, 232 F13
Middle Cove NSW 85 M5
Middle Creek Vic. 220 E9, 227 L2
Middle Dural NSW 86 B4
Middle Indigo Vic. 233 O4, 234 A2
Middle Island Qld 527 N6
Middle Park Qld 512 C1
Middle Park Vic. 204 G12, 206 A5
Middle Point NT 426 F3
Middle River SA 302 G12
Middle Swan WA 375 Q7
Middle Tarwin Vic. 224 H10
Middlemount Qld 527 K9
Middleton Qld 532 I8
Middleton SA 297 H7, 273
Middleton Tas. 578 G11, 583 L11
Middlingbank NSW 101 H8, 126 E11
Midge Point Qld 527 K4
Midgee Qld 527 N11
Midgee SA 302 H4
Midland WA 375 Q9, 376 D4, 325
Midway Point Tas. 577 R3, 579 K5, 583 M8
Miena Tas. 583 J2, 585 J12, **560**
Miepoll Vic. 232 I7
Miga Lake Vic. 228 E11
Mil Lel SA 226 A5, 301 I12
Mila NSW 103 E12, 235 N8
Milabena Tas. 584 E5
Milang SA 301 C3, 303 L11, 255, 263, 275
Milawa Vic. 222 G1, 233 N6, 152, 153, 177, 184
Milbong Qld 517 A10

Pillar Valley NSW 107 P6
Pilliga NSW 106 E8
Pillinger Tas. 582 E4
Pilot Hill NSW 126 A5
Pimba SA 304 F6
Pimlico Qld 520 A9
Pimpama Qld 517 F9
Pimpinio Vic. 228 G8
Pindar WA 386 C3
Pine Creek NT 426 I13, 430 F8, 394, 404, **413**
Pine Hill Qld 526 G11
Pine Lodge Vic. 232 I5
Pine Point SA 302 I8
Pine Ridge NSW 106 I12
Pinery SA 296 A2, 303 K7
Pingaring WA 386 F9
Pingelly WA 384 F5, 386 D9, 330, **356**
Pingrup WA 386 F10
Pinjarra WA 376 C10, 384 C6, 386 C9, **356**
Pinkenba Qld 511 K5
Pinnacles, The WA 386 B6, 330, 346, 362
Pinnaroo SA 110 A11, 230 A10, 301 I3, 303 R10, **272**
Pioneer Tas. 585 P6
Pioneer Bend SA 302 H12
Pipalyatjara SA 308 B2, 389 R11, 434 B13
Pipers Brook Tas. 581 O3, 585 M6, 549, 554, 558, 560
Pipers Creek Vic. 210 G2, 221 Q8
Pipers Flat NSW 90 E3
Pipers River Tas. 581 N4, 585 L6
Pira Vic. 110 G10, 231 M10
Piries Vic. 211 R1, 222 D11, 233 L11
Pirlangimpi NT 430 C3
Pirlta Vic. 230 F4
Pirron Yallock Vic. 210 A11, 216 H7, 227 M9
Pichi Richi Railway SA 299 B12, 272, 274, 285
Pithara WA 386 D6
Pitt Town NSW 91 L6
Pittong Vic. 210 A5, 220 G13, 227 M4
Pittsworth Qld 525 N9, **489**, 495
Pittwater NSW 87 P4, 91 P6, 94 G11, 13
Plainland Qld 516 A13
Platts NSW 100 A11, 103 F12, 235 N8
Pleasant Hills NSW 104 A13, 111 P11, 49
Pleasure Point NSW 88 D7
Plenty Tas. 578 E3, 583 K7, 559, 561
Plenty Vic. 205 M2
Plush Corner SA 300 H4
Plympton SA 292 F8
Plympton Park SA 292 F9
Pmara Jutunta NT 434 I5
Poatina Tas. 583 K1, 585 K11
Point Clare NSW 91 P4, 94 F7
Point Cook Vic. 208 G12
Point Labatt Conservation Park SA 311 P13, 251, 276, 280
Point Leo Vic. 211 K12, 213 K10, 170
Point Lonsdale Vic. 210 H11, 212 A6, 217 Q6, 224 B7, 142, 184
Point Lookout Qld 517 I5, 525 R9
Point Nepean Vic. 212 B6, 224 B7, 186, 193
Point Pass SA 303 M6
Point Piper NSW 85 P10
Point Samson WA 385 G1, 388 A1, 358

Point Talburpin Qld 517 G7
Point Turton SA 302 H9
Pokataroo NSW 106 D5
Pokolbin NSW 97 A10, 102 A8, 14, 40
Police Point Tas. 578 E11, 583 K11
Policemans Point SA 301 E5, 303 N13
Polkemmet Vic. 228 F9
Pomborneit Vic. 216 G6, 227 M9
Pomborneit East Vic. 216 H6
Pomborneit North Vic. 216 G6
Pomona Qld 516 E1, 519 B1, 525 P6, **489**
Pomonal Vic. 226 I1, 228 I12
Pompapiel Vic. 229 Q7, 232 B6
Pompoota SA 296 I10
Pondalowie Bay SA 250
Ponde SA 296 I10
Pondooma SA 302 G4
Pontville Tas. 578 H3, 583 L7, **561**
Pontypool Tas. 583 O5
Poochera SA 302 A1, 304 A12, 311 R12
Pooginagoric SA 301 H7
Poolaijelo Vic. 226 B2, 228 B13, 301 I10
Poona National Park Qld 525 P4
Pooncarie NSW 110 E4
Poonindie SA 302 D8, 273
Pooraka SA 295 J10
Pootilla Vic. 210 D4, 221 L11
Pootnoura SA 309 P9
Poowong Vic. 211 O11, 224 G8, 174
Poowong East Vic. 211 P11
Popanyinning WA 384 F6
Popran National Park NSW 91 O3, 94 B6
Porcupine Flat Vic. 221 N4
Porcupine Gorge National Park Qld 526 A3, 533 P3, 479
Porcupine Ridge Vic. 210 E2, 221 O8, 227 Q1, 229 Q12, 232 C11
Porepunkah Vic. 223 L5, 233 P8, 234 C6, 163
Pormpuraaw Qld 528 D1, 530 A13
Porongurup WA 381 O9, 384 H12, 327, 353
Porongurup National Park WA 381 N9, 384 H12, 335, 353, 362
Port Adelaide SA 294 D11, 296 A8, 301 B1, 303 K9, 240, 244, 245
Port Albert Vic. 225 L10, 156, 157, **182**
Port Alma Qld 527 O11
Port Arthur Tas. 579 N10, 583 N10, 540, 545, 546, 547, 557, **562**, 567, 569
Port Augusta SA 299 A13, 304 I11, 252, 272, 285, 408
Port Bonython SA 302 I2, 304 I12, 278
Port Broughton SA 303 J4, **272**
Port Campbell Vic. 216 E10, 227 K11, 143, **182**, 196, 198
Port Campbell National Park Vic. 216 E10, 227 K11, 143, 182, 194, 200
Port Clinton SA 303 J7
Port Davis SA 302 I3, 303 J3, 304 I13
Port Denison WA 386 B4, 343
Port Douglas Qld 523 C4, 529 M5, 461, 462, **490**, 502
Port Elliot SA 297 H8, 301 C3, 303 L11, 263, **273**
Port Fairy Vic. 226 G9, 143, **182**, 198, 200
Port Franklin Vic. 225 J10, 170
Port Gawler SA 296 A6, 303 K8
Port Germein SA 303 J2, 304 I13, 250, 274
Port Gibbon SA 302 G5

Port Hacking NSW 89 K13, 11
Port Hedland WA 388 C1, 390 B13, 334, **357**
Port Hughes SA 302 I6
Port Huon Tas. 578 E10, 583 K10, 557, 559
Port Jackson NSW 85 O9, 91 O8
Port Julia SA 302 I8
Port Kembla NSW 99 H7, 105 K10, 1, 25, 70
Port Kenny SA 302 A3, 311 Q13, 276
Port Latta Tas. 584 E4, 564
Port Lincoln SA 302 D8, 251, **273**, 283
Port MacDonnell SA 301 H13, 254, **273**
Port Macquarie NSW 95 G7, 107 P12, 17, **61**
Port Melbourne Vic. 204 F11, 139
Port Minlacowie SA 302 H9
Port Neill SA 302 E6, 276
Port Noarlunga SA 296 A12, 297 E3, 298 B5, 301 B2, 303 K10, 255, 267, 278
Port Noarlunga South SA 298 B6
Port Pirie SA 303 J3, 304 I13, 250, **273**
Port Rickaby SA 302 H8, 269
Port Sorell Tas. 580 G5, 585 J6, **562**, 573
Port Stephens NSW 97 G2, 105 N4, 14, 15, 58, 73
Port Victoria SA 302 H7, 250, **274**
Port Vincent SA 302 I9, 269
Port Wakefield SA 303 J6, 258
Port Welshpool Vic. 225 K10, 190
Port Willunga SA 296 A13, 297 E4, 298 B10, 255, 257
Portarlington Vic. 210 H9, 217 Q4, 224 B6, 167
Porters Retreat NSW 90 D10, 103 G1, 104 H8
Portland NSW 90 E3, 104 I6
Portland Vic. 226 D9, 143, **183**
Portland Roads Qld 530 F7
Portsea Vic. 210 I11, 212 C7, 217 R7, 224 B8, 155, 186
Portsmith Qld 522 E12
Potato Point NSW 100 I1, 127 N10
Pothana NSW 102 C1
Potts Point NSW 81 I8, 85 N10, 9
Pottsville NSW 107 Q1, 525 Q11
Pound Creek Vic. 224 H10
Powelltown Vic. 211 O7, 224 G4, 189
Powers Creek Vic. 226 C1, 228 C12
Powlett Plains Vic. 229 P8, 232 A6
Powlett River Vic. 211 N13
Powranna Tas. 583 L1, 585 M10
Pozieres Qld 107 M2, 525 N11
Prahran Vic. 204 H12, 206 B5, 134, 137, 138, 139
Prairie Qld 526 B4, 533 P4, 479
Prairie Vic. 229 Q6, 232 C5
Pranjip Vic. 232 I8
Pratten Qld 525 N10
Precipice National Park Qld 525 J3
Premaydena Tas. 579 M9, 583 N10, 569
Premer NSW 106 G12
Preolenna Tas. 584 E6
Preston Tas. 580 A7, 584 H7, 566
Preston Vic. 204 I6
Preston Beach WA 376 A12, 384 C6
Pretty Gully NSW 107 N3, 525 O12
Prevelly WA 377 B10, 379 B8, 351
Price SA 303 J7
Priestdale Qld 513 O4
Primbee NSW 99 H7
Primrose Sands Tas. 579 L6, 583 N9

Princetown Vic. 216 F11, 227 L11, 200
Priors Pocket Qld 512 A4
Priory Tas. 585 Q8
Prooinga Vic. 231 K8
Propodollah Vic. 228 D6
Proserpine Qld 527 J3, **490**
Prospect SA 292 H2
Prospect Tas. 581 O10
Prospect Hill SA 296 C13, 297 H4
Proston Qld 525 N5
Puckapunyal Vic. 232 G10, 185
Pudman Creek NSW 103 E3, 104 F10
Puffing Billy Railway Vic. 214 B12, 151, 169
Pukanja Qld 523 C8
Pullabooka NSW 104 C7
Pullut Vic. 228 G4
Punchbowl NSW 84 E13, 88 H3
Punchmirup WA 381 L2, 384 G9
Punthari SA 296 I8
Punyelroo SA 303 N8, 276
Pura Pura Vic. 216 E1, 227 L5
Puralka Vic. 226 B6, 301 I12
Purfleet NSW 105 P1, 107 N13
Purga Qld 515 B12, 517 A8
Purlewaugh NSW 106 F11
Purnim Vic. 226 F6, 226 I9
Purnong SA 301 E1, 303 N9, 268
Purnululu National Park WA 383 P8, 391 Q8, 333, 346, 349, 363
Purrumbete South Vic. 216 F7
Putney NSW 84 H7
Putty NSW 105 K5
Pyalong Vic. 211 J1, 232 F10
Pyap SA 303 Q7
Pyengana Tas. 585 P8, 548, 563
Pygery SA 302 C2, 304 B13
Pymble NSW 85 J2, 86 H12, 91 N7
Pyramid Qld 523 G10
Pyramid Hill Vic. 110 I13, 229 Q5, 232 B4, **183**
Pyrmont NSW 81 A7, 85 L10

Quaama NSW 100 F5, 103 G9, 127 L13, 235 Q4
Quairading WA 384 G4, 386 E8, 361
Quakers Hill NSW 91 L7
Qualco SA 303 O6
Quambatook Vic. 110 H12, 229 N4, 173
Quambone NSW 106 B10
Quamby Qld 532 G3
Quamby Brook Tas. 580 I13, 585 J9
Quandary NSW 104 B9, 111 R7
Quandialla NSW 103 A1, 104 C8, 47
Quandong Roadhouse NSW 108 C12
Quantong Vic. 228 F9
Queanbeyan NSW 103 E5, 104 G13, 123 G4, 126 H3, **61**
Queens Park WA 373 M7
Queenscliff NSW 85 Q4
Queenscliff Vic. 210 H10, 212 B5, 217 R6, 224 B7, 142, 155, 167, **183**, 196
Queensport Qld 511 J7
Queenstown SA 294 C12
Queenstown Qld 523 C12
Queenstown Tas. 582 E3, 584 E12, 551, **562**, 565
Quellington WA 376 I3, 384 F3
Quilpie Qld 535 O7, **490**
Quinburra NSW 103 E12, 235 M9
Quindalup WA 377 C7, 379 D2, 343
Quindanning WA 384 E7
Quingilli Qld 523 G11
Quinninup WA 380 D7, 384 D11, 350

Viking

Published by the Penguin Group
Penguin Books Australia Ltd
250 Camberwell Road, Camberwell, Victoria
   3124, Australia
Penguin Books Ltd
80 Strand, London WC2R 0RL, England
Penguin Putnam Inc.
375 Hudson Street, New York, New York
   10014, USA
Penguin Books Canada Limited
10 Alcorn Avenue, Toronto, Ontario,
   Canada M4V 3B2
Penguin Books (N.Z.) Ltd
Cnr Rosedale and Airborne Roads, Albany,
   Auckland, New Zealand
Penguin Books (South Africa) (Pty) Ltd
24 Sturdee Avenue, Rosebank,
   Johannesburg 2196, South Africa
Penguin Books India (P) Ltd, 11,
   Community Centre, Panchsheel Park
   New Delhi 110 017, India

This twenty-first edition published by
   Penguin Books Australia Ltd, 2002
First published by George Phillip &
   O'Neil Pty Ltd, 1980
Second edition 1981
Third edition 1983
Reprinted 1984
Fourth edition 1985
Fifth edition 1986
Sixth edition published by Penguin
   Books Australia Ltd, 1987
Seventh edition 1988
Eighth edition 1989
Ninth edition 1990
Tenth edition 1991
Eleventh edition 1992
Twelfth edition 1993
Thirteenth edition 1994
Fourteenth edition 1995
Fifteenth edition 1996
Sixteenth edition 1997
Seventeenth edition 1998
Eighteenth edition 1999
Nineteenth edition 2000
Twentieth edition 2001

Copyright © Penguin Books Australia Ltd, 2002

ISBN 0 670 04013 4

Printed in China by Midas Printing (Asia) Ltd

Publisher's Note: Every effort has been made to
ensure that the information in this book is
accurate at the time of going to press.
The publisher welcomes information and
suggestions for correction or improvement.
e-mail: cartog@penguin.com.au

Disclaimers: The publisher cannot accept
responsibility for any errors or omissions.
The representation on the maps of any road
or track is not necessarily evidence of public
right of way.

Acknowledgements

General Editor
Astrid Browne

Design
Cover and preliminary pages by Lynn
Twelftree; internal pages by John Canty,
Penguin Design Studio

Page layout and typesetting
Andrea Williamson, P.A.G.E. Pty Ltd; Michael
Kuszla, J&M Typesetting

Cartography
Penguin Cartographic: Michael Archer,
Colin Critchell, Paul de Leur, Damien Demaj,
Bruce McGurty, Julie Sheridan

Writing
Journey through Australia, State Introductions
and Touring Regions written by Ingrid
Ohlsson with assistance from Tony Ohlsson

Copy editing
Saskia Adams, Jenny Lang, Susan McLeish,
Heidi Marfurt

Picture research
Simon James, Susan McLeish, Heidi Marfurt

Map and text research
Saskia Adams, Damien Demaj, Simon James,
Jenny Lang, Paul de Leur, Bruce McGurty,
Susan McLeish, Heidi Marfurt, Ingrid Ohlsson,
Julie Sheridan

Assistance with research
This edition was produced with assistance from
regional tourism associations and local visitor
information centres throughout Australia.
The publisher would like to thank the following
organisations and individuals:
Australian Bureau of Statistics (for assistance
   with population figures)
Australian Council of the Royal Flying Doctor
   Service
Bureau of Meteorology (for climate information)
Commonwealth Department of Transport
   & Regional Development
National Road Transport Commission
   (for information on road rules)
Surf Life Saving Victoria (for information on
   water safety)

New South Wales
Big Sky Country Regional Tourism Organisation
Blue Mountains (Regional Tourism Organisation)
Capital Country (Regional Tourism Organisation)
Central Coast Tourism
Coffs Coast (Regional Tourism Organisation)
Explorer Country Regional Tourism
   Organisation
Geographical Names Board
The Holiday Coast Regional Tourism
   Organisation
Hunter Regional Tourism Organisation
Illawarra & Southern Highlands Regional
   Tourism
Lord Howe Visitor Centre
The Outback Regional Tourism Organisation
National Parks and Wildlife Service
Northern Rivers Regional Tourism
Riverina Regional Tourism
Roads and Traffic Authority
South Coast Regional Tourism Organisation
Sydney Convention & Visitors Bureau
Tourism Mid North Coast
Tourism Murray
Tourism Snowy Mountains

Australian Capital Territory
Canberra Tourism & Events Corporation

Victoria
Alpine Regional Tourism Organisation
Ballarat Tourism
Bendigo Tourism Board
Bright Visitors Centre
City of Melbourne
Delatite Shire Council
Discovery Coast & Hinterland Tourism
Geelong Otway Tourism
Geographic Names Victoria
Grampians National Park Visitors Centre
Greater Shepparton Tourism Committee
Hepburn Shire Tourism
Lakes & Wilderness Tourism Association

Latrobe Shire Council
Mildura Murray Outback Tourism
Mornington Peninsula Tourism
Mt Alexander Marketing & Promotions Board
Northern Grampians Shire Council
Parks Victoria
Phillip Island Visitor Information Centre
Shipwreck Coast Tourism
South Gippsland Shire Council
Southern Grampians Shire Council
Tourism Murray
Tourism Victoria
VicRoads
Woodend Visitor Information Centre
Yarra Valley & Dandenong Ranges
   Tourism Board

South Australia
Adelaide Convention & Tourism Authority
Adelaide Hills Tourism Marketing
Barossa Wine & Tourism Association
Clare Valley Tourism Marketing
Department of Environment & Heritage
Eyre Peninsula Tourism Association
Fleurieu Tourism Marketing Board
Flinders Ranges & Outback South Australia
   Tourism
Geographical Names Advisory Committee
Limestone Coast Tourism
Murraylands Tourism Marketing
Riverlands Tourist Association
South Australian Tourism Commission
Tourism Kangaroo Island
Transport SA
Yorke Peninsula Tourism Marketing

Western Australia
City of Perth
Department of Conservation & Land
   Management
Esperance Region Tourism Association
Geographic Names Committee of
   Western Australia
Goldfields Tourism Association
Heartlands Regional Tourism Association
Kimberley Tourism Association
Main Roads Western Australia
Mid-West Tourism Promotions
Mundaring Information Centre
Outback Coast Tourism Association
Peel Region Tourism Association
Pilbara Tourism Association
Rottnest Island Tourism
South-West Regional Tourism Association
Southern Regional Tourism Association
Swan Valley Tourism
Western Australia Aboriginal Lands Trust
Western Australian Tourism Commission

Northern Territory
Central Australian Tourism Industry
   Association
Department of Transport and Infrastructure
Kakadu National Park
Katherine Tourism
Northern and Central land councils
Northern Territory Tourist Commission
Parks & Wildlife Commission of the
   Northern Territory
Parks Australia
Place Names Committee
Tourism Top End

Queensland
Brisbane Marketing
Bundaberg District Tourism & Development
   Board
Capricorn Tourism & Development
   Organisation
Department of Main Roads
Department of Natural Resources
Fraser Coast South Burnett Regional
   Tourism Board
Gladstone Area Promotion & Development
Gold Coast Tourism Bureau
Gulf Savannah Tourism
Mackay Tourism & Development Bureau
Outback Queensland Tourism Authority
Queensland Parks & Wildlife Service
Southern Downs Tourist Association
Toowoomba & Golden West Regional
   Tourist Association
Tourism Queensland
Tourism Sunshine Coast
Tourism Tropical North Queensland
Tourism Whitsundays
Townsville Enterprise

Tasmania
Cradle Coast Tourism
Department of Infrastructure, Energy
   & Resources
Flinders Island Tourism Association
Forestry Tasmania
Gateway Tasmania
Martyn Cove
Nomenclature Board of Tasmania
Parks and Wildlife Service
South Regional Tourism Association
Tourism Tasmania

Photography
Back flap
Murchison, 669 km north of Perth,
Western Australia
© Telstra Corporation Limited
Half-title page and spine
Bollards on the Geelong waterfront, Victoria
John Meier
Title page
Glass House Mountains, Queensland
Nick Rains
Contents pages
Bronte Baths near Bondi, New South Wales
John Meier
Introductions
p. viii Ted Mead; p. xxiv AUSCAPE (Jean-Paul
Ferrero); p. 112 Penguin Books Australia
(J.P. & E.S. Baker); p. 128 John Meier; p. 236
Australian Picture Library (Nick Rains); p. 312
Jonathan Marks; p. 392 John Meier; p. 436
John Meier; p. 536 Geoff Murray; p. 586
Penguin Books Australia (Ken Stepnell)

Other photography credits
All Saints Estate; Allsport (Blair Hamish);
AMP Tower Centrepoint; Anangu Tours (Laurie
Berryman); ANT Photo Library (Kelvin Aitken,
Jutta Hosel, Chris & Sandra Pollitt, Klaus
Uhlenhut); Michael Archer; AUSCAPE (Tim
Acker, John Cancalosi, Jean-Paul Ferrero, Jeff &
Sandra Foott, Brett Gregory, Jean-Marc La
Roque, Mark Newton, David Parer & Elizabeth
Parer-Cook, Jaime Plaza Van Roon, Glenn
Tempest); Australian National Botanic Gardens
(M. Crisp, Murray Fagg, D. Greig, R. Hotchkiss);
Australian Picture Library (Robin Bickford, Roy
Bisson, John Carnemolla, Craig Lamotte,
Lightstorm, Ian Lloyd, Leo Meier, Photo Index,
Nick Rains, Redferns, Steve Vidler, Volvox, Gerry
Whitmont); J.P. & E.S. Baker; Canberra Tourism
and Events Corporation; Andrew Chapman;
Cloudehill Gardens; Douglas Coughran; Jeff
Drewitz; Fremantle Tourism; Great Southern
Railway; Andrew Gregory; Richard I'Anson;
Murray Jones; Alex Julius; Gary Lewis; Lochman
Transparencies (Bill Belson, Mike Braham, Nick
Gales, Jiri Lochman, Peter & Margy Nicholas,
Col Roberts, Dennis Sarson, Alex Steffe, Len
Stewart, Geoff Taylor); Jonathan Marks; John
McLeish; McWilliam's Wines; Ted Mead; John
Meier; Geoff Murray; Pajinka Wilderness Lodge;
Penguin Books Australia (J.P. & E.S. Baker,
Ricky Eaves, Chris Groenhout, Graeme &
Margaret Herald, Leon Kowalski, John Krutop,
Gary Lewis, Heidi Marfurt, Nick Rains,
Julie Sheridan, Don Skirrow, Ken Stepnell,
John & Jan Tait); photolibrary.com
(Claver Carroll); Bruce Postle; Queensland
Museum (Museum of Tropical North
Queensland); Nick Rains; Christo Reid; Don
Skirrow; Robin Smith; South Australian Tourism
Commission; Sovereign Hill, Ballarat; Sport The
Library (Matt Darby, Greg Epperson); Ken
Stepnell; Stock Photos (Kelvin Aitken, Bill
Bachman, Diana Calder, John Carr, Chris Clark,
Bette Devine, Roger du Buisson, Excitations,
Robert Fox, Andy Game, Ted Grambeau, Great
Western Images, Owen Hughes, Noeline Kelly,
Gary Lewis, Pauline Madden, Nadish Naoroji,
Lance Nelson, Otto Rogge, David Scaletti,
David Simmonds, Don Skirrow, Paul Steel,
Ken Stepnell, Stocktake, Tim Vanderlaan, James
Walshe, Michael Wennrich); Steve Strike;
Tandanya Aboriginal & Cultural Institute;
Tourism New South Wales (Nick Rains);
Tourism Queensland (Peter Lik, Susan Wright);
Tourism Tasmania (George Apostolidis, Richard
Bennett, John de la Roche, Richard Eastwood,
Dennis Harding, Ray Joyce, Steve Lovegrove,
Geoff Murray, Gary Myros, Nick Osborne, Joe
Shemesh, Peter Whyte); Tourism Victoria;
Trezise Bush Guide Service

SUGGESTION FORM

This 21st edition of *Explore Australia* is updated from information supplied by consultants, tourist organisations and the general public. We would welcome suggestions from you.

SUGGESTED AMENDMENT OR ADDITION

TEXT

Page no.	Amendment/Addition

MAPS

Page no.	Grid	Amendment/Addition

GENERAL COMMENTS

OPTIONAL

Name: _____

Address: _____

_____

Phone no.: _____ email address: _____

Place of purchase (shop name and suburb): _____

Date of purchase: _____

Age group:
20 and under ☐   20–29 ☐   30–39 ☐
40–49 ☐   50–59 ☐   60 and over ☐

I would like to receive information on new and updated guides, maps and atlases in the *Explore Australia* range:
YES/NO (please indicate).

Please cut out and send to: Cartographic Publications Manager
250 Camberwell Road, Camberwell Vic. 3124. Alternatively, email your comments to cartog@penguin.com.au

ACCIDENT ACTION

Simple first aid can save a life.

When you approach the scene of an accident, remember to follow the DRABC action plan:

D DANGER
R RESPONSE
A AIRWAY
B BREATHING
C CIRCULATION

1. Check for DANGER –
to yourself and others.

- Do not touch occupants or vehicle if live wires are in contact with car.

- Turn off ignition of crashed car.

- If power lines are causing sparks nearby but not touching car, remove people quickly in case spilt petrol is set alight.

- Ensure no one is smoking.

- Station people to warn oncoming cars and people of the danger ahead.

- At night, light up area and use flashing indicators on vehicles as additional warning.

- Where possible, people, vehicles and debris should be cleared from roadway.

- Only move victim when in danger (e.g. from fire, traffic or burns from hot roadway) or when victim's position makes it impossible to carry out essential treatment (such as stopping bleeding).

- If you do have to move victim, get three or four people to help if possible. Avoid bending or twisting neck or back – keep them straight. Support any injured limbs.

REMEMBER: Most casualties will be suffering some degree of shock. One of the best ways of treating this is by reassuring them – but never give alcohol. Keep casualties calm and protect them from uncomfortable weather conditions, particularly hot sun.

2. Check for RESPONSE –
see if the casualty is conscious.

- Gently shake and ask 'Can you hear me?'.

- If conscious, check for bleeding (see Stopping Bleeding on opposite page).

3. Check and clear AIRWAY –
if unconscious, ensure airway is not blocked.

- Remove any obstructions, such as blood, vomit, loose teeth or broken dentures and teeth.

- Lie victim on side and tilt head back to clear airway.

- Quickly clear mouth, using fingers if necessary. If breathing, leave on side.

- If victim is trapped in car, tilt head back and support jaw to clear airway.

4. Check BREATHING –
see if casualty is breathing.

- Look, listen and feel for breathing.

- If breathing, leave on side and check for other injuries.

- If not breathing, turn on to back and commence Expired Air Resuscitation (see opposite page).

5. Check CIRCULATION –
check for pulse.

- Feel for pulse by placing end of your finger in groove behind the Adam's apple, on either side of neck.

- If no pulse, perform cardiopulmonary resuscitation, if you have been taught this procedure (15 compressions to 2 breaths in 15 seconds).

LEARN BASIC FIRST AID

There are several organisations including St John Ambulance Australia that teach cardiopulmonary resuscitation and how to handle emergencies.